Short Story Criticism

Guide to Gale Literary Criticism Series

For criticism on	Consult these Gale series
Authors now living or who died after December 31, 1999	*CONTEMPORARY LITERARY CRITICISM (CLC)*
Authors who died between 1900 and 1999	*TWENTIETH-CENTURY LITERARY CRITICISM (TCLC)*
Authors who died between 1800 and 1899	*NINETEENTH-CENTURY LITERATURE CRITICISM (NCLC)*
Authors who died between 1400 and 1799	*LITERATURE CRITICISM FROM 1400 TO 1800 (LC)* *SHAKESPEAREAN CRITICISM (SC)*
Authors who died before 1400	*CLASSICAL AND MEDIEVAL LITERATURE CRITICISM (CMLC)*
Authors of books for children and young adults	*CHILDREN'S LITERATURE REVIEW (CLR)*
Dramatists	*DRAMA CRITICISM (DC)*
Poets	*POETRY CRITICISM (PC)*
Short story writers	*SHORT STORY CRITICISM (SSC)*
Literary topics and movements	*HARLEM RENAISSANCE: A GALE CRITICAL COMPANION (HR)* *THE BEAT GENERATION: A GALE CRITICAL COMPANION (BG)*
Asian American writers of the last two hundred years	*ASIAN AMERICAN LITERATURE (AAL)*
Black writers of the past two hundred years	*BLACK LITERATURE CRITICISM (BLC)* *BLACK LITERATURE CRITICISM SUPPLEMENT (BLCS)*
Hispanic writers of the late nineteenth and twentieth centuries	*HISPANIC LITERATURE CRITICISM (HLC)* *HISPANIC LITERATURE CRITICISM SUPPLEMENT (HLCS)*
Native North American writers and orators of the eighteenth, nineteenth, and twentieth centuries	*NATIVE NORTH AMERICAN LITERATURE (NNAL)*
Major authors from the Renaissance to the present	*WORLD LITERATURE CRITICISM, 1500 TO THE PRESENT (WLC)* *WORLD LITERATURE CRITICISM SUPPLEMENT (WLCS)*

ISSN 0895-9439

Volume 74

Short Story Criticism

Criticism of the
Works of Short Fiction Writers

Joseph Palmisano
Project Editor

Detroit • New York • San Francisco • San Diego • New Haven, Conn. • Waterville, Maine • London • Munich

Short Story Criticism, Vol. 74

Project Editor
Joseph Palmisano

Editorial
Jessica Bomarito, Kathy D. Darrow, Jeffrey W. Hunter, Jelena O. Krstović, Michelle Lee, Ellen McGeagh, Linda Pavlovski, Thomas J. Schoenberg, Lawrence J. Trudeau, Russel Whitaker

Data Capture
Francis Monroe, Gwen Tucker

Indexing Services
Synapse, the Knowledge Link Corporation

Rights and Acquisitions
Margie Abendroth, Peg Ashlevitz, Edna Hedblad

Imaging and Multimedia
Dean Dauphinais, Leitha Etheridge-Sims, Lezlie Light, Mike Logusz, Dan Newell, Christine O'Bryan, Kelly A. Quin, Denay Wilding, Robyn Young

Composition and Electronic Capture
Kathy Sauer

Manufacturing
Rhonda Williams

Product Manager
Janet Witalec

LIBRARY OF CONGRESS CATALOG CARD NUMBER 88-641014

ISBN 0-7876-8871-1
ISSN 0895-9439

Printed in the United States of America
10 9 8 7 6 5 4 3 2 1

Contents

Preface vii

Acknowledgments xi

Literary Criticism Series Advisory Board xiii

Preface

Short Story Criticism (*SSC*) presents significant criticism of the world's greatest short-story writers and provides supplementary biographical and bibliographical materials to guide the interested reader to a greater understanding of the authors of short fiction. This series was developed in response to suggestions from librarians serving high school, college, and public library patrons, who had noted a considerable number of requests for critical material on short-story writers. Although major short-story writers are covered in such Thomson Gale series as *Contemporary Literary Criticism* (*CLC*), *Twentieth-Century Literary Criticism* (*TCLC*), *Nineteenth-Century Literature Criticism* (*NCLC*), and *Literature Criticism from 1400 to 1800* (*LC*), librarians perceived the need for a series devoted solely to writers of the short-story genre.

Scope of the Series

SSC is designed to serve as an introduction to major short-story writers of all eras and nationalities. Since these authors have inspired a great deal of relevant critical material, *SSC* is necessarily selective, and the editors have chosen the most important published criticism to aid readers and students in their research.

Approximately eight to ten authors are included in each volume, and each entry presents a historical survey of the critical response to that author's work. The length of an entry is intended to reflect the amount of critical attention the author has received from critics writing in English and from foreign critics in translation. Every attempt has been made to identify and include the most significant essays on each author's work. In order to provide these important critical pieces, the editors sometimes reprint essays that have appeared elsewhere in Thomson Gale's Literary Criticism Series. Such duplication, however, never exceeds twenty percent of an *SSC* volume.

Organization of the Book

An *SSC* entry consists of the following elements:

- The **Author Heading** cites the name under which the author most commonly wrote, followed by birth and death dates. Also located here are any name variations under which an author wrote, including transliterated forms for authors whose native languages use nonroman alphabets. If the author wrote consistently under a pseudonym, the pseudonym will be listed in the author heading and the author's actual name given in parentheses on the first line of the biographical and critical introduction. Uncertain birth or death dates are indicated by question marks. Single-work entries are preceded by the title of the work and its date of publication.

- The **Introduction** contains background information that introduces the reader to the author and the critical debates surrounding his or her work.

- A **Portrait of the Author** is included when available.

- The list of **Principal Works** is ordered chronologically by date of first publication and lists the most important works by the author. The first section comprises short-story collections, novellas, and novella collections. The second section gives information on other major works by the author. For foreign authors, the editors have provided original foreign-language publication information and have selected what are considered the best and most complete English-language editions of their works.

- Reprinted **Criticism** is arranged chronologically in each entry to provide a useful perspective on changes in critical evaluation over time. All short-story, novella, and collection titles by the author featured in the entry are printed in boldface type. The critic's name and the date of composition or publication of the critical work are given at the beginning of each piece of criticism. Unsigned criticism is preceded by the title of the source in which it appeared. Footnotes are reprinted at the end of each essay or excerpt. In the case of excerpted criticism, only those footnotes that pertain to the excerpted texts are included.

- Critical essays are prefaced by brief **Annotations** explicating each piece.

- A complete **Bibliographical Citation** of the original essay or book precedes each piece of criticism. Source citations in the Literary Criticism Series follow University of Chicago Press style, as outlined in *The Chicago Manual of Style,* 14th ed. (Chicago: The University of Chicago Press, 1993).

- An annotated bibliography of **Further Reading** appears at the end of each entry and suggests resources for additional study. In some cases, significant essays for which the editors could not obtain reprint rights are included here. Boxed material following the further reading list provides references to other biographical and critical sources on the author in series published by Thomson Gale.

Indexes

A **Cumulative Author Index** lists all of the authors that appear in a wide variety of reference sources published by Thomson Gale, including *SSC.* A complete list of these sources is found facing the first page of the Author Index. The index also includes birth and death dates and cross references between pseudonyms and actual names.

A **Cumulative Nationality Index** lists all authors featured in *SSC* by nationality, followed by the number of the *SSC* volume in which their entry appears.

An alphabetical **Title Index** lists all short-story, novella, and collection titles contained in the *SSC* series. Titles of short-story collections, separately published novellas, and novella collections are printed in italics, while titles of individual short stories are printed in roman type with quotation marks. Each title is followed by the author's last name and corresponding volume and page numbers where commentary on the work is located. English-language translations of original foreign-language titles are cross-referenced to the foreign titles so that all references to discussion of a work are combined in one listing.

In response to numerous suggestions from librarians, Thomson Gale also produces an annual paperbound edition of the SSC cumulative title index. This annual cumulation, which alphabetically lists all titles reviewed in the series, is available to all customers. Additional copies of this index are available upon request. Librarians and patrons will welcome this separate index; it saves shelf space, is easy to use, and is recyclable upon receipt of the next edition.

Citing *Short Story Criticism*

When citing criticism reprinted in the Literary Criticism Series, students should provide complete bibliographic information so that the cited essay can be located in the original print or electronic source. Students who quote directly from reprinted criticism may use any accepted bibliographic format, such as University of Chicago Press style or Modern Language Association (MLA) style. Both the MLA and the University of Chicago formats are acceptable and recognized as being the current standards for citations. It is important, however, to choose one format for all citations; do not mix the two formats within a list of citations.

The examples below follow recommendations for preparing a bibliography set forth in *The Chicago Manual of Style,* 14th ed. (Chicago: The University of Chicago Press, 1993); the first example pertains to material drawn from periodicals, the second to material reprinted from books:

Morrison, Jago. "Narration and Unease in Ian McEwan's Later Fiction." *Critique* 42, no. 3 (spring 2001): 253-68. Reprinted in *Short Story Criticism.* Vol. 57, edited by Janet Witalec, 212-20. Detroit: Gale, 2003.

Brossard, Nicole. "Poetic Politics." In *The Politics of Poetic Form: Poetry and Public Policy,* edited by Charles Bernstein, 73-82. New York: Roof Books, 1990. Reprinted in *Short Story Criticism.* Vol. 57, edited by Janet Witalec, 3-8. Detroit: Gale, 2003.

The examples below follow recommendations for preparing a works cited list set forth in the *MLA Handbook for Writers of Research Papers,* 5th ed. (New York: The Modern Language Association of America, 1999); the first example pertains to material drawn from periodicals, the second to material reprinted from books:

Morrison, Jago. "Narration and Unease in Ian McEwan's Later Fiction." *Critique* 42.3 (spring 2001): 253-68. Reprinted in *Short Story Criticism.* Ed. Janet Witalec. Vol. 57. Detroit: Gale, 2003. 212-20.

Brossard, Nicole. "Poetic Politics." *The Politics of Poetic Form: Poetry and Public Policy.* Ed. Charles Bernstein. New York: Roof Books, 1990. 73-82. Reprinted in *Short Story Criticism.* Ed. Janet Witalec. Vol. 57. Detroit: Gale, 2003. 3-8.

Suggestions are Welcome

Readers who wish to suggest new features, topics, or authors to appear in future volumes, or who have other suggestions or comments are cordially invited to call, write, or fax the Product Manager:

Product Manager, Literary Criticism Series
Thomson Gale
27500 Drake Road
Farmington Hills, MI 48331-3535
1-800-347-4253 (GALE)
Fax: 248-699-8054

Acknowledgments

The editors wish to thank the copyright holders of the excerpted criticism included in this volume and the permissions managers of many book and magazine publishing companies for assisting us in securing reproduction rights. We are also grateful to the staffs of the Detroit Public Library, the Library of Congress, the University of Detroit Mercy Library, Wayne State University Purdy/Kresge Library Complex, and the University of Michigan Libraries for making their resources available to us. Following is a list of the copyright holders who have granted us permission to reproduce material in this volume of *SSC*. Every effort has been made to trace copyright, but if omissions have been made, please let us know.

COPYRIGHTED MATERIAL IN *SSC*, VOLUME 74, WAS REPRODUCED FROM THE FOLLOWING PERIODICALS:

Book World—The Washington Post, April 23, 1990 for "Vietnam, Carried On" by Josiah Bunting; May 19, 1991 for "Never Done" by David Streitfeld. Copyright © 1990, 1991 Washington Post Book World Service/Washington Post Writers Group. Both reproduced by permission of the respective authors.—*Classical and Modern Literature,* v. 20, spring, 2000 for "'Afraid to Admit We Are Not Achilles': Facing Hector's Dilemma in Tim O'Brien's *The Things They Carried*" by Christopher Michael McDonough. Copyright © 2000 by Classical and Modern Literature, Inc. Reproduced by permission of the author.—*College Literature,* v. 29, spring, 2002. Copyright © 2002 by West Chester University. Reproduced by permission.—*Contemporary Literature,* v. 39, spring, 1998. Copyright © 1998 by the Board of Regents of the University of Wisconsin System. Reproduced by permission.—*Critique,* v. XXXV, fall, 1993; v. XXXVI, fall, 1994; v. XXXVI, summer, 1995; v. XL, spring, 1999. Copyright © 1993, 1994, 1995, 1999 by the Helen Dwight Reid Educational Foundation. All reproduced with permission of the Helen Dwight Reid Educational Foundation, published by Heldref Publications, 1319 18th Street, NW, Washington, DC 20036-1802.—*Essays in Criticism,* v. LI, April, 2001 for "Beckett and the Joycean Short Story" by Adrian Hunter. Reproduced by permission of the publisher and the author.—*The Explicator,* v. 57, spring, 1999. Copyright © 1999 by the Helen Dwight Reid Educational Foundation. Reproduced with permission of the Helen Dwight Reid Educational Foundation, published by Heldref Publications, 1319 18th Street, NW, Washington, DC 20036-1802.—*The International Fiction Review,* v. 16, winter, 1989; v. 17, winter, 1990. Copyright © by the International Fiction Association. Both reproduced by permission.—*Journal of Arabic Literature,* v. VI, 1975; v. XV, 1984; v. XVI, 1985. All courtesy of Brill Academic Publishers.—*Journal of Evolutionary Psychology,* v. XIII, March, 1992. Reproduced by permission.—*Journal of the American Research Center in Egypt,* v. XXVII, 1990 for "Egyptian Tales of the Fantastic: Theme and Technique in the Stories of Yusuf Idris" by Mona N. Mikhail. Reproduced by permission of the author.—*Journal of the Short Story in English,* autumn, 1991. Copyright © 1991 by Presses de l'Universite d'angers. Reproduced by permission.—*The Journal of the Utah Academy of Sciences, Arts, and Letters,* v. 70, 1993. Reproduced by permission.—*The Massachusetts Review,* v. XLII, winter, 2001-2002. Copyright © 2002 by *The Massachusetts Review.* Reproduced from *The Massachusetts Review,* by permission.—*Modern Fiction Studies,* v. 44, fall, 1998. Copyright © 1998 by Purdue Research Foundation, West Lafayette, IN 47907. All rights reserved. Reproduced by permission of The Johns Hopkins University.—*Notes on Modern Irish Literature,* v. 13, 2001. Copyright © 2001 by Edward A. Kopper, Jr. Reproduced by permission of E. A. Kopper.—*Research in African Literatures,* v. 28, fall, 1997. Copyright © 1997 by Indiana University Press. Reproduced by permission.—*Samuel Beckett Today,* v. 7, 1998; v. 9, 2000; v. 11, 2001. Copyright © Editions Rodopi B. V. All reproduced by permission.—*Studies in Short Fiction,* v. 29, summer, 1992. Copyright © 1992 by *Studies in Short Fiction.* Reproduced by permission.—*Style,* v. 36, spring, 2002 for "The 'Moreness' or 'Lessness' of 'Natural' Narratology: Samuel Beckett's 'Lessness' Reconsidered" by Jan Alber. Copyright © *Style,* 2002. All rights reserved. Reproduced by permission of the publisher and the author.—*The Turkish Studies Association Bulletin,* v. 16, April, 1992. Reproduced by permission.—*Twentieth Century Literature,* v. 46, spring, 2000. Copyright © 2000 by Hofstra University. Reproduced by permission.—*WLA: War, Literature & the Arts,* v. 10, fall-winter, 1998 for "Conversation Across A Century: The War Stories of Ambrose Bierce and Tim O'Brien" by Christopher D. Campbell; v. 10, fall-winter, 1998 for "*The Things They Carried* as Composite Novel," by Farrell O'Gorman; v. 11, spring-summer, 1999 for "Challenging the Law of Courage and Heroic Identification in Tim O'Brien's *If I Die in a Combat Zone* and *The Things They Carried*" by Carl S. Horner; v. 11, spring-summer, 1999 for "Telling the 'Truth' about Vietnam: Episteme and Narrative Structure in *The Green Berets* and *The Things They Carried*" by Jon Volkmer. All reproduced by permission of the respective authors.—*World Literature Today,* v. 55, winter, 1981; v. 63, spring, 1989; v. 75, spring, 2001. Copyright © 1981, 1989, 2001 by *World Literature Today.* All reproduced by permission of the publisher.—*The Yearbook of English Studies,* v. 30, 2000. Copyright © 2000 by The Modern Humanities Research Association. Reproduced by permission of the publisher.

Thomson Gale Literature Product Advisory Board

Samuel Beckett
1906-1989

(Full name Samuel Barclay Beckett) Irish-born French short-story writer, dramatist, novelist, scriptwriter, poet, essayist, and translator.

The following entry provides criticism on Beckett's short fiction from 1991 through 2002. For criticism of Beckett's short fiction published prior to 1991, see *SSC*, Volume 16.

INTRODUCTION

One of the most celebrated writers in twentieth-century literature, Beckett is known for his significant impact on the development of the short story and novel forms as well as on contemporary drama. His works expound a philosophy of negation through characters who face a meaningless and absurd existence without the comforts of religion, myth, or philosophical absolutes. Often described as fragments rather than stories, his short fiction in particular evidences his use of sparse, economical language and stark images of alienation and absurdity to present truths that are free of rhetorical embellishment.

BIOGRAPHICAL INFORMATION

Beckett was born on April 13, 1906, and raised in Foxrock, near Dublin, Ireland. In 1927 he received his B.A. in French and Italian from Trinity College in Dublin. Beckett taught French for a short period in Belfast before receiving a fellowship to the École Normale Supérieure in Paris. There he met James Joyce, who had a profound influence on Beckett's early writing. Beckett returned to Trinity College in 1930 for his M.A., after which he accepted a position as a French instructor at the college. In 1932 he resigned his post at Trinity to move back to Paris and concentrate on his writing. When World War II began, he worked for the French Resistance and was forced to flee Paris when the Nazis discovered his activities. After the war, Beckett began writing almost exclusively in French and translating his work into English, beginning his most prolific and, according to many commentators, his most artistically complex period. In 1969 Beckett received the Nobel Prize for literature. He died in Paris in 1989.

MAJOR WORKS OF SHORT FICTION

Beckett published *More Pricks than Kicks,* his first collection of short stories, in 1934. A series of related epi-

sodes describing the adventures of a fictional Irishman named Belacqua Shuah, *More Pricks than Kicks* derived in part from Beckett's unpublished novel *Dream of Fair to Middling Women* (1992). In the collection, Beckett used an elaborate prose style and language derivative of Joyce. Most of Beckett's subsequent works of short fiction were originally written in French and translated into English by Beckett. *Nouvelles et texts pour rien* (1955; *Stories and Texts for Nothing*) consists of three stories and thirteen prose fragments. The three stories feature protagonists whose lives are desolate and at the same time highly comic. The prose fragments are rhetorically formalized vignettes with minimal narrative characterization. Beckett's style reached the extremes of minimalism in the 1960s and 1970s when he abandoned both conventional plot and conventional syntax, stripping his language down to fragmented phrases and one-word expressions to mirror what he considered the difficulty, if not impossibility, of human communication. *Imagination morte imaginez* (1965; *Imagination Dead Imagine*) takes place in an abstract rotunda, "all white in the whiteness," where two bodies reside in a state of minimal existence. *Bing* (1966; *Ping*) uses depersonalized, machine-like language to describe a box containing a faceless and nameless figure. In *Assez* (1966; *Enough*), Beckett returned to a more traditional prose style. The first person monologue combines romantic and scientific language to describe a lost relationship. *Sans* (1969; *Lessness*) is perhaps the most extreme example of Beckett's experimentation with language in his short fiction. Beckett wrote sixty sentences, placed each in one of six groups containing ten sentences, and drew sentences randomly to create a work of art ordered by chance. *Le dépeupleur* (1970; *The Lost Ones*) examines the possibility that those who stop struggling against hopelessness will be the most content. *Companie* (1979; *Company*) depicts the thoughts of an individual lying in bed alone in the dark.

CRITICAL RECEPTION

Initial response to *More Pricks than Kicks* was mixed. While the book received positive reviews outside of Ireland, Irish commentators found its ornate style distasteful. Several commentators have investigated the influence of Joyce's *Dubliners* on the collection. Beckett's later short works fared better with critics as the critical schools of Post-structuralism and Deconstruction complemented his linguistic experimentation. Some commentators have applied the linguistic theory of Jacques Derrida to Beckett's work and have explored the role of theology in his shorter texts. Recent criticism has focused on his short story "First Love" and its significance in Beckett's short fiction oeuvre. While generally not as highly regarded as his novels—particularly the trilogy *Molloy* (1951), *Malone meurt* (1951; *Malone Dies*), and *L'innommable* (1953; *The Unnamable*), considered his masterpiece—Beckett's short fiction is acclaimed for its verbal experimentation and artistic formalism. Although some commentators have debated the genre of some of his short prose works—classifying them alternatively as dramatic fragments, poetry, or short stories—most recognize the immense value of Beckett's short fiction and view him as a distinctive and innovative short-story writer.

PRINCIPAL WORKS

Short Fiction

More Pricks than Kicks 1934
Nouvelles et textes pour rien [*Stories and Texts for Nothing*] 1955

Imagination morte imaginez [*Imagination Dead Imagine*] (drama and prose) 1965
Assez [*Enough*] (novella) 1966
Bing [*Ping*] (novella) 1966
No's Knife: Collected Shorter Prose, 1945-1966 (dramas and short stories) 1967
Sans [*Lessness*] (novella) 1969
Le dépeupleur [*The Lost Ones*] (novella) 1970
Premier amour [*First Love*] (novella) 1970
First Love, and Other Shorts (short stories) 1974
Foirade [*Fizzles*] 1976
Four Novellas; also published as [*The Expelled and Other Novellas*] (novellas) 1977
Companie [*Company*] (novella) 1979
Mal vu mal dit [*Ill Seen Ill Said*] (novella) 1981
Worstward Ho (short novel) 1983
Stirrings Still (novella) 1989
As the Story Was Told: Uncollected and Late Prose (prose) 1990
Nohow On (novella) 1993
Collected Shorter Prose, 1945-1988 (prose) 1995
Samuel Beckett: The Complete Short Prose, 1929-1989 (prose) 1995

Other Major Works

Whoroscope (poetry) 1930
Proust (essay) 1931
Echo's Bones, and Other Precipitates (prose) 1935
Murphy (novel) 1938
Malone meurt [*Malone Dies*] (novel) 1951
Molloy (novel) 1951
En attendant Godot [*Waiting for Godot*] (drama) 1953
L'innommable [*The Unnamable*] (novel) 1953
Watt (novel) 1953
All That Fall (radio drama) 1957
Fin de Partie [*Endgame*] (drama) 1957
Krapp's Last Tape (drama) 1958
Comment c'est [*How It Is*] (novel) 1961
Happy Days (drama) 1961
Poems in English (poetry) 1961
Comédie [*Play*] (drama) 1964
Va et vient [*Come and Go*] (drama) 1966
Eh Joe, and Other Writings (drama and screenplay) 1967
Film (screenplay) 1969
Mercier et Camier [*Mercier and Camier*] (novel) 1970
Not I (drama) 1971
Breath and Other Shorts (drama) 1972
All Strange Away (prose) 1976
Ends and Odds (drama) 1976
Footfalls (drama) 1976
That Time (drama) 1976
A Piece of Monologue (drama) 1979
Ohio Impromptu (drama) 1981
Rockabye (drama) 1981
Texts for Nothing (drama) 1981

CRITICISM

Francis Doherty (essay date autumn 1991)

SOURCE: Doherty, Francis. "Paf, Hop, Bing and Ping." *Journal of the Short Story in English,* no. 17 (autumn 1991): 23-41.

[*In the following essay, Doherty provides a stylistic examination of* Ping *and traces its revisions to gather further insight into the story.*]

Beckett's short prose work, *Ping,* of 1967 is a complex text which presents the reader with many difficulties. In the first place, the sentences which the reader has to confront are daunting in their tonelessness, their fragmentariness and their apparent randomness. Repetition of over-repeated collocations seems to have the effect of neutral counters endlessly shifted in patterns, without the usual comforting illusion of a voice apparently speaking through language and of some kind of a story being told. We seem to have come into a world of language stripped of significance with a slab of text which refuses the conditions of narrative. Readers have grown used over time to a narrative voice which is their link to a shared humanity, and any story which is read is one which takes place in time, and some kind of teleology will take the reader to an "end", and, equally, the story will engage with some of the small range of human emotions and with a relatively small number of situations and relationships which might be expected to engage a reader's attention. But Beckett's text, at first encounter, seems to be devoid of a human voice and of any human story, to be instead an aleatory dealing out of chance-delivered collocations.

However, many readers from David Lodge in 1967 on, have felt that, after reading the piece with care, some meaning and some human concerns not only emerge, but, paradoxically, are very powerfully communicated, albeit through what seems to be an inhuman and mechanically articulated text. The early conclusion that this was a literary text much like other literary texts, being "like any literary artefact, a marriage of form and meaning", and that, after close reading, "the rewards are surprisingly great" might still seem worth confronting and questioning.[1]

Beckett's short work at first reading seems to discard so much that is necessary for a fiction; it seems to abandon narrator, jettison plot, erase human emotions, limit human actions to their possibly barest minimum, reduce the multiplicity of the created universe to a body in a box in a larger box of a room. All movement (nearly) gone; all colour (nearly) gone; all events (nearly) gone, and nothing left of interest for a reader.

But this is not the outcome of immersing oneself in the repetition of those staccato fragments enclosed between full stops. There is, indeed, something going on within the text which raises important questions about Beckettian narrative and his creative enterprise in short prose works.

In their early bibliographical study of Beckett, Raymond Federman and John Fletcher have an "Appendix II" which gives the texts of *Bing* and *Ping,* preceded by the ten variant stages of the French text.[2] It may be possible to arrive at some clearer understanding of this puzzling text by making use of those early drafts. However, any attempt to come to a clearer understanding by reading through those successive versions carries its own problems when we can only guess at the changing conceptions of the author, and we have to acknowledge too that a critic cannot simply follow ideas or images from beginning to end if a writer's inner conceptions change en route, though using apparently the same words or formulations. Nonetheless, reading the drafts does yield something, however fraily hesitant the reader might feel about claiming to upgrade Lodge into "Some Ping More Understood".

As the text is problematical in its relation to common expectations of narrative, I should like to begin with the obvious questions about the "Ping" element and with the analogous words which are used in both the final French Text, *Bing,* and the drafts which precede it. It is important to be as precise as I can about this, as I believe a good deal depends on the use of this word (and its predecessors and counterparts) in our understanding of what Beckett was concerned to express about the creative act and the meaning of literary texts. A careful reading of the drafts of the short text is helpful and instructive, but especially so when we add to our reading a knowledge of Beckett's themes and artistic concerns, and this should help towards some initial understanding of what this kind of emptied, staccato prose might be accomplishing.

The text is plainly a reductionist text, and is something which at first sight seems to be inhuman and devoid of readerly interest, claiming a territory of pure text for its operation. Still, I would claim, it possesses all the elements of fiction, even all elements of discourse, but stamped down to the smallest compass which the artistic abilities can manage for them ('All I could manage and more than I could'). The questions about who writes and what is written and the ends for which writing exists are all raised by this text. In it we are shown at work a fastidiousness of manner which seems to forbid not only what must have been deemed an excess, but demonstrates a sensibility which jettisons what would previously in classical fiction have been taken as minimal requirements for both creating and being created. To a great extent, this is what Beckett was making his own especial artistic task, a special kind of minimalist writing which, while aiming at existing purely as a text, a construct, nonetheless could never escape the tragedy of the human plight, could never escape from the long tradition that human suffering has its central significance for the artist.

To begin with a simple observation: we have here an example of the Beckettian parody of Cartesian reductionism. We have a situation where, rather than show an attempt being made to build up the whole system of thought and reality from an irreducible and ultimately self-evident "truth", "je pense donc je suis", we see attempt after attempt in later Beckettian prose to find ways of reducing all systems of thought and reality to an irreducible minimum, getting as close to absolute zero as can be contrived, getting as near silence as possible and wishing to stay there or end there—and never again to build up a system. For at least forty years Beckett worked his themes of impotence and ignorance, and pursued his art which turned its back on reality, "the plane of the feasible", "weary of puny exploits, weary of being able, of doing, of doing a little better the same old thing, of going a little further along a dreary road", preferring the paradoxical state of

> The expression that there is nothing to express, nothing with which to express, nothing from which to express, no power to express, together with the obligation to express.[3]

The problem, of course, is that such a logic would seem to demand silence, a void—and absolute zero yields absolutely nothing. But just how close can you get to absolute zero, how near to silence can you take your art and still be heard? This seems to be the enterprise, and it is emphatically anti-Cartesian, at least in this sense: Descartes's reductionism concealed a sublime confidence and optimism which allowed the fiction of a *ne plus ultra,* the fiction of a thinking being conscious of itself thinking, where all the problems associated logically and philosophically with such a formulation in language are both embedded and overcome. Beckett's reductionism is always within a given, a formula which defies logic, and which is, literally, meaningless. An

urge to write is a *donnée.* You cannot write without appearing to say something, without in that sense communicating, given that writing means using structures of language (already given) and words (which usually pre-existed the present user), & c.

What this particular text of Beckett's shows clearly, especially when read in its drafts, is that part of the text's complex procedure is to focus on *obligation,* and it does this by introducing prompting or urging words at a variety of junctures. The text may be said to give a kind of account of a state or situation rather than being a straightforward narrative of events. The reader is given staccato bursts on "how it is". These bursts, or "reports", start their textual life as details accumulatively delivered about the precise (?) state of existence of a creature in a situation which is non-real, a situation which for the literary reader will parody other situations which we either knew from experience or from the experience of reading, say, Dante's created worlds of the *Purgatorio* and *Inferno.* The details of the Beckett world are progressively but discontinuously delivered. Standard classical texts are content to give "factual" details about the fictional world being created for the reader and then to pass on, and consequently readers would be very disconcerted to find themselves repeatedly being given (as they are in Beckett's text) expressions which might be held to represent "facts" about the physical features of the fictive universe over and over again. Readers would feel that some kind of contract had been broken, that they were being asked to read something that was not "literature". Such readers would, I assume, give up and throw away the text as "mad", not worth the time and effort needed to persevere with it. It is hard to be precise about how Beckett does persuade the reader to continue with the enterprise of reading his text, but I believe that he does.

In the first attempt at the creation of this work, the text is organised so that we are gradually led in Text I from a located situation to the "person" within that situation, and the "person" is then systematically presented, moving from the head, through the limbs, cylindrical trunk, arms, penis, feet. The rudimentary "voice" of the piece which has done its best, it would seem, to exclude emotion or genuine readerly interest from itself, does, however, come through to the reader when there is a strong interest shown in mathematics, in figures, but oddly, with a kind of mad precision. Characteristically, after hearing "Largeur un mètre. Hauteur deux mètres", we have "Mesures approximatives comme toutes à venir", a voice which is very like the deranged voice of Lucky's speech in *Waiting for Godot:*

> . . . the dead loss per caput since the death of Bishop Berkeley being to the tune of one inch four ounce per caput approximately by and large more or less to the nearest decimal good measure round figures . . .[4]

This version of the text seems to have a rudimentary "voice", shown through what might seem to be a simple and neutrally "scientific" interest in the penis: "Membre glabre. Brèves demi-érections spontanées". The neutral term "membre" (for *membrum virile*) might seem fussy and remote from ordinary humanity, and yet the enjoyed rhythm of "membre glabre" is, in its turn, strangely removed from medical neutrality (where "glabre" might be more commonly encountered in expressions like "visage glabre"—"clean-shaven"). Smuggled in, then, against what seems to be the text's "factual reporting", is a something more, and that "something more" is what, were it sustained and built on might, make the artful. But this interesting "sign of life"—both in the text and in the object presented—might well have seemed excessive, as it is removed from all succeeding versions of the text. All must be controlled, deadened.

Proceeding with its account of the state of affairs, the text seems, much like the earlier novel, *Watt,* to delight in spending time and energy in an exhaustive and exhausting enumeration of what seem to be the possibilities of the ways in which the several named physical states which are listed may be combined one with another. These states are, it is said, "Non liées". So: "Chaleur lumière. Chaleur noir. Froid lumière. Froid noir." are perfectly acceptable as possible states of affairs in a world like our own, but the text gets more from the list than this limited set of combinations. It asserts the reality of

> Chaleur lumière et noir.
> Froid lumière et noir.
> Lumière chaleur et froid.
> Noir chaleur et froid.

It can only have these logically possible (but practically impossible) combinations if the rules which govern the meanings of words (or those laws which govern the state of the universe as we know it) are changed. This is implicitly accepted but at the same time is circumvented. What is said to be a state of affairs with all elements co-existing at the same time, is said to be so, but not so at the same time, because these conditions are subject also to the modifier, "Changements foudroyants". This last qualification might be calculated to persuade a reader that we can have both "light" and "dark" coexisting by the expedient of having changes in the basic states as "lightning-flash-like". This, then, is a text which tries to remain both within a world which is a possible world which the reader would feel comfortable with and yet within another one which, though mathematically logical within a system of permutations, is practically impossible. It is at this point that the text is punctuated by its first three encouraging or urging expression, "Paf". This expression is allowed into the sentence without any signal that it might belong to another level of discourse.

This word, which other more standard texts might well have given an exclamation mark to, and which might be rendered as "Slap!" or "Bang!", presents the reader with initial problems. It cannot exist at the same level of meaning as its context, and it needs, for a full sense of its meaning in its operation its own context and voice. It is a word which has no dictionary definition other than its being noted as a word which accompanies an act. Its reference is beyond the context of the words as they are presented on the page, and it demands to be understood in its own way. It is an alien, and we could allow it into the text only if we had the necessary conditions for its inclusion made plain to us. But no such conditions are ever going to be made plain, and hence it is one of the many sources of puzzlement for the reader trying to negotiate the text.

Readers of Beckett are, of course, well used to his characters being manipulated by outside forces, the reluctant being forced into speech, "quod erat extorquendum".[5] So, if we try to associate the usage of the "paf" with some violence, some blow, however unemphatically allowed into the text, however unattached to context and shorn of a voice, then we do land ourselves with problems. These problems which are created for the reader partly derive from the elision of levels of discourse in the text, flattening the plane of the "speaker" or "voice" from which we have been taught by the text's procedures so far how to read, how to try and hear the words, and from which we are used to hearing that which may be believed (or that which we allow, having suspended our disbelief, to count as believable) with another plane, that of a (possibly violent) controller who is demanding from the voice something which the voice and only the voice can give. We would then have a kind of dramatic situation being enacted within the text.

We could go on to observe that any tyrannous demands are met with an incompetent instrument. The "controller" has no articulated language, utters no real word, is present only by inference from the "paf" it might be held to make. It has to use the only instrument which exists to have said what it wants to have said, though it has no control in the end over what is said. The only user of language, the instrument, is the text, and this is worn out, beyond interest, incompetent. The almost exact analogy might be Lucky as "thinker" in *Waiting for Godot,* where "thinking" is one of his noted skills (like his equally worn-out "dancing") and is offered as one of the entertainments which Pozzo can offer his guests, Vladimir and Estragon. Presumably the audience is to be appalled that this "thinking" represents what has happened to that capacity which has so often been held to mark man from beast ("What a piece of work is man!"), that "thinking" has been so eroded into this farrago. Again, there are many ways in which the *Trilogy* tries hard to give an account of this process which seems necessary to be ascribed to a controller or tor-turer. Of course, to attribute purpose and intelligence, even to a tormenter, is to invent the resolution as part of the perceived problem, to give a spurious meaning to the activity of issuing words to that "issueless misery". If something is perceived as a task, there must be a taskmaster.[6]

In this text the "Paf"s selem to be there to make further demands on the voice, to stimulate it to further efforts. So, while it is only able to elicit "noir" from "noir" (there seems to be no further intensity of "black" pos-sible, even when the voice seems madly to being urged on to find one), it does manage to stimulate "éblouisse-ment" from "blanc", and "fournaise et glace" from "chaleur et froid", but there is no further to be gone than rhetorical exaggeration of what is already elemen-tal, "black, white, hot, cold". The voice can do no more with what it has got. It might seem that it wanted to es-cape from the figure, the "character", to spend some of its energies in the dubious delights of mathematical per-mutations. But it seems that there is no avoiding the figure and what must be constantly reported about it. And here arises one of the text's central ambiguities. When, driven back to the body and its eyes, the text presents certain details, the reader is unsure of the source of those details. We cannot know whether these details come from a narrator or whether they represent the unspoken voice of the "body", whether we attribute them to a "creator" or to one we might call the "crea-ture", or whether it makes no difference which. We might have to come to terms with this truism, that it is a vain question, as all artists can ever really do is to write themselves out of themselves. There is never, ac-cording to this view, any real distinction to be drawn between creator and creature. But this is to go too far too quickly. In this text we are presented with this kind of problem when we read the expression, "Brefs mur-mures de loin en loin". Does what follows this phrase include something of what the "creature" murmurs; are some of the staccato escapes his? If so, how do we know which ones? Is there a way of knowing?

In standard texts there are ways of declaring voices, of showing differing states of consciousness, of dreaming, of fantasising, of a pre-birth or post-death condition, and so on, and a reader will cope quite happily with a variety of pretended states of existence when the text gives what are perceived as adequate signals, even when such signals are given retrospectively.

There are many instances, of course, but we can think of the fantasy opening of *Billy Liar,* for instance, and the whole of William Golding's *Pincher Martin* where we find that we have been reading the contents of a dead man's mind with its fears, hopes, anguishes and terrors. But Beckett's text is dumb.

However, in later versions of the text we do have some help. This is when a decision has been made by the au-thor to use the "Bing" interjection or interruption. We must come to that in its place. But in this first version the possibility is that we do hear some of a voice's murmurs, but murmurs which are endlessy boring for the reporting voice, as boring as the voices of *Play:* "Toujours les mêmes" . . . "Ils sont sus." But one of the possible murmurs which be said to escape could well be the expression

> Il manque un échelon.

This would sound very much like a remark of someone trapped who might be searching for a way out, as hap-pens, for instance, in the slightly later text of 1970, *Le Dépeupleur (The Lost Ones,* 1972), or any of those texts of Beckett which owe much to Dante's *Inferno.* Looking for a ladder as a means of possible exit has many echoes in Beckett, and yet we know that the pos-session of a ladder does not carry any entailment that there will be a way out for the ladder to reach. On the whole, human life's evidence would seem to suggest the opposite, adding another part to the generic tragic story of the "vanity of human wishes". To have a ladder but not to have a way out would be one thing, to judge that you would need a ladder to escape might be an-other; but not to be able to find any directions, even were you to have a ladder, just because all signs are obliterated, all being reduced to "blanc sur blanc invis-ible", so that even were there anything to be found, they could never be found, would be still another. Equally, and very naturally, being human, we can be presented with a total blankness and yet project upon that blankness human needs for shape, balance, symme-try, beauty, order, direction, meaning; and, being hu-man, we will create them where they do not exist. The poet is the maker. But the text here insists that there is "Rien de repérable", no guidance, nothing from which to take directions. It declares that there is a ladder: "Echelle blanche invisible" . . . "Dressée contre le mur sous l'une ou "autre niche"". There would be no way of recovering by sight anything which was so de-scribed, and it would be no good to anyone knowing that, were he so immobile as he is, and unable to verify even the assertion that there is an invisible ladder there. Standard texts would emphasise pathos or tragedy or irony; we should have some guidance as readers as to how to respond to the situation. To have the human re-sponse swamped by a mode of indifferent, even mad, reporting is insupportable. We are given the neutral tones which declare that universal whiteness has ab-sorbed all the colours, aside from the just distinguish-able body: "D'un autre blanc le corps à peine", and in that body a touch of colour left in the eyes: blue, but a blue which is hardly in normal parlance to be allowed as blue at all: "Yeux bleu de glaire"—"blue like the white of an egg". As only the eyes have remnants of a coloured universe, so only they have the remnants of movement: "Seuls les yeux et encore. Déplacements très soudains et rapides. Tout à coup de nouveau immobile ailleurs." But there is a final use of "Paf" in the text which damages the apparent indifference and neutrality. It ensures that the eyes are not directed at the presumed controller or prompter. The last "Paf" generates:

A peine les yeux. Paf ailleurs. Vers d'autres traces.

Finally, the eyes are directed "elsewhere" after the blow of "Paf" has fallen, but the voice is reaching its limits of competence, and it cannot give an account of what the eyes are directed towards as completely as it seemed to be able to do earlier in the text. It is failing, and it can only do in fragments what it formerly did more competently (though incompetently enough for the ordinary reader). Beckettian "fatigue and disgust" has set in. However, it is equally possible that the eyes must not be allowed to look at the one who is reporting, must never communicate with the recorder of it all, but must always be directed elsewhere to another reality.

The importance of the interrupting word was increased by Beckett in the second version of the text. Here he crossed out each of the four "Paf's", replacing them with the stronger "Hop", at the same time that he was making many other verbal minor changes. I suppose that "Hop" would be seen as a more urging word, encouraging someone jumping, say, to jump quicker or higher.

The third version keeps the basic form of the first two up to the fourth "Hop"; here the eyes are "Hop ailleurs. Vers d'autres traces". The rest of the text elaborates on the physical states of the elements which compose the scene, insisting on shades of white as the qualities which allow distinctions to be made and discerning to be achieved. But the questions remain: for whom are the "traces" "visibles"? Are the eyes of the body still capable of a minimal discernment; is it a discernment which starts with some kind of distinctness, then, due to its internal inefficiency, witnesses a rapid fading into blankness; or is it the creator who has created such a universe of fadingness, where all is fading into blankness with an inexorability which is the physical lot of the creature. Is this is what is commonly taken to be the state of *entropy*? Take:

Traces seules inachevées noires jadis pâlies pâlissant gris pâle presque blanc sur blanc ou effacées.

The French allows the "unover" ("inachevées") traces to be black (once upon a time, having become pale, and then a single blur—presumably represented by the singular form, "pâlissant"—growing paler), then pale grey, then white, or, instead, simply obliterated. What would

be the difference? Presumably in the end it would matter nothing; whether a process of degeneration had been managed over time (an unspecified duration) or whether the "traces" had been simply wiped away, the result would be the same. But human stories, conducted over time, are just such events which "leave not a wrack behind", and it is as though they have never been, and yet memories linger on. Being human, however, all this does mean something to us, and it *does* make a difference to us. We value history, inherited myths, stories, memories. So, while these "traces" are problematic for the texts, and this version tries to give an account of them, and though this account lasts until the fifth version, they are finally jettisoned, presumably as too resonant, too rich with potential significance, and against the spirit of spareness and desperation which the the text increasingly seems to aim at. But for the moment, we have an evocative image of

Traces éclaboussures larges à peine comme la main humaine lorsqu'un petit œuf s'écrase.

Though these "splashes as big as a human hand and as though a little egg has been smashed" must have seemed too loaded for the text, there is another expansion which continues through the remaining versions and gathers increasing importance, and that is the "murmure". Here, in Text 3 it starts life as

Bref murmure de loin en loin que peut-être pas seul.

There is no way of knowing whether these "murmurs" are in direct or reported speech, and the elision of the two possible voices is important for the overall exploitation of ambiguity in the text. But the third voice, the voice represented by the interruptive signs of "Paf" and "Hop", insists on an attempt being made to end the "story" with a more heroic end that simply acquiescing in the existence "amid th'encircling". "Hop", "Paf", "Hop" try to stimulate an ending. The first "Hop" startles the text, which had successfully insisted on immobility and near-stasis, into

l'échelon à la main et paf toute volée mur sol colère sans bruit très bref. Hop de nouveau immobile lâche l'échelon sans bruit qui fuseau roule un instant sans bruit invisible.

This remarkable statement that all of a sudden a hand is on the rung of the ladder and all is gone for a moment, noiselessly (and who or what is "without anger, with a display of anger" is unknown), is again stimulated into its negation by "Hop" as all is still again, with the exception of the telling detail of the noiseless spinning for a moment of the rung of the ladder. In the impossible way of this syntax you have an image which demands both that it be visible in order to be an image, and at the same time to be invisible, and an image which demands time for it to exist, spinning like a spindle, but which is only allowed the barest moment for its exist-ence—and so cannot, by any definition, be held to spin—and an image which demands to be heard, the rung of a ladder rotating in its sockets, but a the same time being inaudible.

The succeeding text, 4, carries on this impossible image of the hand and the rung and its collapse into immobil-ity, but this is the text which first adds "Bing" to the repertoire of interruptive words. It is brought in at the ending of the text where "Paf" amd "Hop" seem to have exhausted their potency. We might therefore see "Bing" as the strongest of the three, and, in a standard discourse might have been said to stand for an exclama-tory "smack" or "thwack". The text brings together the two murmurs which were in the previous text, but puts them earlier in the discourse, with an interval between them, and now reversed:

> Bref murmure de loin en loin que peut-être pas seule.
> Bref murmure de loin en loin que peut-être une issue.

Then we have the new, stronger, interruptive:

> Bing murmure. Bing long silence.

The "thwack", it would seem, can only generate the noun, "murmure", with no heard content. A further "thwack" yields only silence. Everywhere a law of di-minishment operates; stronger and stronger stimulation is needed, but the effects of even the strongest stimula-tion wear away quickly. You could say, I think, that having heard the escaping murmurs about "perhaps there might be a way out, and perhaps I am now quite alone", the text is prompted to try and elicit more by increasing the violence which it can use, but unavail-ingly. But whether it is that the creator can find no more to murmur about, or whether the creature is now beyond torment, it is hard to say. What we can say, un-fortunately, is that Beckett certainly would have been able to empathise with those of his friends and acquain-tances who had been taken by the Gestapo and tortured for the information which they might have locked within them, so the idea of a series of systematic "thwacks" to generate more murmurs cannot be a comfortable one. The penultimate sentence uses a "Bing" to find a new murmur:

> Bing murmure de loin en loin que peut-être une nature.

I suppose that we could find many ways of translating that—"perhaps, after all, there is such a thing as na-ture"; "perhaps there is a natural world in spite of what I seem to be immersed in"; "maybe not all is artificial"; and so on. But the final sentence leaves the reader with the head where the murmur might be said properly to belong, as a pathetic object in space:

> Petite tête boule bien dans l'axe yeux droit devant.

Such is the head which contains the material from which the murmurs are made, and that must always mean the survival of some sort of hope, even when all the evi-dence directs us to deny the rational possibility of hope. In this case the pathos of the "peut-être" signals what it is to be human. It is human to seek for fellow—crea-tures ("peut-être pas seul") when there can be no-one but yourself, to search for a way out of situations which trap or imprison us ("peut-être une issue"), and, finally, when all has faded almost to nothing still to be able to hope that, in spite of all the overwhelming evidence of annihilation, there might still be a system, "nature", or-ganised by what we choose to think of as its "laws of nature". That is what it means to be human, it would seem, and it represents another version of Johnson's "Vanity of Human Wishes", that theme to which Beck-ett so constantly returned. It is this text's sense of the doomed hope of the lost creature, reduced to the mini-mum space and almost completely arrested in move-ment, which leads towards the final horrors of Beckett's tormented presentation of the body reduced to its box, everything nearly obliterated into whiteness, a Shel-leyan radiance of eternity where the body's eyes are the last parts of the body for a watcher to observe which have any motion left at all, and yet where this motion and all its resonant possibilities must be denied as nearly as possible. The eyes have to be said to be "hardly"—"à peine"—and their mention usually prompts a "Hop" to make sure that they are directed "ailleurs. Vers d'autres traces." A taboo exists which must not be broken. So far and no further with empathy with suffering or with humanity. A soured version of the Flaubertian or Joycean artist indifferent to his creation.

The next version, Text 5, takes a step towards further enlarging the content of the "murmures". The second and third murmurs, "que peut-être pas seul" and "que peut-être une nature", now have the insertion, "avec bref image", which is qualified again immediately by "Ça de mémoire de loin en loin". "Brefs murmures" later brings a "thwack" which is inserted into the text:

> Brefs murmures bing de loin en loin seuls inachevés.

And, unusually in the texts, the murmurs all come to-gether, and are then increased by one further murmur—"Peut-être un sens" (later translated as "perhaps a meaning"):

> brefs murmures *bing* de loin en loin seuls inachevés.
>
> *avec* xxxxxx *image.* [Que] [p]*P*eut-être une issue.
>
> [Que] [p]*P*eut-être une nature avec [brève] image.[7]
>
> [Que] [p]*P*eut-être pas seul
> [Que] [p]*P*eut-être un sens.

The "brève" has been taken out, and duration is now given in temporal form, but not in our earth time, but rather stellar time, time presumably measured in "light-seconds":

> Une deux secondes temps sidéral.

Thereafter, in this very much longer and expanded text, there is a working distinction to be drawn between the interruptive set of "Hop's" and the stronger "Bing's". "Bing" is always associated with the murmurs. The text replaces "temps sidéral" before "murmures" by a "Bing", so that "thwack" will yield murmurs, as when it prompts the first intimation of an actual image, a situation which will be retained in all the succeeding sequence of texts:

> Bing peut-être une nature une seconde deux secondes avec image même temps un peu moins ciel bleu et blanc.

This characteristically gnomic and non-specific flash of something from the memory, stimulated by the "thwack" with its generation of "peut-être une nature", will be the very most (and the very least) that can be allowed in this minimal world. But the text is not allowed to get carried away into the image and its potential; it is succeeded immediately by the doubly urgent "Hop hop"; and the narrative is restimulated into its task and its apparently endless account of the physical situation and its conditions: "le long des murs seul plan à l'infini sinon que non". As well as never letting itself dwell on what might be taken as the emotional contents of memory or the remnants of feeling, always being prodded into its drained and flattened account of the final conditions of the final body, the text is never allowed to explore the actual cause or determining conditions of the fixedness of the body. As soon as it tries to assign the fixedness to a time or place, then "hop" generates a kind of denial, "fixe ailleurs"—fixed elsewhere. This makes no sense when the text is absolutely precise about the ways in which the parts of the body are immobile, as though sewn together; but somehow the final cause of the "fixe" must always be located "ailleurs". This refusal to allow the actual cause to be named is strategic for the text, and an insertion in the text at this point of the voice's attempt to assign fixedness seems very significant:

> *Fixe là de tout temps là où hop fixe ailleurs* sinon su que non.

The text reports the contents of the murmurs and yet is prevented from getting too involved with them, showing that there is a kind of contradiction between the operations of "hop" and "bing". "Bing" stimulates the murmurs, "hop" stimulates the text to carry on enunciating the physical properties and to chart the vanishing of all into a final eclipse into a total whiteness. In one

sense we might say that there seems to be a kind of collusion between an apparently neutral report and the murmuring of the creature in its box. This would seem to be the last vestige of the relationship between the creative artist and his creature, just enough and yet too much. It seems that, try as the text will, there is no escaping human empathy, even as the task seems to be the creation of impersonal and mechanical works.

The "Bing" has a range of success from "silence" to a final image which has appeared so often in Beckett (as in the aural images in *Eh Joe* of 1967 and *Krapp's Last Tape* of 1960, for example), that haunting image of the imploring eye. This becomes both the triumph of the work of "Bing", and would in a more pointedly ironic work become the climax of the piece, and there would be no more that could be said after that. But, given the nature of our text, struggling to undermine the nature of the narrative enterprise, and yet all the time confirming it, we have two occurrences of the climatic image, separated by only a few sentences. The separation is enough to do the trick. Prolonged torments of "Bing"s has produced this final image:

> Bing peut-être pas seul une seconde deux secondes avec image même temps un peu moins œil noir et blanc mi-clos cils implorant ça de mémoire de loin en loin.

But the tormentor, "Bing", can do no more with fading realities than stimulate two further murmurs which are qualified deliberately by the insertion of *sans image,* until the final sentence when the "final murmur" is stimulated, an ironic image nonetheless, even though the text has prevented it from being a climax and has tried to smother it. The text still manages to present the final image in such a way that it will allow itself to achieve some kind of completion, to be "achevé", and will allow both the tormentor and tormented to rest in peace. We cannot, as human readers, but be moved by this image, conspicuous among so much dessicated and uncaring presentation of the last conditions of the last creature, and we are left with the unresolved image of human suffering pleading for recognition, for relief, and the painful realisation of the impossibility of any such relief:

> Boule blanche unie bien haute dans l'axe yeux fixe devant vieux bing murmure dernier peut-être pas seul une seconde deux secondes avec image même temps un peu moins œil embu noir et blanc mi-clos long [sic] cils importants bing silence hop achevé.

This time, alarmingly, the eye is "embu" and in a process of decline. Its state is "clouded" (though *Ping* translates it as "unlustrous"), but in this text with its diction being kept normally as distant from emotions as possible, apparently, "embu" has a sudden surge of power which it might never have in a less impoverished context. The word, when used of a painting, would mean "flat or dull" (from *emboire*, "to smear or coat with grease, with wax"), but eyes could well expect to have a different modifier, *embué* (from *embuer*, "to dim, cloud—of a glass, etc.").[8] Then we should have "yeux embués de larmes", "eyes dimmed with tears", a much more pathetic image, of course. It is hard not to feel, when reading the text, that there is a tug towards *embué* in *embu,* as we import some of the pathos and heightened emotional charge illegally into this image, occurring as it does in a work so apparently emptied of the human, so seemingly unresponsive to suffering, and yet which includes the unemphasised but genuinely present buffets and blows represented by "Paf", "Hop" and "Bing". Yet the text has found its ending, and no amount of prompting from "hop" can do other than produce the "completed" of "achevé" ("all over"). *Consummatum est,* we might say, irreverently, had not Beckett himself been beforehand with the blasphemy by the opening of *Endgame* with Clov's "Finished, it's finished, nearly finished, it must be nearly finished". But here it is as though there had been a point to this narration all along, but what the point would be would not be known until it was stumbled on, but too late to exploit or explore or put better. Just faithfully trying, in weariness and with failing capacities both of mind and language, to chart the final moments of the final creature, yields the unexpected and unplanned final release.

However, this is no comfort, no consoling moment. We have returned to the condition of light, absolute white, utterly unqualified white (Shelley's "white radiance of eternity", perhaps, without the "stains", perhaps), that condition of the divinely created first stage in the Genesis post-void creation of the universe. We have not achieved the complete and final reversal; we have not returned to the void:

> And the earth was without form, and void; and darkness was upon the face of the deep. And the spirit of God moved upon the face of the waters.

> And God said, Let there be light: and there was light.

In Beckett's text all returns to or goes into the blank uniformity of white light, the created which is now the uncreating, almost as in a parody of creation as uncreation, as in Pope's ending of *The Dunciad.* There Pope had savagely parodied Genesis in his attempt to signal what he saw as the death of civilization and culture in his time:

> Lo! thy dread Empire, CHAOS, is restor'd;
> Light dies before thy uncreating word:
> Thy hand, great Anarch! lets the curtain fall;
> And Universal Darkness buries All.

> (Book IV, 653 - 6.)

Notes

1. David Lodge, "Some Ping Understood", in *The Novelist at the Crossroads and Other Essays on Fiction and Criticism,* London, Routledge & Kegan Paul, 1971, 172-183.

2. "Variants in the Works of Samuel Beckett with Special Reference to *Bing*", in *Samuel Beckett: His Works and His Critics: An Essay in Bibliography,* University of California Press, 1970, 325-343.

3. "Tal Coat", *Proust & 3 Dialogues with Georges Duthuit,* London, John Calder, 1965, 103. First published in *Transition,* '49, no. 5.

4. ". . . la perte sèche par tête de pipe depuis la mort de Voltaire étant de l'ordre de deux doigts cent grammes par tête de pipe environ en moyenne à peu près chiffres ronds bon poids . . ." is the French original.

We must remember, too, in addition to the many measurements in the *Bing* drafts, the many instances of computation and approximation in his writing, his fascination with mathematics in general (witnessed by so many of the doodles on his manuscripts, for example), his cultivation of "irrational numbers", π especially, and the expressed view in *Murphy* of life as "a matrix of surds".

5. A famous instance of this would be Lucky being made to "think" in *Waiting for Godot,* and we should also think of the reported training sessions with Pim instructing him how to respond to the stimuli inflicted with a tin-opener in *How It Is,* teaching him the arts of communication by torment:

> with the handle of the opener as with a pestle bang on the right handier than the other from where I lie cry thump on skull silence brief rest jab in arse unintellible murmur bang on kidney signifying louder once for all cry thump on skull silence brief rest

> (*How It Is,* London, Calder & Boyars, 1964, 75.)

6. An idea from Schopenhauer, no doubt, but occurring in many places, for instance in Strindberg's memories of his schooldays:

> It was regarded as a preparation for hell and not for life; the teachers seemed to exist in order to torment, not to punish. All life weighed like an oppressive nightmare, in which it was of no avail to have known one's lessons when one left home. Life was a place for punishing crimes committed before one was born, and therefore the child walked about with a permanently bad conscience.

> (Quoted in L. Lind-Af-Hageby, *August Strindberg: The Spirit of Revolt: Studies and Impressions,* London, Stanley Paul & Co., 1913, 28.)

7. "Typescript matter in the original is printed here in normal roman characters; manuscript additions are printed in italics. Matter struck through is en-

closed within square brackets, and, where this is illegible, a series of x's gives some guidance as to the extent of the erasure." (Federman and Fletcher, 324.)

8. This image is perhaps somewhere in the background to Beckett's last, moving poem recorded for *The Great Book of Ireland,* and written out three weeks before his death in December, 1989:

Redeem the surrogate goodbyes
who have no more for the land
the sheet astream in your hand
and the glass unmisted above your eyes.

Robert Cochran (essay date 1991)

SOURCE: Cochran, Robert. "The Short Fiction." In *Samuel Beckett: A Study of the Short Fiction,* pp. 3-20. New York: Twayne Publishers, 1991.

[*In the following excerpt, Cochran surveys Beckett's early short fiction, including his short story collection* More Pricks than Kicks.]

"ASSUMPTION"

Samuel Beckett was 23, a scholar in the making recently arrived in Paris as *lecteur* at the École Normale Supérieure, when his first published study appeared in the spring of 1929. An auspicious debut, it was the lead essay in the imposingly titled *Our Exagmination Round His Factification for Incamination of Work in Progress,* a collection of essays in promotion and defense of what became *Finnegans Wake.* The young Beckett's work was titled "Dante . . . Bruno. Vico.. Joyce," and it was soon printed separately in the literary journal *transition,* along with another effort by the author. This other was no learned article, however, but a short story. Titled **"Assumption,"** it was brief, running only four pages in print, and riddled with typos. It opened as in retrospect it needed to open, as if art imitated criticism, in brazen contradiction: "He could have shouted and could not."[1] Later, in more famous formulations, this trick will seem a badge of the author's presence, so much so that one instance will be a title, *Imagination Dead Imagine,* and a sampler of his work will utilize another, *I Can't Go On I'll Go On,* for its title.

"Assumption" centers its attention on a doomed figure, an adept of silence who is "partly artist" (269) by virtue of his "remarkable faculty of whispering the turmoil down" (268), but who is also, and fatally, partly man by virtue of a "wild rebellious surge that aspired violently toward realization in sound" (269). The most rigorous self-control has been necessary, and a terrible price has been exacted: "He felt he was losing, playing into the hands of the enemy by the very severity of his restric-

tions" (269-70). Not only will the unruly urge not subside—"He felt its implacable caged resentment, its longing to be released"—he is not even sure he wants it to: "he felt compassion as well as fear; he dreaded lest his prisoner should escape, he longed that it might escape; it tore at his throat and he choked it back in dread and sorrow" (269). Perhaps this incertitude is responsible for his status as less than wholly artist, as if the artist as artist can only exist in a relationship of hostility to the artist as man or woman.

This, then, is the troubled situation at the story's opening, and also at the story's midpoint, for action, here, has taken a definite backseat to description. But action there is, finally, in the classic sense. Even for this Adam there is an Eve, identified here merely as "the Woman," who intrudes one evening at dusk, speaking: "It was the usual story, vulgarly told: admiration for his genius, sympathy with his suffering, only a woman could understand" (270). The isolato's first reaction is fury, but soon he is "struck in spite of himself by the extraordinary pallor of her lips" (270). Other, similar attractions are described, including "a close-fitting hat of faded green felt" (270). The total ensemble rouses the until recently immured semiartist to something like oxymoron: "he thought he had never seen such charming shabbiness" (270).

The woman stays, and returns on subsequent evenings. Her initial departure is attended by ambivalent reflections that are reported in detail: "When at last she went away he felt that something had gone out from him, something he could not spare, but still less could grudge, something of the desire to live" (270). These losses accumulate, each evening with "this woman" costing him "a part of his essential animality" (270), and thus hastening the day when the "implacable caged resentment" (269) within will overwhelm him.

The end, apparently, for the prose here is at once turgid and oblique, a strange mélange, arrives in two stages. The first seems to be sexual: "Until at last, for the first time, he was unconditioned by the Satanic dimensional Trinity, he was released, achieved [*sic*] the blue flower, Vega, GOD." It sounds glorious, but the morning after is a very different matter: "he found himself in his room, spent with ecstasy, torn by the bitter loathing of that which he had condemned to the humanity of silence" (271). This cycle, too, is repeated, so that "each night he died and was God, each night revived and was torn, torn and battered with increasing grievousness" (271).

They could not go on like this, that is clear enough, and stage two of the end arrives in the penultimate paragraph. The woman is looking at "the face that she had overlaid with death" when suddenly "she was swept aside by a great storm of sound," a "triumphant" cry that shook the house, "climbing in a dizzy, bubbling scale, until, dispersed, it fused into the breath of the forest and the throbbing cry of the sea." The final paragraph, after all this rattle and purple, caps the story nicely: "They found her caressing his wild dead hair" (271).

Given some experience with Beckett's later, better known work, it is possible to discern recurrent elements here receiving early exercise. An isolated central character divided against himself and devoted to the "imposition of silence" understood as a specifically artistic feat, a figure "partly artist," partly misogynist, and almost wholly self-absorbed, a deliberately rudimentary "plot" hardly deserving of the word—such features appear again and again in his work. But **"Assumption"** does not prefigure this later work by any unmistakable sign. It is in every way a young man's story, a young artist's story, a young intellectual's story, brimming with suffering and apotheosis and determinedly transcendent sexuality.

More Pricks than Kicks

Beckett published two stories and one "prose fragment" in 1932. The latter and one of the former are extracts from the unfinished, never published novel *Dream of Fair to Middling Women,* and the other story is an early version of **"Dante and the Lobster,"** which in 1934 would open his first collection of stories, ***More Pricks than Kicks.* "Dante and the Lobster"** was followed there by nine others, connected each to the other in several ways. All share, for example, their central character, one Belacqua Shuah, who gets his surname from the Bible and his cognomen from Dante's *Purgatorio,* and their physical setting, Dublin and environs. Temporally, they are arranged in sequence, leading from the death of a lobster to the death of the hero, with many deaths in between. Tonally, they are united by a highly self-conscious, allusive style—arch, aggressive, comic.

The stories are mostly comic, in a manner that begins to seem recognizably the author's. "He was telling a funny story about a fiasco" says the narrator of a later story, but the reference to the stories of ***More Pricks than Kicks*** is precise.[2] They are stories about fiascos—deaths and dismemberments are everywhere in them—and they are very funny. Things begin promptly in **"Dante and the Lobster"** with the hero, Belacqua, "bogged" in his reading of the opening cantos of the *Paradiso.*[3] Specifically, he cannot follow Beatrice's explanation of moon spots to Dante the pilgrim, and his efforts to do so bear so little fruit that noon, with its call to other duties, comes to him as a relief from this "quodlibet" (a philosophical or theological disputation).

Three obligations organize the remainder of Belacqua's day: "First lunch, then the lobster, then the Italian lesson" (*MPTK,* [*More Pricks than Kicks*] 10). Lunch,

first in line, is presented as a delicate affair, fraught with perils. Many things can go wrong, and if they do, "he might just as well not eat at all, for the food would turn to bitterness on his palate" (*MPTK,* 10). In the first place, he must not be disturbed by any "brisk tattler" bearing either "a big idea or a petition" (*MPTK,* 10); in the second place the bread for his sandwich must be properly toasted, for if there was "one thing he abominated more than another it was to feel his teeth meet in a bathos of pith and dough" (*MPTK,* 11); and in the third place the cheese for the sandwich, to be called for on the way to the "lowly public where he was expected, in the sense that the entry of his grotesque person would provoke no comment or laughter" (*MPTK,* 15), must be not just any cheese but "a good green stenching rotten lump of Gorgonzola cheese" (*MPTK,* 14).

But in the matter of lunch, unlike the matter of Dante's moon spots, Belacqua is successful. He avoids disastrous encounters, with their accompanying "conversational nuisance" (*MPTK,* 13), and the sandwich, cheese, toast, and appropriate spices, no butter, is perfection itself: "his teeth and jaws had been in heaven, splinters of vanquished toast spraying forth at each gnash. It was like eating glass. His mouth burned and ached with the exploit." The lunch, obligation number one, is such a success that "it would abide as a standard in his mind" (*MPTK,* 17). He moves on to obligation number two, the lobster, where other dangers threaten. His "lousy old bitch of an aunt" may not have placed her order in time; the fishmonger may delay him by failing to have the lobster ready. "God damn these tradesmen," Belacqua thinks, "you can never rely on them" (*MPTK,* 16).

But here, again, he is pleasantly surprised—"The lobster was ready after all, the man handed it over instanter"—and he proceeds to obligation number three, the Italian lesson, "quite happy, for all had gone swimmingly" (*MPTK* 17). Of this obligation he has no fears, only eager anticipations. His teacher, Signorina Adriana Ottolenghi, is "so charming and remarkable" that Belacqua has "set her on a pedestal in his mind, apart from other women" (*MPTK,* 16). He is eager to impress her, to "frame a shining phrase" (*MPTK,* 16) in Italian for her, to don "an expression of profundity" in responding to her suggestion that he "might do worse than make up Dante's rare movements of compassion in Hell" (*MPTK,* 19). But these gestures, one begins to notice, are superficial, mere phrases and expressions, far from the heart of the matter, which has to do with "movements of compassion." For in fact Belacqua responds to the Ottolenghi's suggestion with an incomprehension only exacerbated by his "expression of profundity," quoting what he calls a "superb pun" from the *Inferno*'s twentieth canto: *"qui vive la pieta quando e ben morta"* (here pity/piety lives when it is thoroughly/better dead). This gem, of course, has no relation whatever to any of "Dante's rare movements of compassion in hell." Belacqua, busy with his phrases and expressions, preening in the rigged mirror of his mind, has clearly not heard the Ottolenghi. She has tried to teach him, even to teach him more than Italian, but without success, as her response to his citation makes clear:

> She said nothing.
>
> "Is it not a great phrase?" he gushed.
>
> She said nothing.
>
> "Now" he said like a fool "I wonder how you could translate that?"
>
> Still she said nothing.
>
> (*MPTK,* 19)

But Belacqua, poor student, is not the Ottolenghi's only auditor, fortunately, since her suggestion is preserved in Beckett's story, and, in fact, broaches that story's major theme. Readers, here as so often in fiction, drama, and poetry, have the opportunity to be superior to the hero. In the story's title, Dante shares top billing with a lobster, already introduced as delivered fresh and on time to the happy Belacqua on his way from lunch to lesson. In the story's final episode, Belacqua brings the lobster to his aunt, only to be shocked to learn that it is still alive and that lobsters are customarily so when cooked. "Have sense," says his no-nonsense aunt, "lobsters are always boiled alive. They must be" (*MPTK,* 22).

The title now makes sense, and the Ottolenghi's lesson deepens. From Dante's moon spots to the lobster in the pot, from the story's beginning to the story's end, the message is the same. The moon with its spots was Cain, "seared with the first stigma of God's pity, that an outcast might not die quickly" (*MPTK,* 12). The lobster does not die quickly either. Belacqua, seeing it "exposed cruciform on the oilcloth" in preparation for the boiling water, consoles himself: "Well, . . . it's a quick death, God help us all." This easy shuffle, however, equally available to all eager to distance themselves from the suffering of others, is emphatically rejected in the story's last, stark line: "It is not" (*MPTK,* 22).

A quick death—its desirability is a hoary theme, found in Sophocles. Beckett will make its unavailability a cornerstone of his work. In *Waiting for Godot,* for example, Estragon appalls fellow tramp Vladimir by judging his own misfortunes as greater than Christ's. Not only did the latter live in a warm, dry climate, but in that climate "they crucified quick."[4] This advantage is not available in **"Dante and the Lobster,"** not to Cain, not to the lobster, not to the condemned murderer McCabe, the rejection of whose petition for mercy was news that "further spiced" (*MPTK,* 17) Belacqua's lunch, and not to Signorina Adriana Ottolenghi, either, whose final line in the story is a bitter, deep response to Belacqua's casual question, following an interruption:

> "Where were we?" said Belacqua
>
> But Neapolitan patience has its limits.
>
> "Where are we ever?" cried the Ottolenghi "where we were, as we were."
>
> (*MPTK,* 20)

Where we are, ever, in this story, and in the world Beckett will establish with increasing authority from here on out, is a purgatory verging on hell, a place of more pricks than kicks. This, then, is the basic situation, the given, a world chock-full of suffering and decline, slow decline. When Belacqua returns home to his aunt, she is busy in the garden, "tending whatever flowers die at that time of year" (*MPTK,* 21). She embraces him, and "together they went down into the bowels of the earth, into the kitchen in the basement" (*MPTK,* 21). This is not especially oblique. Even the bread used in preparation of Belacqua's lunch at the beginning of the story is subjected to a slow death. Before toasting, the bread is "spongy and warm, alive." Knowing that toasting "must not on any account be done too rapidly," lest "you only charred the outside and left the pith as sodden as before" (*MPTK,* 11), Belacqua lowers the flame and by his patience produces the desired result, "done to a dead end, black and smoking" (*MPTK,* 12).

In such a world, and to its denizens, various attitudes are possible. The Ottolenghi, against the grain, counsels compassion, and her student, though he misses the lesson, is provoked to introspection by her despairing cry. On his homeward walk, he ponders her words: "Where we were . . . Why not pity and piety both, even down below? Why not mercy and Godliness together? A little mercy in the stress of sacrifice, a little mercy to rejoice against judgment" (*MPTK,* 21). But Belacqua is not ready for such wisdom. Here, as in other stories, he is the receiver of compassion, not the giver, and his aunt is right to scorn his squeamishness. "You make a fuss," she says, "and upset me and then lash into it for your dinner" (*MPTK,* 22). No, the "shining phrase" and the "expression of profundity" are the summits of Belacqua's attainment. The shining action, profundity itself, the true phrase that does not shine—these come (when they come) from others, from the Ottolenghi or the aunt, who appears to provide for Belacqua even as she apparently receives poor gratitude from her nephew, or even from the tradesman (whose "little family grocery" [*MPTK,* 13] supplies Belacqua with his Gorgonzola) who "felt sympathy and pity for this queer customer who always looked ill and dejected" (*MPTK,* 15).

Other stories follow a similar pattern. In **"Fingal,"** the second story, Belacqua concludes a country excursion by abandoning his girlfriend of the moment, Winnie Coates, and fleeing to a pub on a stolen bicycle. The story is memorable for the bicycle, since bicycles fascinate many of Beckett's protagonists, for its introduction of the Portrane Lunatic Asylum as part of the landscape (Belacqua, as he points it out, tells Winnie his heart lives there) since asylums and their inmates reappear even more often than bicycles, and perhaps most of all for one moment between Winnie and Belacqua when she extends to him a compassion that, being unearned, must come as a kind of secular grace.

Learning that a rash on his face is in fact impetigo, Winnie is angered that he has nevertheless kissed her. He offers the excuse of passion, recognizing it as lame:

> "I forgot" he said. "I get so excited you know."
>
> She spittled on her handkerchief and wiped her mouth. Belacqua lay humbly beside her, expecting her to get up and leave him. But instead she said:
>
> "What is it anyway? What does it come from?"
>
> "Dirt" said Belacqua, "you see it on slum children."
>
> A long awkward silence followed these words.
>
> "Don't pick it darling" she said unexpectedly at last, "you'll make it worse."
>
> This came to Belacqua like a drink of water to drink in a dungeon. Her goodwill must have meant something to him.
>
> (*MPTK,* 24-25)

It did mean something, perhaps, but not enough to keep him from abandoning Winnie later when the bicycle beckoned.

"Ding-Dong," the collection's third story, features a first-person narrator who identifies himself as Belacqua's former close friend. Following an opening disquisition on Belacqua's devotion to peripeteia—"He was pleased to think that he could give what he called the Furies the slip by merely setting himself in motion" (*MPTK,* 36)—the story is told of an evening made memorable by his purchase, while seated in a pub, of four seats in heaven from "a woman of very remarkable presence" (*MPTK,* 44). This strange event seems consciously to echo *The Tempest,* whence comes also the title, perhaps, from Ariel's song, with Belacqua as the charmed Ferdinand. Certainly the story's close, in which Belacqua "tarried a little to listen to the music" (*MPTK,* 46), encourages the parallel. **"Ding-Dong"** seems a lighter, even a warmer story than its two predecessors, though here, too, there are crucifixions both fast and slow. Among these are the "trituration" (*MPTK,* 43) of a little girl by a bus and the evening departure of "the blind paralytic who sat all day" (*MPTK,* 39) in his wheelchair, begging alms with the aid of a "placard announcing his distress" (*MPTK,* 40). But the story ends with the woman of "remarkable presence," her countenance "full of light" and bearing "no trace of suffering." From others she had "met with more rebuffs than pence" (*MPTK,* 44), but Belacqua for once responds

positively. Perhaps it is significant, too, that his self-centeredness, here called "Ego Maximus, little me" (*MPTK,* 39), is so far moderated that his purchases are on behalf of others—friend, father, mother, mistress—rather than for himself.

"A Wet Night," next in the collection and one of two salvaged more or less directly from *Dream of Fair to Middling Women,* is one of the volume's longest (only **"What a Misfortune"** is comparable). Its central event is a holiday party, "claret cup and intelligentsia," attended by, among others, Belacqua, late and in sad disrepair, and, arriving earlier, his "current one and only" (*MPTK,* 51), Alba Perdue. The party gathers under one roof a diverse collection of Dublin's poseurs and failures, and all—except the Alba, queen of this and any likely ball—are treated with the narrator's contempt. The hostess, for example, Caleken Frica, first described as a "throttled gazelle," possesses a face "beyond appeal, a flagrant seat of injury," and resembles at last nothing so much as a "martyress in rut" (*MPTK,* 61). Her party, attended by many in the hope of free eats and drinks, and these are disappointed by the meagre spread, soon degenerates into a "sinister kiss-me-Charley hugger-mugger" that "spread like wildfire throughout the building, till it raged from attic to basement" (*MPTK,* 76). Alba, however, holds herself apart from all this.

Meanwhile, Belacqua, moving unsteadily from pub to party in a bitter rain, suddenly feels "white and clammy" (*MPTK,* 70) and leans against a wall. Soon he is accosted by a policeman, only to embarrass himself and anger the lawman by throwing up, "with undemonstrative abundance, all over the boots and trouser-ends of the Guard," who promptly knocks him down "into the outskirts of his own offal" (*MPTK,* 71). Beckett, in passages like this, is finding his voice.

At last Belacqua reaches the party, where "the Alba thought she had never seen anybody, man or woman, look quite such a sovereign booby" (*MPTK,* 78). This is saying something, given the present company, but it does not stop her next movement, any more than his impetigo had earlier stopped Winnie's:

> In an unsubduable movement of misericord the Alba started out of her chair.
>
> "Nino" she called, without shame or ceremony.
>
> The distant call came to Belacqua like a pint of Perrier to drink in a dungeon.
>
> (*MPTK,* 78)

"A Wet Night," as several critics have pointed out, is on one level an obvious parody of Joyce's famous *Dubliners* story "The Dead," which it echoes in both structure and detail. But the reference—this is important—is not so much a gesture of homage as a comic declaration of independence. The new man, it says, will be doing things differently. Consider the most obvious instance, the echo of Joyce's famous closing description of the "softly falling" snow that is "general all over Ireland," falling "faintly through the universe . . . like the descent of their last end, upon all the living and the dead."⁵ **"A Wet Night"** features rain instead, and it falls not softly but with "a rather desolate uniformity," and not upon the whole universe of the quick and dead but "upon the bay, the littoral, the mountains and the plains, and notably upon the Central Bog" (*MPTK,* 83). What is more, as if the cool, almost meteorological note introduced by "littoral," "uniformity," and "notably" did not sufficiently undercut the lyricism of the original, Beckett makes sure to deprive the passage of the dignity conferred by closure. The last word is given, instead, to Belacqua's early morning departure from the Alba's home, a less than dignified exit in which he throws away his boots—years later, in *Waiting for Godot,* Estragon will also struggle with boots—and is for the second time ordered to move on by a policeman.

"A Wet Night" is notable also for its praise of silence, given as a clinching general question following a relentless savaging, complete with instances of awful conversation, of the Frica's party. "Who shall silence them, at last?" the narrator wants to know; "Who shall circumcise their lips from speaking, at last?" (*MPTK,* 79). Good question, and Beckett has made it his own, has made it of himself, in a tone hovering exactly between assertion and despair.

"Love and Lethe," story number five, is built like **"Ding-Dong"** on a foolish act that ends in music. Belacqua and yet another lady in his life, this one named Ruby Tough (she is mentioned before her time, in violation of all the norms of sequence and without the slightest apology, in **"A Wet Night"**), agree to a dual suicide and make careful plans. In this purpose, of course, Belacqua is the instigator, and he "cultivated Ruby" as he cultivates the others, as one cultivates a garden for its calories, "for the part she was to play on his behalf" (*MPTK,* 89). But he is richly supplied with reasons; Belacqua lacks many things but reasons he has aplenty—in this instance "Greek and Roman reasons, Sturm und Drang reasons, reasons metaphysical, aesthetic, erotic, anterotic and chemical, Empedocles of Agrigentum and John of the Cross reasons" (*MPTK,* 90). All of these are false, but Ruby, "flattened by this torrent of incentive" (*MPTK,* 90), agrees anyway, secure in her possession of "an incurable disorder" (*MPTK,* 89) and sensing in Belacqua's silly plan "a chance to end with a fairly beautiful bang" (*MPTK,* 90).

But the plan goes awry, as plans do, especially plans on these pages. The "swagger sports roadster, chartered at untold gold by the hour" (*MPTK,* 90), the aged whis-

key purchased "on tick" (*MPTK,* 96), the revolver, ammunition, and poison, all these are squandered to rather more usual ends when "the revolver went off, harmlessly luckily, and the bullet fell *in terram* nobody knows where" (*MPTK,* 99). Instead of dying gloriously under the motto "TEMPORARILY SANE" (*MPTK,* 97) lettered on an old license plate, the would-be self-slaughterers "came together in inevitable nuptial" as the delicate narrator moves "away on tiptoe" (*MPTK,* 99), ending his story in benediction: "May their night be full of music at all events" (*MPTK,* 100). This same narrator recurs more frequently than his predecessors to direct asides, if such things are possible, to the reader. Sometimes these provide helpful information: "Reader, a rosiner is a drop of the hard" (*MPTK,* 86), or, "Reader, a gloria is coffee laced with brandy" (*MPTK,* 87). Sometimes they urge the adequacy of explanations already tendered to the needs of "even the most captious reader" (*MPTK,* 89).

Story number six, **"Walking Out,"** is most memorable for the tramp already extolled, the "real man at last" whose gentle "smile proof against all adversity" (*MPTK,* 104) so abashes the "wretched bourgeois" (*MPTK,* 103) Belacqua. But this is mere interlude in a rush of events "One fateful fine Spring evening" (*MPTK,* 101) that leave that paltry hero beaten and his latest girl Lucy crippled. The beating, a "brutal verberation" (*MPTK,* 113) richly deserved, is administered by an "infuriated Tanzherr" (*MPTK,* 112) on behalf of himself and his "pretty little German girl" (*MPTK,* 109). The walk of the title is at least in part a voyeur's reconnaissance; Belacqua, as Lucy's "horrible diagnosis" (*MPTK,* 109) has only just this same evening made clear, is a "creepy-crawly" (*MPTK,* 108), a "trite spite of the vilest description." The crippling, undeserved, is administered by "a superb silent limousine, a Daimler no doubt, driven by a drunken lord" (*MPTK,* 110), which runs down Lucy, a devoted equestrienne, and her "magnificent jennet" (*MPTK,* 104), as she rides, her mind a court for "cruel battledore" (*MPTK,* 110) between the image of the old Belacqua, loved, and the new, despicable, to the place of their scheduled rendezvous.

Neither arrives, Lucy because of the lord in his Daimler, Belacqua because of the "brutal verberation" of the Tanzherr. But the ending, at least of this story, is all Pippa Passes and Pangloss, since "now he is happily married to Lucy and the question of cicisbei does not arise" (*MPTK,* 113). The question had arisen earlier only at Belacqua's insistence—he had urged her to infidelity on his behalf, even prior to matrimony, just as he had earlier urged Ruby to share his suicide. He knows no other behalf, it seems. These recondite terms, rare even in dictionaries, culled from Latin, Italian, German, "battledore" (Oriental game, source of badminton), "verberation" (lashing with a rod or stick), "cicisbi" (lovers of a married woman or women) and the like—do not worry, reader, they will soon abate.

"What a Misfortune," announcing Lucy's death in its first paragraph, speedily introduces another love (the term is used loosely, as is customary), Thelma bboggs. She is the fifth, after Winnie, Alba, Ruby, and Lucy (the Ottolenghi does not count). Thelma and Belacqua also marry; the preparations for this event occupy the greater part of the story. The parents of the bride, Mr. and Mrs. Otto Olaf bboggs, her sister, Una, "for whom an ape had already been set aside in hell: (*MPTK,* 118), the lover of the bride's mother, Walter Draffin, the groom's best man, Capper Quin, known as Hairy on account of his baldness, the remainder of the groom's entourage, two "deadbeats" (*MPTK,* 128) named Jimmy the Duck Skyrm, "an aged cretin," and Hermione Nautzsche, "a powerfully built nymphomaniac" (*MPTK,* 138)—all these and still more make up the cast of this funniest (and, with **"A Wet Night,"** the longest) story in this funny collection.

And also it's most horrifying—the gentle humor of **"Ding-Dong"** and **"Love and Lethe"** are replaced here with something much more harsh. The "misfortune" of the title refers, among other things, to the story's central event, a wedding. To Belacqua, at the moment of falsehood (he is marrying Thelma for her "promissory wad" [*MPTK,* 116]), the church itself is a "cruciform cage, the bulldogs of heaven holding the chancel, the procession about to give tongue in the porch, the transepts cul de sac" (*MPTK,* 138). Except for **"Dear Otto Olaf"** (*MPTK,* 123), whose gratitude to Walter Draffin for years of service earns him the narrator's respect and sympathy, the story's major characters come in for scathing contempt. Here, for example, is Una, Thelma's older sister: "Think of holy Juliana of Norwich, to her aspect add a dash of souring, to her tissue half a hundredweight of adipose, abstract the charity and prayers, spray in vain with opopanax and assafoetida, and behold a radiant Una" (*MPTK,* 121). Disaster reigns, from large event to small. Thelma dies on her honeymoon, and a nameless car park attendant sustains a broken arm attempting to assist Capper Quin with the borrowed honeymoon car. Alba Perdue, not seen since **"A Wet Night,"** is enlisted as a bridesmaid—an act of deliberate cruelty protested only by Otto Olaf and compounded by her subsequent pairing with Draffin. This is, indeed, a funny, sad story about a fiasco, and this yoking begins to seem increasingly central to Beckett's design. This story, more than the others, begins to resemble the deceptive offering of Prometheus, in Hesiod's *Theogony,* where bare bones are concealed beneath an alluring surface of choice cuts. Under its lavish and exaggerated language, **"What a Misfortune,"** in grotesque characters like Skyrm and Nautzsche, for example, begins to offer that scorched and diminished earth later made fa-

mous in *Godot* and *Endgame.* The title, an allusion to Voltaire, is a phrase much loved by the author—he had used it before, in Italian, in a poem, and would use it later, in French, in *Malone Dies.*[6]

The next story, number eight, **"The Smeraldina's Billet Doux,"** is the volume's least impressive and its briefest. It came, like **"A Wet Night,"** from *Dream of Fair to Middling Women,* and before that apparently from a personal letter, the use of which was reportedly resented by the sender's family. (There exists, unfortunately, a biography of Beckett whose author meant the subject no good; she discusses this matter in a shocked, eager tone and in highly speculative detail, asserting, for example, the "verbatim" use of a letter not itself cited.[7] But this sort of thing can only increase one's sympathy for the Tanzherr of **"Walking Out."** Certainly no one should be encouraged to read the letter—or **"The Smeraldina's Billet Doux,"** for that matter.) It is, as the title suggests, a letter, addressed to Belacqua and written in a mad misspelled sludge of English and German, rich in exclamation, capitalization, and other excesses. The content is simple: the Smeraldina describes her activities and her loneliness, recommends films, and tells Belacqua repeatedly and insistently that she craves his body. Bad news, this, to the Belacqua who considered the crippled Lucy a perfect mate, but prior to her injury considered her so dangerous that he repeatedly urged her to "establish their married life" on what he called the "solid basis" (*MPTK,* 103) of cuckoldry. A similar attitude is one of Otto Olaf's wisdoms, too, in **"What a Misfortune."** Olaf's horns "sat easily upon him," and he feels nothing but gratitude to Walter Draffin: "Any man who saved him trouble, as Walter had for so many years, could rely on his esteem" (*MPTK,* 120). For a man like Belacqua, the Smeraldina is far too robust, and surely he regarded himself fortunate to have her in Germany, where space could serve the present as injury had served the past.

The two final stories, **"Yellow"** and **"Draff,"** deal, respectively, with Belacqua's death and burial. The death is by medical misadventure and follows immediately upon the physician's confident self-evaluation, while the burial is by none other than the Smeraldina, now Mrs. Shuah number three, assisted by none other than Capper Quin, the best man of **"What a Misfortune,"** now reduced to successor, after the manner of Walter Draffin.

"Yellow" is devoted mostly to Belacqua's hospital meditations, his search for mental equipoise in a time of stress. He is in for operations on nape and toe, amputations both, and he is frightened: "At twelve sharp he would be sliced open—zeep!—with a bistoury. This was the idea his mind for the moment was in no fit state to entertain" (*MPTK,* 159). In his distress, a paradox from Donne, heaven-sent, reminds him at once of

Heraclitus and Democritus, and these in turn provide him with two potential aids. "Was it to be laughter or tears?" (*MPTK,* 163) he asks, and at last he chooses the former, reasoning that the latter would be more open to misinterpretation, ascribed not to a considered philosophical position but "rather to the tumour the size of a brick that he had on the back of his neck" (*MPTK,* 164).

This choice once made, even undermined as it is by second thoughts, "the idea" can be confronted successfully. When Belacqua, like the lobster of the opening story, has only seconds to live, he is at his best: he "swaggered through the antechamber" and "bounced up on the table like a bridegroom" (*MPTK,* 174). An ominous simile, this last, in Mr. Beckett's emerging world. We know by now what happens, and soon, to brides and grooms. It is only part, though a vivid part, of a larger lesson on well-laid plans. Plan to die, says **"Love and Lethe,"** and end up with "inevitable nuptial" (*MPTK,* 99); plan a nuptial and end up dead.

"Draff" concentrates its attention not on Belacqua, who begins the story laid out with a Bible under his chin and ends it laid in a grave "upholstered" with bracken and fern, "all lush, green and most sweet smelling" (*MPTK,* 182), but on his widow, the Smeraldina, who has lost all trace of the German accents so pronounced in **"The Smeraldina's Billet Doux."** Things end as they began, with references to Dante prominent, though a definite turn for the worse is indicated by their tenor. Where **"Dante and the Lobster"** opened with Belacqua "stuck in the first of the canti in the moon" (*MPTK,* 9), that is, however stuck, in Paradise, **"Draff"** has his corpse first measured and dressed by a Mr. Malacoda and later conveyed to its resting ground by a driver named Scarmiglione.

But here, as in Dante, commedia prevails. The Smeraldina soon has Capper Quin in tow, Belacqua himself is laid to rest in the "loveliest little lap of earth you ever saw" (*MPTK,* 182), and the cemetery groundskeeper, who gets the book's last scene, is contented: "He sang a little song, he drank his bottle of stout, he dashed away a tear, he made himself comfortable" (*MPTK,* 191). Even Belacqua's house, which is set ablaze by the gardener during his funeral, turns out to be insured. An obnoxious Parson is abandoned on the road after the burial, evicted from the car by Quin, and the servant Mary Ann is raped by the pyromaniac gardener, but these are small matters, that are given short shrift in the story's economy. "Little remains to be told," says the narrator, moving to wrap things up: "On their return they found the house in flames, the home to which Belacqua had brought three brides a raging furnace. It transpired that during their absence something had snapped in the brain of the gardener, who had ravished the servant girl and then set the premises on fire" (*MPTK,* 189).

It is, of course, a part of the story's harsh comedy to undercut such melodrama by so offhanded an introduction, presenting it as the draff of **"Draff."** ("Draff" is dregs, slop for hogs, lees, what is left of malt after brewing, garbage.) The reader, shocked by a narrator not so much unreliable, though he is that, as unfeeling, may think back to other matters judged too "little" to be told at all. What happens, for example, to the aunt who provided shelter and dinner in **"Dante and the Lobster"**? Or to the Ottolenghi? Or to Alba Perdue, perhaps aptly named, who after disappearing with Walter Draffin in **"What a Misfortune,"** is mentioned briefly as dead "in the natural course of being seen home" (*MPTK,* 175) at the beginning of **"Draff"**? This closing story is also notable for the volume's most savage image, a description of the Smeraldina and Quin embracing in shared grief, meeting for the first time after Belacqua's death. They embrace to console, widow and exbest man, but also in self interest, Wife of Bath to Jenkin, and the narrator seems to view this development with extreme distaste: "Capper Quin arrived on tiptire, in a car of his very own. He grappled with the widow, he simply could not help it. She was a sensible girl in some ways, she was not ashamed to let herself go in the arms of a man of her own weight at last. They broke away, carrot plucked from tin of grease" (*MPTK,* 179-80). Amidst his many bows to Dante, Beckett includes more than one nod to Swift's darker muse.

More Pricks than Kicks, oscillating between such varying shades, from a gentle humor praised in one review as "the profound *risolino* that does not destroy"[8] to the harsher genres characterized in *Watt* as "modes of ululation,"[9] offers two basic challenges to readers. The first is superficial, having to do with the volume's recondite, multilingual vocabulary, the youthful author wearing his learning like a sash of medals, and requires only a bank of dictionaries for its solution. (A branch of this challenge, even less important than the main trunk, has to do with the thick, if not rich, allusiveness of the young man's exuberant prose. If you have read "The Dead," recognize the Beresina as a Byelorussian river and Dr. Petrie as Flinders, archaeologist and Egyptologist, and/or can boast familiarity with the landmarks of Dublin and environs—you may applaud yourself. If you have not, do not worry. Little is lost, in your reading of these stories, and their teller, finding his own voice, his own world, will soon lighten the allusive and referential load.)

The second challenge, anyway, is more worth one's time, as it gets to the heart of not only these but later, better stories. It has to do with tone, with that tightrope along pain and pleasure, tragedy and comedy, pricks and kicks, which is even here Beckett's special métier. Already present, for instance, at the extreme of distance and frigid authority, is that impersonal voice out of the heavens, speaking in fiat and inquisition, that in the beginning rejects Belacqua's sorry bromide on the lobster's death and in the end gives similar brief shrift to his anticipated posthumous encounter with "the girls, Lucy especially, hallowed and transfigured beyond the veil. What a hope!" sneers the voice, "Death had already cured him of that naivete" (*MPTK,* 181). Subsequent works will further embody this imperious otherness—it acquires female gender in *Eh Joe* and even shifts from speaking to listening in *Not I.*

Slightly more personal but no less authoritative is the voice occasionally heard in direct address to the reader in mockery of storytelling's conventions, as, for example, in the instances already cited from **"Love and Lethe,"** or this, from **"Dante and the Lobster"**: "Let us call it Winter, that dusk may fall now and a moon rise" (*MPTK,* 20). This is also the voice of the mock-helpful, mock-learned footnotes, five in number. Finally, as noted and emphasized here by way of compensation for usual neglect, there is the very occasional voice of open and undisguised affirmation, as in the sketch of the tinker in **"Walking Out."**

Hearing these voices, learning to discount them, when and by how much, learning, too, to notice the omitted voice, the discarded character, the unstated conclusion and unspoken judgment—these are the skills to cultivate when exploring Beckett's stories. For the considerable armamentarium deployed so ostentatiously and aggressively in *More Pricks than Kicks* is radically curtailed in its successors. Before those successors, however, with their very different delights, there is one last early story to consider.

"A Case in a Thousand"

"A Case in a Thousand" appeared in the August 1934 issue of *The Bookman* and has never been reprinted. Like the earlier **"Assumption,"** it moves through a series of mostly unhappy events to an obliquely triumphant conclusion. A young doctor named Nye, identified at the beginning as "one of the sad men," is summoned for consultation by a surgeon colleague named Bor. The patient, after Bor had "operated with the utmost success," had exhibited "an unfathomable tendency to sink."[10] But here is the complication, a coincidence: the patient, a boy named Bray, is the son of Nye's "old nurse," a woman "whom as a baby and small boy he had adored" (242). And in this old relationship there was a moment that still lives, the memory of which stirs "shame" in Mrs. Bray and makes Dr. Nye's initial recognition something to be "feared" (242). A later story, **"The Expelled,"** refers in passing to a similar situation: "He gave me a woman's name that I've forgotten. Perhaps she had dandled me on her knees while I was still in swaddling clothes and there had

been some lovey-dovey. Sometimes that suffices" (*STN* [*Stories and Texts for Nothing*], 19). But this very likely has little bearing, if any, on Mrs. Bray and Dr. Nye.

The events of the present are no better. Bor will operate again only at Nye's urging, and "from the strictly pathological point of view there was as much to be urged on the one side as there was on the other" (242). Nye, therefore, is "outside the scope of his science" but obliged nonetheless to reach a decision. His procedure in this difficult situation is described at some length: "He took hold of the boy's wrist, stretched himself all along the edge of the bed and entered the kind of therapeutic trance that he reserved for such happily rare dilemmas" (242). His expression at this time, "at once aghast and rapt," is witnessed by Mrs. Bray and triggers her recollection of their previous intimacy. The "trance" results in a decision to operate again, but young Bray's lung collapses and he dies. The mother, who has watched at her son's bedside (and outside the hospital in the intervals between visiting hours) throughout his illness, offers Dr. Nye her thanks, but despite "great efforts to speak their minds," they can share only "silence." Nye then leaves for "a short holiday at the seaside" (242).

He is soon called back, however, by a note from Bor, who tells him Mrs. Bray is back at her stand, maintaining the same vigil she had earlier mounted on behalf of her son. He goes to see her and at last broaches the subject that matters: "There's something I've been wanting to ask you." She answers, "I wonder would that be the same thing I've been wanting to tell you ever since that time you stretched out on his bed." (242). It is, of course, and when he replies only by asking if she can "go on," that bedrock question, she relates "a matter connected with his earliest years, so trivial and intimate that it need not be enlarged on here, but from the elucidation of which Dr. Nye, that sad man, expected great things" (242). Unlike Nye, we do not learn what the matter is, but we do know what we need to know: that Mrs. Bray and Dr. Nye, by their persistence and courage, quite outside the scope of his science or any science, have earned their communion. The patient dies, and the doctor is cured. "Thank you very much" he says when Mrs. Bray finishes, "that was what I was wondering" (242). It is a case in a thousand, take that either way—that it is just one case of a thousand equally compelling, emphasizing its universality, or that it is a rare and unique occurrence, emphasizing its rarity, like what happened to Hamlet or Oedipus. Or take it both ways, as intended, no doubt.

Critics have mostly ignored this story, and such comment as it has elicited has focused on its possible sources in Beckett's relationship with his analyst and/or his mother.[11] This is lamentable, since **"A Case in a**

Thousand" presents its muted personae, Dr. Nye and Mrs. Bray, in a style at great remove from the "white voice" (*MPTK,* 148) and "shining phrase" (*MPTK,* 16) of Belacqua. Silence, as a voice in Beckett's writing, is ascending its footstool. In his sympathy with such creatures, with their tendency to stasis and vigil, their stammering difficulty in the attempt to "speak their minds" (242), he is finding a way to speak his own mind, or perhaps merely to speak.

In the big world, however, as the 1930s end and the fledgling author gets his first novel published (*Murphy,* in 1938), a war is coming on. Beckett's life will be spared, but it will be a near miss. Close friends will perish. He will find it necessary to flee his home. All this will affect his work much as the soft bread in **"Dante and the Lobster"** is changed at Belacqua's hand: "But he would very soon take that plush feel off it, by God but he would very quickly take that fat white look off its face" (*MPTK,* 11). Beckett's next short fictions, four stories written in 1945 and 1946, are harrowed and muted far beyond anything envisioned in *More Pricks than Kicks* and give a "fat white look," indeed, to their prewar predecessors. **"A Case in a Thousand"** is a step, a modest step, in that direction.

Notes

1. "Assumption," *transition* 16-17 (1929): 268; hereafter cited in the text.

2. "The Calmative," in *Stories and Texts for Nothing* (New York: Grove Press, 1967), 29; hereafter cited in the text as *STN.*

3. *More Pricks than Kicks* (New York: Grove Press, 1972), 9; hereafter cited in the text as *MPTK.*

4. *Waiting for Godot* (New York: Grove Press, 1954), 34b; hereafter cited in the text as *G.*

5. James Joyce, *Dubliners* (New York: Penguin, 1976), 223.

6. The poem is "Che Sciagura," a juvenile effort first published in *T.C.D.,* a Trinity College weekly, in 1929. Malone, in the French original of *Malone Dies,* says "*quel malheur*" [what a misfortune] when he loses his stick. The phrase closes the eleventh chapter of *Candide,* spoken by the Eunuch before the naked Cunegonde. "*O che sciagura,*" he says, "*d'essere senza coglioni*!" (What a shame to have no balls!).

7. Deirdre Bair, *Samuel Beckett* (New York: Harcourt, Brace, Jovanovich, 1978), 146.

8. "An Imaginative Work!" review of *The Amaranthers* by Jack B. Yeats, *Dublin Magazine* 11 (1936): 80.

9. *Watt* (New York: Grove Press, 1959), 48; hereafter cited in the text as *W.*

10. "A Case in a Thousand," *The Bookman* 86 (1934): 241; hereafter cited in the text.

11. See, for example, Bair, *Samuel Beckett,* where an especially fuzzy sentence opens with the character Dr. Nye in the subject chair but substitutes the author Beckett at an indeterminate middle point to close in psychological rather than literary analysis: "Dr. Nye's fascination with Mrs. Bray as a mother-sweetheart, his longing for his childhood and the curious womblike evocation of the bizarre incident of the bed all seem to be clumsy attempts to integrate his real-life attitudes towards his mother with his fiction" (185).

Robert J. Kloss (essay date March 1992)

SOURCE: Kloss, Robert J. "The Turning Point at Last: Beckett's 'First Love' There is a Choice of Images." *Journal of Evolutionary Psychology* 13, nos. 1-2 (March 1992): 21-33.

[*In the following essay, Kloss identifies four short stories—"The End," "The Calmative," "The Expelled," and "First Love"—as the turning point in Beckett's artistic career and provides a close reading of "First Love" to gain insight into the images, themes, and characterizations that came to preoccupy Beckett.*]

In her biography of Samuel Beckett, Deirdre Bair vividly depicts a vision he had during one of his late-night, non-stop, drunken prowls that finished on the end of a Dublin jetty in the midst of a March snowstorm. Here, apparently in an epiphany, Beckett envisioned in an instant the direction his writing should take, the form it should have; he had come, in his own words, to "the turning point at last." "All his writing," Bair declares, "would henceforth begin from within himself, with his memories and dreams, no matter how ugly or painful; . . . no clearly defined fictional character would be needed to tell these stories, as no distancing is necessary between the teller and the tale."[1]

Subsequently, Beckett no longer wrote in his native English but in French and turned from traditional narrative to what has since become a distinctive feature of his style, the anguished dramatic monologue. Immediately following this revelation, during 1945-46, he produced four short stories or *nouvelles* which stylistically and thematically mark the most distinct transition in his entire career. Although he had already written novels and short stories (e.g., *Murphy, Watt,* **More Pricks than Kicks**), the four stories—**"The End," "The Calmative," "The Expelled,"** and **"First Love"**—introduce characterizations, themes, and motifs that preoccupied their author till his death.[2]

These tales are narrated by a first person speaker, who is quite forgetful. He is a derelict, a wanderer, often evicted from his lodgings for inexplicable reasons, usually seeking a haven or attempting to reach an unattainable goal. He makes no progress in these attempts, no real gain in any respect, and his life is much the same at the end of his story as at the beginning. From start to finish, the narrator has as his only possessions the words with which he tells his tales. Physically, he is disabled, diseased, afflicted grievously in one way or another; and he is under siege by a nameless "they" who expel him or evict him, persecute him, trouble him continuously. Many, if not all, of the preceding situations are in, for instance, *Molloy, Malone Dies, The Unnamable, Endgame,* and *Waiting for Godot.*

Stylistically, other changes at this time are noteworthy. Syntax, for example, remains clear, but coherence becomes problematical. Ruby Cohn has summarized the major differences: "Besides the important shift from English to French, Beckett achieves a tonal shift from the stylistic elegance of *Murphy,* or the labored exactitude of *Watt,* to a comic of the colloquial. The Bergsonian comic roster virtually disappears; learned allusion is drastically reduced; misquotation and erudite jargon vanish; so, too, do most of the monotonous repetitions, series, permutations and combinations, of *Watt.*"[3]

Further, she remarks, there is a greater concern with "the obscene, the physically disgusting," and "visceral and sexual parts and processes" (109). As Bair observes (118), however, Beckett's fascination with the expression of natural functions in literature had actually begun more than fifteen years earlier, when he read the works of Jules Renard, who wrote freely and bluntly of such matters. Scatological references, as any reader can testify, permeate Beckett's work from 1945-46. Both John Weightman and Sandra Gilbert have made much of *Krapp's Last Tape* in this regard, the former calling it "an anal work,"[4] the latter elaborating more specifically: "Krapp's compulsive hoarding of his tapes is a kind of classically Freudian anal eroticism. . . . The old man's attachment to his memories, like the artist's attachment to his art—the production of excretion of his mind—is, after all, again in Freudian terms, strikingly similar to the 'maker's attachment of a child to his stools." His constipation, Gilbert maintains, "develops in the course of the short work into a physical matter of almost metaphysical importance, a symbol . . . at once grotesque and serious. . . ."[5]

The symbolic force of such scatology operates, too, throughout the *nouvelles.* The narrator of **"The Expelled,"** for instance, relates that "I had then the deplorable habit, having pissed in my trousers, or shat there, which I did fairly regularly early in the morning, about ten or half past ten, of persisting in going on and finishing my day as if nothing had happened. The very ideas of changing my trousers, or of confiding in mother, who goodness knows asked nothing better than to help me, was unbearable, I don't know why, and till bedtime I dragged on with burning and stinking between my thighs, or sticking to my bottom, the result of my incontinence."[6] Indeed, it is to this reluctance to change trousers that he attributes his distinctive peculiar gait. His analogue, the narrator of **"The End,"** having taken refuge in a boat, at least lets down his trousers, but then lies in the waste: "To contrive a little kingdom, in the midst of the universal muck, then shit on it, ah that was me all over. The excrements were me too, I know, I know, but all the same."[7]

Thus thirteen years before Krapp, Beckett's monologists, symbolizing their relationship with humanity at large, saw themselves as feces. Indeed, the closer we look at the *nouvelles,* the more we see them as microcosms of the larger worlds yet to emerge: those of Molley, of Krapp, of Godot. G. C. Barnard has argued that the characters of Beckett's novels and plays are, fundamentally, "schizophrenic, in the accepted clinical sense of the word, or at the least are definitely schizoid types."[8] In substantiation, he cites such symptoms as their withdrawal from the outside world into inner fantasy, emotional poverty, discordant parental relationships, thought and speech disorders, and others typical of the syndrome (5-7). Unfortunately, he omits the *nouvelles* from his consideration, perhaps because they do not neatly fit the character type of the other works. They do, however, represent another character type clinically definable, the obsessive, and this syndrome, I contend, explains in large part the characters' behavior, fantasies, and preoccupation with bodily functions. Indeed, they act most like those particular obsessives whose behavior reflects derivatives of what Freud called "anal eroticism" in an essay written in 1908.[9]

The prominent characteristics of anal erotics, their orderliness, stubbornness, and miserliness, Freud inferred to be sublimations of the original sexual aims, derivatives of the conflicts often inherent in toilet training. As well as sublimations, these permanent character traits, he theorized, could alternately be perseverations of the original instincts or reaction-formations against them. Other components of the anal character are rage, defiance alternating with submission, sadomasochistic tendencies, and, because of less adequate defenses available to the child, intense ambivalence—originally expressed toward the mother in the struggle for separation, individuation, and independence.

Obsessive-compulsive behavior, which all the narrators of the *nouvelles* exhibit, results from a regression from Oedipal conflict to the anal sadistic phase and reliance upon the characteristic defenses of isolation (splitting off the idea or object from the feeling toward it), reaction-formation (turning the feeling into its opposite), and undoing (a two-part act which symbolizes first hostility, then the undoing of its feared effects). Heightened ambivalence toward the mother expresses itself in this undoing but, primarily, in the obsessive's being consumed by doubt. He is perpetually indecisive, seeking some kind of rule or principle as guidance, and, seldom finding one, leaping impulsively to some conclusion in order to gain security. His need to keep his conflicted feelings hidden, even from himself, leads to the defense of isolation and the resulting presentation of himself as a "cold" person, emotionally constricted or, as we sometimes aptly say in recognition of his conflict, "tight-assed." He is especially eager to avoid warm feelings, which he mistrusts since they originally arose in a context of dependency relations that in his experience led to conflict and fears of rejection. These fears, always imminent, lead him to become depressed frequently.

Interestingly, the obsessive uses words in order not to communicate, either flooding the listener with detail but little substance or employing reaction-formation and remaining defiantly silent. His obsessional ideas are, of course, derivatives of the original anal impulses, conflicts, and fantasies, as are the compulsive acts he feels constrained to perform. Some of the most common of these are washing rituals which replace fears of dirt and walking rituals which replace inhibitions in walking.[10] The gait of all the narrators of the *nouvelles,* is important enough for them to reflect on it. Indeed most of the images and concerns of each are virtually identical so that scrutiny of one can serve as a paradigm for scrutiny of all four.

"First Love," for example, reveals quite clearly the obsessive character of its narrator, whose adventures can be succinctly recounted. An old, unnamed man tells of his first love. He remembers visiting his father's grave ostensibly to determine the date of his own marriage from the tombstone since the two events are somehow associated in his own mind. After his father's death, he recalls, a mysterious They expel him from his house, throwing him and all his belongings into the street while he is engaged in using the outdoor toilet. He moves on and eventually shares a bench with a woman named Lulu, whom he meets there several times afterward. He goes off to the countryside to think things over, spending some time in a deserted cowshed where he comes to the conclusion that he loves Lulu or rather Anna, as he now begins to call her. He meets her again, she takes him in, and seduces him. He discovers shortly that she is a prostitute and, after some time, that she is pregnant by him. Unable to face the birth, he wanders off, a derelict again at story's end.

In the brief opening paragraph of **"First Love,"** the narrator presents himself at the outset as a typical obsessive, paralyzed by doubt, measuring human relationships with a calendar or watch rather than intensity or

variety of feelings: "I associate, rightly or wrongly, my marriage with the death of my father, in time. That other links exist, on other planes, between these two affairs, is not impossible. I have enough trouble as it is in trying to say what I think I know."[11] The prepositional phrase with which the speaker ends the first sentence—already qualified by the interjected adverbs—restricts the meaning of two of the most important events in a man's life to a purely temporal plane, isolating them from the feelings which normally accompany them, respectively joy and sorrow. These feelings, however, still lie just below the surface, as Beckett hints in the next sentence, which, while purporting to affirm, syntactically denies a continuation of the ambivalence manifested in the opening statement. The final sentence then discloses the narrator's doubt and hints at his difficulties which become progressively more evident: both verbal and emotional constipation.

His denial of feeling becomes manifest as he explains his reason for coming to the cemetery—merely, he asserts, to determine the date of his father's death from the tombstone, and then a few days later, to confirm the date of his father's birth. Ostensibly, he needs these two figures to compute his own age at the time of his marriage (twenty-five), although why we need this information we are never to learn, for it plays no integral part in the story. His attraction to his father's grave would thus seem to lie elsewhere, on one of the "other planes" whose possibility he admits. Presently he reveals his preoccupation with excretion and decay as he extolls "the smell of corpses" around him in comparison to "what the living emit, their feet, teeth, armpits, arses, sticky foreskins and frustrated ovules" (11). In this encomium, though, he again betrays the powerful feelings he is defending against when he remarks, "And when my father's remains join in, however modestly, I can almost shed a tear" (11-12). He does not, however, cry. He continues only to speak, for like all other Beckettian narrators from the "turning point" on, he will proclaim that words are all he has.

Indeed he now strolls about to read words, those available on tombstones, invigorated and amused by them. Of his own epitaph, he states, "Mine I composed long since and am still pleased with it, tolerably pleased. My other writings are no sooner dry than they revolt me, but my epitaph still meets with my approval" (12). For the first time we discover he is a writer—perhaps—and we discern as well what appears to be a character trait, a self-deprecatory attitude toward his own productions. He here prefigures Molloy who believes that "you would do better, at least no worse, to obliterate texts than to blacken margins. . . ."[12] As innocent as our narrator's words appear, though, they still continue the excretory theme in a highly disguised form. Like an infant who produces feces, usually on demand by the mother, he is at first pleased by his creativity and the product, when they appear to displease the mother who, paradoxically, discards immediately what she had earlier pleaded for, they become revolting.

Beckett's use of language to represent excretion is persuasive. Leo Bersani, who felt such use was leading the author to a dead end, remarked twenty years ago that "I know of no writer who has come closer than Beckett in his novels to translating the rhythm of defecation into sentence structure, or to find a doughy, thick, smirching prose to suggest the monotonous pleasure of a baby playing in his own excretions." Bersani, too, notes the narrator's anal compulsive traits, especially their miserliness with respect to "their very being, which they try desperately to prevent from escaping into communicable meanings of dramatic self-projection."[13] The narrator of **"First Love"** is most certainly an ideally anal character, for beyond his obsession with smell and decay, he often speaks of the significant events of his life in suitable anal imagery.

When he is evicted from his father's house, for example, he graphically portrays the scene in terms of expulsion. One day when he returns, fittingly, from the outdoor toilet where he has experienced difficulty, unsure—in his own words—whether he was constipated or diarrheic, he finds himself locked out by the unnamed others. He tries all doors, but none is open to him. "I think if I'd found one open I'd have barricaded myself in the room, they would have had to gas me out. I felt the house crammed as usual, the usual pack, but saw no one. I imagined them in their various rooms, all bolts drawn, every sense on the alert. Then the rush to the window, each holding back a little, hidden by the curtain, at the sound of the street door closing behind me, I should have left it open. Then the doors fly open and out they pour, men, women and children, and the voices, the sighs, the smiles, the hands, the keys, in the hands, the blessed relief, the precautions rehearsed, if this then that, but if that then this, all clear and joy in every heart, come let's eat, the fumigation can wait. All imagination to be sure, I was already on my way, things may have passed quite differently, but who cares how things pass, provided they pass." (15-16). Clearly this lengthy passage illustrates that prose of which Bersani speaks, and this expressive imagery is that of a man who sees himself as treated literally like shit.

When he moves into Lulu/Anna's small quarters and discovers them densely packed with furniture, he rearranges it to suit himself: "I put it out piece by piece, and even two at a time, and stacked it all up in the corridor, against the outer wall. They were hundreds of pieces, large and small, in the end they blocked the door, making egress impossible, and *a fortiori* ingress, to and from the corridor. The door could be opened and closed, since it opened inwards, but had become impassable" (29). This externalized attempt at an expul-sion which results in a retention is a derivative of compulsive ambivalence. It repeats the narrator's earlier confusion about his constipation and/or diarrhea and foreshadows the end of the tale since it represents as well his emotional constriction, his inability to give, and his stubborn insistence on having things his own way.

For Beckett's narrators, words and feces are intimately related, a relationship that is a commonplace in psychoanalytic theory. Joel Kovel has elaborated on the psychic intertwining of word and feces during the earliest phase of language learning: "What is good in the world is identified with what is good in the person—not his body, but his mind. Thus, within anal symbolism, mental contents come to be considered especially pure and perfect differentiations. Words themselves achieve a magic power, which stems from the infant's magical preoccupation with feces; when the feces are repudiated as filthy, their power to represent the whole universe becomes displaced on the mental product which represents the universe. The mind, good, makes words and thoughts; the body, bad, makes shit and filth. And words are placed in the service of aggression toward the natural world, just as feces had been instruments of aggression toward the mother."[14] In *How It Is,* Beckett's narrator himself makes this vital connection between words, feces, and his very identity: ". . . Nothing physical the health is not in jeopardy a word from me and I am again I strain with open mouth so as not to lose a second a fart fraught with meaning issuing through the mouth no sound in the mud."[15]

Like all of Beckett's compulsive narrators after his turning point, the narrator of **"First Love"** is afraid of his emotions and, consequently, of those things that arouse his emotions. Fleeing the external macrocosm, he attempts to create an internal microcosm of words, repeating the process whereby, as an infant, one learns to master anxiety and anger, retreating from the world of immediate experience into a distant world of abstractions. Cohn has observed how all of Beckett's narrators are characteristically prone to erupt at unpredictable points into "irrational rage."[16] Yet even this defensive maneuver of using abstractions such as words instead of feeling is destined to fail, for words themselves quickly become invested with the emotional attitudes one has toward the things to which they refer and must be dealt with accordingly. A careless word, for instance, might precipitate the sadism which has been so carefully warded off. Thus the narrator of **"First Love"** notes that his writings "revolt" him once, like stool, they are externalized and "dry" (112). What Barbara Shapiro has said of Molloy's self deprecating attitudes about his productions is pre-figured here in this man: "Himself a turd, he produces work which is no better."[17] Here in **"First Love"** Beckett presents for the first time the fully-realized image of narrator as feces, the waste of the world: if you would, pre-Krapp crap. Alain Bosquet remarks of this character that "this man does not lie in the sewer: that would be too easy; he *is* the sewer."[18]

Beyond the connections Bersani perceived, Beckett's characters also exhibit tendencies to extremes of domination and submission in relation to whatever has symbolic reference to feces. That is, they will try to frustrate the world with their dirt, stubbornness, miserliness, and lack of punctuality (*vide* Godot!) or, on the other hand, gain its approval by displaying exactly the opposite characteristics. Typically, after being evicted peremptorily from his father's house, the narrator submissively accepts his fate rather than act on the justifiable indignation or rage a normal person would feel in similar circumstances. Fenichel, in elaborating on such passivity, notes that anal eroticism "is always bisexual in nature, the anus being simultaneously an active expelling organ and a hollow organ which may be stimulated by some object entering it. Vacillation between the original masculine attitude, now reinforced and exaggerated by the active-sadistic component of anal eroticism, and the feminine attitude represented by the passive component of anal eroticism forms the most typical conflict in the unconscious of the male compulsion neurotic. The phallic Oedipus attitude is inhibited by the idea that gratification means the loss of the penis. The regression imposes a feminine attitude, yet does not entirely destroy the original masculine one" (277).

The narrator passively accepts, as well, the actions of They, who claim that he has been left a small sum of money, pay him, but refuse to let him see the will. To assert himself against the provider would be to jeopardize his shaky psychic security even further, so he causes no trouble. Later we discover that although a vagrant on the streets, he has done nothing with this inherited money but keep it in his pocket (19). "What money and feces have in common is that they are deindividualized possessions; and deindividualized means necessarily losable. Thus money, in the same way as the feces previously, is estimated and watched over as a possession which is in constant danger of losing its ego quality."[19] As a result of this psychic equation, the narrator, in a typically anal way, has firmly retained that which to him symbolizes feces and is in danger of being lost.

Once evicted, he takes to wandering, and Beckett, as we know, makes much of the way his characters walk or move, whether on foot, crutches, or bicycle. Gilbert Rose, in an exploration of creative function, has concluded that the body is the model on which we construct the world as a whole, a general schema in which we tend to see in outside objects reflections of our own bodies. Of walking he specifically states that "the total movement of one's body bears such an intimate and ba-

sic relationship to one's concept of self that it is the key factor in recognizing oneself on movie film when all other cues are blocked out. In now classic experiments, subjects failed to identify their own voices, pictures of their hands, and even their profiles. But they promptly recognized their own gait. This is particularly striking since one seldom sees oneself walk. Apparently the person unerringly identifies him- or herself with the total movement of trunk and limbs."[20] The narrator of **"First Love"** in his wandering is less concerned with his gait than is the narrator of **"The Expelled,"** who, as we have already seen, specifically attributed his way of walking to poor toilet habits in childhood. Again we see in the conjunction of gait, feces, and identity, Beckett's intuitive recognition of anal conflict and its consequences in his characters' psychic lives.

The narrator's wandering soon after his eviction takes him to the place he will meet his first love, Lulu, "a bench, on the bank of the canal, one of the canals, for our town boasts two, though I never knew which was which. It was a well situated bench, backed by a mound of solid earth and garbage, so that my rear was covered" (16). Anal references, both overt and covert, continue to multiply. The confusion over the two canals, while reflecting the narrator's obsessive ambivalence, also serves another purpose, that of revealing an infantile cloacal fantasy. A child's ignorance of the female reproductive system leads to an inability to distinguish the excretory from the birth channel, giving rise to fantasies of anal birth. Indeed when Lulu/Anna eventually does become pregnant, the narrator substantiates the existence of this fantasy by suggesting to her, despite the evidence of his own eyes, that "perhaps it's mere wind" (34). Here again he prefigures Molloy, who has great difficulty sorting such matters out, believing that his own mother "brought me into the world, through the hole in her arse if memory serves me correct. First taste of the shit" (16). Later, after he has had intercourse *a tergo* with Ma Lousse, he is uncertain as to whether he entered her vagina or her rectum and declares indifference yet wonders, "But is it true love, in the rectum?" (57)

The narrator of **"First Love"** is himself aware that he is beleaguered by doubts. As he strains to listen to Lulu's song at the bench, trying to hear the words, he can't tell whether she has stopped or he is out of hearing range. "To have to harbour such a doubt was something I preferred to avoid, at that period. I lived of course in doubt, but such trivial doubts as this, purely somatic as some say, were best cleared up without delay, they would nag at me like gnats for weeks on end" (25-26). What he calls "trivial" is of course central; obsessives displace onto small details which under analysis turn out to be substitutes for crucial issues.[21] By this means the person shifts the threat of emotional intensity to the periphery and deems it inconsequential. This defensive maneuver explains the characteristic of Beckett's work after the turning point which Cohn has termed "events" lacking proportion."[22] Often these displacements result in excessive concern with the physical rather than with the more important emotional states, hence the obsessive's characteristic hypochondriacal complaints and Beckett's characters' fascination with their boils, cysts, headaches, toothaches, bursitis, etc., *ad infinitum.*

The narrator of **"First Love,"** for example, when perplexed by the question of love, takes refuge in a deserted cowshed, ruminating on his feelings while poking his finger in "dry and hollow cowclaps" which remind him that his country is completely derelict, "with the sole exception of history's ancient faeces. These are ardently sought after, stuffed and carried in procession. Wherever nauseated time has dropped a nice fat turd you will find our patriots, sniffing it up on all fours, their faces on fire" (21). Clearly time and feces are linked in his mind and somehow, both of them connected to love, for he says immediately by way of denial, "I see no connexion between these remarks. But that one exists, and even more than one, I have little doubt, for my part. But what? Which? Yes, I loved her, it's the name I gave, still give alas, to what I was doing then. I had nothing to go by, having never loved before" (21-22). He then finds himself "inscribing the letters of Lulu in an old heifer pat or flat upon my face in the mud . . . Perhaps I loved her with a platonic love? But somehow I think not. Would I have been tracing her name in old cowshit if my love had been pure and disinterested? And with my devil's finger into the bargain, which I then sucked" (22).

This scene echoes that of the narrator of **"The End"** taking refuge in a similar shed where "The floor was strewn with excrements, both human and animal, with condoms and vomit. In a cowpad a heart had been traced, pierced by an arrow" (61). There he tries to nourish himself, sucking directly from a cow's teat, but ". . . without much success. Her udder was covered with dung" (*Ibid.*). Both scenes reverberate with the equation of food=milk=mother=love, but anal conflicts keep contaminating its purity and creating intense ambivalence in the narrators. The repugnant image of eating feces most likely represents as well a compensatory infantile defense. If a child experiences defecation as a loss of narcissistic integrity, he will engage in coprophagia, "which represents both an undoing of the defecation and an oral-anal pleasure."[23]

After scrawling Lulu's name in the cowpat, the narrator suddenly decides to change it to Anna, perhaps because "Lulu" reiterates the common European word for toilet, i.e., loo-loo. Trying to disguise the conflict by rechristening her "Anna" is only partially successful, however, for the new name itself suggests "anal." After the re-

naming, he begins to think of her in a particular way, "long long sessions, twenty minutes, twenty-five minutes and even as long as half an hour daily. I obtain these figures by the addition of other, lesser figures. That must have been my way of loving" (23). His concern with numbers immediately after admitting his love for Anna reveals the compulsive's special cognitive style, his attempt to deal with a failure of defenses. He must now magically "undo" what has been done. Having felt, he must now "unfeel" by intellectualization and manipulation of numbers, entities which, unlike his emotions, he can control.[24] Fenichel writes, "What was once done with an instinctual intention must be repeated with a superego attitude. The warded-off instinct, however, tends to enter the repetition also; thus the repetition has to be repeated. Usually the number of necessary repetitions quickly increases. 'Favorite numbers,' the choice of which may have their separate unconscious meaning, are set up and determine the number of necessary repetitions; eventually the repetitions may be replaced by counting."[25]

Molloy, we recall, is involved in at least two remarkable episodes of magical, symmetrical undoing, both of which end in denial. Upon reflecting that his farts are unable to break through the newspaper he keeps in his pants for warmth, and perhaps having become somewhat aware of the symbolic anal hostility, Molloy reveals that he counted 315 farts in 19 hours and by subdivision and averaging concludes that he produces "not even one fart every four minutes. It's unbelievable. Damn it, I hardly fart at all, I never should have mentioned it. Extraordinary how mathematics helps you to know yourself" (30).

Later in the journey, Molloy devotes a lengthy obsessive monologue to his dependency needs as he recounts the famous "sixteen sucking stones to be divided among the four pockets" problem. Having gathered these stones from the seashore and feeling compelled to suck on one constantly, yet at the same time insure that he does not suck the same one again prior to having sucked each of the others in its turn, he systematically rotates them from pocket to pocket and at great length (six textual pages) details the procedure. Ultimately he concludes, "And the solution to which I rallied in the end was to throw away all the stones but one, which I kept now in one pocket, now in another, and which of course I soon lost, or threw away, or gave away, or swallowed" (74). Thus is an emotional mountain made into an emotional molehill.

The dependency needs of the narrator of **"First Love"** also are prominent throughout and become especially striking when he moves in with Anna. As he was during their "courtship," he is yet the passive member of the relationship, acting as if he were an infant taken care of by his mother: "She brought my meals at the appointed hours, looked in now and then to see if all was well and make sure I needed nothing, emptied the stewpan once a day and did out the room once a month" (31). He has been using the stewpan as a bedpan because, as he himself puts it, "To relieve oneself in bed is enjoyable at the time, but soon a source of discomfort" (30). She is the active partner too in intercourse, apparently raping him: "My night was most agitated. I woke next morning quite spent, my clothes in disorder, the blanket likewise, and Anna beside me, naked naturally. One shudders to think of her exertions. I still had the stewpan in my grasp. It had not served. I looked at my member. If only it could have spoken! Enough about that. It was my night of love" (31).

His relationship with her, however, soon becomes "seriously disturbed by other sounds, stifled giggles and groans, which filled the dwelling at certain hours of the night, and even of the day" (32). Though he eventually discovers her to be a prostitute, it is probable that the events described here are manifestations of a primal scene fantasy, in which a child imagines its parents in the act of intercourse, often misinterpreting it because of the actions and noises as an act of hostility or even violence. The narrator has hinted that he imagines sex to be dangerous earlier when first confronted with Anna's nakedness: "Fortunately, she was not the first naked woman to have crossed my path, so I could stay, I knew she would not explode" (28).

Unfortunately for him, though, she does "explode," eventually giving birth to a child she claims is theirs, but which he refuses to acknowledge, using the anal birth rationalization mentioned earlier, that the pregnancy is "mere wind." Indeed, the impending birth threatens the narrator's dependency needs so that in anticipating competition from the child, he first attempts to deny it: "From that day forth things went from bad to worse, to worse and worse. Not that she neglected me, she could never neglect me enough" (34); then, when the birth creates an actual rival, he flees rather than face his aggressive impulses toward it and its mother. Significantly, his flight is described in anal imagery. "I crept out over the back of the sofa . . . and opened the door to the corridor. A mass of junk barred my way, but I scrabbled and barged my way through it in the end, regardless of the clatter" (35). Like all other Beckettian narrators to follow, he "must go on," exhibiting what David Shapiro has designated the most conspicuous fact about the obsessive's activity—"its sheer quantity and, along with this, its intensity and concentration . . . a more or less continuous experience of tense deliberateness, a sense of effort, and of trying."[26]

The narrator's last words, as he retreats listening to the newborne's cries, are "I could have done with other loves perhaps. But there it is, either you love or you don't" (36). Though the option reflects the ambivalence of the obsessive and neat symmetry of his thought processes, it is not necessarily true—except for obsessives. To love, one must give, not merely take. To love, one must not be afraid of feeling. But the narrator of **"First Love"** will neither give nor allow himself to feel. When he first reacts to Anna's stroking his ankles on the bench, he gets an erection and is disturbed by his loss of control. "One is no longer oneself, on such occasions, and it is painful to be no longer oneself, even more painful if possible than when one is. For when one is one knows what to do to be less so, whereas when one is not one is any old one irredeemably. What goes by the name of love is banishment . . ." (18).

Here the narrator reveals what David Shapiro has termed the obsessive's need to be always "aware that he is a 'this' or a 'that,'" that is, to establish firmly a role which becomes a general directive for behavior; otherwise, he is lost.[27] Love alienates the narrator by putting him, in his eyes, at the mercy of his feelings. He is right: to love is to lose oneself to some degree in the other. But it is not to lose identity entirely, as he implies; and though the degree to which one is hurt by the loss of love is proportionate to the degree to which one invests in it, this does not always imply banishment or total abandonment. It is only in infancy that one gets such impressions, creates such fantasies, harbors such fears.

The narrator here seems to have done just that—carried oral and anal conflicts into his adult life so that they impair significantly his adult relationships with women, all of whom symbolize mother. On several occasions, for example, as he tries to visualize Anna's face, he finds her image "might have been anything or anyone, an old woman or a little girl" (24-25) and "It looked neither young nor old, the face, as though stranded between the vernal and the sere" (27). She is, it would appear, an imago, an infantile image projected upon reality and reacted to. The narrator of **"The Expelled"** at one point observes that "Memories are killing. So you must not think of certain things, of those that are dear to you, or rather you must think of them, for if you don't there is the danger of finding them, in your mind, little by little" (9).

In their need to think of certain things, their scatological preoccupations, their verbosity, their passivity exploding into rage—in short, in their obsessive-compulsive behavior, the narrators of the *nouvelles* become prototypes of the men and women who are to people Beckett's works for the next forty years. These engrossing creations act out their unconscious infantile fantasies before our eyes and in the bizarreness of their speech and behavior literalize internal emotional states. Bersani saw this technique as a dead end for Beckett, declaring that "extreme fixation at least saves Beckett the embarrassment of being 'representative' of all humanity" (263).

Raymond Riva, however, has attempted to account for Beckett's popularity by arguing the opposite, that the artist allows us to relive a long repressed life and "see ourselves more as we actually are than we know."[28] As if in response to Bersani, Riva contends that "Not any single character or situation can be taken to depict any single situation in life, but certainly all of these strange creatures—and even the earlier, more normal ones—all combine into one complex and disturbing hieroglyph connoting contemporary man and his condition" (132).

This assertion, not Bersani's, better accounts perhaps for Beckett's endurance as an artist. Up until his recent death in his early eighties, he continued to produce work of note, preoccupied still with many of these same themes. Whatever the source of his revelation on that lonely jetty at his turning point, Samuel Beckett persevered. His work itself endures, fascinating readers and audiences still with his remarkable facility to express the elemental unconscious concerns of humanity, however, infantile, scatological, or repugnant they maybe. He has in this, indeed, found common cause with Freud.

Notes

1. Deirdre Bair, *Samuel Beckett: A Biography* (N.Y.: Harcourt Brace Jovanovich, 1978), p. 357. All references are to this edition.

2. Though all written in French in 1945-46, the order of their composition and the year the author translated them is as follows: "The End" (1954), "The Expelled" (1962), "The Calmative" (1967), and "First Love" (1972). The first three appeared originally in the U.S. in *Stories and Texts for Nothing* (N.Y.: Grove Press, 1967) and the last in *First Love and Other Shorts* (N.Y.: Grove Press, 1974). All references are to these editions.

3. Ruby Cohn, *Samuel Beckett: The Comic Gamut* (New Brunswick, N.J.: Rutgers Univ. Press, 1962), p. 105. All references are to this edition.

4. John Weightman, "Spool, Stool, Drool," *Encounter,* 40, No. 4 (1973), 37.

5. Sandra Gilbert, "All the Dead Voices," *Drama Survey,* 6 (1968), 249.

6. *Stories and Texts for Nothing,* p. 14.

7. *Ibid.,* p. 70.

8. G. C. Barnard, *Samuel Beckett: A New Approach* (N.Y.: Dodd, Mead, 1970), p. 32.

9. "Character and Anal Erotism." *The Standard Edition of the Complete Psychological Works of Sigmund Freud,* trans. and ed. James Strachey and others (London: The Hogarth Press, 1966-74), 9 (1908), 167-75.

10. Otto Fenichel, *The Psychoanalytic Theory of Neurosis* (N.Y.: Norton, 1945), p. 268. All references are to this edition.

11. *First Love and Other Shorts,* p. 11.

12. Samuel Beckett, *Three Novels: Molloy, Malone Dies, and The Unnamable* (N.Y.: Grove Press, 1965), p. 13.

13. Leo Bersani, "No Exit for Beckett," *Partisan Review,* (Spring, 1966), p. 263. All references are to this article.

14. Joel Kovel, *White Racism: A Psychohistory* (N.Y.: Random House, 1970), p. 132.

15. *How It Is* (N.Y.: Grove Press, 1964), p. 26. Equations of and confusions between the mouth and the anus are common in Beckett's work. See, for instance *Molloy,* pp. 117, 151, and 161.

16. Ruby Cohn, *Back to Beckett* (Princeton: Princeton Univ. Press, 1973), p. 75.

17. Barbara Shapiro, "Toward a Psychoanalytic Reading of Beckett's *Molloy,*" *Literature and Psychology,* 19, No. 2 (1969), 80.

18. Alain Bosquet, "Combat," *Samuel Beckett: The Critical Heritage,* eds. Laurence Graves and Raymond Federman (London: Routledge and Kegan Paul, 1979), pp. 318-19.

19. Fenichel, p. 281.

20. Gilbert Rose, *The Power of Form: A Psychoanalytic Approach to Aesthetic Form. Psychological Issues.* Monograph No. 49 (N.Y.: International Universities Press, 1980), p. 99.

21. Fenichel, p. 290.

22. Cohn, *Back to Beckett,* p. 75.

23. Fenichel, p. 155.

24. Fenichel, p. 154.

25. Fenichel, p. 288.

26. David Shapiro, *Neurotic Styles* (N.Y.: Basic Books, 1965), p. 31. All references are to this edition.

27. Shapiro, *Neurotic Styles,* p. 38.

28. Raymond Riva, "Beckett and Freud," *Criticism,* 12 (1970), 122.

Nicoletta Pireddu (essay date summer 1992)

SOURCE: Pireddu, Nicoletta. "Sublime Supplements: Beckett and the 'Fizzling Out' of Meaning." *Studies in Short Fiction* 29, no. 3 (summer 1992): 303-14.

[*In the following essay, Pireddu considers the disjointed and confused nature of the short texts in* Fizzles, *arguing that these texts "exhibit the idea of aborted endeavor as their constitutive element."*]

"Perhaps there is no whole, before you're dead" (Beckett, *Molloy* 35), meditates Molloy while lying in the ditch without remembering how he left town. If his name suddenly comes to his mind as in an epiphany, the purpose of his visit to his mother inevitably escapes him: "My reasons? I had forgotten them" (35). For each detail brought to light, other particulars are reabsorbed into forgetfulness. The activity of memory never provides the character with the total picture of his own self. Its discrete nature frustrates the need to continuity; its inability to fill the gaps opened up by oblivion reveals the arbitrariness of any attempt to master reality, and the inconclusiveness of Molloy's writing registers exactly the failure of such an effort.

If in *Molloy* the protagonist narrates the story of a fiasco, Beckett's *Fizzles* represent the fiasco of narration itself. Starting from their titles, both the English and the French version of these short texts exhibit the idea of aborted endeavor as their constitutive element. Voices with no faces recite confused monologues in the hopeless attempt to put order into their past lives; third-person accounts on the verge of syntactical disintegration describe endless wanderings not redeemed by any promise of final revelation; physically impaired bodies struggle against a hostile nature, in the awareness of an impending death. The topology of *Fizzles* is a paradoxical middle ground between defeat and accomplishment. Far from implying total renunciation, the failure announced at the opening of the collection triggers an attempt at depiction that is doomed to incompleteness: to the danger of silence and of annihilation, Beckett's texts oppose a fictional world of traces that hint at wholeness without ever granting to it. Ruins, decaying bodies, and blurred memories materialize the interplay of presence and absence of meaning that the language of *Fizzles* reproduces with its imminent and yet never-achieved dissolution.

Through their conceptual and structural fragmentation, the *Fizzles* dismantle exactly what Adorno defines as art's "unfulfilled (and imprescriptible) longing for perfection," and by articulating the unresolved struggle between destructive forces and self-preservation they meet the "challenge of the irreconcilable" (Adorno 271). Beckett's literary "fiascos" belong, for this reason, to the category of the sublime, the ascendance of which—according to Adorno—coincides with "the need for art to avoid 'playing down' its fundamental contradictions but to bring them out instead" (Adorno 282). In *Fizzles,* the disruption of form and meaning under the effect of such a clash of forces reveals an essential feature of the contemporary sublime, namely, its being latent. If "the traditional concept of the sublime as an infinite presence was animated by the belief that negation could bring about positivity" (Adorno 282), the irreconcilable conflicts of Beckett's texts break this illusion and offer an example of "radical negativity" (Adorno 284). No longer associated with the sense of awe and of subsequent power that defined it in the Kantian version, the sublimity of a literary work like *Fizzles* derives precisely from its margin of unrepresentability, and from the inadequacy of any attempt to penetrate it. Deprived of the aggrandizement that characterizes the Romantic participation in the source of the sublime, these texts rather involve the agonizing experience of characters suspended between physical destruction and recovery of integrity, between oblivion and memory.

With the frantic activity of recollection recurring and yet failing throughout *Fizzles,* Adorno's "radical negativity" merges with Lyotard's notion of the unrepresentable as "Forgotten," as something that remains immemorial and unthought. Beckett's "imperfect" texts express the sublime by calling attention to an excess of meaning and of reality that cannot be recuperated but only evoked through its absence; their words represent precisely

> what every presentation misses, what is forgotten there: this "presence" . . . which persists not so much at the limits but rather at the heart of representation; this unnameable in the secret of names, a forgotten that is not the result of a forgetting of a reality . . . and which one can only remember as forgotten "before" memory and forgetting, and *by repeating it.*
>
> (Lyotard, *Heidegger* 5; my emphasis)

1. RE-MEMBERING/DIS-MEMBERING

It is exactly the notion of a perceptual reenacting that animates Beckett's *Fizzles,* in spite of the failure to which these texts are doomed by definition: the repetitive pattern described by Lyotard sustains the collection as a whole and is epitomized in the title of the last Fizzle, "For to end yet again" (Beckett, *Fizzles* 55).[1] Far from granting a stronger mastery of reality and of meaning in the narration, the dynamics of endless repetition that truncates the texts before they attain a logical conclusion or a potential revelation implies exactly an act of *re*-presentation deprived of presentation and of presence.

The movement suggested at the opening of Fizzle 1 is immediately reduced to a mere act of oscillation that anchors the subject to its initial position: "he is forth again, he'll be back again" (7). However, in spite of this yoke, the subject gropes his way in the dark and starts a quest set in a labyrinthine site that is both material and mental. Proceeding along a zigzag path—that is, not sustained by the teleological linear progression toward a target—and frustrated in his "effort to pierce the gloom" (9), he manages to relive some episodes of his past life but without ever being able to give a global shape to his history. As in Molloy's experience, the unearthing of a detail from oblivion implies the burial of other elements, and reveals simultaneously the inefficacy of the quest and the impossibility of putting an end to it. Similarly, after a series of encounters with Horn and an investigation into the past through his notes, the speaker of the monologue in Fizzle 2 has to acknowledge his failure and, still confused about time and temporal relations, avows the need for a new beginning:

> I thought I had made my last journey, the one I must now try once more to elucidate, that it may be a lesson to me, the one from which it were better I had never returned. But the feeling gains on me that I must undertake another.

(22)

The paradoxical coexistence of renunciation and undertaking of new endeavors persists in Fizzes 3 and 4, where the first-person speaker "gave up before birth" (25) and declares his impotence by emphasizing his lack of voice and of thought, but still sets himself the task of narrating the story of the "other" consciousness in the piece: "I'll tell the tale, the tale of his death" (31)—a tale and a death that never take place. All these aborted attempts and their reiterated necessity are absorbed in the closing statement of Fizzle 8, which strengthens the process of *re*-presentation implied by the title and provides no alternative to eternal beginning: "Through it who knows yet another end beneath a cloudless sky same dark it earth and sky of a last end if ever there had to be another absolutely had to be" (61).

The act of writing and the performance of the characters in Beckett's texts are in the service of a mechanism of *re*-membering which is at the same time a *dis*-membering. In *Fizzles,* memory cannot reestablish a peaceful continuity between past and present; no edifice of totality can be reconstructed from the fragments of their topology. It is primarily the additional connotation of the words *fizzles* and *foirade*—as well as the status of these texts vis-à-vis Beckett's literary production as a whole—that throws further light upon the role of traces and remains, and consequently upon their relation with Lyotard's treatment of the sublime. Actually, the idea of failure in both the English and the French headings is combined with a reference to excrements and to uncontrolled corporal functions that establish the *residual* nature of this collection with respect to the *body* of the author's work. These texts are condemned—by definition—to occupy a marginal place in Beckett's aesthetic project, since they are conceived as excretions that can no longer be integrated within the original source that generated them. Therefore, they constitute an example of "radical fragmentation, pursued to its logical end of dispersion and multiplicity" (Hill 175). Given their shattered structure, the failure of these "fizzles" is extended to their lack of "organic self-coincidence" (Hill 176): they do not merely stand for the expelled remainders of a nonexistent whole, but they are also residual in relation to their own self-containedness.

The title of the collection, in this respect, anticipates the "supplementary" quality of the ruins and traces upon which memory inscribes its project of reconstruction. As in the text of the Freudian unconscious, the fragments that recur throughout Beckett's texts are residual in themselves: far from functioning as synecdoches for a totality that asks to be retrieved, they are "repositories of a meaning which was never present" (Derrida, *Writing* 211).[2] Being "always already" incomplete, these supplements cannot but compensate imperfectly for the lack of plenitude they decree. Like Lyotard's notion of "the jews" (Lyotard, *Heidegger* xxiii) as those devoid of self-identity and of mythical origin, the residues in *Fizzles* stimulate and frustrate the desire for a wholeness and a presence that cannot be *re*-collected, neither through the material assemblage of the fragments, nor through an act of memory. The Forgotten plenitude—the source of the sublime—has to remain forgotten, but it needs memory in order to be remembered as such. It must not be naturalized by representation, nor suppressed and effaced by oblivion, but rather venerated through the aborted efforts to appropriate and represent it. In the agonizing space of Beckett's texts, the condemnation to eternal beginning becomes the only way to maintain this precarious balance of annihilation and preservation. By endlessly reenacting a drama of disintegration that does not culminate with death, Beckett can avoid concluding, since "to terminate"—to put an end to his "fizzles"—would coincide with "to exterminate"—namely, to destroy the "place of remains" (Beckett, *Fizzles* 55), the locus of the conflictual forces that allow the sublime to come into being. With the extermination of these traces, *anamnesis* would turn into *amnesia*. Representation would still belong to the realm of the beautiful; it could still rely on "the solace of good forms" (Lyotard, *Postmodern Condition* 81), but only through an arbitrary act—through the exclusion of those residual elements whose formlessness evokes exactly the unpresentable, the sublime.

The failed attempt at recollection and the material presence of remainders as supplements for the unpresentable emerge from the opening page of Fizzle 1—where "none of [the character's] memories answer" (7)—and are reinforced in its closing comment—with the surfacing of bones as the "fresh elements" that "contribute to enrich" (15) the impossible reconstruction of the character's past history. Bones are combined with "grit" (27) and "dust" (32) to anticipate the physical consumption of the two voices in Fizzles 3 and 4, but—together with the ruins of the landscape—they simultaneously affirm their material presence as opposed to the total effacement implied by death. Nature joins man in the process of mechanical decay, and—as shown in Fizzle 5—can be remembered only through "dead leaves," "not rotting" (39)—since this would reaffirm a form of life, though elementary, and therefore a positive, organic principle of reconstruction—but rather "crumbling into dust" (39). The "place of remains" (55) in Fizzle 8 "where once used to . . . glimmer a remain" best epitomizes the supplementary nature of these texts by indicating exactly the lack of initial plenitude and presence in a kind of *mise en abîme*. Equally, through the reference to "the expelled" (56) that is engulfed in dust mingling with the remainders of buildings, Beckett reinstates precisely the idea of detachment from an original totality and the impossible reintegration that define the residual quality of *fizzle* and *foirade*.[3]

This process of inexorable fragmentation is inscribed in the image of the agonizing skull to which Fizzle 8 reduces its protagonist: the mind that in the Romantic sublime should struggle against a prostrating experience and ultimately regain its power and integrity is metonymically translated into its material container, which acts as a *memento mori*. Death as forgetfulness can only be remembered through a perishable relic; the activity of memory that should re-collect the *disjecta membra* of Beckett's characters can only be "laughable" (58): the unpresentable—the "Forgotten"—needs remembrance in order to be saved from oblivion, but at the same time it decrees the uselessness of any attempt at representation. If the ritual of turning the light on and off seems to grant the characters the restoration of their past (Rabinovitz 318) and of their sense of selfhood, it actually provides only disconnected flashes of memory: the "electric torch" (19) does not clarify the forgotten details of the past contained in Horn's notebook; the light of the bulb is equally ineffective to unify the "faces, agonies, loves, . . . moments of life" (44) recalled by the protagonist of Fizzle 6; the glimmering "remains" of subjectivity, of monuments and of the "light of the day" (55), are the metaphors through which memory exhibits its inadequacy to illuminate the shadow surrounding it.

2. A WRITING OF SURVIVAL

"The understanding"—observes Lyotard—"imposes its rules on to all objects, even aesthetic ones. This requires a time and a space under control" (*Heidegger* 41). *Fizzles* shrinks from such kind of naturalization by altering precisely these two parameters: time acquires the value of Heideggerian temporality—thus reducing the character to being-toward-death—and space is threatening in its vastness and monotony.[4] Like a parodic double of Ishmael meditating upon the whale's "dumb blankness full of meaning" (Melville 199) the "little body" in Fizzle 8 is also confronted with a "whiteness to decipher" (58), but there is no ultimate revelation of its nature or of its origin: the "distant whiteness *sprung from nowhere*" (59; my emphasis) takes the shape of two dwarfs who—although possible

harbingers of death—are not unmasked in their function, and do not hinder the protagonist's slow but endless fall. He sees them with his eyes, eyes that "the fall has not shut nor yet the dust stopped up" (60); therefore he believes in them. However, the sense of sight is actually entrusted to the mere "gaping sockets" of a "sepulchral skull" (60). The ability to master reality through visual perception is thus affirmed and immediately denied: the protagonist's empty sockets put into question understanding and representability.

Through the physical and mental deterioration of its characters, *Fizzles* dramatizes the second phase of the Kantian sublime—that is, it describes the annihilation of the subject under the effect of an overwhelming experience. Actually, the *Critique of Judgment* already presupposes the mind's inadequacy to grasp the source of the sublime (Kant 99): the unattainability of the object decrees precisely the failure of representation. Beckett's texts are founded upon a similar disproportion between the inner and the outer realm, between powerless bodies and minds on the one hand, and uncontrollable destructive forces on the other. The characters face an external reality that is in *excess* with respect to them: memory is no refuge from dissolution—since it fails to provide a reassuring and organic image of the past—and the present is absorbed by the threat of an imminent extinction. With the depiction of bodies in the ditch, Fizzle 5—which significantly bears the title "Se voir" in the French version (Beckett, *Pour finir* 51)—almost invokes death through its material ritual of burial, since the actual occurrence of death would at least redeem the purposeless agony of the characters by inserting it in a design. Similarly, the apostrophe at the beginning of Fizzle 6 turns the mythical image of the earth as source of regeneration into a metonymy for decease: "old earth, no more lies . . . You'll be on me" (43). However, the closing image in the collection frustrates once again this longing for resolution. The "little body" sinking into a wasteland of ruins and dust is "prostrate" and constantly falling "as though pushed from behind by some helping hand" (60), but if there seems to be "no fear of [his] rising again," the logic of *Fizzles*—"to end yet again"—does not rescue him from life.

Nevertheless, whereas Kant's treatment of the sublime involves a subsequent reactive phase that reestablishes the balance between the mind and the object, Beckett's texts endlessly expand the moment of ego-loss without allowing any recovery. *Fizzles* neglects the aggrandizement that in the *Critique of Judgment* derives from the subject's identification with the transcendent source of the sublime: the sky has been "forsaken of its scavengers" (59) and, all the more reason, it is no longer the locus of the divine as a force granting self-preservation and transcending human limitations. In the place of the *leap* of faith with which Kantian subjects can be *el-*

evated and have a revelation of their own sublimity, Beckett's characters experience a *downfall:* the unpresentable haunts and *prostrates* them. Far from providing empowerment through identification, the sublime functions as a term of comparison against which skulls and little bodies can measure their own inadequacy and failure. In this respect, the etchings that Jasper Johns combines with one of the editions of *Fizzles* are symptomatic. The several images of legs that the painter juxtaposes to Beckett's words reinforce the very idea of powerlessness that characterizes the second stage of the Kantian sublime and that accounts for *Fizzles* as a whole. Actually, if the violent excitation aroused by the sublime experience can be equaled to sexual orgasm, the phallic aspect of the legs in John's illustrations invalidates precisely such an idea of energy: it rather suggests flabby and inoperative organs, detached from the body and doomed to impotence and to fiascos.[5]

In the world of *Fizzles* the "grey cloudless sky" (57) conceals no transcendency; no Oversoul can elevate the self after its loss into a sublime Romantic nature. The unpresentable and the threat of annihilation are therefore far from having a metaphysical origin: in their pathetic condemnation to a perennial purgatorial state, the little bodies and the skulls of *Fizzles* are rather deferring to disintegration that in postmodern, post-Hiroshima decades can be more easily associated with an atomic catastrophe. They are thus waiting for a Godot that does not possess any phonetic or intrinsic affinity with God: instead of reassembling their mortal remains after their physical death in the resurrection of body and soul, the nuclear destruction that haunts them will dissolve any trace. The distinction made by Burke and Kent between love for the beautiful as something that the subject can dominate and admiration for the sublime because of its crushing impact upon the mind cannot subsist in the nuclear age. The instinct of self-preservation that arouses the resistance to the overwhelming forces of nature fails to master the threat of an irreversible annihilation with no remainders: obviously, the nuclear sublime does not afford the "empowerment of selfhood" (Wilson 236) entailed by natural phenomena in the Romantic aesthetic tradition. What the nuclear sublime lacks is the "safety distance" that allows the ultimate recuperation of mental power. Actually, in line with the impulse of self-preservation, the "delight" that for Burke is produced by the natural sublime derives not so much from the presence of pain and danger as from their removal: if they "press too nearly" (Burke 34)—as in the case of the nuclear sublime—they are merely "terrible."

Therefore, the dust, bones and ruins that constitute the fictional space of Beckett's texts, as well as the logic of eternal beginning that frustrates closure, assert themselves as a way of resisting the danger involved in an atomic holocaust—namely, that of utter effacement with no remainders and no continuation. The falling fragments of buildings and bodies superimposing layer after layer in the wastelands of these stories create a testamentary *palimpsest* that—despite the failure inscribed in its texture—strives to dissipate the specter of the *tabula rosa* resulting from a nuclear devastation. To the amnesia of the nuclear fire—the physical abolition of all that came before and its parallel elimination of all possible "after"—*Fizzles* opposes anamnesis—the thwarted but always renovated attempts at recollection that the characters make in the stories, and that the author undertakes through his own writing.

In the context of an impending risk of total abolition, Beckett's words are really an example of "writing of survival" (Lyotard, *Heidegger* 44), of an art that implies not so much a positive, life-affirming image—which would be related to the reassuring category of the beautiful—as an unresolved struggle for life, an effort to withstand hostile forces. Confronted with a negative excess, overwhelmed by a "too much," Beckett reacts with a "syntax of weakness" (Harvey 249) that articulates this life-and-death conflict. The act of writing—although doomed to create mere "fizzles"—exorcises the failure of imagination by exploiting imagination to depict failure. It is only through words that the reality of the nuclear disintegration can be evoked, and it is simultaneously through their inadequacy that the sublimity of this phenomenon can emerge. As an event that has not yet taken place, the nuclear conflict is "fabulously textual" (Derrida, "No Apocalypse" 23); it is a trope re-presenting a referent that is unfigurable and threatening in its unpresentability.

Through his inexhaustible depiction of prostration in *Fizzles,* Beckett rhetorically simulates the stage of ego-shattering under the burden of the impending danger of its effacement and puts off the actual experience of general destruction, which is incommensurate to language and thought. Far from attempting to unveil an event whose first occurrence would also be the last (Derrida, "No Apocalypse" 30), *Fizzles* proclaims that "There is nothing but what is said. Beyond what is said there is nothing" (*Fizzles* 37). The "ditch" that circumscribes the "closed place" (37) of Fizzle 5 also describes cognitive limits: "nothing" (37) lies beyond it, "no more" can be known. To jump over the ditch—namely, to enact the experience of boundary crossing implied by the logic of the sublime—in order to represent a nuclear catastrophe becomes an impossible task: the only condition for its realization is actual experience, but the price for such an irreversible step would be absolute destruction "without apocalypse, without revelation of its own truth" (Derrida, "No Apocalypse" 27), ultimately without knowledge. The "day after"—like the "after Auschwitz" for Lyotard—has to be remembered as "Forgotten": *Fizzles* "does not say the unsayable but says that it cannot say it" (Lyotard, *Heidegger* 47).

3. BECKETT "THE EXPELLED"

Nuclear annihilation extends to a universal level the paradoxical coincidence of meaning and inexpressibility that is inherent in death. With the destruction of the "entire archive" and of "all symbolic capacity" (Derrida, "No Apocalypse" 28) no "writing of survival" could be possible: there would be no relic upon which remembrance could inscribe its mourning. *Fizzles* emphasizes the sublime nature of death as an inaccessible moment of revelation and as the repository of unattainable meaning, but with its material and linguistic debris it resists precisely the threat of total silence.

In line with the interpretation of the sublime experience in terms of an Oedipal struggle followed by the identification with a father-figure, Kristeva assimilates death to the realm of the paternal symbolic order and defines Beckett's reaction to it as "an 'unnameable' interplay of meaning and jouissance" (148). Actually, the fragmented syntax of *Fizzles* is not merely an example of counter-symbolic writing totally oblivious of the paternal function: it rather re-members the father-figure as the guarantor of meaning in order to reduce it to a dismembered corpse, and mingles the veneration for the vestiges of meaning with the bliss of disruption. With its logic of eternal beginning, *Fizzles* does not exterminate the father once and for all: rather, it endlessly reiterates his ritual murder. On the other hand, the jubilation over having eliminated this linguistic authority does not imply total freedom. The banishment that is supposed to relieve the character—as well as the author—of the oppressing yoke of paternity and of the threat of death rather leads to the mourning for this lost presence.

However, no surrogate figure can replace this vacancy in the world of *Fizzles,* especially not the maternal image that in other texts by Beckett "becomes a mirage of serenity, shielded from death" (Kristeva 157). In the disintegrating space of Fizzle 8, the mother is a crumbling "ruin" (*Fizzles* 58) in the process of pulverization, and the only other reference to this figure deprives it of identity and of any relevant role: "he'll confuse his mother with whores, his father with a road-man named Balfe" (27). With the elimination of these two vertices of the Oedipal triangle, Beckett is left with a "balance of nothingness" (Kristeva 152) suspended between a return to the womb—perhaps evoked through the collapsing "refuge" (*Fizzles* 56) to which the character does not wish to go back—and the introjection of paternal authority. He therefore partakes of the supplementary nature of "the expelled" as deprived of an origin and of a destination, and shares with him a middle ground "where all the footsteps ever fell can never fare nearer to anywhere nor from anywhere further away" (60)—where neither nostalgia for the beautiful nor euphoria for a new source of self-elevation reigns.

The ritual of deterioration and the logic of the supplement materially embodied in the "remains" of Beckett's *Fizzles* replace the aggrandizement of the subject in the Romantic sublime with a sense of exhaustion and of belatedness that is typical of post-modernism. Instead of gaining self-empowerment through the identification with a sublime paternal figure, Beckett exhibits his epigonic status as a "son, who never enunciated himself as anything else," as "a false father who doesn't want to be a father" (Kristeva 150-51). If Wordsworth in Paris is overwhelmed by a French Revolution that possesses all the qualities of the Burkean sublime and that is thus identifiable with an ideology of power and originality, the post-Kantian sublime of Beckett's *Fizzles* is precisely the negation of such an ideology, and rather works to challenge its pretensions.

Notes

1. If in the English version the idea of endless repetition emphasized in the title of the last text seems to throw light retrospectively upon the development of the collection as a whole—thus still hinting at a possible teleology—the French edition of *Fizzles* connects these texts in a different order. Significantly, "Pour finir encore"—the French equivalent of *Fizzle 8*—is located at the opening of the collection: in this way, it anticipates the structural and conceptual inconclusiveness that sustains the work in its entirety. In addition, by collapsing the distinction between the starting and the terminal point, the title reinforces the idea of aborted attempt that defines these texts. Cf. Beckett, *Pour finir.* It is in the interplay of the two versions that Beckett's problematization of the act of writing and of representation emerges in its most disruptive aspect.

2. For the notion of ruins as supplements and for their connection with the impossible project of restoration through memory—as shown in *Fizzles*—see Derrida, *Mémoires* 68-71.

3. Because of these connotations, the "expelled" can also be defined in terms of Lyotard's "the jews."

4. The lack of control over time and space in Beckett's texts establishes a symptomatic contrast with the power that Marinetti proclaims over reality by taming exactly these two variables: "Human energy centupled by speed will master Time and Space." By glorifying "the beauty of speed" and the subsequent divine authority it provides, the avant-garde repudiates the weakness and the sense of exhaustion that characterize Beckett's postmodern universe. The "Futurist morality" aims at defending man "from decay caused by slowness [and] by memory," the specters that 50 years later would haunt the fiction of *Fizzles*. Cf. Flint 94-95.

5. The legs separated from the body, as well as all the other corporal fragments in John's etchings, partake of the supplementary aspect of "fizzles" and "foirades": because of their discrete nature—as revealed from one of the illustrations—they cannot be made to cohere into a whole. They express the lack of self-identity and the residual quality that characterize the traces in Beckett's texts. For the collaboration of Beckett and Johns cf. Prinz 480-510; Shloss 153-68

John Fletcher (essay date 1992)

SOURCE: Fletcher, John. "Joyce, Beckett, and the Short Story in Ireland." In *Re: Joyce 'n Beckett,* edited by Phyllis Carey and Ed Jewinski, pp. 3-20. New York: Fordham University Press, 1992.

[*In the following essay, Fletcher finds similarities between Beckett's "Fingal" and James Joyce's "Ivy Day in the Committee Room."*]

In freshman classes, I tend to define the short story as a short prose narrative of concentrated effect, complete within its own terms, showing a firm story-line and often an abrupt ending, limited in its temporal and spatial location and in the number of characters deployed, and tending to work through understatement and humor rather than explicit comment.

Joyce's *Dubliners* is one of the greatest short-story collections ever published. Beckett's **More Pricks Than Kicks,** an early book—one he refused for many years to allow to be reissued—is far from being in the same league. Still, they are worth comparing in the light of the above definition for a number of reasons. The first, and most obvious, is that the young Beckett greatly admired his older compatriot and sought to imitate him. Secondly, they are both set in Dublin and feature Dublin people, as Joyce's title explicitly acknowledges. Thirdly, they both deploy a particular sense of humor—at once intellectual, sardonic, and self-consciously literary—which readers tend to associate with Irish writing in general.

I would like in this essay to look closely at their art of the short story with particular reference to "Ivy Day in the Committee Room" from *Dubliners* and to the second story, **"Fingal,"** in **More Pricks Than Kicks.** I have deliberately chosen, as being more typical of their respective authors, stories that are less frequently discussed than, say, "The Dead" in Joyce's case or than **"Dante and the Lobster"** in Beckett's collection; because they are not perhaps the "best" story by either writer, they are, arguably, more representative of each collection taken as a whole.

"Ivy Day in the Committee Room" is set, as its full title implies, in an electoral ward committee room in Dublin as dusk falls on October 6 (Ivy Day, the anniversary of the death of Parnell) in a year early in the present century. A motley group of canvassers and election workers enter the room to warm themselves by the fire, to drink stout, and to chat. Warmed by liquor and fellowship, the half-dozen men become a trifle sentimental about their great hero, Parnell, and one of them, Joe Hynes, is prevailed upon to recite a piece of mawkish doggerel verse that he has written, being, in the eyes of his companions, "a clever chap . . . with the pen" (*D* 125). In an interesting use of what we now call intertextuality, Joyce gives the poem in extenso, all eleven stanzas of it. Deeply touched, Mr. Hynes's listeners give him a spontaneous round of applause. So moved is the poet himself that he pays no heed to the popping of the cork in his bottle of stout, and another prominent character (prominent in that he is present in the room throughout), Mr. O'Connor, starts to roll himself a cigarette, "the better to hide his emotion" (135). Even Mr. Crofton, who represents the Conservative interest (for the men, although in temporary electoral alliance, do not belong to the same political party), agrees that Hynes's panegyric is "a very fine piece of writing" (135). Joyce's irony is all the sharper for not being spelled out: drink and national sentiment temporarily unite these men who, otherwise, have little in common and who indeed (as their sarcastic remarks behind each other's backs reveal all too plainly) do not even greatly care for one another. They have, in other words, about as much charity as they have literary taste: precious little.

In Beckett's story, **"Fingal,"** the hero Belacqua takes his girlfriend Winnie on a walk in the countryside near Dublin. Because she is "hot" (**MPTK** [**More Pricks Than Kicks**] 23) (a sexist epithet that the author did not permit himself in later years), they take advantage of the fine spring weather to make love a couple of times. When not embracing, they gaze upon the Irish landscape in general and upon the Portrane Lunatic Asylum in particular, where Belacqua declares his heart to reside, and Winnie, a doctor friend of hers; so they agree to make for there. But Belacqua, his immediate sexual needs having now been gratified, abandons Winnie to her friend Dr. Sholto. He infinitely prefers to her company—now that the baser lusts of the flesh have been satisfied—that of a bicycle, which he steals from a farmworker. Much to Winnie's annoyance, he gets clean away on it, and the author leaves him drinking and laughing in a roadside pub. This is the "memorable fit of laughing" (23) referred to in the opening sentence of the story, a fit which, we are told, incapacitated Belacqua from further gallantry for some time.

The style throughout **"Fingal"**—indeed throughout the entire collection—is marked by elaborate and calculated allusiveness combined with extensively developed verbal irony. At its best this can give rise to suggestively witty prose, as in the coy way the sexual act is referred to: "They had not been very long on the top [of the hill] before [Belacqua] began to feel a very sad animal indeed" (23). This is an erudite allusion to a saying usually attributed to Galen, the most famous physician of ancient Rome, to the effect that every creature suffers depression after intercourse ("*omne animal post coitum triste est*"); and the bawdy innuendo here is that the first act of love must have been intensely pleasurable for Belacqua since it leaves him feeling particularly sad, whereas the second embrace, on the top of another hill, makes him only plain sad. (What Winnie experiences is not specified, unless we are meant to understand something quite abstruse from the assertion that, after the first occasion, she appears to Belacqua to be in high spirits; following the same logic, the author may be implying that she did not have an orgasm and so escaped Galen's depression. But this may be carrying obscene interpretation further than even this witty author intends.)

At less than its best, this kind of writing is pedantry pure and simple, arrogantly disdaining simple formulations and cloaking a banal idea in an esoteric manner. On the second page of the story, for instance, there is elaborate and rather fatuous play on the name of the French poet Alphonse de Lamartine, and on the third, some toying with Latin and Roman history. This is neither funny nor particularly clever, unlike the rather effective joke upon Galen's aphorism.

All the stories in **More Pricks Than Kicks** are set in Dublin and its environs and are, like *Dubliners,* permeated with the atmosphere of the Irish capital. In snatches of dialogue that anticipate the elegant Irishisms of *Waiting for Godot,* we hear the authentic brogue of the people, which Beckett sometimes helpfully translates ("Now would they¹ do him the favour to adjourn . . . ? This meant drink" [31]), and their characteristic accent ("Dean Swift" pronounced "Dane Swift" [33], for instance). Nevertheless, Belacqua is something of an outsider as far as ordinary Irish people are concerned: he is idle, he is educated, and above all, he is a Protestant, a "dirty lowdown Low Church Protestant highbrow" (172). Inevitably, then, one does not find in **More Pricks Than Kicks** the same intimate familiarity with Dublin life—the sense of belonging to a society that is unique with its particular customs, humor, and myths—as one experiences in *Dubliners.* The country and its people are contemplated in Beckett's collection from a certain distance, which is perhaps not so surprising in the work of a Protestant Irishman, but, for all that, the feeling of alienation cannot be explained solely in terms of religion and ethnic origin. Belacqua is not only a member of the "Protestant Ascendancy," which ruled Ireland until independence; he is also the first in a line of Beckettian heroes whose condition of exile becomes gradually more painful. He is, in fact, the natural precursor of Molloy and of the Unnamable.

Physically, indeed, Belacqua appears a bit of a clown, an early version of the Chaplinesque figures in *Waiting for Godot.* It is easy, for instance, for Dr. Sholto to give a "brief satirical description" (**MPTK** 34) of his person, which would run on these lines: a pale fat man, nearly bald, bespectacled, shabbily dressed, and always looking ill and dejected (he is suffering from impetigo on his face in "Fingal," much to the disgust of Winnie, who has been kissed by him). His appearance is in fact grotesque enough to provoke comment and even laughter in all places except where he is well known. He is a total eccentric; we have already noted his habit of preferring bicycles to women. This oddity in his reactions (or, rather, his incapacity for registering the normal reactions expected of him) is coupled with a faculty for acting with insufficient motivation, which his creator maintains is serious enough to make a mental home the place for him (hence his avowal that his heart resides in the Portrane Lunatic Asylum). But, even more than a padded cell, what Belacqua really longs for is to return to the womb, where he fantasizes about lying on his back in the dark forever, free from "night sweats" (i.e., sex). In default of such a refuge, Belacqua enjoys to the full a melancholy indulged in for its own sake: landscapes, such as Fingal, are of interest to him only insofar as they furnish him "with a pretext for a long face" (30).

Beckett uses this oddity—a person not quite at one with his fellow men, often more an onlooker than active participant in what goes on in the stories—for satirical ends. Inspired caricature fixes the less amiable aspects of a person in few words as is the case in **"Fingal"** with Dr. Sholto, "a pale dark man with a brow" (31) who feels "nothing but rancour" (32) toward Belacqua, evidently because Winnie prefers him to Sholto (which may indicate that what made Belacqua "sad" was pleasurable for her, after all). This is all the more galling to the pompous, prissy doctor in that Belacqua patently prefers his own company, laughing out loud alone in the pub, to getting "sad" with Winnie: his "sadness" falls from him "like a shift" (32) as soon as he finds the bicycle, we are told. Despite an unsightly rash on his face, we are meant to understand that Belacqua is "sexier" than Sholto, even assisted, as the latter is, by the aphrodisiac of a glass of whiskey.

Belacqua's compulsive urge to retreat from the body and its "night sweats" into the wider freedom of the mind springs from a dualistic conviction that he shares with his successor-heroes in the Beckett canon. They, too, are lovers of bicycles; man and machine together form what Hugh Kenner calls, in an arresting phrase, a "Cartesian centaur" (Kenner 132), from Descartes, whose thought deeply influenced the young Beckett who wrote **More Pricks Than Kicks.** In all his writing, indeed, Beckett advances his own version of Cartesianism, in which the mental part of his heroes seeks continually to escape from the physical part. In this early story, therefore, there is already discernible a theme—not quite drowned by the academic wit and the tiresome allusiveness—which becomes increasingly central in Beckett's fiction: the radical split between body and mind, a disconnection that allows the mind to retreat progressively into itself, into an isolated life of its own. In the later works, the body is left to break down, like a worn-out piece of machinery, while the mind, panic-stricken at the prospect of cessation, chatters on, rehashing continually its never-changing futilities.

Thus the seeds of *For to End Yet Again* were sown forty years earlier in **More Pricks Than Kicks,** just as the long road to *Finnegan's wake* starts out from the committee rooms and parlors of the Dubliners whom Joyce portrays so deftly in "Ivy Day" and the other stories. Just as the bicycle that enables Belacqua to escape from Winnie is the twin of the one that leads Molloy into his disastrous encounter with *his* mistress, Lousse, so the Liffey, which the friends cross in a ferryboat in the second story of *Dubliners,* is the same "riverrun," the same Anna Livia's "hitherandthithering waters of" *Finnegans Wake.*

Both writers, then, are supremely consistent with themselves: just as both—the senior, a Catholic; the junior, a Protestant—are intensely, politically, Irish. The political dimension is less in evidence in **"Fingal,"** but it is there, discreetly, in references to Swift and to the potato famine (the tower near which Belacqua and Winnie make love the second time was, they learn, "built for relief in the year of the Famine" [28]). The Fingal landscape stretching out before them is, Belacqua asserts in stoutly patriotic tones, a "magic land" comparable at least to Burgundy and far superior to Wicklow (24).

But Beckett does not—perhaps understandably, given his background—comment upon or even reflect contemporary Irish political concerns: there is no trace in his work of any reference to the Easter Rising or to the civil war; his criticisms are purely social and cultural in nature. Developments like literary censorship or the ban on contraceptives[2] he does satirize and debunk, but he eschews party politics and above all the bitter struggles surrounding the birth of the Irish Republic. Joyce, as a member of the majority community, feels no such inhibitions about expressing his feelings in *Dubliners.* There is telling satire in "The Dead" of the kind of nationalist virago who hurls the insult "West Briton!" at anyone who does not wear his shamrock heart on his sleeve, and in "Ivy Day in the Committee Room," as we have seen, mawkish patriotism is ridiculed in Mr. Hynes's ghastly doggerel. At the same time, the men's emotion is genuine enough, even if its expression is inflated and

pretentious. The figure of Parnell himself, it is important to note, is not ridiculed; if anything, it emerges enhanced by the extremes of devotion to which his admirers will go, composing and applauding bad verse in homage to their "dead King," felt so much more truly to be their sovereign lord than Edward VII, who is about to pay a visit to his "wild Irish" subjects (132) and who is derisively referred to as "Eddie" (124) for his pains. Insofar as the views of the implied author can be surmised, they are those of moderate nationalism, unemphatic patriotism, and temperate republicanism. This tolerant, non-extremist position stands in sharp contrast to the intolerance of the harpy in "The Dead" and to the naïve hero-worship of Mr. Hynes in "Ivy Day in the Committee Room."

Thus far, for the purposes of comparison, I have been treating **"Fingal"** and "Ivy Day in the Committee Room" as more or less of equal interest, but, as I made clear at the outset, the two stories are not of equal merit. Joyce's story, even though not the finest story in *Dubliners,* is markedly superior to **"Fingal."** For one thing, Beckett's story is slighter, shorter than Joyce's by about a third, and it deploys fewer and less interesting characters. Belacqua engages our sympathy, no doubt because the author tends to treat him indulgently, but Winnie is not very plausible, and Sholto is no more than sketched. Joyce, by contrast, introduces seven main characters and brings them on like a competent dramatist at different points in the narrative. Old Jack and Mr. O'Connor are present as the story opens and remain in the room throughout; Mr. Hynes the poet enters, leaves, and re-enters later to deliver his composition; Mr. Henchy enters about one-third of the way through; Father Keon puts in a brief, rather sinister appearance at about the half-way mark; and Mr. Crofton and Mr. Lyons walk in shortly afterward and remain to the end. This deployment of characters gives a much tauter feel to the story than Beckett's does. The effect (to return to my simple definition of the genre outlined at the beginning of this essay) is therefore more noticeably concentrated in "Ivy Day in the Committee Room," and the story line is appreciably firmer, the end coming precisely when it should, with the emotional responses to Hynes's elegy undercut by the implied author's discreet mockery of the enterprise when he gets Mr. Crofton (normally a political opponent) to concede that it is "a very fine piece of writing." The manner in which the end of **"Fingal"** refers back to the beginning (confirming the previously enigmatic allusion to Belacqua's fit of laughing) is competent enough but feels rather contrived in comparison with the ending of "Ivy Day in the Committee Room."

Both stories are sensibly limited in terms of temporal and spatial location, each covering a few hours in real time and a single setting, the committee room in Joyce's case and the vicinity of the Portrane asylum in Beckett's. The closed space of the committee room symbolizes the inward-looking nature of the men's political and social concerns—parochial and mundane—just as Beckett's outing to the country in fine weather is the objective correlative of Belacqua's escaping from convention and flouting of social niceties. And, last but not least, both writers work their effects by understatement and humor rather than explicit comment, although Beckett is, rather curiously, more old-fashioned than Joyce in his occasional, admittedly muted, use of the authorial aside to the reader, a device that the modernist Joyce eschews altogether. Not only that, but the Beckettian asides reveal the writer's unease: he is not really at home in the short-story form, and rhetorical questions like "Who shall silence them, at last?" (26) betray his discomfort. We are, after all, nearly half a century away from the great brief texts *Imagination Dead Imagine, Lessness, Still* and the others, texts that are Beckett's supreme, unique contribution to the short prose form. The classic short story, on the other hand, the kind that Chekhov, Henry James, D. H. Lawrence, and Joyce himself developed to such a high pitch of aesthetic perfection and emotional power, was never (to use an apt colloquialism) Beckett's "scene," any more than the play in several acts was: he wisely abandoned about the same time an attempt to write a stage work in four acts, one act devoted to each of the four years between the widowing and the remarriage of Mrs. Thrale, Dr. Johnson's friend. In the only section actually composed, Act One, Scene One, the tone is already at odds with the realistic, historical material that Beckett was trying manfully to shape into dramatic form. The pauses, repetitions, and formal patterns in the fragment that survives are precisely those which he was to hone later, in *Waiting for Godot,* into a style that, even as early as 1937, is characteristically Beckettian. But the form available to him in the '30s was not suitable to his purposes, and he abandoned the project (*Disjecta* 155-66). He did not abandon *More Pricks Than Kicks,* but he did, as we saw earlier, refuse for many years to have it reissued. In his eyes the book was juvenile stuff, and although that judgment was not fair, he was correct in accepting that, as examples of the short story form, his collection did not begin to match up to those of his great mentor Joyce.

The difference is highlighted by the humor. In both cases, as I said at the outset, this is intellectual, sardonic, self-consciously literary, and characteristically Irish in manner. But in Beckett's case the intellectualism is just too clever by half, the wryness veers disturbingly close to spite, and the literary self-consciousness borders on the arch. The difference between a master of the form and an apprentice who is trying hard to do well can be seen in sharp focus if two characteristic passages of humorous dialogue are compared in detail. In *Dubliners* Joyce wrote:

> The old man watched him attentively and then, taking up the piece of cardboard again, began to fan the fire slowly while his companion smoked.
>
> "Ah, yes," he said, continuing, "it's hard to know what way to bring up children. Now who'd think he'd turn out like that! I sent him to the Christian Brothers and I done what I could for him, and there he goes boozing about. I tried to make him somewhat decent." 5
>
> He replaced the cardboard wearily.
>
> "Only I'm an old man now I'd change his tune for him. I'd take the stick to his back and beat him while I could stand over him—as I done many a time before. The mother you know, she cocks him up with this and that. . . ." 10
>
> "That's what ruins children," said Mr. O'Connor.
>
> "To be sure it is," said the old man. "And little thanks you get for it, only impudence. He takes th'upper hand of me whenever he sees I've a sup taken. What's the world coming to when sons speaks that way to their fathers?" 15
>
> "What age is he?" said Mr. O'Connor.
>
> "Nineteen," said the old man. 20
>
> "Why don't you put him to something?"
>
> "Sure, amn't I never done at the drunken bowsy ever since he left school? 'I won't keep you,' I says. 'You must get a job for yourself.' But, sure, it's worse whenever he gets a job; he drinks it all."
>
> Mr. O'Connor shook his head in sympathy, and the old man fell silent, gazing into the fire 25.
>
> [119-20]

Beckett's humor is quite different, as the following passage from *More Pricks Than Kicks* reveals:

> A stout block of an old man in shirt sleeves and slippers was leaning against the wall of the field. Winnie still sees, as vividly as when they met her anxious gaze for the first time, his great purple face and white moustaches. Had he seen a stranger about, a pale fat man in a black leather coat. 5
>
> "No miss" he said.
>
> "Well" said Winnie, settling herself on the wall, to Sholto, "I suppose he's about somewhere."
>
> A land of sanctuary, he had said, where much had been suffered secretly. Yes, the last ditch. 10
>
> "You stay here" said Sholto, madness and evil in his heart, "and I'll take a look in the church."
>
> The old man had been showing signs of excitement.
>
> "Is it an escape?" he enquired hopefully.
>
> "No no" said Winnie, "just a friend." 15
>
> But he was off, he was unsluiced.
>
> "I was born on Lambay" he said, by way of opening to an endless story of a recapture in which he had distinguished himself, "and I've worked here man and boy."

"In that case" said Winnie "maybe you can tell me what the ruins are." 20

"That's the church" he said, pointing to the near one, it had just absorbed Sholto, "and that" pointing to the far one, "'s the tower."

"Yes" said Winnie "but what tower, what was it?" 25

"The best I know" he said "is some Lady Something had it."

This was news indeed.

[32-33]

Both writers feature characters who speak in Dubin dialect, but Beckett catches it less accurately (lines 17-19, 22-24 and 26) than Joyce does: the syntax in Joyce is exact and plausible, fully characteristic of the Dublin working class (in standard English "only I'm" in line 10 would be "if I were not," and "while" in line 11 would be "until," with "I could no longer" replacing "I could"; and "amn't I never done at" in line 22 would be "do I ever stop remonstrating with"). At the lexical level, words like "cocks up" (12-13), "sup" for "drink" (17), and "bowsy" (22) are authentic Irish idioms, nonstandard English, as "somewhat" (7) would be "into someone" in standard speech. Grammatically, "done" for "did" (6) and "says" for "say" (23) are examples of dialectal deviations.

What these contrasted examples really show, of course, is not so much that Beckett could not reproduce dialect authentically as that he was not greatly interested in doing so. He was not concerned with realism at all, in fact, as is revealed stylistically by his use of non-realist features like free indirect speech (4-5), self-quotation or self-intertextualization (9-10), and authorial asides (16, 27).

This crucial difference between Beckett's approach and Joyce's affects the nature of their humor. Joyce's is mimetic; Beckett's is self-reflexive. Joyce's is satirical, that is, extroverted, while Beckett's is self-conscious, that is, introverted. Joyce's suits admirably the short-story form; Beckett's does not. Both men are great writers, but Joyce is already working at the peak of his form in *Dubliners,* whereas for Beckett, the works of his maturity have still to be written when ***More Pricks Than Kicks*** is composed. Had Beckett died in the same year as Joyce did, he would now be remembered, if at all, as a mere promising disciple of a great Irish writer. The world is fortunate that he lived, in fact, much longer than Joyce (who died at the age of fifty-eight) and became a great Irish writer in his turn. We, their readers, able to re-Joyce 'n Beckett, are thus doubly blessed.

Notes

1. The phrasing "Now they would do . . ." is a misprint in the original. The order as printed makes no sense in Anglo-Irish. Also the question mark indicates an interrogative order.

2. See "Censorship in the Saorstat" (*Disjecta* 84-88), and *Watt* for an extended joke about the aphrodisiac Bando which, like the humble condom, "cannot enter our ports, nor cross our northern frontier, [but] is immediately seized, and confiscated, by some gross customs official half crazed with seminal intoxication . . ." (170).

Works Cited

Kenner, Hugh. "The Cartesian Centaur." *Perspective* 11 (Autumn 1959): 132-41.

John P. Harrington (essay date 1992)

SOURCE: Harrington, John P. "Beckett, Joyce, and Irish Writing: The Example of Beckett's 'Dubliners' Story." In *Re: Joyce'n Beckett,* edited by Phyllis Carey and Ed Jewinski, pp. 31-42. New York: Fordham University Press, 1992.

[*In the following essay, Harrington investigates the influence of James Joyce on Beckett's short fiction, arguing that "A Case in a Thousand" is "the most apparent adoption in Beckett's early fiction of the style of Joyce's own early work."*]

After his work had taken on characteristic form and after he had acquired the public stature usual on winning the Nobel Prize, Samuel Beckett described his younger self of the 1930s as "'a very young writer with nothing to say and the itch to make'" (Harvey 273). The itch to make without anything much to say is, of course, no specifically Irish phenomenon, but it was a particularly acute and a particularly dismal predicament in Ireland in the 1930s. The predicament was not lack of models, for there was a wide choice of exemplary figures as well as regular public debate over the quest for that fabulous Irish chimera, a unified national aesthetic. Rather, the predicament lay in the embarrassment of conveniently located riches. Writing on this in 1976 when, presumably, that predicament remained a current concern, Denis Donoghue concluded that "the price we pay for Yeats and Joyce is that each in his way gave Irish experience a memorable but narrow definition . . . the minor writers of the Irish literary revival were not strong enough to counter Yeats's incantatory rhetoric: no writer in Ireland has been strong enough to modify Joyce's sense of Irish experience in fiction" (131). Donoghue's "no writer in Ireland" qualification here may be a deliberate exclusion of Beckett. But most often Beckett is excluded from discussions of Irish writing by unexamined convention. However, Beckett offers the way out of memorable but narrow definitions of Irish experience. He offers no incantatory rhetoric or distinctly negative sense of Irish experience. Rather,

Beckett's work offers a view of Irish experience that is not narrow, exclusionist, or otherwise provincial. Yeats and Joyce, of course, are not predominantly provincial, but the subsequent example of Beckett does throw into interesting relief the provincial strain of their work and that of others associated with the Irish literary revival and its aftermath.

The young Beckett seems to have dealt expeditiously with the spell of Yeats's incantatory rhetoric. Nevertheless, Beckett's Irish past is one of the more untidy areas of record. Richard Ellmann's recent revelation in *Nayman of Noland* (26) that Yeats himself praised and quoted *Whoroscope* to Beckett in Killiney in 1932 hints at passing literary relations then between Ireland's Nobel past and Nobel future. A fairly recent reminder of that relation's likely complexity was the basis of Beckett's 1976 teleplay ". . . but the clouds . . .," an allusion to Yeats's "The Tower."

Young Beckett's fancy for cosmopolitanism and newness meant that the cost of being Irish and literary was to be exacted first by Joyce. Though by now Beckett has in many ways matched the stature of Joyce as a figure on the literary landscape, Beckett's first reception often included an almost persecutorial sort of circumstantial association with Joyce. At one time part of that association was rumored identity as "Joyce's secretary"; later that was improved to the now familiar "*not* Joyce's secretary." The sense of Beckett as formed by Joyce persisted even after he got as unlike Joyce as possible, even after he chose French over English and drama over fiction, changes as radical as possible but liable to perception as overreaction. Among the early responses to Beckett's first produced plays, for example, was Lionel Abel's commentary in 1959 on *Godot* and *Endgame* in an essay called "Joyce the Father, Beckett the Son": "Joyce is present in Beckett's plays; he is confronted and he is vanquished, though Beckett, whether as Lucky or Clov, is never shown to be victorious" (27).

In early critical apprehension of Beckett as epigone of Joyce and often in critical consensus today, that confrontation and vanquishment were not of Joyce as overbearing personal example, or of Joyce as formulator of Irish experience in fiction, but of Joyce the author of *Finnegans Wake*. This notion was epitomized in the Shenker "interview" in 1956 when Beckett was characterized as saying "'The kind of work I do is one in which I'm not master of my material. The more Joyce knew the more he could. He's tending toward omniscience and omnipotence as an artist. I'm working with impotence, ignorance'" (3). The emphasis on the amount Joyce "knew," presumably cumulative, and the omnipotence to which Joyce was "tending" imply preoccupation with Joyce's last work. Even Beckett's decision to write in French is phrased and depreciated by

Ellmann in terms of Joyce and *Finnegans Wake:* Beckett's "boldness was almost without precedent. It freed him from literary forefathers. It was a decision only less radical than Joyce's in inventing his extravagant *Finnegans Wake*-ese" (16). The Shenker portrayal of Beckett's work as mired in a kind of inverse relationship to Joyce's, tending to ignorance while Joyce's tended to omniscience, encouraged perception of Beckett's early work in terms of Joyce, in terms of *Finnegans Wake* and in terms of *Finnegans Wake*-ese as a great mistake. Vivian Mercier, an acquaintance of Beckett's and an estimable commentator on Irish letters, reiterated this view in the late 1970s: Beckett's "greatest folly consisted in attempting to imitate James Joyce: not the earlier work, either, but *Work in Progress,* the drafts of *Finnegans Wake*" (36).

There is some reason to see Beckett in the 1930s as largely motivated by emulation of and slow progress away from what was then Joyce's *Work in Progress.* Chronologies of his work, of course, usually begin with publication in 1929 of "Dante . . . Bruno. Vico . . . Joyce" both in *transition* and in a celebratory volume of essays in anticipation and encouragement of Joyce's work. Beckett's first publications in Dublin, in *T.C.D.: A College Miscellany,* were the fragmentary, anonymous dialogues called **"Che Sciagura"** (1929) and **"The Possessed"** (1930). These were seen in Dublin as quite obviously written under the spell of Joyce and the style of *Work in Progress:* "'In the Joycean medley,'" *T.C.D.* later commented on the second of these early works, "'its anonymous author performs some diverting verbal acrobatics, but in the manner of a number of *transition*'s offspring, is too allusive to be generally comprehensible'" (quoted in Bair 131). Indeed, Beckett cultivated this association with Joyce by appending to his poems for a 1931 anthology called *The European Caravan* a contributor's note that read in part: "'Samuel Beckett is the most interesting of the younger Irish writers. . . . He has a great knowledge of Romance literature, is a friend of Rudmose-Brown and of Joyce, and has adapted the Joyce method to his poetry with original results'" (quoted in Bair 129-30). The Joyce method of greatest interest then was the method of *Works in Progress,* which began sporadic publication in *transition* in 1927 as vanguard of its self-proclaimed revolution of the word. In this example of rather Whitmanesque arrogance, Beckett points to Rudmose-Brown, his mentor at Trinity College, as his background and to the Joyce method as his means to originality. The influence of *Work in Progress* is also clear in the excerpts from *Dream of Fair to Middling Women* published in 1932 under the titles **"Sedendo et Quiescendo"** in *transition* (misprinted as **"Quiesciendo"**) and **"Text"** in *The New Review.* In Dublin, such progress as Beckett had made in freeing himself from *Work in Progress* as he refashioned material from *Dream* for **More Pricks Than Kicks** was seen as only a slight inverse movement through Joyce's works. "'Mr. Beckett is an extremely clever young man,'" concluded *The Dublin Magazine* in its review of **More Pricks Than Kicks** in 1934, "'and he knows his *Ulysses* as a Scotch Presbyterian knows his *Bible*'" (quoted in Bair 179).

However, the tendency to view the young Beckett as devoted exclusively to Joyce's last works oversimplifies Beckett's critique of his predecessor. Though "Dante . . . Bruno. Vico.. Joyce" was of necessity devoted almost entirely to *Work in Progress*, Beckett's essay also refers familiarly to *The Day of the Rabblement*, which was Joyce's own 1901 declaration of independence from Irish literary predecessors. Furthermore, early in this essay Beckett discusses Stephen Dedalus' attitude in *A Portrait of the Artist as a Young Man*, and later in it he quotes part of Stephen's assertions to Lynch on the aesthetic image. David Hayman, in "A Meeting in the Park and a Meeting on the Bridge" (373), has pointed to echoes of *Portrait* and of *Exiles* in Beckett's first published short story, **"Assumption,"** which appeared in *transition* in 1929 in the same issue as "Dante . . . Bruno. Vico.. Joyce." Even **"Sedendo et Quiescendo,"** which is obviously derived in style from *Work in Progress*, alludes in "art thou pale with weariness" (13) and in "a pale and ardent generation" (14) to Stephen's poem in *Portrait* and derivation of it from Shelley's "To the Moon." In addition, **More Pricks Than Kicks**, however stridently it demonstrates its author's knowledge of *Ulysses*, also includes a story, **"A Wet Night,"** that gives its attention to *Dubliners* and in particular to "The Dead." Beckett's story, like "The Dead," describes a Christmas season party in Dublin hosted and attended by Dubliners who anxiously exude continental sophistication while showing irritability with Gaelic aficionados. At the end of Joyce's *Dubliners* story, of course, Gabriel Conroy approaches new self-knowledge as he views the snow from the window of his room in the Gresham Hotel: "It was falling on every part of the dark central plain, on the treeless hills, falling softly upon the Bog of Allen and, farther westward, softly falling into the dark mutinous Shannon waves" (223). In Beckett's **More Pricks Than Kicks** story, it is rain, not snow, that falls, and the character, Belacqua, is oblivious to rather than intent on the rain that "fell upon the bay, the littoral, the mountains and the plains, and notably upon the Central Bog it fell with a rather desolate uniformity" (83). Nevertheless, Beckett's reference to Joyce's story is scarcely devoted imitation. That clear echo of Joyce is followed in Beckett's story by an obviously parodic approach to self-knowledge by Belacqua: "What was that? He shook off his glasses and stooped his head to see. That was his hands. Now who would have thought that!" (83).

More Pricks Than Kicks was published on May 24, 1934. In July it was reviewed in *The Bookman* by Francis Watson, who, having mentioned Beckett's mono-graph on Proust and his involvement in the translation into French of portions of *Works in Progress*, asserted that "The influence of Joyce is indeed patent in **More Pricks Than Kicks** but Mr. Beckett is no fashionable imitator. Like Joyce he is a Dubliner and an exile, and Dublin has for him that peculiar compulsion which it exercises upon all Irishmen except Bernard Shaw" (219-20). Watson's laudatory review, which praised **More Pricks Than Kicks** as "one of those rare books to be read more than once" (220), may have provided Beckett with the opportunity to contribute to the "Irish Number" of *The Bookman* in August of 1934. That issue included single essays by Stephen Gwynn, Lennox Robinson, and Sean O'Faolain. Beckett contributed two pieces to the issue. One was a review essay, now well known and reprinted, called "Recent Irish Poetry." The other was a short story, not well known and not reprinted, called **"A Case in a Thousand."**

"Recent Irish Poetry" unambiguously categorizes Irish poets as the "antiquarians" or the "others." The antiquarians are those working poets who adhere to "accredited themes" derived from the Irish literary revival's formulation of a national literary identity and sustained by Yeats. The "others," notably Thomas McGreevy and Denis Devlin, friends of Beckett's and within the brood *T.C.D.* called "*transition*'s offspring," pursue instead "awareness of the new thing that has happened, or the old thing that has happened again, namely the breakdown of the object, whether current, historical, mythical or spook" (*Disjecta* 70). Beckett had already reviewed a collection of McGreevy's poems in the July 1934 issue of *The Dublin Magazine*, and he would articulate his admiration for Devlin in a review for *transition* in 1938 (both reviews have been reprinted in *Disjecta*). In "Recent Irish Poetry," McGreevy, Devlin, and Brian Coffey are decreed "the nucleus of a living poetic in Ireland" (76). The bulk of the review, though, is given over to evisceration of the "antiquarians," including less than admiring references to fellow contributors to this special issue of *The Bookman*. One fellow contributor was Frank O'Connor, the only one other than Beckett with two pieces in the issue. Though no associate of *transition*, O'Connor was as effective as Beckett in lampooning the forms of antiquarianism in Ireland in the 1930s; his essay describes how nativism and the state revival of Gaelic in combination with censorship of writers like O'Faolain and Liam O'Flaherty had the result of government sponsorship of Gaelic translations of Emily Brontë, Dickens, and Conrad. Like Beckett, O'Connor signed his two contributions differently. O'Connor's story, "The Man That Stopped," appeared under the pseudonym he would maintain, while his essay, "Two Languages," appeared under his own name, Michael O'Donovan. Beckett's essay, "Recent Irish Poetry," appeared under a pseudonym he would never use again, "Andrew Belis," while his story, **"A Case in a Thousand,"** appeared under his own name. One imagines that the short story of Samuel Beckett should not be construed as wholly apart from the living poetic in Ireland proclaimed by Andrew Belis.

"A Case in a Thousand" is the most apparent adoption in Beckett's early fiction of the style of Joyce's own early work. It is written with a scrupulous meanness uncharacteristic of Beckett's other early fiction, including precise but understated attention to descriptive details of principal and minor characters. Forms of address, variations in Anglo-Irish dialect, and trivial mannerisms indicate social distinctions among characters. The Dublin setting at a nursing home beside The Grand Canal is established unobtrusively and without the sort of painful and scatological imagery common in Beckett's Dublin poems of this period, such as "Eneug I." The narrative, in the third person, proceeds without the allusiveness and obfuscation usual in Beckett's *"transition*'s offspring" fiction.

The story concerns a Dr. Nye and his treatment of a tubercular boy who is worsening since surgery by another doctor. Dr. Nye's treatment of the case is complicated by his discovery that the boy's mother, who watches the hospital room window from the bank of the canal outside, is in fact his own former nanny, a Mrs. Bray. Soon Dr. Nye must make a decision on a second operation. He chooses surgery, the boy dies, and Dr. Nye feels compelled to confront Mrs. Bray with his memory of infantile eroticism. Mrs. Bray clarifies the memory for Nye, in a conversation denied the reader, and they part: "Mrs. Bray to go and pack up her things and the dead boy's things, Dr. Nye to carry out Wasserman's [*sic*] test on an old schoolfellow" (242).

As the title suggests, Beckett's story echoes in important instances Joyce's "A Painful Case" story from *Dubliners*. Beckett's story opens with great economy and asserts in the opening of the second paragraph that "Dr. Nye belonged to the sad men, but not to the extent of accepting, in the blank way the most of them do, this condition as natural and proper. He looked upon it as a disorder" (241). Joyce's story opens with a more elaborate exposition of setting and scene and asserts in the opening of the second paragraph that "Mr. Duffy abhorred anything which betokened physical or mental disorder. A medieval doctor would have called him saturnine" (108). Both characters are troubled by women characters, who threaten the males' assumed roles and assured selves. Mr. Duffy's relationship with Mrs. Sinico begins when "little by little he entangled his thoughts with hers" (110). Beckett's character resists his thoughts and entanglement with Mrs. Bray when "little by little Dr. Nye reintegrated his pathological outlook" (242). The entanglements in both stories are confessional. "With almost maternal solicitude," Mrs. Sinico encourages Mr. Duffy "to let his nature open to

the full; she became his confessor" (110). Mrs. Bray offers to Dr. Nye the opportunity to "disclose the trauma at the root of this attachment" (242). In Joyce's story, the relationship ends on a trivial indelicacy, and years later Mr. Duffy learns in reports about Mrs. Sinico's death that she had become one of "the hobbling wretches whom he had seen carrying cans and bottles to be filled by the barman" (115). In Beckett's story, the relationship ends in Dr. Nye's childhood, and years later he is "troubled to find that of the woman whom as baby and small boy he had adored, nothing remained but the strawberry mottle of the nose and the breath smelling heavily of clove and peppermint" (242). Near the end of "A Painful Case" Mr. Duffy is revolted by "the threadbare phrases, the inane expressions of sympathy, the cautious words of a reporter" (115) used in the newspaper report of Mrs. Sinico's death. At the end of **"A Case in a Thousand"** such words are elided: Mrs. Bray "related a matter connected with his earliest years, so trivial and intimate that it need not be enlarged on here, but from the elucidation of which Dr. Nye, that sad man, expected great things" (242).

Both stories pivot on moments when the male characters recoil from their women confessors; when, in Beckett's words and in both cases, "he really could not bear another moment of her presence" (242). The consequence of Mr. Duffy's withdrawal is the eventual realization that he has sentenced himself, that his own "life would be lonely too until he, too, died" (116), and so, finally, that "no one wanted him; he was outcast from life's feast" (117). In **"A Case in a Thousand"** Dr. Nye has a comparable revelation, but at the beginning of the story and without context: "Without warning a proposition sprang up in his mind: Myself I cannot save" (241). Beckett's story most resembles those in *Dubliners* in the occurrence of such an epiphany, such a sudden perception of limitation. In the Beckett story, however, that epiphany is preliminary, not conclusive, and it is not explicitly connected with the subsequent events in the story. **"A Case in a Thousand"** demands comparison with "A Painful Case" in title, narrative, and style, but it manipulates the poetics of the Joycean model in a fashion that disrupts representation of oppressive determinacy. Beckett's story is an ironic form of this "Joyce method," as indeed his earlier use of the "Joyce method" of *Work in Progress* is ironic, though perhaps insufficiently so if it seems to later commentators a great mistake.

"A Case in a Thousand" is of interest in several respects other than the parallel with "A Painful Case." Deirdre Bair, for example, finds it most significant because it "seems in many respects to be Beckett's way of using his analysis creatively" and because "the story contains the same equivocal erotic attitudes toward women first introduced with Belacqua in *Dream* and *More Pricks Than Kicks*" (185). Eoin O'Brien, in *The*

Beckett Country, identifies the setting of the story as the Portobello Nursing Home. O'Brien discusses that nursing home along with the Merrion Nursing Home, which is only two bridges away on the canal (195-201). At the Merrion Nursing Home Beckett attended his mother's final illness in 1950, and *Krapp's Last Tape* evokes the experience of watching a hospital room window from outside, like Mrs. Bray's. The setting of **"A Case in a Thousand"** is an early, more easily identifiable appearance in Beckett's work of the canal on the south side of Dublin, which reappears in many later works—for example, in *That Time.* Also, in this story Dr. Nye weighs the charms of a meditative life that spares the feet and thinks in bed in the fashion of Malone. Mrs. Bray is introduced into the story with an emphasis on hat and bosom and umbrella suggestive of Winnie in *Happy Days.*

Biography, autobiography, and portents of later work aside, **"A Case in a Thousand"** remains of interest for its indication of the kind of influence on Beckett's work of Joyce's work and for its appearance in a special issue on Irish writing. In the same "Irish Number" of *The Bookman* Norreys Jephson O'Conor, writing on "The Trend of Anglo-Irish Literature," offered the opinion that "younger [Irish] writers, brought up in the atmosphere of what is euphuistically called the 'trouble,' in their search for realism turned towards Russian and other Continental authors—an attitude strengthened by the experimentation and growing reputation of James Joyce" (234). O'Conor was no doubt thinking of Irish writers, such as Frank O'Connor, who advertised their admiration of the Russian short story. But Norreys Jephson O'Conor's observation indicates that Joyce's example could then, in 1934, be one of experimentation, including forms of realism like *Dubliners* and not only the polyglot allusiveness of *Work in Progress.* Consideration of **"A Case in a Thousand"** beside "Sedendo et Quiescendo" indicates the extent to which Joyce's example was less than monolithic, less a limitation than a liberation, and less one of a single experiment than one of the enterprise of experimentation. It is entirely in keeping with such an example that Beckett's **"A Case in a Thousand"** is less imitation of "A Painful Case" than ironic manipulation of its method. The effect of such use of a well-known model is a story that is a critique—in this case a commentary on the poetics and representation of contingent entrapments central to Joyce's story. **"A Case in a Thousand"** certainly is not the only critique of a model in Beckett's early fiction, or even the only critique of Joyce's works. But Beckett, as the prescient Francis Watson recognized as early as 1934, was "no fashionable imitator." **"A Case in a Thousand"** is an early instance of the project central to Beckett's later work, the play with epistemology—the project that propels the narratives of Molloy, Malone, and the Unnamable and preoccupies the characters waiting on stage for Godot.

The example of Joyce for a writer like Beckett in the 1930s ("nothing to say and the itch to make") entailed the influence of Joyce's work both in itself and as exemplar of new Irish writing. In the 1930s, when most apparently conscious of Joyce's work, Beckett was also most conscious of being an Irish writer. Soon after writing these two pieces for the "Irish Number" of *The Bookman,* Beckett wrote "Censorship in the Saorstat," an essay on the absurdity of the Irish Censorship of Publications Act of 1929. Derision of that piece of legislation was then a favorite pastime of Irish writers both "antiquarian" and "other," as witness Frank O'Connor's essay for the "Irish Number." Furthermore, writing on that subject gave Beckett the opportunity to include himself and *More Pricks Than Kicks* in the group of Irish writers and works, including Joyce and *Ulysses,* for whom and for which being banned at home was a badge of honor. "Censorship in the Saorstat" was prepared for *The Bookman,* but the journal ceased publication before that essay could appear.

Joyce could sustain younger writers in many ways, but for Beckett in the 1930s an important part of that sustenance lay in Joyce's example for consciously Irish writers. Irish writers younger than Beckett testify to the liberating effect of the example of Joyce and the connection of that example to Beckett. Thomas Kinsella, casting the influences on Irish writers in the same Yeats/Joyce terms as Denis Donoghue, concludes that "Yeats stands for the Irish tradition as broken; Joyce for it as continuous, as healed—or healing—from its mutilation" (65). The mutilation in question here is precisely the rigidity of conventions, or imitation, termed antiquarianism by Beckett in "Recent Irish Poetry." Aidan Higgins, in the course of asking "Who follows Beckett, himself following so closely on Joyce?" characterizes those works not following Joyce and Beckett as "linear, traditional, benign, and dull" (60). Just those qualities were circumvented in Beckett's **"A Case in a Thousand"** because the story followed from, and did not merely imitate, Joyce's "A Painful Case." In David Hanly's novel *In Guilt and in Glory* two characters discuss Joyce and then continue, with ambivalent sarcasm, to Beckett: "'He's a Protestant of English blood,'" says one, "'educated at Trinity, a cricket player who lived in Paris and writes in French. Of course he's Irish'" (99). These approach definitions of Irish experience that are not narrow.

These examples, like that of **"A Case in a Thousand,"** point to the interesting dimension of Beckett's work in the context of Irish writing. He is a complicated and enriching addition to the local literary history. In turn, Yeats helped define Ireland as a positivistic literary subject, Joyce offered a scrupulous critique of Ireland, and Beckett adumbrated the luxury of aloofness to Ireland. This last is, too, a liberation. **"A Case in a Thousand"** is a significant example of the extent to which the young

Beckett was most conscious of himself as an Irish writer and, like many others, one most conscious of Joyce's own early work. In extricating himself from inherited cultural and national contexts, Beckett began the critique that extended to literary form and language in his major works. Though close attention to Irish literary precedents is for the most part a feature of Beckett's early work, the examination of inherited premises in **"A Case in a Thousand"** and other early pieces is compatible with the analysis of *Godot* or *How It Is.* Just that continuity and relevance of early work to late is one sense of the words of the narrator of *Company,* written in English and published in 1980: "Having covered in your day some twenty-five thousand leagues or roughly thrice the girdle. And never once overstepped a radius of one from home. Home!" (60).

Works Cited

Abel, Lionel. "Joyce the Father, Beckett the Son." *The New Leader* 14 December 1959: 26-27.

Bair, Deirdre. *Samuel Beckett: A Biography.* New York: Harcourt Brace Jovanovich, 1978.

Beckett, Samuel. "A Case in a Thousand." *The Bookman* 86 (1934): 241-42.

———. "Sedendo et Quiesciendo" [sic]. *transition* 21 (1932): 13-20.

Donoghue, Denis. "Being Irish Together." *The Sewanee Review* 84.1 (1976): 129-33.

Ellmann, Richard. *Samuel Beckett: Nayman of Noland.* Washington, D.C.: Library of Congress, 1986.

Hanly, David. *In Guilt and in Glory.* New York: Morrow, 1979.

Harvey, Lawrence. *Samuel Beckett: Poet and Critic.* Princeton: Princeton University Press, 1970.

Hayman, David. "A Meeting in the Park and a Meeting on the Bridge: Joyce and Beckett." *James Joyce Quarterly* 8 (Summer 1971): 372-84.

Higgins, Aidan. "Tired Lines, or Tales My Mother Told Me." *A Bash in the Tunnel: James Joyce by the Irish.* Ed. John Ryan. Brighton: Clifton, 1970. 55-60.

Irish Number. Special Issue of *The Bookman* 86 (1934).

Kinsella, Thomas. "The Irish Writer." *Davis, Mangan, Ferguson? Tradition and the Irish Writer.* By W. B. Yeats and Thomas Kinsella. Dublin: Dolmen, 1970. 57-66.

Mercier, Vivian. *Beckett/Beckett.* Oxford: Oxford University Press, 1977.

O'Brien, Eoin. *The Beckett Country: Samuel Beckett's Ireland.* Monkstown, Co. Dublin: Black Cat Press, 1986.

Shenker, Israel. "Moody Man of Letter." *The New York Times* 6 May 1956: sec. 2; 1,3.

Watson, Francis. Review of *More Pricks Than Kicks. The Bookman* 86 (1934): 219-20.

Michael J. Noble (essay date 1993)

SOURCE: Noble, Michael J. "Speaking the Same Language: Samuel Beckett, Jacques Derrida and Vice Versa." *The Journal of the Utah Academy of Sciences, Arts, and Letters* 70 (1993): 81-90.

[*In the following essay, Noble underscores the common characteristics of the language in Beckett's short stories and Derrida's language theory, contending that "the texts of Derrida and Beckett speak the same ideological and theoretical language."*]

The title page of an English edition of a work by Samuel Beckett or Jacques Derrida is likely to include a translation credit because these writers originally wrote in French. But French is not the only common characteristic of the language of these two writers; the texts of Derrida and Beckett speak the same ideological and theoretical language.

Derrida, as a reader of his own writings and those of Beckett, describes such a theoretical language when he answers a question posed to him in an interview by Derik Attridge. Attridge asks Derrida why he does not write about Beckett, and Derrida replies that he does not feel enough distance from Beckett to write about him:

> This is a writer to whom I feel very close, or to whom I would like to feel myself very close; but also too close. Precisely because of this proximity, it is too hard for me. . . . I have perhaps avoided him a bit because of this identification. Too hard . . . because he writes—in my language, in a language which is his up to a point, mine up to a point (for both of us it is a "differently" foreign language)—texts which are both too close to me and too distant for me even to be able to "respond" to them.
>
> (Acts 60)

Derrida recognizes a shared language with Beckett. If "language" may be broadly defined as a means of representation, what Derrida suggests is that his own texts and those of Beckett represent in similar ways. In addition to explaining the close proximity of their systems of representation, Derrida goes on to explain a simultaneous distance, a "differently foreign" language. It is this paradox that makes it impossible for Derrida to "respond" to Beckett; to do so would be, at once, redundant because of the similarity of the two modes of representation and unworkable because of the distance that necessarily divides the two. Derrida cannot escape his own language to comment on Beckett, and because he sees his language as so similar to Beckett's, it is impossible for him to "respond." What then is this "differently foreign" language? Can we write about such a language without speaking it ourselves?

Translating the "differently foreign" language of Beckett and Derrida reveals a language both foreign in different ways and different from foreign (or the same). It is this language's difference from other modes of representation that allows it to be defined; however, it is not simply the manifestation of difference itself which connects the texts of the two writers. More significantly, these texts represent differently in the same ways. In the interview with Derrida already mentioned, Attridge goes on to suggest why Derrida might find it difficult to write about Beckett. Attridge asks, "Is there a sense in which Beckett's writing is already so 'deconstructive,' or 'self-deconstructive,' that there is not much left to do?" (Acts 61). Attridge proposes that Beckett's writing already deconstructs, even self-deconstructs. Perhaps, the texts perform on themselves the very operations Derrida's texts might seek to perform. However, if this is true, contrary to Attridge's question, there is "much left to do"; such texts resist closure and by their open nature invite discussion rather than deny it. For example, if Beckett and Derrida both work within similar systems of representation, then traditional boundaries between literature and literary theory are breached—two languages cease to be different and their definitions blur.

Beckett's texts may be read a number of ways as deconstructive or self-deconstructive. In his short story **"Dante and the Lobster,"** the text not only self-deconstructs but, consequently, deconstructs Dante and traditional cultural values. The text presents the reader with a protagonist who is not a protagonist, ritual which is not ritual, and plot which is not plot. Belacqua, who serves the textual function of the main character in the story, could not be considered its hero in any traditional sense of the word because he possesses none of those qualities that would usually be associated with heroism. He remains the protagonist of the story only because he is the primary source for its action; he is the hero by default. Rather than some noble quest, Belacqua delights in the basest of activities and goes about them in the most ordinary fashion. For example, much of the story highlights a sandwich Belacqua constructs from two cold, burnt pieces of toast and the rottenest piece of cheese imaginable:

> The lunch had been a notable success. . . . Indeed he could not imagine its ever being superseded. And such a pale soapy piece of cheese to prove so strong! He must only conclude that he had been abusing himself all these years in relating the strength of cheese directly to its greenness. . . . Also his teeth and jaws

> had been in heaven, splinters of vanquished toast spraying forth at each gnash. It was like eating glass. His mouth burned and ached with the exploit.

(15)

Belacqua triumphs through failure; instead of desiring pleasure from his meal, Belacqua desires pain. This passage demonstrates how Beckett's language represents real challenges to traditional values. Belacqua defines the lunch as a success because the cheese was more rotten than he'd thought; he had been "abusing" himself by eating cheese that wasn't as rotten. Though on one level, this text simply replaces a traditional aesthetic with one valuing other ideals, on another level, this reversal subverts established literary conventions. The above passage, for example, serves the textual function of an epiphany in the story, and, yet, the ordinary and banal aspects of the action taking place subvert this function. Is epiphany defined by that which is glorious and inspired, or can it be reduced to that which degrades and pollutes? Who has set such definitions? In Beckett's text, the epiphany and the anti-epiphany become the same thing. The story both is and isn't a short story because in many ways the conventions for short stories exist within the text, and, in other ways, these conventions are violated in irreconcilable ways. What the text represents, therefore, becomes its binary. That which is not literature is literature, etc.

In such a manner does the text deconstruct itself; it climaxes in its anticlimax. At the end of **"Dante and the Lobster,"** Belacqua becomes physically ill at the thought of eating a lobster that had been boiled alive. The irony of the situation is that throughout the story, Belacqua has demonstrated a marked taste for that which is grotesque. This is the point in the story at which the reader would expect some sort of climax; however, because nothing really *significant* occurs, the climax might be better labeled an anticlimax. The story undermines itself because the events of the day, though they have seemed *significant* to the main character, lead to that which ultimately does not satisfy the reader just as Belacqua himself is left unsatisfied. It is not that the story does not signify—it simply signifies in ways which reveal the nature of language itself. **"Dante and the Lobster"** is a very self-conscious text because it is very aware, even hyper-aware, of its own construction. The narrator of the story says, "Let us call it Winter, that dusk may fall now and a moon rise" (18). At times in the story, another persona enters the narrative, interrupts it, and dispels any pretense or illusion of reality which the reader might be constructing. If the narrator calls it "Winter," then the reader will supply a dusk and moon. One aspect, therefore, of the language Beckett speaks is that this language speaks about itself.

Through its self-referentiality, **"Dante and the Lobster"** also deconstructs other texts; in this sense, the text goes beyond its metadiscourse to become metatextual. Beckett's short story does not treat substantively the subject of Dante or his works; rather, the text represents metonymically through allusion rather than allegorically or metaphorically. Beckett counterfeits the names of Dante's characters to represent characters that the reader, because of a familiarity with these names, relates to whatever knowledge he or she may already have of Dante. In other words, the deconstruction of Dante does not occur directly on the page but within the larger contextual margins of the text.

Another aspect of language Beckett shares with Derrida is a defiance of the classification of genre. Critics such as Martin Esslin have placed works by Beckett among those composing the *Theatre of the Absurd* (24). In the introduction to his book *The Theatre of the Absurd,* Esslin provides a comprehensive explanation of absurdist theatre in which he classifies this type of theatre as striving "to express its sense of the irrationality of the human condition and the inadequacy of the rational approach by the open abandonment of rational devices and discursive thought" (24). Esslin contrasts this technique of the absurdists with that of the existentialist theatre in which the meaninglessness of existence is presented "in the form of highly lucid and logically constructed reasoning" (24). Esslin has set up these two dramatic traditions in opposition to each other. Beckett's work goes beyond the merely absurd or existential by embracing both. The duality of his texts allows not only for the depiction of the "senselessness of life" which characterizes the absurdists but also for the emergence of a reasoned, logical understanding of the "irrationality of the human condition" which characterizes the work of existential thinkers.

Crucial to Esslin's argument is a dichotomy between the different modes of representation employed by theory and art. In order to keep these two languages different, Esslin chooses to hierarchize the artistic embodiment of existentialist thought in the text to the more theoretical existential argument of Beckett's work. According to Esslin. "The Theatre of the Absurd has renounced arguing about the absurdity of the human condition; it merely presents it in being—that is, in terms of concrete stage images" (25). Beckett has not "renounced" the argument. Though the play does present the absurdity of life in being and form, the argument over the absurdity of the human condition continues throughout Beckett's work. In *Waiting for Godot,* for example, an important aspect of the play's premise is that two vagabonds discuss the meaning of existence. Vladimir, one of these tramps, contemplates:

> Tomorrow, when I wake, or think I do, what shall I say of today? That with Estragon, my friend, at this place, until the fall of night, I waited for Godot? . . . Probably, but in all that what truth will there be? . . . He'll know nothing. . . . Astride of a grave and a difficult birth. Down in the hole, lingeringly, the grave-digger

puts on the forceps. We have time to grow old. The air is full of our cries. . . . But habit is a great deadener. . . . At me too someone is looking, of me too someone is saying, He is sleeping, he knows nothing, let him sleep on. [*Pause.*] I can't go on! [*Pause.*] What have I said?

> (83)

Because Vladimir does reason about his existence, Esslin's argument, that *Godot* merely represents absurdity through form, is undone. Esslin has hierarchized the form of Beckett's play because of the false dichotomy between theory and art and has, consequently, neglected the strong existential argument of the play. Vladimir challenges his own notions of truth and recognizes its elusive nature. Even distinguishing between life and death becomes difficult because the world created by the text is one in which everything deconstructs. If death is defined as a loss of life and life can be defined only as that which is not yet dead, then they become essentially the same thing. As in **"Dante and the Lobster,"** *Waiting for Godot* refuses to fulfill the conventions of its genre in the standard manner. Though *Godot* does possess the aesthetic form a literary work usually emphasizes, it also treats, through its subject manner, the concerns of theory. In this sense, *Godot* is bilingual; it speaks both the language of literature and the language of literary theory.

The writings of Derrida demonstrate a system of representation very similar to that of Beckett; Derrida's texts are also bilingual in the sense that they speak both the language of literature and the language of literary theory. Because Derrida's writings are primarily concerned with theoretical issues, the more literary aspects such as form are often ignored. As an example of Derrida's concern with representation through form as well as through argument, this passage about Mallarmé emphasizes the spaces between the words and the significance of the blank space:

> One no longer even has the authority to say that "between" is a purely syntactic function. Through the remarking of its semantic void, it in fact begins to signify. Its semantic void *signifies,* but it signifies spacing and articulation; it has as its meaning the possibility of syntax; it orders the play of meaning. *Neither purely syntactic nor purely semantic,* it marks the articulated opening of that opposition.

> (Acts 176)

According to Derrida, everything contributes to the meaning ascribed to a particular text. Even the spaces contribute because they serve a function vital to the construction of meaning. The white space to the left of the above quote, for example, signifies that the words to the right are quoted from someone besides the author of the text you are reading. Derrida plays with spaces so that their significance becomes even more important to the meaning of the text. In *Glas,* for example, the words are organized on the page in unique columns and boxes. The columns do not read like those of a newspaper; rather, different subjects are treated in each column. Some columns are typeset larger than others, and different fonts are used. The spaces help "open" the text to a plurality of readings. Derrida explains:

> The white of the spacing has no determinate meaning, it does not simply belong to the plurivalence of all the other whites. . . . As the page *folds* in upon itself, one will never be able to decide if *white* signifies something, or signifies only, or in addition, the spacing of writing itself.
>
> (Acts 115-16)

The spacing of the words on a page can increase the play of a text. Because the exact meaning can never be interpreted, the text is never exhausted, it is never stale, and it can never be completely deciphered. Derrida's text speaks the language of theory as it discusses the use of space; however, once it practices the use of the blank space, it crosses over into the realm usually reserved for literature. Therefore, Derrida's particular process of representation is "foreign" to that used more often by theory. Similarly, Beckett's language is "foreign" to that commonly used by literature. The two languages are "differently foreign" because they would usually be placed on opposite sides of the border between theory and literature; however, since their systems of representation both pull towards this boundary, they could be named the same language.

Another force which helps to deconstruct barriers placed between the language of Derrida and of Beckett is that the theoretical issues dealt with and the forms employed by both authors are strikingly similar. Not only do both tug at the boundaries of genre, but they tug in the same ways. Beckett, for example, shares a concern similar to that of Derrida regarding the significance of absence and the blank space. In his short novel *Molloy,* Beckett's character debates over the nature of language.

> And once again I am I will not say alone, no, that's not like me, but, how shall I say, I don't know, restored to myself, no, I never left myself, free, yes, I don't know what that means but it's the word I mean to use, free to do what, to do nothing, to know, but what, the laws of the mind perhaps, of my mind, that for example water rises in proportion as it drowns you and that you would do better, at least no worse, to obliterate texts than to blacken margins, to fill in the holes of words till all is blank and flat and the whole ghastly business looks like what it is, senseless, speechless, issueless misery.
>
> (*Three* 13)

Molloy recognizes the crucial nature of the space and the value of the absence. Without the spacing, the words lose all of their meaning and are destroyed. The white on the page is as "significant" as the black because if we fill in the spaces in the words, all meaning is lost. There is the potential in the absence for meaning—it defines and gives birth to the active presence. Spacing goes beyond the visual in this passage; the many commas in the text require the reader to pause before continuing; this creates a space in the continuity of the sentence/phrase as well. This focus on absence is very similar to that already discussed in relation to Derrida. Both texts stress the essential nature of absence, and its crucial role in permitting meaning and understanding.

The texts of both Derrida and Beckett represent this idea of space and absence in similar ways. The theoretical concerns of *Molloy* are as lucid (if I may use that word) and valid as those of works such as Derrida's, which usually remain in the realm of theory. However, the more narrow definition of theory fails to describe works such as *Glas* which embody the very theoretical principles they espouse. These works combine content and form in much the same way Beckett does. Derrida doesn't simply write about space and absence, he creates it in his texts. Not only do his texts deconstruct through argument, they also deconstruct through form. This passage from *Glas,* for example, is very open in its theoretical meaning because of its more literary form. This is the last paragraph of the text; it takes us to the beginning of the text just as Beckett's *Godot.* The end circles around to the beginning:

> It is very arid on the endless esplanade, but it (Ça) does nothing but begin, the labor, here, from now on. As soon as it (Ça) begins to write. It (Ça) hardly begins. No more than one piece is missing.
>
> It (Ça) grates. Rolls on the tree trunks lying down (couchés). Pulleys. The greased ropes grow taut, they are all you hear, and the breathing (souffle) of slaves bent double. Good for pulling. Proofs ready for printing. The cracking whip (fouet cinglant) of the foreman. A regaining of bound force. Thing is oblique. It forms an angle, already, with the ground. Slowly bites again (Remord) its shadow, dead sure (death) of (it)self.
>
> (262)

Here, Derrida describes the circular nature of the text, but simultaneously creates a text which functions in such a way that it harmonizes with the ideology it expresses. Not only does Derrida write about a text ending in its beginning, his texts embody this idea by beginning again. The question is one of perspective. Readers can see the beginning as just so much end, or vice versa.

Translating texts such as those by Beckett and Derrida requires different operations from those usually performed by literary criticism. Because of the generic labels applied to writers such as Beckett or Derrida, other aspects of the text become subjugated to either theoretical or artistic concerns. By highlighting the difference between the two systems of representation and by using these differences as defining characteristics of a particular text, genres inevitably privilege these defining traits over other aspects of the text; this is the violence of generic labels. They propagate such dichotomies as those between theory and literature. Other criteria for judging these types of works is possible, however. Wayne Booth couples these two writers' works based on ambiguity and openness. He writes that questions of genre and classification are often inappropriate in regards to contemporary literature and theory:

> Consider . . . whatever you see as the most ambiguous or "open" work you know—Beckett's *The Unnamable,* perhaps, or Derrida's *Glas.* However indeterminate the work, it will still ask us to rule out certain inappropriate questions. *Glas,* for example, which is difficult to classify according to any traditional literary or philosophical category, insists that we not ask it to answer the "Three Little Pigs" kind of questions ("Who will do what to whom"). It also insists that we finally reject such questions as "in what traditional literary genre shall I place you?"
>
> (24)

In order to avoid doing violence to the text, the groupings and classifications of literary criticism must be fluid enough to allow readers to ask the text different questions. Instead of asking a Derrida text all of the questions a reader would usually ask of a theoretical work, why not ask the questions one might ask of literature? By failing to recognize the "theory" implicit in the literary work, the reader constructs a fallacious hierarchy between theory and art. It is not a simple binary in which one text is consistently valued over the other; rather, the theoretical text is privileged for its ideological content while the art is privileged for whatever aesthetic principles a reader values. If we group Derrida and Beckett together on the basis of how and what they represent, a more equal relationship can be established between the texts.

Ultimately, translating Derrida and Beckett requires the creation of another language or system of representation—one that does not limit the possibilities of a text based on the prejudices of genre. This frees the reader to create her or his own criteria for judging the text. The language of Beckett and of Derrida is one that is very aware of its own existence. Both modes of representation rely on a consciousness of their own operations; both deconstruct and self-deconstruct; both rely on the absence as much as the presence of their language; and both use artistic and theoretical conventions to communicate. Reading the texts of these two writers in the same context underscores the properties of the languages they speak: finally, complete and absolute translation is impossible. The reader/critic cannot write about any particular language without speaking it herself or himself. However, meaning is still created through the text, and the reader does construct a system of representation from the text. The impossibility of complete translation does not cripple the reader or rob the reader of the pleasure of reading: rather, it liberates the reader to read in ways others may not have read and to speak in languages in which others may not have spoken.

Works Cited

Beckett, Samuel. "Waiting for Godot." *The Complete Dramatic Works.* London: Faber & Faber, 1986. 7-87.

———. *Three Novels by Samuel Beckett:* Molloy, Malone Dies, *and* The Unnamable. New York: Grove Weidenfeld, 1958.

———. "Dante and the Lobster." *I Can't Go On, I'll Go On.* Ed. Richard W. Seaver. New York: Grove Weidenfeld, 1976. 7-20.

Booth, Wayne C. *Critical Understanding: The Powers and Limits of Pluralism.* Chicago: U of Chicago P, 1979.

Derrida, Jacques. *Acts of Literature.* Ed. Derik Attridge. New York: Routledge, 1992.

———. *Glas.* Trans. John P. Leavy, Jr., and Richard Rand. Lincoln: U of Nebraska P, 1986.

Esslin, Martin. *The Theater of the Absurd.* Harmondsworth: Penguin, 1980.

Harry Vandervlist (essay date 1994)

SOURCE: Vandervlist, Harry. "Nothing Doing: The Repudiation of Action in Beckett's *More Pricks than Kicks.*" In *Negation, Critical Theory, and Postmodern Textuality,* edited by Daniel Fischlin, pp. 145-56. Dordrecht, The Netherlands: Kluwer Academic Publishers, 1994.

[*In the following essay, Vandervlist identifies the repudiation of action as a unifying theme of the stories in* More Pricks than Kicks.]

Samuel Beckett's early stories may not appear, at first sight, to share the kind of negative strategies characteristic of the better-known prose works, dating from the trilogy, *Molloy, Malone Dies, The Unnamable.* Yet his 1934 collection of stories, **More Pricks Than Kicks,** provides an early example of Beckett's fruitful use of an apparently perverse negative stance: **More Pricks Than Kicks** repudiates one of fiction's fundamental aspects, the presentation of action. Beckett's early protagonists aim not to act, yet fail to avoid action, and the texts themselves echo this failure, succumbing to something less—but also more—than the simple negation of narration. An impulse to escape the necessity to "do something next" exists from the beginning of Beckett's career and "evasive strategies" similar to those described in Beckett's later prose[1] are in fact at work in the 1934 collection, as I will show by way of a reading of the volume's opening story, **"Dante and the Lobster,"** supplemented by brief references to other stories from the collection.

In Beckett's early work an outwardly conventional fiction tries both to tell and to deny its stories, finally yielding an indeterminacy Wolfgang Iser describes as "a structure bringing forth—at least potentially—infinite possibilities" (707). There are two levels to such a denial: the level of represented action within a narrative, and the level of the action of narrating. **More Pricks Than Kicks** stresses the first level, while moving toward the second. No doubt, there is something admittedly preposterous about the notion of deliberately avoiding action. In life, real or represented, the most radical way to shun action is never to have been born; in writing, the pragmatic way to shun action is to leave the page blank. Even Beckett's early protagonists such as Belacqua in **More Pricks Than Kicks** revile themselves for having failed on one or both of these counts. This anxiety begets characters who strive not to act, and a narrative that cancels itself. Readers may be prompted to ask why such texts, in order to be most faithful to their own sense of the futility of action and narration, might not have been best left unwritten. Yet an action or a narrative that "takes itself back" or cancels itself is not the same thing as non-action, or as a narrative that is absent. The apparently perverse strategies of self-cancelled action and narrative give rise to a third thing, which is perhaps the closest fiction can come to evoking negativity, what Iser names "the ceaseless rejection and denial of what has just been said" (707). Through strategies of negation, Beckett's stories privilege possibility over action, and create a space of unfulfilled potential.

Already in **More Pricks Than Kicks,** then, Beckett explores an impulse to evade the element of *mythos*—the mimetic representation of human action—and to deny the grounding aspects of figuration, empirical representation, and allusion.[2] However, where the later texts fragment and hollow out the surface of the text itself, the earlier work uses its protagonist to enact such a process within a (reluctantly) represented world. In **More Pricks Than Kicks** we can see the struggle *against* the presentation of action in Beckett's very choice of a protagonist, for the protagonist of the stories is not invented but chosen, purloined from Dante. We see it also in the narrative shapes of these stories, with their elaborate static structures of undermined allusions, evasive and abortive voyages, missed appointments, broken vows, and illusory endings.

More Pricks Than Kicks enacts the aimless wanderings of the indolent Belacqua, a character improbably lifted from Dante's *Purgatorio* and dumped in Dublin where he acquires the surname Shuah. To choose Dante's Belacqua as protagonist indicates Beckett's fundamental lack of interest in **More Pricks Than Kicks** as a portrayal of action. Dante's indolent spokesman for the late-repenting, trapped in the perfectly circumscribed world of the *Purgatorio,* can accomplish nothing by his own efforts. His existence is reduced to a long waiting:

> Brother, what's the use of going up? For God's angel who sits at the gate would not let me pass to the torments. First must the heavens revolve around me outside it, so long as they did during my life, because I delayed good sighs until the end—unless prayer first aid me which rises from a heart that lives in grace. . . .
>
> (*Purgatorio* 43)

Dante's Belacqua dramatizes *Geworfenheit,* the condition of being *thrown into being:* he is unready for his second "birth" into Purgatory, unprepared by repentance, unsuited to any effective existence there. Belacqua is a type of the ironic character, in Frye's sense of being limited in power and scope (34), useless to all but the most perverse builder of narratives. He does nothing, he has no power to do anything, he does not belong in the world in which he finds himself. He has next to no history. In his life he did *almost* nothing: in his death he is condemned to do *absolutely* nothing.

Dante's Belacqua awaits a progression toward an absolute which is merely postponed. He waits, as Walter Strauss puts it, "in eternity, but not eternally" (252). Beckett's Belacqua, though, waits in an absolute absence of the absolute. Beckett, then, has recast a hiatus in Dante's progressive narrative, and turned this static moment into an entire narrative event. Dante's Belacqua provides a provocative opportunity for Beckett: here is a protagonist who can only do nothing for the present lifetime, whose story is to be without a story. He embodies the stasis that Joyce's Stephen Dedalus associates with the response to art. Belacqua offers the writer a perversely inactive protagonist who subverts the whole game from the outset.

The narrative structures of the stories in **More Pricks Than Kicks** further illuminate Beckett's interest in the possibility of a fiction that negates the necessity of action. **"Dante and the Lobster"** illustrates the sort of narrative movement typical of these stories. The story's opening image is one of doubled immobility. Belacqua, reading Dante's *Purgatorio,* is immobile both physically and mentally: "It was morning and Belacqua was stuck in the first of the canti in the moon. He was so bogged that he could move neither backward nor forward" (9). Belacqua is saved from "running his head against this impenetrable passage" (9) by the striking of a clock which signals midday. It becomes clear that the progress of Belacqua's daily itinerary is governed not by accomplishments, but by the cycle of clock time and the enactment of rituals. Noon strikes and Dante is punctually abandoned: the passage of time does not resolve the enigmas of Dante, but it does allow Belacqua to feel he is moving on. Belacqua's attitude to clocks and time is as contradictory as his feeling about movement in space: eventually he "would not tolerate a chronometer of any kind in the house" and for him "the local publication of the hours" becomes "six of the best on the brain every hour" (129). Here, however, the striking clock temporarily permits him to think himself freed from futility and inaction.

Belacqua orders his day according to considerations of "what he had to do next. There was always something one had to do next" (10). His immediate obligation is to have lunch—and this is not merely a matter of locating and ingesting nutriment. Belacqua's lunch is clearly a sacred ceremony, and the description of it is one of the most carefully constructed comic passages in ***More Pricks Than Kicks***. Ritual purity is a condition attached to the act of lunching: there must be no contamination by other action; the world must be held at arm's length:

> if he were disturbed now, if some brisk tattler were to come bouncing in now big with a big idea or a petition, he might just as well not eat at all, for the food would turn to bitterness on his palate, or worse again, taste of nothingness.
>
> (10)

Belacqua's ritual seeks to avoid this "taste of nothingness." His sandwich—Gorgonzola, mustard, salt, and cayenne pepper, on burnt toast—is exaggeratedly pungent. But the sandwich is an elaborate avoidance ritual: the food itself is really *nothing,* the act of preparation *everything.* And the act of preparation is, above all, not-studying-Dante, not-talking-to-anyone.

Every part of Belacqua's Gorgonzola-and-mustard-on-toast must answer to rigid conditions: the toast must be burnt all the way through, the Gorgonzola must be "rotten." If all of the conditions can be met, the result will be a comical triumph:

> he would devour it with a sense of rapture and victory, it would be like smiting the sledded Polacks on the ice. He would snap at it with closed eyes, he would gnash it into a pulp, he would vanquish it utterly with his fangs.
>
> (13)

The language of this passage suggests a satirical metamorphosis in which Belacqua becomes Hamlet's father or Fortinbras, a conqueror, smiter of Polacks. While this may seem to be one case where allusion grounds a particular interpretation, the result could hardly be less defined, as the allusion evokes one of the most notoriously disputed actions in the canon of English literature. What is it to smite sledded Polacks? Or should

that be Poleaxe?[3] If, through this allusion, Belacqua becomes a man of action as he eats his lunch, then it is a kind of action that trails off into indeterminacy.

Typically, one strategy available to readers confronting such an elaborately presented non-event is the search for these sorts of seemingly helpful allusions, or the search for an entire pattern of imagery that would imply another level of significance. And apparently no toil has been spared in the effort to build up a ludicrously elaborate structure of imagery and allusions around the sandwich and its manufacture. When this structure becomes (hilariously) excessive, however, its parodic nature is made clear. The Christian imagery of the *Purgatorio* presumably lingers in Belacqua's mind and merges with the current events narrated in the newspaper spread on the table (and the events themselves reflect the hanging episode in Joyce's *Ulysses*). Even the name of the paper plays into this structure: it is a "Herald" which Belacqua "deploys" on the table. The main story in the newspaper is that of "McCabe the assassin," whose "petition for mercy" has been rejected. Belacqua learns this as he eats his sandwich in a pub, after hardening himself against any "petitions" that would interrupt the enjoyment of his lunch.

The condemned McCabe and Belacqua's sandwich are identified with one another throughout the passage, and both are linked to the sacrificed Christ. The slices of bread for toast emerge from "prison" and are sawed off "on the face of McCabe" (11). Belacqua says of the bread that "he would very quickly take that fat white look off its face" (11), personifying the bread and allowing it to merge more fully with the murder suspect. The untoasted slices of bread are called "candidates," an allusion to the Latin *candidus,* denoting purity and whiteness, and also one elected or chosen (in this case, as a sacrificial victim). The grocer who supplies Belacqua with "a good stenching rotten lump of Gorgonzola cheese, alive" to place between the burnt slices of toast, gives up the cheese with Biblical gestures:

> The grocer, instead of simply washing his hands like Pilate, flung out his arms in a wild crucified gesture of supplication.
>
> (14)

Finally, the punishment of the murderer and the enjoyment of the sandwich merge as "Belacqua, tearing at the sandwich . . . pondered on McCabe in his cell" (17).

The lunch episode is the core of the story, occupying seven of its thirteen pages. Although it elaborates a structure of imagery which will extend to link the lobster eaten for dinner, with Dante's sufferers, the murderer McCabe, and the Gorgonzola sandwich, the story narrates only the most mundane dramatic events. It is the pretext for a static fabric of imagery and allusion deployed for their own sakes in a parody of master craftsmanship. What is there in the episode that motivates the weighty commentary it must bear? Belacqua's main action—making lunch—is comically inflated by such means as the allusion to Shakespearian "men of action," then dwarfed by the significances thrust upon it by way of the narrative's elaborately structured imagery. As in mock epic, the banality of the action undermines the seriousness of the figurative freight, and as the image-structure collapses, its implied significance is cancelled. Here, however, it is not the high seriousness of epic tradition which is undercut. Instead, Beckett mocks the imputation of significance to everyday actions through the kind of literary presentation that makes the ordinary epiphanic, and clothes the mundane in a fabric of borrowed symbolism. Certainly aspects of the story echo the three-part structure of Dante's *Commedia:* the story does evoke suffering, sacrifice, and the struggle to understand their necessity, as well as the triumph of pity. But it is, nonetheless, primarily a recipe for an exotic and pungent sandwich.

The sandwich, in contrast to Belacqua's deliberations over Dante, is a "notable success" (17). Belacqua's day is redeemed by it, and is going "swimmingly" (17) as he arrives at his Italian lesson after lunch. "Where were we?" he asks of his teacher. "Where are we ever?" she replies, "where we were, as we were" (20). It is a reply he is still pondering as he totes home a lobster for supper:

> Where we were, thought Belacqua, as we were . . . [A]nd poor McCabe, he would get it in the neck at dawn. What was he doing now, how was he feeling? He would relish one more meal, one more night.
>
> (21)

Even for those facing execution, "there is always something one has to do next" (10). Relishing a meal, as Belacqua extravagantly does in the story, is one such thing, but behind it is a strong sense of futility, of avoiding something—the passage of time, and, ultimately, death—to which a reply is impossible. Success, for Belacqua and for *More Pricks Than Kicks,* means filling plot-time and text-space with something approaching non-action, or at least with a kind of self-consuming action described in ways that both assert and retract significance.

That point is reconfirmed in Belacqua's second meal of the story, the lobster. Surprised, he cries out when he unwraps his lobster, "My God . . . it's alive, what'll we do?" (This is, after all, how Beckett's characters generally react to the unwelcome surprise of their own existence.) Belacqua's aunt does what one does next, hurls the lobster into boiling water: "Well, thought Belacqua, it's a quick death, God help us all. It is not" (22).

The story ends with this flat denial from the narrator—"[i]t is not"—made as if "over the head" of Belacqua. Indeed the lobster—"cruciform on the table"—is linked to Christ, as Belacqua's sandwich was linked to McCabe, none of whom, it is suggested, enjoys the mercy of a quick death. Perhaps Belacqua senses that to act, to "relish one more meal," is to join in this chain of murder which so appalls him. He strives never to move beyond his paralysed question, "It's alive—what'll we do?"

His solution, in **"Ding-Dong,"** is to avoid doing anything in particular, since he cannot avoid doing. He seeks to balance action and inaction, movement and stasis, in a mutually cancelling fashion. He would enact oxymoron. **"Ding-Dong"** offers many formulations of Belacqua's self-cancelling evasiveness. For example, Belacqua has a taste for pure movement, which he calls "moving pauses," or "gress" (38).

> Not the least charm of this pure blank movement, this "gress" or "gression," was its aptness to receive, with or without the approval of the subject, in all their integrity the faint inscriptions of the outer world. Exempt from destination, it had not to shun the unforeseen nor turn aside from the agreeable odds and ends of vaudeville that are liable to crop up. This sensitiveness was not the least charm of this roaming that began by being blank, not the least charm of this pure act the alacrity with which it welcomed defilement. But very nearly the least.
>
> (38)

Belacqua sees this "gress" as an equivalent to stasis. On the one hand, Belacqua is "by nature sinfully indolent, bogged in indolence, asking nothing better than to stay put" (37). On the other, "the best thing he had to do was to move constantly from place to place" (36). While he lacks the funds to roam endlessly "[h]ither and thither on land and sea" (36), neither has he "the means to consecrate his life to stasis, even in the meanest bar" (42). In fact Belacqua "had a strong weakness for oxymoron" (38), and he relishes "a double response, like two holes to one burrow" (42). When he attempts to describe all of this to the narrator, he takes pleasure in the failure of his explanations: "All this and much more he laboured to make clear. He seemed to derive considerable satisfaction from his failure to do so" (43). All of the story's formulations of Belacqua's attempts to enact inaction fail. This very failure succeeds in producing another sense of the double movement of the stories: they both present and withdraw, both clarify and obscure.

The exasperated narrator responds to Belacqua, as perhaps we do ourselves, with the judgment:

> he wriggled out of everything by pleading that he had been drunk at the time, or that he was an incoherent person and content to remain so, and so on. He was an

impossible person in the end. I gave him up in the end because he was not serious.

(38)

Like its contradictory protagonist, *More Pricks Than Kicks* is openly exasperated with its own procedures, yet offers itself to readers nonetheless, as if there were no *choice* but to present the stories in this unsatisfactory condition. In the end, this is a fiction that tries, like its protagonist, to be nowhere for as long as possible.

The text shares with Belacqua an anxious self-directed dissatisfaction, an incipient rejection of its own form. Beckett's fictional procedures enact a sort of evasive narrative strolling, wriggling out of the tiresome conventions of storytelling, enduring the parodic or otherwise humorous "bits of vaudeville" that come up along the way. The result is a self-rejecting fiction, uncomfortable with the way it must feed upon that which it hopes to afflict—the endless round of human action in the world, and its presentation in fiction. The image of Belacqua's enormous boil, treated with comic affection and horror, is an example of the way this fiction turns its characters into grotesques, and is also an expression of its own bitterly ambivalent self-consciousness.

The arbitrary narrative movement of *More Pricks Than Kicks* parodies the narrator in Joyce's *Dubliners,* who purposefully roams Dublin in search of epiphanic episodes. In Beckett's narratives, we encounter apparent purposelessness: for example, in **"Fingal," "Love and Lethe,"** and **"Walking Out"** a walk into the countryside ends in a missed appointment or a broken vow. This pattern figures a narratological inconclusiveness or evasiveness that structures Belacqua's and the reader's experience; Beckett's narrator behaves "impossibly" (38), as the narrator of **"Ding-Dong"** puts it. The reader of *Dubliners* is offered an experience of gradual coalescence as the stories accumulate to portray the city. Though Joyce's characters are alienated, isolated, and paralyzed, the life of the city is multiform, and in "The Dead" one senses a general tone of culmination and of charity towards the represented world. The levelling of the living and the dead under the general covering of snow may suggest the frozen, paralyzed life of the city and nation, but it may also imply (positive) continuity between past and present, a sense of community. In any event this ambivalence ought not to be discounted. Either alternative offers a totalizing view of the story which satisfies, as Iser states, "an expectation we all have about the meaning of works of art: that meaning should bring the resolution of all the disturbances and conflicts which the work has brought into being." Iser points out, however, that "this view of meaning constitutes an historical but by no means normative expectation, and Beckett . . . is concerned with a very different sort of meaning" (715).

More Pricks Than Kicks struggles to be a different kind of fiction and offers no such coalescence. What

Iser writes of Beckett's trilogy applies to *More Pricks Than Kicks* as well:

> in this narrative process we experience an increasing erosion of what we expect from a narration: the unfolding of a story. This expectation is actually encouraged by the many fragments of stories, but these serve only to show up the narrative process as one of continual emptying out.
>
> (713)

Fragmentation and hollowing out are embodied in the figure of Belacqua. If *More Pricks Than Kicks* tolerates any "inscription" on its digressive, evasive "pure blank movement," it is the inscription of Belacqua's disintegration. Beginning with his identification with the lobster, first "crucified," then tossed into a pot of boiling water, the stories trace Belacqua's disintegration either directly or, in the later stories in the collection, by proxy in the death or disablement of his spouses. At the hospital he is to undergo a double amputation—of his great toe and of the "baby anthrax" on his neck. He requests that the severed toe be given to the cat, thus paralleling what was almost the lobster's fate. The image of dispersion, of a body-in-pieces, is the state to which Belacqua has ultimately regressed, before a negligent anaesthetist confers upon him his abrupt, arbitrary end. Thus "the perpetual effort to retract what has been stated" (Iser 717) plays itself out physically as well.

We might echo Dante's Belacqua, and ask of such a narrative, "Brother, what use . . . ?" *More Pricks Than Kicks* refuses many of the conventional pleasures of narration—a sense of linear direction, the satisfaction of a journey accomplished, the epiphanic "discovery" of coherences. Beckett's stories clearly address readers who are schooled in these pleasures, but who are able to undo their delight and enjoy the irony of a narrative that unexpectedly rejects them. A different kind of pleasure results from the surprise and humour evoked when these "impossible" stories reveal the conventional nature of "possible" and gratifying narratives.

So does *More Pricks Than Kicks* merely allow us to see that purposeful and complete narratives make something out of nothing, imposing, perhaps, their structures and their completeness? If so "the time and energy spent [reading them] . . . would be out of all proportion" (Iser 716). Does *More Pricks Than Kicks* in turn seek to make nothing out of something? Or simply to avoid making something? That isn't the case either, since we have the stories to read and comment upon. By either set of criteria, then, the stories fail. Belacqua's quest to "be nowhere for as long as possible," to make of his story a blank sheet, is always frustrated by "inscriptions." What are the implications of this double negative, the desire to evade narrative and the failure of this evasion? The accomplished incompetence of Beckett's protagonists, and of their narratives, develops beyond the point of merely undoing expectation. *More Pricks Than Kicks* shows, twenty-two years before Beckett gave the idea a clear formulation in *Three Dialogues,* the struggle to construct the minimal artistic expression. In the collection Beckett outlines the situation of an artist for whom "there is nothing to express, nothing with which to express, nothing from which to express, no power to express, no desire to express, together with the obligation to express" (103). Belacqua's relation to action is the same as that of Beckett's relation to expression.

More Pricks Than Kicks is an early manifestation of Beckett's attempts to reduce fiction to the paradoxical presentation of *no one, nothing, nowhere,* a negative complement to the vision of *everyone, everything, everywhere,* evoked in Joyce's *Finnegans Wake.* If *Finnegans Wake* gains its encyclopedic scope by multiplying the possibilities it affirms in each of its sentences, words, or syllables, then Beckett's characters and narratives demonstrate an inverse procedure. For Belacqua, and later Murphy and others, *not* to act is a way of keeping all possible alternatives intact, in the realm of pure potential. To preserve the idea of potentially infinite possibilities Beckett's protagonists refrain from acting.

Beckett "constantly takes language at its word, and as words always mean more than they say, all statements must be qualified or even cancelled" (Iser 715). Beckett's narratives cancel themselves to avoid saying more than they mean, and thus open up the enormous indeterminate possibilities of meaning. In employing these strategies, *More Pricks Than Kicks* activates the "play of negativity" Iser sees in the later prose, in which "finiteness explodes into productivity" (718). We must be careful, however, not to mistake this productivity for action: it is an endless production of discourse, and an endless production of the self by the negative strategy of stating, cancelling, and then further cancelling the seemingly positive act of correcting an error. All of these strategies issue from a source who, like Dante's Belacqua, is going nowhere. Georg Lukács, in *The Meaning of Contemporary Realism,* castigated Beckett for presenting an endless abstract potential that is never realisable, that goes nowhere and does nothing (66). Beckett's fiction implies that if we think we are going somewhere or doing something, it is always in fiction, within those necessary fictions that allow us to act. In the unspeakable space outside these necessary fictions, however, we remain like Belacqua, "where we were, as we were."

A text like *More Pricks Than Kicks* ultimately demands an inversion of the hierarchy that sees action as more interesting and more meaningful than inaction. Beckett's early novels, in their radical skepticism about action and meaning, in their flight from the rewards and the necessary illusions of a masterful competence, ruthlessly present us with an emptiness where we are conditioned to find the utopia of artistic coherence and wholeness. This fiction exposes the involuntary nature of our attempts to see this utopia as merely deferred, but still recoverable, so that our helpless insistence that "this must mean" becomes comically repetitive. In the end, Beckett places his readers in the same position as his protagonists, and we become the victims rather than the masters of meaning. *More Pricks Than Kicks* anticipates the motif of the inescapable and thus compulsory meaning which the text seeks hopelessly to elude, through the protagonist's similarly hopeless evasion of action. Beckett's later works will refine their focus upon the compulsory aspect of meaning, and place it at the level of the act of narration itself. Belacqua, an actor rather than a narrator, struggles to avoid "doing something next," yet can only cancel or repudiate the actions he cannot help but perform. Molloy, Malone, and others will struggle to end their narration, and succeed only in producing more narrative, more words that "mean to mean," in spite of the qualifications, cancellations, and repudiations attempted by those who speak them.

Notes

1. Two of these strategies, the denial of figuration and evasion of allusion, have already been described in the later work by Wolfgang Iser and Shira Wolosky.

2. Frye uses *mythos* to refer to a work's narrative element, the representation of action as opposed to *dianoia,* the representation of thought (52-53).

3. See, for instance, Harold Jenkins' two page note on this "much-disputed phrase" in his edition of *Hamlet* (425-27).

Works Cited

Aligheri, Dante. *The Divine Comedy: Purgatorio.* Tr. Charles S. Singleton. Princeton: Princeton UP, 1973.

Beckett, Samuel. *More Pricks Than Kicks.* N.Y.: Grove Press, 1972.

———. *Proust. Three Dialogues.* London: John Calder, 1965.

Frye, Northrop. *The Anatomy of Criticism: Four Essays.* Princeton: Princeton UP, 1957.

Iser, Wolfgang. "The Pattern of Negativity in Beckett's Prose." *The Georgia Review* 29 (Fall 1975): 706-19.

Joyce, James. *Dubliners.* N.Y.: Viking, 1969.

———. *Finnegans Wake.* Harmondsworth: Penguin, 1982.

Lukács, Georg. *The Meaning of Contemporary Realism.* London: Merlin Press, 1963.

Shakespeare, William. *Hamlet.* Ed. Harold Jenkins. London: Methuen, 1982.

Strauss, Walter. "Dante's Belacqua and Beckett's Tramps." *Comparative Literature* 11. 3 (Summer 1959): 250-61.

Wolosky, Shira. "Samuel Beckett's Figural Evasions." *Languages of the Unsayable: The Play of Negativity in Literature and Literary Theory.* Eds. Sanford Budick and Wolfgang Iser. N.Y.: Columbia UP, 1989: 165-89.

S. E. Gontarski (essay date 1995)

SOURCE: Gontarski, S. E. "From Unabandoned Works Samuel Beckett's Short Prose." In *Samuel Beckett: The Complete Short Prose, 1929-1989,* edited by S. E. Gontarski, pp. xi-xxxii. New York: Grove Press, 1995.

[*In the following essay, Gontarski assesses Beckett's achievements as a short fiction writer.*]

While short fiction was a major creative outlet for Samuel Beckett, it has heretofore attracted only a minor readership. Such neglect is difficult to account for, given that Beckett wrote short fiction for the entirety of his creative life and his literary achievement and innovation are as apparent in the short works as in his more famous novels and plays, if succinctly so. Christopher Ricks, for one, has suggested that the 1946 short story **"The End"** is "the best possible introduction to Beckett's fiction,"[1] and writing in the *Irish Times* (11 March 1995), literary editor John Banville has called **"First Love"** "the most nearly perfect short story ever written." Yet few anthologists of short fiction, and in particular of the Irish short story, include Beckett's work. Beckett's stories have instead often been treated as anomalous or aberrant, a species so alien to the tradition of short fiction that critics are still struggling to assess not only what they mean—if indeed they "mean" at all—but what they are: stories or novels, prose or poetry, rejected fragments or completed tales. William Trevor has justified his exclusion of Beckett from *The Oxford Book of Irish Short Stories* (1989) by asserting that, like his countrymen Shaw and O'Casey, Beckett "conveyed [his] ideas more skillfully in another medium" (p. xvi). But to see Beckett as fundamentally a dramatist who wrote some narratives is seriously to distort his literary achievement. Beckett himself considered his prose fiction "the important writing."[2] The omission is all the more curious given that Beckett's short pieces exemplify Trevor's characterization of the genre as "the distillation of an essence." Beckett distilled essences for some sixty years, and through that

process novels were often reduced to stories, stories pared to fragments, first abandoned then unabandoned and "completed" through the act of publication. When that master of the Irish short story Frank O'Connor noted that "there is something in the short story at its most characteristic[—]something we do not often find in the novel—an intense awareness of human loneliness,"[3] he could have been writing directly about Beckett's short prose. As Beckett periodically confronted first the difficulties then the impossibility of sustaining and shaping longer works, as his aesthetic preoccupations grew more contractive than expansive, short prose became his principal narrative form—the distillate of longer fiction as well as the testing ground for occasional longer works—and the theme of "human loneliness" pervades it.

Beckett's own creative roots, furthermore, were set deep in the tradition of Irish storytelling that Trevor valorizes, "the immediacy of the spoken word," particularly that of the Irish *seanchaí.* Although self-consciously experimental, self-referential, and often mannered, Beckett's short fiction is never wholly divorced from the culturally pervasive traditions of Irish storytelling. Even when his subject is the absence of subject, the story the impossibility of stories, its form the disintegration of form, Beckett's short prose can span the gulf between the more fabulist strains of Irish storytelling and the aestheticized experimental narratives of European modernism, of which Beckett was a late, if formative, part. Self-conscious and aesthetic as they often are, Beckett's stories gain immeasurably from oral presentation, performance, and so they have attracted theater artists who, like Joseph Chaikin, have adapted the stories to the stage or who, like Billie Whitelaw and Barry McGovern, have simply read them in public performance.

Much of Beckett's short prose inhabits the margins between prose and poetry, between narrative and drama, and finally between completion and incompletion. The short work "neither" has routinely been published with line breaks suggestive of poetry, but when British publisher John Calder was about to gather "neither" in the *Collected Poems,* Beckett resisted because he considered it a prose work, a short story. Calder relates the incident in a letter to the *Times Literary Supplement* (24-30 August 1990): He had "originally intended to put ["neither"] in the *Collected Poems.* We did not do so, because Beckett at the last moment said that it was not a poem and should not be there" (p. 895). The work is here printed for the first time corrected (q.v. "A Note on the Texts") and without line breaks, the latter to reinforce the fact that at least Beckett considered "neither" a prose work.

"From an Abandoned Work," furthermore, was initially published as a theater piece by the British publisher Faber and Faber after it was performed on the BBC

Third Programme on 14 December 1957 by Patrick Magee. Although "From an Abandoned Work" is now generally anthologized with Beckett's short fiction, Faber collected it among four theater works in *Breath and Other Shorts* (1971). That grouping, of course, punctuated its debut as a piece *for* performance.[4] It might be argued, then, that "From an Abandoned Work" could as well be anthologized with Beckett's theater writings. It is no less "dramatic," after all, than "A Piece of Monologue," with which it shares a titular admission of fragmentation. Even as Beckett expanded the boundaries of short fiction, often by contracting the form, his stories retained that oral, performative quality of their Irish roots. Many an actor has discovered that even Beckett's most intractable fictions, like *Texts for Nothing, Enough,* or *Stirrings Still,* share ground with theater and so maintain an immediacy in performance that makes them accessible to a broad audience.

With the exception, then, of *More Pricks Than Kicks,* which with its single, unifying character, Belacqua Shuah, is as much a novel as a collection of stories,[5] and the 1933 coda to that collection, **"Echo's Bones,"** which Beckett wrote as the novel's tailpiece but which was rejected first by the publisher, Chatto and Windus, then by Beckett himself for subsequent editions, and most recently by the Beckett Estate for this collection, this anthology gathers the entire output of Beckett's short fiction from his first published story, **"Assumption,"** which appeared in *transition* magazine in 1929 when he was twenty-three years old, to his last, which were produced nearly sixty years later, shortly before his death. In failing health and stirring little from his Paris flat, Beckett demonstrated that there were creative stirrings still, the title he gave three related short tales dedicated to his friend and longtime American publisher, Barney Rosset. In between, Beckett used short fiction to rescue what was in 1932 a failed and abandoned novel, *Dream of Fair to Middling Women,* salvaging two discrete segments of that unfinished and only recently published (1992) work as short fiction, adding eight fresh, if fairly conventional, tales (or chapters) to fill out *More Pricks Than Kicks* (1934), a work whose title alone, although biblical in origin, ensured its scandalous reception and eventual banning in Ireland. In 1945-46 Beckett turned to short fiction to launch "the French venture," producing four *nouvelles:* **"Premier Amour"** (**"First Love"**), **"L'Expulsé"** (**"The Expelled"**), **"Le Calmant"** (**"The Calmative"**), and **"La Fin"** or **"Suite"** (**"The End"**). These stories, "the very first writing in French,"[6] seemed to have tapped a creative reservoir, for a burst of writing followed: two full-length plays, *Eleuthéria* and *En attendant Godot (Waiting for Godot),* and a "trilogy" of novels, *Molloy, Malone meurt (Malone Dies), L'Innommable (The Unnamable).* When the frenetic creativity of that period began to flag, Beckett turned afresh to short fiction in his struggle to "go on," producing thirteen brief tales

grouped under a title adapted from the phrase conductors use for that ghost measure which sets the orchestra's tempo. The conductor calls his silent gesture a "measure for nothing"; Beckett called his prose stutterings *Texts for Nothing.* For Beckett these tales "express the failure to implement the last words of *L'Innommable:* 'il faut continuer, je vais continuer'"[7] ["I can't go on, I'll go on"].

By the 1940s Beckett had apparently abandoned the literary use of his native tongue. Writing to George Reavey about "a book of short stories," Beckett noted on 15 December 1946, "I do not think I shall write very much in English in the future."[8] But early in 1954 Beckett's American publisher, Barney Rosset, suggested that he return to English: "I have been wondering if you would not get almost the freshness of turning to doing something in English which you must have gotten when you first seriously took to writing in French."[9] Shortly thereafter, Beckett began a new English novel, which he first abandoned then published in 1958 as "From an Abandoned Work." In a transcription of the story, a fair copy made as a gift for a friend, Beckett appended a note on its provenance: "This text was written 1954 or 1955. It was the first text written directly in English since *Watt* (1945)."[10] Almost a decade intervened between "From an Abandoned Work" and Beckett's next major impasse, a novel tentatively entitled *Fancy Dying,* portions of which, in French and English (with German translations of both), were published as "Faux Départs" to launch a new German literary journal, *Karsbuch* in 1965.[11] That abandoned novel (q.v. Appendix II) developed into **"All Strange Away"** (where although "Fancy is her only hope," "Fancy dead") and its sibling, *Imagination Dead Imagine,* but was the impetus for several other *Residua* as well. Although these works were apparently distillations of a longer work, Beckett's British publisher treated the 1,500-word *Imagination Dead Imagine* as a completed novel, issuing it separately in 1965 with the following gloss: "The present work was conceived as a novel, and in spite of its brevity, remains a novel, a work of fiction from which the author has removed all but the essentials, having first imagined them and created them. It is possibly the shortest novel ever published."

In between Beckett completed an impressive array of theater work, including *Fin de partie (Endgame)* (1957), *Krapp's Last Tape* (1958), *Happy Days* (1961), and *Play* (1964), and another extended prose work, *Comment c'est (How It Is),* itself first abandoned, then "unabandoned" in 1960. A fragment was published separately as **"L'Image"** in the journal *X* in December 1959. The English version, **"The Image,"** is here published for the first time in a new translation by Edith Fournier (q.v. "Notes on the Texts"). Another segment of *How It Is* was published as "From an Unabandoned Work" in *Evergreen Review* in 1960.[12] For the next three decades, the post-*How It Is* period, Beckett would write, in French and English, denuded tales in the manner of **"All Strange Away,"** stories that focused on a single, often static image "ill seen" and consequently "ill said," *Residua* that resulted from the continued impossibility of long fiction. As the titles of two of Beckett's late stories suggest, these are tales "Heard in the Dark," stories that were themselves early versions of the novel ***Company.*** And in a note accompanying the French manuscript of ***Bing,*** translated into English first as "Pfft" but quickly revised to the equally onomatopoeic ***Ping,*** Beckett noted: "***Bing*** may be regarded as the result or miniaturization of ***Le Dépeupleur*** abandoned because of its intractable complexities." Abandoned in 1966, ***Le Dépeupleur*** was also unabandoned, "completed" in 1970, and translated as ***The Lost Ones*** in 1971. Throughout this period Beckett managed to turn apparent limitations, impasses, rejections into aesthetic triumphs. Adapting the aesthetics of two architects, Mies van der Rohe's "less is more" and Adolf Loos's "ornament is a crime," Beckett set out to expunge "ornament," to write "less," to remove "all but the essentials" from his art, to distill his essences and so develop his own astringent, desiccated, monochromatic minimalism, miniaturizations, the "minima" he alluded to in the "fizzle" called "He is barehead." As Beckett's fiction developed from the pronominal unity of the four *nouvelles* through the disembodied voices of the *Texts for Nothing* toward the voiceless bodies of **"All Strange Away"** and its evolutionary descendant ***Imagination Dead Imagine,*** he continued his ontological exploration of being in narrative and finally being as narrative, producing in the body of the text the text as body. If the *Texts for Nothing* suggest the dispersal of character and the subsequent writing beyond the body, **"All Strange Away"** signaled a refiguration, the body's return, its textualization, the body as voiceless, static object, or the object of text, unnamed except for a series of geometric signifiers, being as mathematical formulae. The subject of these late tales is less the secret recesses of the repressed subconscious or the imagination valorized by Romantic poets and painters than the dispersed, post-Freudian ego, voice as alien other. As the narrator of **"Fizzle 2,"** "Horn came always," suggests, "It is in the outer space, not to be confused with the other [inner space or the Other?], that such images develop."

Despite such dehumanized immobility, these figures (one hesitates to call them characters) and their chronologically earlier disembodied voices retain a direct and fundamental dramatic quality of which Beckett was fully aware. Despite occasional protestations to the contrary, Beckett encouraged directors eager to stage his prose and developed several thematically revealing stage adaptations of his short narratives. When the American director Joseph Chaikin wrote for permission to stage ***Stories and Texts for Nothing,*** for example, Beckett encouraged him in a letter of 26 April 1980 to mount a single *Text,* for which he proposed a simple, precise staging: a single figure, "[s]eated. Head in hands. Nothing else. Face invisible. Dim spot. Speech hesitant. Mike for audibility." Beckett wrote again on 1 August 1980 developing his adaptation:

> Curtain up on speechless author (A) still or moving or alternately. Silence broken by recorded voice (V) speaking opening of text. A takes over. Breaks down. V again. A again. So on. Till text completed piecemeal. Then spoken through, more or less hesitantly, by A alone.
>
> Prompt not always successful, i.e., not regular alternation VAVA. Sometimes: Silence, V, silence, V again, A. Or even three prompts before A can speak.
>
> A does not repeat, but takes over where V leaves off.
>
> V: not necessarily A's voice. Nor necessarily the same throughout. Different voices, 3 or 4, male and female, might be used for V. Perhaps coming to A from different quarters.
>
> Length of prompt (V) and take over (A) as irregular as you like.
>
> V may stop, A break down, at any point of sentence.

Chaikin ultimately rejected Beckett's staging, preferring his own vision of a medley of texts, and Beckett conceded in a letter of 5 September 1980, "The method I suggest is only valid for a single text. The idea was to caricature the labour of composition. If you prefer extracts from a number of texts you will need a different approach." Chaikin finally chose another, more "theatrical" approach, but Beckett's adaptation of his story remains astonishing, a dramatic foregrounding of the mysterious voices, external to the perceiving part of self. What is caricatured in Beckett's adaptation is at least the Romantic notion of creativity, the artist's agonized communion with his own pure, uncorrupted, inner being, consciousness, or imagination. In Beckett's vision the author figure "A" has at least an unnamed collaborator, an external Other. "A" is as much audience to the emerging artwork as its instigator, as he folds the voices of Others, origins unknown, into his own.

Shivaun O'Casey, daughter of dramatist Sean O'Casey, worked with Beckett to dramatize *From an Abandoned Work,* and Beckett likewise detailed a staging for her. O'Casey's initial impulse was to mount the work on the analogy of *Play,* but Beckett resisted. "I think the spotlight face presentation would be wrong here." He went on to offer an alternative that separated speaker from spoken: "The face is irrelevant. I feel also that no form of monologue technique will work for this text and that it should somehow be presented as a document for which the speaker is not responsible." Beckett's outline is as follows:

> Moonlight. Ashcan a little left of centre. Enter man left, limping, with stick, shadowing in paint general lighting along [sic]. Advances to can, raises lid, pushes

about inside with crook of stick, inspects and rejects (puts back in can) an unidentifiable refuse, fishes out finally tattered ms. or copy of FAAW, reads aloud standing "Up bright and early that day, I was young then, feeling awful and out—" and a little further in silence, lowers text, stands motionless, finally closes ashcan, sits down on it, hooks stick round neck, and reads text through from beginning, i.e., including what he had read standing. Finishes, sits a moment motionless, gets up, replaces text in ashcan and limps off right. Breathes with maximum authenticity, only effect to be sought in [*sic*] slight hesitation now and then in places where most effective, due to strangeness of text and imperfect light and state of ms.[13]

In such an adaptation the narrative offered to the audience is, as Beckett says, separated from the stage character, who is then only an accidental protagonist in the drama, more messenger, say, than character. It was a form of staging that Beckett preferred for most of his prose, a compromise between an unadorned stage reading and a full, theatrical adaptation where characters and not just the text are represented on the stage. When the American theatrical group Mabou Mines requested permission through Jean Reavey to stage *The Lost Ones,* Beckett approved at first only a "straight reading." In rehearsals, however, the work developed into a complex, environmental adaptation with a naked actor "demonstrating" the text with a host of miniature figures. Beckett's comment on the adaptation was finally, "Sounds like a crooked straight reading to me."[14] With O'Casey, Beckett resisted the resurrection of a dramatic structure he himself had by then rejected, the monologue, a form he developed in prose with the four *nouvelles* in 1947 and adapted to the stage with *Krapp's Last Tape* in 1958. The monologue form embraced an ideology of concrete presence, a single coherent being (or a unified ego or, in literary terms, a unified character), an idea with which Beckett was increasingly uncomfortable (witness the tapes themselves in *Krapp's Last Tape*) and all pretense to which was finally abandoned in the "trilogy" and the subsequent *Texts for Nothing.* In the theater Beckett gave full voice to that disintegration of character and the fragmentation of monologue in *Not I* and with the incorporeal, ghostly figure of May in *Footfalls.* When consulted about stagings of his prose, Beckett invariably rejected, as he did with Shivaun O'Casey, adaptations that posited a unity of character and narrative that the monologue form suggests. When I prepared with him stagings of first his novella **Company** and then the story **"First Love,"** he offered possibilities almost identical to those for Chaikin and O'Casey respectively.[15] The central question to Beckett's dramatization of **"First Love,"** for instance, was how to break up an unrelieved reading of the text, again discovered in a rubbish heap:

> The reading can be piecemealed by all kinds of business—such as returning it to bin (on which he sits to read)—exiting and returning to read to the end—look-

ing feverishly for a flea or other vermin—chewing a crust—getting up to piss in a corner with back modestly to audience—etc. etc. making the poor best of a hopeless job.[16]

Actors, then, have intuited what literary critics have too often failed to articulate, that even Beckett's most philosophical and experimental short fictions have an immediacy and emotional power, "the immediacy of the spoken voice," which makes them accessible to a broad audience and places them firmly within a tradition of Irish storytelling.

Beckett's first short stories, **"Assumption," "A Case in a Thousand," "Text,"** and **"Sedendo et Quiescendo,"**[17] however, retain the rhetorical ornament and psychological probing characteristic of much high modernism. These stories, the latter two fragments of a then-abandoned novel, are finally uncharacteristic of the narrative diaspora Beckett would eventually develop, but they are central to understanding its creative genesis. Beckett's first two stories, for instance, were written as if he were still preoccupied with literary models. In the first case Beckett seems to have been reading too many of Baudelaire's translations of Poe; in the second, too much Sigmund Freud. But it was with such derivative short fiction that Beckett launched a literary career in 1929, less than a year after having arrived in Paris, in Eugene Jolas's journal of experimental writing, *transition.* Jolas was in the midst of championing James Joyce's *Finnegans Wake* by publishing not only excerpts from the *Work in Progress* but essays about it as well. Beckett had impressed Joyce enough that he was offered the opportunity to write an essay comparing Joyce to three of Joyce's favorite Italian writers, Dante, Bruno, and Vico, for a volume of essays defining and defending the *Work in Progress.* Jolas (and evidently Joyce himself, for the essay would not have appeared without Joyce's approval) thought enough of the essay to reprint it in *transition.* Along with the essay, Jolas accepted a short story from Beckett, **"Assumption,"** which opens with the sort of paradox that would eventually become Beckett's literary signature, "He could have shouted and could not."

The story details the fate of a young, anguished "artist" who struggles to retain and restrain "that wild rebellious surge that aspired violently towards realization in sound." The silent, unnamed protagonist, however, commands a "remarkable faculty of whispering the turmoil down." He can silence "the most fiercely oblivious combatant" with a gesture, with "all but imperceptible twitches of impatience." He develops as well an aesthetic that separates Beauty from Prettiness. The latter merely proceeds "comfortably up the staircase of sensation, and sit[s] down mildly on the topmost stair to digest our gratification." More powerful are sensations generated when "[w]e are taken up bodily and pitched breathless on the peak of a sheer crag: which is the pain of Beauty." The remainder of **"Assumption"** develops just such an aesthetic of pain, which echoes the German Romanticism Beckett never quite purged from his art. As the artist struggles to restrain the animal voice that "tore at his throat as he choked it back in dread and sorrow," an unnamed Woman enters. She flatters and finally seduces the artist manqué, and "SO [sic] each evening in contemplation and absorption of this woman, he lost part of his essential animality." After he is seduced, "spent with extasy [sic]," the dammed "stream of whispers" explodes in "a great storm of sound." The story ends with the sort of epiphany that Beckett would recycle in the final line of **"Dante and the Lobster"**: "They found her caressing his wild dead hair." **"Assumption"** works through (and finally against) the image of a Promethean artist: "Thus each night he died and was God [the Assumption of the title?], each night revived and was torn, torn and battered with increasing grievousness. . . ." But whether the artist transcends the worldly through this experience to unite with something like the Idea, or pure essence, transcends Schopenhauer's world of representation to achieve the pure will, or whether the title refers simply to the arrogance of such desire may be the crux of the story. The protagonist's romantic agony (in both senses of that phrase) may simply describe postcoital depression, and so travesty the belabored agonies of a would-be artist.

When Beckett came to publish another story in *transition* in March 1932, he selected an excerpt from the stalled novel *Dream of Fair to Middling Women,* which he called **"Sedendo et Quiescendo"** (but which appeared as **"Sedendo et Quiesciendo"**). The story includes a sonnet from the protagonist, Belacqua Shuah, to his lover, the Smeraldina, which developed the same sort of yearning for transcendence and union with the "Eternally, irrevocably one" evident in **"Assumption."** The means to this end was to "be consumed and fused in the white heat / Of her sad finite essence. . . ." In the sonnet the speaker claims that he "cannot be whole . . . unless I be consumed," which consumption provides the climax to **"Assumption."** The parallels between story and sonnet extend to the recycling of imagery and phrasing: "One with the birdless, cloudless, colourless skies" (untitled sonnet to the Smeraldina); "he hungered to be irretrievably engulfed in the light of eternity, one with the birdless cloudless colourless skies" (**"Assumption"**). Even the image of the "blue flower" reappears: "Belacqua . . . inscribed to his darling blue flower some of the finest Night of May hiccupsobs that ever left a fox's paw sneering and rotting in a snaptrap" (**"Sedendo et Quiescendo"**); "He was released, achieved [sic], the blue flower, Vega, GOD . . ." (**"Assumption"**).

Beckett's fourth published story, **"A Case in a Thousand,"** appeared in *Bookman* in August 1934 along with his critical article "Recent Irish Poetry," the latter, however, signed with the pseudonym Andrew Belis. **"A Case in a Thousand"** features one Dr. Nye, who "belonged to the sad men." Physician though he is, Dr. Nye "cannot save" himself. He is called in on a case of surgeon Bor who had operated on the tubercular glands of a boy named Bray, who had then taken a turn for the worse. "Dr. Nye found a rightsided empyema," and then another on the left. He discovered as well that the boy's mother, who has been barred from the hospital excepting an hour's visit in the morning and another in the evening but who maintains a day-long vigil on the hospital grounds until her appointed visiting hour, is actually Nye's "old nurse," who on their meeting reminds him that he was "'always in a great hurry so you could grow up and marry me.'" Mrs. Bray, however, "did not disclose the trauma at the root of this attachment." There are then at least two patients in this story, the Bray boy and Dr. Nye. As the boy's condition worsens and a decision about another operation must be made, the doctor regresses, "took hold of the boy's wrist, stretched himself all along the edge of the bed and entered the kind of therapeutic trance that he reserved for such happily rare dilemmas." At that moment Mrs. Bray "saw him as she could remember him," that is, as the boy she had nursed. The young Bray does not survive the operation, but after the funeral the mother resumes her vigil outside the hospital as if her child were still alive—as in a sense he is. When Nye appears, "she related a matter connected with his earliest years, so trivial and intimate that it need not be enlarged on here, but from the elucidation of which Dr. Nye, that sad man, expected great things." The undisclosed incident, at once a "trauma at the root of this attachment" and an incident so "trivial and intimate that it need not be enlarged on here," is at the root of the story as well. The matter is certainly sexual, particularly Oedipal, and at least one critic, J. D. O'Hara, has surmised that the "trivial and intimate" incident involves the young Nye's curiosity about female anatomy, in particular whether or not women have penises. Dr. Nye's nurse may have answered the question by anatomical demonstration, and the unexpected disclosure may have left the young Nye impotent, which condition would help explain why as an adult Nye was "one of the sad men." The **"Case in a Thousand,"** then, is not (or not only) the young boy's empyema but Nye's disorder, impotence perhaps, as well.

Thereafter, Beckett returned to his stalled and incomplete novel, *Dream of Fair to Middling Women.* Having published two excerpts as separate stories, **"Text"** and **"Sedendo et Quiescendo,"** he now cannibalized two of its more detachable pieces, **"A Wet Night"** and **"The Smeraldina's Billet-Doux,"** retaining the protagonist, Belacqua Shuah, to develop an episodic novel, *More Pricks Than Kicks,* whose lead story, **"Dante and the Lobster,"** was published separately in *This Quarter* in

December 1932. (The story **"Yellow"** was also published separately in *New World Writing* but not until November 1956, twenty-two years after the publication of the novel.)

Beckett's subsequent venture into short fiction began just after the second World War, after the writing of *Watt,* when he produced four stories in his adopted language. Originally, all four of the French stories were scheduled for publication by Beckett's first French publisher, Bordas, which had published his translation of *Murphy.* But Bordas dropped plans to issue *Mercier et Camier* and *Quatre Nouvelles* when sales of the French *Murphy* proved disastrous. Subsequently, Beckett suppressed for a time the French novel and one of the stories. The remaining three *nouvelles* of 1946 were finally published in France by Les Editions de Minuit (1955) and in the U.S. by Grove Press (1967) in combination with thirteen *Texts for Nothing* (**"First Love"** being published separately only in 1970). Although conjoined, the two sets of stories remained very separate in Beckett's mind, as he explained to Joseph Chaikin. Beckett resisted Chaikin's theatrical mixing of the stories, noting that *"Stories* **and** *Texts for Nothing* are two very different matters, the former the beginning of the French venture, the latter in the doldrums that followed the 'trilogy.'" When Chaikin persisted, arguing that *Stories and Texts for Nothing* could all be read as tales for "nothing," Beckett corrected him by return post: "Have only now realized ambiguity of title. What I meant to say was *Stories. Followed by Texts for Nothing."*

The four stories, **"First Love," "The Expelled," "The Calmative,"** and **"The End,"** written before, almost in anticipation of, the "trilogy" of novels, and the thirteen *Texts for Nothing* form the bookends to Beckett's great creative period, which has memorably been dubbed the "siege in the room" and which in some regards was anticipated by the final two paragraphs of **"Assumption."** The "trilogy" seems almost embedded within the *Stories and Texts for Nothing,* as Beckett's first two full-length plays, *Eleuthéria* and *En attendant Godot (Waiting for Godot),* are embedded within the novels, the plays written, as Beckett confessed, "in search of respite from the wasteland of prose" he had been writing in 1948-49. In fact, the unnamed narrator of this four-story sequence, almost always suddenly and inexplicably expelled from the security of a shelter, an ejection that mimics the birth trauma, anticipates the eponymous Molloy, even in the postmortem story **"The Calmative,"** and remains a theme through *Fizzles,* where in "For to end yet again," "the expelled falls headlong down." In these four stories what has been and continued to be one of Beckett's central preoccupations developed in its full complexity: the psychological, ontological, narratological bewilderment at the inconsistency, the duality of the human predicament, the experience of existence. On the one side is the post-

Medieval tradition of humanism, which develops through the Renaissance into the rationality of the Enlightenment. Its ideology buttresses the capacity of humanity to know and adapt to the mechanism of the universe and understand humanity's place in the scheme. This is the world of the schoolroom and laboratory, the world of mathematics and proportion, the world of Classical symmetry, of the pensum. For Beckett's narrators, the punctum, the lived, sentient experience of existence, the being in the world, punctures and deflates that humanistic tradition, the empiricism of the classroom, although the latter never loses its appeal and is potentially a source of comfort (although it apparently destroys Watt). The opening of **"The Expelled,"** for instance, focuses not on the trauma of rejection and forcible ejection but on the difficulty of counting the stairs down which the narrator has, presumably, already been dispatched. There is little resentment here at the injustice of having been ejected from some place like a home. The focus of injustice in Beckett is almost never local, civil, or social, but cosmic, the injustice of having been born, after which one finds one's consolations where one may—in mathematics, say. As the protagonist of **"Heard in the Dark 2"** (and *Company*) suggests, "Simple sums you find a help in times of trouble. A haven. . . . Even still in the timeless dark you find figures a comfort." The experience of living is dark, mysterious, inexplicable, chthonic, in many respects Medieval but without the absolution of a benign deity. Such a dissociation had preoccupied Beckett in his earlier work, chiefly in *Dream of Fair to Middling Women, Murphy, Watt,* and the long poem "Whoroscope," through the philosophical meditations of the seventeenth-century philosopher and mathematician René Descartes, that is, in terms of the conflict between mind (pensum) and body (punctum), although Schopenhauer's division of the world in terms of the will and its representations is never very far from the foreground. Here the hormonal surges in even a spastic body like Murphy's conspire against the idealism and serenity of mind (or soul or spirit). But in the four *Stories* [*Stories and Texts for Nothing*] Beckett went beyond Descartes and descended further into the inchoate subconscious of existence, rationality, and civilization, beyond even the Freudian Eros and the Schopenhauerian Will into the more Jungian Collective Unconscious of the race, and the four separate narrators (or the single collective narrator called "I") of these *Stories* confront those primeval depths with little sense of horror, shame, or judgment. The stories retain an unabashedly Swiftian misanthropy: "The living wash in vain, in vain perfume themselves, they stink" (**"First Love"**). In **"The Expelled"** grotesqueries acquire comic effect even as they disclose psychoanalytic enigmas: "They never lynch children, babies, no matter what they do they are whitewashed in advance. I personally would lynch them with the utmost pleasure." The theme will resurface in the

1957 radio play *All that Fall* when Dan Rooney asks wife Maddy, "Did you ever wish to kill a child. . . . Nip some young doom in the bud." This is depersonalized humanity sunk in on itself: "It is not my wish to labour these antinomies, for we are, needless to say, in a skull, but I have no choice but to add the following few remarks. All the mortals I saw were alone and as if sunk in themselves" (**"The Calmative"**). It is a descent, most often into an emblematic skull, from which Beckett's fiction, long or short, will never emerge. The image anticipates not only the skullscapes of the "trilogy," but the dehumanized, dystopic tale *The Lost Ones,* and what is generally called the post-*How It Is* prose. Such a creative descent into "inner space," into the unconscious, had been contemplated by Beckett at least since the earliest stages of *Watt.* In the notebook and subsequent typescript versions of the novel, Beckett noted, "the unconscious mind! What a subject for a short story." **"The Expelled"** seems a fulfillment of that wish to plumb "perhaps deep down in those palaeozoic profounds, midst mammoth Old Red Sandstone phalli and Carboniferous pudenda . . . into the pre-uterine . . . the agar-agar . . . impossible to describe."[18]

But while character names may shift in the four stories (Lulu, for instance, becomes Anna in **"First Love"**) the narrating consciousness, the "I" of these stories, remains more or less cogent, intact, coherent, psychologically and narratologically whole, and at least pronominally namable. And something like representable external reality still exists, even as it is folded in on itself and therefore inseparable from the consciousness perceiving it. Writing subsequently three interrelated and sequential novels dubbed the "trilogy," Beckett continued to probe the "pre-uterine." It is a period during which Beckett pushed beyond recognizable external reality and discrete literary characters, replacing them with something like naked consciousness or pure being (living or dead is not always clear) and a plethora of voices.

The *Texts for Nothing* are then, as Beckett tried to explain to Chaikin, a major leap beyond the four *Stories.* To use the current historical markers, they represent a leap from Modernism to Post-Modernism, from interior voices to exterior voices, from internality to externality. Beckett's fragments are in fact no longer "completed" stories but shards, aperçus of a continuous unfolding narrative, glimpses at a never to be complete being (narrative). The *Texts for Nothing* would redefine at least Beckett's short fiction, if not the possibilities of the short story itself, as narrative per se was finally discarded (as it was for the most part in the "trilogy" of novels), replaced by attempts of consciousness to perceive, comprehend, or create first a life, then a more or less stable, static image, an essence, failing at the latter no less often than at the former. "No need of a story," says one of the voices, "a story is not compulsory, just

a life, that's the mistake I made, one of the mistakes, to have wanted a story for myself, whereas life alone is enough" (*Text* IV). The struggle of the protean narrators of the four *Stories* and the three novels was to create a narrative to capture or reflect, to represent at least a segment of a life in a work of art—that struggle has been abandoned with the *Texts for Nothing.* If "life," and so story, assumes character, the voice has made yet another mistake, for the coherent entity that in literature we call "character" is itself disbursed amid a plurality of disembodied voices and echoes whose distinctions are unclear and whose sources are unknowable. The disembodied voice captivated Beckett from his earliest creative years when he took the image of Echo as the literary emblem for his first collection of poems, *Echo's Bones.* Echo, an Oread or mountain nymph, pined away for the love of Narcissus until all that remained of her was her voice. *Texts for Nothing* could as easily be called *Echo's Bones* as well, and from there on Beckett would never again create anything like literary characters save for an unnamed (even unnamable) narrator straining to see images and hear sounds, almost always echoes—bodiless voices or later voiceless bodies, origins unknown. In Beckett's tribute to painter and friend Bram van Velde, the *témoignage* **"La Falaise"** (**"The Cliff,"** published here in a translation by Edith Fournier), the window through which the observing "you" views the cliff both separates him from and joins him to the cliff in a process that blends perception and imagination. In these late works the artist figures inhabit a no-man's-land, "an unspeakable [because unnamable?] home" in "neither," which is neither wholly self nor wholly other. In theatrical adaptations of his prose, Beckett retained such paradoxes of self by insisting on the separation of character and narrative, and such separation was evident in almost every stage adaptation of his prose works that he himself had a hand in. These, then, are the limitations, the necessary incoherence and fragmentation within which the writer is obliged to work in the post-Auschwitz era in order to convey the punctum, the experience of living in the world: "I'm here, that's all I know, and that it's still not me, it's of that the best has to be made" (*Text* III). Because of such an impasse, narrative (at least as we've known and expected it, even amid the more experimental Modernists) "can't go on," and yet somehow is obliged to "go on." How it goes on is in fits, sputters, and not so much starts as re-starts, in imaginative ventures doomed to failure. As it had been in *The Unnamable,* all pretense to artistic completion was abandoned even in the titles of these later works to suggest not only that the individual works are themselves incomplete, unfinished, but that completion is beyond human experience. The thirteen *Texts for Nothing* are merely numbered, for instance, and Beckett went on to write stories with titles like *Lessness,* **"From an Abandoned**

Work," *Fizzles* (*foirades* in French), and *Residua.* But these tales are no more unfinished works of art than those paintings by Matisse that retain raw, unpainted canvas.

What one is left with after the *Texts for Nothing* is "nothing," incorporeal consciousness perhaps, into which Beckett plunged afresh in English in the early 1950s to produce a tale rich in imagery but short on external coherence. **"From an Abandoned Work"** deals with three days in the life of the unnamed narrator, an old man recalling his childhood. That childhood was as uneventful as it was loveless, except, perhaps, for words, which "have been my only loves, not many."[19] The father died when the narrator was young, and he lived with his mother until she died. The narrator's life is ordered by the daily journey and return: "in the morning out from home and in the evening back home again." He had taken long walks with his father, and those have continued even after the father's death. His motion, however, is directionless, "I have never in my life been on my way anywhere, but simply on my way." In contrast to his own patterned motion, he retains, "Great love in [his] heart for all things still and rooted." There is, however, a great deal of hostility in the parental relationship: "ah my father and mother, to think they are probably in paradise, they were so good. Let me go to hell, that's all I ask, and go on cursing them there, and them looking down and hear me, that might take some shine off their bliss." In fact, his admission that he may have killed his father, "as well as [his] mother," suggests a consciousness permeated with guilt. The events of the days grow more bizarre. There is "the white horse and white mother in the window." Another day, "I was set on and pursued by a family or tribe of stoats." The narrator, moreover, experiences inexplicable periods of rage: "The next thing I was up in the bracken lashing out with my stick making the drops fly and cursing, filthy language, the same over and over, I hope nobody heard me." The most comprehensive reading of this enigmatic text is one offered by J. D. O'Hara in which he sees the word "work" of the title as referring not to a work of art, the story itself, but to a session of psychotherapy. Freud often spoke of his therapy sessions, for instance, as working through psychological problems. What is abandoned for O'Hara, then, is not a narrative or story, which is in this reading complete, but the therapy, which is never completed and so abandoned. The emotional tensions are never resolved, the anxiety never relieved, the personality never integrated. For O'Hara:

> the protagonist has divided his feelings for his parents into love and hatred, has expressed that hatred to us while concealing it from the world, and has repressed his love and displaced it into a love of words, of animals, of this earth, etc. In all this he has expressed his love of self while expressing his hatred of that self by youthful punishment in the walks, by future punish-

ment in hell, and by present punishment among the rocks, isolated from all humans.

It took almost a decade for Beckett to put such psychological strangeness away. When he returned to short fiction in the early 1960s it was to reshape the remains of aborted longer fiction yet again, a work tentatively entitled *Fancy Dead,* a short excerpt of which, in French and English, was published in 1965 as **"Faux Départs."** The work suggests, however, less a false start than a major aesthetic shift, a rejection of the journey motif and structure (incipient in *Murphy* and *Watt* and fully developed in **"First Love"** and the fiction through **"From an Abandoned Work"**), a return to which might have signaled the death of creative imagination: "Out of the door and down the road in the old hat and coat like after the war, no, not that again." Instead, Beckett (or the narrator) announced a new literary preoccupation, "A closed space five foot square by six high, try for him there" in which he would conduct exercises in human origami, all with a rechristened pronoun through which to tell his story, "last person." For the opening of **"All Strange Away"** Beckett would delete the first three words of the sentence above, but "A closed space" ("Closed place" opens **"Fizzle 5"**) would come close to describing the creative terrain that Beckett's short fiction would thereafter explore. And if an impasse were reached in such imaginative spelunking, the light (of imagination?) go out, "no matter, start again, another place, someone in it. . . ."

The British novelist David Lodge's analysis of one of Beckett's "closed space" tales, *Ping* (*Bing* in French), originally a segment of *Le Dépeupleur (The Lost Ones),* is a cogent reading of this cryptic tale, and so of much of Beckett's late prose: "I suggest that *Ping* is the rendering of the consciousness of a person confined in a small, bare, white room, a person who is evidently under extreme duress, and probably at the last gasp of life."[20] Such is what passes for plot in Beckett's late prose, and Lodge goes on to suggest that:

> *Ping* seems to record the struggles of an expiring consciousness to find some meaning in a situation which offers no purchase to the mind or to sensation. The consciousness makes repeated, feeble efforts to assert the possibility of colour, movement, sound, memory, another person's presence, only to fall back hopelessly into the recognition of colourlessness, paralysis, silence, oblivion, solitude.

Lodge struggles to situate *Ping* within a more or less traditional, realistic frame: an expiring consciousness in search of meaning. The questions that Lodge defers, however, are the narratological ones: Who is the figure to whom all is "known"? By whom is the image described "never seen"?; to whom is it repeatedly "invisible"? Certainly not the reader, to whom even these white-on-white images are strikingly visible, for the reader, like the narrator, sees them clearly if fleetingly in his mind's eye through the imaginative construct we call literature, fiction. The figure described, the narrator hints, is "perhaps not alone," and so the possibility exists of others, whose perceptions fail as well. Although the story lines of the late tales are fairly simple, as Lodge suggests, narratologically they are more complex. The reader's focus is not only on a figure in a closed space, but on another figure and a narrator imagining them. We have, then, not just the psychologically complex but narratologically transparent image of a self imagining itself, but a self imagining itself imagining itself, often suspecting that it is being imagined itself.

In these late tales the mysterious narrator is often recorded in the midst of the fiction-making process. Beckett's subject here is, therefore, less the objects perceived and recorded, a process, of necessity, "ill seen" and so "ill said," but the human imagination. In his seminal study, *The Sense of an Ending: Studies in the Theory of Fiction,* critic Frank Kermode quotes Hans Vaihinger on the human impulse of fiction making; fictions are "mental structures. The psyche weaves this or that thought out of itself; for the mind is invention; under the compulsion of necessity [in Beckett, the "obligation to express"], stimulated by the outer world, it discovers the store of contrivances hidden within itself."[21] Beckett's late short fiction, the post-*How It Is* prose, constitutes a record of those discoveries, and so the late work may have more in common with that of American poet Wallace Stevens than with any of the writers of short fiction.

Such then is the rarefied world of Beckett's late short fiction, from **"All Strange Away"** to *Stirrings Still,* short tales that in fundamental ways are almost indistinguishable from the late novels—as the late prose is almost indistinguishable from the late theater. Despite his early insistence on keeping "our genres more or less distinct,"[22] Beckett seemed in this later phase of his work to have stretched beyond such limitations, beyond generic boundaries to examine the diaphanous membrane separating inside from outside, perception from imagination, self from others, narrative from experience, "neither" wholly the one nor wholly the other. Despite such psychological and philosophical flux, an almost frustrating thematic irresolution, the literary oscillation between waves and particles, these stories retain a direct dramatic and poetic simplicity as if they had been spoken into a tape recorder. Taken together, Beckett's short prose pieces not only outline his development as an artist, but suggest as well Beckett's own view of his art, that it is all part of a continuous process, a series. Writing to George Reavey on 8 July 1948, for instance, Beckett noted, "I am now retyping, for rejection by the publishers, *Malone Meurt* [*Malone Dies*], the last I hope of the series Murphy, Watt, Mercier & Camier, Molloy, not to mention the 4 Nouvelles &

Eleuthéria."[23] That series did not, of course, end with *Malone Meurt.* It continued for another forty years to *Stirrings Still.* The post-*How It Is* stories were just the latest in a series whose end was only Beckett's own. In these generically androgynous stories Beckett produced a series of literary hermaphrodites that echo one another (and the earlier work as well) like reverberations in a skull. Taken together the stories suggest the intertextual weave of a collaboration between Rorschach and Escher.

Notes

1. "Mr. Artesian," *The Listener* (3 August 1967): 148-49. Reprinted in *Samuel Beckett: The Critical Heritage,* ed. by Lawrence Graver and Raymond Federman (London: Routledge & Kegan Paul, 1979), 286-291.

2. *No Symbols Where None Intended: A Catalogue of Books, Manuscripts, and Other Material Relating to Samuel Beckett in the Collection of the Humanities Research Center,* Selected and described by Carlton Lake (Austin, TX: Humanities Research Center, 1984), 133.

3. *The Lonely Voice: A Study of the Short Story* (New York: Harper & Row [Harper Colophon Books], 1985), 19.

4. The work finally seems to have wound up anthologized with Beckett's prose via an exchange between publishers. The dramaticule "Come and Go" was originally published in the U.K. by John Calder, to whom the work is dedicated. Faber has subsequently published "Come and Go" in anthologies of Beckett's drama, and Calder published "From an Abandoned Work" in anthologies of Beckett's prose.

   Beckett's short story "Lessness" was also performed on the BBC, on 25 February 1971 with Donal Donnelly, Leonard Fenton, Denys Hawthorne, Patrick Magee, and Harold Pinter.

5. Even Beckett's earliest critics like Dylan Thomas referred to *More Pricks Than Kicks* as a novel; see *New English Weekly* (17 March 1938): 454-55.

6. Letter to American publisher Barney Rosset dated 11 February 1954.

7. *Ibid.*

8. *No Symbols Where None Intended,* 81.

9. Rosset letter to Samuel Beckett, 5 February 1954.

10. *No Symbols Where None Intended,* 90.

11. A reference to this abandoned work appears in "Why Actors Are Fascinated by Beckett's Theater," *The Times* (27 January 1965): 14: "Mr.

Beckett is at present finishing a novel called *Fancy Dying,* and also writing a play"—the latter presumably *Play.* The source of the information is apparently Jack MacGowran, who was not only playing in *Endgame* at the time but also preparing a one-man performance of Beckett's prose writings, which became *Beginning to End.*

12. "From an Unabandoned Work," *Evergreen Review* 4.14 (September-October 1960): 58-65.

13. Deirdre Bair, *Samuel Beckett* (New York: Harcourt Brace Jovanovich, 1978) 578.

14. *No Symbols Where None Intended,* 140.

15. For further discussion of adaptation of Beckett's prose to the stage see my "*Company* for Company: Androgyny and Theatricality in Samuel Beckett's Prose," *Beckett's Later Fiction and Drama: Texts for Company,* ed. James Acheson and Kateryna Arthur (London: Macmillan Press, 1987), 193-202.

16. Samuel Beckett letter to the editor dated 12 September 1986.

17. The title alludes to Dante's *Purgatorio,* "Sedendo et quiescendo anima efficitur prudens" (roughly, sitting quietly the soul acquires wisdom).

18. Cited by Chris Ackerley, "Fatigue and Disgust: The Addenda to *Watt,*" *Samuel Beckett Today/ Aujourd'hui: Beckett in the 1990s* II: 179.

19. Some twenty-two years later, directing his play *Footfalls* in Germany, Beckett returned to this theme as he told the actress playing May, "Words are as food for this poor girl. . . . They are her best friends" (Walter D. Asmus, "Rehearsal Notes for the German Premiere of Samuel Beckett's *That Time* and *Footfalls,*" *On Beckett: Essays and Criticism,* ed. by S. E. Gontarski [New York: Grove Press, Inc., 1986], 339).

20. "Some Ping Understood," *Encounter* (February 1968): 85-89. Reprinted in *Samuel Beckett: The Critical Heritage,* 291-301. The original publication of the essay, however, contains line numberings to the original publication of "Ping" in *Encounter* 28.2 (February 1967): 25-26.

21. Hans Vaihinger from *The Philosophy of As If,* cited in Kermode (New York: Oxford University Press, 1979), 40.

22. This oft-quoted letter to Barney Rosset of 27 August 1957 objects to a staging of *All that Fall.* Beckett's full wording is: "If we can't keep our genres more or less distinct, or extricate them from the confusion that has them where they are, we might as well go home and lie down." Beckett subsequently authorized several stage versions of *All that Fall.*

23. *No Symbols Where None Intended,* 53.

Robert Scholes (essay date 1998)

SOURCE: Scholes, Robert. "Playing with the Cries." *Samuel Beckett Today* 7 (1998): 379-90.

[*In the following essay, Scholes approaches "First Love" as a hypertext and recommends that the reader explore links found in the story.*]

There is a page on the World Wide Web called "Play It Again, Sam". If you should visit that page, you will find a sold black background, with the words "I Can't Go On" written there. If you click on those underlined words, you will find yourself on another black page, on which the words "I Must Go On" appear. A click there and you are back to the black page with "I Can't Go On" inscribed thereon. You can continue this as long as you wish. Play it again, Sam, indeed. The URL for the first page, for those interested in experiencing this phenomenon, is

<http://www.soros.org/kfish/gogo.html>

I mention these pages because they afford some insight into the way that Beckett appears in the modern cultural text—and because, like the words of any durable writer—they speak *for* us as well as *to* us. In my case, they speak for me. I have read this text, Beckett's **"First Love",** many times, and I have nothing to say about it. And yet I must. I am back in school, a place I never really cared for, and the class is waiting for my book report. I am stalling, of course, trying not to begin, but I must begin. I have undertaken to write about **"First Love",** and to write "semiotically", if possible, so here I am, about to begin, which I shall certainly do—in a moment or two.

Actually, I would rather write about my own first love, and would certainly do so if I were sure which one it was. I think it must have been Carrie, who worked for my parents, was beautiful, I believe, and made wonderful cookies—of that I am certain. Yes, Carrie and her cookies would be a much pleasanter subject than Beckett and his **"First Love",** but, come to think of it, Carrie left me—I must have been eight years old at the time—for a man. She married, had a child, and that was that. As Beckett says at the end of **"First Love",** "either you love or you don't".

I seem to have begun speaking of Beckett and his story (though perhaps not "semiotically"), but not because I promised do so. No, it is rather because Beckett is insisting. His words, as he almost said himself, can be applied to our situations. Yes, despite everything, these disgusting and somewhat boring post-Kafkaesque narratives of despair and degradation have something to say to us about our ordinary lives. And what's more, they are often funny—yes, amusing. You have to like a man who can say, "I have no bone to pick with graveyards". What, then, is Beckett saying to us in **"First Love"**? How should we read this text?

We can take what we might call the pigeon's-eye view, flying high over this story, noting its broad outlines, and dropping our little messages upon the text, as pigeons do with monuments, thereby obscuring some of its words and meanings. Or we can take the worm's-eye view, grubbing around in the mouldering text, chewing on this or that bit to see if there is anything in it that can nourish us, but never seeing the whole picture. Let us not, however, get too caught up in our own grubby metaphors. Let us be eclectic—a little flying and dropping, with a little grubbing and chewing. From up above, we can see that this text has just seven paragraphs. Let me, like a good semiotician, list them, in order, with their size noted, and their opening phrases:

> 1. (four lines) I associate, rightly or wrongly, marriage with the death. [. . .]
>
> 2. (fifteen lines) I visited, not so long ago, my father's grave, [. . .]
>
> 3. (a page and a half) Personally, I have no bone to pick with graveyards [. . .]
>
> 4. (almost two pages) But to pass on to less melancholy matters, [. . .]
>
> 5. (over nine pages) But to pass on to less melancholy matters, [. . .]
>
> 6. (almost three pages) There were in fact two rooms, [. . .]
>
> 7. (about three pages) Gradually, I settled down, in this house.

Very irregular paragraphing, notes our pigeon: Splat! In fact, the fifth paragraph is just about as long as all the others combined? Splat! A semiotician might find these matters interesting and revealing—but not this semiotician, at this moment. Our pigeon's flight over the text has not been in vain, however, for it has called our attention to the fact that the two central paragraphs in this text begin with exactly the same phrase: "But to pass on to less melancholy matters." Given what is recounted in these paragraphs, it is clear that we are in a universe divided between more and less melancholy matters, like that Hegelian night in which all cows lose their colours. This repetition is also a clue, however, as to how we should be reading this text. It suggests that we should attend to repetition—of which, it turns out, there is a lot in these few pages. Let us return, then, by this commodious vicus of recirculation, to the beginning.

The first words of the text, after the title, are: "I associate." Stop right there, please. Hold that phrase. (The semiotician, as Roland Barthes told us too long ago, breaks up the text! And where is our Roland? Where is the author of "A Lover's Discourse" and other lovelorn, melancholy texts? Where is the great apologist for écriture? He sleeps with kings and counsellors and other scriveners, including our Sam, whose corpse, if I may borrow some words from our narrator at the end of paragraph 4, has finally come "up to scratch". Am I being macabre? Am I being impious to our great dead writers? I am being nothing that Samuel Beckett has not taught me to be, and my point is that these lessons are useful. Sam carried his heavy burden lightly, which is why he could indeed play it again and again.) But back to those first words: "I associate"—indeed you do, Sam, indeed you do—and so, then, must we, your readers, in our own attempts to come up to scratch. The first paragraph, I am suggesting, is, among other things, telling us how to read this text and others: by associating, by finding links. Even, as the text suggests, "other links on other levels".

Finding links! How hypertextual! Like other postmodernist writers, Beckett seems to have been writing for hypertext *avant l'ordinateur.* Let us try to come up to scratch ourselves, however, and attend to our own itches. This text offers us—nay, insists upon—two orders of association, which semioticians once liked to call the metaphorical and the metonymical. Unhappy with the confusions evoked by those two terms, I shall refer to these two orders of association as simply the semantic and the syntactic. The semantic is based upon words, as they lie quietly in dictionaries and thesauruses—words, that is, referring to one another by similarity or opposition of meaning, like *live* and *quick* (semantic, based on similarity), or *quick* and *dead* (semantic, based upon opposition). The syntactic order, on the other hand, is based upon linkages established outside the dictionary, in the world and its texts, like death and the grave, the grave and the tombstone. I would say, "Let us get back to Beckett", but death and graves and tombstones have already brought us back. Let us, in any case, look more closely at the words of **"First Love"**.

The first paragraph begins not with narration, as the seventh paragraph does ("Gradually, I settled down"), nor with description, as the sixth paragraph does ("There were, in fact, two rooms, separated by a kitchen"), but with a meta-discursive statement (that is, a statement about the discourse itself): "I associate." The one who is recounting this narrative (the author? the speaker? the narrator?) is telling us how his mind and, by extension, his text, work. And what does this "I" associate? He—let us call him "he", for various reasons—He associates marriage with death. Marriage and death—not your standard pairing of concepts—or mine either. This unusual combination, because of its oddity, offers us food for thought. The text, as early as the next paragraph, clarifies this odd association by supplying a middle term: birth. The entire narrative has in fact been organized as a working out of variations on the themes of death, marriage, and birth, in their various combinations and permutations—and Beckett, as a reading of *Watt* will remind us, is a virtuoso of the *combinatoire*. He takes pleasure—perhaps gives it, too, to readers who share his own combinatorial perversion—in expressing all the possible combinations of a few simple elements—often playing them over, again and again. At the beginning of **"First Love",** however, Beckett's narrator poses for us the problem of what death and marriage may have to do with one another, and, in particular, what his father's death may have to do with his own marriage. Our reading thus becomes motivated by the desire for answers to these questions—which the text will indeed supply.

(Dear old Roland, in the heady days of early structuralism, when narratologists were scrambling around, pasting labels on every narrative device or code, offered us a name for this kind of motivation—but I have forgotten it. Does this mean that Barthes and other laboured in vain? No more than we all do, no more than we all do. The codes offered to us in *S/Z* could never be the last word in the study of narrative. Like other rhetorical and critical terms, they serve to call our attention, as readers, to certain aspects of texts that might otherwise escape us. Breaking up the text, as Barthes did in that justly famous reading of Balzac's *Sarassine*, also serves a great interpretative purpose, in that it forces us to awaken from our narrative slumbers, induced by the teleological charms of realistic narration. By breaking up the text arbitrarily we experience the kind of alienation or estrangement that enables us to stop, for a moment, reading, and start, for a while, thinking. A late (or post-) modernist writer like Beckett, however, is likely to alienate us himself, needing no critic to break up his text. Beckett, needless to say, is very good at this. Having broken up my own text, which was never seductive enough to lull the critical faculties of its audience, though perhaps capable of lulling in a more somatic sense, I must now find my way back to Beckett's. Ah, yes, we were talking about the way that the opening conundrum of **"First Love"**—that association of marriage and death—works to rouse a curiosity that only the text could supply.)

These supplements begin in the second paragraph, in which the narrator recounts his visits to the graveyard, to read a tombstone and thus obtain the dates of his father's death and birth. He does so, apparently, by way of research for the account he is offering us, in order to ascertain his own age (about twenty-five) at the time of his marriage. Knowing that he married shortly after his father's death, he will be able to calculate his age by subtracting his birth date from his father's death date. But he can look at no tombstone to find the date of his own birth. Where, then, does that date repose? It is, he

tells us, "*graven* on my memory". You will forgive the semiotical "aha" which caused me to emphasize that word "graven". To engrave is to scratch, to dig, and, of course, to write in a durable way, to produce writing that cannot be easily erased, like the words scratched upon tombstones. If you look for me tomorrow, says the dying Mercutio to Romeo, you will find me a grave man. Well, this is a grave man who is writing our story here, a man who believes that, if his dead Papa could see him, he would find his "corpse not yet quite up to *scratch*".

To "come up to scratch" is a term from the old days of bare knuckle boxing. It referred to a line scratched in the earth, to which a fighter who had been knocked down had to return or lose the fight. In English idiom now, it signifies, loosely, being ready, measuring up. In Beckett's text, the dead father, "in his great disembodied wisdom", may see "further than his son, whose corpse was not yet quite up to scratch". The living son is, paradoxically, a corpse, but not yet a finished one, not yet perfected, not yet ready to be disembodied, to cross the line graven between life and death—"not yet quite up to scratch". "Scratch", then, signifies, at this textual moment, a line between being bodied and being disembodied, corpsed and decorpsed. One thinks of Yeats and his soul, "sick with desire and fastened to a dying animal"—that is the line of thought embodied or engraved in Beckett's prose, here. To be alive, in this textual universe, is to be a corpse, dragging the flesh around, whereas to be dead is to be disembodied, freed from the drag of the flesh, which prevents one from "seeing". And the drag of the flesh is very much what this story is about. It is also, of course, about scratching, engraving, in a word: writing.

(Semioticians are always finding out that texts are about writing, about how they were written. How boring! How stultifying! And yet—Look! I have nothing up my sleeve. The references to writing are *in* Beckett's text. *He* put them there. And this is important. If *I* were bringing these meanings to the text all by myself, the whole process would be trivial and silly. Why bother? Interpretation is a game in which both the writer and the reader are players. "No symbols where none intended", says Beckett at the end of *Watt,* knowing full well that intention is a slippery notion, extending, as it does, from conscious purpose to unconscious revelation. In the third paragraph our narrator concentrates on graveyards, telling us he prefers the scents of the dead to the odours of the living, but we mustn't let the shock of this revelation distract us from the attention paid to writing in this paragraph. For it is here that we discover our narrator to be a writer. He enjoys, he tells us, wandering among the slabs, "culling inscriptions". He never wearies of these, since he always finds a few that are so amusing, "of such drollery", he says, that he has "to hold on to the cross, or the stele, or the angel, so as not to fall". More important for our interpretative purposes, however, is the revelation that the narrator has composed his own epitaph, which he inscribes not on stone but in our text, and that he has written other things that he finds revolting as soon as they are "dry". This is a curious moment, for the narrator's life, as revealed in the subsequent paragraphs, seems to be that of a homeless person, expelled from his father's house after his father's death, briefly taken in by a woman, driven out again at the moment of his own dubious paternity by the cries of his new-born of his child. There seems to be no place in this life for pen, ink, and paper—for "writing" in the physical sense suggested by that expression: "My other writings are no sooner dry than they revolt me."

I am inclined to read this curious allusion to "other writings" as a kind of break in the text, in which the author's voice is inscribed over that of the narrating character. If we attend to what I have called the "circumstantial" evidence about this text, we can note that Beckett did not like it very much when he wrote it in French, nor, again, when he translated it into English. This story, **"First Love",** is, no doubt, one of the "other writings", that our narrator/author finds revolting. Of this paring, author/narrator, it is the author, Sam, who writes on paper. Our narrator, who tells us that he should have made a note "on paper" of Lulu's proper name, did not in fact do so, though, in the throes of first love, he finds himself "inscribing the letters Lulu in an old heifer pat", or, as he also puts it, "tracing her name in old cowshit" (paragraph 5). When our narrator writes (inscribes, traces—how many words he has for writing!), he writes on dung. But who has written this story—and on what? There are other moments, as well, when what we might call the register of this account shifts from the abjection of a dispossessed vagabond, to a different level, where the abjection and dispossession are on a grander scale, seeming to mirror, in however distorted a manner, the life of a citizen of modern Europe, who is, in fact, an exiled (self-exiled, like Joyce, no doubt) Irish writer, who has wandered through Europe, writing, in a foreign language, texts he finds revolting.

Our narrator is not the only one whose words are writ in cowshit, and cowshit is not the only kind of shit in this text. It seems that history also excretes. In one of the few passages that serve to locate these events in a specific place, the narrator speaks of his native land in this way:

> What constitutes the charm of our country, apart of course from its scant population, and this without the help of the meanest contraceptive, is that all is derelict, with the sole exception of history's ancient faeces. These are ardently sought after, stuffed and carried in procession. Wherever nauseated time has dropped a nice fat turd you will find our patriots, sniffling it up on all fours, their faces on fire.

> ("First Love," 33-34)

Many a nation, not excluding my own, has had its moments of worship for the droppings of history. But that scant population, achieved without birth control, seems to point to Ireland more clearly than to anyplace else. (The text's most specific geographical reference, of course, is to the Ohlsdorf graveyard, in Hamburg, which is present by association, as the complete opposite of the graveyard visited by our narrator. Beckett, of course, did indeed spend some time in Hamburg early in his career.) The mask of this character/narrator is being worn loosely by the author, whose voice repeatedly makes itself heard, though the story is clearly too absurd, too beautiful, too neat—to be literally his. History's "ancient faeces", of course, are themselves signs, already traces, inscriptions—which is why they are worshipped. By positioning them within his account of inscribing the word Lulu on cow pats, the author/narrator compares his own behaviour, when crazed by "first love" to the behaviour of his crazed compatriots, sniffling up the droppings of history: "Would I have been tracing her name in old cowshit if my love had been pure and disinterested? And with my devil's finger into the bargain, which I then sucked? Come now!" He sucks his sticky finger, the devil's finger, too, like the patriots, sniffling up the faeces of history with their faces on fire.

A pretty pass, to which our narrator was led by the events that took place on a bench by one of the town's two canals. These events, narrated in paragraph 5 (the second devoted to "less melancholy matters") may be said to reach a climax when he stretches out, with her "fat thighs" under his "miserable calves". Let us follow the event in his own deadly prose. (I will need to quote at some length, here.)

> She began stroking my ankles. I considered kicking her in the cunt. You begin to speak to people about stretching out and they immediately see a body at full length. What mattered to me in my dispeopled kingdom, that in regard to which the disposition of my carcass was the merest and most futile of accidents, was supineness in the mind, the dulling of the self and of that residue of execrable frippery known as the non-self and even the world, for short. But man is still today, at the age of twenty-five, at the mercy of an erection, physically too, from time to time, it's the common lot, even I was not immune, if that may be called an erection. It did not escape her naturally, women smell a rigid phallus ten miles away and wonder, How on earth did he spot me from there? One is no longer oneself on such occasions, and it is painful to be no longer oneself, even more painful if possible than when one is. For when one is one knows what to do to be less so, whereas when one is not one is any old one irredeemably. What goes by the name of love is banishment, with now and then a postcard from the homeland, such is my considered opinion, this evening. When she had finished and my self been resumed, mine own, the mitigable, with the help of a brief torpor, it was alone.

> ("FL" ["First Love"], 31)

One may pause to note the misogyny of this text. Our narrator, like many male modernists and postmodernists, wants to associate the female with the body and the male with the mind or soul. Unfortunately for him, however, he has a phallus, which ties him to woman, reminds him that he has a body, that he shares "the common lot". "Even", he says, "even I was not immune". Of course, this narrator and his world being what they are, his erection is nothing to brag about—"if *that* may be called an erection". But this is a strangely philosophical passage, is it not. The actual physical act, to which the title of the story may refer, seems to have taken place here, somewhere in or behind this paragraph, between the erection and the torpor, while the narrator was philosophising about the self and the non-self in his enervated existentialist jargon. "What goes by the name of love is banishment", says this Irish exile. And he says it at the present moment, "this evening". And which evening is that? We may well ask. Is it the evening of this first act of "love"? Probably not. That would be "then". This is now, *this* evening. But the text also situates this moment as "today, at the age of twenty-five", the age, that is, which the narrator was *then*. Uh-oh! Beware, interpreters! Traps and snares are being set for you. Is it the evening of the act of narrating? Perhaps. Is it also the evening of the writing? Possibly. Or of the translating? Maybe. Or is it no actual evening at all, but just the word "evening", a signifier, with a signified, but no referent? Almost certainly. And yet, to read is to assign not only signification but reference to words, even if to read fiction is to assign fictional reference.

It is possible that this particular reference to "today, at the age of twenty-five" is intended only to describe how men in general, at the age of twenty-five, even in the present era still behave. But "today" and "this evening", in association, reinforce one another in their apparent reference to a present time. This is a text that both invites and undoes the assignment of specific reference to its significations. But let us look more closely at certain other features of this paragraph. "She began stroking my ankles. I considered kicking her in the cunt. You begin to speak to people about stretching out and they immediately see a body at full length." Notice first the pronouns: She, I, You, they. Two sentences of narration, referring to the two characters in this little drama, followed by two clauses of generalization, in which "you" and "they" have replaced "I" and "she". This late modernist narrator generalizes almost as much as Balzac or George Eliot. But these generalizations do not reach us with the same ethical authority, because the narrator is neither steady nor reliable, and the author has been contaminated by the narrator—or vice versa.

That "stretching out" should lead visions of "a body at full length", should come as no surprise to any late modernist with T. S. Eliot's "The evening is spread out against the sky / Like a patient etherized upon a table" always hovering in the intertextual background. Which ought to remind us that another major intertext for Beckett's story is "The Waste Land".

> While I was fishing in the dull canal,
> Musing upon the king my brother's wreck
> And on the king my father's death before him.
> White bodies naked on the low damp ground. [. . .]

(ll. 189-192)

In Eliot's world, however, one doesn't consider kicking one's neighbour in the cunt. Such are the advances of late modernism over its predecessor. The narrator of **"First Love",** in his own "dispeopled kingdom", is not fishing in the canal near which he is positioned. He becomes, rather, to his own disgust, one of the "white bodies", though neither naked nor on the ground. Unlike Eliot's mythical Fisher King with his sterilizing wound that will not heal, our narrator's wound is precisely his unsterility—that is, both his erection and his potency, his ability to engender. Or, perhaps better, his *in*ability *not* to engender, his inability to terminate the absurd dance of corporeality so as to avoid passing it on to the next generation. His corpse, unable to come up to the scratch of decomposition, must continue to itch with the fever of procreation—and of composition. He must, in short, fuck and write.

He, that is his consciousness, cannot remain in the realm of pure thought but is "banished" by love to the badlands of the body, where his active corpse continues the gross joke of human existence. This is why the birth of his child is the final, unendurable indignity. Before that dreadful event, things had begun to get better for our narrator: "Already my love was waning [. . .] Yes, already I felt better, soon I'd be up to the slow descents again, the long submersions, so long denied me through her fault." At this time he also began to hear his voice uttering unintended sentiments: "I was so unused to speech that my mouth would sometimes open, of its own accord, and vent some phrase or phrases, grammatically unexceptionable but entirely devoid if not of meaning, for on close inspection they would reveal one, and even several, at least of foundation [. . .]." He does not say what his words are devoid *of*. Which makes this particular utterance, written not spoken, grammatically exceptionable. But here again, where there is no narrative need for a discussion of expression and interpretation, the text finds it necessary to introduce the topic—and to leave it very much up in the air. The utterances of this speaker are alien to him, they may be full of meanings but they are (a) not really his, and (b) only "foundational"—whatever that may mean. I take it to mean that interpretation, working on these "foundational" meanings may indeed rise to others, but that these other meanings will be doubly detached from the author of the words being interpreted. Another warning from the author. Not only, no symbols where none intended, but also a guarantee that the utterances are cut off from any intention whatsoever. They will be the interpreter's responsibility. We must respect that thought, I believe, and take responsibility for our interpretations of this text and others—but we must also try to pin them on the author as a blindfolded child tries to pin a cardboard tail on a cardboard donkey—which means that we may pin out interpretative tails to the author's ear, or his haunch, or completely off the authorial image, but the goal is clearly to pin the tail to the author's ass, where it belongs.

Coming back from this metadiscursive excursion into the larger topic of interpretation, I want to pick up the interpretative thread of the birth/death connection. After Lulu/Anna begins speaking about "our" child in her womb, the narrator tells us that, "From that day things went from bad to worse, to worse and worse". And then, the worst happened—not something like the death of mother and child that gives a modern novel like Hemingway's *A Farewell to Arms* its pathetic ending, but a perfectly normal live birth: "But I did not know yet, at that time, how tender the earth can be for those who have only her and how many graves in her giving for the living. What finished me was the birth. It woke me up." He leaves a house for the second time in this narrative, driven out of his first home by the death of his father, and out of the second by the birth of his child. From this second house, however, he takes something with him—or rather something accompanies him. He is pursued by the cries of the new-born. He looks to the stars for orientation, if not for consolation, but he cannot even find the one he used to remember out of the many that his own father had shown him. He discovers that he cannot hear the cries when he is walking. His footsteps drown them out. But, whenever he stops he hears them. Then, he tells us, he "began playing with the cries"—playing a kind of fort-da game, "on, back, on, back, if that may be called playing". The cries became fainter as he distanced himself in space and time from the dreadful event of the birth, but, like the beating of the telltale heart in Poe's gothic tale, they never stopped altogether. And what, he asks, does it matter, that they grew fainter: "cry is cry, all that matters is that it should cease. For years I thought they would cease. Now I don't think so any more. I could have done with other loves perhaps. But there it is, either you love or you don't".

With these final words the narrator brings us up to the present again, and the author's voice once again seems to be heard. "Playing with the cries" is an apt description of everything this author has written, text after text, in which we are allowed to hear the cries of corpses who have not yet come up to scratch. All of which would be unbearable for us as readers, if it were not for the fact that Beckett is indeed playing, that the texts are

full of jokes and other verbal gifts, and that this author does not stand aside and sneer at his characters, nor blame the cosmos for its structure, but recognizes his own implication in his texts and allows us to see and share it, too. For this kind of playing with the cries of human existence, however, imperfect, however, in Beckett's own word, "revolting", we must simply be grateful. There is much more to be said about a rich text such as this one. There are scenes and episodes I have left unconsidered, and I have not said nearly enough about "the dread name of love". But limits are limits, and I must now abandon my own text, which I assure you, revolts me as much as Beckett's revolted him.

Carolyn Jursa Ayers (essay date 1998)

SOURCE: Ayers, Carolyn Jursa. "An Interpretive Dialogue: Beckett's 'First Love' and Bakhtin's Categories of Meaning." *Samuel Beckett Today* 7 (1998): 391-405.

[*In the following essay, Ayers applies Mikhail Bakhtin's theory of dialogue to "First Love."*]

Discussing Beckett and Bakhtin together presents a challenge, to say the least; it seems remarkable that two men who led somewhat parallel lives could come to such diametrically opposed conceptions of man's place in the world. They were, after all, rough historical contemporaries (Bakhtin's dates are 1895-1975, Beckett's are 1906-1989), and lived through some of the same experiences of the twentieth century. Both survived in precarious conditions during the Second World War, and although neither was inclined toward political activity, both occasionally found themselves objects of political suspicion. Furthermore, they both endured painful and debilitating illness over the course of many years. Both men were highly educated, very much at home in the Western literary tradition, and widely read. And they were, I think, both acutely aware of the collapse of coherent meaning systems in the twentieth century. They experienced the tension of the thinking individual whose relationship with the world is insecure and fragile. And yet the conclusions they drew from all this point in entirely different directions: Beckett's textual world is profoundly pessimistic, while Bakhtin's displays all the optimism inherent in the idea of open-endedness.

All the more interesting, then, to bring these two strong voices into dialogue with each other. Beckett's story cannot be "explicated" by applying Bakhtinian terms or concepts. Yet the two voices, one artistic and imaginative, the other philosophical and scholarly, can be brought together so that they enrich each other. Reading Beckett with the help of Bakhtin should, in Bakhtin's words, "renew" the literary event of the Beckett story. I would like, then, to propose an interpretation of **"First Love"** that is "many-sided". I will use Bakhtin's categories of genre, chronotope, and dialogue, and his words about them, to explore the story from various perspectives, at least some of which should shed some light on Beckett's dark narrative.

According to Bakhtin, much of the meaning that adheres to a literary work is contained in its *genre*. Every literary work has roots which extend backwards into time. Formal principles of organization, when they exist together in certain relationships with typical topics and devices, carry echoes of meaning from the distant past; these represent some of the semantic possibilities that the artist has at his disposal to exploit.[1] On the other hand, "semantic phenomena can exist in concealed form, potentially, and be revealed only in semantic cultural contexts of subsequent epochs that are favourable for such disclosure".[2] Thus, different elements of any generic complex might be dominant at different historical moments.

Among the generic categories Bakhtin describes, the one that seems to resonate most in **"First Love"** is the *menippea*. Menippean satire originated in the third century BC, an era which witnessed the decline of the tragic and epic, an era which, as Bakhtin says, ceased to recognize "the wholeness of a man and his fate".[3] In the tradition of the menippea, the follies of men are related in a mixture of prose and verse, often interlaced with a high degree of the comic. Free from the limitations of memoir and history, the menippea allows extraordinary range for invention. Beckett's narrator enjoys just this sort of freedom. In fact, he insists on it; he constantly reminds the reader that he is relating events only as he imagines them. His family's relief at his departure from the house, for instance, "may have passed quite differently" than the scene he describes. It is clear, however, that the narrator is deliberate in his imagination and conscious of his narrative control. Later in the story, he muses, "But I have always spoken, no doubt always shall, of things that have never existed, or that existed if you insist, no doubt always will, but not with the existence I ascribe to them."

Why should the narrator wish to ascribe an existence to things which might never have happened, or to ascribe a different existence to them than that which they actually had? The historical characteristics of the menippea offer some possibilities. In the menippea (as Bakhtin describes it), extraordinary situations often serve as tests for philosophical truths or ideas. "The genre contains the capacity to contemplate the world on the broadest possible scale. [. . .] everywhere one meets the stripped-down pro et contra of life's ultimate questions" (Bakhtin, *Problems of Dostoevsky's Poetics*, 115-16). Certainly the narrator of **"First Love"** does confront the basic mysteries of life; his story concerns precisely death, birth, love, and existence.

Yet the circumstances in which the narrator, and, ultimately, Beckett, consider these questions are, to say the least, strange. Graveyards conventionally provoke contemplation of the transience of life, but a bench with garbage strewn around it? A deserted cowshed? A prostitute's room? These are not the circumstances under which we would normally expect to confront life's ultimate mysteries. Yet, Bakhtin continues, "a very important characteristic of the menippea is the organic combination within it of the free fantastic, the symbolic, at times even a mystical-religious element with an extreme and (from our point of view) crude *slum naturalism* [italics Bakhtin's]. [. . .] the adventures of truth on earth take place on the high road, in brothels, in the dens of thieves, [. . .]. The idea here fears no slum, is not afraid of any of life's filth" (*Problems,* 115). Thus when the narrator withdraws to contemplate his situation in a deserted cowshed in a field of mud and nettles, even though he could by his own account afford other lodgings, he is living out the conditions of the menippea. Or, to be more accurate, he is writing of his experience in the terms of the menippea, for, as he says, things may in fact have passed quite differently.

The narrator, then, seems drawn to the menippea as a form potentially able to accommodate the expression of both his ideas and his mental state. Bakhtin says, "In the menippea there appears for the first time what might be called moral-psychological experimentation: a representation of the unusual, abnormal moral and psychic states of man—insanity of all sorts [. . .], split personality, unrestrained daydreaming, unusual dreams, passions bordering on madness, suicides, and so forth. These phenomena do not function narrowly in the menippea as mere themes, but have a formal generic significance" (*Problems,* 116). The function of these altered mental states is to reveal the possibilities of another person within the character. The character loses his finalized quality and ceases to mean only one thing; he ceases to coincide with himself. What Bakhtin describes in theoretical terms is realized vividly by the narrator of **"First Love",** for example, in his account of his sexual experience with Lulu on the bench ("One is no longer oneself on such occasions, and it is painful to be no longer oneself"). Indeed, the propensity the narrator displays throughout the story for contradicting himself may be interpreted as an act of resistance to finalization that borders on the insane. Scandal scenes, eccentric behaviour, inappropriate speeches and performances, however, are all typical of the menippea, and not in spite of their incongruence with philosophical speculation, but because of it. In the framework of the menippea, there is no contradiction between the mental instability of the narrator and the extraordinary philosophical range of his thinking.

Also characteristic of the menippea are unexpected juxtapositions and contrasts. These are indeed realized at every level of Beckett's narrative, from the association the narrator draws in his mind between his marriage and the death of his father, to the abrupt shifts in stylistic conventions that pop up in his speech. "I am thus in a position to affirm that I must have been about twenty-five at the time of my marriage", he asserts in legalese, only to lapse a short while later into the lyrical mode, recalling that the woman's voice "breathed of a soul too soon wearied ever to conclude." The dynamic of the narrative, in fact, seems to consist of a continual jarring shifting among stylistic levels, from the crudest slang, to the cleverest wordplay, to scholarly pedantry. This is heteroglossia both compressed and underscored.

I think it would be highly speculative, and probably wrong, to suggest that Beckett consciously adopts the framework of the menippea for his story of first love. Nevertheless, it is useful to know that Beckett's modernist prose (abrupt shifts in stylistic levels, unexpected juxtapositions, and so forth, are, after all, hallmarks of modernism as well as of the menippea) has relevant parallels in literary history. These parallels suggest that some of the oddities of Beckett's prose may be strategic.

Our next question, as we probe deeper into **"First Love"**, must be: to what end are the strategic possibilities of the narrative employed? What are these "ultimate philosophical positions", as it were, that are being tested? The narrator, it seems to me, is unusually concerned with defining his own position in terms of space and time. He forgets things, he remembers, he lies down flat, he wanders. He keeps alive the memory of his father, but is compelled to actually visit the graveyard in person to fix the date of his death. And all the time he struggles to fix his own position: he jots down dates, and he specifies thoughts and impulses as belonging to "that period" or "this juncture." He negotiates with the woman over how often exactly she is to look for him. It seems clear that the narrator's extreme difficulty in connecting with other people is part and parcel of his own ontological uncertainty. He vacillates (a temperamental tendency which has already been remarked in the other interpretations in this collection) among various ways of configuring, or ordering, his experience in space and time.

This, of course, brings us to Bakhtin's formulation for the literary expression of the interconnection of space and time, namely the *chronotope*. In his essay "Forms of Time and the Chronotope", Bakhtin identifies eight basic chronotopes, each of which expresses a particular historical experience of time in spatial terms. The delimitation of eight, however, in no way precludes the possibility of more. It is important to realize that for Bakhtin none of the chronotopes is a closed or self-fulfilled system; they can overlap, coexist, and contain any number of minor chronotopes. Furthermore, as literary history evolves, they "find themselves in ever more complex interrelationships" ("Forms of Time", 252).

In **"First Love"**, the narrator seems to be engaged in a conscious effort to unravel the "complex interrelationship" of space and time surrounding his experience of life. He himself can recognize many such connections ("that other links exist, on other levels [. . .] is not impossible"), but he is not satisfied with any of them. Indeed, he seems unsettled by the conflicting value systems that different attitudes toward space and time represent. He gives us clues to the rejected possibilities, however. For example, in labelling the field of mud and nettles in which he takes refuge after his encounter with Lulu the "Elysium of the roofless", the narrator ironically evokes the chronotope of the *idyll*.

Bakhtin describes the idyllic chronotope (in its pure form) as a nostalgic representation folkloric, or unified time. In this chronotope, literature represents temporal unity (the coherence of life's events) through unity of place. Unity of place "weakens and renders less distinct all the temporal boundaries between individual lives and between various phases of one and the same life. The unity of place brings together and even fuses the cradle and the grave . . . and brings together as well childhood and old age . . . the life of the various generations who had also lived in that same place ("Forms of Time", 224). According to Bakhtin, the idyll is "limited to only a few of life's basic realities. Love, birth, death, marriage, labour, food and drink, stages of growth [. . .]" (224). Human life is joined with the life of nature. Sexuality and other details of everyday life, on the other hand, appear softened and to a certain extent sublimated in the idyllic chronotope.

The stable, organic environment of the idyll has been realized differently throughout literary history. It has served as the basis for endowing everyday life with significance (in the provincial novel); it has been invoked to criticize society (by, for example, Rousseau); it has been contrasted with its destruction by the forces of the capitalist world. In the domestic novel, it has been represented by the (family) house. The essential problem the idyll raises is: what is the status of idyllic time/place conditions in relation to life as it is presently experienced?

For our narrator, the idyll seems to represent some desired level of comfortable stasis. But he takes the experience of stasis to the extreme. His taste for graveyards, for instance, is indicative of his wish to unify life and death, but under the conditions of the latter. Thus he prefers to take his refreshment "sitting on a tomb", and he associates his marriage with the death of his father. Likewise, he wants to stay in the family house, not so as to be in a community with his family, but so he can lie flat on his back, immobile. I think the narrator takes his desire for stasis to these extremes because he recognizes that an unchanging, stable environment is basically a self-deception. Hence also his sarcastic reference to the Irish obsession with local history, another manifestation of the desire for idyllic time: "[. . .] history's ancient faeces [. . .] are ardently sought after, stuffed, and carried in procession. Wherever nauseated time has dropped a nice fat turd you will find our patriots, sniffing it up on all fours, their faces on fire."

The impossibility of realizing the idyllic chronotope becomes immediately obvious when the narrator has to leave his room to go to stool. This physical necessity results in his being ejected from his "Garden of Eden", and confronts him with elements of a different, opposing chronotope: that of the *Rabelaisian world*. This chronotope, which Bakhtin identifies with the work of the sixteenth-century writer and humanist François Rabelais, involves a productive and generative "folk" time, one based on the whole man, body and soul. With its roots in the preclass agricultural stage of human societies, when the means of production, ritual, and everyday life had not yet differentiated into the private and public spheres, it represents a reaction to the Medieval rejection of vulgar, crude physical licentiousness ("Forms of Time", 171). For Rabelais, the world is structured around the human body; the world is a zone of physical contact with the body, but infinitely wide. Only scattered remnants of the Rabelaisian chronotope survive in modern times, according to Bakhtin; they are often rendered as carnivalesque episodes, or the grotesque.

The narrator of **"First Love"** displays a decidedly ambivalent attitude toward the physical side of life. He feels it to be real, at times he revels in it (pissing on gravestones is almost a textbook example of a realization of carnivalesque humor), but he is at the same time repulsed. He resists defecation, but later traces the Lulu's name in cowshit. Some of the qualities of the Rabelaisian chronotope appear in his consciousness apparently for the first time during this episode of **"First Love"**. On the night he meets Lulu, for instance, she sings folk songs under her breath, "without the words fortunately [. . .] and so disjointedly, skipping from one to another and finishing none [. . .] The voice, though out of tune, was not unpleasant [. . .]" Yet he is dismayed that "you speak to people about stretching out and they immediately see a body at full length". The way he describes Lulu's body borders on the grotesque; he singles out her fat thighs, her squint, and eventually "the side view of her belly". Likewise, he is ambivalent about the cycle of the seasons, another intrinsic part of the Rabelaisian chronotope. His first instinct is to protect himself against the elements, to save his money for the onset of cold weather. Finally, however, he recognizes that "one should not dread the winter, it too has its bounties [. . .]".

Beckett may have had a natural affinity for a "medieval" configuration of man's relationship to the world. We know that he understood it, at least; he knew Provençal poetry well and was expert in Medieval French poetics. Some of the very qualities of Beckett's writing that have been associated with modernism—a circularity defying logic and linearity, a negation of the individual personality, a vision of man as insignificant in the universe, the juxtaposition of the sacred and the profane—have been remarked to have medieval associations as well (see Kern). Likewise, Ann Beer remarks on Beckett's "almost medieval quality of fatalism and austere compassion" (Beer, 165), and his "almost medieval world-view" (169). Again, what interests us is not the possibility of proving direct sources, but the insight we can gain, the potential meanings we can draw out through the process of dialogue.

Yet the Rabelaisian chronotope, like the idyllic one, has been evoked only to be denigrated. The narrator of **"First Love"** expresses both worldviews, as it were, in a voice laced with irony. This voice of the narrator's, in fact, resists material embodiment in any overarching, pre-existing framework of meaning. Indeed, he is a slippery character, resorting to all the means at his disposal to keep us, the readers, at a distance. One device that he adopts to this end is the figure or mask of *the clown*. The clown figure, of course, is a familiar one in Beckett's writings, with perhaps the most memorable examples in the characters of *Waiting for Godot*. Crucial as well in Bakhtin's theory, the clown (or rogue, or fool) is capable of performing a number of functions. Most importantly for our purposes, he resists the principle of material embodiment, and represents instead its direct opposite in the notion of *potential*.[4] The clown does not have his own fixed place; he passes through several. Thus his own personality is never finalized, but always open to future development.

One important quality of the clown is his right *not to understand*. Because the clown figure is not subject to the conventions which govern proper behaviour, because he does not have a serious role in society, he is not constrained from expressing natural and instinctive reactions. The narrator of **"First Love"** exploits this stance, and represents himself (somewhat disingenuously, perhaps) as completely passive throughout his amorous encounter. He allows himself to be approached, he seems not to know at first what the woman does for a living, and claims astonishment when he finally accepts the news that she is pregnant. This assumed naivety allows him to question each of these circumstances, and to avoid conventional ways of verbalizing and dealing with them. In this way, the clown figure is able to lay bare conventions: notunderstanding is a great "organizing factor" (device) in exposing vulgar conventionality. We see this, for example, in the narrator's reaction to the song the woman sings. Very likely this song about orange trees is from Goethe's Romantic *Wilhelm Meister*, a very "high romantic" representation of love. The narrator pretends not to recognize it; nonetheless he testifies to its effect.

The passive figure of the clown, however much it suits his purpose, is evidently a conscious strategy for our narrator, part of his resistance to embodiment. Throughout the story, it is clear that he is driven ultimately not by his naivety, but rather by acute *self-consciousness.* The narrator is well aware that any position he takes is false. But his use of various fictional devices—and his continual pointing to them—are attempts to bring his false situation under his own control. He is extremely— even morbidly—sensitive to the fact that he is not completely autonomous in the world. The worst possibility, to him, is that others may "complete him" or, in his view, appropriate him, in a way which he is unable to control or dictate. Yet this sort of completion, according to Bakhtin, is exactly the essence of life; this is Bakhtin's principle of *dialogue.*

The narrator's relationships, interestingly enough from a Bakhtinian point of view, are described in terms of voices. As he says more than once, he is surrounded by voices, living and dead. His profound discomfort with being in this position provokes in him two reactions: On the one hand, he resists dialogue, and attempts to stay within his own world of signification. At the same time, he acknowledges the dialogic position in which he finds himself, but reacts by trying to control the dialogue. His response to the threat of the Other's voice alternates rather compulsively between withdrawal and attack.

The Other whose voice the narrator resists, we must realize, exists on many levels and is ultimately abstract— this is reflected in the entire plan of the work. The hero has a family, but the individual (living) members of it are obscure; the only real Other represented in the hero's perception is his father, who is dead. Lulu too, of course, is a genuine Other, but the narrator is astonishingly reluctant to acknowledge her as such. "Shapeless, ageless, almost lifeless, it might have been anything or anyone, an old woman or a little girl", he says, and here he is describing his "First Love!" The most disturbing Other for him, of course, is the one who is literally abstract: the reader. The narrator's antagonistic one-sided dialogue with the reader recalls the attitude of a notorious literary ancestor, who also happened to be familiar to Bakhtin. I am referring to Dostoevsky's Underground Man, who shares a number of personality traits with Beckett's narrator.[5] For each of these disturbed characters, the voice of the Other is not discrete; in Bakhtin's words; "A real-life other voice inevitably fuses with the other voice already ringing in the hero's ears" (*Problems*, 253).

Beginning, as it were, with the idea the "I am alone, and they are everyone else", the narrator of **"First Love"** must nevertheless contend with a few voices individually. The first voice mentioned in the text is that of the narrator's father, whom he overhears saying "leave him alone".[6] This voice seems to comfort him, but perhaps this has to do with the fact that he is no longer compelled to respond to it, and he is (now) able to control the context in which the voice speaks. Later, he hears Lulu's singing, later still the sounds of the men who come to her, and finally the cries of the woman in childbirth and presumably those of the baby. As the story unfolds, the narrator becomes more and more resistant to all these voices; when he finally leaves Lulu in childbirth, he can no longer even find the Wains that his father had pointed out to him. At the same time, he is forced through his own narrative process to recognize these voices. More importantly, he gradually acknowledges the inevitability of his own position in life's dialogue.

Lulu surprises him from the first, putting him, as he sees it, in a position of vulnerability: "[. . .] the risk of surprise was small. And yet she surprised me." He tries to gauge the distance at which he must stand in order not to hear her. Unsuccessful at eliminating her voice outright, his next move is to try to anticipate her response to him, while simultaneously trying to flout any possible expectations she might have. "[. . .] I asked her to sing me a song. I thought at first she was going to refuse, I mean simply not sing, but no, after a moment she began to sing [. . .]" And later, "I thought she would say she had nothing to say, it would have been like her, and so was agreeably surprised when she said she had a room, most agreeably surprised, though I suspected as much". When he arrives at Lulu's rooms, "I began putting out the furniture [. . .] She asked me what I was doing. She can't have expected an answer".

The narrator may have been surprised at first by Lulu's voice speaking and singing to him, but one way to turn the situation around is precisely by narrating it as part of his experience. Throughout the story, he tries to appropriate her speech by reporting it very much in his own language, with his own commentary (in fact, much as he had appropriated the literary expressions of the idyll and the Rabelaisian world). "So you don't want me to come anymore, she said. It's incredible the way they repeat what you've just said to them, as if they risked faggot and fire in believing their ears." He mocks her: "I don't need the lid, I said. You don't need the lid? She said. If I had needed the lid she would have said, You need the lid?" Meanwhile, he himself returns her words to her: "You have no current? I said. No, she said, but I have running water and gas. Ha, I said, you have gas. She began to undress. When at their wit's end they undress, no doubt the wisest course."

Like his literary predecessor the Underground Man, Beckett's narrator chooses to enter a relationship with a prostitute. The strategy seems obvious: this ought to be a dialogue he is able to control. Each hero tries to assert his dominance in this relationship according to the historical and philosophical possibilities of his own era. In the nineteenth century, then, the Underground Man performs an act of charity and compassion. His complacent assumption that the woman he rescues will be grateful, subservient, and dependent on him doesn't work because he unintentionally exposes himself (his insecurities, his desperate pride), and becomes instead the object of her compassion. Beckett's twentieth-century hero, in contrast, has no qualms about accepting and even abusing the generosity of "such a creature". Instead, he tries to dominate verbally. He insults her, calling attention to her fat legs and her squint—which, incidentally, he suddenly notices only when she begins to undress. He seems to be in danger of losing control of the situation here, and is casting about for a point on which to defend himself from an assault on his self.

The narrator claims the greatest power over Lulu when, exercising his authorial privileges, he renames her. The name by which he introduces his **"First Love"**, Lulu, is the one by which she has introduced herself to him. (In fact he is reluctant to take even this utterance of hers at face value: "So at least she assured me and I can't see what interest she could have had in lying to me, on this score. Of course, one can never tell. She also disclosed her family name, but I've forgotten it.") Yet at another crucial point in the story, just when he acknowledges that what he feels for her is love, just when he begins to feel her power over him, he suddenly imposes his own choice of a name: "Anyhow I'm sick and tired of the name Lulu, I'll give her another, more like her, Anna for example, it's not more like her but no matter." Whether it is like her or not really doesn't matter to the narrator; what matters is that he chooses it for her.

Despite all his efforts to forestall the woman's autonomous voice, however, the "plot" of the story depends very much on her voice intruding. She is the first to say "Shove up", and she is the one to say she has rooms, setting the scene for their "night of love." In his hyperconscious mental state, the narrator recognizes very well that not only his control over the Other, but his control over his own voice is at peril in this encounter: "I seemed not to grasp the meaning of these words, nor even hear the brief sound they made, till some seconds after having uttered them . . . Never had my voice taken so long to reach me as on this occasion." Lulu seems to foil all the narrator's moves to appropriate her, even at one point bettering him in wits: "So you live by prostitution, I said. We live by prostitution, she said."

If the narrator is more or less able to block out the disturbing voices of the woman's clients, it is because these voices (like his father's instructions to his siblings) are overheard and demand from him no direct response. Eventually, however, Lulu comes to him with an utterance that absolutely requires an answer: "One day she had the impudence to announce she was with child." At this point he actually does make an attempt, of sorts. "I summoned up my remaining strength and said, Abort, abort [. . .]" When he cannot impose his version of "how things are passing" on the obvious physical reality of her advancing pregnancy, things go "from bad to worse, to worse and worse." Finally, he is utterly overwhelmed by the sound of her cries when she is giving birth. He flees the house, driven again from his self-styled idyllic stasis by the intrusion of the physical.

Yet having once entered into this dialogue, he cannot escape the other's voice. The cries pursue him out into the street and even down through the years. Silence, he acknowledges, will not come. The only possible way for him to appropriate this voice is to incorporate it into his written monologue; indeed, we might now guess that this is his principle motivation for writing.

Even in writing, however, the narrator must confront an Other in the person of his reader. And here he is at his most confrontational, perhaps because he perceives here the greatest threat to his autonomy. Like the Underground Man, he attempts throughout the narrative to anticipate what the reader will think, and then pre-empt the reader's response. He responds in turn to the reader's imagined objections, often trying to shock or insult. We see him justify himself over plot details: "were you to inquire, as undoubtedly you itch, what I had done with the money my father had left me [. . .]" Later, he hints that he is withholding information: "for other reasons better not wasted on cunts like you." This sudden spasm of narrative authority is apparently provoked by his too-open "confession" of leaving the bench. Still later in the story, he tries to distance himself even from his own written record: "Are we to infer from this I loved her with that intellectual love which drew from me such drivel, in another place? Somehow I think not."

The narrator is so defensive, perhaps, because here as in the rest of his narrative he is fighting a losing battle. The more he tries to resist dialogue, the deeper into it he is drawn. His very ability to identify what he experiences as love, the very basis for his narrative, is, he realizes, already determined largely by the voices of others. He himself calls upon these voices to establish his credentials in the eyes of the reader ("[. . .] of course [I] had heard of the thing, at home, in school, in brothel and at church, had read romances, in prose and verse, under the guidance of my tutor, in six or seven languages, both dead and living, in which it was handled at length"), to prove that he is educated and sophisticated. Yet in the next breath he denies the authority of these voices over his own experience.

Why is the narrator compelled to assert the autonomy of his voice? Clearly, he is deeply concerned with the integrity of his selfhood. His effort to define his essential self involves stripping away, excluding everything that comes from other subjects, and then "barring the door" against all "intrusions." We find literal enactments of this in the text: rooms, the bench "protected" on three sides, the removal of all furniture from the room and blocking the entryway, turning the sofa around. The crisis point is reached at the birth of the baby, because reproduction is the ultimate expression of connectedness, of surrender of autonomy to a greater organic whole, which the narrator resists with all his strength: "[. . .] if it's lepping, then it's not mine." His whole impulse is to identify and then deny everything that is *not* part of him, just as he rejects all previous definitions of love.

But somewhere in the course of asserting his own autonomy, the narrator comes to realize that he cannot silence the voices of the Other, whether the Other takes the shape of his father, on whose directions he relies in order to map the stars, the woman (whether she is Lulu, Anna, or simply Woman), or his reader. Looking back on the events recounted in **"First Love"**, the narrator recognizes that his efforts to remove himself from the organic wholeness of humanity are doomed to fail. As Bakhtin maintained, the self is made only through dialogue with the world around him. And while the physical movement of the story, the plot, involves an increasing withdrawal and flight from the voices surrounding the protagonist, his consciousness of the inevitability of dialogue grows. If he begins by attempting to write the final word about himself—his epitaph, and next asserts that he has "found the winning system at last", one which will carry him at any rate until the "curtain drops" on his life, he acknowledges by the time he hears the woman's song about the orange trees that

> of all the other songs I have ever heard in my life, and I have heard plenty, it being apparently impossible, physically impossible short of being deaf, to get through this world, even my way, without hearing singing, I have retained nothing, not a word, not a note, or so few words, so few notes, that, that what, that nothing, this sentence has gone on long enough.
>
> **("FL" ["First Love"]**, 37)

By the close of the story, he admits in a rather melancholy tone that the voice of one Other, at least, remains with him and has become part of him, "but there it is, either you love or you don't."

Yet the voice of this strange narrator remains with us as well. A voice emerging out of an obviously impoverished life experience, yet richly resonant nonetheless. To end this interpretation I would like to invoke one last category of meaning from Bakhtin: that of *laughter.*

Laughter, as Bakhtin sees it, is a positive life force, one that functions to destroy "false verbal and ideological shells" ("Forms of Time", 237).

> We have in mind here laughter not as a biological or psycho-physiological act, but rather laughter conceived as an objectivized, sociohistorical phenomenon, which is most often present in verbal expression [. . .] Alongside the poetic use of a word 'not in its primary sense', that is, alongside tropes, there exists in addition a multiplicity of forms for the various indirect linguistic expression of laughter: irony, parody, humour, the joke, various types of the comic, and so forth. [. . .]
>
> (Bakhtin, "Forms of Time", 237)

We have mentioned already Beckett's mastery of all these, and we seem to agree that these are some of the most rewarding moments in the text. Yet Beckett's laughter seems to be directed exactly counter to what Bakhtin had in mind, which was a sort of organic, subversive force rising out of the depths of humanity. I think Henk Hillenaar[7] is on to something with his suggestion that with Beckett, the laughter seems to be going in the other direction, from the verbal realm to the existential, physical one. If the narrator of **"First Love"** has any integrity, it is the integrity of his wit, his use of language.[8] He is able to employ his narrative strategically to expose the weaknesses of all sorts of conventional thoughts, and while the systems fall away, his wit never deserts him. We ought to end our interpretative dialogue, I think, by granting Beckett the last laugh, if never the last word.

Notes

1. I use the masculine pronoun throughout my paraphrasing of Bakhtin's ideas not simply for grammatical simplicity, but also to foreground—in an admittedly underhanded way—Bakhtin's notorious exclusion of any mention whatsoever of female artists. While deploring this "oversight", I think we have little choice but to take Bakhtin at his word that his system represents only the rudiments of a philosophy, and that in principle the open-endedness of the "human sciences" extends to female voices as well as male. Here Beckett's narrative has it over Bakhtin, as we shall see.

2. "Response to a Question from the Novy Mir Editorial Staff", in *Speech Genres*, 5.

3. Bakhtin lists the characteristics of the menippea in *Problems of Dostoevsky's Poetics*, 114-121.

4. In their study *Mikhail Bakhtin: Creation of a Prosaics*, Gary Saul Morson and Caryl Emerson discuss embodiment and potential as two apparently conflicting value systems: "Alongside of this principle of direct material embodiment (and as if on the same plane), Bakhtin introduces the idea of potential [. . .] Embodiment makes a body and its

size all, whereas potential makes it not all, and not what it appears to be" (436). Thus the figures of the clown, the rogue, and the fool avoid embodiment; they can move in and out of various chronotopes, and "the body we see at any given time and space is *not* wholly representative of a personality [. . .]" (436).

5. Thanks to Barend van Heusden for suggesting the resemblance.

6. The position of the "third" in a dialogue is an important one for Bakhtin, but it would be digressive to pursue that topic here.

7. In his psychoanalytical interpretation of "First Love", elsewhere in this volume.

8. This despite the two languages of the text, evidence of what Beer calls Beckett's "ancestry of doubleness" (164)

Works Cited

Bakhtin, M. M., "Forms of Time and the Chronotope in the Novel", in *The Dialogic Imagination: Four Essays,* ed. Michael Holquist, trans. Caryl Emerson & Michael Holquist (Austin: U of Texas P, 1981).

———, *Problems of Dostoevsky's Poetics,* ed. and trans. Caryl Emerson (Minneapolis: U of Minnesota P, 1984).

———, *Speech Genres and Other Late Essays,* trans. Vern W. McGee (Austin: U of Texas P, 1986).

Beer, Ann, "'No-Man's-Land': Beckett's Billingualism as Autobiography", in James Noonan, ed., *Biography and Autobiography: Essays on Irish and Canadian History and Literature* (Ottawa: Carleton UP, 1993), 163-78.

Kern, Edith, "Beckett's Modernity and Medieval Affinities", in Morris Beja, S.E.

Gontarski, Pierre Astier (eds) *Samuel Beckett: Humanistic Perspectives,* (Columbus, OH: Ohio State UP, 1983).

Morson, Gary Saul, and Caryl Emerson, *Mikhail Bakhtin: Creation of a Prosaics* (Stanford: Stanford UP, 1990).

Willie van Peer (essay date 1998)

SOURCE: van Peer, Willie. "Beckett's 'First Love' and Cynical Philosophy." *Samuel Beckett Today* 7 (1998): 407-17.

[*In the following essay, van Peer places "First Love" within the philosophical tradition of cynicism.*]

My interpretation of **"First Love"** forms part of a larger argument, that sees all interpretation, contrary to present-day fashionable theories, as a quest for truth, guided by specific methodological rules. There is no space to expound on this matter here, so let me restrict the issue with a reference to an article where I have developed this matter in more detail; see Van Peer (1998). As a brief illustration, however, I would like to point out one of the specific methodological rules we employ when we interpret a work. I am sure that we all follow some of these rules, and that if we didn't, our colleagues would not take our work seriously. This creates a strange schizophrenia in current literary studies: theoretically the existence of rules is vehemently denied, but when it comes to practice, nearly all scholars scrupulously stick to very traditional rules. One of these is quite evident in the materials to which we have access surrounding the story at hand. These contain the editorial history of Beckett's story, including an account of the different extant versions. We learn in *Notes on the Texts,* for instance, that the phrase "to put it wildly" in the first English and American editions of **"First Love"** contained an error, which was later corrected to "to put it mildly". Why should we take these materials into account? Why shouldn't we be free to use any edition of the text whatsoever? Or why shouldn't we remain comfortably in the dark about these different textual variants? We should look at these materials, I surmise, because we adhere to an important rule of interpretation, the rule namely that one has to base one's interpretation on a full and non-deficient token of the text. I cannot make sense of this enterprise other than that.

Julie Bates Dock and her co-authors in *PMLA* have recently documented a nice illustration of the kind of biased interpretations that get produced when this methodological rule is ignored or violated. They convincingly show how many feminist interpretations of Charlotte Perkins Gilman's story "The Yellow Wallpaper" are based on editions that deviate from the author's own intended text—and of earlier editions. For instance, after declaring that there is 'something queer' about the house in which the newly married couple have arrived, the female character remarks, "John laughs at me, of course, but one expects that in marriage". The text editions that follow Lane's, which reproduces the 1933 *Golden Book* version of the story print the following: "John laughs at me, of course, but one expects that." As Julie Bates Dock and her co-authors point out: "Omitting 'in marriage' radically transforms the line. [. . .] More important, these two changes distort the author's focus: Gilman is bashing marriage in particular, not men in general" (Dock et al. 1996, 55). The conclusion from Bates Dock's exercise will be clear, I hope. In spite of all assertions to the contrary, the community of literary scholars is still dedicated to certain rules of conduct in interpreting literary texts. If it were not, there would be no point in arguing about interpretation at all.

But back now to Beckett's text. What can or should one say about it? At a first level, one observes two characters, one (the male) internally focalized, the other (the female) only externally characterized, interacting with each other. Their behaviour is somewhat unusual and may cause surprise, if not aversion in the reader. But what does the story mean? My proposal is to situate the text within a specific literary or philosophical tradition, and to work out its *Sitz im Leben* from this general analysis. Although superficially the work narrates a somewhat bizarre concatenation of non-events, at a deeper level I see the text as taking its place in the Western tradition of *cynicism*. I am using the term 'cynicism' here in its philosophical meaning, indicating the movement or the way of life named after Diogenes of Sinope (second half of the fourth century BCE), more specifically after his nickname, *Kuon,* the dog.[1] To the cynics, in the opposition between "*nomos* versus *physis* ('custom' or 'convention' versus 'nature')", preference was to be given to physis, to nature (Höistad 1973, 629). The aim of human life is happiness, and this is achieved by becoming self-sufficient: to live in accordance with nature, exemplified in the numerous (mostly apocryphal) stories about Diogenes, such as the one in which, when Alexander the Great promised to grant him whatever favour he requested, Diogenes replied: "Stand out of my light." My interpretation of Beckett's text boils down to the hypothesis that the characters, their behaviour, their motives, and their emotions are a direct heir to the cynics' worldview. But there is more to it: the hypothesis also asserts that Beckett's texts in general, and **"First Love"** specifically, aim to express and pass on the cynical philosophy.

This interpretation of Beckett's work can also be related to the personality of the author. This is not to revive the debate over authorial intention,[2] but I believe that in interpreting literary works we should take the author's intentions into account—which is not the same as accepting them as a verdict. It seems to me that Samuel Beckett, the man, comes close to being a twentieth-century cynic, and the recent biographies by Anthony Cronin, Lois Gordon, and James Knowlson provide ample support for this view. He did not cling to money, success, or outward appearance, or to fine etiquette, "balls" being a favourite Beckett word. Such a man need not, by the way, be unattractive: Susan Sontag called him the sexiest man she had ever met. He did not seek status or prestige, and cared little for his reputation. He was fearless (and joined the Resistance during the war), yet pessimistic and misanthropic. One is reminded also of his preference for the things in his mind over the disturbances of what he called "this bitch of a world". He saw his fame as a curse, the 1969 Nobel Prize award a "catastrophe" (in Suzanne's, his wife's, words): he anonymously gave away the money it earned him. He had little respect for institutions, and all favours by him were given solely on the basis of individual friendship. Yet he was not a traditional saint. The numerous love affairs, and Cronin's account that he preferred masturbation to 'the real thing', show his cynic attitude also in this.

Now compare all this with the method singled out by the cynic in classical antiquity, "actively to dissociate himself from any influence, external or internal, whose ties, responsibilities or distractions might fetter his individual freedom" (Urmson & Rée 1991, 67). Material prosperity is approached with downright hostility, property is seen as the source of all evil. Life should be lived at the level of the bare minimum necessary for existence, stripped of all conventional values of status, power, class, influence, or reputation. The cynic had to be ready to face insult to keep his emotional resistance against conventional culture fit. Diogenes Laertius relates of Diogenes: "He once begged alms of a statue, and, when asked why he did so, replied, "To get practice in being refused" (VI, 49; 51).

It is clear, then, that in real life Beckett the man displayed many characteristics of the cynical sage. That in itself does not suffice to interpret his texts, but it does help us to figure out the relation between author and work at a deeper level.

Indeed, Beckett's works, including **"First Love"**, also testify to the cynic attitude. According to the cynics, precepts of virtue came from the personal example of the cynic's life and from "illustrations of the uninhibited behaviour of animals and the example of Heracles of virtue in endurance. But Cynics were principally characterized by a fearless, shameless freedom of speech in criticism, a mordant wit and repartee", (Urmson & Rée, 68) as the cynic "was something akin to a god, and something akin to a beast" (ibid.). That seems most applicable to the protagonist of **"First Love"**: human existence shrivels until it attains doglike qualities. Eating is like swallowing down whatever you can find to feed yourself. Beverages are uninteresting unless alcoholic. All characters are homeless, or if they have a home it is nothing but a den, a mere shelter against the enemy that nature can be. Clothing is unimportant, looks are irrelevant, excretion a natural and simple part of life, nothing to be ashamed of, sometimes even something to revel in. And in this list, love, too is reduced to canine proportions. It is stripped of all idealism and romanticism; it is virulently anti-platonic, anti-petrarchan. It is love, as dogs love each other: transient, though intense; free and fast, obscene only for the non-dogs.

Here I would like to briefly comment on an aspect of Beckett's work that I think deserves some attention. One may recall that some scholars have advanced a 'Christian' interpretation of Beckett's work. Especially after the first performances of *Waiting for Godot,* some critics saw Christ-like figures in the characters. Maybe this is no longer a fashionable interpretation of Beckett's works, but there is a sense in which such interpretations are less far-fetched than it may seem nowadays. Research by New Testament scholars has revealed the extent to which the sayings of Jesus stand in relation to the philosophical traditions of his time. They have also been able to reconstruct the sayings of the historical Jesus, allowing the reconstruction of the *Book of Q*,[3] a hypothetical, but highly reliable collection of the sayings of Jesus that must have circulated prior to the writing of the gospels. Over the past decades, it has become apparent that the teachings of Jesus of Nazareth form part of the movement of the Cynics. Let me quote from Burton Mack's recent study of the *Book of Q*:

> The crisp sayings of Jesus in Q1 [one of the variants of the Book of Q] show that his followers thought of him as a Cynic-like sage. Cynics were known for begging, voluntary poverty, renunciation of needs, severance of family ties, fearless and carefree attitudes, and troublesome public behaviour. Standard themes in Cynic discourse included a critique of riches, pretension, and hypocrisy, just as in Q1. The Cynic style of speech was distinctly aphoristic, as is that in Q1. And Cynics were schooled in such topics as handling reproach, nonretaliation, and authenticity in following their vocation, matters at the forefront of Jesus' instructions in Q1.

(Mack 1993, 115)[4]

Hence it must be clear that those critics favouring a Christian interpretation were not altogether off the track: Beckett's texts are indeed similar to the original kernel of cynic philosophy in the early Jesus movement; the interpretation runs into difficulties when Christianity is applied wholesale to them—then discrepancies do appear. But to say that Beckett's work evokes a Christian spirituality—insofar as this is qualified as the views and methods of the cynic sages—is, I would argue, a good approximation of truth.

Perhaps readers find this interpretation rather general or somewhat vague, and still underdetermined by textual evidence. Those readers are right. Let me therefore come down now to some more concrete textual evidence corroborating my interpretation. I will enumerate these under the heading of some four different themes (using the term in a rather loose sense).

The first, and most evident, theme that speaks for the cynical interpretation, is the theme of *vanitas:* the idea that life is vain, and that our actions are irrelevant. The cynic wants to confront his audience with the futility of our aspirations and the emptiness of human strife. In **"First Love",** this theme opens the story, with the comparison between the living and the dead. The latter are said to be in a much better position: "The living wash in vain, in vain perfume themselves, they stink." The dead are to be envied, their company sought, we are told by the protagonist: "My sandwich, my banana, taste sweeter when I'm sitting on a tomb." The theme also resonates in the protagonist's own epitaph, where it says that he "hourly died". In all this, the protagonist takes on a detached viewpoint from which he surveys human vanity, and declares: "their little gimmick with the dust is charming." Human action is largely irrelevant to the cynic, of course. The protagonist makes no secret of his position: "Lie down, all seems to say, lie down and stay down." And he adds: "The mistake one makes is to speak to people." When it really comes to speaking, however, the usual patterns of communication break down, heard in the protagonist's ruminations that it is "incredible the way they repeat what you've just said", concluding: "that's what you get for opening your mouth."

A second theme that presents itself is that of the *outsider:* the cynic is conscious of being a misanthrope, and wants to be one. I hope it will be clear without further elucidation that this theme pervades the whole story. The protagonist does not belong to any group; he is expelled from his family home. Initially, he had a wish to stay. "But they refused", the story says twice. And that was that: "One day, on my return from stool, I found my room locked and my belongings in a heap before the door." Those belongings aren't much, presumably, though at this point I must confess that there is at least one thing in the text that is problematic for my interpretation. That concerns the money the protagonist inherits after his father's death. It seems not really to fit the general scheme of a cynic to just keep the money for old age, as he states. The money certainly is a detail that is difficult to incorporate in my view that the story evokes a cynic's world view, perhaps not even so much the fact that the character still *has* the money, as his motivation for keeping it: we do not expect cynic philosophers to plan their old age and retirement.

To come back to the theme of the outsider: the female protagonist has no relatives or friends either; she is visited regularly, but apparently because she works as a clandestine prostitute. In short, both protagonists in the story are outcasts, as indeed most of Beckett's characters are. We may see in this theme a correlation to the semantic field of *detachment,* as it has been described by Fokkema and Ibsch in their study of European Modernism (Fokkema & Ibsch, 1988). This detachment is certainly applicable to the male protagonist, who overtly refuses to attach himself to any other being (except perhaps for the memory of his father), and is incapable of remembering even the most basic facts about other humans. He even does not know his love's name: "She also disclosed her family name, but I've forgotten it". And since he does not like her first name, Lulu, he simply changes it into Anna. Can one be more detached?

Another theme often associated with cynicism is that of *scatology* and intentional obscenity: remember the story of Diogenes publicly masturbating in a square in Athens. There is no lack of this in Beckett's story: explicit descriptions of the protagonist defecating, the exuberant love invocations in the cow-shed among the nettles and the cow shit, in which the protagonist inscribes his beloved's name with his finger, the description of how it feels to relieve oneself in bed, and more sexually tainted, his confession of being "at the mercy of an erection", or the double entendre: "it is with the heart one loves, is it not, or am I confusing it with something else?"

One could interpret this preoccupation with scatological themes from a psycho-analytic perspective, describing it as a form of regression. That certainly is an option, and there can be little doubt as to the protagonist's profound regression taking place in the story. Such an interpretation, however, may add little if it is not simultaneously able to explain why the character regresses in the first place. The interpretation I have advanced, by contrast, is in a position to do so, and therefore is more parsimonious than a psychoanalytic approach. The reason why the story contains so much regressive material lies, I propose, in the intimate relation cynicism entertains with regression. Regression seems to be an integral part of cynical philosophy from ancient time onwards.

A very powerful theme in this story is that of *demystification* of love, or of anything deemed of high value in our culture at large. What are the first words that the beloved utters? "Shove up!" But then the male lover is not very gallant either: "I asked her if she was resolved to disturb me every evening." This sounds more as the kind of thing that gets said in fights between partners who have been together for some years, than the kind of interchange one expects between new lovers. She is also the opposite of most fictional loves: she is reported to have "fat thighs", has a squint, sings out of tune, and prostitutes herself. The male's emotions are far removed from those associated with courtly love too, for instance when he assures us: "I considered kicking her in the cunt." The protagonist pronounces his own verdict on love when he asserts: "What goes by the name of love is banishment, with now and then a postcard from the homeland, such is my considered opinion." The musings of the male protagonist regularly take the form of explicit misogyny, as when he says of women: "When at their wit's end, they undress."

At this point it is worth mentioning an intertextual relationship that Beckett's story entertains, and which may further clarify the extent to which his is an effort at demystification. Beckett's text forms the antipode of Petrarch and Dante, especially of the latter's *Vita Nuova*. Remember that Beckett studied French and Italian, and that the works of Dante were a source of inspiration to him all his life. In the *Vita Nuova*, the central topic is

that of the first encounter with the beloved. The differences with Beckett are very deep, of course: while the whole episode lasts only a couple of months in Beckett's case, Dante's first meeting with Beatrice will be the beginning of a life-long dedication to love, tenderness, and poetry. In both texts, the lovers' meetings are iterative, and the protagonists hear 'voices' in their head (Dante, 59, 79); "I heard the word fibrome, or brone . . .". In Dante, memory is an important vehicle to communicate to the reader what he has gone through; in Beckett, on the contrary, the reader faces dramatic forms of amnesia. In Beckett, there is a strong predelection of the protagonist for the dead. But such an affinity is also recorded in the *Vita Nuova*: "Dolcissima Morte, vieni a me e non m'essere villana; però che tu dei essere gentile, in tal parte se' stata!" (Dante, 101).[5] Death, in Dante's work, is the deepest relationship to the (mortal) love one can have. Compare, for instance, the first encounter of the protagonists in this work:

> ne l'ultimo di questi die avenne che questa mirabile donna apparve a me, vestita di colore bianchissimo, in mezzo di due gentili donne, le quali erano di più lunga etade; e passando per una via, volse li occhi verso quello parte ov'io era molto pauroso, e per la sua ineffabile cortesia [. . .] mi salutò molto virtuosamente; tanto che me parve allora vedere tutti li termini de la beatitudine. [. . .] e però che quella fu la prima volta che le sue parole si mossero per venire a li miei orecchi, presi tanta dolcezza che, come inebriato, mi partio da le genti [. . .]
>
> (Dante, 26-28)[6]

Here we have all the ingredients of courtly love, inscribed in the description of the first meeting of the two lovers. The retreat from his surroundings will now be the occasion to record the incident and further write about Beatrice. Compare this to Beckett's scene:

> Is it on my account you came? I said. She managed yes to that. Well here I am, I said. And I? Had I not come on hers? Here we are, I said. I sat down beside her, but sprang up again immediately as though scalded. I longed to be gone, to know if it was over.
>
> ("FL" ["First Love"], 21)

The retreat from her follows here too, as in Dante, but her name will now be written, remember, in cowshit. The contrast can hardly be more dramatic. Sure, this is not the first time that courtly love has been debunked. Already Francesco Berni (1497-1535) did so, and so did Cervantes when he had Don Quijote finally meet his Dulcinea (after his descent into the cave of Montesinos), only to have her ask him to lend her some money. But Beckett's demystification takes place in a serious context, not in a comic one. Or does it?

There certainly is a level at which the text can be seen as undermining the credibility of our everyday categories, and as such it resembles comedy: since human toil is ridiculed as irrelevant and megalomaniac, it acts as a mirror comically distorting our self-image. In this sense, Beckett is essentially a *comic* writer. (I can testify that I burst out laughing on several occasions when reading **"First Love".**) This may be the source of the sympathy that readers develop for Beckett's characters, in spite of their repugnant behaviour or their alienating ideas. In Beckett's work, entrenched categories and established views are attacked straight between the eyes, and are given a proper shake-up. For me, personally, reading the story as a comedy is one of the easiest ways to render it meaningful and accessible. But the odd thing is that there usually is not much to interpret in comic texts: they are perhaps the purest cases where we can dispense with post hoc interpretation altogether. Comic texts allow us to follow Susan Sontag's maxim—to erotically enjoy rather than to interpret unproblematically: one surrenders to the body, and enjoys.

What I have proposed here is that to read Beckett properly is to read him in the tradition of cynic philosophy.[7] This may not be a very systematic philosophy, and it certainly has its limits, but in Beckett's hands it exploits the major stratagems for making us see the world in a new way. What are the roots of cynicism? According to Schischkoff (775) these are a sense of failure of life, a certain self-styled arrogance, and an invincible resentment against life as it is lived by the majority of us. It seems to me that much of this applies to Beckett's oeuvre, thus being a rich resource for the cynic way of life. Beckett's characters are full-grown, often also old, dogs. The reader is a young dog, sniffing and following the old dogs' trails. The result is: comic relief.[8]

Notes

1. For further information on cynical philosophy, see Branham & Goulet-Cazé, Largier, Navia.

2. But see Barnes, Iseminger, and Stecker for reappraisals of authorial intention.

3. *Q,* from the German *Quelle,* 'source.'

4. For further references asserting the interrelationship between collections of Cynic sayings and the collections of traditions about Jesus, see Bracht Branham & Goulet-Cazé (229), and the literature mentioned there.

5. "Sweet Death, come to me and do not fret—you have to be gentle like the place you come from." (All translations are mine.)

6. "On the last of these days it happened that this fair lady appeared to me, dressed in the purest white and walking between two distinguished ladies older than she; and striding through the street she turned her eyes to the side where I watched shyly, and in her ineffable eminence [. . .] saluted me so sweetly, that it then appeared as if my gaze had reached all limits of beatitude. [. . .] and since this was the first time that her words moved to come to my ears, I tasted such ecstasy that, intoxicated, I turned away from people [. . .]."

7. A similar interpretation may be found in Rosen.

8. I would like to thank the organizers of the Groningen workshop for their kind invitation to exchange ideas on this topic. I am especially grateful to Henk Hillenaar, Hanneke Hoekstra and Robert Scholes for critical remarks on my paper.

Works Cited

Barnes, Annette, *On Interpretation* (Oxford: Basil Blackwell, 1988).

Branham, R. Bracht, and Marie-Odile Goulet-Cazé (eds), *The Cynics: The Cynic Movement in Antiquity and Its Legacy* (Berkeley, CA: U of California P, 1996).

Cronin, Anthony, *Samuel Beckett: The Last Modernist* (New York: HarperCollins, 1996).

Dante, Alighieri, *La Vita Nova,* ed. and trans. H. W. J. M. Keuls (Den Haag: Bert Bakker, 1964).

Diogenes Laertius, *Lives of the Eminent Philosophers,* trans. and ed. R. D. Hicks, vol. II. Cambridge, MA: Harvard UP, 1991. (Loeb edition; first edition 1925).

Dock, Julie Bates et al., "'But One Expects That': Charlotte Perkins Gilman's 'The Yellow Wallpaper' and the Shifting Light of Scholarship", in *PMLA* 111, no. 1 (1996), 52-65.

Fokkema, D. W. & E. Ibsch, *Modernist Conjectures. A Mainstream in European Literature 1910-1940* (New York: St. Martin's P, 1988).

Gonkarski, S. E. (ed.), *Samuel Beckett: The Complete Short Prose 1929-1989* (New York: Grove P, 1995).

Gordon, Lois, *The World of Samuel Beckett, 1906-1946* (New Haven, CT: Yale UP, 1996).

Höistad, Ragnar, "Cynicism", in *Dictionary of the History of Ideas,* ed. Philip P. Wiener (New York: Charles Scribner's & Sons, 1973), vol. I, 627-634.

Iseminger, Gary (ed.), *Intention and Interpretation* (Philadelphia: Temple UP, 1992).

Knowlson, James, *Damned to Fame: The Life of Samuel Beckett* (New York: Simon and Schuster, 1996).

Largier, Niklaus, "Diognes der Kyniker", in *Exempel, Erzählung, Geschichte im Mittelalter und Früher Neuzeit. Mit einem Essay zur Figur des Diogenes zwischen Kynismus, Narrentum und postmoderner Kritik* (Max Niemeyer, 1997).

Mack, Burton L., *The Lost Gospel. The Book of Q & Christian Origins* (New York: Harper San Francisco, 1993).

Navia, Luis E., *Classical Cynicism: A Critical Study* (Greenwood P, 1997).

Peer, Willie van, "Truth Matters. A Critical Exercise in Revisionism", in *New Literary History* (1998; in press).

Rosen, Steven J., *Samuel Becket and the Pessimistic Tradition* (New Brunswick, NJ: Rutgers UP, 1976).

Schischkoff, Georgi (ed.), *Philosophisches Wörterbuch* (Stuttgart: Kröner, 1978).

Stecker, Robert, *Artworks: Definition, Meaning, Value* (University Park, PA: The Pennsylvania State UP, 1997).

Urmson, J. O. & Jonathan Rée, *The Concise Encyclopedia of Western Philosophy and Philosophers* (London: Routledge, 1989).

Henk Hillenaar (essay date 1998)

SOURCE: Hillenaar, Henk. "A Psychoanalytical Approach to Beckett's 'First Love'." *Samuel Beckett Today* 7 (1998): 419-37.

[*In the following essay, Hillenaar provides a psychoanalytical reading of "First Love."*]

"First Love" is the first soliloquy that Beckett wrote, just after World War II. It has the characteristic features that we find in all his novels, plays or short stories. Especially striking is the combination of a strongly structured, and often comical language, which presents the thinking of a very "adult" person, on one side, with descriptions of very elementary sensations and feelings—those of an earlier life—supporting and feeding this adult thought on the other. In this story, a highly intelligent person is looking back to a highly regressive world, his own inner world, where he behaves again as a child, a baby, now and then even as a foetus.

Such behaviour reminds us very strongly of what happens in the consulting room of a psychoanalyst. Certainly, when the writer is talking about the way to interpret feelings of love, about "money", "the bench" or even "sessions", the reader he is addressing seems to resemble a psychoanalyst. The slightly or openly aggressive tone he likes to adopt towards the reader—"Come now!"—confirms the latter in this feeling. And we know the author didn't like psychoanalysts very much. Still, it seems rather clear that he is using psychoanalytic experience when he writes about the difficulties his character has in coping with life and love. The very first words of the text: "I associate" can be considered as referring not only to one of the main lit-

erary figures in **"First Love"**, but also to the most important skill in the psychoanalytical praxis. From the very beginning until the end of this short story we realize that the philosophy that underlies it has been fed by psychoanalytical concepts. Curiously enough, this fact might not facilitate an interpretation that is thinking in those same terms.

Beckett's story is built around two fantasies, which are also the two fundamental fantasies recurring in most psychoanalytical treatments: the father and the mother. The first is actually called "my father". The second is not called "my mother", but she is presented as the "first love", and as the woman who feeds him and takes care for him in so many ways, she is a very motherly figure. We recognise in her the mother who is going to be also one of the main figures in Beckett's *Molloy,* two years later. There she will be constantly referred to as "my mother", because she actually is the real "first love", the real mother. Here, as so often in a psychoanalytical context, "mother" refers to someone who assumes the role of a mother towards the main figure.

Speaking about a story in which the father and mother figures play such an outstanding part, we are inclined to refer to Freud's well known "family romance", to the urge we all experience, first as children, later also as adults, to give ourselves in our imagination different parents, a nicer father, a lovelier mother, in order to make our whole life more acceptable. Literature must have one of its main sources in this universal phenomenon. The family romance may be cast into many different moulds—including negatively inspired moulds, as it is certainly the case in this Beckett story. Not only the very regressive form of the text, where the mother invades all the space, contributes to that effect, but even more significantly that the father and mother are never represented or even mentioned together. The only link between the two characters is made in the very first sentence of the story, which is also the author's good-natured scoffing at the Oedipus complex: "I associate, rightly or wrongly, my marriage with the death of my father."

The family romance has in fact everything to do with our attitude towards both parents. In the eyes of Freud it is an "Oedipal" adventure, but with Beckett we are definitely in a pre-Oedipal setting. The conditions for a family romance seem to be present, but remain unrealized. However, there is an attempt. The whole text seems to focus on the going to and fro between the father and the mother. Its starts with the fantasies around the father figure, then jumps without much transition—"but to pass on to less melancholic matters"—to the story round the mother figure. At the end, if we may call it so, we attend another departure into the world of the father. We seem to be caught in a circle.

Even though father and mother are treated separately, their stories have much in common. Firstly in structure: both stories bring us from outdoors—a cemetery and a bench in the park—to a room indoors. In both episodes, but for different reasons, this room is again abandoned for another life outside. The two scenes also share the contrast made by the narrator between an upright position and lying down on a bed, a bench, a sofa. Anal images and associations, referring to the pleasures and displeasures of the first activities in life, are, also in various ways, very abundant in this pre-oedipal universe. The author maintains throughout the same mixture of involvement and irony that is so typical of his style.

THE FATHER

Let us first turn to the fantasies regarding the father, which take approximately a fourth of the text. The narrator's father is only a happy memory, some remains in a graveyard that he likes to visit and even to smell, but for the rest this beloved man is no longer available. The narrator uses actually two adjectives to describe him: he is called "a strange man", and "a poor father"—even "poor Papa". Strange, because loving this father doesn't end up in pain as it does with Lulu. He likes "to feel (his son) under his roof", understands his needs, and says to those in the house that share the same heritage: "Leave him alone." He and his son are the only ones in the household "to understand tomatoes". Still he is also a "poor father", because like his son, he is the victim of his family: "Yes, he was properly had, my poor father, if his purpose was really to go on protecting me from beyond the tomb."

This father was actually a rather motherly figure who had taken over more than one of the tasks of his absent wife. He fed his son, protected him, and kept him in his neighbourhood. But on the whole he seems also to have accomplished his task as a father. As we will hear at the end of the story, he has shown the world to his son, who is longing to see the lighthouses and lightships and even the Wains in the sky, which his "father had named" for him. He has taught him also how to behave with his siblings, at least how to be generous with them, if they leave him alone, and even to be ready to do the "odd maintenance jobs every dwelling requires".

In the house of his father his anal difficulties are also reduced to constipation, whereas, dreaming of the love of his mother he will be playing with faeces and remember how enjoyable it can be "to relieve oneself in bed". But life is cruel and precisely this grown-up constipation makes him linger too much while excreting, allowing "the others"—"those hearts that had loved me [. . .] those hands that had played with mine"—to close his room and throw him out of the house. It is also in the company of his father—his dead father—that we

see the narrator in the upright position befitting an adult, developing even some activity, while in his mother's company he will nearly always lie down or try to do so, remaining most of the time completely passive. This upright position allows him to wear a hat, symbol of fatherly authority, and also of the identification of the narrator with his father: "I have always had my own hat, the one my father gave me, and I have never had any other than that hat."

This leads us to what the narrator considers certainly as the main activity he pursues in his father's company: writing, which is also a way of excreting. Whereas, in that most important field of human language, the mother will mainly appear to the narrator as a voice that sings and cries, his father's company, albeit that of a dead body in his grave, makes him write, and write with pleasure. He composes his own epitaph, with which he is "tolerably pleased". It is one of the happiest moments of his story. Therefore he "hastens to record it for the reader":

> Hereunder lies the above who up below
> So hourly died that he lived on till now.
>
> ("**FL**" ["**First Love**"], 26)

This little poem whose second line, according to its creator, "limps a little perhaps" includes more than one paradox that we will have to explain. However, the biggest paradox is certainly that the desire for language which pervades the whole text—the mother representing the original sound created by the voice, the father the elaborate, spoken and written language—should originate in a graveyard, in the proximity of the dead body of the father. The father figure who normally contributes to the moulding, in his son's mind, of a conscience, making him aware of values, giving him a sense of responsibility in life, is doing here something like the contrary. Values and responsibility are rather absent indeed in the mind of the narrator. In his regressive mood he is longing for what he calls "slow descents and long submersions". Such behaviour brings us to notions like the Freudian "death instinct", or to the "principle of an active Nothing" that Wilfred Bion—Beckett's psychoanalyst—often referred to. Perhaps there is also Beckett's flirtation with Gnostic heresy, when he speaks of the "great disembodied wisdom" of his father.

Later in the text, the narrator becomes even clearer about this choice for such a backward moving life, when he evokes his preference in aesthetics:

> [. . .] my father's face, on his death-bolster, had seemed to hint at some form of aesthetics relevant for man. But the faces of the living, all grimace and flush, can they be described as objects?
>
> ("**FL**," 38)

This kind of consideration explains the long scene in the graveyard where the narrator also objects to the living. Therefore he enjoys the smell of the death, "infinitely preferable to what the living emit", his meal and his watering on the graves, the old biblical sayings he hears about the dust to which we all return, and the show of the widow, the "odd relict [. . .], trying to throw herself into the pit". Would this after all be an appearance of the mother in the proximity of the father? We don't know, but it's true that after this moment the narrator feels afraid to die, vomits and envies the dead.

Be that as it may, in this story the world of the father is not like the ones encountered in most other stories we read. Since the father has himself returned to the motherly earth, he is no longer able to point out to his son the way out of the world of the mother, at least not to what we call an adult world of values, shared lives, shared responsibility. In spite of himself, he makes the narrator play the game of the mother. However, from his grave he teaches him to write, and this writing will help him to survive, albeit in the world of a child, of birth and death, of care and protection, to which he seems to be sending him back. It is extremely difficult not to long for that world but also, once you have reached it, not to feel the opposite longing, to detach yourself from it. This seems to be his fate: as long as the narrator is not himself part of the graveyard, as long as he continues to speak, he has to move; he will desire his mother while at the same time he will always want to leave her.

THE MOTHER

Let us see now what the second volet of this diptych is telling us. As we might expect, the regressive mood inspired in the narrator by his father's dead body becomes now even more serious. He describes his "first love" with no rival present. Lulu or, as he wants to call her, Anna, lives alone. We already saw how a father alone can behave in a very motherly way, in the same way a mother alone can adopt the initiatives or activities of the father. But with her, things are more threatening. At the end mothers are inclined to devour the children who cannot part from them.

The author of **"First Love"** seems to be very aware of all this, and doesn't stop playing games with the contrast between the world of the father and that of the mother. All the important themes he deals with—time and space, sexuality, love and language—are affected by this contrast. When, for instance, the narrator speaks about time, the reader is struck by the struggle with dates and numbers on the first page, where we learn with more or less accuracy how to discover somebody's age. Fathers participate and make their children participate in society and its chronology, whereas in the case of the mother we leave this domain of certainty. We no longer know about age; Lulu is without age, and we have to be satisfied with "the odd time" that causes so much embarrassment to both protagonists. Only at the end of the story when the work of the father is again mentioned, the narrator tells us about the nine months of pregnancy, ending in the birth that "finishes" him.

The same contrast can be found, even more clearly, in the writer's arrangement of the spaces where he imagines the encounters with the father and the mother. The father is found in an open space by daylight. The narrator is walking around or sitting on a tomb, having a rather good time, and even laughing at the drollery of the inscriptions. Later in the text he will dream about the open adventurous space his father once showed him and that he is longing for from the sofa of his first love. The first meeting with Lulu is also outdoors, but the bench where this big event takes place is described as a shelter; a rather primitive one, it is true, made of dead trees and garbage, but a real shelter:

> It was a well situated bench, backed by a mound of solid earth and garbage, so that my rear was covered. My flanks too, partially, thanks to a pair of venerable trees, more than venerable, dead, at either end of the bench.
>
> ("FL," 30)

In his craving for regression, the narrator must be happy with such a setting, "empty" as a cradle or perhaps the womb of a pregnant woman. Later, when the bench has been replaced by a sofa in a real room, which happens to be a parlour crammed with "hundreds of pieces" of furniture, the narrator suddenly reacts hyperactively: he throws out all these things as if such products of civilisation were an illness. That is at least what he makes us understand, for, as he is taking them down, he hears the word "fibrome, or brone", which actually refers to a benign growth in the womb. This is one more confirmation that the writer of this very elaborate story is taking us back to experiences of a time when nothing in our inner and outer life was at all complex.

Even the lullaby isn't lacking. Lulu sings and her voice is what most attracts and seduces the narrator. He is like one of Beckett's most famous characters, Belacqua, in *More Pricks than Kicks,* "waiting for a voice that sounds". As we have already said, for Beckett, the voice is the essential prerogative of the mother, language coming from a distance being that of the father. He most probably owes these ideas to his psychoanalyst, Bion, whose contribution to analytical theory is primarily concerned with ideas regarding the support of the mother, her eyes, voice and "reverie" creating thought and mental health for her child. A mother who doesn't offer sufficient support may cause considerable emotional damage, and we feel such danger in a series of nearly tragic remarks of the narrator concerning the eyes, such as: "What could she see in me?" or "I might as well never have laid eyes on her before." Besides, it is difficult to see "because of the dark". No wonder he concludes that she has "crooked eyes"; one is looking at him, the other at some one or something else, here for instance at a hyacinth. The voice seems less problematic. For Beckett, it is the "voice that gives you life" (*Comment c'est*). The narrator likes her singing; it seduces him: "The voice, though out of tune, was not unpleasant [. . .] I asked her to sing me a song [. . .] I did not know the song [. . .] It had something to do with lemon trees or orange trees." Only when, at the end of **"First Love"**, the same voice starts crying and crying, because Anna is giving birth, he leaves the house, and this seems to be the end of the affair.

Between the narrator and Lulu/Anna a true love affair has taken place. A strange affair, sure enough, but a real one, although the narrator is inclined to consider human sexuality as a bad fate or an accident, whereas what he regards as more essential always happens in the mind. Sexuality only occurs really in the room next to his, where Anna is selling her body to her giggling and groaning clients. As far he himself is concerned, he gets excited, but never really or never completely. First, on the bench, he allows her, in spite of himself, to masturbate him. Later he gets excited by her naked body, but avoids every reaction or activity. Finally, during his "night of love", it is Anna who takes advantage of his body, while he is sleeping. In answer to this amorphous or polymorphous sexuality—that of children—Beckett pursues another aim, mysteriously called "supineness", which should permit him to have access to a subtle regressive state of the mind, where his "carcass" wouldn't even count any more:

> What mattered to me in my dispeopled kingdom, that in regard to which the disposition of my carcass was the merest and most futile of accidents, was supineness in the mind, the dulling of the self and of that residue of execrable frippery known as the non-self and even the world, for short.
>
> ("FL," 31)

This original but rather upsetting mysticism doesn't prevent the narrator from really loving the woman he meets in the park. She disturbs him at first, but what would he do with himself if he were not disturbed? Even though he doesn't understand women, her "disturbances" help him to think of his pains, that is, of himself. Such a way of thinking reminds us again of the basic ideas of Bion, which the author seems to represent in this scene in a rather original way, telling us also that he is "not all pain and nothing else". As for the pleasures he relates, they too are those of the beginning, when, strangely enough, love and faeces had still much to do with each other.

> Yes, I loved her, it's the name I have given, still give alas, to what I was doing then [. . .] Would I have been tracing her name in old cowshit if my love had

been pure and disinterested? And with my devil's finger into the bargain, which I then sucked. Come now! My thoughts were all of Lulu, if that doesn't give you some idea nothing will.

> ("FL," 34)

Listening to her voice, the narrator had already noticed, in the same anal register, that this sound was coming from "perhaps the least arse-aching soul of all". However, this very physical love, totally different from the more distant love that the narrator pursues, is far from simple. "Love brings out the worst in a man", he concludes, referring to his strange behaviour. Love also brings many practical problems, like the emptying of the room, his struggle against the light, and so on. However, the biggest problem with which he sees himself confronted is not only practical or sentimental, but also philosophical. This once more reminds us of Bion's theories. This is probably the most complex issue that preoccupies the mind of the narrator and, in my view, one of the keys to the whole text. The narrator experiences this difficulty on several levels, which is also a sign of its central importance. First in the sphere of his feelings: the reader is struck how they change every time the narrator moves: When he is away from Lulu/Anna, he strongly longs for her, but as soon as they are together, he wants to leave, having no feeling for her any more, except one, to escape.

After the first performance of *Waiting for Godot,* the French playwriter Jean Anouilh said that what he had seen were the *Pensées* of Pascal played by a couple of clowns. If he was right—and I think he was—then **"First Love"** must be a (rather unorthodox) comment on Pascal's famous "thought" about man's unhappiness caused by his restlessness or, as Pascal writes, by the fact that "he is not able to stay at rest in his room": "Tout le malheur des hommes vient d'une seule chose, qui est de ne savoir pas demeurer en repos dans une chambre" (*Pensées,* 168). This "thought" of Pascal could be seen as a device in **"First Love"**. Therefore, when he settles in her house, one of his first questions is "Try and put me out now". This paradoxical situation occurs at every meeting:

> Here we are, I said. I sat down beside her but sprang up immediately as though scalded. I longed to be gone, to know if it was over.
>
> ("FL," 36)

> Already my love was waning and that was all that mattered. Yes already I felt better, soon I'd be up to the slow descents again, the long submersions, so long denied me through her fault.
>
> (Ibid., 41)

He doesn't seem to be able to find a good distance in his love life, to control the situation. He even needs a second name for her: in addition to "Lulu", which sounds like a pet name she has given to herself, he invents "Anna". The two names could account for the difference that lies between too much presence and a secure distance. It seems scarcely possible that the writer did not think here of the two opera figures bearing these names: Lulu, the prostitute who is killed in Alban Berg's opera, and Anna, the victim of Mozart's hero Don Giovanni.

However, these rather problematic feelings of the narrator wouldn't be interesting for his creator if they didn't have their philosophical extension. For feeling and thinking are never separated in this text. Consequently, when the narrator gets the idea of moving in with Anna during a conversation "at last worthy of that name", he comes to the following considerations, which are striking indeed:

> I did not feel easy when I was with her, but at least free to think of something else than her, of the old trusty things, and so little by little, as down steps toward a deep, of nothing. And I knew that away from her I would forfeit this freedom.

> ("**FL**," 39)

What Beckett is telling us in these sentences (which, in my view, are among the most important of the text), should be easy to follow for those acquainted with psychoanalytical theory. He is speaking of the two fundamental tendencies or aspirations that govern our psychic life: first our longing for physical presence and love, everything we experienced and learned in the beginning with our mother or the one(s) that took her place. Second, our desire to turn to the outside world, away from her. There the "father" should have taught us how to keep the best distance from all those things the mother has first told us to love or to hate, to accept or to reject. That is what thinking is all about, and science, art and religion. They all belong to the realm of the symbolic father.

In our daily lives, all of us are continuously engaged in this double movement: back to the mother—to food, care, presence, love (or their contraries)—and at the same time, following the frustrating but also gratifying lessons of the father. Psychoanalytical literature has even invented names for these two ideals we must accommodate in our inner life. In the realm of the mother, that of our egocentric, narcissistic self we speak of "ideal ego". In the realm of the father, where we are submitted to the laws of his and later our conscience, it is called just the reverse (at least in English): "ego ideal." However, terminology is not so relevant here. What matters is that, thanks to the long training called childhood, most of us are able to combine, many times even rather easily, these two very complicated movements. Thus we are able to accomplish that difficult thing we call life.

It may be clear by now that the narrator of this story doesn't belong to that happy crowd. He is apparently not able to live, not able to combine the teachings of the mother with those of the father. His feelings as well as his thinking are continually disturbed, lurching from one side to the other. He seems unable to take another road, or something like the middle of the road, where father and mother, ideal ego and ego ideal would find the compromise that life seems to be all about.

Writing this story, Beckett indicates what we all experience at times, when life is quite intense, and when we want to get everything or nothing out of it. In that sense, the narrator must be recognisable for many of us. The text of "**First Love**," however, seems to point also in another direction. What the voice of the mother sings and speaks of with her child are the things she cares for, and those things are everything she shares with the father. Symbolically speaking, the father in childhood represents that what the mother desires. Also for that reason, a dead father presents an insurmountable problem for the child: the desire of the mother, which is transmitted to him by her voice, might be reduced to "nothing". That is precisely what the text I just quoted was telling us: the narrator felt finally free "to think [. . .] of the old trusty things, and so little by little, as down steps toward a deep, of nothing".

The text represents this in a beautiful image as well. While the singing voice desires lemon trees or orange trees, he appropriates one of her more modest wishes: a hyacinth. After having given birth to new flowers, it dies and becomes something like a little graveyard in the narrator's room. As such it remains for him a source of desire: desire of death, the wish he was already cultivating in the first half of the story and which we understand to have been also the wish of the mother. Here, and at many places in the text, the "ideal ego" seems to have no other choice left than the "nothing" his father has become. "I who had learnt to think of nothing, nothing, except my pains." Hadn't he noted, in a very melancholy mood, in his father's graveyard, that his own "corpse was not yet quite up to scratch?"

However, all this brings us back to the mother, much more than to the father. It is her lack of desire—or inner life, or real contact—that must make things difficult. A mother without the desire of another being, usually the father, somewhere at the horizon or in her mind at least, cannot be a good enough mother. It is as if this story, consciously or unconsciously, tells us, and not only tells but also shows us precisely that. We see this in two of the story's more enigmatic episodes, initially difficult to understand. First, the narrator's preoccupation with the voice of the singing mother: does he still hear it or not?

> I heard her singing [. . .] fainter and fainter the further
> I went, then no more, either because she had come to

an end or because I was gone too far to hear her. [. . .]
So I retraced my steps a little way and stopped. At first
I heard nothing, then the voice again, but only just
[. . .].

("FL," 37)

Later, at the very end of the story, it is Anna, crying
while giving birth, who allows him to repeat the same
"game": "I began playing with the cries, a little in the
same way as I had played with the song, on, back, on,
back, if that may be called playing." This is yet another,
more symbolic way to present the same issue: how to
go away from the mother while staying attached to her?
All in all the writer makes us understand, representing
things as he does, that his story is indeed a philosophical tale, but with this difference: that the ideas he tries
to reshape into a scenario are not philosophical ideas,
as in the case of, for instance, Voltaire, Sartre or Bataille, but the psychoanalytical insights of Freud and his
successors. As we have seen, among the latter, Wilfred
Bion might well be playing the biggest part.

It may be clear that this story about **"First Love"**—a
title that, as far as psychoanalysis is concerned, can
only refer to the mother—doesn't intend to illustrate the
Oedipal complex. The rather evocative first sentence
doesn't correspond to the real issue of the text, although
we know that Oedipus is also trying to find his way between his parents. The difference is that in the old tragedy the parents are a couple, both being involved for
instance in the initial banishment of the child, whereas
in Beckett's much more regressive story, the father is
absent, and the mother to whom the narrator goes, "on,
back, on, back", turns out to be a prostitute. Still there
is an analogy, the inner conflict around a first love being central in both "stories", Sophocles' and Beckett's.

Freud, in one of his later publications, in the second
chapter of *Jenzeits des Lustprinzips,* from 1920, tells us
a story that has become very popular since, about what
we somewhat paradoxically might call, a "pre-Oedipal
Oedipus complex". It is about one of his grandchildren,
whom he watches playing with a reel of yarn that his
mother uses for her needlework. The child throws the
reel still attached to the thread over the edge of his bed
that is hanging from the ceiling, to make it disappear in
the bed. Doing this he utters a very long o-o-o-o in
which Freud recognises the German "*Fort*", meaning
"away". After that he pulls the thread and the reel at its
end towards himself, out of the bed, and when it comes
into sight again, he emits a joyful "*Da*": there it is!
Then he repeats his game, again and again, as children
do.

Freud's interpretation of his grandson's behaviour will
probably not surprise the reader of Beckett's story. The
two episodes actually have much in common. Freud
recognises in this game an enjoyable way to get through

and master a painful situation that the child is daily
confronted with and that at first sight he seems to accept without too much difficulty: his mother's leaving
for her work every day. The inner conflict of Freud's
grandson was easier to resolve than that of the young
child whose presence we perceive at the horizon of
Beckett's feelings and fantasies. This child didn't find
his reel of yarn, but did manage to create a whole
thought system to master his misery. Mastery, however,
doesn't give other feelings. In this story nothing really
changes. The narrator is only busy repeating the same
experiences. But he succeeds in writing them down
and, we may suppose, in living with them. "Man is
only a reed", says Pascal, "but a reed that can think".
And write, we might add. Writing allows the narrator to
master the inner conflict he is caught in, this "to and
fro, "away and back", all of us are caught in, one way
or another. That is what he is doing here: describing,
very playfully, this "articulation", this movement, between presence and absence, retention and expulsion,
singing and crying, that life seems to be all about: As
long as we keep moving—there is no other movement
than this—and speaking—there is no other story than
this—we keep living.

The last key to his thought is also in the last sentence:
"either you love, or you don't". You love her, your first
love, when she is away, and you don't when you are
with her. For the narrator, there is no alternative, no escape to the father, for there has been not enough of a
father in his mother's mind.

I would like to suggest that the "ideal ego" of the beginning has two components: the child wants the
mother, but he also wants the things he notices she herself wanting. That is how a child learns to cope with
the two sides of existence: with her, the mother, and
with the other she loves, the father. But the writer creates a narrator whose father is in the graveyard. It is
true that there are some memories of him, a lighthouse
and even the Wains in the sky, but that isn't enough to
keep the narrator going in that direction. Like the
mother, he does not want the Unknown, he wants
"Nothing": Nothingness, graveyards and tombs may
also become a source of pleasure, of wit. Masochism,
even nice, funny masochism is never absent in these
pages. For there is no father, only a limping to or from
the mother: "either you love or you don't."

Limping: isn't that also what the epitaph tells us, giving
to our inner motions their most radical expression, between life and death:

> Hereunder lies the above who up below
> So hourly died that he lived on till now.

The original French version of this epitaph is rather different, and speaks in a slightly more ironic way of "escaping" life:

Ci-gît qui y échappa tant
Qu'il n'en échappe que maintenant

We might wonder if Beckett's coming and going between his two languages, English and French, is not also a way to perform the same movement. French was for him the language of distance, of mental abstraction. English evoked much more the memory of the motherly voice. Now and then, the reader notices the difference. He writes in French, for instance: "les dérangements, les arrangements, bientôt on n'en parlera plus, ni d'elle ni des autres, ni de merde, ni de ciel." His English version seems to be more forceful: "No more tattle about that, all that, her and the others, the shitball and heaven's high halls."

Be that as it may, both his little epitaphs limp, as does in its turn the hyacinth in the story, first putting forth some blooms and ending up as "a limp stem with limp leaves". That is what their creator wants: that they limp a tiny bit like Oedipus did. He is after all, since the beginning, at the horizon of the text. And although death seems to be more present in it than birth, the story ends with a birth, that, although the narrator tries to escape it, should be understood as the beginning of a new movement in the narrator's endless story: "either you love or you don't . . ."

There is a last question that, if we are pursuing a psychoanalytical approach, we cannot evade: are we, the interpreters, able to indicate or to at least suggest some unconscious elements in the text? The answer is not easy, the author himself being so obviously involved in psychoanalysis. But there are two or three suggestions possible. First, the fact that the writer keeps the father and mother figures separated in his text, avoiding every kind of physical or other contact between them—something that occurs equally in other Beckett stories—might be an obsessional pattern in his mind explaining much about his uneasiness, problems and negative choices. Without a more Oedipal "family romance", the writer's fantasies assume very unreal, regressive colours. He gets into the "you love or you love not" dilemma, a movement which doesn't allow any escape. My second observation could be more to the point, and concerns the fact that Beckett uses his feelings to build up a system of thought. However, in narrative literature feelings are generally used to tell a story. The story may have one or several meanings, but it remains a story, not philosophy. In **"First Love,"** the reader gradually realizes that this story serves mainly as an illustration of the psychoanalytical thought behind it. And even psychoanalysis used as a literary formula can become a way to resist certain feelings. In this case, knowing of Beckett's refusal of so many aspects of the father's realm, we are inclined to believe this. Most writers use literary form to evade or to obscure their regressive feelings. In the case of Beckett the contrary could be

true. If he is avoiding or hiding something in his text, then it must be the non-regressive, adult side of his feelings. The only thing he wants to reveal us is what the Germans sometimes call our *Ursuppe* (the "primal soup" from which we are born). This one-sidedness makes the reader feel uneasy indeed, but that, fortunately, is not all. For the rational and logical part of our being has its glorious, sublimated comeback in all the humour Beckett provides in his story. But even his laughter may seem suspect here. Whereas others hide behind the literary form of a joke to speak of regressive and forbidden feelings—especially sex and violence—the opposite occurs in Beckett's story: he seems to use laughter above all to hide the absence of what we call adult feelings, or to make this absence more acceptable.

Insofar as Beckett is also hiding regressive feelings, we should probably consider the lack of violence in the text. Violence remains an unexplored area in this and other stories, although the inner conflicts of the narrator can only originate from all the violence that his psyche must have undergone. The main blind spot, however, in this text, seems to be the lack of "ego ideal" of the narrator. That explains the absence of more positive values or sense of responsibility, which he avoids thanks to a system of thought, only focused on (even caught in) regressive feelings, in "Nothing". This fixation is also noticeable in the style of the narrator, particularly in his use of literary imagery. In literature, the metaphor has always been the sign and realisation of a writer's relationship with the unknown, and therefore of his inner freedom. Looking at Beckett's story, we must conclude that the metaphor has a rather secondary place in the text. There are actually some very beautiful metaphors—for example, love is called "banishment with now and then a postcard from the homeland", and still water "athirst", "reaching up to that of the sky"—but the main images are all symbols—fixed images—and symbols of a more metonymical order: bench, graveyard, mountain, epitaph. Nearly all of them lead us back to one of the parental figures. What the reader feels about this story of Beckett is that here the language that sets him free is not a free language. It is a marvellous language, but it doesn't really have the freedom of Joyce's or Proust's prose. Its main function is to help the author to survive, thanks to an exercise of what we could call sublime—or sublimated—masochism.

PROBLEMS AND METHODS

As far as my interpretation of the text is concerned, I still owe you some explanation of my approach, my way of using psychoanalysis in literature. How does one arrive at such interpretation? For a start, I must remind you, perhaps unnecessarily, of two tendencies we have to avoid: first, we can not take the author as our subject. Beckett is not the subject, and he is certainly not on the couch. However, that does not mean that we should behave, rather hypocritically, as if we didn't know anything about him. We are aware that for several years Beckett underwent psychoanalysis, even with one of the most famous analysts of his time, Wilfred Bion. He does not seem to have been very satisfied about what happened between him and Bion, but—and this is important for us—Beckett knew very well what psychoanalysis was, even to such an extent that, writing this story about a man on a bench and later on a sofa, the association with the couch must have been present in his mind. However, all this does not mean that we want to take the place Bion had. Beckett is dead. He will not answer our questions. We should speak about the text, not about the writer.

A second inclination that we must avoid is to treat this story as a case study, as the description of a mental disturbance—a neurosis, or even a psychosis that an unfortunate childhood with unfortunate parents can provoke. Such an approach would be another way to subordinate the text to non-literary considerations; not to the writer's life experience, but to our interest in a particular case-study. Yet such an interest could be justified, for Beckett himself told critics that he was the child of a religious and rather cold mother and of a nice father whose death, when his son was 27, affected him profoundly. Both parents seem to play a part in the fantasies that inspired **"First Love",** but all this should not make us forget that literature is something different from clinical language. Literature is language in freedom, its structure and style are suited to tell us more about ourselves, our world and how we experience it, than scientific or common language can ever do. The mastery Beckett shows when he plays with the author's distance, going from tragic involvement in his fantasies to uproarious laughter about them, is the best proof of this kind of freedom. Therefore, we don't aim for biographical discoveries or case-studies. In our view, the only objective we should pursue while working in a psychoanalytical perspective is to clarify the text, with the help of psychoanalytical theory and its concepts. Above all, it is not psychoanalysis but the text itself that, at every stage of our research, should remain our central preoccupation.

Our method, then, takes three different points of departure: First, it is useful to understand and formulate the reaction(s) the text provokes in us, the readers. Such reactions, which will change after each reading of the text, are important, for they determine to a large extent how the rest of the research will be pursued. This involves the Freudian concepts of transference and counter-transference. Knowing that writers and readers are inclined to repeat, consciously and unconsciously, former experiences in life, by projecting them or finding them back in what we write or read, we should always be aware of this mechanism of the mind, for it

might also mislead us. Psychoanalysis can teach us what in our fantasies about a work of art originates only in our own inner world, and what we really share with the creator of this work.

What were my reactions when I read **"First Love"**? Initially, melancholy, for sure. It is not a very happy family romance that inspires Beckett in **"First Love"**: lack and emptiness are everywhere. It seems preferable for the man who is speaking in this soliloquy to exist with a dead father than with a living mother, although he loves both. But more than melancholy, I felt uneasiness being confronted with experiences that are so regressive that I could and can not pretend to understand them all. What I also continually experience is the decision of the writer to tell us all of his feelings, in his case, all his regressive feelings, those that psychoanalysts are so fond of, because they seem to reach the foundations of our psychic life. But, like so many great writers, he dominates what we call regression, he plays with it, in language, not as a victim but as a winner, or at least as an exorcist. It is possible that his success in this respect is due partly to his psychoanalysis. Beckett owes a lot to Freud and his successors, without whom he probably wouldn't have done with language what he has done here. But he uses psychoanalytical concepts above all in a meta-psychological way, the feelings of the man who is telling his story appearing as much as anthropological ideas as they are psychological descriptions. What remains, when we read this and many other texts of Beckett, is, rather paradoxically, above all, an immense admiration for the artist who writes such French and English, equally intense, equally rhythmic and rhetorical, exploring with unequalled mastery the deepest layers of our psychic reality. Here literature can be seen to be teaching a lesson to psychoanalysis. Literary texts should be able to open theory as much as theory can open texts.

A second step in approaching the text is the reading and rereading of it with "suspended attention" ("gleichschebende Aufmerksamkeit"), with no other purpose than to catch the creative, frequently hidden, dimensions of the text. Together with transference an intimately linked to it, suspended attention has always been considered as the main and most productive attitude for the psychoanalyst. Thanks to this "free listening", a story or a play may reveal its secrets, instantaneously or gradually. Suspended attention is an effort to reach the primary process of the making of the text, before it assumes its elaborate—secondary—form: the fantasies that underlie the text, the obsessive themes and repetitions that leave their marks on it, the incongruities or details that, despite their apparent insignificance, might reveal themselves as essential for the origins of the text.

Therefore I have tried to answer this question: What does our "suspended attention" perceive, when we try to listen to the voice speaking here? What fantasies, obsessions, or even "voices" have contributed to the creation of this story? What do we see, what do we hear, when we let this story invade us, our mind and our body? What struck me at the first or the second reading were the following items, randomly, which I later put into the ideas expressed earlier in these pages: the separation of the two parents, all the regression, the movement and its different levels, "to and fro", "away and back", the two forms of anal obsession (expulsion and retention), the absence of violence, the epitaph as symbol of the writing process, the limping, the importance of the voice. What I first didn't understand was the game with the voice, singing and then crying. I wondered what Ohlsdorf was (apparently it was Germany's most famous cemetery near Hamburg), and who Reinhold was (a German philosopher who studied human consciousness, 1758-1823), and so on.

A third approach, after the questions about transference and the necessarily chaotic results of the "suspended attention", is a more systematical one. It uses all these and tries to put them together in a structure, studying what may be called the "narrative quality" of the text: should this text be characterized as mainly Oedipal, or do its content and style point to a more pre-Oedipal background? Both categories are inevitably present in any text, as we are always engaged, in literature as well as in real life, in swaying between two poles: pleasure and reality, a motherly world and a fatherly world. Of this "articulation" inside us, Beckett's story offers an example that is perhaps too obvious, because it even turns out to be its main theme. But in any literary text we can find it back, on different levels and often as a surprise: in the way the different characters of the story have been chosen, or time and space are presented, in its atmosphere, in the use of description and narration, in the presence or absence of other voices and opinions—is "the other as other" really taken into account?—in the sexual interest of the narrator—is he describing an adult sexual life or more the polymorphous sexuality of a child?—in the use of images—metaphors and metonyms—or of other style figures.

These are the kind of questions raised by a psychoanalytical approach in literature. I hope to have demonstrated that such an approach can open and clarify Beckett's story in a gratifying way.

Works Cited

Beckett, Samuel, *Premier Amour* (Paris: Editions de Minuit, 1970).

Bion, Wilfred, *Learning from Experience* (London: Basic Books, 1962).

Sigmund Freud, *Jenseits des Lustprinzips*, in *Gesammelte Werke*, Bd. 6 (Frankfurt am Main: S. Verlag, 1964), 191ff.

Gontarski, S. E., *Samuel Beckett: The Complete Short Prose 1929-1989* (New York: Grove P, 1995), 25-45.

Pascal, Blaise, *Pensées. Editions Classiques Garnier* (Paris: Bordas, 1991).

Peter Boxall (essay date 2000)

SOURCE: Boxall, Peter. "'The Existence I Ascribe': Memory, Invention, and Autobiography in Beckett's Fiction." *The Yearbook of English Studies* 30 (2000): 137-52.

[*In the following essay, Boxall maintains that "First Love" signals a turning point in Beckett's writing style with his employment of the monologue form as well as his "oscillation between remembrance and invention as a form of storytelling."*]

BECKETT, MODERNISM, AND AESTHETIC
AUTOBIOGRAPHY

This essay takes as its starting point what I suggest is a seminal moment in Beckett's fiction. In his 1946 novella, **"First Love,"** the narrator draws attention for the first time to an opposition between two categories of thingness which persists as a foundational structural distinction for the remaining four decades of Beckett's prose writing career. Talking of the objects, people, and places that from the subject matter of his stories, the narrator claims: 'I have always spoken, no doubt always shall, of things that never existed, or that existed, if you insist, no doubt always will, but not with the existence I ascribe to them.'[1] From this point on, the movement of Beckett's writing is structured around this reluctantly conceded distinction. His narrators repeatedly claim absolute imaginative control over the non-existent world that they invent, whilst equally repeatedly, if unwillingly, allowing that the things of their stories share their existence with objects that are located in a remembered world beyond them. It is this vacillation that becomes one of the most characteristic features of Beckett's fiction. The prose is caught, from **"First Love"** onwards, in a ceaseless oscillation between remembrance and invention as a form of storytelling, and this oscillation controls the peculiar mode of reference that Beckett develops throughout his mid and late work. As the narrators vacillate between memory and invention, they seek both to refer to a remembered landscape, and to invent a new landscape that owes nothing to a reality that precedes it or constrains it. The things of the stories are both identical with the 'existing' things to which they partly refer, and different from them, as the narrators declare their simultaneous belonging to and freedom from the world of which they write.

This adoption, in **"First Love,"** of a mode of reference which is to become a major characteristic of Beckett's fiction coincides with another sea change in his writing: the adoption of the monologue form in which almost all his remaining prose is written. These departures in Beckett's writing are finely interwoven, and are related in turn to the tenacious but subtle autobiographical register that stretches throughout his fiction. The narrator's claim that he invents the things of his stories, his insistence that he is able to drag the objects on the storyscape to a new literary geography where they are freed from the reality that they share with things that exist, is complicated by the monologue form. As the narrator himself acts as an object upon the storyscape, his tendency to deny his own existence as character threatens to undermine the very reality effect upon which the primacy of his narrating voice is based. The freedom of the narrator's vacillating movement between memory and invention as a mode of storytelling is compromised and limited in important ways by his own presence as character upon the storyscape whose mimetic status he seeks to manipulate. This freedom is further compromised by the relationship between the writing of memory as a formal strategy, and its characteristic autobiographical connection with the geography of Beckett's own memory. The autobiographical status of Beckett's fiction, at least from *Watt* onwards, is always subject to narrative uncertainty, but that the remembered selves and objects that people the majority of his landscapes have some autobiographical content is beyond serious doubt. This essay seeks to address the political implications and possibilities of the relationship between memory, invention, and autobiography as it plays itself out in Beckett's fiction. If the things of his stories both share their existence with a political reality, and negate political referents in a statement of the narrator's imaginative freedom to invent a non-existent world, what is the political value of this dialectical movement between statement and denial? If Beckett's prose moves from reference to an autobiographical self to a form of aesthetic self invention, to what extent can this writing of identity be understood to be politically motivated? Can we read the **"First Love"** narrator's promise to ascribe his own existence as contributing anything to the ongoing attempt to understand the promise and limits of the literary in re-imagining the postcolonial consciousness?

The semi-autobiographical mode of self-invention that Beckett appears to adopt in the stories of the **Novellas** [**Four Novellas**] is not, of course, unique to him. The difficulties and possibilities of a modernist aesthetic of autobiographical self-creation are well marked out by the major modernists before him. Proust's monumental exploration of the relation between remembrance and aesthetics, Yeats's preoccupation with the contradiction between worldly self and mystical, poetic anti-self, and Joyce's partial self-portrait in Stephen Dedalus, exemplify a form of writing which is dedicated to an exposition of the relationship between non-fictional autobiography and fictional self-creation. This writing is driven by irreconcilable but irreducible certainties: the certainty that one is bound to the political world, and the certainty that one is free from it. The modernist autobiographical aesthetic is both formed by the contradiction between these certainties, and, in the form that results, gestures towards a resolution of the contradictions that generate its becoming. A politics of modernist literary representation can thus be found in the movement of the writing between the poles of non-fictional reference and fictional self-invention. The shift in register between autobiography and fiction controls the movement of the writing from the faithful representation of existing relations of production to the invention of a literary space which resists cultural inscription. The contradiction between memory and invention functions as a struggle between an existing false consciousness, and a creative imagination that remains beyond the reach of ideological inauthenticity, and it is partly in this struggle that the political value of modernist self-fashioning is to be found.[2]

The relation of Beckett's work, however, to the politics of modernist autobiography is ambiguous. To draw a politics of representation from the relation between memory and invention in Beckett's writing presents the critic with difficulties that may be different from those posed by the work of Joyce or Proust, and that seem to be related in some degree to the uncertain location of Beckett's writing in the distinction which is in any case uncertain between modernism and postmodernism. Where the relationship between memory and invention in Joyce's semi-autobiographical work displays a contradictory tension typical, for some critics, of a modernist aesthetic that is partly generated by the dialectic between binary oppositions,[3] in Beckett's writing the two modes of representation do not seem so ready to engage in a dialogue that could yield a political content. Whilst the work of modernists such as Joyce, Proust, Yeats, Stein, and Woolf has conventionally been read as being engaged with a set of political concerns, even if that engagement is regarded by some as critical or dismissive of certain political practices,[4] Beckett's work has been widely received as denouncing the political altogether. This perceived resignation from any form of commitment to or interest in the cultural politics that fuelled the work of his major influences has contributed to the characterization of Beckett as a nascent postmodernist who is a central figure in the drift away from modernist literary production. A symptom and a cause of this renunciation of the political, it could be argued, is the failure of the opposition between memory and invention to engage in a generative dialogue. The pairing of memory and invention in Beckett's work is perhaps characteristic, in Frederic Jameson's terminology, more of the postmodern antinomy than of the contradiction that is the driving force in modernist literature.[5] For Jameson, contradiction is distinct from antinomy in that the former names an opposition whose antithetical halves are held in place by a tension which has the potential to lead towards resolution, whereas the latter consists of two statements whose opposition is so complete and fundamental as to defy any attempt to find even a notional common ground or covert compatibility. Consequently, 'contradictions are supposed, in the long run, to be productive; whereas antinomies—take Kant's classic one: the world has a beginning, the world has no beginning—offer nothing in the way of a handle, no matter how diligently you turn them around and around' (p. 2). Joyce's work, at least up to *Ulysses,* can be seen to be driven by what Jameson regards as modernist contradictions: his writing has one foot planted in the intricately described autobiographical geography of Dublin, and another foot in a geography of pure literary invention. The writing pulls hard in these contradictory directions, but this antagonism is organized around the push towards a new place where the antagonists can come together. In Beckett's writing, however, this opposition arguably loses such dialectical tension; the writing of memory and the writing of invention fall into antinomial halves whose difference from each other is such that it is inconceivable that they should move towards resolution. It is indeed difficult to imagine a Beckett narrator promising to forge any form of racial authenticity in the luke-warm smithy of his soul. The narrator moves between recounting past lives and denying their reality with an abandon which may suggest a loss of faith in the transformative power of art to bridge the distance between the creative mind and the political world. Memory and invention as oppositional modes of writing seem to drift from the moorings that, in Joyce's work, hold them both apart and together. Just as the narrator's memories seem not to plant him firmly in a space which has reference to a specific non-fictional geography, so the shift of register to the writing of pure invention seems not to introduce any oppositional tension into Beckett's writing. Rather, memory and invention can appear as empty categories that are drained of their political energy, and merely mark the failure of a residual autobiographical aesthetic to offer any potential release from the problem of the self's simultaneous belonging to and freedom from the world of which s/he writes.

A sign that the relation between memory and invention in Beckett's writing may indeed exemplify antinomy rather than contradiction is the tendency of thesis and antithesis to collapse into each other. For Jameson, antinomy names a relationship between concepts that are so extremely and abstractly opposed that, in their opposition, they betray a sameness which brings any dialogue to a standstill. Jameson's example is that between identity and difference, the 'grandest and most empty of all abstractions' (p. 7): when these concepts have been re-leased from any specific content and thought to their abstract limits, absolute sameness becomes indistinguishable from absolute difference, just as the concept of continual change collapses into the absolute stasis that is its direct opposite. As Estragon wryly observes of the geography of *Waiting For Godot,* where space tends towards abstraction in its denial of contingency or content, 'everything oozes [but] it's never the same pus from one second to the next': the constantly changing meets, as it reaches the limits of its constancy, the constantly the same.[6] This dizzying movement between implacable opposition and sudden conflation characterizes the relation between memory and invention as it is developed in Beckett's fiction. The distinction represents an absolute opposition that forms the structural framework upon which several of the fictions are based, but the coherence that the distinction offers is repeatedly undermined as the poles both move too far apart to sustain any form of narrative tension, and collapse into each other as they reveal their identity. The **"First Love"** narrator's distinction between two categories of thingness, things as they 'exist' and things as they are 'ascribed' by the narrator, persists as a structural device from the *Novellas* to the short fictions collected in the *Nohow On* trilogy. The device is set up partly to allow the narrator as creating unself to free himself from narrator as remembered self. But as Beckett's fiction forces the writing of invention further and further apart from the writing of memory, as the halves of the distinction are pushed to the limit of their difference from each other, each insists upon folding back into the other as memory becomes invention, and invention becomes memory. The narrator of *Molloy,* for example, seeks to separate memory from invention by writing a novel whose circular structure closes around a remembered landscape, and seals it off to allow the creating unself to sever the bonds that hold him to the partly autobiographical self. The second section of the novel, in which the quasi-detective Moran sets out to track down his quarry Molloy, opens with the first words of Moran's 'report' on the progress of his search: 'It is midnight. The rain is beating on the widows.'[7] At the end of the novel, as Moran comes to the close of his report, he finishes his narrative with a description of his coming to write the beginning of his report: 'I went back into the house and wrote, It is midnight. The rain is beating on the windows. It was not midnight. It was not raining' (p. 162). This hijacking of the reality effect upon which the truth value of the entire narrative is based has two consequences. It serves, in one register, to allow the narrative voice that has been speaking as Moran throughout the report to close his narrative with a flourish that dispatches Moran, Molloy, the country that they share, and even the report itself to the realm of falsehood, leaving the unnamed voice that reveals the fictionality of Moran's report to emerge as the only survivor of the novel's wreckage. The report, which by its very nature is a faithful, journalistic record of events, closes upon itself to free the inventing 'I' from the yoke that had chained it to reportage. In another register, however, the narrator's attempt to separate report from invention clearly has the effect rather of collapsing altogether the distinction between the two forms of writing that provides the structural basis of the novel. As the unnamed narrating 'I' moves beyond the reach of the 'I' in whose name he narrates, it simultaneously transgresses and undermines the limit that sustains the distinction in the first place. The narrative device by which inventing consciousness appears in extreme opposition to remembered self leads equally to the loss of narrative energy by which invention is able to fling itself clear of memory.

As the novels of the trilogy progress, this insistent separation and conflation of remembered self and invented self becomes increasingly exposed, and increasingly compressed. In the last pages of *The Unnamable,* the narrator struggles inexorably towards the deadlock in which the contradictions that fuel a modernist aesthetic of self creation appear finally to freeze over. The narrator is driven to impasse by his frantic and impossible attempt to invent in his writing the place in which he writes. The moment he allows himself to speak by conceding the reality of the place and the body which contain him, he seeks to deny the reality of place and body as contingent to his freely creating consciousness. He allows that he is writing in a 'place', but immediately undoes his placedness, insisting that 'I'll make [the place] all the same, I'll make it in my head, I'll draw it out of my memory, I'll gather it about me, I'll make myself a head, I'll make myself a memory'.[8] The narrator's desperate push to cleanse his inventive powers of the contingency of memory leads to a blatant deadlock between I and not-I, where negation is so complete as to appear virtually indistinguishable from affirmation. The movement between statement and denial has become so stark and unproductive as to lead to the eventual, unbridgeable antinomy that closes the trilogy, and brings Beckett's prose writing to a virtual half for over a decade: 'I can't go on, I'll go on' (p. 382). It is perhaps at this point in Beckett's *œuvre* that the relation between memory and invention seems furthest from yielding any sort of politics. The gulf between things as they exist and things as the narrator invents them seems both too wide and too narrow to offer any movement away from an unbearable status quo, the representation of which many critics consider the sole purpose of Beckett's writing.

It is the central argument of this paper, however, that Beckett's dramatization of the struggle between memory and invention does not at any point constitute an abandonment of a political aesthetic. It is clear that the dialogue between created and remembered self in Beckett's fiction, as a residue of the more robust modernist

self-fashioning of Joyce and Proust, nears the point of collapse. But to infer from this near breakdown of negotiations that Beckett's writing resigns and limits itself to an expression of a fundamental and unsolvable difference between self and world would be to consign it prematurely to a form of political redundancy. When reading Beckett as a pioneer of an apolitical postmodern aesthetic, his representation of the relation between memory and invention appears as an antinomial relation between empty categories. The struggle between I and not-I, drained of all contingency and content, exemplifies the 'free play of masks and roles without content or substance' that Jameson identifies as 'postmodernity itself' (p. 18). I suggest, however, that even at the barest and emptiest moments of the relation between self and unself, even during the last pages of *The Unnamable,* memory and invention are not in free play. Indeed, it is difficult to think of a less appropriate term to describe the frantic final throes of the unnamed narrator. The movement between worldly 'I' and invented 'not-I' is not entirely emptied out in a final ghastly parody of modernist self-invention, but remains held in place by a residual autobiographical vein that runs through Beckett's writing. The persistence of autobiography both energizes and constrains the relation between memory and invention, and provides the tension that keeps the unnamable narrator screaming. It is partly in this tense and difficult relation between memory and invention, as it is organized around a tenacious autobiographical referentiality, that I suggest the political promise of Beckett's work may be found. I do not argue that this relation leads to any form or promise of sublation or reconciliation in the fiction: on the contrary, it is necessary to understand the process by which progression by contradiction becomes unlikely in the Beckettian universe. But it seems equally important to understand how and why the inventing 'I' does not entirely succeed in abstracting itself from the autobiographical register which chains it to a non-fictional, culturally specific moment. The oscillation between affirmation and negation refrains from becoming a purely formal strategy, and negation maintains political potency in Beckett's writing, because the texts remain bound, however tenuously, to a political reality beyond them which prevents memory and invention from turning into each others' opposites.

Memory and invention in the 'Novellas'

In order to suggest ways that this relation between memory, invention, and autobiography in Beckett's writing may offer a handle on the political dynamic in his work, I will return to the *Novellas.* All four stories are organized around the narrator's depiction of his banishment and expulsion. They all start with a forcible expulsion of the narrator as character from his family home on the death of his father, and the main focus of the four 'plots' is the wandering of the homeless narrator across the geography of what he describes as the 'city of my childhood' in the search for a new shelter. But this exile takes two forms: the banishment of the narrator as character from his home within the geography of the story, and the banishment of the narrator/character from the narrator as narrator across the geography of the text itself. It is in the precisely choreographed economy of this four-way banishment, and in the nature of the relationship between the city of the narrator's childhood and the non-fictional city of Dublin, that the stories' engagement with a political landscape can be found.

The divide between the narrator and the narrator/character is structured around the relationship between memory and invention. The banishment from self that the narrator suffers upon the writing of the stories is banishment across the distinction between things as they exist beyond the narrator's reference to them, and things as they exist with the existence that he ascribes. In her essay on **"First Love,"** Julia Kristeva refers to this banishment in terms that are helpful, but which I think need to be adjusted. For Kristeva, the narrator's writing of the story is an 'attempt at separating oneself from the august and placid expanses where the father's sublime Death, and thus *Meaning,* merges with the son's self'.[9] In this schema, the narrator inhabits a geography of pure invention, which he shares with the unsullied spirit of his dead father. It is a post-mortem place, located beyond life and beyond contact with the story's grubby urban landscape. The moment of writing, however, is a moment of banishment from this space of serene selfhood to a material geography that tears the narrator away from his disembodied peace. Writing, for Kristeva, condemns the narrator to a 'banishment robbing this sensible but always already dead, filial self of its silence on the threshold of a rimy minerality, where the only opportunity is to become anyone at all' (p. 150). I agree that this expulsion of the writing and inventing narrator, from his primary location in a sublime literary geography beyond the horizons of the text to a secondary material storyscape in which he appears as character, is one of the directions in which the banishment between narrating 'I' and narrated 'I' takes place. The narrator of **"The Calmative,"** for example, refers rather proudly to this inaugurative moment of banishment when he announces, at the opening of his story, 'I'll tell myself a story, I'll try and tell myself another story, to try and calm myself, and it's there I feel I'll be old' (*N* [*Four Novellas*], p. 51). But, in **"The Calmative"** as in the other stories of the *Novellas,* the narrator's prioritization of writing self over self as character is shadowed and undermined by moments in the text when the banishment appears to be operating the other way around. Kristeva's emphasis on the movement by which the writing son is banished from a sublime negative geography into the 'rimy' world of the story makes light of the opposite movement in which the narrator as

character casts himself forward, from the geography of the story, towards the space from which the narrator as narrator writes. Kristeva's suggestion, borrowed from the narrator of **"First Love"** himself, that the character to which the narrator is banished should be thought of as 'anyone at all', obscures one of the central difficulties of the novella: that the character with whose voice the narrator speaks is, by virtue of the monologue form adopted by the narrator, his own. The narrator is not banished, as he claims, to act as 'any old one irredeemably' (*N,* p. 15), but rather the monologue form condemns him to act, very specifically, as himself. Because in all the *Novellas* both narrator and character share the same pronoun, the narrator cannot comfortably sustain the primacy of his location in a negative geography of pure invention beyond the text. He has not, as Kristeva claims, always been already dead. Rather he is both the same as the character in whose name he speaks, and different from him; the character who wanders across the storyscape is both the narrator as he remembers himself at a former time, and an imaginary character that the narrator invents from the geography of his calm negativity. As a result of sharing the pronoun that designates them, the narrator as character and the narrator as narrator are mutually dependent: they are joined by the text which divides them. The narrator creates the story that he tells (without his narrative voice, the text would not come into being at all) but he is also created by it. Without the text and the pronoun that contain him, the narrator would be robbed of his means of speech. The act of writing may, as Kristeva suggests, banish him from the negative geography of his 'paternal country', his 'dispeopled kingdom'. But he is equally banished to his magisterial position beyond the text from the rimy geography of the story that he shares with the 'I' of his creature.

It is in the separation and convergence of these two mutually dependent and hostile 'I's, that the storyscape comes into being. The details and objects that make up the story are all caught in the ripples caused in the reality effect by the narrator's attempt simultaneously to create the story and to be created by it. The story is told both as a memory and as a fable, and the ground of the story is caught in the mercurial shifting of the narrator between remembrance and fabulation. As the narrator seeks to ground the reality of his speaking voice in the story of which he speaks, whilst dismissing the story as a product of his own creative whim, the space of the story rhythmically hardens to a reality to which the narrator must make an accurate reference, and dissolves to a random figment of the narrator's restless imagination. So the ground upon which the **"First Love"** narrator first falls in love with Lulu/Anna fluctuates in this dizzying movement between memory and invention. The narrator/character and Lulu/Anna meet for the first time on a bench by a canal, and the geography of their meeting point is described in detail:

I met her on a bench, on the bank of the canal, one of the canals, for our town boasts two, though I never knew which was which. It was a well situated bench, backed by a mound of solid earth and garbage, so that my rear was covered. My flanks too, partially, thanks to a pair of venerable trees, more than venerable, dead, at either end of the bench.

(*N*, pp. 13-14)

This meticulously described landscape provides the stage for the drama of the narrator's loving. It is to this 'beastly circumstantial'[10] landscape that the narrator as character is banished upon his falling in love with Lulu/Anna. The narrator complains that, before falling in love, he had been able to indulge freely in the solipsism of which Murphy before him was so fond. Before meeting Lulu/Anna, the narrator claims:

What mattered to me in my dispeopled kingdom, that in regard to which the disposition of my carcass was the merest and most futile of accidents, was supineness in the mind, the dulling of the self and of that residue of execrable frippery known as the non-self and even the world, for short.

(*N*, p. 15)

On falling in love with Lulu/Anna, however, the narrator/character is robbed of his ability to spurn the world of bodies and things, and he 'who had learnt to think of nothing' is forced to think of her (*N*, p. 19). Thinking of Lulu/Anna means returning repeatedly to this bench by the canal, where he is trapped in a world of material surfaces that will not be blunted or dulled. The narrator's accurate reference to this material space to which the reluctant lover is banished, however, is repeatedly undermined by the slippage in his mode of reference from memory to invention. As the narrator/character drags himself to the bench for the 'fourth or fifth time' in pursuit of his loved one, the narrator as narrator writes 'Let us say it was raining, nothing like a change, if only of weather' (*N*, p. 22). At moments such as these, which recur throughout the text, the narrator as narrator can be felt, from the other side of the text, picking at the reality effect that holds it in place, reminding us that the bench, the canal, the love, the narrator/character's banishment, are all pure figment. The bench which holds the narrator/character unwillingly to his love suddenly wobbles and flickers as the narrator kicks out one of the props that hold it in place. As if to make up for this mischievous waywardness, the rain that the narrator adds as an afterthought is quickly absorbed into the register that casts the story as a remembered event. Three lines later, the narrator asserts, back in chaste reportage mode, 'the bench was soaking wet' (*N*, p. 22), and the effects of this invented rain falling over the landscape of the narrator's love crop up sporadically throughout the remainder of the story.

Three pages and several hours later, as the narrator/character settles into his new residence with Lulu/Anna, he complains that 'my hat was still wringing' (*N*, p. 25).

Perhaps the most striking of these moments in **"First Love,"** in which a constraining material reality is made to carry within it the negation of its own constraint, occurs with the narrator's reference to the prostitute herself, for love of whom the narrator as character forsakes the peace of his solipsistic 'dispeopled kingdom'. The woman herself that draws the narrator towards thingness is caught, like all the other objects in the story, in the shifting of register between memory and invention. This movement can be seen most precisely as the narrator first feels the yearnings of love. He realizes that he has fallen in love, he recognizes the symptoms most definitively, when he finds himself 'inscribing' the letters of her name in an 'old heifer pat' (*N*, p. 18):

Perhaps I loved her with a platonic love? But somehow I think not. Would I have been tracing her name in old cowshit if my love had been pure and disinterested? And with my devil's finger into the bargain, which I then sucked. Come now! My thoughts were all of Lulu, if that doesn't give you some idea nothing will. Anyhow I'm sick and tired of this name Lulu, I'll give her another, more like her. Anna for example, it's not more like her but no matter. I thought of Anna, then, I who had learnt to think of nothing.

(*N*, p. 19)

This outrageous manoeuvre cuts across the reality effect of the story in a number of ways, and strikes at the heart of the text's ongoing concern with the relationship between writing and space, between existence and ascription. The correspondence between Lulu/Anna's name, and the bodily person to whom the name refers, is strung here across the economy of banishment that holds the story in place. The letters that make up her name appear both in the text, and as objects upon the storyscape, engraved in the shitty, miry ground of the geography to which the loving narrator is banished. As the narrator shifts register, these letters traced in the cowpat, and the printed letters that designate the prostitute in the text itself, metamorphose from Lulu to Anna, in a move that threatens to bring the space of the novella tumbling. The narrator's sudden decision to change the name works partly as his declaration of freedom from his memory, from the story, and from the text that contains and constrains him. His freedom to do so, the implied lack of a demand that he must refer accurately to a preexisting reality, points towards a collapse of the tension between remembered and invented selves that provides the foundation of the story. It is the truth value of the text that condemns the inventing narrator to share his pronoun with his earth-bound character. As the demands of accurate reference give way to narrative whim, in which it would be impossible for reference to fail, the narrator seeks to free himself to his prior space beyond the storyscape and beyond the text, where he is untroubled by shitty fields and inky letters. But even as the inventing 'I' declares his freedom from the text that he invents, he is forced to retract this freedom. The lurch towards pure invention promises to free the inventing 'I' altogether from remembered 'I', but it also threatens to collapse the reality effect that sustains them in different geographies. Even as the narrator chooses imperiously to change Lulu's name to Anna, in a display of his ability to make this story whatever he wants it to be,[11] he blends this demonstration of his inventive freedom with a concession to the demands of referential accuracy: the narrator changes Lulu's name to Anna, because he says it is more like her. The moment that he empties the text of reference to a remembered geography, he claims that his textual sleight of hand is geared towards an approximation of a reality to which the text is struggling to remain faithful. Of course, as soon as the narrator has made this concession to narrative fidelity, he seeks to undermine it with the disclaimer 'it's not more like her, but no matter', but the extent to which it matters whether the words of the text are involved in a referential relationship with an existence beyond them has already become clear. Despite the narrator's disingenuous reversals, he knows that it both matters and does not matter, as his freedom to deny is caught inexorably in the demand that he must affirm.

It is this comic but excruciating movement between affirmation and denial, between sustaining and undermining mimetic security, that leads eventually to the aporia that grinds the narrative of *The Unnamable* to a halt. The narrator of **"First Love"** already anticipates the unnamable narrator who starts his novel with the promise that 'I will proceed by aporia pure and simple [. . .]. Or by affirmations and negations invalidated as uttered [. . .] I say aporia without knowing what it means' (p. 267). In **"First Love,"** the convergence and separation of inventing and remembered 'I's has the effect of pulling apart the text that joins and divides them, consistently threatening to stall the narrative which continues, sometimes, only by virtue of pure momentum. Each statement that the narrator utters to explain or to describe or further to consolidate a narrative situation or moment is undermined by his desire to negate the text that holds him, to undo its demands and its constraints. His anxious attempts to make his story accurate and clear are shadowed by his equal insistence that he has no reason to care whether they are accurate or not. He sweats to ensure that his story is proof against inaccuracy or unbelievability, whilst demanding always that 'there is nothing I wish to prove' (*N*, p. 16). The possibility of remembered and inventing 'I's, in a text such as this, engaging in any kind of dialogue that could generate a solution to the problem of their simultaneous difference and sameness, seems remote. The geography

of the text seems to form and to dissolve in the space of a banishment between self and unself whose mutual difference is so extreme as to appear both unbridgeable and on the point of collapse. The narrator's resolute refusal to concede the purity of his inventing consciousness to the griminess of the text is countered by the narrator/character's demand that he must, and the fluctuating, unstable, consistently collapsing storyscape as I have described it is the result of these irreconcilable demands. In this absolute stand-off between memory and invention, Stephen Dedalus's youthful faith in the power of the artist to 'forg[e] anew in his workshop out of the sluggish matter of the earth a new soaring impalpable imperishable being' seems a long way off indeed.[12] Memory and invention, as contradictory or antinomial modes of representation, consistently fail to enter into any form of progressive dialectic in this text that can sometimes appear above all to be a symptom of their absolute, incompatible hostility.

However, to draw from this apparent failure the conclusion that Beckett's writing abandons struggle in favour of resignation to undecidability and indifference, as many have, is, in terms of this argument, to privilege one economy of banishment over another.[13] The storyscape may be formed in the space of the banishment between narrator as narrator and narrator as character, but the space of the story itself is a geography upon which the narrator as character suffers a different form of banishment. As the narrator/character is expelled from his father's house in **"First Love,"** to the bedsit that he shares with Lulu/Anna, the roofless wandering to which he is condemned takes him across a partly autobiographical landscape that is pitted throughout with details that make it poignantly recognizable as a Dublinesque geography of Beckett's memory. The site itself where the bench on which the lovers meet is situated, and which is subject to the forms of narrative uncertainty that I have described, is a space which has resonances as a Dublin space in Beckett's prose. The narrator says that he met Lulu/Anna 'on a bench, on the bank of the canal, one of the canals, for our town boasts two, though I never knew which was which' (*N*, pp. 13-14). Dublin has two canals running through the town, the Royal Canal and the Grand Canal, and these canals appear in several other of Beckett's works, such as *Mercier and Camier,* and *Molloy,* where they are made to designate a 'Dublinness' in storyscapes whose geographical location is otherwise uncertain.[14] As the narrator makes his way from the bench to Lulu/Anna's flat, these Beckettian/Dublinesque features gain weight and resonance, until the moment at which she reveals to him that she is pregnant with their child, whereupon these autobiographical locating details burst in an extraordinary Proustian moment of remembrance. Lulu/Anna, in order to prove to the doubting, misogynistic narrator that she is indeed pregnant as she claims, stands in the light of the window, and the narrator in exile gazes past the pregnant woman whose physicality has deprived him of his solipsistic ease, at a Dublinesque landscape that is figured, throughout Beckett's writing, as home:

> She had drawn back the curtain for a clear view of all her rotundities. I saw the mountain, impassible, cavernous, secret, where from morning to night I'd hear nothing but the wind, the curlews, the clink like distant silver of the stone-cutter's hammers. I'd come out in the daytime to the heather and the gorse, all warmth and scent, and watch at night the distant city lights, if I chose, and the other lights, the lighthouses and lightships that my father had named for me, when I was small, and whose names I could find again, in my memory, if I chose, that I knew.
>
> (*N*, pp. 28-29)

To a reader familiar with Beckett's prose, and with the unnamed autobiographical Dublinesque landscape that grows in poignant resonance from text to text, this passage comes as a wave of yearning for homeland, for the end of exile. The music of the stone-cutter's hammers, which refers partly to the sound of stone-cutters working in the Glencullen granite quarries that Beckett could hear from his Foxrock home as a child, drifts from text to text, from *Watt* to *Malone Dies* and *How It Is,* carrying with it Proustian memories of childhood and home.[15] The Dublinesque mountains studded with burning gorse, and the lighthouses and lightships given names and significance by the narrator's absent father, throw their shadows and their light in virtually every work of fiction Beckett has written.[16] The narrator/character's exile to and from this evocative geography is controlled by the relationship that stretches across the story between his spiritual love for his dead father, and his sexual love for Lulu/Anna, whose physicality is connected at several points in the story with the father's corpse. The narrator loses his father's protection, upon his death, and as the paternal guiding spirit is withdrawn, he is condemned to wander across an *unheimlich* landscape that has become, as a result, both familiar and alien. It is in this landscape that the love for his father is written: the burning mountains and the clinking hammers are containers of the narrator's cherished identity that he shares with his father, that he was given and taught by his father. But as a gap opens up at the beginning of the story between the father's 'great disembodied wisdom' (*N*, p. 13) and his putrefying corpse, the landscape that presents such comfort and self-knowledge becomes simultaneously alien and threatening. As David Lloyd has convincingly and eloquently argued, this condition of alienation and inauthenticity is 'equally the perpetual condition of the colonized: dominated, interpreted, mediated by another'.[17] As the narrator as character is banished from his father's house to the arms of a woman who holds him to her and his own materiality,

and to the materiality of the text, the landscape and storyscape across which he is banished is a political geography, whose features are both absolutely his, and absolutely not his.

It is in the story's manipulation of the layered relation between this banishment and the banishment that operates between inventing and remembered narrators, that the political meaning and potential of *Novellas* can be found. The two forms of banishment modify and inform each other, and prevent the agonizing relation between memory and invention, statement and denial, from drifting into indifferentiation and generality. The landscape is never designated by name as an Irish landscape, and the solidity of this space that is made to carry the weight of Beckett's remembrance of an autobiographical, Dublinesque geography of childhood, is caught in the fluctuation between the narrator who refers and the narrator who invents. The narrator's stretching and tearing at the limits of his imaginative control over the world he describes is organized around an impossible attempt to refer to a political geography, to absorb a loved country and a loved life into the space of his writing, whilst detaching it from that which the world dictates it should mean. A piece of verbal ingenuity in **"The Calmative"** economically and brilliantly captures the engagement of the narrator's tortuous movement between affirmation and negation with a nonfictional landscape that informs it and locates it. As the narrator as character approaches the city of his childhood, upon which his search for calm is to take place, his description of the familiar Dublin landscape is inhabited by the peculiar mixture of memory and invention that is so characteristic of Beckett's writing:

> I was no sooner free of the wood at last, having crossed unminding the ditch that girdles it, than thoughts came to me of cruelty, the kind that smiles. A lush pasture lay before me, nonsuch perhaps, who cares, drenched in evening dew or recent rain.
>
> (*N*, p. 53)

In this passage, the narrator refers to a remembered, partly autobiographical detail, with the very noun that dismisses the detail and negates its evocative power. The description here of the country that surrounds the Dublinesque city comes up time and time again in Beckett's fiction, most notably in *Molloy,* and the description of the pasture of nonsuch corresponds to the nonfictional geography that the narrator is partly describing and remembering: nonsuch is an Irish dialect term for a form of trefoil that is found abundantly on the grassy plains near the sea coasts of Wicklow and Dublin. But of course, the term nonsuch also suggests, as it names the damp, lush field through which the narrator as character prepares to walk, that there is no such field; it works, as so often, to remind us that the scene the narrator as narrator is describing is pure invention—hence the 'who cares'. As also happens so often in these stories, the field of nonsuch re-emerges later in the story, stripped of some of its mimetic ambiguity. As the distressed narrator/character is stranded in the unfamiliar familiar urban landscape to which he has turned for solace, he admits that 'I longed for the tender nonsuch, I would have trodden it gently, with my boots in my hand, and for the shade of my wood, far from this terrible light' (*N*, p. 63).[18]

It is this engagement of the negativity of Beckett's prose with a characteristically evoked autobiographical political geography that has so far been largely overlooked by Beckett's critics. The political in Beckett's work remains situated, as Leslie Hill has recently commented, in a commitment debate derived from that between Lukács and Adorno: between a critique that accuses it of or congratulates it for complacent apoliticism, and one that sees it, in its resolute denial of a stable or recognizable political agenda, as bearing mute witness to 'the deficient and tawdry emptiness of post-historical, post-political, even post-modern capitalist Europe'.[19] David Lloyd's elegant and compelling essay on **"First Love"** exemplifies the persistence of these parameters, in that his reading does not progress beyond a certain parallelism that tends towards a universalization of the colonial situation and of Beckett's representation of it. Lloyd defines Beckett's writing as an 'aesthetic [which] writes out the inauthenticity enforced upon the colonial subject' by developing a 'narrative mode which refuses any single model of integration' (p. 55). This is indeed one of the powerful drives in Beckett's writing, but the potency and the poignancy of this rejection is found partly in its fundamental co-existence with an opposite drive towards integration and belonging. To free Beckett's writing from the terms of the commitment debate that has contained it for so long, I suggest that we need a politics of reading that can elucidate the process by which Beckett's aesthetic strains to release itself from memory whilst writing memory. Beckett develops a mode of reference that struggles to give expression both to the lure and to the constraint of an autobiographical, political geography, whilst allowing a voice to speak from a utopian space beyond the nation, the culture, and the text that produced it. A critical language that can cast light on this writing will contribute much to our understanding of the possibilities and limits of the contemporary aesthetic in re-remembering and rewriting the nation space.

Notes

1. *First Love,* in Samuel Beckett, *The Four Novellas* (Harmondsworth: Penguin, 1980), p. 19. Further references are given after quotations in the text, preceded by the abbreviation *N*.

2. For a sustained analysis of the capacity for works of art to give expression to a utopian 'ideological surplus' that 'allows for a so-called true consciousness to form itself in the mere false consciousness of ideology', see Ernst Bloch, *The Utopian Function of Art and Literature,* trans. by Jack Zipes and Frank Mecklenburg (Cambridge, MA: MIT Press, 1988), p. 36.

3. For a representative example of a dialectical reading of modernity and modernism, see Marshall Berman, *All That is Solid Melts Into Air: The Experience of Modernity* (1982; repr. London: Verso, 1983).

4. Joyce's work, for example, has been widely read as being hostile to Irish nationalism in its championing of cultural pluralism, but has nevertheless been regarded as being concerned with the politics of Irish colonialism and postcolonialism. For a critical reading of the interpretative tradition that has (mistakenly) stressed Joyce's antipathy to Irish nationalism, see Emer Nolan's recent work, *James Joyce and Nationalism* (London: Routledge, 1995).

5. Jameson, rather dangerously, anchors his fragile distinction between contradiction and antinomy in the equally fragile distinction between modernism and postmodernism: 'Contradiction stand[s] for the modernist option perhaps, while antinomy offers a more postmodern one' (*The Seeds of Time* (New York: Columbia University Press, 1994), p. 4).

6. *Waiting for Godot,* in Samuel Beckett, *Complete Dramatic Works* (London: Faber, 1986), p. 55.

7. *Molloy,* in Samuel Beckett, *The Beckett Trilogy* (1950; repr. London: Picador, 1979), p. 84.

8. *The Unnamable,* in Samuel Beckett, *The Beckett Trilogy,* pp. 378-79.

9. 'The Father, Love and Banishment', in Julia Kristeva, *Desire In Language: A Semiotic Approach to Literature and Art,* ed. by Leon S. Roudiez, trans. by Thomas Gora, Alice Jardine and Leon S. Roudiez (Oxford: Blackwell, 1981), p. 149.

10. See Samuel Beckett, *Murphy* (1938; repr. London: Picador, 1973), p. 12.

11. See Samuel Beckett, *Malone Dies* (1956; repr. London: Picador, 1979), where Malone, in a richly comic moment, asserts his imaginative control over the geography of his room, and concedes such control, in the same sentence: 'After all, this window is whatever I want it to be, up to a point, that's right, don't compromise yourself' (p. 217).

12. James Joyce, *A Portrait of the Artist as a Young Man* (1916; repr. London: Paladin, 1988), p. 173.

13. The best study of Beckett's indifference is Leslie Hill, *Beckett's Fiction: In Different Words* (Cambridge: Cambridge University Press, 1990).

14. For example: 'The canal goes through the town, I know I know, there are even two' (*Molloy*, p. 26).

15. Beckett himself, in letters to Eion O'Brien among others, has located the stone-cutters as referring to workers at the Glencullen quarry. See, for example, Eion O'Brien, *The Beckett Country* (Dublin: Black Cat Press, 1986), p. 59.

16. For an example of these features coming together at another moment of intense autobiographical remembrance, see *Malone Dies:* 'Lemuel watches the mountains rising behind the steeples beyond the harbour, no they are more / No, they are more than hills, they rise themselves, gently faintly blue, out of the confused plain. It was there somewhere he was born, in a fine house, of loving parents. Their slopes are covered with ling and furze, its hot yellow bells, better known as gorse. The hammers of the stone-cutters ring all day like bells' (p. 262).

17. *Anomalous States: Irish Writing and the Post-Colonial Moment* (Dublin: Lilliput Press, 1993), p. 54.

18. The geography of this passage is given an extra resonance by the reference here to the wood in which Dante the pilgrim finds himself at the beginning of *Inferno,* contributing to a network of references to the *Divine Comedy* strung throughout *The Calmative.*

19. Leslie Hill, "Up the Republic!": Beckett, Writing, Politics', in *MLN,* 112 (1997), p. 909.

Birgitta Johansson (essay date 2000)

SOURCE: Johansson, Birgitta. "Beckett and the Apophatic in Selected Shorter Texts." *Samuel Beckett Today* 9 (2000): 55-66.

[*In the following essay, Johansson explores Beckett's utilization of the apophatic approach, which is the theory that God is unknowable, in his short texts.*]

Samuel Beckett's rambling discourses play with boundaries between the sacred and the secular. His protagonists can represent voices that pray, although they may not always be conscious of this. At least, praying does not appear to be their main objective in life, if one can speak of objectives or volition in their case. As Lawrence E. Harvey puts it, "renunciation of personal will" in *Watt,* for example, "is couched in religious language that suggests the ascetic preliminaries to mystic experience" (Harvey 1970, 364). This is an initial implication of a bond between Beckett and theology.

Scholarly studies such as Laura Barge's, *God, the Quest, the Hero: Thematic Structures in Beckett's Fiction* (1988), Jean van der Hoden's, *Samuel Beckett et la*

question de Dieu (1997), and Mary Bryden's, *Samuel Beckett and the Idea of God* (1998) analyse Beckett's tragi-comic vision of circumstances and of the relationship between human beings and the conceptualisation of God. There are, however, also studies that stress Beckett's idiosyncratic approach to theology. Thus, Gabriel Vahanian attacks Beckett for flaunting his atheism, and for ironising the Christian faith. For him, Beckett's *Waiting for Godot* represents the notion that God is dead and the corollary to this premise is that here faith is ridiculed. The play is "constructed around the irrelevance of Christian concepts and especially around the nonsensical or quixotic quality of Christian existence", he states (Vahanian 1957; 1967, 120). In addition, there are scholars, such as T. R. Wright, who present the complex juxtaposition of scepticism and spirituality in Beckett. On the one hand, Wright notices "spiritual cravings and the unaccommodating world" in this play, which deals with "the desperate but unfulfilled desire to be saved" and with the longing for redemption. Beckett's tramps "call out to be saved, to be heard and comforted by an omnipotent and benevolent Father", he adds. On the other hand, he reveals that Beckett's plays are "pervaded by irreverent, even blasphemous references to biblical myths, in particular that of the crucifixion and resurrection of Christ (Wright 1988; 1989, 188, 189, 193, and 197). Wright's stance illuminates the oscillation in Beckett's work between what we, for want of better terms, call "the sacred" and "the secular".

It is true that Beckett's œuvre shows that human expectations are often thwarted and that our intellectual lives are permeated by vain expectations, but this does not single out a certain group of people and has little to do with Christian ethics. Hence, it would be naive to think that *Waiting for Godot,* which is symptomatic of his œuvre as a whole, can be classified as a devout text. Beckett rather deals with how human consciousness fails, but is obliged, to handle issues involving the existence of God and the meaning of existence. He shows how earthly trivialities invade the human mind, whereas fragments of thoughts provide it with ontological insights. Similarly, his prose works extend the modernist literary project by experimenting with fragmented narrative techniques or arrangements and by focusing on the workings of the mind. My paper will discuss this Beckettian approach to life in the light of apophaticism or negative theology.

Earlier studies on Beckett and negative theology have stressed the connection between Beckett's texts, negative theology, and the use of silence or of language. Thus, Hélène L. Baldwin studies the concept of silence in *Samuel Beckett's Real Silence* (1981) and Shira Wolosky examines Beckett's "defense of language as the medium in which, against and through all negation, we go on" in *Language Mysticism: The Negative Way of Language in Eliot, Beckett, and Celan* (1995) (Wolosky, 134). Such readings ignore the creative aspect of Beckett's negative theology. My paper will argue that his way of employing the apophatic approach adds a new dimension to mysticism in that it acknowledges and accepts the limitations and restrictions of the human mind, but that it also enables the reader to identify with those Beckettian speakers who are searching for the mystical Other in an endless vicious circle. Here, the discourse hinges on the search and the wait *per se,* which characterises the limbo in which Beckett's protagonists are usually placed. They employ the methods of negative theology when articulating a never-ending desire for clarity and meaning in life. It is true that they constantly fail and are compelled to start anew, but these failures provide them with certain opportunities, such as accepting their own limitations, receiving fragmented truths about the unnameable Other, and pointing to a dimension beyond the circumscription of language.

The concept of apophaticism, the notion that God is unknowable, indescribable, and unnameable, can be traced back to early theology and the Church Fathers. For example, in *The Life of Moses* (?early 390s), Gregory of Nyssa sees Moses entering "the very darkness itself and [. . .] the invisible things" and perceiving "the Invisible" (Gregory 1978, 43). Similarly, in his treatise "The Mystical Theology", Pseudo-Dionysius (sixth century AD) analyses how Moses plunged into "the truly mysterious darkness of unknowing" (Pseudo-Dionysius 1987, 137). That is to say, the concept of God is beyond comprehension. It represents the mystical Other, whose existence we cannot define or grasp, but if the aim of all knowledge is to classify that which is, then the aim of belief is to accept the concept of God, which is "the infinity beyond being", preferably by way of unknowing. It is true that for Dionysius both the cataphatic and the apophatic are necessary approaches for an optimal theology, but he advocates the latter approach, since it best alludes to the essence of God, as he puts it in his "The Divine Names", "The Celestial Hierarchy", and in letters to the monk Gaius (Pseudo-Dionysius 1987, 49-50, 108-09, 130 and 150). In addition, St. Thomas Aquinas (?1225-1274) reduces the *via remotionis* or the *via negativa* and *via positiva* to one method of knowing God in his *Summa Theologica, Summa contra Gentiles,* and *Compendium Theologiae.* Thomist apophaticism involves removing concepts about God in verbal terms; here, negative theology becomes a corrective to affirmative theology. One cannot form concepts about God. It is not possible for "us to know God", Aquinas maintains, for "we have no way of knowing what remains unknown to us at the peak of our knowledge". Furthermore, the greatness of God is unfathomable, and words are therefore inadequate to describe such a Being. On the other hand, he suggests, human beings can know aspects of God, since otherwise they will not be able to

appreciate or believe in the divine. The cataphatic or the *via affirmativa,* which conceptualises God, therefore complements the apophatic or the *via negativa* in Thomist theology, as it does in Dionysian theology (Aquinas 1987, 19-23).

Beckett's rhetorical style articulates the realisation that everything in the end leads to a state of nothingness and unknowing. What is more important, he deals with how this process develops in the minds of human beings. His approach is ambiguous in that it both sympathises with the human predicament and speaks ironically of the limitations of the mind. It would therefore be incorrect to say that Beckett explores the concept of God *per se.* As mentioned, he rather deals with the way in which the human mind wrestles with, among other concepts, the concept of God. In other words, he articulates and deconstructs the intellectual circumstances surrounding the human condition.

One prominent aspect of this articulation of the condition of being-in-the-world deals with frustration or failure. That is to say, in his works Beckett maps the way in which human beings search for, but fail to find, a further dimension. He thus examines aspects that often have been neglected in literature so far: the attitudes of those who are searching, but whose search does not come into fruition. Beckett's protagonists lead their spiritual lives in a limbo or a no-man's-land, where an unheroic quest for insight continues, but where there is no final answer to be had. They probably demand too much of their senses or it can also be that their scepticism hampers their search. In any case, the result is that they are plunged into depression. Julia Kristeva's notion of "the speech of the depressed [as] repetitive and monotonous" is enlightening in relation to Beckett's texts (Kristeva 1987; 1989, 33). Her diagnosis about the behaviour of the depressed that follows reminds the reader of many a frustrated Beckettian character.

> Faced with the impossibility of concatenating, they utter sentences that are interrupted, exhausted, come to a standstill. Even phrases they cannot formulate. A repetitive rhythm, a monotonous melody emerge and dominate the broken logical sequences, changing them into recurring, obsessive litanies. Finally, when that frugal musicality becomes exhausted in its turn, or simply does not succeed in becoming established on account of the pressure of silence, the melancholy person appears to stop cognizing as well as uttering, sinking into the blankness of asymbolia or the excess of an unorderable cognitive chaos.
>
> (Kristeva 1987; 1989, 33)

The opening lines of **"Texts for Nothing"** (1958)—one of the more extensive pieces in Beckett's selection of shorter prose with its thirteen monologues—provide an example of this type of discourse. Here, the depressive speaker makes numerous efforts to express his dejection and despondency, and he succeeds to articulate a sense of failure by producing those incomplete or unutterable sentences, interruptions, repetitions, and monotonous melodies that Kristeva discusses in her diagnosis:

> Suddenly, no, at last, long last, I couldn't any more, I couldn't go on. Someone said, You can't stay here. I couldn't stay there and I couldn't go on. I'll describe the place, that's unimportant. The top, very flat, of a mountain, no, a hill, but so wild, so wild, enough. [. . .] How can I go on, I shouldn't have begun, no, I had to begin. Someone said, perhaps the same, What possessed you to come? I could have stayed in my den, snug and dry, I couldn't. My den, I'll describe it, no, I can't. It's simple, I can do nothing any more, that's what you think.

> (Beckett 1984, 71)

Beckett's protagonists are often, as in this case, entrapped by temporal and spatial confinement. They lead their lives as if they had died and then been resurrected in the textual space which they now inhabit. Here, they ramble on about their existential circumstances and their corporeal and spiritual suffering. This passage plays with contrasts by juxtaposing active and passive expressions interspersed with curbing negations, such as "suddenly", "no," "couldn't go on", "I shouldn't have begun, no, I had to begin." The sentences in this passage represent, what Kristeva in a psychoanalytic context calls, "recurring, obsessive litanies." Such an allusion to a series of petitions usually recited by the clergy and responded to in a recurring formula by the congregation in churches or processions is apt in this context, since a liturgical register permeates Beckettian language. His ruptured register may thwart any smooth transitions from the nameable to the unnameable, but it is precisely in this limbo of despair and nothingness that Beckett's protagonists belong. In the eyes of the reader, their way of clutching at illusions or mirages is tragi-comical and moving, but unmistakably human. Striving for coherence and meaning in life, these speakers are reduced to trying, failing, and beginning afresh on a never-ending continuum.

If Beckett's protagonists suffer severe depressions in their Sisyphean predicament, however, they invariably find ways of using their negative stance in constructive ways. For example, negative ways of thinking in Beckett agrees with apophatic notions of God as indefinable, but there is also the idea that negativity and depression contain comic aspects. In my opinion John Calder misses this point, when he concentrates on Beckett's serious approach to "the horrors of human existence [sic]", since his texts are equally poised between the tragic and the comic. The oscillation between these perspectives produces an alternative rhetorical model when describing existential possibilities and predicaments. The reader may laugh at the unfortunate Malone, but at the same time he or she recognises or, rather, realises

truths about the human condition in Malone's monologic discourse. As Martin Esslin puts it, the difference between the classical heroes and Beckett's anti-heroes is that the former are aware of the extent of their crisis or dilemma, whereas the latter "are mostly unaware of the depth of their predicament" (Calder 1986, 12 and 17). Beckett's favourite rhetorical images, the mind and the mouth, are thus tools for expressing the anxieties of our time. His protagonists are figures of thought, which represent mental conditions or perspectives. They are Cartesian in their individualism, since thinking equals being in Beckett, but also in their constant inquiring into their circumstances.

Lance St. John Butler discusses this ontological condition in his *Samuel Beckett and the Meaning of Being* (1984). He employs philosophical approaches developed by Martin Heidegger, Jean-Paul Sartre, and Friedrich Hegel on Beckett's works. In the course of his Heideggerian analysis, he mentions Beckett's preoccupation with the concept of "nothingness". Butler argues that his

> fiction in particular abounds with characters terrified of "nothing", depending on "nothing", needing "nothing" in a way that makes it quite plain that this nothing is not just a "not something". And the state of mind of the Beckettian narrator is rarely specific fear of things within-the-world, but it is not comfort and freedom from everything like fear either; it is *Angst*.

> (Butler 1984, 47)

Butler devotes five pages of his book to discussing this aspect of Beckett's work. He refers to nothingness in *Murphy* (1938), to the character Mr. K*not*t [italics added] in *Watt* (1953), to *Texts for Nothing* (1958), and to "a scatter of references to nothingness in most of the work" (Butler 1984, 49). This Heideggerian approach to *Angst* and *Nichts* is apt, and may be developed in various ways. Bryden, for example, touches on the "desert experience" of Beckett's speakers in her book on Beckett and the idea of God (Bryden 1998, 164). She emphasises the atmosphere of calm suffering that these speakers experience in their sparse circumstances (Bryden 1998, 163-88).

In my opinion, Beckett's recurring preoccupation or obsession with the concept of nothingness can also be a secularised and tentative search for the concept of God. His speakers' cry for nothingness may appear desperate and dry in the light of modern agnosticism and atheism, but it is a powerful articulation of hope, and strikes me as one of the most moving and provocative of prayers. The remainder of my paper will examine Beckett's concentration on nothingness in selected shorter texts to see if it overlaps with questions about the negative theological concept of apophaticism and of the absence of God.

As mentioned, **"Texts for Nothing"** involves a series of monologues.[1] Here, the presence of life and the absence of God converge in certain eternal questions. Beckett frequently articulates these questions by way of negations. There are negative analyses of the concept of being as in the eighth text: "I'm a mere ventriloquist's dummy, I feel nothing, say nothing, he holds me in his arms and moves my lips with a string, with a fish-hook, no, no need of lips, all is dark, there is no one." Furthermore, there are reflections on prayer and belief as in the ninth text: "If I said, there's a way out there, there's a way out somewhere, the rest would come. What am I waiting for then, to say it? To believe it? And what does that mean, the rest? Shall I answer, try and answer, or go on as though I had asked nothing?" Beckett also expresses the notion that human beings can never rule out the possibility of living by, through, and for a Deity in the eleventh text: "What am I saying, scattered, isn't that just what I'm not, I was wandering, my mind was wandering, just the very thing I'm not. And it's still the same old road I'm trudging, up yes and down no, towards one yet to be named, so that he may leave me in peace, be no more, have never been" (Beckett 1984, 97, 100, and 107). The unknowable and unnameable figure in this passage can represent the concept of God. He has "never been", that is to say, he represents Nothingness, and yet the speaker is constantly searching for this elusive figure.

"Texts for Nothing" articulates the idea that although human beings live in a lonely void, they are constantly reaching out for someone or something that is Other. Further down in the eleventh text, for example, Beckett's speaker talks about the loss of contact and the urge to communicate: "I don't speak to him any more, I don't speak to me any more, I have no one left to speak to, and I speak, a voice speaks that can be none but mine, since there is none but me" (Beckett 1984, 109). This inevitable urge to communicate in Beckett can represent a conscious or unconscious urge to pray. Such an urge includes the constant but vain search of the ultimate expression for the meaning of existence. As the speaker puts it:

> No, something better must be found, a better reason, for this to stop, another word, a better idea, to put in the negative, a new no, to cancel all the others, all the old noes that buried me down here, deep in this place which is not one, which is merely a moment for the time being eternal, which is called here, and in this being which is called me and is not one, and in this impossible voice, all the old noes dangling in the dark and swaying like a ladder of smoke, yes, a new no, that none says twice, whose drop will fall and let me down, shadow and babble, to an absence less vain than inexistence.
>
> (Beckett 1984, 109-10)

Nothingness and absence are thus two concepts that express the inexpressible in Beckett. Human language, with its possibilities and its limitations, demands explanations, but Beckett's apophaticism tells the reader that the inability and the refusal to explain and to depict can provide a more truthful picture than any description. If we accept that notions of "Being" or of "God" can best be expressed by silence, for example, then this admission provides us with further insights about these elusive concepts.

The apophatic or negative approach will enable us "to make possible a deeper birth, a deeper death, or resurrection in and out of this murmur of memory and dream", to quote the speaker in the twelfth text of **"Texts for Nothing"**. It will help us see the invisible, or as the thirteenth text in this collection puts it: "there's a voice without a mouth, and somewhere a kind of hearing, something compelled to hear, and somewhere a hand, or if not a hand something somewhere that can leave a trace, of what is made, of what is said, you can't do with less, no, that's romancing, more romancing, there's nothing but a voice murmuring a trace" (Beckett 1984, 111 and 113). This is probably an apophatic assessment of the Divine in our age. Here, Beckett articulates the Heideggerian or Romantic contention that today we can merely see traces of the Deity. There are allusions to, and echoes of, biblical notions in contemporary Western culture, for example, but the idea of God as the centre is now largely deconstructed and dispersed. In our Derridean age, we are reduced to analysing the remaining trace itself. Beckett's texts often allude to the detrimental effects of such a circumscription.

Furthermore, Beckett's shorter texts **"The Lost Ones"**, **"Afar a Bird",** and **"Closed Space"** (1984) extend his references to the apophatic.[2] **"The Lost Ones"** focuses on the way in which human beings are constantly searching for another indefinable dimension. The first sentence articulates this sense of loss: "Abode where lost bodies roam each searching for its lost one" (Beckett 1984, 159). It talks about searching eyes and about souls entrapped in enclosed spaces. In brief, it discusses the ubiquitous concept of longing and waiting in society. Beckett's clinical analysis of the human condition in **"The Lost Ones"** may not literally revolve around the spiritual poverty or search, but by concentrating on the practical or prosaic qualities of life, he makes it abundantly clear that there is an existential dimension missing here.

"Afar a Bird" includes the enigmatic words: "something divines me, divines us" (Beckett 1984, 195). The ambiguity of these words lies in the way in which the verb "to divine" means "to discover" and "to bless". Still, Beckett's statement converges in evoking the notion that we may not be alone, after all, and that there may be a force that affects our lives. This presumptive link between humankind and an invisible, unnameable source is, I find, the crucial centre around which Beckett's œuvre revolves. The human search may appear banal and worldly, as in Winnie's self-comforting monologue about the trivialities of life in *Happy Days,* but it reaches out to an invisible "ear" and "hand". Beckett employs the deluded voice of Winnie to represent the extensive degree of deception in wordly existence. In addition, however, Winnie's monologue points to our compulsion or urge to communicate and to be seen. This aspect of the Beckettian discourse can remind us of the secular need for communication and intimacy, but it can also remind us of our need for prayer and divine intervention.

To return to Beckett's short story **"Afar a Bird",** the expression "something divines me, divines us" is a cataphatic admission that there is an active intelligence beyond ours. Further on in the same sentence, the speaker reveals that "I can see him in my mind, there divining us, hands and head a little heap, the hours pass, he is still, he seeks a voice for me, it's impossible I should have a voice and I have none, he'll find one for me". Moreover, the reader here learns that the face of the one who divines the world is hidden, which refers to the apophatic notion of the invisibility of God. Additional allusions, this time to an interaction between a Christlike figure, who takes on the sins of the world, and a suffering human being appear in the passage that follows: "he is fled, I'm inside, he'll do himself to death, because of me, I'll live it with him. I'll live his death, the end of his life and then his death, step by step" (Beckett 1984, 195-96). This passage alludes to how the Passion of Christ epitomises the failures and the weaknesses of humankind, but that it also provides meaning to such shortcomings. Christ's sufferings remind us of our own predicaments, but they also comfort us, as Beckett's passage shows. There may be no God on earth, since "he is fled", but the myth of Christ lives on. The statement "I'll live it with him" suggests that human suffering is inevitable and inextricably linked with the Passion, but that it becomes bearable through this notion of sharing the pain with fellow sufferers.

Stirrings Still and **"What is the Word"** make up parts four and five in *As the Story Was Told: Uncollected and Late Prose* (1990). In these his last two texts, the preoccupation with limitations in this worldly existence, with repetition, with longing, with searching, with waiting comes to a head. As I see it, the concepts of absence and of nothingness are the underlying essential concepts behind all these various activities. The fact that the speaker here addresses, denies or curses an absent force, which cannot be expected to appear and which is nothing, but which never ceases to be the object of desire and longing, suggests a concern with the apophatic.

Stirrings Still is atypical of Beckett in that it deals with a human being, whose spirit moves to a point "high above the earth" (Beckett 1984, 113-14). It is typical of Beckett, however, in that it concentrates on the interaction between a human being and the quest for a further dimension. As the speaker informs us, it "was [. . .] in the guise of a more or less reasonable being that he emerged at last he knew not how into the outer world" (Beckett 1990, 121). *Stirrings Still* also alludes to how a search for further spiritual dimensions can be made visible by using negatives, such as dwelling on the concepts of "darkness", "death," "decay", and "despair". For example, references to the "fleeting dark of night" here reminds the reader of the dark night of the Spanish Carmelite St. John of the Cross (1542-1591). The latter dark night is a metaphor for the darkness of the soul, which the Christian has to experience, before he or she can enter the condition of divine light in a spiritual sense. As in the apophatic tradition, human language fails to define the human condition in Beckett's shorter texts, but the protagonists may approach its meaning by acknowledging aspects of "limitation", "negation" and "renunciation", which are inevitably part of the human condition. The mystery of this search can thus be experienced as the "dark night of the soul", in John of the Cross, or as absence, as in Walter Hilton (c. 1340-1396). Human life becomes a long wait for *deus absconditus,* and this tallies with the fact that the concept of "waiting" is the warp and woof of Beckett's œuvre.

The last shorter text that Beckett published, **"What is the Word,"** reminds the reader of a modernist poem and articulates the way in which existence, perception, and inspiration peter out and leave a void in the twilight zone of old age. The last few lines read as follows:

> glimpse—
> seem to glimpse—
> need to seem to glimpse—
> afaint afar away over there what—
> folly for to need to seem to glimpse
>   afaint afar away over there what—
> what—
> what is the word—
> what is the word [.]

(Beckett 1990, 134)

From a theological point of view, this passage exemplifies how some of Beckett's final words play with the dichotomy between the apophatic and the cataphatic. Our need for verbalising and visualising an absent Other, which attracts us, but which, we think, constantly eludes and evades us and the futility of these attempts crystallise in the fragments "need to seem to glimpse" and "folly for to need to seem to glimpse". This stanza-like text again stresses the way in which human beings cannot but pose questions, which never lead to any conclusive answers, about the characteristics and the whereabouts of, say, God.

The recurring term in this prose poem, "the word", is ambiguous. It alludes both to the Johannean metaphor "the Word" as Christ—one aspect of a triune God—and to the secular meaning of language and the notion of the creative word. The sacred aspect of the question "what is the word" involves the idea that God is absent, unknown, and unnameable from a human perspective. As my paper has shown, these adjectives "absent", "unknown", and "unnameable", constantly recur in the writings of Beckett. The apophatic approach therefore throws light on the mechanics behind the Beckettian discourse.

Notes

1. Samuel Beckett's "Texts for Nothing" were originally published in French in *Nouvelles et textes pour rien* (1958). They were then published in the USA in an edition which also included "The Expelled", "The Calmative", and "The End", entitled *Stories and Texts for Nothing* (1967).

2. Samuel Beckett's "The Lost Ones" and "Afar a Bird" were originally published in French as *Le Dépeupleur* (1970) and *Au loin un oiseau* (1973), and "Closed Space" was included in *Pour finir encore et autres foirades* (1976). These texts were subsequently published in English by John Calder in Beckett's *Collected Shorter Prose 1945-80* (1984).

Works Cited

Aquinas, St. Thomas, *Faith, Reason and Theology: Questions I-IV of his Commentary on the De Trinitate of Boethius* [*Expositio super librum Boethii De trinitate*] trans. with intro and notes by Armand Maurer (Toronto: Pontifical Institute of Mediaeval Studies, 1987).

Baldwin, Hélène L., *Samuel Beckett's Real Silence* (University Park: Pennsylvania State UP, 1981).

Barge, Laura, *God, the Quest, the Hero: Thematic Structures in Beckett's Fiction* (Chapel Hill: North Carolina Studies in Romance Languages and Literatures, 1988).

Beckett, Samuel, *Collected Shorter Prose 1945-1980* (London: John Calder, 1984).

———, *As the Story Was Told: Uncollected and Late Prose* (London: John Calder, 1990).

Bryden, Mary, *Samuel Beckett and the Idea of God* (London: Macmillan, 1998).

Butler, Lance St. John, *Samuel Beckett and the Meaning of Being: A Study in Ontological Parable* (London: Macmillan, 1984).

Calder, John (ed.), *As No Other Dare Fail: For Samuel Beckett on His 80th Birthday by His Friends and Admirers* (London and New York: John Calder and Riverrun P, 1986).

Gregory of Nyssa, *The Life of Moses*, trans., intro, and notes by Abraham J. Malherbe and Everett Ferguson, preface by John Meyendorff (New York, Ramsey, Toronto: Paulist P, 1978).

Harvey, Lawrence E., *Samuel Beckett: Poet and Critic* (Princeton: Princeton UP, 1970).

Hoeden, Jean van der, *Samuel Beckett et la question de Dieu* (Paris: Les Editions du Cerf, 1997).

Kristeva, Julia, *Black Sun: Depression and Melancholia* [*Soleil Noir: Dépression et mélancolie*], trans. by Leon S. Roudiez (1987; New York: Columbia UP, 1989).

Lossky, Vladimir, *The Mystical Theology of the Eastern Church*, trans. by Members of the Fellowship of St. Alban and St. Serguis. [*Essai sur la Théologie Mystique de l'Eglise d'Orient*] (1957; Cambridge and London: James Clarke, 1968).

Pseudo-Dionysius, *The Complete Works*, trans by Colm Luibheid (New York and Mahwah: Paulist P, 1987).

Vahanian, Gabriel, *The Death of God: The Culture of Our Post-Christian Era* (1957; New York: George Braziller, 1967).

Wolosky, Shira, "The Negative Way Negated: Samuel Beckett, Counter-Mystic", in *Language Mysticism: The Negative Way of Language in Eliot, Beckett, and Celan* (Stanford: Stanford UP, 1995), 90-134.

Wright, T. R., *Theology and Literature* (1988; Oxford: Basil Blackwell, 1989).

Julie Campbell (essay date 2001)

SOURCE: Campbell, Julie. "'Echo's Bones' and Beckett's Disembodied Voices." *Samuel Beckett Today* 11 (2001): 454-60.

[*In the following essay, Campbell situates Beckett's unpublished story "Echo's Bone's" within his earlier and later texts.*]

> The dead die hard, trespassers on the beyond, they must take the place as they find it, the shafts and manholes back into the muck, till such time as the lord of the manor incurs through his long acquiescence a duty of care in respect of them. They are free among the dead by all means, then their troubles are over, their natural troubles. But the debt of nature, that scandalous post-obit on one's own estate, can no more be discharged by the mere fact of kicking the bucket than descent can be made into the same stream twice. This is a true saying.

These are the first lines of **"Echo's Bones"**, an unpublished short story, which was originally planned as the final story of ***More Pricks Than Kicks*** (1934), but which did not appear, after all, in the published text. It relates Belacqua's adventures after the death that occurs in the penultimate story **"Yellow"** of *More Pricks* [*More Pricks Than Kicks*]. Here we see that death isn't the end of it all for Belacqua. Perhaps fittingly, as his name is borrowed from Dante, we are introduced to an after-life in which a "debt" must "be discharged"; "natural troubles" are over, but new, posthumous troubles begin.

Belacqua seems to be revisiting the living world as a ghost. He can smoke (Romeo and Juliet cigars), drink (rum and champagne), eat (garlic), but he cannot see his reflection (this is not Narcissus), and he throws no shadow. Nor has his death removed women's fascination for him. He is discovered, sitting on a fence, "picking his nose between cigars", and wondering "if his lifeless condition were not all a dream and if on the whole he had not been a great deal deader before than after his formal departure, so to speak, from among the quick" (1). He has been enjoying, since death, "a beatitude of sloth [. . .] in the "womb-tomb", but on his return to the world as a ghost he finds, "My soul begins to be idly goaded and racked, all the old pains and aches of my soul-junk return!" (2). It is as if it is in the living world, rather than the afterlife, that torment exists, and he has been returned there for "major discipline" (2).

However, if this is the living world that Belacqua now inhabits, it has a strange and dreamlike quality. Zabbrovina, the woman he first encounters after he has been dead for at least forty days, turns, suddenly, into a Gorgon, even as she is seducing him: "She tossed back the hissing vipers of her hair, her entire body coquetted and writhed like a rope, framed into a bawdy akimbo [. . .]" (6). Belacqua appears to be facing a number of heroic tests, for his next encounter is with Lord Gall of Wormwood, a giant, who carries him off to a nest high in a tree. Yet again, it is his sexual prowess (not one of the living Balacqua's most salient features) which is required. Lord Gall requires him to impregnate Lady Gall with a son and heir to ensure that Wormwood does not fall into the hands of his arch-enemy, the Baron, who will otherwise inherit it by default. They travel to the castle on the back of an ostrich; Belacqua fulfils his function, we are told, but sires a girl rather than the required boy. We seem to have entered a fairy-tale world, reminiscent of Lewis Carroll's Wonderland or Looking-Glass World, with additional bawdy developments (echoing Boccaccio's *Decameron*), where birds speak and characters transform and nothing seems to be as it should be.

At the end of the story, Belacqua is shown suddenly sitting on his headstone, a scene described as "classico-romantic" (19). A man, Mick Doyle (the groundsman from **"Draff"**, the narrator tells the reader), is digging up Belacqua's grave, in order to "snatch" the body. In this scene, Belacqua reflects upon his life: "I daresay my life was a derogation and an impudence [. . .] which it was my duty, nay should have been my pleasure, to nip in the womb" (22). The scene begins to take on a distinctly Gothic air:

> What a scene when you come to think of it! Belacqua petrified link-boy, the scattered guts of ground, the ponderous anxiomaniac on the brink in the nude like a fly on the edge of a sore [. . .] in the grey flows of tramontane, the hundreds of headstones sighing and gleaming like bones, the hamper, mattock, shovel, spade and axe, cabal of vipers, most malignant, the clothes-basket a coffin in its own way, and of course, the proscribed hush of great solemnity broken only by the sea convulsed in one of those dreams, ah one of those dreams, the submarine wallowing and hooting on the beach like an absolute fool, and dawn toddling down the mountains. What a scene!
>
> (27)

There is no body in the coffin, but this mystery is not resolved. The story finishes with the enigmatic "So it goes in the world" (28).

The fact that this story did not get published does mean that the very special quality of its humour and strangeness has been shut out of the Beckett canon. The Lewis Carroll quality of the world depicted is also present in the early manuscripts of *Watt* that feature a big bird and transformation scenes. But it is these episodes that Beckett omitted from the final version of the novel, thus choosing to suppress the fantastic elements in the earlier manuscripts that feature the protagonist Quin. *Watt* is a strange and perplexing text as it survives, and it could well be that Beckett wanted to preserve this very particular kind of mystery, which has far less recourse to rather more obviously fantastic situations.

Fantastic or Gothic elements are treated quite differently in *More Pricks* and the unpublished story. In *More Pricks*, the demarcation between life and death is often left intentionally vague, whereas in **"Echo's Bones"** Belacqua's death is made certain and often referred to in the story. The kind of 'this world/other world' that **"Echo's Bones"** borrows from Carroll and Gothic is, in *More Pricks*, a suggestion of a purgatorial afterlife, with a different kind of mystery and strangeness. Beckett can be seen to be challenging the life/death divide in a new and disturbing way, and thus circumventing the 'naturalisation' that the familiarity with existing conventions allows. There is also the question of tone. Although there are many funny moments in *More Pricks*, **"Echo's Bones"** treats death and purgatory with such lightness—more so than anywhere else in Beckett—that it would perhaps have given the volume of stories too bathetic a conclusion. Death, of course, is often treated humorously by Beckett—the narrator of **"First Love"** declares that "Personally I have no bone to pick with graveyards" (1984, 1)—but the humour always has a distinct edge to it, a darkness and a serious quality that are not found in **"Echo's Bones"**.

Many elements of **"Echo's Bones"**, however, are shared with Beckett's later writings: the strong focus on death and the afterlife; the lament of having been born; the oxymoronic "womb-tomb" (in one place referred to as "the lush plush of the womby-tomby", 7); the torments of living and the simultaneous desire for and dread of non-existence. Belacqua inhabits the story in an "in-between" space, dead but within the living world, re-calling those interstitial spaces, where characters are somehow in between life and death that haunt Beckett's work. This story points to directions Beckett did not follow while also containing essential features that appear in later works.

The title **"Echo's Bones"**, of course, comes from Ovid's story of Narcissus and Echo in the *Metamorphoses*. Thomas Hunkeler has recently discussed the importance of the Echo myth in Beckett's work, emphasising, for example, the associations evoked by the term 'Echo's bones' throughout Beckett's oeuvre. The use of the myth is clearly apparent in work dating from the thirties: alongside the unpublished story, there is another "Echo's Bones", the title poem of *Echo's Bones and Other Precipitates*. Although it could be argued that Beckett's play with the Echo myth is primarily 'intertextual play', I aim to show that it is the source of recurrent intratextual images in Beckett's works, such as closed spaces or refuges, the limbo world of neither life nor death, and the disembodied voice. Echo can also be seen to stand for repetition with a difference, an essential strategy of Beckett's intratextual play.

In Ovid's story, Echo is called "resounding Echo, who could neither hold her peace when others spoke, nor yet begin to speak till others had addressed her" (7). She is punished by Juno for her talkativeness, and as a result can only repeat the last words she hears. Her rejection by Narcissus causes her to hide "her shamed face among the foliage, and [she] lives from that time on in lonely caves":

> But still, though spurned, her love remains and grows on grief; her sleepless cares waste away her wretched form; she becomes gaunt and wrinkled and all moisture fades from her body into the air. Only her voice and her bones remain: then, only voice; for they say that her bones turned to stone. She hides in woods and is seen no more upon the mountain sides; but all may hear her, for voice, and voice alone, still lives within her.
>
> (Ovid, 8)

This image of Echo fading away to voice and bone, voice and stone seems to have fascinated Beckett. Echo's plight highlights an important area of intratex-

tual play, or "recollection by invention" in H. Porter Abbott's terms (28). The bone and stone of the Echo story can be recognised in the 'skullscapes' that seem to represent, in part, the lonely cave to which Echo withdraws, as well as the refuge inside the head from which the Beckettian voices speak echoing other voices. In *The Unnamable* the voice speaks of "a head . . . [of] solid, solid bone, and you embedded in it, like a fossil in the rock" (1979, 361-2), whereas in *Texts for Nothing* there is mention of an "ivory dungeon" (1986, 76). Then, too, *The Unnamable* partially echoes the works that went before and is echoed by those that follow.

These spaces, or skullscapes, link up with "the Limbo and the wombtomb" of *Dream of Fair to Middling Women* (121) as well as **"Echo's Bones"**. Phil Baker has discussed this as a kind of "narcissistic self-containment (Beckett's 'womb/tomb' in the head)" (118). Angela Moorjani describes this space as "the tomblike womb and the womblike tomb in the darkness of the mind in which the living are unborn and the dead do not die" (21). What Baker has described as the "withdrawal of interest from the outside world" (119) or "inward turning of the libido" (115) is apparent in many of Beckett's characters. Such withdrawal can be read as a response to the kind of rejection by others suffered by Echo. For example, the protagonist in **"First Love"** is expelled from his secure space in the family home and seeks refuge again with Lulu; he makes a "womb/tomb"-like space by turning the sofa around: "Then I climbed back, like a dog into its basket" (1986, 14).

There is an important connection between stones and death, so essential in terms of Echo's story, in Beckett's own life:

> Beckett's relationship to stones, which he called "almost a love relationship," was associated by Beckett himself with death [. . .]. As a child he frequently picked up stones from the beach and carried them home, where he built nests for them and put them in trees to protect them from the waves and other dangers. On the same occasion, Beckett mentioned Sigmund Freud, who had once written that man carried with him a kind of congenital yearning for the mineral kingdom.
>
> (Büttner, 163, n. 200)

In a sense Beckett's childhood play with stones continues in his adult creativity. Daniel Albright speaks of how in Beckett's narratives "every identity, every predicated self is a stone" (181). Malone speaks of the imaginary play space he creates "with my little suns and moons that I hang aloft and my pockets full of pebbles stand for men and their seasons" (1979, 217). Molloy, famously, plays with his sucking stones: creating a long and elaborate system only to, characteristically, explode this time-consuming play with self-mockery: "I didn't give a tinker's curse" (1979, 69).

A voice coming from somewhere unknown, a disembodied voice, is encountered with increasing frequency in Beckett's works. Eventually Echo is no more than a disembodied voice: "Only her voice and her bones remain: then, only voice; for they say that her bones were turned to stone [. . .] all may hear her, for voice, and voice alone, still lives in her" (Ovid, 8). Echo's voice emanates from her bones, and then from stone; it is a voice from the dead that "still lives" and echoes the voices of the living, and thus is somehow simultaneously dead and alive. Interesting, too, is the fact that Echo's punishment does not end with her death: she is still forced to repeat the voices of others. In *The Unnamable,* the disembodied voice resembles Echo's, and indeed there is nothing else: "all is a question of voices" (1979, 317).

One intriguing element of this play with the voice is the way in which it is intimated that it is repeating what it is told, an essential feature of Echo. This is a recurring phenomenon; Molloy speaks of such a voice: "I heard a voice telling me not to fret, that help was coming. Literally" (1979, 84). Moran, too, reports about "a voice telling me things. I was getting to know it better now, to understand what it wanted" (1979, 162). These voices bring "comfort", or tell the recipient "to write a report" (1979, 162). In *The Unnamable* there is the recognition that, like Echo, "there are no words but the words of others" (1979, 288); "I'm in words, made of words, others' words" (1979, 355). This turns the voice into a passive receiver: "a transformer in which sound is tuned" (Beckett 1979, 327) or into "a mere ventriloquist's dummy" (1986, 97), as the voice of *Texts for Nothing* VIII says of itself. *How It Is* reiterates this passivity: "I say it as I hear it" (7) as do **Company** and the short pieces **"Heard in the Dark I and II",** in which the voice speaks to a passive receiver addressed as "you". The opening line of **Company**: "A voice comes to one in the dark" gives the voice a sense of being disembodied, a ghostly emanation. With **Fizzle** 4, "I gave up before birth", there is a movement from the undead, still living voice of Echo, intoning, "he [. . .] will die, I won't die [. . .] I'll be inside, he'll rot, I won't rot, there will be nothing of him left but bones, I'll be inside [. . .]", to an unborn voice that declares "I gave up before birth [. . .] I didn't have a life" (1984, 197). These passages recall Beckett's own feeling that he had never really been born (see Harvey, 247). The voice seems to live in an unreal, twilight space: a narrative play space of impossible existence/nonexistence. If we relate this space to Beckett's own words about creation, "You hear it a certain way in your head" (qtd. in Knowlson, 596), then the resemblance to Echo as a 'passive receiver' becomes apparent. "In the end," Beckett said, "you don't know who is speaking" (qtd. in Juliet, 157). And with his contention that "you write in order to be able to breathe" (qtd. in Juliet, 152f.), there is a strong sense of the imperative that seems to lie behind the voice in *The Unnamable:* at a loss as to where the words come from, but under the obligation to repeat them.

Works Cited

Abbott, H. Porter, *Beckett Writing Beckett: The Author in the Autograph* (Ithaca, NY: Cornell U P, 1996).

Albright, Daniel, *Representation and the Imagination* (Chicago: U of Chicago P, 1981).

Baker, Phil, *Beckett and the Mythology of Psychoanalysis* (London: Macmillan, 1997).

Beckett, Samuel, *Echo's Bones and Other Precipitates* (Paris: Europa P, 1935), reprinted in *Poems in English* (London: John Calder, 1961).

———, "Echo's Bones", typescript B389/122, Beckett Collection at the Baker Library, Dartmouth College, New Hampshire.

———, "Watt" manuscript, composite T and Tccms/inc with A revision and A note S, Harry Ransom Humanities Research Center, U of Texas at Austin.

———, *Watt* (London: John Calder, 1963).

———, *More Pricks Than Kicks* (London: Calder and Boyars, 1970).

———, *Murphy* (London: Picador, 1973).

———, *Mercier and Camier* (London: Picador, 1974).

———, *The Beckett Trilogy: Molloy; Malone Dies; The Unnamable* (London: Picador, 1979).

———, *Company* (London: John Calder, 1980).

———, *Collected Shorter Prose* (London: John Calder, 1984).

———, *How It Is* (London: John Calder, 1985).

———, *Dream of Fair to Middling Women* (London: Calder, 1993).

Büttner, Gottfried, *Samuel Beckett's Novel "Watt"* (Philadelphia: U of Pennsylvania P, 1984).

Harvey, Lawrence E., *Samuel Beckett: Poet and Critic* (Princeton: Princeton UP, 1970).

Hunkeler, Thomas, *Echos de l'ego dans l'oeuvre de Samuel Beckett* (Paris: L'Harmattan, 1997).

Juliet, Charles, *Conversations with Samuel Beckett and Bram van Velde,* trans. by Janey Tucker (Leiden: Academic P, 1995).

Knowlson, James, *Damned to Fame: The Life of Samuel Beckett* (London: Bloomsbury, 1996).

Moorjani, Angela, "Beckett's Devious Deictics", in *Rethinking Beckett: A Collection of Critical Essays,* ed. by Lance St. John Butler and Robin J. Davis (London: Macmillan, 1990), 20-30.

Ovid, "Narcissus and Echo" from the *Metamorphoses,* trans. by Frank Julius Miller, qtd. in *The Narcissus Theme in Western European Literature up to the Early 19th Century,* by Louise Vinge, trans. by Robert Dewsnap et al. (Skånska Centraltryckeriet, Lund: Gleeerups, 1967).

Joseph F. Connelly (essay date 2001)

SOURCE: Connelly, Joseph F. "The Shared Aesthetic of Jack Yeats and Beckett: *More Pricks than Kicks*." *Notes on Modern Irish Literature* 13 (2001): 47-54.

[*In the following essay, Connelly investigates the relationship between the short stories in* More Pricks than Kicks *and the visual arts, particularly the work of the Irish painter Jack Yeats.*]

When the Irish short story comes under scrutiny, Samuel Beckett's collection *More Pricks than Kicks* (1934) is neither at the forefront nor, at least, even mentioned. As a writer of prose fiction, Beckett is an anomaly as he is considered more French than Irish, and his reputation rests in theater and the novel originally in French and later translated into English. The collection *MPTK* [*More Pricks Than Kicks*] is regarded as apprentice work, a curiosity that interests a handful of readers who then may label the stories as neglected in light of the later and more thought provoking fiction.

My approach in examining *MPTK* as short pieces that constitute a whole is twofold: to analyze Beckett's relationship with the visual artists, and to establish an aesthetic from which the stories may have evolved. The Irish painter Jack B. Yeats, whom Beckett befriended in 1931, demonstrates the major connection between Beckett and the visual artists, in particular their shared aesthetic, which various commentators have acknowledged.[1] This early attitude he brings to the writing of fiction does not readily apply to the later and longer works whose character portrayal becomes almost exclusively interior, unlike the combination of narrative and still worked throughout *MPTK.* The analysis of the short fiction in this manner suggests an awareness that enhances appreciation of the collection based in visual perspectives. When placed against the framework of the visual artists, the stories emerge more formally and less avant garde than previously considered.

Anne Cremin's article "Friend Game" establishes a beginning in this study by outlining Beckett's numerous associations with European visual artists and by focusing on themes, styles, and in general the modernist mode of abstract imagery and thought associated with Beckett's chosen contemporaries. She uses a quotation from Beckett's review of Thomas MacGreevy's monograph, *Jack B. Yeats: An Appreciation and an Introduction* (1945), to show Beckett's emphasis on artistry when he ranks the painter

> . . . with the great of our time, Kandinsky and Klee, Bellmer and Bram van Velde, Rouault and Braque, because he brings light as only the great dare to bring light, to the issueless Predicament of existence, reduces the dark where there might have been, mathematically at least a door.
>
> (85)

In disagreeing with MacGreevy's praise of Yeats' nationalism and citing "the issueless Predicament of existence," Beckett notes the objectivity and the disengagement of the artist from his or her subject matter, and in listing Yeats among the recognized moderns. He brings the painter to the forefront when he is just becoming known on the continent while MacGreevy places Yeats within the literary revival, viewed by Beckett as restrictive.[2]

Commentators have noted the relationship of writer and painter in their depictions of figures on the edge of society, the pairing of characters and the subtle humor in their handling.[3] More recent studies focus on the nature and effect of their relationship. Hilary Pyle, in *Yeats: Portrait of an Artistic Family* (1997) explains ". . . the young writer was immediately impressed, as much by Yeats' self-reliance in his work and determination to remain independent, as by the individual canvases which became a constant visual stimulus to him" (232). He purchased three Yeats' paintings, as well as other artists' over his lifetime, and his studied interest in the visual arts displays a broad and meticulous knowledge. In the late 1920s, as Lois Gordon notes, Beckett kept a notebook of the design of paintings he had studied which were later used in stage settings (33). More important to the considerations of this paper are the seven sketchbooks of Yeats, on display in his studio where Yeats, Beckett, and others met on a regular basis. They have practical considerations in the painter's development as individual pictures and in their narrative qualities. As Bruce Arnold states:

> They have the realization of his art and not its starting. Something has happened to him as a storyteller . . . in the way his books are narratives, a succession of images running through the individual pages and from page to page, even from book to book, for the total work consists of no less than seven volumes of drawings. He achieves a creative transmutation, from the static singleness of the moment with no before or afterwards, which is peculiar to painting, towards the progression of narrative idea, the moment through a tale or story, a sequence of events, peculiar to writing. He comes near to achieving the virtually impossible synthesis of two quite different forms.
>
> (259)

The relationship begins at an opportune time when Beckett is writing and publishing *MPTK;* their developing friendship displays mutual appreciation and discovery of like sensibilities. Yeats is painting hybrid picture-narratives at the same time that Beckett is writing narratives that employ detailing and positioning of imagery associated with the visual arts.

Beckett maintains his friendship with Yeats despite long separations during the war and Beckett's permanent residence in Paris. While abroad, his circle of companions includes the visual artists Avigdor Arikha, Bram van Velde, Alberto Giacometti, Jasper Johns, and Stanley William Hayter. He did collaborative projects with some, and also purchased individual works that he gave away as personal gifts. What characterizes the varied relationships is a common taste among the contemporaries based on the mystery of human existence and more particularly on the space and silence that encompass and separate individuals. This distancing also marks the modernist principle of artistic detachment from the matter of the work as Beckett wrote of Hayter: "[the] bare presence of he who does, bare presence of what is done. Impersonal, unreal work . . . Everything is recognizable, but not to be known. Strange order of things made from an order lacking objects, from objects without order" (qtd. in Cremin 87).

Commentators on Yeats emphasize his working from memory, rather than from model (Pyle, *JBY* 127-29) which may also be compared to Beckett's desire to draw from his creative imagination and not copy life. Yeats' sketchbooks and Beckett's notebooks, along with careful meditations,—perhaps silences—serve as selected memory from which painter and writer work. In relying on memory, years preceding the sketchbooks, Yeats is able to paint watercolor illustrations for Canon Hanny's *Irishmen All* (1913), by working from the chapter titles alone. They collaborated without meeting or reviewing each other's contribution (Pyle, *JBY* 105-06). In Yeats' scholarship, the watercolor "Memory Harbor" (1920), set at Rosses Point in Silgo, becomes the representation of his memory.

From childhood and during student years, Beckett is remembered for a remarkable memory from which he later develops keen awareness of and response to the difficult lives of the lower class. Sharing middle class upbringings, Beckett and Yeats observed and depict the marginalized, travelers, circus performers, laborers, and the rootless in general. Their working from memory differs in the degree each relies on it. The painter's early work as illustrator caused him to follow more faithfully external reality than did Beckett whose sympathies, formed from the past, permeated his characterizations, without reproducing types he encountered or recalled from memory. At the beginning of their friendship, Yeats' style and tone have undergone alteration. Like Beckett he visions the limitations of the human condition in light of changing world events, and the paintings reflect these complexities, especially the poverty and violence of the lower class. The overwhelming space on many of the canvases expresses the vast universe that diminishes the individual, and the flash of color and thick brush strokes points to the unknown that likewise burdens humankind. Beckett's almost total depiction of his major figures from within, especially the later fiction in French, indicates a more philosophical approach than the traditional characterization, while

spacing and positioning of image and secondary characters, presented by the distant and omniscient author, reflect little reliance on memory's storehouse. Though Bair explains that four of the ten stories of *MPTK* employ personal material (161-64), the overall portrayal of Belacqua is the creation of imagination focused on his singularity. He is neither traditional nor unique in his portrayal. The later major figures and pair of figures have less active lives than Belacqua.

The concept of space and distance identified with the creative powers is also necessary in collaborative efforts, such as *Still* (1973), with William Stanley Hayter. Out of respect for Beckett's work methods, the engraver-artist estimates seven years to complete the project, though much of the writing is already done. Over four years they meet, and except for the change of one face Beckett judged as too particular each worked independently and without editorial oversight. This collaboration differs from Yeats and Hanny's; both reveal the dependence on memory as the repository of the other artist's work, but more importantly both conserve the awareness and sensitivity of each other's approach to the completed book.

Aside from memory, collaboration requires the ability to combine, abstract, and correlate. These basic characteristics of the creative mind are extended by Yeats and Beckett in melding picture and narrative in their respective media. Arnold refers to this junction in describing Yeats' sketchbooks, while Pyle cautions the viewer to give attention to the titles of paintings as Yeats is a literary painter (Pyle *JBY*, 129). In the fragmented pieces of *MPTK,* Beckett has Belacqua alert the reader to the narrative method when he labels it "moving pauses" which he rightly judges to be an oxymoron (38). This occurs in **"Ding-Dong",** story three, that ends in the hero's flight from the woman selling prayers for her customers' salvation. The author gradually works in characters of greater eccentricity than Belacqua, such as the revelers in **"A Wet Night."** They further isolate him, as he is more thoughtful and perceptive, but still erratic and asocial, though not a figure of satire. The best synthesis of Belacqua comes from the omniscient narrator of **"What a Misfortune,"** who comments: "Say what you will, you can't keep a dead mind down" (140). While not an oxymoron, it contains a similarly dual effect that evokes the image of the lobster, from story one, and the idea that if his mind is dead, what are the minds of the others. Are they more dead?

One of Beckett's purchases, "A Morning" (also cited as "A Morning in Silgo" 1935), provides insight into their shared aesthetic. The top of the painting is bright sky, creating a clear space that becomes a characteristic of Beckett's work. The reader notes this as early as *MPTK,* in the story "yellow," when Belacqua desires to curtail the dawn, as if to stop time in his hospital room because it activates the mind. As in the Yeats' painting, the morning brings anticipation in the horseman ready to embark. Though the horseman's eyes convey apprehension, the horse and a cat have a moment of communication. This note of humor is reinforced by the pose of rearing horse and rider looking back, from the popular westerns of the time. The prelude to the action has resonance in the lives of both the painter and writer. While Silgo connotes Yeats' formative years, the date and purchase of the painting signify for Beckett the deepening of their friendship and recognition of their shared aesthetic. For Belacqua, in **"Dante and the Lobster,"** the discovery that the lobster is alive indicates his own movement to death and beyond, encapsulated in the nine stories that follow.

Yeats painted a number of singular works in series. "On the Broads" (1899) are three watercolors of the sailing vessel "The Broads," distinguished in the titles by numbers and in content by perspectives. Two are above deck, the first from behind the boat and the second on mid-deck. The third is below deck looking out at a passing ship and shore. Each is self-contained; together they form a series of stills in motion. No person is present. In **"Love and Lethe,"** the fifth story, Beckett writes the basic three scene story: post mid-day dinner conversation of mother and daughter, Belacqua's calling on Ruby and departure with her, and the stayed double suicide which the narrator explains: ". . . on this occasion, if never before or since, he achieved what he set out to do; *car,* in the words of one competent to sing of the mother: *L'Amour et la Mort-caesura-n'est queune mesme chose*" (100). Belacqua, the romantic, has resisted intimacy, accidentally firing the weapon, and tuned their quest into a non-scene worked in parody. Beckett consciously plays with the reader's anticipation when he intervenes and warns about prescribing motivations, at the end of scene one: "How he had formed this resolution to destroy himself we are quite unable to discover. The simplest course, when the motives of any deed are found subliminal to the point of defying expression, is to call that deed *ex nihlo* and have done. Which we beg leave to follow in the present instance" (89). We are asked to take in the scenes and their lively humor, and suspend judgment to the end of the story or the book or both. Beckett's building of parody through the story's rising action, the hero's bungling of its purpose, and Ruby's vision of "her life as a series of staircase jests" (88) reminds the reader of a Charlie Chaplin film with its dualities of joys and sorrows, misconceptions and unrealized achievements. While Yeats' scenes of the sailboat look to the late modern number paintings or Marilyn Monroe faces by Jasper Johns, Beckett's vignettes of Ruby and Belacqua culminate in his later dramatic work of the two tramps.

"Love and Lethe" prepares us for the next two linked stories, **"Walking Out"** and **"What a Misfortune,"**

connected by Belacqua's marriages, first to the bedridden Lucy and then to Thelma Bloggs. As in Yeats' rose paintings and those depicting performing clown and equestrian, where image or characters serve the narrative function, the sequence or movement has little consequence in that each incident is separate and contained. Yeats states his intent in a letter to Thomas Bodkin: ". . . I painted the rose alive and then followed it into the ante room of the Rose's Shadow Land, and painted another little panel of it departing. But there's nothing piano about it, not yet fussy digame" (White 151). In plan and execution his emphasis is series, not sequence, and as such discourages allegorical interpretation.

The most revealing series is the clown and the equestrian, whose relationship extends beyond their singular performance. In the first painting, "The Haute École Act" (1925), the rider and horse appear to be leaving the performance; as she rides side saddle, cradles a rose in her left arm, her eyes are lowered. The title is important as it indicates the social distinction of performance in the world of circus. In "This Grand Conversation was under the Rose" (1943), the title and picture convey the conversation's intimate nature, as it occurs *sub rosa,* the rose above their heads. The horse seems to be listening adding a note of humor. The last painting, "When the Cat's Away" (1949), further carries the humor when the clown now rides the horse; his face appears masked like Pan in a Greek drama, as she watches, relaxes, her riding hat removed, and holds what looks like a bouquet. Their roles are reversed as the horse is actively at play and enjoying the light reprieve from their usual routine. Their privacy is secure for no others are present as they are in the foreground or background of the other paintings. The title reveals what they are doing is not what the viewer has come to expect. Clown and horse are centered in a shift from their previous stances, and the imagery is less clear as Yeats now works with more vibrant coloration, whirling brush strokes, and feelings that direct the eye, in the substantive change from the earlier linear and more representative approach. Not only does the rose image indicate the private relationship of equestrian and clown; it has permanently become the painter's signature of how he works *sub rosa.* In the series' last painting, the equestrian is the onlooker, who offers her bouquet in homage to clown and horse, a gesture of mutual recognition. The depth of feeling sets off this series from the previous sailboats and roses.

A similar and gradual shift in *MPTK* comes through in "yellow," the next to last story. In the placement of stories, Beckett causes the reader to reconsider Belacqua's character as he dies in bed prior to surgery. He is now more thoughtful, though no less humorous, as he thinks of death and his various ways to handle it. His only human contacts are the nurses who remain distant. His wife, the Smeraldina, whom we learn of in the concluding story, is not by his side, as Beckett centers on Belacqua's aloneness and singularity. Statements like "The mixture is too rich," referring to the anesthetic, and "His heart was running away, the terrible yellow yerks in his skull" (174) indicate how unsuited his person is among the flow of humanity and his uniqueness in dealing with what his nature will allow. The quotations taken metaphorically lead naturally to the concluding sentence that affirms his neglect. "They had clean forgotten to osculate him" (174)! His death is an ironic compliment that raises Belacqua in the reader's esteem, as do the words of the surgeon overheard by the hero. "One of the best . . ." (174), though not spoken about him.

Amid these ironies and the compacted comic imagery of the closing pages of "yellow," Beckett prepares the reader for the fiction's final irony, which is another reconfiguration of Belacqua after his demise in the previous story. To the person Harry Capper Quin, whom we meet as the hero's best man in **"What a Misfortune,"** Beckett gives another chance on a new life and one to Belacqua also.

> . . . (Hairy) seemed to have taken on a new lease of life. . . . Perhaps the explanation of this was that while Belacqua was alive Hairy could not be himself, or, if you prefer, could be nothing else. Whereas now the defunct, such of his parts at least as might be made to fit, could be pressed into service, incorporated in the daily ellipses of Capper Quin without having to face the risk of exposure. Already Belacqua was not wholly dead, but merely mutilated.
>
> (187)

Whether the characters undergo a reversal or one character assimilates into another, Belacqua now can continue though cold in the ground in an added twist reminiscent of Yeats' clown and equestrian, in "When the cat's away." Though in different media, writer and painter retain common human nature shared by very different characters and a comic rendering that borders on the burlesque. They employ imagery of a similar nature that meets the materials of their chosen arts well. Brush strokes and words, scenes and stories, make for lively narratives that are singular moments as well; Harry as Belacqua, clown as equestrian, and vice versa heighten the liveliness.

The principle supporting the twists and turns of the stories and paintings is basic irony. Beckett works the technique to its full extent by cloning character from a different character, and in the process of Belacqua's dying integrates the imagery of marriage and holy orders. The hero's passing is a multisided and broad comedy without the crudity of slapsticks or the harshness of parody. Its realism is absurd and differs from Yeats' as the painter is less fanciful than the writer is, at this stage of development, though his works will gradually become more visionary.

A good example of a painting that coincides with the development of *MPTK* is "The Clown among the People" (1932). Leaving the performance, the clown is portrayed centering the picture in ironic position to those he passes, two of whom are distinguishable as they look contentedly at him. His face has a preoccupied look in contrast to theirs, and though he is among spectators he is alone. A tent pole behind the figure on the right is the only identifiable object except for the three figures. Short and overlapping brush strokes, among muted shadowy coloring, create a weight as if the clown is burdened. Sadness and joy mingle in the perfectly executed composition. A slight note of humor in the scene is the one figure's glance of satisfaction and admiration beside the clown who passes her and ironically may not even notice. James White commends the characters' universal quality and the significance of the human condition (14). At the time of the painting and stories of *MPTK* viewers and readers were accustomed to Yeats' subtle form of realism and confused by Beckett's convolutions which he will temper and simultaneously deepen the complexities in later writings.

In analyzing the aesthetics of Yeats and Beckett, the paper examines the backgrounds of each, and in selected paintings of Yeats interprets their approaches and concepts with those of Beckett's writing in *MPTK*. In placing pictures and stories in relative position to each other, the artists' shared and modernistic sensibilities come through. The principle of distance, so important to early modernists, is consciously maintained in the respective works at the onset of their relationship. Though neither artist is a social reformer, their blend of realism and humor suggests more than a passing interest in the human condition, as both deal sympathetically with the outcasts and rootless who people their work. They portray humanity in acts of sustaining itself, rather than justifying and evoking moods of pity and despair.

In contrast to mirroring, their realism represents as both rely on active and disciplined imaginative memories as the source of their artistry. I have attempted to present Beckett's stories as the visual artist may approach a canvas by exploring and creating scenes that utilize imagery, color and form in detailing the pictures. The latter is important in *MPTK* as the collection appears chaotic and lacking causation, and in hindsight alone are our apprehensions rectified when they are least appropriate, such as the death of Belacqua in "yellow," preceded by the lamenting **"The Smeraldina's Billet Doux."** The conscious detailing and positioning of stories and characters create a sense of detachment, like pictures in a museum, while serving the humorous tone and ironic coherence that surprise and delight the reader. In Beckett's words about Yeats' paintings, "(they reduce) the dark where there might have been . . . a door" which is also applicable to the writing of *MPTK*.

The 1930s are the appropriate decade for the young writer and seasoned painter, in the process of stylistic and conceptual adjustments, to come together and discover their mutual working endeavors. What more can we expect of consummate artists in their respective media than their unique excellences!

Notes

1. Dierdre Bair refers to the relationship as father-son (119). The Yeats commentators, Hilary Pyle in both citations and Bruce Arnold, rely on the writing of Yeats in dealing with their friendship, as does Marilyn Gaddes Rose in "Solitary Companions in Beckett and Jack B. Yeats." *Eire Ireland IV* (Summer 1969): 66-80.

2. Brian Fallon. *Irish Art 1830-1990.* Appleton, 1994, uses the term "painter of Literary Renaissance" to describe Yeats. He agrees with McGreevy in placing the nationalist tag on the painter.

3. Marilyn Gaddes Rose is the first to make the comparison.

Works Cited

Arnold, Bruce. *Jack Yeats.* New Haven: Yale UP, 1998.

Bair, Deirdre. *Samuel Beckett: A Biography.* New York and London: Harcourt Brace and Javanovich, 1978.

Beckett, Samuel. *More Pricks Than Kicks.* New York: Grove, 1972.

Cremin, Ann. "Friend Game," *Art News* 84 (May 1985): 82-89.

Gordon, Lois. *The World of Samuel Beckett, 1906-1946.* New Haven: Yale UP, 1996.

Pyle, Hilary. *Jack B. Yeats, A Biography.* London: Routledge and Kegan Paul, 1970.

———. *Portrait of an Artistic Family.* London: Merrell Halberton, 1997.

White, James. "Memory Harbor": Jack B. Yeats's Painting Process." *Yeats Studies* 2 (Bealtaine 1972): 9-17.

———. Ed. *Jack B. Yeats: Drawings and Paintings 1871-1951 A Centenary Exhibition.* London: Martin Secker and Warburg, 1971.

Adrian Hunter (essay date April 2001)

SOURCE: Hunter, Adrian. "Beckett and the Joycean Short Story." *Essays in Criticism* 51, no. 2 (April 2001): 230-44.

[*In the following essay, Hunter determines the influence of Joyce's* Dubliners *on* More Pricks than Kicks.]

Reviewing *More Pricks than Kicks* in 1934, Edwin Muir identified a Beckett very much at home in Bloom's kitchen: 'the toasting of a slice of bread, or the purchase and cooking of a lobster, can become matters of intellectual interest and importance to him'.[1] For Muir, the influence of Joyce was no cause for concern, though he was firm in his conclusion that, as yet, Beckett's work '[did] not nearly come up to' the standard of the master. Other reviewers at the time were not so forgiving, blaming the waywardness, incontinence and 'verbal aggravation' of Beckett's prose on his obvious enthralment to 'Mr. Joyce's latest work' (i.e. 'Work in Progress'), a book which for any young writer was bound to prove 'a dangerous model'.[2] While it is not surprising to find reviewers connecting the two authors, it is nevertheless odd that they should identify Beckett's debt as owing to *Ulysses* and the 'Work in Progress' and not to Joyce's volume of similarly interconnected short fictions, *Dubliners*. As John P. Harrington points out, if one reads the *More Pricks* [*More Pricks Than Kicks*] stories alongside *Ulysses* and 'Work in Progress' then the portrait of Beckett as 'epigone of Joyce',[3] his loyal secretary, is quickly drawn. It is only when we compare them with *Dubliners* that the critical and parodic intelligence of Beckett's stories begins to emerge.

An important document in Beckett's response to his modernist precursors is the first of the three dialogues with 'George Duthuit', concerning Tal-Coat. The dialogue is frequently cited for the vision it offers of an expressionless art of the future: 'The expression that there is nothing to express, nothing with which to express, nothing from which to express, no power to express, no desire to express, together with the obligation to express'.[4] This statement is generally taken as Beckett's commitment to an art of radical indigence from which all of 'nature' will disappear, all white in the whiteness. However, Beckett is stating here his disappointment with the 'revolutionary' art of the present: Matisse and Tal-Coat, for all their 'prodigious value', are still for him artists of 'nature' enlarging upon that fundamental 'composite of perceiver and perceived' to which all art of the past has appealed. Modernism continues to patrol 'the field of the possible . . . the plane of the feasible', and so to understand it, to assimilate it, requires only some realignment by the viewer. Faced with the work which foregrounds its incompleteness, we learn to read silence and absence: 'Total object, complete with missing parts, instead of partial object. Question of degree' (*Proust* and *Three Dialogues*, pp. 101-3).

In recent criticism of *Dubliners* there has been much discussion of the indeterminacy generated by Joyce's 'missing parts', his 'scrupulous meanness'.[5] Irritated by realist and symbolist readings which seek 'verifiable facts and incontrovertible conclusions' (Bašić, p. 351), critics have tried instead to reckon with the destabilising effects of the stories' gaps and withholdings, rather than attempting to explain these features away. Instead of reading *Dubliners* as a complex symbolist puzzle wanting a few key thematic pieces (one named 'Irish paralysis', for example), we are encouraged to celebrate, as readers of *Ulysses* and *Finnegans Wake* have been doing for years, the text's ellipses, to deal with it not as a partial object, but as a 'total object, complete with missing parts'.

Beckett's phrase offers a useful formula for viewing Joyce's stories because it treats reticence and fragmentariness as, in Elizabeth Bowen's word, 'positive'[6] qualities, and not as obstacles to satisfactory interpretation. It suggests that we should frankly acknowledge the disruptive effects of what is missing from the stories, rather than try to gloss what isn't there. When one considers the extent to which the *Dubliners* stories are indeterminate, the value of approaching them in this spirit becomes clear. To take an obvious example, 'The Sisters' is maddeningly full of apertures and evasions. Its boy narrator in many ways mirrors the reader's attempts to find meaning in the utterances of Old Cotter and the sisters themselves, utterances more notable for what they keep back than what they avow (Joyce's ellipses throughout):

> —No, I wouldn't say he was exactly . . . but there was something queer . . . there was something uncanny about him. I'll tell you my opinion . . .[7]

> —I have my own theory about it, he said. I think it was one of those . . . peculiar cases . . . But it's hard to say . . .
>
> (p. 8)

> —Wide-awake and laughing-like to himself . . . So then, of course, when they saw that, that made them think that there was something gone wrong with him . . .
>
> (p. 17)

That last statement is the story's conclusion and comes amid a silence which has taken possession of the house as it has the dead priest. The 'something' that went wrong with Father Flynn looks back to Cotter's 'something uncanny' (literally 'unknown') at the beginning of the story. Similarly, the narrator feels that he 'has been freed from *something*' (p. 11; my emphasis) by the priest's death. What these 'somethings' are is not made clear. Even if Cotter's 'something' could be identified, it would still be 'unknown'. As with the trio of baleful words that trouble the boy on the first page of the story—*paralysis, gnomon, simony*—we are left to infer meaning and significance from the contexts of reference and utterance. But although the narrator studies the language of Cotter and the sisters, as he attempts to piece together meanings in the adult world in the same way as the reader does, there is an important difference be-

tween their positions in relation to the facts of the case. The narrator may indeed be left to study the silences of the other speakers in the story, but the reader is doubly distanced because he has to cope with the narrator's silences too. The narrator plays the same game of withholding from the reader as do the adults with him. What is the 'something' (p. 11) the narrator feels freed from? What is the nature of his interest in the news of Father Flynn's death? Why is he so hostile to Old Cotter? Is it because the old man knows or suspects that the boy's relationship with the priest was 'unhealthy'? Why does he think the priest in his dream smiles? What relation, if any, does he perceive or intend between the strange words in the first paragraph? Why does his story peter out in the weightless coffin-side chatter of the two sisters? What has he got to hide? The narrator neither explains nor clarifies any of the questions about his situation that he himself prompts. Although he implies that he is, like the reader, involved in a process of learning and acquiring knowledge, he fails, or refuses, to interpret his own story.

The uncertainties of 'The Sisters' arise because Joyce withholds crucial evidence from the narrative, a method he employs throughout *Dubliners*. Sometimes the omissions can seem wilfully interdictive until the story is seen as a whole. When, in 'The Boarding House', for example, Mrs. Mooney interviews Polly concerning Doran, we are told that 'Things were as she had suspected: she had been frank in her questions and Polly had been frank in her answers' (p. 69). What the questions and answers were, and what Polly's frankness revealed, are matters for conjecture. It is only when we reach the end of the story that we see why Joyce has held back this information, for he has succeeded in making Polly his suspect as the prime mover in the whole affair—so that she becomes the controlling centre of the narrative—without revealing anything about her desires or motivations. When the story moves to the climactic interview between Mrs. Mooney and Doran, we are not told what transpires between them. Instead, we join Polly in Doran's room for a final scene which, while resolving matters on one level, generates deeper puzzles on others. The narrative deliberately shifts its focus to an inscrutably impersonal centre:

> Polly sat for a little time on the edge of the bed, crying. Then she dried her eyes and went over to the looking-glass. She dipped the end of the towel in the water-jug and refreshed her eyes with the cool water. She looked at herself in profile and readjusted a hairpin above her ear. Then she went back to the bed again and sat at the foot. She regarded the pillows for a long time and the sight of them awakened in her mind secret amiable memories. She rested the nape of her neck against the cool iron bedrail and fell into a revery. There was no longer any perturbation visible on her face.
>
> (pp. 74-5)

The description of Polly in Doran's room directs attention to the hitherto suppressed layer in the narrative which concerns Polly's true feelings. But instead of elaborating this or offering any explanation through *indirect libre*—a privilege we have enjoyed in relation to the thoughts of Mrs. Mooney and Doran—the narrative withdraws here into an uninflected third-person mode. When thoughts come, they seem to act upon Polly, not the other way round; Polly is only active when she is physically doing something. A notion of interiority is played with here, but the focus remains resolutely on the surface, the performative. We now view Polly without any interpretative commitment from the narrator: her 'amiable memories' and 'intricate' 'hopes and visions' remain 'secret' because the narrative, which has up to this point allowed the reader access to character motives, now pointedly refuses any such intimacy. This refusal can only strike us as forbidding because the text has hitherto deliberately prompted questions about Polly's enigmatic mentality, for instance through the song she sings, 'I'm a . . . naughty girl',[8] and her saying that she would 'put an end to herself', a comment clearly made for effect given her light-heartedness once Doran has gone downstairs. At the crucial point, and in respect of the central character, the narrative has become reticent.

Elsewhere, Joyce's prefers free indirect speech to omniscient narration, as in 'Clay', 'A Painful Case', 'Eveline', and 'A Little Cloud', where a superintending, explicatory perspective in the narrative is refused. As recent critics of *Dubliners* have been at pains to point out,[9] this technique complicates Joyce's epiphanies by allowing the possibility that they may be fabricated or delusory aspirations toward feeling rather than genuine occurrences of it. Take, for example, the final paragraph of 'A Little Cloud':

> Little Chandler felt his cheeks suffused with shame and he stood back out of the lamplight. He listened while the paroxysm of the child's sobbing grew less and less; and tears of remorse started to his eyes.
>
> (p. 94)

Dominic Head considers this scene 'staged', the language belonging to Chandler's 'own "poetic" turn of phrase . . . chosen for its alliteration, without regard for the weariness of its cadence which is inappropriate for a scene of highly charged emotion' (p. 62). Joyce's deployment of free indirect speech makes it possible to read Chandler's epiphany—like those of Duffy in 'A Painful Case' and of Eveline in her story—as falsified, his tears as crocodile, or at least as tears of self-pity for his failure in both art and life. After all, Chandler has been seen constructing such 'poetic' scenes for himself throughout the story, as when he wonders whether to

write a poem about the tramps and beggars while crossing Grattan Bridge: 'the thought that a poetic moment had touched him took life within him like an infant hope' (p. 79).

Like Little Chandler, Duffy, in 'A Painful Case', is conscious of language. However, he is unwilling to give his ideas expression in written form because this would bring him into debasing contest with 'phrasemongers, incapable of thinking consecutively for sixty seconds' and subject him 'to the criticisms of an obtuse middle class' (p. 123). Convinced of the superiority and singularity of his thought, Duffy finds himself 'listening to the sound of his own voice' when conversing with Mrs. Sinico. His decision finally to break with her is taken in part because her 'interpretation of his words disillusioned him' (p. 124).

On the face of it, Duffy's epiphany at the end of the story involves his coming to appreciate the extent of Mrs. Sinico's loneliness and his own culpability in her death. Sonja Bašić sums up Duffy's insight as the point where 'the theme—the rejection of life and love—is not only clearly outlined but also firmly related to character motivation' (p. 20). In other words, the story achieves thematic and structural unity in its ending. But in order to read it in this way we need to accept that Duffy achieves some degree of self-realisation, that he does indeed feel that his 'moral nature [is] falling to pieces' (*Dubliners*, p. 130). That means ignoring what Joyce has told us about Duffy earlier in the story:

> He had an odd autobiographical habit which led him to compose in his mind from time to time a short sentence about himself containing a subject in the third person and a predicate in the past tense.
>
> (p. 120)

The whole of the epiphany scene is conveyed through free indirect speech, much of it in the kind of short sentences described here. The final paragraph reads:

> He turned back the way he had come, the rhythm of the engine pounding in his ears. He began to doubt the reality of what memory told him. He halted under a tree and allowed the rhythm to die away. He could not feel her near him in the darkness nor her voice touch his ear. He waited for some minutes listening. He could hear nothing: the night was perfectly silent. He listened again: perfectly silent. He felt that he was alone.
>
> (p. 131)

The possibility remains, tantalisingly, that Duffy's epiphany is one of his constructions. Certainly, that would seem to be what Joyce is suggesting by the preponderance here of short sentences containing a third-person pronoun and a predicate in the past tense. The effect is to threaten any certainty of attribution in the language. We do not know that these constructions originate in Duffy, nor do we know that they do not.

In his early story, **"A Case in a Thousand"** (1934), Beckett too can be found experimenting with the suppression of information and the occlusion of perspective. John Harrington has described it as Beckett's 'most apparent adoption . . . of the style of Joyce's own early work' (p. 36). For Harrington, however, the correspondences between Beckett's text and Joyce's are thematic; he takes no note of any affinities of form. The story concerns a young physician, Dr. Nye, who finds himself having to treat his former nanny's gravely ill son. The young boy dies during surgery but weeks later the mother is still to be seen every day lingering in the hospital grounds. The final scene of the story involves an enigmatic encounter between the mother and her former ward, Dr. Nye:

> 'There's something I've been wanting to ask you,' he said, looking at the water where it flowed out of the shadow of the bridge.
>
> She replied, also looking down at the water:
>
> 'I wonder would that be the same thing I've been wanting to tell you ever since that time you stretched out on his bed.'
>
> There was a silence, she waiting for him to ask, he for her to tell.
>
> 'Can't you go on?' he said.
>
> *Thereupon she related a matter connected with his earliest years, so trivial and intimate that it need not be enlarged on here, but from the elucidation of which Dr. Nye, that sad man, expected great things.*
>
> 'Thank you very much,' he said, 'that was what I was wondering.'
>
> (my italics)[10]

Gaps in Joyce are precisely that—apertures, silences which do not threaten the illusion of objectivity in the presentation. In Beckett's story, however, the narrative voice advertises what it leaves unsaid. There is no effort here to maintain an objective stance, to disguise the authorial sleight of hand. Beckett's candour of procedure here demonstrates his divergence from what is perhaps the defining mannerism of Joyce's short fiction. The narrator's refusal to tell all is revealed at the same time as it is enacted; Beckett is not willing to adopt uncritically the Joycean persona of the artist 'refined out of existence'.

Throughout *More Pricks Than Kicks,* Beckett picks up on aspects of *Dubliners,* making explicit that which is normally implicit in the Joycean story. Linda Hutcheon's description of postmodernist parody as 'repetition with critical distance', an 'ironic signalling of difference at the very heart of similarity' which allows the writer to 'speak *to* a discourse from *within* . . .',[11] usefully indicates how Beckett's irony functions. As Hutcheon implies, parody here acts not to diminish, or reveal

the fallibility of, the text to which it refers. Rather, it infiltrates the language of its predecessor in order to conduct an ironic rearticulation of it.

When we read the following passage in **"Draff"**, for example, we are struck not by the sense that it ridicules the kind of epiphanic moment experienced by, say, Chandler in 'A Little Cloud', but by the way in which Beckett gives playful voice to the agonised suppressions of the Joycean story as a whole:

> Hairy, anxious though he was to join the Smeraldina while his face was at its best, before it relapsed into the workaday dumpling, steak and kidney pudding, had his work cut out to tear himself away. For he could not throw off the impression that he was letting slip a rare occasion to feel something really stupendous, something that nobody had ever felt before. But time pressed. The Smeraldina was pawing the ground, his own personal features were waning (or perhaps better, waxing). In the end he took his leave without kneeling, without a prayer, but his brain quite prostrate and suppliant before this first fact of its experience. That was at least something. He would have welcomed a long Largo, on the black keys for preference.[12]

The irony directed at Hairy and his lusting after a certain melancholy depth of feeling is also aimed at the structural device of the epiphany and the way in which it sets itself up as a moment of illumination. Hairy's appearance is actually 'waning', but the scene demands a dilation of feeling, a 'waxing'—lyrical and lachrymose. Where Joyce's epiphanies are insidiously qualified, if not undermined, by suggestions that they may be fabricated or delusory, Beckett is blatant about the constructed nature of the epiphanic moment: 'Hairy', we are told, 'felt it was up to him now to feel something' (p. 194). Beckett's irony works not by supplying a superior rendering of the epiphany, but by exposing the implicatory sleight of hand by which the Joycean story achieves its complexity of effect.

"Draff" ends in a spirit of mild suspensefulness as Hairy and the Smeraldina try to think of an inscription for Belacqua's headstone: 'He did mention one to me once', Hairy says, 'that he would have endorsed, but I can't recall it' (p. 204). In typically Joycean fashion, no effort is made to recall it: instead the narrative shifts its focus, in a manner similar to 'Clay' and 'The Boarding House', to a deliberately unrevealing figure—that of the groundsman. 'So it goes in the world' (p. 204) is the final line of the story, but it is not made clear whether this sentiment emanates from the groundsman (perhaps in relation to his own emotion at the 'little song' he is humming to himself), or whether it is meant by the narrator to be the missing epitaph for Belacqua. It might also be read as an oblique acknowledgement of the story's own failure to provide the inscription for Belacqua's headstone. Like Joe's comments on Maria's singing at the end of 'Clay', and like Crofton's opinion of

Hynes's poem in 'Ivy Day in the Committee Room', and like the inscrutable thoughts of Polly which conclude 'The Boarding House', the statement hovers interrogatively. Beckett's ending, however, openly signals its ironic self-consciousness about its method:

> The groundsman stood deep in thought. What with the company of headstones sighing and gleaming like bones, the moon on the job, the sea tossing in her dreams and panting, and the hills observing their Attic vigil in the background, he was at a loss to determine off-hand whether the scene was of the kind that is termed romantic or whether it should not with more justice be deemed classical. Both elements were present, that was indisputable. Perhaps classico-romantic would be the fairest estimate. A classico-romantic scene.
>
> Personally he felt calm and wistful. A classico-romantic working-man therefore.
>
> (p. 204)

Again, Beckett is simultaneously presenting an epiphany and exposing its inner workings as a device. The groundsman is a figure from the margins, a representative of that 'submerged population group' in which Frank O'Connor says the short story specialises.[13] As with Joyce's endings, there is a refusal to synthesise the various elements of the plot here; instead the narrative shifts to an impressionistic soft focus. But Beckett applies one more twist by ironically signalling his own contrivance in the scene—its 'classico-romanticism'.

Beckett draws attention in this way to the act of narration itself throughout his early stories, particularly at structural points. In **"A Wet Night"**, the broad parody of the end of Joyce's 'The Dead' climaxes in this passage:

> But the wind had dropped, as it so often does in Dublin when all the respectable men and women whom it delights to annoy have gone to bed, and the rain fell in a uniform and untroubled manner. It fell upon the bay, the littoral, the mountains and the plains, and notably upon the Central Bog it fell with a rather desolate uniformity.
>
> (p. 87)

The parody here functions on many levels. The second sentence ostentatiously fails to follow Joyce's famous original where it leads—from 'treeless hills' and the Bog of Allen, through images of Calvary, to the 'universe', with all its living and its dead (pp. 255-6). On the Central Bog it's only raining, not snowing. Hugh Kenner has written of how in Joyce's original snow 'rhymes with the uniform inevitability of human stasis', of how it 'levels and unifies all phenomena' in Gabriel's sight.[14] In Beckett's parody, this effect of uniformity, of the levelling of the gravestone, the mountains, Dublin, is toyed with, but the rain's uniformity is grey and mundane and transfigures nothing. Beckett's reit-

erative use of rain throughout the ruminative last parts of the story imitates Joyce's technique of narrow semantic repetition ('falling softly', 'softly falling', 'falling faintly', 'faintly falling'). Beckett's reiteration, however, plays on a word that has been explicitly de-poeticised: 'Now it began to rain upon the earth beneath and greatly incommoded Christmas traffic of every kind by continuing to do so without remission for a matter of thirty six hours' (pp. 86-7). Furthermore, he does not allow the parodic epiphany to conclude his story.[15] Belacqua leaves his girlfriend's house (having enjoyed the kind of passionate intimacy denied to Gabriel Conroy) in the pitch-dark small hours. The street lamps, which in Joyce's story provide the 'ghostly' twilight shrouding Gretta and also prompt Gabriel's vision of Michael Furey, are extinguished.

In **"Love and Lethe"** the crucial scene is again exposed, though in a somewhat different way:

> Who shall judge of his conduct at this crux? Is it to be condemned as wholly despicable? Is it not possible that he was gallantly trying to spare the young woman embarrassment? Was it tact or concupiscence or the white feather or an accident or what? We state the facts. We do not presume to determine their significance.
>
> 'Digitus Dei' he said 'for once.'
>
> That remark rather gives him away, does it not?
>
> (p. 104)

Beckett's narrator makes explicit the uncertainties which the narrative itself has prompted concerning the motives of the central character—the kinds of questions that Joyce's stories by their reticence cause us to ask. The comment 'That remark rather gives him away, does it not?' makes explicit the relationship the reader typically finds in Joyce: in the absence of a superintending, directive presence, we are obliged to supply our own provisional confirmation of the meaning of the various textual details. Earlier in **"Love and Lethe"** the narrator was similarly benighted concerning the recurring question in the book, why Belacqua wishes to kill himself:

> How he had formed this resolution to destroy himself we are quite unable to discover. The simplest course, when the motives of any deed are found subliminal to the point of defying expression, is to call that deed ex nihilo and have done. Which we beg leave to follow in the present instance.
>
> (p. 95)

More than comically disingenuous, this disclaimer again parodies the kind of narratorial withholding which we find repeatedly in Joyce's short fiction. It does so not by revealing Joyce's blind spots or expediencies but by uncovering the full complexity of his practice. All Beckett's early stories, in fact, can be read as counterpoints to Joyce's. In the treachery of apprenticeship, Beckett voiced the Joycean story's scrupulously unarticulated knowingness. As the narrator says at one point of Belacqua, 'Notice the literary man' (p. 101). Indeed we do.

Beckett's sensitivity to the devices of *Dubliners* is perhaps best borne out by the opening story from *More Pricks Than Kicks,* **"Dante and the Lobster".** The story begins with Belacqua worrying over an 'impenetrable passage' in Dante—Beatrice's explanation, in *Paradiso* ii. 52-148, of why the moon has dark patches. He can follow her 'refutation', but is bemused by the 'proof' because it is delivered as 'a rapid shorthand of the real facts'. Still, he 'pore[s] over the enigma' of the passage, endeavouring to understand 'at least the meanings of the words'—as monads, one presumes, rather than as a connected sequence delivering a singular 'meaning' (p. 9). Later in the day, at his Italian lesson, Belacqua asks the Ottolenghi about the passage, but she defers an explanation of its sense: 'It is a famous teaser. Off-hand I cannot tell you, but I will look it up when I get home' (p. 18).

To these puzzles and textual enigmas is added, finally, Dante's pun, 'qui vive la pieta quando e ben morta'. In English the pun on 'pieta' (meaning both 'pity' and 'piety') is lost, which leads Belacqua to wonder if the line is really translatable at all. At any rate this textual enigma patterns his subsequent thoughts: 'Why not piety and pity together both, even down below? Why not mercy and Godliness together? A little mercy in the stress of sacrifice, a little mercy to rejoice against judgment' (p. 20). As he approaches his aunt's house at the end of the story Beckett conspicuously shifts the scene, preparing us for the epiphanic moment and the emergence of the story's deep-laid significance: 'Let us call it Winter, that dusk may fall now and a moon rise' (p. 20). Once at his aunt's house Belacqua is horrified by the realisation that the lobster she is about to cook will be boiled alive. There it lies, 'cruciform on the oilcloth', having 'about thirty seconds to live': '"Well, thought Belacqua, it's a quick death, God help us all". It is not' (p. 21). That final line—sounding as an 'impersonal voice out of the heavens'[16]—strikes many readers as a false note, an unnecessary and heavy-handed narratorial intervention. Indeed, John Fletcher takes the presence of this and other 'Beckettian asides' as evidence that the author was unsuited to the short story—a genre, Fletcher explains, in which writers must 'work their effects by understatement and humour rather than explicit comment'.[17] This is to miss the point of Beckett's irony. His story proceeds as though about to reach a highly inferential and impressionistic ending which will bring together, at some deep metaphorical level, the 'meanings' of all its enigmatic details. The last line seems incongruous because instead of the characteristic short story withdrawal at the point of closure, Beckett allows the blatant intrusion of a voice signalling over

the characters' heads. He blows the cover under which the story operates, exposing the narrator's presence by making it explicit. It is as though he wishes to terminate the kind of 'lost' or indeterminate endings which characterise the Joycean story. As with **"A Case in a Thousand"** and **"A Wet Night",** he is unwilling to allow the naturalistic illusion of the inconspicuous or objective narrator to predominate, signalling instead an ironic awareness of how Joyce defers meaning and creates an enigmatic openness in his texts by suppressing the personality of the narrator. As Hugh Kenner put it in his 'Progress Report' some years later, 'To play one more game by the old rules would merely be competence'.[18]

John Pilling suggests that Beckett's criticism of Maupassant, made during a lecture entitled 'Naturalists', that he contained 'no subjectiveness' comparable to the great European novelists, is evidence of Beckett's lack of interest in Maupassant and, by extension, the short story.[19] But Beckett's complaint might also be read positively, as a declaration of intent. The intrusive 'It is not' sums up the break he is attempting throughout these early works with the aesthetic of the modernist short story as he inherited it from Joyce. The line brings to bear on the story a 'subjective' narratorial voice which exposes, plays with, the conspicuous detachment and 'objectivity' upon which the short form seemingly depends for its effects. Indeed, all Beckett's stories examined here contain this narratorial self-consciousness, this voice that reads as it writes.

Notes

1. Edwin Muir, *Listener,* 4 July 1934, p. 42.

2. Unsigned review, *Times Literary Supplement,* 26 July 1934, p. 526.

3. John P. Harrington, 'Beckett's "Dubliners" Story', in Phillis Carey and Ed Jewinski (eds.), *Re: Joyce'n Beckett (New York, 1992),* p. 32.

4. Samuel Beckett, *Proust* and *Three Dialogues with George Duthuit* (1965), p. 103.

5. See for instance Phillip Herring, *Joyce's Uncertainty Principle* (Princeton, 1987); Dominic Head, *The Modernist Short Story: A Study in Theory and Practice* (Cambridge, 1992); Sonja Bašić, 'A Book of Many Uncertainties: Joyce's *Dubliners', Style,* 25 (1991), 351-77.

6. 'The Faber Book of Modern Short Stories', in *Collected Impressions* (1950), p. 39.

7. James Joyce, *Dubliners,* ed. and corr. Robert Scholes (1967), p. 7.

8. As Zack Bowen illustrates, the song from which she sings describes a situation very close to that narrated in the story, prefiguring, among other

things, 'impish Polly's contentment on Doran's bed' (*Musical Allusions in the Works of James Joyce: Early Poetry Through* Ulysses (Dublin, 1975), p. 17).

9. See Head, *Modernist Short Story, passim,* and also Zack Bowen, 'Joyce and the Epiphany Concept: A New Approach', *Journal of Modern Literature,* 9 (1981), 103-14.

10. Samuel Beckett, *The Complete Short Prose, 1929-1989,* ed. S. E. Gontarski (New York, 1995), pp. 23-4.

11. Linda Hutcheon, *A Poetics of Postmodernism: History, Theory, Fiction* (New York and London, 1988), pp. 26, 35. The same point is made by Robert Alter, who describes parody as a mode which 'fuses creation with critique' (*Partial Magic: The Novel as a Self-Conscious Genre* (Berkeley and Los Angeles, 1975), p. 25), and by Matei Calinescu, who argues that a successful parody should 'offer the possibility of being mistaken for the original itself' (*Five Faces of Modernity: Modernism Avant-Garde Decadence Kitsch Postmodernism* (Durham, NC, 1987), p. 141).

12. Samuel Beckett, *More Pricks Than Kicks* (1970), p. 195.

13. Frank O'Connor, *The Lonely Voice: A Study of the Short Story* (1963), p. 18.

14. Hugh Kenner, *A Reader's Guide to Samuel Beckett* (Syracuse, NY, 1996), p. 54.

15. The word 'epiphany' is in fact slyly inserted just before the scene in question: 'A divine creature, native of Leipzig, to whom Belacqua, round about the following Epiphany, had occasion to quote the rainfall for December . . .' (p. 87).

16. Robert Cochran, *Samuel Beckett: A Study of the Short Fiction* (New York, 1991), p. 18.

17. 'Joyce, Beckett, and the Short Story in Ireland', in Carey and Jewinski (eds.), *Re: Joyce'n Beckett,* p. 27.

18. Hugh Kenner, 'Progress Report, 1962-65', in John Calder, (ed.), *Beckett at Sixty: A Festschrift* (1967), p. 61.

19. John Pilling, *Beckett Before Godot* (Cambridge, 1997), p. 94.

Jan Alber (essay date spring 2002)

SOURCE: Alber, Jan. "The 'Moreness' or 'Lessness' of 'Natural' Narratology: Samuel Beckett's 'Lessness' Reconsidered." *Style* 36, no. 1 (spring 2002): 54-75.

[In the following essay, Albert utilizes "Lessness" to test the narratological approach of Monika Fludernik's Towards a 'Natural' Narratology.*]*

1. INTRODUCTION

According to J. E. Dearlove, the fragmentary short prose works that Samuel Beckett produced in the period following the publication of *Comment C'est* (1961), i.e., **"All Strange Away"** (1963-64), ***Imagination Dead Imagine*** (1965), ***Enough*** (1965), ***Ping*** (1966), ***Lessness*** (1969), and ***The Lost Ones*** (1966, 1970), might strike readers as "utterly alien and incomprehensible," and by thrusting the burden of creating order and meaning on readers, "demand a new critical response" ("Last Images" 104, 116). Similarly, Mary Bryden points out that some readers have reacted adversely to Beckett's later prose, seeing it as "perversely uncommunicative" and "teasingly mysterious" (137). The short prose work ***Lessness*** is definitely one of the most enigmatic texts of the period after *How It Is*. Because of the initial shock that this strange and incomprehensible prose work might produce in readers, it may be used as a case to test the new narratological approach Monika Fludernik puts forward in *Towards a 'Natural' Narratology* (1996).

Fludernik attempts to counteract some of the shortcomings of classical narratology and other traditional approaches to narrative theory. Her aim is the radical "reconceptualization of narratology" and "the creation of a new narrative paradigm" (xi), a paradigm, however, that despite its interdisciplinary make-up, will still be identifiable as narratological. As Gibson notes, Fludernik sets out to redefine narrativity in terms not of plot but of cognitive or what she calls "natural" parameters. These parameters are based on our experience, on our sense of embodiedness in the world ("Review" 234). Whereas structuralist narratology employs formal categories defined in terms of binary oppositions, Fludernik wishes to institute organic frames of reading. She reconstitutes narrativity on the basis of experientiality, a feature derived from research on oral narrative established by Labov (*Language*). At the same time experientiality relates to Käte Hamburger's thesis that narrative is the only form of discourse that can portray consciousness, particularly the consciousness of someone else (83). Since, for Fludernik, the prototypical case of narrative is given in its oral version (textual make-up is considered to be a variable), the "natural" narratological paradigm, as Ronen suggests, identifies narrativity with conversational parameters in a storytelling situation (647). Furthermore, Fludernik wishes to institute a reconceptualization of the term "natural" within a more specifically cognitive perspective. She argues that "natural" narratives, i.e., narratives of spontaneous storytelling, cognitively correlate with perceptual parameters of human experience. According to her, these parameters are still in force even in more sophisticated written narratives like those in many experimental twentieth-century texts. Fludernik subsumes the experientiality of "natural" narrative and the cognitive parameters that are based on "real-life" experience in the process of "narrativization," i.e., a reading strategy that naturalizes (Culler 134-60) texts by recourse to narrative schemata. She argues that inconsistencies of strange and incomprehensible texts cease to be worrisome when we can read them as a series of events, a story, or when we can explain them as the skewed vision of a ruling consciousness, that of a teller, or that of a reflective or "registering" mind. Such reading processes that manufacture sense out of apparent nonsense are observed to apply even more radically when experimentation touches the core of narrative: the establishment of a fictional situation and/or the very language of storytelling. Fludernik argues that "natural" narratology is sorely tested at points where the oddities of experimental texts like "Lessness" obstruct readers' attempts to narrativize on the basis of "natural" parameters.

Fludernik's reconceptualization of narrativity allows us to define a great number of plotless narratives from the twentieth century as narratives fully satisfying the requirement of experientiality, since such texts operate by means of a projection of consciousness without necessarily needing any actantial base structure. In contrast to this, the traditional definition of narrative in terms of (a series of) action(s) (Genette, *Narrative Discourse* 30; Rimmon-Kenan 15; Stanzel 150; Prince, *Dictionary* 58; Genette, *Revisited* 20; Bal 16) does not cover plotless experimental twentieth-century texts like Beckett's later prose. Although all of these texts have *discourse* reference, what precisely (if anything) is their *story* (or plot) frequently cannot be determined with any clarity. Events and stories are simply no longer central to the focus of what these texts are about. Interestingly, Gérard Genette points out that "for Beckett," 'I walk' would already be "too much to *narrate*" (*Revisited* 19). Since Beckett, for example in *Ping* and *Lessness*, does not rely on Genettean minimal forms of narrative, action or event sequences, his experimental texts do not qualify as narratives in the traditional sense. Nevertheless, Genette's statement implies that Beckett narrates, i.e., produces a narrative. The central question, then, is the question of what constitutes Beckett's narrative. An obvious theoretical solution to this problem is to deny the label *narrative* to such texts, to say, that is, that the norm for twentieth-century fiction is no longer instantiated by the narrative discourse type, and consequently to marginalize such texts. The predominantly negative characterization of experimental fiction as contravening traditional story parameters (Hassan 9) points in this direction, as does the prevalence of the labels "anti-narrative" (Chatman 56-59; Prince, *Dictionary* 6) and "anti-literature" (Dearlove, "Last Images" 117; Buning 102; Hassan 3) among both traditional narratologists and Beckett critics, as well as in M.-L. Ryan's proposal of the term "antinarrativity" (379-80). Fludernik offers an entirely different solution to this problem. Rather than pointing out the negative features of this kind of narra-

tive, Fludernik's approach describes its structure in terms of experientiality (Lieske 374). Therefore, in the present paper I wish to treat *Lessness* in so far as it relates to the visualizing of a story (plot) situation and/or a storytelling situation (Fludernik, *Towards* 269). More precisely, in my "natural" narratological analysis I shall concentrate on the establishment of story-world, that is, on characters, setting and plot, as well as on the storytelling frame and the language of storytelling. According to Fludernik, a text like "Lessness" does not completely disrupt the process of narrativization, but "merely dilute[s] constants of mimetic conceptualization to the point where realist frames become tenuous and are reduced to the notions of malleable or inconstant character, setting and event outlines" (273).

The purpose of the present paper is threefold. First, I wish to demonstrate the superiority of Fludernik's "natural" narratology to structuralist narratology in accounting for marginally narrative texts like Beckett's *Lessness*. Second, I shall illustrate the utility of Fludernik's new paradigm for the literary interpretation of such an incomprehensible avant-garde text. Third, I will discuss some of the shortcomings or what I call the "lessness" of "natural" narratology.

2. The "Natural" Narratological Paradigm

2.1. The Redefinition of Narrativity in Terms of Experientiality

In *Towards a 'Natural' Narratology,* Fludernik rejects all traditional plot-based concepts of narrativity, i.e., the quality of "narrativehood," as Prince calls it ("On Narratology" 80), and equates narrativity with experientiality. "*Narrativity is a function of narrative texts and centres on experientiality of an anthropomorphic nature*" (26). According to Fludernik, experientiality involves "the quasi-mimetic evocation of 'real-life experience'" (12) and is established by readers in the reading process (36). Experientiality includes a sense of moving with time, of the *now* of experience (Ricoeur 62-65). In contrast to Ricoeur, Fludernik supplements this almost static level of temporal experience by more dynamic and evaluative factors. Within her model, temporality is a constitutive aspect of embodiment and evaluation, but it is secondary to the experience itself. For her, experience cannot be subsumed under the umbrella of temporality. Rather, experience includes temporality as one of its parameters. Human experience typically embraces goal-oriented behavior and activity, with its reaction to obstacles encountered on the way. She argues that unexpected obstacles dynamically trigger the reaction of the protagonist. According to Fludernik, the three-part schema of "situation-event (incidence)-reaction to event" constitutes the core of all human action experience (29). Moreover, whereas in oral narrative, narrated experience always tends to be related to incidence, more extended narrative ventures frequently reproduce quite uneventful experiences and tend to center on the narrator's mental situations. Thus, the dynamics of experientiality reposes not only on the changes brought about by external developments or effected through the goal-oriented actions of a central intelligence. Rather, it is related particularly to the resolution effect of the narrative endpoint and to the tension between tellability and narrative "point" (Labov, *Language* 366; Fludernik, "Historical" 374-77). In other words, for Fludernik, the emotional involvement with an experience and its evaluation provide cognitive anchor points for the constitution of narrativity (*Towards* 13). She argues that embodiment constitutes the most basic feature of experientiality; specificity and individuality can in fact be subsumed under it. Embodiedness evokes all the parameters of a "real-life" schema of existence in a specific time and space frame. Experientiality combines a number of cognitively relevant factors. The most important of these is the presence of a human protagonist and his experience of events as they impinge on his situation. Experientiality always implies the protagonist's consciousness. "Narrativity can emerge from the experiential portrayal of dynamic event sequences which are already configured emotively and evaluatively, but it can also consist in the experiential depiction of human consciousness *tout court*" (30). Fludernik demotes the criteria of sequentiality and logical connectedness from the central role they usually play in most discussions of narrative. For her, the bounded sequentiality of "The king died and then the queen died of grief" (Forster 87) holds little or no interest as narrative. In Fludernik's model there can be narratives without plot, but there cannot be any narratives without a human experiencer at some narrative level. The fictional existence of an anthropomorphic experiencer is the *sine qua non* for the constitution of narrativity. In contrast to traditional narratologists, who endow plot-oriented narratives with proto-typical narrativity (Prince, *Narratology* 146), Fludernik argues that events or actantial and motivational parameters in and of themselves constitute only a zero degree of narrativity, a minimal frame for the production of experientiality. I also wish to note that Fludernik refuses to locate narrativity in the existence of a narrator (*Towards* 26). For her, all narrative is produced through the mediating function of consciousness. According to Fludernik, consciousness is the locus of experientiality and can surface on several levels and in different shapes.

2.2. The Three Ingredients of "Natural" Narratology

Since William Labov and Joshua Waletzky (1967) hypothesized that narrative structures can be found in oral accounts of personal experience, conversational storytelling, as Minami notes, has received much attention (467). Fludernik has been influenced by "natural" narra-

tive and relies on the results of research in discourse analysis established by Labov in *Language in the Inner City* (1972). In her approach, "natural" narrative includes only spontaneous conversational storytelling (*Towards* 13-14). According to Fludernik, one has to conceptualize the move from orality to literacy as a continuum that affords the narratologist interesting insights into the various functions of elements within their narrative pattern (53). Fludernik views "natural" narrative as a prototype for the constitution of narrativity and argues that narrative is always "natural" in the sense that, as Ronen suggests, it is anchored in human everyday experience (647).

The second basic ingredient of Fludernik's model is "natural" linguistics. For instance, she mentions Wolfgang Dressler and his *Natürlichkeitstheorie* ("theory of naturalness"). Dressler judges "natural" those elements of language that appear to be regulated by cognitive parameters based on man's experience in the "real world" (5). "Natural" linguistics attempts to locate linguistic processes within more general processes of cognitive comprehension: the general parameters of language relate to human embodiedness in "natural" environments; metaphors of embodiment serve as the basis for describing them. The central insights that Fludernik adopts from these approaches for her narratological paradigm are that cognitive categories are embodied and that higher-level symbolic categories rely on embodied schemata. The question of how human embodiment in the environment is reflected in readers' cognitive categories and schemata interests her most (*Towards* 19).

The third basic ingredient of Fludernik's model is the concept Jonathan Culler calls "naturalization." Culler came up with this concept in order to account for readers' interpretative strategies when encountering initially odd or inconsistent texts. According to Culler, readers attempt to recuperate inexplicable elements of a text by taking recourse to available interpretative patterns. In naturalizing a text we give it a place in our cultural world (137). Culler's naturalization in particular comprises the familiarization of the strange. Fludernik redeploys and redefines Culler's concept as "narrativization," that is to say, as a reading strategy that naturalizes texts by recourse to narrative schemata (*Towards* 34). She argues that whenever readers are confronted with potentially unreadable narratives, they look for ways of recuperating them as narratives. In the process of narrativization, something is made a narrative by the sheer act of imposing narrativity on it. Readers attempt to re(-)cognize texts in terms of the "natural" telling, or experiencing, or viewing parameters; or they try to recuperate inconsistencies in terms of actions and event structures at the most minimal level. In the process of narrativization, readers engage in reading texts as manifesting experientiality, and therefore construct these texts in terms of their alignment with experiential cognitive parameters (313). According to Pier, the dynamics of narrative are set into motion in this process. These dynamics are largely absent in the static models proposed by classical narratology (557).

2.3. Mimesis and Realism

Fludernik conceives of mimesis in radically constructivist terms. According to her, we must not identify mimesis as the imitation of reality. Rather, we should understand mimesis as the artificial and illusionary projection of a semiotic structure. Readers recuperate this structure in terms of a fictional reality. Since this process of recuperation takes place within the cognitive parameters of the readers' "real-world" experience, every reading experience in terms of making sense of a text inevitably results in an "implicit though incomplete homologization of the fictional and the real world" (*Towards* 35). With regard to experimental narrative. Fludernik suggests to read it as a kind of "intertextual play with language and with generic modes" (35). In this analytical context, as Lieske notes, experimental texts are not mimetic in terms of reproducing a prototypical version of narrative experience but in their structured anticipation of the readers' attempts to reinterpret them mimetically, if only at the level of an explicitly "anti-mimetic" language game (374).

Similarly, Fludernik develops a constructivist concept of realism. She does not relate realism to the nineteenth—century movement of realism. Rather, she links it with the specific mimetic evocation of "reality" and specific forms of the mimetic representation of individual experience. Fludernik sees realism as an interpretational strategy. In the process of narrativization, readers make texts conform to "real-life" parameters. Realism in Fludernik's sense closely corresponds to "a mimetic representation of individual experience that cognitively and epistemically relies on real-world knowledge" (38). The process of reading narratives as narratives inevitably involves an activity of narrativization on the readers' part. Readers project a realistic frame on the text and its enunciational properties. Fludernik demonstrates that the wide range of anti-illusionistic techniques radically disrupts conventional realistic story parameters and does not allow readers a realist mode of understanding. At the same time, as Lieske points out, she stresses that such disruptions do not inevitably destroy narrativity *per se* but deconstruct the overall narrative coherence of the text and affect the most fundamental properties of narrative discourse (374).

2.4. The Four-Level Model

Fludernik summarizes the cognitive categories and criteria of "natural" narratology in a four-level model. This model runs somewhat parallel to the three *Mimeses* developed in Ricoeur's *Time and Narrative*. *Mimesis I* relates to prefiguration (54-64), *Mimesis II* to configuration in the shape of emplotment (64-70), and *Mimesis III* to reconfiguration (70-87). Fludernik's *level I* is identical to Ricoeur's *Mimesis I*. It includes the pre-textual "real-life" schemata of action and experience such as the schema of agency as goal-oriented process or reaction to the unexpected, the configuration of experienced and evaluated occurrence, and the "natural" comprehension of observed event processes as well as their supposed cause-and-effect explanations. Furthermore, on this level, teleology, i.e., temporal directedness and inevitable plotting, combines with the narrator's after-the-fact evaluation of narrative experience, as is typical of "natural" narrative, and with the goal-orientedness of acting subjects. Fludernik's *level II* introduces the "natural," macro-textual schemata or frames of narrative mediation. On this level she distinguishes between the "real-world" scripts of TELLING and REFLECTING,[1] the "real-world" schema of VIEWING, and the access to one's own narrativizable experience (EXPERIENCING). Further, Fludernik situates the schema of ACTION or ACTING on *level II* (*Towards* 43-44). Fludernik's *level III* constitutes a fine-tuning of *level II* through well-known "naturally" occurring storytelling situations, generic criteria and narratological concepts. At this point I wish to emphasize that Fludernik's *levels II* and *III* do not reproduce Ricoeur's *Mimesis II*. Rather, they characterize features that are partially relevant for Ricoeur's reconfiguration on the level of *Mimesis III*. In contrast to the cognitive parameters on *levels I* and *II,* which are basic-level experiential frames, the categories on *level III* are culturally determined. One might argue that they are metaphorical extensions of concepts from *levels I* and *II*. Nevertheless, they are "natural" because they operate in a non-reflective manner and relate to one's experience of hearing and reading stories. I also wish to note that readers' interpretations do not (yet) constitute the cognitive parameters on *level III*. Rather, they provide cognitive tools *for* the interpretation of narrative texts (45). Finally, Fludernik's *level IV* is that of narrativization, the level on which the "natural" parameters from *levels I* to *III* are utilized in order to grasp, and usually transform textual inconsistencies and oddities. Narrativization is the process of naturalization that enables readers to re(-)cognize as narrative texts that appear to be non-narrative according to the cognitive parameters on *levels I* and *II* or *III* (46). The "natural" frames on *levels I* to *III* do not *effect* narrativization. Rather, narrativization utilizes "natural" parameters as *part of* the larger process of naturalization applied by readers. Although narrativized non-"natural" text types do not *become* "natural," a new cognitive parameter may become available (330). For instance, second-person fiction (Fludernik "Introduction," "Second," "Second-Person Narrative") does not become "natural" in the process of narrativization. Rather, a semantic and interpretative perspective renders this type of narrative recuperable, because readers have recourse to "natural" categories. It may institute a new genre or a new narrative mode and will then have to be included as a reference model on *level III*.

I shall now turn to my own "natural" narratological analysis of Samuel Beckett's *Lessness*. I am of course aware that other readers might narrativize the text differently.

3. "Natural" Narratology and Beckett's "Lessness"

3.1. The "Setting"

Lessness is set in a container. At some point, this enclosure must have resembled the box-like chamber in Beckett's *Ping* and the first two stages of the shape-shifting container in Beckett's **"All Strange Away."** At the time of narration in *Lessness,* the four walls of the container of this piece have fallen open into "scattered ruins" (197); "Blacked out fallen open four walls over backwards true refuge issueless." The whiteness of *Ping,* i.e., the image of "four square all light sheer white blank planes," is "gone from mind" (*Lessness* 197). Moreover, the narrative voice of *Lessness* abandons the fluctuations of light and darkness in **"All Strange Away"** and *Imagination Dead Imagine,* and reduces them to a pervasive and passive grey (Dearlove, "Last Images" 121). The container is "ash grey" like "the sand" (197). Earth and sky have the same color as the enclosure: "ash grey sky mirrored earth mirrored sky" (197). From our "real-world" knowledge we can infer that since the world of *Lessness* is not black but grey, a dim light has to emanate from somewhere. But the text does not contain any information about the source of the light. Moreover, as in **"Enough,"** there is "no stir," that is no wind, in the world of *Lessness,* and, as in *Ping,* the silence of this world is unbroken: "no sound" (197). "Day and night" (198) appear to be abandoned in *Lessness.* The piece is "timeless" (199), and the narrative voice characterizes the world of "Lessness" in terms of "changelessness" (197). Philip H. Solomon argues that the hour in question must be 6 a.m. or 6 p.m. "Each is a moment of transition with respect to light and dark—the grey of dawn or the grey of dusk" (66). In *Lessness,* time seems to have come to rest in a transitional period.

The "setting" of *Lessness* resembles places in the "real world." The scattered ruins of this piece may consist of stone. Indeed, the narrative voice mentions sand, earth, and sky. Since there is no wind and no sound, however, the world of *Lessness* also differs from "real-world" settings. Moreover, *Lessness* makes it impossible to differentiate between earth, sky, and the scattered ruins,

because they are all ash grey. In contrast to the other "Residua," which are set in a measurable container, the narrative voice of this piece does not give us any information as to the size of the enclosure in *Lessness.* The only hint we get is the phrase "the ruins flatness endless" (199). Spatial structure appears to be lacking altogether. Furthermore, the fact that there is no movement with time seriously impairs a "realistic" reconstitution of story-world.

3.2. The Future

The enclosure of *Lessness* contains an immobile "little body ash grey locked rigid" (197). The body's contours have been eroded: "Legs a single block arms fast to sides little body face to endlessness" (198). The figure's sex is undecidable. The "genitals" of this "little block" are "overrun" (198) and its features are barely defined: "grey face features crack and little holes two pale blue" (197); "grey smooth no relief a few holes" (198). The body is incapable of action: "Face to white calm touch close eye calm long last all gone from mind" (198). In a very ambiguous manner, the text indicates that the figure is alive: "Grey face two pale blue little body *heart beating only upright*" (197). This might imply that the body is the only constituent of story-world in an upright position, and consequently that the figure is alive, or that the body's heart beats only in an upright position. The figure is grey like the rest of this world. Furthermore, the narrative voice refers to the figure's past and to a possible future. I wish to note that in such instances, the voice refers to the figure in terms of the personal pronoun "he." Additionally, the text presents the future as a return to past possibilities: "*He will curse God again as in the blessed days* face to the open sky the *passing* deluge" (197); "On *him will rain again as in the blessed days* of blue the *passing* cloud" (197). Later on, the references to past and future turn out to be dreams and figments: "Never was but grey air timeless no sound *figment the passing light*" (197); "Never but this changelessness *dream the passing hour*" (197). Susan Brienza and Enoch Brater point out that in the two sentences containing the personal pronoun "he," which I have quoted above, the past is superimposed on the indefinite future by using the phrase "as in the blessed days" (250-51). They argue that a cycle of endlessness in time results, because both the "deluge" and the "cloud" will not pass nor have they passed. The present participle "passing" creates an action suspended in time, which is endless, like the "waiting" in *Waiting for Godot* (1985).

The figure in *Lessness* is most radically dehumanized. The narrative voice describes the little body exclusively in terms of bodily fragments. Additionally, its bodily parts are not recognizable. Readers will hardly confuse the block-like figure with inhabitants of the "real world." This figure is indistinguishable from the box-like chamber. In fact, it seems to have become a brick of the scattered ruins.[2] In other words, one cannot possibly differentiate between the figure and the "setting." The only "features" that distinguish the body from the rest of story-world are pale blue eyes, and its possibly upright position. Moreover, the figure does not express any signs of intentionality or goal-orientedness in terms of Fludernik's cognitive *level I.* Its "life signs" are reduced to its upright position or the beating of its heart. I do not think that the figure's "eyes" can be seen as a life sign, since a dead body may (at least for some time) have pale blue eyes as well. Furthermore, the figure's past and future turn out to be mere illusions. The body is trapped in the timeless zone of fiction.

At this point, I wish to note that both the "setting" and the figure in *Lessness* differ from familiar narratological concepts on Fludernik's cognitive *level III.* But in contrast to Buning, who merely points out the "absence" of traditional story parameters and characterizes *Lessness* in terms of an "anti-literary tendency" (102), "natural" narratology takes a closer look at such allegedly absent constituents. On the basis of experientiality, "natural" narratology attempts to explain *why* these constituents are so different from traditional concepts. I would argue that the description of the "setting" and the figure in *Lessness* are reminiscent of the perception of an insane person or a person on drugs. We should keep this in mind while looking at other aspects of *Lessness.*

3.3. THE "PLOT"

The body in *Lessness* is incapable of action, and the "setting" undergoes no noticeable transformation. The narrative voice presents us with repeated descriptions of the rudimentary features of the strange world of this piece. Indeed, the voice postulates an imaginative realm of dreams and future possibilities. *Lessness* consists of 120 sentences, and is divided into twenty-four paragraphs. Upon closer inspection, we realize that the text consists of sixty sentences, each of which occurs exactly twice. There are sixty sentences in the first twelve paragraphs. Later on, they are repeated in a different order. Ruby Cohn divides the sentences thematically into the following six groups or families (265): (1) the ruins as "true refuge"; (2) the endless grey of earth and sky; (3) the little body; (4) the space "all gone from mind"; (5) past tenses combined with "never"; (6) future tenses of active verbs and the "figment" sentence "Figment dawn dispeller of figments and the other called dusk" (199; 201). Martin Esslin uses the following categories for the same groups: (1) the ruins; (2) the vastness of earth and sky; (3) the little body; (4) the fact that the enclosed space is now forgotten; (5) a denial of past and future; (6) an affirmation of past and future.[3] J. E. Dearlove points out that the titles of the first four families are fairly consistent, whereas the last two groups are

more enigmatic because they deal with daydreams and figments in reference to past and future. For Cohn, the distinction is one of tense, whereas for Esslin, the difference is one of assertion ("Last Images" 120). Beckett's method of composition in *Sans* (1969), the original French version of *Lessness,* is extremely creative. Cohn reports that

> Beckett wrote each of the sixty sentences on a separate piece of paper, mixed them all in a container, and then drew them out in random order twice. This became the order of the hundred twenty sentences in *Sans.* Beckett then wrote the number 3 on four separate pieces of paper, the number 4 on six pieces of paper, the number 5 on four pieces, the number 6 on six pieces, and the number 7 on four pieces of paper. Again drawing randomly, he ordered the sentences into paragraphs according to the number drawn, finally totaling one hundred twenty.

(265)

According to Poutney, *Lessness* confronts us with the fact that an arbitrary and capricious world of chance lies beyond man-made, imposed order (56). "The confusion is not my invention," Beckett told Tom Driver. "It is all around us and our only chance is to let it in" (Finney, "Assumption" 63). The formal patterning in *Lessness* may give readers the impression that a random number generator produced the text. This is, to some extent, true.[4] Furthermore, there is a complete absence of memorable events in *Lessness.* Nothing happens at all in it. Events most certainly do not constitute the primary focus of this text. Hence, we are not in a position to reconstruct a proper event-series in terms of the ACTION schema on Fludernik's cognitive *level II.* Since there is a complete elimination of "plot," the text exclusively consists in (vague and distorted) descriptions. Moreover, *Lessness* lacks teleology and closure. In contrast to Brienza and Brater, who argue that "the abrupt last line does not leave us with the impression that the piece might go on indefinitely" (254), I would argue that the cyclical way in which the narrative voice describes the central "situation" of *Lessness,* in combination with the final sentence ("Figment dawn dispeller of figments and the other called dusk" [201]), which is circular in itself, suggests that this short prose work may indeed continue forever. Whereas Mood simply argues that *Lessness* is "plotless" (78), "natural" narratology concerns itself with whether there is not a different story buried under the (admittedly quite) uneventful cloak.

3.4. THE LANGUAGE OF STORYTELLING

The syntax of *Lessness* is most radically disrupted. The piece shares with *Ping* its sentence style and structure as well as the absence of any punctuation except periods. The "scattered ruins" (197) might be a description of the words themselves. The narrative voice uses verbs sparingly; present tense verbs are entirely absent. The personal pronoun "he" occurs only in connection with sentences dealing with the past or the future. This voice gives us the impression that human existence is possible only in the past or in the future. Later on, however, the voice reveals this to be a mere illusion. Occasionally, it also drops articles and prepositions. Its radical reductionism generates a terse, staccato-like style, and is reminiscent of a computerized programme. Moreover, the reduced syntactical form creates pseudo-independent phrases like individual images. Thus, Murphy argues (114) that the words may be said to face on "all sides endlessness." For instance, as I have shown above, we can read the phrase "heart beating only upright" in several different ways. Likewise, in the sentence "little body little block genitals overrun arse a single block grey crack overrun" (198), it remains unclear whether the genitals, or the arse, or both are overrun, and the "grey crack" is ambiguous (eye, tip of penis, vagina, or anus?). Additionally, in all but two of the twenty-four paragraphs, we come across words containing the suffix "-less" or the suffix "-lessness" ("endless," "timeless," "issueless," "endlessness," "changelessness"). These words, like the neologism *Lessness,* stand out and set up a network of tenuous meanings. Furthermore, we are faced with a mass of repeated elements in which no clear subordination of one to another is established (Knowlson and Pilling 176), so that we may concentrate on different elements each time we read the text. There are thirty-eight phrases containing "all," as in "all sides" (198) or "all light" (197), that seem to be cancelled out by the thirty-four occurrences of "no," as in "no sound" (197) or "no hold" (198) (Brienza and Brater 252), and a number of contradictory constructions like "all gone" and "never but" are used. This may give readers the impression that the narrative voice constructs a rudimentary world, and, at the same time, deconstructs it.

The language of *Lessness* is reminiscent of a person in a state of shock, or a madman, i.e., the babbling of a deranged person. This piece most radically foregrounds the linguistic medium. The construction of "sentences" is so awkward that it seriously impairs the reconstruction process. Hence, the text draws our attention to the "sentence"-structure itself. The narrative voice reduces language to repetitious echoings in a syntaxless chain of words and phrases. The deliberate nonfluency, in combination with the repetitive structure of this piece and the proliferation of conspicious "less(ness)" words, generates a style in which the words draw attention to themselves more as signifiers than as signifieds. The language is free-floating in proper Derridean fashion. Indeed, the strategy of constructing and simultaneously deconstructing is reminiscent of Robbe-Grillet's "mouvement paradoxal" (130).

3.5. THE STORYTELLING FRAME

While Ruby Cohn argues that in *Lessness* we are confronted with an observant third-person narrator (262), Mary F. Catanzaro thinks that the narrative voice should be attributed to the "little body," the faceless storyteller of this piece ("Musical" 47). Although I find both accounts of the text convincing, one might argue that since the personal pronoun "he" occurs several times, Cohn's interpretation makes much more sense. The dispassionate depiction of the rudimentary world of this piece is reminiscent of third-person neutral narrative. We get, Fludernik suggests, the typical "camera-eye" effect of the mechanical shutter that registers incoming stimuli but does not interpret them (*Towards* 175). Since the depicted images are distorted ones, however, we get the impression that there has to be something wrong with the "camera." Further, I wish to note that the non-figural "camera-eye" cannot convincingly be ascribed to any position of fixity. Throughout, the text gives a sense of two distinct points of view operating, namely the point of view of the body, on the one hand, and the point of view of the "narrator," on the other (Murphy 113). In this piece, the subject-object division is made obsolete. The disembodied voice may simultaneously be related to both points of view, that is to "narrator" and narrated alike. Hence, we may be confronted with first-person or third-person neutral narrative. The deliberately defocalized presentation of *Lessness* constitutes a serious problem for "natural" narratology not only because it rules out possible anchor points for experientiality but also because the narrative voice remains covert and impersonal (Chatman 197) throughout the piece. Is it then possible to establish experientiality anywhere in the text?

I think that we can read *Lessness* as the projection of the consciousness or imagination of the "character," the "narrator," or both, the "narrator"-narrated. To begin with, the human faculty of imagination plays a crucial role in the depiction of story-world. One can only distinguish between the sand, the sky, the ruins, and the figure with the "eye of imagination," not with the "eye of flesh." Furthermore, the piece evokes desire for a state where time has come to rest or where the mind enjoys "the blue celeste of poesy" (199). I would argue that the projected mind in *Lessness* carries out a mental experiment, namely the experiment of imagining the end of time. Like the attempt to imagine the death of imagination in Beckett's *Imagination Dead Imagine,* this mental experiment is based on a paradox, since time is ultimately necessary to imagine a state in which time has come to rest. As the work unfolds, the projected consciousness realizes that the experiment of imagining the end of time is doomed to failure. The form of *Lessness,* that is the repetition of the sixty sentences, which constitutes the most outstanding feature of the text, contradicts the subject matter of this piece. "The passing hour" (197) is not a "dream" but the ultimate reality of human existence. "Dusk" and "dawn" are not "figments" but "dispeller[s] of figments" (201). This short prose work is not "timeless" and cannot be characterized in terms of "changelessness" because the mind it projects moves within time, and, in doing so, changes the order of the sixty sentences. The "true refuge," in which one can have the illusion of an eternal present, is ultimately "issueless" (197) since time will always go on.

In terms of "natural" narratology, this problem is handled by the REFLECTING frame on Fludernik's cognitive *level II*. This script tends to project a reflecting consciousness (*Towards* 44). The ruminations of the projected mind in *Lessness* might be directed at imagining the end of time, and are ultimately dependent on the "real-world" parameter of time. To sum up, in this piece, we may establish experientiality in terms of the necessity of the human faculty of imagination for depicting a story-world, in terms of the human wish to stop the stream of infinite time, and in terms of the "real-world" knowledge that stopping time is ultimately impossible. Thematically, human time seems to have been central to the composition of *Lessness.* Without coming to this conclusion, Ruby Cohn points out that although *Lessness* is almost bare of figures, it compels calculation. She notes that the resultant numbers serve to call attention to human time: "The number of sentences per paragraph stops at seven, the number of days in a week. The number of paragraphs reaches twenty-four, the number of hours in a day. The number of different sentences is sixty, the number of seconds in a minute, of minutes in an hour" (263).

Moreover, we can read *Lessness* as the projection of the readers' consciousness. Readers are brought into this text, as they must join the narrative voice in imagining whatever may be going on in its mind. When we read Beckett's *Lessness,* we get the impression that we (as readers) have the same "dream" as the narrative voice of this text. Therefore, one may argue that there is a large degree of involvement in *Lessness* (Opas and Kujamäki 287). This effect is extremely disconcerting since the narrative voice cannot be pictured as directing or directly addressing readers. Because there is no corresponding use of the first person, no deictic locus of utterance, *Lessness* lacks a first-person narrator, a speaker with whom we might identify.

4. Consequences and Conclusions

"Natural" narratology provides only a partially satisfying analysis of Beckett's *Lessness.* Problems center on the redefinition of narrativity in terms of an experientiality that turns out to be a vague criterion. One may refer to the points mentioned below as the "moreness" or "lessness" of "natural" narratology. I shall begin with what I call the "moreness" of the new paradigm.

One might argue that Fludernik's redefinition of narrativity is useful, because it allows us to define a great number of experimental and plotless texts as narratives fully satisfying the requirement of experientiality, since they operate by means of a projection of consciousness—the character's, that of the narrative voice, or the readers'. Traditional narratologists like Gérard Genette, Gerald Prince, and Franz Karl Stanzel can only read such texts as contravening traditional parameters. They would ultimately have to deny the label *narrative* to such texts, and consequently marginalize them. For instance, Stanzel explicitly states that there is "no place" for Beckett's **Ping** in his typological circle (236), and this claim is obviously also true for *Lessness.* Additionally, Genette discusses very little experimental writing in any of the three books I have cited and mentions postmodernist texts merely in passing. As Lieske points out, Fludernik's approach is particularly important in the context of poststructuralist debates about the end of narrative or the death of the author because it reclaims postmodernist fiction for narratological analysis despite this fiction's lack of conventional plot or logical coherence (374).

Moreover, Fludernik's narrative paradigm has helped this essay to an entirely new interpretation of *Lessness.* One might argue that "natural" narratology paves the way for a new reading of this initially alien and uncommunicative text. I have utilized the following schemas, frames, or scripts as parts of a larger attempt to narrativize Beckett's *Lessness.* First, I have employed the schema of temporal directedness and that of agency as a goal-oriented process on Fludernik's cognitive *level I* for the context of a thought experiment. Second, I have referred to the REFLECTING frame on *level II,* which turns the act of telling into a process of self-reflexive rumination, for the mental activity in the course of a thought experiment. Third, I have utilized narratological concepts and familiar knowledge about first- and third-person neutral narrative on *level III* in order to establish a storytelling situation. As I have shown, narrativization by means of the consciousness factor acquires a central status in experimental writing like *Lessness* where the readers' establishment of experientiality serves to identify some sort of teller-figure, a registering mind. Even though the readers' attempts to establish experientiality are seriously impaired, we may read *Lessness* as the projection of the readers' consciousness or of the consciousness of the block-like figure, the "narrator," or both, the "narrator"-narrated. One might argue that the projected mind carries out a mental experiment that is similar to the attempt to imagine the death of imagination, namely the experiment of imagining the end of time. Further, I would argue that the projected consciousness in this piece struggles with its imaginings in the course of the mental experiment and realizes that the task of imagining the end of time is ultimately impossible. Hence, we can read *Lessness* as the agonized ruminations of a mind that struggles with some kind of traumatic experience. I think that the projected consciousness realizes not only that its own existence but also that its "heroic" attempt to break out of the stream of infinite time are nothing but insignificant ripples on the surface of infinite time. Time imprisons us all. The mind begins to understand that while the stream of infinite time will never stop, both its existence and the mental experiment will sooner or later end. This quasi-traumatic experience of feeling the ultimate meaninglessness of one's own existence could, in a way, account for why the images that can be reconstituted on the basis of the information given in the text are very distorted ones. One might argue that the projected mind finds itself in a state of shock. Consequently, the language of this mind is syntaxless and its perception, deranged. It may experience feelings of terror, hallucinations, or psychosomatic disturbances. I suspect that we are all more or less familiar with such disruptions of ordinary human experience. As far as *Lessness* is concerned, Fludernik suggests, embodiment is reduced to consciousness with the setting dwindling to rudimentary implied contiguities (*Towards* 311). Furthermore, I would like to argue that after paragraph twelve, the projected mind ends the mental experiment because it is overwhelmed by the stream of infinite time, and decides to do nothing but move passively within time. It decides to invent nothing new but to merely reshuffle old material. This decision could account for the repetitive structure of this short prose work, i.e., the repetition of the first sixty "sentences" in the second half of the piece. Since I feel that there are also problems with this new interpretation of *Lessness,* I shall now turn to what I call the "lessness" of Fludernik's new paradigm.

Despite my (more or less) desperate attempts to make Beckett's *Lessness* more readable, I wish to note that this text constitutes a borderline case. *Lessness* challenges narrativization and the whole "natural" narratological project. My analysis of this piece is obviously a strategy radically appropriated to the mimetic project, a move to make sense contrary to all linguistic evidence. When reading this text, we are confronted with a slippery boundary on which we may hesitate to tread for fear of losing our mental balance.

We have to situate *Lessness* at the boundary between the genres of narrative and lyric. In the realm of extremely experimental writing, the traditional distinctions between genres become erased. Fludernik argues, indeed, that where narrativity can no longer be recuperated by any means at all, the narrative genre merges with poetry (*Towards* 310). This obviously raises the question of what it takes for a text to project experientiality but still remain narrative and not lyrical. Fludernik

speaks of "poetry's typical lack of experientiality (and hence narrativity)" (355). I do not see why, according to Fludernik, poetry's typical "preoccupation with *sensibilia*" (356) should have nothing to do with experientiality. Furthermore, she argues that the boundary between poetry and narrative is permeable (356). That is to say that, for her, there are degrees of narrativity. In contrast to her, I think that it is impossible to distinguish between narrative and lyrical texts, or to determine the different grades of narrativity, on the basis of experientiality, i.e., "the quasi-mimetic evocation of 'real-life experience'" (12). For such a distinction, categories like plot, action, character, "real-world" setting, all of which Fludernik attempts to play down in her paradigm, turn out to be crucial after all. Interestingly, she claims that in her redefinition of narrativity in terms of experientiality she insists on such essentialities as plot, character, and voice in the constructivist interpretation of their cognitive foundation (305). For Fludernik, such categories can be subsumed under experientiality and embodiment. In contrast to her, I think that the categories of plot and "real-world" setting should play a crucial role in the definition of narrative as a distinguishing feature, because according to the approach taking "experientiality first, plot later," almost every poem qualifies as a narrative. Furthermore, not only would almost every poem be a narrative but even almost every *text*. For instance, according to the experientiality criterion, inarticulate screams of horror would qualify as narratives. Fludernik's definition of narrative is thus too broad. Because she attempts to include almost every text in her definition (347ff.), the term "narrative" becomes meaningless. The more a term includes, the less it means. And this is the "lessness" of "natural" narratology.

Another problem is, of course, that the new paradigm is supposed to deal with an incredibly large number of "narrative" texts. I doubt that Fludernik's quasi-universal naturalizing mode of reading can do justice to all these texts. As I have shown, if one is willing to, it is even possible to narrative a machine-generated text like *Lessness,* actually structured by a throw of the dice, as the expression of a subject's thought. A "natural" narratological analysis ultimately has to ignore certain aspects, like the mechanical structure of *Lessness,* in order to make a text fit into its new consciousness-oriented paradigm. Such a piece calls for another mode of reading than the naturalizing mode prescribed by "natural" narratology. By narrativizing *Lessness,* we miss the central point of a postmodernist text that foregrounds ontological chaos, i.e., ontological questions concerning the self, or the mode of existence of the self (McHale 9-11); we impose a normalizing strategy on the text rather than deal with its fundamental otherness. Throughout the writing of this paper, I had the odd sensation that the easier it is to narrativize Beckett's *Lessness,* the more modernist the text becomes or seems.[5]

To put this slightly differently, I thought that my consciousness-oriented, "natural" narratological analysis ultimately involves some kind of modernist reading strategy. It is obviously much easier to establish a consciousness factor in a kind of writing that deals excessively with the depiction of consciousness (e.g., in texts by James Joyce, Virginia Woolf, Ernest Hemingway, or William Faulkner) than it is to do so in a kind of writing that calls the very existence of consciousness into question. There is a fundamental contradiction between the aims of postmodernist literature, i.e., pieces like *Lessness* and texts written by experimentalists like B. S. Johnson, Christine Brook-Rose, Alasdair Gray, or Brigid Brophy, on the one hand, and Fludernik's attempt to narrativize them on the other. In *Towards a 'Natural' Narratology,* Fludernik postulates something like a biological core, a minimal cognitive basis.[6] In contrast to this, both postmodernist literature and poststructuralist thought (in Jacques Derrida, Michel Foucault, Julia Kristeva, et al) call the very existence of a biological core and a minimal cognitive basis into question, and look at human beings as free-floating signifiers. One can of course argue that such self-reflexive word-gaming constitutes a last-ditch scenario for narrativization in terms of "natural" cognitive parameters, and that it ultimately has its roots in the "real world." Nevertheless, I think that where experientiality resolves into words, "natural" narratology finds its ultimate horizon. Where language has become pure language, structured by a machine, or free-floating in Derrida's sense, disembodied from speaker, context, and reference, both human experience and Fludernik's concept of narrativization by means of human experience become redundant.

Since narrativity (in both the traditional and Fludernik's sense) is not a necessary condition of inclusion in the literary canon (one need only consider the mass of "non-narratological" Beckett scholarship), narratologists do not *have* to deal with avant-garde texts like Beckett's *Lessness* and may leave such texts to other approaches, perhaps of a more poststructuralist or even musicological orientation. A reading of *Lessness* should be liberated from the confines of experientiality, i.e., the feasible, the logically consistent, and humanly plausible, and instead concentrate on the text's otherness, on its monstrosity, on the role of chance and chaos. Reading *Lessness* draws the recipient "forwards towards the new, into strange, unfamiliar and monstrous compounds" (Gibson, *Towards* 272). *Lessness* deconstructs the categories of the anthropological and the textual, the human and the material. The disembodied voice of this text constitutes itself in and through the text and arrives at a new identity that has to be located in a counterworld, a limbo between *signifiant* and *signifié*. We should allow this limbo-world to seep into our "real world" and not attempt to explain this different counterworld by means of our "real-world" knowledge. Gibson

argues that one should register elements of monstrous deformation and explore their implications (259). I wish to note that the word-stock in *Lessness* is finite and structured by chance. For me, *Lessness* implies that we attempt to define and redefine ourselves with regard to the limits of our discourses and that chance is actually the sole criterion that imposes a structure on our limited possibilities. Given the choice between taking Fludernik's approach to fiction, which is based on order and meaning, and Gibson's approach, which is based on chaos and confusion, with regard to *Lessness,* I prefer Gibson's, because, as Beckett puts it: "The confusion [. . .] is all around us and our only chance is to let it in" (Finney 63).

Finally, there are also problems with the rather ahistorical conception of Fludernik's cognitive four-level model. If one accepts the redefinition of narrativity in terms of experientiality, I feel that it is necessary to investigate whether there are not *different types of embodiment* (and hence narrativity) in different centuries, i.e., the question whether one can distinguish between something like realist, modernist, and postmodernist experientiality. Additionally, we should address the difference between male and female experientiality. I agree with Gibson, who points out that Fludernik takes the concept of "embodiedness" to be an unproblematic given ("Review" 237). For instance, dehumanization, fragmentation, perspectivism, decentering, and self-reflexivity, e.g. in MTV video clips, which are arguably part of our everyday experience, play a much more crucial role in forms of postmodernist than of modernist experientiality, whereas an interest in consciousness and subjectivity and the assumption that there is something like a minimal cognitive basis is a more integral part of modernist than of postmodernist experientiality. Consequently, readers nowadays may consider postmodernist texts to be much closer to their everyday experience, and they may feel that they have to narrativize (in a postmodernist sense) earlier texts to make them "natural." Irrespective of texts like *Lessness,* which are to be located beyond the scope of both experientiality ("natural" narratology) and plot-orientation (classical narratology), what is at stake, with regard to diachronic narratological projects, is the creation of a new narrative paradigm, one that subsumes "natural" narratology as the special case of an extended application of realist parameters or that is able to account for realism differently within its own framework. Experientiality thus remains a problematic criterion. On the one hand, it does not allow us to distinguish between narrative and lyrical texts; on the other, it does not address whether embodiment, i.e., humanity's being in the world, has not changed fundamentally over the centuries. I consider this paper to be a first step toward a larger investigation of the "moreness" and/or "lessness" of "natural" narratology.

Notes

1. "Reflecting" refers to the mental activities outside utterance that turn the act of telling into a process of recollection and self-reflective introspection or rumination (44).

2. The body in "Lessness" is reminiscent of the figures in *Play,* where we are confronted with *"three identical grey urns."* We learn that *"from each a head protrudes, the neck held fast in the urn's mouth"* (147).

3. Esslin's list is from his introduction to the BBC Radio 3 production of "Lessness" (25 February 1971) and is quoted by Brian Finney (*Since* 39-40).

4. J. M. Coetzee uses the computer program Univac 1106 to deal with the combination of sentences in "Lessness." His results verify mathematically that no significant ordering principle governs the arrangement of phrases, sentences, or paragraphs (195-98).

5. As far as modernism is concerned, I refer to Brian McHale's distinction between modernist and post-modernist fiction. According to McHale, modernist fiction, particularly the stream-of-consciousness novel, foregrounds epistemological questions, i.e., questions of knowledge and consciousness, whereas postmodernist fiction foregrounds ontological questions, i.e., questions of modes of existence (9-11).

6. Experientiality is an essentialist notion; Fludernik assumes that experience is the same for everyone.

Works Cited

Bal, Mieke. *Narratology: Introduction to the Theory of Narrative.* Second Ed. Toronto: U of Toronto P, 1997.

Beckett, Samuel. "All Strange Away." *Samuel Beckett: The Complete Short Prose, 1929-1989,* 169-81.

———. *Comment C'est.* Paris: Les Editions de Minuit, 1961.

———. "Enough." *Samuel Beckett: The Complete Short Prose, 1929-1989,* 186-92.

———. *How It Is.* London: Calder & Boyars, 1964.

———. "Imagination Dead Imagine." *Samuel Beckett: The Complete Short Prose, 1929-1989,* 182-85.

———. "Lessness." *Samuel Beckett: The Complete Short Prose, 1929-1989,* 197-201.

———. "The Lost Ones." *Samuel Beckett: The Complete Short Prose, 1929-1989,* 202-23.

———. "Ping." *Samuel Beckett: The Complete Short Prose, 1929-1989,* 193-96.

———. *Play. Collected Shorter Plays of Samuel Beckett.* London: Faber and Faber, 1984. 145-60.

———. *Samuel Beckett: The Complete Short Prose, 1929-1989.* Ed. S. E. Gontarski. New York: Grove, 1995.

———. *Sans.* Paris: Les Editions de Minuit, 1969.

———. *Waiting for Godot.* London: Faber and Faber, 1985.

Brienza, Susan D., and Enoch Brater. "Chance and Choice in Beckett's 'Lessness.'" *English Literary History* 43.2 (1976): 244-58.

Bryden, Mary. *Women in Samuel Beckett's Prose and Drama: Her Own Other.* Lanham: Barnes & Noble Books, 1993.

Buning, Marius. "'Lessness' Magnified." *From Caxton to Beckett: Essays Presented to W. H. Toppen on the Occasion of his Seventieth Birthday.* Ed. Jacques B. H. Alblas and Richard Todd. Amsterdam: Rodopi, 1979. 101-21.

Catanzaro, Mary F. "Musical Form and Beckett's Lessness." *Notes on Modern Irish Literature* 4 (1992): 45-51.

———. "Song and Improvisation in 'Lessness.'" *Beckett in the 1990s: Selected Papers from the Second International Beckett Symposium held in The Hague, 8-12 April, 1992.* Ed. Marius Buning and Lois Oppenheim. Samuel Beckett Today/Aujourd'hui. An Annual Bilingual Review/Revue Annuelle Bilingue. Amsterdam: Rodopi, 1993. 211-18.

Chatman, Seymour. *Story and Discourse: Narrative Structure in Fiction and Film.* Ithaca: Cornell UP, 1978.

Coetzee, J. M. "Samuel Beckett's *Lessness:* An Exercise in Decomposition." *Computers and the Humanities* 7 (1973): 195-98.

Cohn, Ruby. *Back to Beckett.* Princeton, NJ: Princeton UP, 1973.

Culler, Jonathan. *Structuralist Poetics: Structuralism, Linguistics and the Study of Literature.* London: Routledge & Kegan Paul, 1975.

Dearlove, J. E. "'Last Images': Samuel Beckett's Residual Fiction." *Journal of Modern Literature* 6.1 (1977): 104-26.

———. *Accommodating the Chaos: Samuel Beckett's Nonrelational Art.* Durham, NC: Duke UP, 1982.

Dressler, Wolfgang. *Semiotische Parameter einer textlinguistischen Natürlichkeitstheorie.* Österreichische Akademie der Wissenschaften. Philosophisch-Historische Klasse. Sitzungsberichte, 529. Vienna: Verlag der ÖAW, 1989.

Finney, Brian. *Since 'How It Is': A Study of Samuel Beckett's Later Fiction.* London: Covent Garden P, 1972.

———. "Assumption to Lessness: Beckett's Shorter Fiction." *Beckett the Shape Changer.* Ed. Katherine Worth. London: Routledge & Kegan Paul, 1985. 61-83.

Fludernik, Monika. "The Historical Present Tense Yet Again: Tense Switching and Narrative Dynamics in Oral and Quasi-Oral Storytelling." *Text* 11.3 (1991): 365-97.

———. "Introduction: Second-Person Narrative and Related Issues." *Style* 28 (1994): 281-311.

———. "Second Person Fiction: Narrative *You* as Addressee and/or Protagonist." *Arbeiten aus Anglistik und Amerikanistik* 18.2 (1993): 217-47.

———. "Second-Person Narrative as a Test Case for Narratology: The Limits of Realism." *Style* 28 (1994): 445-79.

———. *Towards a 'Natural' Narratology.* London: Routledge, 1996.

Forster, E. M. *Aspects of the Novel.* London: Penguin, 1990.

Genette, Gérard. *Narrative Discourse: An Essay in Method.* Trans. Jane E. Lewin. Ithaca, NY: Cornell UP, 1980.

———. *Narrative Discourse Revisited.* Trans. Jane E. Lewin. Ithaca, NY: Cornell UP, 1988.

———. *Fiction and Diction.* Trans. Catherine Porter. Ithaca, NY: Cornell UP, 1993.

Gibson, Andrew. Rev. of *Towards a 'Natural' Narratology,* by Monika Fludernik. *Journal of Literary Semantics* 26.3 (1997): 234-38.

———. *Towards a Postmodern Theory of Narrative.* Edinburgh: Edinburgh UP, 1996.

Hamburger, Käte. *The Logic of Literature.* Trans. Marilynn J. Rose. Bloomington: Indiana UP, 1973.

Hassan, Ihab. "The Literature of Silence." *The Postmodern Turn: Essays in Postmodern Theory and Culture.* Ed. Ihab Hassan. Columbus: Ohio State UP, 1987. 3-22.

Knowlson, James, and John Pilling. *Frescoes of the Skull: The Later Prose and Drama of Samuel Beckett.* London: John Calder Publishers Ltd, 1979.

Labov, William. *Language in the Inner City: Studies in the Black English Vernacular.* Philadelphia: U of Pennsylvania P, 1972.

———, and Joshua Waletzky. "Narrative Analysis: Oral Versions of Personal Experience." *Essays on the Verbal and Visual Arts.* Ed. J. Helms. Seattle: U of Washington P, 1967. 12-44.

Lieske, Stephan. Rev. of *Towards a 'Natural' Narratology,* by Monika Fludernik. *Zeitschrift für Anglistik und Amerikanistik* 46 (1998): 373-75.

McHale, Brian. *Postmodernist Fiction.* London: Methuen, 1987.

Minami, Masahiko. Rev. of *Towards a 'Natural' Narratology,* by Monika Fludernik. *Narrative Inquiry* 8.2 (1998): 467-72.

Mood, John J. "Samuel Beckett's Impasse—Lessness." *Ball State University Forum* 14.4 (1973): 74-80.

Murphy, Peter. *Reconstructing Beckett: Language for Being in Samuel Beckett's Fiction.* London: U of Toronto P, 1990.

Opas, Lisa Lena, and Joensuu Kujamäki. "A Cross-Linguistic Study of Stream-of-Consciousness Techniques." *Journal of the Association for Literary and Linguistic Computing* 10.4 (1995): 287-91.

Pier, John. Rev. of *Towards a 'Natural' Narratology,* by Monika Fludernik. *Style* 31 (1997): 555-60.

Pountney, Rosemary. "The Structuring of Lessness." *The Review of Contemporary Fiction* 7.2 (1987): 55-75.

Prince, Gerald. *A Dictionary of Narratology.* London: U of Nebraska P, 1987.

———. "On Narratology: Criteria, Corpus, Context." *Narrative* 3.1 (1995): 73-84.

———. *Narratology: The Form and Functioning of Narrative.* New York: Mouton, 1982.

Rabinovitz, Rubin. *Innovation in Samuel Beckett's Fiction.* Urbana: U of Illinois P, 1992.

Ricoeur, Paul. *Time and Narrative.* Vol. 1. Trans. Kathleen McLaughlin and David Pellauer. Chicago: U of Chicago P, 1984.

Rimmon-Kenan, Slomith. *Narrative Fiction: Contemporary Poetics.* London: Methuen, 1983.

Robbe-Grillet, Alain. *Pour un nouveau roman.* Paris: Editions du Minuit, 1963.

Ronen, Ruth. Rev. of *Towards a 'Natural' Narratology,* by Monika Fludernik. *Journal of Pragmatics* 28.5 (1997): 646-48.

Ryan, Marie-Laure. "The Modes of Narrativity and Their Visual Metaphors." *Style* 26 (1992): 368-87.

Solomon, Philip H. "Purgatory Unpurged: Time, Space and Language in 'Lessness.'" *Journal of Beckett Studies* 6 (1980): 63-72.

Stanzel, Franz Karl. *A Theory of Narrative.* Trans. Charlotte Goedsche, with a Preface by Paul Hernadi. Cambridge: Cambridge UP, 1984.

FURTHER READING

Criticism

Amiran, Eyal. Review of *Samuel Beckett: The Complete Short Prose, 1929-1989,* by Samuel Beckett. *Studies in Short Fiction* 34, no. 4 (fall 1997): 523-25.

Laudatory review.

Cathleen Culotta, Andonian, ed. *The Critical Response to Samuel Beckett,* Westport, Conn.: Greenwood Press, 1998, 428 p.

Collection of critical essays.

John, Pilling, ed. *The Cambridge Companion to Beckett,* Cambridge: Cambridge University Press, 1994, 249 p.

Collection of essays on Beckett's work.

Additional coverage of Beckett's life and career is contained in the following sources published by Thomson Gale: *British Writers: The Classics,* **Vol. 2;** *British Writers Retrospective Supplement,* **Vol. 1;** *British Writers Supplement,* **Vol. 1;** *Concise Dictionary of British Literary Biography, 1945-1960;* *Contemporary Authors,* **Vols. 5-8R;** *Contemporary Authors New Revision Series,* **Vols. 33, 61;** *Contemporary Authors–Obituary,* **Vol. 130;** *Contemporary British Dramatists;* *Contemporary Literary Criticism,* **Vols. 1, 2, 3, 4, 6, 9, 10, 11, 14, 18, 29, 57, 59, 83;** *Dictionary of Literary Biography,* **Vols. 13, 15, 233;** *Dictionary of Literary Biography Yearbook,* **1990;** *DISCovering Authors 3.0;* *DISCovering Authors: British Edition;* *DISCovering Authors: Canadian Edition;* *DISCovering Authors Modules: Dramatists, Most-studied Authors,* **and** *Novelists;* *DISCovering Authors;* *Drama Criticism,* **Vol. 22;** *Drama for Students,* **Vols. 2, 7, 18;** *Encyclopedia of World Literature in the 20th Century,* **Ed. 3;** *Guide to French Literature,* **1789 to the Present;** *Literary Movements for Students,* **Vol. 2;** *Literature and Its Times Supplement,* **Ed. 1;** *Literature Resource Center; Major 20th-Century Writers,* **Eds. 1, 2;** *Reference Guide to Short Fiction,* **Ed. 2;** *Reference Guide to World Literature,* **Eds. 2, 3;** *Short Stories for Students,* **Vol. 15;** *Short Story Criticism,* **Vol. 16;** *Twayne's English Authors; Twentieth-Century Literary Criticism,* **Vol. 145;** *World Literature and Its Times,* **Vol. 4; and** *World Literature Criticism.*

Yusuf Idris
1927-1991

(Transliterated as Yūsef Idrīs, Youssef Idris, and Yûsuf Idrîs) Egyptian short-story writer, novelist, playwright, travel writer, editor, essayist, and critic.

The following entry presents criticism on Idris's short fiction from 1975 through 2001.

INTRODUCTION

Regarded as one of the best short-story writers in contemporary Egyptian literature, Idris is lauded for his stories and novellas that portray the changing values of Egyptian society during the twentieth century. Critics note that he was one of the few Arabic authors to realistically address issues of homosexuality, sexual impotence, poverty, sexual and cultural mores, and the dangers of religious fundamentalism.

BIOGRAPHICAL INFORMATION

Idris was born in Bairum, Sharqiva Province, in Egypt, on May 19, 1927. He was educated at Cairo University, where he received an M.D. in 1952. Soon after graduation, he became a medical inspector in the Department of Health, a position that involved working with the urban poor. His concern for the poor and disenfranchised became a recurring theme in his work. While in college, he began to write stories. In 1954, he published his first collection of short stories, *Arkhas layālī* (*The Cheapest Nights and Other Stories*). The volume was hailed as a major literary contribution to Egyptian short fiction. He worked as a physician and a psychiatrist for over a decade, but gave up his medical practice in the mid-1960s to focus on his literary career. His interest in science is reflected in his fiction and journalism. In 1967 Idris was awarded the Naguib Mahfouz Medal for Literature for his collection of short stories *Qissat hubb* (*City of Love and Ashes*). He later became politically active, and his leftist political views resulted in several arrests and brief imprisonments. In the mid-1970s he began focusing on journalistic work for the newspapers *Al-Jumhūriyya* and *Al-Ahrām*. Later though, Idris redirected his attention to short fiction as well as critical essays. He died in August 1991.

MAJOR WORKS OF SHORT FICTION

Idris was a prolific short fiction writer whose work focuses on such themes as love, repression, poverty, alienation, and the concept of masculinity. Sex is a central theme in his work, particularly the various sexual mores in the villages and in urban areas. Several stories explore the inherent iniquity in sexual relationships between men and women from different sociopolitical backgrounds. For example, *Qā'al-Madīna* (1959; *City Dregs*) chronicles the story of 'Abd Allah, a judge, who confronts his servant and lover, Shuhrat, when he discovers his expensive watch missing. Although he had once felt guilty because of his powerful position and her vulnerable one, her theft now frees him from any emotional and sexual connections to her; however, he also becomes aware of how illogical and hypocritical his own values are. In "Akbar al-Kabā'ir" ("The Greatest Sin of All"), as Shaykh Sadiq becomes increasingly devout, he neglects his farm and wife. She eventually seeks comfort in the arms of a young, poor man named Muhammad. Idris also touched on the theme of homosexuality in a few of his stories—a subject taboo in Egyptian literature. "Abū al-Rijāl" ("A Leader of Men") depicts the shocking realization of Sultan, a married, powerful, masculine man, that he has been repressing his homosexuality during his entire life. When he pressures one of his young male servants to have sex with him—and take the dominant role in the sexual encounter—his façade as a strong, virile leader has completely overturned.

Many of Idris's stories reflect his concern with such issues as Egypt's soaring birth population, the denial of civil liberties in a repressive society, the growth of religious fanaticism, and the devastating poverty and hopelessness in urban areas. In "Arkhas Layālī" ("The Cheapest Nights"), a middle-class man walks disoriented through the streets of a busy village. Annoyed by the mass of poor children teeming around him, he wonders why there are so many children and speculates with satisfaction that many of them will die of crime or starvation. Finding his way home, he crawls into bed and has sexual relations with his wife. Nine months later, he is congratulated on the birth of his child. In "Al-Mahfaza" ("The Wallet"), Sami, a young boy, is resentful of his family's poverty when he can't afford to go to the movies with his friends. One night, he sneaks into his parents' room while they are sleeping to steal money from his father's wallet. When he finds the wallet empty, he is overcome by shame and resolves to find a job to help his family with expenses. Other stories reflect the changing political and social situation in Egypt as well as the relationship between the individual and society. In "Alif al-Ahrār," a man obsesses about his loss of individuality in a job that demands conformity. When he refuses to use his typewriter in an act of defiance, he is fired and told that he is expendable.

CRITICAL RECEPTION

Idris is viewed as one of Egypt's finest short-story writers. His prolific output of short stories, particularly in the mid-1950s, was welcomed as a new direction in Egyptian fiction. Critics point to his rejection of the romantic tendencies of Arabic literature at the time in favor of a realistic portrayal of Egyptian society—especially the poorer and disadvantaged classes—as innovative and authentic. Idris utilized colloquial language in his dialogue to mixed reviews among Arab commentators: some critics derided it as lazy and inferior; others saw it as an authentic reflection of the changing Egyptian culture. His incorporation of political and cultural themes have led some critics to view his stories as shrewd reflections of the state of Egypt as it struggled to become an independent modern nation. Reviewers have praised his fantastic tales for their adept utilization of fable and myth. He is deemed a pioneering writer based on treatment of such sensitive topics as homosexuality, sexual impotence, and the danger of religious fundamentalism. Several critics have discussed Idris's stories within the development of the Egyptian short story genre and have traced his development as a short fiction writer. Moreover, critics often compare Idris's short stories to the short fiction of the Egyptian Nobel writer Naguib Mahfouz. Idris is viewed as a gifted and important short-story writer who made a valuable and influential contribution to Arabic literature.

PRINCIPAL WORKS

Short Fiction

Arkhas layālī [The Cheapest Nights and Other Stories] 1954
Jumhūriyyat Farahāt [Farahat's Republic] 1956
A-Laysa kadhālik? [Is That So?] 1957
Al-Batal 1957
Hādithat sharaf 1958
Al-Harqām (novella) 1959
Qā'al-Madīna [City Dregs] (novella) 1959
Akher al-Dunya [The End of the World] 1961
Al-'Askarī al-aswad [The Black Soldier; also translated as The Black Policeman] 1962
Al-'Ayb [Sin; also translated as Shame] (novella) 1962
Lughat al-āy āy 1965

Qissat hubb [City of Love and Ashes] 1967
Al-Mukhattatīn [The Striped Ones] 1969
Al-Naddāha [The Siren] 1969
Al-Baydā' [The White Woman] 1970
Mashuq al-Hams [Ground Whispers] 1970
Al-Mu'allafāt al-kā milah 1971
Bayt min lahm [House of Flesh] 1971
In the Eye of the Beholder: Tales from Egyptian Life from the Writings of Idrīs 1978
Anā Sulṭān qānūn al-Wujūd [I am the Lord of the Law of Existence] 1980
New York 80 (novella) 1981
Uqtulhā [Kill Her] 1982
Rings from Burnished Brass 1984
Al-'Atb 'ala al-nazar [Vision at Fault] 1987
Abū al-Rijāl / A Leader of Men [translated by Saad Elkhadem] (novella) 1988
The Piper Dies and Other Stories 1992

Other Major Works

Al-Lahza al-harija [The Critical Moment] (play) 1957
Al-Harām [The Sinners; also translated as Taboo] (novel) 1959
Al-Farāfīr [The Farfurs; also translated as The Little Birds] (play) 1964
Al-Mahzala al-ardiyya [The Terrestrial Comedy] (play) 1966
Bi-sarāhah ghayr nutlaqah (essays) 1968
Al-Jins al-thālith (play) 1971
Iktishāf qārrah (travel book) 1972
Al-Irada [Will Power] (essays) 1977

CRITICISM

Catherine Cobham (essay date 1975)

SOURCE: Cobham, Catherine. "Sex and Society in Yusuf Idris: 'Qā'al-Madīna'." Journal of Arabic Literature 6 (1975): 78-88.

[In the following essay, Cobham examines the theme of sex in Qā'al-Madīna, contending that Idris "discusses sex because it is such an important part of the differences in culture between different social groups, not for the sake of his own erotic fantasies."]

Yūsuf Idrīs shows his most shrewd understanding of Egyptian society and its changing values through his stories of sexual relationships and his exploration of the nature of love, need, desire, repression, frustration, and masculinity and femininity themselves within these relationships. In his tales of village life, like **"Ḥādithat Sharaf"**,[1] he demonstrates with lucid simplicity the workings of the process by which the community forces its members to conform to accepted standards of behaviour. Sex is the touchstone of social intercourse, and the attitude of a community to sexual relationships is most expressive of its culture; in the village masculinity and femininity are prized but, to appearances at least, they must be put to their designated uses in work and marriage. In a city the sexual code is more complex, and it is more difficult to confine the subject of sex within narrative patterns, but in *Qāʾal-Madīna*[2] (and also in **"al-Naddāha"**[3] and **"Ḥalqāt al-Nuḥās al-Nāʿima"**[4]) Idrīs describes specific sexual relationships between men and women from different social backgrounds in a way which shows the interrelation of their positions in society with their attitudes to sex, and so imposes a pattern on elusive but crucial aspects of Egyptian life and creates a starting-point for thought and understanding.

Shaykh ʿAlī in the story **"Ṭabliyya min al-Samā"**[5] and Nāʿisa in **"Al-Shaykh Shaykha"**[6] rebel involuntarily against the laws of behaviour in the village, but these stories do not, as Theodore Prochazka maintains (in his Ph. D. thesis "Treatment of Theme and Characterisation in the Works of Yūsuf Idrīs", London 1972) "underline the author's view that life in the country is balanced" and therefore desirable, a life "from which a foreign body must be extruded".[7] Shaykh ʿAlī and Nāʿisa are protesting at the inappropriateness and inequity of the laws, but themselves lack the perspective and awareness which Idrīs' stories are able to impose on their actions. In the cities, where it must be assumed that most of Idrīs' readers live, the laws of behaviour are less clearly defined. Sexual codes of different classes and cultures overlap and conflict, and inevitably those rich enough to afford secrecy and a "private life" are able to escape much external condemnation, while many servants, and other working-class people with whom they come into contact, are emigrants from the countryside and are confused by the varying standards of behaviour and the changes which city life creates in them.

Qāʾal-Madīna is the story of the judge ʿAbd Allah who loses his watch, suspects his servant Shuhrat of having stolen it and makes a journey to "the bottom of the city" to catch Shuhrat red-handed with the watch and accuse her face to face. The plot itself is ironic: a judge who sits in court and passes judgment on all kinds of people every day, who has it in his power to adjourn a sitting to suit himself when the defendant pauses "to swallow his saliva",[8] rarely leaves the green riverside quarter of Cairo where he lives, but when the crime is committed against himself he is intoxicated by the idea of confronting the criminal in her own house in the poorest area of the city.[9] He rejoices at the opportunity

to point to guilt in an individual who has personally threatened the ideas with which he protects himself and justifies his way of life.

ʿAbd Allah is a skillfully drawn caricature:

> "His life was filled with the numbers 3445, 299876, 10031, 66, 8345. They were the numbers of his car, his refrigerator, his life insurance, his flat and his bank account . . . He was a man of medium estate, and was in fact average in all things. He was not tall, but you could not possibly have called him short. Similarly he was neither thin nor fat, and his skin was neither white nor brown. In brief, if we took the average height, weight and colouring of a hundred men . . . we would have before us ʿAbd Allah. Even in the sweetness of his tea—Mme. Shanadī would say to him as she put sugar in the cups: 'How many, ʿAbd Allah *bayk*?', then normally she would supply the answer herself and say: 'Ah, I know. You like it medium . . . One and a half, isn't it?', whereupon he would smile and say, as he prepared to play trumps, for they were in the middle of a game of bridge, 'You know, Madame, I am a moderate sort of man.' Everybody would laugh then as if he had made a joke, for the judge's jokes were themselves always average, and moderately funny."[10]

His behaviour is portrayed with delicate satire, not with facile or clumsy sarcasm, so that the reader is led to stand back with the author and understand it, not to join with him in ridiculing the judge. Idrīs describes ʿAbd Allah searching for his watch when he first discovers its loss:

> "During the search operation he had taken off his trousers and jacket and remained only in his shirt and shoes and socks so that he could bend down and look under beds and chairs . . . and in all those places that always spring to a man's mind the moment he loses anything . . . although in the majority of cases all that he finds there is dust and spiders . . . Then he sat down on a chair and placed one bare white leg on top of the other and began to think and wonder. A man like ʿAbd Allah is confronted by problems of every shape and size, but to lose his wrist watch is an unusual problem which only arises—if it arises at all—once in the whole of his life."[11]

ʿAbd Allah is so perplexed by the loss of his watch that he decides to smoke:

> "[He] did not smoke, but he had a packet of cigarettes which he kept in the desk drawer to offer to visitors, and very occasionally he smoked, once a month perhaps or every two months. He stood up to get a cigarette and returned to his former position, sitting with one leg crossed over the other. This movement revealed to him that he was almost completely naked and he hurried to put on his pyjamas before anyone saw him. Not that there was anyone else in the flat, for he was a bachelor and lived by himself, having decided upon his thirty-fifth year as the appropriate time to get married."[12]

With descriptions like this the author accumulates details which gives indications of ʿAbd Allah's attitude to sex. His pragmatic reasons for his abstinence from sex are in retrospect an ironic comment on his relationship with Shuhrat:

> "'Abd Allah was upright, not because it was forbidden (*harām*) not to be upright, or because these 'things' were not right . . . but because on one ill-fated occasion he had gone with a student friend and they had picked up a girl from the street in his friend's big car and had taken her on to the Alexandria road, and the next day he had been terrified by the appearance of ominous symptoms. Of course he had been completely cured but he had sworn to himself never to go near a woman until he got married."[13]

By the time he is thirty his resolve has weakened and he determines to enjoy the five years before he gets married, but although he takes the initial step of ordering his manservant to come only in the mornings, still the flat does not "fill up with women", and he has recourse to Mme. Shanadī's salon to meet girls in keeping with "the dignity of his position" as a judge. The author's very brief sketch of Mme. Shanadī and her salon is like a vivid cartoon for a situation in a novel by Maḥfūz: Mme. Shanadī is "a widow in her fifties whose passion for bridge reached the bounds of madness". Among her friends are "great men of the state" who meet in her salon where she skilfully directs the conversation and "excels in listening to troubles and giving understanding smiles." She is significantly different from the delicate pale-skinned girls and women who frequent her salon, although she partakes of some of their affectations: "her skin was deep brown and she could have come from the heart of the Ṣa'īd, but she said herself that she was Turkish."[14] At her soirées and card-parties 'Abd Allah gradually learns the conventions of behaviour with girls of his own class and is surprised to meet girls from the families of other judges when he visits a cabaret, but secretly these conventions, the need to be "polite and refined and say nice things to them,"[15] irk him and inhibit him, and he is constantly insecure in their company and in the places where he is obliged to go with them. He chooses a place far from Cairo and makes sure that none of his friends or acquaintances or the lawyers from the court knows it, but still he is perpetually ill at ease and "he does not breathe freely until the girl gets out of the car, after tweaking his hand and saying 'Bye Bye' [in English]". The most disturbing aspect of his relations with these girls is that he only has to touch their hands and they start away from him, and finally need forces him to try Mme. Shanadī herself, who "responds to him as if it were a routine procedure, and treats him like an overgrown naughty child", so that his shame and resentment at his unjust deserts increases.[16]

The circumstances in which he engages Shuhrat are themselves satirised. In what is described ironically as "one of the revolutions which 'Abd Allah made against himself, or more precisely against his friends", he makes an arbitrary decision to try and change the pattern of his life and his relationships, quite unaware of the real nature of his dissatisfaction. This expresses itself in a complaint about "the crisis of servants" and an attack on their bad ways to the accomodating Farghalī, the doorman at the court, "who inclined his head, and sometimes his whole body, as a sign of his complete agreement with everything that the judge said." He asks Farghalī to find a woman willing to work for him and, perhaps hardly acknowledging his intentions to himself, he starts by stipulating that she should be old, and finally decides that she should be young, "since the servants' staircase was steep and the flat was on the seventh floor", at which Farghalī smiles, "realising the implied meaning" of the judge's conditions.[17]

The satire, with its sporadic levity, fades when Shuhrat enters the story, and the meaning of the confrontation between her and 'Abd Allah stands clearly on the page. He interrogates her, as master to servant, but she is "polite rather than humble and submissive", and he is disconcerted by her assurance and independence. He remembers his real interest in her: "Would he be able to? He was frightened. It needed a hard struggle to overcome innocence." He stares at her impudently, perhaps searching for "that thing which experience had taught him to look for every time he met a woman, which meant she had no objection, but he did not find it", and she returns his look without embarassment. Although he recognises her innocence instinctively he cannot acknowledge it for long, and is almost jubilant when he thinks he has found out dissimulation in her. When she tells him that she has never worked for anyone before, he thinks disbelievingly that she "must want to appear in his eyes like the lady of the house whom need has forced out to work".[18] Again he cannot believe that she does not partake of the hypocrisy of the girls he is used to, when, shortly after he has finally forced her to submit to him, he returns to her to "look at those strong features, to see what had happened to them", and finds her "with resentful eyes and shining cheeks", upset by her first rude experience of infidelity to her husband. Roughly, he presses her to tell him what is wrong, but she remains silent until he insists:

> "He shook her shoulder with some pity and much irritation:
>
> 'What's the matter?'
>
> She said, 'I've never done it before', and the tears sprang into her eyes. He did not believe her for a moment. That was an old trick . . . she must be trying to make him look ridiculous, if she thought she could convince him that this was her first time. She must think him stupid and naive, or no doubt she wanted a rise for it."

After Shuhrat had refused to submit to him at his first diffident sallies, he had felt the ignominy of his weakness: "A woman like her and he wasn't strong enough to get her . . . and the flat was empty, and although he was young he had social standing, and yet he couldn't do it!", but when he has succeeded, he is seized by an unprecedented awareness of his physical power, for "it had not been his money or his manners or his standing in society which had got her, but his own strength."[19]

For a time he enjoys this new consciousness of his virility which he had never experienced with prostitutes, nor in the emasculated intercourse of Mme. Shanadī's salon, but soon the spectre of Shuhrat's husband rises to the surface of his consciousness, and although he barely allows himself to consider their respective relationships to Shuhrat, he is forced to consider the differences between their ways of life. Momentarily he desires equality with her, and wants to convince himself that she submits to him and tries to please him "for himself and for his manhood". Not knowing whether he is serious or in fun he asks her if she loves him, and the exchange which follows his question is a set-piece between the intellectual who has forgotten how to respond to his feelings, but has "read about love . . . and been deeply involved in discussions about the meaning of love . . . with other educated people like himself", and an illiterate woman who knows what love is intuitively, but when forced to give an explanation answers: "Love is sent by God".[20]

He is consistently preoccupied by the financial aspects of their relationship, although only when he has determined to get rid of Shuhrat and she has faded to the peripheries of his experience does a distant, elegiac sympathy for her poverty become possible, as it occurs to him to wonder how the family will live when she no longer works for him.[21] As his confidence in himself and his contempt for her increases, he changes from proving himself to testing the nature of her dependence upon him, unscrupulously, by lowering her wage. This has the unexpected and undesired effect of bringing her world closer to his imagination, because when she complains to him he learns details of her poverty, and his jealousy of her husband turns to distaste: "His disgust reached its limit when he learnt that her husband worked in the tannery. Many impressions merged into one another in his mind . . . dirty hide, the smell of cattle and glue, Shuhrat's embrace and his bed."[22]

The signs of the change that Shuhrat has undergone at 'Abd Allah's hands begin to irritate him, and as he was instinctively aware of her innocence when she first came, he begins to notice signs of a loss of her former naivety and honesty, "even in her smiles" and in her "languid, theatrical gesture" as she looks at herself in the mirror. He determines most firmly to dismiss her when she changes her *milāya* for a cheap blouse and skirt and goes bare-headed, with a light red colour on her lips "perhaps made by a red biro". He explains his distaste to himself with unconscious hypocrisy and puritanism mingled:

> "Why did she insist on wearing clothes like these when she looked much prettier in a *milāya*? . . . What would she do when she had stopped working for him, and how would they eat? She would have to go out on the streets, and the ones that wore *milāyas* couldn't be worth so much, so that was why she wanted a skirt and blouse, to raise her price."

He does not want to pursue his thoughts too far, and besides, "Shuhrat as far as he was concerned was finished. Only a few days and he would drive her out for good, then let her do whatever she pleased." He is aware that he is responsible for the changes in her, but his recognition of his guilt is short-lived because he, the judge, has no fear of punishment or recrimination for what he does in the privacy of his flat. Since Shuhrat has changed into "a woman who can be bought and sold", he is preoccupied by feelings of jealousy "not of the lover for his beloved" but, since he has reverted to identifying his virility with his social status, the jealousy of "the master for his servant, or the master for himself. He had a terrible fear that Shuhrat would put him on the same level as a youth who did the ironing or sold bread on the street."[23]

The emphasis in the description of 'Abd Allah's journey from the pleasant areas of Cairo by the Nile to the poorest areas behind al-Azhar is strikingly different from that in, for example, Yaḥya Haqqī's description in *Qindīl Umm Hāshim* (Cairo, 1944) of Ismā'īl walking through the square of Sayyida Zaynab, or al-Manfalūṭī's account of his hero wandering in "a lonely, desolate quarter . . . the dwelling-place of *jinns*" in the story 'urfat al-Aḥzān'.[24] With a powerful, evocative conceit Idrīs describes each stage of the journey in terms of the width and surface of the roads, the age of the houses and the type of windows they have, the shops which are replaced by booths and eventually by hand-barrows, and the features and clothes of the people and the way they speak and move, as all these things are modified, and degenerate; the reduction of humanity suggested by the description of the change in the people's language and movement is particularly effective.[25] The complete interdependence and unity of life at the last stage of the journey, potentially a source of strength to the people, and a dramatic contrast to 'Abd Allah's way of life, is represented as a desperate clinging on to subsistence:

> "The houses leant against one another so that they would not fall down, and so did the people. The old man struggled along helped by the young man, the blind man was led by a youth and the sick man was propped up by a wall . . . and a hidden thread joined them together as if they were the beads of a rosary, one spirit inhabiting many different bodies."[26]

'Abd Allah, accompanied by Farghalī and a friend, becomes the centre of apprehensive attention and "women sitting in doorways weaving gossip out of their boredom . . . saw them and wondered, and heads were bent together and the whisper passed from doorway to doorway and they said to one another, 'Police'."[27]

'Abd Allah's expedition to Shuhrat's quarter of the city is as much to restore his dignity and to assert his superiority over her to his own satisfaction, as to find his watch. He has a fleeting, ecstatic vision of asserting his physical power over her again: "if only he could strangle her . . . yes, if he could entwine his fingers around her neck and press and press upon her throat",[28] but as he descends through the city, growing subdued and then benumbed by the unfamiliar surroundings, the gulf between him and Shuhrat becomes increasingly apparent. When he finally confronts her, "he assumes the role of the prosecuting attorney, and she that of the accused . . . and he shouts like the robbed master and she cringes like the thieving servant", but all savour of victory has gone out of the occasion and he is "like a sleep-walker", anaesthetised to the poverty and misery around him, as well as to any sensation of triumph at the sight of his rival, "something moving on the mattress . . . a tall, brown-skinned man, with a head like the tall clay jar that stood beside it, sleeping there . . . his clothes loosened and his worn, grimy underclothes showing through the opening in his trousers."[29]

'Abd Allah's bemused relief as he emerges from the "nightmare" and returns to familiar sights and sounds is conveyed by the imagery which the author uses, and by the description of the intense contrast of the sensuous experience as they leave the poor quarters and approach the Nile and 'Abd Allah's flat:

> "Breezes began to blow and faces revived from the day's heat, and the bridge was filled with groups of people strolling along. There was so much water, and the distant white buildings were like dovecotes, and the city was so beautiful, more beautiful than he had ever seen it . . . He took avid gulps of the air and his head spun."[30]

That evening he sits on his balcony as the sun sets:

> "Night would have engulfed the city if millions of tiny lights had not been sown over the surface of the earth, and these grew and changed the darkness as they bloomed, shining and twinkling. Then they burst into flower, and red and green and blue and yellow lights of different shapes and names and varieties suffused the air of the city, and the darkness was transformed into a carnival."

Still he has not quite regained his peace of mind and "he tries to concentrate his eyes on a spot wavering in the shadows of the night, far from the lights, behind the minaret of al-Azhar."[31]

The point of view expressed by Prochazka that Idrīs' "stories on sex are on the whole a form of erotic daydreaming" must be discounted most vehemently since it altogether misrepresents the nature of the stories. Prochazka writes:

> "Sexuality is . . . only one side of human existence, but Yūsuf Idrīs' characters are overwhelmed by sex, not because their sexual desire is so powerful, but because Egypt's sexual code is so strict."[32]

His remarks would suggest that Idrīs only reflects the tensions and conflicts of sexual behaviour and his own confusion about them, rather than understanding the reasons for them, and standing back from them for the duration of his narrative, while he describes his characters' actions and implicitly or explicitly shows the roots of these actions in the society.

The particular structure of *Qā'al-Madīna* demonstrates that the story is not concerned primarily with the sexual relationship for its own sake. Prochazka discusses in particular **"Ḥalqāt al-Nuḥās al-Nā'ima"** and **"Al-Naddāha"** in relation to these comments, but I would argue that the points made here about *Qā'al-Madīna* apply equally to these stories: Idrīs discusses sex because it is such an important part of the differences in culture between different social groups, not for the sake of his own erotic fantasies.

Qā'al-Madīna takes the shape of a detective story: the judge discovers the loss of his watch, eliminates the suspects until he decides that Shuhrat must be guilty, and then plans his journey to recover it, with the help of his friend Sharaf, an impoverished actor who is to pretend to be a policeman, and Farghalī, who comes from the same area as Shuhrat. The description of his sexual relationship with Shuhrat only forms the recapitulation in the centre of the narrative but it explains, most pertinently, the exact nature and extent of his separation from Shuhrat and all the people like her, and demonstrates the emptiness and hypocrisy of his own values. The natural climax of the story is not in the death of their sexual relationship, but in their confrontation in Shuhrat's house, when he "takes her to the window, and he looks out, and she looks out, and he says, 'Officer', and Sharaf says, 'Yes, sir' . . . and almost laughs", and then they go back into the room, and he threatens her with "a year in prison" if she does not hand back the watch, and in the end she takes it from a broken glass in the cupboard and gives it to him.[33]

Idrīs traces the intricacies of cause and effect in the details of the relationship between Shuhrat and 'Abd Allah, a relationship which is more a confrontation, and has its blueprints in stories like **"Al-Ḥāla al-Rābi'a"** (where a complacent young doctor has his first contact with a woman "criminal").[34] Then with a skilled and delicate sense of proportion he steps back to describe the complete and tragic division between their ways of life with the dispassionate intensity of one who has been involved with, and has identified with, both sides and is able to create an image which does not impart a subjective impression, but forces the reader to imagine those aspects which he does not know from experience, and to share in the conflict.

Notes

1. *Al-Mu'allafāt al-Kāmila*, Cairo 1971, pp. 94-123 (originally published in the collection *Ḥādithat Sharaf*, Beirut 1958).

2. *Qā'al-Madīna* Cairo n.d., pp. 216-287 (originally published in *A-Laysa Ka-dhālika?*, Cairo 1957).

3. *Mashūq al-Hams*, Beirut 1970, pp. 6-46 (originally published in the collection *Al-Naddāha*, Cairo 1969).

4. *Ibid.*, pp. 160-197 (originally entitled 'Dustūr yā Sayyida').

5. *Al-Mu'allafāt al-Kāmila*, pp. 52-65.

6. *Ibid.*, pp. 390-405.

7. Prochazka, p. 38.

8. *Qā'al-Madīna, op. cit.*, p. 217.

9. *Ibid.*, p. 270.

10. *Ibid.*, p. 220.

11. *Ibid.*, p. 218.

12. *Ibid.*, p. 221.

13. *Ibid.*, p. 222.

14. *Ibid.*, pp. 223-4.

15. *Ibid.*, p. 232.

16. *Ibid.*, p. 226.

17. *Ibid.*, pp. 232-3.

18. *Ibid.*, pp. 236-7.

19. *Ibid.*, pp. 240-2.

20. *Ibid.*, pp. 245-8.

21. *Ibid.*, p. 258.

22. *Ibid.*, pp. 251-4.

23. *Ibid.*, pp. 255-261.

24. In *Majallat al-Ḍād*, Aleppo, March-April 1950, pp. 149-153.

25. *Qā' al-Madīna*, pp. 271-6.

26. *Ibid.*, p. 275.

27. *Ibid.*, p. 276.

28. *Ibid.*, p. 272.

29. *Ibid.*, p. 279.

30. *Ibid.*, p. 284.

31. *Ibid.*, pp. 285-6.

32. Prochazka, p. 167.

33. *Qā'al-Madīna*, pp. 280-1.

34. *Qā'al-Madīna*, pp. 7-20.

Roger Allen (essay date 1978)

SOURCE: Allen, Roger. Introduction to *In the Eye of the Beholder: Tales of Egyptian Life from the Writings of Yusuf Idris*, edited by Roger Allen, pp. vii-xxxix. Minneapolis: Bibliotheca Islamica, 1978.

[*In the following essay, Allen traces Idris's development as a short fiction writer and assesses his contribution to modern Arabic fiction.*]

Yūsuf Idrīs is one of the most famous Egyptian writers of the latter half of this century, and his fame transcends national boundaries within the Arab world itself. He has written short stories, novels and novellas, and plays; to each of these genres he has made important contributions. Through his writings he has urged fellow authors to experiment with both form and content, and he has produced innovative works of his own. On the political and cultural planes, he has been in a real sense a member of the *avant-garde* and on several occasions this has brought him into conflict with the authorities in Egypt. It is then a famous and complex personality whose works are represented in this collection.

Idrīs was born in May, 1927, and spent his early childhood in the village of Al-Bayrūm in Sharqiyya province which is part of the Nile Delta. He received his secondary education in the town of Zagāzīg (to the Northeast of Cairo) and then studied medicine in Cairo, graduating from the Qasr al-Aynī hospital in 1951. Soon after his graduation, he became a medical inspector in the Department of Health, a post which gave him ample opportunity to observe the terrible conditions of the urban poor. He had apparently been writing stories for his own amusement while still a student, and in the early 1950s he was encouraged to submit some of them for publication in newspapers. One of those who seems to have given him some encouragement at this time was the writer, Abd al-Rahmān al-Khamīsī. Idrīs' first collection of short stories, **Arkhas Layālī,** was published in 1954 and attracted immediate attention among critics and reading public alike for its intense and often bitter realism. Since that time, his great success as a writer has led him away from the practice of medicine (which he has, to all intents and purposes, given up) and into the realm of creative writing and journalism. Both these latter activities have, of course, also allowed him to express his own views on current political and social issues. He has been a writer for the newspaper *Al-Jumhūriyya* and now writes for *Al-Ahrām*.

Although he is no longer in practice as a medical doctor, his training has left him with an abiding interest in scientific matters and this is reflected in the subject matter (and indeed the vocabulary) of many of his writings; see, for example, the story **"In Cellophane Wrapping"** in this collection which will be discussed in detail below. While Idrīs has kept up his interest in scientific writings, his decision to devote himself to creative writing also led him to read a great deal of *belles-lettres* in both Arabic and Western languages. He had, of course, read the usual store of Arabic classics taught at school (The *Thousand and One Nights* and the almost perversely difficult *Maqāmāt* of Al-Harīrī, which must be equally as troublesome to recalcitrant Egyptian schoolchildren as, say, Chaucer is to their English counterparts). He then began to read modern authors of Arabic fiction, such as Mahmūd Taymūr, Yahyā Haqqī and Nagīb Mahfūz. He also read the works of several Western writers, chief amongst whom seem to have been Poe, Hemingway, Dostoevsky and Chekov.

Idrīs has now published nine collections of short stories,[1] eight novels or novellas and seven plays. Recently, ill health has led to a substantial reduction in his output, and one can imagine the effect which such circumstances may have on someone who is not only a creative artist, but also a doctor by training. Hopefully, a recent operation has improved the situation. At any rate, Idrīs' recent (1976) announcement that he is working on a sizeable novel (tentatively entitled *Iftah al-Qalb—Open the Heart*) may be encouraging to his many admirers.

Idrīs' writing career began in the early 1950s. He thus falls into the period following the Second World War, when an earlier generation of writers had tackled some of the more basic problems of style and content in each of the genres represented in this collection and laid some, if not most, of the groundwork for the emergence of a thriving literary tradition. Needless to say, the course of this process varied from one genre to another. In the short story, for instance, the Arabs had known an anecdotal tradition of story-telling for many centuries. During the 1920s, several writers expanded this base by introducing themes and techniques from several European models such as Guy de Maupassant and the Russian school (Gogol and Turgenev, for example). They began to produce in Arabic works of fiction which turned away from the more sentimental and moralistic tales of earlier writers such as Gibrān and Al-Manfalūtī and concentrated more on succinct character sketches and economy of description. Many famous Egyptian littérateurs, Mahmūd Taymūr, Yahyā Haqqī, Ibrāhīm al-Māzinī and Nagīb Mahfūz, to name just a few, had made important contributions to the genre by the end of the Second World War. Yūsuf Idrīs, as we shall see, was to carry the development forward in several significant ways.

The history of the development of a novelistic tradition within the modern Arabic renaissance (*nahda*) goes back to the later decades of the nineteenth century, when a number of writers produced examples of historical fiction, often with intrusive elements of romance, melodrama and moralizing. While the historical and romantic novel traditions developed in their own ways, there grew up alongside them a realistic tradition, the culminating point of which thus far has been the earlier works of Nagīb Mahfūz and, in particular, his *Trilogy* (*Al-Thulāthiyya*, 1956-7). Since that time, Mahfūz has written novels, short stories and a few plays, concentrating and perhaps excelling in the novel genre (at least until the 1967 War). Idrīs has contributed to the same genres, while the bulk and the best of his output may perhaps be found in the realm of the short story. These two men stand in the very front rank of writers of Egyptian fiction.

Idrīs has also made important contributions to the theatre, and, while they are not represented in this collection, a few remarks should be made about his place in the modern history of this genre. The Arabic drama had faced other problems of acculturation and artistic development in its early modern history. Several critics have suggested that some forms of drama were known in the Arab world, and specifically Egypt, before the modern renaissance; Idrīs is one such writer.[2] Whatever tradition did exist came into contact with the European dramatic tradition during the nineteenth century. Performances took place in both Syro-Lebanon and Egypt. However, largely because of the civil strife in Syria during the 1850s, the majority of proponents of the genre fled to the more conducive environment of Egypt under the rule of the Khedive Ismā'īl. The tradition which developed proceeded initially along the path of vaudeville and slapstick farce to a large degree, although there were also early attempts to translate the European dramatic classics into Arabic. It was the great contribution of Tawfīq al-Hakīm (born in 1898) to write a series of dramas which are essentially *littérature des idées,* based on themes from Greek literature, the Qurān and the *Thousand and One Nights,* to name just three. Furthermore, the historical verse dramas of the poet, Ahmad Shawqī, also contributed to the important process of raising the dramatic medium to a more serious literary and philosophical plane. During the last three decades, the Egyptian theatre has witnessed a great deal of development, both as a contribution to the written literature of the country and in the realm of stage performance. During the period of the revolution (after 1952), the drama has become a natural outlet for discussion and argument on political and social concerns of the Egyptian intelligensia, and the immediacy of its impact on the public has often made it a potent weapon for those for and against the policies of the regime in power. Needless to say, this has frequently resulted in altercation and outright conflict. Apart from its tremendous social importance, the drama has also been a medium of artistic experiment for many writers. One of the most common problems to which dramatists have addressed themselves is the often discussed question of the use of language. If the drama is to have its desired impact on a contemporary audience and deal with social, moral, educational and political questions of the day, can the written language be an effective means of communication; conversely, can the colloquial language (the language of communication among Egyptians) come to be accepted as a valid literary medium? Until recently, the colloquial seemed indeed to have won acceptance among the vast majority of writers and critics, but more recently a more conservative element has been in control of Egyptian cultural activities and a significantly large number of plays are being produced in the written language. The themes of such plays are often excessively moral and religious, so that the use of the written language may lend an appropriate atmosphere of allegory or the "unreal" to such plays. But, whatever the case may be, the two-fold nature (diglossia) of the Arabic language continues to make its presence felt in the dramatic medium.

Having introduced the author of the works in this collection, let us turn to a consideration of Idrīs' contributions to modern Arabic fiction and, within that context, offer some comments on the particular works which have been translated.

. . . . .

The title story of Idrīs' first published collection of short stories, *Arkhas Layālī* (*The Cheapest of Nights*) appeared in 1954, but its subject is as relevant today as it was over two decades ago.[3] A man has emerged from a mosque in a provincial village after the evening prayer; he has had a cup of tea which was especially strong, and his brain is racing. As he wades his way down an alley full of children, he mingles curses against the man who gave him such strong tea with nasty but realistic thoughts about the teeming mass of young humanity all around him, many of whom, as he notes, will die of starvation for sure. As he wanders around the village in search of companionship, he begins to feel both cold and lonely. With another curse on the man who gave him the tea, he turns round and heads for home. There he crawls over the bodies of his six children in order to find the warmth and consolation of his somnolent wife, whom he arouses. Nine months later, he is being congratulated on the birth of yet another child, while he wonders all the while where all these children could possibly come from!

The perennial problem of Egypt's increasing population and a doctor's concern with ignorance of birth control methods are here combined in a short story which amply demonstrates the qualities which made Idrīs' initial short story collections both popular and admired by critics. In the first place he is concerned to portray the poorer classes of Egyptian society as accurately as possible. Previous writers had also concerned themselves

with such people, but it was frequently within the context of general philosophical discussions on such topics as the futility of life. Idrīs presents the poor people as he finds them and allows the bald facts and their implications to speak for themselves. In this he is helped considerably by his use of language which is uncomplicated and explicit. An inherent part of this process involves the use of the spoken language, the colloquial dialect of Cairo or the provinces, when his characters speak. This lends a special vividness to the curses and invocations found in this and many other of Idrīs' stories. But, apart from the use of the colloquial, Idrīs showed in this collection the ability to create cameo-portraits with an economy in the use of language. His descriptions show the character living in his own surroundings; but there is no moral at the end, and indeed, few, if any, of the characters emerge any better off than they were at the beginning of the story.

This "cameo" aspect is well illustrated by the story from this collection which has been selected for inclusion in this anthology, **"A Stare"** (**"Nazra"**). A narrator describes in the first person a chance encounter with a little girl who is carrying a tray full of food on her head. The tray is about to slip, and she asks him to adjust it on her head for her. He watches anxiously as she crosses the street, deftly weaving her way through the traffic. She stops, and he imagines that the tray is about to fall off once again. Rushing across the street, he is almost knocked down himself. But all she is doing, he discovers, is watching some other children playing with a ball. Then, with a final wistful stare, she is "swallowed up" by the street. Here, in a few short paragraphs, we see some of the contrasts in Egyptian society expressed—perhaps unconsciously—through the emotions of the narrator. While the girl goes on her way regardless, the narrator becomes very anxious. One wonders whether he realizes that his advice to her to return to the oven, his surprise at her asking a complete stranger to help her, his comments on her appearance, all these things reflect on him. Is there not perhaps some hidden moral in the fact that she, a personification of the burdens of poverty in Egypt, crosses the street unscathed—no small achievement in Egypt—while the narrator, rushing over impetuously to help her, is almost knocked down? But she is not in any trouble; she is merely staring longingly at a group of children luckier than herself.

The collection, *The Cheapest of Nights,* is full of stories about Egyptians like this little girl, from the poorer classes. Some of them are portrayed at their work in the provinces, others confront the features of modern life during brief visits to Cairo, still others live in the slums of the big city itself. In **"Incident"** (**"Al-Hādith"**) we follow some provincials on a visit to Cairo; they see the sights about which they have heard so much and we hear their comments, frequently not very complimentary, on the conduct of Cairenes. **"A Quarter of a Jasmin Patch"** (**"Rub' Hawd"**) tells the story of Ismā'īl Bey, a landowner who suddenly decides one day to inspect his property. He scolds a peasant who is not hoeing his jasmin patch properly and demands a hoe to do it himself. He cannot even break up the hard ground with the implement he is given, and then suddenly his heart flutters. As he is carried back to the house, the sardonic peasant takes the hoe and breaks the ground apart with his first blow.

Idrīs' second collection appeared under the title *Jumhūriyyat Farahāt* (*Farahāt's Republic*) and contained three short stories and the novel, *Love Story* (*Qissat Hubb*). "Farahāt's Republic" is set in a Cairene Police Station where a Station Sergeant, Farahāt, presides over all the chaotic goings-on with an iron hand and a loud voice.[4] Into this scene comes the narrator. He is obviously from a higher class than most of Farahāt's other customers or victims, but he too has been arrested on some charge or other. Farahāt does not realize this and soon engages the narrator in conversation; in fact, he essentially becomes the narrator himself. While Farahāt intersperses his narrative with staccato orders, insults and curses to all comers, he paints a picture of a dreamworld which he envisages. Inside the gruff and callous exterior of the man who metes out such instant and apparently indifferent justice there resides the heart of a dreamer. When at the end of the story Farahāt discovers that the man with whom he has been sharing his dream is under arrest too, his whole mood changes and his dreams for the future vanish.

I am grateful to one of our translators for this volume, Trevor Le Gassick, for the information that Idrīs originally entitled the story "Abd al-Bāqī's Republic." It would not have been lost on the Egyptian reading public so used to reading between the lines of works of literature that the name "Abd al-Bāqī" consists (as do several Muslim names) of the word *"abd"* (meaning "slave, servant") and one of the epithets used to describe God in the Qurān (the so-called "beautiful names"); the name thus means literally "servant of the One who remains." Exactly the same features are found in the name Abd al-Nasīr (Nasser). The fact that the tale has the word "Republic" itself in its title and that the name of the chief character was changed before publication gives this work a particular significance; beyond the purely local social implications of the events which it reveals to the reader there lies a wider, political message.

This work gives us a convincing picture of a mercurial character dealing with his fellow human beings in an exasperated fashion. The grandiose dreams which he envisions disappear abruptly at the conclusion of the story. Other projects actually implemented by the government of Egypt during the revolutionary period may

not vanish so quickly; the results of building that modern Pyramid, the High Dam at Aswān, are only now beginning to be realized. . . .

The next two selections in this anthology of Idrīs' works are from the collection which appeared originally (1957) under the title *Isn't That So?* (*A Laysa Kadhālik?*), but which reappeared subsequently (1970) named after the novella which it contains, *City Dregs* (*Qā' al-Madīna*). The short story, **"The Wallet"** (**"Al-Mahfaza"**), treats in a very effective fashion one of Idrīs' most common themes, poverty and its effects on an Egyptian family. The availability of primary education to the younger generation in Nasser's Egypt means that Sāmī, the young boy in the story, is able to go to school. However, he is too ashamed to tell his colleagues who keep asking him to go to the cinema with him that he cannot accompany them because he has no money. His father and mother both refuse his requests for the necessary ten piasters; they claim that they have none to give him, but he cannot and does not believe them. The core of the story relates to Sāmī's attempt to get some money from his father, by theft from his wallet at night while the household is asleep. Sāmī's thoughts and reactions are described as he steals into his parents' bedroom, and the tension is built up by the skillful switching of tenses from the narrative past to the vivid present. In attempting to take money from his father's wallet, Sāmī is regarding his father as the all-powerful figure who can do anything; he regards it as inconceivable that his father has no money to give him so that he can go to the cinema. When Sāmī discovers that his father's wallet is indeed empty, his first reaction is one of resentment. Where else could he keep his money? If there is none, where does it all go? But then, he sees his father lying asleep in his bed, his hair dishevelled and his mouth open. The feeling of resentment turns to one of pity. Sāmī feels that he himself should be aspiring to earn a living so that he can give his father some money, instead of vice versa. After replacing the wallet, he steals back to his own room. When his younger brother asks for the inevitable drink of water, he gets him one willingly instead of ignoring him as he has usually done before. An awareness of the real situation of his family and the sight of his sleeping father have aroused a sense of family responsibility in him. Yet again, Idrīs succeeds in this story in showing the plight of the poorer classes through the depiction of a single character who is endeavoring to change his lot on however small a scale; Sāmī emerges no better off at the end of the story, but he has learned a lesson.

With *City Dregs* we come to one of Idrīs' most successful longer works of fiction. In the form of a novella, it treats yet again, as the title implies, the conditions of the urban poor. In this case, that is achieved not only by some masterly description of the poorer quarters of Cairo, but also by a noticeable contrast in treatment of the characters from different classes within the story itself. The character who remains in the center of the action throughout the work is the judge, "Maitre" Abdallāh, but the real force and impact of the narrative focuses on the figure of Shuhrat who comes to his house as both servant and mistress.

In the first chapter we are introduced to the Judge and his trusty servant, Farghalī; the picture is pure caricature. The Judge, for example, is shown to be a totally mediocre, average person:

> His life is full of numbers: 3445, 299876, 10031, 66, 8345—these are the numbers of his car, of his refrigerator, of his life insurance policy, of his apartment, of his bank account . . . he is a man of average circumstances. Indeed it can almost be said that he is average in everything.

So petulant is he that he thinks nothing of cancelling a session of the court merely because he is preoccupied with the problem of the loss of his watch. So orderly is his life, at least on the surface, that he has "decided" that he will marry at the age of thirty-five; that seems to be the right time to do it. However, his experiences with women up till now have been either too risky or else too unstimulating. Within this thoroughly routine, pedestrian existence the Judge has at his beck and call the obsequious Farghalī, and it is to him that the Judge turns with the problem of his sexual frustration, albeit expressed in a request for a young girl to help with the housework.

The loss of the watch, the elimination of all the other possibilities and suspects, the Judge's failure to find a "suitable" woman for himself outside the apartment, all these strands lead to the splendidly abrupt beginning of the second chapter: "It must have been Shuhrat." Up till this point, Shuhrat's name has not been mentioned once. But, now that the situation has been set out and the Judge's life and habits have been described with a detached but forceful caricature, Idrīs now devotes the next four chapters to Shuhrat's position in the Judge's apartment and the development of their relationship. At the beginning of the second chapter, we are introduced to Sharaf, an actor friend of the Judge, and his role is to be that of "a good listener." Through this device, Idrīs proceeds to trace for us the Judge's initial inability to force his attentions on Shuhrat, his "wave of joy" when he finally overpowers her, his desire to make her love him, and then his increasing feeling of boredom with her. As he begins to test her feelings and his own revulsion becomes stronger, she in turn becomes more brazen and starts asking for "loans" to pay for the European-style clothes which she has started wearing. He decides that he must dismiss her but keeps postponing the inevitable. However, his refusal to give her the loan for which she is asking seems to give her an inkling of his intentions. The actual theft of the watch

brings us back to the present again, with Sharaf listening to the Judge and helping him decide what is to be done. We have now had presented to us the basic frame story and a retrospective account of the events which led up to it. The final two chapters move towards the climax and then the conclusion.

In Chapter 7 the Judge concocts a plan whereby his actor friend, Sharaf, is to play the part of a detective when they go to confront Shuhrat with her crime, and, with Farghalī to guide them to her home, they set out for the poorest parts of the city. The description which follows must surely be one of Idrīs' finest literary creations; in it he makes use not only of his intimate knowledge of the poorer quarters of Cairo and their inhabitants, but also his ability to use a succession of images to create a tremendous tension. The party travels from the airy quarter where the Judge lives through the streets of the modern part of the city which are teeming with cars and people. Thereafter, the atmosphere becomes more and more stifling, physically and psychologically as the car is hemmed in by more and more people and eventually abandoned in favor of walking. The streets become narrower and narrower, and Idrīs differentiates the various levels of poverty and squalor in a masterly fashion, using visual images such as shops, street signs and houses and sensual ones such as smells and even changing language-patterns. With each paragraph, they advance further. As they do so, the Judge comes to realize what his relationship with Shuhrat has really involved. He was able to conquer his initial misgivings about her wearing a native wrap when she first came to his apartment and thus succeeded in satisfying his sexual desires for a while. But this journey to the home of Shuhrat shows him with brutal clarity the huge gulf which separates them. His initial desire to punish her for stealing his watch becomes a need to restore his own self-respect. As they reach the "City Dregs", the place where Shuhrat lives, the houses and people lean against each other for support, children play in heaps of garbage, women sit chatting on thresholds, and flies are everywhere, particularly in children's eyes. At last comes the confrontation, the culmination of this graphic and horrifying journey. The Judge ignores Shuhrat's children and sleeping husband and asks his rehearsed question. He is aware that she is trying desperately to support her family and wonders to himself why he is behaving as he is; "he is acting a part and she is not." At first, Shuhrat pretends innocence, but Sharaf plays his detective role at the right moment and her resistance crumbles. But there is no sense of victory for the Judge. He questions her as to why she took the watch, but then her husband begins to wake up and the Judge goes on his way.

The description of the return journey is considerably shorter, but is no less effective for that. We can, of course, imagine all the visual detail of the first journey in reverse, but this time Idrīs concentrates on the sensual. As they approach the modern city, there are the vehicles as before, but this time there is a feeling of air, of breadth. Breezes begin to blow and water is plentiful; the world blossoms and the city looks beautiful. Back in his apartment at the beginning of Chapter 8, the Judge watches the city as the lights are being turned on in the evening, and his eyes follow the lights to the point where the old city lies, where Shuhrat must still be. At this point, the narrative switches from the story of this particular episode to the present. The Judge still wears the watch, and the manner in which he recovered it has become one of his anecdotes; he does however curtail the part dealing with the actual recovery. He spots Shuhrat on a street, obviously soliciting. Above all, he notices that she is wearing a new blouse. As a result of her new profession, she can now afford the kind of clothing which her relationship with him led her to believe was necessary and which made her steal his watch in the first place.

City Dregs is one of Idrīs' most successful essays in fictional form beyond that of the short story. Within the framework of a crime narrative involving the loss of a watch and its recovery, he portrays the development and breakdown of a tragic relationship, one which leads Shuhrat from poverty into depravity and which shows the Judge how illogical and hypocritical his own values and standards are. When we have finished reading this novella, we too, like the Judge, are left with the memory of the journey to the very dregs of the city.

The next short story collection by Idrīs to appear after *City Dregs (Qa' al-Madīna)* was *An Affair of Honor (Hādithat Sharaf)* which was published in 1958. The title story (already available in translation as **"Peace With Honor"**[5]) is set in a provincial farm estate *(izba)*. Fātima, generally acknowledged as being the prettiest girl on the estate, is caught in a field with Gharīb, a young man who can succeed in making any woman swoon just at the sight of him. Fātima has been warned all along to beware of the 'shame', and the whole community is convinced that it has now happened to her. The two most handsome inhabitants of this microcosm become the focus of the jealousies and instinctive suspicions of the community. While Gharīb flees the estate, Fātima is subjected to the humiliation of an 'examination'. When she is found to be safe, everyone rejoices; the honor of the estate has not been sullied. For a while, Gharīb abandons his rakish ways, but he cannot keep it up for long. Fātima on the other hand has lost some of her innocence and is even capable of a certain amount of defiance. At the end of the story, she is still unmarried, a forbidden fruit too luscious for any of the villagers to allow anyone else to marry.

The question of societal attitudes and especially taboos on the individual is a theme to which Idrīs has fre-quently addressed himself, and especially in matters of sex. In an article in the periodical, *Mawāqif* (no. 9, 1970), Idrīs has the following to say on the subject:

> I choose woman as being the best expression of frankness in society . . . I can say that I write about sex as being part of life. Sex for me equals life. As far as I am concerned, any other significance is invalid . . . the relationship between men and women is in need of a revolution. They are not two different, separate and distant entities. They are very close to each other . . . a single entity, a single human being . . . Thus, sex does not imply men coming to women and vice versa, but rather the desire of both to plunge deeper and deeper into life and to embrace the continuity of mankind.

Idrīs' concern with attitudes to the subject of sex in Egyptian society can, of course, be readily seen in the immaculate and futile planning of the Judge Abdallāh in *City Dregs* which leads him to hire Shuhrat in the first place. It emerges too in the story, **"An Affair of Honor"**, and we shall see it as a central theme in some of his more recent stories to be discussed below.

In the story, **"The Big Hand"** (**"Al-Yad al-Kabīra"**) from this same collection we find another situation which Idrīs uses on several occasions in his short stories, namely the implications of the presence or absence of a father-figure to a particular family. Other examples are **"The Seesaw"** (**"Al-Marjīha"**) from *The Cheapest of Nights* and **"House of Flesh"** (**"Bayt min Lahm"**) from the collection of that name, to be discussed below. In **"The Big Hand"**, the narrator describes in the first person his reactions on returning to his village, the walk from the railroad station to his house, the comments of the villagers whom he passes, but above all the greetings from his father and mother. On one occasion however, he returns to find the atmosphere very different. His father has just died; the house is empty, and the rest of the family are at the cemetery. He himself goes to the cemetery and communes with his dead father. After reminiscing for a while, the narrator engages his father in a conversation, expressing the love which the whole family feels toward him and the anguish which he himself feels because his father has died while he was away. When the narrator returns home, the whole family sits in silence. Then suddenly, everyone bursts into tears. They have all faced the reality that the head of the household is now dead and gone forever.

. . . . .

The works which we have described thus far constitute a remarkable outpouring of literary effort. In the years between 1954 and 1958, Idrīs published five collections of stories and three plays, and all that by the age of thirty. These years coincided with the first decade of the Egyptian Revolution, and the heady experiences of the Czech arms deal, the withdrawal of European and Israeli forces after the Tripartite Invasion of 1956, and the attempts at the unification of a "United Arab Republic" with Syria. At the same time, tight control began to be exercised on the publication media in Egypt, and writing was kept under strict censorship. Apparently, the collection, **An Affair of Honor,** suffered as a result of this process and was eventually published for the first time in Lebanon.

It is perhaps only after the advent to power of Anwar al-Sādāt in 1970 and the so-called "correctional revolution" *(thawra al-tashīh)* that it has been fully possible to discover quite how capricious was the observance of civil liberties in Egypt during the period of the 1960s up till the fateful debacle with Israel in 1967. Nagīb Mahfūz has recently discussed this period with remarkable candor in his novel, *Al-Karnak* (the name of a ficticious café), but both he and Yūsuf Idrīs began to address themselves to the problems of contemporary man and of the individual in society (often in unfavorable circumstances) during the 1960s. Both used symbolism and even surrealism to couch their thoughts in terms which could be understood by their readership and yet survive the attentions of the censor. In Idrīs' case, there continue to be stories which reflect the social concerns treated in his earlier collections, but these are juxtaposed with other stories which reflect the absurd and illogical aspects in the existence of contemporary man.

These points can best be demonstrated by describing the two stories from Idrīs' next collection, **The End of the World** (*Ākhir al-Dunyā*—1961), which are included in this anthology. The first, **"Playing House"** (**"La'bat al-Bayt"**), takes us into the world of two children at play and into the mind of one of them, Samīh, the little boy who loses his temper with Fātin, the girl with whom he is "playing house", wishes her good riddance, but then rapidly comes to hope that she will return. The portrayal of such childish petulance is well managed as we follow Samīh's changes of mood from initial exasperation, through boredom, to regret and a desire for reconciliation. But, in spite of the charming children's environment within which the story is convincingly set, we may still note that such instant flashes of temper and almost immediate regret are not confined to the world of children!

With **"The Omitted Letter"** (**"Alif al-Ahrār"**) we come to one of Idrīs' most effective expressions of the conditions of modern man; it is a veritable tragicomedy about his position in and response to the kind of existence governed by the demands of technology and administrative bureaucracy. There is much in this story which is amusing. It is a flea which keeps Ahmad Rashwān, the ultimate in punctilious civil servants, awake and thereby provokes the incredible and crucial question as to how he differs from his own typewriter. Everything about the company, from its fancy glass doors,

to the posturings of Ahmad's boss and the upward and downward movement of the mouse-like figure of the Director-General as he swivels his chair, all these things are portrayed with a generous dose of sarcasm. And yet, the essential question is a real and critical one: is modern man being dominated by the machines which are supposed to help him; does he have any freedom of choice, can he exert any initiative? These are the issues which Ahmad resolves to settle for himself when he refuses to insert into a typed document a letter which he has deliberately left out as an assertion of his own individuality. Needless to say, the company bureaucracy, in the form of Abd al-Latīf, his boss, is quick to inform Ahmad that he has no individuality. Abd al-Latīf makes no concessions to Ahmad's feelings as he makes this fact brutally clear to him, but the Director-General tries a more gentle approach. Everyone has to obey orders, he tells Ahmad, even the Director-General himself. But by now, Ahmad has become obsessed by the notion of the dignity of mankind and his own superiority over his colleagues, and continues his defiance. After he is fired, he discovers that the typewriter key for the letter which he has deliberately left out is not working and rushes to tell his boss. As a final blow to Ahmad's crusade for individual rights, his boss tells him that machines can be repaired; we are left to infer that defiant employees who insist on asserting their individuality are fired.

Idrīs' output continued at the same rapid pace during the early part of the 1960s, and the year 1962 saw the appearance of not only the novel, *Shame (Al-Ayb)* but also a collection of lengthy short stories under the title **The Black Soldier** (*Al-Askarī al-Aswad*). This latter volume contains three long works: the title story, **"Lady Vienna"** (**"Al-Sayyida Fiannā"**) and **"Men and Bulls"** (**"Rijāl wa Thīrān"**). It has to be admitted that in all three works, the artistic dimension tends to take a back seat while the author indulges in some writing which shows clear journalistic tendencies. In **"Lady Vienna"** an Egyptian finds himself in Vienna and searches for a woman who will satisfy his needs; he encounters a woman who feels a similar need for an African man. One has only to read Yahyā Haqqī's *The Lamp of Umm Hāshim* (in translation, *The Saint's Lamp* tr. Mustafa Badawi, Leiden: Brill, 1973) or Al-Tayyib Sālih's *Season of Migration to the North* (translated with the same title by Denys Johnson-Davies, London: Heinemann, 1970) to realize that the theme of cross-cultural encounters such as these can be much more successfully and artistically handled than is the case in **"Lady Vienna"**. The same may be said about **"Men and Bulls"** which is essentially a description of the life of a bullfighter in Spain, full of long depictions of bullfights and the reactions of the narrator to the events which he witnesses and the people whom he meets.

The story of **"The Black Soldier"** suffers from some of the faults which we have just outlined. The desire to produce a work which will be a direct commentary on the human condition seems to have been very much in the forefront of the author's consciousness. **"The Black Soldier"** is undoubtedly the best of the works in this volume because it shows Idrīs, the committed Egyptian writer of fiction, addressing himself to a question which has only recently shown itself with full clarity to have been one of the central issues of Egyptian society during the decade of the 1960s, namely personal liberty, the psychological effect of internment on intellectuals and other members of society, and the generally reticent attitude of society at large to the seemingly random arrest of its members by the state security forces. Like *City Dregs,* **"The Black Soldier"** is told in retrospect. The two works share something else too, in that, just as Shuhrat is the real heroine of *City Dregs,* so Shawqī, the doctor who spends time in prison and is tortured at the hands of the Black Soldier, is the real hero of the latter story. And yet, whereas *City Dregs* succeeds in blending the core of the story and the characters in it into a background almost cinematic in its vividness, in **"The Black Soldier"** there is a heavy emphasis on description of past events at the expense of characterization of even the major figures in the story. What emerges therefore is a tale of immense power, one which fully reflects Idrīs' close involvement in the struggles for personal freedoms during the 1960s and shows his own considerable courage in even broaching such a theme, but, at the same time, one which lacks the artistic subtlety of some of his earlier works. Idrīs here allows his overwhelming concern for his fellow human beings to come entirely to the fore; we are therefore presented with an important document, but one which lacks some of the artistic qualities of his other fictional works.

Idris' last three collections of short stories appeared over a period of nine years: *The Language of Screams* (*Lughat al-Ay Ay,* 1965) contains stories written between the years 1957 and 1965; *The Clarion* (*Al-Naddāha,* 1969) contains those written between 1965 and 1969; and *The House of Flesh* (*Bayt min Lahm,* 1971) those written in 1970 and 1971, along with a couple from an earlier period. For an author who had previously been so noticably prolific in his fictional output, this may seem to represent a considerable change on the author's part. The causes are no doubt as complicated as the personality of our subject, but they seem to be made up of some combination of the following factors. In the first place, Idrīs began to take an intense interest in the theatre during the 1960s. We have already noted that he had published two plays in the 1950s and that he advocated in a series of articles in 1963 a completely new approach to the drama and indeed the creation or revival of indigenous Egyptian dramatic forms. To emphasize his points, Idrīs composed his highly successful and controversial play, *Farāfīr* (in translation, *Farfoors* tr. Farouk Abdel Wahab, in *Mod-*

ern Egyptian Drama, Minneapolis: Bibliotheca Islamica, 1974), which was performed for the first time in 1964. It should also be remembered that Idrīs gave up his medical career during this period and, as many creative writers in Egypt do, turned to journalism, working first for *Al-Jumhūriyya* and then for *Al-Ahrām.* On the more negative side, we have already noted the extremely difficult conditions under which Egyptians had to carry out their lives during the oppressive years of the 1960s up till 1967. The June War of that year was, of course, a setback for the Arab world as a whole and something which caused intellectuals in particular to indulge in a great deal of thought about the very bases of their society and its attitudes to itself and others. This general unease in the immediate aftermath of June 1967 continued until the death of Abd al-Nāsir in 1970. The first years of the Sādāt regime have seen some superficial freedoms restored to the press and other writers, but at the same time have witnessed the appearance or reappearance on the cultural scene of some extremely reactionary figures with whom Idrīs can feel little sympathy. In fact, he and several of his fellow writers were deprived of their jobs early in the Sādāt regime and the situation does not seem to have improved within the last few years. All these factors, positive and negative—to which can be added a debilitating heart condition—have made the last decade a particularly trying one for Idrīs, as for many creative writers in Egypt. This may perhaps account for the slower rate of publication during these years.

Some of the stories in the collection, *The Language of Screams,* reflect the wide variety of themes found in Idrīs' earlier collections. **"Because Judgement Day Will Not Happen"** takes us, like **"Playing House"**, into the world of children. **"Caught in the Act"** is a particularly successful description of a brief encounter. The Dean of a university college is initially outraged when he sees a girl student smoking in secret as he looks out of his window. His anger is put aside as he watches the young girl enjoying every puff of the cigarette, and he almost comes to participate vicariously in her feelings of relaxation and pleasure. As she finishes the cigarette, he comes to himself again. The girl suddenly feels a sense of danger, and their eyes meet. She realizes that she has been "caught in the act."

Alongside these stories we find others (the most recently composed of those in the collection) which stress a new theme, Man's lack of concern for his fellow human beings. The title story deals with a successful man who is made aware by the chronic illness of his old school friend, Fahmī, of his separation from the plight of other people less fortunate than himself. In an ending the implications of which are too clear to miss and in fact expressed with an insufficient sense of artistry, Al-Hadīdī, the successful man carries Fahmī out of the house on his shoulders; they are going on "another, more difficult path." His wife asks him if he has gone mad as she refuses to go with him.

The story from **The Language of Screams** collection included in the present anthology is certainly the best in the set and must be reckoned one of Idrīs' most powerful examples in the short story genre. If human indifference is the theme of **"The Language of Screams"**, then **"The Aorta"** deals with the subject of human oppression and cruelty. In an opening passage of considerable impact, the author builds up a picture of the human herd instinct, as people swirl around a square like ants, following anyone who seems to have any goal and then reverting to their lemming-like rush to nowhere as the goal proves not to exist. In the midst of all this, the first-person narrator suddenly comes face to face with Abduh whom he suspects of stealing money. We are made aware of the narrator's total lack of any human feelings towards this man: as he contemplates the possibility of chewing him up while throttling him, all he can comment on is the man's "repulsive" habit of bursting into tears. The animal hatred and callousness of the narrator proves contagious, and the people around him join in the insane hunt for the money which, they believe, is hidden on Abduh's person. Abduh pleads in vain that he has had an operation to cure "a dangerous disease that threatened to infect all Egyptians," and that he has had his aorta removed. The similarities of the crowd in this story to those of a lynch mob are now further emphasized as they hoist Abduh up on to a butcher's hook and then proceed to strip him. When they discover that he is indeed covered in bandages, they still do not believe Abduh's story; by now, the herd instinct is at its fullest frenzy. Only when the bandages are finally off and Abduh's aorta dangles in the air does the crowd finally realize that Abduh was telling the truth. He has been done to death for something which he never had.

This story is one of the most impressive and forceful of Idrīs' more recent compositions, in some of which there is a conscious withdrawal from reality in order to address himself to various profound and disturbing issues of the day. Indifference and human cruelty were indeed apt subjects for discussion in Egypt during the 1960s, and they were not irrelevant elsewhere. Idrīs' treatment of them before the June War of 1967 is not a little prophetic. Many authors touched upon this theme in the aftermath of the war, including playwrights like Saʿdallāh Wannūs and Muhammad al-Māghūt. Naġīb Mahfūz devoted a considerable amount of attention to it in a series of compositions written immediately after the War. The impact of stories such as **"Under the Bus Shelter"** and **"Sleep"** may have been more noticable directly after such a defeat, but the implications of the often grotesque events which take place in their surreal environment find an earlier echo in these stories of Idrīs.

This combination of themes based on both the real and surreal is carried on into the next collection of short stories, **The Clarion** (**Al-Naddāha**—1969). The title story again deals, like **City Dregs**, with the impact of the big city and those who live there on the fate of a woman. Fathiyya, a country girl, is seen in her village by Hāmid, who serves as a doorman in the big city. She feels attracted towards the metropolis and agrees to marry him. He takes her back to live in his small room in the building where he works. Hāmid has to be away a great deal, Fathiyya feels alone, disoriented and bored, and the inevitable happens. Fathiyya gives in to another man, and they are caught *in flagrante* by Hāmid. The latter takes Fathiyya back to the station, intending to send her back to her village. However, she manages to escape from him in the crowd and returns to Cairo. The conclusion of the story makes it clear that this time she is taking on the city on her own terms.

One of the stories in this collection with a non-realistic frame of reference is **"The Wonder of the Age"** (**"Muʿjizat al-Asr"**), in which a midget mastermind with tremendous talents and potential is unappreciated by his own people, but finds encouragement elsewhere. Another is **"The Point"** (**"Al-Nuqta"**), a brief impression with no plot in which the narrator describes his relationship to his own environment. But the shortest story in the collection, perhaps Idrīs' shortest short story, is the one chosen for this anthology. **"The Concave Mattress"** (**"Al-Martaba al-Muqaʿ ʿara"**) is a telling commentary on the routine, even the monotony, of married life for certain couples. The sting is in the tail, so to speak, in that the wife only comes to realize the fact after her husband's corpse has bounced on the hard ground below the window beside which she has been standing.

The comment of Idrīs cited above about sex and the importance of the relationship between men and women continues to find an application in these latest collections of short stories. In those already analysed, we have seen the subject presented in a variety of contexts and through a variety of approaches, ranging from the bitter and sarcastic to the purely tragic. But Idrīs' repertoire on this topic is far from expended, and we find new examples in his most recent collection, **House of Flesh (Bayt min Lahm)**. In four of the stories included in this anthology Idrīs illustrates further the frustrations, the temptations and even the loneliness involved in the relationship between a man and his wife, and indeed between men and women outside marriage. The title story, **"House of Flesh"**, is a very forceful case in point. Here the author takes his reader back to one of the themes to which he had addressed himself on more than one occasion in earlier stories: the problems of the family without a father figure, or, in more sexual terms, the emotions and tensions inside a house full of women, a widowed mother and her three growing daughters. Society here works in a vicious circle, since the mother does not wish to remarry before her daughters have settled down and yet the lack of a man in the house means that no men ever have the pretext to go there. The only exception is the blind Qurān reader. Anything is better than nothing, it is decided, and the mother marries him at her daughters' urging. The mother puts on her wedding ring at night as the couple go to bed and then make love. The daughters lie awake in the same room, following every sigh and groan. Even with a man in the house now, no men come to ask for the girls' hands. As they grow up and reach maturity, they plead with their mother to help them. In resignation, she lets them put on the ring. Each daughter in turn sleeps with her mother's husband, the ring becoming a passport for the relief of their sexual frustration. And, as the author tells us at the end of the story, the blind man knows nothing about what is going on; or does he?

In the story **"In Cellophane Wrapping"** (**"Alā Waraq Sīlūfān"**) we have another instance of sexual frustration. The gorgeous and bored wife of a celebrated surgeon visits the operating theatre where her husband is performing for the first time a pioneering operation. She is confronted by the fact that in this situation he is far from being the quiet, submissive creature which he seems to be at home; he is in fact an utter tyrant who loses his temper, throws things around and yells at his subordinates. Seeing this aspect of him which she has never seen at home arouses all the basic impulses towards him which she has been transferring, albeit diffidently, to another man. Idrīs here succeeds in conveying through the stream of consciousness technique the feelings of this spoiled and petulant woman as she enters her husband's working environment, her initial resentment at her husband's lack of concern for her and her gradual realization in the operating theatre itself that he does in fact become a completely different person at home, someone who allows her considerable latitude and freedom. Even though she really feels the need for him to exhibit at home the same character traits as he displays at work, she comes to be aware of her own selfishness. The "other man" vanishes into thin air as she watches the miraculous skill of her husband at work.

In two of the stories from this same collection, sexual relationships are treated in a more sardonic fashion. In **"The Greatest Sin of All"** (**"Akbar al-Kabā'ir"**) Shaykh Sādiq becomes increasingly devout and this leads him to neglect not only his farm but also his wife, Umm Gād. She however finds consolation with the eighteen year-old Muhammad on the roof of the house, while her husband below is involved in his religious rituals. This story begins with a short commentary from the author to the effect that most people find the whole tale very amusing and burst into laughter, while Muhammad himself cannot see anything funny about it at

all. The insertion of this tale-telling description at the beginning of the story lends a certain folkloric touch (presumably deliberate); this, we presume, is the kind of story which people like to be able to tell each other. The same is true of another story, **"Lily, Did You Have to Put the Light On?"** (**"A Kāna Lā Budda Yā Lī-Lī An Tudī' al-Nūr"**). Once again, we are told at the beginning of the story that this is the kind of anecdote which people like to gossip about, and we are even told that in this case certain types, when sufficiently stoned, like to improvise variations on the basic theme. This story also has an amusing side to it, and again the butt of the humor is religion, or the outward practice of it. The gradual build-up of the present shape of the story and the assumption that many tongues have participated in the process of its composition is further aided by the structure of the story. It begins with the description of the quarter and the kinds of people who live there and then proceeds to describe the scene as the newly attracted mosque congregation is stuck in the position of prostration during their prayers, not daring to move. We then retrace in retrospect the arrival of the young Imām and his initial failures, then his technique for scoring some success and his final defeat as he falls victim to the charms of the gorgeous Lily, a child of an Egyptian mother and English soldier father. This defeat, eventually acknowledged by the Imām, explains the terrible dilemma of his congregation whom he leaves stranded in the prostration position. That provokes the laughter of the listeners to the tale, but it is not the last laugh. The young Imām follows the Devil's lead and goes to Lily's room. But she no longer needs the lessons which she has previously requested on how to pray; the Imām is finally thwarted, since she has been instructed in prayer by a phonograph record.

If sexual themes are a common theme in these stories, they are not the only ones; for Idrīs continues right up till the present his wide choice of subject matter. **"The Chapter on the Cow"** (**"Surat al-Baqara"**) presents us with an amusing, rustic tale, full of lively colloquial dialogue and touches of local description. In it we trace in simple chronological sequence the responses of a peasant who is leading a cow home from market to importunate questions from all and sundry as to how much he paid for the animal. These responses change from initial politeness to exasperation, anger, outright assault and finally the uncontrolled outbursts of a lunatic.

Two other stories show a continuation of Idrīs' use of a suspension of reality to paint an allegory of modern life. In **"The Journey"** (**"Al-Rihla"**), translated by the editor in the *Journal of Arabic Literature,* Volume 3, 1972), a man carries the dead body of his father around in a car. He proclaims his continuing love for him and his great debt to him for the way he has cared for him while a child. To those who ask, the son vehemently denies that there is an unpleasant smell in the car. However, the stench gradually becomes more pervasive, and even the narrator has to admit that his father's body is the thing which is smelling. He abandons both the car and the body on the road. One may interpret this story as a statement that the younger generation is rejecting the old, and such a literal interpretation may be all that is intended. However, in a country like Egypt in which any work of literature is minutely examined for its possible political and social implications, wider implications have been suggested for this story. These are further underlined by the publication date of the story in *Al-Ahrām* (5 June 1970). According to such interpretations, the dead father is intended to represent Abd al-Nāsir (rendered effectively "dead" by the June War of 1967 and its results), and the message of the story is thus that the time had come to abandon even such a beloved figure as one's own (the country's) father figure.

Another short short story (like **"The Concave Mattress"** discussed above) is **"The Little Bird on the Telephone Wire"** (**"Al-Usfūr wa l-Silk"**). Here the style is more cursive and indeed almost poetic in comparison with the deliberate terseness of the dialogue in **"The Concave Mattress."** A little bird lives his life of flying, perching on a telephone wire and making love to his paramour, blissfully unaware of the electronic pulses of modern life going back and forth within the wire which he is clutching. Deceits, blandishments, love, hatred, heroism, cowardice, all these things are blended into the same electronic pulses which succeed in eradicating all differentiations. As modern technology reduces everything to the same level, the little bird, with its "innocent" claws, carries on unawares, and the picture which results presents the reader with a forceful contrast between the guileless values of nature and the normalizing reductions brought about by modern technology and the existence which it creates.

"The Chair Carrier" places the narrator of the story in a crowded street, as in **"The Aorta".** But this time, he is not participating in their activity; in fact, he is exasperated by their total lack of interest or concern. Once again, the theme of total indifference to others is introduced. A man is carrying a gigantic chair around. He has been carrying it since the Pharaonic period, even though a notice is pinned to it saying that the Pharoah has given it to him and he should take it home and sit on it. The narrator is almost beside himself with frustration as he reads the message to the porter. The latter listens patiently but with scarcely concealed annoyance. He tells the narrator he cannot read and in any case he needs the proper "authorization." The narrator has no such authorization, and so the porter goes on his way, grumbling that he has to earn a living and has been delayed for nothing. As the narrator watches him slowly disappearing into the crowd, and as people continue to speed by in total disregard of the man and his huge chair, the narrator is left with a vestigial feeling of guilt

because he did not have the authorization. Perhaps he is implying thereby that the modern world feels no sense of the meaning of and need for a historical perspective, and thus the man and his chair must continue to wander in search of someone with the proper "authorization."

In the preceding pages we have placed the works of Yūsuf Idrīs included in this anthology within a chronological framework. The content and structure of each composition has been analysed within the context of other works written at about the same time as the work in question. Such a diachronic presentation of this author's works runs the risk of viewing each work in isolation from others with similar themes, relying on the logic of chronological order rather than more literary criteria. However, the decision to follow this pattern was based partially on the fact that this anthology includes works from different genres, the novella and the short story. We were also motivated to follow this approach by the fact that Idrīs, perhaps to an extent greater than any modern Arab writer of comparable stature and quality, displays a development in both style and narrative technique which can be well illustrated through a diachronic perspective. However, now that we have described and analysed the works included in this anthology and other works from the same periods, an attempt will be made to essay some general remarks about the different facets of Idrīs' artistry.

As the contents of the anthology will show, the short story is the genre with the greatest representation. That is no accident, in that this genre constitutes the greater part of Idrīs' output. Indeed, we may perhaps go even further than that and suggest that the short story is the genre with which Idrīs feels most at home and to which he has contributed his most noteworthy works. In this Introduction we have not commented upon his novels. There are two reasons for that decision: in the first place, their length precludes the inclusion of anything but a short extract in a book such as this, and they have thus been eliminated from consideration. But secondly and more importantly for our general comments on Idrīs' writings, many of his novels (and indeed his longer plays) tend to show a distinct lack of cohesion in their later sections. Even such an exciting and brilliant play as *Farfoors* suffers from this in its second act, but in novels like *Shame* (*Al-Ayb*) and *The White Woman* (*Al-Baydā'*) the portrayal of character development is often subordinated to the expression of views on society and politics through lengthy descriptions which remain external to the development of the narrative structure of the work. Perhaps only in *Taboo* (*Al-Harām*) among the novels does Idrīs succeed in producing a convincing novelistic structure, even though here too there are problems of emphasis between the two groups described, the inhabitants of the village itself and the migrant workers (*tarāhīl*).

Having said this about Idrīs' longer works, we must immediately point out that his concentration on the short story has been of the greatest benefit to modern Arabic literature. After all, the genre must be considered one of the most difficult from the point of view of the use of language. Anyone who writes on a regular basis will know that it is much easier to spread one's thoughts over several pages with no constraints on space than to put on paper everything one wants to say in a restricted number of words or in some kind of precis form. The short story is, of course, in no way a precis, but it does involve the use of words to their maximum semantic capacity and the economical application of the various facets of the fictional art. It is in this regard that Idrīs' genius comes to the fore, and we become aware that his own experiments with language constitute a real contribution to the development of the short story in modern Arabic literature. Idrīs himself has always been extremely modest about this and has even described the process as an unconscious one:

> Renewal of writing is a natural, spontaneous and ingrained process which the author pursues unconsciously, because that is actually what art is. Writing is not a process of abandoning one mode and starting another; it's an attempt to get at the real "me" . . . Put differently, my struggle with myself is the worst one I have; it's a struggle with my-own inner, animal self . . . I try to get close to this inner "me" and write from the inside. Thus, I can say that development in writing does not come about one day through the dissemination of some specific (intellectual) school of thought, even though the experience of others can be useful to you because it shows you how other people view themselves. Development in writing will only occur as the consequence of this struggle with oneself, and of its receptivity to and desire for development.

> (*Mawāqif* 9 (April-June 1970), 51 ff.)

We noted at the beginning of this introduction that from the beginning of his writing career Idrīs insisted on the use of the colloquial in written form to convey his dialogue. The descriptions meanwhile were written in a style which observed most of the grammatical and stylistic conventions of the written language.[6] To be sure, Idrīs' style was the object of criticism from the beginning of his career. In the Introduction to the collection, **Farahāt's Republic**, Tāhā Husayn, that stalwart foe of the use of the colloquial as a literary language, suggested that Idrīs should abandon his use of the colloquial while complimenting him on his undoubted contribution to the development of the short story. Another critic, Fu'ād Duwwāra, has the following to say about the use of language in the novel, *Taboo:*

> I am one of those who have no doubts at all concerning Yūsuf Idrīs' great talent and the excellence of his writings. However, I have the feeling, especially after reading this novel, that he is a lazy writer who does not write or revise his works with the care they deserve

> . . . Among signs of laziness in this novel is a disjointed and poor use of style in a number of places. This is in spite of the fact that the author has demonstrated in numerous other works that he is quite capable of producing a neat and genuinely expressive style.

> (*On the Egyptian Novel (Fī al-Riwāya al-Misriyya),*
> Cairo: Dār al-Kātib al-'Arabī, 1968, p. 86)

At this point in our discussion, we can gain further insight into the questions of the coherence of structure and use of language in Idrīs' works through another quotation:

> I personally regard the language problem as a burden on me. But I'm very content when writing in Egyptian Colloquial . . . Personally, I cannot write in the classical written language (*fushā*). I can do it and it may turn out fine, but at the crucial moment of composition, I am not in a position to choose between what is suitable and what is not. The writing is almost dictated to me. I am the means, not the writer himself. Introducing the force of will here impairs the entire process. Perhaps it is better to interfere later with a conscious mind and through the author himself.

> (*Mawāqif* 9, ibid.)

From this, it seems clear that Idrīs relies a great deal on the inspiration of the moment when writing. It is hardly surprising therefore that, of all the possible literary genres, the short story is the one which best suits his genius. In this respect, he would seem to differ widely from his famous colleague, Nagīb Mahfūz, who readily admits to being the most methodical writer. His huge *Trilogy (Al-Thulāthiyya),* a group of three novels, involved years of planning and research followed by many years of writing. Furthermore, Mahfūz writes for a specific number of hours each day and then stops. Everything we know about Yusūf Idrīs suggests that, when he has an idea, it keeps hold of him until he has finished what he wishes to say. This comparison no doubt contains elements of exaggeration or simplification, but the writings of the two authors seem to bear out its major implication. Mahfūz' works have passed through a number of phases, and yet his mode of writing and especially his themes have changed relatively little. He has continued to reflect the life-style, the values and the aspirations of the middle class of Egyptians to which he himself belongs. This he has done in a grammatically correct style which has made few compromises with the colloquial dialect. Idrīs, on the other hand, has gradually broadened the scope of his themes and has stretched written literary Arabic to remarkable limits.

In this context, Idrīs' remark about his discomfort with the written language and his preference for the colloquial is significant. For, as his writing career has developed, his short stories have shown increasing signs of the influence of the colloquial language, both in its structures and its vocabulary. As Somekh points out in his article mentioned above, this does not mean that Id-rīs writes his stories in the colloquial, but rather that he is expanding the manner through which the written language may express accurately (and stimulatingly) the language, the thought processes, the interior monologues, the streams of consciousness of contemporary man, all these being most naturally conceived in the colloquial parlance of the country concerned. In a recent comment, the Egyptian story writer and critic, Sulaymān Fayyād, suggests that Idrīs' ability to use language in this way to illustrate character is one of the main reasons for his mastery of the short story genre; by contrast, he finds Mahfūz' style almost bland by comparison. (*Arabic Books / Kutub Arabiyya*/no. 1 (Jan. 1977,) 1)

Yusūf Idrīs remains one of the most famous creative writers in the Arab world today, and arguably its finest writer of short stories. We have suggested that some of his works show certain flaws, but that is comforting in its own way; the world might well be intolerable with too many Mozarts. Idrīs' writing career has been seriously impaired over the last decade for reasons which have been mentioned above. One thing we can be sure is that, when his next works are published, they will continue to be provocative and often extremely moving, they will show a continuing concern for man and his existence on earth, and they will arouse both admiration and opposition for their experiments in theme and style. Such is the essence of Yūsuf Idrīs.

Notes

1. It should be noted that at least two collections have been published in more than one edition with different titles in each case.

2. Idrīs published a series of articles in 1963 in the magazine, Al-Kātib, in which he expresses his views. Two references on this subject in English are: Farouk Abdel Wahab, *Modern Egyptian Drama,* Minneapolis: Bibliotheca Islamica, 1974, 9-18; and Alī al-Rā'ī, "Some Aspects of Modern Arabic Drama," in *Studies in Modern Arabic Literature,* ed. R. C. Ostle, Warminster, England: Aris and Phillips, 1975, 172ff.

3. It is translated in the collection, *Arabic Writing Today: The Short Story,* ed. Mahmoud Manzalaoui, Cairo: Dār al-Ma'ārif, 1968, p. 227.

4. The short story version of this work (it has also been adapted by the author as a play) has been translated in *Modern Arabic Short Stories,* trans. Denys Johnson-Davies, Oxford: Oxford University Press, 1967.

5. See *Arabic Writing Today: The Short Story,* ed. Mahmoud Manzalaoui, Cairo: The American Research Center in Egypt and Dar al-Ma'ārif, 1968.

6. There are two excellent studies on Idrīs' style in English: Jan Beyerl, *The Style of the Modern Arabic Short Story,* Prague, 1971 (this includes linguistic analyses of the writings of other writers also), and S. Somekh, "Language and Theme in the Short Stories of Yūsuf Idrīs," *Journal of Arabic Literature* VI (1975), 89 ff.

Mona Mikhail (essay date 1979)

SOURCE: Mikhail, Mona. "Love and Sex: A Study of the Short Fiction of Naguib Mahfouz and Yusuf Idris." In *Images of Arab Women: Fact and Fiction,* pp. 91-111. Washington, D.C.: Three Continents Press, Inc., 1979.

[*In the following essay, Mikhail finds parallels in the portrayal of sex and love in the short stories of Idris and Naguib Mahfouz.*]

The short stories of Naguib Mahfouz and Yusuf Idris, and indeed a great many stories of other Egyptian writers, do not present any systematic love ethic by which they can be characterized or measured. They tend to embody perhaps more of a romantic yearning for absolutes than a traditional notion of love. The romantic treatment of love has been, as it were, exhausted by such writers as Ihsan'Abd Al-Quddus and others whose versions have been interpreted by all the means of mass media, radio, television, and cinema.

A large portion of Idris' early stories deal with love in its initial stages. He seems more preoccupied by the phenomenon of the loss of innocence in his characters—boys and girls, men and women—than by the actual love encounters themselves. As in the early Hemingway stories, there is an attempt to control the destructive forces of life. Stories like **"Al-Gharab"** (The Stranger) trace the initiation to maturity of a young boy thrown into the snares of a gang of thieves and the wily arms of a fickle woman. On a lighter note, in the collection *Hadithat Sharaf* (Incident Involving Honor) the story **"Mahatta"** (Bus Stop) is an amusing rendition of a nascent romance taking place on a bus ride. The title story of the collection by the same name is a violent denunciation of a society that denies love. However, Fatma, the heroine who has lost her "honor," evolves as the defiant free agent. She has lost her innocence but has gained self-assurance in the process. The metaphors and symbols are used very effectively to convey this change in her. In a more recently published collection, *Bayt min Lahm* (House of Flesh), the story **"Hiya"** (She) is an absurd tale playing on the theme of the unknown. Appearances and reality, the duality of the nature in the beautiful woman who turns out to be the image of a repellent beast, is an intriguing view of the male female relationship.

It is this "severely modern" and "unromantic idiom" that Idris and Mahfouz share with Hemingway. Like Hemingway, of whom it has been said that his female characters are not lifelike, Idris' and Mahfouz' women tend to embody ideas and ideals. However, some of Idris' women (and there are not too many) are very much in love with life. They, too, like his men, are in pursuit of the absolute. They are ready to pay any price for authenticity. **"Al-Naddaha"** (The Siren) does not merely respond to the luring, lulling call of the wild in her. Like a true existentialist, she searches for truth. The middle-aged woman in **"Halaqat al-Nuhas-al-Na'ima"** (Rings of Smooth Brass) is not merely gratifying her sexual desires but, after a long exile, comes to grips with her real self, knowing full well that her bliss and happiness will not continue; consequently, she never lets go of any opportunity to know herself better.

In the case of Idris' and Mahfouz' short stories, the question is treated differently. Indeed the image of woman in their fiction is surprisingly forceful, given the traditional conservatism expected. Although one could equally say that Idris on the whole writes of a world only inhabited by men, the few women who make an appearance are certainly not easily forgotten. Mahfouz' classical "putain respecteuse" of Bidaya-wa-Nihaya or that of "Miramar" represents an always illusive truth. In one of his more recent short stories, "Harat-al-'Ushshaq" (Lover's Lane), Mahfouz situates his search for love and communication within the confines of the city and a prison cell.

Idris' hero is the Absurd man in that he experiences most of the accepted truths of Camus' *Le Mythe de Sisyphe*. In his work, Camus discusses ways in which the individual should react to anxiety, a sense of estrangement, and the horror of death. The solution he suggests is that one should accept the paradox of life as the mind experiences it. This is what the imprisoned man in the story **"Mashuq al-Hams"** (Ground Whispers) attempts to do in his isolation. The most acute instance of experiencing the absurd is his realization that he is isolated from the other human beings he believes to be in the prison. He desperately tries to overcome this "anguish" by reaching out to the other, even if he had to create him from a heap of "ground whispers."

The hero of **"Ground Whispers"** in an attempt to overcome his "absurd" situation defies it and rebels against it. The title story of the recent collection *Mashuq al-Hams*[1] (Ground Whispers) is an interesting innovation on the theme of love. It is more a study of the basic human need to communicate. The interchangeability of the two themes, love and communication, make up the design of the story.

The hero who narrates the story in the first person is a political prisoner detained in one of Egypt's large prisons where both men and women, common criminals, serve their various sentences. Idris leaves no doubt in the reader's mind that the central theme is love, since he establishes it from the beginning.

In the first paragraph, the narrator equates his joy at being transferred to another wing of the prison to that of a young boy's first encounter with the naked body of a beautiful woman, and his inability to relate to the situation. Such was the overwhelming state he was in, especially when he realized that his cell was situated in the midst of others, therefore not isolated, and also that he was within close proximity to the women's section of the prison. Idris proceeds to an almost clinical study of the state of incarceration and confinement. Indeed the story can be considered an indictment of the penal system which denies the human being's right to fulfill himself through love and/or communication. The narrator examines the meaning of liberty and its subsequent loss, what is entailed when it is lost and the continual unaccountable hope that it will be regained. However, real prison life, according to him, only begins when that hope completely dies, and despair sets in. Time in prison is irrelevant, thus one's activities in prison are carried outside normal perspectives. The need to communicate is seen in the narrator's desperate attempts to decipher a German newspaper in which the warden would sometimes smuggle in some food. The day he managed to understand one word of German from his meager knowledge of English, French and Egyptian, and guessed it meant freedom, his joy was unlimited.

Being imprisoned, according to Idris (a medical doctor who in fact experienced prison life), does not necessarily mean that one has to live like a disabled person or a mental retard. According to the author, one can fill one's life—people it—with the characters one once knew, but somehow they acquire new dimensions. The traditionally boring person becomes a clown and acquires the reputation of a great joker whose company is sought by all. The frightened, horrified person is turned into a frightened, helpless mouse. There can be variations of these characters, of course, and idiosyncrasies can be added to them. One thing, however, cannot be easily replaced in a prison through one's imagination, and that is a woman.

Here it is interesting to note how Idris has symmetrically inserted the word *women* after certain paragraphs emphasizing the underlying theme of the story—love between a man and a woman. Therefore in the structure of the story the one word paragraph carries with it a weighty effect. On page fifty, line seventeen echoes line sixteen by simply repeating the word *women*. This is immediately followed by a declamation on the word *liberty*. On page fifty-three, line ten, the one word *women* symmetrically divides the page, and immediately follows the word *liberty* he had guessed as being the meaning of the German word *Freiheit*. Again, on page fifty-four, line four, we see the word *women,* the only dream which transforms prison into a bearable reality.

Hence we can see how both the content and the form of the story enhance each other in underlining what was to follow. In this manner, the writer was preparing the way for the extraordinary relationship which was to grow and blossom between our imprisoned hero and a woman convict temporarily placed in a neighboring cell.

For by some stroke of unexplainable luck he had been placed in the most coveted cell of all, for which wardens received rich bribes from prisoners wanting to occupy it and which carried an eventful history of daring ventures. For one convict had managed to dig his way to the other side with a pen knife and his bare hands, and to socialize with the three women on the other side. Consequently the wall was so securely built that nothing short of dynamite could let anyone through. The euphoria he experienced from being so close to women, hundreds of them, did not make him lose complete control over himself for he had to investigate the situation cooly. He knew that the first thing he was going to do after curfew would be to knock on that wall. For life only begins for prisoners when they are permitted to talk to their fellow inmates once they have all reported back to their respective cells.

During those stolen moments before curfew is sounded, and the tyrannical presence of the jailors is momentarily averted, the prisoners would attempt to establish channels of communication with inmates of neighboring cells by knocking and beating on their cell walls. In very perceptive detail, Idris analyzes the mental state, the almost pathological need to reach out to the other, the basic need to be heard, recognized, accepted and wanted.

So our prisoner lives through the agony of doubt for two long days, pounding on deaf walls. His frustration is so great that he is often tempted to dash his brains against them. For after that glimmer of hope, being moved close to the women's quarters, it appears that no one is there to respond to his call for life. Death slowly grows from despair.

Suddenly, prison life is transformed. Someone on the other side of his cell seems to be attempting to communicate with him. Hushed noises begin to surface, as if emanating from the heart of the earth. Hope creeps into his heart, and he responds with regular beats:

> And my ears captured the voices, translated them, purified them and transcribed them into a language; from a language spoken by the hand to a language sensed by the feelings, grasped by the mind. She too like me is alone. Those two quick, simultaneous knocks mean

that she too is worried, afraid like me that something may happen to cut communications. This single knock after which the hands were not removed from the wall, is a reassured smile I notice, for as her worrying reassures me, no doubt my worrying reassures her.

(p. 64)

Thus, on this desert island, our friend finds an oasis where some signs of civilization still persist. He finds a mate to knock to him so that he in turn may knock to her, and thus a real world is recreated, one with the real world emotions of fear, affection, doubt and need for steady reassurance. Gradually he realizes that he is experiencing *the* one great passion of his life. For he has lived through many a love story of the same stuff which drove Kais mad, and Werter to commit suicide, and Juliet to be killed. This time he has no doubt that he has finally met the woman of his dreams, in spite of the fact that he felt she would somehow destroy him:

> This time no struggle, or continuous struggles to back out, I'm in it with all my being. And I knock, and I almost die from the pleasure, and the answer comes back to me, feminine, surrendering, hushed. I see the hand delivering it, white, small, with microscopic yellow hairs, and nails the pale color of gazelle blood. A hand I know and kiss, and kiss every finger of, and with my tongue lick what is between the fingers.

(p. 35)

The sexual imagery in those lines and in several other descriptions of similar "encounters" abound in the story. Idris thus succeeds in creating this verisimilitude of a love affair through his poetic use of prose. Beyond that "encounter" Idris is, I think, investigating something fundamental, the principle of being, the ineluctable principle of life, Man and Woman inevitably and irresistably drawn to one another, needing one another, complementing one another. This instinctive, Adamic impulse is obviously not so much a physical necessity as it is a spiritual *must*. This is sustained to the end of the story, for their physical contact never goes beyond a heap of unintelligible words, depicted as "ground whispers."

The ground whispers reduce language to its essential purpose, that of communication. The relationship goes through initial stages of courtship and flirtation. Through the various ground whispered conversations, he *creates* her, full blown woman, sees her, embraces her. He models her into a petite woman with the top of her head barely touching his nose. He *makes* her deep black eyes and soft black hair framing her long face. He breathes life into his model, has no doubt that her name is Fardus (Paradise), that she has bedouin blood, and has a tattoo just above her dimple in the exact middle of her chin, a faded greyish three dots. Her mouth is not small like a girl's, but full with a curling upper lip. She has been in prison for three years, her husband having forced her to smuggle drugs. She was caught with the merchandise on the express train to Alexandria.

The relationship takes a more serious turn once the narrator puts the finishing touches to his companion and now their love is to be consummated. The Man and the Woman become two charged currents, attracting one another, engulfing one another. Idris indulges in the repetition of love scenes and presents a variation of circumstances which effect a semblance of reality.

However, the narrative is intended to establish this intimate familiarity between the two lovers. They are destined to enact the drama of life, with its tediousness as well as its unpredictability. For the day comes when this affair comes to an end. She responds no longer to his call. But Idris does not end the story on this sad note. With a last touch of cynicism, he leaves the reader with the lingering doubt as to the identity and sex of the lover.

For the prisoner, bereaved by his loss, manages to learn in a rare moment of communication with the warden that the adjacent cells have not been women's quarters for quite some time, but have served as temporary dwellings for both men and women awaiting more permanent destinations. And, too, very often they were left vacant. Thus the tortured narrator-prisoner lives with the agonizing doubt that he may have been in love with a man, and that he may have been mistaken for a woman. In spite of this possibility, however, his love for Fardus remains as alive as ever, much to his amazement, more so than for any woman he had known. Further, in spite of the seeming importance he gives to sex in this story, he succeeds in transcending the mere physical, although he neither denies nor denigrates it. The narrator discovers that a willingness to share one's very being is the secret to realizing our humanity, even if appearance and reality twist and confuse the visions of those involved.

From the sketchy figures of the early stories of initiation, to the more developed characters in stories like **"Halaqat al-Nuhas al-Na'ima"** (Rings of Smooth Brass) and **"Bayt min Lahm"** (House of Flesh), Idris presents women who show remarkable determination to pursue their search for self-awareness and self-fulfillment. They stand out as strong and willful, yet not "bitchy," as do some of Hemingway's characters.

In fact the only negatively depicted woman in the stories examined here is Al-Hadidi's wife (nameless) in **"Lughat Al-Ay Ay"** (Language of Pain). She is incapable of understanding her husband's crises and unsuccessfully tries to keep him prisoner at her side. He rejects what she stands for and realizes she has been stunting his growth and subsequently opts for his freedom, leaving her behind.

Fathiyya, the heroine of **"Al-Naddaha"** (The Siren), is one of the most interesting delineations of character Idris ever attempted. The naive romantic peasant sustained by her dream stubbornly remains true to the call of authenticity within her. Undaunted by the wickedness and treachery she discovers in the city of her dreams, Fathiyya takes the great leap into the unknown by abandoning her husband and child in search of herself. The development and radical change Fathiyya undergoes takes place before our very eyes. Idris' skillful narrative techniques make us partake in that change, however extraordinary its consequences may seem. She is by no means an aggressive or oppressive female, nor is she a castrating figure like the wife in Idris' **"Language of Pain."**

Hamid, her husband, is shattered by her actions, although she expected, even desired at the start that he might end her miserable life. Fathiyya on the other hand brought about a change in him at the beginning of their marriage—made him into a livelier, more sociable and energetic person, and he had become the happier for it. The fact that she leaves him is not so much that she feared he would eventually kill her, as much as it is that she did not want to escape her "destiny," that "voice" that had beckoned deep inside her which she tried in vain to stifle.

In **"Bayt min Lahm"** (House of Flesh) a group of women, a mother and her daughters, are determined to fulfill their humanity at the extreme price of incest. The remarkable woman is the mother who will close her eyes on what she surmises is happening and will not deprive her "own flesh and blood" from the enjoyment of life. This is an extreme, unlikely situation to be sure, but Idris is merely emphasizing his point about the centrality of love and communication and its importance for the discovery of the "other."

Though Idris' use of love and sex as themes in his works is rare, his story **"Halqat al-Nuhas al-Na'ima: Qissa fi Arba'Murabba'at²** (Rings of Smooth Brass: Story in Four Squares), however, is a departure from the usual Idris work in this respect. The story, divided into four parts, each carrying the title "First Square" and so on, uses the square as a recurring motif in the story.

The story is simple. It is that of a middle-aged woman, who having sacrificed her youth in the service of a much older husband and sons and daughters, realizes that she is unwanted and unneeded by those same children to whom she had given so much. After their father died, she had refused to remarry, and had thus buried her youth and chance for happiness. Her children, now successful and with their own families, visit only on holidays, and no matter how much love and affection they express for her, she knows she is marginal to their existence. It is this feeling that Idris studies and analyzes in great depth and sympathy.

Her children, aware of their mother's malaise, suggest she visit the shrine of the venerated Sayyida Zaynab, as it becomes ladies of her age and standing. Sayyida Zaynab, also known as "Mother of the Old" (and Umm Hashim) was sought by young and old for her miraculous intercessions and doings.

So one Friday she goes to the shrine, and there the miracle happens. Among the crowds of people who attempt to get as close as possible to the shrine and tomb in order to hold on to the brass rings handing from the sides of the tomb is a young man who helps her from slipping to the ground. Something sparks immediately between the two, so different in background, age and status; yet a love relationship blooms. Idris displays his genius as he analyzes and explores this love within the limits of his four squares. He delves into deeper realms of archetypal nature. He touches upon the Oedipal complex and incorporates it into the framework of his story.

The attraction between the respectable, middle-aged grandmother and the twenty-year old motherless boy is mutual, animal in its primitiveness, yet also real and noble. Idris traces in an effective stream of consciousness the reactions of the woman to the initial encounter with the touch of the young man:

> By what force can she inform him of that feeling she can no longer fight, which made her forget everything but the fact that she had found him, and that at this specific moment he was dearer to her than the whole world.
>
> (p. 164)

This sudden, violent attraction of two people, who are themselves unloved, unwanted, and unneeded, is stronger than all conceivable societal objections. The woman is careful to remind the boy that she is like his mother, and encourages him to treat her as such. Our young man, aware of the fact but starving for affection, was ready to draw it from any source, especially from a mother-figure. The natural forces which draw them together have been suppressed for years by the woman:

> Since the call, a genii had awakened in her, capable of everything alive, a genii she had ignored, and tried to kill, ignored by her children and all those around her, and by all the values and mores and advice tried to strangle him, imprison him so that he may die from neglect and want.
>
> (p. 174)

We thus see in action the tremendous change this restrained and conventional middle-aged woman undergoes. She is fully aware and in control of her feelings and actions, however strange they may appear:

> Aware of it being a risk, she was confident that her opinion, judgement was right, confident that in the end she would give him the "mother" in her were it only for a few hours and take from him, maybe against his wish, the "son" were it only for a few minutes, and that she could never, never escape this fate.
>
> (p. 175)

So she accompanies him to his shack of a home and cleans the abandoned place and cooks him a hearty meal, as she would have done for her own child. She then bathes him:

> And what she had expected exactly happened. For the mother in her found the child in him, and the child in him brought back certain touches and features of her motherhood that had long withered, and died, and she seemed to become a mother for the very first time.
>
> (p. 177)

Thus, a complex relationship develops between these two people hungering for love and affection. The mother/son initial contact metamorphoses into rare love between man and woman:

> And so, in spite of their close clasp, there started to grow and spread an emotional cloud that totally enveloped them, and completely bound them. A cloud secreted by their bodies, to excite all that is not possible for the body to excite. Can it be love?
>
> (p. 182)

So ends the first square in which the designs of this extraordinary relationship have been drawn. The "Second Square" is an elaboration of the motifs painted in the first. Here are presented the detailed analysis of this attraction of opposites. Idris probes the depths of human psyche and links this act to something primeval, which reaches far back in the human consciousness. Their movements reflect that primal desire of man to return to the womb and of woman to absorb and contain. Idris compares this attraction to yet another immutable pattern. He explains the attraction of opposites in terms of the principle governing planets and the solar system:

> Attraction generating attraction, this wide universe capable of suspending our planet, our sun and thousands others in its frightening space with nothing but the attraction of gravitation, and attraction of opposites. Attraction of which no one knows the secret till now: that which attracts especially the woman to the man so as to use him as a means to reproduce a copy of her own making of that same man, to have a son, and how marvellous would it be if he came to be exactly like the father, and she would do anything for his love; and if it were permissible to choose that same son to produce for her, from her own self also another son: closer to what she wants and desires.
>
> (p. 185)

Idris further elaborates on this planet/solar system imagery when in the third part, the third square, he describes how this youth orbited round his star, became

part of her whole system ineluctably moving in her or-
bit. However Idris constantly reminds us of the reality
of the situation. He does not remain in these high
spheres, but periodically brings the mother/son axis into
play. This is in spite of her discovery that the female in
her has bloomed and flourished to extents she never realized she was capable of, and in spite of her giving of
herself without guilt or shame. The specter of her social
being experiencing all this bliss, however, suggests the
love/incest complex. For the moment, though, their
communion transcends all possible obstacles—social,
moral and religious. "And between the two great poles
a welding spark generated like a bolt, a thunderbolt that
made the square tiles in the room tremble, and the windows shake." (p. 192)

The fourth and last part of the story completes the symmetry of this mosaic-like design. For although the
miracle had happened and her children marvelled at her
newly found vitality, and her total devotion to Sayyida
Zaynab, she knew that it would come to an end. The
day comes when the young man loses interest, having
satisfied his hunger for a motherly love, and turns to a
younger, prettier girl:

> She felt that she did not want to moan, and that she
> could put an end to her dizziness, for she is not sad nor
> reproachful, nor is she surprised or even bitter towards
> him or the girl. She realized through an indefinable
> feeling, without any begrudging that she too had noth-
> ing to give or bestow, neither a surplus of motherhood
> nor an excess of affection; the green active volcano did
> not have one drop left in it.
>
> (p. 165)

With this sense of emptiness, she turns to Umm Hashim
the Sayyida Zaynab, Mother of the Old. For she realizes that from now on, she is doomed to a life of soli-
tude and loneliness; she felt unwanted and unneeded
and therefore clung with whatever energy she could
summon to the rings around the marble tomb—rings
that had become worn, eaten up by God knows how
many thousands of people who, like her, in utter desperation, had turned to the shrine of the holy woman:

> There she was like the precursor of winter, without
> noise she came . . . true loneliness without any kind of
> escape . . . a loneliness like a demarcation line be-
> tween being a son, and becoming a father. Her mother-
> hood had been exhausted to the very last, or seemed to;
> and her becoming once more a child, a daughter to a
> mother that does not exist, maybe that is why she has
> been named "Mother of the Old," for the human being
> cannot survive as a human unless he be a father or a
> son. If his virility comes to an end he resumes being a
> son, and if motherhood is no more, the woman be-
> comes a daughter once more, a rule without exceptions
> . . .
>
> But now she is in a decisive moment of loneliness,
> loneliness like that of Sayyida Zaynab herself, with
> people crowding around her, holding on to the rings

> round her tomb, men and women, each and every one
> lonely like herself, all with one hope—to once again be
> sons and daughters to Mother of the Old. Lonely in her
> tomb in spite of the crowds around. Each one trying to
> grasp one of those rings, insistent to the point of tears,
> and moans, and succeeding for a brief moment in leav-
> ing his state of loneliness and touching his mother,
> mother of all, she may be, but in spite of everything is
> lonely.
>
> (p. 197)

A long short story in the collection entitled *"Hikaya
bila bidaya wala Nihaya,"* deals with a study of a fundamental aspect of love, namely doubt. "Harat al-
'Ushshaq" (Lover's Lane) is the enactment of a philosophical treatise on doubt. It is, however, clothed in the
robes of a love story. The characters are a middle-class
government clerk, his very attractive wife, and a series
of other local stereotypes ranging from Shaykh Al-Hara
(the neighborhood mayor) to the school teacher passing
by the baker's. The story is divided into seven parts,
each narrating an episode which is usually a consequence of the part preceding. We soon discover that
there is an underlying pattern which repeats itself and
helps create a total impact at story's end.

Mahfouz' extensive use of dialogue to move the story
forward is effectively used here, giving it Socratic overtones.

The story opens on a scene of conjugal felicity. Husband and wife are congratulating themselves on the
bliss they have lived in for the past five years. They can
still remember distinctly their courting days before marriage, then the first years of their happy union:

> He sighed, then a glimmer appeared in his dreamy look
> and said:
>
> "Those days, I was just a clerk in the archives . . .
> poor, hard-working, a husband passionately in love,
> even children we had decided to relegate to later times,
> no time for thinking, no time to look, work, work,
> work . . . no thoughts, no worries, a limitless faith in
> everything, in you, in myself, in God, endless confi-
> dence in you, in myself, in God; everything was con-
> stant, solidly built.[3]

This seemingly idyllic scene is soon interrupted with
the husband's growing querulousness. He hints that he
has been noticing certain goings-on in their alley. They
apparently are willing to continue to gossip about their
fellow neighbors; no one seems to escape their gossip.
He then tells his wife of his growing sense of indignation with the rumors he has been hearing. This first part
ends with a heated discussion between the two in which
he announces his decision to divorce her.

The second scene recapitulates the first, and now the
once happy husband is alone and very sad. The Imam,
Shaykh Marwan, visits him and offers to comfort 'Abd-

Allah. Furthermore, he intervenes in favor of the divorced wife and protests her innocence. In a question-answer repartee, he succeeds at the end of the conversation in convincing the doubting husband of the integrity of the wife. Using such convincing arguments as the following, the Imam brings about the change:

> I know not where to begin, shall I tell you that the men of God have perceptions of the heart that by far supercede the proofs of logic? But I fear that your faith in the force you imagine is not so. Many like to believe that they have faith, then you see them fall apart in face of their first trial. The true believer, O Abd-Allah, moves mountains, overcomes death, shakes life itself . . .

> (p. 113)

Thus through similar religious and philosophical arguments, Shaykh Marwan brings peace once more to the tortured existence of 'Abd Allah who bursts out saying at the end of part two:

> God bless you Shaykh Marwan, you have saved me from darkness, and opened the doors of happiness and guidance.

> (p. 118)

It is significant to note that all seven parts, like scenes of a play, open on the same setting. The alternating scenes of the husband and wife reconciled occur in the same living room which had witnessed their initial happiness. The wife always makes her appearance in a house coat, combing her hair, indicative of the relaxed atmosphere reigning in the household. During their conversations we learn that the husband has begun to be very critical of the Imam, and refuses to go to his sessions of Qur'an:

> I do not deny that I was fascinated by him, but he proceeded to unveil his true self. I have resisted boredom for months, waited in vain for him to say something new, but there was nothing different. A man who does his duty without putting any soul in it calls out his merchandise like a potato vendor.

> (p. 112)

And, again, he explains when he discovered this change:

> a short while ago, but it is not easy to change and deny what we are used to believing in

> (p. 120)

With such hints strewn all about the narrative one cannot help but note the philosophical processes here at play. On the one level the story is simply that of a marriage in danger of collapsing and, on a deeper level, the writer is investigating fundamentals. He questions matters involving faith, appearance and reality. For once he had highly considered the Imam, named his son after him, and now doubts his motives, actions, and accuses

his wife outright of have had some kind of illicit encounter with Shaykh Marwan on their stairway. The outraged wife denies his allegations and once more leaves, a divorced woman for the second time.

In the fourth part, 'Abd Allah listens to the logic of 'Antar, the respected grade school teacher. He intercedes in favor of Shaykh Marwan whom 'Abd Allah had shamelessly thrown out of his house. The school teacher is forced to make a revelation concerning the Imam which is intended to efface any doubts of the beguiled husband. 'Abd Allah is shocked to hear that the shaykh had been undergoing some treatment to cure him of a case of sexual impotence that had befallen him a year ago. So in part five, Haniyya, the wife, is lovingly cajoling her new baby whom they named this time after the teacher, 'Antar.

The ensuing part comes up with some disturbing revelations about the once trusted friends of 'Abd Allah. Shaykh Al-Hara, shunned by all, accused of being the official informer to authorities, interrogates 'Abd Allah on the nature of his relationship with the teacher and the Imam. When asked what topics were usually discussed in their meetings, 'Abd Allah explains:

> Indeed they are serious subjects, like liberty and the daily bread, good and evil; will immortality involve the soul only or both soul and body; do spirits exist in effect or merely symbolically.

> (p. 138)

Shaykh Al-Hara proceeds in his investigation trying to corroborate some information he had collected concerning the two men, then just before leaving, announces that the two have been arrested.

This totally unexpected turn of events greatly disturbs 'Abd Allah and his wife. Once more 'Abd Allah's faith is shaken, once more he loses his bearings. He is left alone in this dilemma as the Shaykh Al-Hara refuses to supply him with any incriminating evidence as to the alleged guilt of the once trusted friends. 'Abd Allah is once more in doubt and is left tormented by conflicting impulses.

The whole Hara (alley) reacts in shock to the news; the inhabitants feel that they too have been cheated. Their heated arguments do not resolve the question and they by no means reach a consensus as to whether the informer, Shaykh Al-Hara, was solely to blame for his treachery, or whether the two culprits deserved their fate.

It is precisely that uncertainty that eats away at 'Abd Allah. The incident brings back a horde of suppressed doubts and emotions that had once troubled him so. Sensing his mood, Haniyya turns to her husband pleadingly:

H: Here we are gradually returning to hell . . .

A: The important thing is that my life be built on a clear truth.

H: What's more important than all this is to appeal to wisdom during crises, and to always remember that you are a father.

He answered with bitter irony:

A: Indeed, I am the father of Marwan, and 'Antar . . .

H: And it is a truth more important than anything else . . .

And he said perturbed:

A: No, there exists a higher truth, which should not be undermined and I want to face it as it really is, even if it throws me in a circle of fire.

H: I fear that our quest will lead us at the end to burning fire.

(p. 149)

The growing doubts that assail 'Abd Allah give him no peace. He is forever questioning and in search of truth. He is aware of the inherent contradictions of his life. He is "'Antar's and Marwan's father," the namesakes of two highly respectable men, and yet today both stand accused. Maybe after all they both have had affairs with his wife, and he was fooled all along?

Beneath all this commotion, Mahfouz' clear voice speaks. 'Abd Allah (Slave of God) is a man, like many, confronted with the eternal quest for truth. As a final resort, 'Abd Allah turns to Shaykh Al-Hara seeking elucidation on the question of the arrest and its implications. The man who has the answer brings no relief. He is implacable in his stance in refusing to release any information that could be interpreted one way or another. He merely fulfills the function of supplying and collecting pertinent data which will eventually and hopefully lead to some truth. The author depicts the shaykh as a teacher who knows all the facts, but wishes to see people search out the facts themselves and draw their own conclusions. 'Abd Allah wants immediate satisfaction:

A: Then how can one know the truth?

S: I know not what to say, but it is not enough to depend on others, you must exploit your personal talents and past experience . . .

'Abd Allah sighed deeply and said:

A: The truth is I used to find ready answers from these men, answers that were decisive and comforting whenever I needed them.

(p. 156)

Undaunted, 'Abd Allah persists in wanting to know whether the two men are completely guilty and hence the possible guilt of his wife. Insisting on not committing himself, Shaykh Al-Hara informs him that chances are fifty-fifty that they are guilty, upon which 'Abd Allah finally resolves on a different course:

A: If my wife be guilty in the percentage of fifty percent she is at the same time innocent in the percentage of fifty percent.

S: And so?

A: And because I love her more than life itself, and because I can not do without her unless I go mad, or commit suicide, I will therefore admit the possibility of innocence . . .

(p. 159)

And so ends 'Abd Allah's story. A compromise reached after long deliberations, trials and falterings. As he said at the end, he expects to be happy, however sadly, and indicates that he estimates his happiness not to be less than a fifty percent possibility. (p. 199)

Mahfouz thus succeeded in subtley camouflaging his philosophical treatment of the question of Truth, in the guise of a simple story involving the love of a man for a woman. One can speculate on the symbolic significance of the characters, and how the author infuses life and credibility into them. Haniyya (happiness), the beautiful wife who is at the center of the conflict, is happiness itself. Without her 'Abd Allah finds life intolerable; madness and death are the only possible alternatives. Haniyya is inscrutable, evanescent; like happiness she appears and disappears almost at will. Once he starts doubting her, life is never again the same. "Where ignorance is bliss, 'tis folly to be wise," Mahfouz reiterates.

'Abd Allah seeks with all his might to recapture his old happiness when he lived in an ordered universe and neither questions nor doubts disturbed him. That was a time of innocence, before the fall. His lot henceforth is to live with knowledge that fills him with doubts and never again will he regain his "paradise lost."

Shaykh Al-Hara, traditionally and proverbially the one who "knows absolutely everything about everybody," is appropriately chosen by Mahfouz as the informer. He *informs* not in a pejorative sense, although on the surface structure of the story he is considered as such, an agent or a squealer. However, on the deeper level, he leads 'Abd Allah, informs him of a way to some form of happiness. The all-knowing Shaykh Al-Hara's refusal to give pat answers to the naive husband forces the latter to come to grips with the reality of his existential being.

Yusuf Idris' treatment of love is radically different from that of Mahfouz. The philosophical investigations and allegorical classifications of Mahfouz are far removed from Idris' approach. **"Hadhihi al-Marra"** (This Time) in the collection *Lughat Al-Ay Ay* is an interesting illustration which may be compared to Mahfouz' "Harat al-'Ushshaq." Both stories are concerned with the examination of the relationships between a man and his wife, and the central theme to both stories is that of doubt. Mahfouz conveys suspicion through devices such as an allegorical framework for the story, sets of characters stereotyped to a degree and a recurrent pattern of behavior reminiscent of traditional folktale narratives. He immerses his material in philosophical inquiries which finally evolve into some hypothesis that presumably solves, at least temporarily, the dilemma of his protagonists.

Idris proceeds from a different premise altogether. He is more prone to delving into the psychological ramifications of problems and then linking them to cosmic essences. His characters, although symbolic, are more easily identifiable as individuals undergoing specific experiences and changes. The story **"Hadhihi al-Marra"** is one such story.

Imam is one of those people who survives long stretches of time in prison in the hope of seeing Suhair, his wife. Idris here is examining at great length the love of this incarcerated man and the doubts that assail him. During one of Suhair's visits he senses an almost imperceptible change that has come over her; hence his tormented state. Idris expands the moment and, as it were, anatomizes it in an effort to pin-point where things went wrong. This trivial change that has come over Suhair is of central importance to the story—and Idris analyzes in great detail the nature of Imam's love for his wife. Their love for one another was not the common garden variety. In spite of the facts that they had been married for many years and had a daughter, their passion for each other was still as strong as it had been in the beginning:

> He loved her and loved his daughter from her, their daughter was part of that love, as if she were the palpable proof, and renewal of unseen and unevaluative feelings. His daughter was wholesome, beautiful, blooming, merry, and was charming and coy; coy exactly like her mother to the extent that one would wonder whether she was replica of the mother who loved him and whom he loved, or was she the image of the love that was theirs; and fear was also there.[4]

In similar terms the author reiterates that unique love, that withstood long deprivation and was sustained and nurtured behind the walls of a prison. Idris in this story merely relates the inner workings of Imam's mind, like the eye of a camera which closely scrutinizes the outward movements of a character. Delimited by time and space, the camera's eye has no other alternative but to plunge vertically. It follows in slow motion the imperceptible changes in an effort to isolate and hopefully neutralize that intruding element of doubt.

Within the structure of the story we notice a rising progression in the intensity of Imam's feelings for Suhair, especially as the anticipated time of her visit draws near:

> He no longer felt her separate from himself . . . or a different independent being . . . as if she had become the female principle in him, or as if he had become her male component . . . she is with him, in him, inside of him and he is aware of himself there, in her soul, in the depths of her looks, inside every contraction and detraction of her slender ribs, while she inhales and exhales, he can even feel himself within his feeling of her. A whole that is amalgamated, like a live being impossible to separate, and any attempt at separation or fission merely adds life, and strength and continuum to it.
>
> (p. 265)

To counterpoint these abstract feelings, the writer juxtaposes these passages with ones dealing with real body contact:

> And without realizing it, they drew nearer, and clung together, as it always happens, every time they drew close and clung to one another, and he held her arms in his clutch, and from the first touch, he felt this thing that he had to become aware of immediately.
>
> (p. 267)

Thus Imam becomes aware through sensory perception of some change in his beloved one. This gradually develops into an almost obsessive awareness of the other. He grows conscious of her presence with literally every cell of his body; a body which is as it were transformed into a highly sensitive apparatus of reception and emission; a synthesizing electronic set emitting signals, and receiving vibrations:

> Each one scrutinizing the other with apparatuses that have no names, that measure every minute, to reassure him that he is the same unchanged, or if he had changed, then it would be to a stronger love, closer bond, boundless attachment. Small, all-encompassing apparatuses scattered in all directions, receiving and emitting, absorbing and selecting every cell in the body seeking assurance from its counterpart.
>
> (pp. 267-68)

Here it is interesting to note the "mechanistic" imagery Idris uses very effectively to convey the "état d'âme" of his tormented hero. This imagery functions in the structure of the story by supporting a parallelism of a visual sequence, which subsequently takes over in the story. Wordsworth's words here seem very apt:

> The eye—it cannot choose but see;
> we cannot bid the ear be still;
> our bodies feel, where'er they be,
> against or with our will.

Idris goes one step further in itemizing the parts of the body that see and feel:

He desired her with all his being, with his hands and with his nose, with his kinky hair . . . with his shaven moustache, with the black beauty spot on his ear.

(p. 268)

The "mechanistic" imagery mentioned earlier is seen then functioning alongside the visual perceptions:

Each time his mind continued repeating these words till the apparatuses of his body were satisfied, and in turn gave him a hidden signal that it was done, then the mind would start its work, and become capable of comprehending and seeing, scrutinizing, and meditating, then begins the second look. The slowed down, investigating look, which bears no trace of worry.

(p. 268)

and again:

Since that morning he had dreamed of how their expressions would follow quickly and ever more easily— the first a stunned look, the second pleasure, the third at the zenith of sensuality, and the fourth pure dream— floating both of them through and beyond those once locked doors to the empyrean spaces of the universe . . .

(p. 269)

By breaking down this encounter into a series of frames, as it were, in time-lapse fashion, the author is concretizing to a remarkable degree the experience of his hero. Idris here is superbly illustrating his skillful use of cinematic techniques. Hence we see how love as a means of communication is offered as the only alternative for the loss of faith in formalized religion, "the only life-force that has a future in this age of death:"[5]

Eros is not merely a demoniac power who creates chaos and destruction . . . In all ages, this same power has been a source of irresistible energy . . . (It) is also one of the greatest inspirations of human culture.[6]

These stories of Idris discussed above have in different ways attempted to isolate and escape, if even for a brief moment, the coldness and loneliness of life by reaching out to the "other" and trying to merge with the mystery of the universe.

In both the stories of Mahfouz and Idris we have time and again seen how human contact, love and warmth are the essence of real generosity. The ability to feel and respond to the needs of others is the goodness sought, while lack of communication and misunderstanding represents evil. Like other existential writings of Camus, Sartre and Hemingway, these stories have addressed themselves to different aspects of the dilemma of existential man.

Janine, the middle-aged woman of "La Femme Adultère," is reminiscent of Idris' heroine of **"Rings of Smooth Brass,"** who likewise had led a sterile life until she met the youth who for a brief moment shared with her the real meaning of life. Janine, accompanying her husband on trips to villages in southern Algeria, is mysteriously attracted by the "free lords" of the desert and realizes that she must seize a meaning to her otherwise sterile life, led in exile and deprivation. She, too, succeeds for a brief interval to neutralize her loneliness when she merges in communion with the surrounding universe, thus commiting "adultery."

"What do you value most?" asks Count Greffi of Lieutenant Henry in *A Farewell to Arms,* to which Henry answers: "Someone I love."[7] Hemingway time and again emphasizes the importance of love. Though, in his case, there is a definite role for love in that his women are easily categorized according to how they affect their men's lives. Yet he is invariably seeking in his love encounters some transcendent mystical union. Like Hemingway, Idris seems to attain this idealistic union through the physical (sexual) encounter. This is consistent with an existential view of life which emphasizes a "carpe diem" theme of love of the earth and the moment.

Notes

1. Idris, "Mashuq al-Hams," in *Mushuq al-Hams,* p. 64.

2. Idris, "Halaqat al-Nuhas al-Na'ima: Qissa fi Arba'Murabba'at" in *Mashuq al-Hams,* p. 164.

3. Mahfouz, "Harat-al-'Ushshaq," in *Hikaya bila bidaya wala Nihaya,* p. 102.

4. Idris, "Hadhihi al-Marra," in *Lughat Al-Ay Ay,* p. 264.

5. Victor White, "Anathema-Marantha," in *Love and Violence,* trans. George Lamb (London: Sheed and Ward, Inc., 1954), p. 233.

6. August Adam, *The Primacy of Love* (Westminster, Maryland: Newman Press, 1958), p. 130.

7. Hemingway, *A Farewell to Arms* (New York: Charles Scribners' Sons, 1929), p. 271.

Roger Allen (essay date winter 1981)

SOURCE: Allen, Roger. "The Artistry of Yūsuf Idrīs." *World Literature Today* 55, no. 1 (winter 1981): 43-7.

[*In the following essay, Allen maintains that Idris's short fiction effectively conveys his social and political concerns, especially his focus on the urban poor.*]

Yūsuf Idrīs's first published work, a collection of short stories entitled *Arkhas Layālī* (*The Cheapest Nights*), appeared in 1954. He is perhaps the most prominent of a number of younger Egyptian writers whose vitality and forcefulness at that time reflected their sense of identification with the course of events in their country during the 1950s, and particularly the Revolution of 1952. On the broader political plane 1954 was also the year in which Jamāl 'Abd al-Nāsir (Gamal Abdul Nasser) became the de facto ruler of the country. The years that followed were heady ones indeed for both Egypt and its younger generation of intellectuals and writers. Agricultural reform laws were introduced which radically altered the power structure of rural society, while on the international level Egypt signed an arms agreement with Czechoslovakia, obtained financial and technological aid from the Soviet Union to build the High Dam at Aswān (after the United States had refused to do so) and nationalized the Suez Canal in 1956, in the process witnessing the acute embarrassment of Britain and France at the withdrawal of their forces in the face of adverse international opinion. These events brought 'Abd al-Nāsir to a prominence which made him a natural focus of pan-Arab sentiment, and the movement culminated in the unification of Egypt and Syria as the United Arab Republic.

This series of events was different indeed from those of earlier decades in this century, when Arab aspirations for independence and social and cultural progress had seemed to promise a happier future, mostly however at the pleasure of the English and French occupying forces. But that future seemed to be continually thrust just out of reach by developments both internal and external. On the pan-Arab level the end of World War II had seen the foundation of the Arab League with headquarters in Cairo, but that token of a growing sense of unity was almost immediately confronted with the reality of the creation of the state of Israel. The year 1948 saw the first of a series of defeats which have punctuated the recent history of the Arab world—1948, 1956, 1967 and, to a certain extent, 1973—and which have had a considerable impact on much modern Arabic literature. In fact, the 1948 defeat provided a number of junior officers in the Egyptian army with clear proof of the corruption of the country's ruling elite at the highest level. This fact, along with increasing governmental chaos, political terrorism and social unrest, contributed to the organization and eventual success of the 1952 Revolution.

These were also the years during which Yūsuf Idrīs, born in May 1927 in a village on the Nile Delta, was a student in Cairo. He involved himself in demonstrations during this turbulent period and has continued to express his political views through his writings ever since. This has often brought him into conflict with the regime, and he has been arrested and imprisoned on more than one occasion for his leftist views, particularly during the 1960s when, as recent investigations have revealed, the observance of civil liberties was especially capricious. It was the early creative years of Idrīs which were his most productive, and in the 1970s he has written hardly any works of literature. His latest anthology of stories, **Bayt min Lahm** (House of Flesh), appeared in 1971, but some of the selections were written much earlier than that. He continues to serve as one of the "writers in residence" at *al-Ahrām,* Cairo's most famous daily newspaper, where among his colleagues are Tawfīq al-Hakīm, the acknowledged doyen of Arab dramatists (see *BA* [*Books Abroad*] 50:1, p. 99 and *WLT* [*World Literature Today*] 53:4, pp. 601-605), and Najīb Mahfūz, the Arab world's most famous novelist (see *BA* 46:2, pp. 236-37). A further contributory factor to his meager output in recent years has been his health: he has been suffering from a serious heart condition. One must hope therefore that the title of a new and as yet unfinished work, *Iftah al-Qalb* (Open the Heart), is symbolic of a new period of creativity.

Between 1954 and 1958 Idrīs published no less than five collections of short stories, some including works of novella length. This outpouring of creativity was welcomed by critics as a new direction in Egyptian fiction, and indeed it was. For Idrīs eschewed the more romantic tendencies of some of his immediate predecessors and chose to present his subjects in a direct and attractive realism. Furthermore, his own village origins allowed him to bring an authentic touch to the village scenes which formed the background to many of the stories. In this case the life in the provinces was not the romanticized world of Muhammad Husayn Haykal's early novel *Zaynab* (1913), but an uncompromisingly accurate and sympathetic portrait of the life of the peasantry. From the first collection, the story **"Mishwār"** (A Trip), in which a Delta village policeman takes a mad woman to an asylum in Cairo, is an effective mirror both of provincial attitudes to the allures of the big city and of the callous indifference of a variety of urban officials to the plight of this country yokel policeman and his insane charge.

Besides his childhood experiences in a rural village, Idrīs brought to his short stories another unique qualification, that of a practicing doctor who, upon graduation from Cairo's Qasr al-'Aynī Hospital, had spent some time as medical inspector in one of the poorest quarters of the city of Cairo. The title story of the first collection, **"Arkhas Layālī"** (The Cheapest Nights), shows his acute concern with his homeland's most pressing problem, that of overpopulation. Once again the setting is a village. 'Abd al-Karīm leaves the mosque after evening prayer and wades his way toward the center of the community through hordes of children, all the while cursing the unknown source which brought them to life and comforting himself with the thought that half of them will die of starvation. None of his friends are out and about, and so, cursing the tea-seller whose strong brew is making his head spin, he returns to his cold house and, clambering over his sleeping children, makes love to his wife. Before long he is once again being congratulated on the addition of another mouth to his family.

If this story represents a cri de coeur from an Egyptian doctor, a vastly different mood is conveyed by one of the stories from the collection *A Laysa Kadhālika* (Isn't That So?; 1957), which was later republished under a different title, *Qā'al-Madīna* (City Dregs). The story entitled **"Abu al-Hawl"** (The Sphinx) is a somewhat sardonic and ghoulish tale about an arrogant medical student who is always called "doctor" by the respectful peasantry and who is sufficiently carried away one day that he communicates the medical student's need for corpses to his admiring audience, whereupon late that night one of them obliges him by arriving at his doorstep with a body allegedly washed up in the river.

However, no work of fiction by Idrīs makes more brilliant use of his experiences among the urban poor than *City Dregs* itself, a novella which succeeds superbly in manipulating the narrative point of view. The beginning of the work is a wonderful portrait of Judge 'Abdallāh, a man who is stubbornly insistent on being as average as possible. The mysterious loss of his watch allows the author to trace in retrospect the Judge's relationship with Shuhrat, a married woman whom he has hired purportedly as a housecleaner but in fact as a mistress. The climax of the work comes when the Judge, together with a friend and his faithful retainer Farghalī, goes by car from his own airy, modern part of town across Cairo to the old city where Shuhrat's abode lies. The increasing sense of constriction and tension is captured in a spectacular piece of word-painting which makes the work, in my opinion, among Idrīs's most successful essays in fiction. At the end of the story the Judge has his watch back, but one day he catches sight of Shuhrat obviously soliciting on the street. If the title does not suggest it to us with sufficient clarity, we now come to realize that this is the story of Shuhrat, the poor mother fending for her family; the Judge has merely served as the agent of her downfall.

The poorer classes of both city and countryside, these are Idrīs's major topic in these collections. Some stories provide unforgettable cameos: 'Abduh in **"Shughlāna"** from *Arkhas Layālī*, for example, who is delighted to be able to make some money by giving blood, until he becomes anemic and is not allowed to give any more; the little girl in **"Nazra"** (A Stare), from the same collection, who can weave her way deftly through the Cairo traffic with a tray of food on her head while the worried narrator who is watching her is almost mowed down; and one of the most touching, **"Mārsh al-Ghurūb"** (Sunset March; from *A Laysa Kadhālika*), which paints a picture of a vendor of licorice juice desperately trying to sell some of his wares to people rush-

ing home after work. In this last story language is used with great effect to link together the falling expectations of the vendor and the sounds he produces on the two small cymbals which he uses—like all such vendors—to attract the attention of would-be customers. The story ends with the sound's disappearing gradually into the distance in a verbal diminuendo which is most effective.

The poor are also the sufferers in the title story of *Jumhūriyyat Farahāt* (Farahāt's Republic; 1956). It too gives us an unforgettable cameo sketch, but in this case there is also a political statement scarcely concealed beneath the surface. The narrator is brought to a police station under arrest, and it is soon obvious that he possesses a much higher level of education than the majority of petty criminals who are dragged into the station in a never-ending stream to face the summary justice of Farahāt, the station sergeant. This local tyrant mistakes the narrator for a visitor to the station and intersperses his callous, cursory remarks and yells to the accused who stand before him with a remarkable picture of an idealized world which he reveals to the narrator, one with modern factories, nice houses for everyone and a cinema on every street. At the climax of his account of this dreamworld, the constable informs Farahāt that the narrator is under arrest. The bubble bursts, and Farahāt resumes his customary demeanor. Even so, at the story's end we realize that this petty tyrant, who can be so gruff and apparently insensitive to the poor people of his district, is actually a rather naïve dreamer with little appreciation of the intricacies of modernization. And when we observe that the title of the story refers to the police station as a "republic," it becomes clear that we are dealing with a portrayal of a microcosm of the larger reality of Egypt and perhaps a not entirely complimentary portrait of its leader.

The story **"Jumhūriyyat Farahāt"** brings us to another literary genre with which Idrīs has been closely connected, namely the drama. In 1957 he adapted and expanded the story into a most successful play and also published *Malik al-Qutn* (The Cotton King), a drama which illustrates the exploitation of the peasantry—this time cotton growers—by the landowning class. However, both the theme and manner of presentation of these two plays make it clear that they are extensions or adaptations of ideas for short stories, that being the medium in which his immense creativity was being best displayed at the time. His major contributions to the development of Egyptian drama were to come in the next decade.

If **"Jumhūriyyat Farahāt"** leads us naturally to the mention of the beginnings of Idrīs's dramatic oeuvre, then the title story of the last of the early collections of short stories, *Hādithat Sharaf* (A Matter of Honor; 1958), leads us in another direction. This story is set, like many others of this period, in the provinces. The scene is an *'izba,* a large country estate, a veritable societal fishbowl with its fixed codes of morality and a thousand eyes to oversee it. Idrīs manages to capture brilliantly the feelings of jealousy, spite, prudery and hatred when the two most beautiful young people in the community, Fātima the girl and Gharīb the boy, are "caught" in a field in an ambiguous situation which affords the village gossips and crones a positive orgy of suspicion and speculation. This portrayal of the tensions within a small, rural society structure at which Idrīs excels is carried yet farther in what is, in my opinion, his best novel, *al-Haram* (The Taboo; 1959).

This novel seems significantly to have been written at or around the same time as the short story. (I should, however, add at this point that the exact dates of composition of the stories in the earlier collections of Idrīs could only be checked by consulting the author himself; but, as becomes clear in referring to the later collections, it is not unknown for him to forget some of his stories with the passage of time and only publish them years later. In this case, however, the connection between the backgrounds of **"Hādithat Sharaf"** and *al-Haram* does not seem fortuitous.) In the novel too we are dealing with the fishbowl society of a village confronted with the discovery of an abandoned newborn baby in its midst. To the tensions which this event arouses in the village are added the innate suspicions of this small society at the coming of the *tarāhīl,* the migrant workers on whom suspicion—almost inevitably—falls. Even the beautiful and chaste Coptic girl Linda does not escape her father's suspicions in these circumstances of panic; but when the mother is discovered to be the poor 'Azīza who has been raped and subsequently dies, the sadness of the occasion brings about a rapprochement between the two traditionally antagonistic groups. The somewhat idealistic ending thus contrived is further emphasized by a reference to the Agricultural Reform Law, to which I have drawn attention earlier. The conclusion here is just a little too happy, and the intrusion of politics into this tale of the rural countryside lessens the impact of an otherwise effective novel.

This very same criticism may be leveled at Idrīs's other novels with even more justification, for in *al-'Ayb* (The Sin; 1962) and *al-Byadā'* (The White Woman; 1970, but written, so the author tells us, in 1955) societal and political issues are allowed to dominate two situations involving a man and a woman. In the first the major theme is the attitude of women toward going to work and toward their male colleagues, and also the attitude of those colleagues toward them. The chief female character allows her sense of propriety to be compromised, and once having accepted a bribe as her male counterparts regularly do, she loses her sense of morality. In the second novel Idrīs seems (in his introduction) to

identify himself closely with the hero Yahyā, who finds himself wrestling with the demands of local political realities in his homeland and of the universal, international causes in which he believes. All this unfolds within the context of his frustrating pursuit of "the white woman" of the title.

Thus, while these novels continue to demonstrate Idrīs's concern with the political and social problems of his countrymen, the artificial nature of their narrative thread often seems subordinated to the overt political or social message, suggesting that we are dealing with a writer whose sense of commitment is most forcibly and effectively conveyed in the shorter genres.

. . . . .

The 1960s were not a happy decade for Egypt, culminating early in the disastrous defeat of June 1967 and the ensuing period of self-examination, criticism and recrimination. The period began with the dissolution of the United Arab Republic in 1961 and the instigation of a yet more rigorous form of socialism. Within this milieu writers were soon made aware that, in the words of the Egyptian critic Sabrī Hāfiz, "the years of fear and lack of security had returned in a severer version." Idrīs's short story collection *Ākhir al-Dunyā* (The End of the World; 1961) contains works written during the period from 1958 to 1961, and in the main the stories are similar to those of previous collections in theme and technique. **"La'bat al-Bayt"** (Playing House), for example, is a charming and perceptive portrait of two children at play, squabbling and then making up. One story however, **"Alif al-Ahrār"** (The Letter *alif* in the Word *Ahrār*), has a more universal theme, what one might term the dehumanization of bureaucratic man. The story is a veritable tragicomedy, told with a generous dose of sardonic humor, about an educated clerical office worker who comes to believe that he is no different from a machine; he protests and is eventually fired for his pains. As he proclaims his humanity to the world outside, his countrymen simply pass him by as yet another madman.

This last story is a good illustration of a trend which is distinctly visible in the works of Idrīs and other writers in this decade, one which Sasson Somekh describes in his book on Idrīs's colleague and countryman, the novelist Najīb Mahfūz, as being "into the labyrinth." This labyrinth is the existential quest for a meaning in life and for an escape from the alienation resulting from the realities of life in a modernistic society. Idrīs and others portray these feelings in symbolistic works which serve two separate functions, as Idrīs himself has observed: in the first place, they provide the most appropriate artistic mode through which to address such issues; and secondly, they afford a means by which to avoid the ravages of the censor's blue pencil. Both writers and censors may have been completely familiar with "the code," but through some generally tacit truce the status quo was allowed to prevail.

This disturbing view of reality is nowhere more evident than in the short story collection *Lughat al-Āy-Āy* (The Language of Screams; 1966). While **"Li'anna al-Qiyāma la Taqūmu"** (Because the Day of Judgment Will Not Come) may deal with a subject which Idrīs has touched on before, the life of a family where the father is either unable to provide support or else dead (see, for example, the earlier stories **"al-Mahfaza"** [**The Wallet**] and **"al-Yad al-Kabīra"** [**The Big Hand**]), we now find **"Lughat al-Āy-Āy"** itself and **"al-Aurtā"** (The Aorta), the latter being surely one of the most nightmarish visions to emerge from Egypt during this most unsettled period. A terrifying study of mass hysteria and man's cruelty to his fellowman, this story starts with a passage which, like the one mentioned earlier in **City Dregs,** seems almost visual in its ever closer view of a mass of humanity swirling around a square until it finds its target, the luckless 'Abduh, who has had an operation to sever his aorta because he has "a dangerous disease that threatened to infect all Egyptians." At the end of this story the crowd is left standing in horror and disbelief at the sight of 'Abduh strung up by the neck on a meat hook, with his severed aorta waving in the air. The frightening anonymity of the tale and the total vagueness of the background—so untypical of Idrīs's earlier short stories—give this modern parable an immensely powerful impact.

If Idrīs's output of short stories diminished during the 1960s from the remarkable levels of the previous decade, this was not because there was any diminution in creativity, but rather that it was turned in a different direction, most notably the drama. In 1963 Idrīs published a series of articles in the Cairo cultural monthly *al-Kātib* under the title "Nahwa Masrah 'Arabī" (Toward an Arabic Drama). What he advocated was the need to look into the traditional Arab forms of drama culled from folkloric sources, rather than relying on the European model which had formed the basis of works up until that time. Within Egypt he proposed a revival of the form known as *al-sāmir*, a *théâtre en ronde* approach culled from provincial evening entertainments, with no formal stage as such and few, if any, props. In the following year he provided a convincing illustration of his ideas with the play *al-Farāfīr* (The Farfurs) and with it contributed one of the most important works to the history of modern Egyptian drama. The play is a raucous, witty and irreverent exposé of a whole series of societal and personal foibles, but within this farcical milieu there is a serious investigation of the nature and rights of authority, both between individuals and on the larger national and international level. At the conclusion of each of the two acts of the play no solution has been found to the problems of the necessity and rights of master and servant, of ruler and ruled. This led to criti-

cism of the play for its nihilism and even possible advocacy of anarchy. However, whatever the import of the work, there can be no doubt that it represents a significant new step in modern Egyptian drama.

Having made this important gesture in both theory and practice of experimental drama, Idrīs appears to have decided to leave the elaboration to others, among whom we would mention Mahmūd Diyāb, the late Najīb Surūr and Shawqī 'Abd al-Hakīm as the most consistent and successful. He himself chose a more orthodox framework for his next play, *al-Mahzala al-Ardiyya* (The Terrestrial Comedy; 1966), which is something of a morality play about family feuds and the evils of cupidity and which loses a sense of focus in its tendency to digress and its attempt to combine the themes of greed and madness within one artistic mold. However, another play, *al-Mukhattatīna* (The Striped Ones; 1969), did apparently share with *al-Farāfīr* the theme of a concern with the relationship between ruler and ruled and the quest for an ideal society. I use the past tense in referring to this play because it was one of a number of plays which were censored during the 1969-70 season, when several playwrights composed works in which they vented their spleen on the subject of the events of 1967 and the implications of those events for the Arab world. Idrīs's play has never been performed, to my knowledge, to this day.

In 1966 Idrīs finally gave up his medical career altogether. Since then he has served as a journalist with *al-Jumhūriyya* and, more recently, *al-Ahrām.* If anything, this has caused a further reduction in his output, at least by the yardstick of his remarkable early outpouring of creativity. In 1969 there also appeared his collection of short stories *al-Naddāha* (The Siren), also published as *Mashūq al-Hams,* and in 1971 there appeared his most recently published literary work, the collection of short stories *Bayt min Lahm* (House of Flesh). Many of Idrīs's favorite subjects are to be found here. There is the country setting of **"Sūrat al-Baqara"** (Chapter on the Cow) from the latter collection, with its amusing description of a man returning from market and gradually losing patience and sanity at mankind's insatiable curiosity about the price he has paid for a cow; and "al-Naddāha" itself, a most successful exploration of the lure of the big city to a girl from the countryside. There are some extremely effective parables too, including two stories which must be among his shortest: **"al-Martabat al-Muqa"ara"** (The Concave Mattress), a rather bitter view of the relationship between married people and of life in general; and **"al-'Usfūr 'Alā al-Silk"** (The Little Bird on the Wire), an effective juxtaposition of the antics of two birds on a telephone wire and the business of the world going on through the wire itself.

The title story **"Bayt min Lahm"** harks back to Idrīs's earlier descriptions of families which are without a father figure; but in this case a theme which has made itself increasingly evident in his stories, the role of sex in society, plays a major part in the narrative, as the widowed mother, despairing of finding husbands for her three daughters, allows them to commit incest with her second husband in order to satisfy their sexual desires. Other stories too explore the sexual theme from a variety of perspectives, from the almost sardonic folk narratives such as **"Akbar al-Akābir"** (The Greatest Sin of All) to the frustrated and pampered surgeon's wife in **"'Ala Waraq Sīlūfān"** (In Cellophane Wrapping).

. . . . .

From the preceding description certain salient features of Idrīs's approach to writing have, it is hoped, become clear. Firstly, there is his abiding concern with humanity and its problems. His major themes remain the people of the city and countryside and, most especially, the poorer classes. Stories about the middle, bourgeois class (such as **"In Cellophane Wrapping"**) are relatively rare, considering his total output of stories. The description of these people is wholly realistic and unsentimental. The author allows us a brief glimpse into the life of a particular individual or group and then leaves them as he finds them; there is rarely any change or improvement in their lot. Even when realism gives way to a more symbolistic approach and the application is more universal than local, the same concern with the issues of man's existence and survival shines through the layers of meaning, whether they are piled up to convey the complicated nature of the problem or to play the games of the censor.

Ever since Idrīs's first collection appeared, he has been criticized for his style, at least by the more conservative critics. He has, of course, insisted on using the colloquial dialect of his country in composing dialogue for his works of fiction and drama, but it is not to that aspect that these critics are referring (although not a few of them disapprove of that too). They are rather taking Idrīs to task for his extreme waywardness with vocabulary and syntax. In the former regard, Idrīs's style shows an ever-increasing tendency to use individual dialect words even in sections in which dialogue is not involved. Idrīs's countryman Mahfūz has also done this, but with great discretion, retaining a predominantly standard written form of vocabulary and syntax even for dialogue. With Idrīs, on the other hand, not only is the dialogue in his works in pure colloquial, but one finds speech patterns, lexical items and whole elements of syntax intruding from the colloquial into passages of cursive, descriptive prose. This feature earns him the reproach of a number of critics, but it also lends his works an unmistakable air of spontaneity and authenticity which few of his contemporaries in Egypt can rival.

Above all, a study of the development of Idrīs's use of language gives his readers a clear indication of a writer who is developing, changing and reacting to events and people as they have an effect on him. In fact, the author himself admits to this spontaneity when he tells us that he writes his works when his imagination catches fire. There is very little planning to it—again a contrast with Mahfūz—and, if feasible, the whole work is composed at a single sitting. This feature may also help to explain the faults in construction which are often to be found in some of his more lengthy works. Many of these, the play *al-Farāfīr* and the novel *al-Haram,* for example, are extremely important components of his total oeuvre; but in the case of these two and other longer works the reader is left with the impression that more concern with overall structure and a sharper sense of focus would have produced works which may have been somewhat shorter but would have gained in quality for what they lost in quantity. This said, however, we should immediately add that it is this very quality of spontaneity which gives Idrīs's short stories so many of their virtues and so much of their variety. The short-story genre is, of course, one which requires that words be used judiciously and economically, and within the milieu of the vignette Idrīs comes into his own. He is, in a word, one of the two or three greatest short-story writers who have written and are writing in Arabic.

As noted earlier, Idrīs has not written a great deal of literature in recent years, being involved more in journalism and bureaucracy. His works have contributed to modern Arabic literature some masterpieces which will almost certainly stand the test of time. Let us hope that the novel on which he is now working will see the beginning of a new period in his literary career.

P. M. Kurpershoek (essay date 1981)

SOURCE: Kurpershoek, P. M. Introduction to *The Short Stories of Yusuf Idris,* pp. 1-18. Leiden: E. J. Brill, 1981.[1]

[*In the following essay, Kurpershoek traces the development of the short story genre in Egypt and locates Idris's place within that tradition.*]

Ever since his first collection of short stories appeared in 1954, Yūsuf Idrīs has been generally recognised as the genre's leading representative among the artists who rose to prominence with the 1952 Revolution.[2] Therefore it is all the more astonishing that his production in this field by no means received the earnest attention from Egyptian critics which, by their unanimous judgement, it deserved;[3] and what they wrote on this subject pales into insignificance beside the amount of criticism devoted to his theatrical works.[4]

In showing comparatively little interest in the short story (*uqṣūṣa, qiṣṣa qaṣīra*), while acknowledging Idrīs' mastery of it, the arbiters of literary taste perhaps reflected the widespread opinion that its very shortness and 'journalistic' character make it doubtful whether it quite belongs to the realm of serious literature.[5] That there was, and probably still is, a tendency among the Egyptian reading public to judge the merits of one's writings by the criterion of length may be gathered from the fact that Idrīs himself thought it necessary to uphold the short story against the supposedly superior qualities of the novel.[6]

Nevertheless the Egyptian *uqṣūṣa* has made great strides towards artistic maturity since in the early part of this century some magazines classified translated and adapted stories as 'amusing matter' (*bāb al-fukāha*).[7] The main credit for this goes to a number of authors who, themselves not contented with merely translating foreign authors, consciously strove to create a national art of the short story, as a brief survey of its emergence will show.

The sketches in 'Abdallāh Nadīm's paper *at-Tankīt wa-t-Tabkīt* (1881)[8] and the attempts of classicists like Muḥammad al-Muwailiḥī[9] at resuscitating the ancient Arabic *maqāma* style[10] have sometimes been mentioned as an indication that a rudimentary form of short story already existed in Egypt independently of the mainstream of world literature, or that, given time, an authentically Arabic equivalent might have developed. But most students of the subject agree that the *uqṣūṣa* in its present form is the product of a literary development which drew its inspiration directly from European sources, foremost among them De Maupassant and Chekhov.[11]

This interest in foreign literary forms was closely bound up with the remarkable cultural revival (*an-nahḍa*) which started during the reign of Muḥammad 'Alī (1805-1848) and increased in momentum in the last decades of the 19th century when a new national press, largely founded by Lebanese and Syrian émigrés, channeled European ideas and knowledge to a growing Western-educated middle class of professionals in a simple, fluent language without the flourish that used to be considered as the hallmark of literary excellence. The importance of the press to the later emergence of the Egyptian short story can hardly be overrated.[12] In the early stages newspapers and magazines like *al-Ahrām*, Ibrāhīm Muwailiḥī's *Miṣbāḥ ash-Sharq*, *al-Laṭā'if*, *aḍ-Ḍiyā'* and *Fatāt ash-Sharq* began to present *riwāyāt*, translated and adapted stories and novels written by unnamed foreign authors.[13] These *riwāyāt* were mostly moralising and romantic in tone and, due to the fact that many of them were, evidently, abridged versions of originally longer stories or novellas, loosely knit and crammed with events.[14] These artistic deficiencies, however, in no way diminish their importance as the forerunners of a new sort of fiction.[15]

A more scrupulous approach towards foreign literature won through with the appearance of the cultural magazines *al-Bayān* (1911-1919) and *as-Sufūr* (1915-24). The translations by 'Abbās Ḥāfiẓ, Ibrāhīm 'Abd al-Qādir al-Māzinī and Muḥammad as-Sibā'ī in the English oriented *al-Bayān*, edited by shaikh 'Abd ar-Raḥmān al-Barqūqī, marked a definite improvement over the previous periods of adaptation, though as-Sibā'ī could not refrain from adding an occasional line of Arabic verse.[16] *As-Sufūr*, founded by 'Abd al-Ḥamīd Ḥamdī, rather took its cue from French literature and, contrary to *al-Bayān*, also made room in its columns for the work of Egyptian *uqṣūṣa* writers, such as the brothers Muḥammad and Maḥmūd Taimūr, Ḥasan Maḥmūd and Maḥmūd 'Izzī;[17] indeed Muḥammad Taimūr's *Mā Tarāh al-'Uyūn* (What Eyes See), which it published in 1917, is often taken as the starting point of the Egyptian short story,[18] in the same manner as Muḥammad Ḥusain Haikal's *Zainab* (1913) passes as the first Egyptian novel.[19] Small wonder, therefore, that above all it is the influence of Guy de Maupassant, the French master of the short story, that makes itself felt in the early production of this generation.[20]

Although Muḥammad Taimūr (1892-1921) died prematurely and his chief interest was with the theatre, his name remains indissolubly linked with the genesis of the Egyptian short story. This reputation is due not only to his own stories but also because his younger brother Maḥmūd (1894-1973), a much more prolific writer, carried on his brother's ideas.[21] Maḥmūd and others still doted on the mawkish themes and sweet-sounding prose rhythms of al-Manfalūṭī's collection *al-'Abarāt* (Tears), published in 1915,[22] but the literary principles advocated by Muḥammad already foreshadowed the next stage in the development of the *uqṣūṣa*, and these were once more adopted in part by the realist movement of the fifties. He was one of the first authors to call for a "local Egyptian literature that, being truthful in expression, was not to borrow its images from the desert (i.e., the Arabic classics) or from the West".[23] Muḥammad found the lacrymose romanticism of al-Manfalūṭī and the rather chaotic adapted stories little to his taste. Though himself the scion of an aristocratic family, he took to haunting lower-class quarters and mixed with the common people in search of new inspiration and of "the Egyptian national character" (*ash-shakhṣiyya al-miṣriyya*)[24] which, he maintained, had so far only been portrayed with any success in al-Muwailiḥī's *Ḥadīth 'Īsā Ibn Hishām* (1906) and Haikal's novel *Zainab* (1913).[25]

In the flare-up of nationalist sentiment that culminated in the revolutionary events of 1919, the aim of creating an independent national literature (*adab qawmī mustaqill*),[26] impregnated with the Egyptian spirit and true to nature in its descriptions, became the banner round which rallied the adherents of the so-called New

School (*al-Madrasa al-Ḥadītha*). The idea that guided them was that the movement for political independence, which was then gaining momentum under the national leadership of Saʿd Zaghlūl, ought to have its counterpart in the cultural domain; this was expressed in their catch-phrase 'intellectual independence' (*istiqlāl fikrī*).[27] The School's main contribution was in the realm of literature and music, but it also had its ramifications in architecture and the dance. Those who were engaged in literature lived their version of the roaring twenties in the coffee-houses of Cairo, among which "The Cosmograph" in ʿImād ad-Dīn street, subsequently renamed "Art Café," was their favourite meeting-place.[28] After closing-time they went to the house of Ibrāhīm al-Miṣrī,[29] one of the most fervent advocates of the New School, who had started publishing short stories in *as-Sufūr* shortly after Muḥammad Taimūr.[30] There they would often spend the whole night reading to one another their latest productions.

The group's hub and intellectual mentor was, it appears Aḥmad Khairī Saʿīd, who coined the slogan "Up with originality, up with creativity, up with renewal and reform!"[31] Together with his *alter ego,* the talented short-story writer Maḥmūd Ṭāhir Lāshīn,[32] he issued in 1925 the magazine *al-Fagr* which, during the two years of its existence, served as the mouthpiece of the New School. With Aḥmad Khairī Saʿīd as its principal editor, the paper adopted the radical view that the Arab heritage should be abandoned as a source of inspiration and that those who wished to create a modern national literature worth its name should turn to European examples in order to "destroy the corrupt and reactionary and to build that which is useful and necessary"; accordingly *al-Fagr* was given the subtitle "Journal of Demolition and Construction" (*Ṣaḥīfat al-Hadam wa-l-Binā'*).[33]

Much more than in its predecessor, *as-Sufūr,* or any other contemporary paper, the emphasis in *al-Fagr* was on the short story, both Egyptian and in translation.[34] In the latter field a significant shift occurred when the translators, who till then had limited their activities almost exclusively to French and Anglo-American authors, began to acquaint themselves with Russian literature, to which they had access through their knowledge of English or French. This discovery had immediate and far-reaching consequences for the further development of the Egyptian short story itself. The rapid increase in the number of Russian works, many of them translated from English by Muḥammad as-Sibāʿī, and articles on Russian literature in magazines like *as-Sufūr* and *al-Bayān,* and later *Wādī an-Nīl, al-Balāgh al-Usbūʿī, as-Siyāsa al-Usbūʿiyya* and *al-Fagr,* was avidly absorbed by the disciples of the New School. For them the writings of authors like Gogol, Pushkin, Tolstoy, Dostoyevsky, Turgenev, Chekhov and Gorky were eye-openers on to a new, remarkably congenial world.[35] Their refreshing realism, the torrential, passionate emo-

tions, the manifest sympathy for the fate of the downtrodden, the psychological depth, the violent extremes of exuberant joy and deep affliction, sin and remorse, all this was, as Yaḥyā Ḥaqqī later recounted, breathlessly taken in by the young Egyptian iconoclasts. They were enraptured to find that "this atmosphere corresponds to the fervid, emotional nature of the Oriental young man, who is deprived of love." "Therefore," Ḥaqqī continues, "I am not far from the truth when I give most of the credit for the production of the members of the New School to Russian literature. So, after the story had undergone the influence of French literature through Haikal, it came under the influence of Russian literature through the New School."[36]

Ḥaqqī's opinion that the Egyptian short story is especially indebted to the great Russians is borne out by the subdivision of *al-Fagr,* the magazine which more than any other contributed to bringing about its breakthrough: the first part of the paper's story section was reserved for Egyptian production, the second for translated works, practically all Russian, and the third for serialised Egyptian stories.[37] The magazine's editor, Aḥmad Khairī Saʿīd, was already in 1920 so transported by what he read of the Russians that he called Egypt "the nation most akin to Russia."[38] The merits he attributed to Russian literature were exactly those that he and his friends grievously missed in the Arab tradition and the sentimentalism (*wigdāniyya*) of al-Manfalūṭī: "(Russian literature) has reputedly a standing all its own. Its chief characteristics are that it analyses the various inclinations of the human soul, pictures human life as it is, complete with its painful and evil aspects and calls for freedom in every domain."[39]

Realism geared to the exposure of class differences, ignorance, social injustice and abuses, the creation of convincing, true-to-life characters and defiance of what was felt as undue reverence for the institutions of the past were, in fact, the values most cherished by the New School and again by the angry young men of the late forties and the fifties. In championing realism, or 'the school of facts' (*madhhab al-ḥaqā'iq*), as it was then often dubbed,[40] the adherents of the New School and others generally professed to have been motivated by considerations which lay outside the sphere of aesthetics pure and simple. The reasons most frequently given in explanation of their preferences are national pride, a craving to secure for Egypt a place among the civilised nations—and in their opinion the possession of a great literature was the unmistakable sign of national pre-eminence—and the need for social reform. In their judgement this was the first prerequisite for any progress.

The idea that literature has primarily an enlightening function, that it should be useful rather than sweet, was carried to an extreme by the brothers ʿĪsā and Shaḥāta

'Ubaid, who were Christians of Syrian extraction.[41] Their failure to win literary recognition was, it would seem, largely due to their excessive zeal in applying their naturalistic views, a tendency which detracted seriously from the readability of their stories and was perhaps related to the fact that they were not in touch with literary circles but worked in frustrating isolation.[42] Nevertheless their observations reflect to a great extent the opinions current among their colleagues of the New School. In imitation of the French naturalists they considered that an author should make a 'dossier' of his characters, taking duly into account the peculiarities of their make-up, hereditary factors and milieu.[43] They predicted that, when 'the school of facts' overcame the inbred conservatism of the Egyptian public and triumphed over "the idealism of the sentimental school," many advantages would accrue to Egypt from their approach: "If we succeed in this then we have achieved something of which Western authors have no knowledge because they are not in a position to study our psyche and social order. Then the day will arrive when they start translating our stories into their languages, considering that they delight in everything Egyptian, especially so after Egypt's glorious national movement has caught the attention of the whole world. Then, only then, the Egyptian nation can be considered one of the independent, advanced nations, whatever its political system, for literature is the measure of a nation's degree of development. Egypt's progress and precocious maturity certainly entitle it to its own artistically sophisticated, independent literature."[44]

Maḥmūd Taimūr (1894-1973), an incomparably more successful pioneer of the Egyptian short story, shows in his early work a similar concern for "the usefulness of story-writing."[45] Though he also considered it a disgrace that the national Renaissance had not yet produced a distinctively Egyptian literature,[46] he appeared less chauvinistic than 'Īsā 'Ubaid and more inclined to stress the social function of the author. Citing Zola's words, "Clean your houses, then I will clean my pen," he argued in the preface to the second edition of his collection *Shaikh Gum'a* (1927) that only realism (*al-madhhab al-wāqi'ī*) serves a useful purpose, because "if vice remains hidden it tends to grow rampant and becomes difficult to eradicate . . . We are in need of men who tell us the truth about our life and ourselves, however hard and painful that may be, not of men who paint our milieu in delusive, false colours."[47]

Social criticism had become a recurrent theme in Egyptian literature ever since the Islamic activists Gamāl ad-Dīn al-Afghānī (1838-97) and his famous Egyptian disciple Muḥammad 'Abduh (1849-1905) had propagated the view that only all-embracing reform (*iṣlāḥ*) could counter the undermining penetration of Western influence and thought into Muslim society.[48] Already audible in the work of al-Muwailiḥī and al-Manfalūṭī, one of

'Abduh's pupils, the call for *iṣlāḥ* was given a new impulse by the 1919 revolution, though it took a different, definitely secular shape. Discarding both the classical tradition and romanticism, the writers of the New School opted instead for the realist approach which, they believed, would be more effective than the moralising, preachy tone of some of their reform-minded predecessors. Moreover, they did not take the existing social stratification for granted. The role of the working classes in the disturbances and Wafdist agitation of 1919 evoked their admiration, whereas the picture they drew of the aristocracy, and even of the middle class, is on the whole highly unflattering.[49] As we have seen they came to cultivate a Bohemian life-style and revelled in frequenting popular coffee-houses where they discussed literature passionately and cracked jokes till well into the night. Yaḥyā Ḥaqqī describes in his *Fagr al-Qiṣṣa al-Miṣriyya* (Dawn of the Egyptian Short Story, 1960) how the revolutionary turmoil of 1919 induced Muḥammad Taimūr and Ḥusain Fawzī to transfer their meetings from the stately mansion of the Rashīd family to the 'Art Café', where they joined the inseparable Aḥmad Khairī Sa'īd and Maḥmūd Ṭāhir Lāshīn.[50] The latter two reportedly conceived the idea of founding *al-Fagr* during one of their frequent ramblings through the ebullient bazaar-quarter round the Ḥusain mosque, an *ambiance* they much preferred to "the meetings of the educated in the upper-class areas."[51] Thus it could happen that, among the members of the New School, the aristocratic brothers Taimūr, having eagerly imbibed European thought and the atmosphere of the Egyptian street, "showed themselves most zealous in depicting the repugnant greed of the rich and the destitution of the poor."[52] But, no doubt due to the fact that none of them came from a lower-class family, Egyptian readers have not always found their portrayal of popular life convincing.[53]

Among the various forms of social corruption (*fasād*) they singled out for criticism, the relation between the sexes is certainly the theme on which they dwelled most frequently. Here one is often under the impression that they, like the subsequent generations of story writers, adopted a tone of moral indignation as a convenient cover for writing with the more freedom on a subject they found most stimulating. The pages of their work are crowded with profligate young men from wealthy families and civil servants chasing and seducing innocent damsels, Casanovas who discover that their conquest is the spouse of one of their close friends, cruel fathers who force their daughters to marry much older partners they do not love,[54] and despotic husbands who happily surrender themselves to debaucheries, unaware that their locked-in wives avenge themselves by cuckolding them in secret. Other themes that figure prominently are the morbid distrust young whore-mongers later harbour as to their wives' fidelity and the social harm resulting from the imposition of the veil upon women. It should be pointed out, however, that they did not confine their criticism to this aspect of *fasād;* the unscrupulous attempts of middle-class people to climb the social ladder and the abuse of power by civil servants were equally pilloried.[55]

Though the pioneers of the New School were at one in their preference for realism, their views inevitably differed and fluctuated on the point of language. The bilingual situation in Egypt and other Arab countries automatically faced them with the fundamental dilemma whether to abide throughout by the rules of the traditional written language (*fuṣḥā*), or to enhance the naturalistic colouring of their work by employing the vernacular (*'āmmiyya*) in dialogue and perhaps even in the narration in the form of scattered colloquialisms. The New School's aversion to uncritical imitation (*taqlīd*) of classical examples and to the Arab cultural inheritance (*at-turāth*) in general, coupled with its emphasis on the need for a local Egyptian literature and realism, would lead one to expect a clear-cut choice in favour of the second of these alternatives. Indeed it was the prevailing opinion among its members that "the characters should be made to use the same expressions as people do in real life,"[56] but this principle was not uniformly complied with. Muḥammad Taimūr, for instance, kept to *fuṣḥā* Arabic in the dialogues of *Mā Tarāh al-'Uyūn* and only employed the vernacular in his "contemporary Egyptian plays."[57] But even this was considered by 'Isā 'Ubaid "an extremist, dangerous view."[58]

Though not a member of the New School in a narrower sense, the 'Ubaids were inspired by very much the same ideals and were almost dogmatic in their advocacy of realism in art. In Shaḥāta's opinion a writer should work upon the same principles as a photographer: "Just as the accomplished photographer shows his skill by making pictures conform to the original, so the proficient writer portrays life as he sees it."[59] This rigid view led him to conclude: "Stories should be based on naked facts and accurate observations without any interference of the imagination."[60] 'Isā made an exception, however, for the language used by the characters which, as he saw it, ought to be "an intermediate form of Arabic without archaic constructions, though it is permissible to intersperse it with some colloquial expressions in order to avoid the impression of stiffness or affectation."[61] In this he professed himself motivated by fear lest Egyptian literature isolate itself from the Arab context, a danger of which he may have been more acutely aware because of his Syrian origin.[62] Nevertheless he failed to act upon his own advice, for the characters of his stories sometimes speak a curious hotchpotch of French, *fuṣḥā* and *'āmmiyya,* while colloquial words even occur in the narration.[63]

A well-known example of an author who, after initially having accepted, albeit with some hesitation, the *'āmmiyya* as the only suitable vehicle for the dialogue, but who eventually came over to quite the opposite view, and even took the trouble to rewrite parts of his early work into *fuṣḥā*, is Maḥmūd Taimūr. In the preface to his first short-story collection *Shaikh Gum'a,* he wrote: "It is universally accepted that the dialogue (the conversations) should be in the tongue of the speakers, because thus reality is most faithfully rendered."[64] But two years later, in the second edition, he argued that the two languages were in fact incompatible. He had therefore arrived at the conclusion that "since classical Arabic is the written language we must write the whole story, both the descriptive parts and the dialogue in this language . . . though there is no objection to employing, if necessary, some colloquial words and phrases."[65]

Others, like Yaḥyā Ḥaqqī and Ḥusain Fawzī, continued writing their dialogues in *'āmmiyya,*[66] but the latter's limited production of short stories terminated with his departure for Europe in 1925,[67] and Ḥaqqī only joined the group of the New School in its second stage, that is towards the end of 1926.[68] Moreover, both felt ill at ease with the straightforward realism then in vogue with some of their colleagues and experimented with a more subjective style that left little scope for the introduction of characters through their direct speech. Even Maḥmūd Ṭāhir Lāshīn, who together with Aḥmad Khairī Sa'īd formed the soul of the magazine *al-Fagr,* returned in his later short stories to *fuṣḥā* after an intermediate stage in which he tried to give his work a more realistic hue by drawing freely upon the vernacular.[69]

Al-Fagr was discontinued in 1927, only two years after its first issue had appeared, but its contributors seem to have entertained little doubt that during this brief span they had made great strides towards their aim of creating a national, realistic art of short-story writing. Its editor, Aḥmad Khairī Sa'īd, proudly pointed out that the sort of short stories published in *al-Fagr* were being imitated in rival magazines such as *al-Muqtaṭaf, al-Hilāl* and *al-Kashkūl,*[70] and Ḥaqqī felt that it was definitely the New School that "established the short story as a respectable genre, propagated the realist approach and rid us of the sobs of romanticism."[71]

With the disappearance of *al-Fagr,* the New School gradually dispersed. Some of its members ceased writing short stories altogether, others did so temporarily or, like Ḥaqqī, Sa'īd and Lāshīn, took increasingly to the novella. New authors came to the fore and another pioneer from outside the New School, Sa'īd 'Abduh, continued writing short stories and polishing his style well into the fifties. But on the whole, the thirties saw a drift away from realism towards a more self-reflexive, romantic or philosophical style of story-writing.[72]

The decline of realism and, according to the critic Ṣabrī Ḥāfiẓ, of the Egyptian art of the short story in general, lasted till the late forties.[73] Then the political and social unrest preceding the military coup of 1952 brought forth a new generation of talented, revolutionary-minded authors who took up the thread of the realist story from where the New School had left it.[74] Their most prominent representative was Yūsuf Idrīs. During the past twenty-five years or so of his career, this versatile artist has ceaselessly experimented with new forms, whether in the domain of the short story, the novel or the drama, developing ever more idiosyncratic forms of expression in the process. His work as a whole, therefore, does not fit into the scheme of one particular school or concept of art. Yet the fact that he kept insisting on the subject of an authentically Egyptian art of the short story, his crucial role in revitalising and restoring the predominance of the realist trend in the fifties, while steering clear of the preconceived patterns of socialist realism—all this tends to confirm that his early artistic views and taste are firmly rooted in the new literary tradition established by the Taimūrs, Lāshīn, Aḥmad Khairī Saʿīd and others.

Like members of the New School, Idrīs reacted against the romantic or sentimental treatment of the short story by some of his contemporaries, against the blatantly un-Egyptian elements in their work and against what he felt as the shackling influence of the cultural heritage and its modern defenders. The similarities do not stop here. Probably under the influence of translations he read in magazines like *al-Qiṣṣa,* edited by the poet Ibrāhīm Nāgī (1898-1953), who introduced him into the literary world, Idrīs also displayed a marked taste for Russian authors, especially Chekhov, Gorky and Dostoyevsky.[75] His readings in the work of Chekhov confirmed in him the belief, spread by the amateurs of the New School, that only by giving an artistically satisfactory, faithful picture of local reality could the Egyptian short story hope to gain international recognition. Hence his constant search, in the footsteps of Muḥammad Taimūr,[76] for the 'national character,' and his stubborn defence of the literary value of the *ʿāmmiyya* in the face of purist opposition. Again, many of his stories focus on the more reprehensible aspects of the social situation in Egypt, such as the unsatisfactory marital relations and the arrogant, selfish conduct often met with in the upper classes.[77] Though Idrīs does not seem well-informed on the role of the New School, his expressed opinions on the nature and purpose of the short story, and on the literary trade in general, are remarkably close to those of its members. He would have had no difficulty in subscribing to Ḥusain Fawzī's judgement that "a work of art, to deserve its name, should first of all be free from the reactionary ideas that hamper the progress of this country. Besides, it must be untainted by foreign influence and blind imitation of the Arabic classics. It rather should give candid expression to our feelings and boldly expose our shortcomings."[78] Some of Idrīs' artistic views are also strikingly similar to those advanced by the School's principal theorist,

Aḥmad Khairī Saʿīd (1894-1962), a kindred spirit, with whom he has moreover his medical background in common. Creativity and originality are the values both of them appreciated most in an artist. Even Idrīs' pet opinion, that of the superiority of the visionary author, the discoverer of truths, over the uninspired craftsman,[79] appears like an echo at almost forty years' distance of Saʿīd's definition of the authors task: "The author, whether he writes plays or stories, observes life from a distance, using his imaginative insight to penetrate into the essence of its characters and events . . . in order to discover what is commonly called the obvious, yet hidden truth."[80]

In the years that elapsed after *al-Fagr* ceased appearing and the friends of the 'Art Café' went their various ways, plotting activists took the place of the gentle Bohemians of old and revolutionary socialist propaganda howled down the modest call for reform. But when the changes that occurred in the country's social and political physiognomy are allowed for, it is perhaps not too daring, on this showing, to conclude that the idea of the truly Egyptian short story, as conceived by the enthusiasts of the so-called New School, was taken up again and given new substance by Yūsuf Idrīs.

Notes

1. The main sources of this chapter are 1) Sayyid Ḥāmid an-Nassāg, *Taṭawwur Fann al-Qiṣṣa al-Qaṣīra fī Miṣr,* Cairo 1968, 2) ʿAbbās Khiḍr, *al-Qiṣṣa al-Qaṣīra fī Miṣr,* Cairo 1966, 3) Yaḥyā Ḥaqqī, *Fagr al-Qiṣṣa al-Miṣriyya,* Cairo 1960 (repr. in *Muʾallafāt Yaḥyā Ḥaqqī* 2, Cairo 1975); they will be referred to respectively as *Nassāg, Khiḍr* and *Ḥaqqī.*

2. Cf. e.g. Ṣabrī Ḥāfiẓ, "Innovation in the Egyptian Short Story" in *Studies in Modern Arabic Literature,* ed. R. C. Ostle, London 1975, 104; Lewīs ʿAwaḍ, "Cultural and Intellectual Developments", in *Egypt since the Revolution,* ed. P. J. Vatikiotis, London 1968, 151; Ghālī Shukrī, *Azmat al-Gins fī-l-Qiṣṣa al-ʿArabiyya,* Cairo 1971, 241; ʿAlī al-Gangīhī, "Malik fī Gumhūriyya!," *Ākhir Sāʿa,* (15 May 1957); Fuʾād Dawwāra, "Li-mādhā Tadūr Adabunā fī Ḥalqa Mufragha," *Al-Idhāʿa,* (5 Nov. 1960); ʿAbd al-Aẓīm Anīs, "Khawāṭir," *Al-Gumhūriyya,* (17 Nov. 1965), M. J. L. Young, "ʿAbd al-Salam al-ʿUjaili and his maqamat", *Middle Eastern Studies* 14 (May 1978), 205-10.

3. In a recent interview Idrīs observed with some bitterness that in his opinion the most penetrating analysis of his short stories had not been written by an Egyptian critic but by Sasson Somekh, the Israeli scholar who selected and prefaced the anthology *Dunyā Yūsuf Idrīs* (Tel Aviv, 1976), "Al-ghām Gadīda Yufaggiruhā Yūsuf Idrīs", *Rūz al-Yūsuf,* 23 Jan. 1978, 44-7.

4. Cf. bibliography, 209-11.

5. An-Nassāg writes that he was struck by the fact that in Egypt no academic study dealing in a serious manner with the art of the short story appeared until the end of the forties. Even today, he continues, now that the short story has gained such popularity, "it is still considered unfit as a subject for scholarly studies . . . while the critics content themselves with writing occasional articles which only serve to acquaint the readers with the new collections of stories that keep appearing, or with a new author. None of the students (of literature) has yet thought of making thorough researches into this art!", *Nassāg,* 1-3.

6. E.g. Ragā' Shāhīn, "Yūsuf Idrīs: Uḥiss bi-r-Rahba wa Akhāf al-'Agz," *Ākhir Sā'a,* (3 Nov. 1965).

7. *Khiḍr,* 24.

8. 'Abdallāh Nadīm (1845-1896), the legendary orator of the 'Urābī revolt, satirical playwright, journalist, editor and co-founder of several short-lived newspapers like *Miṣr al-Fatā, aṭ-Ṭā'if, al-Ustādh,* who gradually turned from a political agitator into a reforming educational writer. In his paper *at-Tankīt wa-t-Tabkīt,* which first appeared 6 June 1881, he lampooned, among other things, the decay of Islamic society and the corruptive influence of the West. Cf. Aḥmad Amīn, *Zu'amā' al-Iṣlāḥ fī-l-'Aṣr al-Ḥadīth,* Cairo 1949, 213-9.

9. *Ḥadīth Ibn Hishām aw Fatra min az-Zamān* (1907) by Muḥammad al-Muwailiḥī (1868-1930) was originally serialised in the weekly *Miṣbāḥ ash-Sharq,* edited by his father, the erudite journalist Ibrahim al-Muwailiḥī (1846-1906), see R. Allen, "Hadith 'Isa Ibn Hisham by Muhammad al-Muwailihi," *Journal of Arabic Literature,* i (1970), 88-108.

   Other attempts at reviving the *maqāma* genre were *Layālī Saṭīḥ* (1907) by the poet Ḥāfiẓ Ibrāhīm and Muḥammad Luṭfī Gum'a's *Layālī ar-Rūḥ al-Ḥā'ir* (1912).

10. *Maqāma* (assembly), a kind of dramatic anecdote in the telling of which the author subordinates substance to form and does his utmost to display his poetical ability, learning and eloquence. Its creator is presumed to be Badī' az-Zamān al-Hamadhānī (968-1008).

11. *Nassāg,* 51; *Khiḍr,* 80; *Ḥaqqī,* 20; Lewīs 'Awaḍ, *Al-Adab wa-th-Thawra,* Cairo 1967, 336. A dissentient view is expounded in the introduction to Fārūq Khūrshīd, *Fī-r-Riwāya al-'Arabiyya,* Cairo 1959.

   On the popularity of De Maupassant and Chekhov see e.g. J. Brugman, "Muhammad al-Siba'i and the Egyptian literary renaissance" in *Akten des VII. Kongress für Arabistik und Islamwissenschaft,* Göttingen 1974, 91; *Nassāg,* 360-1.

12. "(In my study) I dealt only with the press, for the press and the short story are inseparable", *Nassāg,* 3. Cf. also P. J. Vatikiotis, *The Modern History of Egypt,* London 1969, 431.

13. In the early part of this century the term *riwāya* was indiscriminately applied to every type of story and even to plays, cf. Maḥmūd Taimūr, *Wamīḍ ar-Rūḥ,* Cairo 1971², 62: "Muḥammad Taimūr was one of the partisans and founders of the 'Egyptian *riwāya*' or, as some prefer to call it, 'the Egyptian theatre'"; cf. also 'Abdel 'Aziz 'Abdel Meguid, "A survey of the terms used in Arabic for 'narrative' and 'story'", *The Islamic Quarterly* i (1954), 195-204. Besides adapted *riwāyāt,* some of these magazines depended to a considerable extent on what now would be called 'popular science'. *Aḍ-Ḍiyā'* (Magazine for Science, Literature, Health and Industry), for instance, treated its readers in its first year of issue (1898-9) to such appetizing topics as, "The widespread belief that new-born babies should not be bathed for one year as a precaution against hereditary syphilis," "How to remove ink-blots from clothes," "Blanching negroes by means of electricity."

14. *Khiḍr,* 41.

15. Ib., 69.

16. Ib., 106.

17. *Nassāg,* 59.

18. Ib., 86-104; Maḥmūd Taimūr, *Shaikh Gum'a,* Cairo 1927², 8.

19. E.g. H. A. R. Gibb, *Studies on the Civilization of Islam,* London 1962, 291, 294; H. Kilpatrick, *The Modern Egyptian Novel,* London 1974, 21, 26; Ḥamdī Sakkūt, *The Egyptian Novel and its Main Trends,* Cairo 1961, 11; Maḥmūd Taimūr, *Shifā' ar-Rūḥ,* 12-3.

20. *Nassāg,* 59; 'Īsā 'Ubaid, *Iḥsān Hānom,* Cairo 1921, 17; Maḥmūd Taimūr, *Shifā' ar-Rūḥ,* 13.

21. *Nassāg,* 333.

22. Maḥmūd Taimūr, *Shifā' ar-Rūḥ,* 9; *Nassāg,* 328. The titles of Maḥmūd Taimūr's early sketches, which were partly written in rhymed prose, and his brother's poetry works, clearly exhibit the rather maudlin tone made fashionable by al-Manfalūṭī (1876-1924): "Love between a Tear of Despair and the Kiss of Hope" (Maḥmūd Taimūr, 1916), "The Blooming Narcissus on the Grave of the Poet," "The Setting Star on a Girl's Grave" (*Wamīḍ ar-Rūḥ,* 104, 115).

Muṣṭafā Luṭfī al-Manfalūṭī's chief contribution to modern Arabic literature are two collections of essays and stories, *an-Naẓarāt* (1910) and *al-'Abarāt* (1915). In his preface to *an-Naẓarāt* he declared that he greatly relished "poetic expressions of grief and sorrow, miserable and distressing situations, stories of suffering, fate-stricken people." His romantic wails, shot through with superficial criticism of what he saw as the depravity of modern man, were couched in a rhythmical language which combined traditional rhetorical display with a certain modern smoothness. Both his style and penchant for tearful subjects were later sharply censured and ridiculed by the New School, 'Īsā 'Ubaid (*Iḥsān Hānom,* 7) and Ibrāhīm 'Abd al-Qādir al-Māzinī (al-Māzinī and 'Abbās Maḥmūd al-'Aqqād, *ad-Dīwān,* Cairo Feb. 1921, 3-32). But at the time al-Manlafūṭī was generally admired and his work held up as an example of eloquence (*Nassāg,* 82; *Khiḍr,* 56; Maḥmūd Taimūr, *Fir'awn Ṣaghīr,* Cairo 1939, 12; Aḥmad Ḥasan az-Zayyāt, *Wahy ar-Risāla,* Cairo 1957[6], vol. i, 386-7). Al-Manfalūṭī also adapted a considerable number of French romantic nineteenth-century works, distorting them beyond recognition, probably because he was unversed in foreign languages and received his materials at second hand (*Nassāg,* 62; *Wahy ar-Risāla,* vol. i, 390).

23. *Ḥaqqī,* 62.

24. Ib., 66; *Wamīḍ ar-Rūḥ,* 20.

25. Maḥmūd Taimūr, *Shifā' ar-Rūḥ,* 12.

26. H. A. R. Gibb, *Studies on the Civilization of Islam,* 294, considers that *Zainab* (Tableaux and Morals of the Countryside, written by an Egyptian of peasant stock) foreshadowed this strengthening of the national consciousness. This opinion is quoted with approval and elaborated upon in D. Semah, *Four Egyptian Literary Critics,* Leiden 1974, 89, 76. Muḥammad Ḥusain Haikal (1888-1956) was strongly influenced by Aḥmad Luṭfī as-Sayyid, the editor of the moderate, reformist newspaper *al-Garīda* (1907-19). Due to the educative force of his writing and his long connexion with the University of Cairo Luṭfī was called 'the teacher of the generation'. He, and his friend Fatḥī Zaghlūl, believed that "the start of a real reform of society was reform of the national character"; therefore much of his work deals with "first, the Egyptian character as it was at the time, and secondly, the type of ideal character which he considered necessary for progress," J. M. Ahmed, *The Intellectual Origins of Egyptian Nationalism,* London 1960, 91. According to Semah "Haikal seems to have been the first writer of the group (i.e., round Luṭfī) to draw practical conclusions concerning the future of modern Egyptian literature,

which he saw as an influential factor in the attempt to create and promote national self-consciousness," *Four Egyptian Literary Critics,* 76.

But Gibb gives Muḥammad Taimūr the credit for having first "touched the central difficulty, that of presenting a realistic representation of contemporary social life, in vocabulary, forms of expression, and especially in the dialogue", *Studies,* 299.

27. "The young authors of the New School were the first to proclaim that Egypt should be intellectually independent," "al-Istiqlāl al-Fikrī," *al-Fagr,* 27 Jan. 1925, 1.

28. The School's nucleus was made up of Muḥammad Taimūr, Muḥammad Rashīd, Aḥmad 'Allām, Zakī Ṭulaimāt, Maḥmūd 'Aẓmī, Fā'iq Riyāḍ, Ḥusain Fawzī, Ibrāhīm al-Miṣrī, Ibrāhīm Ḥamdī, Aḥmad Khairī Sa'īd, Maḥmūd Ṭāhir Lāshīn, Ḥasan Maḥmūd and others. Cf. *Nassāg,* 166; *Ḥaqqī,* 75-8.

29. Maḥmūd Taimūr's preface to Lāshīn's collection *Yuḥkā Ann,* repr. Cairo 1964, b., *Nassāg,* 166.

30. *Khiḍr,* 256.

31. Aḥmad Khairī Sa'īd, "Ṣawt al-Mi'wal", *al-Fagr* (20 Jan. 1925), 1.

32. Maḥmūd Taimūr, preface to *Yuḥkā Ann,* a; *Ḥaqqī,* 77-8.

33. Aḥmad Khairī Sa'īd, *al-Fagr* (20 Jan. 1925), 1.

34. *Nassāg,* 176.

35. But the Taimūrs, who received a French education, valued De Maupassant beyond all others, Maḥmūd Taimūr, *Shifā' ar-Rūḥ,* 13. Muḥammad Taimūr acknowledged that he borrowed one of his stories, *Rabbī li-Man Khalaqt Hādhā an-Na'īm* (1917) from De Maupassant, *Wamīḍ ar-Rūḥ,* 252. Yaḥyā Ḥaqqī maintains that Russian authors were more popular with the members of the New School who had a better command of English than of French, cf. *Ḥaqqī,* 82. The question seems largely academic, however, in view of the increasing number of Arabic translations both groups had at their disposal. For example, Maḥmūd Ṭāhir Lāshīn's *al-Infigār,* published in the collection *Sukhriyyat an-Nāy* (1926), was avowedly adapted from one of Chekhov's stories, according to Khiḍr the same one that Muḥammad as-Sibā'ī had translated and included in his collection *Mi'at Qiṣṣa* under the title *Zawba'a Manziliyya, Khiḍr,* 241-2.

36. *Ḥaqqī,* 82.

37. *Nassāg,* 176.

38. Aḥmad Khairī Sa'īd, "Al-Madhāhib al-Kitābiyya", *ash-Shabāb* (April 1920), 7.

39. *ibidem.*

40. E.g. ʿĪsā ʿUbaid, *Iḥsān Hānom*, 8.

41. ʿĪsā died towards the end of 1922, Shaḥāta in 1961, *Nassāg,* 121.

42. Cf. *Ḥaqqī,* 101.

43. *Mizāg ash-shakhṣiyya, al-muʾaththirāt al-wirāthiyya, ẓurūf ḥayātihim (Iḥsān Hānom,* 4, 5, 9).

44. ʿĪsā ʿUbaid, *Iḥsān Hānom,* 14.

45. *"Fāʾidat al-balāgha al-qiṣaṣiyya", Shaikh Gumʿa,* Cairo 1927[2], 11.

46. Ib., 10.

47. Ib., 13-4.

48. Another view, as set forth in Elie Kedourie, *Afghani and ʿAbduh, an Essay on Religious Unbelief and Political Activism in Modern Islam,* London 1966, has it that both men were in fact political agitators and rather subverters than reformers of Islam.

49. Cf. *Khiḍr,* 99-100; ʿAbd al-Muḥsin Ṭāhā Badr, *Taṭawwur ar-Riwāya al-ʿArabiyya al-Ḥadītha,* Cairo 1968, 233. ʿĪsā Ubaid dedicated *Iḥsān Hānom* to the leader of the Wafd party, Saʿd Zaghlūl.

50. *Ḥaqqī,* 77.

51. Maḥmūd Taimūr, preface to *Yuḥkā Ann,* b.

52. *Khiḍr,* 99.

53. Ib., 102.

54. Nassāg credits Ḥasan Maḥmūd with the introduction of the unequal marriage as a popular theme in the Egyptian short story, *Nassāg,* 156.

55. *Khiḍr,* 100-1, 232.

56. Ḥusain Fawzī, "Kitāb Gadīd wa Adab Gadīd", *al-Fagr* (8 May 1925), 2.

57. *Wamīḍ ar-Rūḥ,* 63; admittedly *Mā Tarāh al-ʿUyūn* was written well before the 1919 revolution and before the New School took shape.

58. ʿĪsā ʿUbaid, *Iḥsān Hānom,* 17-8.

59. Shaḥāta ʿUbaid, *Dars Muʾlim,* repr. Cairo 1964, d.

60. Ib., h.

61. ʿĪsā ʿUbaid, *Iḥsān Hānom,* 18.

62. *Ibidem.*

63. Cf. *Nassāg,* 143-4.

64. He made the reservation, however, that "because this is a new trend in Egypt I did not wish to apply it in all my stories. It is an experiment which, I hope, will prove successful," *Khiḍr,* 199.

65. *Shaikh Gumʿa*[2], 15.

66. *Nassāg,* 305.

67. Ib., 278.

68. Ib., 282.

69. Ib., 215-6.

70. Aḥmad Khairī Saʿīd, *al-Fagr* (26 June 1925), 1.

71. Yaḥyā Ḥaqqī, preface to Lāshīn's *Sukhriyyat an-Nāy,* y.

72. *Nassāg,* 4.

73. Ṣabrī Ḥāfiẓ, "Innovation", 103.

74. Ib., 103; Ṣ. Ḥāfiẓ makes a global distinction between two new schools: the realistic mainstream represented in the work of authors like Yūsuf Idrīs, Shukrī ʿAyyād, Ṣalāḥ Ḥāfiẓ, ʿAbd al-Ghaffār Makkāwī, ʿAbd ar-Raḥmān ash-Sharqāwī and others, whom he considers as the continuators of the work of Lāshīn, Ḥaqqī and Maḥmūd al-Badawī; and a second, less important trend with a more experimental character, "containing a blend of symbolic, expressionistic and surrealistic traits" (102), with as its exponents Yūsuf ash-Shārūnī, Fatḥī Ghānim, Edward al-Kharrāṭ, ʿAbbās Aḥmad and Badr ad-Dīb.

75. In this Idrīs shared the tastes of his generation, see R. Makarius, *La Jeunesse Intellectuelle d'Êgypte,* Paris, La Haye 1960, 93. Moreover Idrīs may have felt drawn to the great Russian writers because they were frequently associated with the conception of the author as a 'prophet' with a lofty mission (*risāla*) in life (see pp. 52-3). As early as 1929 Muʿawiyya Muḥammad Nūr wrote in *as-Siyāsa al-Usbūʿiyya* (23 Nov. 1929), 17, an article entitled "Al-Adab al-Wāqiʿī" (Realistic Literature), in which he praised Russian literature for its "veracious description of life" and called Tolstoy, Turgenev and Dostoyevsky "prophets and at the same time artists, who have a moral message for the damned." Ibrāhīm Nāgī in his booklet *Risālat al-Ḥayā* (undated) devotes a chapter to "The Mission of Russian Literature." His conclusion is that Russian literature, through its ultimate reconciliation of violent extremes, "prophesies that we are moving towards the creation of a world where harmony will prevail for ever," *Risāla al-Ḥayā,* 142. In the fifties Shukrī ʿAyyād was still haunted by the same *idée fixe:* "The Russian writer came close to being a prophet or visionary. He was an artist with a mission. The art-for-art's sake theory never obtained a firm footing in Russia." Like Aḥmad Khairī Saʿīd (cf. p. 8), he was struck by what he saw as the fundamental congeniality of the Russian and Egyptian national characters:

"(The Russians) were rather simple in manner . . . Their character had a streak of sadness in it, mingled with a sense of humour . . . a rather trenchant, pungent sort of humour . . . In their emotional life Russians . . . were usually patient and devout," "Iktishāf al-Adab ar-Rūsī," *al-Ādāb* (Sep. Oct. 1957), 383-5.

76. Cf. *Wamīḍ ar-Rūḥ*, 20, 31.

77. This affinity also shows in the use of corresponding themes. The orphan child in Idrīs' short story *an-Naẓra* who, unable to participate in other children's games, bitterly realises her derelict position in society is earlier found in *Ṣaffārat al-'Aid* by Muḥammad Taimūr; the first sexual experience of an adolescent with a woman who initially felt only maternal love for him, described in *Dustūrak yā Sayyida* is reminiscent of Muḥammad Taimūr's *Kān Ṭiflan fa-Ṣār Shābban;* and despite the difference in dénouement, the story of the disaster that befalls the doorman Ḥāmid in *an-Naddāha* when his attractive wife rouses the sexual appetite of a wily effendi is strikingly similar to the sad story of the doorman 'Abd as-Samī' in Lāshīn's *Ḥadīth al-Qarya.*

78. Ḥusain Fawzī, "Kitāb Gadīd wa Adab Gadīd," *al-Fagr* (1 May 1925), 2.

79. Cf. p. 52.

80. Aḥmad Khairī Sa'īd, "Ḥayātunā al-'Aqliyya", *al-Gadīd* (12 Nov. 1928), 4.

Dalya Cohen (essay date 1984)

SOURCE: Cohen, Dalya. "'The Journey' by Yusuf Idris." *Journal of Arabic Literature* 15 (1984): 135-38.

[*In the following essay, Cohen offers a psychoanalytical interpretation of "The Journey."*]

I. INTRODUCTION

"The Journey" is a short story which is included in Yūsuf Idrīs's tenth collection called ***House of Flesh*** (Cairo, 1971). The story is written in the form of a monologue and in the technique of the stream of consciousness.

It starts with a confession of love to a man. In the beginning it is not clear who the speaker is and the reader is tempted to think that it is a woman addressing her lover. Only later, as the monologue unfolds, the reader discovers that it is rather a son talking to his father. The son tells his father about a secret journey that they are going to undertake. He carefully dresses his father, then sneaks him into the elevator and right into his car.

Thereafter they take off. The presence of the father in the car fills the son with ecstasy. He reveals all his feelings towards his father and lapses by flashing back into scenes from his childhood. Strangely enough, wherever they arrive people stare at them in terror and complain of a terrible smell. They point to the father and scream of a corpse. The son is so happy he smells nothing. Then, little by little, he becomes aware of the stench. At first he ignores it and attempts to continue the ride anyway, but later the stench gets so strong that he is unable to put up with it any longer. Exhausted he pulls up and abandons the car with his father on the road. Then he continues the journey by himself.

II. PSYCHOANALYSIS

This is a patient with a neurotic disturbance narrating a fantasy to his psychiatrist. In his fantasy there are two psychoanalytic cycles: 1) the existentialist cycle, relating to his existence, in which there are some normal patterns; 2) the sexual cycle, which is grossly abnormal. The first indication to its being abnormal is the fact that no woman at all is mentioned in the fantasy, not a mother, not a sister, not even a girlfriend. The patient talks about his brothers, but no mention is made of a female whatsoever,

What we have here is a description of a homosexual experience. A son committing incest with his father. The father is dead and may have been dead for some time. The son is not aware of this. He takes him to his car which functions as the bed, and has intercourse with him. Immediately afterwards he is filled with a strong sense of shame and guilt—that is when he starts smelling the terrible stench. He then runs away from the scene of crime, deserting his dead father buried in the car like in a grave.

If we follow the text we see that first there is an erotic description of the father by the son: his clothes, the way he dresses, his hair, his mustache. It sounds almost like a woman talking to her lover.

The son touches the father, dresses him, brushes his hair and all the time repeats the words: "Don't be afraid, don't be afraid. We are going on a secret journey. No one will ever know or will ever find out. I have taken all the precautionary measures . . .".

Another erotic description follows when the son describes how he used to receive his father coming home from work. Together with his brothers (again, no mention of a female in the house) he would massage his father's toes, but he alone would work on the *big toe*. In psychoanalysis, the big toe is a recurrent symbol for the male sex organ.

Then we are told of how much he loved the physical touch with his father, being carried on his arms, faking sleep. This is considered a normal sensation with a child if he also has an emotional contact with his father, if he has love, care and understanding. In such a case the child will develop normally. But if the physical touch is the only touch between a son and a father, and the father is a dominant, omnipotent figure, strict, hard and uncompromising, then the child will have a neurotic disturbance in his development and will later try to find the love he missed in his father in another man—namely, display homosexual tendencies.

The father in this monologue is a very dominant, strict and uncompromising figure. The son says about him that he was the only person in the world that he used to fear. The father would often argue with his son and would make him give up his opinions and accept his own. He would not let him smoke. Smoking is an important symbol in psychoanalysis for sex.

Inevitably the oppressed son develops a rebellious spirit. He hates his father and at the same time still loves him. Such ambivalent feelings of love and hatred are common characteristics of a neurotic disturbance.

So the son takes all the precautionary measures and finally succeeds in getting his father into his car, namely, into his bed. Then follow passionate confessions of love and exclamations of tremendous pleasure. The son feels so high he can almost fly. In the car-bed, all the disagreements and arguments between the father and the son disappear and they become one, completely united. The car-bed is their island. People surround them like dinosaurs because they do not approve of such sexual intercourse—an incest. It is pathological and against the social code. They threaten them, they want to drown them, devour them. The policeman, like the stoplight, is a symbol of the social order. He is in charge of keeping the order, and he is suspicious. He sniffs the air with his nose and almost discovers the truth, but then the son succeeds in deceiving him.

All along the son fears the end. Apparently he has been there before. The beginning is the best part. The end is the worst. The sobering up after the sexual climax feeling shame, guilt and disgust is shattering. Suddenly, the fear of the consequences becomes the fear for his life. He panics and runs away, leaving his father behind. In his flight there is pain but also much relief. He is free now . . . until the next time.

III. Interpretation

"The Journey" is a story of a strong social and political criticism. For example, Yūsuf Idrīs singles out the generation gap. The son belongs to the generation of the car and of freedom. The father belongs to the generation of the train and of slavery. The society is a patriarchal society, the mustache being the symbol of it.

Yūsuf Idrīs, himself at one time a physician and psychiatrist, shrewdly uses psychoanalytic motives for the purpose of exposing the malaise of the social political order of his time.

The story was written in June 1970—the third anniversary of The Six-Day War with Israel which ended in a terrible defeat. The main attack is on Nasser, who in spite of the calamity of the war which he brought on Egypt, remained in power.[1] Nasser is the father in the story, the omnipotent patriarch who has a complete domination over his son. The oppressed son is Egypt, or the Egyptian people. The message is that Nasser brings death to them—the stench of a decaying corpse. He wears a red tie—an indication of his strong affiliation with Communist Russia. The relationship between the father and son which knew some tender and affectionate moments, gradually developed a pathological character, an abnormal pattern. It takes the son a long time to realize that there is something wrong with his father, namely, to smell the stench. At first, he even denies there is a stench and it is only after the stench almost suffocates him that he realizes that he must get rid of its source or else die. There is simply no choice. The father must come to an end so that he can begin and as much as this end is painful it is inevitable. So he buries the father in the car and walks away, breathing the fresh air in a new sense of freedom.

That Yūsuf Idrīs was one of Nasser's opponents is well known. In the beginning he supported Nasser's rise to power, but like many others soon got disillusioned. The clash with Nasser came in 1954, when it became clear that the revolution had accomplished few of its promises. Yūsuf Idrīs was arrested and imprisoned. During his detention he joined the Communist Party only to resign later, when he realized that he could not accept the totalitarian side of communism. In 1969, a year before **"The Journey"** appeared, Idrīs wrote **"The Schemers"**, a play which was banned by the censor in Egypt for being highly critical of Nasser's regime. Nevertheless, Idrīs's short stories and "non-political" works continued to appear.

What gives **"The Journey"** its Arab coloring is the name Abdallah. Abdallah is the doorman who helps the son get his father into the car. It is the *only name* mentioned in the story therefore it is significant. Abdallah means "The Servant of God". Why would Idrīs give the only name in his story to the doorman, and of all Arab common names choose this specific one with its religious connotation? The answer is probably to create *Koranic allusions*.

In the Koran, the theme of The Day of Judgment occupies a central place. On The Day of Judgment all the dead will be resurrected and then brought before the Almighty on trial. The righteous will be rewarded, the evil-doers will be punished. God's servants—the angels, assist him in conducting the trials.

In Idrīs's story, the father who is in fact dead, is resurrected. He is being dressed up, walked out of his lodging place and taken on a journey. The journey is the trial. At the end of it, the father is found guilty and sentenced to death—that is when he is being dumped in the car.

Surat *Qāf* in the Koran which deals with The Day of Judgment speaks of the following: "And the trumpet is blown, this is The Threatened Day. And every soul cometh along with it *a driver* and a *witness,*" Verses 20, 21. "And the day when they hear the cry in truth, that is the day of coming forth (from the graves). Lo, we it is who quicken and give death and unto us is the *journeying.*" Verses 42, 43.[2]

The words driver, witness and journeying[3] are significant. In Idrīs's story, the son functions as his father's driver. He takes him on a journey. All along their way they encounter witnesses who raise an accusing finger against the father. This is Reckoning Day.

Thus, Idrīs's **"The Journey"** is maintained on four levels: the individual, the psychological, the socio-political and the religious. They are skillfully layered one beneath the other. As a result, Idrīs manages not only to explore the complex motivation that underlies human behavior, but also to reveal his shrewd understanding of his society and its changing values.

Notes

1. Nasser died abruptly in September 1970.

2. *The Meaning of the Glorious Koran,* an explanatory translation by Mohammed Marmaduke Pickthall.

3. [It must be remembered, however, that the Koranic word which Pickthall translates as "journeying" is *'al-maṣīr!*—Editors].

Sasson Somekh (essay date 1985)

SOURCE: Somekh, Sasson. "The Function of Sound in the Stories of Yusuf Idris." *Journal of Arabic Literature* 16 (1985): 95-104.

[*In the following essay, Somekh considers acoustic and rhythmic elements of Idris's short stories.*]

I

During the last three decades, Yūsuf Idrīs (b. 1927) has established himself as a major figure in Arabic literature. He is first and foremost a writer of short stories, of which he has published twelve volumes between the years 1954-81.[1] The bulk of his work undoubtedly constitutes a landmark in modern Egyptian fiction; and the influence of his art is very much in evidence in the writings of younger Arab storytellers.

Regrettably, his works were for many years beyond the reach of readers who have no command of Arabic. It is therefore gratifying that in 1978 two volumes of his stories were published in English translation.[2] Furthermore, a scholarly work dealing with several aspects of his life and art appeared in English in 1981.[3]

II

Idrīs' mastery of storytelling is manifest in many ways, not the least of which is his handling of the language. Admittedly, critics with a partiality for classical stylistic norms often complain that Idrīs' language is "lax" or "untidy".[4] Others regret the excessive use of the dialect in his dialogue, as well as in the narrative sections.[5]

However, the art of fiction is not commensurate with linguistic "tidiness" or on its texts being written in an "exemplary" language. The ultimate test of the language of a story is in whether it is conducive to the modulations of the artistic text. In this sense Idrīs is undisputedly a master. His language, though constantly changing in the course of his career, is impressively rich, his imagery original, and above all, the different levels of contemporary Arabic are fully utilized in the service of his story.

In the following pages, which draw on a more comprehensive study of Idrīs' style,[6] we shall concern ourselves with one of the manifestations of the art of language in his fiction. By analyzing one of his short stories, and comparing it to two longer ones, we shall try to illustrate the employment of sound and rhythm as elements of structure. In so doing, we hope to call attention to one feature which might prove significant, indeed crucial, in the study of Idrīs' narrative art.

III

The first story in question is entitled **"Mārsh al-Ghurūb" ("Sunset March",** the English translation of which is given in this issue).[7] It first appeared in the Cairo monthly *al-Hadaf* in May 1957[8] and was later incorporated in the volume *Alaysa Kadhālika* ("Isn't That So?" 1957).[9] In point of fact, the title of the story, when it was first published, was **"Laḥn al-urūb" ("Sunset Tune").** The significance of the change of the title will be commented upon later in this paper.

Thematically, this story is in line with most of the author's early sketches, which mostly draw their subject matter from the life of the impoverished masses in Cairo and in the Egyptian countryside. In these stories, however, the description is not naturalistic, nor is it neutral in tone. The point of view is, more often than not, identical with that of the simple and down-trodden characters; and a great sympathy with their predicament is always evident, although it is sometimes mingled with a tinge of irony.

In **"Sunset March"** we are presented with a story of one of the wretched; and although we are not directly in touch with the inner feelings of this sole character, the seller of liquorice juice (*'irqsūs*), we are definitely made to identify with his plight.

Two questions pose themselves at this juncture. The first: Is the man's unhappy lot the main theme of the short story? Indeed, at first sight it impresses its reader as nothing but a portrait of a hapless vendor of cold drink on a cold day. It has no plot in the usual sense of the term, and we hardly know anything about the personal background, problems and thoughts of the vendor. Which brings us to the second question: Is there a "story" in **"Sunset March"**?

We shall first try to answer the latter question, and then go on to consider the thematic essence of our short story.

IV

Admittedly, we are presented with a portrait. But it is by no means a static picture. Although most of the text presents the man in a stationary position, he is in fact constantly changing in relation to the background scene. Furthermore, there is a constant "inner movement" which amounts to a "plot".

At first we have a scene in which "it was . . . wintertime, and the sun had just set. The whole universe was reeking of that sickly atmosphere which immediately follows sunset till it gets dark. People were proceeding in silence across the bridge; their haste reflected all the gloom of a dying day and all the cold of winter."

Later on, the seller "looked around him and noticed people disappearing into the distance, slinking by as though they were being swallowed up by some hidden lair or other. He noticed the bloody wound which the sun had left in the sky as it made its way into the world of darkness."

Still later—"It was getting dark and gloomy everywhere. The chill in the heavens now began to settle on the earth. People dwindled away. Everything assumed a greyish-blue hue and looked cold and lifeless."

And again—"It was getting darker and darker as the heavens continued to impose themselves on the earth. By now, the wound in the sky had healed and the red sky of twilight had vanished. People were being transformed from beings into spectres."

Towards the end of the story we note the image of the juice-seller turning into a spectre too, and deserting the scene. "His figure melted away into the night and disappeared . . . And there was nothing in the world, big, so big; and the darkness so plentiful."

This succession of scenes, portraying, as they do, the passing of day and the arrival of evening, do not fail to lend the setting itself a dynamic feature, and remind one of such impressionist painters as Claude Monet in his Rouen Cathedral series of paintings. The changing scenery is not a sheer "setting". It reflects and amplifies the vendor's anxiety and his growing desperation until he finally leaves the Shubra Bridge.

However, while the changing background is instrumental in lending the character a measure of life, it is the variety of noises that turns the text into a *story*. In other words, the noises constitute a major structural device. At least two kinds of noises are involved: Those produced by the man's cymbals, and those of his own voice. The combined operation of these two types is modulated to produce a reflection of the man's fluctuating moods. In fact, we have four stages in the inner psychology of the protagonist, all reflected "acoustically".

Stage I: The man is hoping against hope. He is well aware that to sell juice on a cold day is next to impossible, and that it is only by intensifying the clatter of his cymbals and by raising his voice that he can hope to attract some passers-by. At this stage the cymbals produce loud and strident noises, coming in spurts rather "like the call of a turkey cock." In the story these noises have yet another function: To reflect the man's fears and doubts. Every time he looked at the same setting sun "the intervals between the cymbal clashes became shorter, and the sound they made was louder and sharper."

Stage II: This starts with the words "The minutes went by quickly. Time was rushing by just like people . . ." The cymbal clashes are now shrill and hysterical. His calls include an appeal to God (*yā karīm satrak*—"Your protection, generous God") and not just the words *yām-na'nish* ("Delicious" or, rather: "How refreshing", the reference being, of course, to the quality of the juice), as in the first stage. This pious formula, coming straight from the man's heart, is elongated "as though he wished to make a thin rope out of it to stretch over the bridge and stop people."

Stage III: This stage also begins with words denoting the passage of time—"Time slipped by, and the number of passers-by diminished." The man has not given up hope completely. His submissive appeal to God now fully replaces the reference to the juice. The same submissiveness and despair applies to the music of the cymbals. "They sounded like the heartbeat of someone close to death, quiet for a long time and then suddenly bursting into action in some final struggle against the oblivion of death."

Stage IV: The words "A total despair now came over him" introduce this part. In fact, we are now witnessing a stage which is *beyond despair*. In this final part of the story, "The cymbal clashes, which had been well-spaced, become frequent again and even harmonious. But now there was a strange timbre to the sound . . . , a kind of melody, subdued, lilting and sorrowful. The man's hands were working unconsciously, and the melody came out the same way, pianissimo, and shrouded in darkness. No one else could hear it."

But the spontaneous, indeed unconscious, effort soon gives way to a more elaborate one: "He began to apply himself wholeheartedly to the process. He was a virtuoso at cymbal clashing, and set about timing and improving the melodic line . . . It made him feel so overjoyed that he started nodding his head sedately to the beat. Soon the nods spread to the hairs in his beard which started an undulating dance of their own." Finally, he departs from the bridge to the beat of the hushed melody of the cymbals, "one step per clash, a mournful, aching sound; one per step, with a deal of sorrow in each gentle clash."

In other words, we witness a gradual but acute psychological change: From hope against hope, to alarm, to despair, and finally to *catharsis*. All these stages are conveyed chiefly by means of acoustic references. The language is studded with sounds and metaphors denoting the various qualities of sound.

It will now be clear why the author, in an afterthought, decided to change the title of the story from "Sunset Tune" to **"Sunset March"**. In fact, the word "march" is not only designed to underline the final stage, that of the man's self indulgence in reflective music, or his rhythmic departure from the scene. It is also instrumental in foregrounding the role of acoustics and rhythm in the story. In replacing "tune" by the more technical term "march" the author is calling our attention to this aspect of his text.

As for the thematics of our story—it does not now seem proper to speak of the "social" theme in isolation. The story, as we have seen, portrays a series of psychological shifts, of anguish, fear and relief; and we would do the author an injustice if we excluded these aspects from the "theme" of his work. Furthermore, the final stage, as demonstrated above, suggests yet another thematic element: that of art as a soother and redeemer. For in the first three stages of the story, the "art" of the cymbal clashes is directed towards the passers-by, and is meant to help bring about a material relief. However,

it produces few if any results. In the last stage (and in certain parts of the third stage) the music generated by the cymbals is inwardly oriented, and directed at the "soul". This music has no other function than soothing the man's anguished self by means of beauty and harmony. At least in this pursuit he proves to be a "successful" artist.

In other words, we have a triple thematic construct, which might be schematically designated as destitution → trepidation → art. It is this multi-layered thematic structure, combined with the rich acoustic texture, that gives the story its human depth and poetic richness.

V

"Sunset March" is by no means the only work by Yūsuf Idrīs wherein acoustic and rhythmic elements feature so prominently. In many of his other stories the sensitivity towards such elements, and the manner in which they feature, amount to a major artistic hallmark. In fact, these elements seem to occupy an even more central role in Idrīs' later works, those written in the 1960s and 1970s.[10] His recourse to the world of voices can be further demonstrated by the sheer mention of the titles of two of his more recent collections of short stories: *Lughat al-Ay-Ay* ("The Language of Ay-Ay", 1965), and *Mashūq al-Hams* ("Crushed Whispers". 1970).[11]

To return to the use of the acoustic and rhythmic devices in the texts of the stories, I would like to refer to two more examples which might further illustrate my point. In discussing **"Sunset March"** we have seen that the rhythmic and acoustic components were instrumental in reflecting a succession of psychological stages. In **"The Black Policeman"** ("al-'Askarī al Aswad"), a story published in 1961,[12] we are presented with another example of the use of similar elements in a psychological context, though not necessarily in an identical fashion. Here the noises are not produced by a protagonist, but by an external agent. They serve to reflect and progressively enchance the feeling of tension among the characters of the story (as well as in the reader).

The protagonist of **"The Black Policeman"** is a young physician, shawqī, who has been imprisoned and tortured by the secret police. Accompanied by a friend (the narrator) and a male nurse, he pays a visit to the house of a retired policeman who served for many years as a master torturer, notorious for his sadistic treatment of prisoners. The expoliceman was afflicted by a hideous malady. On entering the policeman's shoddy residence shawqī and his friend are extremely uneasy. Dreadful memories from the past are no less tormenting than the apprehension that precedes the renewed meeting with the bestial man. An interval lapses before they are finally allowed into the policeman's bedroom. During this period the tense and melancholic atmosphere that surrounds shawqī and the narrator is conveyed in the text by means of a rhythmic device:

> Near the middle of the courtyard there was an over-turned metal washbasin, on which stood a chicken pecking in staccato jerks with its beak at the bits of dirt and mud clinging to the underside of the basin, in hopes of finding food. But its pecking only served to clash its beak against the washbasin which rang in reverberating regular and tedious knocks. The knocking rose, resounding in a ceaseless and obstinate ringing, only augmenting the gloom in the large, bare courtyard.[13]

Later on the policeman's wife emerges from the room, but soon disappears. Here the narrator remarks:

> She left us standing there, looking around the courtyard, rather surprised. Before long, the chicken, which had been startled and scared off by the woman, re-emerged and once again mounted the wash-basin and its beak began again to produce that gloomy, regular, resounding knocking.[14]

After a while the woman makes another appearance, but once again re-enters the bedroom. As for the three men, that narrator now tells us:

> All was blanketed in a silence which was broken only by the chicken's steady pecking on the surface of the wash-basin. Now the woman's coming and going no longer disturbed or interrupted its knocking.[15]

The chicken's rapping is mentioned again for the fourth and last time as follows:

> We had no idea why we were made to wait. There must have been some reason for it. The most embarrassing thing was the silence which engulfed us, and which expanded and spread to the point of even absorbing the chicken's rapping. We no longer noticed it.[16]

The scene in question, burdened as it is with a tense anticipation, is a crucial juncture in the story, and the employment of the rhythmic-acoustic devices which serve at once to enhance the anxiety of the narrator and his friend shawqī, and to convey the feeling of these men. It is to be noted, in passing, that here, as in **"Sunset March"**, we have four "beats" or "waves" of reference to the noise, although in **"The Black Policeman"** they do not necessarily convey distinct psychological phases.

VI

A third story worth mentioning in the context of our study is ***City Dregs***[17] (*Qāʿ al-Madīna*), a long short story, incorporated in ***Alaysa Kadhālik*** (this volume also includes **"Sunset March"**). Here we also find the recurring appearance of voices (again, in four or five separate "waves"), punctuating a crucial (or transitional) stage in the story.

The protagonist in ***City Dregs*** is a young Cairene judge, ʿAbdallah, who suspects his former housemaid, Shuhrat, of having stolen his wristwatch. He therefore decides to make a surprise visit to her house. Accompanied by a friend and a doorman, he proceeds from his own affluent quarter to the slums where Shuhrat lives. The journey, which begins as a frivolous adventure, turns into a nightmare. The fastidious young judge discovers a horrible urban scene of which he knows nothing. He is dismayed by what he sees and hears in the shabby, narrow alleys. However, far from commiserating with the fate of the dwellers of the alley, Abdallah is filled with disgust and rage. His malice towards Shuhrat is multiplied by his "ordeal". The growing rage is reflected in the text by a series of passages describing the reception of the unsavoury scenes in Abdallah's mind. The scenes are depicted by a variety of artistic means, making use of a number of different senses: sight, smell, and most remarkably, the aural sense. Naturally it is the latter which concerns us here. To return to the story: soon after the three men leave behind them the clean and quiet residential quarter where Abdallah lives, a crowded and tumultuous city begins to emerge. When their car reaches al-Azhar Street, "the bustle becomes intense. In the road all mingle; this one and that, those mounted and those on foot. One hears the screech of wheels, the wails of motor-horns, the tinkle of horses' bells, the whistles of traffic policemen, the cries of street vendors and passersby. The heat reaches its peak, the throng its thickest."[18]

But these scenes prove to be only the beginning. As the men proceed on foot into the narrow alleys, the scenery becomes progressively more depressing. At first the alleys are straight. The houses are decent and the people relatively well-dressed. At this stage the language spoken is refined (*rāqiya*), made up of coherent words and sentences.[19]

But as they advance the scene becomes uglier, the noise less pleasant. There are four different passages, each describing a further step into the heart of wretchedness. I shall quote from each stage those sentences relating to the realm of language:

Stage 1. "Language disintegrates; it becomes single words, calls, insults."[20]

Stage 2. "Language crumbles to half words or even quarters, to locutions that only the speakers understand."[21]

Stage 3. "Language becomes hisses (*sarsaʿa*), vowels and consonants arising out of greatly protuberant larynxes."[22]

Stage 4. "Staccato mutterings merge into the barking of dogs and into the creaking of great doors as they are pushed open."[23]

Now the judge's march into this unfamiliar territory constitutes, as I have pointed out, the backbone of the story and this is also suggested by its title. It is in this section that Abdallah's towering egotism is brought out, and it is through what he sees and hears and smells that he is incensed. The constant references to human and other noises in **City Dregs** is yet another example of the centrality of acoustic and rhythmic elements in the art of Yūsuf Idrīs. The recurrence of these elements in clusters (often consisting of some four components) demonstrates that they are definitely used as a structural device.

VII

In section III and elsewhere in this paper, we have seen how Idrīs produces concatenations of astounding similes in order to portray the acoustic universe in a literary text. Furthermore, the passages quoted from **City Dregs** demonstrate the rich "meta-language" that he concocts to describe the speech and hubbub of people.

There is, however, another feature which Idrīs uses in abundance, and which is not usually discernible through translation. That is the onomatopoeia. The sheer quantity of sound-imitating morphemes in his stories is dazzling. No less impressive is their variety.

In the chapter of **City Dregs** discussed above we find, among many others, the following "acoustic" words: 1. *ḥafīf* ("rustling"), 2. *za'īq* ("screaming"), 3. *hamhama* ("mumble"), 4. *sarsa'a* ("hisses"), 5. *habhaba* ("barking") and many others. Elsewhere in the stories discussed we find such words as: 6. *qazqaza* ("cracking [nuts]"), 7. *sakhsakha* ("titter"), 8. *ṭarqa'a* ("crackle").

This list constitutes but a fraction of the rich onomatopoeic inventory to be found in Idrīs' stories. However, this random sample does demonstrate one more characteristic of the author's style. Some of these words, (e.g. the first three) may be considered to belong to a classical *fuṣḥā*, or at least to the modern *fuṣḥā*. But most of the others do not come from the classical inventory, and can hardly be found in dictionaries of the classical or modern *fuṣḥā*.[24] In fact they are drawn chiefly from the spoken language of Cairo.

It will be remembered that Idrīs has been often taken to task for his "excessive" use of the dialect in his stories. Such criticism seems to imply that the *fuṣḥā* is equipped with all the necessary linguistic and lexical elements necessary for modern fiction. However the case of the onomatopoeia proves that there are certain linguistic items of the spoken language that are not readily replaceable by *fuṣḥā* equivalents. It also indicates that the use of *'āmiyya* items by Idrīs (and others) is not necessarily haphazard, neither is it a private whim. At least in the case of "acoustic" items, the author resorts to vernacular items as part of his efforts to portray "local reality". In so doing he is definitely enriching the language of fiction, rather than damaging it, as certain critics seem to imply. The *fuṣḥā*, which is basically a written language,[25] can hardly be expected to provide the author with all the onomatopoeic items which the modern reader regards as reflecting "real" voices. If he is to render the "local colour" or rather the "local vocality", he has little choice but to fall back on the spoken variety of language, which is infinitely richer in items pertaining to local *realia* and *vocalia*.

Notes

1. A list of Idrīs' short-story volumes can be found in my article "Language and Theme in the Short Stories of Yūsuf Idrīs", *Journal of Arabic Literature*, Vol. VI (1975), pp. 89-100. In recent years Idrīs has published two new volumes of short stories: *Anā Sulṭān Qānūn al-Wujūd* (1980) and *Uqtulhā* (1982) as well as a novella, *New York 80* (1981).

2. Roger Allen (ed.), *In the Eye of the Beholder: Tales of Egyptian Life from the Writings of Yusuf Idris*, Minneapolis and Chicago (Bibliotheca Islamica) 1978; and: Yūsuf Idrīs, *The Cheapest Nights and Other Stories*, translated by Wadida Wassef, London (Peter Owen) 1978. A list of other stories in translation can be found on p. 195 of Kurpershoek's book (see next footnote). In 1984 another volume of Idrīs' stories appeared in English translation: Yusuf Idris, *Rings of Burnished Brass*, translated by Catherine Cobham, London and Washington (Heineman and Three Continents Press). This volume includes four novellas, one of which is "The Black Policeman", discussed in section V of this article.

3. P. M. Kurpershoek, *The Stories of Yūsuf Idrīs: A Modern Egyptian Author*, Leiden (Brill) 1981.

4. See, for instance, Muḥammad Zaghlūl Salām, *Dirāsāt fī al-Qiṣṣa al-'Arabiyya al-Ḥadītha*, Alexandria 1973, p. 368.

5. See, for instance, Ṭāhā Ḥusayn's introduction to Idrīs' second volume of short stories, *Jumhūriyyat Faraḥāt*, Cairo 1956.

6. S. Somekh, *Lughat al-Qiṣṣa fī adab Yūsuf Idrīs*, Acre 1984.

7. I am grateful to Dr. Roger Allen for his translation. He has made every effort to produce an English version reflecting, as far as possible, the text of the Arabic story, at times sacrificing an elegant English phrase.

8. See the bibliographical list in Sayyid Ḥāmid al-Nassāj, *Dalīl al-Qiṣṣa al-Miṣriyya al-Qaṣīra*, Cairo 1972, p. 176, also Kurpershoek, p. 191.

9. The subsequent editions of this book were published under the title *Qā' al-Madīna.*

10. Cf., e.g., the clear structural function of the word "silence" (*ṣamt*) and its derivatives in the title story of *Bayt min Laḥm* (1971). This story ("House of Flesh") was skilfully translated into English by Denys Johnson-Davies and included in his book *Egyptian Short Stories,* London and Washington (Heinemann and Three Continents Press) 1978, pp. 1-7.

11. *Mashūq al-Hams* is, in fact, a second edition (with only one story omitted) of *al-Naddāha* ("The Clarion" or "The Voice"), which is also of a somewhat "communicative" connotation.

12. This story "al-'Askarī al-Aswad" was originally published in the Cairene monthly *al-Kātib,* June 1961, and incorporated in a volume bearing the same title which appeared in 1962.

13. *Al-'Askarī al-Aswad,* Cairo 1962, p. 43. I am grateful to Carol Bardenstein for translating the four quotations from this story.

14. Ibid., p. 44.

15. Ibid., p. 46.

16. Ibid., p. 46.

17. An English translation of this story by Pierre Cachia, can be found in Roger Allen's anthology (referred to in fn. 2 *supra*), pp. 17-77. My quotations are based on Prof. Cachia's translation (hereafter referred to as "trans.").

18. Orig. (= *Alaysa Kadhālika,* Cairo 1957), p. 344; trans. p. 62-3.

19. Orig. 346; trans. 64.

20. Orig. 346; trans. 64.

21. Orig. 347; trans. 64-5.

22. Orig. 347; trans. 65.

23. Orig. 348; trans. 65.

24. None of the words listed here appears in *al-Mu'jam al-Wasīṭ,* a dictionary of *fuṣḥā* published in 1960-1961 by the Cairo Language Academy.

25. The oral use of *fuṣḥā* is becoming widespread, mainly under the impact of mass communication. See: Al-Sa'īd Muḥammad Badawī, *Mustawayāt al-'Arabiyya al-Mu'āṣira fī Miṣr,* Cairo 1973; Gustav Meiseles, "Educated Spoken Arabic and the Arabic Language Continuum", *Archivum Linguisticum* 11 (N.S.), pp. 89-106.

Issa J. Boullata (review date winter 1989)

SOURCE: Boullata, Issa J. Review of *A Leader of Men,* by Yusuf Idris. *The International Fiction Review* 16, no. 1 (winter 1989): 82-3.

[*In the following review, Boullata provides a reading of the story "Abû al-Rijâl."*]

Youssef Idris, born in Egypt in 1927, is one of the most prominent Arab writers today. Originally a medical doctor, he has dedicated himself to literature and written some thirty books in various genres, including short stories, novels, plays, and essays.

One of his recent stories, published in the Egyptian magazine *October* (November 1, 1987, pp. 40-45), is entitled **"Abû al-Rijâl."** It is reprinted in Arabic in this book [*A Leader of Men*] with an excellent English translation.

The story is not primarily constructed as a plot of events but rather as an exploration of a main character's inner depths. The tensions that sustain its continuity and keep the reader riveted till the end derive as much from Idris's masterful narrative art as from his choice of an unusual subject matter. In fact the subject matter is normally regarded in the Arab world as one about which feelings, thoughts, and words ought to be repressed. Idris brings them out into the open in this story as he deals with a married, virile, and macho man who, in his early fifties, discovers his latent homosexuality and is made to face up to it in the story.

The protagonist, whose name is Sultan, sits on his veranda at some distance from the handsome young man in tight pants whom he summoned. In silence he reviews his past full of heroic and manly acts in order to understand how his earlier macho self slipped imperceptibly into his present state. Memory takes Sultan back to his poverty-stricken childhood which, notwithstanding, was dignified and proud. He remembers his school days as an intelligent boy, with a strong personality and clear leadership traits, who did not permit other boys even to touch him. He recalls his university years during which he shared his bursary with his family as he earned two degrees, one in economics and the other in history, and won the respect of everybody through his call for social justice and his readiness to serve everyone in need.

Sultan then gradually becomes aware that he began to lose respect when, for no known reason, he did not immediately rise to help and defend his community at the village against an obvious aggression in which he was expected to act but counseled caution and preparation for a future encounter with the enemy. And when he was challenged by a young man who did not accept being insulted or ridiculed by him on account of his uncle being a well-known effeminate person in the village, Sultan lost all his self-respect on being pulled to the ground and forced to say in public that he was a woman or else die at the point of the sicle the young man pushed into his neck. After this incident in which he yielded, Sultan became the object of whispers, and he sank further in his shame. Finally he stopped caring as he accepted to act like a woman in homosexual relations, but continued to savor the hypocritical courtesy people still showed him as a champion of their causes.

In his English translation, Elkhadem captures not only the rhythm of the Arabic sentences but also the author's extreme caution in avoiding vulgar expressions and his care not to offend the sensibilities of readers exposing themselves to a controversial subject. He also parallels the author's flair for exactitude in his deep psychological analysis of the characters and his apt wording for vivid descriptions of situations and moods.

Roger Allen (review date spring 1989)

SOURCE: Allen, Roger. Review of *A Leader of Men*, by Yusuf Idris. *World Literature Today* 63, no. 2 (spring 1989): 360-61.

[*In the following review, Allen asserts that the publication of an English translation of* A Leader of Men "*is of great benefit to students of modern Arabic and especially Egyptian fiction.*"]

It was in the 1950s and 1960s that the Egyptian author Yusuf Idris established his reputation as a short-story writer of genius (see *WLT* [*World Literature Today*] 55:1, pp. 43-47). His ability to encapsulate realistic "slices of life" and more symbolic and nightmarish visions within the tight strictures of the genre, his profound psychological insights into a variety of human dilemmas, and perhaps above all his intuitive and often wayward use of numerous levels of language in creating his fleeting yet memorable world—these qualities were combined into short stories which made up a large number of collections and were to prove a significant factor in raising the Arabic short story to new levels of artistry (see *WLT* 60:2, pp. 199-206 on this general topic). Although other Arab writers have also made notable contributions to this fictional genre, Idris's talent has given him a particularly important place not only within the Arab world but also on a much-larger plane.

Three collections of Idris's stories are available in English: ***The Cheapest Nights*** (1978), translated by Wadida Wassef; ***In the Eye of the Beholder*** (1978; see *WLT* 53:4, p. 739), edited by Roger Allen; and ***Rings of Burnished Brass*** (1984; see *WLT* 60:1, p. 171), trans-

lated by Catherine Cobham. There also exist numerous isolated translations, but little attention has been devoted to Idris's recent output. It should immediately be added that, quite apart from the reduced size of that output when compared with earlier years, there is considerable debate within Egypt itself concerning the role and quality of works written by an older generation of writers—thus including Idris and Najib Mahfuz (see *WLT* 63:1, pp. 5-9)—at a time when more than one further generation is adding to the narrative tradition and "demanding a place in the sun." With such debates in mind, the availability of **"Abu al-Rijal"** (originally published in Arabic in the magazine *October* on 1 November 1987) is of great benefit to students of modern Arabic and especially Egyptian fiction.

The story is divided into ten sections, some of which involve retrospect. The translator points out that the work numbers among the very first in modern Arabic fiction which investigate the inner trauma of a man with a reputation for toughness (as implied in the title) who finds himself relentlessly faced with the reality of his own homosexual inclinations. Although the handling of the psychological dimension has always been one of Idris's strong points, it is not treated with any great subtlety here; the causality presumably to be inferred from the description of the strong-willed mother in section 6, for example, is patent enough to become almost trite. On other levels, however, the story works well. The creative use of time change, the switching of venues, and, above all, Idris's remarkable usage of contemporary Arabic style (which Sasson Somekh has investigated in a series of studies) provide welcome evidence of the author's continuing creativity. If this is not among his greatest contributions to the modern Arabic short story, it is certainly worthy of note for both its theme and technique.

The translator notes in his preface the difficulties involved in rendering Idris into English (or any other language), something of which I myself am well aware. Although the translation flows in many places with considerable facility, it cannot as a whole be said to represent a genuinely finished piece of work. Problems arise at the word level: "hymns" (*tasabih*) in the context of the call to prayer sounds incongruous, whereas "a masticatory" (*madgha*) will not be understood far beyond the pharmacy (why not "[chewing-]gum"?); the notion of riding around the Egyptian countryside in a "surrey" (*karta maftuha*) is not a little comic. Tenses manage to cause their usual problems, exacerbated perhaps by Idris's deliberate manipulation of time frames. What works in Arabic, with its notions of "complete" and "incomplete," sounds unnatural in English: "He rose, rebelliously; rose as if he would incite a rebellion. No! He won't put on his suit. He will wear his coarse woolen galabia." The use of *would* in place of the English future here could provide at least one solution to the awkwardness of the English.

The text of a new story by Idris on a rarely broached topic, translated into readable if not idiomatic English, is a useful addition to the library of students of modern Arabic literature. York Press's very reasonably priced volume is therefore to be welcomed.

Abu al-Ma'ati Abu al-Naja (essay date 1989)

SOURCE: al-Naja, Abu al-Ma'ati Abu. "The Short Story Collection, *Vision at Fault.*" In *Critical Perspectives on Yusuf Idris,* edited by Roger Allen, pp. 97-104. Colorado Springs: Three Continents Press, 1994.

[*In the following essay, which was originally published in 1989, al-Naja considers the main thematic concerns of* Vision at Fault.]

Even if we overlook the explanations that Yusuf Idris has proffered in a number of newspaper statements regarding the reasons for his preference for writing journalistic articles in recent years, the reader of this latest collection finds himself—perhaps unintentionally—posing himself a question as he considers the stories included: Is there a connection between the current small output of this story writer and the kind of experiments which he now considers worthy of being couched in short story form? Expressed differently, has short story writing, as far as Yusuf Idris is concerned, turned into a kind of quest for a rare pearl, however much time and effort may be involved?

Everybody realizes that the writer's career—any writer's—may take a number of different directions. It may take the form of an exploration of new positions on the larger map of society, the mind, or life in general; it may happen as the natural result of a growth in experience and knowledge and everything that that implies by way of a change in the mode of comprehending the human experience and crafting it into an artistic entity, even though it be on the basis of the self-same old situations!

Whatever its method, what does this new collection, *Vision at Fault,* have to offer that is new? Does it offer any kind of explanation for the small output of this short-story writer who built his reputation in Arabic literature on his brilliant creativity in the genre?

GENERAL FEATURES OF A NOTABLE JOURNEY

Anyone who follows the course of Yusuf Idris's long journey with the short story—starting with *The Cheapest Nights* in the 1950s and then a whole series of other excellent collections, of which the most important are *An Affair of Honor, The End of the World, The Sin [sic], The Language of Screams, The Siren, House of Flesh, Kill Her,* and so on, will notice that at first his particular artistic vision sprang from his powerful and explosive sense of the profound effect that social problems have on the behavior of his heroes and the way that their fate is determined. In later collections however, the horizon broadens to reveal the effect of more psychological and cosmic issues on the heroes' behavior. As a result, his technique has developed from an initial sharp focus on societal issues, in which the vision relies on a good deal of conviction, to something different, with a considerably reduced element of certainty. Confronted with deep-rooted psychological issues and a larger, cosmic intellectual vision, the storytelling technique prefers to suggest, to disclose, to allude. Sometimes it makes use of the language of images and symbols, but, for all that, it remains within the general framework of a realistic vision, if one can use such a term!

Anyone following Idris's long journey, be it through his short stories, plays, or novels—and, however different the forms may be, it is still essentially one and the same journey—will, I assume, be confronted with its immense wealth, its breadth and depth, and will come to realize the seriousness of the challenge that faces a writer who is determined to transcend his own oeuvre with every new work he produces. Has Yusuf Idris, I wonder, fallen into the trap presented by such a challenge? Every time he has been on the point of writing a new story or approached the narrative moment, has he remembered that he has written the story before or already come to the same point in one form or other? Has he ever felt that all the good stories have been written already, either by him or someone else, and that searching for new sources in the recesses of the human mind or on the horizons of society, the cosmos, or nature, all this represents a dilemma exactly like the one faced by the hero in the superb story in this collection, **"Way Out"**?

About this hero, Idris has the following to say:

> "For a long time he had had the impression that life was no longer synonymous with happiness. This had all occurred a long time ago, after he had savored all the first fruits available, first success, first pound, first flirtation, first night with a woman. There had been a time when his ultimate dream was to have a monthly salary of a hundred and fifty pounds; when he spent that amount on a single day, the goal had increased to five thousand. He had wanted a son; he now had three of them, and a daughter too. He had wanted them to get an education and be graduated; they had. The goal had been changed again: for them to get married; now he had grandchildren."

He had everything he wanted, but life was no longer synonymous with happiness.

"He used to be able to face the world with a pocketful of piastres. Now he went into a panic if there was a figure missing from the check. When he had threatened to leave home, he had done so in the absolute confidence that he could start life afresh; now he was scared even to go out of the house."

This then is the serious existential dilemma facing the hero of **"Way Out."** How can a man over fifty recover his sense of surprise and confidence at the same time? Lurking behind every new sensation he lives and experiences there lurks the specter of the old. He learns the lesson from a new-born chicken which bores at the shell of its own egg. Feeling constricted by its environment it keeps chipping away at the shell without even realizing that, beyond the narrow prison in which it is confined on all sides, there lies a wide cosmos that is stupendous and formidable. The hero manages to assert himself when he realizes that he will only be able to find this stupendous fresh resource—life being synonymous with happiness—when he can learn to respond to the same internal call that motivates the new-born chicken. He too must keep on chipping away until he breaks out of the walls of prison, whether that prison consist of family, society, or even nature itself if that becomes a prison!

While reading this story, I do not know why I kept having the strong feeling that the author of this collection is placing himself at the ultimate edge of things. He bores at the walls of the impossible, searching for a way out of this wide formidable universe, somewhere that life can be synonymous with happiness! I am not suggesting that I know why a great writer should stop writing for a while, nor indeed what the secret of writing is. Even so, let us endeavor to take a comprehensive look at the stories in this collection and see if the author really has tried to bore through the walls of the impossible, to place himself at the beginnings and ends of things in a quest for wonder or an aperture through which to survey a wide, formidable universe, something we can hardly see even though we are only separated from it by a thin shell, something we have to smash through. After all, you will never get anything unless, when the moment of decision comes, you are prepared to risk everything!

Unusual Experiences

In the title story, the narrator meets the old peasant who asks for his help in making some spectacles for his donkey; its eyesight has gotten very weak. The problem, which is a real joke at the start, is carried to a conclusion. In theory a weak-sighted donkey can see better if a way can be found to put the appropriate strength spectacles in front of its eyes. Practically speaking however, how can you measure how weak the donkey's vision is without any indications from the animal itself? Horse, donkeys, it makes no difference. The solution to

the problem emerges from its point of origin. The donkey's owner finds out that the animal's eyesight is weakening when it does not respond to the sight of the neighbor's female donkey as it has always done in the past. Now, if we can put the donkey at a certain distance from the neighbor's female donkey and then put a series of different strength lenses in front of the donkey's eyes, the most appropriate lenses will be the ones that make the donkey respond to the presence of the female! All this takes place, of course, in front of a crowd of folk from the village, old and young. Using the plot development in this story that begins with an utterly weird and comic situation, the author cajoles his readers into discovering a moment of explosive and spontaneous sex that impinges not only on the animal world where the social conventions regarding sex do not apply but also on the group as a whole. This is how Yusuf Idris records the effect of the surprising turn of events on the crowd:

"Nature unabashed, in the raw, yelling out in a loud voice: You put the earthquake inside our bodies, and within us the volcano burst. Disorder in the universe, or is it providing order? Sanity or madness to the utmost degree. Bodies thrashing excitedly, nectar pouring forth with all the primitive power of sun-spots, the pull of the full moon, hurricanes at their savage height. If human spectacles can help donkeys, I wonder if donkey's spectacles can do the same for humans"?

Here the author breaches the walls of societal convention; through the aperture we are given a look at the world of explicit sex. He places himself at the extreme edge between man as social and natural animal. The basic question is this: when did social man lose the feeling of innocence towards sex and why? But there's another question; in fact, two. Was humor the only and inevitable reason for selecting such a weird event as the vehicle for this story? Was the colloquial dialect in which the story is couched the only possible choice for an experience which lies on the extreme edge between social and natural man?!

"His Mother"

In this story we approach a rare moment in an unusual relationship between a vagrant boy and a tree. First the boy loses his father, and then his mother too, when she marries someone else. Hunger is not his most dogged foe either, since he can fend for himself by pilfering in garbage cans. No, his worst foe is the long, cold, rainy winter night when he is chased away from any place where he might be able to find some shelter. Every place has an owner, even the rusty, abandoned railroad wagons from which the police keep chasing him away. Then one night he comes across this tree, called "Mother of Feelings." It's a huge, non-fruit-bearing tree; its long branches hang down and come together at the base to form a trunk. Naturally enough, this trunk has apertures in it and is hollow on the inside. The boy takes refuge inside the trunk and discovers that this time there is no owner to throw him out. So he becomes the owner; it becomes his home in the big city. If Idris had written this story in the 1950s, he may well have given us a wonderful portrait of this boy's personal tragedy, but here the story is presented with no background. The real story starts when the boy senses that the tree has also become his friend, as though it is a mother with no children who then finds her child. He is scared he will come back one night and find someone else occupying his home inside the trunk, but removes his fears by lowering fresh branches to cover up the aperture so that no one else can see it. The tree keeps him warm, and, since the inside is cold, his breath also keeps the tree warm. The sharp protuberances inside the tree turn into blossoms to form a soft cushion.

Idris handles skillfully this rare relationship between boy and tree, the attractive connection between the different levels of life that stem from the kinship bonds between them. The boy grows up and becomes big and strong, too large to fit in the space inside the tree. He goes out into society, now able to argue with it on equal terms. He gets a house and a job. One day, he walks past the tree again and sees that it has become withered; the leaves have all dried up. For a few moments, he stands in front of it crying for his "mother."

Here too, we are placed on the edge of a society, with no place for a young boy who is unable to protect himself. By boring through the shell, this boy manages to open a crack in nature's prison and emerges into a wide universe of affection hiding in the trunk of a tree!

"Leader of Men"

If the story **"Way Out"** represents the key to this collection, then **"Leader of Men"** is the jewel. It's a story about a man who starts at the bottom and reaches a summit he never even dreamed of; in this long journey the secret password is man's ability to face challenges and make decisions. Through a long journey of fifty years,

> "he proceeded like a genuine colt, never tiring or running out of steam. He had set himself no particular goal, just the sheer process of moving ahead. He was not after money. Political ambition was not his motivation, nor was he seeking some place in history. Some of this, even all of it, might come to pass because of his perseverance and insistence. His goal was that his society should be a just one, not one filled with wronged people none of whom had anything more than the single gallabiyyah their father had had."

When had the first breakdown in his life come? He could not remember the time. It's certain there was such a time, but he couldn't recall it now. There had been a man, a call for help. The person who made it realized he wasn't directing his cries to the wrong man. He had had to make a decision on the spot. In no time at all he would have considered the odds. For him, sedate, reasonable behavior was not the sensible way of doing things. There were times when, if circumstances dictated, the craziest and most unusual decisions had to be made.

The assault had happened in front of everyone; the people who did it must have been mad. The response, everyone realized, would be instantaneous and brutal.

But, in spite of all that, he remained silent for a long time while he made a number of mental calculations. In place of the usual roar his voice came out sounding puny:

> "This time I think we should withdraw and allow ourselves to select the best time and place for the confrontation. Everyone—above all, he himself—was fully aware that this very hour, high noon, was the best time (he could remember it in every detail). Getting his men together for the face-off was best done on the spot.
>
> How had it all happened? For several years, day and night, he had been analyzing the recesses of his own mind. He had been wheedling his interlocutors into telling him why, in their view, he had done what he had."

Let's leave this question, which represents the core of the story, and follow the path of the hero's fall. It had all happened in phases. He had started off as a major boss in the capital city, but then Sultan—that is his name—had returned to his birthplace in order to become the "leader of men," leader of a group of considerably less import; an illegal gang to be sure, but at least its existence was enough to preserve his self-esteem and give the appearance of being in charge of something.

But then comes the major fall, in his own village and among his own kith and kin. This time the challenge comes from a young boy who scarcely knows who he is or anything about his legendary strength and brutality. This young man refuses point blank to allow Sultan to insult him by making crude remarks about his uncle who, according to the wagging tongues in the village, is a pervert. The young man starts a fight with Sultan, and this time the result is a foregone conclusion. The young man is in his twenties, while Sultan is in his fifties. The young man throws Sultan to the ground, puts the blade of his scythe on his neck and utters a solemn oath not to take it away until Sultan has admitted in front of everyone there that he is a woman. If anyone comes too close, he will bury the blade in Sultan's neck!

Then comes the end, or rather the beginning of the story. We find that, perhaps as a result of the public acknowledgment he has made in order to save his own skin, Sultan has in fact turned into a kind of woman. His relatives can think of only one way to rid themselves of the scandals he is causing, and that is to kill him.

STRUCTURE OF THE STORY

How does Yusuf Idris present this story, one that manages to cover a complete lifetime, a journey to the top and back down again? He starts it at the end, from the point where Sultan is scraping bottom, when he begins to feel the urge actually to become something like a woman, his discovery of this cataclysmic sensation in the presence of the nephew who is most impressed by his uncle's personality. Sultan had called him "the bull," but, when he invites him that night, he has no idea why. The young man sits in front of his uncle, waiting to see what he would ask him to do. The events in the story begin from this meeting and almost finish there too. Sultan resists his deadly feelings, and it is to the pulse of their ebb and flow that the story is constructed.

As Sultan resists these perverted sensations we live through some moments of his rise to power; when he surrenders, we see aspects of the downfall as well, as we share Sultan's secrets with him. In fact, the skillful way in which Yusuf Idris spreads them through the story affords the reader a greater perspective or Sultan's downfall than he himself has.

SIGNIFICANCE OF THE DOWNFALL

Sultan's personality is that of a noble dictator or a just tyrant who is carried to the top by a formidable rebellious power. But he comes from the bottom, and the journey is long and hard. As a result, he has no time to catch his breath or look around him. His first point of weakness is that his strength refuses to come to terms with his own weaknesses and fears, nor is it prepared to compromise with the strengths and fears of those around him. In his arrogance he refuses to consider minor details and intermediate goals on the long journey; he is for ever plunging ahead "as though continuing was everything, in quest of a distant, obscure goal named justice."

The second point of weakness is that he is content to rely on the sense of power that stems from the legend of his power. It does not come from his own internal strength, something that has already been exhausted by self-reliance and ignoring everyone else. When he finds himself confronted for the first time by someone who believes for a moment that he has nothing to fear from his own legend, indeed who senses that deep inside he is scared to death and exhausted, he suffers his first fall and fails to make a firm decision. After that, he can no longer be either noble dictator or just tyrant. Instead he turns into a mere dictator who conceals his own internal depravity by humiliating an innocent young man who is in no way to blame for the imputation that his uncle is a pervert!

With the second fall Sultan realizes that he has been stripped bare; all he can do now is to punish himself, a totally just punishment by becoming just like the boy's uncle whose perversion he made public and laughed at.

BETWEEN THE TWO WAYS OUT

Isn't the journey of Sultan, "the leader of men," a kind of "way out" from the bottom to the very top? How is it that the hero of **"Way Out"** manages to make a decision to leave the prison of his own family and the role of father when he suddenly discovers he no longer is a father or has any real role, whereas Sultan fails to find a way out and actually returns to a bottom level that is even lower that the one from which he started? It may be because, while the hero of **"Way Out"** is an ordinary kind of person, he allows himself to talk, sometimes to himself, or others to people around him. When the main event happens, it is not a complete surprise to him; he has been spotting warning signs for some time and has even come to terms with them. His strength has not dwindled to the point of utter exhaustion. So he is able to take the "way out" and grab life's most valuable prize—even for someone over fifty—when life becomes synonymous with happiness.

Sultan by contrast prefers to be a dictator and to carry all the burdens of the journey up (or the "way out") on his own. The burden wears him out. His initial triumphs for which he alone wins the laurels give him exceptional power. However, when the first breakdown occurs, he finds himself, by sheer logic, bearing the burden of shame on his own. The weight crushes him, and the long journey down has begun. His attempts to conceal his own weakness lead him to expose the weaknesses of other people and to despise them, even if they themselves are not responsible for the point of weakness (for example, the way he scoffs at Al-Tahhan's nephew). A hidden force explodes inside the young boy, just like the force he himself used to feel and applied whenever people made fun of his father when he was a boy. He sinks so low that there is only one way out, and that is for his closest relatives to kill him.

Saad Elkhadem (essay date winter 1990)

SOURCE: Elkhadem, Saad. "Youssef Idris and His Gay *Leader of Men*." *The International Fiction Review* 17, no. 1 (winter 1990): 25-8.

[*In the following essay, Elkhadem views Idris's treatment of homosexuality in "Abû al-Rijâl" as pioneering.*]

Most Arabists and literary historians agree that Youssef (Yûsuf) Idrîs (b. 1927) is one of the most accomplished, if not *the* most accomplished, short-story writer in Arabic literature today. Although he has written six novels and seven plays, Idrîs's mastery is most evident in the shorter forms. His first collection of short stories, *Arkhas Layâlî* (*The Cheapest Nights*), which was published in 1954, established him as one of the leading "realist" writers in Egypt. **"Arkhas Layâlî,"** the title story, which appeared earlier in the Cairene newspaper *al-Misrî,*[1] and which deals with the sad and depressing life of the downtrodden fellahin, was immediately recognized as a pioneering work. This instant acknowledgment encouraged Y. Idrîs, who has a medical degree from the University of Cairo, to dedicate most of his time and energy to creative writing. Beside his belletristic works, Mr. Idrîs has published a great number of essays on literary and social topics; when collected and republished, his non-belletristic writings occupy seven volumes.[2]

While contributing regularly to *al-Ahrâm,* the leading Egyptian newspaper, and speaking on radio and appearing on television, in November 1987, Mr. Idrîs, now one of the most-celebrated literary figures in the Arab world, ended a creative lull that had lasted several years, and published his short story **"Abû al-Rijâl"** in the Cairene magazine *October.*[3] Literally translated, "Abû al-Rijâl" means "The Father of Men." However, because the story deals with the latent homosexuality of a strong and virile man who has an exaggerated sense of masculine pride, the title must be understood as an ironic comment on the tragic dilemma of the protagonist. Originally, Y. Idrîs called his story "al-Kumûn," meaning "latency"; however, because the same word could be also read as "al-Kammûn," which means "cumin," since, in Arabic, both words have the same spelling, Mr. Idrîs was persuaded by Salâh Muntassir, the magazine's editor, to give his story a new title.[4]

"Abû al-Rijâl" is the story of a man from a poor and humble family who, after many bitter and heroic fights against poverty and prejudice, succeeds in establishing himself as a scholar, a moral leader, and a social reformer, "the pride and joy of his generation, and of all the following generations."[5] However, it must be noted now that while he is being praised as a self-made man who overcame poverty and obscurity by his own efforts, some passages of the text depict him as a gangster, a thug, and a ruthless opportunist, "A leader of a gang, but it is a gang of rebellious insurgents, of bloodthirsty murderers and habitual criminals" (3). This striking discrepancy is never cleared up or justified. Some of the critics who unreservedly admire the artistry of Mr. Idrîs would do their best to overlook this obvious inconsistency; but some will feel obliged to point out this unmistakable contradiction, and, in vain, try to find a convincing explanation for it.

"Abû al-Rijâl" depicts the dilemma which an intelligent, powerful, and aggressively virile man in his early fifties faces when he suddenly discovers that, up until now, his life has been nothing but a sham, and that his extremely masculine attitude is nothing more than a hypocritical imitation of his strong and proud father. In ten short scenes, the author depicts how Sultan, the protagonist, forces himself to analyze, confront, and come to terms with his latent homosexuality. When he discovers that the odd feelings and bizarre sensations that have been tormenting him lately are the symptoms of his suppressed sexual desires, Sultan proceeds to adjust to this ignominious reality. This confrontation between his tormented soul and the sources of its agony is triggered by a meeting that takes place late in the evening between Sultan and Bull, one of the young handsome men who serve him. After summoning Bull to the veranda of his country villa, Sultan orders the young man to sit in silence and wait while he contemplates his next move, and explores how to approach Bull, and how to make it clear to him that his strong and frightful master wants to have sex with him.

While sitting there waiting for his master's orders, "the boy began to wonder what . . . Sultan might want of him; he even went as far as to assume that Sultan might want to do to him what men do to women; and he wondered what he should do" (19). After long hours, during which Sultan has reviewed his life, and analyzed several significant incidents that took place during his childhood, puberty, and manhood, he comes to the conclusion that he must submit to his true nature, lift up this hypocritical facade, and disclose his sexual preference. He then decides to "advance towards the boy . . . he advances and advances; and the boy has reconciled himself to compliance, for what else can he do? but he was stunned with what had happened and what is happening, for he was asked to do the opposite of what he had reconciled himself to accept" (19). After this encounter, Sultan, the mighty lord and proud master, the leader of men, realizes that, from now on, none of his followers and admirers will appreciate his manliness and courage, or treat him with the same reverence and devotion as they used to do in the past. However, "not caring anymore about whatever they would say, or whatever they would hide, or suppress, or reveal, because after the veil of masculinity was removed from him, he himself removed the veil of shame" (19).

In one of his earlier stories, Youssef Idrîs dealt with another daring subject matter, namely sexual impotence. The middle-aged protagonist of **"Abû Sayyid"** is a virile man with a strong sense of masculine pride. When he is suddenly afflicted with sexual impotence, he suffers greatly and is deeply humiliated; however, his loving and understanding wife helps him to overcome this serious psychological crisis. But compared to **"Abû al-Rijâl," "Abû Sayyid"** is—in spite of its somewhat daring topic—moderate indeed. For Islamic Egypt, sex is not a popular subject that can be discussed in the open or treated in literature, let alone homosexual relationships which have been ignored and avoided on grounds of religion, morality, and taste. Remembering that Egypt—as well other Islamic countries of the Middle East—has been lately pressured into conservatism by the new Fundamentalists, one realizes the risk Mr. Idrîs has taken by depicting the emotions and the sexual desires of a homosexual without condemning, or even reprehending them. On the contrary, he even lets his protagonist voice his dissatisfaction with the stringent ethical norms of his society when he says: ". . . indeed, why is it wrong for a human being to be a [homosexual]?" (18). Also considering the fact that in spite of the relatively enlightened periods which some of the Arab countries have experienced during their long history, never before has any author dared to deal seriously with this extremely sensitive subject. Of course, some early Arabic poets may have alluded to homosexuality in their works (e.g., Abû Nuwwâs), and a few contemporary authors may have referred to it, or dealt with it superficially (e.g., Najîb Mahfûz), but no one before Y. Idrîs has probed so deeply in the mind and soul of a homosexual.

It must also be stated that although Y. Idrîs deals here with the fleshly desires of a homosexual, he never uses a vulgar expression, or depicts an obscene situation. His choice of words and selection of scenes are done with the utmost care and caution, so that no situation in his story could be construed as pornographic or even erotic. Words and phrases that may sound offensive have been rigorously avoided. For instance, when he depicts how Sultan approaches the young man and forces him to have sex with him, Y. Idrîs stops before the sexual act begins, but then resumes his description after it has taken place, in order to record the thoughts and detail the feelings of the protagonist after he has fulfilled his wishes and gratified his desires: "Everything ended; the sticky sweat reeking of the smell of a shattered pride, a torn dignity, and a degradation he relishes and enjoys; nauseous odors when mixed together, but they never made him nauseous" (19). Or, when he introduces the motif of bestiality into his story, Mr. Idrîs does it in such a way that it does not offend the sensibilities of his readers: "No, his mother had never impugned his masculinity, on the contrary, she was always proud of him; he only remembers an infamous day when his mother entered the cattle pen on a summer day when everyone else was resting or having a nap, to find him alone in the pen with the she-ass of his uncle . . . he still remembers the way his mother acted; and he must confess now that her behavior was the epitome of worldly wisdom; as if she were a psychiatrist, because when she opened the door of the pen and saw him, she said, while turning back fast: 'How could you mount your uncle's she-ass without a saddle, you young donkey?'" (12). Also, when Mr. Idrîs incorporates the popular, but vulgar proverb, "'Iryân al-Tîz wa yuhibb al-Ta'mîz" (literally translated it means: "With a naked

ass, but likes to prance") in his story, he rewords it so that it does not sound coarse or tasteless: "'Iryân al-Mu'khkhirah wa yuhibb al-Fashkharah" (meaning, literally, "His posterior is naked, and he is fond of boasting," which was translated in this edition as: "Although he is too poor even to cover his behind / He brags like a man who is wealthy and refined" [7]).

These, and other concessions made by Mr. Idrîs while dealing with this highly controversial subject matter, have enabled him to publish his story in one of the leading magazines in Egypt without arousing the ire of the conservative circles in his country or endangering his reputation as the leading short-story writer of the Arab World. While there may be some minor reservations regarding the literary and artistic merit of this work, there should be no doubt that, because of its daring topic, **"Abû al-Rijâl"** will remain one of the most pioneering works in Arabic fiction.

Notes

1. *Al-Misri* 14 March 1953.

2. For a complete bibliography of works by, and about, Y. Idris, see H. al-Sakkut and M. Jones, "Bibliographi Yusuf Idris," in *Adab wa Naqd* (Cairo), 34 (Dec. 1987): 125-215.

3. *October* 1 Nov. 1987: 40-45.

4. *October* 1 Nov. 1987: 4.

5. Youssef Idris, *A Leader of Men / Abû al-Rijâl*, trans. S. Elkhadem (Fredericton, N.B.: York Press, 1988) 10. All references are to this bilingual edition.

Mona N. Mikhail (essay date 1990)

SOURCE: Mikhail, Mona N. "Egyptian Tales of the Fantastic: Theme and Technique in the Stories of Yūsuf Idrīs." *Journal of the American Research Center in Egypt* 27 (1990): 191-98.

[*In the following essay, Mikhail offers a thematic and stylistic examination of Idris's short fiction.*]

When Naguib Mahfouz was awarded the 1988 Nobel Prize for Literature, he immediately paid tribute not only to the generations of great Arab writers that came before him, but was quick to point out that several of his contemporaries were well-deserving candidates. He cited amongst others his countrymen Yahia Haqqi and Yūsuf Idrīs as two of the most important innovators in the realm of Arabic literature.

Yūsuf Idrīs, one of Egypt's most talented writers, has been writing novels, plays, and short stories, as well as contributing editorials on varying social and political

subjects for leading daily and weekly papers and magazines in the Arab world, for over four decades. He has
been showered with honors and literary prizes throughout his career, receiving last year the coveted Saddam
Hussein Literary Prize. A physician by training, he early
on abandoned that career to devote himself to writing.
After an extended phase of writing novels and collections of stories in the vein of social realism, Idrīs successfully experimented with the theater of the absurd
and, as we shall see in the ensuing stories, delved into
exploring tales of the fantastic. He has written a collection of strange and powerful stories that are steeped in
fable and myth.

FOLKTALE: TECHNIQUE AND THEME

Folktale time and again recurs in the writings of Yūsuf
Idrīs. With great subtlety and depth of perception he
draws upon some of the well known themes of Egyptian folklore and incorporates them in the modern mold
of the short story. The folktale as a form is cleverly
used to give shape to the content which is also inspired
by the traditional lore. He thus starts the story **"Al-
Shaykh Shaykha"** in the collection *'Ākhir al-Dunyā:*

> God's lands are wide and many, and each place is self-
> sufficient, has its big and small; boys and girls, peoples,
> families, Muslims and Copts, large fortunes governed
> by laws; laws governing every aspect of life, and some-
> times there is an exception, an anomaly to the rule, as
> in our village, unique amongst other lands of God for
> having this living creature who cannot be classified
> amongst the people and humans of our village—and by
> the same token cannot be classified with the animals.
> He also is not the lost chain between them; a creature
> unique to himself, nameless, sometimes they call him
> Shaykh Muḥammad, sometimes Shaykha Fāṭima, only
> sometimes, for the sake of simplification; for the truth
> is that he is a nameless shadow, fatherless, motherless;
> no one knows from where he comes, who endowed
> upon him this strongly built body. As for human fea-
> tures he did have them, he had two eyes, two ears and
> a nose. He walked on two feet. . . .[1]

Here we immediately notice a predominant characteristic of folklore and that is its adherence to form. The
pattern adopted here is one fairly common in the narratives that have survived both in oral and written legend.
What Idrīs does in this story and others of the same category is to create most interesting relationships between
folklore and literature. We will try to see to what extent
the formal features of the folktale are found in his sophisticated writings.

As Axel Olrik tells us in his article on "Epic Laws of
Folk Narrative,"

> With its single thread, folk narrative does not know the
> perspective of painting; it knows only the progressive
> series of bas-reliefs. Its composition is like that of
> sculpture and architecture; hence the strict subordina-
> tion to number and other requirements of symmetry.[2]

So we can try to see what Idrīs does with a folktale,
giving it added dimensions which render it quite a sophisticated piece of literature.

The story is that of a weird creature, almost unclassifi-
able:

> . . . his short, thick rough brushlike hair creates a
> problem worthy of notice. He shows no feminine signs,
> nor does he show any male propensities . . . .

> (p. 391)

The writer then enumerates the rest of his features,
which do not differentiate between male and female.
The very ambiguity of the sex of the character is a
mythic category. Finally this hermaphrodite seems to be
feared and yet in a strange way revered by the villagers
as some kind of a deity. For he or "it" was deaf and
mute; and therefore they never hesitated to unveil their
innermost secrets before him, assured that he could
never disclose the shame, treachery, or ignominious doings that he witnessed daily. This wild creature, this
anomaly of nature, had grown to be accepted as a reality amongst the villagers, although his mode of life was
forever shrouded in rumors. They never were sure about
his comings and goings, never knew exactly what he
ate or drank; some believed he ate only wild weeds
from the fields as he never touched food offered to him.
No one could ascertain anything about him; it was always a matter of guessing, and mostly rumors. Thus the
narrator of the story tells us that his fellow villagers accepted Al-Shaykh Shaykha without question. Indeed he
was a phenomenon; and who were they to question the
Creator's will? Here Idrīs lets the mentality of the average peasant speak for itself, the resigned acceptance of
the will of God:

> If the Creator so wishes there is no way but his wish.
> The slave has no right to object to his scheme, even if
> his scheme is anomalous . . . the pattern of life be-
> comes anomalous so that the universe may appear or-
> derless, how many lunatics, crazy people, disfigured
> and madmen run around . . . they all live, and all must
> live all part of this slow, awesome convoy leading them
> towards the end where there is no end . . . .

> (p. 392)

The story teller proceeds with his yarn, from time to
time bringing in wise sayings and depicting the attitudes of the people, young and old, vis à vis this strange
creature. So the years go by; and as time passes, rumors
come and go about the strange things surrounding this
strange person. (He brings to mind Fellini's hermaphrodite in the *Satyricon.*) Some of these rumors had it that
he had some shameful, incestuous relations with Nā'isa,
the old lame woman, who was also believed to be his
mother, and was caught many a time leaving his favorite hiding place—a barren strip close to the village
mosque. She too was a strange, repulsive woman. The

only sign of her femininity was the *khulkhāl* (bracelet or anklet). For a living, she carried heavy sacks of flour, which men often hesitated to lift, and huge sheaves of fodder for the animals.

And so the rumors multiplied and grew round Shaykh Shaykha: some believed a monkey had fathered him; some that a gypsy had given a remedy to a sterile woman who unfortunately had borne this result.

Life could have gone on forever, and Shaykh Shaykha could have continued being the classical figure of "the present absent, riding walking, being not being crea-ture" (p. 397), were it not for a strange happening which broke this seemingly never ending cycle of life in the village. Our narrator tells us that one of the young vil-lagers overheard the deaf-mute shaykh speak. This was of course an earth-shaking revelation which was ini-tially dismissed as heretical. For, could they face one another if that were proved to be true? Will the husband be able to look the wife in the eyes, the mother her son, the neighbor his neighbor, if all got to know the real person they were living or dealing with?

> Major catastrophe if the rumor were true, or even the slightest possibility of its truth, this wouldn't be merely demolishing walls interior that surround and divide them, but will be an opening in every wall—an open-ing from whence it is possible to move to the other all that the inside contains; and then the day of chaos ar-rives, which must be by far worse and more horrific than the Day of Judgement.
>
> (p. 400)

In a most sensitive and perceptive fashion Idrīs pro-ceeds to analyze the psyche of the villagers and exam-ine their behavior when faced with imminent danger. Here the story deviates from the single strand to acquire the more sophisticated depths of psychological investi-gation. The folktale becomes co-opted into the modern mold.

Here it is impossible to miss the interplay between ap-pearance and reality in the choice of characters, the am-biguity of the whole setting, and the nature of the awe-some creature, the hero of the story. The threatened villagers, once their faith is shaken, are conditioned to find more evidence against the "treacherous" creature living amongst them. So the evidence multiples until they are convinced of having heard him pronounce full articulate sentences in their presence. For fear had taken hold of the whole village, fear of being exposed before one another. The fear took the form of almost mass hysteria, for each one realized that he had spoken much and done even more to be ashamed of in the presence of the once believed deaf-mute creature. They thus sought to see him once more, hoping that his familiar sight would reassure them of his innocence and appease their fears. But he had disappeared and was nowhere to be found, taking with him their secrets.

However after some time he reappears led by Nā'isa, the lame one:

> No sooner had the news spread, than the whole village, big and small, and especially its women who seemed stunned and trembling with fear and anger, all forming a big black spot in the human enclosing, circle round Shaykh Shaykha and Na'isa.
>
> (p. 403)

Nothing had basically changed in his appearance other than that his twisted neck seemed a little straighter, and he produced sounds like laughter every time one asked him a question, "a laugh which sounded more like it was uttered" (p. 403). Nā'isa in a protective gesture tries to ward off the belligerent villagers and vents her insults and wrath upon them, telling them that she had tried to have him cured in the city, and that whatever secrets he may have seen or heard of any one of them could be applicable to the others. For in her fury she told them that he was her son, and was even ready to name the father too. In the face of her passion, and the laughs of Shaykh Shaykha, the people were bemused, but the doubts continued to grow:

> And the people began realizing more and more that the feared had happened, and that the laughs of Shaykh Shaykha is the gap that has opened in every wall and the items of their hidden secret safes were in danger. They were naked in the presence of Shaykh Shaykha, naked of all that covers and protects and gives them dignity and status . . . and they realized that they could no longer live in the same village with one who knew everything about them . . . one who faces them with his strange, horrible laugh wherever they may be.
>
> (p. 405)

And so one day the villagers awake to the frightened cries of a bereaved, wounded mother bemoaning her dead child. They discover it is Nā'isa the lame, harsh woman, throwing stones at the onlookers and bitterly crying, saying that her son had been deaf and mute all his life, and now lay drowned in his blood with a smashed head.

Thus ends the gory tale. Like most of the traditional stories the "monster" has been killed; and no one has to fear him any more (and everyone else lives happily ever after, and the children go to bed). But obviously Idrīs was saying much more in this tale. What has been touched upon earlier in reference to appearance and re-ality is certainly an aspect of the story which has been incorporated in both the form and content. The very un-certainty as to the nature of the creature, the ambiguity surrounding its presence amongst the villagers, all are part and parcel of this theme. The real and pretended lives of the villagers, their secrets and shame as op-posed to their status in everyday life, is the underlying motif of the story.

On another level Idrīs is using the traditional set of characters to serve his own ends. For instead of being the monster of the folktale, Shaykh Shaykha is made to personify the "Truth" one never wants to face. He becomes that disturbing alter ego everyone has to suffocate to be able to live his own life. He may be also our bad conscience which we would like to still for fear of its bothering us one day. As long as that conscience remained mute, we could coexist; but once a shade of doubt arose that it might verbalize, then it had to be made quiet forever.

ANALYSIS OF THE TREATMENT OF DEATH IN SELECTED SHORT STORIES

Death is one of the recurrent themes in the short stories of Yūsuf Idrīs. In other collections, death of the "father" treated as an archetype reappears with mythical dimensions. In an earlier collection *Ḥādithat Sharaf* (*Incident Involving Honor*), the story, **"Al-yadd al-Kabīra"** (**'The Big Hand'**) deals with the subject in traditional fashion. The son returns to his home town after the father's death; and an interplay of past and present takes place in the mind of the narrator, who relives with great intensity moments of family closeness, warmth, and love, now all gone. Through the use of a continuous present tense, we share in the actuality of the scene:

> We sit there a family facing life . . . in a moment when sorrows and worries evaporate . . . and the family is small and life out there is big and the coach is overcrowded, and in the summer we sit on the porch, and my father is happy sitting amongst us like a god, we all love him, and we melt in his talk.[3]

The evoked scene, intensely lived by the returning son is enhanced by the contrasting surroundings—desolate and bare. The poetic usage of the language succeeds in creating the effect of loss and pain. This scene of a family clinging together, as it were, seeking the father's guidance and protection, permeated by a sense of warmth and love, is immediately followed by a scene of desolateness. "The sun was strangled by the narrow evening," the place was deserted, the doors to the house squeaking; the rooms now look bigger, and the dominating color is yellow. In fact the whole story is dyed in deathly paleness but for that one isolated scene of family togetherness. "The sun, yellow in its yellowness lies silence, silence and sickness; and our village also lies yellow with its yellow mudhuts" (p. 66). And again: "The sun's rays piercing through the stairway fall on the tiles of the entrance hall making small yellow circles" (p. 74). The cumulative effect of all this is climaxed by the sudden realization that the father is irrevocably dead.

> My father, then, lies here in this grave, under those piles of stone and dust and cement, he who could never stand being in a room with closed windows; my father sleeps here, wrapped in his funeral garments made of

striped linen, covered with white sheets surrounded by all this wasteland, and his eyes are closed. My father is here; no, he couldn't be lying down he must be sitting up, sitting cross-legged reading 'Salutations' and his big foot bent under him and his toe wriggling and his eyes looking downwards as if praying, and there he just finished his prayers, and I said 'Peace be with you' and he didn't answer.

> (p. 77)

It is as if he fully realizes the reality of the death only when he relives the scene. The story abounds in "death" images such as the ones mentioned above, as well as recurrent images of void, emptiness, and hollowness, all of which successfully create an atmosphere of great loss. "The light from the lamp was choked," "the sun was strangled by the narrow evening," "the long, lonely bare trees," the shadows and whisperings all contribute to that total effect of death.

In a variation on the theme, a few years later, Idrīs in his latest collection *Bayt min Laḥm* (*A House of Flesh*), in the story entitled **"Al-Riḥla"** (**"The Journey"**) we see a more complex treatment. In this story Idrīs is very clearly dealing with Freud's myth of the rebellion of the sons against the father. The internal monologue is used throughout the story, revealing the subconscious of a son transporting his dead father seated next to him in his car as if alive, across the city. This "journey" of death is also one of life. The son re-examines the eternal father/son relationship in its mythical dimensions. At first, the death of his father appears to him as a liberation from paternal despotism: "Either my life, or your death. . . . You must end, so that I may begin."[4] Here Idrīs is dealing with the archetypal pattern of father/son relationship. "You would I were you, I would you were I." The interchanging of roles, "The King is dead, Long live the King," is an aspect extensively used in this story. On the other hand, we also get the traditional filial love, pain, and sorrow at the loss of the father, the sense of the superego.

Here both the form and content of the story combine to create and enact the theme: the journey of death, death in general, and the particular death of the old, the father, the paternal power, travel side by side with the successor, the continuation of life, the refutation of death:

> And I left you, on purpose I left you on the road, I left you in the car, alone, the car as your grave, and I continue the journey alone on foot, grieving at the separation, but, and this is what is painful, happy to be rid of you, happy to have left you, and the car to you . . . breathing air, the fresh air which doesn't have this cursed, dear smell . . . your smell.

> (p. 80)

In this story written in June of 1970 and published a year later we can clearly see a different approach to the subject matter from earlier treatments. Here Idrīs is preoccupied with a suprahistorical archetype, the primal father ousted and overthrown by the son. He succeeds in presenting this myth in the modern, everyday language of a Cairene businessman driving his dead father from one end of the city to the other, trying to avoid red lights and questions by the traffic officers along the way. Like Joyce in *Dubliners,* Idrīs places his stories in the city; in the story "The Dead" the protagonist Gabriel Conroy is exposed to death, and consequently achieves a new vision of himself. In both stories the main characters retire to contemplate the universality of death, death which has liberated them.

Joyce deals with death from different angles of vision. In "The Sisters," death has not had its anticipated effect on the boy, for he becomes aware of life rather than death, of sunlight drowning the candlelight, and the odor of flowers overpowering the smell of death. On the other hand, the old priest loosely holding in death a chalice that he could not hold in life, or dribbling snuff down a cassock, is not mystical priesthood, but its pathetic reality. To the boy the death of the priest has meant the death of religion in him; the national myth of the perfection of the priesthood has been forever damaged in his mind. The motif of paternal authority simultaneously rejected and desired is taken up time and again in both Joyce and Idrīs.

In the collection entitled *Ḥādithat Sharaf* (*Incident Involving Honor*), Idrīs gives us several variations on the theme. The story **"Shaykhūkha Bidūn Junūn"** (**"Died of Old Age: No Proof of Insanity"**) is a poignantly touching plea for the unwanted and unclaimed of this earth. Idrīs is here drawing on his earlier career as public health doctor, which provided him with a wealth of experience from which he frequently draws material for his fiction. In this story he treats death as a daily reality, a routine that flows simultaneously with life. The doctor, who narrates the story, strikes the tone saying, "On such a morning 'Amm Muḥammad[5] died . . . that same morning I started my day by signing birth certificates."[6] In bitter tones he proceeds to tell us of the red tape involved in bureaucratic procedures for the dead. "For the dead too, have a world of their own." 'Amm Muḥammad, now dead, suddenly acquires great importance in the eyes of the administration. While no one was ever aware of his sorry existence all those long years when he was alive, now they are reluctant to let him go to his final abode, to some peace at last. For 'Amm Muḥammad, ironically, all through his life dealt with death. He was an undertaker, who made a living from the dead, who was himself a precursor of death, who did not speak but rather croaked through his dried-out vocal chords. Death to 'Amm Muḥammad was, in effect, his familiar ambience, where he felt most comfortable. He had become such an expert that he often would volunteer to save the doctor a trip to the death-bed of some wretched creature in some God-forsaken alley of the old city and would himself verify whether the cause of death was natural or otherwise. Then the doctor would authorize burial and sign the death certificate. 'Amm Muḥammad, that illiterate practitioner, had won the love and confidence of all those around him, especially the doctor who that morning discovered that he had permanently lost his friend. He was to sign his death certificate to certify that 'Amm Muḥammad had died of old age and had shown no sign of insanity. The undertaker, known for his sagacity amongst his colleagues, today was under a shadow of doubt, just because the law had to be satisfied and reassured that he died sane. Idrīs is extremely cynical about the situation and is vigorous in condemning the state of things. The simple facts are turned into a highly charged story. His characters, an undertaker and a doctor, are well chosen to investigate the subject of death. The story may not have a plot in the traditional sense but does rotate around the axis of death. It is an impressionistic rendition of a state, the doctor's reckoning with death when it strikes someone close. He somehow had always taken 'Amm Muḥammad for granted, had never thought of the possibility of his death. Then one day after signing a series of birth certificates, he is confronted with the fact that his companion now needs his signature to finally go. His confrontation this time with death has a real meaning. It is not a faceless, lifeless corpse, but a being he had known well and worked with, and even grew to like and cherish—a reality. Idrīs succeeds in making out of this simple fact an impressive, moving moment. He goes further and makes the story a forum from which he condemns this *condition humaine* which is merciless towards its own. Like Docteur Rieux in Albert Camus' *La Peste,* the doctor here is simply recording facts in a cold, detached manner. He is not making any moral judgments, at least not outright. With Rieux he sides with the unwanted, the unclaimed, the plagued. He also realizes that we all are carriers of the plague of death, but we never stop to take stock of that reality. Like Camus, Idrīs is here dealing with death as the inevitable fact of life which we have to face daily and come to grips with. They both treat their subject matter with detachment. They both are giving a deliberate impression of uninvolvement but being in fact totally committed to showing and exposing the wounds of a wretched humanity. Idrīs in his stories deals therefore with the plight of man in an absurd world. The plight of the doctor is as poignant as a Meursault's realization of the absurdity of man's lot; in both cases resulting from their awareness of their mortality. For as Camus points out in *Le Mythe de Sisyphe,* we are all calculated, as it were, by "the bloodstained mathematics which dominate the human lot." The doctor in Idrīs's story, like Camus' heroes, is the everyday man who before his discovery of the absurd, had hopes and ambitions and the belief that he was free to order his life; he comes to realize however, that all that he had believed is disproved in one sweep of the absurdity of death. "What is absurd," writes Camus, is "the clash between its irrationality and the desperate hunger for clarity which cries out in man's deepest soul:"

> Mais ce qui est absurde, c'est la confrontation de cet irrationel et de ce désir éperdu de clarté dont l'appel résonne au plus profond de l'homme. L'absurde dépend autant de l'homme que du monde.[7]

The absurd also results from the conflict between our awareness of death and our desire for life, from the clash between our demand for explanation and the essential mystery of all existence.

"Al-Ma'tam" (**"The Funeral"**) in the collection *Arkhas Layālī* (*Cheapest Nights*) is another short story with vitriolic overtones. This time it is an undertaker who stands bargaining with the neighborhood shaykh over the number of funeral "services" the latter has performed. Abū al-Mitwallī insists that he had brought over only seven dead infants whereas the miserable shaykh insists that there were eight. Haggling over the difference of a few piasters and a few more "ardent" prayers, Idrīs launches his bitter attack and denounces a state of things that reduces life to such paltry dimensions. Abū al-Mitwallī reminds the shaykh that summer is at hand and soon the number of casualties will rise and he will have a handsome revenue. Here again the juxtaposition of life and death is highly effective. While the shaykh mumbles the prayers that will carry the soul of that suckling babe straight to heaven, the undertaker entertains himself by watching life go on in the streets. He quenches his thirst with some refreshing drink while making sure that the shaykh is not cheating on the number of "right" prayers. Idrīs's characterization of both the money-grubbing shaykh and the pragmatic unemotional undertaker is given with extreme economy. He neither condemns nor disdains those two otherwise contemptible characters. With the inquisitive eye of a camera zooming in on its objective, Idrīs captures indicative and revealing moments:

> And shaykh Muḥammad hesitated, while his hand opened and then closed (on the five piasters note), and he placed his faith in God, and felt the five piasters and his head disappeared in his old cassock . . .[8]

While he peered through "his clouded eyes" and asked for an extra piaster he decided to be less exigent, but Abū al-Mitwallī snatched his little bundle and disappeared in the bustling crowds. Here the callousness and the greed of the two characters invites our compassion rather than contempt. Their misery and destitution somehow justify their behavior. Idrīs seems to say that wretchedness begets wretchedness, misery lives off misery; here the author is condemning a human condition which makes such misery possible. Again his choice of character, incident, and setting, as well as his narrative technique, all contribute in the effective treatment of the theme. Again Idrīs sides with existential man, with the here and the now.

In **"Jumhūriyyat Faraḥāt,"** a story of the same collection, we move toward a more symbolic treatment of the theme of death. Here we "live" a state of confinement, and we go through a dantesque experience of death. Events take place in a police station, a drab, gloomy place which gradually metamorphoses before our eyes into an Inferno inhabited by *'afārīt*,[9] and wrongdoers and sinners of all kinds.

The police station, a dimly lit sullen hall of judgment, is governed by Faraḥāt and his *'afārīt*. Faraḥāt is described as being old and decrepit, "sealed in his red tarbuush (fez)." His job is to write by hand reports in duplicate of each and every case that occurs in his precinct. An eerie atmosphere permeates the whole story through the light imagery, the absurd dialogues, and hovering spirits of death. The scant light that escapes the oil lamp is more of a protective veil than any attempt to dispel darkness. The shadows formed by it are like faceless creatures prancing around the place. Objects suddenly become alive, the rifles standing against the walls are hollow eyes peering into a vacuum. Words uttered are like "whips" lashing in the darkness. In this underworld atmosphere Faraḥāt has to sit in an everlasting posture, listening and recording accusations, lies, allegations, and grievances of all kinds; in short, all the ugliness, injustices, and breaches of faith of humanity. This garishness is relieved as it were for a brief moment by a "dream" which lasts only momentarily. So Faraḥāt dreams of an ideal world where order, justice, harmony, and above all logic will reign. But he very quickly realizes that it is only wishful thinking, for he has to face his reality of utter sordidness.

The story is given through the point of view of a narrator who happens to be taken by some mistake to the police station. He is thus a spectator witnessing events and incidents, yet definitely a participator and creator; for it is through him that we are immersed in that atmosphere. We may deduce that the vision is not a totally pessimistic one, if we consider the "hope" in the dream as being a possibility of an orderly, harmonious world. but the dream never materializes and thus remains a fantasy. The choice of the name "Faraḥāt," connoting joy or happiness, constitutes a built-in irony which enhances the point of the story.

Notes

1. Idrīs, "Al-Shaykh Shaykha," in *'Ākhir al-Dunyā* (Cairo: Mu'asasat Ruz al-Yūsuf, 1961), 390.

2. Axel Olrick, "Epic Laws of Folk Narrative," *Form in Folklore,* vol. 51 (n.p.: 1909), 1-2.

3. Yūsuf Idrīs, "Al yadd al-Kabīra," from *Ḥadithat Sharaf,* in *Al-Mu'allafāt-al-Kāmila* (Cairo: 'Ālam al-Kutub, 1971), 73.

4. Idrīs, "Al-Riḥla," in *Bayt min Laḥm* (Cairo: 'Ālam al-Kutub, 1971), 79.

5. 'Amm: term of respect used for the elderly; literally means "uncle," a regionalism, in certain cases used in the same manner as the French "le père Michel," etc.

6. Idrīs, "Shaykhūkha Bidūn Junūn" in *Ḥādithat Sharaf*, 28.

7. Camus, *Le Mythe de Sisyphe* (Paris: Gallimard, 1942), 37.

8. Idrīs, "Al-Ma'tam," in *Arkhaṣ Layālī* (2d ed.; Cairo: Dār Al-Kātib al-'arabī, 1967), 146.

9. 'Afrīt (plural: 'afārīt): An evil spirit of the dead who maliciously returns to the world of the living to unnerve mortals, or to seek revenge. Here the policemen clad in black are the 'afārīt—ghostlike figures.

John M. Crofoot (essay date April 1992)

SOURCE: Crofoot, John M. "Rhythms of the Body, Rhythms of the Text: Three Short Stories by Yusuf Idris." *The Turkish Studies Association Bulletin* 16, no. 1 (April 1992): 34-6.

[*In the following essay, Crofoot argues that by examining the rhythm of three Idris stories—"Summer's Night," "Daood," and "Sunset March"—illustrates "how consciousness or a sense of self depends on the interplay of the body and discourse."*]

This paper is part of a larger work in progress on narrative rhythm and community formation in works by Ahmet Mithat, Yusuf Idris, Kateb Yacine and Muhammad Barrada. Each of the stories in the present discussion explores the formation of a community through process involving rhythm. **"Summer's Night"** treats transformations in a group of adolescent boys; **"Daood"** deals with the parallels between feline and human reproductive cycles; and **"Sunset March"** presents a performance in which a juice vendor becomes an artist. Examination of rhythm in these stories shows how consciousness or a sense of self depends on the interplay of the body and discourse.

The analytical method of the study concentrates on alternations of register, voice and setting as keys to narrative rhythm. Bakhtin discusses alternation in the terms of dialogism, i.e., the intermingling of social classes, linguistic registers and literary genres in a single work. Genette outlines a narratological method for analyzing the alternations in temporal order, spatial setting, tempos of narration, etc. Combining these discussions of

alternation with Arab critics' assessments of rhythm in phrase structure and Chernoff's study of African musical rhythms, I devise an approach that designates the bases of narrative rhythm. Drawing on theories of reading (Iser, Valdes, Fish, etc.,), I demonstrate how rhythm at once structures the reading process *and* requires the reader to participate in the enactment of the text.

In **"Summer's Night"** a group of adolescent boys gathers on a haystack outside their village to talk of themselves, their bodies and their sexual fantasies. Idris's use of succinct, repetitive phrase structure in both narration and dialogue brings the reader to participate in the same cadences through which the boys establish a pact of confidence with each other. In the opening, the reader encounters the rhythmic techniques of repetition, syntactical patterning and punctuation: *al-'ashâ walâ, wa-al-tibn bârid, wa-kûmatuhu 'âliyya, wa-al-dunyâ layl, layl mufaddad . . .* (The evening is over, and the hay is cold, and its mass is high, and the world is darkness, a silvery darkness . . .) The ubiquitous commas require pauses and ensure the cadence of the reader's silent yet vocal enactment of a written text.

Idris alternates back and forth between the registers of standard and Egyptian colloquial Arabic. The linguistic shift occurs most frequently in the movement from diegetic narration to mimetic dialogue and contributes to the broader rhythms of narrative structure. Within passages of colloquial dialogue, alternation, repetition and patterning continue the rhythms of reader enactment. In a litany of the storytelling pact of confidence, the alternation of antiphonal voices repeats succinct oaths of secrecy. While the representation of performative dialogue portrays the way friends establish a sense of group solidarity, the reader not only witnesses the scene but participates in the pact through reenactment of the cadences of the stylized mimetic passage. Thus, the reader and the adolescent group are subject to the same discourse, and the reader eagerly anticipates the subsequent act of storytelling just as the boys do. Sensuality is a prevalent theme in **"Summer's Night"** and in much of Idris's writing. Sensuality is also a consequence of Idris's prose style, for the rhythms of the text extend to the discursive engagement of the reader.

In **"Daood,"** linguistic sensuality underscores the physiological bases of communication. This story depicts repetitive cycles in the body as the constitutive aspect of a family of three members: wife, father and cat. The familial bonds are affirmed through the common gender and reproductive function shared by cat and mother and the proto-linguistic dialogue between cat and husband. The cat's newborn kittens are thought to pose a rivalry for survival with the wife's infant. When the husband goes to get rid of the kittens, he is powerless until his body completes a dialogical progression from heartbeat, to fear, to reflex, and finally to conscious, willful action. Ironically, the cat responds to his declaration of "scat" with "spitting." The irony draws attention to the interconnection of body, consciousness and communication in discourse—discourse which is more than "linguistic." While the entire passage is narrative diegesis, each bodily movement is retold succinctly in a separate line as a reply in a dialogue. This format underscores the process of rhythmic alternation, where the body's internal dialogue gives rise to language and consciousness, just as for Kristeva biological drives are the basis of semiosis.

Through textual rhythm, Idris links the sensual being of his readers with that of his characters, thus forming a community among his readers and the characters. This process of reader-affiliation with the social space projected in the narrative has the potential to reform the reader's consciousness of his or her relation to society. In **"Sunset March"** such a change in consciousness and identity takes place through performance. Frustrated by the pedestrians' lack of interest in his drink, the vendor, dancing and singing, strikes a groove with his castanets. Performance enables the juice vendor to become an ascetic artist. Idris portrays rhythm here as a bodily movement that leads to a different function of the individual in relation to the social environment.

In Western literary theory, the concept of prose rhythm encompasses familiar narrative operations such as *leitmotif,* polyphony, chronology and syntactical patterning. However, none of these terms adequately describes the complex interconnection of operations in the performance of narrative. My analysis of rhythm in Middle Eastern narrative goes beyond this conceptual limitation of Western theory. By analyzing the thematic and technical uses of rhythm in these three stories, it is possible to advance a hypothesis about the relation between structural patterning and the process of reading. The merger of textual and corporeal rhythms in the reader's performance of narrative brings the reader into the text's discursive domain and interpretive community. Rhythm reflects the continued influence of oral storytelling on written narrative and the importance of audience participation in the enactment and dissemination of texts in cultural economies where access to written texts is still limited.

Sasson Somekh (essay date 1993)

SOURCE: Somekh, Sasson. "Structure of Silence: A Reading in Yûsuf Idrîs's 'Bayt min Lahm' ('House of Flesh')." *Writer, Culture, Text: Studies in Modern Arabic Literature* (1993): 56-61.

[*In the following essay, Somekh explores how silence plays a key structural role in "House of Flesh."*]

I

In an article published previously,[1] I attempted to demonstrate some of the ways in which rhythm and sound (such as onomatopoeia) are functionally employed in the short stories of the Egyptian writer Yûsuf Idrîs (1927-1992).[2] My contention was that these elements, besides representing voices, human or otherwise, serve as distinct structural devices in many of his stories. The present paper further elaborates on some of these "acoustic" devices, although in this case the absence of sound rather than sound itself is discussed. One of Idrîs's stories in particular illustrates how words and phrases denoting "silence" play a major structural role in it.

The story in question is **"Bayt min Lahm"** (**"House of Flesh"**).[3] This short story is interesting because rather than being typical it constitutes one of its author's most original works. Indeed, it was translated into several languages,[4] and critics in Egypt and elsewhere have repeatedly commented on it. However, most of these comments pay scant attention to the story's language. Without such attention, the dynamics of the story are overlooked, and any discussion of its thematic foci will probably miss the mark.

II

"House of Flesh" tells the story of a poor widow, fairly young, living with her three unmarried daughters. The daughters prevail upon their mother to marry the blind Koran reciter whom she pays to come to their house once a week to pray for her deceased husband. The marriage takes place, and the young reciter moves in with the four women in their one-room apartment. The mother indulges in the pleasures of marital life. Before long, however, she discovers to her horror, that at least one of her daughters has been slipping into the blind man's bed in her absence. She overcomes her wrath, because she is aware of how frustrated her daughters are. They are ugly and impecunious orphans, and in a society like theirs, they have no chance whatever of marrying. Their need for sex is no less pressing than for food. She therefore tacitly allows them to pursue "the ring game," whereby each daughter, in her turn, wears her mother's wedding ring and enters the marital bed. The blind husband keeps quiet about the matter. He sets about assuring himself that "she who shared his bed was always his wife, all proper and legitimate, the wearer of the ring. Sometimes she grows younger or older, she is soft-skinned or rough, slender or fat—it is solely her concern, the concern of those with sight, it is their responsibility alone in that they possess the boon of knowing things for certain; it is they who are capable of distinguishing, while the most he can do is to doubt, a doubt which cannot become certainty without the boon of sight, and so long as he is deprived of it just so long will he remain deprived of certainty, for he is blind and no moral responsibility attaches to a blind man. Or does it?"[5]

This short outline is sufficient to illustrate the great thematic difference between this story and those written by Idrîs earlier in his career. For one thing, the social ingredient (poverty, low social status), plays only a marginal role here. The main theme of **"House of Flesh"** is clearly not the privation of its characters, but rather the sexual imperatives that transcend social taboos and mores. This thematic axis is evident in many of the author's stories published in the 1960s and the 1970s. Among these stories are: **"The Greatest Sin of All," "Lily, Did you Have to Put the Light On?," "The Siren,"** and **"Rings of Burnished Brass."**[6] Although the sexual dimension was not absent from Idrîs's earlier stories, those written in the 1950s and early 1960s, it was not then portrayed as being above social realities; indeed it was treated within the framework of these realities. At times it was even cloaked in negative terms (for instance in his story **"The Cheapest Nights"** [1954],[7] in which sex is presented in the context of unchecked population growth and destitution). In **"House of Flesh"** and other later stories, Idrîs seems to have developed a different kind of philosophy. On one occasion he formulated his "existentialist" view of sex as follows: "I can say that I write about sex as being part of life. Sex for me equals life. As far as I am concerned, any other significance is invalid . . . Thus, sex does not imply men coming to women and vice versa, but rather the desire of both to plunge deeper and deeper into life and to embrace the continuity of mankind."[8]

III

We shall refer to the thematic aspects of **"House of Flesh"** later in the discussion. But let us first cast a glance at its style and structure, which are also shared by many of Idrîs's "existentialist" stories. The style is far removed from the "prosaic" or "linear" language encountered in the author's earlier stories. It is infinitely more evocative and rhythmic. The rhythm is created by, among other things, a series of recurrent words, phrases, and short sentences that punctuate the entire text. Thus the chain of words *al-khâtim bi-jiwâr al-misbâh, al-samt yahullu fata'mâ al-âdhân, fi al-samt yatasllalu al-'isba', yada'u al-khâtim* (The ring is beside the lamp. Silence reigns and ears are blinded. In the silence the finger slides along and slips on the ring) occurs not only at the beginning of the story, but also towards its end. However, the repetition is not static. In the second occurrence of this four-sentence concatenation, two words (*sâhib al-dawr* [whose turn it is]) are appended to the third sentence indicating that the conspiracy of silence has engulfed all five of the story's protagonists, or at least its four feminine characters. The same applies to the clause *wa al-baytu hujrah* (and the house is

but a room), appearing at the beginning of the story and repeated towards its end, giving the other occurrences of the word *hujrah* (as well as *bayt* and *dâr*, both meaning "house") an added sense of narrowness, at once cramped and cozy.

The textual composition of **"House of Flesh"** is circular. This time-structure enhances the rhythmic quality of the verbal texture. Furthermore, the story itself contains several explicit references to the recurrence of events and words, such as: *sawtu al-tilâwati yatasâ'du fi rûtîn la jiddatah fîhî* (the sound rises up, with dull, unimpassioned monotony) or: *Bi al-ta'awwud yajî bi al-ta'awwud yaqra', wa-bi al-'âdati yamdî* [By habit he comes, by habit he recites, by habit he takes himself off].

IV

By far the most conspicuous case of reiteration is that of the word *samt* (silence) and its derivatives, as well as other items denoting silence. *Samt* occurs as many as forty-three times in this very short story. As the story evolves, "silence" acquires a variety of connotations, giving the entire text its special flavor and meaning.

The opening section of the text (i.e., of the "*sjuzet*"), as we have just seen, is located in a point in time that is different from the beginning of the story (the "fabula"), and we shall come back to it in due course. In the second section, which introduces us to the beginning of the story, the word *samt* denotes mourning and desolation. Even the weekly visits of the Koran reciter do not constitute a true interruption of that silence. Then it is "like silence broken by silence" (*qat'al-samt bi al-samt*).

However, when the reciter disappears from the house after his arrangement with the woman ends, the four women realize that, in fact, "it was not merely that his was the only voice that broke the silence, but that he was the only man, be it only once a week, who knocked at the door." Here we have the first occurrence of the word "silence" side by side with the word "man," foreshadowing some ensuing correlation between the two.

After the marriage of the mother and the blind man, we discover that silence has vanished (*al-samt talâshâ*, repeated twice). The *man* (and, of course, sex) has turned the mourning, despairing widow into a boisterously happy wife. But no sooner does she discover that one of her daughters has sinned with her blind husband than she is once again engulfed in total *silence*. This time, silence is to be attributed to a combination of horror, shame, confusion, and helplessness. Before long, however, the sinning daughters in turn, also become silent. Theirs is, conceivably, a silence indicating sin and shame. The only one who remains noisy is the blind husband. But at some point he senses what is happening, and he too joins the ranks of the silent. His silence is that of connivance, but probably also the outcome of his fear that the "house of flesh" might fall into ruin if silence does not reign.

To return now to the opening paragraph, describing as it does the state of affairs in the house *after* the "conspiracy of silence" has become all-pervasive, we read the following: "Silence reigns and the ears are blinded." Silence now represents the essence of the life of a community that practices incest and, in fact, delights in it. Silence is sex emancipated from social, moral, or religious shackles. The women's ears are "blinded" so as not to hamper the blind man in his industry of ecstasy.[9]

"Silence," then, signifies in our text a variety of situations and thematic foci. At each stage of the story the word *samt* and its derivatives reflect a different set of meanings, relating sometimes to one of the protagonists, sometimes to the whole "commune." "Silence" thus becomes a key structural device, encompassing a whole range of relationships (character-character; character-situation; situation-situation), determining the configuration of the entire text as well as its thematic bearings.

V

It is to be emphasized that in the context of the story, *samt* is not merely a lexical term denoting silence. It has been transformed into an "acoustic" word in the sense that it denotes absolutely no noise. In other words, **"House of Flesh,"** along with many other stories by its author, is a text in which an acoustic signifier is employed as a major structural element. Furthermore, it is in the nature of things that silence is, physically speaking, of one variety, while noise is multifarious. Languages, including Arabic, have therefore devised a plethora of words, onomatopoeic or otherwise, to represent different noises. In those stories in which positive acoustic elements are instrumental in indicating different psychological stages (e.g., **"Mârsh al-Ghurûb"** (**"Sunset March"**[10] or **"Al-Umniyyah"** [**"The Wish"**]),[11] Idrîs was able to employ an astonishing array of words, connotations, and similes to indicate these different stages. In **"House of Flesh"** too, such "acoustic" terms are in evidence, although to a considerably lesser extent than *samt*. Futhermore, the former do not function as cardinal motivators of the story. Their main function is contrastive, in other words they are employed to enhance the word *samt* in several sections of the story by occasionally providing one or more of its antonyms. In the first stage of "silence," for instance, the main sound figuring in the text is that of knocking (on the door). Two expressions are used with this meaning: *daqq al-bâb* and *naqr al-bâb*. "Knocking" refers twice to the actual knocking on the door of the little house by the blind man upon arriving to perform his

Koran recitation. The third occurrence of a "knocking" expression is used metaphorically, but here too it is related to marriage: *wa man al-majnûn alladhî yaduqqu bâb al-faqîrât al-qabîhât, wa bi al-dhât idhâ kunna yatîmât* (and what madman would knock at the door of the poor and ugly, particularly if they happen to be orphans [1]). In all these cases, the noise in question connotes the possibility (or impossibility) of terminating the silence through the appearance of men. Other sounds that occur before the blind man's joining the family are those of *tilâwah* (recital) and *anfâs . . . 'amîqât al-shahîq* (breathing . . . deeply drawn) on the part of the deprived daughters.

After the marriage takes place and silence is temporarily dispelled, the text, relating the advent of cheerfulness, is studded with "acoustic" words and collocations. "Silence vanished, as though never to return, and the clamour of life pervaded the place" (4). The daughters are amazed to hear their mother's loud laughter and womanly guffaws (*sakhsakhât imra' ah*), especially during and after sex, practiced by the married couple at night in the small room in which the daughters also sleep. Noises also emanate from the blind man. He cracks jokes and sings, imitating such popular singers as Umm Kulthûm and 'Abd al-Wahhâb. His voice is loud, raucous with happiness, booming (*sawtuhu 'âlin, ajashshu bi al-sa'âdah yula'li'*). Among the other words describing his noisy happiness mention should be made of nouns and verbs derived from *sakhab* (three times) and *dajjah*. The daughters are ostensibly happy for their mother, hoping indeed, that the laughter of their stepfather will attract men, for "men are bait for men." Nevertheless, their true feelings are represented at this stage, namely immediately after their mother's marriage, with onomatopoieac words and similies connoting suppressed sexual yearning: "[Their] disturbed breathing changes into a hissing sound (*fahîh*), a hissing like the scorching heat spat out by thirsty earth. The lump in the throat (*gussah*) sinks down deeper, becomes stuck. What she hears is the breathing of the famished . . . They are all famished; all scream and groan (*tasrukh wa ta'inn*), and the moaning breathes not with breathing but perhaps with shouts for help (*istijârat*) . . ." (5). In the third stage, the four women are silent, while the man is still noisy. This stage comes to its end when he too falls silent upon becoming cognizant of the peculiar silence of the women.

The interplay of silence and noise in our story can be summed up as follows:

Stage	Mother	Daughters	Blind Man	Situation
1	*silence*	*silence*	reciting, tapping	mourning
2	noise	"hissing"	noise	marital joy
3	*silence*	*silence*	noise	horror/conspiracy
4	*silence*	*silence*	*silence*	house of flesh

It is only when total silence reigns that a kind of harmony is achieved. The house of flesh withdraws into itself to celebrate, in silence, the victory of sex over a host of worldly concerns.

Notes

1. Sasson Somekh, "The Function of Sound in the Stories of Yûsuf Idrîs," *Journal of Arabic Literature* 16 (1985): 95-104; *Genre and Language in Modern Arabic Literature* (Wiesbaden: Harrassowitz, 1991) 83-91.

2. On Yûsuf Idrîs and his works see: P. M. Kupershock, *The Stories of Yûsuf Idrîs: A Modern Egyptian Author* (Leiden: Brill, 1981); Sasson Somekh, *Dunyâ Yûsuf Idrîs min khilâl Aqâsîsihi,* (Tel Aviv: 1976), 3-29. For a list of critical works discussing Idrîs's stories see Kupershoek, 208-15; see also the special Idrîs issue of the Cairo monthly *Adab wa Naqd 'Alam al-Kutub* (Dec. 1987): 152-215 (a bibliography prepared by Hamdi al-Sakkut and Marsden Jones).

3. Appearing in Idrîs's book *Bayt min Lahm* (Cairo, 1971) 5-13.

4. At least two translations of "House of Flesh" are available in English: by Denys Johnson-Davies in his *Egyptian Short Stories* (London: Heinemann, 1978) 1-7; and by Mona Mikhail in Roger Allen (ed.), *In the Eye of the Beholder: Tales of Egyptian Life from the Writings of Yûsuf Idrîs* (Minneapolis and Chicago: Bibliotheca Islamica, 1978) 191-98. The quotations in this article are from Johnson-Davies's excellent translation. Numbers placed after English quotations refer to Johnson-Davies's anthology.

5. *Bayt min Lahm,* 166; Denys Johnson-Davies's translation, p. 7. The words "no moral responsibility is attached to a blind man" are a rendering of *wa laysa 'alâ al-a'mâ haraj,* an explicit reference to the Koran, *Surat al-nûr,* 61. But while the word *haraj* in our text retains its basic koranic undertones (prohibition, legal or moral), it also carries the weight of its usage in modern Arabic denoting "embarrassment" or "objection." This is an excellent example of Idrîs's simultaneous evocation of the different levels of meaning, especially in words drawn from the classical inventory.

6. The first two stories (titles "Akbar al-Kabâ'ir" and "Akân Lâ budd yâ Lîlî an Tudî'î al-Nûr?") appear in *Bayt min Lahm* (Cairo: 1971), and their English translation can be found in Roger Allen's anthology; the last two ("al-Naddâhah" and "Halaqât al-Nuhâs al-Nâ'imah") appear in *Mashûq al-Hams,* Beirut: Dâr al-Talî'ah, 1970, and their translation is included in Catherine Cobham's anthology, Yûsuf Idrîs, *Rings of Burnished Brass,* (London: Heinemann, 1984) 99-122 and 123-42.

7. This is the title-story of Idrîs's first book, published in Cairo in 1954; its English translation can be found in Wadida Wassef's anthology, *The Cheapest Nights and Other Stories* (London: Peter Owen, 1978) 1-6.

8. Quoted from Roger Allen's introduction to his anthology, xx-xxi; originally published as a part of an interview in the Beirut quarterly *Mawâqif* 9 (April-June 1970): 51 ff.

9. The four stages or situations stipulated here in conjunction with *samt,* namely: mourning→joy→ horror/conspiracy→house of flesh (see section V), tally with the four-tier pattern that I discerned in other stories of Idrîs, including "Mârsh al-Ghurûb" (Sunset Marsh), "al-'Askarî al-Aswad" (The Black Policeman) and "Qâ'al-Madînah" (City Dregs); see my article in *Journal of Arabic Literature* 16 (1985): 98, 101, 102-03. It is remarkable that Idrîs himself often uses the number "four" conspicuously in some of his stories. Note the titles of such stories as "al-Hâlah al-Râbi'ah" (Case No. Four), in *Alaysa Kadhâlik* 1957), and "Qissah fî Arba'at Murabba'ât: Halaqât al-Nuhâs al-Nâ'imah" (A Story in Four Squares: Rings of Burnished Brass), in *Mashûq al-Hams,* 1971; English translation in Cobham's anthology, 123-42.

10. See the preceding footnote. An English translation of this story by Roger Allen was published in *Journal of Arabic Literature* 16 (1985): 92-94.

11. Originally published in *Arkhas Layâlî,* 1954. For a discussion of its acoustic elements, see: Sasson Somekh, *Lughat al-Qissah fî Adab Yûsuf Idrîs* (Tel Aviv: Tel Aviv University, 1984) 25-26.

Rasheed El-Enany (essay date 1997)

SOURCE: El-Enany, Rasheed. "The Western Encounter in the Works of Yusuf Idris." *Research in African Literatures,* 28, no. 3 (fall 1997): 33-55.

[*In the following essay, El-Enany examines the East-West theme in two Idris stories, "Madame Vienna" and* New York 80 *in order to discuss his "preoccupation with this theme at various stages in his career."*]

The theme of the Arab in Europe, with all its cultural implications, is one that has found expression in Arabic fiction from a relatively early period in the evolution of the genre. The earliest mature attempts at treating the subject were those made by Tawfiq al-Hakim and Yahya Haqqi in *'Usfur min al-sharq* (1938; trans. as *A Bird from the East*) and *Qindil 'Umm Hashim* (1944; trans. as *'Umm Hashim's Lamp*), respectively. Since the appearance of these two Egyptian works, which more or less established the theme in Arabic fiction, fresh approaches to it by later Egyptian and other Arab writers have not ceased.[1] To this theme Yusuf Idris has made two major contributions in the form of two long short stories separated by a time gap of some twenty years. The first is **"Al-Sayyida Vienna"** (**"Madame Vienna"**),[2] first published in 1959, and the second is *New York 80,* published in 1981.[3] I shall attempt here to describe Idris's attitude to the cultural encounter as it emanates from the two works, as well as the techniques he uses to render it. I shall also attempt to examine whether the twenty-year gap between the stories and the change of setting from Europe to America has served to modify the author's vision in any way. Having done that, I shall then proceed to deal with a number of other stories by the author some of which may not fit neatly with the two already mentioned, nor indeed with the general norms of the fictional tradition in Arabic dealing with the East-West theme, but which, nevertheless, represent in their own right further demonstrations of Idris's continuing preoccupation with this theme at various stages in his career.

In common with both earlier and subsequent treatments of the theme, Idris portrays the cultural issue in both stories in terms of a sexual encounter between a male Egyptian and a female Westerner. In **"Madame Vienna,"** however, Idris digresses from the near consensus in the genre that allocates these roles to the intellectual class, the Arab being almost always a student sent to study abroad, with the European often being a fellow student. Here, Idris, while sticking to the middle class, presents the encounter in terms more raw and basic, by making his Egyptian protagonist, Darsh, a minor civil servant on a few days' official mission in Europe, while giving the woman a small secretarial job in some company. These, then, are fairly ordinary representatives of their respective cultures, lacking the knowledge and sophistication of intellectuals—even their knowledge of English, the language through which they communicate, is fairly basic. This fact, while broadening the scope of any conclusions about the cultural encounter drawn from the story, helps throughout against turning what is a very lively and self-sustaining story into an allegorical situation bedraggled with intellectual juxtapositions and lengthy discussions, as happens, for instance, in al-Hakim's treatment of the subject.

Darsh, a married man, father, and great womanizer all his life, is tired of the women of his country. He may have been sent to Europe on an official mission, but he had only one personal motive: "to try a European woman . . ." (77). The cultural dimension to his sexual curiosity is hinted at in his definition of his personal mission as that of "conquering Europe, the woman" (79). As he roams the streets of Vienna, he is dazzled by the beauty and variety of Austrian women in whom

"the spirit of Europe is concentrated" (80). But Darsh is not just after any European woman—he is adamant not to have anything to do with street girls. He wants the encounter to be "with a true European lady of character, who wants him, and not his money, and who would give him herself of her own free will . . ." (86). It is more than sexual knowledge, then, that he is after; he is after knowledge of the European "other." And when American sailors suddenly flood the streets, he fears no competition because he knows they are after "the frivolous Europe," whereas he is looking for "Europe, the lady" (87).[4]

After many failed attempts, Darsh manages in the nick of time, on his last night in Vienna, to make the contact he had so much feared he would have to go back without. His persistence, daring, humor, and past expertise in female conquests pay off when he chats up a beautiful and respectable woman on her way home after a long day's work and an evening at the opera with friends. Like him she is married and has children, though her husband is briefly away on business. Throughout, Darsh maintains a tentative approach toward the woman and is not quite sure how to handle her. As he puts it, "his brain has nearly exploded with bewilderment" on her account: "Is she a devil or an angel? Naive or cunning? Is she making fun of him or has she really fallen for him?" (126). Her neutral smile puzzles him and the way she shakes her head could mean "yes" as much as "no" (127). All these seemingly innocent details appear to be spontaneously coded with a reflection of the historical suspicion and uncertainty that characterize the attitude of East towards West. On the other hand, when he holds her tightly and kisses her for the first time, she groans, "You are going to break my back, African!" (127), addressing him generically by the name of the different race he belongs to. Nor is it an oversight on the author's part that Darsh never learns her name, nor she his. Each of them is to the other a representative of a whole opposite culture and not just an individual, and it is perhaps to draw attention to this fact that Idris leaves them unknown to each other. Significantly again, he gives his protagonist the name Darsh, which is uniquely Egyptian. The woman, on the other hand, is referred to in the title by the name of the very city whose culture she embodies.

As the situation develops, it transpires that **"Madame Vienna"** was no less curious about the otherness of Darsh than he about hers, nor any less eager to discover him:

> "We here in the West hear a lot about the East, its mystery, its men, and its charm. I have always dreamt of a brown Eastern prince, as a teenager and even as a wife and mother. When I saw you I thought I had found him and that it was a chance in a lifetime. . . ."

(141)

Darsh is thus made aware that her expectations of him are no less than his expectations of her, and is determined "to raise high Africa's head," to use the author's sexually suggestive phrase (146). Idris then develops the situation in such a way as to suggest that our unfounded expectations of the "other," our misconceptions or fanciful ideas about other cultures, can only hamper a genuine encounter.

Through a series of little details and situations, the *reality* of the European woman, and by implication her whole culture, gradually displaces her mythologized image in Darsh's head. When he holds her hand, he experiences a feeling of fellowship with her as he notices "her thin fingers, made strong through hammering at typewriter keys" (129-30). Again, when he enters her apartment, he is struck by its narrowness and the numerous familiar little objects that he can see all over the place. But when he enters the tiny bathroom and spots there an extended washline, like the one used by his wife in their own apartment, and with children's underwear hanging from it, too, he is genuinely shocked, and he asks himself the seemingly naive but enormously significant question: "What use is Europe, then, if her people use the same objects as we do?" (144). What shocks Darsh here is the ordinariness, the familiarity, the ultimate similarity of the "other."

On the other hand, when some of his idealized conceptions about the other are proven in reality, he is, ironically, frustrated rather than gratified. When the woman returns his sexual passion with equal panache, he is at first excited: "This is how a woman should be," he tells himself. "In the East, women are like corpses . . . but here when you kiss a woman, she kisses you; you hug her, she hugs you; you take her, she takes you. This is how it should be . . ." (129). But soon enough, he shrinks before her activeness and reciprocality: "Why doesn't she lie submissively and let him do the man's job?" he thinks to himself. "Why can't she be a little shy? Shyness makes a woman more feminine and a man more masculine . . ." (147). So disturbed is he by the very fulfillment of his previous fantasy, he cannot muster an erection. Ironically, it is only when he closes his eyes and begins to fantasize about his own wife that he can function properly.

What is it that Yusuf Idris is saying here? Does he want to say that a culture can only fulfill itself against the "other" through full acceptance of the "self"? This would indeed appear to be his vision, especially if we also take into account the woman's view of things. For after the lovemaking, she picks up her husband's picture and kisses it, admitting to a horrified Darsh that all the time as they made love she had been thinking of him: "I didn't know that he *is* my African man for whom I've been searching," she says (162). Idris here is obviously at pains to appear even-handed, but he is

also underlining his artist's vision. This can perhaps be summed up in the thesis that our misconceptions and exaggerated ideas about another culture stem essentially from the inadequate understanding of our own and that no authentic encounter of cultures is possible without first a full realization of the potential of the self. A perfectly rational vision, admittedly, but beneath its sobriety, there is, I believe, a deep sense of pessimism emphasizing that East is East and West is West and never the twain shall meet, to use Rudyard Kipling's famous phrase.[5]

The ultimate similarity of the other to the self, an idea that comes across clearly in **"Madame Vienna,"** a similarity that is easy to realize once experience and knowledge allow us to penetrate beyond the crust of popular beliefs and exaggerated misconceptions, is further emphasized in an early play by Idris, *Al-Hahza al-harija* (The critical moment), first published in Cairo in 1958,[6] that is, around the same time as **"Madame Vienna."**

The play is set in the Egyptian city of Port Said in the period immediately prior to and during its Anglo-French occupation in the aftermath of Nasser's nationalization of the Suez Canal in 1956. The central character in the play is a young man called Sa'd who enrolls in the popular resistance movement and receives military training in anticipation of the expected attack. The play is centrally concerned with Sa'd's inner conflict. On the one hand he is a devoted nationalist who wants to defend his country, but on the other hand he is afraid of death, a highly likely outcome of the violent confrontation with the invading other. When the "critical moment" arrives, however, Sa'd's father, whose protective instinct toward his son overrides any sense of patriotic duty, locks him up in a room of the house to stop him from going out to join the resistance. Soon after, a British soldier by the name of George forces his way into the house in search of resistance fighters. In the ensuing confusion, he shoots Sa'd's father. Sa'd meanwhile is petrified by fear behind his locked doors, and although he has a gun and could shoot his way through the door and confront the enemy, he quickly changes out of his uniform and hides under the bed. Indeed, we later know that the door lock did not work and that the whole household, including Sa'd, had known this for years. Sa'd chooses to forget this fact because it offers him a way out of the call of duty and the much-feared confrontation with the other.

It is not, however, in Sa'd's predicament that we are interested here, but rather in that of the British soldier, George. Considering the nationalist background to the play, and particularly the fact that it was written shortly after what went down in Arab history books as the Tripartite Aggression, referring to the collusion against Egypt among Britain, France, and Israel, Idris would have been more than excused if he had portrayed the

British soldier in a totally unsympathetic light as an evil aggressor. But he does nothing of the sort. In a conversation between him and another soldier, before attacking the house in act three of the play, George, like Sa'd, is shown to be prone to fear of death and thoughts of cowardice; he too is afraid of confronting the other. Indeed the conversation between him and the other soldier mirrors geometrically an earlier one in act two that took place between Sa'd and a friend of his also in the resistance. This parallelism between scenes is no doubt a technical device intended by the playwright to show the essential human sameness of self and other, even when a particular historical circumstance pitches them in mortal opposition to each other.

Idris sustains his sympathetic attitude toward the British soldier throughout. Even when he kills Sa'd's father, it is out of fear and confusion rather than in cold blood. In his apparent concern to show the sameness of self and other, Idris pushes the situation beyond what is realistically acceptable when he makes George, in his distraught state of mind after the shooting, confuse the wailing young daughter of the dying man with his own Shirley whom he left behind in Southampton and is keen to get back to alive. Although the soldier and the girl do not understand each other's language, the pathos of the situation is shown to transcend language, and the soldier ends up asking the girl for forgiveness. The scene is brought to an end when other British soldiers arrive and carry off their mentally devastated comrade.

Sa'd eventually is released by his young sister from incarceration to confront, as it were, the consequences of his fear of confrontation with the other. The reality of his failure weighs down heavily on him and he tries to blow his own brains out, but again cannot muster enough courage. Meanwhile, George, now totally unhinged, staggers back on stage raving about his daughter, Shirley. This time the confrontation takes place. Sa'd and George fire at each other. Predictably, George is killed and Sa'd, now reconciled to himself, joins the larger battle for the homeland. Given that the essential sameness of self and other is made so much of in the play, and that the British soldier is portrayed in such humane terms, one may be tempted to think that the ending of the play is somewhat forced for patriotic or didactic reasons. But this is not so, to my mind. An essential factor to recollect here is that at no time does communication take place between the British soldier and Sa'd, nor any other member of the family. The barriers of language, fear, and animosity are all too solid for that. The emphasis on the ultimate sameness is thus there only by way of dramatic irony for our benefit, the spectators. A further irony built into this situation is that self and other are hopelessly unaware of their essential similarity, and that while they remain so they can only continue to destroy each other. This is an important aspect of this play, which critics, however, have tended

not to notice in their eagerness, perhaps, to pursue psychological and other themes in the play.[7] **"Madame Vienna"** and *The Critical Moment,* different works as they are, appear to share the same general vision, namely, that although East and West are ultimately similar, they are nevertheless incompatible because of the complexities of history, geography, and human nature.

That Idris means for **"Madame Vienna"** and *New York 80* to be viewed together as his contribution to the subject is evident from his including **"Madame Vienna"** in the same volume as *New York 80* and retitling it **"Vienna 60,"** an obvious attempt to parallel the title of the newer story and to indicate the time gap between the two stories through the titles. As a work of art, *New York 80* is inferior in quality to **"Madame Vienna."** It reads very much like an extended essay juxtaposing the different value systems of the two cultures through, again, a sexual situation. But unlike in the earlier story, the situation has no life of its own and serves only as a thin fictitious apparel to clad the author's thoughts on the subject, which are given through lengthy tracts of dialogue. In fact, the story consists largely of dialogue interspersed with short pieces of narrative. The fact that the story was written in the middle of the last twenty-odd years of the author's life, during which he had mainly expressed himself through the journalistic essay rather than any creative art form, should go perhaps some way towards explaining the poor quality of the story, which is totally uncharacteristic of the work of this great writer.

New York 80 is different in many ways from **"Madame Vienna."** One obvious difference is that it is set in America rather than Europe. America is of course the farthest west part of the West, geographically as well as culturally, in the sense that the harshest and least acceptable values of the West are more poignantly represented by it than by Europe, which is physically nearer to the East and, like it, is part of the Old World. This fact is only tacitly attested to in Idris's treatment of the subject, as he displays in *New York 80* a tone of cultural repulsion and harsh indictment totally absent in **"Madame Vienna."** Again in **"Madame Vienna"** there is an attempt at evoking a sense of place describing with empathy some of the features of the old city and its streets. No such attempt is made in *New York 80,* where the story is set between a public bar and a hotel room that could have been anywhere. This total defacement of the city is itself an unspoken statement reducing it to the set of repugnant values which the story unfolds.

The most important difference between the two stories lies perhaps in the nature of the protagonists in *New York 80.* In **"Madame Vienna"** the encounter, as we have seen, was between a decent working woman with a family who represents "the spirit of Europe" and a typical Egyptian man who represents the East. In the present work, however, the West is represented by a whore who takes great pride in her profession, while the East is represented by the narrator/protagonist who is a professional writer and is evidently a persona for Yusuf Idris himself.[8] As if to ensure intellectual parity between the two characters in the endless arguments they have, Idris qualifies the woman above what is normal for a prostitute, giving her a PhD and making her a psychologist and sex therapist who wilfully chooses prostitution simply because it pays better. One wonders again whether Idris's representation of Europe as a decent ordinary woman and of America as a sophisticated whore is yet another manifestation of the fact that his Eastern man's view of Europe is not identical with that of America.

Another essential difference between the two stories is the reversal of sexual-cum-cultural roles. In **"Madame Vienna"** the initiator of the situation was the Eastern male, though he was soon to meet with a more than enthusiastic response. In *New York 80,* by contrast, it is the call-girl who persistently chases the protagonist to the point of offering to pay him for sex instead of being paid by him. In **"Madame Vienna"** we have seen how Darsh was adamant not to know Europe through a whore. In *New York 80,* the protagonist is equally revolted by the idea of tradeable physical pleasure. His rejection of it, in spite of his evident physical attraction to the woman, is symbolic of a rejection of a materialistic, dehumanized culture where everything can be valued in terms of dollars (e.g., 32, 55). Her judgment of him, and by implication of the culture he stands for, is no less dismissive; she labels him a "child, emotionally and psychologically" (25). She explains to him that a purely physical relationship is evidence of a maturity that he has yet to reach and offers to help him out of what she sees as emotional underdevelopment (32-33). Their polemical exchange ends abruptly when the woman appears to break down under the force of the protagonist's rejection of her and leaves the cafe after making a scene. The end is forced on the story and entirely unconvincing. Throughout, both sides have appeared equally dogmatic about their beliefs and outlook on life and shown themselves to be intellectual peers able to give as much as they take in terms of polemic support for their cultural stances. Thus, although Idris can only have meant us to interpret her eventual collapse as a triumph for the Eastern argument, it does not work. The admirable even-handedness in vision that he had shown in **"Madame Vienna"** is lost here, together with artistic quality. The vision here has no shades of gray at all: the West is all black and the East is all white, and as the encounter, unlike in **"Madame Vienna,"** is never sexually consummated, the previous message that "never the twain shall meet" is even more rudely forced.[9] The question remains: why has the writer's vision been so radicalized in the course of twenty years? Is his rejection of the West total? Or is this harshness of tone reserved for the "new West" (i.e., America), as opposed to the "old West" (i.e., Europe)? During those twenty years, the United States had been politically at loggerheads with progressive regimes in the Arab world, particularly Nasser's Egypt. Could this offer some background explanation, even though *New York 80* deals with a cultural clash and not a political one?

In order to answer this question or at least to examine the extent to which the artist's vision agrees with his explicitly stated views, we need to turn to his vast output of journalism, which comprises no fewer than eleven collections of essays, not to mention uncollected ones, spread over a period of four decades (see *Yusuf Idris: 1927-1991*). But first I will quote, by way of introducing the subject, a key passage from one of the writer's novels that amounts to a direct statement on the issue. The novel concerned is the admittedly autobiographical *Al-Bayda'* (The white woman) written in 1955 but not published until 1970.[10] The passage, reproduced here, is fully quoted in P. M. Kurpershoek's study of the author:

> It was a really confusing situation, but that is the way it was. By nature I was fond of everything European, particularly of European women, why I do not know. On our visits to Ismailia or Port Said, for instance, we noticed the European character of these cities and of the Canal Zone in general: bungalow-style houses with sloping roofs stoves and chimneys; and of course the tidiness, calm and order. Order, so distasteful to us, becomes in their hands an art. The art of order: orderly eating, orderly warfare, orderly loving. It made me feel sad to see those things and deep in my heart I wished that all of us could become like that white, complicated being with its ruddy face. But amazingly enough I never wanted to become a European. I dreamt of possessing their wonderful inventiveness, cleanliness and sense of order, but possessing them myself as an Arab, for I was not prepared to have one single hair of my head changed. Sometimes, when taking part in demonstrations against the British occupation, I noticed to my surprise that I shouted our slogan "Down with England!" with as much rancour and disgust as I admired what I saw of them in Ismailia, Alexandria and Port Said. . . .
>
> (66-67; for the original, see *Al-bayda'* 181-82)

This revealing confession by the protagonist/narrator who is obviously a persona for the author is symptomatic of the ambivalent love-hate or fascination-repugnance sentiment that almost every Arab intellectual has experienced toward the West from the time of al-Jabarti down to the present day. Idris's admiration here is the unqualified one of a young man still in his twenties. It extends from urban planning and architecture down to such qualities as order, cleanliness, and inventiveness. The irony in the situation is that the object of his fascination is a colonial power that he is fighting to eradicate from his country. Another characteristic factor in the relation raised by the passage is that of identity: how to adopt the European way of life and value system while remaining an Arab, or as the author puts it, without having "one single hair of my head changed"—a question that still confounds Arab societies. In the last decade or two, this question has tended to find violent political expression in movements opposed to the process of Westernization, which, in two centuries, does not yet seem to have rooted itself deep enough in the fabric of Arab, and indeed other, Muslim societies.

We can now proceed to review Idris's attitude toward the West and particularly the United States in his polemical writing. In *Iktishaf qarra* (Discovering a continent), an intellectual travelogue written after a tour of some Asian countries and published in 1972, Idris makes a scathing attack on America. Written at the height of America's involvement in Vietnam and against a background of its continuing anti-Arab policies with regard to the Palestinian question, or to put it in more general terms, at the height of the Cold War years when to most Third-World countries America was the symbol of capitalist reaction and neocolonialism working against progressive powers the world over, it is not difficult to understand Idris's anti-American rhetoric. After arguing that the role of European civilization had receded since the Second World War to allow American civilization to come to the fore, he defines the mission and means of that civilization. America's mission is to block the progressive current of history and the means to do that is the technology developed from the European science that America inherited (18-27).

In another anthology of articles, entitled *Al-Irada* (1977) (Will power), several articles are devoted to America. In one of them with the title "The Decision," he talks of conflict and power being the foundation of American society, "the power of money, influence, or guns," and contrasts this with what he describes as the "gentle, easy-going life" of the Egyptians (39). He describes the preparations for heart surgery that he underwent there, and while expressing admiration for American medicine, he laments the industrialization of the treatment process in such a way that dehumanized it and made it comparable to the production line in a car factory. At the end he wonders whether he should not have gone to England instead: "Is England not closer to us and to our nature than those enormous human treatment factories?" (40). This last question should perhaps serve to justify my earlier proposition that Idris's attitude towards Europe is a mellower one than his attitude towards America.

In an article entitled "America 1976," he describes the difficulty he encountered in obtaining a visa to visit the USA. The Consul tells him that he is blacklisted on ac-

count of his anti-American writings, and he uses the occasion to rail at America for being "very democratic with its own citizens but suspicious and dictatorial towards others . . . regarding every revolutionary in the world as an inevitable threat to American security . . ." (82-83). In yet another article, which he titles "America, the Mystery of Modern Times," he again extends a comparison with Europe in which the latter is the favorite: "In European countries you do not see capitalism in its reality. Rather you see it trimmed with state interference . . . but here [in America] you are at the heart of a purely capitalist world . . ." (93). In *'An 'amd isma'tasma'* (Listen intently and you will hear), he includes an article, dated 1974, in which he reviews America's relations with Nasserite and post-Nasserite Egypt and holds the nation responsible for the 1967 war, which he describes as "a war to assassinate 'Abd al-Nasir personally" as a punishment for his nationalist policies (51).

An article written in the 1960s and included in *Jabârtialsittinat* (A Jabarti of the sixties) shows the extent to which Idris could get carried away in his politically motivated polemic. The article entitled "An American Asks: Do We Have Freedom (of Expression)?" denies the existence of press censorship in Egypt and argues that the absence of any criticism of Nasser and his policies does not indicate repression but simply that the whole nation is totally behind him! Indeed, he goes further by arguing that, if anything, Egypt was more democratic than America because for all America's claims of democracy, the massive popular opposition to the Vietnam War did not succeed in stopping it.[11]

In articles written in the eighties, Idris appears to be trying to strike a more balanced attitude towards America, but his sentiment remains basically the same.[12] For once he makes the distinction between state policies and society at large: "What deserves to be fought against in American society," he writes, "is not society itself, but rather the aggressive way in which it is administered so that its enormous advancement is directed toward the repression of the peoples of Latin America and the Middle East and the support of dictators . . ." (*Intiba'at Mustafizza* 10). In another article he argues that America with her wealth and technology is in an ideal position to become a great humanitarian power with a major civilizing role to play in the world. He wonders in a tone of wishful thinking whether America would ever assume that role (22). Meanwhile, however, Idris has no illusions about relations with the West: "We are in a state of confrontation which is in the very least a cultured one." Did he have any counsel for his nation on holding their own in this confrontation? Yes, and that consists in "adopting and assimilating American and European technology, while retaining and strengthening our own spiritual, national, and cultural wealth" (23). The question of identity is obviously uppermost in his thinking here, as it was in the passage quoted from *Al-Bayda'* written almost thirty years earlier. In his writings in that late period one can indeed detect a sense of weariness of the West. "We Arabs," he writes, "have looked up to the West for much longer than we should have . . . our fascination with it approaches the point of sanctification. We still look on what happens in Paris, London, or New York as if they were our emotional and intellectual capitals. The West, on the other hand, has nothing for us except scorn and never thinks of us except to exploit or subjugate us or to deprive us of the last dirhem in our wallets . . ." (*Faqr al-fikr wa fikr al-faqr* 45).

This brief review of Idris's attitude toward the West in his journalism will, if anything, serve to underline the ambivalence of his vision as expressed in his artistic works. The West appears simultaneously attractive and repellent. The fascination with its achievements is counterbalanced by the resentment of its political opposition to Arab national ambitions, while the desire to borrow and learn from it is tempered by an almost paranoid fear for identity. Another factor that becomes clear from the writer's articles is that he keeps his harshest thoughts and words for the United States; he has an empathy with Europe that he never shows in his comments on America.

After such a digression that was necessary to place the author's vision in perspective and to explain the difference in tone between **"Madame Vienna"** and *New York 80,* further artistic treatments of the theme by the author may be considered. Idris's story **"'Akana labudd 'an tudi'i al-nur ya Li-Li?"** (**"Did You Have to Turn on the Light, Li-Li?"**), first published in 1971 in *Bayt min lahm,* falls right in the middle between the earlier **"Madame Vienna"** and the later *New York 80.* At the center of the event in **"Did You . . ."** [**"Did You Have to Turn on the Light, Li-Li?"**] is the seduction of the young Imam of a small back street mosque by a half-Egyptian, half-English cabaret dancer who is something of a prostitute specializing in foreign customers only. This much detail alone is enough to take us some distance on the way to an interpretation of the story along the terms already used in this study: the Imam of a mosque lends himself naturally to a role whereby he can represent traditional culture, whereas the woman with her alluring beauty, foreign name, sinful ways, and, above all, half-Englishness seems a perfect candidate to stand for Western culture. Idris then has stuck here also to the familiar pattern of male representing East, female representing West and the theme being explored through a sexual encounter. The main deviation within this pattern is that rather than taking us to Europe or America, the scene is set in the popular, lower-class quarter of al-Batiniyya in the heart of old Cairo, where the oldness is an ideal background for the interplay of old and new, fixity and mutability, self and other.

Batiniyya is the "den of opium, seconal and hashish," as Idris defines it in his story, and as it has long been known in reality. Its inhabitants are made up largely of drug traffickers and addicts and, according to the Imam/protagonist, their heads are "foggy with dope" even when they come to the mosque to pray (trans. Wadida Wassef 121). The story opens dramatically with a congregation of worshipers performing the dawn prayer at the mosque. The worshipers are in the final stages of the second prostration, with their bodies arched and their foreheads stuck to the ground between their hands. It only remains for the Imam to utter the words "God is the greatest!" for them to sit up, recite the "salutation," and end the prayer. They wait and wait, but the words of the Imam never come. Their heads are still dizzily laden with dope from the previous night, and they are isolated from reality in their uncomfortable prostrate position and unable to raise their heads in order to investigate the matter, as this would annul their prayer; they thus remain stuck in this position. As for how long this prostration continued, the story is uncertain. Two minutes, half an hour, until the noon prayer of the following day—these are some of the various reports given, but most telling of all is the account of "those who insist they are still prostrate to this moment" (122). As the congregation continue in their prostrate position, they each begin to ponder their predicament:

> What exactly should he do now, and what do the laws of religion say with regard to a situation like this? If one of them were to move and raise his head, would that annul his prayer, and possibly that of the entire congregation? And would he alone take the blame?
>
> (123)

The situation is absurd, surrealistic, and very funny indeed, but behind its hilarity is, I believe, a profound hidden indication. Idris is presenting here a metaphor for a community living in a kind of time warp, a community fixed in a time that is past, isolated from reality, and frightened to face it, a community paralyzed under a spell without hope of release. The fact that the community is arrested in a posture of religious worship and that their inability to deal with the situation is entirely due to fastidious jurisprudent considerations is, on a symbolic level, an embodiment of a culture so much inward-looking, so much cocooned from external reality, so much enslaved by its own traditions, its self-generated doubts, its own oldness and incompatibility with any situation at variance with itself and its own predictability.

But what actually happens to the Imam? If one does not forget the title of the story during the first few breathtaking paragraphs, one might guess that the enigmatic silence of the Imam must have something to do with the eponymous Li-Li and her "turning on the light." The suspicion is then strengthened by the subsequent use of the words of the title in the manner of a refrain at certain junctions in the narrative. It is not, however, until the denouement of the story that the feverish narrative, suspense-laden and endlessly delayed by flashbacks and soul-searching by the Imam/narrator, finally yields its secret. The Imam's defenses, long sustained against many temptations in the sin-immersed quarter, collapse dramatically before the sight of Li-Li's semi-naked flesh sprawled on her bed in her deliberately (?) well-lit room in the middle of the night. The window of the room is only across the narrow street on a level with the balcony of the minaret from which the Imam calls for prayer. Li-Li had approached him before with the unusual request of giving her private lessons on how to pray. Conscious of her real motive and steadfast in his resistance to seduction, he dismisses her. But then one day he climbs, in the small hours of the morning, to the minaret's balcony to call the sleeping for the dawn prayer. The sight of her in the manner described above drives the chaste Imam out of his mind. His eyes are nailed to her body and for the first time he understands the extent of his own weakness. The words of the call to prayer turn into a desperate plea to God to come to his help, and in one final act of resistance he descends to the mosque and leads the prayer. He faces the *kibla* and starts the prayer, but before his eyes he can only see Li-Li's naked form, "throbbing, voluptuous, her silken hair fallen in ripples down her sides" (134). He abandons his congregation, prostrate in the middle of the prayer, and steals to the second floor of the house across the way. He knocks on Li-Li's door and tells her that he has come to teach her to pray. "Sorry, I bought the English record that teaches prayer. I found I understand it better" is what she says to him in answer as she "switches off the light" (134).

The irony of the denouement is so powerful. She has led him on only to turn him down the moment he surrenders, and the magnitude of his collapse is matched only by the total indifference of her dismissal of him. Now is the time to go back to our interpretation of the story in cultural terms. If we take the prostrate posture in prayer as a quintessentially representative moment of a traditional, acquiescent, religiously oriented culture, then the Imam's abandonment of prayer at this particular moment before its termination can only be more telling in its symbolic quality as an act of surrender to the promise or allure of a different culture—one more worldly, more earthy, more sensual, i.e., the culture of Western modernity for which Li-Li appears to stand. The author is indeed at pains to stress the "otherness" of Li-Li in spite of her being the daughter of a poor Egyptian woman who conceived her after an amorous night with a British soldier during World War Two. She

is seen by the people of Batiniyya as a *khawagaya*, that is, a European, or foreigner. Her hair is red and her skin milk-white. She drinks alcohol and works as a cabaret dancer with visiting foreign groups. And above all she remains sexually inaccessible though highly desirable to the men of the area who in the end accept that she only sleeps with foreigners. Her seduction of the Imam is then more than what meets the eye on the realistic level, which clearly treats the familiar theme of saint enticed by whore. Any fallen woman of Batiniyya would have sufficed here without being a half-English *khawagaya*, and the story mentions many of them who tried but failed to seduce him.

The seduction of the Imam can then be seen as a cultural one in a symbolic reading of the story. And it is in this context that the interplay of darkness and light in the story may best be understood. The Imam climbs to the balcony of the minaret in the dead of night to be "blinded" by "a window of shining light" (129). The experience is rendered in epiphanic terms:

> I gazed in. One look swept me up like a whirlwind from the *pit* of *somnolence* to the *peak* of *awareness*. An awareness full of terror, as I realized I was facing something wondrous and overwhelming.
>
> (129; emphases added)

The darkness here can be that of ignorance of the self's weakness, of isolation from reality and complacency, all of which are terms that simultaneously apply to the Imam as an individual as well as to the culture he stands for collectively. The epiphanic terms are dictated by the glorious experience of discovering a whole new world. The journey is tellingly described as one from the pit (*qa'*) to the peak (*qimma*) and from somnolence (*ghafwa*) to awareness (*yaqza*)—terms that can adequately, though in a rather generalized way, describe the Arab nation's encounter with Western modernity, which shook it out of medieval "obscurantism." Such experience, again as the passage shows, is as much one of "wonder" as it is one of "terror."

The Imam, however, though totally overpowered by Li-Li's charm, is not unaware of her threat. He sees her as a "snare" (*sharak*) in which he is caught and the very devil who, contrary to common belief, is the very incarnation of beauty (130). He tries hard to ward her off but all he has for a weapon is his voice and the sound of his own plaintive pleas going up to heaven. Face to face with the "devil" in a fight for survival, as he puts it, he dashes into battle armed only with his voice: "The voice is my weapon. I am the voice and the voice is all that is left in my soul. The voice is my only hope . . ." (30; my own trans.)[13] The story, in fact, makes a good deal of his voice. It is a voice whose mellowness, when he reads the Quran or calls to prayer, has become proverbial in the neighborhood—it is his only power of attraction over a community who otherwise care little for him. But the voice is of no avail to him at his hour of trial. And no wonder, for he is the personification of a hollow, verbal culture, enamored of its own vocality and unable to listen beyond its own intonations. Such a culture cannot withstand the lurid and more fleshy temptation of the Western model, any more than the Imam can find shelter from Li-Li's flesh in the sonority of his prayers.

Finally, one must not fail to remark on Li-Li's treatment of the Imam at the end. Having seduced him, the seduction remains, as it were, tantalizingly unconsummated. She had no genuine interest in him. It was a power game: she only wanted to subjugate and humiliate him. He was interesting while he resisted, but the moment she had him at her feet, there was no longer a point in offering him anything—she switches off the light. And has this not been the story of East-West relations since colonialism and indeed until today as many in the East would see it? The story ends at this point when the light is switched off and the door is shut in the face of the Imam. One can imagine his despair standing there in the *dark,* at once denied the *light* for which he had made an enormous sacrifice and unable to return to his congregation to save them from the darkness of their eternal prostration.[14] In **"Did You Have to Turn On the Light, Li-Li?"** Idris appears to have stumbled on the perfect metaphor for the East-West "thing"—a metaphor so perfect it can almost be mistaken for something else.[15] Its subtlety, complexity, and indeed profundity are on a scale that neither its antecedent, **"Madame Vienna,"** nor, needless to say, its successor, *New York 80,* has approached.

Idris's latest and final approach to the theme in art form can be seen in the story **"Al-Sigar"** (**"The cigar"**), which appeared in his late collection *'uqtulha* (*Kill her!*).[16] The story, which barely has a plot and in which very little happens, is written in the first person and has the hallmarks of being based on an incident that happened to the author personally or at least is narrated in such a way as to create this impression. On a flight from Beirut to Cairo, the Egyptian narrator has the extremely good fortune of being seated next to a dazzlingly beautiful European woman—a queen from Bavaria, he calls her. Why especially from Bavaria is not clear, unless it is a reflection of the common belief in Germanic physical perfection. They start talking and she tells him that she had always dreamt of visiting the East and that Cairo had always been at the center of her dreams. She enlists his help in finding a suitable hotel, stressing her repugnance for big, posh places like the Hilton and the Sheraton. She wanted a hotel with character, one whose rooms were tents, whose courts were the desert, and where food was cooked on fire in the open, a fire stirred by a youthful brown Bedouin with a black beard and an *'iqal,* or Arab headgear, hanging

down on one side carelessly but elegantly. . . ." And what is more, she wanted the Bedouin, after grilling the meat, to devour it with her under the moonlit sky (6).

The author here is obviously caricaturing the West's old, romanticized picture of the East. His hero listens with horror to the details of the Bavarian's stereotyped expectations of the East as he, who has dreams of bedding her, knows all too well that neither he nor the Cairo she is going to has anything to do with Bedouins and deserts. Thus, he immediately sets out with "cruel eloquence," as he puts it, to "demolish the revolting, primitive picture [i.e., of the East] that apparently had stuck in her mind since childhood" (10). The story, which is of mediocre artistic quality, depends unfortunately on reportage rather than presentation. Thus, we are told eventually that the narrator succeeded in converting the woman to a more realistic picture of the East, though we are not told how he did that. But as he puts it: "The tent turned into a room in a luxurious hotel and the brown, bearded Bedouin into my very person, prim, eloquent, and elegant as I am" (13).

They have dinner together and everything appears to be going just fine and according to plan until he takes out his cigarette pack and offers her one. She declines politely and instead opens her handbag and takes out of it an enormous cigar (a Churchill, we are told specifically), unwraps it, and places it between her lips. She then inclines her head toward the narrator, asking for a light (14). It was as if his Bavarian queen had suddenly grown a phallus. Indeed, the ritualistic description of her movements are evocative of an unfolding penis. Our hero immediately loses his desire for her. He comments that although he had succeeded in dispelling her false dreams about the East, that "accursed cigar" then came and grew a mustache above her lips. And when she says to him that she hoped he believed in sexual equality and did not mind her smoking a cigar, he comments silently that indeed they had become equals: two men (15).

The attitude of the narrator/protagonist here is perhaps not unlike that of Darsh in **"Madame Vienna,"** written some twenty years earlier. Darsh too was disturbed by the audacity of the Austrian woman in bed, which detracted from her femininity, as he remarked. But **"The Cigar,"** as mentioned earlier, is not a good short story. It begins and proceeds almost all the way in the direction dictated by an East-West theme, but it ends simply on what sounds like an anti-feminist note. It is as if the author wants to denounce female emancipation if in the end it is going to turn women into men. But this development is thrown at us suddenly at the end and apparently at the expense of jettisoning the original theme. On the other hand, we are shown that the European has some cultural misconceptions about the East that the hero put right, as we are told. The picture remains unbalanced, however, because we are not quite sure what the Eastern man's misconceptions about the West are, except that his Bavarian beauty queen metamorphosed into a phallus-endowed monstrosity. But we cannot make much out of this because the story is too superficial and lacking in a sense of purpose to allow an interpretation beyond the immediate realistic level.

We can now return, following the chronology of Idris's work, to what is perhaps his earliest treatment, in his fiction, of the theme under discussion. By this I mean a long short story of some 70 pages, with the title **"Sir-ruhu al-bati"** (**"The secret of his power"**), which first appeared in the collection *Hadithat sharaf* (*An incident of honor*), published in 1958.[17] I have kept this work until so late in my discussion because it stands apart in Idris's fiction in that it does not approach the East-West theme through a sexual metaphor.

The story is set mainly in an unnamed Egyptian village of the Nile Delta, and the protagonist is a child whom we watch growing to manhood as the plot develops. The time span may thus seem too long for a short story but as it happens the plot is endowed with a strong sense of purpose that sustains interest without abatement throughout the extended narrative and until its denouement. This sense of purpose is imparted by the obsessive nature of the protagonist's quest, powerfully rendered by Idris's racy narrative and endless delaying techniques.[18] The child is intrigued, from early in his life, by the mystery of Sultan Hamid, the village saint, whose shrine stands on the edge of the local cemetery outside the village. The saint is revered by the villagers and his holiness taken for granted, although nobody knows anything about his history or origin. When the child passes his primary school examinations, his grandfather urges him to go light the six candles previously promised for Sultan Hamid. The child cannot convince himself that he saint could have had anything to do with his success, but still he honors the age-old tradition, albeit after cheating the saint out of three candles and buying sweets with the rest of the money.

From that day on, the saint begins to dominate the boy's thoughts. After his initial sense of awe, the shrine with its dilapidated walls fails to impress him. What is inside those walls, he wonders, to make the villagers cherish him so in their hearts and talk about him as if he were an enormous being living somewhere? (132). He begins making rounds among the old people of the village, asking them about the family origins of Sultan Hamid, but they all assure him that the saint was not related to anybody in the village. However, no one but the protagonist seems to wonder how he came to be buried in the village (138). In his bewilderment, the boy seeks the help of the Shaykh of the *Kuttab,* or Quranic school, who tells him that the secret of Sultan Hamid may only be reached through *dhikr,* or the ritualistic repetition of

God's name. He thus begins to frequent the weekly *dhikr* ring at the Shaykh's house. But having never liked the idea in the first place, he soon realizes that *dhikr* cannot solve his problem. Another logical discovery follows: that Sultan Hamid cannot be a saint since the epithet usually added to saints' names is that of "shaykh" and not "sultan" (140-42).

He soon makes yet another more radical and more bewildering discovery. One Friday he travels to a neighboring village to watch a soccer match between its team and that of his own. During the game, one of the opponent team's players kicks the ball so high, it lands on the roof of an elevated stone structure beyond the fields. That turns out to be the shrine of Sultan Hamid, to the amazement of the protagonist who, on further inquiries, establishes that many other villages in the province had their own shrines of Sultan Hamid (147-48). The boy's obsession with the mystery wears him out. His health deteriorates and he is obliged to draw back from the brink and forget about Sultan Hamid. Years pass and he grows up and leaves the village and settles in Cairo. But one summer, while on a visit to the village, he returns home one evening to find a stranger sitting there busy tucking into a huge meal. Hosting strangers passing through the village and listening to their stories was a hobby of the protagonist's grandfather. On this occasion, the stranger had the appearance of a dervish, but on being asked to what sūfī order he belonged, he proclaims: "We are not an order. We are the Children of Sultan Hamid . . ." (155).

With these words, the protagonist's quest is revived again with renewed vigor after years of dormancy. After an initial reluctance, the stranger is drawn to speak about the so-called saint. He explains that his hallowed status was gained on account of "his scattering of the enemies, his defeat of the infidels," without specifying who those were or when that happened (157). In fact, he tells a long story steeped in legend and miraculous acts about how Sultan Hamid confronted the enemy when they arrived in Egypt like a colossus, his feet dug into the earth and his head high up in heaven. Scores of men were unable to make him budge and swords broke on him, leaving him unscathed. Finally an old soldier realizes that the secret of his invincibility is the purity of his body and that the way to defeat him is to defile him first (cf. Lancelot of the Arthurian legend). Thus the old soldier begins to urinate on different parts of Sultan Hāmid's body, which immediately becomes vulnerable to sword strokes. Sultan Hamid is thus cut up into millions of pieces, but each piece turns into a man who rises to fight the enemy until the land is cleared of them (157-58). The protagonist does not simply dismiss this account as the ravings of a dervish. He realizes that behind the legend some reality must lie. But his extensive research at the National Library in Cairo leads him nowhere: he finds no sultan by the name Hamid ever to have ruled Egypt.

The breakthrough happens, however, by sheer accident. He makes the acquaintance of an eccentric European woman known as Madame International because of her extensive travels worldwide. On one occasion, he tells her the story of Sultan Hamid and his obsession with him, which fascinates her. Eventually she leaves for Europe and he forgets all about her. But many months later he receives a letter from her and it transpires that she, too, had become obsessed with Sultan Hamid and that together with a group of friends she spent months investigating the matter. Eventually she came across a book containing the letters of a certain Roger Clément, sent from Egypt to his friend in Paris, Monsieur Guy de Rouen. Clément, we are told, was one of the archeologists who accompanied Napoleon's campaign in Egypt and is thought to have donned the national dress and settled in Egypt. In her letter, Madame International includes the last few pages of the book containing Clément's last letter from Egypt.

The letter is dated 20 June 1801. It contains the writer's impressions of Egypt and the Egyptians, and an account that solves once and for all the mystery of Sultan Hamid, bringing the story to its conclusion. The letter is rather long, occupying the last 23 pages of the story. Here is a summary of it: M. Clément describes how on arrival in Egypt he first thought he had come to bring the flame of civilization to a dark African land, but that he soon found that he was to be touched by its magic and miraculous powers (170). He sets out to correct some of his Parisian friends' misconceptions about the Egyptians: "The Egyptians . . . are not as you say. They do not dance around a fire at night, and their women are nothing like the harem of the *Thousand and One Nights* . . ." (171). In words obviously put into his mouth by Idris, he argues that it was easy to conquer Egypt at the start, but that problems came later. He is held in awe in particular by Egyptian peasants whose mystique he cannot fathom.

To illustrate to his friend what he means, he begins to tell him the story of Hamid, one of those peasants who had been the talk of the French army in Egypt for many months. He was an ordinary *fellah* from the Delta village of Shatanuf where the French built a garrison. Now, although the garrison's policy was to avoid harassing the *fellahin,* a soldier loses his nerve one day under the hostile gaze of a *fellah* and shoots him dead. The villagers go to the captain and demand the life of the murderer. When their demand is rejected, a member of the garrison is found dead the following day. The captain arrests the chief of the village and threatens to have him killed unless the assassin surrenders. A *fellah* by the name of Hamid gives himself up before the end

of the day and the chief is released. The captain decides to hang Hamid after a mock trial, but at the eleventh hour the men of the village attack the garrison and free the man. When the French regain control, the captain executes the chief. A rumor goes round that the escaped Hamid has sworn to kill the captain. Soon enough the captain's horse brings its master's body back to the camp. By this time the news has reached Napoleon himself, who orders no less an officer than his second-in-command, Kléber, to capture Hamid. Overnight, the entire Delta becomes a safe haven for Hamid. Peasants everywhere have their little fingers amputated and their cheeks tatooed to give themselves two of the most distinguishing physical characteristics of Hamid, and to further confuse the French. Gangs form up and down the country who call themselves Children of Hamid and engage in waylaying the French. Gradually Hamid's name acquires the epithet "the sultan" among the people as a token of respect. M. Clément comments breathlessly that the Egyptians "were not a people, but a mass [*kutla*] which merged into Hāmid and made even the General [i.e., Napoleon] look like a dwarf beside him" (184).

The French succeed in the end, however, in finding and killing Hamid. M. Clément speaks of the rage that shook the whole country and attributes to the incident the second uprising of Cairo. Hamid's body is not moved from the spot where he was killed, and in no time a shrine with a large dome is built over him and crowds without number begin to visit every day. Kléber realizes that in his death Hamid has become more dangerous than in his life. Again breathless with admiration, M. Clément is made a mouthpiece for Idris's almost mystical belief in his people:

> We have conquered these people with our superiority, our guns, our brass music, our printing press, and our chemical science, but where can we get their supernatural power to stick together like a solid mass, to love one another, and to survive? Where can we have faith like that? . . .
>
> (187)[19]

Kléber destroys the shrine, exhumes the body, and has it thrown into the Nile. But before he is aware, the body is picked up from the water and a new shrine, larger than the first, is built over it, again attracting crowds of pilgrims in their thousands. Almost driven to madness, Kléber decides, after consultation with his general staff, to exhume the body again, cut it up into small pieces, and scatter them all over the country. (Idris is obviously utilizing the Osiris myth here to give some depth to his theme.) Little did Kléber know what he was letting himself in for. For the news starts to arrive that in every spot where a part of the body was found, a shrine was built over it. Thus instead of just one, hundreds of shrines were erected up and down the country.

At this point in the letter, the mystery of Sultan Hamid, which has baffled the protagonist all his life, can be said to have been solved. The saint turns out to have been a patriotic hero who fell in the fight against foreign aggressors a century and a half earlier and around whom popular imagination had woven stories elevating him to a saintly, supernatural status—not an uncommon practice in all cultures. That of Joan of Arc is an example that French history itself has to offer. The story could have ended here, the protagonist's quest having reached its culmination and the Egyptians' ability to hold their own and assert their identity and unity before the European other, in spite of the other's superior power and technology, established. But Idris keeps the story going a little longer, giving it a significant though unconvincing twist. The focus of attention is now turned to M. Clément, who becomes obsessed with the phenomenon of Sultan Hamid in his own time, as much as the protagonist was to become 150 years later. He disguises himself in the Egyptian national dress and is subsumed in the crowd at one of the many shrines built for Hamid. In his letter he describes the experiences in highly romanticized, almost mystical terms, strongly reminiscent of the words of the French archeologist Monsieur Fouquet in Tawfīq al-Hakim's *'Awdat al-ruh* (1933) (The return of the spirit):

> It was as if those rough bodies, sticky and dusty, exuded a substance superior to life, the essence of life, the totality of all that is powerful and triumphant in it; of all that is invincible, the supreme miraculous power, the very secret of life. . . . Hamid's shrine was the focus at which individual wills converged, a focus that concentrated the will to eternity and turned it into a magical elixir able to achieve it. . . .
>
> (190)[20]

M. Clément is humbled by the experience to the point of wanting to "prostrate himself before the crowds and ask their forgiveness," and for the first time in his life he feels "the greatness of life and the splendor of being a human possessed of that miraculous power, the power to come together with other humans in order to produce something greater than the life of each of us" (191). It is amazing that as Yusuf Idris put these words in the mouth of M. Clément, he was able to be totally oblivious of the fact that his character was a contemporary of the French Revolution, a great popular movement that changed human history once and for all through "the convergence of individuals in order to produce something greater than their separate selves." Someone in M. Clément's position should have had little to learn from the Egyptians in this particular connection and at that particular time, but Idris allows credibility to be swept away by the tide of his patriotic passion.

M. Clément's letter, and with it the whole story, ends on a note of total cultural surrender, total abnegation of the self, and subsumption into the other. Here is how he describes his agony to his friend:

> I am afraid, Rouen. I feel an overwhelming power drawing me to those people and calling upon me to know their secret. . . . I am resisting violently. My education, my cultural heritage, my intellect—should all hold me back from their mass when they come together but I am no longer myself. . . . I fear that today or tomorrow I may sneak off to one of the many shrines of Sultan Hamid . . . and light a candle for him as I used to do for the Virgin Mary at church. . . . I can feel myself walking powerless towards that fate. I car feel my resistance diminishing and coming to an end. Help, Rouen!
>
> (191-92)

This vision is unique in Idris's renderings of this recurrent theme. The cultural attraction here is completely one-sided with the French archeologist seen to be drawn toward the East to the point of losing his identity. It is also unabashedly romantic in its idealization of the Egyptians, and intellectually naive in using a Frenchman as a vehicle for the expression of this idealistic view. The influence of al-Hakim's equally romantic view of Egypt in *'Awdat al-ruh* is undeniable here on the much younger Yusuf Idris. It may also be that Idris had at the back of his mind the model of Nasser. For in the late 1950s, when this story was written, a period of national euphoria, when the newly independent Egypt seemed to be making headway in every direction, Nasser seemed indeed a focal point that brought together the mass of Egyptian people as an unstoppable force in their confrontation with the West.

In conclusion, it would appear that the cultural encounter between East and West is an issue that preoccupied Yusuf Idris throughout most of his career from the 1950s to the 1980s. It comes up repeatedly in his fiction and in his journalism, though not significantly in his theater. His favorite medium for treating the theme appears to be, in common with other Egyptian and Arab writers, through the exploration of a metaphorical sexual relation between an Eastern man and a Western woman. His artistic achievement varies in quality. He appears at his best in a story like **"Did You Have to Turn On the Light, Li-Li?"** where the metaphorical and realistic planes of the work are merged inseparably, while *New York 80* shows him at his worst with the novella often reading like a tract on the opposed value systems of the two cultures.

Does the writer bring a profound vision to his treatment of the theme? This is a question that I think must now impose itself on us, and to which I believe the answer will generally be negative. The profoundly of vision and originality of thought that often characterize the work of this great artist in his examination of the human condition through the medium of the Egyptian social scene, are not, alas, to be found here. His metaphors appear to revolve round the stereotypical notion of the spirituality of the East and the materialism of the

West. No attempt is made at redefining or genuinely delving into the values of either culture. Nor is the complexity of the clash/encounter explored beyond the outer veneer. The ultimate mutual rejection in **"Madame Vienna"** is oversimplified, while, to take the other extreme, the total surrender by West to East in *The Secret of His Power* defies credibility. The incompatibility of the visions of these two stories in particular, written more or less at the same period of the author's career, calls into question the consistency of his thought on the issue. Current politics, nationalist pride, and resentment of the West's colonial past in the East, as well as lack of real experience of the West may all be factors in accounting for what we must describe as the general mediocrity of the artist's representations of the encounter.

Notes

1. A most recent example is a long short story titled "Layla Yahudiyya" (A Jewish night) by the Egyptian Fu'ad Qindil, included in his collection *'Asal al-shams* (Honey of the sun).

2. "Al-Sayyida Vienna" was first serialized in weekly installments in the Cairene daily *Al-Masa'* between 17 July 1959 and 7 August 1959, and was later included in the collection *Al- 'askari al-aswad wa qisas 'ukhra.*

3. The book also includes "Al-Sayidda Vienna" retitled "Vienna 60." It is this edition of both stories that I use here and all page references in the text are made to it.

4. The contemptuous view of the Americo-European encounter is somewhat anticipatory of the author's harsh dismissal of American culture in *New York 80.*

5. For a different view of the ending of "Madame Vienna," see al-Qitt 200-01. Al-Qitt holds that the ending is forced in order to point out the impossibility of separating oneself from one's own cultural environment. The fact that the rejection is mutual rather than one-sided forces the point even more in his view.

6. Reference here is made to Idris's collected plays, *Nahwa masrah 'Arabi.*

7. For a detailed study of this play, see Rudnick-Kassem 77-92.

8. Details abound in the story that tally with known facts about Yusuf Idris's career and character. See, for example, pp. 28, 38-40, 56-57. Even the color of the protagonist's eyes is given as green, though this is very unusual among Egyptians, of whose cultural identity he is supposed to be a typical representative: Idris had green eyes! See p. 42.

9. For a somewhat amorphous discussion of *New York 80,* see Najib. Najib also briefly discusses the story "Did You Have to Turn On the Light, Li-Li?"

10. According to the author, the novel was written in the summer of 1955 and serialized in part in the Cairene daily *Al-Jumhuriyya* in 1960. See his short preface to the novel.

11. For further commentary on this article and the background to its authorship, see Kurpershoek 67-69.

12. This is in contradiction to Kurpershoek's claim that in 1976 Idris "buried the hatchet [i.e., in his war with America] . . . thus bidding farewell to the three decades of his anti-imperialist struggle" (70-71). As I have shown here, *New York 80* and many of the articles written during the 1980s were to prove that the writer's basic antagonism towards American culture and policies were still in place.

13. This part is my own translation from the Arabic text (p. 30). For some reason, Wadida Wassef omits it from her translation (p. 131). Roger Allen, however, retains it in his own translation of the story, for which see Idris, *In the Eye* 149-67.

14. Apparently Idris himself had a most bizarre interpretation of his own short story. In an interview given to Kurpershoek in June 1978 he reveals that he was prompted to write the story by Nasser's acceptance in 1970 of the American peace initiative that came to be known as the Rogers Plan after the name of the then-US Secretary of State. Kurpershoek reports that Idris was indignant at Nasser's readiness to compromise and quotes him as saying: "For twenty years Nasser preached hatred of the United States and kept the people prostrated (in this position). Then he jumped through the window in order to meet Rogers. So why did he inveigh against America? That is the reason why I put all the blame on the preacher." Kurpershoek rightly comments that such an implication can only elude the reader without the author's additional comment. I must add here that while possibly useful in some respects, the author's own comment should not be taken as a prescription for a uniform interpretation of the story, preempting other readings. Authors sometimes know least about their work! See Kurpershoek 160-61.

15. For a view of the story from a feminist angle, see Wise. Wise sees the story as a description of "the prototype of male seduction by female exposure" (180-84). She also discusses briefly "Madame Vienna" and "Al-Sigar," all from a purely feminist point of view (110-18).

16. The story "Al-sigar" was first published in the Qatari magazine *Al-duha* 5 (1981). See bibliography in 'Uthman.

17. Reference here is made to *Al-mu'allafat al-kamila li Yusuf Idris* 124-92.

18. This view of mine is in sharp contrast with that of 'Ali al-Ra'i, who holds that the excessive length of the story deprives it of artistic and intellectual concentration. He writes: "The experience of the peasant child with Sultan Hamid turns with deadly slowness into a national lyric in praise of the inner qualities of the Egyptian people and the insuppressible ability to conquer their enemies" (92-93).

19. In a different context, Kurpershoek comments, "Idris's articles exhibit an almost mystical faith in the simmering potential of the Egyptian people . . ." (57).

20. The idea of a worshiped hero round whom the Egyptians merge into a powerful mass is central to the French archeologist's argument, as he again expresses himself in romantic, quasi-mystical terms. Idris evidently models his M. Clément on al-Hakim's M. Fouquet (vol. 2, ch. 25, pp. 37-56). For an English translation of the novel see al-Hakim, *The Return of the Spirit* (trans. W. M. Hutchins).

Works Cited

al-Hakim, Tawfiq. *'Awdat al-ruh*. Cairo: Matba'at al-Ragha'ib, 1933. Trans. in English by W. M. Hutchins as *The Return of the Spirit*. Washington, DC: Three Continents, 1990.

———. *'Usfur min al-sharq*. 1938. Trans. in English by Bayly Winder as *Bird of the East*. Beirut: Khayats, 1966.

Al-Qitt, 'Abd al-Hamid. *Yusuf Idris wa al-fann al-qasasi*. Cairo: Dar al-Ma'arif, 1980.

Al-Ra'i, 'Ali. *Yusuf Idris bi-qalam ha'ula'*. Cairo: Maktabat Misr, 1986 (?).

Haqqi, Yahya. *Qindil 'Umm Hashim*. 1944. Trans. in English by M. M. Badawi as *The Saint's Lamp and Other Stories*. Leiden: Brill, 1973.

Idris, Yusuf, *Al-Lahza al-harija* (The critical moment). Cairo, 1958.

———. *Hadithat Sharaf* (An incident of honor). Beirut: Dar al-Adab, 1958.

———. *Al-'Askari al-aswad wa qisas 'ukhra*. Cairo, 1962. Collected short stories.

———. *Al-Bayda'* (The white woman). 1955. Beirut: Dar al-Tali'a, 1970.

———. "'Akana labudd 'an tud'i al-nur Ya Li-Li?" *Bayt min lahm*. Cairo: 'Alam al-Kutub, 1971. Trans. into English as "Did You Have to Turn On the Light, Li-Li?" in *The Cheapest Nights and Other Stories*. London: Peter Owen, 1978.

———. *Al-Mu'allafat al-kamila li Yusuf Idris*. Cairo: 'Alam al-Kutub, 1971.

———. *In the Eye of the Beholder*. Ed. Roger Allen. Minneapolis: Bibliotheca Islamica, 1978.

———. *Iktishaf qarra* (Discovering a continent). Kitab al-Hilal 255. Cairo: Dar al-Hilal, 1972.

———. *Nahwa masrah 'Arabi*. Beirut: al-Watan al-'Arabi. 1974. Collected plays.

———. *Al-Irada* (Will power). Cairo: Maktabat Gharib, 1977. Collected articles.

———. *New York 80*. Cairo: Maktabat Misr, 1981. Includes "Al-Sayyida Vienna" retitled "Vienna 60."

———. *'Uqtulha* (Kill her!). Cairo: Maktabat Misr, 1982 (?).

———. *Faqr al-fikr wa fikr al-faqr*. Cairo: Dar al-Mustaqbal al-'Arabi, 1985.

———. *Intiba'at Mustafizza*. Cairo: Al-Ahram, 1986.

———. *'An 'amd isma' tasma'* (Listen intently and you will hear). Cairo: Maktabat Misr, n.d.

———. *Jabarti al-sittinat* (A Jabarti of the sixties). Cairo: Maktabat Misr, n.d.

Kurpershoek, P. M. *The Short Stories of Yusuf Idris*. Leiden: Brill, 1981.

Najib, Naji. "Al-Bu'd al-khamis lil-insan wa al-ittisal bil-mawjudat." 'Uthman 101-85.

Qindil, Fu'ad. *'Asal al-shams* (Honey of the sun). Cairo: al-Hay'a al-Misriyya al-'Amma lil-Kitab, 1990.

Rudnick-Kassem, Dorota. "Egyptian Drama and Social Change: A Study of Thematic and Artistic Development in Yusuf Idris's Plays." Diss. Institute of Islamic Studies, McGill U, 1992.

'Uthman, I'tidal, ed *Yusuf Idris: 1927-1991*. With an introduction by Samir Sarhan. Cairo: al- Hay'a al-Misriyya al-'Amma lil-Kitab, 1991 (?).

Wise, Renata Clara. "The Concept of Sexuality in the Short Stories of Yusuf Idris." Diss. U of Texas at Austin, 1992.

Renate Wise (essay date 1998)

SOURCE: Wise, Renate. "Subverting Holy Scriptures: The Short Stories of Yûsuf Idrîs." In *The Postcolonial Crescent: Islam's Impact on Contemporary Literature*, edited by John C. Hawley, pp. 140-54. New York: Peter Lang, 1998.

[*In the following essay, Wise investigates the Islamic influence on Idris's short fiction.*]

I. Introduction

Since the seventh century Arabic literature has been greatly influenced if not dominated by Islam. While literary critics have elaborated amply on the impact of Islam on medieval Arabic literature,[1] they have for the most part ignored the Islamic influence on modern Arabic literature. Instead, when analyzing this literature, critics are quick to point to the influence of Western literature: "Modern Arabic literature took shape as a result of increasing contacts with Europe and, as a result, has been highly influenced by Western literary models and concepts" (Somekh 4). This proves true also for the short stories of the prominent Egyptian author Yûsuf Idrîs (1927-1991). The influence of Western writers, especially the Russians Chekhov, Gorky, and Dostoyevsky, and of Western concepts on Idrîs's short stories has been illustrated by several critics.[2] An assessment of the influence of religious scriptures on, and their exploitation by, these stories warrants an exploration of *terra incognita*.[3] And it is a territory gladdened by plenty.

The uniqueness of Idrîs's fiction, however, does not derive from its overt demonstration of religious and literary inseparability in an Egyptian context. We find this inseparability just as pronounced in, for example, the fiction of the Nobel Prize laureate Naguib Mahfouz. What is unique to Idrîs's short stories is a hidden agenda that is based on subversions of Qur'anic injunctions, iconoclasm, blasphemy and reinterpretations of hadiths, and that serves to justify sexual illicitness.

II. Disobeying Qur'anic Injunctions

As true master of the literary craft, Yûsuf Idrîs employs subversions of Qur'anic injunctions as well as prevailing stereotypes about sexuality in order to give sexual illicitness an aura of innocence. The short story **"Akbar al-Kabâ'ir"** is a telling example. The commands which are violated in this story are those concerning adultery; for example, "and come not near adultery. Lo! it is an abomination and an evil way" (Pickthall, Sura 17:32) and also "the adulterer and the adulteress, scourge ye each one of them (with) a hundred stripes" (Sura 24:2). The story implies that its heroine Umm Jâdd al-Mawlâ, wife of Shaykh Siddîq, has been sexually frustrated for years, ever since her husband had decided that divine and not sexual fusion will make him eternal. Sexually deprived, Umm Jâdd al-Mawlâ looks at the legs of the manure carrier Muhammad with "her gaze fixed on his black legs made muscular by hard work and covered with hair" (Idrîs, Akbar 62). She was looking at something in his calves which "had suddenly hardened . . . as if it were a piece of iron" (Idrîs, Akbar 62). She agrees to meet him at night on the rooftop of her house when her husband goes to yet another *mawlid*.[4] Scared, she thinks about calling the rendezvous off:

A thousand voices kept urging her to get up and leave, but iron chains kept her riveted to the rooftop. Overwhelming forces like Time and Fate made her ears deaf and her eyes blind to everything. A voice made her go and put the ladder up. She tightened the white veil around her and massaged her face with a few drops of borrowed rose water. All this she did as though she were hypnotized, driven to an inevitable fate.

("Bayt" ["Bayt min Lahm"] 66-67)

Overwhelming forces like Time and Fate make her go to the rooftop, deafening and blinding her to the sin of adultery which she is about to commit. By emphasizing the urgency of her sexual desires, the narrator exploits traditional notions of female sexuality. Lacking moral responsibility or a *superego,* to use Freud's psychoanalytical terminology, the heroine submits to her animal instincts, to the Freudian *id,* supporting once again the claim of the Sufi Jalâluddin Rûmî (1207-1273) that "the animal qualities prevail in women" (Rûmî 2465). Unrestrained by moral and religious considerations, the heroine obeys the voice which "made her go and put the ladder up." She has the potential to cause *fitna,*[5] since the gratification of her Dionysian desires becomes her *telos.*

As for the manure carrier Muhammad, he also submits to his sexual desires once he has sensed the woman in Umm Jâdd:

His arm touched her arm, his undershirt her dress, and in particular, the calf of his leg the side of her leg. Suddenly, Muhammad's heart started pounding, as if someone had caught him unawares and suddenly thrown him into the canal. At that moment, he had realized that the Shaykha Umm Jâdd al-Mawlâ was a woman.

("Bayt" 65)

Even though caught off guard by his libido, Muhammad, unlike Umm Jâdd al-Mawlâ, has the luxury of choice either to submit to his desires or to listen to God's laws forbidding adultery. He is aware of the risks he is taking, since he is scared not only of Shaykh Siddîq's coming home unexpectedly but also of God's wrath. The narrator's prioritizing of things to be feared by Muhammad is indicative of the manure carrier's concern for religious commands. He fears first and foremost for his physical existence threatened by the anger of the husband and then for his spiritual well-being. Yet neither physical nor metaphysical threat deter him from feeling an "all-encompassing joy" (**"Bayt"** 67). "His whole being was vibrating powerfully and intensely."

They meet and make love to the rhythm of the resounding voice of Shaykh Siddîq. Their movements are synchronized with the swaying of the bodies of the dervishes who participate in Shaykh Siddîq's *mawlid.* The narrator in this short story is not the first who has compared sexual intercourse with the dance of the Sufis.

Annemarie Schimmel explains that sterner Sufis have warned against the practices of *samâ'*. They thought that "in music and dance powers are at work which belong to that dangerous, uncontrollable zone of eros which the pious had to avoid or, at best, to strictly regulate" (Schimmel 139). Unable to control this erotic zone, the lovers decide to meet every time Shaykh Siddîq goes to a *mawlid*. Whenever Muhammad hears Shaykh Siddîq calling people to prayer, "he would feel this thing throbbing in his body, making his blood boil and almost blinding him" ("**Bayt**" 70). Indeed religious rituals of the Sufis, vocalized by Shaykh Siddîq, become a powerful aphrodisiac for the hero. The protagonists not only commit fornication but also desecrate religious rituals. The subversion of Qur'anic injunctions forbidding adultery and the hero's abuse of the sacredness of Sufi rituals originate in, and are euphemized by, the overwhelming desire to fuse in the protagonists. Replacing religious rituals and defying taboos and divine laws, sex becomes the driving force in their lives.

The sin of adultery has been committed but the participants are not to be faulted since they are not to be blamed for a sexuality which is beyond their control. Who is to be blamed? Who has committed "the greatest sin," as the Arabic title of the short story translates? The story points to Shaykh Siddîq who failed in his marital duties. As the Muslim scholar al-Ghazâlî (d. 1111) explains in his work *Ihyâ' 'Ûlûm ad-Dîn,* the stilling of a woman's sexual hunger is an important duty of the husband:[6]

> It is just for a husband to have sexual intercourse with his wife at least every fourth night if he has four wives. To be sure, he should increase or decrease the frequency of intercourse according to the woman's needs so as to secure her virtue. Indeed her virtue is his duty. If he does not oblige her sexually, he will cause her distress and jeopardize her fidelity.
>
> (al-Ghazâlî 64)

Thus, according to al-Ghazâlî, Shaykh Siddîq jeopardized Umm Jâdd's fidelity and is to be blamed for her adultery. Totally devoted to his prayers, he neglected his marital obligations. The narrator of this story comes to the same conclusion when he assures us that "Shaykh Siddîq will surely enter hell, and through its widest gate" (Idrîs, Akbar 70). This finale shifts the focus from the sin of adultery to the even greater sin of not stilling a wife's sexual hunger. Faulted is the one who prefers divine pursuits to earthly pleasures.

The short story **"Bayt min Lahm"** is also based on the assumption that leaving a woman sexually hungry is more sinful than the violation of Qur'anic injunctions. It depicts a widow and her three unattractive, unwed daughters whose only male visitor is a blind Qur'an reciter. Urged by her daughters, the widow marries the blind man. By taking turns in putting on their mother's wedding ring, the three daughters are able to dupe the sightless man into having sexual intercourse with them.

The religious ramifications are obvious. In addition to violating Qur'anic laws forbidding adultery, the blind reciter disobeys the law forbidding the father to have sexual intercourse with his stepdaughters. While the Qur'an allows a Muslim up to four wives, "And if ye fear that ye will not deal fairly by the orphans, marry of the women, who seem good to you, two or three or four" (Sura 4:3) it also commands:

> Forbidden unto you are your mothers, and your daughters, and your sisters, and your father's sisters, and your mother's sisters, and your brother's daughters and your sister's daughters, and your foster-mothers, and your foster-sisters, and your mothers-in-law, and your step-daughters who are under your protection (born) of your women unto whom ye have gone in—but if ye have not gone in unto them, then it is no sin.
>
> (Sura 4:23)

Since the blind Qur'an reciter shares the marital bed with the daughters' mother, the daughters are forbidden to him. The story's plot violates Qur'anic injunctions, commands of God. Can these violations be justified and on what bases?

The Qur'an reciter knows about the daughters' ruse but hides behind his blindness. He convinces himself

> that his partner in bed was always his legitimate wife, the bearer of his ring, young sometimes or old at other times, soft or coarse, thin or fat. It was nobody's business but hers. Nay, it was the business of the people who could see, their responsibility alone.
>
> (Idrîs, **"Bayt"** 13)

The denouement of the short story which, as the critic Sasson Somekh has pointed out (Somekh 18), represents a Qur'anic reference, casts doubt on his innocence: "He was blind, after all, and there is no fault in the blind. Or is there?" (Idrîs, **"Bayt"** 13). The critic Fedwa Malti-Douglas points out that the last sentence represents in itself a subversion of the Qur'an since it questions the text of the Qur'an. She argues that the "fault in the blind" does not refer to a lack of moral responsibility, but, in keeping close to the Qur'anic text, to the notion "that the visually or other physically handicapped are in some sense accursed or punished" (74). Then, what the subversive last sentence questions is some curse supposed to afflict the blind. Again Malti-Douglas points in the right direction when she explains that from a traditional Islamic perspective blind men are the most virile of men. Thus it is the virility of the Qur'an reciter and not his moral irresponsibility which leads to his violation of Qur'anic commands. Assuming that sexual vigor in the blind is excessive, the obedience of Qur'anic commands which restrict sexual choice would demand excessive, "superhuman" moral strength. Although the sightless hero had the opportunity to obey God's commands, since he was clearly able to distinguish between his sexual partners, his disobedience of these commands meets with mitigating circumstances.

With the protagonist victimized by the virile nature of the blind, and thus nearly absolved from sin, can the daughters be faulted? Not really, since their sexual misbehavior is justified by the fictional equation of sexual hunger with physical hunger. This description of the female libido as physical hunger gives female sexuality the same urgency as the concept of a virility excessive in the blind gives to male sexuality. Interestingly enough, while blindness nearly exculpates the Qur'an reciter from moral responsibility, femaleness acquits the daughters.

The only other participant in this *ménage à cinq* who cannot be excused on the basis of excessive sexual urges is the mother who is aware of her daughters' artifice. However, by equating physical with sexual hunger and emphasizing the nurturing duties of a mother, she washes her hands of sin. She muses:

> The girls are hungry; the food is forbidden, that is true, but hunger is still more sinful. There exists nothing more sinful than hunger. Indeed she knows hunger and it had known her. It had drained her spirit and sapped her marrow. She knows it. She had her fill of it. She will never forget its taste. They are hungry! She who used to take food out of her mouth to feed them, whose only concern was to feed them even if she had to go hungry herself, she, the mother, did she forget?
>
> (Idrîs, **"Bayt"** 11)

Not differentiating between sexual and physical hunger, the mother provides her daughters with food out of her mouth to still their physical hunger and with the virility of her blind husband to satisfy their sexual hunger. Sexual deprivation, as the mother reasons, is more sinful than the disobedience of a Qur'anic command. The subversions of the Qur'nic injunctions dictating sexual choices are accomplished on three premises: Muslims are allowed up to four wives; blind men are cursed with more virility than other men; and sexual and physical hunger are equivalent.

III. THE DESTRUCTION OF ICONS: THE LUSTY VIRGIN MARY AND HER CONCUPISCENT CHRIST

While the theme of uncontrollable sexuality dominates the stories **"Bayt min Lahm"** as well as **"Akbar al-Kabâ'ir,"** the destruction of the sacred images of the Virgin Mary and Christ becomes the leitmotif in the short story **"Jiyûkûndâ Misriyya."** In Mariology the Virgin Mary's relationship with her son Christ presents the apogee of pure nurture and self-sacrificing love. She

is an object of love without being subjected to the endurance of bodily pleasures. The Virgin fulfills nurturing and protective needs without the threatening aspects of concupiscence and defilement afflicting the terrestrial female. Mother of a deity, immaculately conceived, pregnant without sexual intercourse, she ascended bodily into heaven. Purged of the defiling horror of female procreative functions, the purity of her body is even safeguarded from the putrefaction of death.[7]

It is this Christian Virgin Mary—idealized in her asexuality and purity—to whom the hero in the short story **"Jiyûkûndâ Misriyya"** compares the Christian heroine Hanûna. She is fifteen or sixteen years of age while the hero is fourteen years old. She is taller but weaker than he (**"Jiyûkûndâ"** [**"Jiyûkûndâ Misriyya"**] 29). The hero walks by her window and waits for her to notice him: "But she was silent and still. She looked exactly like the Virgin Mary, as if the picture [of the Virgin Mary] which hung in her room were hanging now in the window" (**"Jiyûkûndâ"** 33). This picture symbolizes for the hero the happiness mother and son find in the embrace of maternal love. Mary's pictorial smile of maternal bliss reminds one of the smile of Mona Lisa whose French name 'La Joconde' becomes part of the title of this short story, translated as the "Egyptian Mona Lisa." Interestingly, many admirers of Mona Lisa contend that her famous smile radiates the solipsism of a pregnant woman.

The adolescent hero models the heroine Hanûna after the picture of the smiling Virgin Mary who represents the nurturing mother but lacks the concupiscence and threatening impure aspects of the terrestrial woman. He craves to be her son Christ, protected in her embrace: "I am Christ and you are the Virgin. Think of me as your Christ and of yourself as my Virgin" (**"Jiyûkûndâ"** 34). He wants to be extremely close to her (**"Jiyûkûndâ"** 35) and to fuse with her (**"Jiyûkûndâ"** 30). However, the hero's desire to fuse with the holy mother can be accomplished only on a sexual level:

> But that day when I asked her to be my Virgin and to accept me as her Christ, I was not doing this while transforming myself in my mind into a small child whom the mother embraces. A strong, ancient, tempestuous wish to embrace Hanûna lay dormant behind my question and desire.
>
> (**"Jiyûkûndâ"** 35)

The psychoanalyst Michael Balint argues that the return to the experience of primary love—the possibility of regressing to the infantile stage of a sense of oneness, and a tranquil sense of well-being in which all needs are satisfied—is a main goal of adult sexual relationships.[8] The hero's sentiments support Balint's statement: "I wanted to encompass her completely and make her smaller so that I could introduce her to my core in some way. This was the only way I knew to silence this continuous desire to be close to her and to be permanently joined with her" (**"Jiyûkûndâ"** 35). Since this fusion can only take place during coitus, men according to Balint, come closest to a refusion with the mother during intercourse: "The male comes nearest to achieving this regression during coitus: with his semen in reality, with his penis symbolically, with his whole self in phantasy" (Chodorow 194).

As long as the hero wants to be the Christ who finds nurturance in the arms of the Virgin Mary, he will not be able to fuse with Hanûna in order to fulfill his "strong, ancient, tempestuous wish." His sexual desires cannot be satisfied if he continues to regard himself as Christ and Hanûna as the pure holy mother. Since the women in the world of the short stories are endowed with an "out-of-bounds" libido, the metamorphosis of the Virgin Mary into Eve the temptress is predictable:

> Suddenly Hanûna embraced me with a trembling, urgent, sudden strength. She placed a quick kiss on my forehead. My face must have turned crimson. I raised my head and my face came to face hers. We were both breathing heavily when a second wonderful surprise came. I found her bending down to me—for I was a little shorter than she—and kissing me on my lips. It was another quick kiss, enormously confusing.
>
> (**"Jiyûkûndâ"** 36)

The transformation is complete when the hero realizes that Hanûna "had in her the thing which makes the breasts protrude, the skin soft like silk, and gives the voice this fine timbre" (**"Jiyûkûndâ"** 37). Hanûna embodies no longer the pure Virgin Mary glorified in her asexuality but a concupiscent woman trying to seduce him.

The hero is caught between his need to play the child Christ in order to be nurtured and affirmed by Hanûna, the holy mother, and his sexual needs which Hanûna in the role of the Virgin Mary cannot fulfill:

> Whenever I remembered that I had tried to imagine her as girl and female, I would have felt like I was on the verge of inciting a rebellion which would shake the earth and the heaven. I would have felt as if I were on the verge of committing the greatest sin—the greatest sin a human being can commit.
>
> (**"Jiyûkûndâ"** 38)

Having sex with Hanûna, the imagined holy mother, becomes "the greatest sin." The story **"Jiyûkûndâ Misriyya"** deconstructs the archetype of the pure, holy mother as well as the image of the asexual Christ. When the adolescent hero constructs his ideal woman, a replica of the Virgin Mary in order to satisfy his narcissism, he changes into her child Christ. He chooses the Virgin Mary because she radiates holiness and purity,

attributes which the terrestrial mother lacks. When his sexual urges triumph over his infantile narcissism, the hero erases his image of the extraterrestrial mother and admits to his human nature. He realizes that he was attempting the impossible "for all the sanctities of the world cannot keep apart the two strongest of life's forces when they come together—that of the man and the women—since the third force is that Satanic law which cannot be disobeyed" (**"Jiyûkûndâ"** 37). With this claim the narrator reinterprets the hadith "when a man and a woman are isolated in the presence of each other, Satan is bound to be their third companion" (al-Tirmidhî 120-21). While this hadith warns of a strong possibility of succumbing to Satan, it does not discount the possibility of human steadfastness when faced with divine punishment. The narrator's modification of this hadith contends that sexual illicitness and disobedience of holy scriptures are human certainties, since the desire to fuse in man and woman is an all-binding, Satanic law. Forced by their human nature, the protagonists obey the Satanic law and destroy virginal icons. The virgin Hanûna tumbles from the pedestal of holiness to the quagmire of the concupiscent terrestrial woman. Expelled from Platonic paradise, the heroine gets married off to her cousin when her father catches her *in flagrante delicto* with the hero. As for the lusty hero, when realizing that he has lost his nurturing "mother," he is consumed with remorse wondering "Did I have to go to that highest level? Was not closeness, mere closeness, a thousand times easier to bear than the complete severance of any ties with her?" (**"Jiyûkûndâ"** 41).

In this story the Virgin Mary as well as her son Christ are endowed with concupiscence. Yet this iconoclasm is justified by an all-too-human weakness of the hero striving for nurturance and love. Assuming that this kind of nurturing love can be found in sexual fusion alone, the hero's destruction of sacred images is only human.

IV. THE BLASPHEMY OF GOD'S SERVANT

The Satanic law of **"Jiyûkûndâ Misriyya"** dictates the plot of the short story **"A-Kâna Lâ Budda Yâ Lîlî An Tudî' an-Nûr."** Its hero Shaykh 'Abd al-'Al loves God and thinks that "he is the only thing which deserves to be alive" (**"A-Kâna"** [**"A-Kâna Lâ Budda Yâ Lîlî An Tudî' an-Nûr"**] 21) in the universe. He assumes the challenging position of Imâm of the Shabûkshî Mosque in the Bâtiniyya Quarter which was a "den of opium, seconal and hashish" (**"A-Kâna"** 15). Already the introduction smacks of blasphemy since some of the worshippers "were half stoned as they performed the prayer," thus disobeying the command "O ye who believe! Draw not near unto prayer when ye are drunken, till ye know that which ye utter, nor when ye are polluted save when journeying upon the road, till ye have bathed" (Sura 4:43).[9] The impious plot thickens when the heroine Lîlî is introduced as the offspring of a week-long marriage between her Egyptian mother and an English soldier named Johnny (**"A-Kâna"** 24). Furthermore, Lîlî makes her living as a prostitute. To sum up, the characters display major *desiderata* for a sacrilegious climax: Set in an atmosphere of sin, the pious Imâm steadfast in his devotion faces the beautiful harlot impudent in her sexual quests.

Becoming an exercise in blasphemy, the story continues to describe Lîlî's attempts to seduce the hero Shaykh 'Abd al-'Al by trying to entice him to give her private lessons in praying. The hero refuses. Nevertheless he succumbs to "the Satanic law" when he looks into Lîlî's bedroom window. He explains: "I rubbed my eyes and took one look which pulled me out of the depth of my slumber to a climax of wakefulness like a raging hurricane" (**"A-Kâna"** 27). What he sees is a white-skinned woman asleep on the bed with the top half of her body uncovered. For the first time in his life the hero looks at "that amazing mass of flesh which is a woman's body." Lîlî becomes the embodiment of Satan:

> But listen, Satan! . . . While you knew where I was, I did not know who and where you were. How they used to engrave on our minds such a false image of you. We always pictured you as a man, an ugly man. Not once did they think to compare you to beauty, even though nothing delights you more than to lie in wait surrounded by beauty, especially in a woman's form.
>
> (**"A-Kâna"** 27-28)

The heroine incarnates Satan: "There she was, all of her, Satan personified and perfect in every detail. All the temptation was there too" (**"A-Kâna"** 29). The hero perceives the Dionysian force in him (his libido) as satanic force outside of him. Once the heroine fuses with Satan, the short story represents the dialectic between the hero and Satan. It portrays the struggle of the Dionysian and the Apollonian forces in the hero.

Idrîs conveys masterfully the hero's agony by polarizing his inner struggle through contextualization. Frequent introjections of "My Lord!," "Satan!," and "Lîlî, why did you have to turn on the light?" build the story's frame. After the Lîlî who exposes herself and Satan have become synonymous in the hero's mind, the introjections become metaphysically antipodal entities. The context which links them is one of sin. Since Idrîs's protagonists are denied control over their libido, the victory of Satan becomes a foregone conclusion. The hero leaves his congregation bent over in prostration waiting for the "God is greatest" to conclude the prayer:

> I faced the qibla and stated my intention to pray . . . I opened my eyes . . . Right there in the middle of the qibla I saw Lîlî, asleep, naked, stretched out, open, with her hair spilling in waves across her body and then pulled back . . . Forgive me, God! . . . I hid the truth from You . . . Satan won!
>
> (**"A-Kâna"** 34)

The hero runs to Lîlî and tells her that he will teach her how to pray. Whereupon she informs him that she has bought an English record which teaches her how to pray. Then she turns off the light and the hero's fate can be best described by the exclamation of Rûmî: "First and Last my fall is through woman!" (Schimmel 124).

Again, Satanic law is stronger than divine law. Confronted by a beautiful naked woman, the hero deserts his congregation while bent over in prostration. Considering the worshippers' position—vulnerably risqué in Idrîs's world of sin—the Shaykh's action seems even more blasphemous. Yet, since in Idrîs's fiction the law between man and woman becomes, according to the short story **"Mashûq al-Hams,"** "the most binding sacred law" (**"Mashûq"** [**"Mashûq al-Hams"**] 84), the hero cannot be reproached for obeying. This theory of the human libido is similar to the iron-magnet attraction theory of the medieval Muslim scholar Ibn Hazm (994-1064) who explains that "the energy of the iron, left to itself and not prevented by obstacles, seeks what resembles it and hastens towards it blindly, naturally and necessarily, not out of free choice and intention" (Hazm 23). Just as the hero in **"Jiyûkûndâ Misriyya,"** Shaykh 'Abd al-'Al does not have a choice but to hasten blindly to the magnet. Although Ibn Hazm mentions possible obstacles which could stop the iron in its magnetic attraction, neither violations of Qur'anic injunctions nor iconoclasm and blasphemy can stop Idrîs's heroes in their libidinous pursuits.

V. REWRITING A HADITH

While the narrators of the short stories **"Jiyûkûndâ Misriyya"** and **"A-Kâna Lâ Budda Yâ Lîlî An Tudî' an-Nûr"** subvert the hadith "when a man and a woman are isolated in the presence of each other, Satan is bound to be their third companion," the narrator of the short story **"Al-'Amaliyya al-Kubrâ"** rewrites this hadith to read "when a man and a woman are isolated in the presence of each other, 'death is their third companion'" (**"Al-'Amaliyya al-Kubrâ"** 179). This substitution presupposes that on a certain symbolic level Satan and death are interchangeable. When considering that Satan is man's worst enemy in the spiritual kingdom as death is man's worst enemy in the surgical kingdom, we can establish a first rationale for this substitution. The Shaykh in **"A-Kâna Lâ Budda Yâ Lîlî An Tudî' an-Nûr"** faces his worst enemy when he meets Lîlî, the embodiment of Satan. The surgeon Doctor 'Adham in **"Al-'Amaliyya al-Kubrâ"** faces the challenge of his life when trying to save the life of a female patient. Both lose, the Shaykh to Satan, the surgeon to death.

Furthermore, profiled by events and characteristics associated with not only Satan but death, two of the *dramatis personae* efface the distinction between Satan and death. Doctor 'Adham severs the aorta of a female patient on whom he was performing exploratory surgery. Cutting a piece of vein out of the woman's thigh, he tries to repair her aorta. However, his attempt fails because he does not have the right needle and a thread strong enough to withstand the pressure of the blood pumping from the patient's heart. The patient dies. Since he is depicted as "a terrifying Satan" in his dealings with his nurses and assistants (**"Al-'Amaliyya"** [**"Al-'Amaliyya al-Kubrâ"**] 178) and since he causes the death of his female patient, he personifies Satan and death. The polysemous nature of another protagonist's name includes meanings associated with Satan as well as death. The nurse and sexual interest of the surgeon's assistant is named "Inshirâh." "Inshirâh" in this morphological form means "joy, delight, relaxation." Since Idrîs exploits mental structures which equate sexual desire (the force from within) with Satan (the force from without), Inshirâh by promising sexual fulfillment is synonymous with Satan. The root of "inshirâh," however, means in other morphological forms "cutting open, dissection, autopsy"—meanings associated with death.

Idrîs's masterful exploitation of intertextuality makes death and sex, the submitting to the Satanic law, almost indistinguishable. The description of the process of surgery is frequently interrupted by the depiction of the courtship between the surgeon's assistant and the nurse Inshirâh. Ultimately, the patient's death is sexualized since it is synchronized with the sexual climax of the surgeon's assistant. The dying of the female patient serves as powerful aphrodisiac for the surgeon's assistant. In a blood-splattered hospital-room, the female patient lies in the throes of death while the surgeon's assistant and his nurse who have been instructed to take care of the dying patient strip off their clothes, and their bodies catch on fire in a naked embrace on the bed next to the bloodstained bed of the dying unconscious woman. Before the assistant loses his consciousness in *la petit mort,* the female patient regains consciousness for a split-second in order to glance at the copulating couple right next to her. The surgeon's assistant explains that

> before he lost his awareness of her existence he felt that the woman had surely regained consciousness for a moment. It seemed from the way she looked at them that she saw them for the first time and that she realized what was happening. Indeed she almost did not regain consciousness until it was too late. One glance, however, was enough to put something of a smile on her face—a little surprised smile, like the smile of a child who opens his eyes for the first time to the world and finds what he sees surprising.

(**"Al-'Amaliyya"** 206)

The female patient regains consciousness just in time to watch his orgasmic throes. While the intertextuality of conversation fragments between the assistant and the nurse Inshirâh sexualizes the atrocity of the surgery,

their copulation sexualizes the death throes of the female patient. The childish smile of the female patient suggests that watching the copulating couple rejuvenated her, that she was reborn. While Freud regards human history as a struggle between the life instinct, embodied in the pleasure principle, and the death instinct *Thanatos,* such struggle does not exist in the world of the short stories. The pleasure principle is the only driving force; it becomes the *telos* of the protagonists.

VI. CONCLUSION

In the short stories sexual desire becomes the driving force of the protagonists, the *raison d'être.* While the heroines are not plagued by moral and religious considerations and obey their animal instincts without a moment's hesitation, the heroes demonstrate a moral consciousness. Sooner or later, however, they submit to their desires. The hero's attraction to the heroine is stronger than the fear of divine punishment. Disobeying Qur'anic injunctions forbidding adultery and incestuous relationships, desecrating sacred images and committing blasphemy—Idrîs's hero continues in his libidinous quest. Not even death stops the protagonist in this quest. While sex replaces religious rituals in **"Akbar al-Kabâ'ir,"** the pleasures of voyeurism replace the agony of death in **"Al-'Amaliyya al-Kubrâ."** Watching the copulating couple next to her, the female patient smiles like a child awakening innocently to the world's realities, to life. Her childish smile reveals Idrîs's hidden agenda. Once sexual desire has become identical with life itself[10] by defeating death, is then sexual illicitness and the disobedience of divine laws not justified?

Notes

1. See, for example, among more recent works John Renard, and Mustansir Mir.

2. P. M. Kurpershoek discusses the influence of Western writers on Idrîs's fiction. For surrealist and Marxist interpretations of Idrîs's short stories, see Dalya Cohen-Mor. Mona Mikhail gives an existentialist interpretation of Idrîs's short story "An-Naddâha."

3. A notable exception is Fedwa Malti-Douglas, "Blindness and Sexuality: Traditional Mentalities in Yûsuf Idrîs's 'House of Flesh.'"

4. In Egypt the term *mawlid* is used to denote a feast held in honor of a saint. For a historical background of the *mawlid* and its diffusion through the Islamic world, see the *Encyclopaedia of Islam,* 2nd ed. (Leiden: E.J. Brill, 1960-): 895-897.

5. *fitna* is polysemous. Among its many meanings are: A burning with fire; affliction, distress, or hardship; punishment; discord, dissension among the people; madness, insanity. For more meanings

see Lane, 2336-37. Here I use *fitna* to mean "chaos provoked by women's sexuality." Fatima Mernissi elaborates on this meaning of *fitna;* see 31, 39, 41-42, 53-54, for example.

6. Ghassan Ascha discusses the issue of woman's sexual rights according to Islamic jurisprudents, 52-58.

7. For a critical discussion on the virtues of the Christian Virgin Mary, see Warner.

8. Michael Balint as quoted by Chodorow, 194.

9. Although the Qur'an addresses the use of wine only, the majority of Muslim jurists include the use of drugs since drugs like wine have an intoxicating effect. For an interesting discussion of the legality of the use of hashish, see Rosenthal, chapter 4.

10. Yûsuf Idrîs himself considered sex equal to life. See al-Sâ'igh: 54.

Works Cited

Allen, Roger, ed. *In the Eye of the Beholder: Tales of Egyptian Life from the Writings of Yûsuf Idrîs.* Minneapolis and Chicago: Bibliotheka Islamica, 1978.

Ascha, Ghassan. *Du statut inférieur de la femme en Islam.* Paris: L'Harmattan, 1989.

Chodorow, Nancy. *The Reproduction of Mothering: Psychoanalysis and the Sociology of Gender.* Berkeley and Los Angeles: U of California P, 1978.

Cohen-Mor, Dalya. *Yûsuf Idrîs: Changing Visions.* Potomac, M.D.: Sheba, 1992.

Al-Ghazâlî, Ihyâ'. *'Ulum ad-Dîn.* Cairo: Mu'assasat al-Halabî wa Shurakâ'uhu li an-Nashr wa at-Tawzî', 1967.

Hazm, Ibn. *Tawq al-Hamâma.* Cairo: Dâr al-Ma'ârif bi-Misr, 1975.

Idrîs, Yûsuf. *Bayt min Lahm.* Cairo: 'Alâm al-Kutub, 1971).

———. "Akbar al-Kabâ'ir," in *Bayt:* 59-70; trans. as "The Greatest Sin of All" by Mona Mikhail in Allen: 121-32.

———. "Bayt min Lahm" in Idris, *Bayt,* 5-13, trans. by Roger Allen as "House of Flesh," in Allen, 191-98.

———. "A-Kâna Lâ Budda Yâ Lîlî an Tudî' an-Nûr," in Idrîs, *Bayt,* 15-35, trans. by Roger Allen as "Lili, did you have to turn the light on?" in Allen, 149-67.

———. "Mashûq al-Hams," in *An-Naddâha.* Cairo: Dâr Gharîb lit-Tibâ'a, n.d.: 59-98.

———. "Al-'Amaliyya al-Kubrâ" in *An-Naddâha:* 169-206.

———. "Jiyûkûndâ Misriyya" in *Anâ Sultân Qânûn al-Wujûd.* Cairo: Gharîb lit-Tibâ'a, n.d., 27-42, trans. by Dalya Cohen-Mor as "Egyptian Mona Lisa" in Dalya Cohen-Mor, *The Piper Dies and Other Stories.* Potomac, MD: Sheba, 1992: 1-23.

Kurpershoek, P. M. *The Short Stories of Yûsuf Idrîs: A Modern Egyptian Author.* Leiden: E. J. Brill, 1981.

Lane, Edward William. *Arabic-English Lexicon.* New York: Frederick Ungar, 1956.

Malti-Douglas, Fedwa, guest ed. *Critical Pilgrimages: Studies in the Arabic Literary Tradition* Austin: U of Texas P, 1989.

Al-Marsot, Afaf Lutfi, ed. *Society and the Sexes in Medieval Islam.* Malibu, California: Undena, 1979.

Mernissi, Fatima. *Beyond the Veil: Male-Female Dynamics in Modern Muslim Society.* Bloomington and Indianapolis: Indiana UP, 1987.

Mikhail, Mona. *Images of Arab Women.* Washington, D.C.: Three Continents Press, 1979.

Mir, Mustansir, ed. *Literary Heritage of Classical Islam: Arabic and Islamic Studies in Honor of James A. Bellamy.* Princeton: Darwin P, 1993.

Pickthall, Muhammad. *The Glorious Qur'an: Text and Explanatory Translation.* Elmhurst, NY: Tahrike Tarsile Qur'an, 1992.

Renard, John. *Islam and the Heroic Image.* Columbia, SC: U of South Carolina P, 1993.

Rosenthal, Franz. *The Herb: Hashish Versus Medieval Muslim Society.* Leiden: E. J. Brill, 1971.

Rûmî, Jalaluddin. *Mathnawî-yi ma'nawî,* ed., trans., and commented upon by Reynold A. Nicholson, 8 vols. London and Leiden, 1925-1940. V:2465.

al-Sâ'igh, Samîr. "Yûsuf Idrîs: al-Kitâba, al-Thawra, al-Jins," *Mawâqif,* 9, May-June (1970): 54.

Schimmel, Annemarie. "Eros in Sufi Literature and Life," in Al-Marsot, 139.

Somekh, Sasson. *Genre and Language in Modern Arabic Literature.* vol. 1. Studies in Arabic Literature, Sasson Somekh and Alexander Borg, eds. Wiesbaden: Otto Harrassowitz, 1991.

———. *Lughat al-Qissa fî Adab Yûsuf Idrîs.* Leiden: E. J. Brill, 1981.

al-Tirmidhî, *Sahîh al-Tirmidhî,* vol. 5. Cairo: al-Matba'a al-Misriyya bil-Azhar: 120-21; and vol. 9. Cairo: Matba'a al-Sâwi, 1934:8-10.

Warner, Marina. *Alone of All Her Sex: The Myth and the Cult of the Virgin Mary.* New York: Vintage, 1976.

M. Akif Kirecci (essay date winter 2001)

SOURCE: Kirecci, M. Akif. "Political Criticism in the Short Stories of Yusuf Idris: 'Innocence' and '19502'." *The Massachusetts Review* 42, no. 4 (winter 2001): 672-88.

[*In the following essay, Kirecci contends that "Innocence" and "19502" "strongly reflect the author's perception of Egyptian political life."*]

This article analyzes two short stories by Yusuf Idris (1927-1991), commonly regarded as Egypt's master of this genre. These two stories, **"Innocence" ("Bara'ah")** and **"19502,"** not only vividly represent the relationship between literature and politics, but also are fine examples of Idris' artistic style. Indeed, his literary works as a whole reflect Egypt's culminating experiences and struggles along the path to becoming an independent modern nation. I thus argue that an intellectual can assert his political views via literature as effectively as by engaging in politics itself—if not more so.

In **"Bara'ah,"** Idris visualizes the visit of Egyptian President Anwar al-Sadat to Israel. The message is clear: he does not favor the idea of such a visit, nor does he approve of the peace initiative. Instead, he apparently tries to warn al-Sadat of the consequences of the course he has chosen. The assassination scene is the most interesting aspect of the story as the vision was later realized in October 6, 1981, with the actual murder of the president while reviewing a military parade celebrating the 1973 war.

In the other story considered here, **"19502,"** Idris turns his criticism upon the 1952 Egyptian revolution. The title itself carries a loaded message: by inserting a zero between the digits of the date of the revolution, Idris indicates that the revolution achieved nothing. We will deal with this story first—after a brief excursion into the development and role of the short story genre in the Arab world.

THE SHORT STORY IN ARABIC LITERATURE

To understand these stories, one must first know the tradition from which they come. According to some historians, Arabic literature has its own tradition of the story form, which *The Thousand and One Nights* and *Maqamat* exemplify. This approach has usually been taken by the apologetic to show that there was a unique tradition of the "short story" within Arabic literature, and that the modern Arabic short story is a continuation or transformation of this trend. However pleasing this argument might be, it is unjustifiable to argue that *The Thousand and One Nights* and *Maqamat* form the basis of today's modern short story as a different genre. Instead I would argue that they provided a solid background for the modern Arabic story to emerge in its present form.

When the first Arabic short story appeared in 1870, it sparked a lengthy debate as to whether its emergence owed its existence to the impact of Western culture. But if the Arab reader became acquainted with this modern genre first through translations of short stories from Western literature,[1] this decreases the validity of the earlier argument that it emerged from within Arabic narrative tradition. It must be remembered, however, that translations from Western languages into Arabic mark the importance of the language as a communicative device; with the barrier removed it was the Arabic language that provided the impetus for the development of the new genre.

The next step in the establishment of this new genre was the creation/emergence of the audience. The importance of newspapers and magazines in the birth of the short story is also accurate for the Arab world.[2] The increase in the numbers of daily newspapers and periodicals, the development of the printing press, the spread of education, and the psychological preparedness of the educated circles to read Western fiction, all contributed to the emergence of the "modern Arabic short story." Thus by the end of the century it was common to find newspapers and magazines in Egypt and Syria publishing stories or sections of novels, both in translated and original form.[3]

Due to the youth of this literary genre, some terminological disparity has been witnessed both in Western and Arabic literature.[4] Arabic has a variety of different terms to denote different types of narratives and stories (*qissah, sirah, hadith, hikayah, samar, khurafah, usturah, riwayah, nadirah, khabar* and *mathal*), all of which have historical connotations. As Abdel-Meguid claims,[5] there was still not an agreement on the terminology during the 1920s. Arab writers then used different terms variably (i. e., *riwayah, qissah* and *hikayah*) to denote what is today known more generally as the short story. The project of identifying the new genre by using old terminology with a new understanding of its concepts developed gradually.

As the short story and its techniques evolved, so the terminology used to describe it has also been clarified. In the first stage, during the 1870s, "*riwayah*" was used for both the novel and the short story, especially in the literary journal *Jinan*. Alternately, in the journal *al-Hilal* around 1890 the expression "*riwayah*" was always used to denote only the novel, while "*qissah*" indicated the short story. In his preface to the first collection of short stories *al-Shaykh Jum'ah wa Qisas Ukhra* (1925), Mahmud Taymur suggested a new term, "*uqsusa*," for the short story, while reserving "*qissah*" for the novel. In his book *Fann al-Qisas*, Mahmud Taymur proposes the following terms: "*uqsusa*" for short story/*conte;* "*qissah*" for long short-story/novella; and "*riwayah*" for novel/*roman.*[6] His involvement in the discussion, however, could not solve these terminological difficulties. Nevertheless, through the development of literary criticism, today it is accepted by the majority of both publishers and writers that the term "*qissah qasirah*" in Arabic signifies "short story," although it would appear to be a direct translation from English.[7]

The evolutionary stages of the Arabic short story can be classified in three different periods, as Abdel-Meguid suggests in his book *The Modern Arabic Short Story*.[8] "The Embryonic Stage" dates from the beginning of the nineteenth century to 1914. The first Arabic short stories appeared in the magazine *al-Jinan* (founded in 1870) to which Salim Al-Bustani made a considerable contribution with both original and translated short stories.[9] The works of Labibah Hashim and Mash'alani, writers who published their stories in the magazine *al-Diya'*, also belong in this period. Egyptian Mustafa Lutfi Al-Manfuluti and his Lebanese-American fellows Jubran Khalil Jubran and Mikha'il Nu'aymah are also representative of this stage. Although Manfaluti's *Nazarat* and *'Abarat*'s primary aim was "moral uplift,"[10] and though they were described as melancholic they put a certain group into contact with this young genre. The work of the writers in this stage was usually considered an adaptation effort from Western short stories. It is well known that al-Manfaluti often had somebody translate the stories from French for him, after which he wrote his own versions. Nevertheless, these efforts made the Egyptian readership love this new genre and prepared them for the next stage.

"The Trial Stage" dates from 1914 to 1925. The father of the modern Egyptian short story Muhammad Taymur (1892-1921) is the best representative of this stage. Tahir Lashin, Khayri Sa'id, the 'Ubayd brothers and Ibrahim Al-Misri are also considered to be in this stage. This period is characterized by a certain immaturity in narrative techniques. For this reason, writers of this new genre felt the necessity of studying its techniques in Western literature. They attempted to approach the subject in a more unconventional way than the previous generation. We may also call this the transitional stage in which we witness the attempts for authentic voices.

It was Mahmud Taymur who opened the third stage, "The Formative Stage," which extends from 1925 to the present, by publishing his collection *al-Shaykh Jum'ah wa-qisas ukhra'*. During the early period of this stage, a new narrative style emerged, to be perfected in the years to come. An emphasis on development and psychological analysis of the characters in the stories and a realistic approach are typical aspects of this stage.

Since World War II, the Arabic short story has gained much popularity and has ceased to be a genre reserved for the social elite. It is from this perspective that Idris embodies a high level of maturity in the developmental stages of the Arabic story. His name became virtually associated with this genre in Egyptian literature. As Egypt was passing through a set of historical, political, and social struggles during the nineteenth century, Idris became a witness of society reflecting the experiences of these turbulent phases into his art. It can be safely stated therefore that he is the master of the Arabic short story, bringing this literary genre to the masses.

YUSUF IDRIS (1927-1991)

In modern Arabic literature no one's name has been associated more frequently with the short story than Yusuf Idris. It is not only his genius and powerful pen that are appealing to me, but also his role as a participant in the events of history. He was arrested and imprisoned more than once because of his left leaning opinions,[11] and his criticism of the government in his literary works. That is what makes him controversial, and indispensable in understanding Egyptian culture and the plight of the Egyptian people in the grip of societal transformation.

The first decade of Idris's literary work (1954-1964) is marked by social realism. His later work in (1965-1982) along with this realism demonstrates highly symbolic and surreal features. It is noteworthy that while critics have studied his realistic stories, his symbolism and surrealism have not been carefully evaluated.

Egypt's experiences along the path to becoming a modern nation are voiced in Idris' stories. This voice sometimes appears in the form of political critique, sometimes in the form of interpreting modernity; sometimes mirroring the sorrow of suppressed classes, at other times emphasizing the value of freedom. However, his stories are always the product of a "committed" intellectual.

He began his writing career in the early 1950s. In 1952, one of his stories was published in a leftist magazine, *al-Tahrir*. In 1953 he was appointed to one of the most widely read daily periodicals, *al-Misri,* where he published his first short story. In late 1953 he became responsible for the literary section of the weekly *Ruz al-Yusuf,* a position which allowed him to publish the short stories of that generation's youth.[12] Idris made his livelihood as a medical doctor, but that did not prevent him from becoming a notable literary figure. His medical practice gave him the chance to see and analyze his people from a different perspective. Social and psychological analyses of his characters are usually a salient feature of his writings. Later in his life he gave up medicine to focus solely on his writing. He then began to write for newspapers, first *al-Jumhuriyyah* (established by the revolutionary leadership) and later *al-Ahram,* the nation's paper of record, and the Arab world's largest daily. When he became a journalist he became more involved with political and social issues, a new profession the impact of which was reflected in his literary works, as the stories **"Bara'ah"** and **"19502"** clearly demonstrate.

Idris published his first collection of short stories, **Arkhas Layali (The Cheapest Nights)**, in 1954. This collection was defined as "intense" and severely realistic.[13] His use of language demonstrated a shift from earlier generations' complex and complicated use of Arabic. He employed a clear and "uncomplicated"[14] Arabic, which helped in spreading the genre to a wider audience. His second book, **Jumhuriyyat Farahat (Farahat's Republic)** appeared in 1956. In this collection Idris again chose his characters from among society's poor and gave a realistic depiction of their lives. Oftentimes, He adopted a style against conventional attitudes in society. His two collections, **Qa' al-madinah (City Dregs)** and **Hadithat sharaf (A Matter of Honor,** 1958) especially brought issues considered "taboo," such as sex and individuality, into the foreground. His later works became increasingly concerned with the plight of the modern man. **Akhir al-dunya (The End of the World,** 1961) is a case in point. His later works [including **al-'Askari al-aswad (The Black Soldier,** 1962), **Lughat al-ay-ay (The Language of Ay-Ay,** 1965), **al-Naddaha (Inevitability,** 1969), **Bayt min al-lahm (House of Flesh,** 1971)] dealt with a variety of topics ranging from social and political problems to the psychology of his heroes. His works were also profoundly concerned with poor country folk and their struggle for survival, a distinctive feature of the so-called "committed" literature of the time. His subject matter, including poverty and class struggle, may be seen as reflections of his political perspective.

One of the most controversial issues in his writing is his use of colloquial language. For example, his play **al-Farafir (The Little Birds)**, one of his best known works, is regarded by most critics as a masterpiece of Egyptian colloquial writing.[15] The different forms of Egyptian colloquial language in Idris's stories forcefully verbalize the existential anguish of his characters,[16] although Kurpershoek states that this does not apply to his later works which, according to him, are "wordy."[17] Nevertheless, his skillful use of colloquial Egyptian paved the way for generations to come. For Idris, the decision to use Egyptian dialect was a natural inclination, since his aim was to reach out to society and nudge it towards modernity. However, his extensive use of colloquial Arabic left him subject to severe criticism by traditional literary figures, like 'Abbas Mahmud Al-'Aqqad, the champion of "literary Arabic." In this instance, he was indeed involved in a struggle between tradition and modernity. He was caught between **al-thabit** (the static) and **al-mutahawwil** (the dynamic), in Adunis's terms. The involvement of Taha Husayn (another and even more influential pioneer of literary Arabic) in the discussion perhaps provides us a better

understanding of these two contesting views in Arabic literature. Husayn suggests that Idris uses a colloquial style whenever he deems it is necessary to "authenticate" a character or an event.[18] Taha Husayn even praises Idris' use of language, saying that it is impossible to remove a single superfluous word from his sentences. This statement may be interpreted as a support for Idris' use of the colloquial, which would seem contradictory to Husayn's call for the use of literary Arabic (**fusha**). However, supporting Idris, who was also a modernist, would fit well with Husayn's position *vis-a-vis* the static and the dynamic—using Adunis' terms—since he was also a representative of the modernist school in Arabic literature. Therefore, both Idris and Husayn should be seen as representatives of the dynamic trend. As Allen asserts, the contribution of Yusuf Idris to modern Arabic literature shows his successful role in significantly advancing the achievements of the early generations' (i.e., Taymur, Haqqi, and Mahfuz), further helping modern Arabic literature reach 'a harmony between form and content.'[19]

Yusuf Idris is a "natural" story-teller, in its traditional and modern sense. Traditional, because he writes with such ease that his writings give the impression that they have never been reworked or rearranged before publication, drawing—perhaps—more on the oral tradition of *The Thousand and One Nights*. He is natural in the modern sense because he uses such complicated themes, metaphors and techniques making his audience believe that he is the master of the modern literary art.

"19502"[20]

The 1952 coup, under the leadership of Jamal 'Abd al-Nasir, can be interpreted as the starting point of the social and political upheavals in Egypt that soon followed. The Free Officers wanted to shatter British control over Egypt, compelling them to seek new alliances and try alternative policies, eventually changing the balance of power in the Middle East through a series of internal and external crises. Among these were the March 1954 Crisis, 'Abd Al-Nasir's policy of Non-Alignment, the 1956 Suez War, the 1959 anticommunist campaign, the 1961 Socialist Laws, the 1967 national defeat, and the 1968 popular uprising. Egyptian intellectual discontent, however, was not due to the political crises that Egypt experienced, but rather the unfulfilled promises of the 1952 revolution, seen in a set of insecure policies (e.g., censorship) against the intellectuals. The change of leadership after 'Abd al-Nasir apparently was not enough to change the status quo, since Anwar al-Sadat was also a member of the Free Officers. The erosion of intellectual enthusiasm towards the 1952 revolution (and thus towards the government) was a salient feature of the later decades that Idris's story **"19502"** mirrors.

Idris uses stream-of-consciousness technique in portraying his character in this story. A man suddenly realizes that no one notices him. He feels that he is alive, talking, moving, thinking; but no one sees or hears him. It is as if he has suddenly moved to another level where he is able to see others, but others cannot see him. He notices this while peering in a looking glass which does not reflect his face. The narrator, therefore, starts with a hero who is invisible, a hero whose voice cannot be heard, a hero whose scream arouses no one.

The man tries to make sure then that his consciousness is in its place. He makes no sense of his situation and starts examining items and people around him. These items the narrator mentions while passing by seem unimportant. Nevertheless, when we read the story to the end, these seemingly insignificant items have intruded into the man's consciousness enough to bother him. An expensive bar of soap, the Managing Director's towel, the gleaming tiles and a tape recorder that an employee listens to throughout the day: although these items cannot be attributed to his literal loss of face, their disturbing presence is clearly noted. After examining his surroundings he realizes that his consciousness is in its place. In fact, everything is in its place except his *face*.

The man begins checking his identity, asking questions to himself. He remembers who he is and what he does. He is sure that he is in full possession of his reason, but the world around him gets more and more remote as he inquires about his mental state. His reality does not match the one surrounding him; he is increasingly bothered by his failed efforts to make the two come closer. He is lost. At this point he says to himself "I will do it."

The reader then realizes that the man is ill. He takes his clothes off as if to symbolize the naked truth that he is lost, helpless to connect with reality again. With the introduction of "I will do it," the story's pace accelerates. His visit to his house deepens his depression. He finds his wife and his son with another man, as a family. Nobody recognizes him; in fact no one even sees him. He is an alienated person even in his own house.

In his search of his face—or his identity—the narrator mentions several officials (Director, The Managing Director, Public Relations Deputy, and Chairman of the Board) who do not see him or recognize him or even hear him. Even a woman he pinches on the bus has no reaction. A set of "officials" who make no move to recognize or understand the man is a tool for showing the narrator's discontent with those "public" officials. They dwell in their own world, making no effort to reach out to the people. The fact that the man works for one of those public offices presents an ironic criticism of the government.

Identity loss therefore can be interpreted from two different angles. One is that an ordinary citizen loses his identity, and the public officials do not care about it.

The alternative is that a government officer loses his identity and the government pays no attention to it. In both cases the impact of the identity loss cannot be confined to one realm, since the man is depicted as having two roles, as a public employee and as an ordinary citizen.

Carefully chosen scenes of bureaucratic environments give the narrator ample opportunity to construct his criticism. It is not only senseless people that bother the man, but his surroundings as well. "The dark wall behind" the man marks the series of pessimistic thoughts and nightmares that plague him. He also has some degree of discontent with other ordinary people around him. The woman who listens to the tape recorder all day in the office, his wife and his son, and even the woman in the bus who shows no reaction when he pinches her, show the dissemination of senselessness around him which triggers his anger.

All of these events accumulate and return the reader to an earlier mentioned promise: "I will do it." The psychological state of the hero in the story is so well-portrayed—a legacy of Idris' medical background—that suicide seems the only choice. He makes his last efforts to reach out to the reality in which he labored, but, again, no one hears his yelling. He goes to the top of the building and—without hesitation—he jumps.

Only then, when the man commits suicide, do people notice him. At the story's close, the police and an ambulance arrive. They need to file a report on the incident. "They have written: 'Identity unknown.'" After the file is transferred to the district attorney and the corpse is buried, the incident is listed as "anonymous." No one knows who the man was.

Most tellingly, the police file the incident under the number 19502, an ingenious allusion to the 1952 Egyptian revolution. Inserting a zero in the middle of the date says more than can be conveyed in a hundred pages of criticism. An identity-less man, whose reality reaches out to his surroundings and the "public officials" only when he dies, indicates, as Dalya-Cohen's analysis also confirms,[21] how the revolution has departed from the true goals and principles that had inspired it. For Idris, the end of the revolution is a catastrophic one, as the inserted zero implies.

The political message of the story lies in the acts of the government officials. The officials label the man's identity "unknown." At this point, Idris ironically ties the dilemma to the identities of both the man and the revolution. The man, representing the real people, cannot be identified by his own government. Thus Idris switches the theme around, turning the table on the government. The real identity crisis lies not in the man who commits suicide, but in the government who recorded the incident under the number 19502. By the symbolic use of this file number, Idris wields a very pointed critical weapon against the government and the revolution. The loss of identity in a regular citizen represents that revolution.

Innocence ("Bara'ah")[22]

"Bara'ah" was published in the collection *Ana Sultan qanun al-wujud* (*I am the Lord of the Law of Existence*) in 1980. Critics usually consider this collection as one of his surrealist and allegoric works. **"Bara'ah"** may be read as a prophetic dream predicting Sadat's assassination even before his visit to Israel. Bringing the date of its publication (1972) into our attention, Dalya-Cohen assumes that Idris knew that Sadat was planning to visit Israel,[23] and it seems that he was trying to warn him of the consequences.

In the first sentence we are introduced to a General who occupies a central position throughout the story: "The smile of the General, the boat and the invitation" (71). While there is no specific mention of either the people or the countries involved, it is not hard to understand from the upcoming lines that Idris symbolically questions the possible visit of Egyptian leader Anwar al-Sadat to Israel. In this reading, the General represents President Anwar al-Sadat. Al-Sadat was a member of the Free Officers—a group of military men who launched a *coup d'état* under the leadership of Jamal Abd Al-Nasir, deposing King Farouq in 1952.[24] "The smile of the General" as a recurring leitmotif draws a connection between themes such as the words "smile," "boat," and "invitation," which are introduced in different contexts in the story.

In **"Bara'ah,"** Idris uses an omniscient narrator. He picks and describes the scenes and he controls the flow of the story. In a few places, though, the narrator states that he is "only watching" and there is "no sin in watching" (72, 77, 79). This withdrawal of the usually omnipresent narrator from the scene on certain occasions can be a useful strategy for criticizing an action with which he does not concur. In doing so, the narrator clearly marks the line between the two different groups of people. One is the General with his old enemies and new friends. The second is the narrator himself, who is present with the others. They do nothing but watch. This is a very innovative set-up for criticizing those in the first group. The two conflicting sets of people—the rulers and those that they rule—ready the ground for a class-based critique of political leaders and their deeds.

It is on account of this perspective that we find no sympathy for Sadat's "possible" visit to Israel in the story. For many Arab nationalists, no matter how important a step it was towards peace in the Middle East, Sadat's visit to Israel was a betrayal. It was not only a devia-

tion from 'Abd Al-Nasir's policy, but also from the Arab cause. Bearing in mind that Idris was an ardent supporter of Arab nationalism, we should not then be surprised that he denounces the peace initiative. "How can I shake hands when their hands are full of snakes, serpents and scorpions?" (72). It is obvious from the choice of metaphors that the narrator has little sympathy for either the initiative or the General. A few pages later, when the General stretches out his hand, the narrator refuses. "No General, even with you I will not shake hands" (76). The narrator further explains his fear of death or disaster, as if saying that something bad is going to happen. The sense of political foreboding in the story, therefore, stems from Sadat's betrayal.

When the narrator's discontent with the main figures in the scene reaches its utmost level, he switches from a description of the crowd, to himself. Then he suddenly turns to the people in the scene and criticizes them. Actually, it is more an accusation of hypocrisy:

> "The wigs are more beautiful than the original hair a thousand and one times. The artificial eyes are sweeter and more charming than natural ones a million times."
>
> (78)

The narrator has switched the mood; he is no longer satisfied with watching. "It is no longer humanly possible for me to stay and watch" (79). He then introduces the theme of "the silence of the Judgment Day" (79), which leaves the reader in the throes of anticipation. Again the narrative mood changes. The reader's attention is caught by an unknown person's action. At this point, when the story reaches its peak, the assassination happens.

The title **"Bara'ah"** is designed to underline the position of the first person; that is, the intellectual himself, as opposed to politicians and those who supported, or did nothing to prevent, this political act. The narrator frequently maintains that "There is no sin in watching," "watching is not a sin," "I will remain watching." Indeed, the repetition of the same theme over and over again builds a concept of sin. If you are not watching, it means that you are involved with this political action. According to the narrator, if you are involved with the visit, if you are shaking hands with "the scorpions," this makes you guilty and sinful. If you are only observing, then you are innocent. "What is the crime in watching? My heart is as clean as white Mahalla calico" (81).

Toward the end of the story, it becomes more evident that the narrator assumes another role: "It is no longer humanly possible for me to stay and watch." A few steps further he dreams an assassination scene, but does not forget to deny that he was part of the act. His son appears to be accusing the narrator of being involved. The narrator replies as if his son is interrogating him.

"No! I did not touch anything, my son. You are crazy. I was watching, like all these people . . . What is the crime in standing and watching? My heart is as clean as white Mahalla calico, like the hearts of these people. I did nothing but watch . . . What is the crime in watching, you fool?"

(80-1)

It seems that in the first scene Idris is trying to disassociate himself from this action. Nevertheless, I would argue that he criticizes Egyptian intellectuals who watch government policies and do nothing. It is also worth noting that the expression "like all these people" again implies that intellectuals do not behave as they are supposed to, and choose instead to act like ordinary people.

Through the use of an oral "paternal" narrative,[25] we get the sense that there is a story being told, not in the very beginning, but only later, as the monologue unfolds. The narrator refers to his relationship in an intimate manner, calling out "my son," instead of a definite name. The father tells his story variably, sometimes complaining, sometimes in an angry manner, and sometimes just as a story. The son occupies a very passive position, which suggests that he symbolizes the public attitude.

The Day of Judgment theme does not occupy as central a place in **"Bara'ah"** as it does in his other story **"al-Rihlah" ("The Journey")**.[26] It is interesting that Idris mentions the Day of Judgment twice with "the silence of Judgment Day." "They stare in silence, the silence of astonishment, the silence of curiosity, the silence of Judgment Day" (72), ". . . and silence—the silence of curiosity, the silence of joy, the silence of Judgment Day" (79). By doing so, he implies that the righteous will be rewarded and the evildoer will be punished. It seems that Idris' judgment for this action is assassination or death for the main sinner.

Stages in the psychology of the narrator reflect the intellectual's perception of this visit. We can classify these levels as follows:

STAGE I

He simply watches as an eyewitness to the events of his society, of history. He does not agree with what is happening in the scene, but does not have the power to control the scene. He does not interfere to change it. He is only an observer.

STAGE II

"It is no longer possible for me to stay and watch" signals the change of position in Stage II. Given this statement, the reader expects that something is going to happen; even the narrator is involved in the anticipated action. He draws the conflict to the level of apprehen-

sion of misfortune. Nonetheless, the narrator does not give any clue what is going to happen next. He leaves the crucial point of the story in obscurity, making the audience question their expectations and frustrating them with the question: "Why did nothing happen?"

STAGE III

In this last stage the narrator seems very concerned to establish his own innocence. The act of watching the events, even if he does not support them, is an innocent action. But after the assassination has taken place, the narrator's concern with regard to being innocent does not change, but rather intensifies. There are two actions in this stage, which are represented almost in the same context. The narrator is innocent in both cases. In the first one, the sin is to go there and shake hands. As I have already mentioned, the narrator has disassociated himself from this action, therefore he should be regarded as "innocent" because, he neither participated nor gave his approval. In the second one, the General is assassinated by someone that the narrator does not know. Even the narrator himself is surprised. Although he admits that it is not possible for him to watch anymore, he does not know who committed the killing. Therefore, since he remains out of the picture in both cases, he must be innocent.

We can interpret the theme of innocence from two different perspectives. The first one is that the narrator emphasizes the fact that he was not involved in the act of "handshaking" and "assassination." He is not an active participant in either of the two events. Therefore he cannot be blamed for anything. The second reading of the theme concerns his criticism of the intellectual and public, and their passive stance regarding the government or Sadat's possible visit to Israel (in reality still five years in the future). The role of the intellectual can not be restricted to that of a passive bystander, but rather he should take action regarding matters that effect the country and the people. In both cases the political message of the story is clearly expressed.

CONCLUSION

In these two short stories it seems as if Idris seeks answers to the questions regarding the position of the intellectual *vis-à-vis* Egyptian political life. "What role should the intellectuals assume and how they are accountable? Should an intellectual be a passive bystander or an active participant?"[27] Idris, by his clear messages in **"19502"** and **"Bara'ah,"** emphasizes the role of intellectuals in society, urging them to take a stance, to be a part of political decisions. The intellectual is the voice of society, and should act accordingly. Despite the potential dangers of being prosecuted for criticisms addressed to the leaders and the government, as Idris proved in his own life, the intellectual can make a difference.

Much evidence has been reported regarding Idris' opposition to Egypt's administration in general and Sadat's visit to Israel in particular.[28] Rather than focusing on the accounts of these sorts of opposition, an assessment of the political aspects of his writings will reveal Idris' real legacy. After all, it was not just his desire to seem "avant-garde"[29] that put him in opposition with the leaders of his country, but rather his genuine conviction that a committed intellectual cannot be in alliance with the government.

Therefore, the narratives in these stories strongly reflect the author's perception of Egyptian political life. Through them, we can witness a vivid portrayal of the emotional conflicts that arise from the psychological impact of political and social issues. As I have argued earlier, the political content of Idris' short stories, and his position in the canon of Arabic literature as a whole and Egyptian literature in particular, illustrate the intimate relation between literature and politics. His writings also reflect the perception of the state among the different levels of society.

Notes

1. Abdel-Maguid, Abdel-Aziz, *The Modern Arabic Short Story* (Cairo: Al-Maaref Press, 1954), 64.

2. Beyerl, Jan, *The Style of the Modern Arabic Short Story* (Prague: 1971), 4. See also Abdel-Maguid, *op. cit.*, 9.

3. Abdel-Maguid, *ibid.*, 70

4. For further discussion see: Roger Allen, "The Novella in Arabic: A Study in Fictional Genres," *International Journal of Middle Eastern Studies*, 18, (1986), 473-484, and, by the same author, "Narrative Genres and Nomenclature: A Comparative Study," *Journal of Arabic Literature*, XXIII (1992), 208-214.

5. Abdel-Maguid, *ibid.*, 11-27.

6. Mahmud Taymur, *Fann al-Qasas, Dirasat fi-al-qissah wa-al-masrah* (al-Matba'at al-Namuzajiyyah), 99-111, Abdel-Maguid, *ibid.*, 27 and Jan Beyerl, *ibid.*, 7.

7. I have found interesting that even a modern author such as Abdel-Aziz Abdel-Meguid uses a term *short story-tellers* instead of short-story writers when he is addressing some contemporary writers, such as Tawfiq al-Hakim and al-Mazini. I wonder if this approach—if not accidental—could be related to the legacy of *The Thousand and One Nights*.

8. Abdel-Maguid, *ibid.*, 77-132.

9. Jan Beyerl, *ibid.*, 5-6.

10. John A. Haywood, *Modern Arabic Literature 1800-1970* (London: Lund Humphries, 1971), 127.

11. Roger Allen, "The Artistry of Yusuf Idris," *World Literature Today*, Vol. 55 No. 1, (Winter 1981), 43-47.

12. P. M. Kurpershoek, *The Short Stories of Yusuf Idris* (Leiden: E. J. Brill, 1981), 27.

13. Roger Allen, ed. *In The Eye of the Beholder: Tales of Egyptian Life from the Writings of Yusuf Idris* (Minneapolis & Chicago: Bibliotheca Islamica, 1978), vii.

14. Roger Allen, "Yusuf Idris's Short Stories: Themes & Techniques," in *Critical Perspectives on Yusuf Idris* (Washington D.C.: Three Continents Press, 1994), 15-6.

15. See Nada Tomiche, "Niveaux de langue dans le théâtre egyptien," *Le Theatre Arabe* (Paris: UNESCO, 1969).

16. Mona N. Mikhail, *Studies in the Short Fiction of Mahfouz and Idris* (New York: New York University Press, 1992), 146.

17. Kuropershoek, *ibid.*, 98.

18. Mona N. Mikhail, *ibid.*, 145.

19. Roger Allen, *In the Eye of the Beholder*, ix.

20. Yusuf Idris, *al-A'mal al-Kamilah: al-Qisas al-qasirah* (Dar al-Shuruq, 1990), 603-609. The story was first published in the collection *Uqtulha* (*Kill Her*) in 1982. An English translation of the story can be found in Dalya Cohen Mor's translation of a collection of stories from Idris. Yusuf Idris, *The Piper Dies and Other Stories* (Potomac, MD: Sheba Press, 1992), 71-81.

21. Dalya Cohen Mor, *Yusuf Idris: Changing Visions* (Potomac, MD: Sheba Press, 1992), 126.

22. Published first time in *Al-Adab: The Journal of Literature* in 1972 and later on published in *Ana Sultan Qanun al-Wujud* (Cairo: Maktabat Garib, n. d. 43-50. My page references to the story are based on Dalya Cohen Mor's translation in her previously mentioned work, *The Piper Dies* (1992).

23. Dalya Cohen Mor, *ibid*, 126.

24. P. J. Vatikiotis, *The History of Modern Egypt: From Muhammad Ali to Mubarak*, 4th Ed. (Baltimore: The Johns Hopkins University Press, 1991), 376-384.

25. A theme that he also used in the story, "The Journey," published in the Cairo daily *al-Ahram* in 1970.

26. A translation of the story by Dalya Cohen is published in the *Journal of Arabic Literature*, Vol. XV (1984), 135-138.

27. Dalya Cohen Mor, *Yusuf Idris,* xvii-xviii.

28. In a later interview, Idris explains his feelings about Sadat's visit to Israel in detail. See Mahmud Fawzi, *Yusuf Idris: 'Ala fawhat al-burkhan.*

29. Roger Allen, *ibid.,* vii.

Ramzi Salti (essay date spring 2001)

SOURCE: Salti, Ramzi. "A Different Leader of Men: Yusuf Idris Against Arab Concepts of Male Homosexuality." *World Literature Today* 75, no. 2 (spring 2001): 247-56.

[*In the following essay, Salti elucidates the sociopolitical implications of Idris's depiction of homosexuality in* A Leader of Men.]

When Yusuf Idris (1927-91) published his controversial story **"Abu al-rijal"** (Eng. **"A Leader of Men"**) in the Egyptian magazine *October* in 1987, it was immediately hailed by scholars as the first and only work in modern Arabic literature to probe "so deeply in the mind and soul of a latent homosexual" (Elkhadem, 1988, 1). Consequently, many critics praised the story for daring to broach a subject that "is normally regarded in the Arab world as one about which feelings, thoughts, and words ought to be repressed" (Boullata, 83), one that is "regarded by the great majority in Islamic Egypt as repugnant and distasteful" (Elkhadem, 1). Even those scholars who did not perceive the work as a significant contribution to Arabic short fiction tended to emphasize that the story was nevertheless noteworthy "for both its theme and technique" (Allen, 360).

Although critics seem unanimous in praising Idris for daring to broach the sensitive and controversial topic of homosexuality, few have attempted to engage the subject as it may relate to notions of gay liberation and homophobia in the Arab world. In fact, many critics of the work seem to have opted for a stylistic critique, thus marginalizing and diffusing the very heated subject that is at the heart of this story. For instance, in his review of the 1988 book version of *A Leader of Men,* Roger Allen mentions only in passing that the work is about a man "who finds himself relentlessly faced with the reality of his own homosexual inclinations," dedicating the bulk of his review instead to matters of translation and general stylistics. Like most other critics, Allen avoids addressing the sociopolitical implications of the work and expresses no opinion as to the many ways in which homosexuality is represented throughout it. Is the reader to deduce from the fact that Idris has "probed so deeply in the mind and soul of a latent homosexual" (Elkhadem, 1988, 1) that he is necessarily attempting to dispel existing negative stereotypes of the homosexual in Egyptian society? Or is Idris in fact reaffirming social views that aim at persecuting and oppressing homosexuals? Is Idris's work homophobic or is it enabling to gay movements, however obscure, in the Arab world? Is Sultan represented as a victim of bigotry and homophobia or as a man who has strayed from "tradition" and "goodness" and is punished accordingly?

Clearly, the answers to such questions are far from obvious. Some may argue that Idris is attempting merely to present the plight of a homosexual without making a judgment—be it negative or positive—on the very topic he is broaching, as if the writer were somehow able to detach himself completely from his reality and give readers an untainted and completely objective account of homosexuality. In addition to ignoring the fact that Idris himself is a participant in his society, such a view also overlooks the very basic question concerning the (mis)representation of the homosexual protagonist in the work. A detailed analysis of the story would therefore not only shed further light on Idris's genius, but would also prove enabling for any discourse centering on homosexuality and homophobia in the Arab world. Such an examination will necessarily and appropriately attempt to engage sociopolitical issues that are of central importance to the text—issues that have been dismissed thus far by a majority of critics dealing with the work.

The protagonist in Abu al-rijal is Sultan, a man who, in his early fifties, begins to confront his homosexuality after many years of hidden torment and repression. Yet what is most significant about Sultan's character, at least in the way he is presented at the beginning of the story, is that he does not in any way live up to the stereotypical image of the homosexual in society. Instead of being predictably represented as passive, victimized, and weak, Sultan is initially depicted as an overly macho, dominating, tough individual who is respected and feared by almost everyone in his village.

As the story progresses, however, Sultan finds himself confronting feelings that he has long repressed, emotions that, once faced, eventually lead to some sort of demise in his social standing—i.e., in the way in which people start to view him as well as in the way he comes to see himself. At fifty-one, Sultan is finally toying with the idea of "coming out," if not to society then at least to himself. Once he makes that decision, he seems willing, and ultimately able, to cross the line between theory and practice, between exploring his homosexual desires and acting on them. Theory, in this novella, precedes practice, and Sultan's coming-out process, as convoluted and complex as it may be, is nevertheless carefully planned out, with little or no spontaneity accompanying his actions. Consequently, each of the ten sections contained in the story may be thought of as a step toward self-acknowledgment and self-acceptance.

On the other hand, each section may also be considered as a step toward Sultan's demise.

At the beginning, we are presented with Sultan, who at "fifty-one and three months" seems to be in a state of delirium, as if some power had suddenly overtaken him, forcing him to look at his own body with new eyes. Standing in his room and dressed only in his underwear, he observes the natural effects of age on his once hairy and muscular body, which has now become much less hairy and also fat. This loss of body hair, emphasized in detail throughout the opening sections of the story, is not only significant but pivotal to Sultan's consequent realizations. Aging here is recounted as a loss, never as a gain. Sultan does not realize that the years have enabled him to acquire wisdom and power, but rather that they have taken away many of the things that had defined him as a manly man, nay "a leader of men." The most obvious and visible of these is facial and bodily hair, for in Sultan's society a moustache and a hairy chest determine a man's virility and masculinity. Instead of his hairy body, Sultan notes "a frightening effeminate smoothness" (3), and his instinctive action of running his fingers over his moustache, which he had recently shaved, causes him to panic and grow angry. In his rage, he calls out to one of his many faithful followers, nicknamed Bull, summoning him to his room. At this point, the reader is alerted to another loss, that of a manly voice; Sultan's shout, which "used to shake the house" (4), has grown faint.

It is interesting to note that, from the opening passages onward, homosexuality is introduced as a loss of masculinity—here a loss of physical masculine traits that make a man a man—in order to separate, as Arno Schmitt puts it, "the Man from the non-Man" (19). In order for Sultan to begin accepting his homosexuality, he must face up to his being a "non-man." Only then, it seems, will he be able to take the next step, in which he sets the stage for his eventual sexual encounter with Bull. It is also his rage at his perceived losses that, ironically, gives him the courage to invite a real man, appropriately named Bull (Thawr), into the scene.

If the first part of the narrative deals with Sultan's mental readiness for a further exploration of his homosexuality, the second part sets the stage for the actual realization of Sultan's fantasy, for it is at this point that a real man is called into the picture. Bull is described as "handsome and attractive in spite of his untidy hair and clothes," conjuring up an image of great contrast to Sultan's perfumed body and tidy attire. The man and the non-man are now in the same room, and the anticipation continues to mount.

The third section of the narrative is devoted solely to a description of the encounter between the two main characters, a scene engulfed in darkness, silence, and tension. In discussing *A Leader of Men,* Elkhadem notes that "no situation in [Idris's] story could be construed as pornographic or even erotic" (1990, 27), yet this section of the story, which (like all others) does not employ any profane language, seems to be filled with homoerotic elements, as Sultan's fantasy is recounted in detail:

> A dark, deserted place; touching ensues; a feverish groping that makes his hands shake and his whole body shiver as he swoops down on the young man, squeezing the powerful muscles of his arms and the bulging muscles of his legs, and his desire is becoming mightier, and inside him yearning howls boldly and madly unleashing a wailing cry that represents his masculinity.
>
> (5)

Although, as Elkhadem states, Idris seems to be consciously avoiding graphic descriptions and language, this scene is far from tame in its account of Sultan's attraction to Bull's body, and although the elusive line between pornography and eroticism may or may not have been crossed at this point (depending, of course, on the reader), it would be difficult to dismiss this scene as completely devoid of eroticism. After all, the setting itself and the anticipation alone have already contributed to the establishment of a stereotypical homoerotic encounter.

The fourth segment of the story finds Sultan wondering about the cause or origin of his homosexuality, triggering memories that center on his childhood years, his parents, and his upbringing in general. He remembers being raised in a large poor family, being "an outstanding pupil" at school, shying away from other kids who sought some sort of sexual gratification by touching each other, "emulating his father, whom he regarded as the manliest of all men" (7) at a very young age, and working very hard in order to contribute to his family's finances.

At this point in the narrative, it is crucial to note the way in which Idris turns from the microcosm (Sultan's specific reality in his village) to the macrocosm (a homosexual's reality in a homophobic society). It is perhaps here, for the first time, that the author hints at some sense of commonality in the struggle for liberation by homosexuals everywhere—a sort of universal homosexual plight that transgresses borders, cultures, and religions, yet one which is only able to function at a macrocosmic level. For although homophobia takes on different disguises in relation to the (homophobic) society at hand, it is nevertheless united in its hatred of homosexuality; and although the laws, attitudes, and customs regarding homosexuality vary enormously according to each respective society (even within the entity that we call the Arab world), they are all based in a common desire to uproot, cure, punish, or otherwise marginalize homosexuals. Consequently, the fact that a homosexual views his homosexuality in relation to his own (homophobic) society does not—should not—detract from the common bond he shares with homosexuals everywhere, if only in his desire to be with someone of the same sex.

If the first five segments of Idris's story hint at Freudian views of homosexuality, the sixth focuses strictly on the mother-son relationship during Sultan's childhood. Here, Idris seems determined to dive into the question of whether a domineering mother can influence her son's sexual orientation. Sultan's mother is described as having "a special brand of love that aims at making men out of boys . . . for all a mother wants is to create men and not toys to play with nor dolls to cuddle" (12).

This presentation of the mother as being full of "tenderness and steadfastness," with an "unadulterated Egyptian temperament," is seen by some critics as a much too obvious attempt on Idris's part to link Sultan's homosexuality with his mother's character. In his review, Roger Allen notes: "Although the handling of the psychological dimension has always been one of Idris's strong points, it is not treated with any great subtlety here; the causality presumably to be inferred from the description of the strong-willed mother in section 6, for example, is patent enough to become almost trite" (Allen, 360). Although on the surface it may seem that Idris is merely reiterating existing social and psychological views that blame a male child's homosexuality on his mother's temperament, a closer analysis of this sixth section may actually prove that, far from being "trite," the mother-son relationship is problematized and complicated in a way that paradoxically upholds existing stereotypes while simultaneously chipping away at their very core.

The portrayal of Sultan's mother is far from two-dimensional, for she cannot be said to fall neatly within a stereotypical classification. She is presented as tender and steadfast at the same time, without being more one than the other. Yet she also never pampered her child at all, instead giving him his privacy, respecting his manhood, and never "impugning his masculinity" (12). In this way, she is neither domineering nor stifling in her treatment of her child, and no indication is given that she was overprotective of Sultan in any way. So what is to be inferred from this paradoxical representation? That her strong character, coupled with Sultan's father's unwillingness to beat him, caused or contributed to his homosexuality? Or that her tenderness and the remarkable way in which she dealt with discovering her son committing bestiality somehow turned him into a sissy?

It may be due to Idris's genius that the above two questions cannot be answered easily. The lack of pampering on the mother's part may, on the one hand, be seen as a

subversion of the mother-spoils-son, son-turns-to-sissy (gay) model. On the other hand, the fact that she is an intelligent woman who is far from submissive may be regarded as a reaffirmation of the stereotype of the domineering mother who impugns her son's masculinity at an early age, a point that Allen seems to have opted for. Either way, the fact that the mother-son relationship is presented in such complexity makes it difficult to dismiss the story's psychological dimension as insignificant.

This sixth section of the novella is also crucial because it introduces readers to Shahin al-Tahhan, the village's well-known homosexual. Shahin al-Tahhan lives up to the stereotype of the homosexual who is out of the closet in every sense, a fact that puts him in sharp contrast with the rugged Sultan. The first time he is described, it is in the following manner:

> This Shahin al-Tahhan was one of the many phenomena known in some villages of Lower as well as Upper Egypt. A man who was always clean-shaven and who had the appearance of a man, but was effeminate in everything else; the way he walked and talked, his closeness to women socially and even in his work.
>
> (12)

It is interesting to note first of all that, being a homosexual, Shahin al-Tahhan is necessarily "clean-shaven." Not unlike Sultan, who had shaved his moustache upon his decision to deal with his repressed desires, Shahin al-Tahhan is presented as having lost an essential part of his manhood, a loss which contributes to the rumor that he is a homosexual.

At first glance, it may seem disturbing that homosexuality, here as elsewhere in the story, is recounted strictly in terms of a loss—a point that will have been exhausted by the end of the text. Yet this stereotypical presentation may also prove functional in subverting some common views of the homosexual as necessarily effeminate. In addition to the obvious dimension of questioning gender roles in society, one must bear in mind that Idris's protagonist himself is presented as overly macho to start with.

Another problematic aspect of the story which needs to be addressed at this point concerns Sultan's history of attraction toward males. Here the text seems to be sadly lacking in recounting past (probably potential) sexual encounters between Sultan and other men. While Sultan's past is constantly recalled—presumably to dismiss and/or reinforce governing views of a man's sexual orientation as attributable to his upbringing—the reader is never given an account of his desires' having significantly surfaced in the past. Furthermore, the fact that he is involved in a heterosexual marriage, and has many children, is never addressed on any large scale. Did

Sultan only become aware of his "latent" homosexuality in his fifties? Or was it at that age that he was no longer able to contain it? Few clues are given by Idris regarding this crucial point, and the reader is left to wonder—perhaps rightly so—about when the process began on a conscious level.

Shahin al-Tahhan is also significant, because it is through him that the reader is given a concise view of Egyptian social attitudes toward homosexuality. After all, this is a man who was known to seduce young boys by paying them for their services—a point that would presumably ignite hatred and fear in the hearts of many. Yet al-Tahhan, as despised as he may be, is nevertheless accepted as a "natural" part of society. Although the implications of such a statement are many, the crucial point remains that al-Tahhan has never been run out of town, or worse, for his behavior or his very existence. Instead, he is left to himself even by religious leaders in the village: "He was loathed by the prudish and religious people, but, because of his notoriety and long history, ordinary people took him as a normal phenomenon that did not evoke any loathing; he only became the object of ridicule to some, and an example given by mothers to their sons when they wanted to warn them of the consequences of being soft" (12). True, had al-Tahhan not belonged to a well-known family in the village, the consequences of his homosexuality might have been different. Yet, as things stand, there may actually be a hint of social tolerance in this paragraph, though any discussion of the legal ramifications of homosexuality—which might have been relevant at this point—is absent.

The seventh section traces a recent event that contributed greatly toward Sultan's "metamorphosis." It also attempts to trace the roots of his forthcoming demise. The recounted incident centers on Sultan's failure to respond to a cry for help by one of his supporters (who was being assaulted by thugs) in his legendary manner—i.e., spontaneously and ferociously. Instead of his customarily manly cry urging his supporters to lash back at the aggressors, Sultan informed them in a *soft* voice that they would delay the confrontation until later, a statement which bewildered both his supporters and his enemies.

This scene is of extreme significance for many reasons. First, it equates Sultan's refusal to commit violence with cowardice and nothing but; second, it deeply roots his homosexuality in a domain of weakness and frailty. After all, as Sultan's stream of consciousness informs us, it was at that moment that he began feeling his manliness slip away, leading him to the realization that "he was nothing but a lie" (14). The most obvious reading of this incident, of course, would equate homosexuality with effeminacy and consequently with a lack of courage. Yet there is more to this scene than a mere reaffirmation of preconceived notions of gender. It must

be remembered that in facing up to his true self, Sultan is also succumbing to existing social views on the topic and to fallacies that he himself may be adopting as a necessary prerequisite for anyone on his way to becoming another Shahin al-Tahhan: "The great tragedy was that he believed it, and because of his strong conviction, the others believed him . . . and because he was not sure that they would fear him, or, indeed, that they might even hurt him, he stepped out of his role as a lion and showed them that he was nothing but a mouse" (14).

Thus there may be a suggestion here that it is not homosexuality that renders the individual weak but rather the way a homosexual perceives himself and his sexual orientation that ultimately causes his demise, even within a certain solitary imaginary space that excludes social views. Did Sultan become a coward as a direct result of his acknowledged homosexuality, or did the realization that he was gay cause him to perceive effeminacy as the only way of liberating himself from the confinements of a traditionally defined heterosexual role? Clearly, the answer here lies in self-esteem and the ways outward behavior affects the manner in which one is viewed by others and by oneself. Even if Idris is suggesting that cowardice may be an essential component of homosexuality, the fact that Sultan was able to translate his inner self into his outward behavior in a credible manner for most of his life points to the power of the mind. A reversal of the inward-outward model would then conclude that when Sultan ceased to believe in himself—when he began to hate his self—that lack of self translated into everyday-life situations, leading to his downfall (in society's eyes as well as his own).

Sultan's metamorphosis from "lion" to "mouse" did not happen overnight, as the eighth section is quick to affirm. The incident involving the failure to respond to the cry for help seemed an isolated one, for "in the morning he became his same old self again" (15). In the eyes of society, however, the incident did not pass unnoticed, and it was at this point that some people began looking at Sultan differently, though no one dared verbalize such thoughts.

In addition to foregrounding the beginning of Sultan's downfall, this section also provides a powerful commentary on homophobia, pointing to the fact that homophobia is often deeply rooted in self-hatred. By ridiculing (other) homosexuals, the closeted homosexual hopes not only to fool society, but also to disassociate himself from what he hates most about himself. In order to illustrate this notion, Idris stages a confrontation between Sultan and Ahmad al-Tahhan (Shahin's nephew), wherein the former begins to ridicule the latter not for being gay, but *for being related to a gay person,* going so far as to declare, "By God, we will never stop until we make you do it openly with your uncle tonight!" (17). Yet Sultan's plans to regain acceptance and respect from his followers backfire on him, for, in an unprecedented move, Ahmad rebels against Sultan, wrestling him to the ground with a sickle at his throat, forcing him to say "I am woman!" To the shock of everyone watching the scene, Sultan actually utters the words—presumably to save his own life—causing the crowd to moan "as if the sky had fallen down" (17). Then, to seal Sultan's defeat, Ahmad spits at him as he walks away.

By the end of this section, Sultan's downfall seems to be complete. He has been humiliated, degraded, and forced to admit to being a woman—a fate worse than death, it seems—in front of everyone in the village. He has chosen dishonor over death in a society that has always preached to the contrary. Yet this admission on Sultan's part is also significant at another level, for his defeat somehow proves liberating for him: "The thing that amazed him most was that he said it without having the feeling of yielding or surrendering to an unchangeable situation, but as if he were uttering a sigh of relief: 'I am woman!'" (17). Once again, homosexuality is equated with *being a woman* and consequently linked to weakness, helplessness, and dishonor in the eyes of society. Sultan is freed of his torment when he speaks the words of truth, and, despite society's rejection, he feels that he is now able to face up to his true self.

The connection and affinity between the status of women and that of homosexuals in a patriarchal society is quite clear in this section. Both are marginalized segments of society that traditionally have been dominated by heterosexual males in power. Subsequently, there may be a strong suggestion to equate the struggle and situation of gays and lesbians in the Arab world with existing feminist struggles for equality and recognition. Thus it may be argued that homosexual men (in this case) have to *become* women, or at least adopt traditionally defined roles for women, in order to achieve some sense of comfort and relief, if not some vague notion of identity or agency. Gay Arab empowerment would then be linked to preexisting feminist struggles in the Arab world and not seen primarily as an autonomous struggle for freedom.

If one is to subscribe to the view that homosexuality is constantly recounted as a loss in *A Leader of Men*—a loss of virility, strength, respect, and leadership abilities—then the title gains another significant dimension. In his essay on the story, Saad Elkhadem discusses the significance of Idris's title by noting that, "Literally translated, 'Abu al-rijal' means 'The Father of Men.' However, because the story deals with the latent homosexuality of a strong and virile man who has an exaggerated sense of masculine pride, the title must be understood as an ironic comment on the tragic dilemma of the protagonist" (25). Although Elkhadem's comment is undoubtedly valid, there may also be an additional significance to the title, if the novella is read as an attempt to subvert existing social views of the homosexual in society. Is homosexuality necessarily related to a lack (or loss) of leadership abilities, or is society's conjured-up image of the homosexual man as *woman*—and thus as lacking within male-dominated domains—determinant in its insistence on removing homosexuals from positions of power? Could Idris be scrutinizing society for upholding appearances over content in its adoration of conceived idols (broaching a debate that is very much alive in both Western and Eastern societies)? If so, then may the former (now deposed) Leader of Men now be seen as a new kind of leader of men, one who heads a new social movement that calls for reform and equality by challenging certain existing prejudices?

If Sultan's "emerging" homosexuality has been thus far linked with shame and dishonor, the story's ninth section—the shortest one of all—manages to turn the argument around by questioning the very roots of homophobia. This recuperated sense of self-pride and self-acceptance comes in the form of a rhetorical yet central question that asks, "But, indeed, why is it wrong for a human being to be a Tahhan?" (18). This question becomes more poignant when read in the original Arabic, for, literally speaking, Sultan does not actually question what is wrong (*khata'*) in being a Tahhan (gay), but rather what is "shameful" (*'ayb*) about being a Tahhan. Clearly, the word *'ayb* in this context is significant, for it shows that, instead of merely questioning and/or accepting notions of right and wrong, Sultan is for the first time directly broaching social notions of shame and honor, and the way these two concepts relate to what he and others perceive in terms of such Manichean opposites as wrong and right, black and white, et cetera.

Admittedly, the line between what is shameful and what is wrong may be muddled in this instance, as indicated by the translator's choice to translate the Arabic word *'ayb* as "wrong" (perhaps for contextual or even idiomatic reasons). Yet that translation here seems to diffuse the subtle rebellious tone of the question, which aims at challenging notions of "shame" in society and not "right" and "wrong." After all, what is perceived as shameful is not necessarily always perceived as wrong (depending, of course, on the perceiver). Thus, although society may see homosexuality as "shameful" and therefore as "wrong," the rhetorical question comes from Sultan, who is actually trying to separate what he had previously considered to be shameful from what, in his mind, is truly wrong.

This subversive question is, significantly, left unanswered. It is presented as part of Sultan's new view of himself and his acknowledged homosexuality, yet it also represents his first attempt, however feeble, to challenge existing social views rather than succumb completely to the shame they inflict on anyone who is perceived as going against the norm. In fact, it may not be an exaggeration to state that, in this question, one can trace a faint cry for gay liberation and a plea for social tolerance. On the other hand, the question, as central as it may be to a discourse centering on homosexuality, remains isolated within the boundaries of a work that consistently represents homosexuality as a loss, as seen in the very next paragraph which, stresses yet again Sultan's shame at his now nearly hairless body.

In his essay "Homosexuality and Islam," Khalid Duran discusses the Qur'an and the *shari'ah* and the way they relate to homosexual behavior by noting that, although homosexual acts are strictly forbidden in Islam, they are only punished when they move from the private to the public space: "Like fornication, homosexuality has to assume the character of a public nuisance in order to become punishable. There are, therefore, no self-proclaimed gays in Muslim countries" (183). Although such sweeping statements may be neither entirely valid nor statistically correct, Duran does point to the problematic aspects of moving from the private (secular) space to the public (religious) one. As long as one's comportment is confined to the private, whether in a homosexual or a heterosexual context, society seems much more inclined to acknowledge or even accept "normal deviation." When the private is equated with the secular, neither religion nor the law needs to be addressed, while society itself continues to shape and be shaped by unfamiliar behavior. The danger therefore lies in the transition between the private and the public, and such a transition may only occur once the private space has been educated to understand local concerns by gays and lesbians. On that level, Duran's view seems to coincide with Idris's affirmation that homosexuals (Shahin al-Tahhan) in society may be tolerated as a "normal deviation," situated somewhere between a necessary evil and a fact of life.

The closing section of *A Leader of Men* represents, in more than one way, the climax of the story, since it focuses on Sultan's ultimate demise as he at last engages in sexual behavior with Bull. Yet, although the actual sexual encounter is omitted—as Elkhadem puts it, "Idris stops before the sexual act begins, but then resumes his description after it has taken place" (27)—there are nevertheless striking remarks included that make this scene perhaps the most significant one of all.

The twist in this final scene is described by Idris in a most subtle tone. Bull, who by now has "reconciled himself to accept" playing the passive role in the sexual encounter, is surprised to find that he is asked to play the "opposite" role—i.e., that of the active partner. His reaction is one of surprise and relief: "Happy that he was saved, although he was entrapped in a different way; this is not important; important is that he had reached a stage where this one was the same as the other" (19). Such loaded statements are left ambiguous for obvious reasons. Yet in spite of this ambiguity, or

perhaps because of it, the scene is pivotal to the way homosexual relationships are seen by (Arab) society as it broaches issues of gender, role playing, and traditional notions of masculinity. Bull, who has long looked up to Sultan, automatically assumes that he will be expected to play the "female" role in the encounter, that of the "inferior" party who will serve as woman, as the depository of male aggression desire and lust. The fact that he is asked to play the role of the aggressor, the one who is supposed to be in control, surprises him and completes Sultan's transformation from masculine to feminine, a journey downward whose origin may be traced back to the story's very first section.

In his review of *A Leader of Men,* Issa Boullata does not seem to do justice to this last point when he states that "finally [Sultan] stopped caring as he accepted to act like a woman in homosexual relationships" (83). By equating Sultan's acceptance of his sexuality to "acting like a woman," Boullata seems to reaffirm the stereotype of the homosexual as necessarily lacking in manliness that the whole story is attempting to dispel. Even a superficial examination of such statements as "A man's worth is not dependent on how thick his moustache is" or "A man is a man when he is gallant, generous, courageous, unambiguous, and a savior to those in trouble" (11) leads one to understand that, in this story at least, the stereotypical characteristics of—and alleged explanations for—homosexuality are rendered invalid. It is therefore neither a lack of caring nor "sinking further into shame" that induces Sultan to "act like a woman"; it is rather his acceptance of himself as a homosexual man and his realization that homosexuality is not necessarily equated with femininity that lead him to act upon the feelings and desires he had kept buried within himself for so long. Furthermore, the "shame" in which Sultan "sank" and which Boullata seems to see as a step toward acceptance of acting "like a woman"—note that Boullata is not talking about Sultan's self-acceptance—is actually a "veil of shame" which Sultan willingly drops once he realizes that what he has mistaken for masculinity all his life is nothing more than a veil, the "veil of masculinity" (19).

Several social views of homosexuality surface in this closing section of *A Leader of Men.* Homosexual relationships, when acknowledged, are often nothing more than a replica of traditional heterosexual relationships, where each party is assigned a gender role that she or he must play. As Schmitt notes, male-male sex relations in the Arab world are often seen as a way for one party to establish superiority over the other, or, as in Sultan's case, to reaffirm one's dominant status. Penetration is thus seen as happening "between a Man and a non-Man" (19). Based on this governing social view, it is no wonder that Bull—who in many ways is Sultan's inferior follower—is ready to assume the passive role during the sexual encounter as a means of reaffirming Sultan's superiority over him, sacrificing his body to please

his master without having any desire for sex with another male. It is also due to this social view of homosexuality that Sultan's role reversal gains more impact
and proves so shocking and unexpected, even though
foreshadowed by his imminent loss of masculinity.

In subverting the existing stereotype of the man and
non-man (or "half man"), Idris may be pointing to a notion of desire that has remained unexplored through
centuries of Arabic literary production. Male homosexual relations, when surfacing at all in literature, have
almost invariably been between an adult male and a
youth, where the former is attracted by the latter's femininity, androgyny, and passivity. The erotic encounter
that came to be relatively accepted, and definitely expected, by Arab society for many centuries thus re-
volved around the notion of pleasure and release for the
so-called dominant party, with little regard given to the
notion of pleasure for the penetrated party. Like a
woman, the passive participant is considered a depository of male desire, a tool to be used for the pleasure of
man with no regard to its own desire or consciousness.
These passive participants, regardless of their will to be
penetrated, become accepted, as in Abu Nuwas's time,
as a natural part of society and as another tool to be
used to fulfill the true man's desire. Furthermore, it is
understood that once the youth reaches a certain age, he
becomes no longer desirable and may himself as an
adult turn to a new generation of youths one day.

Sultan's situation in the story's concluding section is
therefore doubly marginalized. His emerging homosexuality, which excludes him from the norm, may
somehow be understood by a society that is more than
familiar with the works of the Abbasid poets, but his
desire to be penetrated excludes him totally from any
existing category and consequently from any notion of
grace and forgiveness that otherwise may have been be-
stowed upon him. Sultan is not attracted to any female
attributes in Bull—who is continually described as rugged, muscular—but is instead drawn to the masculine
qualities that would have repulsed many "gay" Abbasid
poets. His desire to be penetrated, and thus dominated,
is in sharp contrast with accepted social views of any
leader of men.

On the other hand, Idris's attempt at subverting the
view of the manly homosexual as the "buggerer" may
not, in the long run, do much to subvert the traditionally accepted views of homosexual relationships. After
all, Sultan's encounter with Bull is not one that occurs
between two men, but still one that falls within the binary definition of man and non-man, the latter being the
newly emerged and feminized Sultan. It is not until
Sultan completes his journey downward toward feminization—thus becoming a non-man—that he is able to
engage in sexual activity with a man. Consequently, although the roles have been altered, the basic dichotomy
remains, and the possibility of a homosexual relation-

ship involving two men—or, for that matter, two non-
men—remains undiscussed and nonexistent.

Defining homosexual relationships within the narrow
binary opposition of man/non-man is obviously as destructive to postcolonial gay discourse as using the traditionally narrow man/woman gender definitions is to
postcolonial feminist discourse. In both cases, it is not
until traditionally assigned gender roles are reexamined
and subverted that any progress may occur. It is not until patriarchy's two main driving forces (misogyny and
homophobia) are understood and discussed that the road
may be paved for the liberation of those who are not in
the privileged position held by heterosexual males. The
universality of such statements, on a very general level,
rings true for the marginalized elements of any patriarchal society; yet in the specific instance of Sultan, they
gain a new dimension: Sultan is not only combating
reigning social views of the homosexual, but is also going up against neocolonialism, enacted laws, and religion.

Throughout the story, Sultan's loss of masculinity is
constantly juxtaposed with notions of shame and degradation. By the final section, he comes to a kind of self-
acceptance that is the result of refusing to feel shame
for something that is beyond his control. Sultan thus rejects the "hypocritical courtesy" that had long governed
his life, because "after the veil of masculinity was removed from him, he himself removed the veil of
shame" (19). In his process of self-affirmation, he ceases
to care about the way in which society will henceforth
view him and accepts his marginalization as he revels
in his newfound femininity. In this way, he may perhaps join the ranks of al-Tahhan and others like him—
the first step toward gay empowerment—but must shed
his traditional notions of masculinity, thus substituting
essentialist social prerequisites for the homosexual with
a set of new yet equally narrow definitions that will
henceforth govern his life.

Still, it would be difficult if not impossible to dismiss
completely the importance and relevance of Idris's story
in relation to Arab society and to Arabic literature. The
fact remains that this is the first published work in many
centuries to address homosexuality in such a blatantly
noncloseted manner. After all, the work had been first
published in one of Egypt's most popular magazines
and had been read by the public at large. The fact that it
was written by a renowned Egyptian author added to its
importance as a breakthrough in Arabic literature. Yet,
for all the critical acclaim that the novella received, and
as functional as it may be or could have been in initiat-
ing some kind of discourse centering on the state of the
Arab homosexual in Arab society, the story for the most
part was easily dismissed as yet another deliberately
controversial work on the part of writer who had not
only become famous for daring to broach unmentionable topics (Idris had previously published a story which

dealt with male impotence, for example) but also was and is perceived as clearly heterosexual. The combination of the above two elements, and the fact that it was specifically Idris who was writing about homosexuality, may have thus diffused the anger and backlash which might have otherwise occurred had the theme been broached by an unknown or lesser-known author.

Yet, as in the case of other progressive Egyptian writers such as Naguib Mahfouz and Nawal El Saadawi, the main question remains whether the lack of reaction by conservative circles is in actuality beneficial for the author and, in this case, for gay discourse. One is reminded here of El Saadawi's statement that "nothing is more demoralizing for a woman [author] than to produce literary or scientific work which no one feels worthy of criticism" (Tarabishi, 189). Perhaps more than in any other part of the world, censorship in Muslim countries functions as a double-edged sword. In El Saadawi's case, many of her works have indeed been published—albeit in limited quantities—in Egypt, but were deliberately left unreviewed, thus thrusting them into a state of temporary oblivion, only to be (re)discovered later and by subsequent generations. Such works remain virtually unknown to the Egyptian reading public, unlike other El Saadawi books, which were censored and banned, yet, for the most part, continue to circulate in various forms around Egypt and the Arab world.[1]

Note

1. For more on this point, see the interview with Nawal El Saadawi, "Hadith ma' imra'ah ghadibah," published in *Zahrat al-Khalij,* no. 609 (24 November 1990), pp. 35-37. Also see my essay, "Paradise, Heaven, and Other Oppressive Spaces: A Critical Examination of the Life and Works of Nawal el-Saadawi," *Journal of Arabic Literature,* 25 (1994), pp. 152-74.

Works Cited

Allen, Roger. Review of Yusuf Idris, *Abu al-rijal / A Leader of Men. World Literature Today,* 63:2 (Spring 1989), p. 360.

Boullata, Issa. Review of Yusuf Idris, *Abu al-rijal / A Leader of Men. International Fiction Review,* 16:1 (1989), p. 83.

Elkadem, Saad. Preface to Yusuf Idris, *Abu al-rijal / A Leader of Men.* Fredericton, N.B. York. 1988. Pp. 1-2.

———. "Youssef Idris and His Gay *Leader of Men.*" *International Fiction Review,* 17:1 (1990), pp. 25-28.

Idris, Yusuf. *Abu al-rijal / A Leader of Men* (bilingual edition). Saad Elkhadem, tr. Fredericton, N.B. York. 1988.

Schmitt, Arno. "Different Approaches to Male-Male Sexuality/Eroticism from Morocco to Usbekistan." *Sexuality and Eroticism among Males in Moslem Societies.* Arno Schmitt and Jehoeda Sofer, eds. New York. Harrington Park. 1992. Pp. 1-24.

Tarabishi, Georges. *Woman Against Her Sex: A Critique of Nawal el-Saadawi.* Basil Hatim and Elizabeth Orsini, trs. London. Saqi. 1988.

FURTHER READING

Criticism

al-Mousa, Nedal. "A Social Psychological Interpretation of Yusuf Idris's 'Snobbism'."[1] *Arabic and Middle Eastern Literatures* 2, no. 2 (July 1999): 173-75.
    Provides a social psychological perspective on "Snobbism."

Roger, Allen, ed. *Critical Perspectives on Yusuf Idris.* Colorado Springs: Three Continents Press, 1994, 180 p.
    Collection of critical essays.

Cohen-Mor, Dalya. *Yusuf Idris: Changing Visions.* Potomac, Md.: Sheba Press, 1992, 188 p.
    Examines the central themes of Idris's short fiction.

Mikhail, Mona N. *Studies in the Short Fiction of Mahfouz and Idris.* New York: New York University Press, 1992, 168 p.
    Analysis of the short fiction of Idris and Naguib Mahfouz.

Somekh, S. "Language and Theme in the Short Stories of Yusuf Idris." *Journal of Arabic Literature* 6 (1975): 89-100.
    Offers a thematic and stylistic analysis of Idris's short fiction.

The Things They Carried

Tim O'Brien

(Full name William Timothy O'Brien) American novelist, short-story writer, memoirist, and journalist.

The following entry presents criticism on O'Brien's short-story collection *The Things They Carried* (1990) from 1990 through 2002.

INTRODUCTION

Published in 1990, *The Things They Carried* is regarded as an exceptional fictional work based on the experiences of a dozen American soldiers dealing with the trauma and boredom of combat during the Vietnam War. Reviewers commend O'Brien's innovative combination of fiction, memoir, and nonfiction in the short pieces that comprise the volume. In fact, the interweaving of fact and fiction in *The Things They Carried* has generated much commentary, particularly about the ambiguous nature of his narratives and the metafictional quality of his storytelling techniques. In 1991 the volume was nominated for a Pulitzer Prize and a National Book Critics Circle Award.

PLOT AND MAJOR CHARACTERS

The Things They Carried is comprised of twenty-two interconnected short stories, many of which were published separately in periodicals. These short pieces utilize elements of disparate forms—fiction, nonfiction, fantasy, memoir, author's notations, and literary commentary—and focus on the Vietnam War experience and its traumatic aftermath. The opening piece, "The Things They Carried," is a list that focuses on everything carried into battle by each soldier in the book, ranging from such items as jungle boots and personal letters to feelings like grief, rage, and shame. Critics have praised it as a fitting and insightful introduction to the recurring characters in the book. Many of the pieces explore the process of storytelling and reflect on the confusion of the war experience: several episodes are derived from other sources, or are remembered long after the fact; some are stories overheard and repeated in the oral tradition. Several stories feature a character named Tim O'Brien who comments on the process of writing the stories—twenty years later. The interplay between memory and imagination makes it difficult for the reader to distinguish the truthful elements of the

story. The O'Brien narrator often recalls and elaborates on the scenes in various stories; in other stories, he is not identified as the narrator until after the narrative is complete. In "The Man I Killed," O'Brien revises the story of his mental breakdown after killing an enemy soldier—only to reveal that his revised version is also invented. Other stories are related by other narrators. "Speaking of Courage" chronicles the grief and alienation of Vietnam veteran Norman Bowker, who is unable to articulate his shame over his failure to save his friend from death in combat after he returns home to Iowa. In an addendum to the story, "Notes," the narrator informs readers that the original version of "Speaking of Courage" was written in 1975 at the suggestion of Bowker, who killed himself three years later in Iowa. In "Sweetheart of the Song Tra Bong," Rat Kiley chronicles the strange story of Mary Anne Bell, an Ohio cheerleader who follows her high school sweetheart to Vietnam and transforms into a terrorist herself. By the end of the fantastic tale—as Mary Anne disappears into the jungle wearing a necklace of human tongues—Kiley is relating information from other sources and the story has become a legend. "How to Tell a True War Story" meditates on the relationship of truth to storytelling. In one section of the story, another soldier relates the story of a six-man patrol that is ordered into the mountains and undergoes a traumatic experience. When the soldier tries to apply a moral and revises the story, the narrator recognizes the inherent truth of the first version. For him, a true story is one that isn't based on what actually happened, but the different ways in which the traumatic experience is rewritten and retold. Critics note that traumatic experiences are endlessly filtered and recirculated in the stories. In another section of "How to Tell a True War Story," Rat Kiley cruelly kills a baby water buffalo for no reason—which upsets a listener at one of O'Brien's book readings years later. O'Brien then retells the story, over and over, with each version providing a new perspective on Kiley's own emotional trauma from earlier combat experiences and the murder of the buffalo. Eventually he reveals that it all was a fictional exercise meant to express trauma and its consequences without merely utilizing his own personal experiences.

MAJOR THEMES

Critics assert that the central theme of *The Things They Carried* is the relationship of storytelling to truth. In this vein, they often discuss O'Brien's interest in transcending reality to represent the truths of his traumatic Vietnam War experience as a defining characteristic of the book. Commentators note that for O'Brien, the question of authenticity and verisimilitude when relating war experiences is ambiguous; instead, a story's authenticity is often based on its effect on the reader. As O'Brien states, a story is truthful if it "makes the stomach believe." Reviewers assert that the stories address the effects of combat trauma and the struggle for redemption and recovery. The role of memory is an important theme in the stories in the volume. Another major thematic concern in *The Things They Carried* is cowardice: not only in combat, but also in the narrator's choice to participate in what he feels is an unjust war. Commentators have analyzed the representations of masculinity and femininity in the book. Exile and alienation also figure prominently in the stories, as returning American war veterans feel displaced from their old life and haunted by their wartime experiences.

CRITICAL RECEPTION

A resounding critical success, *The Things They Carried* is considered a valuable contribution to the canon of Vietnam War literature. Commentators often discuss the genre of the book; it is often classified as a composite novel instead of a group of interconnected short stories. Some reviewers regard *The Things They Carried* as a continuation of O'Brien's first two Vietnam narratives: the autobiographical *If I Die in a Combat Zone* (1973) and novel *Going after Cacciato* (1978). The tendency of the stories to reflect upon their own status, format, and function has prompted critics to refer to the volume as a work of metafiction. O'Brien's concentration on storytelling and memory has led critics to compare *The Things They Carried* to the work of Marcel Proust and Joseph Conrad. Moreover, O'Brien's war stories have been compared to the Civil War stories of Ambrose Bierce and the classical stories of Homer's *Iliad*. Mental health professionals have praised O'Brien for his insightful depiction of combat trauma in his stories. Critics applaud his ability to memorialize his wartime experiences and view *The Things They Carried* as his most accomplished work of fiction.

PRINCIPAL WORKS

Short Fiction

The Things They Carried 1990

Other Major Works

If I Die in a Combat Zone, Box Me Up and Ship Me Home (memoirs) 1973
Northern Lights (novel) 1975

Going after Cacciato (novel) 1978
The Nuclear Age (novel) 1985
In the Lake of the Woods (novel) 1994
Tomcat in Love (novel) 1998
July, July (novel) 2002

CRITICISM

Josiah Bunting (review date 23 April 1990)

SOURCE: Bunting, Josiah. "Vietnam, Carried On." *Book World—Washington Post* (23 April 1990): B13.

[*In the following review, Bunting considers the defining and unifying characteristics of the stories in* The Things They Carried.]

A war writer's compulsion to write about why, and how, he writes about war and about what constitutes good war writing is not often resisted successfully. It rises like second growth forest, from soil in which his memory has already quickened and that has nourished his imagination and sometimes its trunks and shoots bristle in the midst of taller usually stronger trees. Too often the consequence is literary criticism, or reflections on the unreliability of memory, or simple assertions about writing about combat, that should have stood alone. It is rare that writers of unusual imaginative powers have critical gifts to match. When the fruits of both are mixed, the result is to diminish each. Perhaps ***The Things They Carried*** deserves a partial exemption from such criticism: It is after all a collection of long stories and memoirs (it is impossible to tell which is which) published over the last 11 years of Tim O'Brien's writing life. What efforts have been made to stitch them together, after the fact, cannot be judged.

Most of these narratives tell stories about the lives and deaths of 19-year-old American boys in the Central Highlands of Vietnam in 1968. The stories are linked in one way or another, through flashbacks, casual anticipations, the reappearance of different characters, all members of an infantry platoon. Episodes in their lives as infantrymen are rendered in an authorial tone, with an evocative, quiet precision not equaled in the imaginative literature of the American war in Vietnam. It is as though a Thucydides had descended from grand *politique* and strategy to the calm dissection of the quotidian effects of war on several individuals—given, particularly, the things they carried with them into combat: their own exhaustion, their few pathetic bibelots, their memories, their weapons. They carried no political sensibility or outrage. "They marched for the sake of the march. They plodded along slowly, dumbly, leaning forward against the heat, unthinking, all blood and bone, simple grunts, soldiering with their legs, toiling up the hills and down . . . but [without] volition, without will, because it was automatic . . . a kind of emptiness, a dullness of desire and intellect and conscience and hope and human sensibility." O'Brien has it just right; and he observes a few pages later that "a true war story is never moral. It does not instruct, nor encourage virtue, nor suggest models of proper human behavior, nor restrain men from doing the things men have always done. If a story seems moral, do not believe it."

Precisely so. Such stories as wars produce must aim only at telling what seems significant in what the participant remembers of what he saw, as his imagination has transmuted such things. What figures most vividly in his mind must not consciously be "moral." The things he carried into the war are very different from what he carried away from it—in O'Brien's case, for example, a conviction that it was a lack of true courage that prevented him from leaping from a rowboat close to the Canadian side of the Rainy River in 1968, a leap that would have made a conviction about the injustice of the war a commitment not to fight in it.

There is a sense in these narratives of elemental fatalism: not unlike that of soldiers of World War I, as they appear in Siegfried Sassoon, Henri Barbusse, Wilfred Owen, Erich Maria Remarque. An American boy in the infantry, from the Minnesota prairie, simply serves to survive; exhausted, private, helplessly clinging to his small baggages against the coming of the distant date of his expected "rotation" home to America. There is no political or moral irruption here; only personal remorse and the lived knowledge that no sense is to be made of the war by those called upon—always the youngest and least knowing—to fight it.

It is now more than 17 years since the departure of the last American soldiers from Vietnam. It is 25 since the commitment of U.S. Army and Marine units to combat. The former lapse of time is greater than that between Hiroshima and the inauguration of John Kennedy. In 1961, not many people were writing about ground combat in World War II; but our absorption in Vietnam remains intense, self-consciously intense, haunting. Novels, memoirs, collections—all pour forth in a thick stream that does not diminish: acts of exorcism, atonement, reconstruction, epiphany. It will never all be said; but it is difficult to imagine that it will ever be set down more accurately, more usefully, than in these narratives. If in form they resist classification, if their facts and their fictions are commingled beyond separate identification, if critical reflection occasionally intrudes unduly, these are small cavils to set alongside a growing body of work about our worst and longest war, by its best and more steadfast chronicler.

David Streitfeld (review date 19 May 1991)

SOURCE: Streitfeld, David. "Never Done." *Book World—Washington Post* (19 May 1991): 15.

[*In the following review, Streitfeld examines O'Brien's revisions to the paperback edition of* The Things They Carried.]

In the hardcover edition of Tim O'Brien's **The Things They Carried**, published last year, there is a scene where the narrator, called Tim, goes back to Vietnam with his 10-year-old daughter Kathleen. They go on a sidetrip to Quang Ngai, where Tim finds the field his friend Kiowa died in—a stretch of ground that for 20 years "had embodied all the waste that was Vietnam, all the vulgarity and horror."

As Kathleen watches, Tim takes Kiowa's hunting hatchet over to where the field dips down into the river. "Right here, I thought. Leaning forward, I reached in with the hatchet and wedged it handle first into the soft bottom, letting it slide away, the blade's own weight taking it under."

In the paperback edition, just released by Penguin, the scene is the same—except for one detail. This time it's a pair of moccasins that Tim buries.

Tim O'Brien, the real Tim O'Brien, explains the switch: "When I was writing the novel, the phrase 'bury the hatchet' didn't occur to me. But when I read it in the hardcover version, I thought 'Ohmigod. That's kind of heavyhanded symbolism.' It hadn't been intended that way, so I changed it to moccasins."

There are a couple of other small changes between the editions—"four or five times," O'Brien says, "I realized I was making a mistake." And even this won't be the end. He'll probably do a substantial rewrite maybe a decade from now. He's already done revisions of his classic early works, *If I Die in a Combat Zone* and *Going After Cacciato*, slipping them quietly into print in recent paperback reissues. (The changes in **The Things They Carried** have been made in so low-key a fashion that the Penguin book doesn't even include a new copyright.)

Nor does the process stop after one revision. The author already has another change to make in *Cacciato* involving the circumference of the table at the Paris peace talks. A physicist recently wrote O'Brien a letter full of equations that said the diameter he had described was impossible, so next time around the figure will be changed.

"I don't look at my work as holy, and I don't think writers should," O'Brien says. "I don't want to leave behind something I know that I'm less than capable of, or something that I know will put off a reader."

Most people thought *The Things They Carried* was pretty fine the first time around. It was a runner-up for both the Pulitzer and National Book Critics Circle awards, while the paperback carries six full pages of endorsements from reviewers totaling 37 separate entries. This is probably a record, and it is going to strike some as overkill.

Still, the book deserves the praise. O'Brien came up with an unconventional way to write about Vietnam that feels right, a hybrid form: neither short stories nor novel, autobiographical in form but not literally. After three novels directly and two tangentially concerned with the war, *The Things They Carried* has the air of reconciliation between the present and the past. This, plus the news that O'Brien is writing a love story next, suggests that he may have come to some conclusions.

Nope. "I don't care about answers," he says. "I care about stories—and there are so many wonderful stories left to tell about Vietnam, both imagined and real, that I'd be crazy not to write about it. I'd be denying the best material I'll ever have. Take a guy like Conrad. Can you imagine someone saying to him, 'Don't write about the ocean anymore, don't set your stories on the sea.' He'd be nuts. Or it'd be like saying to Shakespeare, 'Don't write any more plays about kings,' or to Updike, 'Stop writing about suburbia.'"

The writers who came out of World War II tended to write one book about the struggle: their first. There were exceptions—James Jones continued to write about Army life throughout his career—but generally Norman Mailer, Irwin Shaw, Gore Vidal and their compatriots went on to other things. Vietnam has had a different effect on its writers. "There was something about that period—not just the war itself, but the ambiguous moral issues that surrounded it, to which we're going to keep returning," O'Brien believes. He figures he'll circle back to the war every other book.

His war stories, by the way, aren't designed for those who were there. "I hated most of those guys," O'Brien says, calling them "bullies and showoffs and adventurers" and some unprintable things as well. "I didn't like them then, I don't like them now."

Steven Kaplan (essay date fall 1993)

SOURCE: Kaplan, Steven. "The Undying Certainty of the Narrator in Tim O'Brien's *The Things They Carried*." *Critique* 35, no. 1 (fall 1993): 43-52.

[*In the following essay, Kaplan perceives* The Things They Carried *to be O'Brien's imaginative attempt to reveal and understand the uncertainties about the Vietnam War.*]

Before the United States became militarily involved in defending the sovereignty of South Vietnam, it had to, as one historian recently put it, "invent" (Baritz 142-43) the country and the political issues at stake there. The Vietnam War was in many ways a wild and terrible work of fiction written by some dangerous and frightening storytellers. First the United States decided what constituted good and evil, right and wrong, civilized and uncivilized, freedom and oppression for Vietnam, according to American standards; then it traveled the long physical distance to Vietnam and attempted to make its own notions about these things clear to the Vietnamese people—ultimately by brute, technological force. For the U.S. military and government, the Vietnam that they had in effect invented became fact. For the soldiers that the government then sent there, however, the facts that their government had created about who was the enemy, what were the issues, and how the war was to be won were quickly overshadowed by a world of uncertainty. Ultimately, trying to stay alive long enough to return home in one piece was the only thing that made any sense to them. As David Halberstam puts it in his novel, *One Very Hot Day,* the only fact of which an American soldier in Vietnam could be certain was that "yes was no longer yes, no was no longer no, maybe was more certainly maybe" (127). Almost all of the literature on the war, both fictional and nonfictional, makes clear that the only certain thing during the Vietnam War was that nothing was certain. Philip Beidler has pointed out in an impressive study of the literature of that war that "most of the time in Vietnam, there were some things that seemed just too terrible and strange to be true and others that were just too terrible and true to be strange" (4).

The main question that Beidler's study raises is how, in light of the overwhelming ambiguity that characterized the Vietnam experience, could any sense or meaning be derived from what happened and, above all, how could this meaning, if it were found, be conveyed to those who had not experienced the war? The answer Beidler's book offers, as Beidler himself recently said at a conference on writing about the war, is that "words are all we have. In the hands of true artists . . . they may yet preserve us against the darkness" (Lomperis 87). Similarly, for the novelist Tim O'Brien, the language of fiction is the most accurate means for conveying, as Beidler so incisively puts it, "what happened (in Vietnam) . . . what might have happened, what could have happened, what should have happened, and maybe also what can be kept from happening or what can be made to happen" (87). If the experience of Vietnam and its accompanying sense of chaos and confusion can be shown at all, then for Tim O'Brien it will not be in the fictions created by politicians but in the stories told by writers of fiction.

One of Tim O'Brien's most important statements about the inherent problems of understanding and writing about the Vietnam experience appears in a chapter of his novel, *Going After Cacciato,* appropriately titled "The Things They Didn't Know." The novel's protagonist, Paul Berlin, briefly interrupts his fantasy about chasing the deserter Cacciato, who is en route from Vietnam to Paris, to come to terms with the fact that although he is physically in Vietnam and fighting a war, his understanding of where he is and what he is doing there is light-years away. At the center of the chapter is a long catalogue of the things that Berlin and his comrades did not know about Vietnam, and the chapter closes with the statement that what "they" *knew* above all else were the "uncertainties never articulated in war stories" (319). In that chapter Tim O'Brien shows that recognizing and exploring the uncertainties about the war is perhaps the closest one can come to finding anything certain at all. Paul Berlin, in his fantasy about escaping the war and chasing Cacciato to Paris, is in fact attempting to confront and, as far as possible, understand the uncertainties of the Vietnam War through the prism of his imagination. Once inside his make-believe world, Berlin has the opportunity to explore all of the things that he did not know about the war: The elusive enemy suddenly becomes his partner in a long debate about the meaning of the war; he explores the mysterious tunnels of the Vietcong; one of the victims of the war becomes Berlin's tour guide as he and his fellow soldiers go after Cacciato; and, most important of all, Berlin is given a chance to test and ultimately reject his own thoughts of desertion by imagining how he would react to the desertion of another soldier.

In his most recent work of fiction,[1] **The Things They Carried,** Tim O'Brien takes the act of trying to reveal and understand the uncertainties about the war one step further, by looking at it through the imagination. He completely destroys the fine line dividing fact from fiction and tries to show, even more so than in *Cacciato,* that fiction (or the imagined world) can often be truer, especially in the case of Vietnam, than fact. In the first chapter, an almost documentary account of the items referred to in the book's title, O'Brien introduces the reader to some of the things, both imaginary and concrete, emotional and physical, that the average foot soldier had to carry through the jungles of Vietnam. All of the "things" are depicted in a style that is almost scientific in its precision. We are told how much each subject weighs, either psychologically or physically, and, in the case of artillery, we are even told how many ounces each round weighed:

> As PFCs or Spec 4s, most of them were common grunts and carried the standard M-16 gas operated assault rifle. The weapon weighed 7.5 pounds, 8.2 pounds with its full 20-round magazine. Depending on numerous factors, such as topography and psychology, the rifleman carried anywhere from 12 to 20 magazines, usu-

ally in cloth bandoliers, adding on another 8.4 pounds at minimum, 14 pounds at maximum.

> (*Carried* 7 [*The Things They Carried*])

Even the most insignificant details seem worth mentioning. One main character is not just from Oklahoma City but from "Oklahoma City, Oklahoma" (5), as if mentioning the state somehow makes the location more factual, more certain. More striking than this obsession with even the minutest detail, however, is the academic tone that at times makes the narrative sound like a government report. We find such transitional phrases as "for instance" (5) and "in addition" (7), and whole paragraphs are dominated by sentences that begin with "because" (5). These strengthen our impression that the narrator is striving, above all else, to convince us of the reality, of the concrete certainty, of the things they carried.

In the midst of this factuality and certainty, however, are signals that all the information in this opening chapter will not amount to much: that the certainties are merely there to conceal uncertainties and that the words following the frequent "becauses" do not provide an explanation of anything. We are told in the opening page that the most important thing that First Lieutenant Jimmy Cross carried were some letters from a girl he loved. The narrator, one of Cross's friends in the war and now a forty-three-year-old writer named Tim O'Brien, tells us that the girl did not love Cross, but that he constantly indulged in "hoping" and "pretending" (3) in an effort to turn her love into fact. We are also told "she was a virgin," but this is immediately qualified by the statement that "he was almost sure" of this (3). On the next page, Cross becomes increasingly uncertain as he sits at "night and wonder(s) if Martha was a virgin" (4). Shortly after this, Cross wonders who had taken the pictures he now holds in his hands "because he knew she had boyfriends" (5), but we are never told how he "knew" this. At the end of the chapter, after one of Cross's men has died because Cross was too busy thinking of Martha, Cross sits at the bottom of his foxhole crying, not so much for the member of his platoon who has been killed "but mostly it was for Martha, and for himself, because she belonged to another world, and because she was . . . a poet and a virgin and uninvolved" (17).

This pattern of stating facts and then quickly calling them into question that is typical of Jimmy Cross's thoughts in these opening pages characterizes how the narrator portrays events throughout this book: the facts about an event are given; they then are quickly qualified or called into question; from this uncertainty emerges a new set of facts about the same subject that are again called into question—on and on, without end. O'Brien catalogues the weapons that the soldiers carried, down to their weight, thus making them seem important and their protective power real. However, several of these passages are introduced by the statement that some of these same weapons were also carried by the character Ted Lavendar; each of the four sections of the first chapter that tells us what he carried is introduced by a qualifying phrase that reveals something about which Lavendar himself was not at all certain when he was carrying his weapons: "Until he was shot . . ." (4, 7, 10).

Conveying the average soldier's sense of uncertainty about what actually happened in Vietnam by presenting the what-ifs and maybes as if they were facts, and then calling these facts back into question again, can be seen as a variation of the haunting phrase used so often by American soldiers to convey their own uncertainty about what happened in Vietnam: "there it is." They used it to make the unspeakable and indescribable and the uncertain real and present for a fleeting moment. Similarly, O'Brien presents facts and stories that are only temporarily certain and real; the strange "balance" in Vietnam between "crazy and almost crazy" (20) always creeps back in and forces the mind that is remembering and retelling a story to remember and retell it one more time in a different form, adding different nuances, and then to tell it again one more time.

Storytelling in this book is something in which "the whole world is rearranged" (39) in an effort to get at the "full truth" (49) about events that themselves deny the possibility of arriving at something called the "full", meaning certain and fixed, "truth." By giving the reader facts and then calling those facts into question, by telling stories and then saying that those stories happened (147), and then that they did not happen (203), and then that they might have happened (204), O'Brien puts more emphasis in *The Things They Carried* on the question that he first posed in *Going After Cacciato:* how can a work of fiction become paradoxically more real than the events upon which it is based, and how can the confusing experiences of the average soldier in Vietnam be conveyed in such a way that they will acquire at least a momentary sense of certainty. In *The Things They Carried,* this question is raised even before the novel begins. The book opens with a reminder: "This is a work of fiction. Except for a few details regarding the author's own life, all the incidents, names, and characters are imaginary." Two pages later we are told that "this book is lovingly dedicated to the men of Alpha Company, and in particular to Jimmy Cross, Norman Bowker, Rat Kiley, Mitchell Sanders, Henry Dobbins, and Kiowa." We discover only a few pages after this dedication that those six men are the novel's main characters.

These prefatory comments force us simultaneously to consider the unreal (the fictions that follow) as real because the book is dedicated to the characters who ap-

pear in it, and the "incidents, names, and characters" are unreal or "imaginary." O'Brien informs us at one point that in telling these war stories he intends to get at the "full truth" (49) about them; yet from the outset he has shown us that the full truth as he sees it is in itself something ambiguous. Are these stories and the characters in them real or imaginary, or does the "truth" hover somewhere between the two? A closer look at the book's narrative structure reveals that O'Brien is incapable of answering the questions that he initially raises, because the very act of writing fiction about the war, of telling war stories, as he practices it in *The Things They Carried,* is determined by the nature of the Vietnam War and ultimately by life in general where "the only certainty is overwhelming ambiguity" (88).

The emphasis on ambiguity behind O'Brien's narrative technique in *The Things They Carried* is thus similar to the pattern used by Joseph Conrad's narrator, Marlow, in *Heart of Darkness,* so incisively characterized by J. Hillis Miller as a lifting of veils to reveal a truth that is quickly obscured again by the dropping of a new veil (158). Over and over again, O'Brien tells us that we are reading "the full and exact truth" (181), and yet, as we make our way through this book and gradually find the same stories being retold with new facts and from a new perspective, we come to realize that there is no such thing as the full and exact truth. Instead, the only thing that can be determined at the end of the story is its own indeterminacy.

O'Brien calls telling stories in this manner **"Good Form"** in the title of one of the chapters of *The Things They Carried*: This is good form because "telling stories" like this "can make things present" (204). The stories in this book are not truer than the actual things that happened in Vietnam because they contain some higher, metaphysical truth: "True war stories do not generalize. They do not indulge in abstractions or analysis" (84). Rather, these stories are true because the characters and events within them are being given a new life each time they are told and retold. This approach to storytelling echoes Wolfgang Iser's theory of representation in his essay "Representation: A Performative Act":

> Whatever shape or form these various (philosophical or fictional) conceptualizations (of life) may have, their common denominator is the attempt to explain origins. In this respect they close off those very potentialities that literature holds open. Of course literature also springs from the same anthropological need, since it stages what is inaccessible, thus compensating for the impossibility of knowing what it is to be. But literature is not an explanation of origins; it is a staging of the constant deferment of explanation, which makes the origin explode into its multifariousness.
>
> It is at this point that aesthetic semblance makes its full impact. Representation arises out of and thus entails the removal of difference, whose irremovability trans-

forms representation into a performative act of staging something. This staging is almost infinitely variable, for in contrast to explanations, no single staging could ever remove difference and so explain origin. On the contrary, its very multiplicity facilitates an unending mirroring of what man is, because no mirrored manifestation can ever coincide with our actual being.

(245)

When we conceptualize life, we attempt to step outside ourselves and look at who we are. We constantly make new attempts to conceptualize our lives and uncover our true identities because looking at who we might be is as close as we can come to discovering who we actually are. Similarly, representing events in fiction is an attempt to understand them by detaching them from the "real world" and placing them in a world that is being staged. In *The Things They Carried*, Tim O'Brien desperately struggles to make his readers believe that what they are reading is true because he wants them to step outside their everyday reality and participate in the events that he is portraying: he wants us to believe in his stories to the point where we are virtually in the stories so that we might gain a more thorough understanding of, or feeling for, what is being portrayed in them. Representation as O'Brien practices it in this book is not a mimetic act but a "game," as Iser also calls it in a more recent essay, "The Play of the Text," a process of acting things out:

> Now since the latter (the text) is fictional, it automatically invokes a convention-governed contract between author and reader indicating that the textual world is to be viewed not as reality but as if it *were* reality. And so whatever is repeated in the text is not meant to denote the world, but merely a world enacted. This may well repeat an identifiable reality, but it contains one all-important difference: what happens within it is relieved of the consequences inherent in the real world referred to. Hence in disclosing itself, fictionality signalizes that everything is only to be taken *as if* it were what it seems to be, to be taken—in other words—as play.

(251)

In *The Things They Carried*, representation includes staging what might have happened in Vietnam while simultaneously questioning the accuracy and credibility of the narrative act itself. The reader is thus made fully aware of being made a participant in a game, in a "performative act," and thereby also is asked to become immediately involved in the incredibly frustrating act of trying to make sense of events that resist understanding. The reader is permitted to experience at first hand the uncertainty that characterized being in Vietnam. We are being forced to "believe" (79) that the only "certainty" was the "overwhelming ambiguity."

This process is nowhere clearer than in a chapter appropriately called **"How to Tell A True War Story."** O'Brien opens this chapter by telling us "THIS IS TRUE." Then he takes us through a series of variations of the story about how Kurt Lemon stepped on a mine and was blown up into a tree. The only thing true or certain about the story, however, is that it is being constructed and then deconstructed and then reconstructed right in front of us. The reader is given six different versions of the death of Kurt Lemon, and each version is so discomforting that it is difficult to come up with a more accurate statement to describe his senseless death than "there it is." Or as O'Brien puts it—"in the end, really there's nothing much to say about a true war story, except maybe 'Oh'" (84).

Before we learn in this chapter how Kurt Lemon was killed, we are told the "true" story that Rat Kiley apparently told to the character-narrator O'Brien about how Kiley wrote to Lemon's sister and "says he loved the guy. He says the guy was his best friend in the world" (76). Two months after writing the letter, Kiley has not heard from Lemon's sister, and so he writes her off as a "dumb cooze" (76). This is what happened according to Kiley, and O'Brien assures us that the story is "incredibly sad and true" (77). However, when Rat Kiley tells a story in another chapter we are warned that he

> swore up and down to its truth, although in the end, I'll admit, that doesn't amount to much of a warranty. Among the men in Alpha Company, Rat had a reputation for exaggeration and overstatement, a compulsion to rev up the facts, and for most of us it was normal procedure to discount sixty or seventy percent of anything he had to say.

(101)

Rat Kiley is an unreliable narrator, and his facts are always distorted, but this does not affect storytelling truth as far as O'Brien is concerned. The passage above on Rat Kiley's credibility as a storyteller concludes: "It wasn't a question of deceit. Just the opposite: he wanted to heat up the truth, to make it burn so hot that you would feel exactly what he felt" (101). This summarizes O'Brien's often confusing narrative strategy in *The Things They Carried:* the facts about what actually happened, or whether anything happened at all, are not important. They cannot be important because they themselves are too uncertain, too lost in a world in which certainty had vanished somewhere between the "crazy and almost crazy." The important thing is that any story about the war, any "true war story," must "burn so hot" when it is told that it becomes alive for the listener-reader in the act of its telling.

In Rat Kiley's story about how he wrote to Kurt Lemon's sister, the details we are initially given are exaggerated to the point where, in keeping with O'Brien's fire metaphor, they begin to heat up. Kurt Lemon, we are told, "would always volunteer for stuff nobody else would volunteer for in a million years" (75). And once

Lemon went fishing with a crate of hand grenades, "the funniest thing in world history . . . about twenty zillion dead gook fish" (76). But the story does not get so hot that it burns, it does not become so "incredibly sad and true," as O'Brien puts it, until we find out at the story's close that, in Rat's own words, "I write this beautiful fuckin' letter, I slave over it, and what happens? The dumb cooze never writes back" (77). It is these words and not the facts that come before them that make the story true for O'Brien.

At the beginning of this chapter, O'Brien asks us several times to "Listen to Rat," to listen how he says things more than to what he says. And of all of the words that stand out in his story, it is the word "cooze," (which is repeated four times in two pages), that makes his story come alive for O'Brien. "You can tell a true war story by its absolute and uncompromising allegiance to obscenity and evil" (76). This is just one way that O'Brien gives for determining what constitutes a true war story. The unending list of possibilities includes reacting to a story with the ambiguous words "Oh" and "There it is." Rat Kiley's use of "cooze" is another in the sequence of attempts to utter some truth about the Vietnam experience and, by extension, about war in general. There is no moral to be derived from this word such as war is obscene or corrupt: "A true war story is never moral. It does not instruct" (76). There is simply the real and true fact that the closest thing to certainty and truth in a war story is a vague utterance, a punch at the darkness, an attempt to rip momentarily through the veil that repeatedly re-covers the reality and truth of what actually happened.

It is thus probably no coincidence that in the middle of this chapter on writing a true war story, O'Brien tells us that "Even now, at this instant," Mitchell Sanders's "yo-yo" is the main thing he can remember from the short time encompassing Lemon's death (83). This object, associated with games and play, becomes a metaphor for the playful act of narration that O'Brien practices in this book, a game that he plays by necessity. The only way to tell a true war story, according to O'Brien, is to keep telling it "one more time, patiently, adding and subtracting, making up a few things to get at the real truth" (91), which ultimately is impossible because the real truth, the full truth, as the events themselves, are lost forever in "a great ghostly fog, thick and permanent" (88). You only "tell a true war story" "if you just keep on telling it" (91) because "absolute occurrence is irrelevant" (89). The truth, then, is clearly not something that can be distinguished or separated from the story itself, and the reality or non-reality of the story's events is not something that can be determined from a perspective outside of the story. As the critic Geoffrey Hartman says about poetry: "To keep a poem in mind is to keep it there, not to resolve it into available meanings" (274). Similarly, for O'Brien it is

not the fact that a story happened that makes it true and worth remembering, anymore than the story itself can be said to contain a final truth. The important thing is that a story becomes so much a part of the present that "there is nothing to remember (while we are reading it) except the story" (40). This is why O'Brien's narrator is condemned, perhaps in a positive sense, to telling and then retelling numerous variations of the same story over and over and over again. This is also why he introduces each new version of a story with such comments as: "This one does it for me. I have told it before many times, many versions—but here is what actually happened" (85). What actually happened, the story's truth, can only become apparent for the fleeting moment in which it is being told; that truth will vanish back into the fog just as quickly as the events that occurred in Vietnam were sucked into a realm of uncertainty the moment they occurred.

O'Brien demonstrates nothing new about trying to tell war stories—that the "truths" they contain "are contradictory" (87), elusive, and thus indeterminate. Two hundred years ago, Goethe, as he tried to depict the senseless bloodshed during the allied invasion of revolutionary France, also reflected in his autobiographical essay *Campaign in France* on the same inevitable contradictions that arise when one speaks of what happened or might have happened in battle. Homer's *Illiad* is, of course, the ultimate statement on the contradictions inherent in war. However, what is new in O'Brien's approach in *The Things They Carried* is that he makes the axiom that in war "almost everything is true. Almost nothing is true" (87) the basis for the act of telling a war story.

The narrative strategy that O'Brien uses in this book to portray the uncertainty of what happened in Vietnam is not restricted to depicting war, and O'Brien does not limit it to the war alone. He concludes his book with a chapter titled **"The Lives of the Dead"** in which he moves from his experiences in Vietnam back to when he was nine years old. On the surface, the book's last chapter is about O'Brien's first date, his first love, a girl named Linda who died of a brain tumor a few months after he had taken her to see the movie, *The Man Who Never Was*. What this chapter is really about, however, as its title suggests, is how the dead (which also include people who may never have actually existed) can be given life in a work of fiction. In a story, O'Brien tells us, "memory and imagination and language combine to make spirits in the head. There is the illusion of aliveness" (260). Like the man who never was in the film of that title, the people that never were except in memories and the imagination can become real or alive, if only for a moment, through the act of storytelling.

According to O'Brien, when you tell a story, really tell it, "you objectify your own experience. You separate it from yourself" (178). By doing this you are able to externalize "a swirl of memories that might otherwise have ended in paralysis or worse" (179). However, the storyteller does not just escape from the events and people in a story by placing them on paper; as we have seen, the act of telling a given story is an on-going and never-ending process. By constantly involving and then re-involving the reader in the task of determining what "actually" happened in a given situation, in a story, and by forcing the reader to experience the impossibility of ever knowing with any certainty what actually happened, O'Brien liberates himself from the lonesome responsibility of remembering and trying to understand events. He also creates a community of individuals immersed in the act of experiencing the uncertainty or indeterminacy of all events, regardless of whether they occurred in Vietnam, in a small town in Minnesota (253-273), or somewhere in the reader's own life.

O'Brien thus saves himself, as he puts it in the last sentence of his book, from the fate of his character Norman Bowker who, in a chapter called **"Speaking of Courage,"** kills himself because he cannot find some lasting meaning in the horrible things he experienced in Vietnam. O'Brien saves himself by demonstrating in this book that the most important thing is to be able to recognize and accept that events have no fixed or final meaning and that the only meaning that events can have is one that emerges momentarily and then shifts and changes each time that the events come alive as they are remembered or portrayed.

The character Norman Bowker hangs himself in the locker room of the local YMCA after playing basketball with some friends (181), partially because he has a story locked up inside of himself that he feels he cannot tell because no one would want to hear it. It is the story of how he failed to save his friend, Kiowa,[2] from drowning in a field of human excrement: "A good war story, he thought, but it was not a war for war stories, not for talk of valor, and nobody in town wanted to know about the stink. They wanted good intentions and good deeds" (169). Bowker's dilemma is remarkably similar to that of Krebs in Hemingway's story "Soldier's Home": "At first Krebs . . . did not want to talk about the war at all. Later he felt the need to talk but no one wanted to hear about it. His town had heard too many atrocity stories to be thrilled by actualities" (Hemingway 145).

O'Brien, after his war, took on the task "of grabbing people by the shirt and explaining exactly what had happened to me" (179). He explains in **The Things They Carried** that it is impossible to know "exactly what had happened." He wants us to know all of the things he/they/we did not know about Vietnam and will probably never know. He wants us to feel the sense of uncertainty that his character/narrator Tim O'Brien experiences twenty years after the war when he returns to the place where his friend Kiowa sank into a "field of shit" and tries to find "something meaningful and right" (212) to say but ultimately can only say, "well . . . there it is" (212). Each time we, the readers of **The Things They Carried,** return to Vietnam through O'Brien's labyrinth of stories, we become more and more aware that this statement is the closest we probably ever will come to knowing the "real truth," the undying uncertainty of the Vietnam War.

Notes

1. The reviewers of this book are split on whether to call it a novel or a collection of short stories. In a recent interview, I asked Tim O'Brien what he felt was the most adequate designation. He said that *The Things They Carried* is neither a collection of stories nor a novel: he preferred to call it a work of fiction.

2. In the "Notes" to this chapter, O'Brien typically turns the whole story upside down "in the interest of truth" and tells us that Norman Bowker was not responsible for Kiowa's horrible death: "That part of the story is my own" (182). This phrase could be taken to mean that this part of the story is his own creation or that he was the one responsible for Kiowa's death.

Works Cited

Baritz, Loren. *Backfire: A History of How American Culture Led Us into Vietnam and Made Us Fight the Way We Did.* New York: Morrow, 1985.

Beidler, Philip. *American Literature and the Experience of Vietnam.* Athens: U of Georgia P, 1982.

Halberstam, David. *One Very Hot Day.* New York: Houghton, 1967.

Hartman, Geoffrey. *Criticism in the Wilderness: The Study of Literature Today.* New Haven: Yale UP, 1980.

Hemingway, Ernest. *Short Stories.* New York: Scribner, 1953.

Iser, Wolfgang. *Prospecting: From Reader Response to Literary Anthropology.* Baltimore: Johns Hopkins UP, 1989.

Lomperis, Timothy, *"Reading the Wind": The Literature of the Vietnam War: An Interpretative Critique.* Durham: Duke UP, 1989.

Miller, J. Hillis. "*Heart of Darkness* Revisited." *Heart of Darkness: A Case Study in Contemporary Criticism.* Ed. Ross C. Murfin. New York: St. Martin's, 1989.

O'Brien, Tim. *Going After Cacciato.* New York: Dell, 1978.

———. *The Things They Carried.* Boston: Houghton, 1990.

Lorrie N. Smith (essay date fall 1994)

SOURCE: Smith, Lorrie N. "'The Things Men Do': The Gendered Subtext in Tim O'Brien's *Esquire* Stories." *Critique* 36, no. 1 (fall 1994): 16-40.

[*In the following essay, Smith examines the representations of masculinity and femininity in five of the stories in* The Things They Carried.]

Tim O'Brien's 1990 book of interlocked stories, **The Things They Carried,** garnered one rave review after another, reinforcing O'Brien's already established position as one of the most important veteran writers of the Vietnam War. The Penguin paperback edition serves up six pages of superlative blurbs like "consummate artistry," "classic," "the best American writer of his generation," "unique," and "master work." A brilliant metafictionist, O'Brien captures the moral and ontological uncertainty experienced by men at war, along with enough visceral realism to "make the stomach believe," as his fictional narrator, Tim O'Brien, puts it. This narrator's name and the book's dedication to its own fictional characters are just two indications of how crafty and self-reflexive O'Brien can be about his representational and narrative strategies. By exposing so much of his own artifice, he seems to practice Michael Herr's much earlier recognition that after Vietnam there is "not much chance anymore for history to go on unselfconsciously" (43). Yet, O'Brien—and his reviewers—seem curiously unself-conscious about this book's obsession with and ambivalence about representations of masculinity and femininity, particularly in the five stories originally published during the 1980s in *Esquire*. If this observation is accurate, and if, as one reviewer (Harris) claims, O'Brien's book exposes the nature of all war stories," then we might postulate that "all war stories" are constituted by what Eve Kosofsky Sedgwick calls, in another context, a "drama of gender difference" (6). The book diverts attention from this central play by constructing an elaborate and captivating metafictional surface, but the drama is finally exposed by the sheer exaggeration and aggressiveness of its gendered roles and gendering gestures. "The things" his male characters "carried" to war, it turns out, include plenty of patriarchal baggage. O'Brien purports to tell "true" war stories, but stops short of fully interrogating their ideological underpinnings—either in terms of the binary construction of gender that permeates representations of war in our culture, or in terms of the Vietnam War itself as a political event implicated in racist, ethnocentric assumptions. Hence, the text offers no challenge to a discourse of war in which apparently innocent American men are tragically wounded and women are objectified, excluded, and silenced. My intent in bringing this subtext to light is not to devalue O'Brien's technical skill or emotional depth, but to account for my own discomfort as a female reader and to position

The Things They Carried within a larger cultural project to rewrite the Vietnam War from a masculinist and strictly American perspective.

As much about the act of writing as about war itself, O'Brien's book celebrates the reconstructive power of the imagination, which gives shape, substance, and significance to slippery emotion and memory. We might even say that imagination itself—as embodied in the act of storytelling—plays the hero in this book, countering our national propensity for amnesia and offering the hope of personal redemption. O'Brien has often spoken of the imagination as a morally weighted force shaping the narratives and myths we live by. In Timothy Lomperis's *Reading the Wind,* for instance, O'Brien comments, "It's a real thing and I think influences in a major way the kind of real-life decisions we made to go to the war or not to go to the war. Either way, we imagine our futures and then try to step into our own imaginations . . . the purpose of fiction is to explore moral quandaries" (48, 52). In a more recent interview, he claims "exercising the imagination is the main way of finding truth" (Naparsteck 10). Taking his cue from O'Brien, critic Philip Beidler asserts that form, theme, and moral imperative merge in *The Things They Carried*: "It is at once a summation of Tim O'Brien's rewriting of the old dialectic of facts and fictions and a literally exponential prediction of new contexts of vision and insight, of new worlds to remember, imagine, believe" (32-33).

O'Brien has a genius for making poetry out of such prolix abstractions, and some of the most arresting passages in the book reflect on the craft and epistemology of writing. At some points, the book asserts, with post-structural sophistication, that stories displace and reconstitute reality and define the self: "Stories are for eternity, when memory is erased, when there is nothing to remember except the story" (40). At other points, O'Brien emphasizes the communicative power of storytelling: "The thing about a story is that you dream as you tell it, hoping that others might then dream along with you, and this way memory and imagination and language combine to make spirits in your head" (259). By the end of the book, storytelling even carries the power of salvation and transubstantiation: "As a writer now, I want to save Linda's life . . . in a story I can steal her soul. I can revive, at least briefly, that which is absolute and unchanging. In a story, miracles can happen" (265). Writing, like life, entails choice; unlike life, it also offers endless possibility. Hence, O'Brien's stories often offer multiple versions of "reality," complicating the ambiguously entwined experience, memory, and retelling of Vietnam: "In any war story, but especially in a true one, it's difficult to separate what happened from what seemed to happen. What seems to happen becomes its own happening and has to be told that way" (78). The book insistently asserts that "story-truth is truer sometimes than happening truth" (203) and admits that some stories, are simply "beyond telling" (79), can only be apprehended by those who experienced the event. Storytelling is finally a ritual both private and shared, a yearning toward wholeness, coherence, and meaning even while admitting their elusiveness.[1]

But who is invited to share this ritual? Despite its valorization of storytelling, *The Things They Carried* repeatedly underscores the incommunicability of war. This paradox has been identified by Kali Tal, who defines writing by Vietnam veterans as a literature of trauma, with analogues to writing by survivors of the Holocaust, slavery, incest, rape, and torture. For Tal, "Trauma literature demonstrates the unbridgeable gap between writer and reader and thus defines itself by the impossibility of its task—the communication of the traumatic experience" ("Speaking" 218). Tal challenges critics to account for the "inherent contradiction within literature by Vietnam veterans" by recognizing that "the symbols generated by liminality are readable only to those familiar with the alphabet of trauma" (239). I agree in general with this claim but would qualify it with Susan Jeffords's argument that revisionist cultural and literary productions over the past decade have restored the once-stigmatized Vietnam veteran to a position of power and status. Indeed, thanks largely to Oliver Stone, Sylvester Stallone, and Ron Kovic, veteran writers have increasingly had access to a discourse that is all *too* readable and familiar in our culture. The "alphabet of trauma," that is, has been encoded as a narrative of wounded American manhood that depends, for its meaning—whether tragic, ironic, or redemptive—on the positioning of women and Vietnamese as others.[2]

In an earlier essay, Tal found connections between the aims of feminist criticism and literature of Vietnam combat veterans who choose "to renounce their inherited white male power" ("Feminist Criticism" 199). Such texts, not surprisingly, are rare; more often, veterans' narratives fight bitterly to regain and sustain the power that the war temporarily disrupted. Hence, a consideration of how gender constructs affect the Vietnam veteran's rewriting of trauma opens a deeper gap than Tal identifies, in terms of both textual representation and the position and response of the reader. O'Brien often depicts war as inaccessible to nonveterans, creating a storytelling loop between characters within stories that excludes the uninitiated reader and privileges the authority of the soldiers' experience. But it is important to note that the moments of deepest trauma in the book occur when the masculine subject is threatened with dissolution or displacement. All readers are to some extent subjugated by O'Brien's shifty narrator: however, the female reader, in particular, is rendered marginal and mute, faced with the choice throughout the book of either staying outside the story or reading against her-

self from a masculine point of view. O'Brien repeatedly inscribes the outsider as female, hence reinforcing masculine bonds that lessen the survivor/outsider distinction for male readers. Male characters are granted many moments of mutual understanding, whereas women pointedly won't, don't, or can't understand war stories. In short, O'Brien writes women out of the war and the female reader out of the storytelling circle.

For all its polyphonic, postmodernist blurring of fact and fiction, *The Things They Carried* preserves a very traditional gender dichotomy, insistently representing abject femininity to reinforce dominant masculinity and to preserve the writing of war stories as a masculine privilege. Specifically, O'Brien uses female figures to mediate the process in homosocial bonding, a narrative strategy Sedgwick plots as a triangulation:

> In the presence of a women who can't be seen as pitiable or contemptible, men are able to exchange power and to confirm each other's value even in the context of the remaining inequalities in their power. The sexually pitiable or contemptible female figure is a solvent that not only facilitates the relative democratization that grows up with capitalism and cash exchange, but goes a long way—for the men whom she leaves bonded together—toward palliating its gaps and failures.
>
> (160)

If we transfer Sedgwick's paradigm from the realm of class struggle to the current cultural contest over the meaning, communicability, and "gaps and failures" of the Vietnam War, we can understand how O'Brien's representations of "contemptible" femininity strengthen male bonds and deflect the contemporaneous assaults of an emasculating lost war, the woman's movement, and feminist theory. We might even place the female reader at one corner of the triangle, her exclusion facilitating the bond between male writer and reader. Anxiety over the general incommunicability of trauma is thus greatly eased by the shared language of patriarchy.

Starring the now conventional trope of a democratic platoon of characters, this collection of stories suppresses any signifiers of age, race, class, or ideology to accentuate the common bond of masculinity. O'Brien closes male ranks in this book, celebrating camaraderie and preempting complicity or identification on the part of the female reader. Lavishing sensitive attention to the depth and complexity of men's emotions and rescuing their humanity in the face of a dehumanizing war, O'Brien represents women not as characters with agency and sensibility of their own, but as projections of a narrator trying to resolve the trauma of the war. Although he seems at points to engage and question conventional gender constructions, in the end he does so only to quell threats to masculinity and to re-assert patriarchal order. For all its internal resistance to narrative closure, the book's framing narrative is a hermeneutic circle: men at war act like men at war, and only men can write about it and understand it. Thus, while O'Brien fractures the surface on his stories, discontinuity is finally subsumed by a seamless narrative voiced by a strongly centered masculine subject with the power to construct both masculinity and femininity.

Critics like Beidler who ignore gender can thus read *The Things They Carried* as a high achievement in the cultural project he sees writers of the Vietnam generation undertaking: to "reconstitute [American cultural mythology] as a medium both of historical self-reconsideration and, in the same moment, of historical self-renewal and even self-invention" (5). Such a grand(iose) humanistic accomplishment can only be achieved if we overlook how dominant conceptions of culture, self, and history erase or subjugate the female subject. Once we admit this asymmetry and oppression, totalizing myths of "universal truth" like those Beidler reads in O'Brien and other writers of the Vietnam generation become impossible. A feminist reading of fiction by Vietnam veterans reveals quite a different cultural and discursive project: what I have elsewhere labeled "backlash" and what Susan Jeffords calls "the remasculinization of America." Jeffords details how the proliferation of texts and films about the Vietnam War, especially during the 1980s, has contributed to "the large-scale renegotiation and regeneration of the interests, values, and projects of patriarchy now taking place in U.S. social relations." More specifically, "the representational features of the Vietnam War are structurally written through relations of gender, relations designed primarily to reinforce the interests of masculinity and patriarchy" (xi). Because Tim O'Brien is indisputably canonized as a major "Vietnam author in his generation" and *The Things They Carried* is widely acclaimed, it merits close examination in the context of this larger cultural work of consolidating the masculine subject, cementing male bonds, and preempting or silencing feminist dissent.

II

The core of *The Things They Carried* consists of five long stories originally published in *Esquire* during the late 1980s—the period in which Susan Faludi documents an "undeclared war on American women" and Jeffords locates the rehabilitation of temporarily outcast male Vietnam veterans. (Women veterans, of course, have never been visible enough to be cast out.) Three of these stories play elaborately on gender oppositions: **"The Things They Carried"** (1986), which opens the book, **"How to Tell a True War Story"** (October 1987), and **"Sweetheart of the Song Tra Bong"** (July 1989). **"The Lives of the Dead"** (January 1989), the volume's last story, reaches toward a reconciliation in which both masculine and feminine deaths are redeemed by the storytelling imagination. Read sequentially, these

stories make up an increasingly misogynist narrative of masculine homosocial behavior under fire. Before reading the three central stories to track the book's gendered subtext, however, it is worth looking briefly at patterns of feminine representation in other stories to indicate how pervasively it is used to define masculine bonds and power.

In several stories, O'Brien introduces an invented ten-year-old daughter, Kathleen (a mother and wife is mentioned once but never shown). Her dramatic role is to prompt the writer's memory and reshaping of his Vietnam experiences. Representing both a younger generation distanced from the war and all those excluded from its first-hand experience, Kathleen entreats her father to leave the past behind, forget about the war, get past his "obsession." As someone who cannot "read" his stories, she reinforces the familiar criterion of "being there" and the more implicit criterion of masculinity as qualifications for understanding Vietnam. As a narrative device and muse, Kathleen prompts the narrator's justification for writing war stories. In **"Ambush,"** for instance, she questions whether her father ever killed anyone, jumping in logic from "You keep writing these war stories" to "'so I guess you must've killed somebody.'" This is a familiar question in war literature, usually underscoring the veteran's distance from the uninitiated. Here, the question gives rise to a moral and aesthetic imperative for blurring fact and fiction. To the ten-year-old, he says "what seemed right . . . 'Of course not.'" But "here" in the present-time of the story, he wants "to pretend she's a grown-up. I want to tell her exactly what happened, or what I remember happening, and then I want to say to her that as a little girl she was absolutely right. This is why I keep writing war stories" (147). Although the narrator tries to be kind to his daughter and wrestles with the morality of telling the truth versus doing the right thing, he ends up having it both ways, thus maintaining absolute power. By lying to the young Kathleen, he excludes her from her own awareness of truth; he can only grant that she was right by pretending "she's a grown-up." Truth is established as relative and situational; the (male) writer maintains absolute authority over its manipulation and what story is "right" for the daughter.

In **"Field Trip,"** Kathleen actually accompanies her father on a return trip to the "shitfield" in Vietnam where twenty years earlier he lost his best friend, Kiowa, and where he enacts an ersatz Indian farewell ritual. (Any cultural gap that may have existed is here bridged by ties of camaraderie.) Kathleen is a trooper, yet the war remains "as remote to her as cavemen and dinosaurs" (208), and she finally concludes her father is simply "weird." After wading in the mucky field, father and daughter have an Oedipal moment of complicity in which the mother is excluded and her potential power defused: "'All the gunk on your skin, you look like

. . . Wait'll I tell Mommy, she'll probably make you sleep in the garage.' 'You're right,' I said, 'Don't tell her'" (213). But this moment dissolves into distance again. Looking back at a farmer waving a shovel over his head, Kathleen interprets the man's actions as anger, while the narrator says "No . . . all that's finished" (213). (With the Vietnamese farmer, unlike Kiowa, the cultural gap is unbridged, the narrator rejecting Kathleen's reading that the man might have his own anger.) In the end, the war is closed off to Kathleen and she's merely along for the ride.

"Speaking of Courage," a post-traumatic stress story highly reminiscent of Hemingway's "Soldier's Home," similarly imagines a woman, Sally Gustafson, née Kramer, an old girlfriend of Norman Bowker's "whose pictures he had once carried in his wallet" and whose small-town, middle-class reality is so far from Norman's world of post-traumatic stress that she comes to signify for him the utter impossibility of communicating his experience or closing the breach between his pre- and post-war self. She has no actual agency or dialogue in the story, but lives completely in Norman's mind as a synecdoche for the whole town that "did not know shit about shit, and did not care to know" (163). Did Sally suffer through Norman's absence in Vietnam? Did she have her own traumas and losses because of the war? Such stories aren't told in this book. Norman imagines several conversations with Sally, but each time realizes "there was really nothing he could say to her." He pictures more perfect dialogues with his father, "who had his own war and who now preferred silence," suggesting that understanding might at least be possible with another veteran, though it is never realized. In the end, Norman feels invisible and mute. The commentary, **"Notes,"** following the story, claims that the "real" Norman committed suicide, but not before passing his story on to Tim, who makes it his own and thus "saves" Norman's life just as he saves "Timmy's life with an story" in the book's last line.

Several stories collapse representations of women, death, the enemy, and Asians. In the vignette, **"Style,"** the soldiers come upon a burned hamlet and a teen-aged girl dancing ritualistically in front of her house, in which lie the bodies of "an infant and an old woman and a woman whose age was hard to tell. . . . There were dead pigs, too" (154). Her movements are inexplicable to the men, and this inscrutability leads to the story's real concern: not the grieving girl, whose suffering is beyond the Americans, but American (mis)interpretations of Vietnamese culture. Azar, the book's hypermacho fool, mocks her movements, but Henry Dobbins opposes Azar and insists he "dance right." The girl is given no motive, voice, or selfhood; she exists to dramatize an aesthetic and moral point about proper "style." She is pure spectacle and performance, symbol of a whole culture's incomprehensible otherness. As with all the other women in the book, there is no reconciling the gap of gender and, here, culture.

The only other detailed representation of a Viet person is the dead boy in **"The Man I Killed,"** which circles obsessively around the final fact and fetish of war: the dead and mutilated body. Here, the unrepresentable—death, Asian, enemy—is distinctly feminized, as if to underscore its absolute otherness. The story focuses on the narrator's speechlessness and his imaginative projection of the boy's life. True to his mission, he "saves" the soldier's life by dreaming it in a story, turning the screw even further to imagine "He knew he would fall dead and wake up in the stories of his village and people" (144). The description of the body emphasizes feminine characteristics: he appears as "a slim, dead, almost dainty young man. He had bony legs, a narrow waist, long shapely fingers. His chest was sunken and poorly muscled—a scholar, maybe. . . . His eyebrows were thin and arched like a woman's, and at school the boys sometimes teased him about how pretty he was, the arched eyebrows and long shapely fingers, and on the playground they mimicked a woman's walk and made fun of his smooth skin and his love for mathematics" (139, 142). Presumably, this feminization serves to express the man's ill-suitedness for war, and it helps humanize the enemy. Ultimately, though, the narrator's task is to harden himself to guilt and horror, to "pull your shit together . . . talk," in the words of Kiowa. The almost homoerotic fixation on the dead men's body suggests the narcissism Eric Leeds, referring to Klaus Theweleit's study of *Freikorps* troops, finds at the heart of warrior culture. In one of the blurrings of the book, the narrator recognizes himself in the dead man but also makes him absolutely other, that is, womanly. Recovery from this trauma (conceived explicitly in the story as regaining a voice) rests on asserting the living, masculine self in opposition to the dead, silent, feminine other.

III

Representations of woman as inscrutable, uncomprehending, and dangerous are more fully developed in the longer *Esquire* stories. As the book unfolds, in fact, the masculine subject is constituted in opposition to femininity that becomes increasingly other: the woman who must be rejected because she cannot understand the male experience of war in **"The Things They Carried,"** the woman rendered both pitiable and contemptible because she does not understand in **"How to Tell a True War Story,"** and the woman who understands war too well, hence threatening male hegemony and phallic power in **"Sweetheart in the Song Tra Bong."** It seems more than coincidental that the stories that most deeply probe and most emphatically reassert masculinity should appear in this glossy, upscale men's magazine famous, as Faludi puts it, for its "screeds against women." The intended audience for this magazine (subtitled "Man at His Best") is unabashedly male, and though O'Brien's stories rarely show men at their best, they do speak to a self-conscious and perhaps threatened masculinity. (Anyone familiar with Vietnam studies will also associate *Esquire* with a controversial and often-quoted article by William Broyles entitled "Why Men Love War.") As with *Playboy,* the female reader opening these pages ventures into alien and dangerous territory. Ultimately, reading war, like experiencing, remembering, and writing it, is constructed as a masculine rite.

The narrative structure of these stories is very similar: alternating radically disjunctive passages of past and present, fiction and commentary, war and memory. The force that presumes to reconcile these dualities and overcome the confounding incommunicability of war is the writer's imagination, articulated from a masculine point of view. In both the opening and closing stories of the volume, imagination is linked to an idealized, unattainable woman—Martha, a girlfriend at home, and Linda, a childhood sweetheart who died at nine. The first story plays one of the many variations on the imagination-reality motif and picks up where O'Brien's earlier novel, *Going After Cacciato,* left off, with Paul Berlin imagining himself pleading for peace at the Paris Peace Talks but admitting: "Even in imagination we must be true to our obligations, for, even in imagination, obligation cannot be outrun. Imagination, like reality, has its limits" (378). **"The Things They Carried"** goes further to limit the imagination, asserting that in battle, "Imagination was a killer." What this means, on one level, is that the nerve-wracking tension in the field could lead soldiers to imagine the worst or make a fatal mistake. But the story also establishes an inexorable equation: imagination = women = distraction = danger = death. The story's dramatic resolution turns on recovering masculine power by suppressing femininity in both female and male characters. Survival itself depends on excluding women from the masculine bond. In this first story, the renunciation of femininity is a sad but necessary cost of war, admitted only after real emotional struggle. It establishes a pattern, however, for the rest of the book.

"The Things They Carried" introduces the cast of Alpha Company and establishes their identity as a cohesive group, each manfully carrying his own weight but also sharing the burden of war. The story features Lieutenant Jimmy Cross, the platoon's 24-year-old C. O., who fell into the war via ROTC. He is presented as a man of integrity, honesty, and deep compassion for his men, a cautious, somewhat stiff and unseasoned commander with no inherent lust for death and destruction. The story is fundamentally an initiation narrative whose tension lies in Jimmy Cross's need to deal with guilt

and harden himself to battle realities, which are here distinctly differentiated from the realm of imagination. Jimmy Cross's story alternates with lyrical passages cataloguing all the "things" men at war carry, including "all the emotional baggage of men who might die." These passages, echoing O'Brien's earlier constraints of "obligation," insistently repeat the idea that "the things they carried were largely determined by necessity. . . . Necessity dictated" (4, 5).

Lieutenant Jimmy Cross's survival and his coming of age as an effective soldier depend on letting go of all that is not necessary and immediate—here equated completely with the feminine, the romantic, the imaginary. Becoming a warrior entails a pattern of desire, guilt, and renunciation in relation to a woman. The story opens by describing in detail Jimmy Cross's most precious cargo:

> First Lieutenant Jimmy Cross carried letters from a girl named Martha, a junior at Mount Sebastian College in New Jersey. They were not love letters, but Lieutenant Cross was hoping, so he kept them folded in plastic at the bottom of his rucksack. In the late afternoon, after a day's march, he would dig his foxhole, wash his hands under a canteen, unwrap the letters, hold them with the tips of his fingers, and spend the last hour of light pretending. He would imagine romantic camping trips into the White Mountains in New Hampshire. He would sometimes taste the envelope flaps, knowing her tongue had been there. More than anything, he wanted Martha to love him as he loved her, but the letters were mostly chatty, elusive on the matter of love. She was a virgin, he was almost sure.
>
> (4)

Martha's writing—and, implicitly, her reading of his war experience—are sexualized through association: her inability to respond to his love and his longing suggest the blank page of virginity in patriarchal discourse. Though Jimmy Cross tries to realize a connection with Martha through this sacramental/sexual ritual, she is represented as aloof and untouchable, a poet with "grey, neutral" eyes inhabiting "another world, which was not quite real." Martha's words are never presented directly, but are paraphrased by the narrator, who reminds us twice that she never mentions the war in her letters. Like other women in the book, she represents all those back home who will never understand the warrior's trauma. In addition to the letters, Jimmy Cross carries two pictures of Martha and a good-luck charm—a stone Martha sent from the Jersey Shore, which he sometimes carries in his mouth; he also "humped his love for Martha up the hills and through the swamps." As the story progresses, Martha—rather these metonymic objects signifying Martha—becomes a distraction from the immediate work of war and caring for his men. His mind wanders, usually into the realm of sexual fantasy: "Slowly, a bit distracted, he would get up and move among his men, checking the perimeter, then at full dark he would return to his hole and watch the night and wonder if Martha was a virgin" (4). Memory and desire intertwine in a fantasy that fuses courage and virility and, by extension, fighting and writing upon her blank virgin page. In one of the book's several retrospective "should haves," Jimmy Cross remembers a date with Martha and thinks "he should've done something brave. He should've carried her up the stairs to her room and tied her to the bed and touched that left knee all night long. He should've risked it. Whenever he looked at the photographs, he thought of new things he should've done" (6). We are meant to see the move from chivalry to sado-masochistic erotica as natural and understandable, because "He was just a kid at war, in love," after all. That Jimmy Cross's sexual "bravery" might have been earned through violation and coercion is not considered in the story. The focus is on the male's empowering fantasy.

Jimmy Cross's distraction climaxes with the sniper shooting of Ted Lavender "on his way back from peeing." Just before this incident, the company had waited tensely for Lee Strunk to emerge from clearing out a Vietcong tunnel. The language of sexual desire and union, coming just before Lee Strunk's "rising from the dead" and Lavender's death, links Jimmy's imagination of Martha—his merging with the feminine—with annihilation of the self. As he gazes suggestively down into the dark tunnel, he leaves the war and succumbs to a fantasy of perfect union between masculine and feminine, death and desire:

> And then suddenly, without willing it, he was thinking about Martha. The stresses and fractures, the quick collapse, the two of them buried alive under all that weight. Dense, crushing love. Kneeling, watching the hole, he tried to concentrate on Lee Strunk and the war, all the dangers, but his love was too much for him, he felt paralyzed, he wanted to sleep inside her lungs and breathe her blood and be smothered. He wanted his to be a virgin and not a virgin, all at once. He wanted to know her.
>
> (12)

Such unraveling of gender duality, however, is dangerous, such paradoxes unsustainable. At the moment of Jimmy's imagined dissolution, Ted Lavender is shot, As if to punish himself for daydreaming and forgetting "about matters of security"—but more deeply for abandoning his men in the desire to know the feminine—Jimmy Cross goes to the extreme of rejecting desire for Martha altogether. He reacts to the trauma of Lavender's death in two significant ways. The first is one of the book's parallel scenes of My Lai-like retribution, here bluntly told but not shown: "Lieutenant Jimmy Cross led his men into the village of Than Khe. They burned everything" (16). The second is guilt, entangled with anger that his love for Martha is unrequited. He reverts to a familiar binary choice—either Martha or his

men: "He felt shame. He hated himself. He had loved Martha more than his men, and as a consequence Lavender was now dead, and this was something he would have to carry, like a stone in his stomach for the rest of the war" (16)—his good luck charm transformed to the weight of guilt. That night he cries "for Ted Lavender" but also for the realization, or perhaps rationalization, that "Martha did not love him and never would." Jimmy Cross regains a "mask of composure" necessary to survive war's horror, burns Martha's letters and photographs in a purgative ritual reversing the opening blessing, and wills himself to renounce Martha and all she signifies: "He hated her. Yes, he did. He hated her. Love, too, but it was a hard, hating kind of love" (23). With this rejection and a newly hardened, terse idiom, Jimmy Cross completes his transformation: "He was a soldier, after all. . . . He was realistic about it. . . . He would be a man about it. . . . No more fantasies . . . from this point on he would comport himself as an officer . . . he would dispense with love; it was not now a factor" (23-24). His survival as a soldier and a leader depends upon absolute separation from the feminine world and rejection of his own femininity: "Henceforth, when he thought about Martha, it would be only to think that she belonged elsewhere. He would shut down the daydreams. This was not Mount Sebastian, it was another world, where there were no pretty poems or midterm exams, a place where men died because of carelessness and gross stupidity" (24).

How are we meant to read this rejection? O'Brien is not blaming Martha for male suffering, for of course, the story isn't *about* Martha at all, though she introduces the book's protypical figure of the woman incapable of understanding war. Rather, he uses her to define "necessary" codes of male behavior in war and to establish Jimmy's "proper" bond with his men. We are given no rationale for why Jimmy perceives his choice in such absolute terms, nor are we invited to critique Jimmy for this rigidity, though we do pity him and recognize his naivete. Jimmy Cross's rejection of the feminine is portrayed as one of the burdensome but self-evident "necessities" of war, and O'Brien grants Jimmy this recognition: "It was very sad, he thought. The things men carried inside. The things men did or felt they had to do." Most sad and ironic of all, Jimmy ends up suffering alone because of his status as an officer: "He would show strength, distancing himself." Jimmy Cross's allegorical initials even encourage us to read his youthful renunciation in Christian terms.

At the very end, however, masculine bonds prevail and compensate for Jimmy's losses. O'Brien places the men of Alpha Company in a larger cultural landscape of men without women by alluding to cowboy movies and Huckleberry Finn: "He might just shrug and say, Carry on, then they would saddle up and form into a column and move out toward to villages west of Than Khe."

The narrative voice here is very carefully distinguished from the characters, and it is hard to know how to take the conditional "might" and the self-conscious diction: as parody? as straight allusion? as Jimmy Cross's self-deluding macho fantasy? One possibility is that O'Brien means to expose and critique the social construction of masculinity, suggesting that soldiers' behavior in Vietnam is conditioned by years of John Wayne movies, as indeed numerous veterans' memoirs attest is true. Likewise, the story unmasks the soldiers' macho "stage presence," "pose," and "hard vocabulary": "Men killed, and died, because they were embarrassed not to"; they do what they "felt they had to do." But these constructions are inevitably converted into behavior that seems natural and inevitable—"necessary"—within the ur-story underlying all war stories: the tragic destruction of male innocence. O'Brien's depth as a writer allows him to reveal the socialized nature of soldiering and to show compassion for the vulnerable men behind the pose. But he stops short of undoing and revising these constructions. In the end, men *are* how they act, just as they *are* their stories and culture *is* its myths. The story rescues the humanity of men at war and consigns femininity to the margins, thus assuring the seamless continuity and endless repetition of masculine war stories.

Because Tim O'Brien's characters live so fully for him he is impelled to follow up the story of Jimmy Cross and Martha with a vignette, **"Love."** Like George Willard, the lonely but ever-receptive narrator of *Winesburg, Ohio,* O'Brien portrays himself as the burdened repository of other people's stories. Here Jimmy Cross comes to visit character-narrator Tim O'Brien "many years after the war" to talk about "all the things we still carried through our lives." One thing Jimmy Cross still carries is a torch for Martha, and he shows the narrator a copy of the same photograph he had burned after Ted Lavender's death. The story embedded in the story concerns his meeting with Martha at a college reunion. Now a Lutheran missionary nurse serving in Third World countries, she responds to Jimmy with the same friendly but aloof demeanor that marked her letters during the war. She gives him another copy of the photo to gaze at and reveals "she had never married . . . and probably never would. She didn't know why. But as she said this, her eyes seemed to slide sideways, and it occurred to him that there were things about her he would never know" (30). Despite her continuing inscrutability and distance, Jimmy risks telling Martha that "he'd almost done something brave" back in college, and he describes his knee-stroking fantasy. Martha's ambivalent reaction widens the gulf between men and women and hints, with Hemingway-like ellipses, that she is either repressed, fearful, uninterested, or a lesbian; in any case, she is unreceptive to Jimmy's advances, which absolves him from any failings or flaws as a masculine sexual being:

Martha shut her eyes. She crossed her arms at her chest, as if suddenly cold, rocking slightly, then after a time she looked at him and said she was glad he hadn't tried it. She didn't understand how men could do those things. What things? he asked, and Martha said, The things men do. Then he nodded. It began to form. Oh, he said, those things. At breakfast the next morning she told him she was sorry. She explained that there was nothing she could do about it, and he said he understood, and then she laughed and gave him the picture and told him not to burn this one up.

(31)

What are "the things men do?" In the context of this pair of stories, these things are both sexual and violent. Jimmy passes this story on to the narrator, joking that "Maybe she'll read it and come begging." But he leaves more concerned about the reader's response than Martha's, with a plea that Tim depict him positively, as if he still hadn't exorcised his guilt over Lavender's death: "'Make me out to be a good guy, okay? Brave and handsome, all that stuff. Best platoon leader ever.' He hesitated for a second. 'And do me a favor. Don't mention anything about—' 'No,' I said, 'I won't'" (31). O'Brien teases us with an indeterminate ending; if he is true to his word, then he hasn't revealed "anything about—" Jimmy's secret, and we are left wondering. If the writer has, in fact, betrayed Jimmy in the course of the retelling, we cannot be sure what it is we were not meant to know and why Jimmy wants to suppress it. In either case, the men wordlessly understand each other, and the reader is an outsider. Like Jake Barnes hungering impotently after Lady Brett, Jimmy continues to suffer from Martha's unattainability. As in the previous story, we are allowed to glimpse the gap between the mask and the face, the wounded man behind the masculine pose. But Martha is barely more than a plot device signifying Jimmy's life of virility and innocence destroyed by the war.

IV

If traditional manhood is tenuously constructed and tragically vitiated in these first two stories, it is ferociously reasserted in **"How to Tell a True War Story."** This story replays a version of the retribution scene first enacted after Ted Lavender's death. Again, the objective is deep compassion for the anguish and loss the men feel. And once more, male powerlessness is overcome through the repulsion of femininity. Here, though, the characters cope with lost innocence through explicitly misogynist reactions. It is as if the deeper men get "carried" into war (and the deeper we get into the book), the more they define themselves in opposition to the feminine.

The most self-reflexive story in the volume and the most confrontational toward the reader, O'Brien's narrative oscillates here between a core war story ("This is true"), stories within the story ("I had to make up a few things"), and aphoristic reflections on truth and fact ("A thing may happen and be a total lie; another thing may not happen and be truer than the truth"; "truths are contradictory"). The central story presented from several overlapping perspectives, concerns Rat Kiley's re-action to the sudden death by booby trap of his friend, Curt Lemon. Again, the medium of misreading is a let-ter—that important signifier of connection to "the world" in so much war literature. In his grief, Rat "pours his heart out" in a letter to Curt's sister: "So what happens? Rat mails the letter. He waits two months. The dumb cooze never writes back" (76). At this point, the narrator is paraphrasing Rat's language. In the metafictional section immediately following, the narrator ascribes the obscenity directly to Rat Kiley and analyzes it:

> . . . you can tell a true war story by its absolute and uncompromising allegiance to obscenity and evil. Lis-ten to Rat Kiley. Cooze, he says. He does not say bitch. He certainly does not say woman, or girl. He says cooze. Then he spits and stares. He's nineteen years old—it's too much for him—so he looks at you with those big sad gentle killer eyes and says *cooze*, because his friend is dead, and because it's so incredibly sad and true: she never wrote back.
>
> (76-77)

Stepping outside the story to give us a lesson in mime-sis, the narrator's rationale for "obscenity and evil" is that he's simply telling it like it is, realistically render-ing the soldier's idiom. Yet matter-of-fact description turns to sympathy, and then to blame, as he aligns him-self with Rat while cautioning the uninitiated (implicitly female) reader: "If you don't care for obscenity, you don't care for the truth; if you don't care for the truth, watch how you vote. Send guys to war, they come home talking dirty." (Dirty, of course, means derogatory refer-ence to the female body.) It turns out that Rat Kiley's propensity for aggressively sexist language is *our* fault. Within the story, the blame certainly lies with the sister: "The dumb cooze never writes back." He is excused, like Jimmy Cross and many other characters, because he's "just a boy"—a recurring line throughout the book that manages to convey both irony and sympathy.

Retribution in this story gets played out against an im-age of suffering innocence—a "baby VC water buf-falo"—which Rat Kiley slowly tortures by shooting it body part by body part until "Nothing moved except the eyes, which were enormous" (echoing the descrip-tion of Rat's own "big sad gentle killer eyes"). The men stand by watching and then dump the baby buffalo into the village well, a symbol of devouring feminine sexuality as menacing as Jimmy Cross's tunnel. "We had witnessed something essential, something brand-new and profound, a piece of the world so startling that there was not yet a name for it" (86). Mitchell Sanders

comments, "that's Nam . . . Garden of Evil. Over here, man, every sin's real fresh and original." Such hyper-bole makes for a good war story, but one might ques-tion whether such "evil" in a war is in fact anything new and why its discovery is always a revelation. In any event, the question of evil as a moral category is rendered moot by narrative commentary that insists in the amorality of war stories (this dialectic between Mitchell Sanders and the narrator is a continuing thread in the book): "If a story seems moral, do not believe it." Instead, we are asked to contemplate the "aesthetic purity of absolute moral indifference." War is presented as a self-contained, inevitable, a-political, and purely "essential" masculine reality; all the imagination can do here is play endless riffs on its themes and images. For Sanders, the "moral" is that "Nobody listens. Nobody hears nothin'. Like that fatass colonel. The politicians, all the civilian types. Your girlfriend. My girlfriend. Ev-erybody's sweet little virgin girlfriend" (83). Such dis-tinctions preserve the absolute dichotomy of masculin-ity and femininity and perpetuate a mystique of war that only male comrades can comprehend.

We might forgive Rat Kiley for being young, hurt, ig-norant, and an unwitting product of his culture, as we are asked to forgive Jimmy Cross for being "just a boy." But as Lynne Hanley points out, the appeal to such sympathy, one recurrent strategy upholding masculine innocence in war literature, rests on "the idea that men go to war not *really* knowing that killing other people is what war is all about. And the story that keeps this idea alive and close to our hearts is the story of the soldier's tragic discovery on the battlefield that what he is a part of is killing. . . . This fiction of the independent agency of war . . . lifts the burden of guilt from the men who declare and organize war, as well as from those who ac-tually carry the guns and drive the tanks and drop the bombs" (27, 29). Such an unraveling, however, does not seem to be O'Brien's intent. As in **"The Things They Carried,"** recuperation of masculinity is achieved through the third-party mediation of a woman outside the war zone—first the sister who didn't write back, then the reader who doesn't listen. The coda compli-cates our response to the story's obscenity and reiter-ates hostility against women, who are categorically de-nied the ability to understand war. O'Brien deliberately calls attention to gender difference in this passage, put-ting the female reader in the uncomfortable position of being told she has no hope of grasping the "true war story," let alone learning "how to write" it. Her reading up to this point is thus invalidated, and she is cast out along with Kathleen, Martha, and Sally, Curt Lemon's sister and the older woman at the reading:

> Now and then, when I tell this story, someone will come up to me afterward and say she liked it. It's al-ways a woman. Usually it's an older woman of kindly temperament and humane politics. She'll explain that as a rule she hates war stories; she can't understand

why people want to wallow in all the blood and gore. But this one she liked. The poor baby buffalo, it made her sad. Sometimes, even, there are little tears. What I should do, she'll say, is put it all behind me. Find new stories to tell.

I won't say it but I'll think it.

I'll picture Rat Kiley's face, his grief, and I'll think, *You dumb cooze.*

Because she wasn't listening.

(90)

The sole function of this postscript is to solidify the male bond and ridicule and reject the feminine, which it does with stunning hostility. The woman's "kindly temperament" and "humane politics" are rendered naive and unrealistic; her sadness at the death of the baby buffalo is simplistic and sentimental; her "little tears" are diminutive, inappropriate. The narrator closes the male storytelling circle by appropriating Rat Kiley's obscene term to create his own bond with his comrade-characters and his male audience and to put distance between himself and his female reader. "A true war story," we are informed, is a "love story," which, according to this story, can only tell of love between men. The narrator asserts unequivocally in the last line that "a true war story" is "about sisters who never write back and people who never listen" (91).

V

Rat Kiley figures prominently again as the authoritative witness of the book's most disturbing story, **"Sweetheart of the Song Tra Bong."** Premised on an elaborately far-fetched "what if," the story unsettles and stretches our ability to suspend disbelief precisely *because* it is calculated to overturn conventional gender roles: suppose a soldier were to "ship his honey over to Nam . . . import [his] own personal poontang." The absolute incongruity of having a woman enter the male sanctuary of war reinforces the extent to which culture constructs war as an all-male activity. The story counts on the reader's cognitive dissonance when faced with this image and trades heavily on its novelty and shock effect. As usual, O'Brien layers and fractures his narrative and mixes tones—strategies that mask the gender drama with a struggle over epistemological uncertainty and aesthetic indeterminacy. Framed by the narrator but close to Rat's perspective, the story follows Rat's effort to get it right, to "bracket the full range of meaning" for his incredulous friends. But Rat's story, part of which he heard second-hand and part of which he experienced, comes with the narrator's disclaimer that Rat has a reputation for "exaggeration and overstatement" and may be biased because he "loved her." By the end, the story has the feel of a truth-is-stranger-than-fiction tale in the oral culture of soldiers—the kind of story usually punctuated at the end with the enigmatic "there

it is." Within the self-reflexive frame of the story, the actions Rat recounts for the narrator may or may not have happened; as always in this book, we are cautioned against looking for mimetic or factual truth and led toward accepting the emotional truth constructed by the imagination. To the interlocutors within the text, and to the narrator who is almost always complicit with his own characters, this has the ring of a "true war story" because it solidifies the masculine hegemony of war and casts out the monstrous woman who dares to appropriate masculine codes of behavior.

"Sweetheart of the Song Tra Bong" is further complicated by its literary self-consciousness, for it can be read as a gendered and perhaps parodic version of *Heart of Darkness* and its derivative retelling, *Apocalypse Now*—those explorations of the imperialist male psyche gone off the deep end. Here, inscrutable evil and cultural otherness are collapsed into the figure of a woman. The story is less concerned with what motivates the Kurtz figure, however, than with defending men's homosocial bonds against all threat of feminine invasion. As in other *Esquire* stories, the figure of a woman is the other against which masculine identity and innocence are sympathetically defined. Here, though, the woman is distinctly not, as Rat points out, like "all those girls back home, how clean and innocent they all are, how they'll never understand any of this, not in a billion years" (123). O'Brien's ingenious twist is to create a woman who understands war because "she was there. She was up to her eyeballs in it." Of course, being there and understanding war are only conceived in masculine terms—fighting—rather than any of the other roles women actually did play in Vietnam, for the masculine point of view prevails here. The story appears to be deconstructing gender difference by imagining a woman warrior, suggesting that *even* women can be corrupted by war. In fact, though, it portrays the woman as *more* masculine than the men, hence monstrous and unnatural. She can finally be tamed only within a masculine narrative. Characteristically, Rat gives the story a moral: "You come over clean and you get dirty and then afterward it's never the same. A question of degree" (123). The "degree" to which people are transformed by war, however, turns on the difference of gender in this story. Gender difference temporarily blurs but ultimately gets resolved into the old oppositions, and women are warned against disrupting patriarchal order and assuming power assigned to men.

Rat's story takes place at an obscure outpost where he once served as medic, a liminal place where the men are free to bend military rules, where basketball, beer, and easy camaraderie help pass the time between incoming emergencies. Beyond the medical station is a Green Beret base inhabited by six "Greenies," who are "not social animals." This positioning is significant, for it begins to define "normal" and transgressive behavior in the story. The Greenies are associated with nature; Rat claims they were "animals . . . but far from so-cial." Exuding an almost supernatural aura of power and authority, the special forces disappear and then "magically reappear, moving like shadows through the moonlight, filing in silently from the dense rain forest off to the west." The medics keep their distance and "no one asked questions." The base's NCO, Eddie Dia-mond, sets the plot in motion with a "joke": "What they should do, Eddie said, was pool some bucks and bring in a few mama-sans from Saigon, spice things up." Mark Fossie, a young medic, is taken with the idea, saying that all it would take is "a pair of solid brass balls." The phallic reference is reiterated when Eddie Diamond "told him he'd best strap down his dick." Six weeks later, the men are astonished when Mark's child-hood sweetheart, Mary Anne Bell, shows up. After a heavy silence, someone says, simply, "That fucker."

In the beginning, Mary Anne is represented as a parody of the all-American girl and "sweetheart" pin-up, both innocent and sexual. Seventeen and "just barely out of high school," she shows up in "white culottes and this sexy pink sweater." Rat dwells on the details of her appearance: "long white legs and blue eyes and a complexion like strawberry ice cream." She and Mark dote on each other, sharing their American dream of a perfect house, a perfect family, a perfect future. They set up house "in one of the bunkers along the perimeter," on the border between civilization and the Greenies' wilderness. No mere sex symbol, however, Mary Anne has "a bubbly personality" and "a quick mind," and she quickly develops an interest in the art of jungle warfare. Her interest is seen as naive at first, for she seems comi-cally unaware of danger. Eddie Diamond comments, "D-cup guts, trainer-bra brains" but then warns omi-nously, "this girl will most definitely learn." Unlike all the other women in the book, Mary Anne asks ques-tions and listens carefully. Her interest, however, has nothing to do with strategy or politics. Clearly, she is stimulated by entry to a place both exotic and mascu-line, beyond the constrictive boundaries of conventional society: "The war intrigued her. The land, too, and the mystery." In his description, which reveals a protective sort of love for Mary Anne, Rat simultaneously erases and calls attention to gender difference: "Like you and me. A *girl,* that's the only difference, and I'll tell you something: it didn't amount to jack. I mean, when we first got here—all of us—we were real young and inno-cent, full of romantic bullshit, but we learned pretty damn quick. And so did Mary Anne" (108). Like Con-rad's dark continent, "Nam" is represented as an exter-nal force that changes innocent Westerners forever.

As Mary Anne "learns" about Vietnam, the narrator's descriptions change from conventionally feminine to more masculine terms: she displays "tight, intelligent focus," "confidence in her voice, a new authority in the

way she carried herself." Mark is first proud and amazed at her competence, then uncomfortable and angry. "Her body seemed foreign somehow—too stiff in places, too firm where the softness used to be. The bubbliness was gone. The nervous giggling, too" (110). As in other sto-ries, the male's confusion is explained by the fact that he's "just a boy—eighteen years old" (111). Mary Anne starts helping out in the operating room, learning how to fire an M-16, and eventually disappearing at night. At first Mark thinks she's sleeping with someone else, but eventually discovers the incredible fact that "Mary Anne's out on fuckin' *ambush*" with the Greenies. When she first returns from such a mission, Mark "had trouble recognizing her. She wore a bush hat and filthy green fatigues; she carried the standard M-16 automatic assault rifle; her face was black with charcoal" (113), and from this point on the narrative emphasizes how much she changes and how disruptive these changes are to masculine identity and community. Mark temporarily reestablishes patriarchal order by announcing their en-gagement, but when he starts making arrangements to send Mary Anne home, she disappears for three weeks into "that no-man's land between Cleveland Heights and deep jungle." When she returns, it is as one of the shadows that "float across the surface of the earth, like spirits, vaporous and unreal," disappearing into the Spe-cial Forces hootch. No longer a "social animal," she is "lost" forever to Mark and his control, passing over to the other side where hypermasculinity merges with the mysterious jungle.

Mark becomes emasculated in inverse proportion to Mary Anne's increasing autonomy, as if her transforma-tion deprives him of his own traditional eighteen-year-old initiation into manhood. He makes a final stand one day outside the Special Forces area, telling Rat he'll "bring her out." By nightfall, "Fossie's face was slick with sweat. He looked sick. His eyes were bloodshot; his skin had a whitish, almost colorless cast." At mid-night, Rat and Eddie Diamond find "the kid" transfixed by a weird music "like the noise of nature" accompa-nied by "a woman's voice . . . half singing, half chant-ing . . . the lyrics seemed to be in a foreign tongue" (118). The three men enter the hooch and find Mary Anne surrounded by accoutrements of dark pagan wor-ship: candles, tribal music with "a weird deep-wilderness sound," and a "stench . . . thick and numb-ing, like an animal's den, a mix of blood and scorched hair and excrement and the sweet-sour odor of molder-ing flesh—the stink of the kill." In one corner impaled on a post is "the decayed head of a large black leop-ard." Everywhere there are "stacks of bones—all kinds" and propped against a wall stands a poster: "AS-SEMBLE YOUR OWN GOOK!! FREE SAMPLE KIT!!" This scene invites comparison with Coppola's almost camp representation of Kurtz's jungle com-pound, and one is not sure whether to laugh at the spe-cial effects or take them as serious depictions of trans-gression. In any event, when the men find Mary Anne, it is clear that her change is complete. Not only is she no longer feminine, but she is no longer human, as if a woman "perfectly at peace with herself" is no "person" at all, or no one the men can recognize: "It took a few seconds, Rat said, to appreciate the full change. In part it was her eyes: utterly flat and indifferent. There was no emotion in her stare, no sense of the person behind it. But the grotesque part, he said, was her jewelry. At the girl's throat was a necklace of human tongues. Elongated and narrow, like pieces of blackened leather, the tongues were threaded along a length of copper wire, one overlapping the next, the tips curled upward as if caught in a final shrill syllable" (120).

The necklace of tongues conveys multiple meanings. It is linked with other references to Mary Anne's entry to another language outside patriarchy: "a foreign tongue," "a woman's voice rising up in a language beyond translation." It is clearly part of the animal, natural world, beyond social order. Like Medusa's snakes, the necklace emphasizes an enforcing, stony silence. Mary Anne literally wears her own "gook" parts on her body, an image reminiscent of the more common string of ears collected as souvenirs by soldiers in many Vietnam war stories but more horrific, because they are decoratively flaunted. Tongues carry a multiplicitous sexual charge, suggesting both male and female genitalia, hetero- and homoerotic sexually. Her power is a particularly feminized form of monstrousness, a form of "jewelry" both alluring and threatening to castrate Mark's "solid brass balls." Once the men realize Mary Anne has transgressed the bounds of patriarchal propriety and order, "there was nothing to be done." They leave her in her lair, but not before she is granted one soliloquy that in fact explains nothing to the men except her absolute inscrutability and animalism, the voracious death-loving maw she has become. To the reader—particularly the female reader—the passage inverts the book's repeated pattern of blaming women for not understanding the war; here, the woman knows more than the men, and knowing is essentialized in terms of the female body:

'You just don't *know*' she said. 'You hide in this little fortress, behind wire and sandbags, and you don't know what it's all about. Sometimes I want to *eat* this place. Vietnam. I want to swallow the whole country—the dirt, the death—I just want to eat it and have it there inside me. That's how I feel. It's like . . . this appetite. I get scared sometimes—lots of times—but it's not *bad*. You know? I feel close to myself. When I'm out there at night, I feel close to my own body, I can feel my blood moving, my skin and my fingernails, everything, it's like I'm full of electricity and I'm glowing in the dark—I'm on fire almost—I'm burning away into nothing—but it doesn't matter because I know exactly who I am. You can't feel like that anywhere else. (121)

Indeed, Mary Anne has entered the only place where female language, autonomy, sexuality, and power make sense—beyond culture into an untranslatable heart of darkness and horror. If a reading of the story stopped here, it might appear to be a feminist assertion of semiotic power disrupting patriarchal symbolic order, a deconstruction of the myths of the American sweetheart and the American Dream suggesting that we are all complicit in the fall from innocence into the "Garden of Evil" that is Vietnam. O'Brien sounds theoretically sophisticated in such a passage, as if he's read plenty of French feminism. Rat himself sounds like a protofeminist in his commentary, once again appearing to erase gender difference while in fact emphasizing it: "She was a girl, that's all. I mean, if it was a guy, everybody'd say Hey, no big deal, he got caught up in the Nam shit, he got seduced by the Greenies. See what I mean? You got these blinders on about women. How gentle and peaceful they are. All that crap about how if we had a pussy for president there wouldn't be no more wars. Pure garbage. You got to get rid of that sexist attitude" (117). Aside from Rat's use of sexist language to critique sexism, it is important to note two things. First, Mary Anne's subjectivity, although given brief voice in the preceding passage, is never fully imagined. She is given no motive for her change and exists to register the men's reactions to her—both in the original story and in its retelling by both Rat and the narrator. Ultimately, what we understand about her is that the men do not understand her. Second, she ends up outside the social order altogether, "glowing in the dark" but also "burning away into nothing," her power unassimilated and ineffective: "And then one morning Mary Anne walked off into the mountains and did not come back." Unlike Coppola's Kurtz and Oliver Stone's Barnes in *Platoon,* ritualistically sacrificed because of their transgressions, she disappears into a disembodied spook story: "If you believed the Greenies, Rat said, Mary Anne was still somewhere out there in the dark . . . She had crossed to the other side. She was part of the land. She was wearing her culottes, her pink sweater, and a necklace of human tongues. She was dangerous, She was ready for the kill" (125). O'Brien cannot imagine an ending for such a story; Mary Anne is never elevated to the level of tragic heroine, but remains a sort of macabre, B-movie "joke," good for a nervous laugh among the men. Ultimately, her change changes nothing.

In the end, social order is restored and male homosocial bonds are re-established, exchanged—according to Sedgwick's paradigm—through the medium of Mary Anne's story. Even the segregated medics and the Greenies come together, because the final installment of Mary Anne's story is passed from one of the Greenies and Eddie Diamond to Rat Kiley to the Tim O'Brien narrator. Through storytelling, the men close ranks and banish the woman beyond the periphery of civilization.

Having appropriated masculine power within a female body, she is seen as "dangerous" to the social order and becomes "part of the land." The men are allowed to maintain their image of the war-making female as an aberration from the norm, but Mary Anne is denied the freedom or power to tell her own story. Unlike the ending of *Apocalypse Now,* where Kurtz's embrace of "the horror" brings about either total chaos or cathartic purgation (depending on which version you see), Mary Anne's savagery and monstrousness function to solidify male bonds and validate the humanity of the more "normal" soldiers. She carries to the furthest extreme the book's pattern of excluding women from the storytelling circle.

VI

In the story that closes the book, **"The Lives of the Dead,"** O'Brien makes a turn toward wholeness, closure, and regeneration. Here, for once, the feminine occupies a position in the same precious realm of the imagination as the masculine, although alternating sections again keep the war stories, the childhood stories, and the present-day metafictional commentary separate. The imagination, which was so dangerously distracting in **"The Things They Carried,"** is now a force that keeps the dead alive and integrates the self by mixing memory and desire, "bringing body and soul back together," unifying through the shaping force of language and narrative form, "a little kid, twenty-three-year-old infantry sergeant, a middle-aged writer knowing guilt and sorrow" (265). The narrator alternates in this story two primal experiences of death: his view of a Vietcong corpse on his fourth day in Vietnam, and his experience of love and loss at age nine. The story resurrects Linda, his fourth grade sweetheart, who died of a brain tumor. In retrospect, he imagines their first love as "pure knowing," imbued with the knowledge that "beyond language . . . we were sharing something huge and permanent" (259). At this point in the book, the concept of merging wholly with another through "pure knowing" has accumulated the weight of fear (Jimmy Cross and Martha) and danger (Mary Anne and the war), both of which are also associated with transgressing normal gender codes and dissolving the socially constructed self. Here, the impulse seems to be to idealize youthful passion, distinguishing it from more frightening forms of grown-up "knowing." The narrator remembers that, in fact, his urge to tell stories has always been connected with resuscitating the dead. Grieving after Linda's death, he dreams of Linda coming back to comfort him: "Timmy, stop crying. It doesn't *matter.*" In the months following, he begins to make up elaborate stories to bring Linda alive and call her into his dreams. He writes the stories down and in their vividness they become real. He gives Linda a voice (which of course is only his own dream voice, the feminine within himself) and imagines her expressing herself with a lit-

erary metaphor, once more reinforcing the connection between gender and writing/storytelling, with the female figured as absence: "'Well, right now,' she said, 'I'm *not* dead. But when I am, it's like . . . I don't know, I guess it's like being inside a book that nobody's reading." The strategy stuck with him, for "In Vietnam, too, we had ways of making the dead seem not quite so dead." The most important way, the book makes clear, is to both read and write the dead by telling stories woven "in the spell of memory and imagination."

"The Lives of the Dead" reverses the book's opening story, **"The Things They Carried,"** for here the imagination, linked with the memory of a girl, is not a dangerous force but is redemptive and regenerative. The story also moves beyond the antagonistic polarity of gender that marks the other *Esquire* stories. Linda is forever innocent and forever young, an idealized Laura or Beatrice or Annabel Lee who comes when bidden as muse for the narrator's cathartic stories. Although it sounds ungenerous to critique such a moving and lovely story, one must wonder whether the book's only positive and unthreatening representation of femininity is possible because she is forever pre-pubescent, safely encased in memory, dream, death, and narrative. Unlike Martha or Mary Anne or Curt Lemon's sister, she never grows up to be a castrating "cooze" or savage monster. She never touches the war, thus never intrudes upon his homosocial bonds; rather, the narrator uses her, as male writers have always used female muses, to find his voice and arrive at his own understanding of his traumas. In the context of all the other war stories in the book, Linda still functions as part of a triangle; she is the mediator that facilitates the narrator's reconciliation with his own past in Vietnam and his recovery of a whole self. It is tempting to read that self as universally human, but the force of the whole preceding book cautions us that it is a masculine self wounded in war and recovered in war stories. Woman can only play dead or absent muse to the central masculine subject.

The Things They Carried contributes significantly to the canon of Vietnam War fiction. It is a remarkable treatment of the epistemology of writing and the psychology of soldiering. It dismantles many stereotypes that have dominated Hollywood treatments of the Vietnam War and distorted our understanding: the basket-case veteran (the book's narrator is reasonably well-adjusted), the macho war lover (characters such as Azar are presented as extreme aberrations), the callous officer (Jimmy Cross is fallible and sympathetic), the soldier as victim of government machinations, the peace movement, or apathetic civilians. The book probes the vulnerability of soldiers betrayed by cultural myths and registers how deeply war in our culture is a gendered activity. But O'Brien inscribes no critique of his characters' misogyny or the artificial binary opposition of masculinity and femininity, no redefinition of power, no fissure in the patriarchal discourse of war. However ambiguous and horrible Vietnam may be, and however many new combinations of memory, fact, and imagination O'Brien composes, war is still presented as an inevitable, natural phenomenon deeply meaningful to the male psyche and hostile to femininity. More pernicious, these stories seem to warn women readers away from any empathetic grasp of "the things men do." Feminist playwright Karen Malpede shares Tim O'Brien's conception of the power of stories and the imagination, but she goes further to critique the very structures of thought and social organization that support war: "I mean quite literally that we need new rites, new myths, new tales of our beginnings, new stories that speak of new options open to us. The task before us is a task of the imagination, for whatever we are able to imagine we will also be able to become" (Gioseffi 132). Lynne Hanley echoes this idea, with a warning: "As a product of the imagination, literature has the potential to disrupt and transform the belligerent passions that permeate our culture. But literature also has its feet in the mud, and all too often our books, or our responses to them, encourage us instead to think bayonets" (35). Tim O'Brien's imaginative flights are heady, but his exclusion of women as readers and as characters finally reveals a failure of the imagination and muddy, clay feet.

Notes

1. Like Toni Morrison's *Beloved, The Things They Carried* is fueled by the problem of how to tell stories about unspeakable trauma and how to make peace with the ghosts of the dead. This comparison sheds light on how texts and narrative strategies are gendered. Morrison's narrative of "rememory" circles around the central story in a complex interplay of voices and sub-stories; its impulse is generous, inclusive, and collective, aimed at regeneration for a whole community as well as Sethe and her traumatized family. For a fuller treatment of this idea in Morrison, see Linda Krumholz. O'Brien's stories, as I hope to show, deal with trauma and the threat to the masculine subject by excluding women, both as readers and as characters. Though storytelling often reinforces camaraderie and redeems the solitary narrator, it does not include a whole community traumatized by the Vietnam War, nor does it attempt, as Morrison's story does, to recover a collective repressed history.

2. For elaborations on the ways Vietnam War literature has worked to rehabilitate male veterans and masculinity, see Susan Jeffords, Jacqueline Lawson, and Lorrie Smith. Lynne Hanley explores female alternatives to "belligerent" narratives.

Works Cited

Beidler, Philip D. *Re-Writing America: Vietnam Authors in Their Generation.* Athens: U of Georgia P, 1991.

Broyles, William. "Why Men Love War." *Esquire* (Nov 84): 55-65.

Faludi, Susan. *Backlash: The Undeclared War on American Women.* New York: Crown, 1991.

Gioseffi, Daniela, Ed. *Women on War: Essential Voices for the Nuclear Age.* New York: Touchstone, 1988.

Hanley, Lynne. *Writing War: Fiction, Gender, and Memory.* Amherst: U of Massachusetts P, 1991.

Harris, Robert R. "Too Embarrassed Not to Kill." Review of *The Things They Carried.* New York *Times Book Review* 11 Mar 1990.

Herr, Michael. *Dispatches.* New York: Knopf, 1977.

Jeffords, Susan. *The Remasculinization of America: Gender and the Vietnam War.* Bloomington: Indiana UP, 1991.

Krumholz, Linda. "The Ghosts of Slavery: Historical Recovery in Toni Morrison's *Beloved.*" *African American Review* 26:3 (Fall, 92): 395-408.

Lawson, Jacqueline. "'She's a Pretty Woman . . . for a Gook': The Misogyny of the Vietnam War." In Philip K. Jason, ed. *Fourteen Landing Zones: Approaches to the Literature of the Vietnam War.* Iowa City: U of Iowa P, 1990.

Lomperis, Timothy. *"Reading the Wind": The Literature of the Vietnam War.* Durham: Duke UP, 1987.

Naperstock, Martin. "An Interview with Tim O'Brien." *Contemporary Literature* 32:1 (Spring 91): 1-11.

O'Brien, Tim. *Going After Cacciato.* New York: Dell, 1978.

———. *The Things They Carried.* New York: Penguin, 1990.

Sedgwick, Eve Kosofsky. *Between Men: English Literature and Male Homosocial Desire.* New York: Columbia UP, 1985.

Smith, Lorrie. "Back Against the Wall: Anti-Feminist Backlash in Vietnam War Literature." *Vietnam Generation* 1:3-4 (Summer-Fall, 1989): 115-126. Special issue on "Gender and the War: Men, Women, and Vietnam.

Tal, Kali. "Feminist Criticism and the Literature of the Vietnam Combat Veteran." *Vietnam Generation* 1:3-4 (Summer-Fall, 1989): 190-202.

———. "Speaking the Language of Pain: Vietnam War Literature in the Context of a Literature of Trauma." In Philip K. Jason, ed. *Fourteen Landing Zones: Approaches to Vietnam War Literature.* Iowa City: U of Iowa P, 1991.

Theweleit, Klaus. *Male Fantasies* Trans. Stephen Conway in collaboration with Erica Carter and Chris Turner. Minneapolis: U of Minnesota P, 1987.

Catherine Calloway (essay date summer 1995)

SOURCE: Calloway, Catherine. "'How to Tell a True War Story': Metafiction in *The Things They Carried*." *Critique* 36, no. 4 (summer 1995): 249-57.

[*In the following essay, Calloway provides a stylistic analysis of* The Things They Carried, *regarding the volume as a work of contemporary metafiction.*]

Tim O'Brien's most recent book, **The Things They Carried**, begins with a litany of items that the soldiers "hump" in the Vietnam War—assorted weapons, dog tags, flak jackets, ear plugs, cigarettes, insect repellent, letters, can openers, C-rations, jungle boots, maps, medical supplies, and explosives as well as memories, reputations, and personal histories. In addition, the reader soon learns, the soldiers also carry stories: stories that connect "the past to the future" (40), stories that can "make the dead talk" (261), stories that "never seem . . . to end" (83), stories that are "beyond telling" (79), and stories "that swirl back and forth across the border between trivia and bedlam, the mad and the mundane" (101). Although perhaps few of the stories in **The Things They Carried** are as brief as the well-known Vietnam War tale related by Michael Herr in *Dispatches*—"'Patrol went up the mountain. One man came back. He died before he could tell us what happened,'"(6)—many are in their own way as enigmatic. The tales included in O'Brien's twenty-two chapters range from several lines to many pages and demonstrate well the impossibility of knowing the reality of the war in absolute terms. Sometimes stories are abandoned, only to be continued pages or chapters later. At other times, the narrator begins to tell a story, only to have another character finish the tale. Still other stories are told as if true accounts, only for their validity to be immediately questioned or denied. O'Brien draws the reader into the text, calling the reader's attention to the process of invention and challenging him to determine which, if any, of the stories are true. As a result, the stories become epistemological tools, multidimensional windows through which the war, the world, and the ways of telling a war story can be viewed from many different angles and visions.

The epistemological ambivalence of the stories in **The Things They Carried** is reinforced by the book's ambiguity of style and structure. What exactly is **The Things They Carried** in terms of technique? Many reviewers refer to the work as a series of short stories, but it is much more than that. **The Things They Carried** is a combat novel, yet it is not a combat novel. It is also a blend of traditional and untraditional forms—a collection, Gene Lyons says, of "short stories, essays, anecdotes, narrative fragments, jokes, fables, biographical and autobiographical sketches, and philosophical asides" (52). It been called both "a unified narrative with chapters that stand perfectly on their own" (Coffey 60) and a series of "22 discontinuous sections" (Bawer A13).

Also ambiguous is the issue of how much of the book is autobiography. The relationship between fiction and reality arises early in the text when the reader learns the first of many parallels that emerge as the book progresses: that the protagonist and narrator, like the real author of **The Things They Carried**, is named Tim O'Brien. Both the real and the fictional Tim O'Brien are in their forties and are natives of Minnesota, writers who graduated Phi Beta Kappa from Macalester College, served as grunts in Vietnam after having been drafted at age twenty-one, attended graduate school at Harvard University, and wrote books entitled *If I Die in a Combat Zone* and *Going After Cacciato*. Other events of the protagonist's life are apparently invention. Unlike the real Tim O'Brien, the protagonist has a nine-year-old daughter named Kathleen and makes a return journey to Vietnam years after the war is over.[1] However, even the other supposedly fictional characters of the book sound real because of an epigraph preceding the stories that states, "This book is lovingly dedicated to the men of Alpha Company, and in particular to Jimmy Cross, Norman Bowker, Rat Kiley, Mitchell Sanders, Henry Dobbins, and Kiowa," leading the reader to wonder if the men of Alpha Company are real or imaginary.

Clearly O'Brien resists a simplistic classification of his latest work. In both the preface to the book and in an interview with Elizabeth Mehren, he terms **The Things They Carried** "'fiction . . . a novel'" (Mehren E1), but in an interview with Martin Naparsteck, he refers to the work as a "sort of half novel, half group of stories. It's part nonfiction, too," he insists (7). And, as Naparsteck points out, the work "resists easy categorization: it is part novel, part collection of stories, part essays, part journalism; it is, more significantly, all at the same time" (1).

As O'Brien's extensive focus on storytelling indicates, **The Things They Carried** is also a work of contemporary metafiction, what Robert Scholes first termed fabulation or "ethically controlled fantasy" (3). According to Patricia Waugh,

> *Metafiction* is a term given to fictional writing which self-consciously and systematically draws attention to its status as an artefact in order to pose questions about the relationship between fiction and reality. In provid-

ing a critique of their own methods of construction, such writings not only examine the fundamental structures of narrative fiction, they also explore the possible fictionality of the world outside the literary fictional text.

(2)

Like O'Brien's earlier novel, the critically acclaimed *Going After Cacciato*,[2] **The Things They Carried** considers the process of writing; it is, in fact, as much about the process of writing as it is the text of a literary work. By examining imagination and memory, two main components that O'Brien feels are important to a writer of fiction (Schroeder 143), and by providing so many layers of technique in one work, O'Brien delves into the origins of fictional creation. In focusing so extensively on what a war story is or is not, O'Brien *writes* a war story as he examines the *process* of writing one. To echo what Philip Beidler has stated about *Going After Cacciato*, "the form" of **The Things They Carried** thus becomes "its content" (172); the medium becomes the message.

"I'm forty-three years old, and a writer now," O'Brien's protagonist states periodically throughout the book, directly referring to his role as author and to the status of his work as artifice. "Much of it [the war] is hard to remember," he comments. "I sit at this typewriter and stare through my words and watch Kiowa sinking into the deep muck of a shit field, or Curt Lemon hanging in pieces from a tree, and as I write about these things, the remembering is turned into a kind of rehappening" (36). The "rehappening" takes the form of a number of types of stories: some happy, some sad, some peaceful, some bloody, some wacky. We learn of Ted Lavender, who is "zapped while zipping" (17) after urinating, of the paranoid friendship of Dave Jensen and Lee Strunk, of the revenge plot against Bobby Jorgenson, an unskilled medic who almost accidentally kills the narrator, of the moral confusion of the protagonist who fishes on the Rainy River and dreams of desertion to Canada, and Mary Ann Bell, Mark Fossie's blue-eyed, blonde, seventeen-year-old girlfriend, who is chillingly attracted to life in a combat zone.

Some stories only indirectly reflect the process of writing; other selections include obvious metafictional devices. In certain sections of the book, entire chapters are devoted to discussing form and technique. A good example is **"Notes,"** which elaborates on **"Speaking of Courage,"** the story that precedes it. The serious reader of the real Tim O'Brien's fiction recognizes **"Speaking of Courage"** as having first been published in the Summer 1976 issue of *Massachusetts Review*.[3] This earlier version of the story plays off chapter 14 of *Going After Cacciato*, "Upon Almost Winning the Silver Star," in which the protagonist, Paul Berlin, is thinking about how he might have won the Silver Star for bravery in

Vietnam had he had the courage to rescue Frenchie Tucker, a character shot while searching a tunnel. However, in **The Things They Carried**'s version of **"Speaking of Courage,"** the protagonist is not Paul Berlin, but Norman Bowker, who wishes he had had the courage to save Kiowa, a soldier who dies in a field of excrement during a mortar attack.[4] Such shifts in character and events tempt the reader into textual participation, leading him to question the ambiguous nature of reality. Who really did not win the Silver Star for bravery? Paul Berlin, Norman Bowker, or Tim O'Brien? Who actually needed saving? Frenchie Tucker or Kiowa? Which version of the story, if either, is accurate? The inclusion of a metafictional chapter presenting the background behind the tale provides no definite answers or resolutions. We learn that Norman Bowker, who eventually commits suicide, asks the narrator to compose the story and that the author has revised the tale for inclusion in **The Things They Carried** because a postwar story is more appropriate for the later book than for *Going After Cacciato*. However, O'Brien's admission that much of the story is still invention compels the reader to wonder about the truth. The narrator assures us that the truth is that "Norman did not experience a failure of nerve that night . . . or lose the Silver Star for valor" (182). Can even this version be believed? Was there really a Norman Bowker, or is he, too, only fictional?

Even more significant, the reader is led to question the reality of many, if not all, of the stories in the book. The narrator insists that the story of Curt Lemon's death, for instance, is "all exactly true" (77), then states eight pages later that he has told Curt's story previously—"many times, many versions" (85)—before narrating yet another version. As a result, any and all accounts of the incident are questionable. Similarly, the reader is led to doubt the validity of many of the tales told by other characters in the book. The narrator remarks that Rat Kiley's stories, such as the one about Mary Ann Bell in **"Sweetheart of the Song Tra Bong,"** are particularly ambiguous:

> For Rat Kiley . . . facts were formed by sensation, not the other way around, and when you listened to one of his stories, you'd find yourself performing rapid calculations in your head, subtracting superlatives, figuring the square root of an absolute and then multiplying by maybe.

(101)

Still other characters admit the fictionality of their stories. Mitchell Sanders, in the ironically titled **"How to Tell a True War Story,"** confesses to the protagonist that although his tale is the truth, parts of it are pure invention. "'Last night, man,'" Sanders states, "'I had to make up a few things . . . The glee club. There wasn't any glee club . . . No opera,'" either (83-84). "'But,'" he adds, "'it's still true'" (84).

O'Brien shares the criteria with which the writer or teller and the reader or listener must be concerned by giving an extended definition of what a war story is or is not. The chapter **"How to Tell a True War Story"** focuses most extensively on the features that might be found in a "true" war tale. "A true war story is never moral," the narrator states. "It does not instruct, nor encourage virtue, nor suggest models of proper human behavior, nor restrain men from doing the things men have always done" (76). Furthermore, a true war story has an "absolute and uncompromising allegiance to obscenity and evil" (76), is embarrassing, may not be believable, seems to go on forever, does "not generalize" or "indulge in abstraction or analysis" (84), does not necessarily make "a point" (88), and sometimes cannot even be told. True war stories, the reader soon realizes, are like the nature of the Vietnam War itself; "the only certainty is overwhelming ambiguity" (88). "The final and definitive truth" (83) cannot be derived, and any "truths are contradictory" (87).

By defining a war story so broadly, O'Brien writes more stories, interspersing the definitions with examples from the war to illustrate them. What is particularly significant about the examples is that they are given in segments, a technique that actively engages the readers in the process of textual creation. Characters who are mentioned as having died early in the work are brought back to life through flashbacks in other parts of the text so that we can see who these characters are, what they are like, and how they die. For instance, in the story, **"Spin,"** the narrator first refers to the death of Curt Lemon, a soldier blown apart by a booby trap, but the reader does not learn the details of the tragedy until four stories later in **"How to Tell a True War Story."** Even then, the reader must piece together the details of Curt's death throughout that particular tale. The first reference to Lemon appears on the third page of the story when O'Brien matter-of-factly states, "The dead guy's name was Curt Lemon" (77). Lemon's death is briefly mentioned a few paragraphs later, but additional details surrounding the incident are not given at once but are revealed gradually throughout the story, in between digressive stories narrated by two other soldiers, Rat Kiley and Mitchell Sanders. Each fragment about Curt's accident illustrates the situation more graphically. Near the beginning of the tale, O'Brien describes the death somewhat poetically. Curt is "a handsome kid, really. Sharp grey eyes, lean and narrow-waisted, and when he died it was almost beautiful, the way the sunlight came around him and lifted him up and sucked him high into a tree full of moss and vines and white blossoms" (78). Lemon is not mentioned again for seven pages, at which time O'Brien illustrates the effect of Lemon's death upon the other soldiers by detailing how Rat Kiley, avenging Curt's death, mutilates and kills a baby water buffalo. When later in the story Lemon's accident is narrated for the third time, the reader is finally told what was briefly alluded to in the earlier tale **"Spin"**: how the soldiers had to peel Curt Lemon's body parts from a tree.

The story of Curt Lemon does not end with **"How to Tell a True War Story"** but is narrated further in two other stories, **"The Dentist"** and **"The Lives of the Dead."** In **"The Lives of the Dead,"** for example, Curt is resurrected through a story of his trick-or-treating in Vietnamese hootches on Halloween for whatever goodies he can get: "candles and joss sticks and a pair of black pajamas and statuettes of the smiling Buddha" (268). To hear Rat Kiley tell it, the narrator comments, "you'd never know that Curt Lemon was dead. He was still out there in the dark, naked and painted up, trick-or-treating, sliding from hootch to hootch in that crazy white ghost mask" (268). To further complicate matters, in **"The Lives of the Dead,"** O'Brien alludes to a soldier other than Curt, Stink Harris, from a previous literary work, *Going After Cacciato*, written over a decade before **The Things They Carried.** Thus, the epistemological uncertainty in the stories is mirrored by the fact that O'Brien presents events that take place in a fragmented form rather than in a straightforward, linear fashion. The reader has to piece together information, such as the circumstances surrounding the characters' deaths, in the same manner that the characters must piece together the reality of the war, or, for that matter, Curt Lemon's body.

The issue of truth is particularly a main crux of the events surrounding **"The Man I Killed,"** a story that O'Brien places near the center of the book. Gradually interspersed throughout the stories that make up **The Things They Carried** are references to a Vietnamese soldier, "A slim, dead, dainty young man of about twenty" (40) with "a star-shaped hole" (141) in his face, who is first mentioned in the story **"Spin"** and whose death still haunts the narrator long after the end of the war. Nine chapters after **"Spin,"** in **"The Man I Killed,"** the protagonist graphically describes the dead Vietnamese youth as well as creates a personal history for him; he envisions the young man to have been a reluctant soldier who hated violence and "loved mathematics" (142), a university-educated man who "had been a soldier for only a single day" (144) and who, like the narrator, perhaps went to war only to avoid "disgracing himself, and therefore his family and village" (142).[5] **"Ambush,"** the story immediately following **"The Man I Killed,"** provides yet another kaleidoscopic fictional frame of the incident, describing in detail the events that lead up to the narrator's killing of the young soldier and ending with a version of the event that suggests that the young man does not die at all. The reader is forced to connect the threads of the story in between several chapters that span over a hundred pages; not until a later chapter, **"Good Form,"** where the protagonist narrates three more stories of the event, does the reader fully question the truth of the incident. In the first version in **"Good Form,"** the narrator reverses the details of the earlier stories and denies that he was the thrower of the grenade that killed the man. "Twenty years ago I watched a man die on a trail near the village of My Khe," he states. "I did not kill him. But I was present, you see, and my presence was guilt enough" (203). However, he immediately admits that "Even *that* story is made up" (203) and tells instead what he terms "the happening-truth":

> I was once a soldier. There were many bodies, real bodies with real faces, but I was young then and I was afraid to look. And now, twenty years later, I'm left with faceless responsibility and faceless grief.
>
> (203)

In still a third version, "the happening-truth" is replaced with "the story-truth." According to the protagonist, the Vietnamese soldier

> was a slim, dead, almost dainty young man of about twenty. He lay in the center of a red clay trail near the village of My Khe. His jaw was in his throat. His one eye was shut, the other eye was a star-shaped hole. I killed him.
>
> (204)

But the reader wonders, did the narrator kill the young man? When the narrator's nine-year-old daughter demands, "'Daddy, tell the truth . . . did you ever kill anybody,'" the narrator reveals that he "can say, honestly, 'Of course not,'" or he "can say, honestly, 'Yes'" (204).

According to Inger Christensen, one of the most important elements of metafiction is "the novelist's message" (10). At least one reviewer has reduced O'Brien's message in *The Things They Carried* to the moral "'Death sucks'" (Melmoth H6); the book, however, reveals an even greater thematic concern. "Stories can save us," asserts the protagonist in **"The Lives of the Dead,"** the concluding story of the text (255), where fiction is used as a means of resurrecting the deceased. In this multiple narrative, O'Brien juxtaposes tales of death in Vietnam with an account of the death of Linda, a nine-year-old girl who had a brain tumor. As the protagonist tells Linda's story, he also comments on the nature and power of fiction. Stories, he writes, are "a kind of dreaming, [where] the dead sometimes smile and sit up and return to the world" (255). The narrator of **"The Lives of the Dead"** thus seeks to keep his own friends alive through the art of storytelling. "As a writer now," he asserts,

> I want to save Linda's life. Not her body—her life . . . in a story I can steal her soul. I can revive, at least briefly, that which is absolute and unchanging. . . . In a story, miracles can happen. Linda can smile and sit up. She can reach out, touch my wrist, and say, "Timmy, stop crying."
>
> (265)

Past, present, and future merge into one story as through fiction O'Brien zips "across the surface of . . . [his] own history, moving fast, riding the melt beneath the blades, doing loops and spins . . . as Tim trying to save Timmy's life with a story" (273). His story mirrors his own creative image of history, "a blade tracing loops on ice" (265), as his metafictive narrative circles on three levels: the war of a little boy's soul as he tries to understand the death of a friend, the Vietnam War of a twenty-three-year-old infantry sergeant, and the war of "guilt and sorrow" (265) faced by "a middle-aged writer" (265) who must deal with the past.

In focusing so extensively on the power of fiction and on what a war story is or is not in *The Things They Carried,* O'Brien writes a multidimensional war story even as he examines the process of writing one. His tales become stories within stories or multilayered texts within texts within texts. The book's genius is a seeming inevitability of form that perfectly embodies its theme—the miracle of vision—the eternally protean and volatile capacity of the imagination, which may invent that which it has the will and vision to conceive.[6] "In the end," the narrator states,

> a true war story is never about war. It's about sunlight. It's about the special way that dawn spreads out on a river when you know you must cross the river and march into the mountains and do things you are afraid to do. It's about love and memory. It's about sorrow. It's about sisters who never write back and people who never listen.
>
> (91)

How, then, can a true war story be told? Perhaps the best way, O'Brien says, is to "just keep on telling it" (91).

Notes

1. Biographical information on the real Tim O'Brien is taken from published facts of his life. See, for instance, Michael Coffey, "Tim O'Brien" *Publishers Weekly,* 237, 16 Feb. 1990, 60-61, and Everett C. Wilkie, Jr., "Tim O'Brien," *Dictionary of Literary Biography Yearbook: 1980,* eds. Karen L. Rood, Jean W. Ross, and Richard Ziegfeld. Detroit: Gale, 1981, 286-290.

2. New York: Delta/Seymour Lawrence, 1978. *Going After Cacciato* received the National Book Award in 1979.

3. Vol. 17, pp. 243-253. The earlier version of the story has also been published in *Prize Stories 1978: The O'Henry Awards.* Ed. and intro. William Abrahams. Garden City: Doubleday, 1978. 159-168. A later version of "Speaking of Courage" appeared in *Granta,* 29 (Winter 1989): 135-154, along with "Notes."

4. O'Brien frequently makes changes between versions of his stories that are published in literary magazines and chapters of his books. The version of "Spin" that was published in the Spring 1990 issue of *The Quarterly* (3-13), for example, combines several of the individual stories from *The Things They Carried* into one longer tale. In addition, O'Brien makes changes between the hardback and paperback versions of his books. In both the "Field Trip" chapter of the hardback edition of *The Things They Carried* and the short story version of "Field Trip" (*McCalls* 17, August 1990: 78-79), the narrator returns Kiowa's hatchet to the site of Kiowa's death, but in the paperback edition of *The Things They Carried* (New York: Penguin, 1990), the narrator carries a pair of Kiowa's moccasins. For references to changes in O'Brien's earlier works, see my "Pluralities of Vision: *Going After Cacciato* and Tim O'Brien's Short Fiction," *America Rediscovered: Critical Essays on Literature and Film of the Vietnam War.* Eds. Owen W. Gilman, Jr. and Lorrie Smith. New York: Garland, 1990. 213-224.

5. O'Brien develops the figure of the young Vietnamese youth who opposes the war more fully in *Going After Cacciato,* where Li Van Hgoc, a Vietnamese major, has been imprisoned in a tunnel complex for ten years for fleeing from the war and refusing to fight. The major, in a sense, mirrors Paul Berlin and the Third Squad. Theoretically, the soldiers have one main factor in common with Li Van Hgoc; they are all deserters from the war.

6. This theme is also a main theme of *Going After Cacciato,* which examines issues such as how war affects the imagination and how the imagination affects war, how reality cannot be escaped, even in the imagination, how the imagination is used to invent rather than to discover, how the imagination must be used as a responsible tool, and how the imagination can be a force for remaking reality.

Works Cited

Bawer, Bruce. "Confession or Fiction? Stories from Vietnam." *Wall Street Journal* 215, 23 Mar 1990: A13.

Beidler, Philip D. *American Literature and the Experience of Vietnam.* Athens: U of Georgia P, 1982.

Christensen, Inger. *The Meaning of Metafiction.* Bergen: Universitetsforlaget, 1981.

Herr, Michael. *Dispatches.* New York: Vintage, 1977.

Lyons, Gene. "No More Bugles, No More Drums." *Entertainment Weekly* 23 Feb. 1990: 50-52.

Mehren, Elizabeth. "Short War Stories." *Los Angeles Times* 11 Mar. 1990: E1, E12.

Melmoth, John, "Muck and Bullets." *The Sunday Times* (London) 20 May 1990: H6.

Naparsteck, Martin. "An Interview with Tim O'Brien." *Contemporary Literature* 32 (Spring 1991): 1-11.

O'Brien, Tim. *The Things They Carried.* New York: Houghton, 1990.

Scholes, Robert. *Fabulation and Metafiction.* Urbana: U of Illinois P, 1983.

Schroeder, Eric James. "Two Interviews: Talks With Tim O'Brien and Robert Stone." *Modern Fiction Studies* 30 (Spring 1984): 135-64.

Waugh, Patricia. *Metafiction: The Theory and Practice of Self-Conscious Fiction.* New York: Methuen, 1984.

Tina Chen (essay date spring 1998)

SOURCE: Chen, Tina. "'Unraveling the Deeper Meaning': Exile and the Embodied Poetics of Displacement in Tim O'Brien's *The Thing They Carried.*" *Contemporary Literature* 39, no. 1 (spring 1998): 77-97.

[*In the following essay, Chen asserts that "exile as a fluid and inescapable experience resulting from immersion in the moral ambiguity of the Vietnam War infects all aspects of the stories" in* The Things They Carried.]

Tim O'Brien is obsessed with telling a true war story. Truth, O'Brien's fiction about the Vietnam experience suggests, lies not in realistic depictions or definitive accounts. As O'Brien argues, "[a]bsolute occurrence is irrelevant" because "a true war story does not depend upon that kind of truth" (**Things** [**The Things They Carried**] 89). Committed to examining the relationship between the concrete and the imagined, O'Brien dismantles binaristic notions of "happening-truth" and "story-truth": "A thing may happen and be a total lie; another thing may not happen and be truer than the truth" (89). In order to assess whether he has written fiction that is "truer than the truth," O'Brien singles out the type of reaction his stories should provoke: "It comes down to gut instinct. A true war story, if truly told, makes the stomach believe" (84). This emphasis on the body's visceral response to fiction aptly encapsulates O'Brien's investigation of the literal and metaphoric relationships between stories and bodies, particularly as such affiliations are forged by a psychology of exile and displacement. For O'Brien, the returning veteran's paradoxical desires—a yearning to reverse the unwilling transformations conjured by combat experience; the inexplicable sense of exile that troubles any possibility of an easy return or rest—are best expressed by how a true war story "never seems to end" (83) but can only be told and retold, different each time yet no less faithful to the truths it must convey.

O'Brien's compulsion to revisit his war experience through fiction is not unique. The moral ambiguity and unresolved conflicts characterizing U.S. involvement in Vietnam have made that war a compelling presence in the American literary and cultural imagination.[1] Vietnam did more than redefine the *mythos* of war. According to John Hellmann, it provoked a crisis in the very narrative of nation:

> Americans entered Vietnam with certain expectations that a story, a distinctly American story, would unfold. When the story of America in Vietnam turned into something unexpected, the true nature of the larger story of America itself became the subject of intense cultural dispute. On the deepest level, the legacy of Vietnam is the disruption of our story, of our explanation of the past and vision of the future.
>
> (x)[2]

If the Vietnam War has been figured as a "disruption" of America's self-narration as nation, its rupturing of "our story" has none of the glamour or play that characterizes postmodernism. Rather, it has been cast as psychic trauma, a metaphysical fracture in the body politic that refuses to heal completely.

For O'Brien, the lingering hurts of the war are intimately linked to his stories, which, by virtue of their allegiance to the contradictory truths of war, resist closure. *The Things They Carried,* a collection of related short stories that appears grounded in O'Brien's own "real" combat experience even as it insists upon war as an endless fiction, ponders the complexities of such connections.[3] Written as a series of quasi-memoiristic episodes, the book questions the nature of truth and the possibility of ever having an unchallenged "sense of the definite" (88). Directing readers beyond the stories to the narrative gaps within and between them, O'Brien renders the indescribable experiences of "Vietnam" as moments one may gesture to but never fully represent. After Vietnam, it becomes impossible to "tell where you are, or why you're there, and the only certainty is overwhelming ambiguity." O'Brien's war stories, which are ultimately "never about war," reflect the difficult choices forced upon those who have confronted the contradictions of combat: "There is no clarity. Everything swirls. The old rules are no longer binding, the old truths no longer true. Right spills over into wrong. Order blends into chaos, love into hate, ugliness into beauty, law into anarchy, civility into savagery" (88).

The disorder of a world without rules underlies O'Brien's problematizing of the boundaries between personal memory and official history. O'Brien's vexed preoccupation with the disjunctures that make history

unreliable and memory the condition for narrative is engendered by the impossibility of ever achieving an unproblematic return home—whether that return is to family, community, one's prewar subjectivity, or nation. As such, the stories in *The Things They Carried* reflect the rootless existence of an exile. Marked by a complex understanding of Vietnam and its indelible consequences, the stories demonstrate a preoccupation with the nature of displacement and alienation. While much critical attention has been directed to the idea of the Vietnam veteran who feels exiled from America, O'Brien's work demands a reconceptualization of exile: O'Brien is alienated from his nation, his friends, himself, and, however counterintuitively, Vietnam.[4] Although O'Brien's fictive project centers on the impossibility of ascertaining any one "truth" from the experience of war, *Things* is guided nonetheless by an impulse to tell the truth, "though the truth is ugly" (87). And the ugliness of the truth that Tim O'Brien tells, an ugliness paradoxically sublime in its "largeness" and "godliness," deals much more with perpetual unmooring than it does with any kind of resolution. Exile as a fluid and inescapable experience resulting from immersion in the moral ambiguity of the Vietnam War inflects all aspects of the stories in *Things.*

Exile in *The Things They Carried* is rendered as a multiply located mode of experience; it is a condition both singular and plural in its manifestations. What begins as a fear of exile from a centrally located home, a site firmly identified as the plains of Minnesota, proliferates into multiply situated points of exile upon returning from the war. As a careful reading of *Things* reveals, O'Brien's war stories are not about recovering from trauma or resolving the conflicts contributing to or created by the war in any permanent way; they are about accepting indeterminacy and learning to live not through Vietnam but with it. In a 1991 interview with Steven Kaplan, O'Brien admits: "My concerns as a human being and my concerns as an artist have at some point interesected in Vietnam—not just in the physical place, but in the spiritual and moral terrain of Vietnam. . . . There was an intersection of values, of what was and what was to come, that I'll always go back to," even though the stories "are almost all invented, even the Vietnam stuff" (101, 95). This conscious, deeply intentioned reconstruction of Vietnam invokes Salman Rushdie's concept of "homeland" as one which, for the exiled writer, is always already fictive in nature: "if we do look back, we must . . . do so in the knowledge—which gives rise to profound uncertainties—that our physical alienation . . . almost inevitably means that we will not be capable of reclaiming precisely the thing that was lost; that we will, in short, create fictions, not actual cities or villages, but invisible ones, imaginary homelands" (10). Rushdie's eloquent articulation of an imaginary homeland recognizes the intimate relationship between an exilic longing and storytelling. O'Brien perceives such a connection occurring when "remembering is turned into a kind of rehappening" (36). His contested "confession" to killing someone during the war in **"Good Form"** testifies to the curious relationship between the stories and the idea of return, where each sustains and makes possible the other:[5]

> Here is the happening-truth. I was once a soldier. There were many bodies, real bodies with real faces, but I was young then and I was afraid to look. And now, twenty years later, I'm left with faceless responsibility and faceless grief.
>
> Here is the story-truth. He was a slim, dead, almost dainty young man of about twenty. He lay in the center of a red clay trail near the village of My Khe. His jaw was in his throat. His one eye was shut, the other eye was a star shaped hole. I killed him.
>
> What stories can do, I guess, is make things present.
>
> I can look at things I never looked at. I can attach faces to grief and love and pity and God. I can be brave. I can make myself feel again.
>
> (203-4)

For O'Brien, the epistemology of displacement, mediated by the limitations and possibilities of his stories, registers on multiple levels: geographical, temporal, narrative, social, even moral. Although O'Brien's concept of displacement is predicated upon the impossibility of any permanent return, his work nonetheless insists upon multiple returns, however fleeting or unstable, to the imaginative landscape of Vietnam. These returns produce the stories, which in turn demand the acknowledgment of Vietnam as the central topos and creative core of the fiction. Vietnam exists as both place of estrangement and ironic homeland, a fictive geography acting synchronically as point of return and alienation. Alienation becomes a state of desire producing the stories. Return is figured as momentarily possible, a juncture of time, space, and desire that never offers a definitive resting place.

. . . . .

In his prize-winning *Going After Cacciato,* O'Brien posits a traditional conception of exile as separation from native community. Near the end of *Cacciato,* the protagonist, Paul Berlin, dreams himself at the Paris peace talks and identifies the fear of exile as his original motivation for participating in the war: "I am afraid of exile. I fear what might be thought of me by those I love. I fear the loss of their respect. I fear the loss of my own reputation. Reputation, as read in the eyes of my father and mother, the people in my hometown, my friends. I fear being an outcast" (322). Exile, then, is figured as alienation from members of one's community, both family and friends. This concern reappears in **"On the Rainy River"** when, this time speaking as a narrator named "Tim" who considers evading the draft by fleeing to Canada, O'Brien writes: "I feared the war,

yes, but I also feared exile. I was afraid of walking away from my own life, my friends and my family, my whole history, everything that mattered to me" (48).[6] As with Paul Berlin, O'Brien's narrative persona in *The Things They Carried* suffers from an overwhelming and compelling fear of exile, which is verbalized as a break with the familiar. For both characters, exile is simple in its execution, chilling in its consequences. While this particular paradigm of exile exercises a powerful pull in both works, the fear of exile in its most basic terms that acts as an ending point for *Cacciato* serves as a point of beginnings in *Things.* This specific model of exile, far from governing the consciousness of displacement developed in the later book, instead fractures into more complicated formulations of the experiences of both "home" and alienation. O'Brien's intensely self-conscious meditation on the formative conditions of exile and alienation theorizes displacement as a polyvalent and multiply situated experience.

Although I have used "exile" to denote the state of alienation characterizing O'Brien's narrative voice in *The Things They Carried,* the consciousness and experience reflected in the text differ from traditional definitions of exile in significant ways. In "Reflections on Exile," Edward Said names exile as "the unhealable rift forced between a human being and a native place, between the self and its true home: its essential sadness can never be surmounted" (357). The "native place" of Said's paradigm is somewhat inadequate in representing the point of imaginative grounding that positions a writer like O'Brien, since the invocation of Vietnam—even more than America—as "true home" produces meanings that transcend the signifying capacities of Said's terminology. Mary McCarthy defines exiles as "the banished victims deracinated and tortured by the long wait to go home" (qtd. in Gurr 18). Again, the "wait to go home" figures peculiarly within the context of displacement surrounding the veteran. Already finding the self occupying what is ostensibly "home," the "long wait" becomes less a hope than a state of resignation. However, the eloquence elicited by the exilic experience and by the longing to orient the self toward a place other than where one finds oneself marks O'Brien as a writer who is displaced, if not exiled in the traditional sense. In *Things,* displacement explodes in a doubled movement: the combined impulses of dislocation and reinsertion create the storytelling process. Place as a locus of identity is figured both geographically and metaphorically; Vietnam as imagined and imaginary homeland produces a synchronic process of alienation and return.

As with exile, central to the notion of displacement is the idea of home. Home for the exile is the place of origin, or belonging. Said delineates it as "a community of language, culture, and customs" (359). In a more expansive definition, Michael Seidel describes it as "locus, custom, memory, familiarity, ease, security, sanctuary" (10). In contrast to the connotations of comfort and familiarity that characterize home for the exile, O'Brien as a displaced writer has no "ease," no "sanctuary," no "native place" to which to return. Rather, home becomes a shifting and ambiguous location, simultaneously situated in Minnesota and in Vietnam, constantly mediated and housed in the language of his stories. Despite multiple sites for home, what distinguishes Vietnam from other potential points of orientation for O'Brien's exilic consciousness is the ability of its fictive geography to generate new and sustaining acts of creativity. The imagined spaces of Vietnam act as a metaphor for home, representing less a point of origin than a territory of self-generation and re-creation. Although O'Brien uses the stories in *The Things They Carried* to examine the various homes and acts of alienation that shape a consciousness of displacement, it is Vietnam—invoked through bodies and the fictions of narrative as metonymic substitutions for geography— that emerges as the imagined homeland of the book.

Metonymy, a rhetorical figure designating a relationship of contiguity by substituting a part for a whole, works simultaneously in *The Things They Carried* to mask and expose the construction of Vietnam as imaginary homeland, the trope that governs the consciousness of the work. In *The Location of Culture,* Homi K. Bhabha asserts that metonymy "must not be read as a form of simple substitution or equivalence"; rather, "[i]ts circulation of part and whole, identity and difference, must be understood as a *double movement*" (54-55). In this way, metonymy, even while substituting one term for another, also insistently engages and provokes the recognition of a lack, the replacing term only partially signifying the replaced term. The space of signification left unfilled by the supplantation then acts to destabilize equivalence and subrogation. In *Things,* Vietnam is figured metonymically by the bodies in the text as well as the stories themselves. Both bodies and stories act as substitute terms for Vietnam; the meanings circulating among the three figures continually cross and recross categories of signification, so that it becomes impossible to discuss one term without referring and relating to the other two. Thus the densely reticulated relationship between O'Brien's consciousness of displacement and its orientation toward Vietnam reveals itself as an organic and integral part of the book.

Of critical importance to O'Brien's examination of displacement in *The Things They Carried* is the potential of home to act as a site producing multiple ways of structuring consciousness. The necessity of redesignating home as a generative location collides with figurations of the metonymic relationship between body and place in the title story, which traces Lieutenant Jimmy Cross's crush on Martha, "a junior at Mount Sebastian College in New Jersey" (3). Mesmerized by fantasies of

Martha while partially cognizant of his self-willed delusions about her requiting his love, Lieutenant Cross cultivates within himself an exilic consciousness that continually returns to the idea and image of home as it is embodied in Martha. Martha represents more than the idea of home; she actually figures as a metonym for home and all its attendant images. When Lieutenant Cross receives a good-luck charm from her, it is a pebble:

> Smooth to the touch, it was a milky white color with flecks of orange and violet, oval-shaped, like a miniature egg. In the accompanying letter, Martha wrote that she had found the pebble on the Jersey shoreline, precisely where the land touched water at high tide, where things came together but also separated. It was this separate-but-together quality, she wrote, that had inspired her to pick up the pebble and to carry it in her breast pocket for several days, where it seemed weightless, and then to send it through the mail, by air, as a token of her truest feelings for him.
>
> (9)

Just as the pebble acts as a metonym for the Jersey shoreline (and, by extension, America), Martha's explanation of how she carries the pebble with her and finally sends it to Lieutenant Cross as a "token of her truest feelings" works to figure the pebble as a metonym for her. Cross actualizes this figural relationship when he "carrie[s] the pebble in his mouth" and imagines that it is her tongue (9). Constructing his fictions on a nightly basis, he "spend[s] the last hour of light pretending [. . . and] imagin[ing] romantic camping trips into the White Mountains in New Hampshire" (3). Despite the comforting and romantic nature of his fantasies, Cross's exilic daydreams return him to a center and a home that is depicted as static and lacking in generative potential. Cross's imaginative returns home, to Martha and the Jersey shoreline, to America, always result in the same stories. His romantic fantasies are pitifully inadequate in the face of the ambiguous and dangerous realities of combat duty in Vietnam. Moments before Ted Lavender, a doped-up, sleepy-eyed member of Alpha Company, is shot while "on his way back from peeing," Lieutenant Cross is "not there" because

> [h]e was buried with Martha under the white sand at the Jersey shore. They were pressed together, and the pebble in his mouth was her tongue. He was smiling. Vaguely, he was aware of how quiet the day was, the sullen paddies, yet he could not bring himself to worry about matters of security.
>
> (12-13)

The subsequent death of Ted Lavender jolts him into awareness, forcing the realization that the romantic fantasies produced by an exilic consciousness longing to return home to America are unable to meet the exigencies of combat experience in Vietnam. This perception leads Lieutenant Cross to burn his pictures of Martha, steeling himself with the thought that "[t]his was not Mount Sebastian, it was another world, where there were no pretty poems or mid-term exams, a place where men died because of carelessness and gross stupidity" (23-24).

Although Worthington, Minnesota is represented by the narrator as "everything that mattered to me" in **"On the Rainy River,"** it, too, lacks a certain ability to engender the new ways of reading and writing the world crucial to the consciousness of O'Brien's fiction. His hometown—"a conservative little spot on the prairie"—exemplifies a "blind, thoughtless, automatic acquiescence" that results in "a kind of schizophrenia" (48). When a draft notice forces the narrator to make a choice between fighting a war he believes is wrong or facing the public censure a refusal to fight would provoke, he finds no alternative perspectives in the town to help him in his decision. For all of the "polyestered Kiwanis boys, the merchants and farmers, the pious churchgoers, the chatty housewives, the PTA and the Lions club and the Veterans of Foreign Wars and the fine upstanding gentry out at the country club," war and the decision to fight are matters of utmost simplicity: "it was a war to stop the Communists, plain and simple, which was how they liked things, and you were a treasonous pussy if you had second thoughts about killing or dying for plain and simple reasons" (48-49). The clearly demarcated categories of right and wrong paint over difficult moral choices with a "simple-minded patriotism" and "prideful ignorance" (48). Ironically, his fears of being exiled from his community force the narrator into fighting the war because he "was embarrassed not to," an act which, in turn, alters his notion of exile to the point where he understands that the constant alienation of displacement cannot be eradicated by any journey—whether of escape or return—but instead proves to be his very destination.[7]

. . . . .

To deconstruct the ways in which O'Brien articulates the processual and insistently experimental reality of displacement requires a close examination of how he uses both the human body and the art of storytelling as metonyms for Vietnam. In stories about war, bodies—whether whole or in pieces, alive or dead—figure prominently. The Vietnam War spawned a host of disfigurations, deformations of both body and spirit. Men who shipped over to help "stop the Communists, plain and simple," became avid collectors of Vietcong body parts after experiencing psychological transformations that were anything but simple.[8] The focus on the materiality of the body emerges as an organic expression of the war. In *The Things They Carried,* the rhetorical relationship between bodies and Vietnam works metaphorically as well as metonymically. In **"Night Life,"** a story about night patrol and Rat Kiley's decision to shoot himself in the foot in order to escape the war, Vietnam is personified as a corporeal entity:

> All around you, everywhere, the whole dark countryside came alive. You'd hear a strange hum in your ears. . . . Like the night had its own voice—that hum in your ears—and in the hours after midnight you'd swear you were walking through some kind of soft black protoplasm, Vietnam, the blood and the flesh.
>
> (249)

Depicted as a living organism, "the blood and the flesh" of Vietnam suggests instant connections to the other corporeal entities inhabiting the spaces of the text. However, while Vietnam is marked by its incredible vitality, many of the bodies in *Things* are not alive—at least not at first. As O'Brien makes clear, they are animated by stories, and by desire.

O'Brien makes an important distinction between life and the body: "Inside the body, or beyond the body, there is something absolute and unchanging" (265). Just as the vitality of Vietnam inspires the stories O'Brien has to tell, it is the death of the human body that generates his fiction: "in a story, which is a kind of dreaming, the dead sometimes smile and sit up and return to the world" (255). It is precisely because of the desire to "ke[ep] the dead alive" that the stories are created (267). As such, bodies and the imaginary landscape of Vietnam work in concert to impel the stories and direct the consciousness of displacement.

The story that closes the collection, **"The Lives of the Dead,"** begins with a recitation of the bodies littering the text. The list is both a catalog and a litany of the dead:

> I'm forty-three years old, and a writer now, and even still, right here, I keep dreaming Linda alive. And Ted Lavender, too, and Kiowa, and Curt Lemon, and a slim young man I killed, and an old man sprawled beside a pigpen, and several others whose bodies I once lifted and dumped into a truck. They're all dead.
>
> (255)

By naming the dead, O'Brien's narrative persona acknowledges the inanimate bodies that animate—and, in turn, are animated by—his text(s). Even more important than the actual naming of bodies is the materiality of the body itself, its ability to transform itself into an occasion. By delineating with special care the textures and details of the human body, O'Brien forces the reader to an awareness of how physical particularities assume a metaphysical importance. When Curt Lemon steps on a rigged 105 round and dies while playing a game of chicken with smoke grenades, we are told, with details at once grisly and compelling, about Curt Lemon's individual body parts and how they are blown into a tree.

Ordered to "peel him off," the narrator remembers "the white bone of an arm . . . pieces of skin and something wet and yellow that must've been the intestines" (89). The dismembered body evokes O'Brien's own narrative project, which goes about the job of remembering Curt Lemon as it remembers him for that brief moment before the booby-trapped round explodes.

Detailing the bodies in the text(s) allows O'Brien a concrete way of approaching the ambiguous situations of which he writes. The close attention to the death and transformation of the body lays bare the paradox that characterizes any recounting of the war, emphasizing the very real horror of death even while elevating it into an aesthetic moment. The messiness of bodies, especially in death and metamorphosis, promotes a profound irony: the gruesomeness of the Vietnam experience beckons with an almost overwhelming attraction.

Just as the mutilation and dismemberment of enemy bodies during wartime signifies more than a simple taking apart of bodies, instead denoting a powerful fear and desire to deny the enemy a sense of shared humanity, so O'Brien's focus on the details of the bodies in his text moves beyond the actual bodies to talk about something else. Vietnam, the quiescently generative presence propelling the stories of *The Things They Carried,* emanates from the carefully attended bodies of the text. As Martha becomes, for Lieutenant Jimmy Cross, the embodiment of America as home and haven, the bodies that preoccupy the later stories work metonymically to figure the reticulated relationship between O'Brien's consciousness as a displaced writer and his embrace of Vietnam as an imaginary homeland. One of the most powerful stories in the collection, **"Sweetheart of the Song Tra Bong,"** is a patently improbable tale which, utilizing O'Brien's narratorial skepticism to frame and reframe the embedded narrative, is told primarily by Rat Kiley, the medic of Alpha Company. Kiley "had a reputation for exaggeration and overstatement, a compulsion to rev up the facts" (101). The story that we are asked to believe is simple: as a result of a mad night of brainstorming and late-night drinking, Mark Fossie, a medic assigned to a detachment near Chu Lai, arranges to smuggle his high-school sweetheart into the country. Even more compelling than the metafictive nature of the story is O'Brien's depiction of Mary Anne Bell's physical transformation, which turns her from a "seventeen-year-old doll, . . . perky and fresh-faced, like a cheerleader visiting the opposing team's locker room" (107) into a part of the jungle where "[a]ll camouflaged up, her face smooth and vacant, she seemed to flow like water through the dark, like oil, without sound or center" (124).

When Mary Anne, dressed in "[w]hite culottes and this sexy pink sweater" (102), first steps off the helicopter and into the medical compound at Chu Lai, she is a tempting if somewhat out-of-place representative of "those girls back home [and] how clean and innocent they all are, how they'll never understand any of this, not in a billion years" (123). For the men in the medical detachment, Mary Anne embodies all the best aspects of home; they regard her very much as Lieutenant Jimmy Cross regarded Martha. Her relationship with Mark emblematizes the simple allurements of the American Dream: "From the sixth grade on they had known for a fact that someday they would be married, and live in a fine gingerbread house near Lake Erie, and have three healthy yellow-haired children, and grow old together, and no doubt die in each other's arms and be buried in the same walnut casket" (105-6). However, this vision of life—centered on the image of a profoundly American idea of home—disintegrates in the face of the more compelling dreams embedded in Vietnam. The "mystery" of the land tantalizes Mary Anne. She quickly adapts to the rigors of the war, forgoing touristic excursions through the "ville" in favor of learning "how to clip an artery and pump up a plastic splint and shoot in morphine," as well as how to operate an M-16 (109). These new accomplishments are accompanied by "a sudden new composure," and Mark, somewhat "proud" and "amazed," begins to perceive her as "a different person" (109). This difference is registered gradually, however. The surety of the gingerbread house is replaced by "a new imprecision" as her litotic revisions of what they had imagined as their future foreshadow her transformation:

> Not necessarily three kids, she'd say. Not necessarily a house on Lake Erie. "Naturally we'll still get married," she'd tell him, "but it doesn't have to be right away. Maybe travel first. Maybe live together. Just test it out, you know?"

(110)

Physical changes parallel Mary Anne's shift away from America and her embrace of Vietnam. She falls "into the habits of the bush," and Mark thinks uncomfortably that "[h]er body seemed foreign somehow—too stiff in places, too firm where the softness used to be" (110). When she begins disappearing with the "Greenies" and taking part in night ambushes, she melts into "a small, soft shadow" (115). Rat Kiley notes, "[w]hen she came in through the wire that night, I was right there, I saw those eyes of hers, I saw how she wasn't even the same person no more" (116-17). The substantive difference impressed upon her body speaks to how meaning inheres in the corporeal, which figures metonymically both itself and the jarring awareness of another figural relationship. Mary Anne becomes *other* than Mary Anne, turning instead into some new, unidentifiable entity who simultaneously registers displacement and substitution through her physical transubstantiation into the imaginative landscape of Vietnam.

Mary Anne's metamorphosis stems directly from her relationship with the land; her fascination with "the mountains, the mean little villages, the trails and trees and rivers and deep misted-over valleys" (121) permeates her system until she not only figures Vietnam but actually *becomes* Vietnam:

> Sometimes I want to *eat* this place. Vietnam. I want to swallow the whole country—the dirt, the death—I just want to eat it and have it there inside me. That's how I feel. It's like . . . this appetite. . . . When I'm out there at night, I feel close to my own body, I can feel my blood moving, my skin and my fingernails, everything, it's like I'm full of electricity and I'm glowing in the dark—I'm on fire almost—I'm burning away into nothing—but it doesn't matter because I know exactly who I am.
>
> (121)

Mary Anne's desire to incorporate Vietnam, through ingestion, into herself is ironically contingent upon her own willingness to be consumed, "burning away into nothing." Her internalization of the land and the subordination of the geography to her appetite records, on a narrative level, the actual metonymic relationship O'Brien constructs between the figure of the body and the figuration of Vietnam as homeland, the place from which the stories emerge. At the end of the story, the identification of Mary Anne with Vietnam and all its possibilities is complete. The conjoined voices of Rat Kiley and the narrative persona of Tim O'Brien explicate the phenomenon chorically:

> For Mary Anne Bell, it seemed, Vietnam had the effect of a powerful drug: that mix of unnamed terror and unnamed pleasure that comes as the needle slips in and you know you're risking something . . . you become intimate with danger; you're in touch with the far side of yourself, as though it's another hemisphere, and you want to string it out and go wherever the trip takes you and be host to all the possibilities inside yourself.
>
> (123-24)

It becomes impossible to distinguish between Mary Anne and Vietnam. As woman and land merge, their fusion complicates easy categorical distinctions. Both are alive with possibilities and imbued with the capacity to signify beyond themselves. Mary Anne becomes more than a simple high schooler from Cleveland Heights, Vietnam infinitely more than a small country at the margins of American consciousness.

The female body, originally invested with the responsibility of signifying the comfort and ease associated with romanticized and nostalgic constructions of domesticity and home, instead becomes a way of talking about the disorienting power of Vietnam. The darker elements of the war bleed across boundaries between home and exile, transfusing themselves into a new construct of home-as-displacement, the only construct capable of generating the stories. The last image of Mary Anne captures this new formation perfectly. She slips away from the compound to roam the country, and all that is left are the stories:

> when the Greenies were out on ambush, the whole rain forest seemed to stare in at them—a watched feeling—and a couple of times they almost saw her sliding through the shadows. Not quite, but almost. She had crossed to the other side. She was part of the land. She was wearing her culottes, her pink sweater, and a necklace of human tongues. She was dangerous. She was ready for the kill.
>
> (125)

In the fusion of the land and the woman, Vietnam is figured as the home to which the displaced consciousness of the text returns. The spiritual and emotional terrain of Vietnam begets the storytelling. Figured by Mary Anne, the storytelling possibilities lurking in the shadows are made manifest. The attention to her bodily representation of Vietnam returns the exilic consciousness of the text to its truest center.

"Speaking of Courage," another story exploring the correlation between Vietnam and the body, also depicts the conjunction of place and body, but in a much more literal way. Part of a trilogy of stories about the death of Kiowa, who dies after getting shot in a "shit field" when the Song Tra Bong River floods its banks during a heavy rain, **"Speaking of Courage"** describes Kiowa being sucked into the field during a VC attack: "Kiowa was almost completely under. There was a knee. There was an arm and a gold wristwatch and part of a boot. . . . There were bubbles where Kiowa's head should've been" (168). The story builds off of the metonymic substitutions of bodies for Vietnam in **"The Things They Carried"** and **"Sweetheart of the Song Tra Bong,"** literalizing the connection. Kiowa not only dies in Vietnam; he is incorporated into the texture of the land: "Kiowa was gone. He was under the mud and water, folded in with the war" (185). Kiowa's death actually makes him part of the shit field, "folded in" with not just the war but the land itself. Kiowa's literal incorporation into the land proves significant for a later discussion of the narrator's own feelings of alienation and separation from Vietnam.

In **"The Ghost Soldiers,"** O'Brien's narrative persona, after being wounded twice in combat, is transferred to Headquarters Company—S-4, the battalion supply section. The world of S-4 is completely different from that of Alpha Company: "Compared with the boonies it was cushy duty. We had regular hours. There was an EM club with beer and movies, sometimes even live floor shows" (219). It is a relatively "safe" way to spend time in Vietnam, but when his former comrades in Alpha Company come in for stand-down, O'Brien realizes that he is no longer a member of their fraternity. The solidarity forged between the members of the company by combat experience, the experience enabling the disparate members of a unit to become a "tribe" and "share the same blood" (220), now works to exclude him, exile him:

> In a way, I envied . . . all of them. . . . They were still my buddies, at least on one level, but once you leave the boonies, the whole comrade business gets turned around. You become a civilian. You forfeit membership in the family, the blood fraternity, and no matter how hard you try, you can't pretend to be part of it.
>
> (221)

Here, the narrator's sense of alienation and exile stems from his separation from his platoon. The platoon, figured as a "blood fraternity," is a body from which the narrator is metaphorically amputated. Such an amputation, already painful in light of his earlier injuries, is rendered even more excruciating by the fact that his former comrades do not view Bobby Jorgenson, the inexperienced medic partially responsible for causing his condition, as he does. Mitchell Sanders informs the narrator that while "[t]he kid messed up bad, for sure[,] . . . [p]eople change. Situations change. I hate to say this, man, but you're out of touch. Jorgenson—he's *with* us now" (224-25).

Significantly, the narrator's displaced status registers not simply on a figurative level. His distinction from the rest of the company is marked bodily as well: "Their deep bush tans, the sores and blisters, the stories, the in-it-togetherness. I felt close to them, yes, but I also felt a new sense of separation. My fatigues were starched; I had a neat haircut and the clean, sterile smell of the rear" (221). Given this "new sense of separation," the narrator finds himself pushed ever farther outside the configurations of belonging. Thus the remembering of the dead like Kiowa, who are figured as part of Vietnam itself, establishes an identificatory chain of relation, and it becomes clear that O'Brien's displaced consciousness is oriented toward Vietnam and the brotherhood that it begins to represent. No longer comfortable as a "civilian," he endures the constant sense of loss and alienation characterizing the psychology of the exile. When considered also in the context already established for home—that it act as the orienting place from which stories emerge—the displacement O'Brien experiences stems from his inability to access the ways in which Vietnam acts as both home and land, site of desired return and creative potential. O'Brien's envy and desire are directed toward *the stories* which only a reorientation to Vietnam can effect. The desire evinced by the feelings of loss which separation entails directs itself insistently back toward an imagined home represented by Vietnam, the point of origin for the displaced consciousness that determines the trajectory of *The Things They Carried.*

. . . . .

More than a collection of stories, *The Things They Carried* is a book about the need to tell stories, the ways to tell stories, and the reasons for telling stories. When considered within the framework of exile and displacement, stories invest alienation with a purpose and a direction, even if the knowledge that there can never be a final resting place or point of return renders the experience of displacement a teleological end in itself.[9] The stories serve a double function; they not only redeem the experience of displacement but also, like the bodies discussed earlier, figure as metonymic substitutions for the idea of Vietnam as home. As with so many of the ideas in this work, the connections between the terms are densely reticulated, bound together by a series of sequential substitutions so that it becomes impossible to talk about one figure without invoking the ghostly images of others. O'Brien names the stories as "the real obsession" in **"Spin"** (38), but in **"How to Tell a True War Story,"** the stories, like the bodies, become metonyms for Vietnam. When Mitchell Sanders tries to talk about the eerie experience a six-man patrol undergoes during a listening-post operation, he imbues Vietnam with a polyvocality which then generates his own story. According to Sanders, the men on patrol hear

> All these different voices. Not human voices, though. Because it's the mountains. Follow me? The rock—it's *talking.* And the fog, too, and the grass and the goddamn mongooses. Everything talks. The trees talk politics, the monkeys talk religion. The whole country. Vietnam. The place talks. It talks. Understand? Nam—it truly *talks.*
>
> (81-82)

Sanders, who almost compulsively identifies the moral of every situation, finds himself at a loss to come up with a single, definitive moral for his own story. It becomes a matter of just "*listen*[ing] to your enemy" (83)—or acknowledging the texture of "[t]hat quiet—[and] just listen[ing]" again (84). The focus on the ways in which Vietnam articulates itself transcends the distinctions made between the animate and the inanimate, the stories and the storyteller. The irrevocable blurring of boundaries calls to attention the very nature of relation. In the shifts and substitutions between bodies, stories, Vietnam, and home that function throughout the text, what part of each figure remains untouched by the others? Embedded within Sanders's assertion about the ability of Vietnam to speak rests the figure of the body. The invocation of the body immediately conjures up an attendant vision: the potential of Vietnam to produce acts of storytelling that will orient O'Brien's displacement and enable him, finally, to tell a true war story.

The Things They Carried is a book that turns on a single realization: as part of imagining a return to Vietnam as home to engender a new way of reading and writing the world, distinctions disappear and the impossibility of separating experiences and stories, reality and the imaginary, into orderly categories transcends the desire for neatness and clarity. O'Brien's post-Vietnam world is a confusing, ambiguous place. No hard and fast rules exist; truth is always provisional, waiting to adapt itself to the next story, the next reality. *The Things They Carried* testifies to displacement as a complicated condition; the polyvalent and equivocal nature of its vision and its orientation transforms everything in its scope. As such, the careful detailing of metonymic and metaphoric relationships between the bodies, the stories, home, and Vietnam uncovers Tim O'Brien's own moral, which asserts:

> In a true war story, if there's a moral at all, it's like the thread that makes the cloth. You can't tease it out. You can't extract the meaning without unraveling the deeper meaning. And in the end, really, there's nothing much to say about a true war story, except maybe "Oh."
>
> (84)

The figural relationships in the text make it unimaginable to talk about anything in isolation. The metonymic act of substitution does more than replace one term with another; in the semiotic space between the two signs, meaning explodes beyond the signifying capacities of either figure, revealing the futility of talking about one figure without constantly referring to the other. And it is precisely that movement between tropes—a movement reinforced by the structure of the text as a collection of stories which talk to each other—that produces a more complicated vision of the world. In O'Brien's war stories, the figurations of home/body/Vietnam/stories coalesce to produce an awareness of how no single idea can be unraveled from the cloth woven by the connections between each of them. It is a profound realization, leaving us to say, with wonder and a little awe, "Oh."

Notes

1. In the words of Andrew Martin, "the Vietnam War has maintained a stranglehold on the American imagination" (5). This "stranglehold" manifests itself in both pop cultural and political discourses. The outpouring of books, movies, and television shows, not to mention President Bush's assertion that the Persian Gulf war would "not be another Vietnam," attests to the accuracy of Martin's statement. For an account of Vietnam's influence on American skepticism toward military solutions for third world problems, see Klare. For an interpretive critique of the literature and criticism of the Vietnam War, see Lomperis. For discussions of the representation of Vietnam in popular visual culture, see Martin; Adair; and Dittmar and Michaud.

2. While Hellmann's conception of a national narrative powerfully identifies the continued impact of the war on American political and cultural discourses, it is important to note that the very idea of a single narrative of nation is necessarily a reductive one. For a nuanced study of the disparate and sometimes competing "national" discourses America took into the war, see Milton Bates's *The Wars We Took to Vietnam*. Bates's examination of the war as a collection of America's multiple domestic conflicts—about territorial expansion, race, class, gender, and generational difference—challenges the applicability of single paradigms to complex situations. This recognition of the multiplicity of war is also articulated by Le Ly Hayslip in her memoir *When Heaven and Earth Changed Places:* "Most of you did not know, or fully understand, the different wars my people were fighting when you got here. For you, it was a simple thing: democracy against communism. For us, that was not our fight at all. . . . For most of us it was a fight of independence—like the American Revolution. Many of us also fought for religious ideals, the way the Buddhists fought the Catholics. Behind the religious war came the battle between city people and country people—the rich against the poor—a war fought by those who wanted to change Vietnam and those who wanted to leave it as it had been for a thousand years. Beneath all that, too, we had vendettas: between native Vietnamese and immigrants (mostly Chinese and Khmer) who had fought for centuries over the land. Many of these wars go on today" (xv).

3. In mounting a challenge to the conventions of narrative, O'Brien's project of problematizing truth is embodied by the narrator of *The Things They Carried*. While the narrator is named "Tim," and it is tempting to read him as synonymous with the real Tim O'Brien, there are distinctions between the narrator and the author that prevent any easy assignment of authorial intention or identity.

4. Both Philip D. Beidler in *Re-writing America* and Philip H. Melling in *Vietnam in American Literature* refer to the idea of the veteran as an expatriate or exile in the country of his birth. For a collection of articles exploring this paradigm, see Figley and Leventman.

5. All short stories referred to in the text are names of specific stories in *The Things They Carried*.

6. See Bates 248-52 for a more detailed discussion of the ways in which "Tim" and Tim O'Brien do and do not correspond to each other.

7. This idea of the journey being the destination is reinforced by O'Brien's insistence on the provisionality of truth. In a footnote to his 1994 work *In the Lake of the Woods*, O'Brien couches his refusal to give a conclusive ending to the novel as

one informed by the idea of an uncertain journey with no end: "My heart tells me to stop right here, to offer some quiet benediction and call it the end. But truth won't allow it. Because there *is* no end, happy or otherwise. Nothing is fixed, nothing is solved. The facts, such as they are, finally spin off into the void of things missing, the inconclusiveness of conclusion. . . . Our whereabouts are uncertain. All secrets lead to the dark, and beyond the dark there is only maybe" (304).

8. The idea of mutilation and dismemberment as a way of denying humanity to the enemy is explored in Mark Baker's collection of oral histories, particularly in the chapters "Victors" and "Victims" (167-236).

9. As Theresa Hak Kyung Cha articulates it in *Dictee*, "Our destination is fixed on the perpetual motion of search. Fixed in its perpetual exile" (81).

Works Cited

Adair, Gilbert. *Vietnam on Film: From "The Green Berets" to "Apocalypse Now."* New York: Proteus, 1981.

Baker, Mark. *Nam: The Vietnam War in the Words of the Men and Women Who Fought There.* 1981. New York: Berkeley, 1983.

Bates, Milton J. *The Wars We Took to Vietnam: Cultural Conflict and Storytelling.* Berkeley: U of California P, 1996.

Beidler, Philip D. *American Literature and the Experience of Vietnam.* Athens: U of Georgia P, 1982.

———. *Re-writing America: Vietnam Authors in Their Generation.* Athens: U of Georgia P, 1991.

Bhabha, Homi K. *The Location of Culture.* London: Routledge, 1994.

Cha, Theresa Hak Kyung. *Dictee.* New York: Tanam, 1982.

Dittmar, Linda, and Gene Michaud, eds. *From Hanoi to Hollywood: The Vietnam War in American Film.* New Brunswick, NJ: Rutgers UP, 1990.

Figley, Charles R., and Seymour Leventman, eds. *Strangers at Home: Vietnam Veterans Since the War.* New York: Praeger, 1980.

Gurr, Andrew. *Writers in Exile: The Identity of Home in Modern Literature.* Brighton, Sussex: Harvester, 1981.

Hayslip, Le Ly. *When Heaven and Earth Changed Places: A Vietnamese Woman's Journey from War to Peace.* 1989. New York: Plume-Penguin, 1990.

Hellmann, John. *American Myth and the Legacy of Vietnam.* New York: Columbia UP, 1986.

Klare, Michael T. *Beyond the "Vietnam Syndrome": U.S. Interventionism in the 1980s.* Washington, DC: Washington Institute for Policy Studies, 1981.

Lomperis, Timothy J. *"Reading the Wind": The Literature of the Vietnam War.* Durham, NC: Duke UP, 1987.

Martin, Andrew. *Receptions of War: Vietnam in American Culture.* Oklahoma Project for Discourse and Theory 10. Norman: U of Oklahoma P, 1993.

Melling, Philip H. *Vietnam in American Literature.* Boston: Twayne, 1990.

O'Brien, Tim. *Going After Cacciato.* New York: Delacorte/Seymour Lawrence, 1978.

———. *In the Lake of the Woods.* Boston: Houghton; New York: Seymour Lawrence, 1994.

———. "An Interview with Tim O'Brien." With Steven Kaplan. *Missouri Review* 14.3 (1991): 93-108.

———. *The Things They Carried.* 1990. New York: Penguin, 1991.

Rushdie, Salman. "Imaginary Homelands." *Imaginary Homelands: Essays and Criticism, 1981-1991.* New York: Viking-Penguin, 1991. 9-21.

David R. Jarraway (essay date fall 1998)

SOURCE: Jarraway, David R. "'Excremental Assault' in Tim O'Brien: Trauma and Recover in Vietnam War Literature." *Modern Fiction Studies* 44, no. 3 (fall 1998): 695-711.

[*In the following essay, Jarraway analyzes three examples of O'Brien's depiction of trauma and recovery in* The Things They Carried *and explores the metaphor of excremental waste in relation to O'Brien's war experiences.*]

"'You know something?'" [Azar] said. His voice was wistful. "'Out here, at night, I almost feel like a kid again. The Vietnam experience. I mean, wow, I *love* this shit.'"

—Tim O'Brien, *The Things They Carried*

"The excremental is all too intimately and inseparably bound up with the sexual; the position of the genitals—*inter urinas et faeces*—remains the decisive and unchangeable factor."

—Sigmund Freud, *Complete Letters*

"[Kathy Wade] remembered opening her robe to the humid night air. There was a huge and desperate wanting in her heart, wanting without object, pure wanting."

—Tim O'Brien, *In the Lake of the Woods*

"If at the end of a war story," Tim O'Brien writes in his second Vietnam novel, ***The Things They Carried*** (1990), "you feel uplifted, or if you feel that some small bit of rectitude has been salvaged from the larger waste, then you have been made the victim of a very old and terrible lie" (***Things*** [***The Things They Carried***] 76). O'Brien, of course, has not been the first to remark upon the larger waste that is war. With reference to the Vietnam debacle in particular, Michael Herr's *Dispatches* (1977) sets the tone for the wastage of that "psychotic vaudeville," as he calls it, almost from the beginning:

> [A] Marine came up to Lengle and me and asked if we'd like to look at some pictures he'd taken. . . . There were hundreds of these albums in Vietnam, thousands, and they all seemed to contain the same pictures . . . the severed-head shot, the head often resting on the chest of the dead man or being held up by a smiling Marine, or a lot of heads, arranged in a row, with a burning cigarette in each of the mouths, the eyes open . . . a picture of a Marine holding an ear or maybe two ears or, as in the case of a guy I knew near Pleiku, a whole necklace made of ears, "love beads" as its owner called them; and the one we were looking at now, the dead Viet Cong girl with her pajamas stripped off and her legs raised stiffly in the air.
>
> (Herr 198-99)

In the face of such overwhelming madness, therefore, Tim O'Brien eradicates all possibility for responsive uplift in ***The Things They Carried*** by reducing even the metaphorical import of waste. As the measure of atrocious acts and imbecile events, waste's claim on all concerned, accordingly, is seen to be absolutely *literal*.

At this zero-degree level of rectitude, then, war becomes the equivalent of human waste—"a goddamn *shit* field" (***Things*** 164)—in which an entire platoon must immerse itself in order to register most completely the nauseous vacuity and repulsive futility of their lives at war: "[A]fter a few days, the Song Tra Bong overflowed its banks and the land turned into a deep, thick muck for a half mile on either side. . . . Like quicksand, almost, except the stink was incredible. . . . You'd just sink in. You'd feel it ooze up over your body and sort of suck you down. . . . I mean, it never stopped, not ever" (161). "Finally somebody figured it out. What this was, it was. . . . The village toilet. No indoor plumbing, right? So they used the field" (164). "Rain and slop and shrapnel, it all mixed together, and the field seemed to boil . . . with the waste and the war" (191). "For twenty years," O'Brien's novel's narrator later remarks in hindsight, "this field had embodied all the waste that was Vietnam, all the vulgarity and horror" (210). That the full impact, however, of the "excremental assault" of my title should come to be realized so belatedly—*In Retrospect,* as Robert McNamara most recently puts forward the case—is, ironically, Vietnam's most extravagantly wasteful legacy.[1] But as one of O'Brien's least savory platoon members is given to remark, "'Eating shit—it's your classic irony'" (187).

Irony is the trope of trash or waste. And while it's not central to my purpose to trash or waste some of the more well-known literary theories endeavoring to come to terms with, if not indeed aiming to recover from, that extraordinarily riddling concatenation of events that is "Vietnam," I nonetheless want to cultivate a healthy sense of irony in an effort to disclose what discursive representations of war—theoretical as well as artistic— may actually be endeavoring to cover over or cover up—to re-cover, as it were.[2] The fiction of Tim O'Brien, ***The Things They Carried*** in particular, with its own healthy sense of irony, can gesture toward the shortcomings of theory. But, as I shall argue later, in keeping with that penetrating sense of irony even some of the best insights of *this* work may, too, have gone to waste, driving us on to O'Brien's next and most recent novel, *In the Lake of the Woods* (1994).

Kalí Tal, in her important essay "Speaking the Language of Pain," has been in the vanguard of a number of important writers to locate Vietnam literature in the context of the discourse of trauma.[3] In so doing, Tal underscores the chief failing of most literary theorists attempting to deal holistically with the war, namely, "their inevitable and total reduction of the war to metaphor" (Tal 223), whether this be the war's likeness to the myth-making of classic American literature (Philip Beidler), to the psychic landscape in literature closer to the present (John Hellman), or to the construction of the American self-image in the literature of the future (Thomas Myers).[4] As with all experiences of trauma (Holocaust literature, rape literature, incest literature, etc.), according to Tal, "Reality so violates personal mythologies" that only the example of "the literal immersion of concentration camp victims in shit . . . of being forced to wear, eat, or swim in excrement"—only such "excremental assault" (a phrase she borrows from Terrance Des Pres's *The Survivor: An Anatomy of Life in the Death Camps* [1976])—can approximate the individual's totally abject sense of psychic and social "violation" (Tal 234). Yet the transformation of national or cultural myths is dependent organically upon the revision of personal myths (Tal 243). Hence, any kind of real social or cultural amelioration envisioned in mythically discursive terms is most likely to occur as a consequence of trauma, whose excremental horror "strike[s] at the very core of the victim's conception of self in the world, forcing the most radical restructuring of personal myth . . . to include the previously unthinkable" (234).[5]

What Tal, however, is insistent upon throughout her essay is the almost impossible task to which the trauma author becomes heir. "For if the goal is to convey the traumatic experience," as the explains, "no secondhand rendering of it is adequate. The horrific events which have reshaped the author's construction of reality can only be described [and] not re-created" (Tal 231). Thus, the trauma author appears forever to be laboring in a "liminal state," a kind of "unbridgeable gap between writer and reader" (218) that is bounded, on the one side, by "the urge to bear witness, to carry the tale of horror back to the halls of normalcy" (229), and on the other, by "the truth of the experience" that "in even the most powerful writing . . . language cannot reach or explicate" (222). Working at cross-purposes in this way, the trauma author is rather like O'Brien's Lieutenant Jimmy Cross in *The Things They Carried,* never quite succeeding in having his men "get their shit together, . . . keep it together, and maintain it neatly and in good working order" (*Things* 24).[6]

The closest experience, therefore, that we as readers of Vietnam literature are ever likely to have that might approximate something of its trauma will undoubtedly lie, along with its authors, in that "liminal state" between what we may already know too well, and what we sense is hardly there for us to imagine. The two senses of "recovery" in my title noted previously thus speak to both sides of trauma's liminal divide. Georges Bataille, who perhaps knows more about excremental assault than most, in his *Visions of Excess* gives us the initial sense of a calculated recovery, usually in closed forms of discourse whose economy, in the end, "is limited to reproduction and to the conservation of human life" (116). In more open forms of discourse, however, whose economy of "unproductive expenditure" is likely to include the traumas of "war" and "perverse sexual activity" (118), we have the quite other sense of a more radical form of recovery since expenditure, as revealed in its "excremental symbolism," is mainly "directed toward loss" rather than "the principle of conservation" and the "stability of fortunes" (122).

Recovery from trauma, then, in this more radical form can only proceed, as Tal suggests, by way of a restructuring of personal experience in a wholly *expendable* way. In contrast, the more conservative notion of recovery, by falling back upon the already known and familiar, will negate the reality of trauma by failing to include in personal experience what has been formerly left unthought. And yet the temptation to collapse the former sense of recovery into the latter, in effect, to *cover up* the trauma that is Vietnam, would appear to be overwhelming, as that horror is strikingly rendered in *The Things They Carried:*

> For the common soldier, at least, war has the feel—the spiritual texture—of a great ghostly fog, thick and permanent. There is no clarity. Everything swirls. The old rules are no longer binding, the old truths no longer true. Right spills over into wrong. Order blends into chaos, love into hate, ugliness into beauty, law into anarchy, civility into savagery. The vapors suck you in. You can't tell where you are, or why you're there, and the only certainty is overwhelming ambiguity. In war

you lose your sense of the definite, hence your sense of truth itself, and therefore it's safe to say that in a true war story nothing is ever absolutely true.

> (88)

Nonetheless, O'Brien, like Bataille, will hew to that loss of the definite, and elsewhere insist on the war's "uncertainty" (*Things* 44), its "mystery" (209), and what he candidly admits is sometimes "just beyond calling" (79).[7] For if there is to be any kind of recovery from the trauma that promises no more Vietnams, only the kind of openness and responsiveness to experience that can make what is "absolutely true" quite expendable will do. In place of a character like Rat Kiley whose obsession with "policing up the parts" and "plugging up holes" (249-50) ultimately leads to his turning his own gun on himself as the sure fire method of withstanding change, O'Brien perhaps suggests something more redemptive in the example of an unknown soldier waist-deep back in the shit field: "Bent forward at the waist, groping with both hands, he seemed to be chasing some creature just beyond reach, something elusive, a fish or a frog" (192). Bataille, in a passage that elucidates O'Brien's description of the shit field, writes: "[T]he moment when the ordered and reserved . . . lose themselves for ends that cannot be subordinated to anything one can account for" is precisely that moment when "life starts" (Bataille 128).

Life starts for both the authors and readers of Vietnam literature in those moments when the most authentic form of recovery in the trauma text represents a groping after the unaccountable, the unthinkable, and the unsayable. In the space remaining, I will dwell on three such exemplary moments in O'Brien's work—moments in which the excremental assault of war proves to be almost insupportable. In each case, nothing less than a wholly new conceptualization of subjectivity is called for—a "traumatic moment of epiphany," as it were (Žižek 34) And the recovery's success will largely depend upon the degree to which, translating Tal in the terms of both Bataille and O'Brien, the radical restructuring of personal myth will be carried forward in the direction of "things" that cannot be subordinated to anything one can discursively account for.

My first example of a promised recovery occurs, predictably enough, exactly at that moment, in the **"Sweetheart of the Song Tra Bong"** chapter of O'Brien's *Things,* when the character involved disappears at its end: "She [Mary Anne Bell] had crossed to the other side. She was part of the land. . . . She was dangerous. She was ready for the kill" (125). Mary Anne is the seventeen-year-old girlfriend of Mark Fossie whom he secretly flies from Cleveland to Vietnam to keep him company between battle maneuvers. Scandalously out of place in the battlefield, Mary Anne nonetheless is for a time tolerated by platoon members to the extent that she confirms their sexist myths of the active and aggressive male and the passive and docile female in cultures both home and abroad: "The way she looked, Mary Anne made you think about those girls back home, how clean and innocent they all are, how they'll never understand any of this, not in a billion years" (123).

But very quickly, Mary Anne becomes immersed in the excremental assault of war first hand—"She was up to her eyeballs in it," Rat Kiley acerbically remarks (*Things* 123)—and as a result, gradually begins to alter her sense of self by forming new attachments to the Green Berets, undertaking to assist medically in the fields of combat, and eventually embroiling herself directly in ambush operations, sometimes for weeks at a stretch. The "new confidence in her voice, [and] new authority in the ways she carried herself" (109), in the end, instructively reveals that the trauma of wartime liminality—"that mix of unnamed terror and unnamed pleasure" (123)[8]—can sometimes prove to have beneficial consequences, provided, as Rat Kiley ironically observes, that "you know you're risking something":

> [Y]ou become intimate with danger; you're in touch with the far side of yourself, as though it's another hemisphere, and you want to string it out and go wherever the trip takes you and be host to all the possibilities inside yourself. Not *bad*, she'd said. Vietnam made her glow in the dark. She wanted more, she wanted to penetrate deeper into the mystery of herself, and after a time the wanting became needing, which turned then to craving. . . . She was lost inside herself.
>
> (124)

In losing her self, echoing Bataille, to a host of possibilities not restricted in any sense to the essentializing exclusiveness of culturally approbated gender roles, trauma thus moves Mary Anne into that healthful space that "cannot be condensed into a 'proper locus,'" to borrow the phrasing of Elspeth Probyn, and where the self finds its recovery "as a theoretical manoeuvring, not as a unifying principle" (106). And if Mary Anne Bell disappears at the end of her chapter, it's only because, like Kathy Wade in O'Brien's next novel, *In the Lake of the Woods,* she enters into that permanent state of missing persons where "Mystery finally claims us all" (*In the Lake* 304).

My second unspeakably traumatic moment that promises recovery through subjective enlargement occurs in **"The Ghost Soldiers"** chapter of *The Things They Carried,* when the narrator is wounded from behind, and narrowly escapes death from the incompetent ministradioms of an inexperienced medic terrified by battle:

> So when I got shot the second time, in the butt, along the Song Tra Bong, it took the son of a bitch ten minutes to work up the nerve to crawl over to me. By then I was gone with the pain. Later I found out I'd almost died of shock. To make it worse, [the medic] bungled the patch job, and a couple of weeks later my ass started to rot away. . . . It was borderline gangrene. I spent a month flat on my stomach; I couldn't walk or sit; I couldn't sleep. . . . After the rot cleared up, once I could think straight, I devoted a lot of time to figuring ways to get back at him.
>
> (*Things* 218)

In this passage, what is perhaps more insupportable for the narrator than his weeks of agonizing pain recuperating in a foreign hospital is his enforced removal from a community of men whose fierce loyalty and compassion for each other the shock of war is able to authenticate in any number of passionately charged ways—homosocial possibilities somewhat ironically belied by the narrator's vengeful intention merely to "think straight." When the *worst* thing that Vietnam can do for you is "turn you sentimental," and "make you want to hook up with girls like Mary Hopkin" (235), when the "sense of pure and total loss" in wartime comes down to finding you "didn't fit [in] anymore" (225) with "guys" who "loved one another" (221), abandoning you to "dark closets, madmen, [and] murderers" (231), when even "the clean, sterile smell of [your] rear" can suggest an insupportable "sense of separation" (221) from other men in comparison to "the awful stink of [yourself]" (227)—all of this homoerotic "double talk," in Wayne Koestenbaum's phrase opens up an unspeakable hole in the trauma text into which Freud may have been reluctant to insert his finger (Koestenbaum 30),[9] but which the narrator of *The Things They Carried* shows no hesitation about penetrating:

> I remembered lying there for a long while, listening to the river, the gunfire and voices, how I kept calling out for a medic but how nobody came and how I finally came and how I finally reached back and touched the hole. The blood was warm like dishwater. I could feel my pants filling up with it. All this blood, I thought—I'll be *hollow.* Then the brittle sensation hit me. I passed out. . . .
>
> (*Things* 238)

The extraordinary tension in this passage between abject physical pain and a kind of orgasmic pleasure—"how nobody came" and "how I finally came"—gives considerable weight to O'Brien's previous remark about the only certainty being the overwhelming ambiguity of war. But the ambiguity is there, I think, at least to enlist the possibility of legitimating notions of queer subjectivity in contexts previously unspeakable, so that for one traumatic moment, as O'Brien puts it, "the whole comrade business gets turned around" (*Things* 221).[10]

Koestenbaum observes that "[a]nal secrets filled many of Freud's letters to [Wilhelm] Fliess" (36), not the least among which in that homoerotic correspondence is Freud's excitement over "all the things that resolve themselves into—excrement for me (a new Midas!)" (Freud qtd. in Koestenbaum 36). Daniel Boyarin, more recently, has made explicit even further Freud's "associaton between the anus, anal penetration, shit, and birth-giving," singling out Freud's "excrement babies" as "the necessary condition of sexual satisfaction from a man" (127). What we learn of the excremental privileging of anal sexuality in an early phase of psychoanalytic discourse can perhaps suggest a good deal about O'Brien's own preoccupation with the imagery of waste from the standpoint of trauma's gross re-visioning of personal and national ideologies that the recent controversy over gays in the military, for example, has only slightly begun to gesture toward.

And central to the radical recovery of anality, within a psychoanalytic revisionism at any rate, is the need to give some credence, as Boyarin writes, to the "homoerotic desire . . . for 'femaleness,' for passivity, to be the object of another man's desire, even to bear the child of another man" (129). So that when the whole comrade business gets turned around, as O'Brien puts it, it might be possible at last to "stare into the big black hole at the center of your own sorry soul" (***Things*** 231), much like Mary Anne previously, and discover not the usual "candy-asses" (21) looking to escape the war, or the "damned sissy . . . taken off for Canada" (48), or even the "pussy for president" who might put an end to war (117), but a man who can transcend the homophobia compounded by misogyny in mainstream culture by *the very fact* of his femininity:

> Frail-looking, delicately boned, the young man had never wanted to be a soldier and in his heart had feared that he would perform badly in battle. . . . He had no stomach for violence. He loved mathematics. His eyebrows were thin and arched like a woman's, and at school the boys sometimes teased him about how pretty he was, the arched eyebrows and long shapely fingers, and on the playground they would mimic a woman's walk and make fun of his smooth skin and his love for mathematics. He could not make himself fight them.
>
> (142)

Eventually, this young man will go off to war, and become the single Vietnamese victim of the narrator himself. And his senseless death will prompt the narrator, twenty years later, to return with his young daughter to Vietnam, to immerse himself in what was once the shit field of the Song Tra Bong, and bury the hatchet of a fallen Native American comrade named Kiowa, as an act of reparation and penance for the murder of a man who just possibly might have been the object of the narrator's own desire, if not enduring love.

Still, that rather pat resolution to a quite extraordinary sequence of homosexual tensions throughout ***The Things They Carried*** might suggest that the work of

trauma, most active in its intractable liminality may itself have been too easily buried in the waste of war, if the irony of Rat Kiley's "plugging up holes" (not to mention the narrator's own anal wound) is at all significant. But perhaps it's O'Brien's own fixation on his victim's eyes—"one eye was shut and the other was a star-shaped hole" (***Things*** 140)—where we catch sight of trauma's unfinished business. "I imagined the eye at the summit of the skull," Bataille writes, "like a horrible erupting volcano . . . associated with the rear end and its excretions" (74). The excremental assault fomented by Bataille's pineal eye/solar anus in *Visions of Excess,* so like the "star-shaped hole" of the narrator's victim, will thus have to be resumed in O'Brien's next novel, where John Wade's loss to "the tangle" of selfhood will find an appropriate extension in Wade's desire "to crawl into a hole" (*In the Lake* 296), and disappear like his wife before him. "[T]he eye can only be opened when another eye is closed," is Lee Edelman's extrapolation from a parallel vision of anal desire in Freud ("Piss Elegant" 153; see also 173), which seems to fit the relation between O'Brien's two novels almost precisely.[11]

My final example of trauma, therefore, argues for a kind of ironic recovery somewhere between the success of Mary Anne Bell earlier, and the failure of O'Brien's narrator later.[12] It occurs in the **"Speaking of Courage"** chapter of ***Things*** when Norman Bowker, surprised by sudden mortar fire one dark night, discovers that his friend Kiowa has been swallowed up completely by the waste of the swampy battlefield and for a split second, experiences a failure of nerve: "[H]ow he had taken hold of Kiowa's boot and pulled hard, but how the smell was simply too much, and how he'd backed off and in that way had lost the Silver Star" (***Things*** 172):

> [A]nd then suddenly he felt himself going too. He could taste it. The shit was in his nose and eyes . . . and the stink was everywhere—it was inside his lungs—and he could no longer tolerate it. Not here, he thought. Not like this . . . and then he lay still and tasted the shit in his mouth and closed his eyes and listened to the rain and explosions and bubbling sounds. . . . A good war story, he thought, but it was not a war for war stories, nor for talk of valor, and nobody in town wanted to know about the terrible stink. They wanted good intentions and good deeds.
>
> (168-69)

From that day forward, and for several years thereafter back in Des Moines, Norman Bowker relives that moment of weakness in his father's Chevy by driving it endlessly around a nearby lake, his carefully timed seven-mile orbits performing a kind of expiation for letting down his buddy, for falling woefully short of the expectations of his father and townsfolk, but mostly for failing the promise within himself.

Bowker's car circling the lake thus becomes a powerful metaphor not only for revolving the excremental trauma of war in its suggestive displacement onto the equally punishing domestic contexts of family and community back home—"a nucleus" around which O'Brien, in his following **"Notes"** chapter, would suggest his entire novel turns (*Things* 180). But Bowker's endless circling also brings round once again both the self-preserving and the self-denying forms of recovery at the very catastrophic center of the literature of witness. "In combat," as Judith Herman observes, "witnessing the death of a buddy places the soldier at particularly high risk for developing post-traumatic stress disorder" (54).[13] Three years after Norman Bowker's chapter ends, so the narrator informs us, Bowker commits suicide, an act he seems already to anticipate—"suddenly he felt himself going too"—by relaxing his tolerance for an unfamiliar and fearful circumstance, at the very moment when all of his tenacity and resourcefulness to deal with the shock of the new are needed. Ironically, in saving his own life, he ultimately loses it. Yet those endless repetitions centered on that lake back in Iowa suggest that Bowker is in on the game at quite a different level: a perverse kind of Lacanian "enjoyment" betokened by "the circular movement which finds *satisfaction* in failing again and again to attain the object" (Zitek 48; emphasis added). On that level, the expenditure of effort is not directed toward any self-serving end, but (as in a quite similar Lake of the Woods in O'Brien's next work, "where all is repetition") rather than fall back, one moves forward to a much larger although as yet imperfectly known vision of selfhood, motored, like Kathy Wade, only by "a huge and desperate wanting in her heart, wanting without object pure wanting" (*In the Lake* 257).

In the end, I'm tempted to argue that the liminality of Bowker's knowing just enough to understand practically nothing about himself makes him the ideal witness to trauma.[14] And for the ideal readers of Vietnam literature, he continues to remain, like John Wade in *In the Lake of the Woods,* a little "beyond knowing": "We are fascinated, all of us, by the implacable otherness of others. And we wish to penetrate by hypothesis, by daydream, by scientific investigation those leaden walls that encase the human spirit, that define it and guard it and hold it forever inaccessible" (103). "I prowl and smoke cigarettes. I review my notes. The truth is at once simple and baffling: John Wade was a pro. He did his magic, then walked away. Everything else is conjecture. No answers, yet mystery itself carries me on" (269). This concluding reference to a driving mystery—"a mystery that is simply the world of the beyond" (Caruth, *Unclaimed* 145 n. 15)—perhaps yields the ultimate irony of Tim O'Brien's work, given his stated intention, in a recent *New York Times* interview, "to stop writing fiction for the foreseeable future" ("Doing" 33). This mystery may not be a bad thing if our attention is diverted back to so much else that awaits us in the discourse of trauma, where the mysteries of recovery more properly lie. "The Vietnam experience," as one character from *Things* cryptically attests, "I mean, wow, I *love* this shit" (237).

Notes

1. Indeed, the "belated" recognition of the significance of the whole "Vietnam" experience forms a chief aspect of its conceptualization in the context of psychic trauma as I attempt to locate it here. As Cathy Caruth observes in *Unclaimed Experience,* "Traumatic experience beyond the psychological dimension of suffering it involves, suggests a certain paradox: that the most direct seeing of a violent event may occur as an absolute inability to know it; that immediacy, paradoxically, may take the form of belatedness" (92).

2. Thus, as Tina Chen recently observed, "O'Brien's stories are not about recovering from trauma or resolving the conflicts contributing to or created by the war in any permanent way; they are about accepting indeterminacy and learning to live not through Vietnam but with it" (80).

3. Of the three broad experiences of trauma dealt with in her important *Trauma and Recovery,* namely hysteria, shell shock, and sexual abuse (Herman 9), Judith Herman deals with the particular instance of "Vietnam" throughout her study under the second heading, and refers to O'Brien's *Things* as a leading instance (see 38, 52, 137). For similar treatments of the Vietnam experience in this psychomedical context, see also Kulka et al., Lifton, and Figley and Levantman.

4. Kalí Tal references her comments specifically to Philip Beidler's *American Literature and the Experience of Vietnam* (1982), John Hellman's *American Myth and the Legacy of Vietnam* (1986), and Thomas Myers's *Walking Point: American Narratives of Vietnam* (1988), among other important theoretical works that tend to totalize the experience of the Vietnam War (Tal 218-23).

5. In Lacanian terms, the most radical restructuring of subjective "myth," as Slavoj Žižek points out, "triggering a traumatic crackup of our psychic balance," will come from the direction of the Real as "the previously unthinkable," hence "alien to the symbolic order" (11)—the "life substance [ironically] that proves a shock for the symbolic universe" (22). "What ultimately interrupts the continuous flow of words, what hinders the smooth running of the symbolic circuit, is the traumatic presence of the Real: when the words stay out, we have to look not for imaginary resistances but for the object that came too close" (23)—"an objectival remainder—excrement" (43). Caruth also alludes to the Lacanian address in Žižek to

theorize trauma as "an 'escape' from the real into ideology" (*Unclaimed* 142 n. 9). Žižek also insightfully remarks that suicide is often at the center of subjectivity's encounter with the Real, an important aspect of O'Brien's *Things* that I shall return to later. But on the duplicitous (rather than salubrious) sense of "recovery" just scanned, Žižek notes that we often notice in acts of suicide "a desperate attempt to recover the traumatic encounter of the Real . . . by means of integrating it into a symbolic universe of guilt, locating it within an ideological field, and thus conferring meaning upon it" (42). This last idea will gradually become clearer as we proceed.

6. On language's inablility to "explicate" the trauma of war just noted, Caruth, in her important collection of essays on the subject, remarks generally upon "the way [traumatic experience] *escapes* full consciousness as it occurs," that it "cannot, as Georges Bataille says, become a matter of 'intelligence,'" and that "it seems to evoke the difficult truth of a history that is constituted by the very incomprehensibility of its occurrence" ("Recapturing" 153).

7. I have discussed these aspects of the Vietnam conflict at some length previously in "'Standing by His Word': The Politics of Allen Ginsberg's Vietnam 'Vortex.'" For a further expansion of the Vietnam experience in the context of trauma as a "crisis of truth" and "a crisis of evidence," see Felman 17 and passim.

8. O'Brien's phrase here comes remarkably close to Žižek's unpacking of Lacan's trauma-discourse: "even if the psychic apparatus is entirely left to itself, it will not attain the balance for which the 'pleasure principle' strives, but will continue to circulate around a traumatic intruder in its interior. . . . [T]he Lacanian name for this 'pleasure in pain' is of course enjoyment (*jouissance*) . . . the circular movement [of] which finds satisfaction in failing again and again to attain the object" (48). For the liminal "in-betweenness" of the traumatic experience, Caruth looks before Lacan to Freud, where the "temporal definition of trauma in *Beyond the Pleasure Principle* seems to be an extension of his early understanding of trauma as being locatable not in one moment alone but in the relation between two moments . . . [in] the description of the traumatic experience in terms of its temporal unlocatability" (*Unclaimed* 133 n. 8).

9. Freud's English translator, James Strachey, wrote in a footnote: "At this point (so Freud told the present editor, with his finger on an open copy of the book) there is a hiatus in the text [of Josef Breuer and Freud's collaboration, *Studies on Hysteria*, wherein the hysterical childbirth of Anna O.

had been deliberately omitted by Breuer]" (qtd. in Koestenbaum 29). Comments Koestenbaum: "Anna's unmentionable pseudomotherhood is the hole in Breuer's text; her pregnancy is as unspeakable as the hole in Breuer where Freud inserts his 'finger,' filling up a space that the elder [Breuer] modestly (and flagrantly) leaves open. Leaving holes in his text is Breuer's style of seduction: these blanks encourage Freud's participation" (29-30). Caruth follows Henry Krystal in underscoring trauma as a kind of psychic discourse in which "a void, a hole is found" ("Traumatic" 6).

10. O'Brien's wordplay on "whole" in this passage yields a further means of comprehending the traumatic Real in the context of subjective enlargement, setting us as it does before "[a]n identification with what psychoanalysis calls the 'anal object,' a remainder, an amorphous leftover of some harmonious Whole [for which] Lacan quotes Luther's sermons: 'You are the excrement which fell on the earth through the Devil's anus'" (Žižek 178). Comments Žižek, "[W]hat we have here is the opposition between a harmonious work of art ["straight" readings of O'Brien's novel, perhaps?] and the queer remainder which sticks out" (179).

11. Edelman secures several extraordinary intertextual linkages between Freud and Alfred Hitchcock on the eye as an image of anal desire in the manner of Bataille, and one instance in particular, occurring at the end of Hitchcock's *Psycho,* sets up an uncanny resonance with O'Brien's text on this issue: "But [the film] cannot (a)void the end to which its narrative logic compels it: a vision of the swamp as toilet, as the cavernous place of shit, disclosing the back end of Marion's car, like the eye that emerged from the drain, and with it the winking caption that names this site of waste as 'the end'" ("Piss Elegant" 165). Hence, the problematic of "plugging up holes" in the unfinished business of O'Brien's decidedly anal-oriented text noted previously forms an instructive intersection with Edelman's own conclusion: "Thus Freud, like Hitchcock or like Norman Bates, dreamed of exchanging an eye for an eye, of voiding the telltale stain of the anus staring back from every hole. . . . [Yet,] 'it is not easy for anyone to serve two masters' . . .—insofar, that is, as [normalization] seeks to shut that eye by plugging the anal hole, must only stage anew the vision of anal desire and guarantee the blind logic of its inevitable return" ("Piss Elegant" 173).

12. If irony is the trashy trope of trauma, noted earlier, then in the context of the *fuller* recovery of selfhood in O'Brien's fiction, Paul de Man is enormously instructive on its rhetorical deployments when he asserts, "Irony comes into being when

self-consciousness loses its control over itself. For me, at least, the way I think of it now, irony is not a figure of self-consciousness. It's a break, an interruption, a disruption. It is a moment of loss of control, and not just for the author but for the reader as well" (qtd. in Edelman, *Homographesis* 225).

13. Herman further elaborates:

> Hendin and Haas found in their study of combat veterans with post-traumatic stress disorder ["Suicide and Guilt Manifestation of PTSD in Vietnam Combat Veterans"] that a significant minority had made suicide attempts (19 percent) or were constantly preoccupied with suicide (15 percent). Most of the men who were persistently suicidal had had heavy combat exposure. They suffered from unresolved guilt about their wartime experiences and from severe, unremitting anxiety, depression, and post-traumatic symptoms. Three of the men died by suicide during the course of the study.
>
> (50)

What is more, "Caught in a political conflict that should have been resolved before their lives were placed at risk, returning soldiers often felt traumatized a second time when they encountered public criticism and rejection of the war they had fought and lost" (71).

14. Claude Lanzmann, in his essay-contribution to *Trauma: Explorations in Memory*, cites Lacan precisely to the same effect: "[O]ne of the things which we should be watching out for most, is not to understand too much, not to understand more than what there is in the discourse of the subject. . . . I will even say that it is on the basis of a certain refusal of understanding that we open the door onto psychoanalytic understanding" (qtd. in Lanzmann 204).

Works Cited

Bataille, Georges. *Visions of Excess: Selected Writings, 1927-1939*. Ed. Allan Stoekl. Trans. Allan Stoekl, Carl R. Lovitt, and Donald M. Leslie, Jr. Theory and History of Literature 14. Minneapolis: U of Minnesota P, 1985.

Boyarin, Daniel. "Freud's Baby, Fliess's Maybe: Homophobia, Anti-Semitism, and the Invention of Oedipus." *Pink Freud*. Ed. Diana Fuss. Spec. issue of *GLQ:A Journal of Lesbian and Gay Studies* 2.1-2 (1995): 115-47.

Caruth, Cathy. *Unclaimed Experience: Trauma, Narrative, and History*. Baltimore: Johns Hopkins UP, 1996.

———. Introduction. "Recapturing the Past." *Trauma: Explorations in Memory* 151-57.

———. Introduction. "Traumatic Experience." *Trauma: Explorations in Memory* 3-12.

———, ed. *Trauma: Explorations in Memory*. Baltimore: Johns Hopkins UP, 1995.

Chen, Tina. "'Unraveling the Deeper Meaning': Exile and the Embodied Poetics of Displacement in Tim O'Brien's *The Things They Carried*." *Contemporary Literature* 39.1 (1998): 77-98.

Edelman, Lee. "Piss Elegant: Freud, Hitchcock, and the Micturating Penis" *Pink Freud*. Ed. Diana Fuss. Spec. issue of *GLQ:A Journal of Lesbian and Gay Studies* 2.1-2 (1995): 149-77.

———. *Homographesis: Essays in Gay Literary and Cultural Theory*. New York: Routledge, 1994.

Felman, Shoshana. "Education and Crisis, or the Vicissitudes of Teaching" *Trauma: Explorations in Memory* 13-60.

Figley, C., and Levantman, S., eds. *Strangers at Home:Vietnam Veterans Since the War*. New York: Praeger, 1980.

Freud, Sigmund. *The Complete Letters of Sigmund Freud to Wilhelm Fliess, 1887-1904*. Ed. and trans. Jeffrey Moussaieff Masson. Cambridge: Harvard UP, 1985.

Herman, Judith Lewis. *Trauma and Recovery*. New York: Basic, 1997.

Herr, Michael. *Dispatches*. New York: Avon, 1978.

Jarraway, David R. "'Standing by His Word': The Politics of Allen Ginsberg's Vietnam 'Vortex.'" *Journal of American Culture* 16.3 (1993): 81-88.

Koestenbaum, Wayne. *Double Talk: The Erotics of Male Literary Collaboration*. New York, Routledge, 1989.

Kulka, R. A., et al. *Trauma and the Vietnam War Generation*. New York: Brunner/Mazel, 1990.

Lanzmann, Claude. "The Obscenity of Understanding: An Evening with Claude Lanzmann." *Trauma: Explorations in Memory* 200-20.

Lifton, R. J. *Home from the War: Vietnam Veterans: Neither Victims nor Executioners*. New York: Simon, 1973.

Myers, Thomas. *Walking Point: American Narratives of Vietnam*. New York: Oxford University Press, 1988.

O'Brien, Tim. Interview. "Doing the Popular Thing." *The New York Times Book Review* 9 Oct. 1994: 33.

———. *In the Lake of the Woods*. Boston: Houghton, 1994.

———. *The Things They Carried*. Boston: Houghton, 1990.

THE THINGS THEY CARRIED

—

A WORK OF FICTION BY

TIM O'BRIEN

Houghton Mifflin / Seymour Lawrence
BOSTON · 1990

O'Brien's war stories in The Things They Carried *have been compared to the Civil War stories of Ambrose Bierce and the classical stories of Homer's* Iliad.

Probyn, Elspeth. *Sexing the Self: Gendered Positions in Cultural Studies.* New York: Routledge, 1993.

Tal, Kalí. "Speaking the Language of Pain: Vietnam War Literature in the Context of a Literature of Trauma." *Fourteen Landing Zones:Approaches to Vietnam War Literature.* Ed. Philip K. Jason. Iowa City: U of Iowa P, 1991. 217-50.

Žižek, Slavoj. *Enjoy Your Symptom! Jacques Lacan in Hollywood and Out.* New York: Routledge, 1992.

Christopher D. Campbell (essay date fall-winter 1998)

SOURCE: Campbell, Christopher D. "Conversation across a Century: The War Stories of Ambrose Bierce and Tim O'Brien." *WLA: War, Literature & the Arts* 10, no. 2 (fall-winter 1998): 267-88.

[*In the following essay, Campbell finds similarities between the* The Things They Carried *and the war stories of Ambrose Bierce.*]

There is a certain brotherhood of warriors, a commonality of experience, that transcends time and the differences between individual wars. The decision of whether to go to war or to avoid it, the task of conducting oneself appropriately in situations that have no parallels in peace, the frustrations that result from beholding waste and stupidity and death at close range, and the difficult transition to civilian life (provided one survives) are some of the principal elements that distinguish this fraternity.[1] Frequently, members of this brotherhood will recount their experiences in memoirs or histories, but these accounts tend to be specific, personal, and dated—rooted in and limited by their attempt to recount factual truths. Rarely, however, a former soldier becomes a genuine *writer*—someone capable of translating his mundane reality into a transcendent fiction—someone who understands Tim O'Brien's dictum that "story-truth is truer sometimes than happening truth" (O'Brien 203). Two such men, separated in time by the passage of a century, but linked by their experiences and the art those experiences produced, are Ambrose Bierce and Tim O'Brien.

Their wars and their armies could hardly have been more different. The American Civil War, though it has been called the first modern war (largely for the scale of its destruction and bloodshed), was also the last of another age in its battlefield tactics and organization. The same man who would be dubbed "The King of Spades" for his employment of trench warfare in the defense of Richmond would also order the last Napoleonic charge at Gettysburg. The massed movement of troops in formation on an open field of battle bore little resemblance to the campaign of ambush, containment, and pacification that would be waged in tropical jungles, tunnels, and villages a century later. The largely volunteer army, in which men who had grown up in the same state if not the same town fought side by side on native ground against former countrymen and sometimes still blood kin, was markedly different from the melting pot of largely reluctant draftees that found itself engaged half-way around the world against an enemy as "other" to them as any on earth. Yet, in the literature of these two men, similarities of theme and treatment exist that bridge those differences and more yet to be conceived, and that attest to the universality of the soldier's experience. Likewise, differences of tone and meaning in the tales of each tell us more about contrasts between the philosophies of their authors than the dissimilarities of their wars or times.

The first decision that faces many a fit young man in a time of war is whether or not he will fight. In Bierce's day, that question was sometimes made all the more difficult by the necessity, in choosing to fight, of also choosing a side. Indeed, an unwillingness to fight against one's blood kin or former friends was doubtless a factor in many decisions to avoid military service. The decision to fight, however, was apparently an easy one for Bierce. On 19 April 1861, "Bierce became the second man in Elkhart County [Indiana] to enlist in the Union army" (Morris 19). Indeed, in the most recent contribution to Bierce biography, Roy Morris Jr. covers Bierce's young life before the beginning of the war in a swift nineteen pages, but one gets the sense that had the rest of his family enlisted on the side of the South, Bierce might have been the *first* in his county to join the Union cause. Thus, Bierce's own life holds no parallel to the soul-searching of O'Brien's **"On the Rainy River,"** where the semi-fictional[2] first-person protagonist of *The Things They Carried* must come to grips with his draft notice.

But for many of Bierce's peers, the decision was not so easy. As Morris points out, William Dean Howells, Henry James Jr., Henry Adams, Walt Whitman, and Samuel Clemens all found ways to serve that did not involve putting themselves in harm's way. Or else they avoided the conflict entirely, heading west to the territories or east to Europe, leaving "less gifted, less learned, but physically braver Ambrose Bierce" as "the only one to make anything approaching great art out of the looming national calamity" (23).

Empathy is the strength of the writer, however, and though Bierce did not seem to face any trying decisions about whether to fight or on which side, he could appreciate the dilemma of those who did, as he demonstrated in his story, "A Horseman in the Sky." At the core of this story, Bierce no doubt had Robert E. Lee's momentous decision in mind. A man with absolutely no enthusiasm for secession, Lee was offered command of the Union Army, but when his home state seceded, he could not escape what he felt was a higher obligation to Virginia. The protagonist of Bierce's story, a Virginian named Carter Druse, made the opposite decision, announcing one morning at breakfast, "Father, a Union regiment has arrived at Grafton. I am going to join it" (79).[3] In the scene which follows, one can almost imagine the dialogue with self, the internal war of words that Lee must have waged as he paced the floor all night before his resignation from the Army of the United States. "The father lifted his leonine head, looked at the son a moment in silence, and replied: 'Well, go, sir, and whatever may occur do what you conceive to be your duty. Virginia, to which you are a traitor, must get on without you'" (79). Those citizens of the South whose consciences directed them to take arms against their home states faced a lose-lose decision. A choice to fight on either side left them traitors to either their consciences or their homelands. Likely, many whose sentiments lay with Union or with Abolition ended up fighting on the Southern side, because, as O'Brien puts it in **"On the Rainy River,"** they were cowards. Facing his own demons, O'Brien's narrator explains,

> It was a kind of schizophrenia. A moral split. I couldn't make up my mind. I feared the war, yes, but I also feared exile. I was afraid of walking away from my own life, my friends and my family, my whole history, everything that mattered to me. I feared losing the respect of my parents. . . . I feared ridicule and censure. My hometown was a conservative little spot on the prairie, a place where tradition counted, and it was easy to imagine people sitting around a table down at the old Gobbler Café on Main Street, coffee cups poised, the conversation slowly zeroing in on the young O'Brien kid, how the damned sissy had taken off for Canada.
>
> (48)

Substitute "traitor" and "the North" for "sissy" and "Canada" and you have the dilemma of the Southerner whose heart and conscience are with the Union cause. Follow O'Brien's story to its conclusion, and you find a modern parallel for the Confederate soldier who fights not for The Cause, but to save face. With the Canadian shore in sight, O'Brien's narrator faces a bitter truth:

> Right then . . . I understood that I would not do what I should do. I would not swim away from my hometown and my country and my life. I would not be brave. . . . It had nothing to do with morality. Embarrassment, that's all it was. . . . I would go to the war—I would kill and maybe die—because I was embarrassed not to.
>
> (59-62)

In general, Bierce gives more attention to the opposite side of this dilemma. Rather than exploring the issue of moral cowardice and its role in filling the ranks of the army, Bierce chooses to focus on the price of moral bravery. For O'Brien's narrator the imagined costs of such a choice are overwhelming. He caves. He fights for a cause he does not believe in. At least two of Bierce's stories take as their themes the very real paradoxical costs of moral bravery that can only arise in a *civil* war.

One such story is the already mentioned "A Horseman in the Sky." Bierce continues,

> So Carter Druse, bowing reverently to his father, who returned the salute with a stately courtesy that masked a breaking heart, left the home of his childhood to go soldiering. By conscience and courage, by deeds of devotion and daring, he soon commended himself to his fellows and his officers; and it was to these qualities and to some knowledge of the country that he owed his selection for his present perilous duty at the extreme outpost.
>
> (79)

There is no hint of cowardice here, no irony in Bierce's description of Druse's "brave, compassionate heart" (81). Neither human frailty nor malice form the themes of this story. Rather, the courage to do one's duty and the tremendous cost of that courage in such a war as this drive Bierce's themes. When forced by military necessity to take the life of a Confederate scout who has detected a Union march, the success of which depends on surprise, Druse does so. He pauses, it is true, but finally, "The duty of a soldier was plain: the man must be shot dead. . . . In his memory, as if they were a divine mandate, rang the words of his father at their parting: 'Whatever may occur, do what you conceive to be your duty.' . . . He fired" (81-82). The Confederate scout is, of course, the elder Druse. Duty is Carter Druse's curse and his salvation. Duty demanded he fight in opposition to his homeland and his family, but it is duty which enables him to live with the consequences. He finds resolution and solace in his father's mandate. "He was calm now. . . . Duty had conquered; the spirit said to the body: 'Peace, be still'" (82). The reader may be outraged, but at whom can the outrage be directed? If there is Biercean irony in this story, it is in the final remark of the shocked sergeant as he walks away from the patricide, "Good God!" (85).

An equally illuminating study is "The Affair at Coulter's Notch," a story which takes the dilemma of having chosen the side of conscience still a step further. An artillery officer with the Union Army, Captain Coulter is ordered to silence a Confederate battery positioned near a plantation house. The reader familiar with Bierce's style can see the story's ending coming from the moment a young adjutant remarks to Coulter's colonel that, "there is something wrong in all this. Do you happen to know that Captain Coulter is from the South?" (147). The general who has ordered Coulter to engage the Confederate guns has been insulted by Coulter's "red-hot Secessionist" wife at some earlier date when the division was encamped near Coulter's home. The plantation house is, of course, Coulter's, and the story ends with a fiendishly powder-grimed, bloody, and tear-streaked Coulter cradling his dead wife and child and revealing this truth to the colonel.

The most important theme of "The Affair at Coulter's Notch," however, is not the dilemma of the Southerner fighting against the South. Rather, the central issue of this story is the perfidy of the general who orders Coulter to the task, knowing the house to be Coulter's, expecting Coulter's family to be there, and hoping to dispatch Coulter, wife, and child in a single demonic engagement to assuage his own damaged pride. At one point, the militarily sound option of silencing the Confederate guns with more effective if less destructive fire from Federal infantry snipers is refused. The colonel's answer that "the general's orders for the infantry not to fire are still in force" (147) makes clear the nature of

the engagement as a private vendetta. This sacrifice of human life on the altar of selfish pride is perhaps the bitterest theme of Bierce's war stories. It is one he repeats, even more explicitly in "One Kind of Officer."

Bierce's title invites judgment and demands discrimination. What kind of officer is this? It is the same kind as the general whose wounded pride finds balm in the destruction of the Coulter family. In fact, it is, in some ways, a reversal of that story, and one with a more poetically just outcome. In "One Kind of Officer," it is the subordinate artillerist, Captain Ransome, whose pride is wounded by General Cameron and who seeks revenge by following orders to the letter—orders which result in the senseless slaughter of hundreds of men on his own side. The discriminating factor in determining what *kind* of officer this is, is not whether or not he blindly follows orders. Both Captain Ransome and his subordinate, Lieutenant Price, follow their orders to the letter, and neither does so blindly. Yet one is justified by the outcome and the other is clearly not. Rather, the discriminator here, if there is one, is whether the officers follow their conscience. Informed that he is firing on his own men, Ransome does not cease. At the height of his madness, the captain himself dispatches a Union color bearer with a pistol shot. That Lieutenant Price's "I know nothing" results in the eventual and just execution of Ransome, however, does not make the lieutenant a better officer; it merely demonstrates that his vengeance is better aimed. One mustn't forget that the lieutenant also knew of the mistake and informed the captain of it, and received precisely the same insult that the captain had suffered from the general, "It is not permitted to you to know *anything*. It is sufficient that you obey my orders" (202). Clearly the lieutenant, in informing the captain of his battery's mistaken "friendly fire" (an oxymoron even more profound than "civil war") expected the captain to give the order to cease fire. When the captain did not, that responsibility devolved upon the lieutenant. Though the firing did end almost immediately thereafter, Bierce's simple comment, "The lieutenant went to his post," gives no indication that he was any more likely to countermand an insulting and immoral order and stop the slaughter than was the captain. Thus, his complicity in this crime is only slightly less than the captain's, and if he escapes a firing squad in the end, it is more a comment on the unequal fortunes of war than on his quality as an officer. In these men who follow orders in direct contradiction to the simplest standards of decency, Bierce's tale foreshadows the pleas of the Nazi SS tried in the aftermath of World War II.

Though few reach Captain Ransome's level of heinousness, the role of officers is a frequent theme in Bierce's war fiction. Like many in the Union Army, Bierce blamed the protraction of the war and the profusion of the bloodshed largely on poor leadership. In "An Affair of Outposts" he minces no words in attributing to Grant's "manifest incompetence" (174) the slaughter and near Union disaster that was Shiloh. If Bierce were given the task of writing the Officer's Field Manual, one might gather from his fiction that his first rule would be simply: "Do no harm." The harm that poor officership can and does cause is all too evident in both Bierce's stories and his memoirs. On May 27, 1864, Bierce was present when Generals Wood and Howard sent

> a weak brigade of fifteen hundred men, with masses of idle troops behind in the character of audience, [marching] a quarter-mile uphill through almost impassable tangles of underwood, along and across precipitous ravines, [to] attack breastworks constructed at leisure and manned with two divisions of troops as good as themselves.
>
> (42)

Bierce labels the act a "criminal blunder" and titles his account of it "The Crime at Pickett's Mill."

If Bierce's proscriptive rule would be "do no harm," his prescriptive corollary would condense Robert E. Lee's sublime ruminations on the subject[4] to simply: "Do your duty." Furthermore, Bierce has great disdain for those who expect praise for doing no more than what is necessary and expected, and equal disdain for those willing to heap it on them. The following excerpt from Bierce's commentary in the Sunday, July 31, 1898, San Francisco *Examiner* may be his most thorough expression of this philosophy outside his fiction:

> I venture to submit that the enthusiastic young gentlemen who send us military news from the several war-centers are a trifle too repetitive in their praise of "coolness." In every engagement on sea or land they are profoundly affected by the tranquil self-possession of our officers in the "hail of shot and shell" or "storm of bullets." It would be interesting to know how these admiring scribes think that an officer might naturally be expected to act. Do they look for him to gnash his teeth, tear his hair, roll his eyes and stamp like a bee-herder that has mistaken his vocation? Would it be more in accordance with the laws of nature and the fitness of things for him to pass the few precious moments of actual fighting in dodging bullets and yelling unintelligible warnings to the men whose work he has undertaken to direct and supervise? Possibly the correspondents have not learned that the first and most elementary duty of an officer in action is to keep his head on straight and his heart out of his mouth. For doing so he is entitled to the same praise that is the due of any man who does rather well the work the [sic] he has in hand and to no more. Let us have a rest from the apotheosis of "coolness."
>
> (*Skepticism* 88-89)

Still, though coolness may be what is expected, even Bierce knew too well that men's courage frequently falls short of their own expectations. In "One Officer, One Man," Captain Graffenried, an officer heretofore condemned to safe but inglorious duty at higher headquarters, finally has a chance at combat. "He was in a state of mental exaltation and scarcely could endure the enemy's tardiness in advancing to the attack. To him this was opportunity. . . . Victory or defeat . . . in one or in the other he should prove himself a soldier and a hero" (208). In the end, he thrusts his own sword through his heart, unable to bear the suspense of waiting for an attack that never comes.

O'Brien, too, takes up the theme of how men handle the awesome fear of combat, extending his theory of how they ended up there to begin with in the chapter from which the larger work takes its name. Among the things men carried in Vietnam, O'Brien lists,

> the common secret of cowardice barely restrained, the instinct to run or freeze or hide, and in many respects this was the heaviest burden of all, for it could never be put down, it required perfect balance and perfect posture. They carried their reputations. They carried the soldier's greatest fear, which was the fear of blushing. Men killed, and died, because they were embarrassed not to. It was what had brought them to the war in the first place. . . . They were too frightened to be cowards.
>
> (20-21)

This issue of pride masquerading as courage is one of the points of Bierce's "Killed at Resaca." Lieutenant Herman Brayle is eventually shot and killed, largely because he will never take cover under fire, and as Bierce observes dryly, "He who ignores the law of probabilities challenges an adversary that is seldom beaten" (136). When the narrator of the story, who has come into possession of Brayle's personal effects, finds in them a letter and reads it a year after the war, he finds the reason for Brayle's foolhardy displays of "bravery." The letter, from Brayle's beloved, Miss Marian Mendenhall, reads:

> Mr. Winters, whom I shall always hate for it, has been telling that at some battle in Virginia, where he got his hurt, you were seen crouching behind a tree. I think he wants to injure you in my regard, which he knows the story would do if I believed it. I could bear to hear of my soldier lover's death, but not of his cowardice.
>
> (140)

Brayle has carried his reputation and Miss Mendenhall's letter (later returned to her stained with his blood) to his death. As a whole, however, Bierce's tale is more a misogynistic indictment of those who would incite such vanity of courage rather than an empathetic portrayal of those who display it. The letter carried by Brayle expresses sentiments nearly the opposite of those in letters carried by O'Brien's Lieutenant Jimmy Cross, in which "Martha had never mentioned the war, except to say, Jimmy, take care of yourself" (23).

Lieutenant Cross forms O'Brien's principal treatment of the weight of responsibility that rests on the shoulders of line officers. In general, O'Brien is gentler on the human race as a whole than is "Bitter Bierce," and his portrayal of officers is no exception. We have seen Bierce's attitude toward the treachery of officers who spend the lives of their men for their own private gain or vendettas, and we have seen how clearly Bierce put the blame for most of the Union defeats on failures of leadership. O'Brien's presentation of Cross is far more sympathetic than almost anything in Bierce. When Cross makes costly mistakes, they haunt him terribly, but he learns from them. Similarly, there are no examples in *The Things They Carried* of anyone to match Bierce's Captain Ransome, or the general at Coulter's Notch. These Biercean characters are willful perpetrators—calculating and unremorseful. It may be evidence of another hundred years of progress toward the egalitarian American ideal that O'Brien's officers seem equally victimized by the war as do their men. Speaking of officers in Vietnam, O'Brien has said, "The enlisted men—the common grunts—preferred an officer who put the emphasis of man over mission" (McNerney 6). Accordingly, O'Brien's Cross is another example of how his preference to offer the positive model contrasts with Bierce's satirist's preference for portraying the opposite.

After any war short of total annihilation, a society faces the task of reintegration of the survivors. It is only in the last twenty years, in the aftermath of Vietnam, that the difficulty of this task has begun to receive widespread acknowledgment. Terms such as "post-traumatic stress syndrome" have made their way from the psychiatrist's office into the general vocabulary. O'Brien addresses this theme specifically in **"Speaking of Courage"** and in **"Notes."** In the former, Norman Bowker spends an entire day driving around a lake near his hometown. "The war was over and there was no place in particular to go" (157). Bowker is burdened with memories of the war, with stories, with tortured feelings of personal failure, and has no one to share them with. Like Bierce, who according to Morris, held "an oftenstated belief that part of himself had died in the war" (51), Bowker complains to the narrator of **"Notes,"** "It's almost like I got killed over in Nam . . . Hard to describe" (178). In **"Notes,"** we learn that Bowker eventually hanged himself. We also learn from **"Notes"** something of, if not the motivation, at least the value of writing about one's war experiences:

> I did not look on my work as therapy, and still don't. Yet . . . it occurred to me that the act of writing had led me through a swirl of memories that might otherwise have ended in paralysis or worse. By telling stories, you objectify your own experience. You separate it from yourself. You pin down certain truths. You make up others. You start sometimes with an incident that truly happened . . . and you carry it forward by in-

venting incidents that did not in fact occur but that nonetheless help to clarify and explain.

(179-80)

Although both men spent time as journalists after their respective wars, O'Brien began to publish stories of Vietnam before the war was even fully over and left journalism to write full time following the publication of his memoir, *If I Die in a Combat Zone* (1973). Bierce, on the other hand, spent over a quarter of a century as a journalist and was perhaps the best known satirist of his day by the time he published his first collection of stories, *Tales of Soldiers and Civilians,* in 1892. This marked difference in the two men's careers may account, at least in part, for some of the differences in their fictions.

There is certainly, however, one remarkable parallel in both their lives and their fiction, and that is their visits to their old battlefields after their wars have passed, and the fictional accounts which preceded each. Bierce's "A Resumed Identity" and O'Brien's **"Field Trip"** bear remarkable similarities in both theme and action, but the differences in their meaning and outcome are perhaps as good a contrast of these men's philosophies as can be found. Both penned these pieces in anticipation of their actual visits to the ground. Bierce's visit would not come until the year before his mysterious disappearance, when, en route from Washington to Mexico, he made a tour of his old battlefields (Morris 251), including that of the Battle of Stones River, the setting for the short story. O'Brien's similar return to the fields of Vietnam would not occur until 1994 (McNerney 2), four years after the publication of **"Field Trip"** in *The Things They Carried.*

In a 1994 interview, O'Brien remarks that, "in a large way, the feeling of going back to Vietnam was exactly the way I'd imagined it. That's the power of human imagination. That's why I think we love stories so much. They are future predictors" (4). One must wonder if perhaps it is Bierce's story O'Brien has in mind, for it predicts a significant aspect of O'Brien's experience. Bierce opens his tale with an old man watching an army of ghostly soldiers move silently through the landscape before him. O'Brien does not use ghosts to create his storytruth in **"Field Trip,"** but they were very much a part of his happening-truth when it finally came. Barely a month after his return to the States, O'Brien said of his visit:

> There's nothing left on my firebase in terms of barbed wire or buildings, not a scrap. But the outline of the hills on which the firebase was placed is the outline as it was a long time ago, minus all the buildings. In a spooky way, it looks as if ghosts are inhabiting the place now. . . . The ghosts are still there. It's as if you

close your eyes, you can see the paddies and villages and firebases and so on; you can almost hear the soldiers laughing and drinking. It makes you believe in a spirit world.

(2-3)

In O'Brien's story itself, the parallels with Bierce's, if coincidental, are uncanny. Each story takes place long after the battles have passed. In each, the land and its people have once again returned to agriculture. In Bierce, once the ghost soldiers have passed away and the day begins to dawn, the protagonist surveys the scene before him:

> On every side lay cultivated fields showing no sign of war and war's ravages. From the chimneys of the farmhouses thin ascensions of blue smoke signaled preparations for a day's peaceful toil. . . . A Negro . . . prefixing a team of mules to the plow, was flatting and sharping contentedly at his task.

(241-42)

Compare this to the description O'Brien's protagonist gives when, revisiting Vietnam, he arrives at the site of what is the central traumatic event of *The Things They Carried,* the death of Kiowa:

> No ghosts—just a flat grassy field. The place was at peace. There were yellow butterflies. There was a breeze and a wide blue sky. Along the river two old farmers stood in ankle-deep water, repairing the same narrow dike where we had laid out Kiowa's body after pulling him from the muck. . . . One of the farmers looked up and shaded his eyes, staring across the field at us, then after a time he wiped his forehead and went back to work.

(207)

When Bierce's protagonist thinks himself deaf because he cannot hear the passing troops, he "said so, and heard his own voice, although it had an unfamiliar quality that almost alarmed him" (240). Having spoken in the midst of the field, the fictional O'Brien remarks, "My voice surprised me. It had a rough, chalky sound, full of things I did not know were there" (212).

The parallels seem too extensive to be coincidental, and one could hardly want them to be. The already healing and optimistic conclusion of O'Brien's tale becomes even more so with Bierce's darker finish as a foil. The old Civil War veteran, for he is both old and amnesiac, eventually finds his way to Hazen's monument on the Stones River battlefield. There, faced finally with the reality of a lost lifetime, the old man beholds his reflection in a pool of clear water, and horrified, falls face downward into it and dies. Bierce's old man is the Civil War equivalent of Norman Bowker. But such is not the fate of O'Brien's narrator. Nearly everything is reversed. The fictional O'Brien of the story comes not to find a monument, but to leave one, Kiowa's moccasins, in the field. The pool is not clear; it is sewage. O'Brien does not fall face first in it and die; instead, he sits in it and slaps hands with the water like a child in a bathtub, and feels, "something go shut in my heart, while something else swung open." Finally, he arises to go on with life, telling his daughter at last, "All that's finished" (213).

By this point, it should be clear that whatever the similarities of war that both Bierce and O'Brien beheld, the tinting of the spectacles through which they viewed them was vastly different. It is not without reason that Bierce was nicknamed "Bitter Bierce." The difference in their perceptions is evident throughout their works.

In O'Brien's, there is no less waste of life and potential, but it results from the sheer dumb luck of war. When Kiowa slips under the mud in **"Speaking of Courage"** and **"In the Field,"** Lieutenant Cross eventually rationalizes that "it was one of those freak things, and the war was full of freaks, and nothing could ever change it anyway" (198). In contrast, Bierce's stories, more often than not, revolve around clearly human agency in the perpetration of disaster. Even when there is human agency in O'Brien, as in Cross's choice to set up on the shit field into which Kiowa sinks, the agency is that of stupidity, mistake, or oversight. The key is that it lacks volition. In Bierce the agency is more often human malevolence.

Part of this difference is accounted for by each author's philosophy of fiction. Clearly, Bierce has a moral in mind, something to teach, a judgment to make. For O'Brien, didacticism has no place in a war story. "I pretty much believe," he says in the interview with McNerney, "that war stories don't carry morals. You should keep them as close to the bone as possible without embroidery, without much but the facts" (8-9). This different approach to the purpose of fiction helps to account, as much as the passage of a century, for the marked difference in tone between the works of these two authors. The difference between Bierce's fiction and O'Brien's is the difference between a lesson and the test. O'Brien goes on to say,

> All stories have at their heart an essential moral function, which isn't only to put yourself into someone's shoes, but to go beyond that and put yourself into someone else's moral framework. How would *you* behave in that world? What is the moral thing to do and not to do? . . .
>
> Fiction in general, and war stories in particular, serve a moral function, but not to give you lessons, not to tell you how to act. Rather, they present you with philosophical problems, then ask you to try to adjudicate them in some way or another.

(10)

This attitude accounts for one of the most significant differences in these stories. O'Brien's evoke sympathy. They evoke understanding. One may be overwhelmed with awe at the circumstances O'Brien's characters endured, and though the reader may occasionally feel an urge to pass judgment, it is seldom because O'Brien has invited it. Bierce, on the other hand, is in the business of judgment. The earlier author's greatest successes came not in the field of fiction, but as a journalistic satirist, as one whose daily task was to point out fault, stupidity, corruption, dishonesty, hypocrisy, and all the infinite mundane vices that have plagued the human race from time immemorial. Sympathy was hardly ever Bierce's goal, except when sympathy for the victim of some offense would serve to intensify the condemnation of its perpetrator. Thus, the purpose of Captain Armisted's death in "An Affair of Outposts," his life having been sacrificed in order to save the Governor's, is not meant to evoke sadness at his death so much as to add something like the sin of murder to the Governor's already significant burden of adultery and deceit. Like Carter Druse, who sacrifices his own father, and Captain Coulter, who sacrifices his home, wife, and child, Captain Armisted, who by this point in the story is aware that it is the Governor who has seduced Armisted's wife, sacrifices himself to a sense of duty.

A key to the focus of Bierce's fictions is where credibility lies, and that focus, again, is not on noble sacrifice, but on selfish frailty. It is with some difficulty that the reader accepts the actions of these noble protagonists. Few would be willing or able to make these same decisions, or take these same actions. Few in Carter Druse's position would sacrifice their father. Most in Captain Coulter's position would train their guns on those of the Confederates not so near the house. And most, if not all, with Armisted's knowledge of the Governor's very personal betrayal, would delight in sacrificing him to the grim reaper of war, given half an opportunity to do so. Perhaps this tendency of Bierce's to cause his characters to act in ways contrary to all intuition and most human nature explains his fondness for, even dependence on, the surprise ending. In many cases, his stories would work no other way. The reader would simply reject the actions of his characters as unbelievable at too early a stage in the story for Bierce to make his point. By withholding an essential portion of the truth, Bierce lulls his readers into accepting the story's action before they have reason to question its plausibility.

This failure to evoke lasting empathy in the mind of the reader may explain why of all Bierce's Civil War short stories only "An Occurrence at Owl Creek Bridge" has garnered significant acclaim. Although this story employs the typical Biercean surprise ending, that ending, in this case, does not destroy the credibility of the action. Rather, the reader's identification with the protagonist is actually increased by the revelation of the truth. Whereas Peyton Farquhar's miraculous and heroic escape might stretch credibility for a short while,

the final realization that it has all taken place in his mind leaves the reader with a heightened sense of reality and identification. This is in sharp contrast with the typical Biercean ending, which may occasionally achieve surprise (though only if the reader is new to Bierce), but at the cost of shattering identification, credibility, and catharsis.

Quite the opposite is typical of O'Brien. While treating many of the same themes, O'Brien does so in a manner realistic and simple, without depending on trick endings and without being didactic. The result is an identification with his characters that is lasting. This vicarious immersion in a character is explicitly one of O'Brien's goals as a writer. O'Brien finds great satisfaction in the letters he receives from readers, especially women, who say, "Thank you for writing this book because now I feel something in terms of identification, and in terms of participation that I didn't feel before. My husband can't talk about it, but now I sort of understand why he doesn't, why he can't" (McNerney 24). "The whole creative joy," says O'Brien, "is to touch the hearts of people whose hearts otherwise wouldn't be touched" (25).

In the end, it is their contrasting approaches to fiction, more than the passage of a century, which distinguishes Ambrose Bierce and Tim O'Brien. The goal of the satirist—and it was this role that Bierce was never able to fully escape—is to reform the heart, gaining access through the mind. The goal of a writer like O'Brien is to inform the mind, gaining access through the heart. To borrow a phrase from war, the latter campaign is waged on better ground.

Notes

1. Though we continue to move toward erasing the gender distinction of our warriors, we are not there yet, and for the purposes of this essay, the choice of such gendered terms is conscious. As O'Brien himself notes, "One fact we live with . . . is that women don't serve in combat in western societies, much" (McNerney 18).

2. The copyright page of *The Things They Carried* contains the following disclaimer: "This is a work of fiction. Except for a few details regarding the author's own life, all the incidents, names, and characters are imaginary." I use the term "semifictional" here because part of the genius of *The Things They Carried* is the impossibility of knowing with certainty where those "few details" leave off and "story-truth" picks up.

3. All page references to Bierce's stories are from McCann's 1956 collection.

4. Memorization of Lee's quote is required of every entering class at the United States' military academies: "Duty then is the sublimest word in the

English language. You should do your duty in all things. You can never do more. You should never wish to do less."

Works Cited

Bierce, Ambrose. *Ambrose Bierce's Civil War.* Ed. William McCann. Washington: Regnery, 1956.

———. *Skepticism and Dissent: Selected Journalism from 1989-1901.* Ed. Lawrence I. Berkove. Ann Arbor: Delmas, 1980.

McNerney, Brian C. "Responsibly Inventing History: An Interview with Tim O'Brien." *War, Literature & the Arts* 6:2 (1994): 1-26.

Morris, Roy, Jr. *Ambrose Bierce: Alone in Bad Company.* New York: Crown, 1995.

O'Brien, Tim. *The Things They Carried.* 1990. New York: Penguin, 1991.

Farrell O'Gorman (essay date fall-winter 1998)

SOURCE: O'Gorman, Farrell. "*The Things They Carried* as Composite Novel." *WLA: War, Literature & the Arts* 10, no. 2 (fall-winter 1998): 289-309.

[*In the following essay, O'Gorman examines* The Things They Carried *as a composite novel.*]

> I feel I'm experimenting all the time. But the difference is this: I am experimenting not for the joy of experimenting, but rather to explore meaning and themes and dramatic discovery . . . I don't enjoy tinkering for the joy of tinkering, and I don't like reading books merely for their artifice. I want to see things and explore moral issues when I read, not get hit over the head by the tools of the trade.
>
> (*Anything Can Happen* 269)

> Novels have a kind of continuity of plot or of narrative which this book does not have. But it would be unfair for me to say that it's a collection of stories; clearly all of the stories are related and the characters reappear and themes recur, and some of the stories refer back to others, and some refer forwards. I've thought of it as a work of fiction that is neither one nor the other.
>
> (*Missouri Review* 96)

> It would be more fun, it would be more instructive, it would be more artistic, more beautiful, to include as much as possible the whole of humanity in these stories.
>
> (*Missouri Review* 98)

When Tim O'Brien's *If I Die in a Combat Zone* appeared in 1973, critics lauded the memoir and promptly prepared a place for the new author—three years out of Vietnam—in the ranks of the contemporary war writers who were trying to record what was happening in the bloody quagmire in which America, uncharacteristically, found itself mired. Such a characterization seemed borne out in his next two novels; both *Northern Lights* and *Going After Cacciato* were clearly representative of a new literature of the Vietnam experience. But in each of these works there is also ample evidence of his concern with issues broader than a specific war in Southeast Asia: indeed, even early readers recognized that *If I Die in a Combat Zone* was no mere raw emotional record of war experiences but rather "a spare, poetically allusive, and classically toned personal memoir" (Myers 141).

Such an observation suggests the true scope of O'Brien's interests: in his work there is an abiding concern with the question of battlefield courage, linking him with not only with the best of a tradition of American war writers—Cooper, Crane, Hemingway—but also with the ancients; a more general concern with moral choice and the human capacity for evil which links him to such writers as Conrad (perhaps his most oft-cited influence); and, finally, an explicit interest in storytelling itself, in narrative forms and the power of the imagination, which might connect him to a number of experimental writers, both modern and postmodern. Critics have gradually acknowledged this complexity, and O'Brien has accordingly gained increasing recognition as a writer concerned not only with that war Americans like to think of as so peculiar but also as one whose "fundamental themes . . . grant his work larger, even universal significance" (Myers 141).

O'Brien's own comments strongly support such readings of his work. In interviews he has cited as influences not only fellow Midwestern soldier-novelist Hemingway, but also Fitzgerald, Faulkner, and Joyce. Even more ambitiously, he has acknowledged that "the good writer must write beyond his moment, but he does have to be rooted in a lived-in world—like Conrad, Shakespeare and Homer" (qtd. in Myers 142). While his own "concerns as a human being and concerns as an artist have at some point intersected in Vietnam" (*Missouri Review* 101), those concerns are perennially human ones—with courage, moral choice, storytelling, "mysteriousness," and the experience of "awakening into a new world, something new and true, where someone is jolted out of a kind of complacency and forced to confront a new set of circumstances or a new self" (*Missouri Review* 99). O'Brien, then, rather traditionally sees the writer as communicating age-old themes that are newly manifested in his particular imaginative world; ultimately he sees his own subject matter as bounded not by the events of one war but rather by the full range of human experience itself.

The veracity of such a claim seems more apparent given O'Brien's broadened scope in his later novels, which are more generally about the American experience. *The*

Nuclear Age (1986) is a parody about a nation obsessed with total war and apocalypse; *In the Lake of the Woods* (1994) concerns a husband and wife and the inevitable secrets of married life. But, ironically, it is perhaps in his 1990 publication of *The Things They Carried*—his first full-length return to the terrain of Vietnam in the twelve years since *Going After Cacciato*—that he most fully commits himself to exploring the universal concerns he speaks of so frequently in interviews. In fact, in *The Things They Carried* he is more consciously than ever before coming back to Vietnam with the intention of making it a story about the whole of human experience.

Thomas Myers has claimed with regard to *The Things They Carried* that "in a radically different way from his earlier combat zone narratives, the work depicts Vietnam as both 'this war' and 'any war'"(153). O'Brien would welcome such an observation, for he has maintained that, despite the general American perception of the war as an anomaly, Vietnam was not really an exception. In an interview with Larry McCaffery, he denies that his war was "especially chaotic and formless." He claims that the work of earlier writers—he mentions Siegfried Sassoon, Robert Graves, Rupert Brooke—has enabled him to acknowledge this fact most fully: "Every war seems formless to the men fighting it . . . We like to think our own war is special: especially horrible, especially insane, especially formless. But we need a more historical and compassionate perspective. We shouldn't minimize the suffering and sense of bewilderment of other people in other wars" (*Anything Can Happen* 267). Such a statement encapsulates O'Brien's own commitment to at once capture the unique fury of his own conflict and to communicate it to posterity as something eternally, horribly human.

What is surprising is that he does so most powerfully by moving beyond the battlefield. Readers of *The Things They Carried* are immediately struck its variety of settings—which include not only the killing grounds of Vietnam, but also the small towns and cities of America—and the variety of characters to be found in these settings. Speaking specifically about his unusual choice to place a Midwestern American female in Vietnam in his story **"Sweetheart of the Song Tra Bong,"** O'Brien claimed "it would be more fun, it would be more instructive, it would be more artistic, more beautiful, to include as much as possible the whole of humanity in these stories" (*Missouri Review* 98).

This claim is central to understanding the structure of the work as a whole. For more compelling than any discursive statement about the universal nature of war, or any conventionally presented variety of setting and character, is O'Brien's unconventional choice of form in *The Things They Carried.* Consisting of short stories published separately over nearly a decade, but reworked, reordered, and bound together with various additions, the work defies traditional generic distinctions. O'Brien himself has described it as something of an anomaly:

> Novels have a kind of continuity of plot or of narrative which this book does not have. But it would be unfair for me to say that it's a collection of stories; clearly all of the stories are related and the characters reappear and themes recur, and some of the stories refer back to others, and some refer forwards. I've thought of it as a work of fiction that is neither one nor the other.
>
> (*Missouri Review* 96)

Why this particular form, then? O'Brien has always been distinguished from more pedestrian "war writers" by his technical and stylistic skill, his ongoing interest in metafiction and in the surreal. Yet he was annoyed at having *Going After Cacciato* characterized so strongly as a purely experimental work:

> I feel I'm experimenting all the time. But the difference is this: I am experimenting not for the joy of experimenting, but rather to explore meaning and themes and dramatic discovery. . . . I don't enjoy tinkering for the joy of tinkering, and I don't like reading books merely for their artifice. I want to see things and explore moral issues when I read, not get hit over the head by the tools of the trade.
>
> (*Anything Can Happen* 269)

Given this explicit attitude, one might infer that O'Brien has chosen or "developed" this form—consciously or not—because it best serves his purpose here. O'Brien's narrator persona notes in **"The Ghost Soldiers"** that in Vietnam "we were fighting forces that did not obey the laws of twentieth-century science" (229); and it seems that in describing those forces, as well as the universal forces of the human psyche, he felt compelled to move from the established linear form of the novel to something more complex and potentially richer. *The Things They Carried* is, accordingly, best characterized as neither novel nor collection of short stories, but as what Maggie Dunn and Ann Morris have recently defined as a composite novel. Their definition in *The Composite Novel: The Short Story Cycle in Transition* describes this form as the genre of connectedness: "the aesthetic of the composite novel" is such that "its parts are named, identifiable, memorable; their *interrelationship* creates the coherent whole text" (5-6). O'Brien, it seems clear, is using the composite novel form not for artifice's sake but rather to "explore meaning and themes and dramatic discovery"; and he is writing not just a Vietnam story, not even just a war story (adapting Faulkner, he claims that "war stories aren't about war— they are about the human heart at war" [qtd. in Myers 142])—but rather a story and stories about the whole of humanity, and he has chosen the composite novel as the most appropriate form to do so.

He accomplishes this goal by using the strengths of the composite novel in its ability to link seemingly disparate stories by using some common, recurring focus(es).

Here he develops to the full various latent possibilities of relationship in the composite novel: by using setting as a referential field that includes not only Vietnam but also middle America, linking the two together as a psychically united region; by using character in a similar sense, focusing on both a collective protagonist and an emerging narrator protagonist; by making storytelling, the process of fiction making itself, a recurring focus; and finally—in a strategy all his own—by using the composite novel's heightened possibilities for allusion to make his work part of a broader literary and human endeavor (and for all its alleged novelty, even this seemingly "new" composite novel form is ultimately linked with a tradition, a tradition which O'Brien is tapping into and thereby connecting his work with that larger "historical perspective" of which he spoke).

In O'Brien's return to Vietnam in *The Things They Carried,* then, he shifts to a new form in order to accomplish his broad goal most fully: the composite novel allows him to play with multiple settings, characters, the theme of storytelling, and even allusiveness, in a way that most fully incorporates "the whole of humanity" into his story. Here, using Morris and Dunn's concept as a framework and occasional guide, I want to briefly touch on all of these aspects of the work.

O'Brien has said explicitly that "my concerns as a human being and my concerns as an artist have at some point intersected in Vietnam—not just in the physical place, but in the spiritual and moral terrain of Vietnam" (*Missouri Review* 101). His vision of the war clearly seems to fall within Morris and Dunn's conception of the composite novel that employs setting as a referential field, thereby portraying place as not only "a specific geographical space" reflecting "a common ethos or culture," but also as "less concretely dependent upon physical space and more abstractly dependent upon a historical moment or period" (36).

With regard to the first characteristic, O'Brien's Vietnam is fully a locus *and* an ethos. Indeed, it is so much of an ethos that at times it seems almost a ghost-place, a region of the psyche rather than of Southeast Asia. This characteristic is clear not only in explicit statements about the land being "haunted" (in **"The Ghost Soldiers,"** 229) and even "*talking* . . . the fog too, and the grass and the goddamn mongooses" (in **"How to Tell a True War Story,"** 81), but also in O'Brien's implicit sense of the cultural depth of the country; his sensitivity to the mysterious otherness of Vietnam, and the tragedy of America's failure to recognize it, is revealed in such short vignettes as **"Church,"** in the personal history that makes **"The Man I Killed"** so poignant, and in the fitting metaphor of the centuries-deep cultural quagmire the US so blithely wades into in **"In the Field."**

But O'Brien uses the structure of the composite novel to emphasize more clearly the second characteristic, that which portrays place as less a physical phenomenon and as more "abstractly" dependent upon a specific historical period. Implicit in his comment about the "moral terrain" of Vietnam is the fact that this terrain necessarily includes the United States, for his moral experience in that country was profoundly, definitively shaped by the fact that he was there as an American soldier; the word "Vietnam" in his statement encompasses not merely one place but also a time, an enduring moment in *our* national history, one which spanned the seemingly insurmountable geographical boundary of the Pacific and linked two radically different countries in one horrible experience (and O'Brien has insisted that he cannot write about the war as anything but an American, cannot but superficially attempt to portray what it was like for the Vietnamese people—**"The Man I Killed"** may be as close as he comes to trying to do so). Today many Vietnamese immigrants to this country rightly criticize Americans for still failing to recognize that their country is not a war, but a place; for O'Brien as for many other veterans, however, it was and remains quite inseparably both.

The structure of the composite novel allows O'Brien to connect Vietnam and America more radically than he might have done in a "conventional" novel, to depict artfully the radical connection of the seemingly disparate countries. The first (and eponymous) story, **"The Things They Carried,"** establishes this connection in its first sentence, which links First Lieutenant Jimmy Cross to "Martha, a junior at Mount Sebastian College in New Jersey" (3). The foxholes of Vietnam and this collegiate world in the urban American Northeast are bound together inexorably, and the rest of the story—despite its largely "factual" tone—will suggest that all of what these men carry through this foreign place is ultimately attached to America, whether it be supplies from "the great American war chest," "sparklers for the Fourth of July, colored eggs for Easter," (16) or the bonds of emotion. And **"Love,"** which follows immediately after, suggests that the bonds run both ways through space, and through time as well; set in Massachusetts, the story depicts Jimmy Cross and O'Brien's narrator persona perhaps a quarter century later, remembering Vietnam by remembering the girl from New Jersey.

Similar connections are established regularly throughout the work, next—in another explicit act of remembrance—in **"On the Rainy River,"** where the narrator persona leaps back in time from some indeterminate postwar present to the summer before his entry into Vietnam; before he tells any more about that bloody tropical place he must tell about small-town America and the placid, cold northern woodland that is the border of Minnesota and Canada. Having done so, he leaps back into vignettes set again in the war itself (though interspersed with more letters home; e.g., Rat Kiley's in **"How To Tell a True War Story"**) before attempting what is perhaps his most radical connection of the two countries, in **"Sweetheart of the Song Tra Bong."** Almost midway through the book, this story goes further than any other in drawing America into this violent ghost-place, Vietnam. The war's seduction of Mary Anne Bell, a young girl fresh from Cleveland, bespeaks the fundamental involvement of even the most seemingly innocent Americans in this setting. After a few weeks in the country, she wants "to *eat* this place. Vietnam. I want to swallow the whole country . . ."; and by the story's end, she is in fact "part of the land. She was wearing her culottes, her pink sweater, and her necklace of human tongues" (125).

Then, after O'Brien delves as closely as he might into the Vietnamese experience of the war in **"The Man I Killed,"** he again shifts the next lengthy story in space and time, back to America and after the war. In **"Speaking of Courage,"** Norman Bowker is the returned veteran living in the small town Midwest in the silent aftermath of Vietnam. The ennui of his life here seems diametrically opposed to the anxiety of life in the war; yet, once again, the two experiences are part of the same whole. The ennui of the war itself has been evident in other tales, and the drama of the war intrudes here—in Iowa—as he remembers the night of Kiowa's death. And throughout this story, the lake Bowker circles both serves as the centerpiece of his current mundane existence and suggests the horror of the boggy field, which is only gradually revealed to the reader.

Indeed, in this story and in **"Notes," "In the Field," "Good Form,"** and **"Field Trip,"** O'Brien reveals a single event through glimpses of Norman Bowker's life in 1975 Iowa, the murky "present" of the narrator persona in Massachusetts, the wartime past of Alpha Company, the narrator's Massachusetts present again, and then a few months more into that present—but back in Vietnam. These four adjacent stories, perhaps more comprehensively than any others, encapsulate the scope in space and time of the work as a whole. But then O'Brien, after briefly returning to the familiar (in **"The Ghost Soldiers"** and **"Night Life,"** two more stories set in the conflict itself) performs his most drastic expansion of place and time at the very end of *The Things They Carried,* in **"The Lives of the Dead."** Here the narrator persona begins by recording his first exposure to death in Vietnam, but uses this tale as an occasion to frame his very earliest experience of death. In doing so he returns again to his prewar Minnesota, but not to the time of **"On the Rainy River"**—no doubt just a few months prior to this incident—but rather to an utterly pre-Vietnam era, 1956, and his childhood. His first exposure to death on the battlefield becomes an occasion to reflect on the common human experience of death,

whether it come in a napalmed village in wartime Southeast Asia or in the movie theaters and shopping malls of the peacetime United States. O'Brien here uses a radical shift of setting to suggest finally a truth that transcends place, but only after he has masterfully used the composite novel to render the boundaries between America and Vietnam fluid, to merge both together as not just a "physical place" but also "spiritual and moral terrain," to depict aspects of the experience of a whole American generation, and—even more broadly—that of the whole of humanity.

The previous discussion of setting suggests another manner in which the collected stories in *The Things They Carried* unite to form a composite novel: through their development of both, on the one hand, a clear "collective protagonist," and, on the other, an "emerging protagonist"—a narrator persona who is apparently Tim O'Brien but who is in fact, as the reader discovers, largely invented.

Morris and Dunn define the collective protagonist as "either a group that functions as a central character" or "an implied central character who functions as a metaphor (an aggregate figure who . . . may be . . . archetypal . . .)" (59). In this work the applicability of the first definition seems quite clear; the title, after all, is concerned with a "they" that seems quite clearly delineated in the dedication to the "men of Alpha Company." Yet given O'Brien's statement regarding the appropriateness of including women in the war in **"Sweetheart of the Song Tra Bong"** and the nature of the work itself, we might extend the concept of the collective protagonist even further. The composite novel structure necessarily works against assigning any character a "minor" status, and, as we have seen in the previous examination of the complexities of setting, these stories are painfully inclusive of civilians as well as soldiers—indeed of as much of the whole of humanity as O'Brien can squeeze in. Therefore, not only Jimmy Cross, Norman Bowker, and Kiowa are central characters here, but also Martha, Elroy Berdahl, Mary Anne Bell, even Linda (the first and last names in this list—in the first and last stories—suggest that *The Things They Carried* is as much a story about love as it is about war).

Perhaps a similar observation might also be made regarding the development of a "single" archetypal protagonist here—something like the disillusioned veteran of Hemingway's *In Our Time*—but there is a clearer and more undeniable focus on a shifting persona who is a sort of Tim O'Brien. Morris and Dunn observe in many composite novels "a narrator-protagonist as the focus and significant element of interconnection," (49) and such is clearly the case in *The Things They Carried.* The author has confirmed in interviews what his narrator persona says at the beginning of **"Good Form"**: that, other than the fact that he is a writer and a former foot soldier in Quang Nai province, "almost everything else is invented." Indeed, even as he writes this "I invent myself" (203).

While this ongoing invention serves to unite the various stories here, it might not necessarily entail any sort of positive progression. The narrator persona is a shadowy figure at best, one hard to pin down in space and time; he is perhaps more accessible in telling about himself in the past than he is in talking "bluntly"—as he says he will in **"Good Form"**—in the present. He is a figure who is at once seemingly honest and idealistic (his claim that "this is true" runs like a refrain throughout the work), but also cowardly—as in **"On the Rainy River"**—and crassly vengeful—as in **"The Ghost Soldiers."**

He is also a writer who gives credit to his sources, and in doing so reveals how even in developing this single protagonist O'Brien again bears witness to the experience of the whole of humanity. The work begins with **"The Things They Carried,"** one of the few stories here told entirely in third person; there is no "I" or even "we" here. But immediately following, in **"Love,"** Jimmy Cross—whose story has just been told—comes to visit "me" at home after the war and to tell another story about Martha. The narrator-protagonist has entered *The Things They Carried,* and will remain for almost the duration; but almost always he speaks in collaboration with other storytellers, such as Mitchell Sanders (whose tale is essential to **"How to Tell a True War Story"**) and Rat Kiley (who relates the bulk of **"Sweetheart of the Song Tra Bong"** and others), even Norman Bowker. **"Speaking of Courage"** is in third person but is immediately followed by **"Notes,"** which gives credit for the preceding story to Bowker; and this almost confessional story is in turn followed by a third and final third person narrative. **"In the Field"** shows the narrator—almost certainly—as a young, frightened "boy" (186) amidst a group of not much more secure men, including—once again—Lieutenant Jimmy Cross.

Indeed, this recurrently collaborative storytelling function almost implies an emerging *collective* narrator-protagonist, and suggests as much about O'Brien's concept of narrative as it does about his notions of character. It is noteworthy that in the text itself, in **"The Man I Killed,"** O'Brien writes of his Vietnamese victim: "He knew he would fall dead and wake up in *the stories of his village and people* [emphasis added]" (144). O'Brien sees *The Things They Carried* as to a large extent the story of his own village and people, and so gives his characters their fair share in the telling. As he claims in his essay "The Magic Show," what the writer must do, like the shaman, is to summon "a collective dream" among his people (178).

In some sense, then, the emerging narrator-protagonist of *The Things They Carried* is radically inseparable from the collective protagonist; and yet in **"The Lives of the Dead,"** the focus moves from the men of Alpha Company back to the individual narrator-protagonist Tim, to a quite personal story of his youth in Minnesota. Moreover, this final piece is equally a story about storytelling, about "Tim trying to save Timmy's life with a story" (273). As such it, along with the other complexities of narrative touched on above, suggests a third focus that unifies the work: storytelling itself.

Morris and Dunn claim that storytelling, "the process of fiction making" itself, can become a unifying focus in the composite novel (88); as the previous discussion of the narrator-protagonist indicates, in this metafiction such a process is clearly at the center of the narrative. Indeed, **"How to Tell a True War Story"** may have been an even more appropriate title story for the collection than **"The Things They Carried"**; not only it but also **"Spin," "Ambush," "Notes," "Good Form,"** and **"The Lives of the Dead"** explicitly discuss this particular form of truth-telling, and all of the stories here do so implicitly.

O'Brien's explicit concern with talking about storytelling here, in fact, ultimately calls into question the extent to which he is making up stories at all. His metafiction confuses traditional genre distinctions, so that Dan Carpenter can suggest *The Things They Carried* "evokes the hyperintense personal journalism of Michael Herr and the journalism-as-novel of Norman Mailer," but is in fact both fiction and nonfiction, even "an epic prose poem of our time" (qtd. in Kaplan 190). O'Brien would certainly be pleased with any such suggestion that his work is, far from being merely "postmodern," in fact in the tradition of great modern—and even classical—writers. He has cited the influence of not only Faulkner and Joyce but even Homer in conveying to him the sense of "nonlinear time, the experience of one's life as jumps and starts" (Myers 144); and he has indicated his belief that the great stories are those that are continually "retold" and thereby "carry the force of legend" (156). Even Morris and Dunn speak of the composite novel as achieving the very effect of which O'Brien speaks, precisely by returning to the form of "the sacred composite, the epic cycle, and the framed collection." It is in fact this classical conception of storytelling—if his theme is that of the *Iliad,* his form is that of the *Odyssey*—which most fully allows O'Brien to unite his "Vietnam" stories with the whole human experience, not only with humans alive at this time and place in Viet Nam and America, but all those living and dead.

O'Brien's notion of the writer-shaman summoning a "collective dream" suggests his view that storytelling itself is by nature communal. His entire collective-metafictional technique here is perhaps a way of getting at larger cultural and human truths. In Mitchell Sanders's tale about a "talking" Vietnam in **"How to Tell a True War Story,"** in the tale of the man who "would fall dead and wake up in the stories of his village and people" (144) in **"The Man I Killed,"** and in the generations-deep quagmire of **"In the Field,"** it is clear that O'Brien senses something like an alien collective unconsciousness in Vietnam, a mysterious cultural psyche that is known—albeit only partially—through talk and stories. What he does with the new yet ancient form of the composite novel is to tap into some of the established myths of his *own* culture. In short, he alludes to older stories, stories which bespeak both his own tradition and the perennially human heart—and particularly those told in this century through the form of the composite novel. O'Brien's commitment to the stories of the past, to the dead as well as the living, is established by the beginning epigraph from a Civil War diary (also by a former sergeant from the Midwest, as Philip Beidler notes [37]). But his commitment to a small pantheon of great moderns can be established by briefly examining his allusions—both thematic and formal—to three writers for whom he has repeatedly expressed admiration: Conrad, Hemingway, and Joyce.

O'Brien has expressed his disappointment with the majority of films purporting to chronicle the war in which he served, but he admits an at least partial admiration for *Apocalypse Now,* which places a mad Colonel Kurtz at the end of a river deep in the jungles of Southeast Asia. The idea of enacting *Heart of Darkness* during the Vietnam conflict was, then, not a new one when O'Brien wrote **"Sweetheart of the Song Tra Bong,"** but it certainly seems to be one he draws from with a power all his own. As noted previously, he has spoken repeatedly of Conrad's influence on his work, which is thematically evident throughout all of ***The Things They Carried.*** But it is concentrated in **"Sweetheart"** [**"Sweetheart of the Song Tra Bong"**], and with the brilliant adaptation of not only shifting the setting to Viet Nam but also of characterizing the corruption of a Kurtz who is not a merchant or colonel, but rather an archetypally innocent American female. Although *Heart of Darkness* is obviously not drawn from a composite novel itself, the composite novel form allows O'Brien to—in the middle of a "longer" work—echo one of the greatest works of twentieth-century short fiction.

Carpenter referred to ***The Things They Carried*** as "an epic prose poem of our time," but doubtlessly O'Brien also had in mind one of the great American composite "war" novels of our era: *In Our Time.* The newer work parallels Hemingway's account of the generation that fought the first great war of this century both in its overall form and in individual stories. **"Speaking of Courage,"** featuring a tired veteran returned to his small Midwestern town, almost certainly echoes Hemingway; as Steven Kaplan notes, "Norman Bowker's dilemma is

. . . remarkably similar to that of Hemingway's character Krebs in the story "Soldier's Home." Neither of these men returning from war can tell his story" (189).

Yet while both here and throughout the work O'Brien follows his great predecessor in searching for a definition of courage, he "asserted early in his career that his conclusion could not be a mere restatement of Hemingway" (Myers 144). In his novel *Northern Lights,* for example, there are some forty pages of parody which echo *The Sun Also Rises* (much to the dismay of critics); and while ***The Things They Carried*** is, fortunately, tainted by nothing so distracting, it is not impossible that O'Brien is reacting to Hemingway even in **"On the Rainy River."** O'Brien has stated that the story is a dramatization of the "moral schizophrenia" he felt during the summer of 1968, but that its plot and setting are entirely invented. He saw the river as a concrete means of putting his character "on the edge" (*Missouri Review* 95-6); but it is also difficult to read the story, set in the woods of the northern Midwest and climaxing in a fateful fishing trip, without thinking of "Big Two-Hearted River." The loquacity of O'Brien's narrator persona here, however, could not be further removed from the reticence of Nick Adams and his creator; and his openhearted, anguished concern about the war is emotionally at opposite poles from the ideal of "grace under pressure."

Though he may call Hemingway's ideals into question in **"On the Rainy River,"** O'Brien ultimately emulates the great example of *In Our Time* in this story, in **"Speaking of Courage,"** and in his utilization of the very form of the composite novel. Given the parallels between his theme and that of Hemingway, his choice to do so is hardly surprising; the imaginative leap from World War I to the Vietnam conflict was perhaps even less difficult to make than that from the jungles of Africa to those of Southeast Asia. But in his final story O'Brien moves from his concern with moral corruption and war to one even more universally human: death. In doing so he sets in 1956 Minnesota a brief tale that alludes to another tale in the most surprisingly alien setting yet—turn-of-the-century Ireland. At the close of ***The Things They Carried,*** O'Brien establishes a connection to another of the great composite novels of the twentieth century, Joyce's *Dubliners.*

Like Joyce's "The Dead," O'Brien's **"The Lives of the Dead"** comes at the end of his work and establishes the ongoing presence of the dead in the lives of the living. An individual death in wartime Viet Nam, which introduces the story, is linked in the narrator persona's mind with the death of a young girl in his childhood, in peacetime Minnesota. O'Brien's story, like Joyce's, is one which is about both death and first love, and suggests that the two are necessarily bound together; just as for

Gretta Conroy the love of Michael Furey is bound up with his death, so too the narrator Tim O'Brien cannot think long of death without thinking of his innocent love for lost Linda. Both stories also suggest that what O'Brien called the "whole of humanity" somehow includes "all the living *and the dead* [emphasis added]," as Joyce would say; and the contemporary writer knows that the ranks of "the dead" now include Joyce himself. O'Brien's allusiveness to *Dubliners,* to "The Dead" and the literary tradition Joyce helped to establish, bears witness to this conviction.

And, fittingly, in this last story O'Brien concludes *The Things They Carried* not only by shifting settings and bringing in the character of Linda (who has perhaps been with the narrator all along), not only by once again alluding to the broad literary tradition he seeks to emulate, but also by presenting his strongest vision of storytelling itself. In his essay "The Magic Show" he has discursively suggested something of this vision:

> The process of imaginative knowing does not depend upon the scientific method. Fictional characters are not constructed of flesh and blood, but rather of words, and those words serve as specific incantations that invite us into and guide us through the universe of the imagination. Language is the apparatus—the magic dust—by which a writer performs his miracles. . . . Beyond anything, I think, a writer is someone entranced by the power of language to create a magic show of the imagination, to make the dead sit up and talk, to shine light into the darkness of the great human mysteries . . .
>
> (177)

This vision of the writer again suggests his earlier claim that in Vietnam the United States was fighting forces that twentieth century science could not understand, and that he is committed to exploring the nature of those forces as fully as he can. But even more so it suggests again his vision of the shaman who by telling stories summons "a collective dream"; here, too, O'Brien links storytelling to religion, citing not only the shaman but also Christ as a storyteller and miracle worker in one (177). Writing is, he claims, essentially an act of faith, a way of exploring "that which cannot be known by empirical means" and moving toward "epiphany or understanding or enlightenment" (179).

This vision of the role of the writer is perhaps what most fully elevates O'Brien from mere "war writer" to speaker to and for the whole of humanity. And this language, in both "The Magic Show" and in **"The Lives of the Dead,"** seems allusive again in that it is almost Joycean. The narrator persona here closes in an act of grand affirmation of the powers of the writer to transform lives, to raise the dead, sounding "like a Vietnam version of Joyce's Stephen Dedalus" (Myers 154). Certainly throughout the story—when he speaks of the writer for whom "memory and imagination and language combine to make spirits in the head"—he echoes young Stephen's vision of himself in *A Portrait of the Artist as a Young Man* as a "priest of the eternal imagination, transmuting the daily bread of experience into the radiant body of ever-living life."

Finally, then, **"The Lives of the Dead"** ties together all of the focal elements—setting, protagonists both collective and emerging, storytelling, allusiveness—which O'Brien has been working with all along to bind *The Things They Carried* together as composite novel. The richness and complexity of this book—and the composite novel form—make it difficult to determine where one focal element ends and another begins, where one can examine setting without examining character, or examine an "emerging protagonist" without examining storytelling, and so on. But O'Brien is pleased to have it so, it seems; as many of his statements indicate, he rejects the rigorously analytical vision of the real for one that allows more room for mystery and relatedness. In writing *The Things They Carried,* he has posited his own vision of the real, not just of his experience in Vietnam but of perennial facets of experience that belong to the whole of humanity.

Works Cited

Beidler, Philip. *Re-Writing America: Vietnam Authors in Their Generation.* Athens: University of Georgia Press, 1991.

Dunn, Maggie, and Morris, Ann. *The Composite Novel: The Short Story Cycle in Transition.* New York: Twayne, 1995.

Kaplan, Steven. *Understanding Tim O'Brien.* Columbia: University of South Carolina Press, 1995.

Myers, Thomas. "Tim O'Brien." *Dictionary of Literary Biography.* Vol 152, *American Novelists Since World War II,* fourth series. Ed. James R. Giles and Wanda H. Giles. Detroit: Bruccoli Clark Layman, 1995.

O'Brien, Tim. Interview. *Anything Can Happen: Interviews with Contemporary American Novelists.* Ed. Tom LeClair and Larry McCaffery. Urbana: University of Illinois Press, 1983.

———. "An Interview with Tim O'Brien." By Steven Kaplan. *Missouri Review* 14: 1991: 94-108.

———. "The Magic Show." *Writers on Writing.* Ed. Robert Pack and Jay Parini. Hanover: Middlebury College Press, 1991.

———. *The Things They Carried.* New York: Penguin, 1990.

Rosemary King (essay date spring 1999)

SOURCE: King, Rosemary. "O'Brien's 'How to Tell a True War Story'." *The Explicator* 57, no. 3 (spring 1999): 182-84.

[*In the following essay, King asserts that in "How to Tell a True War Story" O'Brien "lures readers into a debate over fact and fiction that ultimately privileges the latter."*]

The title of Tim O'Brien's short story **"How to Tell a True War Story"** is a pun. On one hand, O'Brien is asking how a listener can distinguish whether a story is a factual retelling of events; on the other he outlines "how to tell" a war story. The meaning of the title depends on the reader's position: If listening to a war story, the title suggests, O'Brien will help you to discern whether the story is real; if telling a war story, the title implies that O'Brien will show you how to narrate a story well. The title, however, defies paradigmatic balance. In other words, the reader is drawn into the role of storyteller as O'Brien works to untangle the relationship between fact and fiction.

O'Brien's word play in the title hinges on the definition of "true," a word he uses alternately throughout the story to mean either factually accurate, or something higher and nobler. He does this through three embedded narratives: Mitchell Sanders's narration of Curt Lemon's death; the narrator's description of hearing Sanders's story; and Tim O'Brien's commentary on how to tell a true war story.[1] Each narrator claims his story is an authentic retelling of events as they occurred in Vietnam, asserting the historicity of their narratives.[2] For example, Sanders introduces his story by claiming it is "God's truth" (O'Brien 79). Then he periodically interrupts the story exclaiming its veracity: "This next part [. . .] you won't believe [. . .]. You won't. And you know why? [. . .] Because it happened. Because every word is absolutely dead-on true" (81). Similarly, in the second embedded narration, the narrator tries to convince the reader that he was in Vietnam listening to Sanders's story firsthand when he blatantly states, "I heard this one, for example, from Mitchell Sanders" (79). He continues by recalling where he heard the story, how night slowly fell, the confines of a muddy foxhole, and the garbling of a nearby river, and concludes, "The occasion was right for a good story" (79). The narrator repeatedly says "I remember" throughout the passage to suggest further that he actually remembers Sanders telling the story. In the third narrative, Tim O'Brien recalls how he narrates the episode to an audience. He says, "I'll picture Rat Kiley's face, his grief," for instance, hinting that he was present at Lemon's death (90). In addition, he states that although he may have warped the details slightly, "it happened in this little village on the Batangan Peninsula [. . .]" (91). Tim O'Brien sug-

gests here that he may have fictionalized past events; even as an eyewitness to Lemon's death, however, the "facts" of the event are unclear at best.

At the same time that O'Brien's characters privilege factual accuracy, they undercut it as well. Sanders, for instance, completes his description of Lemon's death only to add, "I got a confession to make [. . .]. Last night, man, I had to make up a few things" (83). He then tries to recapture his credibility with the listener by pleading, "Yeah, but listen, it's still true" (84). In a sense, Sanders constructs his story (a "way of knowing" in the present) based on what he believes to have happened (a "way of knowing" in the past). As in Sanders's narrative, Tim O'Brien admits fictionalizing "true" war stories as well: "In war you lose your sense of the definite, hence your sense of truth itself, and therefore it's safe to say that in a true war story *nothing is ever absolutely true*" (88, emphasis added). At the end, Tim O'Brien admits that his narration is fictional: "Beginning to end [. . .] it's all made up. Every goddamn detail [. . .]. None of it happened. *None* of it. And even if it did happen [. . .]" (91). The line between fact and fiction in a true war story is more than merely blurred— the line is erased altogether, and fact becomes fiction.

O'Brien's title delivers punch not only through the conflated definition of *true* but also through the distinction of what makes a war story "true." He underscores the importance of manipulating what actually happened to get at the essence of truth.

> Yet even if it did happen—and maybe it did, anything's possible—even then you know it can't be true, because a true war story does not depend upon that kind of truth. Absolute occurrence is irrelevant. A thing may happen and be a total lie; *another thing may not happen and be truer than the truth.*
>
> (O'Brien 89, emphasis added)

"True war stories," then, capture the genuine experience of war because truth registers only through "gut instinct" (84). Again, O'Brien submits that factual events should not be given a degree of authority simply because they occurred in the past; more important than the historical artifact of what actually occurred is the significance, or truth, of the experience. O'Brien's concept has deep implications for story telling because he suggests that altering facts may be more significant than clinging to the story of what actually transpired. Several critics have commented on O'Brien's unique blend of fact and fiction.[3] For example, in *Understanding Tim O'Brien,* Steven Kaplan summarizes: "O'Brien destroys the line dividing fact from fiction, and tries to show [. . .] that fiction (or the imagined world) can often be truer than fact" (171). What is more significant than the "dividing line," however, is the reader's position in this debate as storyteller.

In **"How to Tell a True War Story,"** O'Brien lures readers into a debate over fact and fiction that ultimately privileges the latter. Paradoxically, this debate situates readers as storytellers—even as they read or "listen" to the story—with O'Brien giving advice on "how to tell" a "true war story" by revising factual events. Further, once readers have finished O'Brien's story, they are no longer storytellers but are now listeners—even though they are finished reading or "listening" to the story. The pun of the title thus plays out when the reader tells the story while reading it and listens to the story when finished.

Notes

1. It is questionable whether Tim O'Brien is actually the author or a fictitious character of the same name. A close reading of his short stories "Field Trip" and "The Lives of the Dead," in *The Things They Carried,* suggests that Tim O'Brien is a fictitious character.

2. O'Brien's short story lends itself well to a New Historicist evaluation of the "historicity of texts" and the "textuality of history." See Hayden White's *Metahistory: The Historical Imagination in Nineteenth-Century Europe* (Baltimore: Johns Hopkins UP, 1973) and Louis Montrose's "Professing the Renaissance: The Poetics and Politics of Culture," *Twentieth Century Literary Theory* (New York: St. Martin's, 1997).

3. In addition to the Kaplan article, see Don Ringnalda's *Fighting and Writing the Vietnam War* and Eric Schroeder's *Vietnam, We've All Been There.*

Works Cited

Kaplan, Steven. "The Things They Carried." *Understanding Tim O'Brien*. Columbia: U of South Carolina P, 1995. 169-192.

O'Brien, Tim. "How to Tell a True War Story." *The Things They Carried*. New York: Penguin, 1991. 75-91.

Daniel Robinson (essay date spring 1999)

SOURCE: Robinson, Daniel. "Getting It Right: The Short Fiction of Tim O'Brien." *Critique* 40, no. 3 (spring 1999): 257-64.

[*In the following essay, Robinson investigates O'Brien's approach to the truth in* The Things They Carried.]

> But it's true even if it didn't happen—
>
> —Ken Kesey

In his introduction to *Men at War,* Ernest Hemingway states that a "writer's job is tell the truth. His standard of fidelity to the truth should be so high that his inven-

tions [. . .] should produce a truer account than anything factual can be" (xi). Tim O'Brien, for whose writing the Vietnam War is the informing principle, returns to this notion of truth in his short fiction.[1] His stories revolve around multiple centers of interest—at once stories in the truest sense, with a core of action and character, and also metafictional stories on the precise nature of writing war stories.

For O'Brien, like Hemingway in his introduction, the notion of absolute fidelity to facts almost becomes a non sequitur when considering truth. Facts might provide a chronology of events (and even then, we may disagree on the validity of the facts), but alone they cannot reveal the hidden truths found in a true war story. As Hemingway writes, facts "can be observed badly; but when a good writer is creating something, he has time and scope to make it of an absolute truth" (xi-xii). That is also true for O'Brien: He sometimes writes stories that contradict the facts of other stories; yet the essential, underlying truth of each story is intact and illuminating. Those truths lie as much in the fragmented, impressionistic stories he tells as in the narrative technique he chooses for the telling.

O'Brien does not deliver Vietnam in neatly packaged truisms. The same words that rang obscene for Frederic Henry in Hemingway's *A Farewell to Arms,* "abstract words such as glory, honor, courage, or hallow," become empty in O'Brien's fiction. Those words imply a rational order to war that does not exist, and the absence of those words mirrors the horror of a world at its most irrational. As O'Brien writes in **"How to Tell a True War Story,"** [O]ften in a true war story there is not even a point" (88). What O'Brien prefers are the images that make "the stomach believe" (89), images of men at war who are too afraid not to kill.

The true reasons that bring O'Brien's characters to Vietnam are far from the abstract words that Frederic Henry dismisses and equally far from the Hollywood notion of heroism so prevalent in war movies prior to American involvement in Vietnam. The average age of the company of foot soldiers O'Brien writes about is nineteen or twenty, and most were probably drafted, as is the case of the fictional Tim O'Brien through whom author O'Brien often tells his stories. Thus, we see boys becoming men before they have had the opportunity to understand what manhood involves. And among the many things each soldier carried—the weapons, charms, diseases, and emotions—they "carried the soldier's greatest fear, which was the fear of blushing. Men killed, and died, because they were embarrassed not to" (**"Things"** [**"The Things They Carried"**] 20-21). Even the enemy soldiers, the Viet Cong, exhibit that moral dichotomy and fight out of fear as much as nationalism:

> In the presence of his father and uncles, he pretended to look forward to doing his patriotic duty, which was also a privilege, but at night he prayed with his mother

that the war might end soon. Beyond anything else, he was afraid of disgracing himself, and therefore his family and village.

("Man" ["The Man I Killed"] 142)

However, quite different from most of O'Brien's characters driven by fear is Azar, the nineteen-year-old draftee who straps a puppy to a Claymore antipersonnel mine and blows the dog to pieces. Azar, still a teenager, loves Vietnam because it makes him "feel like a kid again." "The Vietnam experience," he says, "I mean, wow, I *love* this shit" ("**Ghost**" ["**The Ghost Soldiers**"] 237; O'Brien's emphasis). O'Brien's characters choose war for entirely negative reasons, not for unselfish love of country or of basic freedoms but from fear of embarrassment and cowardice or the love of war as if it were a child's game. Even the decision to go to Vietnam is determined not through an examination of positive motives but, again, for negative reasons: "I would go to the war [. . .] because I was embarrassed not to. [. . .] I was a coward. I went to war" ("**River**" ["**On the Rainy River**"] 63).

That inability in O'Brien's characters to establish a positive purpose in their reasons for going to war mirrors the historical ambiguities surrounding American involvement in Vietnam. Like the chaotic and morally ambiguous war they fight, O'Brien's characters are unsure of their purpose or even their actions. Azar explains blowing up the puppy as simple childish exuberance: "What's everybody so upset about? I mean, Christ, I'm just a *boy*" ("**Spin**" 40; O'Brien's emphasis). After one of his men dies, "Lieutenant Jimmy Cross led his men into the village of Than Ke. They burned everything. They shot chickens and dogs, they trashed the village well, they called in artillery and watched the wreckage, then they marched for several hours through the hot afternoon" to a place where they set up camp for the night ("**Things**" 16). Those men act not from forethought but from some measure of selective emotion: Azar, the sadist, experiences delight from torturing the puppy and, in "**The Ghost Soldiers**," torture-prankstering a medic on guard duty who had nearly allowed another soldier to die through inaction; and the troop, following Lavender's sniper-death, razes the nearest village not for some strategic reason but out of an apparent need for revenge. The chauvinistic clichés that so often accompany patriotic fervor are missing. These characters have no center around which they can construct a reason for their involvement, and the only absolute is that resupply helicopters will arrive soon with more things for them to carry: For "all the ambiguities of Vietnam, all the mysteries and unknowns, there was at least the single abiding certainty that they would never be at a loss for things to carry" ("**Things**" 16).

As Lorrie Smith writes in "Disarming the War Story," "The 'story' of World War II [. . .] has meaning for our culture as a heroic quest, and it forms a coherent narra-

tive in which the soldier's sacrifices are redemptive" (90). All of that coherence of purpose is lost in O'Brien's stories of Vietnam, as his characters stumble through a landscape of disjointed experiences and realities. And though we may, as Smith asserts, "feel acutely the disjunction between ideals and realities" (90) when we attempt to consider Vietnam in terms of heroic quests, coherent actions, and redemptive sacrifices, O'Brien's characters seldom articulate any distinctions. For them, the realities are too overpowering to place against any abstract notions based upon cultural and societal ideals. Only Lt. Jimmy Cross, in "**The Things They Carried**," and Tim, in "**On the Rainy River**," consider that disjunction, and then only in personal terms, excluding any real notion of established codes.[2]

One often expects writers of war stories to present antithetical abstractions in a concrete form to establish some moral or ethical base. O'Brien, however, fuses abstracts such as realty and surreality and right and wrong in an effort to emphasize the lack of firm moral ground supporting his characters in a war lacking in definable purposes. To stop his own pain at seeing his best friend blown up, Rat Kiley systematically dismembers a baby water buffalo by shooting pieces from its body—its mouth, tail, ears, nose—until all that remains alive and moving are its eyes. The reaction by Rat's stunned comrades is restrained amazement: "A new wrinkle. I never seen it before. [. . .] Well, that's Nam" (86). A group of Green Berets keep a pile of enemy bones stacked in a corner of their barracks underneath a sign that reads, "ASSEMBLE YOUR OWN GOOK!! FREE SAMPLE KIT!" ("**Sweetheart**" ["**Sweetheart of the Song Tra Bong**"] 119). That distillation of moral or ethical standards, an "aesthetic purity of moral indifference" ("**True**" ["**How to Tell a True War Story**"] 87), illustrates a general loss of humanity in any war, but possibly more so in a war that lacks any underlying absolutes, any real reasons for having gone to war. Thus the moral confusion Tim feels (in "**On the Rainy River**") after finding out he has been drafted becomes a moral indifference once exposed to the brutalities and absurdities of war.

Those apparent indifferences extend even to how the soldiers deal with the death of their comrades. When a man dies, he is not killed, but "greased. [. . .] offed, lit up, zapped." ("**Things**" 19). Somehow, by verbally denying the reality of death through hyperbolic misnomers, they reject the death itself. At one point in "**The Lives of the Dead**," Tim's unit enters a village it has calmly watched being bombed and burned by air strikes for thirty minutes. When the unit enters, the only person in the village is a dead old man who is missing an arm and whose face is covered by swarming flies and gnats. Each man, as he walks past the dead Vietnamese, offers a greeting and shakes the remaining hand: "How-dee-doo. . . . Gimme five. . . . A real honor. . . .

Pleased as punch" (256). After Tim refuses to introduce himself or even offer a toast to the old man's health, he is ridiculed for not showing respect for his elders: Maybe it's too real for you?'" he is asked. "'That's right,'" he replies. "'Way too real'" (256). It is only his fourth day, and Tim soon realizes that he must develop the cynical sense of humor he will eventually need to cope with the realities of death. Paul Berlin, on his first day in Vietnam, in **"Where Have You Gone, Charming Billy?"** watches one of his comrades die of a heart attack brought on by the fear of dying. In his attempt to deal with witnessing his first death, he tries to transform the event into something that had not happened. Eventually, however, as the realities of the experience eat at him, he places the death in comic terms by imagining the official death notification:

> SORRY TO INFORM YOU THAT YOUR SON BILLY BOY WAS YESTERDAY SCARED TO DEATH IN ACTION IN THE REPUBLIC OF VIETNAM, VALIANTLY SUCCUMBING TO A HEART ATTACK SUFFERED WHILE UNDER ENORMOUS STRESS. [. . .]
>
> (130)

Berlin finally concludes that the death will make "a good joke" and "a funny war story" for his father (132). Not superficial male posturing, but overwhelming fear forces O'Brien's characters purposefully to detach themselves from death. They use any method possible, from keeping the dead alive through absurd ceremonial greetings to parodying government form letters to, as Albert Wilhelm writes, "keep the horrors of war at bay" (221).

Ironically, one of the deaths that breaks through the fabricated veneer of insulation is the death of an enemy in **"The Man I Killed."** In explicit detail bordering on the religious, Tim vividly recalls the man he killed—maybe the first man or maybe just the first he had an opportunity to study afterwards. Azar dismisses the death in the common distancing dialogue discussed above, "Oh, man, you fuckin' trashed the fucker. [. . .] You laid him out like Shredded fuckin' Wheat. [. . .] Rice Krispies, you know? On the dead test, this particular individual gets A-plus" (140); And Kiowa tries moving Tim beyond his dumbstruck staring at the bloody corpse to talk about his emotions. Only here and in **"Speaking of Courage,"** where Norman Bowker, back home in Iowa on the Fourth of July, recounts the death of Kiowa in a swampy field, is the examination of death not covered under false layers of fear. O'Brien the writer must now dredge up those deaths that Tim the young soldier tried so hard to bury, which may explain why O'Brien returns to Vietnam in his fiction with such force and passion: he is reliving the horrors he suppressed decades earlier.

As in **"The Man I Killed"** and **"Speaking of Courage,"** O'Brien often uses a spiraling narrative technique to draw out the realism of death, even if this characters continue to refute that death. O'Brien revolves those stories around a specific death, as Joseph Heller revolves the first part of *Catch-22* around Snowden's death, covering the same ground yet illuminating the moment's particular horror with each movement back to the death. The effect is at once numbing and oddly positive. We sense the overwhelming totality of death on the one hand, but we also imagine the narrator attempting to place a new order to his story, one that will somehow exclude the death. In **"The Man I Killed,"** the effect is an increasing horror at seeing the dead man; whereas in **"Speaking Of Courage,"** Norman realizes that he failed to save his friend's life. **"The Things They Carried"** revolves around the sniper death of Lavender, and in so doing shows Lt. Jimmy Cross's movement from the innocence of his insular world in which, to keep the war at a distance, he pretends that a girl back home in the United States is in love with him. However, with Lavender's death, he must face the reality that his lack of focus in leading his men may in part have caused that death. As many initiations do, Cross's initiation into the realities surrounding him result also in his need to destroy something of his past, which he does when he burns Martha's letters and photographs.

Kiowa's death becomes the center point for Norman Bowker in **"Speaking of Courage"** and is also the death around which the action revolves in **"In the Field."** Ironically, here two other soldiers feel the responsibility for Kiowa's death, which adds an interesting layer of multiplicity of perception to O'Brien's stories. O'Brien further explores that notion of multiplicity of perception through Jimmy Cross's drafting a letter to Kiowa's parents. His first draft places blame on some ubiquitous "They" who sent him and his men to bivouac in a tactically indefensible position; in his second draft, he accepts the blame; and finally, he revises the letter to express "an officer's condolences. No apologies necessary" (197-98). All three drafts are accurate and true, underscoring the inability to write about war in absolute terms.

O'Brien's cyclical pattern that places death as the center point around which many of his stories revolve reinforces a permanence to war that a more linear narrative structure would necessarily exclude. O'Brien's characters cannot leave the deaths behind them and trudge on through a strictly chronological story. "The bad stuff," O'Brien writes in **"Spin,"** "never stops happening: it lives in its own dimension, replying itself over and over" (36). And even when the war is over, it is not over; even though "the war occurred half a lifetime ago, [. . .] the remembering makes it now" (40). So the cyclical pattern established in many of these stories continues to revolve long after the story stops, and the things they carried during the war become eclipsed by the things they carry following the war.

The deaths, of course, form the most visually unforgettable parts of O'Brien's stories. They are, first of all, not Hollywood war deaths: They are not scripted to show grace under pressure or to elevate the human reaction to the horrors of war. O'Brien's characters do not die filled with the notions of courage, honor, and camaraderie: they just die. Ted Lavender dies while zipping up his pants after urinating on a bus,"; Kiowa dies from drowning in the muddy human filth of a village's sewage field; Billy Boy Watkins dies of a heart attack brought on by the fear of dying after stepping on a land mine; Lemon dies from stepping on a land mine while playing an innocent game of catch and is literally blown into a nearby tree; and Jorgenson who dies after eluding enemy patrols and taking a mid-night swim, swallows bad water. None of the deaths are the deaths of heroes; and like the ritualized shooting of the water buffalo following Lemon's death, they serve to show a major theme connecting O'Brien's work—how isolated events of cruelty define war. Azar killing the puppy, Bowker shooting the water buffalo, a little girl dancing to an unheard rhythm outside her burned-out hut following a napalm raid, the first enemy killed, and the singular deaths of friends accrue as acts of cruelty to, as O'Brien says, "touch [the] reader's heart more than a grandiose description of the fire bombing of a village, or the napalming of a village, where you don't see corpses, you don't know the corpses, you don't witness the death in any detail. It is somehow made abstract, bloodless" (Kaplan 102). By focusing on the character—the individual coming in close contact with what death looks like—and allowing the surrounding scenes and events to take secondary importance, O'Brien increases the absurdity and horror. His plots are determined not by incident and event, but by the changing moral attitudes and development of his characters.

Likewise, "declarations about war, such as war is hell" (Kaplan 101) or war is immoral seem, in O'Brien's fiction, just as hollow as the declarations of war that place men in battle. These declarations, while possibly true, are little more than abstract generalities that fail to turn something deep within the reader. "A true war story," as O'Brien wrote, "if truly told, makes the stomach believe" (84). A true war story, then, may not have a point, and it certainly does not exist in the narrative vacuum of beginning-middle-end, but it functions at a level of truth beyond that found in the story's words. Often, you doubt whether an O'Brien story can be true. Can a man actually transport his girlfriend to an isolated medical post in the Central Highlands and the lose her to the war as she slowly matriculates into the jungle? Some things, Pederson says in **"Keeping Watch by Night,"** "you just see and you got to believe in what you see" (66). A true war story has no moral, no instruction, no virtue, no suggestion of proper behavior; there is only a revelation of the possible evil in the nature of man: "You can tell a true war story," O'Brien tells us, "by its

absolute and uncompromising allegiance to obscenity and evil" (**"True"** 76). True war stories, as O'Brien writes in his nonfiction narrative *If I Die in a Combat Zone,* offer "simple, unprofound scraps of truth" that lack any lessons to teach about war. The writer, then, according to O'Brien, must "simply tell stories" (32). However, within that apparent lack of pretense to message lies the phenomenological truths of O'Brien's fiction, which strike much deeper than, as Lorrie Smith writes, an exploitation of "war's larger political implications" (94). By suppressing the abstract in favor of the concrete, O'Brien allows his stories to exist as commentary through the "complex tangles and nuances of actual experience" (Calloway 222).

Beyond that, moreover, as O'Brien tells Steven Kaplan, "good stories somehow have to do with an awakening into a new world, something new and true, where someone is jolted out of [. . .] complacency and forced to confront a new set of circumstances or a new self" (99). The archetypal pattern that O'Brien here alludes to of initiation into the complexities of the real world forms an underlying basis of much of O'Brien's fiction. Paul Berlin's witnessing Billy Boy's death signals his loss of innocence, his transition into manhood, and an unwelcome realization of the world's potential for cruelty. And Tim, who may realize that his only options are kill or be killed, cannot be comforted by that knowledge as his world of relative innocence is shattered by the realities of this new world he inhabits. Correspondingly, that separation between men and boys is also shown by the physical appearance of the soldiers as they trudge along under the weight of all they carry: "The most recent arrivals had pasty skin burnt at the shoulder blades and clavicle and neck; their boots were not yet red with clay, and they walked more carefully than the rest, and they looked more vulnerable" (**"Spin"** 36). As their appearance evolves and their movements change, so, too, their character changes in the "effort to establish a new order" to their life (Kaplan 99)—one in which the vulnerability of youth is replaced by the cynicism and hardness of manhood.

That also may be why O'Brien still returns to Vietnam in his fiction—because he is still trying to make sense of the new order established in his life over twenty years ago. In his stories, in the futile attempt to regain what he had before the war he can still dream alive the people who died; unfortunately, though, that also necessitates his reliving their deaths. That need may be what still hits O'Brien: "twenty years later, in your sleep, and you wake up and shake your wife and start telling the story to her, except when you get to the end you've forgotten the point again. And then for a long time you lie there watching the story happen in your head. You listen to your wife's breathing. The war's over. You close your eyes. You smile and think, Christ, what's the point" (**"True"** 88-89)? The point, however, is all in the telling, as is the healing. In his stories, O'Brien answers his characters desire to make sense out of their experiences: Kiowa imploring Tim to just talk after killing an enemy soldier instead of dumbly staring at the corpse, or Rat Kiley—not wanting to have to listen to the silence of the night—asking Kiowa to tell once again how Lavender fell like a sack of cement, or the platoon waiting once more for Rat to tell his story about the sweetheart of Song Tra Bong. O'Brien's characters, like O'Brien himself, carry their stories with them, sometimes damning the unimaginable weight of relived experience and sometimes extolling the outlet allowed through story-telling, which becomes at times a life-support system and a salvation from the moral complexities of the war.

Those moral complexities required of O'Brien "an innovative form rather than the conventional chronological narrative" (Slabey 206). In presenting stories from a war that lacked a traditional progression or a logical structure, O'Brien demands more from his writing than strict realism can provide. He blurs the distinctions in his stories to present truths coalesced in memory and imagination to, "get things right"—not in the absolute terms of packaged truisms and simplistic judgments but through the inner landscape of experiential truth telling.

Notes

1. In this essay, I consider only those stories of Tim O'Brien's that were previously published as separate short stories and are substantially different from any counterparts in later novels. Thus, I exclude stories that appeared in *Going After Cacciato* in much the same form as when they were published earlier as well as those stories in *The Things They Carried* that were not separately published.

2. Any use of "Tim" in this essay refers to the fictional character, and the use of "O'Brien" refers to Tim O'Brien the author. In an interview with Steven Kaplan, O'Brien discusses the similarities and differences between him and his fictional character:

> Everything I have written has come partly out of my own concerns [. . .] but the story lines themselves, the events [. . .] the characters [. . .] the places [. . .] are almost all invented. [. . .] Ninety percent or more of the material [. . .] is invented, and I invented ninety percent of a new Tim O'Brien, maybe even more than that.

(95)

Works Cited

Beidler, Philip D. *Re-Writing America: Vietnam Authors in Their Generation*. Athens: U Georgia P, 1991.

Calloway, Catherine. "Pluralities of Vision: *Going After Cacciato* and Tim O'Brien's Short Fiction." Gilman and Smith 213-22.

Gilman, Owen W., and Lorrie Smith. *American Rediscovered: Critical Essays on Literature and Film of the Vietnam War*. New York: Garland, 1990.

Kaplan, Steven. "An Interview with Tim O'Brien." *Missouri Review* 14.3 (1991): 95-108.

O'Brien, Tim. "The Ghost Soldiers." O'Brien, *Things* 215-44.

———. "How to Tell a True War Story." O'Brien, *Things* 73-92.

———. "In the Field." O'Brien, *Things* 183-200.

———. "The Lives of the Dead." O'Brien, *Things* 253-73.

———. "The Man I Killed." O'Brien, *Things* 137-44.

———. "On the Rainy River." O'Brien, *Things* 41-64.

———. "Speaking of Courage." O'Brien, *Things* 155-74.

———. "Spin." O'Brien, *Things* 33-40.

———. "Style." O'Brien, *Things* 151-54.

———. "Sweetheart of Song Tra Bong." O'Brien, *Things* 99-126.

———. "The Things They Carried." O'Brien, *Things* 1-26.

———. *The Things They Carried*. New York: Penguin, 1991.

———. "Keeping Watch by Night." *Redbook* 148 (Dec. 1976) 65-67.

———. "Where Have You Gone, Charming Billy?" *Redbook* 145 (May 1975) 81, 127-32.

Slabey, Robert M. "*Going After Cacciato*: Tim O'Brien's 'Separate Peace.'" Gilman & Smith 205-11.

Smith, Lorrie. "Disarming the War Story." Gilman and Smith 87-99.

Wilhelm, Albert. "Ballad Allusions in Tim O'Brien's 'Where Have You Gone, Charming Billy?'" *Studies in Short Fiction* 28.2 (Spring 1991) 218-22.

Jon Volkmer (essay date spring-summer 1999)

SOURCE: Volkmer, Jon. "Telling the 'Truth' about Vietnam: Episteme and Narrative Structure in *The Green Berets* and *The Things They Carried*." *WLA: War, Literature & the Arts* 11, no. 1 (spring-summer 1999): 240-55.

[*In the following essay, Volkmer compares and contrasts* The Things They Carried *and Robin Moore's* The Green Berets, *focusing on the way both authors treat the truth about the Vietnam War.*]

Robin Moore's *The Green Berets,* published in 1965, is one of the earliest novels of the Vietnam conflict. Tim O'Brien's **The Things They Carried** (1990), is one of the more recent. Nevertheless, there are many similarities: both are novels-in-short-stories; both focus on American soldiers; both employ mainly jungle settings; and both feature a first-person narrator who is both one-of-the-guys AND separated from them by the status of being a writer. Moreover, each book makes an explicit claim that it tells the "truth" about the Vietnam conflict, a truth which each claims is only accessible through a fictive presentation of action and events.

My purpose is to interrogate the claims to ownership of "truth" in these two novels, and discuss how presumptions about the nature of "truth" affect the fictive shaping of the novel. By this comparison, I hope to show how these two novels form what might be called a set of bookends of the Vietnam era, with Moore's work reflecting the simplicity and naïveté of a country embarking on war, and O'Brien's work living as testament to the complexity and hard-won, although limited, knowledge from the perspective granted by a quarter of a century.

I started with some similarities that make these books ripe for comparison. The rest of my essay is devoted to their differences. A look at the titles reveals much. The synecdoche of *The Green Berets* (GB) is not accidental. Throughout the book, Moore's characters are described solely in terms of their qualifications as fighting men. Hence,

> Sven Kornie was the ideal Special Forces officer. Special Forces was his life; fighting, especially unorthodox warfare, was what he lived for. He had no career to sacrifice; he had no desire to rise from operational to supervisory levels. And not the least of his assets, he was unmarried and had no attachments to anyone or anything in the world beyond Special Forces.
>
> (23)

While man and mission are submerged into the same "truth" in GB, the title of **The Things They Carried** (TTC) signals the separation of man from mission. The war, and all its paraphernalia, are the unhappy load carried on the back of the foot soldiers. The first and eponymous chapter lists pages and pages of things that soldiers carried in the war, listings which are used to highlight the soldiers' individualities as much as their commonalities:

> Henry Dobbins, who was a big man, carried extra rations; he was especially fond of canned peaches in heavy syrup over pound cake. Dave Jensen, who practiced field hygiene, carried a toothbrush, dental floss, and several hotel-sized bars of soap he'd stolen on R&R in Sydney, Australia. Ted Lavender, who was scared, carried tranquilizers until he was shot in the head outside the village of Than Khe in mid-April.
>
> (4)

Later in the chapter, the list of "things they carried" is enlarged to include the abstract and metaphysical. "They carried all the emotional baggage of men who might die. Grief, terror, love, longing" (20). There is one thing they do not carry:

> They had no sense of strategy or mission. They searched the villages without knowing what to look for, not caring, kicking over jars of rice, frisking children and old men, blowing tunnels, sometimes setting fires and sometimes not.
>
> (15)

O'Brien pays little attention to his characters as soldiers. As foreshadowed by the title, O'Brien's truth is always individual; it lies in the idiosyncrasies of individuals. Robin Moore, as I will show, believes in a common and objective Truth; his emphasis is on the soldierly qualities that his characters share, as idealized and symbolized by their head gear.

"The Green Berets is a book of truth." Thus Moore begins his introduction. He explains that while he had originally planned a nonfiction work, two things convinced him that he should employ a fictional presentation. The first is a kind of names-changed-to-protect-the-guilty routine. "Time and again, I promised harried and heroic Special Forces men that their confidences were 'off the record'" (2).

Moore's other reason is more ambitious. He praises other reporters for giving "detailed incidents," but his idea, he says, is to give "the broad overall picture of how Special Forces men operate, so each story basically is representative of a different facet of Special Forces action in wars like the one in Vietnam" (1).

Notice that Moore claims veracity for his portrayal not only of the Vietnam engagement, but of all wars like it. How does he presume to so generalize? Through Cold War Manichaeism, of course. The presumptive "truth" that underlies GB is the vision of the world as a giant struggle between Good (freedom, democracy, America), and Evil (tyranny, Communism, the Soviet Union). Moore is quite happy to employ the metaphor of an encircled jungle outpost for the state of the world, not only in his own time, but seemingly for all time:

> In essence, these stories will be true of the political problems and combat situations Special Forces men are facing in 1965, or for that matter 1975, wherever Americans must fight to keep the perimeter of the free world from shrinking further.
>
> (13)

The crucial failure of the book (and, it might be argued, of America's early involvement in the Vietnam), is a refusal to see or acknowledge how this Manichaean episteme influences the perception and construction of narrative events. Robin Moore was in Vietnam. He claims much firsthand experience of the war, including, presumably, all the ambiguity that accompanies such experience. And yet, when that experience is translated into what the author promises is a higher fictive "truth," the reader finds it first suspiciously, and sometimes laughably, unambiguous.

In Moore's book, shades of gray are strained out in favor of broad swatches of black and white. The Special Forces men are uniformly lionized for their courage, strength, and intelligence, while the North Vietnamese are demonized as vicious and fanatical Communists. The South Vietnamese allies are treated with suspicion and contempt. These sentiments are broadened still further in lines like: "'Now we get the Oriental mind at work,'" Stitch said wearily to the Americans in the room. "'If we stay here twenty years we won't change them, and God save us from getting like them'" (46-7).

While Asians are routinely described in phrases such as "the sinister little brown bandit" (36), the ethnic ideal for the Special Forces men is chillingly Aryan. Talking about "the ideal Special Forces officer," the narrator states with pride that Sven Kornie, "joined the German Army and miraculously survived two years of fighting the Russians on the eastern front" (22). Thus, in the strict dualism of the Cold War, the character's possible Nazi past is not only pardonable but praiseworthy, because he was fighting Communists. Kornie's men—given the names Borst, Schmelzer, Stitch, Bergholtz—seem to have a lot in common with their commander, a fact not lost on the narrator: "He introduced me to Sergeant Bergholtz, and I sensed my guess was correct that a Germanic-Viking crew had indeed been transported intact to the Vietnam-Cambodia border" (25).

Moore's plots are as predictable as his characters. In each of the nine stories, the heroic Green Berets are beset by overwhelming odds, or treachery, or the restrictions imposed by short-sighted career army officers who don't understand the dictates of "unconventional" war. The linear narratives rise to dramatic climaxes that usually take the form of a battle where a smashing victory is snatched from the jaws of near certain defeat.

In one story Moore even employs his own version of a Fisher King myth. "Home to Nanette" has the Green Beret hero, Arklin, sent to singlehandedly transform a peaceful Meo village "into an orderly paramilitary operation" (177). The villagers treat Arklin as a demigod, presenting him the choicest young virgins. He at first resists this heathen practice, but finally "bowed to the inevitable" (173) and accepts a beautiful fifteen-year-old girl "much lighter colored than the others, smaller breasted, and more delicately boned" (172). (She turns out, of course, to be half-French, conveniently blending a Western epitome of sensuality with the native allure.)

Arklin, a married man, stoically refrains from sex with the willing native. However, he finds the Meos surly and uncooperative because of this rejection. So Arklin, a true Green Beret, must do whatever it takes to fulfill his mission. As Moore tells it:

> Out of desperation born of his inability to circumvent his morals and nearly inflexible sense of responsibility, Arklin drank three gourds of Meo liquor. The alcohol produced the release and Arklin consummated his 'marriage' to Nanette. Once breakthrough had been effected, Arklin so thoroughly pleased and satisfied his young bride that the Meos, seeing her the next day, knew at once that the American was finally one of them. . . .
>
> Tasks were accomplished much more quickly now. The weapons room was finished. . . . Sandbags were filled and molded into bunkers, and on the firing range the Montagnards worked hard to improve their marksmanship.
>
> (175-6)

Thus the erect penis of the Green Beret restores vitality to the stagnant community. Besides the poorly concealed prurience, there is also the irony, apparently lost on Moore, that the "fertility" his Fisher King instills portends unmitigated catastrophe for the village. By the end of the story most of the Meos are dead, the village is on the brink of being overrun, and the survivors must be evacuated by airplane. But in the book's perspective, the operation is a success because, in Arklin's words, "They [the Meos] inflicted heavy damage on the Communist buildup" (220).

Robin Moore's fictional imperative, as it turns out, is to strain out the moral ambiguity of war, as well as the tactical ambiguity of jungle warfare, in favor of his vision of Morality (Green Berets are always the good guys), and Justice (they always win). This formula of rendering the Vietnam war as a series of gritty but simplistic action-adventure narratives probably accounts both for the novel's pop culture presence[1], and for its dismissive treatment by scholars of Vietnam war literature.[2]

Robin Moore attempts to use the fictive constructs to present the truth about Vietnam. As I have tried to show, Moore betrays, and is betrayed by, those selfsame constructs. *The Green Berets* is, at best, a part of what Neil Sheehan calls the "Bright Shining Lie" of Vietnam. At worst, it is gruesome comedy, a testament to the naïveté, self-delusion and arrogance that launched the United States into its Vietnam nightmare.

As GB demonstrates, while the traditional plot structure—rising action, climax, denouement—is well suited for war literature, it is not politically neutral. By imposing order and coherence on events, the plot invests them with significance. Whether the plot culminates in triumph or tragedy, the plot tends to bless its subject with meaning, even glamor.

In *The Things They Carried,* Tim O'Brien makes the problem of locating truth the central theme. Instead of promising the truth, O'Brien spends most of his time hacking away at the very idea of "truth" when it comes to war. The term is too closely aligned with "meaning," "coherence," and "significance" for his liking. O'Brien's strategy, throughout the book, is to hook the reader into an engaging story, then radically disrupt the narrative. O'Brien wants to pull the rug out from under the reader, explode the complacencies, keep the reader on edge and guessing. This state of never coming to conclusions, never being allowed to settle into a truth, paradoxically provides a "truer" sense of the experience of Vietnam than a consistent narrative could do. Responding to this point in a letter to me, O'Brien writes, "Thing is, I *do* state conclusions. Many, many conclusions. But as I say at one point, 'the truths are contradictory.' They swirl. There are varieties of truth, angles on truth, reports of truth, etc." He continues:

> In general, I guess, I'm saying that "truth" does not seem to be . . . something we can touch and eat for breakfast. Take a look at the Rat Kiley stuff about story and believability and truth in **"Sweetheart"** [**"Sweetheart of the Song Tra Bong"**]; take a look, too, at the fat bird colonel thing in **"How to Tell a True War Story"**: how we *hear,* what we *bring* to a report of truth (say a story being told) determines in part our judgments about "truthfulness." (How can a thing *be* true if we don't *believe* it's true? No way, unless you accept the notion of noumenon.) The fat bird colonel has wax in his ears, wrong frequency—i.e. military rank and rear-echelon-ness and officerlike values add up to the inability to hear or listen to or believe what those six guys experienced up in the mountains. For the colonel, that cocktail party in the fog *cannot* be true—not literally, not metaphorically. Same-same with Rat's **"Sweetheart"** story: nobody believes him because they've come to the story with certain values and conventions about women and combat. Rat explicitly disputes these conventions, yet doesn't convince his buddies—the guys never do believe him, though he claims to have witnessed certain events with his own two eyes.
>
> (August 1993)

As illustrated in this quote, O'Brien brings an ingenious arsenal of weapons for disrupting reader expectations and complacencies. His narration is recursive rather than linear. He happily contradicts himself.

A strategy which O'Brien uses over and over again is the invitation to and the denial of the authorial fallacy. This begins even before the reader gets to the first story, and discovers that the narrator's name is "Tim O'Brien." The front matter of the book contains the routine disclaimer that, "all the incidents, names, and characters

are imaginary." But a page later, the author "lovingly" dedicates the book "to the men of Alpha Company, and in particular to Jimmy Cross, Norman Bowker, Rat Kiley, Mitchell Sanders, Henry Dobbins, and Kiowa"—that is, to those selfsame names and characters we have just been assured are imaginary.

In many places the narrative claims to be dropping the pretense of fiction in order to tell the reader what "really" happened, only to snap the fictive trap. Nowhere is the reader more thoroughly indicted than at the end of the chapter called **"How to Tell a True War Story."** Here the narration of an episode in the setting of Viet Nam makes one of its frequent meta-narrational jumps into a more familiar time and place, only this time the reader is given an actual stand-in:

> Now and then, when I tell this story, someone will come up to me afterward and say she liked it. It's always a woman. Usually it's an older woman of kindly temperament and humane politics. She'll explain that as a rule she hates war stories; she can't understand why people want to wallow in all the blood and gore. But this one she liked. The poor baby buffalo, it made her sad. Sometimes, even, there are little tears. What I should do, she'll say, is put it all behind me.
>
> I won't say it but I'll think it.
>
> I'll picture Rat Kiley's face, his grief, and I'll think, *You dumb cooze.*
>
> (90)

The meta-narrator's voice continues in this indignant tone, damning the kindly woman (and by extension, all readers) for accepting the writer's earlier portrait of a moving moment in a horrible war. Now he insists, "Beginning to end, . . . it's all made up. Every goddamn detail—the mountains and the river and especially that poor dumb baby buffalo. None of it happened. *None* of it" (91).

And then the O'Brienesque quick reversal: "And even if it did happen, it didn't happen in the mountains, it happened in this little village on the Batangan Peninsula, and it was raining like crazy" (91).

At this point, the poor woman might be forgiven if her temperament became less kindly and she demanded of the author, *What in the hell do you want from me?* It seems that both writer and reader are caught in a double bind. As any Vietnam vet will tell you, you can't know what it was like unless you were there. But O'Brien adds that you can't know what it was like even if you were there, and even when a writer succeeds in touching the reader's emotions, there is still the ever present danger of melodrama and sentimentality. In this section, more than anywhere else in the book, the writer's frustration is evident.

In **"How to Tell a True War Story,"** O'Brien most directly attacks the romantic treatment of war. Here's the plot: a soldier is killed; his friend writes a long letter to the dead man's sister; she never writes back. Interwoven with the fragments of this narrative are didactic pronouncements on the nature of a "true" war story. Among them:

> A true war story is never moral. It does not instruct, nor encourage virtue, nor suggest models of proper human behavior, nor restrain men from doing the things men have always done. If a story seems moral, do not believe it. If at the end of a war story you feel uplifted, or if you feel that some small bit of rectitude has been salvaged from the larger waste, then you have been made the victim of a very old and terrible lie.
>
> (76)

O'Brien is, as usual, talking only indirectly about war itself; his contempt is reserved for the *stories* of war.

Throughout TTC, one finds a preoccupation with epistemology, so that it turns out to be as much a book about a man trying to write a book as it is a book about the war. O'Brien never forgets, or lets the reader forget, that no reader ever has direct experience; the "experience" we read is always mediated through the memory and imagination of the writer, which complicates the search for truth:

> In any war story, but especially a true one, it's difficult to separate what happened from what seemed to happen. What seems to happen becomes its own happening and has to be told that way. The angles of vision are skewed.
>
> (78)

The metaphors weave in and out. In an earlier chapter, **"Spin,"** O'Brien compares the process to a traffic circle:

> You take your material where you find it, which is in your life, at the intersection of past and present. The memory-traffic feeds into a rotary up in your head, where it goes in circles for a while, then pretty soon imagination flows in and the traffic merges and shoots off down a thousand different streets. As a writer, all you can do is pick a street and go for the ride, putting things down as they come.
>
> (38)

In **"How to Tell . . ."** [**"How to Tell a True War Story"**] he employs the metaphor of the weave of cloth:

> In a true war story, if there's a moral at all, it's like the thread that makes the cloth. You can't tease it out. You can't extract the meaning without unraveling the deeper meaning. And in the end, really, there's nothing much to say about a true war story except maybe, "Oh."
>
> True war stories do not generalize. They do not indulge in abstraction or analysis.
>
> (84)

After all the generalization and abstraction, the reader must do a double take at that last line. What then, is O'Brien saying about Truth? Where is the locus of real-ity? I believe O'Brien's book points to a complicated and dynamic version of reality: it can never exist in the details, for details are whimsical and accidental. It can never exist in generalizations, for they are prey to politics and romanticism. And yet, those are the only two choices, the only constructs at hand, so they must be used. But the undercutting of the authority of either one is just as important as its authoritative delivery, and real truth exists, if at all, in glimmers and glimpses, in an unstable ethereal place that occurs just above the rabble of raw detail and below the Olympian realm of generalization and abstraction. There is never a conclusion, there is only endless process: "You can tell a true war story if you just keep on telling it" (91).

In comparing Moore to O'Brien, it is instructive to look at the one story in TTC in which the Green Berets play a prominent role. **"Sweetheart of the Song Tra Bong"** is one of the longest pieces in O'Brien's book, and the one that most resembles a typical "war story." The plot concerns a medic who ingeniously contrives to bring his girlfriend all the way from the United States to the Vietnamese jungle, just to be with him. The girlfriend is happy with him for a while, but then becomes fascinated with Vietnam, with the war, and with the Green Berets who are encamped on the other side of the outpost. Eventually the boyfriend who brought her loses her to the Green Berets. She goes on their ambushes, and goes further, leaving even them in the end, to become a jungle creature, a preying cat almost, that spooks the Green Berets themselves.

O'Brien's book is about grunts, common fighting men who for the most part didn't choose or want to be in Viet Nam, not about elite Green Berets, and it's curious to see how O'Brien presents them in his book as something ghostly, otherworldly. Curiously, the enemy is often referred to in the same terms of ghosts and mystery and otherworldliness. In **"Sweetheart,"** we come the closest to Moore's view: the Greenies, as O'Brien calls them, have adopted the ways of the enemy, and are engaging the enemy in ways that the regular grunts don't know and don't care to know. O'Brien's common soldiers are almost as wary of the Greenies as they are of the enemy. Moore would probably be comfortable with this view.

But O'Brien undercuts this credibility by making **"Sweetheart"** more a story about storytelling than a paean to the Green Berets. The story of the girl who goes native is not presented straight out; the book's first-person narrator gets it from another character, Rat Kiley, who is branded unreliable—an habitual liar and gross exaggerator. Other characters respond to the story as Rat Kiley tells it, providing a metafictional commentary about the story as story, what stories accomplish, and the rules that stories must follow. For example, at the point where Rat Kiley tells the others that the girl has disappeared, he pauses to gauge the audience response:

> When he first told the story, Rat stopped there and looked at Mitchell Sanders for a time.
>
> "So what's your vote? Where was she?"
>
> "The Greenies," Sanders said.
>
> "Yeah?"
>
> Sanders smiled. "No other option. That stuff about the Special Forces—how they used the place as a base of operations, how they'd glide in and out—all that had to be there for a *reason.* That's how stories work, man."
>
> Rat thought about it, then shrugged.
>
> "All right, sure, the Greenies. . . ."
>
> (112)

In this interchange, we see an example of the complicated way that O'Brien sees story and reality working together. Rat has previously sworn again and again this is a true story he's telling, although the narrator has told us not to trust Rat. In his response to Sanders, it is almost as if Rat is making it up, agreeing with Sanders that the facts of the story dictate that the girl ran off with the Green Berets, and so he will agree to that and continue the story with that as a "fact" even if it hadn't occurred to him before. The way O'Brien italicizes the word "reason," it's clear he has Sanders using the word in the sense of "rule," as in the rules of storytelling.

Near the story's conclusion, Rat shrugs and says he doesn't know whatever became of the girl. This infuriates Mitchell Sanders, whom O'Brien uses throughout as spokesman for the rules or obligations of storytelling. These obligations are not only not arbitrary, but alleged to be connected to something essential, to "human nature" itself:

> "You can't do that."
>
> "Do what?"
>
> "Jesus Christ, it's against the *rules,*" Sanders said. "Against human *nature.* This elaborate story, you can't say, "Hey, by the way, I don't know the *ending.* I mean, you got certain obligations."
>
> (122)

Once again, O'Brien is using italics to link the most important parts, "rules . . . nature . . . ending," as if there is some organic, inviolable structure to storytelling.

Rat fulfills his obligation, but of course O'Brien undercuts it with Rat's disclaimer that he doesn't know the conclusion of the story from his own experience, but "I

heard it secondhand. Thirdhand, actually" (124). He then goes ahead and gives the story a most romantic, sensational, and unbelievable ending:

> If you believed the Greenies, Rat said, Mary Anne was still out there in the dark. Odd movements, odd shapes. . . . She had crossed to the other side. She was part of the land. She was wearing her culottes, her pink sweater, and a necklace of human tongues. She was dangerous. She was ready for the kill.
>
> (125)

After reading O'Brien's **"Sweetheart,"** one can't help but think of Moore's earnest narrator as a less self-aware Rat Kiley. The reader is ever more cognizant of Moore's manipulation of details in slavish adherence to conventional rules of narrative structure. Each of Moore's stories rises to such a clear climax, conclusion and closure, with such clear good guys and bad guys, that the reader cannot help disbelieving him, because the shaping hand of the author is too much in evidence making everything come out right for the sake of story every time. In **"Sweetheart,"** O'Brien makes the machinations of storytelling itself the central aspect of the story.

Despite the superficial similarities, *The Green Berets* and ***The Things They Carried*** are novels that come not only from opposite chronological positions, but from opposite ends of the war's epistemological spectrum as well. Robin Moore claims to possess Truth at the cosmic level (Good vs Evil), and at the empirical level. However, he imposes fictive constructs, characterization and plot, with such programmatic rigidity that he violates a reader's common sense apprehension of the ambiguities and chaos of real life, and ends up being disbelieved despite all his claims.

While Moore tries (and fails), to make sense out of the chaos of the Vietnam conflict, O'Brien promises (and succeeds), to portray the war as a cacophony of competing truths, but not one that reduces itself to chaos or meaninglessness. O'Brien writes, "Complication isn't chaos. I was after *clarity,* of a sort" (letter to the author, August 1993). While Moore tries to bring the suspense and satisfaction of traditional plot structure to strengthen his claim on the reader, O'Brien attacks reader expectations. He distrusts any large claim of truth. He distrusts any simple explanations or answers. He even distrusts his own memory.

And yet, for all his disclaimers and disruptions, O'Brien's episteme is not nihilistic. He does believe in truth, but in his conception it's a slippery thing, dynamic, tentative, tenuous, transforming itself into untruth as soon as one gets complacent with it. Whenever he explicitly tells the reader that something is "true," the reader learns to expect that truth to be contradicted or undercut somewhere else in the book.

The transcendent concept for O'Brien is not "truth" but "story":

> Stories are for joining the past to the future. Stories are for those late hours in the night when you can't remember how you got from where you were to where you are. Stories are for eternity, when memory is erased, when there is nothing to remember except the story.

(40)

At the beginning of this essay, I referred to GB and TTH as "bookends" of the Vietnam era. Moore's experience in Vietnam was in the first half of 1964, a time the United States was precisely on the cusp of the massive political and social upheavals often referred to as the counter culture revolution. Domestic opposition to the Vietnam war was central to this inter-generational American conflict, both as a cause and an effect. That Moore's book could be a best seller reflects, I believe, its publication during the last stages of society's WWII-era combination of glorified patriotism and pervasive paranoia over the threat of a worldwide Communist hegemony. A few years later, in 1968, John Wayne's attempt to bring GB to the big screen was a famous flop. The most often cited moment in the movie is the ending, where The Duke, hand in hand with the tiny orphan Vietnamese boy, walks into the sunset on the beach. Except in Vietnam the coast faces east. A western beach sunset could only happen in someplace like . . . California. Which is where, as the wags always say, this movie is really set.

The most serious and successful film statements about the Vietnam appeared in the late 1970s, and tried to make sense of the war in mythical or archetypal terms. Michael Cimino's *The Deer Hunter* (1978) and Francis Ford Coppola's *Apocalypse Now* (1979) cross-reference war scenes with, in the former case, archetypal small-town America, and in the latter, Joseph Conrad's mythical vision of evil and the human heart.

Tim O'Brien's *Going After Cacciato* (1975) fits into this category. In this novel, the scenes of Vietnam warfare are interwoven with a preposterous but almost believable plot of a deserter being tracked, on the ground, all the way from the battlefield in Southeast Asia to Paris, France. Thus the longing of the frightened homesick soldier becomes transmuted into an epic and archetypal quest.

I have noticed, however, that many Vietnam veterans express dissatisfaction with these three highly acclaimed works of art. It's as if the artistic qualities of the construction interfere with the down-to-earth realism that those who experienced the Vietnam war demand. And once again we are back to the conundrum formulated earlier in this essay of generalities versus details. *Apoca-lypse Now* and *The Deer Hunter* and *Going After Cacciato,* although liberally infused with gritty, even gory realism, finally exist more at the level of generalization, of mythic or aesthetic statement. At the other extreme, some of the finer works of journalism, Michael Herr's *Dispatches,* say, offer extraordinary glimpses of the details of the war, but leave it up to the reader to provide any overarching meaning or point.

Which brings me back to **The Things They Carried.** This book arrived on the scene in 1990, coincidental with the fall of the Berlin Wall, the collapse of the Evil Empire, and the end of whole Manicheaen dualism that dominated political discourse since the end of WWII. What is left when the Evil Empire is gone? The story of how some men once believed in it. And how others who didn't were sent to fight a war in a faraway country by those who did. And the Truth, or Truths, or truths of the war can only be found in the reverence for story.

Reverence for story is what ultimately separates GB from TTC, and, I would argue, what raises O'Brien's book above nearly all of the imaginative representations of the Vietnam War. Whereas Robin Moore's book is a failed attempt to make story serve his version of "truth," Tim O'Brien finds truth in allowing it to serve the needs of story. In the narratives that he weaves around "Tim O'Brien," around Jimmy Cross, Norman Bowker, Kiowa, and the rest, without glamorizing the obscenity of war, he achieves the beauty of art, and the ring of truth.

Notes

1. Moore co-wrote the hit song "Ballad of the Green Berets" with Sgt. Barry Sadler; John Wayne starred in the movie.

2. Moore's book is not even mentioned in Arthur Casciato's comprehensive article, "Teaching the Literature of the Vietnam War" (*Review,* Vol. 9, 1987).

Works Cited

Moore, Robin. *The Green Berets.* New York: Ballantine Books, 1983.

O'Brien, Tim. *The Things They Carried.* Boston: Houghton Mifflin, 1990.

———. Letter to Jon Volkmer. 3 August, 1993.

Carl S. Horner (essay date spring-summer 1999)

SOURCE: Horner, Carl S. "Challenging the Law of Courage and Heroic Identification in Tim O'Brien's *If I Die in a Combat Zone* and *The Things They Carried.*"

WLA: War, Literature & the Arts 11, no. 1 (spring-summer 1999): 256-67.

[*In the following essay, Horner maintains that O'Brien challenges conventional ideas about courage and heroism in* If I Die in a Combat Zone *and* The Things They Carried.]

In his autobiographic text, *If I Die in a Combat Zone: Box Me up and Ship Me Home,* and in his novel, **The Things They Carried,** Tim O'Brien questions the presumed sanctity of the oldest male law. Courage and masculinity, so-called "professionalism," the "old order" (*If I Die* 192), grace under pressure, or the collective male psyche could, O'Brien writes, blind a man into stupidity during the Vietnam War. Not that he could always rely on published information or even rationally determine a wise course in the call of duty, but a citizen had the obligation to discover whether business leaders, politicians, and military officers had moral, legal, and therefore truly evident causes for sanctioning violence in Vietnam. Blind or obsessive duty for the sake of honor, God, and country might be bravery to a fault, or nothing more than "manliness, crudely idealized" (*If I Die* 142).

Courage is only one part of virtue, O'Brien explains, alluding to the warnings of Plato. Courage cannot be separated from wisdom, temperance, and justice. Once a man sheds heroic identification and merit deeds; once he refuses either to compromise his morality, to kill illegally, or to entrap himself in the futile sacrifice of "a war fought for uncertain reasons" (*If I Die* 135); once he seeks inwardly and deliberately for the meaning of courage (an obligation more frightening and dangerous than prescriptive duty), he escapes mechanical bravery and the spiritual death that blind conscription can produce. That is, the soldier who responds not to what he really believes but to the expectations of indoctrinated parents, small-town neighbors, sergeants, and lieutenants is charged, O'Brien writes, with the passion, the ignorance "merely" of "a well-disguised cowardice" (*If I Die* 135).

Throughout gender history, men have been pressured to react to deadly crisis according to the sacred rules of a male honor code. From Odysseus to King Arthur, from Ulysses to George Washington, and from Aeneas to Norman Schwarzkopf, clearly the most widely accepted values of integrity, dignity, respect, self-respect, valor, and thus unquestioned masculinity hinge upon a commissioned response to fear and duty. Rational control over the emotion of fear or doubt; strength not only of body but also of mind—the tangential strength, that is, of the gifted athlete and military wizard; appropriate aggression fed by a competitive spirit; full-pitch confidence to win against overwhelming odds; and utter loyalty to duty, to God, to country, to family, and to friends collectively define the classic male hero. Here is the meaning of inventiveness, resilience, and endurance in the male universe. Here is the legendary crisis crusher, the icon of national and international glory and fame, the Captain, my Captain of moral common sense and duty, the human bush hog cutting the memorial path to higher truth. "It's the old story," Major Callicles insists in *If I Die in a Combat Zone.* "Guts to stand up for what's right. . . . It's not standing around passively hoping for things to happen right; it's going out and being tough and sharp-thinkin' and *making* things happen right" (194-195). Clearly, undaunted courage lies at the heart of this "crucible of men" and epic "events" (22-23).

A "blond, meticulously fair, brave, tall, [and] blue-eyed" Captain Johanson would be recognized traditionally and yet blindly as his "nation's pride" for his classic masculinity when in "the steady, blood-headed intensity of Sir Lancelot" (*If I Die* 131, 144) he charges across a rice paddy to kill a Vietcong soldier nearly at point-blank range. Did he act for the benefit or the safety of his platoon? Was his deed an act of self-sacrifice? Was this an "ag-ile, mo-bile, and hos-tile" man "resigned to bullets and brawn" (*If I Die* 44, 91)? Or was this mission nothing more than an adrenalin rush—not bravery, not courage really, but mindless aggression? "It's the charge, the light brigade with only one man" sailing neither with fear nor with regret into harm's way, O'Brien cautions, that typically comes to mind "first" in the classification of heroes. Men who charge the enemy despite their fear of death "are remembered as brave, win or lose." Here are the sacred heroes forever tall, true, and tough—forever rough, ready, and rugged—and men like Johanson confess that they would "rather be brave" in this way "than almost anything" else in life. These men are truly "heroes forever" in war history and in literature, but we must not conclude that "courage" presupposes the bloody "charge" (*If I Die* 131).

"Courage is nothing to laugh at, not if it is proper courage and exercised by men who know what they do is proper" (133), O'Brien writes in *If I Die in a Combat Zone,* arguing that if we are not thinking, we are not human. If we are not thinking, by extension we are not brave in the human dimension. "Proper courage is wise courage," O'Brien explains, alluding to Plato's dialectic of noble bravery in "Laches." "It's acting wisely, acting wisely when fear would have a man act otherwise. It is the endurance of the soul in spite of fear—wisely" (133).

Mindless charge has its place in war—indeed, force can generate the power necessary to win a deadly conflict. But we must not confuse crude aggression with the noble cause enlivened by courage. Doing the best that any individual can do, according to his own conscience, keeps common sense and meaning in the acts of courage. Routine physical acts, the thing to do at the time, raw valor, doing what everyone else is doing to avoid shame, acting bravely "out of a spirit of righteousness . . . necessity . . . resignation" (*If I Die* 45), merely following orders—is that acting gallantly? What might be classified or even decorated with the Congressional Medal of Honor as courageous mentality could like the "endless march" of duty honestly be reduced to a physical response to stressful experience with "no volition, no will, because it was automatic, it was anatomy . . . a kind of inertia, a kind of emptiness, a dullness of desire and intellect and conscience and hope and human sensibility" (***Things*** [***The Things They Carried***] 15).

Human courage comes not from the hypothalamus, not from the anterior pituitary or adrenal glands, and not from any other direct or indirect influence on a fight-or-flight response to stress, including the central nervous system and the testicles, but from the clear thinking cortex of the brain. "Men must *know* what they do is courageous," O'Brien argues in *If I Die in a Combat Zone*—that is, "they must *know* it is right, and that kind of knowledge is wisdom and nothing else" (137). Be it Plato's rationalism or Heidegger's and Sartre's existentialism, acting knowingly and thoughtfully is the human condition.

Within this self-limiting vision of courage, O'Brien hesitates to celebrate many brave men. "Either they are stupid and do not know what is right," including one Alpha Company soldier who had no thoughts about his participation in the war—certainly, no high thoughts about morality or politics—and who only wanted to get out of Vietnam alive. "Or they know what is right and cannot bring themselves to do it. Or they know what is right and do it, but do not feel and understand the fear that must be overcome" (*If I Die* 137). Holding ground on principle, or for no other reason than to hold it, as in the example of a cow taking countless rounds from O'Brien's company in a free-fire zone, is neither courage nor endurance. It is mortal stupidity.

Of course, O'Brien is not the first writer to challenge the law of courage, warning that mindless assault, even for honorable causes, loses the human dimension of bravery. Although Hemingway vehemently opposed the psychoanalytic view popular in his day that each individual suffers a point at which his mind or body will break down under pressure, Colonel Lum Edwards explained that even during the most frightening combat of the 1944 Hurtgen campaign Hemingway was never "impressed by reckless bravado." While he "admired the man who could see clearly what was necessary to do and had the courage to do it, regardless of the percentage of risk involved," never did Hemingway identify "raw courage," or suicidal aggression, as honorable or even as desirable "unless it was the only way of getting

the job done." Impressed by Hemingway's love of direct action over diction, Edwards concluded that his friend practiced his honor code sincerely each of his eighteen days in Hurtgenwald:

> I never saw him act foolishly in combat. He understood war and man's part in it to a better degree than most people ever will. He had an excellent sense of the situation. While wanting to contribute, he knew very well when to proceed and when it was best to wait awhile.
>
> (qtd. in Baker 435)

Despite the attractive filter that Hemingway placed on courage—essentially, that a life-threatening event in war (or in any deadly crisis) is merely a test, a test not only of courage and endurance but also of dignity—O'Brien notes in *If I Die in a Combat Zone* that simple stoicism is not a consistently adequate measure of bravery under any circumstance in war:

> It's too easy to affect grace, and it's too hard to see through it. . . . Grace under pressure means you can confront things gracefully or squeeze out of them gracefully. But to make those two things equal with the easy word "grace" is wrong. Grace under pressure is not courage.
>
> (142-143)

If Hemingway had lived under the daily grind of a combat soldier for a year or more, rather than drifting in and out of deadly conflict as a correspondent, the law of averages would have shattered his stoicism and thus his own law of courage, as the ironies, uncertainties, and cruelties of the war theater would contradict, any man's inflexible belief.

Shoved or hit in his childhood school yard, any man of Alpha Company would fight. Rather than lose dignity or the appearance of courage, he would scream and snarl and flail the air and flail his enemies in the cruel power and glory of male potency. Indeed, public confessions about the fear of death were more than "bad luck" or "the ultimate self-fulfilling prophecy," all of which was strictly "taboo" (*If I Die* 138) for any soldier in any combat platoon during the Vietnam War. The collective male honor code precludes the contemplation of fear. Admitting fear is simply illegal or shameful in the male universe. The men of Alpha Company were nurtured in the same laws of masculinity as any other soldier in any other war. A man must not cry. He must not whine or complain. Worse, he must not lose control over his emotions or run in the heat of crisis. He must at least wear the mask of bravery in all conflict. The burden of fear and the shame that he would have to suffer if he let it creep into his face haunted even the toughest soldier of Alpha Company. Everyone "carried the common secret of cowardice barely restrained, the instinct to run or freeze or hide." Certainly, under the crushing weight of stress, violence, and ordnance, the male role "was the heaviest burden of all, for it could never be put down." Carrying "the soldier's greatest fear," the terror not of death but "the fear of blushing," the men of Alpha Company "were too frightened to be cowards." No high "dreams of glory or honor" threatened their dignity, merely "the blush of dishonor." They might even sneer at death in order not to be embarrassed by it. Indeed, men "died so as not to die of embarrassment" (*Things* 20-21). Here we see to what extent soldiers are driven in war, the bright center stage of the collective male psyche, not only by the Darwinism of androgen, testosterone, and adrenaline that inflames their aggressive spirits but also by the far more imperial grip of social Darwinism.

The "secret" to success in all crises, Bill brags to Jake in Hemingway's *The Sun Also Rises,* is "never be daunted." Of course, we can presume that Bill has been frightened by the violent experiences that any boy or man must endure in social reality, but he must always be politically correct, and thus he will not show his fear. "Not in public. If I begin to feel daunted I'll go off by myself" (73). The silly Lion believes that he will be king over the forests of Oz if he develops not heart and not mind but courage. Ironically, Juno fails to realize in Virgil's *Aeneid* that men value courage over life and safety; thus, her effort to save Turnus from certain death in fated battle with Aeneas only frustrates the man beyond either the fear or the pain of death. "The horror of it!" Turnus shrieks, realizing that he has fled the battlefield in pursuit not of his rival but only of an apparition of Aeneas. Here for the classic soldier is "a fault so grave," a "disgrace" and "shame" so unforgivable and "terrible" (271-272), that only Juno can restrain her mortal from instantly killing himself on his own sword or foolishly attempting to swim back to land in order to regain his dignity in the heat of war.

In order to protect themselves from shame and forbidden fear, some soldiers in Alpha Company "carried themselves with a sort of wistful resignation." Other soldiers wore the masks of "pride or stiff soldierly discipline or good human or macho zeal." All of them were inwardly "afraid of dying," the bravest leaders like Captain Johanson and the toughest grunts like Rat Kiley, "but they were even more afraid to show it" (*Things* 19).

"All of us, I suppose, like to believe that in a moral emergency we will behave like the heroes of our youth," O'Brien writes—that is, "bravely and forthrightly, without thought of personal loss or discredit." Alan Ladd and Humphrey Bogart had impressed O'Brien's childhood dreams in the formidable way in which a hero responds to crisis. In his impressionable childhood, O'Brien incubated the belief that he "would simply tap a secret reservoir" of his "moral capital" (*Things* 43) and conquer mounting evil as if he were the new gen-

eration's Frederick Henry, Captain Vere, or Shane (*If I Die* 139). However, the "old image" of himself "as a man of conscience and courage" (*Things* 60) collided with the Darwinian forces of the Vietnam War. Would his decision to go either to Canada where he could live according to his conscience or to Vietnam where he would answer his call to duty despite his conscience result in an honest act of courage? If he did succumb to national pride, would he find the path to truth and honor promised by his culture or merely kill the citizen's obligation to follow his inner voices in matters of political dispute?

Despite respected warnings from Ezra Pound that soldiers have entrapped themselves in war "from fear of weakness" or "from fear of censure" (qtd. in O'Brien, *If I Die* 37), or from fear of not being manly, and despite O'Brien's research into the political contradictions of Ho Chi Minh, the Gulf of Tonkin, the Geneva Accords, SEATO, and the division, if not the "moral confusion," among "smart" American politicians who "could not agree on even the most fundamental matters of public policy," O'Brien suffered the gnawing pressure to abandon his belief "that you don't make war without knowing why" (*Things* 44). This "moral split," he explains, caused him to experience "a kind of schizophrenia" (*Things* 48), even to the degree of hallucinating the faces and voices of his parents, his hometown friends, alien neighbors and civic leaders, Civil and World War veterans, high school cheerleaders, his best friend who died in her childhood, a memory of his cowboy hat and mask, Jane Fonda, Gary Cooper, and a myriad of other polar impressions. Although the events **"On the Rainy River"** are invented in *The Things They Carried* only to evoke O'Brien's confusion and anguish that he more autobiographically expresses in *If I Die in a Combat Zone,* the feeling of psychic warfare draws us into a haunting truth:

> I couldn't make up my mind. I feared the war, yes, but I also feared exile. I was afraid of walking away from my own life, my friends and my family, my whole history, everything that mattered to me. I feared losing the respect of my parents. I feared the law. I feared ridicule and censure.
>
> (*Things* 48)

Cleanth Brooks writes that moral pressure is exerted as "the essential ether" (52) in American small towns. Indeed, aliens to community codes risk the deadly loneliness not only of spoken and unspoken ridicule but also of self-doubt. Besides his mother and father, whose hurt over a son's resolution to go against the stream he could vividly imagine, O'Brien could picture the emotional violence of town leaders and gossips if they were to discuss his decision to follow his conscience:

> My hometown was a conservative little spot on the prairie, a place where tradition counted, and it was easy to imagine people sitting around a table down at

the old Gobbler Café on Main Street, coffee cups poised, the conversation slowly zeroing in on the young O'Brien kid, how the damned sissy had taken off for Canada. At night, when I couldn't sleep, I'd sometimes carry on fierce arguments with those people. I'd be screaming at them, telling them how much I detested their blind, thoughtless, automatic acquiescence to it all, their simple-minded patriotism, their prideful igno- rance, their love-it-or-leave-it platitudes, how they were sending me off to fight a war they didn't understand and didn't want to understand. I held them responsible. By God, yes, I *did*. All of them—I held them person- ally and individually responsible—the polyestered Ki- wanis boys, the merchants and farmers, the pious churchgoers, the chatty housewives, the PTA and the Lions club and the Veterans of Foreign Wars and the fine upstanding gentry out at the country club. They didn't know Bao Dai from the man in the moon. They didn't know history. They didn't know the first thing about Diem's tyranny, or the nature of Vietnamese na- tionalism, or the long colonialism of the French.

(*Things* 48-49)

Of course, O'Brien could not discuss his inner turmoil with anyone so heavily locked into conservative beliefs about men, heroes, and war. And even though he recog- nized the irony of giving up honest feelings about him- self in order to live a life without conflict with people whom he did not know or care about intimately, he could not tolerate the anticipation that these underin- formed citizens would condemn him to the leagues of cowards and traitors.

When the heart is squeezed, the intellect cannot always make decisions according to what O'Brien idealizes as "an act of pure reason" (*Things* 54). Rather than make decisions inwardly—that is, trusting an internal barom- eter and therefore being true to ourselves—O'Brien learned that fear of public condemnation might deter- mine what we finally do. Under the "terrible squeezing pressure" (*Things* 59) that attacks the human con- science, we can succumb to whatever society says that we must do and thus judge ourselves according to what other people say or do "as we make our choices or fail to make them" (*Things* 62). Under the "great world- wide sadness" that "came pressing down" and the "weight" that kept "pushing [him] toward the war" (*Things* 54, 59), O'Brien suffered "a moral freeze" on the Rainy River. "Canada had become a pitiful fantasy," not a solution to the pressure but a "silly and hopeless" dream of escaping his gnawing pressure:

I couldn't decide, I couldn't act, I couldn't comport myself with even a pretense of modest human dig- nity. . . . Right then, with the shore so close, I under- stood that I would not do what I should do. I would not swim away from my hometown and my country and my life. I would not be brave. That old image of myself as a hero, as a man of conscience and courage, all that was just a threadbare pipe dream. Bobbing there on the Rainy River, looking back at the Minnesota

shore, I felt a sudden swell of helplessness come over me, a drowning sensation.

(*Things* 59-60)

Facing the strange and alien moment in his life when he was "ashamed of [his] conscience, ashamed to be doing the right thing" (*Things* 55), ashamed of the philosophical and political convictions that made him doubt his ability to make a moral decision ironically to fight what he believed to be an immoral war, O'Brien confesses that the boiling rivers of "hot, stupid shame" (*Things* 54) finally determined the currents of his inner struggle. National and hometown patriots would not know that they sent a "coward" to fight their war in Vietnam. "It had nothing to do with morality," good thinking, and courage, O'Brien finally writes. "I would go to the war—I would kill and maybe die—because I was embarrassed not to" (*Things* 62-63).

Although we cannot expect ideal or even rational con- sistency in the contemplation of courage, O'Brien learned first in the war that raged between his heart and his intellect and then in the bush of the Vietnam War "that manhood is not something to scoff at"—indeed, that "soldiering . . . is something that makes a fellow think about courage, makes a man wonder what it is and if he has it" (*If I Die* 136, 202). In the honesty of mental toughness, no man is a total hero. No man is a total coward. Working toward his own perspective on bravery, O'Brien explodes the popular cliché: "A cow- ard dies a thousand deaths but a brave man only once." The error in this false assumption, O'Brien explains, is that no man is either "once and for always a coward" or "once and for always a hero." Operating as a foot sol- dier in the area of Chu Lai, including the villages of My Khe and My Lai one year after the well-known My Lai Massacre, O'Brien learned the tough reality that in the bush

. . . men act cowardly and, at other times, act with courage, each in different measure, each with varying consistency. The men who do well on the average, per- haps with one moment of glory, those men are brave.

(*If I Die* 143)

So ambiguous is the truth about courage, so intense and forgivable are the inconsistencies and contradictions of real men in crisis, a classic honor code—no matter how ideally projected, distorted, and perpetuated in gender history—deconstructs its own pressures in the hideous violence of war. In no literature about the war theater do we come to this intersection of courage more hon- estly than in the example of Alpha Company struggling under the fire of bullets, duty, pride, and self- preservation in *The Things They Carried:*

For the most part they carried themselves with poise, a kind of dignity. Now and then, however, there were times of panic, when they squealed or wanted to squeal but couldn't, when they twitched and made moaning sounds and covered their heads and said Dear Jesus and flopped around on the earth and fired their weapons blindly and cringed and sobbed and begged for the noise to stop and went wild and made stupid promises to themselves and to God and to their mothers and fathers, hoping not to die. In different ways, it happened to all of them.

(18-19)

Unlike the inspiring and yet coolly unrealistic cowboys, soldiers, and celebrated heroes of our childhood dreams and movies, taking fire—actually taking rounds intended to kill us, to kill the trembling flicker of perception that stands between us and dusty death—gives us vision about our vulnerability in crisis. We are never more alive, O'Brien is saying in *If I Die in a Combat Zone* and in **The Things They Carried,** than when we are almost dead. War gives us this mirror of our mortality, this truth about our humanity and courage:

> Afterward, when the firing ended, they would blink and peek up. They would touch their bodies, feeling shame, then quickly hiding it. They would force themselves to stand. As if in slow motion, frame by frame, the world would take on the old logic—absolute silence, then the wind, then sunlight, then voices. It was the burden of being alive. Awkwardly, the men would reassemble themselves, first in private, then in groups, becoming soldiers again. They would repair the leaks in their eyes. They would check for casualties, call in dustoffs, light cigarettes, try to smile, clear their throats and spit and begin cleaning their weapons. After a time someone would shake his head and say, No lie, I almost shit my pants, and someone else would laugh, which meant it was bad, yes, but the guy had obviously not shit his pants, it wasn't that bad, and in any case nobody would ever do such a thing and then go ahead and talk about it. They would squint into the dense, oppressive sunlight. For a few moments, perhaps, they would fall silent, lighting a joint and tracking its passage from man to man, inhaling, holding in the humiliation. Scary stuff, one of them might say. But then someone else would grin or flick his eyebrows and say, Roger-dodger, almost cut me a new asshole, *almost.*

(19)

Works Cited

Baker, Carlos. *Ernest Hemingway: A Life Story.* New York: Scribner's, 1969.

Brooks, Cleanth. *William Faulkner: The Yoknapatawpha County.* New Haven: Yale UP, 1963.

Hemingway, Ernest. *The Sun Also Rises.* New York: Scribner's, 1926.

O'Brien, Tim. *If I Die in a Combat Zone: Box Me up and Ship Me Home.* New York: Delta-Dell, 1989.

———. *The Things They Carried.* 1990. New York: Penguin, 1991.

Plato. "Laches." *The Collected Dialogues of Plato.* Ed. Edith Hamilton and Huntington Cairns. Bollingen Series LXXI. New York: Pantheon-Random, 1961. 123-144.

Virgil. *The Aeneid.* Trans. W. F. Jackson Knight. New York: Penguin, 1956.

Christopher Michael McDonough (essay date spring 2000)

SOURCE: McDonough, Christopher Michael. "'Afraid to Admit We Are Not Achilles': Facing Hector's Dilemma in Tim O'Brien's *The Things They Carried.*"[1] *Classical and Modern Literature* 20, no. 3 (spring 2000): 23-32.

[*In the following essay, McDonough utilizes "the tragedy of Hector" from the* Iliad *to glean insight into* The Things They Carried.]

> "The war, like Hector's own war, was silly and stupid."
>
> —Tim O'Brien, *If I Die in a Combat Zone,* 145

What has Troy to do with Vietnam? In recent years, the pertinence of the one Asian war to the other has been powerfully argued by numerous scholars, notably Jonathan Shay, in his seminal study, *Achilles in Vietnam: Combat Trauma and the Undoing of Character* (New York: Athenaeum, 1994), as well as by various authors responding to Shay in a special issue of *Classical Bulletin* 71.2 (1995), "Understanding Achilles." As can be seen in the titles here mentioned, the critical emphasis has generally been laid on the experience of Achilles, while little attention has focused on what James Redfield once called "the tragedy of Hector." Some discussion of the great Trojan hero might prove useful, however, especially for understanding Tim O'Brien's **The Things They Carried,** one of the finest works of American literature to emerge from the experience in Vietnam: for Hector as well as the protagonist of **The Things They Carried,** both brought to the brink by the necessity of battle, the dilemmas posed by the warrior mentality force unsettling questions about their societies and themselves.

As it was for the many young men who opposed the war in Vietnam, the debate over whether to fight or to flee had been at once a personal and political one for O'Brien. After negatively assessing the justice of the American involvement in Indochina, the narrator wonders whether it would be courageous or cowardly to fight for a cause he believed to be wrong. Although O'Brien elected to go to the war, the quandary remains in the foreground of his work: a central concern of **The Things They Carried,** a quasi-autobiographical work of fiction, is the shifting and indefinite line which divides bravery from cowardice (as well as honor from shame). "For the common soldier," O'Brien remarks in an oft-quoted sentence, ". . . the only certainty is overwhelming ambiguity" (88). Many literary critics have rightly characterized O'Brien's uncertainty as postmodern,[2] but in fact *The Things They Carried* deals with issues of courage as old as war itself—or at least as old as the oldest literature about war. In *If I Die in a Combat Zone,* an earlier work which anticipated many of the themes of *The Things They Carried,* O'Brien often turned to Plato for enlightenment in these matters, citing definitions of courage from both the *Laches* and the *Republic* and applying them to his own situation in Vietnam. But in *The Things They Carried,* and especially in the chapters **"On the Rainy River"** and **"Speaking of Courage,"** O'Brien discusses topics which might more profitably be considered from a Homeric rather than Socratic viewpoint.

As one scholar has noted of *The Things They Carried,* "There is nothing new in what O'Brien demonstrates here about trying to tell war stories . . . and, of course, Homer's *Iliad* is the primal statement on the contradictions inherent in war."[3] Some consideration of Homer's poetry can help to sharpen analysis of combat experience as, in fact, Jonathan Shay has shown in his aforementioned study of post-traumatic stress disorder.[4] While much of *The Things They Carried* likewise deals with the subsequent effects of combat, O'Brien also assesses the soldier's frame of mind *before* going off to war: in the book's first chapter, he lists not just the assorted weapons and supplies each soldier must carry while marching, but also "the emotional baggage of men who might die" (20), thus delineating the things they carried mentally as well as physically. The contours of this state of mind are most vividly portrayed in **"On the Rainy River,"** in which the narrator—"Tim O'Brien," a character distinct from the author—describes what he did after receiving his draft notice, in June, 1968, a few short weeks after his college graduation. At first enraged and then filled with self-pity, he spends an anxious month debating whether he should go to the war or flee his Minnesota home for Canada. One day, he snaps—a matter to be discussed more fully below—and drives north until he reaches the Rainy River; there he stops at the Tip Top Lodge, an abandoned resort on the American side of the border, run by an octogenarian named Elroy Berdahl. It is not anything which the old man says or does that is important for O'Brien during the agonizing days that follow—quite the opposite. Throughout this difficult time, the narrator is especially grateful for the "willful, almost ferocious silence" (52) Berdahl maintains, a reprieve from the pressing voices which are described at various points in the episode. Before his flight north, for instance, he had thought of what might be said by the people of his conservative hometown:

> . . . it was easy to imagine [them] sitting around a table at the old Gobbler Café on Main Street, coffee cups poised, the conversation slowly zeroing in on the young O'Brien kid, how the damned sissy had taken off for Canada.

(48)

It is ultimately in these voices that O'Brien locates the source of his anxiety: in addition to a fundamental disagreement about the war in Vietnam, his dilemma is a struggle between a well-founded fear of death and a profound feeling of being ashamed. As he writes,

> Intellect had come up against emotion. My conscience told me to run, but some irrational and powerful force was resisting, like a weight pushing me toward the war. What it came down to, stupidly, was a sense of shame. Hot, stupid shame. I did not want people to think badly of me. Not my parents, not my brother and sister, not even the folks down at the Gobbler Café.

(54)

To be at odds with public opinion was not an unusual position in 1968, to be sure. But while it would be wrong to reduce O'Brien's objections to the war to the mere desire to save his own skin, his remarks nonetheless take on meaningful perspective when compared with several episodes in the *Iliad* centering on the intertwined notions of glory and shame.

In his ground-breaking study, *The Greeks and the Irrational,* E. R. Dodds has noted, "Homeric man's highest good is not the enjoyment of a quiet conscience, but the enjoyment of *time,* public esteem."[5] This is not to say that the warriors at Troy are mindless automata surrendering all individuality to the whims of the crowd: in fact, they are acutely aware that the needs of the self and the demands of society may well be in conflict. James Redfield aptly puts it, "All men are born to die, but the warrior alone must confront this fact in his social life . . . The greatness of Homer's heroes is a greatness not of act but of consciousness."[6] There is a direct relationship in Homer's world between the risks one is willing to run and the respect society will confer; for this reason, the battlefield, where the threat to life is greatest, is the hero's proving ground. It is important to realize that the hero's status depends upon (and, in fact, cannot exist without) the tension between personal and public impulses: this tension is at the center of the epic. "The wrath of Achilles"—the words with which the *Iliad* famously opens—is directed not at the Trojans but at Agamemnon, the commander who has arbitrarily stripped him of his war-bride, Briseis. As a woman, Briseis means little to the hero, but as a prize he has legitimately earned for valor in battle, her significance is immense. In this foolish exercise of power, Agamemnon unintentionally sets into motion a crisis about the nature of heroism which brings Achilles face-to-face with the hollowness of his shame culture: why should there be any personal risk, if there is to be no public recognition?[7]

In addition to the possibility of winning glory, the Homeric hero is motivated also by *aidos,* "shame." By and large, this aspect of the ancient mentality is typified in the person of Hector, Achilles' great Trojan opponent.[8] More than any other combatant at Troy, Hector is aware of his special status as a warrior: as the greatest hero on the Trojan side, he carries the greatest burden in its defense and has the greatest reputation to lose in any defeat. Nonetheless, Hector is only mortal and cannot overcome Achilles, the son of a goddess; Achilles' withdrawal, however, allows Hector to score enormous victories over the Greeks, culminating in the slaying of Patroclus. When Achilles subsequently rejoins the battle, Hector has grown proud in his achievements and so ignores the advice of his brother Polydamas that he remove the troops from the field. What follows is a complete disaster for the Trojans: those who escape slaughter run headlong back to Troy, leaving Hector alone in Book Twenty-two to face the all-but-invincible Achilles. There, before the gates of Troy as the whole city watches from the walls, harsh reality begins to set in on Hector, who says to himself (22.99-110),

> ὤ μοι ἐγών, εἰ μέν κε πύλας καὶ τείχεα δύω,
> Πουλυδάμας μοι πρῶτος ἐλεγχείην ἀναθήσει, ὅς μ'
> ἐκέλευε Τρωσὶ ποτὶ πτόλιν ἡγήσασθαι νύχθ' ὕπο
> τήνδ' ὀλοήν, ὅτε τ' ὤρετο δῖος' Ἀχιλλεύς. ἀλλ'
> ἐγὼ οὐ πιθόμην· ἦ τ' ἂν πολὺ κέρδιον ἦεν. νῦν δ'
> ἐπεὶ ὤλεσα λαὸν ἀτασθαλίῃσιν ἐμῇσιν, αἰδέομαι
> Τρῶας καὶ Τρῳάδας ἑλκεσιπέπλους, μή ποτέ τις
> εἴπῃσι κακώτερος ἄλλος ἐμεῖο· Ἕκτωρ ἦφι βίηφι
> πιθήσας ὤλεσε λαόν. ὣς ἐρέουσιν· ἐμοὶ δὲ τότ' ἂν
> πολὺ κέρδιον εἴη ἄντην ἢ Ἀχιλῆα κατακτείναντα
> νεέσθαι, ἠὲ κεν αὐτῷ ὀλέσθαι ἐϋκλειῶς πρὸ
> πόληος.

> Ah me, if I go now inside the gates and wall, Polydamas will be the first to reproach me, since he tried to convince me to lead the Trojans back to the city on that fateful night when godlike Achilles rose up. But I would not listen, though it would have been far better had I. Now since I have by my own stupidity destroyed my people, I am ashamed before the Trojans and the Trojan women in their trailing robes, that some lesser man than I will say of me, *Hector put his faith in his own strength, and destroyed his people.* That is what they will say. But for me, it would be much better then to confront Achilles, strike him down, and return, or else to be killed by him in glory before the city.

Generations of readers have rightly admired the determination of Hector to see this heroic challenge through to its fatal end; O'Brien himself writes in *If I Die in a Combat Zone* how hard it is to picture oneself "as the eternal Hector, dying gallantly" (146). Hector's refusal to retreat, however, must not be judged according to a reductive concept of bravery, but rather in terms of competing disincentives, as identified succinctly by Redfield: "Hector's fear of death is overcome by his greater fear of disgrace."[9]

Although a very different set of political circumstances stands in the background, a similar fear of disgrace

overtakes O'Brien as he agonizes on the Rainy River. Like Hector who envisions the ridicule of the Trojans, he imagines his entire community watching and yelling at him, an overwhelming sensation he cannot endure. "I would go to the war," he writes, "—I would kill and maybe die—because I was embarrassed not to" (62). Perhaps somewhat harshly, O'Brien calls himself a coward for giving in to these voices; he knows, though, that he has only chosen the lesser of his fears, stating earlier in the book of soldiers in general, "It was not courage, exactly; the object was not valor. Rather, they were too frightened to be cowards" (21). These thoughts are handled more fully in "Under the Mountain," a chapter from *If I Die in a Combat Zone,* in which the narrator's friend Erik discusses Ezra Pound's "Hugh Selwyn Mauberley" while the pair are still in boot camp at Fort Lewis, Washington. "All this not because of conviction, not for ideology," Erik says,

> rather it's from fear of society's censure, just as Pound claims. Fear of weakness. Fear that to avoid war is to avoid manhood. We come to Fort Lewis afraid to admit we are not Achilles, that we are not brave, not heroes.

(45)

As a consideration of the theoretical roots of heroism shows, the warrior's status is etched round by fears: it is only a matter of which one to give in to, or *not* to give in to, as the case may be. In Book Twenty-two, Hector is quite literally backed up against a wall. Before him lies Achilles and certain doom, behind him the Trojans and intolerable derision. Although he toys temporarily with the fantasy of a settlement, between these options there really is no other—he can be either a dead hero or a live coward. But at the crucial moment, as Achilles bears down, Hector runs. It would be a misinterpretation to see this as the cowardly choice, for it is neither cowardly nor a choice: we must note that, caught between difficult options, Hector does not run back *inside* the walls of Troy but instead *around* them, in this way straddling the line between death and dishonor. Eventually, the goddess Athena fools him into thinking his brother has joined him for the fight; he stops, realizes the trick, and is killed. Nonetheless, Homer's portrait of Hector powerfully captures the unyielding nature of the heroic paradox: the poet renders the warrior's inability to decide in terms of a mad dash around a wall.

Something like this Homeric trope of indecision—Hector's going around in circles—is to be found in O'Brien's work, where it symbolizes much the same thing. In *If I Die in a Combat Zone,* for instance, he writes that, after getting his draft notice in 1968, "Late at night, the town deserted, two or three of us would drive a car around and around the town's lake, talking about the war . . ." (25). O'Brien has employed this image several times in his work, most notably in

"Speaking of Courage" from *The Things They Carried*. In this vignette, the narrator's friend, Norman Bowker, having returned home from the war, spends the Fourth of July driving his father's car around a lake eleven times pondering an important failure of nerve he had experienced in Vietnam. In both places, O'Brien patterns the decision between cowardice or courage in terms much like Hector's run, as a repeated circular motion.[10]

Closer still in spirit to Hector's dilemma is O'Brien's own flight to the Canadian border in **"On the Rainy River."** Throughout the difficult time after getting his draft notice, the narrator feels in himself "a moral split," an overwhelming sensation which, though eventually growing to encompass the world around him, originates in a simple dichotomy: "Run, I'd think. Then I'd think, Impossible. Then a second later I'd think, *Run*." As he continues, "I feared the war, yes, but I also feared exile" (48).[11] Later in the summer, this sense of internal division manifests itself externally, when one day, as he remarks, "I felt something break open in my chest . . . a physical rupture—a cracking-leaking-popping feeling" (49). As a result of this crisis—quite literally a breaking point—O'Brien suddenly takes off, driving north until he reaches Elroy Berdahl's Tip Top Lodge. When O'Brien first sees the old man, his sense of self-division is all the more reinforced, since Berdahl carries a small paring knife, and furthermore, as he notes,

> His eyes had the bluish gray color of a razor blade, the same polished shine, and as he peered up at me I felt a strange sharpness, almost painful, a cutting sensation, as if his gaze were somehow slicing me open.
>
> (51)

While the narrator acknowledges that this sensation is a result in part of guilt, we might also see his description of Berdahl's gaze as the widening of his problem from the personal to the cosmic. So great is the crisis which O'Brien feels—so strong is his sense of the dilemma facing him—that he feels it is visible to the people he meets. Indeed, this "moral split" which has already affected his body he now even senses in the landscape, as he waits for resolution by "the Rainy River, which separates Minnesota from Canada, and which for me separated one life from another" (50).

It is in this ambivalent region, poised between conflicting visions of his future—balanced precariously at the Tip Top, as it were—that O'Brien wrestles with his conscience. Here, where he describes himself as "half awake, half dreaming," his riven mental state is figured strongly by his liminal status: we might recognize that the dilemma which Hector in the *Iliad* faced (and never resolved for himself) was rendered in topographical terms, as it is here by O'Brien, who envisions himself "on the margins of exile," and "[g]etting chased by the Border Patrol" (53).[12] At this excruciating point in the

narrative, Elroy Berdahl takes O'Brien out for a fishing trip on the highly symbolic Rainy River. As the small motorboat makes its way upstream, O'Brien realizes "that at some point we must've passed into Canadian waters, across that dotted line between two different worlds" (58). The narrator surmises that, in bringing the situation to this point, Berdahl had taken him "to the edge" and would watch "as I chose a life for myself" (58). He chooses Vietnam rather than Canada—that is, fight rather than flight—making the same decision Hector did, though by surviving, he avoids Hector's fate. In forcing O'Brien's decision between the difficult options before him, Berdahl re-enacts the role which Athena had played in Hector's final moments, though the old man with the sharp gray eyes is more benevolent to his charge than the gray-eyed goddess had been. "He was a witness, like God, or like the gods," writes O'Brien, "who look on in absolute silence as we live our lives, as we make our choices or fail to make them" (62).

Though these gods seem more Lucretian than Homeric, perhaps the author has consciously drawn on the *Iliad* for these remarks. In this context, it is worth noting Homer's description of the divine audience watching Hector's final moments (22.158-166):

> πρόσθε μὲν ἐσθλὸς ἔφευγε, δίωκε δέ μιν μέγ᾽ ἀμείνων
> καρπαλίμως, ἐπεὶ οὐχ ἱερήϊον οὐδὲ βοείην
> ἀρνύσθην, ἅ τε ποσσὶν ἀέθλια γίγνεται ἀνδρῶν,
> ἀλλὰ περὶ ψυχῆς θέον Ἕκτορος ἱπποδάμοιο.
> ὡς δ᾽ ὅτ᾽ ἀεθλοφόροι περὶ τέρματα μώνυχες ἵπποι
> ῥίμφα μάλα τρωχῶσι· τὸ δὲ μέγα κεῖται ἄεθλον
> ἢ τρίπος ἠὲ γυνὴ ἀνδρὸς κατατεθνηῶτος·
> ὡς τὼ τρὶς Πριάμοιο πόλιν περιδινηθήτην
> καρπαλίμοισι πόδεσσι· θεοὶ δ᾽ ἐς πάντες ὁρῶντο·

> It was a great man who fled, but far better he who pursued him
> rapidly, since here was no festal beast, no ox-hide
> they strove for, which are the prizes that are given men for racing.
> No, they are running for the life of Hector, breaker of horses.
> As when about the turnposts racehorses with uncloven hooves
> run at full speed, since a great prize is laid up for their winning,
> a tripod or a woman, in games for a man's funeral,
> so these two swept whirling about the city of Priam
> in the speed of their feet, while all the gods were looking upon them.

As his moment of crisis, O'Brien feels that he too is surrounded by a roaring stadium crowd "[l]ike some weird sporting event" (60), and that the gaze of a civic pantheon which includes Abraham Lincoln, Saint George, the U.S. Senate, and LBJ, falls upon him. Numbered among these cultural luminaries is "a blind poet scribbling notes" (60). Very likely this description refers to Robert Frost's famous reading at the inauguration of President Kennedy, but does not the epithet "blind" also bring to mind the blind poet of Chios, Homer himself?

As an issue of interpretation, however, it can hardly matter whether or not O'Brien alludes deliberately to Homer. Because all wars result in widespread destruction and death, survivors "shape their own discoveries of war into patterns first to be found in Homer," as classicist James Tatum once noted in *The Yale Review*.[13] Both Homer and O'Brien portray the experience of those who must come to grips with the dilemma courage imposes: on the one hand is the loss of face, on the other, the loss of life. For Homer, the debate which rages within Hector's heart about these difficulties is dramatized as a race around the walls of a city which his hero cannot honorably enter. This same debate is felt inside Tim O'Brien's heart as well and manifests itself bodily, growing so large at last that it requires the natural and political boundary dividing a continent to describe it. In each work, the authors imagine such divisions of self in broadly geographical terms, as their protagonists negotiate the no-man's land between the antitheses described by O'Brien so well: "War makes you a man; war makes you dead" (*The Things They Carried,* 87).

Notes

1. Works of Tim O'Brien which will be referred to *infra* are: *The Things They Carried: A Work of Fiction* (Boston: Houghton Mifflin, 1990) and *If I Die in a Combat Zone, Box Me Up and Ship Me Home* (New York: Dell Pub. Co., 1973). Translations from Greek are the author's own. For their help with this piece, the author would like to thank Kelly Malone, David Gill, S. J., and *CML*'s editor and anonymous referee.

2. See Steven Kaplan, *Understanding Tim O'Brien* (Columbia: U of South Carolina Pr, 1995), 169-192; Don Ringnalda, *Fighting and Writing the Vietnam War* (Jackson: University Pr of Mississippi, 1994), 90-114; and Catherine Calloway, "'How to Tell a True War Story': Metafiction in *The Things They Carried,*" *Critique* 36 (1995): 249-257. For a recent Marxist critique of this postmodern position, see Jim Neilson, *Warring Fictions: American Literary Culture and the Vietnam War Narrative* (Jackson: University Pr of Mississippi, 1998), 191-209.

3. Kaplan (above, note 1) 185.

4. O'Brien has called Shay's book "one of the most original and most important scholarly works to

have emerged from the Vietnam war," although he does not consider his own work to be therapeutic (1990: 179).

5. E. R. Dodds, *The Greeks and the Irrational* (Berkeley: U of California Pr, 1951), 17.

6. James M. Redfield, *Nature and Culture in the Iliad: The Tragedy of Hector,* enlarged edition (Durham: Duke U Pr, 1994), 101.

7. See Achilles' famous response to Odysseus, *Iliad* 9.307-429, especially 318-322.

8. See Redfield (above, note 5) 119, who notes, "Hector is a warrior not because he loves war but because he is before all else a hero of *aidos.*"

9. Redfield (above, note 5) 115.

10. The various revisions of "Speaking of Courage" have been expertly charted by Mark Taylor, "Tim O'Brien's War," *The Centennial Review* 39 (Summer 1995): 213-230, who notes that the

    circles around the lake suggest the endlessness and purposelessness of the Vietnam War to those who fought it . . . and the undifferentiated moments of life afterwards for many veterans. These circles also suggest O'Brien's going round and round the central events of his own wartime experience, and of his imagination, working tirelessly to get it right, to find the truth, to display the meaning he wishes to display.

    (218)

11. On exile in O'Brien's work, see especially Tina Chen, "'Unraveling the Deeper Meaning': Exile and the Embodied Poetics of Displacement in Tim O'Brien's *The Things They Carried,*" *Contemporary Literature* 39 (1998): 77-98.

12. Ringnalda (above, note 1) 101-102 has explicated "On the Rainy River" as a description of "liminal uncertainty" conveying the ambiguity between genres of truth and fiction. Typically, Ringnalda overstates his case: "O'Brien knows that reality is accessible *only* through mediation. That being the case, he spurns the Western paradigm of Manichaean dualism, which convinces most of the people most of the time that they can tell the difference between reality and fiction" (104). Is Manichaean dualism really "Western"? See the penetrating critique of Neilson (above, note 1) 200-203 on this point.

13. James Tatum, "The *Iliad* and Memories of War," *The Yale Review* 76 (1986): 16.

John H. Timmerman (essay date spring 2000)

SOURCE: Timmerman, John H. "Tim O'Brien and the Art of the True War Story: 'Night March' and 'Speaking of Courage'." *Twentieth Century Literature* 46, no. 1 (spring 2000): 100-14.

[*In the following essay, Timmerman compares the conflict between the reality of war and normal life as portrayed in "Night March" and "Speaking of Courage,"* *which appear in* The Things They Carried.]

The Vietnam war story is not simply about the rise and fall of nations (South Vietnam, North Vietnam, Laos, China, Thailand, the United States, the Soviet Union). Rather, it is about the rise and fall of the dreams of individual soldiers—their hopes riddled by disillusionment, their fantasies broken by shrapnel-edged realities. In his *Fighting and Writing the Vietnam War,* Don Rignalda observes that Washington engaged in the war as a clinical and statistical commodity: "We imposed a carpentered reality on a country (South Vietnam) that wasn't a country at all, but merely a recent, diplomatically created abstraction run by a series of corrupt puppets. Oblivious, Americans became 'cartomaniacs' in Vietnam" (14). Having reduced the Washington-created enemy to ciphers, the cartomaniacs did precisely the same thing to the American soldier. In a war fought according to statistics, and where ciphers are thrown against ciphers, who is left to tell the true war story? Who enters the lives and uncovers the dreams, the dark secrets, the fears and the hopes that bestow personality back on the cipher?

Certainly it is possible to engage the experience of war exclusively on scholarly and academic terms, to configure the experience according to statistics and historical accounts. Every time human experience is rendered as fact, however, the human place in was becomes more abstracted and more simplistic. In "We're Adjusted Too Well," Tim O'Brien voiced his dismay that the nation's hope for everything to slide back into some vague state of being "normal"—or "adjusted"—has been fulfilled all too well. For his part, O'Brien says, "I wish we were more troubled" (207). If American society is no longer troubled, if it has exorcised a segment of our historical past, it has also occluded something of our human nature. War stories must evoke the dreams and lives of individual soldiers, as opposed to giving a statistical or historical accounting of data.

This telling raises several aesthetic questions. Can one capture the reality of the event in such a way that the reader imaginatively participates in it? Is there a point where the imaginative life evokes a greater reality than the factual accounting, so that the reader understands not only what happened but also why it happened and how it affected the soldier? Furthermore, as the war recedes into the past, can the writer preserve an authentic memory of it, free from romantic idealism or bitter cynicism? Or are we better off letting it slide, as two of

O'Brien's characters (the fathers of Paul Berlin and Norman Bowker) suggest?

A gap inevitably opens up between the imaginary casting of an event (the fictive event) and the factual details of that event (the historical chronicle). That forces of the First Cavalry Division, for example, combined with CIDG soldiers to kill 753 NVA regulars near Fire Base Jamie on December 6, 1969, is the historical chronicle. What happened in the hearts and minds of the soldiers who fought that battle is not conveyed by clinical data. To uncover that is the task of fiction.

This is precisely the task that Tim O'Brien undertakes.

The essential dialectic of the war story lies in this interplay between reality as data and the reality of the human spirit. O'Brien aims for nothing less than resolving this dialectic into an integrated whole, often by means of a metafictional discourse in which his characters and narrators engage in the dialectic themselves. Two notable examples are his companion short stories **"Night March"** and **"Speaking of Courage,"** both of which pose a fundamental distinction between the fact of what "actually" happened and the reality experienced by the individual.

Examining these two works also raises questions about how the true war story can be told. Is the disparity between personal experience and the historical facticity of war irresolvable? Or is it possible to achieve some integration, and if so, how? Such questions further define the complementary and conflicting elements of these two stories. After examining the stories, therefore, I will consider what in general constitutes the true war story for Tim O'Brien.

"Night March" is O'Brien's most widely anthologized story. It first appeared in *Redbook* in May 1975 under the title **"Where Have You Gone, Charming Billy?"** and was revised to become a chapter of *Going After Cacciato* in 1978. It still stands independently, but in *Going After Cacciato* it is woven seamlessly into the rather wide-ranging plot of one man's imaginary long walk away from war. All the stories in *Cacciato* stem from Paul Berlin's reflections while on observation post. Past horrors and present dreams (echoing the book's epigraph from Sassoon) buckle together at the moment of "observing." But at that moment, Paul Berlin's actual goal, we are told, is simply to live long enough to escape to the real world. What constitutes the real world is the essential issue.

The internal tensions of the war story **"Night March"** may best be understood by comparing it to O'Brien's postwar story **"Speaking of Courage."** First published in the Summer 1976 issue of *Massachusetts Review* and then in *Prize Stories* and *The O. Henry Awards* in 1978, **"Speaking of Courage"** finally became a part of O'Brien's 1990 work *The Things They Carried.* The two stories are connected in several ways. For example, the 1976 version of **"Speaking of Courage"** reprises chapter 14 of *Going After Cacciato,* where Paul Berlin thinks he could have won the Silver Star if he had rescued Frenchie Tucker. In **"Speaking of Courage,"** Norman Bowker thinks he could have won the Silver Star if he had rescued Kiowa. But neither Berlin nor Bowker rescued, and neither won. Like men on plastic ponies at the carousel, they hang suspended, bouncing up and down between reality and fantasy.

More pointedly, however, both stories address a conflict between the reality of war and the reality of normal, civilized life. In **"Night March,"** Paul Berlin tries to deny the reality of the war he is in so that he can survive. He endures his war life by a daily pretending, a fantastic escape not unlike Cacciato's imaginary trip to Paris. He insists that his primary reality lies elsewhere, in what the infantrymen in Vietnam called "the World." The World is a state of mind—an absence of fear and conflict, an idealized place that really exists nowhere. For Cacciato the imaginary utopia is Paris; for the average infantryman like Paul Berlin, it is simply the United States.

This displacement of reality through insistence on the unreality of the war becomes necessary to survive. Each individual is forced to supply his or her own reasons for personal actions and the personal meanings of those actions as well. For example, *The Things They Carried* first introduces a young Vietnamese soldier in **"Spin,"** and then, nine chapters later, in **"The Man I Killed,"** the narrator details killing this soldier and creates a short hypothetical biography for him—a "past" used to escape the reality of his death. The next chapter, **"Ambush,"** suggests that perhaps the man is not really dead after all. Finally, near the end of the book and after three more variations of the event, the narrator's nine-year-old daughter beseeches him, "'Daddy, tell the truth. . . . Did you ever kill anybody?'" The narrator reflects that he "can say, honestly, 'Of course not.'" But then again, he "can say, honestly, 'yes'" (204). The tension is unnerving. There are too many vagaries in war. How then does the writer work toward the "true" war story?

In an interview, O'Brien reflects on the dialectic between reality and fantasy as an essential state of the war novel. The war novel contains an element of surreality in order to deny the horror. O'Brien observes that

> In war, the rational faculty begins to diminish . . . and what takes over is surrealism, the life of the imagination. The mind of the soldier becomes part of the experience—the brain seems to flow out of your head, join-

ing the elements around you on the battlefield. It's like stepping outside yourself. War *is* a surreal experience, therefore it seems quite natural and proper for a writer to render some of its aspects in a surreal way.

(qtd. in McCaffrey 135)

Moreover, citing *The Red Badge of Courage* as an example, O'Brien adds that "Every war seems formless to the men fighting it" (135). So soldiers dream; they pretend and deny in order to diminish the horror. Precisely because it captures that human reality in the midst of war and unbelievable horror, O'Brien claims that "*Cacciato* is the most realistic thing I've written. The life of the imagination is *real*" (142). The life of the imagination is real precisely because it embraces the experience, moving beyond factual data.

"Night March" is an "interior" war story—the story of a combat participant immediately involved in the war. From the outset, the story is couched in denials and pretending. Reality, after all, lies in that ambiguous other place, the World. As the **"Night March"** platoon moves in "the dark, single file," as if in an actual nightmare, the pattern of negation intensifies: "There was no talking now. No more jokes" (*Cacciato* 186). At the same time, Paul Berlin's denial of the fact of war intensifies: "He was pretending he was not in the war. And later, he pretended, it would be morning, and there would not be a war" (186). The negations develop through the early stages of the story, often closing off a paragraph of objective description by the omniscient narrator, as if each stab at engaging the fact of war is deflected by an act of will. The mind of Paul Berlin clutches on the negatives: "There was not yet a moon" (187); "So he tried not to think" (187); "He would not be afraid ever again" (188).

The reality of war that Paul Berlin struggles to avoid, however, will not disappear. O'Brien lets it slip into the first paragraph almost accidentally, as if flitting momentarily through the gates of denial erected in Berlin's mind: "Pretending he had not watched Billy Boy Watkins die of fright on the field of battle" (186). Historical fact keeps leaking through, even as the denials mount. It even comes as snatches of a song: "Where have you gone, Billy Boy, Billy Boy." Bits and pieces of the grim fact keep intruding: this is war; Billy Boy Watkins died.

Denying Billy Boy Watkins's death, however, is necessary in order for Paul Berlin to deny his own relentless fear. Soldiers are supposed to be brave, after all. And Paul Berlin tries mightily to keep the pose of bravery: "He would laugh when the others made jokes about Billy Boy, and he would not be afraid ever again" (188). But like the darkness, fear envelopes him. "The trick," Paul Berlin reflects, "was not to take it personally" (188). But such a trick is impossible.

Paul Berlin wishes that some day he may be courageous enough to laugh at death. Through laughter he might be absolved of fear. It is not coincidental that tragicomedy has surfaced as a subgenre in war literature. Tragicomedy as a literary mode essentially sees the world as an evil place; the necessary human response to it is laughter, for laughter holds evil in abeyance and demarcates the wholeness of the individual human. A good description of the genre arises in Ken Kesey's tragicomic novel *One Flew over the Cuckoo's Nest* where the embattled Randal Patrick MacMurphy, who, incidentally, led an escape from a prison camp during the Korean War, exclaims, "When you lose your laugh, you lose your footing" (65).

A tragicomic scene in **"Night March"** offers contrasting reactions to the reality of war. A "child-faced" soldier (Cacciato), smelling of Doublemint gum—that keen reminder of the World—creeps up to Paul Berlin and offers him a stick of gum. As Cacciato and Berlin relax and chew their gum, Cacciato begins whistling tunelessly. He isn't even aware of his whistling. The whistling is contrasted to Paul's giggling. Whereas Berlin is painfully aware of his own giggling, Cacciato is oblivious to his whistling. While Berlin fights, and fails, to escape the present fact of war, Cacciato seems to do so naturally. He seems to have escaped to his imaginary reality.

The question of time arises. Neither Berlin nor Cacciato has a watch. Cacciato says "Time goes faster when you don't know the time" (215) and remembers that Billy Boy Watkins owned two watches. But Billy Boy is dead. Even with two watches he doesn't know the time. The irony wrenches the two soldiers into a confrontation with the fact of Billy Boy's death.

This was no ordinary death. All along Paul Berlin has been fighting his personal fear, but Billy Boy actually died of fear: "A heart attack! You hear Doc say that? A heart attack on the field of battle, isn't that what Doc said?" (192). The very fear they feared most had, in fact, gripped and killed Billy Boy Watkins. Dozens of horrible ways to die, and he died of fear.

Suddenly Paul Berlin begins to giggle—suffocating, spasmodic laughter that has him helpless in the grass:

> He giggled. He couldn't stop it, so he giggled, and he imagined it clearly. He imagined the medic's report. He imagined Billy's surprise. He giggled, imagining Billy's father opening the telegram: SORRY TO INFORM YOU THAT YOUR SON BILLY BOY WAS YESTERDAY SCARED TO DEATH IN ACTION IN THE REPUBLIC OF VIETNAM. Yes, he could imagine it clearly.
>
> He giggled. He rolled onto his belly and pressed his face in the wet grass and giggled, he couldn't help it.
>
> (193)

To survive his own fear Paul Berlin battles it with laughter. But it is laughter on the verge of hysteria; since nothing makes any sense, all one can do is laugh.

As he lies giggling on the grass, now watching the clouds pass over the moon, marking the passing of time and the nightmare, Paul Berlin now imagines himself talking with his father. As in **"Speaking of Courage,"** the absent father is one of the most important characters in this story. He represents both a confessor figure and also an incarnation of personal and moral values in a war without apparent purpose or value. And now Paul Berlin finds a way to respond to this father:

> Giggling, lying now on his back, Paul Berlin saw the moon move. He could not stop. Was it the moon? Or the clouds moving, making the moon seem to move? Or the boy's round face, pressing him, forcing out the giggles. "It wasn't so bad," he would tell his father. "I was a man. I saw it the first day, the very first day at the war, I saw all of it from the start, I learned it, and it wasn't so bad, and later on, later on it got better, later on, once I learned the tricks, later on it wasn't so bad." He couldn't stop.
>
> (194-95)

The moon clouds up again. The column moves on. Cacciato—to this point unnamed, a scarcely seen visitant called "the boy"—hands Paul Berlin a stick of Black Jack gum—"the precious stuff." And then we learn the boy's name with his ironic jest: "'You'll do fine,' Cacciato said. 'You will. You got a terrific sense of humor'" (195)—ironic in that it was fear, not humor, that provoked Berlin's uncontrolled giggling.

The moral argument that the horrors of war so threaten human sensibility that they must be escaped by fantasy or fought by laughter (both of which Berlin does with only limited success) is precisely reversed by the conditions of the postwar story. Having now arrived back in the World, the ideal world always dreamed of during the war, the veteran discovers that he carries with him the undeniable fact of war. He cannot escape the memory. Oddly, the present world now becomes the fantasy; the past war has become the reality. The fantasy is engendered by the simple fact that people in the world have chosen to deny the reality of the war; they don't want to hear about it. Least of all do they want to hear about it from the returned veteran, which would make their abstracted, statistical notions of war altogether too real.

Other thematic patterns of **"Night March"** survive intact in **"Speaking of Courage."** Norman Bowker was originally Paul Berlin. Like Paul Berlin, he has struggled with courage and cowardice. He too seeks a confessor-father into whose ears he wants to pour his story. But in this carefully crafted tale, all of civilization seems to block the telling, and thereby to deny reality to Norman Bowker.

Such a story requires a different sort of telling. The nightmare of the observation post and the circling memories are now replaced by the tranquillity of the home town and Bowker's circling drive around the lake, encapsulating the weary circularity of his own life and mind. Paul Berlin's desperate effort to escape time in **"Night March"** is replaced by Bowker's uncanny ability to tell time from the feel of the day—or night. Paul Berlin in fact shares Norman Bowker's preternatural ability to "feel" the time. However, during the conflation of memories that occurs during his stint on observation post duty from midnight to 6 a.m., time itself seems suspended as the surreal images glide in and out of his mind. Norman Bowker is never separated from the consciousness of time, now that he has nothing to do, nowhere to go, little to fill up the hours except aimless traveling. While Paul Berlin sought to deny time, Bowker seems trapped in a psychological clock, ticking off meaningless hours.

The difference in how one apprehends time also mirrors the difference between fact and fantasy. Eric Schroeder makes a distinction "between time past and time present and . . . this becomes complicated by the introduction of another temporal dimension: time imagined." The result, Schroeder points out, is an indeterminacy about "not only when a particular event happened, but whether it happened" ("The Past and the Possible" 124). Just as Paul Berlin imagines life in the World occurring simultaneously during his six hours on observation post, so too Bowker attempts to reconstruct his present in the World by conflating past realities and imaginary time—what might have been.

We see, then, several points of comparison developing between the two stories. **"Night March"** shows a soldier, Paul Berlin, during the war; **"Speaking of Courage"** shows a soldier, Norman Bowker, after the war. Paul Berlin attempts to escape the reality of war through fantasy, particularly that of the World; Norman Bowker finds that even though he is in the World, he cannot escape the reality of war. Both characters attempt to escape time; both develop a preternatural ability to "feel" time; and neither can fully escape time imagined—that is, the reality of personal events that shape the entirety of their lives.

Furthermore, Paul Berlin reacts to his immediate world of war by trying to drive back fear with laughter, even though it borders on hysteria. Norman Bowker finds himself in a grim, absurdist world where nobody listens to what he has to say. *The Things They Carried* is very much a novel about telling one's story into an apparent abyss. How does one tell the truth about war when no one wants to listen? Here lies the essential issue for the writer of the true war story. The issue is complicated, however, by the very question of whether language and narrative are adequate to tell the story. Thus the narrative in both stories is roughly circular, replaying events, lurching into indecision, in an effort to get the true story woven into a whole.

"Speaking of Courage" opens on Norman Bowker cruising around the lake one Fourth of July: "The war was over and there was no particular place to go" (*The Things They Carried* [*TTC*] 157). Whereas in **"Night March"** there is a denial of place, in this story there is no place to go. The World is everywhere the same as Bowker remembers it, but it is now perceived as flat—the sameness becomes empty, for all of it is seen through memory shaped by war. Aimlessly, like a patrol without direction, he wheels his father's "big Chevy" on its seven-mile loop around the lake. The lake itself is flatly prosaic—a nondescript midwestern lake that was "a good audience for silence" (158). Thus the central metaphor is established—an aimless, circular traveling around a vast silence. Readers of O'Brien's *If I Die in a Combat Zone* will recognize the same pattern in chapter 3 of that work, where O'Brien recalls driving around the lake before being drafted, weighing his own options, "moving with care from one argument to the next" (25). In **"Speaking of Courage,"** the "smooth July water, and an immense flatness everywhere" (*TTC* 159) suggest the same uncertainty in the returned veteran's life.

As he travels, Norman Bowker's mind aimlessly circles around patterns of recollection. The first involves his prewar memory, imaged specifically in his boyhood sweetheart, Sally Kramer, now Mrs. Sally Gustafson. Norman spots her working in her yard and almost pulls over "just to talk." But knowing "there was really nothing he could say to her" (159), he accelerates past. Sally represents things lost, the way things might have been, and also, perhaps, a measure of Norman's internal change.

So too Norman measures the town by the huge psychological distance he has grown from it. The town is home, but "The town seemed remote somehow. Sally was married and Max [his boyhood friend] was drowned and his father was home watching baseball on national TV" (159). While the World falls into its holiday routines, Norman Bowker wanders slightly apart from it all. He is the Prufrockian man, alone in a world undisturbed by his anguish, and like Eliot's Prufrock, he also finds that "It is impossible to say just what I mean." What he says is that tired phrase that passed the lips of countless Vietnam soldiers when faced with yet one more impossible task—a polite, meaningless phrase rippling with undertones of anguish: "'No problem,' he muttered" (159). No problem: it was an act of denial in order to survive—a lie then, a lie now. His aimless circling works then to demonstrate Norman Bowker's inability to settle back into the routine of the World and exemplifies the psychological distance between his former and present selves.

The second pattern evoked by his aimless wandering is the recollection of war. The imagined meeting with Sally initiates a recollection of Norman's war experience, but like Paul Berlin's, this experience is couched in terms of denial: "He would not say a word about how he'd almost won the Silver Star for valor" (160). The need to speak of it, however, is nearly overwhelming, so Norman Bowker invents a conversation with his father: the way things should have been. The third pattern in the story, then, develops the imaginary confession. The war story is spoken into unhearing ears, signaled by the change in verbs: they all become "might have" or "would have." The discourse takes place wholly in the fantasy world.

What people would have heard, if only they had listened, was Norman Bowker's story of how he had courage, of how he almost saved his friend Kiowa, except for the terrible stink of the shitfield. His father was the appropriate one to initiate the hearing, for his father also knew the truth of war: "that many brave men did not win medals for their bravery, and that others won medals for doing nothing" (160). But his father is a disappeared self for Norman Bowker—the person who, himself having had no one to listen, has buried the stories and adopted the routine manners of the present by no longer listening. Norman Bowker's father is immersed in his own pointless circularity, watching players on TV circle the bases in the great national pastime.

Nonetheless, Norman Bowker mentally relates his story to the imagined confessor-father. Recounting the experience in the muck field, he pauses before the worst parts:

> "Sounds pretty wet," his father would've said, pausing briefly. "So what happened?"
>
> "You sure you want to hear this?"
>
> "Hey, I'm your *father.*"
>
> (162)

This father murmurs, "Slow and sweet, take your time," and Norman slows the big Chevy, the mechanical replacement for his father, on the circular road. He observes the fireworks under preparation for the Fourth of July celebration. Stories start to converge. As he nears the actual fireworks the remembered story of the mortar attack in the muck field intensifies. Oddly, Sally Kramer-Gustafson momentarily intrudes as the imagined listener. But she is too much of the present. She couldn't listen, Norman Bowker realizes, for the reality of war is too powerful, too overwhelming, too *truthful*. She would wince even at the language. But his father, were his father here listening, would understand "perfectly well that it was not a question of offensive language but of fact. His father would have sighed and folded his arms and waited" (165). It is a matter of how to tell a true war story; the facts themselves are offensive, not the language that directs the facts. Finally Norman Bowker, after recollecting Kiowa's death, realizes: "A good war story, . . . but it was not a war for

war stories, nor for talk of valor, and nobody in town wanted to know about the terrible stink. They wanted good intentions and good deeds. But the town was not to blame, really. It was a nice little town, very prosperous, with neat houses and all the sanitary conveniences" (169).

After his seventh circle of the lake, Norman Bowker pulls into a drive-in restaurant for something to eat. Ironically, he is as ignorant of procedures at the drive-in as the patrons there are of his war. The conflict of realities is almost perfectly, heart-breakingly, completed. He honks his horn for the car-hop girl: "The girl sighed, leaned down, and shook her head. Her eyes were as fluffy and airy-light as cotton candy" (170). Condescendingly she points to the intercom and asks, "You blind?" Yes. Indeed. By virtue of his war experience, Norman is now blind to the ways of the world. He'll never see straight again; it will always be circular, through the crooked paths of a memory he can neither deny nor express.

The irony intensifies, for the abstracted voice over the intercom rasps at Norman in field communications from the war. The phrases clip out: "Affirmative, copy clear." "Roger-dodger." "Fire for effect. Stand by." The gulf between the intercom voice and Norman's sensibility is nearly overwhelming. The war reality is reduced to a game.

Nonetheless, the very abstractedness of that voice stirs Norman. It is just a piece of metal and some strange electronics next to the Chevy window. Still, through it a voice asks, "Hey, loosen up. . . . What you really need, friend?" And for a moment, in this weird electronic confessional, Norman almost tells:

> "Well," he said, "how'd you like to hear about—"
>
> He stopped and shook his head.
>
> "Hear *what,* man?"
>
> "Nothing."
>
> (171)

He cannot get it out, not even to this depersonalized voice over the intercom, which, oddly enough, mimics the listening father Norman longs for.

Norman drives slowly away, the longing to tell now a deep, pervasive ache inside:

> If it had been possible, which it wasn't, he would have explained how his friend Kiowa slipped away that night beneath the dark swampy field. He was folded in with the war; he was part of the waste.
>
> Turning on his headlights, driving slowly, Norman Bowker remembered how he had taken hold of Kiowa's boot and pulled hard, but how the smell was simply too much, and how he'd backed off and in that way had lost the Silver Star.

He wished he could've explained some of this. How he had been braver than he ever thought possible, but how he had not been so brave as he wanted to be. The distinction was important. Max Arnold, who loved fine lines, would've appreciated it. And his father, who already knew, would've nodded.

                                                                            (172)

The longing is buried, however, deep in memory. As the war story coils back inside his brain, he stops the Chevy, walks out into the water of the lake like one trying to baptize himself into a new reality, then stands and watches the fireworks, the town's own little fantasy battle. "For a small town, he decided, it was a pretty good show" (173).

"Night March" and **"Speaking of Courage"** represent two angles of vision on the Vietnam war experience. One a war story, the other a postwar story, they are juxtaposed in patterns of denial and affirmation. From the perspective of Paul Berlin, the immediacy of war must be denied in order to retain the reality of a world where sanity and peace still hold sway. From that of Norman Bowker, the world to which he has returned is deaf to his war experience. But the stories are also very much about the literary art of telling a true war story. Examination of the artistry of the stories is incomplete without consideration of the larger aesthetic issue toward which all the elements point. In fact, each story becomes a metafiction: they are about the process of telling war stories as much as they are war stories themselves. This is a fundamental issue that O'Brien has grappled with and cogently defined during the development of his career: how to tell the true war story.

The Vietnam war was different from earlier wars, and so posed challenges to the writer that often pushed him or her beyond the limits of conventional literary stereotypes. Dennis Vannatta remarks that "part of the problem that fiction writers have had is trying to build an artistic structure around a war that lacks the familiar geometry of clearly established battle lines, troop movements, and advances and retreats" (242). Steven Kaplan observes that "almost all of the literature on the war . . . makes clear that the only certain thing during the Vietnam War was that nothing was certain" (43). Oddly, the very uncertainties also provided a certain liberation for the fiction writer. It was possible to speak more freely of courage, of cowardice, of fears and fantasies.

The combat veteran who writes of combat writes from both inside and outside the experience. Chapter 30 of *Cacciato* provides an interesting gloss on this fact, for by that point in the book, the reader understands that the term *observation post* is multidimensional in meaning. Literally it is the elevated spot one climbs to in order to observe possible enemy action. But during the long night hours it is also a spot for reflective observa-

tion on the war itself. And the observation post is also a self-reflective place. In chapter 30, Berlin had been fiddling with the optics on the night-vision goggles but now is playing a time-guessing game. Vision and time unify all the reflections of the observation post. Now Paul reflects: "It was a matter of hard observation separating illusion from reality. What happened, and what might have happened" (247). He goes on to wonder why evil things happen, and never the pretty things, and then agrees with Doc Peret's view "that observation requires inward-looking, a study of the very machinery of observation" (247-48). Insight and vision, and Paul wonders, "where was the fulcrum? Where did it tilt from fact to imagination?" (248). The writer undertakes such observation, trying to balance the outside and inside vision, fact and imagination. Such is also the basic strategy for O'Brien's linking independent stories into the thematically unified novel.

The process of the inside and outside vision bears particular significance for O'Brien's **The Things They Carried,** for here the writer is very much aware of himself writing fiction about a historical reality he himself experienced. The writer abruptly introduces himself into the text—"I'm forty-three years old, and a writer now, and the war has been over for a long while" (36). Of course, this may be construed simply as a narrative pose. As Catherine Calloway has pointed out, substantial biographical details of the author differ from those of the narrator (250). Furthermore, in the concluding notes to **The Things They Carried,** O'Brien again introduces himself as the forty-three-year-old writer, but tells us that "almost everything else is invented." But he insists "it's not a game. It's a form" (203).

Maria S. Bonn points out that "The dizzying interplay of truth and fiction in this novel is not solely aesthetic postmodern gamesmanship but a form that is a thematic continuation of the author's concern throughout his career with the power and capability of story" (13). While soldiers carry many things into battle, as the book's initial chapter details, they also carry many things *from* battle. In this case, the writer carries stories, sometimes "odd little fragments that have no beginning and no end" (*TTC* 39), which, like the fragmented war itself, he seeks to place into some kind of order. The writer observes:

> Forty-three years old, and the war occurred half a lifetime ago, and yet the remembering makes it now. And sometimes remembering will lead to a story, which makes it forever. That's what stories are for. Stories are for joining the past to the future. Stories are for those late hours in the night when you can't remember how you got from where you were to where you are. Stories are for eternity, when memory is erased, when there is nothing to remember except the story.

                                                                            (40)

While bits and pieces of the writer flicker in and out of the narration, at one point O'Brien stops the narration altogether and addresses the act of writing itself in **"How to Tell a True War Story"** (*TTC* 73-91). He establishes several qualities of the true war story, but the first one seems to contradict what he has said elsewhere about the story's engagement with philosophical and moral substance. In one interview, for example, O'Brien claims that "The writer needs a passionate and knowledgeable concern for the substance of what's witnessed, and that includes the spiritual and theological and political implications of raw experience" (qtd. in McCaffery 137). And in another interview, he points out that "My concerns have to do with abstractions: what's courage and how do you get it? What's justice and how do you achieve it? How does one do right in an evil situation?" (qtd. in Schroeder, "Two Interviews" 145).

But there is a difference between exploring the moral meanings of humans confronting battle and the didactic reduction of that confrontation to moral precept. The true war story, O'Brien says, "does not instruct, nor encourage virtue, nor suggest models of proper human behavior, nor restrain men from doing the things men have always done. If a story seems moral, do not believe it" (*TTC* 76). Truth to experience is a higher aesthetic value than moral precept. Moral lessons are not given by the writer. Rather, the writer's task is to represent experience authentically so that others understand the event, and from that understanding they may, if they choose, adduce their own moral lessons.

This is particularly true regarding courage, the vexing issue before Paul Berlin and Norman Bowker. What actually constitutes courage? Perhaps that's the wrong question because it's too easy to give categorical responses. Either Paul or Norman might have won the Silver Star—a physical representation of an act of courage. Much harder is to assess courage as a quality of human nature itself, yet that is the task O'Brien sets for himself. In an interview, O'Brien says that "Courage interpenetrates the whole fabric of a life. To take a strand out and say this is courage and this is something else violates a central humanness" (qtd. in Naparsteck 4). If there is an ethics of writing for O'Brien, it assumes that the highest moral imperative for the writer is an authentic revelation of human nature.

A second challenge to the writer of the true war story arises precisely out of that effort toward authenticity. Every event is recalled by the intellect and as the emotions experienced during the event; writing involves, as Hemingway understood, the head and the heart. O'Brien puts the challenge like this: "In any war story, but especially a true one, it's difficult to separate what happened from what seemed to happen. What seems to happen becomes its own happening and has to be told that way. The angles of vision are skewed" (*TTC* 78). The difficulty is precisely enacted through Paul Berlin in *Cacciato*. The story is as much about the fantasy of war as it is about the so-called reality. Soldiers are dreamers: that dreaming is a part of their reality, what O'Brien calls "that surreal seemingness" (*Cacciato* 78). Paradoxically, as Steven Kaplan has observed, the war fiction becomes "more real than the events upon which it is based" (46) when the life of the imagination arranges the experience of the facts. Literary art is never straightforward fact; rather, it arranges facts to communicate what the author wishes to seem true for the reader.

A third trait of the true war story, according to O'Brien, might be called its fundamental inconclusiveness. "You can tell a true war story," O'Brien writes, "by the way it never seems to end. Not then, not ever" (*TTC* 83). Vietnam gave the lie to tidy endings. It lingers yet in the minds of veterans, sneaking up during unprotected moments. It lingers for them precisely as it does for Norman Bowker. Thus, the true war story resists reduction to generalized moral statements. As O'Brien observes, "In the end, really, there's nothing much to say about a true war story, except maybe 'Oh'" (*TTC* 84).

The true war story tells the things that happen to real people. They might, out of abject fear and loneliness, dream away the hours on observation post, delighting, as Cacciato does, in a stick of Black Jack gum. Or, stricken by the inconsolable loneliness of having a story that no one wants to listen to, they might drive in endless circles around an unruffled lake. Late in *The Things They Carried*, Mitchell Sanders exclaims, "'Hey, man, I just realized something.'" Then, very deliberately, "He wiped his eyes and spoke very quietly, as if awed by his own wisdom." It is the wisdom also conveyed by the true war story. "'Death sucks,' he said" (271).

Works Cited

Bonn, Maria S. "Can Stories Save Us? Tim O'Brien and the Efficacy of the Text." *Critique* 36 (Fall 1994): 2-15.

Calloway, Catherine. "'How to Tell a True War Story': Metafiction in *The Things They Carried*." *Critique* 26 (Summer 1995): 249-57.

Kaplan, Steven. "The Undying Uncertainty of the Narrator in Tim O'Brien's *The Things They Carried*." *Critique* 35 (Fall 1993): 43-52.

Kesey, Ken. *One Flew over the Cuckoo's Nest*. New York: Viking, 1962.

McCaffery, Larry. "Interview with Tim O'Brien." *Chicago Review* 33 (1982): 129-49.

Naparsteck, Martin. "An Interview with Tim O'Brien." *Contemporary Literature* 32 (Spring 1991): 1-11.

O'Brien, Tim. *Going After Cacciato*. New York: Delta, 1978.

———. *If I Die in a Combat Zone*. New York: Dell, 1972.

———. *The Things They Carried*. Boston: Houghton, 1990.

———. "We're Adjusted Too Well." *The Wounded Generation: America After Vietnam*. Ed. A. D. Horne. Englewood Cliffs: Prentice, 1981. 205-07.

Rignalda, Don. *Fighting and Writing the Vietnam War*. Jackson: UP of Mississippi, 1994.

Schroeder, Eric James. "The Past and the Possible: Tim O'Brien's Dialectic of Memory and the Imagination." *Search and Clear*. Ed. William J. Searle. Bowling Green: Bowling Green State UP, 1988. 116-34.

———. "Two Interviews: Talks with Tim O'Brien and Robert Stone." *Modern Fiction Studies* 30 (Spring 1984): 135-64.

Vannatta, Dennis. "Theme and Structure in Tim O'Brien's *Going After Cacciato*." *Modern Fiction Studies* 28 (1982): 242-46.

Mark A. Heberle (essay date 2001)

SOURCE: Heberle, Mark A. "True War Stories." In *A Trauma Artist: Tim O'Brien and the Fiction of Vietnam*, pp. 176-215. Iowa City: University of Iowa Press, 2001.

[*In the following essay, Heberle provides a thematic and stylistic analysis of* The Things They Carried *and locates the book within O'Brien's oeuvre.*]

Recirculated Trauma, Endless Fiction

After publishing his fable of nuclear age trauma in 1985, O'Brien's next novel was to have been *The People We Marry,* a work that eventually appeared as *In the Lake of the Woods* in 1994 (Kaplan 1995: 218). In the interim, however, he published several short stories, some set in Viet Nam and others in the United States but all related to the war. The shorter stories took on a life of their own and eventually a comprehensive form that became *The Things They Carried,* published by Houghton Mifflin in 1990, four years before the novel that was to have followed *The Nuclear Age*. Its award-winning title story, which appeared in 1986, was the first part of the larger work to be published. In 1989, just before its publication, O'Brien called *Things* [*The Things They Carried*] the best thing he had yet written (Naparsteck 8), and he has noted how much he enjoyed putting together the book as a whole. Indeed, reviewers greeted *The Things They Carried* as O'Brien's triumphant return to form after the relatively disappointing achievement of *The Nuclear Age*. The work has received admiring academic critical attention as well.

Calling it a "remarkable text" (28), Philip Beidler used a citation from the title story as an epigraph to his 1991 study of Vietnam authors, and Don Ringnalda referred to *Things* as O'Brien's "ultimate Vietnam War fiction" (105). Even Lorrie Smith, a critic who finds much of the work "pernicious" in its masculinist discourse, concedes that *Things* "contributes significantly to the canon of Vietnam War fiction" and is "remarkable" in its treatment of writing and soldiering (38).

O'Brien has told one interviewer that the genesis of the book was the image of the war as something to be carried, a weight of things that derived from his own experiences: "remembering all this crap I had on me and inside me, the physical and spiritual burdens" (Lee 200). As a work derived from painful memories that must be borne again, *The Things They Carried* has also been admired by mental health professionals for its insightful representation of combat trauma. *Things* is the only work of Vietnam War fiction quoted in Jonathan Shay's comparative study of the *Iliad* and PTSD or in Judith Herman's *Trauma and Recovery*. (And among the jacket blurbs for each book appear commendations by O'Brien.) Shay cites the narrator's insistence in **"How to Tell a True War Story"** that "a true war story is never moral" to argue more generally that trauma can never be easily resolved through writing (183), a point also emphasized by Kali Tal in discussing Lawrence Langer's study of Holocaust literature (Tal 1996: 49-50). Herman . . . cites passages from *Things* to exemplify Vietnam War trauma generally.

As O'Brien's satisfaction with the writing of the book suggests, however, *Things* is a work of recovery as well as trauma. Although "you can tell a true war story by its absolute and uncompromising allegiance to obscenity and evil" (**"How to Tell a True War Story"** 76), yet "this too is true: stories can save us" (**"The Lives of the Dead"** 255). *The Things They Carried* negotiates between these two truths by making storytelling itself the most important subject of the book. Throughout the work, stories are produced through a wide variety of discursive gestures, including recollection, confession, and explanation, as well as explicit storytelling; and many tales are repeated, elaborated by further details, or supplemented by additional explanation or commentary. This ceaseless replication of the fictive process witnesses to the mutual dependence of trauma and narrative as O'Brien reinvents himself as a soldier and as a writer. In the end, the work exemplifies both the need to write one's way beyond trauma and the impossibility of ever doing so.

The Things They Carried as Self-Revision

Composed of twenty-two pieces, beginning with **"The Things They Carried"** and ending with **"The Lives of the Dead,"** O'Brien's fifth book has been characterized both as a collection of short stories and as a novel, but neither classification exhausts its generic range. Among the "things" carried in the volume are apparent fiction and apparent nonfiction, including straightforward realism, fantasy, memoir, author's notes, and literary commentary. In content and form, *Things* revises O'Brien's two previous war-sited works. Like *If I Die in a Combat Zone,* the book originated in a few independently published pieces that prompted a larger structure that would come to incorporate them; as with *Going After Cacciato,* those earliest elements were a series of prize-winning stories.[1] Although closely resembling *Combat Zone* in form and mode, *Things* is not a memoir; and although it includes many interconnected stories, it is not a continuous narrative work like *Cacciato.* O'Brien has called it simply a "fiction," and it is more appropriate to identify its twenty-two "fictions" as "pieces" or "sections" rather than as chapters or stories. For example, **"Spin,"** the third section, merely narrates or recalls a number of short, unconnected sketches, some of them identified as memories, others as stories; the seventh piece, **"How to Tell a True War Story,"** and the last, **"The Lives of the Dead,"** are similarly miscellaneous. Whatever its genre, most of *Things* follows a group of about a dozen GIs who experience the mixed trauma and boredom of combat in Viet Nam and reappear in the various episodes that make up the book. These protagonists are a rewriting of *Cacciato*'s Third Squad, and both groups are fictional versions of the men of Alpha Company with whom O'Brien served in Viet Nam during his year in-country; indeed, the soldiers in *Things* belong to an Alpha Company themselves. As in *Combat Zone,* Tim O'Brien is one of its members, and a great deal of first-person narrative and commentary in the book presents his own point of view.

Revisiting the war through the experiences and point of view of a representative group of GIs is a cliché in American representations of Vietnam (Leland 740), but *Things* is also a self-conscious refashioning of the structure of *Cacciato.* The novel had begun with a list of the dead, followed by a description of the living. The title fiction of *Things* is O'Brien's supreme use of a list, a masterpiece of literary realism and formal patterning that focuses on everything carried by each soldier in the book, from jungle boots, 2.1 pounds; to letters from home, 10 ounces; to grief, terror, love, shameful memories, and "the soldier's greatest fear, which was the fear of blushing. Men killed, and died, because they were embarrassed not to" (20-21). Thus, both works open with a catalog of characters, burdened by personal and collective trauma, who will reappear in the episodes to follow. Like *Cacciato* as well, *Things* goes on to recall the deaths of squad members until all have been recuperated by the end of the book, where they reappear in the oxymoronically titled final piece—it seems that "the lives of the dead" are not over in *The Things They Carried.*

Formally, then, O'Brien's fifth book combines the most obvious features of his two earlier Vietnam narratives: A series of structurally coherent scenarios portray the war through the experiences of a small group of GIs; and the writer represents himself as a protagonist, participant, or commentator in all but three (**"The Things They Carried," "Speaking of Courage,"** and **"In the Field"**). The site of narration thus varies from piece to piece, moving from the first-person point of view of *Combat Zone* (and *The Nuclear Age*) to the third-person intimate perspective of *Cacciato* (and *Northern Lights*). The title narrative, nearly an epitome of the war as it was represented in both *Combat Zone* and *Cacciato,* sometimes takes on an omniscient perspective that reflects what O'Brien has represented in the earlier books about men in combat.

Throughout *The Things They Carried,* O'Brien refashions traumatic experiences that were first represented in *Combat Zone* and rewritten in the later books. Thus, breakdown in combat was briefly described in Chapter XIII (119-20) of the memoir, but its description in **"The Things They Carried"** (18-19) explicitly recalls not only Paul Berlin's experience on Cacciato's hill but also William Cowling's embarrassment in guerrilla training:

> For the most part they carried themselves with poise, a kind of dignity. Now and then, however, there were times of panic, when they squealed or wanted to squeal but couldn't, when they twitched and made moaning sounds and covered their heads and said Dear Jesus and flopped around on the earth and fired their weapons blindly and cringed and sobbed and begged for the noise to stop and went wild and made stupid promises to themselves and to God and to their mothers and fathers, hoping not to die. In different ways, it happened to all of them. Afterward, when the firing ended, they would blink and peek up. They would touch their bodies, feeling shame, then quickly hiding it. . . . After a time someone would shake his head and say, No lie, I almost shit my pants, and someone else would laugh, which meant it was bad, yes, but the guy had obviously not shit his pants, it wasn't that bad, and in any case nobody would ever do such a thing and then go ahead and talk about it.

Whether or not O'Brien personally did "such a thing," he wrote about it in both *Cacciato* and *The Nuclear Age.* The destruction of Tri Binh 4 recalled in the memoir ("Alpha Company") and revised in the obliteration of Hoi An in *Cacciato* ("Fire in the Hole") reappears in the wiping out of Than Khe in **"The Things They Carried."** All three operations are ordered by junior officers during patrols near hostile villages, and the two purely fictional accounts are brutal responses to the death of an American GI, Jim Pederson in *Cacciato* and Ted Lavender in *Things.* Alpha Company's destructive takeover of a Buddhist monastery as a combat base in "July" (*Combat Zone*) is refashioned more positively in

"**Church,**" where the monks' gracious courtesy is reciprocated by some of their guests. In the same chapter of the memoir, Captain Smith's incompetence leads to an American soldier's being buried in mud when a half-track runs over him, and his comrades have to find his corpse and pull it out of the mire. The episode is elaborately expanded and altered in several of the later sections of *Things,* which focus on the fate of Kiowa, an American Indian GI who is lethally buried under mud and human waste during a nighttime mortar attack. In "**On the Rainy River,**" O'Brien refashions his failure to flee from military service when he had a chance to do so, concluding his account with the same moral paradox that had haunted his recollection in *Combat Zone* ("Escape"): "I survived, but it's not a happy ending. I was a coward. I went to the war" (63). And as noted . . . O'Brien's description of the destruction of a water buffalo, recalled in *Combat Zone* (139) and rewritten in both *Cacciato* and *The Nuclear Age,* reappears in "**How to Tell a True War Story.**"

The Things They Carried rewrites O'Brien's earlier work, but it also revises itself as it proceeds, frequently providing multiple versions of a single episode and commenting on its own origins. The work's continual self-reflection upon its own status and purpose as imaginative writing has prompted Catherine Calloway (1995) to label it a metafiction. Perhaps the most comprehensive subject of *Cacciato* is its own making, as represented in the meditations of Paul Berlin. But *Things* is more explicitly metafictional, as the very titles of "**How to Tell a True War Story,**" "**Notes,**" and "**Good Form**" indicate. In the last sentence of the book, O'Brien re-imagines himself as a ten-year-old boy, "skimming across the surface of my own history, moving fast, riding the melt beneath the blades, doing loops and spins, and when I take a high leap into the dark and come down thirty years later, I realize it is as Tim trying to save Timmy's life with a story" (273). The image is a memory, a story, and a metaphor for the story making that has now come to an end—indeed, "**Spin**" is the third piece in *The Things They Carried.*

In this final passage, O'Brien is re-membering himself, an act that combines the roles of artist, character, and audience. Such self-representation is the most striking feature of *The Things They Carried* and its most significant means of making storytelling a crucial subject. Except in *Northern Lights,* the protagonists of his previous books were authorial surrogates, and even Paul Perry shares the quasi-authorial role of meditative observer or narrator that characterizes Berlin, Cowling, and O'Brien himself in *Combat Zone.* In *Things,* however, the author is directly refashioned as the figure whom O'Brien has referred to as "the Tim character" (Naparsteck 7) and "the character Tim O'Brien" (Kaplan 1991: 96-97).[2] We will refer to O'Brien's persona as

"Tim O'Brien" or as "the narrator" to distinguish him from the author. By employing what we may call the *trope of memory,* suddenly recalling and then elaborating in more detail a past scene from the war, this latest version of O'Brien combines his identities as soldier and author, which had been distinct in the earlier books. For example, "**Spin**" consists of eighteen short sections, most of them brief scenes from the war introduced by the simple formula "I remember" or an equivalent. Four sections are prefaced by the reflection that "what sticks to memory, often, are those odd little fragments that have no beginning and no end" (39). The final section identifies O'Brien's authorial role by making explicit the relationship between memory and fiction: "Forty-three years old, and the war occurred half a lifetime ago, and yet the remembering makes it now. And sometimes remembering will lead to a story, which makes it forever. That's what stories are for. Stories are for joining the past to the future" (40). In remembering, the author rewitnesses what the soldier had seen, so that the two selves also merge, like Tim the writer and Timmy the ten-year-old. Both are present even in brief sketches such as "**Stockings,**" which describes Henry Dobbins's unwavering faith in a personal talisman: "Even now, twenty years later, I can see him wrapping his girlfriend's pantyhose around his neck before heading out on ambush" (129). By the end of the piece, which describes Dobbins's decision to keep wearing the stockings for good luck even though his girlfriend has dumped him, the narrator has rejoined his platoon imaginatively: "It was a relief for all of us" (130). As in *Combat Zone,* the use of "we" and "us" incorporates the narrator Tim O'Brien into five other brief war pieces that are not directly presented as memories.

In "**The Things They Carried,**" "**Speaking of Courage,**" and "**In the Field,**" however, the narrator is neither remembering what once happened nor is present when it does. But each of these originally independently published stories is followed by a brief sketch in *The Things They Carried*—"**Love,**" "**Notes,**" and "**Field Trip,**" respectively—that identifies O'Brien's persona as the author of the preceding longer story. Indeed, in these three metafictional appendices and in nine of the other pieces in *Things,* Tim O'Brien is the narrator, remembering, describing, arguing, or explaining things to us in the first person.

Two of the other works, "**Sweetheart of the Song Tra Bong**" and "**Night Life,**" are represented by O'Brien's persona as stories that were narrated by his comrades Rat Kiley and Mitchell Sanders. In "**The Ghost Soldiers,**" Norman Bowker tells how Morty Phillips suffered a lethal infection after taking a swim, and Kiley and Sanders tell additional stories in "**Spin**" and "**How** to Tell a True War Story." Telling stories is thus omnipresent in *Things,* and Tim O'Brien represents himself and his comrades as an eager audience:

> By midnight it was story time.
>
> "Morty Phillips used up his luck," Bowker said.
>
> I smiled and waited. There was a tempo to how stories got told. Bowker peeled open a finger blister and sucked on it.
>
> "Go on," Azar said. "Tell him everything."
>
> ("The Ghost Soldiers"—221)

Tim O'Brien's presence in such scenes enacts a *trope of storytelling* to represent his fiction as simply the transmission of episodes overhead and repeated, just as the act of remembering defines his function as merely recovering and fleshing out actual incidents. In the latter case, he is a witness; in the former, an audience for twice-told tales. The notion of sharing the accounts of others is reinforced by the narrator's general references to the war as a source of stories; for example: "Vietnam was full of strange stories, some improbable, some well beyond that, but the stories that will last forever are those that swirl back and forth across the border between trivia and bedlam, the mad and the mundane. This one keeps returning to me. I heard it from Rat Kiley, who swore up and down to its truth, although in the end, I'll admit, that doesn't amount to much of a warranty" (101). This is the introduction to **"Sweetheart of the Song Tra Bong,"** Rat Kiley's account of Mary Anne Bell, a football cheerleader from Ohio who flies to the war zone to join her high school sweetheart but gradually becomes so enamored of counterguerrilla terrorism that she migrates into the jungle and is last seen prowling about in her pink culottes, wearing a necklace of human tongues. O'Brien has claimed that the story is based on an actual incident (Coffey 61, Baughman 205), so it perfectly exemplifies the convincing lunacy of a true war story that lasts forever.

Insofar as *The Things They Carried* presents itself as a miscellany of overheard and remembered episodes from the war, strikingly mundane and authentically bizarre, the book resembles the method and material of Michael Herr's *Dispatches,* a work and a writer O'Brien greatly admires. But its self-conscious use of remembering and storytelling also recalls Proust and Conrad. The work ends, like *Remembrance of Things Past,* by recalling the originating instance of the narrator's identity as a writer—in Tim O'Brien's case, the death of his childhood girlfriend Linda and his dreams of her continuing presence in his life. And **"Sweetheart of the Song Tra Bong"** is O'Brien's *Heart of Darkness,* Americanized, Vietnamized, and surrealized (and possibly encouraged by Francis Ford Coppola's film version of Conrad,

Apocalypse Now, for which Herr wrote the screenplay). Like Conrad's tale, **"Sweetheart"** [**"Sweetheart of the Song Tra Bong"**] is filtered through three sets of narrators, since Rat Kiley heard the end of the story from a comrade who talked to the Green Berets, and in their account the high school sweetheart is already turning into a ghostly legend: "[A] couple times they almost saw her sliding through the shadows. Not quite, but almost. She had crossed to the other side" (125). The Ohio cheerleader becomes the Kurtz figure who has "crossed to the other side," while the Green Berets practice the barbarous rites that she first emulates and then goes beyond. And both in this story and in those that the other members of Alpha Company tell, O'Brien makes the circumstances of storytelling itself part of the tales, complete with interruptions by listeners and characterizations of his own narrative by GI storytellers, who thus become additional authorial surrogates.

Overall, Tim O'Brien appears in nineteen of the twenty-two pieces that make up *Things* as a participant, audience/observer, or commentator, and he is identified as the author of the other three. Whether as writer or soldier, he is the book's central figure, and his multiple roles as author and character make *Things* a peculiarly Proustian work, despite its subject. But just as Proust's narrator is not the author of *Remembrance of Things Past* but a young man who is about to write it, the Tim O'Brien who appears in *The Things They Carried* cannot be simply identified with the author who has created him. As noted above, O'Brien's book is identified as "a work of fiction" on the title page and in the brief foreword, which notes that "except for a few details regarding the author's own life, all the incidents, names, and characters are imaginary." Although the autobiographical details virtually identify author and protagonist, O'Brien has given himself an imaginary daughter in **"Ambush," "Good Form,"** and **"Field Trip,"** and the last of these pieces details a trip back to Viet Nam with her in 1990 that, needless to say, never happened. There are also less obvious differences between O'Brien and his persona, including some noted by the author: The vengeful behavior of Tim O'Brien in **"The Ghost Soldiers"** represents some of his creator's darker impulses, but the episode never occurred; and O'Brien does not share the narrator's mystification of war's violence (e.g., "For all its horror, you can't help but gape at the awful majesty of combat"—87) in **"How to Tell a True War Story"** (Naparsteck 9). Thus, the Tim O'Brien who appears in the book, a soldier who fought in Viet Nam in Quang Ngai Province and is now a writer and the author of a book called *Going After Cacciato,* is a character created by the Tim O'Brien who wrote *The Things They Carried.*

The narrator provides a confession and a justification for O'Brien's self-fabrication in **"Good Form,"** as if the apparent misrepresentation of the first seventeen sections of *Things* were an act of bad faith with the reader:

> It's time to be blunt.
>
> I'm forty-three years old, true, and I'm a writer now, and a long time ago I walked through Quang Ngai Province as a foot soldier.
>
> Almost everything else is invented.
>
> But it's not a game. It's a form. Right here, now, as I invent myself, I'm thinking of all I want to tell you about why this book is written as it is.
>
> (203)

The narrator then proceeds to revise **"The Man I Killed,"** an earlier piece that seems to recall his emotional breakdown after killing an enemy soldier, by revealing what actually happened, only to confess that the second account is also invented. And both versions are finally revealed to be fictive substitutes for what did *not* happen rather than what did:

> I want you to feel what I felt. I want you to know why story-truth is truer sometimes than happening-truth.
>
> Here is the happening-truth. I was once a soldier. There were many bodies, real bodies with real faces, but I was young then and I was afraid to look. And now, twenty years later, I'm left with faceless responsibility and faceless grief.
>
> Here is the story-truth. He was a slim, dead, almost dainty young man of about twenty. He lay in the center of a red clay trail near the village of My Khe. His jaw was in his throat. His one eye was shut, the other eye was a star-shaped hole. I killed him.
>
> (203-4)

What "really" happened was a failure to feel, an emotional constriction in response to trauma that the narrator associates with moral cowardice. "Responsibility" recalls the narrator's choice to participate in a bad war, represented in *Things* by the account of a traumatic breakdown in **"On the Rainy River"** when he is unable to flee to Canada; "grief" is felt for all the dead, even the enemy, and all the other wasted casualties. **"Good Form"** thus represents Tim O'Brien, the narrator of *The Things They Carried,* as a trauma writer and as a trauma survivor and provides a significant explanation for his rewriting of Vietnam. But although traumatization may be an important source of the writing, the source of the narrator's feelings remains both unspecific and endless, as "faceless" but also as all-embracing as all the things he carried out of the war. By refashioning himself so, O'Brien not only gives his personal traumatization a fictional form but also represents its ineffability.

The recycling in *The Things They Carried* of material from O'Brien's experiences and from his earlier books indicates the persistence of significant war memories in the writer's imagination. Some of them may be the unresolved traces of traumatic experiences, but they are also the inspiration for his writing. In *Things* the distinction between trauma and inspiration is frequently blurred in any case: Many of the pieces dramatize traumatization and various reactions to it, whereas others show how trauma is directly converted into a fiction. But the repetition of incidents and experiences in O'Brien's work also raises issues of authenticity and verisimilitude. War literature has commonly been validated on the basis of its truth to actual experience, but O'Brien's multiple rewritings radically question such assumptions. The problem of authenticity is addressed by Tim O'Brien in **"How to Tell a True War Story,"** which questions the categories of "truth" and "war story" through the communication of unspeakable grief.

"How to Tell a True War Story": Misreading Tim O'Brien

"How to Tell a True War Story" is not only O'Brien's most complex meditation on war literature in general but also a brilliant representation of trauma writing. The work is narrated by the Tim O'Brien who is a fictional persona for the author and who self-reflectively interweaves stories and commentary on his own writing. The longest of its fourteen sections is an actual example of formal storytelling that raises issues that are developed throughout the piece, including, the validity of fiction and its relationship to trauma:

> I remember how peaceful the twilight was. A deep pinkish red spilled out on the river, which moved without sound, and in the morning we would cross the river and march west into the mountains. The occasion was right for a good story.
>
> "God's truth," Mitchell Sanders said. "A six-man patrol goes up into the mountains on a basic listening-post operation. The idea's to spend a week up there, just lie low and listen for enemy movement. . . ."
>
> Sanders glanced at me to make sure I had the scenario. He was playing with his yo-yo, dancing it with short, tight little strokes of the wrist.
>
> His face was blank in the dusk.
>
> (79)

The blank-faced narrator goes on to describe how the six soldiers become so hyperaroused by the sounds emanating from the mountains—Vietnamese music, a cocktail party, a "terrific mama-san soprano . . . gook opera and a glee club and the Haiphong Boys Choir" (81)—that they call in an all-night air strike against the mountains and flee back to base camp in the morning. Asked by a "fatass colonel" what happened, "[t]hey just look at him for a while, sort of funny like, sort of amazed, and the whole war is right there in that stare. It says everything you can't ever say. It says, man, you got *wax* in your ears. . . . Then they salute the fucker and walk away, because certain stories you don't ever tell" (82-83). Sanders then moves off into the dark, his story over. But in the next two sections of **"War Story"** [**"How to Tell a True War Story"**], he returns in the morning to give it a moral ("you got to *listen* to your enemy" [83]) and then later to revise that to "just listen," while confessing to Tim O'Brien that most of the account was made up. "[B]ut listen," Sanders insists, "it's still true" (84).

Mitchell Sanders's fable resembles some of the strange and true stories of the war reported by Michael Herr in *Dispatches* that stand by themselves as comments on its absurd and incomprehensible violence: for example, "Patrol went up the mountain. One man came back. He died before he could tell us what happened" (Herr 6). Like **"Sweetheart of the Song Tra Bong,"** O'Brien's episode mimics Conrad in its careful attention to the narrative situation, metacommentary by the storyteller, and symbolic details (Kaplan [1995] notes that the narrator Tim O'Brien recalls minutely the almost comic icon of the storyteller's magic: "Even now, at this instant, I remember that yo-yo" [183]). Within its fictional setting, this account of American soldiers who go into the mountains, undergo a traumatic experience, but ultimately return safely addresses the anxieties of its listeners, who anticipate their own dreaded mountain mission in the morning. Whether it happened or not, it is true to their fears and hopes. Finally, the survivors' inability to tell others what they have been through suggests that although storytelling is a necessary outlet for traumatization, the trauma event itself is incommunicable. Sanders's attempt to give the tale a moral and to separate "fact" from "fiction" are unnecessary, therefore, as the narrator Tim O'Brien knows and as much of **"War Story"** demonstrates.

Sanders's tale exemplifies that a story can be truer than what actually happened, that it can be more valuable than actual experience, and that it can make the survivor's trauma meaningful, but only to the right audience. O'Brien's representation of his authorial persona in **"War Story"** is concerned with these issues as well, particularly in the account of Rat Kiley's slaughter of a baby water buffalo, the ninth of the fifteen sections that make up **"War Story."** Tim O'Brien introduces this third revision of the water buffalo incident from *Combat Zone* by noting that "I've told it before—many times—many versions—but here's what actually happened" (85). But at the end of **"War Story,"** the Rat Kiley episode—story? memory of actual occurrence?—has become another example of storytelling, a piece that he often reads in public and that is sometimes mistaken for a personal experience still bothering the storyteller, mistaken usually by "an older woman of kindly temperament and humane politics" (90): "She'll explain that as a rule she hates war stories; she can't understand why people want to wallow in all the blood and gore.

But this one she liked. The poor baby buffalo, it made her sad. Sometimes, even, there are little tears. What I should do, she'll say, is put it all behind me. Find new stories to tell" (90). The narrator uses her reaction to denounce two sorts of misreadings of O'Brien's own fiction that derive from the relationship between traumatization and war stories.

On the one hand, a story may be interpreted as an actual experience rather than the fabulation of something that may or may not have happened: "Beginning to end, you tell her, it's all made up. Every goddamn detail— the mountains and the river and especially that poor dumb baby buffalo. None of it happened. *None* of it. And even if it did happen, it didn't happen in the mountains, it happened in this little village on the Batangan Peninsula, and it was raining like crazy, and one night a guy named Stink Harris woke up screaming with a leech on his tongue. You can tell a true war story if you just keep on telling it" (91). The narrator initially uses direct experience to validate the episode, only to deny that it happened; but if it did, he adds, it will be found in *Going After Cacciato!* Even the authenticity of the original account in *Combat Zone* must now be questioned, if what "actually happened" is to be found in **"How to Tell a True War Story,"** or in Chapter Six of O'Brien's second novel. Paradoxically, a "true" story is one that has multiple versions. Ultimately, the greater truth of the revisions depends not on what happened, but on the different ways in which killing a water buffalo is rewritten as a powerfully traumatic experience in *Cacciato, The Nuclear Age,* and **Things.**

Nevertheless, introducing the episode in **"War Story"** as an actual happening has established its credibility and thus met our need to believe that it is literally "true"—the narrator himself uses the mimetic fallacy before he disabuses his sympathetic listener of trusting in it as anything more than a narrative device. And of course the story's authenticity is validated by the listener's concern for the storyteller: She assumes that he has been traumatized because the terrible details are so real, so vivid. Indeed, her response suggests that the story has fulfilled an important criterion of a "true war story, if truly told": It "makes the stomach believe" (84). Whatever her concern about the narrator's obsession with the war, she has enjoyed the story, after all, despite its "absolute and uncompromising allegiance to obscenity and evil" (76), another of the narrator's criteria. In fact, her response is contradictory: Moved by what has been narrated, she exhorts the author to write about something else.

Forced to correct the mistaken assumption that true war stories represent actual experiences, the narrator is even more upset by the notion that their subject is war. If the mimetic fallacy mistakes fiction for fact in a true war story, a second sort of misreading misses the point of the fiction itself. In the first instance, the well-meaning reader or listener misattributes traumatization to the storyteller; in the second, she fails to locate the true fictional source of trauma and its victim. The water buffalo episode is the last of three sections in **"How to Tell a True War Story"** that deal with Rat Kiley, and although all of them take place during the war, their subject is something else.

"War Story" begins with a narrative episode followed by a commentary upon it, a pattern repeated throughout. In the first, Rat Kiley writes a letter to the sister of a good friend who has been killed, filling it with a few dubiously eulogistic stories to illustrate "how her brother made the war seem almost fun, always raising hell and lighting up villes and bringing smoke to bear every which way" (75). At the end of the letter, "Rat pours his heart out. He says he loved the guy. He says the guy was his best friend in the world. They were like soul mates, he says, like twins or something, they had a whole lot in common. He tells the guy's sister he'll look her up when the war's over" (76). But at the end of the section, his war stories are ignored: "Rat mails the letter. He waits two months. The dumb cooze never writes back" (76). In the commentary that follows, Rat's disappointment is used to illustrate that "a true war story is never moral":

> You can tell a true war story if it embarrasses you. If you don't care for obscenity, you don't care for the truth; if you don't care for the truth, watch how you vote. Send guys to war, they come home talking dirty.
>
> Listen to Rat: "Jesus Christ, man, I write this beautiful fuckin' letter, I slave over it, and what happens? The dumb cooze never writes back."
>
> (77)

After two more sections with commentary, Rat's methodical massacre of the baby buffalo is gruesomely detailed, together with the platoon's reaction: "He shot it twice in the flanks. It wasn't to kill; it was to hurt. He put the rifle muzzle up against the mouth and shot the mouth away. Nobody said much. . . . Curt Lemon was dead, Rat Kiley had lost his best friend in the world. Later in the week he would write a long personal letter to the guy's sister, who would not write back, but for now it was a question of pain. He shot off the tail. He shot away chunks of meat below the ribs . . ." (85). By the end of the atrocity, "Rat Kiley was crying. He tried to say something, but then cradled his rifle and went off by himself" (86). The narrator and the platoon have become witnesses of "something essential, something brand-new and profound, a piece of the world so startling there was not yet a name for it. Somebody kicked the baby buffalo" and eventually Kiowa and Mitchell Sanders dump what remains of the animal in the village well. The episode ends with Sanders's commentary: "'Well, that's Nam,' he said. 'Garden of Evil. Over here, man, every sin's real fresh and original'" (86).

The platoon reacts as if it were the audience for the kind of fiction that "makes the stomach believe," according to the narrator: "[I]n the end, really, there's nothing much to say about a true war story, except maybe 'Oh'" (84). By contrast, Tim O'Brien's own listener has tried to interpret the story as personal testimony and so missed its point:

> I won't say it but I'll think it.
>
> I'll picture Rat Kiley's face, his grief, and I'll think, *You dumb cooze.*
>
> Because she wasn't listening.
>
> It *wasn't* a war story. It was a *love* story.
>
> (90)

Keeping his own brutality to himself, the narrator goes on to explain that a true war story is made-up, as we have noted above. But missing its subject is worse than mistaking its fictionality. The story does not represent Tim O'Brien's trauma, but Rat Kiley's. His love for his best friend is displaced through his behavior toward a Vietnamese water buffalo and Curt Lemon's sister; both the little atrocity and the profanity are reactions to combat death, brutal expressions of loyalty to a lost comrade. The atrocity takes crazed vengeance upon the only available trace of the enemy; the letter tries to make something good come out of the waste of his friend, perhaps even to perpetuate his love through someone intimately connected to Lemon. To Rat, the sister is dismissing his love for her brother, even invalidating the Curt Lemon that Rat admired. We can perfectly understand and support her silence, but to the doubly spurned lover her failure to answer is an act of betrayal that leaves his own wound unhealed.

The sister resembles the narrator's well-meaning but theme-deaf listener, who weeps for the baby water buffalo while ignoring the point of the episode: Rat Kiley's pain. But the story does not shrink from exposing the obscenity of the war, a point reinforced by Mitchell Sanders's commentary. Somebody's (i.e., anybody's) kicking the murdered baby buffalo and the poisoning of the village well by the GIs epitomize their everyday brutality toward Viet Nam and the Vietnamese, a destructiveness nakedly celebrated even in Rat's tribute to Lemon. But they, too, have lost a comrade, and Rat's love needs validation, his vengeance and breakdown need closure. Trauma cannot be healed by sympathetic atrocity, of course, which will only make it worse, but destruction seems the only means at hand for these violence-tempered young men. Violence and love depend on each other so closely in the Rat Kiley episodes that as in any "true war story, if there's a moral at all, it's like the thread that makes the cloth. You can't tease it out. You can't extract the meaning without unraveling the deeper meaning" (84). In his fourth version of buffalo hunting, O'Brien nonetheless does produce a love story from the elemental filth of the war, one that avoids sentimentality or a happy ending.

"How to Tell a True War Story" ends with an emphatic denial of the mimetic and thematic limitations of war literature as popularly understood (and written):

> You can tell a true war story if you just keep on telling it.
>
> And in the end, of course, a true war story is never about war. It's about sunlight. It's about the special way that dawn spreads out on a river when you know you must cross the river and march into the mountains and do things you are afraid to do. It's about love and memory. It's about sorrow. It's about sisters who never write back and people who never listen.
>
> (91)

By calling attention to its materials, O'Brien reminds us that **"War Story"** has fulfilled its own criteria. People who never listen include Curt Lemon's sister, Tim O'Brien's audience, and everyone denounced when Mitchell Sanders tries to define the moral of *his* story: "Nobody listens. Nobody hears nothin'. Like that fatass colonel. The politicians, all the civilian types. Your girlfriend. My girlfriend" (83). True war stories are not simply stories about war but fictions of traumatization that require willing listeners as well as skillful storytellers. Nor are they solely narratives of past events: Rat Kiley's breakdown is no more merely a record of some terrible events in the Vietnam War than *Heart of Darkness* is just an account of a trip down the Congo River in 1890. The war is a fictional creation that speaks of important human truths every time it brings together a storyteller and an audience, whether in Quang Ngai Province in 1969 or in a lecture hall in 1990, and that is the ultimate point of O'Brien's fictional essay with examples (or vice versa). The conclusion also reminds us that everything in the piece has been made up, including the narrator Tim O'Brien and the kindly listener whom silently he browbeats. His repetition of Rat Kiley's profanity links them as both storytellers and fictional characters; like Mitchell Sanders, the narrator has had an audience for his story, and he has taken his listener aside to comment on it; and the narrator himself has also been a listener—to Rat Kiley, to Sanders, and even to his audience.

Through fictionalizing himself here as elsewhere, O'Brien is able to represent trauma and its consequences without merely representing his personal experiences. Everything in the work speaks of psychic or moral breakdown, from the listening post soldiers who call in air strikes upon the jungle and abandon their post, to Rat Kiley, crying over a dead friend, a slaughtered water buffalo, and the wasting of himself and others that is the war. But although stories can both replicate and relieve trauma by displacing it formally, they cannot give it closure. By presenting a fable derived from their own nightmares, Mitchell Sanders's story temporarily calms men who will be facing combat the next day in the mountains, but his attempts to censor its falsehood and draw out a moral call attention to the limited magic of fictions.

And Rat Kiley is not the only figure who cannot forget the death of Curt Lemon. The narrator of **"War Story"** is obsessed with this traumatic incident. In the third section of the piece, he identifies Lemon as the friend for whom Rat Kiley wrote his love letter and then describes in detail how he was blown to pieces by a booby-trapped mortar round underneath a giant tree while tossing smoke grenades with Rat. Used to help explicate Kiley's letter writing, the description thus becomes a fragment that chronologically reverses antecedent and consequence, as if it were an afterthought to the letter instead of its cause. While Rat cannot let Lemon's death be the end of the story, the narrator Tim O'Brien cannot introduce it directly. Yet this traumatic incident is the origin of all the storytelling in **"War Story."** Tim O'Brien refers to Lemon in seven of the fifteen sections that make up the work, and he describes his death in four of them. Its continual intrusion suggests an ineffaceable trauma, so that **"War Story"** epitomizes in miniature the recurrence of traumatization characteristic of *Things* as a whole. The first of the descriptions is the longest and most detailed; the second, which repeats phrases from the first, is the briefest: "We crossed that river and marched west into the mountains. On the third day, Curt Lemon stepped on a booby-trapped 105 round. He was playing catch with Rat Kiley, laughing, and then he was dead. The trees were thick; it took nearly an hour to cut an LZ for the dustoff" (85). This account is followed immediately by the baby water buffalo incident, which it motivates; but the battle in the mountains also recalls Mitchell Sanders's story, which is told the night before such a battle, and the cross-references suggest a complex of traumatization that has been fragmented throughout **"War Story."**

The third description of Lemon's death follows the briefest of the fifteen sections in **"War Story,"** a typical combination of metafictional comment with example:

> Often in a true war story there is not even a point, or else the point doesn't hit you until twenty years later, in your sleep, and you wake up and shake your wife and start telling the story to her, except when you get to the end you've forgotten the point again. And then for a long time you lie there watching the story happen in your head. You listen to your wife's breathing. The war's over. You close your eyes. You smile and think, Christ, what's the *point?*
>
> (88-89)

The paragraph itself is a "true war story," of course, even though the episode occurs two decades after the war is over in the domestic security of a couple's bedroom. But here it is impossible to distinguish between story and traumatic intrusion: Whatever is being re-imagined resists even the narrator's attempt at thematic closure, and it cannot be explained, even to his wife. It has no point at which it can be resolved, but it is also pointless to bother her with it—she probably wouldn't be able to listen. (As Jonathan Shay notes, "normal adults do not want to hear trauma narratives" [193].) The third death of Curt Lemon follows immediately in the next section. The narrator introduces it as another example of a "pointless" story, but does so in a way that suggests an unwelcome traumatic intrusion: "This one wakes me up" (89). In this account, Tim O'Brien is involved directly with Lemon's death, for he has to gather the pieces of body left in the trees after the booby trap has detonated, and he uses the trope of memory so chillingly, so tangibly, that story and continued traumatization are indistinguishable: "I remember pieces of skin and something wet and yellow that must've been the intestines. The gore was horrible, and stays with me. But what wakes me up twenty years later is Dave Jensen singing 'Lemon Tree' as we threw down the parts" (89). The last sentence concludes this particular war story but not the nightmare, which now circles back to the dream that wakes him up "twenty years later" in bed with his wife and thus epitomizes the endless recirculation and ineffability of trauma, as well as its asynchronous fragmentation.

"Twenty years later, I can still see the sunlight on Lemon's face" begins the narrator's last description of the death. The "sunlight" will be among the subjects used to illustrate his final assertion that "a true war story is never about war" (cited above). Here, it recalls the moment when the doomed soldier stepped beyond the shade of the trees where he and Rat Kiley were fooling around and onto the booby trap, so that "when his foot touched down, in that instant, he must've thought it was the sunlight that was killing him." "[I]f I could ever get the story right," the witness/survivor/narrator continues, "how the sun seemed to gather around him and pick him up and lift him high into a tree, . . . then you would believe the last thing Curt Lemon believed, which for him must've been the final truth" (90). Here the "right story" would be literally untrue, yet we would believe in it. It might also efface all visible traces of trauma by eliminating the presence of an observer who would watch Curt Lemon die, and then survive to tell about it, dream about it, write a letter about it, and commit atrocities in its name. But the desire to get the story "right" after four accounts of Lemon's death shows that trauma, however displaced, can never be buried: "You can tell a true war story if you just keep on telling it." As Tobey Herzog notes (1997: 29-30), Lemon's obliteration is based on the death of the author's friend Chip Merricks, who stepped on a mine in Pinkville, a traumatic incident that was casually and ironically recorded in Chapter IX of *Combat Zone*. It is also briefly alluded to in "The Vietnam in Me" as the author revisits the site of the fatal ambush. Thus the actual event, nearly irrecoverable for O'Brien and rendered through the register of emotional constriction in both of the autobiographical memoirs, is here replaced and supplemented by a fiction, rendered from four different perspectives, that is more "true" than what actually happened yet remains without closure—and is thus available for additional posttraumatic refabrication. Whether as author or as narrator of **"War Story,"** Tim O'Brien can't get over whatever it was that happened to Chip Merricks or to Curt Lemon.

OTHER REFABRICATIONS OF TRAUMA

Ultimately, the imagined listener is right about the narrator's obsessiveness, wrong about urging him to put the war behind him. Although everything is made up—including Tim O'Brien and the listener herself—the author of *The Things They Carried* has created a true story that shows how trauma may be recycled but can never be closed. **"How to Tell a True War Story"** is O'Brien's most elaborate metafiction of traumatization, but other sections of the work handle the subject with comparable artistry. Besides Lemon's death, the narrator Tim O'Brien witnesses the deaths of Ted Lavender, Kiowa, and an enemy soldier, as well as several other Vietnamese. Lavender's death is represented in **"The Things They Carried,"** Kiowa's in **"Speaking of Courage"** and **"In the Field,"** and the Vietnamese soldier's in **"Ambush."** Traumatic episodes all, their representations are fittingly marked by fragmentation, violation of chronology, instrusiveness, and repetition.

The award-winning title story is a brilliantly organized epitome of O'Brien's representation of the war in *Combat Zone* and *Cacciato*. Written in thirteen sections, it can be seen as a master catalog of combat trauma that combines and refabricates three lists from the earlier novel: the roll call of the dead and living that introduces *Cacciato,* the seriatim characterization of each of the squad members in Chapter 22 ("Who They Were, or Claimed to Be"), and the itemization of ignorance that made Viet Nam and the Vietnamese bewilderingly alien to the GIs who searched and destroyed them (Chapter 39, "The Things They Didn't Know"). The physical, psychological, and moral burdens and the objects of destruction, survival, pleasure, and hope carried by Alpha Company are categorized, section by section, until the war has been established as a site of obscene violence and almost unbearable trauma.

Within the larger catalog, O'Brien weaves two discrete narratives. The first appears only in the middle section, where Lee Strunk goes down an enemy tunnel for what seems to his waiting comrades an eternity and then emerges "right out of the grave," according to Rat Kiley, "grinning, filthy but alive," to hear his friends make "jokes about rising from the dead." This story rewrites the tragic tunnel narratives of *Cacciato* as rough comedy, but we are told that at the moment when Strunk "made [a] high happy moaning sound," Ted Lavender "was shot in the head on his way back from peeing. . . . There was a swollen black bruise under his left eye. The cheekbone was gone. Oh shit, Rat Kiley said, the guy's dead. The guy's dead, he kept saying, which seemed profound—the guy's dead. I mean really" (13).

Lavender's killing interrupts and completely displaces Strunk's survival, a discrete and coherent episode that is buried and isolated in the middle of the narrative. By contrast, the unexpected death reappears throughout the piece from beginning to end. Within the catalog of things carried by necessity, for example, we are told that "Ted Lavender, who was scared, carried tranquilizers until he was shot in the head outside the village of Than Khe in mid-April" and that "until he was shot, [he] carried six or seven ounces of premium dope, which for him was a necessity" (4). And this catalog ends as a parody of an army field issue description with ironic practical application: "Because the nights were cold, and because the monsoons were wet, each [soldier] carried a green plastic poncho that could be used as a raincoat or groundsheet or makeshift tent. With its quilted liner, the poncho weighed almost two pounds, but it was worth every ounce. In April, for instance, when Ted Lavender was shot, they used his poncho to wrap him up, then to carry him across the paddy, then to lift him into the chopper that took him away" (5). These repeated fragments register the persistence of Lavender's death, while their mechanical assignment to the appropriate list suggests emotional constriction.

But Lavender's death also intrudes more dramatically into *Things,* which combines the omniscient narration of lists with the imaginative meditations of Alpha Company's commanding lieutenant, Jimmy Cross, an ironic Christ figure who survives Vietnam and whose men suffer while following him. Cross carries the burden of responsibility for his men, but he also carries ten ounces of letters, two photographs, and a good luck pebble from his virginal girlfriend Martha as well as memories, hopes, and fears about her love for him. Like Paul Berlin or O'Brien himself, Cross is a reluctant warrior, and he dreams of Martha while trying to carry out his duties. He blames his own negligence for Lavender's death, and his hopeless love for his negligence. Alone in his foxhole the night after Lavender is shot, Cross breaks down and cries: "In part, he was grieving for Ted Lavender, but mostly it was for Martha, and for himself, . . . because he realized she did not love him and never would" (17).

Like *Cacciato,* the piece ends with the sacrifice of dreams for duties, but the lieutenant's ironic immolation of his keepsakes will do nothing to efface his guilt:

> On the morning after Ted Lavender died, First Lieutenant Jimmy Cross crouched at the bottom of his foxhole and burned Martha's letters. Then he burned the two photographs. . . .
>
> He realized it was only a gesture. Stupid, he thought. Sentimental, too, but mostly just stupid.
>
> Lavender was dead. You couldn't burn the blame.
>
> (22)

Nor can he efface his love for Martha, since "the letters were in his head," or the realization that "she wasn't involved. She signed the letters Love, but it wasn't love, and all the fine lines and technicalities did not matter" (23). Turning away from both his griefs, he resolves at the end of the story to dedicate the one and sacrifice the other to command responsibility: "He would dispense with love; it was not now a factor. And if anyone quarreled or complained, he would simply tighten his lips and arrange his shoulders in the correct command posture. He might give a curt little nod. Or he might not. He might just shrug and say, Carry on, then they would saddle up and form into a column and move out toward the villages west of Than Khe" (25). But the conclusiveness of this resolution is belied by the play-acting going on inside his imagination, which tries to cover up or replace the death of Lavender and the loss of Martha.

The final reference in *Things* carries us back to other vain attempts to close off the trauma of Lavender's death. Kiowa notes so repetitiously that the dead man went down "like cement" that his fixation irritates Norman Bowker, who makes a crude joke of the death ("A pisser, you know? Still zipping himself up. Zapped while zipping" [17]); waiting for the dustoff, his comrades smoke the rest of the dead man's dope. The most decisive reaction displaces traumatization with futilely murderous devastation: "When the dustoff arrived, they carried Lavender aboard. Afterward they burned Than Khe. They marched until dusk, then dug their holes, and that night Kiowa kept explaining how you had to be there, how fast it was, how the poor guy just dropped like so much concrete. Boom-down, he said. Like cement" (8). The constriction of the atrocity is followed so closely by the reintrusion of Lavender's death that traumatization seems to be feeding on itself. And a more detailed repetition of the sequence reintrudes later, suggesting the recurrence of what has been repressed in the narrative: "After the chopper took Lavender away, Lieutenant Jimmy Cross led his men into the village of Than Khe. They burned everything. They shot chickens and dogs, they trashed the village well, they called in artillery and watched the wreckage, then they marched for several hours through the hot afternoon, and then at dusk, while Kiowa explained how Lavender died, Lieutenant Cross found himself trembling" (16). Cross's trembling initiates the little breakdown noted above; and his tears for Lavender, Martha, and himself show the futility of violence as a remedy for traumatization.

In its original form, **"The Things They Carried"** appeared as a short story in *Esquire* in 1986, and O'Brien's masterpiece has been frequently reprinted in anthologies. By itself, the piece is not explicitly a post-traumatic narrative, and it lacks the presence of the character Tim O'Brien as participant, observer, storyteller, or audience. In *Things,* however, O'Brien adds a first-person postscript that establishes the relationship between traumatization and storytelling which characterizes the book as a whole. This second piece in the volume tells of Lieutenant Cross's postwar visit to the Massachusetts home of the writer Tim O'Brien. Not only does it introduce the figure who will be the chief character in the rest of *Things,* but it also introduces the subject of unresolved trauma and the trope of memory:

> Spread out across the kitchen table were maybe a hundred old photographs. There were pictures of Rat Kiley and Kiowa and Mitchell Sanders, all of us, the faces incredibly soft and young. At one point, I *remember* [emphasis added], we paused over a snapshot of Ted Lavender, and after a while Jimmy rubbed his eyes and said he'd never forgiven himself for Lavender's death. It was something that would never go away, he said quietly, and I nodded and told him I felt the same about certain things.
>
> (29)

They reminisce about happier memories, and Cross goes on to reveal that he met Martha in 1979, when he discovered that she was an unmarried Lutheran missionary, and impulsively revealed his undiminished love for her. Gently but decisively rejected, he explains that he now carries a copy of the photo of her that he had burned in Viet Nam, her farewell gift to him at the end of their final meeting. As his former lieutenant's visit ends, Tim O'Brien gets his approval to write a story about what they have discussed, and Cross jokes about getting Martha back—"Maybe she'll read it and come begging"—and being portrayed positively—"Make me out to be a good guy, okay? Brave and handsome, all that stuff. Best platoon leader ever" (31).

O'Brien's brief narrative, which is titled **"Love,"** thus functions as the inspiration for the longer narrative that precedes it, a truer story than the heroic melodrama requested by its protagonist. Viewed as a unit, the two works become a metafiction representing both the persistence of trauma—Cross is still bothered by Lavender's death and its connection to his unrequited love for Martha—and the reformulation of trauma into a fiction

that transcends and transforms it: Jimmy Cross's double burden becomes the foundation and groundwork of a fiction masterpiece. **"Love"** is also O'Brien's first example in *Things* of a true war story that isn't about war, as its title indicates. Its title identifies as well the thematic significance of Jimmy Cross's traumatization in **"The Things They Carried"**: the conflict between loving his men and loving Martha and the way in which love, like war, can be unbearable.

Although Lavender's death is recuperated fictionally as Jimmy Cross's trauma, the deaths of Kiowa and the enemy soldier, which are narrated in **"Speaking of Courage"** and **"The Man I Killed,"** respectively, continue to haunt the narrator. The Native American, who perished during a horrendous night mortar attack, was his best friend in the war; the unnamed North Vietnamese was killed by Tim O'Brien himself. Like Ted Lavender's, both deaths appear as intrusive fragments that violate chronology. They persist through several different versions, just as Curt Lemon's death is narrated four times in **"How to Tell a True War Story."** Moreover, like Jimmy Cross's obsession with Lavender and Martha, they are not simply past events but remain present in the narrator's imagination.

Like Lavender's death, both traumas are also reconfigured metafictionally in *The Things They Carried.* In contrast to the relatively simple sequence of war story followed by its putative origin "many years after the war" (**"Love"** 29), however, the traumatic origins of **"Speaking of Courage"** and **"The Man I Killed"** are revealed only indirectly and evasively. Their complex representation reflects their deeper level of shock: The narrator cannot get over Kiowa's death or his own killing of the young soldier, whereas Ted Lavender is Jimmy Cross's burden, and **"The Things They Carried"** a finely polished transformation of trauma into a coherent fiction by a former soldier who has become a writer.

The narrator identifies himself also as a trauma survivor in **"Love,"** where he tells Jimmy Cross of his own haunting by unnamed things that cannot be forgotten. Only in the penultimate list of memories in **"Spin"** does Tim O'Brien's traumatization begin to emerge, however, and only as a disconnected series of fragments that intrudes into and concludes a list of remembered images from the war:

> A red clay trail outside the village of My Khe.
>
> A hand grenade.
>
> A slim, dead, dainty young man of about twenty.
>
> Kiowa saying, "No choice, Tim. What else could you do?"
>
> Kiowa saying, "Right?"
>
> Kiowa saying, "Talk to me."
>
> (40)

The full story will finally come out ten pieces later, only to be further explained and justified in **"Ambush"** and **"Good Form."** While the intrusive memory focuses on the man he killed, Tim O'Brien's fixation on Kiowa's presence as comforter significantly ties together this earlier trauma with his friend's horrible death, as if the latter itself were a terrible memory only beginning to emerge from repression.

Like the stories, therefore, the narrator's traumatization only gradually and fragmentarily defines itself. The reference in **"Love"** to experiences that will not go away is more fully realized in **"The Man I Killed,"** the twelfth of the twenty-two sections of *Things*. Occupying the center of the book, it begins suddenly as an image of the narrator's victim that goes on for nearly a full page, an anatomy that begins with the head—"His jaw was in his throat, his upper lip and teeth were gone, his one eye was shut, his other eye was a star-shaped hole"—and ends at his feet—"His rubber sandals had been blown off. One lay beside him, the other a few meters up the trail" (139). Gradually the image becomes an obituary as the narrator imagines the background and circumstances that have led the "slim young man" to his death on a trail outside My Khe. And within another page the characterization has become a memory, a narrative, and a scene of trauma as the narrator squats next to the body while Azar exults ("you laid him out like Shredded fuckin' Wheat. . . . Rice Krispies, you know?" [140]) and then Kiowa tries to talk his friend out of his shock: "Nothing *anybody* could do. Come on, Tim, stop staring (141). . . . You feel terrible, I know that (142). . . . Talk to me" (144). These three final words end **"The Man I Killed,"** but not the trauma, which is presented not as an episode in the past but as an intrusive memory haunting the narrator. Talking only to himself, he never responds to Kiowa; therefore, although he is able to recover this traumatic experience (unlike his part in Kiowa's own death, as we shall see), it remains unexpressed to others. As studies of PTSD survivors have revealed (Shay 115-19), destroying the enemy can be as terrible an experience as the death of one's comrades, but ideological and social codes make the public expression of grief in such cases more difficult. O'Brien's narrator tries to resolve his feelings both by re-creating the young Vietnamese soldier in his own image, especially his sense of obligation to others, and by imagining that his victim's death will find some redemption: "He was not a Communist. He was a citizen and a soldier. . . . He was not a fighter. . . . He liked books. . . . Beyond anything else, he was afraid of disgracing himself, and therefore his family and village. . . . He knew he would fall dead and wake up in the stories of his village and people" (140-44 passim). But however much the narrator refigures his own distress, it can neither be laid to rest nor communicated to others.

The persistent cover-up of trauma is also dramatized in **"Ambush,"** right after **"The Man I Killed"** has dramatically re-created the incident alluded to in the fragments of **"Spin."** When his daughter was nine years old, the narrator begins, she questioned his obsession with Vietnam: "You keep writing these war stories . . . so I guess you must've killed somebody" (147). "Of course not," he answered her then but now relates for the third time the account of his killing a young enemy soldier with a grenade as the latter passed by his ambush position on a trail near My Khe. This is a matter-of-fact, third-person account that rewrites the fragments of **"Spin"** and the direct traumatization of **"The Man I Killed"** as a coherent, cause-and-effect narrative. At the end, however, Tim O'Brien's continued psychic wound is made apparent as he imagines what might have happened if he had simply let his victim pass:

> Even now I haven't finished sorting it out. Sometimes I forgive myself, other times I don't. In the ordinary hours of life I try not to dwell on it, but now and then, when I'm reading a newspaper or just sitting alone in a room, I'll look up and see the young man coming out of the morning fog. I'll watch him walk toward me, his shoulders slightly stooped, his head cocked to the side, and he'll pass within a few yards of me and suddenly smile at some secret thought and then continue up the trail to where it bends back into the fog.
>
> (149-50)

The almost journalistic account of his kill is thus undercut by the persistent trauma that concludes **"Ambush,"** and both seem to make the response to his daughter a lie intended to protect her innocence and his repression of the memory.

As we have noted, however, in **"Good Form"** Tim O'Brien insists that everything in *Things* has been invented and then presents a fourth version of the incident at My Khe, a confession that he was present but did not kill the young man. "But listen"—he warns us after finishing this account—"even *that* story is made up" (203). Finally, we seem to reach an explanation that would respond both to the kindly listener, who would like the narrator to stop writing war stories, and to his daughter, who wonders why he continues to do so: He writes stories not to recall past experiences but to make them up, to overcome the emotional constriction of the past. Stories, he asserts, can "make things present" so that "I can look at things I never looked at. I can attach faces to grief and love and pity and God. I can be brave. I can make myself feel again" (204). In this account, writing transforms Vietnam into morally meaningful fiction through fictional traumatization; but it also functions as therapy for a still-unidentified guilt connected with things that the narrator couldn't carry at the time they occurred. We might associate his grief with O'Brien's own feelings that if he had been brave enough, he would never have even been in the war. But that would be to mistake Tim O'Brien for the author and to analyze a state of mind that the story deliberately leaves undefinable. Just as the various versions of **"The Man I Killed"** deny an authoritative account, the narrator's feelings resist the closure of a final resolution. In fiction, he concludes in **"Good Form,"** his daughter Kathleen can ask,

> "Daddy, tell the truth . . . did you ever kill anybody?" And I can say, honestly, "Of course not."
>
> Or I can say, honestly, "Yes."
>
> (204)

Storytelling thus becomes a vehicle for the endless reproduction of trauma, revealing *and* covering it up, revising what has happened or inventing what has not. The author of **"Good Form"** has no daughter, of course; but that everything in the story and in *Things* as a whole is made up means that O'Brien is representing how guilt and grief are endlessly recycled rather than simply recalling his own.

Such recirculation is also fashioned with authentic complexity in the case of Kiowa's death. The narrator's friend is buried alive within a communal privy where the platoon has camped at night when it is heavily mortared during a rainstorm. Kiowa's death is variously described and revised in four of the pieces in *Things:* **"Speaking of Courage,"** a former comrade's reminiscence of the horror as he drives aimlessly about his hometown's lake on the Fourth of July years after his service in Viet Nam; the appended **"Notes,"** in which Tim O'Brien explains how he came to write the story; the following account, **"In the Field,"** which narrates the platoon's recovery of the body from the mud and filth in which it was submerged; and **"Field Trip,"** a description of the narrator's return to the site of Kiowa's death in Viet Nam twenty years after it occurred. Alternately moving, horrifying, and sardonic, O'Brien's sequence of episodes powerfully examines the persistence of trauma and the attempt to put it to rest.

"Speaking of Courage" is a revision of an earlier, prize-winning story of the same title that O'Brien published in 1976. That first version is an appendage to *Cacciato,* for the soldier who drives aimlessly around his hometown's lake, regretting his failure to be a hero by rescuing Frenchie Tucker from a VC tunnel, is Paul Berlin. Details of the setting are taken directly from O'Brien's hometown, Worthington, Minnesota; moreover, Berlin's circuit replicates the description in *Combat Zone* of O'Brien's own desultory drives around town during the summer before his induction into the army (25). Although its counterpart won an O. Henry Prize, its later refabrication in *Things* is an even stronger work, another of O'Brien's masterpieces. Here, the unhappy veteran is Norman Bowker, traumatized by his

failure to rescue Kiowa from his terrible fate, alienated from the town and his previous civilian life, unable to talk with his father about almost winning the Silver Star by saving his friend's life. The first sentence sums up Norman's condition with eloquent understatement that could be applied to countless other traumatized veterans: "The war was over and there was no place in particular to go" (157). The narrative bleakly mirrors the trauma survivor's isolation and anomie as he circles the lake twelve times, recalling his failure to pull Kiowa out of the mud and excrement along the Song Tra Bong while distantly observing the minutiae of small-town life. The persistence of the traumatic memory is captured by the meaningless circularity of his drive, briefly interrupted at an A&W Root Beer stand, before he immerses himself in the lake and watches the town's Independence Day fireworks display. Unable either to let go of Kiowa or to feel at home, Bowker narrates his war story as an experience that he would like to tell his father if the latter were not at home watching a baseball game on TV and if his son did not feel so guilty and ashamed: "[H]e would have talked about the medal he did not win and why he did not win it. . . . 'So tell me,' his father would have said" (161). His untold tale becomes for him an epitome of the true story of Vietnam, a revelation that he feels would fall on deaf ears: "The town could not talk, and would not listen. 'How'd you like to hear about the war?' he might have asked, but the place could only blink and shrug. It had no memory, therefore no guilt. . . . It was a brisk, polite town. It did not know shit about shit, and did not care to know" (163). The only willing listener is the voice he hears on the A&W squawk box, his only message an order for a Mama Burger and fries. Just before he stops at Sunset Park and stands in the lake, he finally arrives at a dark enlightenment:

> There was nothing to say.
>
> He could not talk about it and never would. The evening was smooth and warm.
>
> If it had been possible, which it wasn't, he would have explained how his friend Kiowa slipped away that night beneath the dark swampy field. He was folded in with the war; he was part of the waste.
>
> (172)

The final personal pronoun is ambiguous, of course, so that the attempt to finally bury Kiowa is not only unredemptive but suggests that Bowker has died in some sense as well.

The **"Notes"** that follow this haunting portrayal of persistent trauma are the closest O'Brien comes to identifying himself directly with the narrator of *The Things They Carried,* who extends Bowker's guilt to his own. Identifying himself as the author of *Going After Cacciato,* Tim O'Brien tells us that the original version of

"Speaking of Courage" was written in 1975 "at the suggestion of Norman Bowker, who three years later hanged himself in the locker room of a YMCA in his hometown in central Iowa" (177). Like **"Love,"** it purports to present the materials from which the preceding story was constructed. Thus, Norman Bowker's long letter to the narrator begins with the confession that "there's no place to go. Not just in this lousy little town. In general. My life, I mean. It's almost like I got killed over in Nam . . . Hard to describe. That night when Kiowa got wasted, I sort of sank down into the sewage with him . . . Feels like I'm still in deep shit" (177-78) [ellipses in the original]. Written originally to give a voice to his former comrade's traumatization, the story disappointed its author as an unfunctional part of the novel—"*Going After Cacciato* was a war story; **'Speaking of Courage'** was a postwar story" (181)—and was published as a short story, we are told. But beyond its formal flaws, the substitution of Paul Berlin for Bowker and the elimination of the terrible night in Viet Nam left it morally flawed as well: "[S]omething about the story had frightened me—I was afraid to speak directly, afraid to remember—and in the end the piece had been ruined by a failure to tell the full and exact truth about our night in the shit field," the narrator confesses to us. Upon its publication, Bowker's reaction, too, was a reproach: "'It's not terrible,' he wrote me, 'but you left out Vietnam. Where's Kiowa? Where's the shit?'"—and "eight months later he hanged himself" (181).

Unlike **"Love,"** this account of how a preceding story was written involves the narrator directly in the consequences of traumatization: Unable or unwilling to represent his own experience, he effaces his former comrade's story. **"Speaking of Courage"** (1976) becomes a "false war story," and Tim O'Brien's failure to refigure the trauma fictionally so that it may be relieved is at least partly responsible for Norman Bowker's final despair. As a result, the narrator is so implicated in Bowker's agony that he identifies the rewritten story as an act of memorialization and deferred obligation: "Now, a decade after his death, I'm hoping that **'Speaking of Courage'** makes good on Norman Bowker's silence. And I hope it's a better story" (181).

Noting how strongly he had been moved by Bowker's original letter, Tim O'Brien states that "I did not look on my work as therapy, and still don't" (179). In revising the earlier story, however, the author of **Things** has represented it as a trebly therapeutic fiction. In finally giving voice to Bowker's repressed trauma, the narrator addresses his feelings of guilt for not doing it originally. But in addition, the end of **"Notes"** reveals that the new story allowed him to give voice to his *own* traumatization: "It was hard stuff to write. Kiowa, after all, had been a close friend, and for years I've avoided thinking about his death and my own complicity in it.

Even here it's not easy. In the interests of truth, however, I want to make it clear that Norman Bowker was in no way responsible for what happened to Kiowa. Norman did not experience a failure of nerve that night. He did not freeze up or lose the Silver Star for valor. That part of the story is my own" (182). As Kaplan notes (1995: 192), the final sentence is ambiguous because of the narrator's peculiar fictional role as both writer and participant in his own scenarios: Has he simply made Bowker feel guilty for Kiowa's death, or does he feel guilty for Kiowa's death himself? If the former, Bowker would have revealed in the letter his failure to save his friend; if the latter, the *narrator* failed to pull Kiowa out of the slime. Of course, both Bowker and the narrator Tim O'Brien may feel guilty about Kiowa's death whether or not they could have saved him because soldiers frequently feel guilt and grief if their own survival of a comrade's death seems unfair or incomprehensible (Shay 69). In any case, Tim O'Brien's personal trauma—his "complicity" in Kiowa's fate—has either been refigured through Norman Bowker or remains something that cannot be told.

"In the Field," the piece that follows **"Notes,"** raises the issue of responsibility and guilt again only to leave it unresolved. The story follows the platoon of eighteen soldiers on the morning after the mortar attack as they comb their excrement- and mud-infested night position for Kiowa's body. Formally, this narrative resembles **"The Things They Carried"** and **"Speaking of Courage"** in that the Tim O'Brien character is absent and the narration is relatively impersonal. But while those works were followed by metafictional accounts of their traumatic origins, **"In the Field"** simply extends the trauma of **"Speaking of Courage"** and **"Notes."** As with the title story, omniscient narration alternates with an intimate third-person perspective as the point of view alternates from the activities of the platoon as a whole to the private meditations of Lieutenant Jimmy Cross and an unnamed younger soldier who are searching the flooded field by themselves. Both feel responsible for Kiowa's death: Although Cross carried out orders in pitching camp atop the communal waste field, he ignored the villagers' warnings and blames himself for the GI's death. The unnamed soldier feels guilty for switching on his flashlight to show Kiowa his girlfriend's picture just before the lethal mortar rounds hit the platoon. But even the normally sadistic Azar feels chastened. Once Kiowa's body has been pulled out of the slime, Azar sees his own jokes about the death ("[e]ating shit" [187], "one more redskin bites the dirt" [188]) as murderous: "[W]hen I saw the guy, it made me feel . . . sort of guilty almost, like if I'd kept my mouth shut none of it would've ever happened. Like it was my fault" (197).

Norman Bowker's response as he looks "out across the wet field" is closest to the truth, however: "Nobody's fault," he said. "Everybody's" (197). As a result, trauma is at least temporarily relieved, not least because Kiowa's corpse undergoes a strange resurrection. His body, though hideously disfigured, is recovered by his comrades, a communal ritual that leaves them peculiarly satisfied: "For all of them it was a relief to have it finished. . . . They felt bad for Kiowa. But they also felt a kind of giddiness, a secret joy, because they were alive, and because even the rain was preferable to being sucked under a shit field, and because it was all a matter of luck and happenstance" (197).

And for the lieutenant and Kiowa's unnamed friend, too, the story ends with ironic absolution. The young soldier is searching for his girlfriend's picture, not his friend's body; after all, "Kiowa's *dead*" he tells the lieutenant (194), who then watches him continue his search, "as if something might finally be salvaged from all the waste," and "silently wishe[s] the boy luck" (195). And when the young GI finally tries to confess his own culpability, the lieutenant "wasn't listening," floating in the muck and meditating on everything that could be blamed "when a man died," from "the war" to "an old man in Omaha who forgot to vote" (198-99). At the end of the piece, the letter of self-incrimination to Kiowa's father that Jimmy Cross has been revising throughout is replaced by a daydream of going golfing "back home in New Jersey": "When the war was over, he thought, maybe then he would write a letter to Kiowa's father. Or maybe not. Maybe he would just take a couple of practice swings and knock the ball down the middle and pick up his clubs and walk off into the afternoon" (199). Perhaps it is the shit field itself, a symbolic paradigm of the ghastly enterprise of Vietnam, that is the final cause of Kiowa's death. O'Brien's ironic title, **"In the Field,"** modulates from a metonym for a battleground to a sense that everyone in the story is "In the Shit," a morass so all-consuming that staying alive is all that matters.

Yet even after this ironic closure to Kiowa's death, O'Brien's fourth handling of the subject suggests that the narrator's own trauma remains unhealed by his writing. **"Field Trip"** begins, in fact, by alluding to the earlier episode: "A few months after completing '**In the Field,**' I returned with my daughter to Vietnam, where we visited the site of Kiowa's death, and where I looked for signs of forgiveness or personal grace or whatever else the land might offer" (207). Although **"Notes"** hinted at Tim O'Brien's feeling some responsibility for Kiowa's death, his own role has been left unclear: Did he freeze when his friend was pulled beneath the slime, like Norman Bowker in **"Speaking of Courage"**? Is the young, unnamed soldier in **"In the Field"** a version of his guilt, as suggested by Mark Taylor (227-28), distorted beyond being recognized by the reader? In any case, the persistence of trauma is explicit in his meditations as he looks at the field of death:

This little field, I thought, had swallowed so much. My best friend. My pride. My belief in myself as a man of some small dignity and courage. Still, it was hard to find any real emotion. It simply wasn't there. After that long night in the rain, I'd seemed to grow cold inside, all the illusions gone, all the old ambitions and hopes for myself sucked away into the mud. Over the years that coldness had never entirely disappeared . . . somehow I blamed this place for what I had become, and I blamed it for taking away the person I had once been. For twenty years this field had embodied all the waste that was Vietnam, all the vulgarity and horror.

(210)

While a government interpreter waits with his ten-year-old daughter, bemused like Cowling's Melinda by the symptoms of her father's traumatization—"Sometimes you're pretty weird, aren't you?" she has observed earlier (209)—Tim O'Brien wades into the muck of the paddy, squats and then sits down in the slime at the place where "Mitchell Sanders had found Kiowa's rucksack." There, he offers his friend's old hunting hatchet to the land beneath him.[3] As "tiny bubbles broke along the surface" (an image associated with the disappearance of Kiowa's head in **"Speaking of Courage"** [168] and **"In the Field"** [193]), his attempt to "think of something decent to say" inevitably settles on the all-purpose GI mantra for the trauma of Vietnam: "'Well,' I finally managed, 'There it is'" (212). This moving scene of expiation and memorialization culminates with the narrator's sense of personal catharsis: "The sun made me squint. Twenty years. A lot like yesterday, a lot like never. In a way, maybe, I'd gone under with Kiowa, and now after two decades I'd finally worked my way out. A hot afternoon, a bright August sun, and the war was over" (212). It also recapitulates but transcends Kiowa's immersion in the field and Norman Bowker's frustrated attempt to cleanse himself—or drown himself—in his hometown lake on the Fourth of July.

This apparent closure of trauma is qualified and decisively undercut by O'Brien, however. The narrator's exact role in Kiowa's death is uncertain, as if that were a story that he can never recount, despite his resolution in **"Notes"** to tell "the full and exact truth." Within *Things,* **"Field Trip"** is followed by **"The Ghost Soldiers"** and **"Night Life,"** two grimly comic accounts of the narrator's wounding and Rat Kiley's self-mutilation in the war, respectively, which is *not* over for his imagination. And **"Field Trip"** itself includes an unresolved source of guilt and remorse. Tim O'Brien's personal ritual is witnessed not only by his daughter and his official guide but also by a farmer whose land was once taken over by the Americans but has now been restored to its communal purposes. Although Kiowa's hatchet has been buried, the narrator cannot so easily translate his personal peace into a wider redemption: "The man's face was dark and solemn. As we stared at each other, neither of us moving, I felt something go shut in my heart while something else swung open. Briefly, I wondered if the old man might walk over to exchange a few war stories, but instead he picked up a shovel and raised it over his head and held it there for a time, grimly, like a flag, then he brought the shovel down and said something to his friend and began digging into the hard, dry ground" (212). The narrator, an intruder in peace as in war, reacts immediately: "I stood up and waded out of the water" (212). His ten-year-old daughter responds instinctively to what she has seen, and the story ends with questions about its apparent resolution:

> When we reached the jeep, Kathleen turned and glanced out at the field.
>
> "That old man," she said, "is he mad at you or something?"
>
> "I hope not."
>
> "He *looks* mad."
>
> "No," I said. "All that's finished."
>
> (213)

This reassurance must depend on the farmer's attitude, of course, which the narrator cannot interpret but would prefer not to think about. Like the barely registered destruction of Than Khe after the death of Ted Lavender or Rat Kiley's enthusiasm about how Curt Lemon "liked testing himself, just man against gook" (75), the trauma of Vietnam involves more than the death of American comrades for the narrator—those are simply the stories he can tell best.

As noted above, **"Field Trip"** is immediately preceded by **"Good Form,"** which reveals that "almost everything" (203) in the book has been invented. This reminder also calls into question the apparent personal recovery dramatized in the subsequent piece. Its soul-baring is so convincing that **"Field Trip"** seems an authentic personal experience rather than the self-confessed fiction of everything that appears before it; yet we can only believe in its authenticity if we believe in the "happening-truth" of the preceding fictions concerning Kiowa. We are left, therefore, with a series of episodes that represents an attempt to write about an experience that never happened as it is described. Yet by inventing a narrator who makes up traumatic experiences and recoveries, O'Brien paradoxically represents the ineffability of such experiences, what Kali Tal (1996) has called "the impossibility of recreating the event for the reader" (121). Whatever the protagonist of *The Things They Carried* has experienced can never be fully represented through writing—and that is why he can never stop writing about it.

"THE LIVES OF THE DEAD": BRINGING THEM BACK ALIVE

The Things They Carried ends with **"The Lives of the Dead,"** an account of how the narrator became a professional writer. Although published as an independent story in the January 1989 issue of *Esquire,* the piece is a deliberate conclusion to the book, incorporating and dramatizing once more what **Things** has exemplified about true war stories and their relationship to traumatic experiences. Beginning with the simple assertion that "stories can save us," this final fiction resurrects Ted Lavender, Kiowa, Curt Lemon, "an old man sprawled beside a pigpen, and several others whose bodies I once lifted and dumped into a truck. They're all dead. But in a story," the narrator's introduction continues, "the dead sometimes smile and sit up and return to the world" (255). Combining the tropes of memory and storytelling, **"Lives"** [**"The Lives of the Dead"**] brings back the war dead in brief episodes that alternate with the narrator's account of his love for his grade-school classmate Linda, their first and only date, her death from brain cancer at the age of nine, and his dreaming her alive thereafter. By combining Vietnam and a love story, soldiers and nine-year-olds, **"The Lives of the Dead"** transcends the war and exemplifies the narrator's earlier insistence that "a true war story is never about war" (91).

The paradox of the title identifies its real subject, a central concern of O'Brien's fifth book as a whole: the ways survivors carry the dead with them through the rest of their lives. **"The Lives of the Dead"** is filled with descriptions of corpses: an old Vietnamese farmer killed by an American air strike on an unfriendly village; Ted Lavender; *The Man Who Never Was,* a dead body dropped along the French coast to deceive the Nazis about the D-Day landings in a movie that Timmy and Linda saw on their one date; Linda's body in her funeral home casket, "bloated," the skin "at her cheeks . . . stretched out tight like the rubber skin on a balloon just before it pops open" (270); twenty-seven "enemy KIAs" [enemy soldiers killed in action] dumped into a truck by Tim O'Brien and Mitchell Sanders after their battle in the mountains—all "badly bloated . . . clothing . . . stretched tight like sausage skins . . . heavy . . . feet . . . bluish green and cold" (271). For Timmy, however, "It didn't seem real. A mistake, I thought. The girl lying in the white casket wasn't Linda. . . . I knew this was Linda, but even so I couldn't find much to recognize. . . . She looked dead. She looked heavy and totally dead" (270). And for Mitchell Sanders, gathering the remains of a great victory that he and the narrator have survived brings a comparably banal enlightenment:

> At one point [he] looked at me and said, "Hey, man, I just realized something."
>
> "What?"
>
> He wiped his eyes and spoke very quietly, as if awed by his own wisdom. "Death sucks," he said.
>
> (271)

The human imagination is unsatisfied with this trite truth, as Timmy's bewilderment and Sanders's tears for the enemy suggest, and O'Brien dramatizes various attempts to supplement or transmute the dead body throughout the story. **"The Lives of the Dead"** begins with a traumatic experience for the narrator, who cannot look at the decaying corpse of the old man who is "the only confirmed kill" (255) of Jimmy Cross's punitive air strike. A newcomer to the war, he is further appalled as his comrades shake the corpse's hand and then prop it up as the guest of honor at a macabre get-acquainted party that gradually turns "that awesome act of greeting the dead" into a ceremony: "They proposed toasts. They lifted their canteens and drank to the old man's family and ancestors, his many grandchildren, his newfound life after death. It was more than mockery. There was a formality to it, like a funeral without the sadness" (256-57). Kiowa comforts him later in the day, praising the courage of the narrator's refusal to participate, wishing that he had done the same but also reassuring him that "you're new here. You'll get used to it," since he assumes that "this was your first look at a real body" (257). The necrology of the scene is not simply repulsive, however, as the narrator realizes. Underneath the GIs' ghoulish humor and postmortem sadism lies an unconscious awareness of the mortality that they share with the Vietnamese farmer and an attempt to imagine beyond it. In **"Night Life,"** the previous piece in ***Things,*** Rat Kiley has a nervous breakdown when he begins to see himself and his comrades as potential corpses, imagining them as a collection of organic body parts rather than as human beings. By contrast, here the narrator's comrades transform a corpse into a life to be celebrated beyond the "real body." Their grotesquerie contrasts strikingly with the sterile funeral home where Timmy is left bewildered and unsatisfied by the reality of Linda's preserved body.

The resurrection of the dead pervades O'Brien's final work. Kiowa comes back here, after all, as the comforter at the end of this first episode. ***Things*** began with Ted Lavender's death, and it ends with his corpse waiting for a medevac but miraculously reanimated as Mitchell Sanders and the rest of the platoon conduct a dialogue with their comrade before sending him home: "'There it is, my man, this chopper gonna take you up high and cool. Gonna relax you. Gonna alter your whole perspective on this sorry, sorry shit.' . . . 'Roger that,' somebody said. 'I'm ready to fly'" (261). The last we hear and see of Rat Kiley's dearest friend is not the obliteration of his body but the full account of his trick-or-treating in the Vietnamese countryside on Halloween, "almost stark naked, the story went, just boots and balls and an M-16. . . . To listen to the story, especially as Rat Kiley told it, you'd never know that Curt Lemon was dead. He was still out there in the dark, naked and painted up, trick-or-treating, sliding from hootch to hootch in that crazy white ghost mask" (268).

It is the resurrection of Linda, however, that has made all the others possible. Although Kiowa assumes that the Vietnamese farmer provides Tim O'Brien's first look at a corpse, he is wrong. "It sounds funny," O'Brien's persona tells him, "but that poor old man, he reminds me of . . . [ellipsis in the original] I mean, there's this girl I used to know. I took her to the movies once. My first date" (257). "[T]hat's a bad date," Kiowa understandably responds, ending the first section of **"The Lives of the Dead."** Most of the rest is taken up with the narrator's memories of his love for Linda, their going off to see *The Man Who Never Was* with his parents as chaperones, the exposure of her fatal illness, her death, and his visit to the funeral home. As he recounts it, his life as a storyteller began when he imagined his love alive the day after Linda died, in "a pink dress and shiny black shoes," all traces of her illness gone, "laughing and running up the empty street, kicking a big aluminum water bucket" (266). Timmy breaks down, knowing that she's dead, but Linda insists that "it doesn't *matter*" (267) and forces him to stop crying. Thereafter, Linda's death and his grief are replaced by dreaming her back to life and his subsequent career as an author: "She was dead. I understood that. After all, I'd seen her body, and yet even as a nine-year-old I had begun to practice the magic of stories. Some I just dreamed up. Others I wrote down—the scenes and dialogue. And at nighttime I'd slide into sleep knowing that Linda would be there waiting for me. Once, I remember, we went ice skating late at night, tracing loops and circles under yellow floodlights" (272). By asking what it's like to be dead, Timmy initially questions the truth of his own imagination, but Linda sets him straight: "'Well, right now,' she said, 'I'm *not* dead. But when I am, it's like . . . [ellipsis in original] I don't know, I guess it's like being inside a book that nobody's reading'" (273).

According to this account, therefore, writing grows directly out of trauma but refashions it beyond the unreality of death. Like the rest of the dead, Linda comes back to life through the narrator's stories, but so does he as he examines a photograph of himself as a nine-year-old:

> [T]here is no doubt that the Timmy smiling at the camera is the Tim I am now. . . . The human life is all one thing, like a blade tracing loops on ice: a little kid, a twenty-three-year-old infantry sergeant, a middle-aged writer knowing guilt and sorrow.
>
> And as a writer now, I want to save Linda's life. Not her body—her life.
>
> (265)

In saving her, therefore, he saves himself. Near the end of **"The Lives of the Dead,"** however, we are reminded that while stories can save lives, what is saved is itself a fiction: "I'm forty-three years old, and a writer now, still dreaming Linda alive in exactly the same way. She's not the embodied Linda; she's mostly made up, with a new identity and a new name. . . . Her real name doesn't matter. She was nine years old. I loved her and then she died" (273). The facts are less important than the truth that the story has compelled us to believe. Employing the tropes of memory and storytelling for the last time as the book comes to an end, O'Brien uses them together not to represent the fact of death—even the dead are fictions in a true war story—but to save the lives of Linda and his other characters forever: "And yet right here, in the spell of memory and imagination, I can still see her as if through ice, as if I'm gazing into some other world, a place where there are no brain tumors and no funeral homes, where there are no bodies at all. I can see Kiowa, too, and Ted Lavender and Curt Lemon, and sometimes I can even see Timmy skating with Linda under the yellow flood-lights. I'm young and happy. I'll never die" (273). Ultimately, of course, by making us believe in the man who never was, fiction can create people who will never die.

O'Brien's great book has certainly done both, but it is O'Brien's persona, a fictional creation, not necessarily O'Brien himself, who seems to have saved his life through writing by the end of **"The Lives of the Dead."** A survivor of trauma who has translated what he could not carry into true war stories, Tim O'Brien resembles the author's other protagonists in passing through fear, guilt, and grief to achieve his own separate peace. The narrator's ability to memorialize a terrible war so masterfully makes **The Things They Carried** O'Brien's most accomplished fiction, and his persona's ostensible resolution of his personal trauma also makes it the most redemptive. Yet Tim O'Brien's sense of well-being in **The Things They Carried** is also a function of his narrow characterization. Except for the relationships with his daughter and Linda, he has no life outside of writing; in fact, everything he does, says, or remembers in the book becomes part of its storytelling. Trauma is endlessly recirculated through the tropes of memory and storytelling or explicitly fabricated in multiple versions, never experienced directly by the fictional protagonist as it is in the three previous novels. Like **Things**, O'Brien's next book will be formidably metafictional, but its hero's inescapable, comprehensive, and endless traumatization will cost him his life, not enable him to save it.

Notes

1. "The Ghost Soldiers" appeared in *Esquire* in 1981 (March) and was reprinted in the 1982 O. Henry Award *Prize Stories* volume. "The Things They Carried" first appeared in the August 1986 *Esquire* and won the 1987 National Magazine Award in Fiction. "How to Tell a True War Story" (October 1987), "The Lives of the Dead" (January

1989), and "Sweetheart of the Song Tra Bong" (July 1989) also appeared in *Esquire,* while four other sections of *Things* appeared first as short stories: "Speaking of Courage" (*Granta,* Winter 1989), "In the Field" (*Gentleman's Quarterly,* December 1989), "On the Rainy River" (*Playboy,* January 1990), and "Field Trip" (*McCall's,* August 1990). Six other shorter pieces in *Harper's* (March 1990) and *Mānoa* (Spring 1990) were to be slightly altered when they appeared shortly afterward in *The Things They Carried.* (For bibliographical details, see Calloway 1991 and 1993.)

2. In turn, O'Brien noted to Martin Naparsteck, "the Tim character" is "transformed again" into the character Norman Bowker (7). Here as elsewhere, O'Brien's self-revisions are at the center of his fiction making. The transformations of O'Brien into Norman Bowker (and Paul Berlin) in "Speaking of Courage" are discussed below.

3. As Calloway (1995) notes, the hunting hatchet in the original 1990 edition of the story is replaced by moccasins in the 1991 paperback editions (Penguin and Flamingo [U.K.]). Perhaps "burying the hatchet" was too flagrant a symbol for the narrator's attempted therapeutic gesture.

Marilyn Wesley (essay date spring 2002)

SOURCE: Wesley, Marilyn. "Truth and Fiction in Tim O'Brien's *If I Die in a Combat Zone* and *The Things They Carried.*" *College Literature* 29, no. 2 (spring 2002): 1-18.

[*In the following essay, Wesley contrasts O'Brien's representation of the truth in* If I Die in a Combat Zone *and* The Things They Carried.]

The requirement of truth as a faithful portrayal of unique experience is the standard most consistently applied to the literature of the Vietnam War. In his discussion of memoirs of the war, J. T. Hansen observes that all the writers he studied shared the objective of "authenticity," an authority based on "knowledge of the war they experienced" (1990, 134-35). Similarly, Donald Ringnalda points out that for the former soldiers, who are the most exacting audience for the Vietnam story, the standard of evaluation is "accuracy, factualness, faithful attention to details" (1990, 65). Nevertheless, as Lorrie Smith argues, verisimilitude has "no inherent value" if the text does not also examine "the cultural assumptions which animate and give meaning to its images" (1990, 90). In *The Body in Pain,* Elaine Scarry theorizes a basis for this discrepancy by explaining that narrative rendition is an integral component of war because the story of war is the exposition of a special kind of violence: deliberate violence that in turn provokes narrative deliberation. For war is the calculated action of a society rather than the random accident of an individual, and, although war is aggression against singular mortal bodies, its effect, according to Scarry, depends on collective fictive interpretations. War, she contends, is a violent contest in which each side tries to out-injure the other to effect "perceptual reversal" from the premise that "physical damage" is "acceptable and ideological and territorial sacrifices" are "unacceptable" to the opposed proposition that more physical damage is unacceptable and sacrifices of territory and belief are acceptable (1985, 89). Although fighting a war is a matter of personal experience—the effect of weapons on bodies—winning that war, the alteration of a society's predominant perceptions about its own purposes, is an effect of shared interpretation—the influence of narrative on minds. War, then, inevitably imposes a compromised version on the interpretation of genuine experience, an effect demonstrated by the literary conventions of Tim O'Brien's *If I Die in a Combat Zone* (1973). In *The Things They Carried* (1990), however, O'Brien has addressed the divergence of values— the contradiction between a standard of literary authenticity and the project of moral evaluation—inherent in the "truth" of his first work. Resisting the cultural closure imposed by the traditional war narrative, the postmodern form of *The Things They Carried* identifies Vietnam as a continuing struggle over representation despite the cessation of military combat.

From his earliest writing, O'Brien, to use the words of one of his more recent titles, has been engaged in the effort to "tell a true war story," but in so doing he has also struggled to evaluate the attitudes that produced and were produced by the Vietnam experience. Although there is no single defining plot for the American war story, there is in works by such writers as Crane, Hemingway, and Mailer an array of typical motifs: the noble example, the test of courage, the battle as initiation, the collective adventure of the platoon, and the disjunctive return to the civilian world. Too often, however, as Lynne Hanley argues in *Writing War,* traditional tropes have been turned into formulas through which violence is encoded as a desirable course of action that presents war experience as male, agentless intensification—the chief social activity through which "winners" are determined. The incidents in *If I Die in a Combat Zone,* O'Brien's collection of autobiographical essays on his experience in Vietnam, do not vary significantly from the incidents fictionalized in the stories of *The Things They Carried,* published seventeen years later. But whereas the first book relies on the standard of the representation of truth, the second, by abandoning literary realism, comes closer to presenting a polemic vision that insists on the problematic nature of the Vietnam experience. While the earlier book clearly intends a criticism of war, that effect is discounted by its reli-

ance on representational codes which annual subversive analysis—especially its characterization of the noble officer, and its preoccupation with the theme of courage—traditional devices which repress the disturbing impact of violence in Vietnam.

The verisimilitude of O'Brien's memoir is a result of his evident eagerness to communicate with his reader through straightforward description of sensations and emotions, thematic self-revelation, translation of the argot of the soldier, and simple organization based on sequential military events: induction, basic training, arrival in Vietnam, experience of battle, term in the rear, and return to the States. This effort to engage the reader is so powerful that O'Brien frequently presents his own experiences in the second person, as in this description of a helicopter-lift into a war zone:

> You begin to sweat. Even the rotor blades whipping cold air around like an air-conditioner, you begin to sweat.
>
> You light a cigarette, trying to think of something to say. A good joke would help, something funny. Laughing makes you believe you are resigned if not brave.

> (O'Brien 1973, 112)

Through its representation of easily identifiable physical and emotional effects—the chill of apprehension and the desire for laughter to relieve tension—the passage insists that the alien experience of war in Vietnam is directly transferable. In fact, the elision of author and reader, insisted upon by grammatical address in which the perspective of an absent "you" substitutes for direct observation of a participant "I," is engineered through the presentation of universal and simple correlatives of shared experience. This sense of apprehensible truth is reinforced through the soldier's engaging confession of weakness. Whatever genuine differences may exist between a non-combatant reader and the veteran writer are denied through the narrative production of verisimilitude. And although the insider's language the author uses to introduce the texture of alternative reality might separate his perspective from that of an outsider-reader, O'Brien cancels this effect through careful translation. "Pinkville," he explains is "GI slang for Song My, parent village of My Lai—the Batangan Peninsula or the Athletic Field, appropriately named for its flat acreage of grass and rice paddy" (1973, 126). And just as the alien geography of Vietnam can be naturalized for American consumption, so too can the chaotic experiences of the soldier be ordered as events in an identifiable succession of incidents from his introduction to the military to his exit, generally presented as historical movement from month to month.

It has long been acknowledged that realism as a literary form does more than record the texture of a setting or set forth believable characters. According to Leo Bersani, mimetic fiction also constructs "a secret complicity between the novelist and his society's illusions about its own order . . . by providing [society] with strategies for containing (and repressing) its disorder within significantly structured stories about itself" (1992, 247). That is, to present war as literary "truth" is to destroy its capacity to challenge the very social expectations that may have produced it.

The formal institution of easy assimilation in *If I Die in a Combat Zone* is reinforced thematically through archetypal representation of the heroic officer and the young initiate. Although O'Brien includes a variety of leaders—the insensitive Colonel Daud; the dangerous, bumbling ROTC-trained Captain Smith; a racist first sergeant fragged by black infantrymen; the maniacal Major Callicles; and the war-loving lieutenant, "Mad Mark"—his most extensive account of an officer is an encomium to Captain Johansen, especially fulsome on the occasion of Johansen's rotation out of Vietnam:

> Captain Johansen was one of the nation's pride. He was blond, meticulously fair, brave, tall, blue-eyed, and an officer.
>
> Standing bare-headed upon a little hill, Johansen said that we were a good outfit, he was proud of us, he was sad that some of the men were dead or crippled. There was a brief change-of-command ceremony. We all stood at attention, feeling like orphans up for adoption.
>
> (O'Brien 1973, 148)

This portrayal records O'Brien's evident admiration through the characterological codes of superiority—those of breeding and bearing—that do not so much describe an individual as enlist him within the ranks of what Martin Green designates as the "aristo-military caste."[1] Thus Johansen's example extends from personal achievement to public principle. As the generic "officer" of traditional war narrative, he embodies the US military project as a form of fairminded paternal intervention, and the affiliative connection explicit in this passage makes it difficult for the "orphaned" son to write about his valiant father's war as an instance of personal and political moral hypocrisy. Nonetheless, that is exactly what O'Brien is trying to do in *If I Die in A Combat Zone.*

The trope for this subversive project is the representation of violence. O'Brien resists the repression of the disturbing "disorder" of the war in Vietnam by revealing the barbarism and carelessness of American power. The display of the battle trophy of a Viet Cong ear as well as the destruction of a peaceful fishing village because of mistaken coordinates for defensive mortar fire are examples which contradict the restraint and concern for others modeled by Captain Johansen's military authority. But the subversive representation of a violence out of ideological bounds is weakened by the memoir's preoccupation with the courage war requires. In formula stories of war, violence provides the primary filter, the test of courage, through which masculine character in a war story may be evaluated. Even though O'Brien redefines that quality as Platonic "wise endurance" (1973, 138), his thematic investment repeats the traditional trope of war as the uniquely desirable setting for the ultimate determination of a young man's mettle.

Although O'Brien writes from the perspective of well-grounded ethical and political objections to the Vietnam war, his challenge is discredited by the effect of the formal realism and the traditional narrative tropes of *If I Die in a Combat Zone,* which transform his memoir into the conventional account of a young soldier within the military tradition. Written almost two decades later, however, **The Things They Carried** impels radical ethical critique. Through the revision of the devices of realism and the omission of codes of complicity, this cycle of stories exploits conflicting codes of violence to get at the disparate "truths" about Vietnam which involve the depiction of process rather than action.

Postmodern Morality in *The Things They Carried*

The title story of **The Things They Carried** invokes and revises two key devices of generic war fiction: the structure of dramatic action and the focal representation of the officer. Buried within this narrative is a conventional plot. A platoon of infantrymen from Alpha Company, led by Lieutenant Jimmy Cross, is on a mission to destroy Viet Cong "villes" and tunnels. The seventeen men—among them, Ted Lavender, Lee Strunk, Rat Kiley, Henry Dobbins, Mitchell Sanders, Dave Jensen, Norman Bowker, Kiowa, and Tim O'Brien, characters who recur throughout the collection—are especially uneasy when they discover a tunnel. Standard operating procedure demands that one of their number, chosen by lot, crawl inside and explore before they blow it up, a maneuver literally dangerous and psychologically unnerving. On the day of the story, Lee Strunk is unlucky enough to have to descend. The others, worried for him and uneasily aware of their own mortality, await his eventual reemergence. Although Strunk returns unscathed, Ted Lavender, the most frightened of the group, is later shot while urinating. A helicopter is summoned to remove his body, and the men respond to his death in a variety of ways: relief, humor, hysterical grief, and the destruction of the nearby village of Than Khe.

This imposed dramatic structure of violation and resolution, which makes violent death and chaotic response comprehensible is not adapted by the story, which is, instead, organized as lists of actual and emotional burdens toted by the soldiers. The things they carry include the accounterments of war, such as steel helmets, which, O'Brien carefully notes, weigh 5 pounds; the particular objects of their military duties, the 23-pound M-60 of the machine gunner or the medic's bag of "morphine and plasma and malaria tablets and surgical tape and comic books . . . for a total weight of almost 20 pounds" (1990, 6-7); and the heavier load of fear and whatever the men rely on to cope with fear, like Ted Lavender's drugs, Kiowa's bible, and Jimmy Cross's love letters.

In *Writing War* Hanley contends that modern military narratives are suffused with a "'secret unacknowledged elation' at the thought of war, with the conviction that war is exciting,"[2] and that this style of representation has promoted war as a desirable societal event (1991, 4). But by presenting violence in terms of burden rather than battle through deliberately non-dramatic structure, by stressing the continuous pressure of war rather than the climactic action of combat through the metaphor of weight to be borne, **"The Things They Carried"** deflates the excitement of traditional portrayal of the violence of the military adventure, and it deflects the ascription of moral purpose to the violent events of war.

Similarly, this story, which foregrounds the reactions of Lieutenant Jimmy Cross, obviates his reception as noble example. Jimmy fights the inexpressible fear the men share by obsessing about a girl he wants to love and substituting the banalities of her letters for the reality of Vietnam. After Lavender's death, Cross digs a foxhole and gives in to uncontrolled weeping. Finally, despite the rain, he burns the letters. Accepting the "blame" for his soldier's death, he resolves to be a leader, not a lover, "determined to perform his duties firmly and without negligence" (O'Brien 1990, 24). He imagines himself, henceforth, an officer in the manner of John Wayne: "if anyone quarreled or complained, he would simply tighten his lips and arrange his shoulders in the correct command posture. . . . He might just shrug and say, Carry on, then they would saddle up and form into a column and move on . . ." (1990, 25). Like the rest of the men, the lieutenant responds to the random violence in largely unproductive ways. He doesn't set any superior standard because, like the others, he can find no relevant standard to set.

Of course, Lavender's death cannot be explained or contained by Cross's pose of heroic responsibility any more than it can be relieved by the unit's destruction of the "chickens and dogs" and hootches of Than Khe (O'Brien 1990, 16). In **"The Things They Carried,"** the unplottable violence of the Vietnam experience is structurally contrasted to the assimilable violence of war as popular fiction. In the space between these two opposed representations—experiential disorder, the way the events of war feel to the soldiers in the field, and fictive order, the way popular representations suggest they should respond—emerges the "truth" about Vietnam as a constant process of "humping" or carrying the impossible responsibility of power through a violent landscape.

The proper treatment of this truth, O'Brien suggests, is storytelling. Conditioned as we are to the designations of "fiction" and "non-fiction," it is easy to imagine that truth and stories are opposite categories. **"How to Tell a True War Story,"** however, dissolves this relation to allow storytelling to emerge as the pursuit of provisional comprehension. Two scenes of graphic violence organize this effect. The first is the death of a young soldier who steps on a mine during a happy moment; the second is the destruction of a baby water buffalo by his best friend:

> 1. In the mountains that day, I watched Lemon turn sideways. He laughed and said something to Rat Kiley. Then he took a peculiar half-step, moving from the shade into bright sunlight, and the booby-trapped 105 round blew him into a tree. The parts were just hanging there, so Dave Jensen and I were ordered to shinny up and peel him off. I remember pieces of skin and something wet and yellow that must've been the intestines. The gore was horrible, and stays with me.
>
> (O'Brien 1990, 89)
>
> 2. He stepped back and shot it through the front right knee. The animal did not make a sound. It went down hard, then got up again and Rat took careful aim and shot off an ear. He shot it in the hindquarters and in the little hump at its back. It wasn't to kill; it was to hurt. He put the rifle muzzle up against the mouth and shot the mouth away. Nobody said much. The whole platoon stood there feeling all sorts of things, but there wasn't a great deal of pity for the water buffalo.
>
> (O'Brien 1990, 86)

The passage continues in this vein. Rat shoots off the tail, then wounds the baby water buffalo in the ribs, the belly, the knee, the nose, and the throat. It is still living when one of the men kicks it, and the group finally dumps it into the village well.

It is impossible to read these two passages without placing them in a causal relationship that induces emotional and political interpretation. The juxtaposition of nature and death is especially shocking. In the first scene the sunlit American boy is wastefully decimated by a hidden explosive device. Rat Kiley and Curt Lemon have just been playing catch with a smoke bomb, turning war, for a few moments of pastoral innocence, into a carefree game.[3] But the Vietnamese have, evidently, broken the rules. An invisible enemy, they not only kill Curt, but cruelly dismember him. Although presented as a kind of hero, Curt is reduced to a substance to be peeled off and scraped away. A similar ironic reversal, Curt's "wet" and "yellow" intestines are converted from organs of life to signifiers of death.

The second scene is, apparently, a direct result of the first. Rat chooses a symbol of Vietnamese innocence, the ubiquitous water buffalo, which is an emblem of the culture, not an agent of war, and a "baby" at that, to mimic Curt, who has been cast as the momentary emblem of youthful American guilelessness. The horrific attack on the body of the animal mimics his friend's fragmentation and evisceration. The biblical motto of vengeance, "an eye for an eye . . . ," is literally enacted in a narrative sequence meant to inscribe the sense of just retribution. Revenge, as David Whillock notes, is a common plot device in film treatments of the Vietnam war which attempt to impose the closure "that was not possible" in actuality (1990, 310). This text, however, will not let the imputed causal attributions stand. At the end of the account of Curt Lemon's death, O'Brien appends a narrative interpolation: "But what wakes me up twenty years later is Dave Jensen singing 'Lemon Tree' as we threw down the parts" (1990, 89). Dave's humor, probably a means of self-protection, nevertheless deflects an automatic assignment of blame. Similarly, previous details about some of Curt's playful "pranks" disrupt his reception as an innocent character. In the condoling letter Rat writes to Curt's sister he describes a terrifying incident he thinks of as funny: "On Halloween night, this hot spooky night, the dude paints up his body all different colors and puts on this weird mask and hikes over to a ville and goes trick-or-treating almost stark naked, just boots and balls and an M-16" (76).

As a conclusion to the description of Rat's actions, O'Brien condenses the general reaction of the men into another gnomic comment by Jensen: "'Amazing,' Dave Jensen kept saying. 'A new wrinkle. I never seen it before'" (1990, 86). The awful humor of Jensen's song and his appreciative acknowledgement of the peculiar novelty of Rat's performance both undercut the causal efficacy of the sequence, which is, in fact, denied sequentiality by its placement within a fiction organized as an essay on writing the war story. And even while reacting with shock and sadness to the extensive catalogue of assaults on the body parts of the baby water buffalo, a reader may respond with irreverence to the exaggeration of the attenuated murder, an unwilling recognition of the kind of overstatement that signals a gag rather than a tragedy. This subversion of narrative causality is further reinforced as O'Brien alternates accounts of action with lectures on the postmodern tests of a "true war story" **"How to Tell . . ."** [**"How to Tell a True War Story"**] exemplifies: it cannot moralize or generalize, it will probably be obscene and most certainly embarrassing, and it will overturn convictions by muddling oppositional categories of truth and fiction, good and evil, and love and war (77, 84, 89, 90). The effect of the true war story will be to replace certainty with confusion.

As parallel scenes of descriptive violence, the deaths of Curt Lemon and the baby water buffalo are meant to suggest opposed explications of guilt and innocence. But the postmodern sabotage of the codes of reception of these scenes confronts the complexity of moral responsibility, which the conventional war story may evade through the narrative attribution of cause and effect. In **"The Things They Carried"** Mitchell Sanders contends that the events of that story imply "a definite moral." When another soldier responds that he cannot extrapolate a meaning—" I don't see no moral," he insists—Sanders counters, "There it *is,* man" (O'Brien 1990, 13-14). The contrasting presentations of thematic and formal violence in **"How to Tell a True War Story"**—evocative description set against subversive representation—substitute ethical uncertainty for the accessible "moral" of traditional story-telling.

O'Brien also gives Mitchell Sanders the last word on the slaughter of the water buffalo: "'Well that's Nam,' he said. 'Garden of Evil. Over here, man, every sin's fresh and original" (1990, 86). For R. W. B. Lewis the quintessential American story begins with a renovated Adam in the "Garden of Innocence" located in the geographic region he imagines is a "new" world, a mythic assumption O'Brien disputes in **"Sweetheart of the Song Tra Bong."** Lewis's Adam is the "hero of a new adventure: an individual emancipated from history . . . standing alone, self-reliant, and self-propelling, ready to confront whatever awaited" (1966, 5). However, O'Brien's protagonists' participation in the violence of Vietnam serves to undermine such self-serving illusions of originality, confident self-control, as well as innocence.

For Tobey C. Herzog, in *Vietnam Stories: Innocence Lost,* the traditional theme of the initiation of a military protagonist into the depravity of war dominates central texts of literature on Vietnam, a premise O'Brien's fiction significantly complicates. The narrative of war, according to Paul Fussell's study *The Great War and Modern Memory,* proceeds in three mythic stages: 1) "preparation" for war, usually based on inappropriate romanticized models; 2) participation in battle, which is "characterized by disenchantment and loss of innocence"; and 3) the resultant "consideration" of the experience of war (1975, 130). O'Brien's representation of the Vietnam War differs from this pattern, first, in that there is never innocence to be lost. In all three of his accounts—the memoir, his novel *Going After Cacciato* (1978), and in **The Things They Carried**—the main character cooperates with the government despite his ethical objections to the Vietnamese conflict because of an inability to face social opprobrium if he does not do so. "It's not a happy ending," the narrator of **"On the Rainy River"** confides, "I was a coward, I went to the war" (1990, 63). Secondly, O'Brien departs from Fussell's schema in that the dehumanizing preparation for the war in the boot camp in *If I Die* is coextensive with, not different from, the war itself; for O'Brien the war in Vietnam is the exaggeration of his nation's basic principles.

Certainly *The Things They Carried,* like the World War I literature Fussell examined, evaluates the experience of war, but O'Brien's evaluation is less decisive and more inclusive. According to Wayne Miller in stories of the Great War the conclusion emerges that it is the social system, not the soldier, that is blameworthy: in "a world in which traditional political and social values have lost meaning . . . one seeks one's separate peace" (1970, 102). Although outraged by war, the literary doughboy emerges morally intact. The contemplation of violence in the **"Sweetheart of the Song Tra Bong,"** however, does not allow the soldier the illusions of separation from a morally deficient culture or abdication of personal responsibility. Postmodern in execution, this story is a compendium of references to other stories, especially those reflecting contemporary ideological assumptions about war. The setting, an encampment containing a small field hospital alongside a tentful of Special Forces soldiers, recalls two popular narratives of the Vietnam period, *M★A★S★H* and *The Green Berets,*[4] which reflect opposite strategies of assimilation of the violence. The first, a movie and a popular television series still re-running, addressed the need to contain the disturbing reality of death and gore, available to stateside civilians in hitherto unknown quantities via television news. The medics of the *M★A★S★H* unit, whose charge is to repair the bodies of wounded men from the distant front-lines of the Korean Conflict, spend most of their time in eccentric and playful disengagement from the expectations and red-tape of the military establishment. Not only does the medical narrative repeatedly suggest that the physical damage inflicted by war can be repaired by well-intentioned Americans, it asserts through the zany antics of *M★A★S★H* characters that even participants in war, like Hemingway heroes, can maintain separate positions of moral integrity.

The second reference is to *The Green Berets,* the 1967 motion picture concocted by Hollywood and Washington in support of the ongoing war in Vietnam. In this update of John Wayne's previous roles, violence was not evaded but embraced. The American soldiers under Wayne, a Special Forces colonel, fight decisively and heroically for democracy, confident that the South Vietnamese support their intervention and that the North Vietnamese deserve technologically sophisticated extermination, certainties not universal among actual soldiers.[5] "Missing from this view," according to Herzog, "are the difficult moral issues involved with war: the moments of self-revelation on the battlefield; the con-

fessions of fear, brutal instincts, and frustrations; and the questions of personal responsibility for violent actions" (1992, 24).

In **"Sweetheart of the Song Tra Bong,"** O'Brien inserts an innocent American girl between these twin idylls of denial and endorsement. Scripting an apocryphal military daydream, O'Brien has one of the young medics transport his seventeen-year-old girlfriend from the States to the war. The point of the story is not just that Mary Anne Bell—"this cute blonde just out of high school" (1990, 102)—loses her innocence, but that her loss speaks to the general ethical confusion of the war in Vietnam.[6]

According to Rat Kiley, who narrates her story, Mary Anne's transformation typifies that of any participant in the war. She begins her visit filled with dreams and goals dictated by American values: "someday they would be married and live in a fine gingerbread house near Lake Erie, and have three healthy yellow-haired children, and grow old together, and no doubt die in each other's arms and be buried in the same walnut casket. That was the plan" (O'Brien 1990, 106). Soon, however, the young woman begins to change. Her immitigable curiosity leads her into contact with the Vietnamese countryside and the practices and procedures of both the camp's medics and its resident green berets. By the end of the second week she has begun to help treat the wounded and later begins to learn the tricks of the military trade. As a result of her new experience, Mary Anne begins to change: "she fell into the habits of the bush. No cosmetics, no fingernail filing. She stopped wearing jewelry, cut her hair short and wore it in a green bandanna" (109). More important than the physical modification is the girl's characterological transformation. She doesn't laugh as often, her voice seems to deepen as she talks less but more forcefully, and even her face takes on a "new composure, almost serene, the fuzzy blue eyes narrowing into a tight, intelligent focus" (O'Brien 1990, 109). Mary Anne no longer expresses the same expectations for the future with her lover, whom she leaves in order to participate in the *Apocalypse Now*-type military exploits of the "Greenies." Finally, she leaves them, too, crossing "to the other side. She was part of the land. She was wearing her culottes, her pink sweater, and a necklace of human tongues. She was dangerous. She was ready for the kill" (125).[7]

Turning the archetypal tale of a young man's initiation into the male mystery of violence into the story of a young girl on a whimsical visit opens it to fresh interpretation. The first explanation supplied by the narrator, follows Fussell's model of the conversion of innocence to experience: "What happened to her . . . was what happened to all of them. You come over clean and you get dirty and then afterward it's never the same" (O'Brien 1990, 123). Thus, in a single stroke, O'Brien demolishes the masculine mystique of the violence of war as the litmus test for manhood. But there are deeper implications. Mary Anne's transformation is the consequence of an appeal that varies among Americans in Vietnam in intensity, but not in kind. She is presumably particularly vulnerable because her circumscribed feminine role as the archetypal American girl-next-door has not allowed her any previous access to "the adrenaline buzz" (109) of the operating theater nor the narcotic "high" of the battlefield: "you become intimate with danger; you're in touch with the far side of yourself," like "the effect of a powerful drug: that mix of unnamed terror and unnamed pleasure that comes as the needle slips in" (123). In place of the ideological containment of violence suggested by the *M★A★S★H* allusion or its sentimental celebration in the John Wayne movie, O'Brien offers an analytic depiction of its appeal that functions, as well, as a powerful critique of normative American values. Besides the rejection of war as masculine ritual, **"Sweetheart of the Song Tra Bong"** posits a kind of falseness of national experience, especially true of feminine socialization, that accounts for the addictive appeal of the existential authenticity encountered in the danger and physical extremes imposed by war. Mary Anne's induction into genuine experience is clearly destructive as well as empowering. That she, or any other American, can only encounter personal potential and visionary "truth" in the national practice of institutionalized death is the story's most disturbing implication. When she accuses her boyfriend of insularity, she expresses a key ethical argument of *The Things They Carried:* "You hide in this little fortress, behind wire and sandbags, and you don't know what it's all about" (121). The concept of innocence—presented as the absence of the experience of moral complexity—is rejected as a legitimate basis for morality.

In the war stories of *The Things They Carried* Tim O'Brien represents violence in terms of opposing narrative possibilities: the unplottable experience contrasting the implicit order of **"The Things They Carried,"** the narrative sequence and the postmodern dislocation of **"How to Tell a True War Story,"** the containing and exploiting myths invoked in **"Sweetheart of the Song Tra Bong."** What emerges is not another ameliorating instance of the "loss of innocence"—war imagined as something imposed on soldiers rather than enacted by them (and us)—nor even a clarification of what is right and wrong. The first story introduces the moral burden of war; the second insists on the provisional nature of

the process of ethical inquiry; and the third deconstructs the categories through which such judgments are conventionally assigned: guilt and innocence, self and other, male and female. O'Brien's contradictory depictions of violence produce the thematic assertion of the moral confusion imposed by the war, and his manipulations of textual conventions violate the comfortable reception of war modeled by its traditional depiction as a test of courage, a mode of heroism, or an assertion of superiority or virtue. Instead, O'Brien's representational divergence demands the possibly impossible ethical interrogation of the violence of Vietnam.

Like Dave Jensen, the soldier amazed by the originality of experience in Vietnam, critics have been astounded by O'Brien's apparent newness. His narratives of war have been variously labeled as postmodern; magic realism; "faction," a combination of fact and fiction; even "fictive irrealism."[8] But these metafictive labels stress his stunning epistemological effects at the expense of his troubling ethical achievement. In "The Vietnam in Me," an essay published in 1994 on the twenty-fifth anniversary of his tour of duty, he emphasizes the disturbing moral legacy of the American war in Vietnam. In addition to revealing the painful symptoms of his own continuing confusion—isolation, nightmares, depression, suicidal impulses—O'Brien expresses his outrage at the massacre at My Lai by soldiers of Charlie Company on March 16, 1968, two years before he served in the same region. But he reserves his severest condemnation for the moral abdication of the US in reaction to such incidents:

> I despised everything—the soil, the tunnels, the paddies, the poverty and myself. Each step was an act of the purest self-hatred and self-betrayal, yet, in truth, because truth matters, my sympathies were rarely with the Vietnamese. I was mostly terrified. I was lamenting in advance my own pitiful demise. After firefights, after friends died, there was a great deal of anger—black, fierce, hurting anger—the kind you want to take out on whatever presents itself. This is not to justify what occurred. . . . Justifications are empty and outrageous. Rather, it's to say that I more or less understand what happened on that day in March 1968, how it happened, the wickedness that soaks into your blood and heats up and starts to sizzle. I know the boil that precedes butchery. At the same time, however, the men in Alpha company [the unit in which O'Brien served] did not commit murder. We did not turn our machine guns on civilians; we did not cross that conspicuous line between rage and homicide. I know what occurred here, yes, but I also feel betrayed by a nation that so widely shrugs off barbarity, by a military justice system that treats murderers and common soldiers as one and the same. Apparently we're all innocent—those who exer-

cise moral restraint and those who do not, officers who control their troops and officers who do not. In a way America has declared *itself* innocent.

(O'Brien 1994, 53)

It is the absolute necessity of moral evaluation that is the central issue of *The Things They Carried.* The moral certainty that assigns absolute righteousness to "us" and complete culpability to "them"—the object of the war narrative Scarry describes—is precisely what O'Brien's strategic sabotage of textual certainty in *The Things They Carried* is meant to forestall. For it is only through the unflinching willingness to evade the consoling simplicity built in to the formulaic war narrative process that genuine responsibility can be attempted. And for O'Brien, author of the war stories in *If I Die in a Combat Zone* and *Going After Cacciato,* as well as those of *The Things They Carried,* it is the telling, the retelling of war stories that leads to the possibility of the scrupulous analysis to which he is committed: "All you can do is tell it one more time, patiently, adding and subtracting, making up a few things to get at the real truth," (1990, 91) which is a truth not just of texture but of accountability.

". . . BECAUSE TRUTH MATTERS"

Because it supports the narrative project of war, the generic story of war is defined by its uncritical manipulation of events of military violence, and the pressure towards simplification and closure imposed by the narrative structure of war is also reflected in influential literary criticism of the Vietnam story. Sandra M. Wittman's *Writing About Vietnam: A Bibliography of the Vietnam Conflict* (1989) has over 1,700 entries, and they are still coming. Yet despite the unprecedented number of texts, which indicate that the question of Vietnam remains vitally open, some important criticism about Vietnam literature promotes the desirability of the military/narrative project of closure. Although Philip Beidler in his 1982 *American Literature and the Experience of Vietnam* observes the "manic contradiction" and "bizarre juxtaposition" of key works (1982, 4), he evidently distrusts the validity of the resulting characteristic openness these devices introduce. Lamenting the inconclusiveness of American responses to the experience of Vietnam, he demands: "How, then, might one come up with some form of sensemaking for this thing—this experience already cast in the image of some insane metafiction recreating itself in actual life—and in the process find some reason to believe that the effort might be of some literary or cultural significance?" (10). Like Philip H. Melling, and Owen W. Gilman, Jr., he settles the problem by grounding the literature of the American war in Vietnam in similarities to the Puritan and classic literature of early American imperialism in

order to locate a "visionary myth" that fixes "memory" of a "Vietnam more real than reality" (85).[9] In fact, Ringnalda describes his *Fighting and Writing in Vietnam* as "atypical" and "dissenting" largely because of his insistence "that the last thing that America needs to do with the experience in Vietnam is to make sense of it" (1994, ix).[10]

In the literature of past wars, the simplified "sense" of the war narrative has been resisted through literary deployments of the very sense-making apparatus used for wartime propaganda. Hemingway's concrete prose style deflates the literary pretension of political rhetoric of World War I. World War II, the first war subject to official narration by the publicity industry, is countered through the exploitation of public forms—the extended treatment of a joke, the "Catch 22" of Joseph Heller's title, and the alternative fantasy of science fiction in Kurt Vonnegut's *Slaughterhouse-Five.*[11] These operations are ironic in that one code of meaning contradicts another. Because the second code in each case is the alternative source of a truth denied by the dominant code, the use of irony re-introduces the possibility of the complex expression it is the purpose of war to rescind. But because the second code also functions as a site of authorizing definition, irony has not been adequate to the essential confusion of the Vietnam experience. *The Things They Carried* resists both the pressure of sense-making and the implicit source of sense irony promises.

Vietnam, mediated by the visual narrative of TV news, as Beidler notes despairingly, was received by its combatants in the narrative formulas of television melodrama: "cartoons, commercials, cowboys, comedians and caped crusaders . . . child-world dreams of aggression and escape mixed up with moralistic fantasies . . ." (1982, 11). This mode of reception conforms to postmodernism, the representational practice, which, according to Peter Brooker's provisional definition, "splices high with low culture," "raids and parodies past art," "questions absolutes" and "swamps reality in a culture of recycled images" (1992, 3). The spirit of popularized representation Beidler deplores is actually the basis for the productive postmodern treatments of the Vietnam War by O'Brien.

In "Postmodernism and the Consumer Society" Fredric Jameson designates Vietnam as the "first terrible postmodernist war [that] cannot be told in any of the traditional paradigms of the war novel or the war movie," witnessing "the breakdown of any shared language through which the veteran might convey such experience" (1992, 176). Vietnam is for Jameson a signal instance of the outer limit of contemporary economic deficiency and social incapacity that it is the painful burden of postmodern art to convey.

On the other hand, Cornell West maintains that for black writers who have had to "come to terms with state-sponsored terrorism" postmodernism may serve, not as the emblem of exhaustion of moral resources Jameson describes, but as a source of social redefinition: "acknowledgement of the reality one cannot not know" (1992, 218). For West as for Scarry, violence provides access to power. Within the narrative structure of war that power is deflected to the service of ideological limitation, but its deployment as a literature of violence treated through the oblique filter of postmodern practice may generate ethical redefinition. In the Vietnam literature of O'Brien the referential sphere of culture is juxtaposed to the experiential sphere of the suffering and death imposed by war. What emerges from the gap between them is indeed "truth," not the reflection of reality but an invitation to engage in the effort of revision.

Notes

1. In *Dreams of Adventure, Deeds of Empire* (1979) Green posits that the representation of the feudal British warrior class was modernized in the imperial eras of expansion dominated by merchant classes as the expression of gentlemanly bearing, an ideological middle ground which combined the noble status of inherited privilege with the aspirations of the bourgeoisie at the same time as it obscured military force as the basis of economic colonization.

2. The quotation Hanley cites comes from Doris Lessing's *Prisons We Choose to Live Inside* (1987), in which Lessing argues for the open acknowledgement of the pleasurable excitement with which many people respond to the activities of war.

3. Fussell notes the constant trope of the game in World War I. Not only did writers compare battles to football, regiments were encouraged into battle by leaders who supplied balls to kick into enemy territory. "Modern mass wars," he explains, "require in their early stages a definitive work of popular literature demonstrating how much wholesome fun is to be had at the training camp" (1975, 18). O'Brien's invocation of this war-as-the-play-of-boys metaphor reverses the assumptions that war, like games, is bound by rules, that winning is what is important, and that the uncomplicated companionship of young males is an important result of military experience.

4. Both of these popular films were adapted from fiction: Robin Moore's best-selling *The Green Berets* (1966) and Richard Hooker's *MASH* (1968).

5. John Wayne's iconic significance in the promotion of male military adventure is widely noted. See Miedzian (1991, 147-48) Gerzon (1992, 30-35).

6. Herzog argues that the moral ambiguity of the American experience of Vietnam resulted from the special circumstances of the war (1992, 51-59). The isolation of individual soldiers created by the practice of separate assignments to military units, limited tours of duty, and rapid transitions from military to civilian life caused many problems. The every-man-for-himself arrivals and departures to and from field units made difficult adjustments the problem of separate individuals rather than obstacles shared with a supportive group, and the limited tours may have encouraged an emphasis on individual survival at the expense of other goals. Widespread American opposition to the war also contributed to a sense of ethical uncertainty, and the dispersion of the enemy throughout the whole country made observable geographical progress impossible. Similarly, since it was frequently difficult to distinguish between friend and foe in field maneuvers, it was often hard to define what was procedurally correct in many circumstances. The measurement of success in body counts, fired by media coverage and political pressures on commanders, was particularly pernicious. An emphasis on score-board numbers, Herzog argues, "led to inflated claims and, at times, American soldiers' callous disregard for civilian lives" (53). The media image of the crazed and bloodthirsty American soldier may have contributed to its occasional reality, as did the general availability of drugs and alcohol.

7. Jacqueline Rose's argument in the title essay of *Why War?* is that war, the paradoxical attempt to arrive at epistemological certainty, is inevitably uncertain. "Death" she explains, "forces us to acknowledge that what belongs to us most intimately is also a stranger or enemy, a type of foreign body in the mind" (1993, 19). Mary Anne's conversion seems to literally enact this confrontation of radical unfamiliarity.

8. See Slabey (1990, 205-10), Calloway (1990, 213), and Smith (1990, 96). Don Ringnalda provides a comprehensive discussion of O'Brien's metafictional practice in chapter five of *Fighting and Writing the Vietnam War* (1994).

9. In *Vietnam in American Literature*, Melling argues that the "key" to understanding Vietnam is pursuing historical continuity in order to "avoid the dead end of absurdity and the postmodern faith of a surrender to fragments" (1990, xiii, 16). Gilman

in "Vietnam and John Winthrop's Vision of Community" urges Americans to discover in the experience of Vietnam something like the affirming "ideal" which "vitalized" the Puritans (1991, 139).

10. Similarly, Kai Tal rebukes four traditional critics for their attempted "total reduction of the war to a metaphor" (1991, 223), comforting in its conformity to previous mythic and historical ideology.

11. Citing *Catch-22,* Fussell comments that irony is the "one dominating form of modern understanding" (1975, 34-35). In *Wartime: Understanding Behavior in the Second World War,* Fussell describes these two texts as primary examples of a literature dependent on a thematics of "blunders" (1989, 31), the ironic exploitation of the distance between right and wrong.

Works Cited

Bersani, Leo. 1992. "Realism and the Fear of Desire." In Chapter 2 of *A Future for Astyanax: Character and Desire in Literature.* 1976. Reprint. New York: Longman.

Beidler, Philip. 1982. *American Literature and the Experience of Vietnam.* Athens: University of Georgia Press.

Brooker, Peter. 1992. "Introduction: Reconstructions." In *Modernism/Postmodernism,* ed. Peter Brooker. New York: Longman.

Calloway Catherine. 1990. "Pluralities of Vision: *Going after Cacciato* and Tim O'Brien's Short Fiction." In *America Rediscovered: Critical Essays on Literature and Film of the Vietnam War,* ed. Owen W. Gilman and Lorrie Smith. New York: Garland.

Fussell, Paul. 1975. *The Great War and Modern Memory.* New York: Oxford University Press.

———. 1989. *Wartime: Understanding and Behavior in the Second World War.* New York: Oxford.

Gerzan, Mark. 1992. *A Choice of Heroes: The Changing Face of American Manhood.* New York: Houghton Mifflin.

Gilman, Owen W., Jr. 1991. "Vietnam and John Winthrop's Vision of Community." In *Fourteen Landing Zones: Approaches to Vietnam War Literature,* ed. Philip K. Jason. Iowa City: University of Iowa Press.

Green, Martin. 1979. *Dreams of Adventure, Deeds of Empire.* New York: Basic Books.

Hanley, Lynne. 1991. *Writing War.* Amherst: University of Massachusetts Press.

Hansen, J. T. 1990. "Vocabularies of Experience." In *America Rediscovered: Critical Essays on Literature and Film of the Vietnam War,* ed. Owen W. Gilman and Lorrie Smith. New York: Garland.

Herzog, Tobey C. 1992. *Vietnam War Stories: Innocence Lost.* New York: Routledge.

Hooker, Richard. 1968. *MASH.* New York: William Morrow.

Jameson, Fredric. 1992. "Postmodernism and Consumer Society." In *Modernism/Postmodernism,* ed. Peter Brooker. New York: Longman.

Lewis, R. W. B. 1966. *The American Adam.* Chicago: University of Chicago Press.

Melling, Philip H. 1990. *Vietnam in American Literature.* Boston: Twayne.

Myriam Miedzian's *Boys Will Be Boys: The Link Between Masculinity and Violence* New York: Dougleday.

Miller, Wayne Charles. 1970. *An Armed America: A History of the Military Novel.* New York: New York University Press.

Moore, Robin. 1966. *The Green Berets.* New York: Avon.

O'Brien, Tim. 1994. "The Vietnam in Me." *The New York Times Magazine.* 2 October, 48-57.

———. 1978. *Going After Cacciato.* New York: Dell Publishing.

———. 1973. *If I Die in a Combat Zone.* New York: Dell Publishing.

———. 1990. *The Things They Carried.* New York: Penguin.

Ringnalda, Donald. 1994. *Fighting and Writing in Vietnam.* Jackson: University of Mississippi Press.

———. 1990. "Unlearning to Remember Vietnam." In *America Rediscovered: Critical Essays on Literature and Film of the Vietnam War,* ed. Owen W. Gilman and Lorrie Smith. New York: Garland.

Rose, Jacqueline. 1993. *Why War?* Cambridge: Blackwell.

Scarry, Elaine. 1985. *The Body in Pain: The Making and Unmaking of the World.* New York: Oxford University Press.

Slabey, Robert M. 1990. *Going After Cacciato: Tim O'Brien's "Separate Peace." America Rediscovered: Critical Essays on Literature and Film of the Vietnam War,* ed. Owen W. Gilman and Lorrie Smith. New York: Garland.

Smith, Lorrie. 1990. "Disarming the War Story." In *America Rediscovered: Critical Essays on Literature and Film of the Vietnam War,* ed. Owen W. Gilman and Lorrie Smith. New York: Garland.

Tal, Kai. 1991. "Speaking the Language of Pain: Vietnam War Literature in the Context of a Literature of Trauma." In *Fourteen Landing Zones: Approaches to Vietnam War Literature,* ed. Philip K. Jason. Iowa City: University of Iowa Press.

West, Cornell. 1992. "An Interview with Cornell West." In *Modernism/Postmodernism,* ed. Peter Brooker. New York: Longman.

Whillock, David Everett. 1990. "The Fictive American Vietnam War Film: A Filmography." In *America Rediscovered: Critical Essays on Literature and Film of the Vietnam War,* ed. Owen W. Gilman and Lorrie Smith. New York: Garland.

Wittman, Sandra M. 1989. *Writing About Vietnam: A Bibliography of the Literature of the Vietnam Conflict.* Boston: G. K. Hall.

Additional coverage of O'Brien's life and career is contained in the following sources published by Thomson Gale: *American Writers Supplement,* Vol. 5; *Authors and Artists for Young Adults,* Vol. 16; *Concise Dictionary of American Literary Biography Supplement*; *Contemporary Authors,* Vols. 85-88; *Contemporary Authors New Revision Series,* Vols. 40, 58; *Contemporary Literary Criticism,* Vols. 7, 19, 40, 103; *Contemporary Novelists,* Ed. 7; *Contemporary Popular Writers*; *Dictionary of Literary Biography,* Vol. 152; *Dictionary of Literary Biography Documentary Series,* Vol. 9; *Dictionary of Literary Biography Yearbook,* 1980; *DISCovering Authors 3.0*; *DISCovering Authors Module: Popular Fiction and Genre Authors*; *Literature Resource Center*; *Major 20th-Century Writers,* Ed. 2; *Reference Guide to American Literature,* Ed. 4; **and** *Short Stories for Students,* Vols. 5, 15.

How to Use This Index

CMW = St. James Guide to Crime & Mystery Writers
CN = Contemporary Novelists
CP = Contemporary Poets
CPW = Contemporary Popular Writers
CSW = Contemporary Southern Writers
CWD = Contemporary Women Dramatists
CWP = Contemporary Women Poets
CWRI = St. James Guide to Children's Writers
CWW = Contemporary World Writers
DA = DISCovering Authors
DA3 = DISCovering Authors 3.0
DAB = DISCovering Authors: British Edition
DAC = DISCovering Authors: Canadian Edition
DAM = DISCovering Authors: Modules
　　DRAM: Dramatists Module; **MST:** Most-studied Authors Module;
　　MULT: Multicultural Authors Module; **NOV:** Novelists Module;
　　POET: Poets Module; **POP:** Popular Fiction and Genre Authors Module
DFS = Drama for Students
DLB = Dictionary of Literary Biography
DLBD = Dictionary of Literary Biography Documentary Series
DLBY = Dictionary of Literary Biography Yearbook
DNFS = Literature of Developing Nations for Students
EFS = Epics for Students
EXPN = Exploring Novels
EXPP = Exploring Poetry
EXPS = Exploring Short Stories
EW = European Writers
FANT = St. James Guide to Fantasy Writers
FW = Feminist Writers
GFL = Guide to French Literature, Beginnings to 1789, 1798 to the Present
GLL = Gay and Lesbian Literature
HGG = St. James Guide to Horror, Ghost & Gothic Writers
HW = Hispanic Writers
IDFW = International Dictionary of Films and Filmmakers: Writers and Production Artists
IDTP = International Dictionary of Theatre: Playwrights
LAIT = Literature and Its Times
LAW = Latin American Writers
JRDA = Junior DISCovering Authors
MAICYA = Major Authors and Illustrators for Children and Young Adults
MAICYAS = Major Authors and Illustrators for Children and Young Adults Supplement
MAWW = Modern American Women Writers
MJW = Modern Japanese Writers
MTCW = Major 20th-Century Writers
NCFS = Nonfiction Classics for Students
NFS = Novels for Students
PAB = Poets: American and British
PFS = Poetry for Students
RGAL = Reference Guide to American Literature
RGEL = Reference Guide to English Literature
RGSF = Reference Guide to Short Fiction
RGWL = Reference Guide to World Literature
RHW = Twentieth-Century Romance and Historical Writers
SAAS = Something about the Author Autobiography Series
SATA = Something about the Author
SFW = St. James Guide to Science Fiction Writers
SSFS = Short Stories for Students
TCWW = Twentieth-Century Western Writers
WLIT = World Literature and Its Times
WP = World Poets
YABC = Yesterday's Authors of Books for Children
YAW = St. James Guide to Young Adult Writers

Literary Criticism Series
Cumulative Author Index

al-Hariri, al-Qasim ibn 'Ali Abu Muhammad al-Basri
1054-1122 .... **CMLC 63**
See also RGWL 3

Ali, Ahmed 1908-1998 .... **CLC 69**
See also CA 25-28R; CANR 15, 34; EWL 3

Ali, Tariq 1943- .... **CLC 173**
See also CA 25-28R; CANR 10, 99

Alighieri, Dante
See Dante

Allan, John B.
See Westlake, Donald E(dwin)

Allan, Sidney
See Hartmann, Sadakichi

Allan, Sydney
See Hartmann, Sadakichi

Allard, Janet .... **CLC 59**

Allen, Edward 1948- .... **CLC 59**

Allen, Fred 1894-1956 .... **TCLC 87**

Allen, Paula Gunn 1939- ..... **CLC 84; NNAL**
See also AMWS 4; CA 112; 143; CANR 63, 130; CWP; DA3; DAM MULT; DLB 175; FW; MTCW 1; RGAL 4

Allen, Roland
See Ayckbourn, Alan

Allen, Sarah A.
See Hopkins, Pauline Elizabeth

Allen, Sidney H.
See Hartmann, Sadakichi

Allen, Woody 1935- .... **CLC 16, 52**
See also AAYA 10, 51; CA 33-36R; CANR 27, 38, 63, 128; DAM POP; DLB 44; MTCW 1

Allende, Isabel 1942- ... **CLC 39, 57, 97, 170; HLC 1; SSC 65; WLCS**
See also AAYA 18; CA 125; 130; CANR 51, 74, 129; CDWLB 3; CLR 99; CWW 2; DA3; DAM MULT, NOV; DLB 145; DNFS 1; EWL 3; FW; HW 1, 2; INT CA-130; LAIT 5; LAWS 1; LMFS 2; MTCW 1, 2; NCFS 1; NFS 6, 18; RGSF 2; RGWL 3; SSFS 11, 16; WLIT 1

Alleyn, Ellen
See Rossetti, Christina (Georgina)

Alleyne, Carla D. .... **CLC 65**

Allingham, Margery (Louise)
1904-1966 .... **CLC 19**
See also CA 5-8R; 25-28R; CANR 4, 58; CMW 4; DLB 77; MSW; MTCW 1, 2

Allingham, William 1824-1889 ...... **NCLC 25**
See also DLB 35; RGEL 2

Allison, Dorothy E. 1949- .... **CLC 78, 153**
See also AAYA 53; CA 140; CANR 66, 107; CSW; DA3; FW; MTCW 1; NFS 11; RGAL 4

Alloula, Malek .... **CLC 65**

Allston, Washington 1779-1843 .... **NCLC 2**
See also DLB 1, 235

Almedingen, E. M. .... **CLC 12**
See Almedingen, Martha Edith von
See also SATA 3

Almedingen, Martha Edith von 1898-1971
See Almedingen, E. M.
See also CA 1-4R; CANR 1

Almodovar, Pedro 1949(?)- .... **CLC 114; HLCS 1**
See also CA 133; CANR 72; HW 2

Almqvist, Carl Jonas Love
1793-1866 .... **NCLC 42**

al-Mutanabbi, Ahmad ibn al-Husayn Abu al-Tayyib al-Jufi al-Kindi
915-965 .... **CMLC 66**
See also RGWL 3

Alonso, Damaso 1898-1990 ...... **CLC 14**
See also CA 110; 131; 130; CANR 72; DLB 108; EWL 3; HW 1, 2

Alov
See Gogol, Nikolai (Vasilyevich)

Al Siddik
See Rolfe, Frederick (William Serafino Austin Lewis Mary)
See also GLL 1; RGEL 2

Alta 1942- .... **CLC 19**
See also CA 57-60

Alter, Robert B(ernard) 1935- .... **CLC 34**
See also CA 49-52; CANR 1, 47, 100

Alther, Lisa 1944- .... **CLC 7, 41**
See also BPFB 1; CA 65-68; CAAS 30; CANR 12, 30, 51; CN 7; CSW; GLL 2; MTCW 1

Althusser, L.
See Althusser, Louis

Althusser, Louis 1918-1990 .... **CLC 106**
See also CA 131; 132; CANR 102; DLB 242

Altman, Robert 1925- .... **CLC 16, 116**
See also CA 73-76; CANR 43

Alurista .... **HLCS 1**
See Urista (Heredia), Alberto (Baltazar)
See also DLB 82; LLW 1

Alvarez, A(lfred) 1929- .... **CLC 5, 13**
See also CA 1-4R; CANR 3, 33, 63, 101; CN 7; CP 7; DLB 14, 40

Alvarez, Alejandro Rodriguez 1903-1965
See Casona, Alejandro
See also CA 131; 93-96; HW 1

Alvarez, Julia 1950- .... **CLC 93; HLCS 1**
See also AAYA 25; AMWS 7; CA 147; CANR 69, 101; DA3; DLB 282; LATS 1; LLW 1; MTCW 1; NFS 5, 9; SATA 129; WLIT 1

Alvaro, Corrado 1896-1956 .... **TCLC 60**
See also CA 163; DLB 264; EWL 3

Amado, Jorge 1912-2001 ... **CLC 13, 40, 106; HLC 1**
See also CA 77-80; 201; CANR 35, 74; CWW 2; DAM MULT, NOV; DLB 113; EWL 3; HW 2; LAW; LAWS 1; MTCW 1, 2; RGWL 2, 3; TWA; WLIT 1

Ambler, Eric 1909-1998 .... **CLC 4, 6, 9**
See also BRWS 4; CA 9-12R; 171; CANR 7, 38, 74; CMW 4; CN 7; DLB 77; MSW; MTCW 1, 2; TEA

Ambrose, Stephen E(dward)
1936-2002 .... **CLC 145**
See also AAYA 44; CA 1-4R; 209; CANR 3, 43, 57, 83, 105; NCFS 2; SATA 40, 138

Amichai, Yehuda 1924-2000 .. **CLC 9, 22, 57, 116; PC 38**
See also CA 85-88; 189; CANR 46, 60, 99, 132; CWW 2; EWL 3; MTCW 1

Amichai, Yehudah
See Amichai, Yehuda

Amiel, Henri Frederic 1821-1881 .... **NCLC 4**
See also DLB 217

Amis, Kingsley (William)
1922-1995 ...... **CLC 1, 2, 3, 5, 8, 13, 40, 44, 129**
See also AITN 2; BPFB 1; BRWS 2; CA 9-12R; 150; CANR 8, 28, 54; CDBLB 1945-1960; CN 7; CP 7; DA; DA3; DAB; DAC; DAM MST, NOV; DLB 15, 27, 100, 139; DLBY 1996; EWL 3; HGG; INT CANR-8; MTCW 1, 2; RGEL 2; RGSF 2; SFW 4

Amis, Martin (Louis) 1949- .... **CLC 4, 9, 38, 62, 101**
See also BEST 90:3; BRWS 4; CA 65-68; CANR 8, 27, 54, 73, 95, 132; CN 7; DA3; DLB 14, 194; EWL 3; INT CANR-27; MTCW 1

Ammianus Marcellinus c. 330-c.
395 .... **CMLC 60**
See also AW 2; DLB 211

Ammons, A(rchie) R(andolph)
1926-2001 ...... **CLC 2, 3, 5, 8, 9, 25, 57, 108; PC 16**
See also AITN 1; AMWS 7; CA 9-12R; 193; CANR 6, 36, 51, 73, 107; CP 7; CSW; DAM POET; DLB 5, 165; EWL 3; MTCW 1, 2; PFS 19; RGAL 4

Amo, Tauraatua i
See Adams, Henry (Brooks)

Amory, Thomas 1691(?)-1788 .... **LC 48**
See also DLB 39

Anand, Mulk Raj 1905- .... **CLC 23, 93**
See also CA 65-68; CANR 32, 64; CN 7; DAM NOV; EWL 3; MTCW 1, 2; RGSF 2

Anatol
See Schnitzler, Arthur

Anaximander c. 611B.C.-c.
546B.C. .... **CMLC 22**

Anaya, Rudolfo A(lfonso) 1937- ...... **CLC 23, 148; HLC 1**
See also AAYA 20; BYA 13; CA 45-48; CAAS 4; CANR 1, 32, 51, 124; CN 7; DAM MULT, NOV; DLB 82, 206, 278; HW 1; LAIT 4; LLW 1; MTCW 1, 2; NFS 12; RGAL 4; RGSF 2; WLIT 1

Andersen, Hans Christian
1805-1875 .... **NCLC 7, 79; SSC 6, 56; WLC**
See also AAYA 57; CLR 6; DA; DA3; DAB; DAC; DAM MST, POP; EW 6; MAICYA 1, 2; RGSF 2; RGWL 2, 3; SATA 100; TWA; WCH; YABC 1

Anderson, C. Farley
See Mencken, H(enry) L(ouis); Nathan, George Jean

Anderson, Jessica (Margaret) Queale
1916- .... **CLC 37**
See also CA 9-12R; CANR 4, 62; CN 7

Anderson, Jon (Victor) 1940- .... **CLC 9**
See also CA 25-28R; CANR 20; DAM POET

Anderson, Lindsay (Gordon)
1923-1994 .... **CLC 20**
See also CA 125; 128; 146; CANR 77

Anderson, Maxwell 1888-1959 .... **TCLC 2, 144**
See also CA 105; 152; DAM DRAM; DFS 16, 20; DLB 7, 228; MTCW 2; RGAL 4

Anderson, Poul (William)
1926-2001 .... **CLC 15**
See also AAYA 5, 34; BPFB 1; BYA 6, 8, 9; CA 1-4R; 181; 199; CAAE 181; CAAS 2; CANR 2, 15, 34, 64, 110; CLR 58; DLB 8; FANT; INT CANR-15; MTCW 1, 2; SATA 90; SATA-Brief 39; SATA-Essay 106; SCFW 2; SFW 4; SUFW 1, 2

Anderson, Robert (Woodruff)
1917- .... **CLC 23**
See also AITN 1; CA 21-24R; CANR 32; DAM DRAM; DLB 7; LAIT 5

Anderson, Roberta Joan
See Mitchell, Joni

Anderson, Sherwood 1876-1941 .. **SSC 1, 46; TCLC 1, 10, 24, 123; WLC**
See also AAYA 30; AMW; AMWC 2; BPFB 1; CA 104; 121; CANR 61; CDALB 1917-1929; DA; DA3; DAB; DAC; DAM MST, NOV; DLB 4, 9, 86; DLBD 1; EWL 3; EXPS; GLL 2; MTCW 1, 2; NFS 4; RGAL 4; RGSF 2; SSFS 4, 10, 11; TUS

Andier, Pierre
See Desnos, Robert

Andouard
See Giraudoux, Jean(-Hippolyte)

Andrade, Carlos Drummond de ..... **CLC 18**
See Drummond de Andrade, Carlos
See also EWL 3; RGWL 2, 3

Armitage, Frank
See Carpenter, John (Howard)

Armstrong, Jeannette (C.) 1948- .... **NNAL**
See also CA 149; CCA 1; CN 7; DAC; SATA 102

Arnette, Robert
See Silverberg, Robert

Arnim, Achim von (Ludwig Joachim von Arnim) 1781-1831 ..... **NCLC 5; SSC 29**
See also DLB 90

Arnim, Bettina von 1785-1859 ...... **NCLC 38, 123**
See also DLB 90; RGWL 2, 3

Arnold, Matthew 1822-1888 ..... **NCLC 6, 29, 89, 126; PC 5; WLC**
See also BRW 5; CDBLB 1832-1890; DA; DAB; DAC; DAM MST, POET; DLB 32, 57; EXPP; PAB; PFS 2; TEA; WP

Arnold, Thomas 1795-1842 .... **NCLC 18**
See also DLB 55

Arnow, Harriette (Louisa) Simpson 1908-1986 .... **CLC 2, 7, 18**
See also BPFB 1; CA 9-12R; 118; CANR 14; DLB 6; FW; MTCW 1, 2; RHW; SATA 42; SATA-Obit 47

Arouet, Francois-Marie
See Voltaire

Arp, Hans
See Arp, Jean

Arp, Jean 1887-1966 .... **CLC 5; TCLC 115**
See also CA 81-84; 25-28R; CANR 42, 77; EW 10

Arrabal
See Arrabal, Fernando

Arrabal, Fernando 1932- ... **CLC 2, 9, 18, 58**
See Arrabal (Teran), Fernando
See also CA 9-12R; CANR 15; EWL 3; LMFS 2

Arrabal (Teran), Fernando 1932-
See Arrabal, Fernando
See also CWW 2

Arreola, Juan Jose 1918-2001 .... **CLC 147; HLC 1; SSC 38**
See also CA 113; 131; 200; CANR 81; CWW 2; DAM MULT; DLB 113; DNFS 2; EWL 3; HW 1, 2; LAW; RGSF 2

Arrian c. 89(?)-c. 155(?) .... **CMLC 43**
See also DLB 176

Arrick, Fran .... **CLC 30**
See Gaberman, Judie Angell
See also BYA 6

Arrley, Richmond
See Delany, Samuel R(ay), Jr.

Artaud, Antonin (Marie Joseph) 1896-1948 .... **DC 14; TCLC 3, 36**
See also CA 104; 149; DA3; DAM DRAM; DLB 258; EW 11; EWL 3; GFL 1789 to the Present; MTCW 1; RGWL 2, 3

Arthur, Ruth M(abel) 1905-1979 ..... **CLC 12**
See also CA 9-12R; 85-88; CANR 4; CWRI 5; SATA 7, 26

Artsybashev, Mikhail (Petrovich) 1878-1927 .... **TCLC 31**
See also CA 170; DLB 295

Arundel, Honor (Morfydd) 1919-1973 .... **CLC 17**
See also CA 21-22; 41-44R; CAP 2; CLR 35; CWRI 5; SATA 4; SATA-Obit 24

Arzner, Dorothy 1900-1979 .... **CLC 98**

Asch, Sholem 1880-1957 .... **TCLC 3**
See also CA 105; EWL 3; GLL 2

Ascham, Roger 1516(?)-1568 .... **LC 101**
See also DLB 236

Ash, Shalom
See Asch, Sholem

Ashbery, John (Lawrence) 1927- .. **CLC 2, 3, 4, 6, 9, 13, 15, 25, 41, 77, 125; PC 26**
See Berry, Jonas
See also AMWS 3; CA 5-8R; CANR 9, 37, 66, 102, 132; CP 7; DA3; DAM POET; DLB 5, 165; DLBY 1981; EWL 3; INT CANR-9; MTCW 1, 2; PAB; PFS 11; RGAL 4; WP

Ashdown, Clifford
See Freeman, R(ichard) Austin

Ashe, Gordon
See Creasey, John

Ashton-Warner, Sylvia (Constance) 1908-1984 .... **CLC 19**
See also CA 69-72; 112; CANR 29; MTCW 1, 2

Asimov, Isaac 1920-1992 ..... **CLC 1, 3, 9, 19, 26, 76, 92**
See also AAYA 13; BEST 90:2; BPFB 1; BYA 4, 6, 7, 9; CA 1-4R; 137; CANR 2, 19, 36, 60, 125; CLR 12, 79; CMW 4; CPW; DA3; DAM POP; DLB 8; DLBY 1992; INT CANR-19; JRDA; LAIT 5; LMFS 2; MAICYA 1, 2; MTCW 1, 2; RGAL 4; SATA 1, 26, 74; SCFW 2; SFW 4; SSFS 17; TUS; YAW

Askew, Anne 1521(?)-1546 .... **LC 81**
See also DLB 136

Assis, Joaquim Maria Machado de
See Machado de Assis, Joaquim Maria

Astell, Mary 1666-1731 .... **LC 68**
See also DLB 252; FW

Astley, Thea (Beatrice May) 1925- .. **CLC 41**
See also CA 65-68; CANR 11, 43, 78; CN 7; DLB 289; EWL 3

Astley, William 1855-1911
See Warung, Price

Aston, James
See White, T(erence) H(anbury)

Asturias, Miguel Angel 1899-1974 .... **CLC 3, 8, 13; HLC 1**
See also CA 25-28; 49-52; CANR 32; CAP 2; CDWLB 3; DA3; DAM MULT, NOV; DLB 113, 290; EWL 3; HW 1; LAW; LMFS 2; MTCW 1, 2; RGWL 2, 3; WLIT 1

Atares, Carlos Saura
See Saura (Atares), Carlos

Athanasius c. 295-c. 373 .... **CMLC 48**

Atheling, William
See Pound, Ezra (Weston Loomis)

Atheling, William, Jr.
See Blish, James (Benjamin)

Atherton, Gertrude (Franklin Horn) 1857-1948 .... **TCLC 2**
See also CA 104; 155; DLB 9, 78, 186; HGG; RGAL 4; SUFW 1; TCWW 2

Atherton, Lucius
See Masters, Edgar Lee

Atkins, Jack
See Harris, Mark

Atkinson, Kate 1951- .... **CLC 99**
See also CA 166; CANR 101; DLB 267

Attaway, William (Alexander) 1911-1986 .... **BLC 1; CLC 92**
See also BW 2, 3; CA 143; CANR 82; DAM MULT; DLB 76

Atticus
See Fleming, Ian (Lancaster); Wilson, (Thomas) Woodrow

Atwood, Margaret (Eleanor) 1939- ... **CLC 2, 3, 4, 8, 13, 15, 25, 44, 84, 135; PC 8; SSC 2, 46; WLC**
See also AAYA 12, 47; AMWS 13; BEST 89:2; BPFB 1; CA 49-52; CANR 3, 24, 33, 59, 95; CN 7; CP 7; CPW; CWP; DA; DA3; DAB; DAC; DAM MST, NOV, POET; DLB 53, 251; EWL 3; EXPN; FW;

INT CANR-24; LAIT 5; MTCW 1, 2; NFS 4, 12, 13, 14, 19; PFS 7; RGSF 2; SATA 50; SSFS 3, 13; TWA; WWE 1; YAW

Aubigny, Pierre d'
See Mencken, H(enry) L(ouis)

Aubin, Penelope 1685-1731(?) .... **LC 9**
See also DLB 39

Auchincloss, Louis (Stanton) 1917- .. **CLC 4, 6, 9, 18, 45; SSC 22**
See also AMWS 4; CA 1-4R; CANR 6, 29, 55, 87, 130; CN 7; DAM NOV; DLB 2, 244; DLBY 1980; EWL 3; INT CANR-29; MTCW 1; RGAL 4

Auden, W(ystan) H(ugh) 1907-1973 . **CLC 1, 2, 3, 4, 6, 9, 11, 14, 43, 123; PC 1; WLC**
See also AAYA 18; AMWS 2; BRW 7; BRWR 1; CA 9-12R; 45-48; CANR 5, 61, 105; CDBLB 1914-1945; DA; DA3; DAB; DAC; DAM DRAM, MST, POET; DLB 10, 20; EWL 3; EXPP; MTCW 1, 2; PAB; PFS 1, 3, 4, 10; TUS; WP

Audiberti, Jacques 1899-1965 .... **CLC 38**
See also CA 25-28R; DAM DRAM; EWL 3

Audubon, John James 1785-1851 . **NCLC 47**
See also ANW; DLB 248

Auel, Jean M(arie) 1936- .... **CLC 31, 107**
See also AAYA 7, 51; BEST 90:4; BPFB 1; CA 103; CANR 21, 64, 115; CPW; DA3; DAM POP; INT CANR-21; NFS 11; RHW; SATA 91

Auerbach, Erich 1892-1957 .... **TCLC 43**
See also CA 118; 155; EWL 3

Augier, Emile 1820-1889 .... **NCLC 31**
See also DLB 192; GFL 1789 to the Present

August, John
See De Voto, Bernard (Augustine)

Augustine, St. 354-430 .... **CMLC 6; WLCS**
See also DA; DA3; DAB; DAC; DAM MST; DLB 115; EW 1; RGWL 2, 3

Aunt Belinda
See Braddon, Mary Elizabeth

Aunt Weedy
See Alcott, Louisa May

Aurelius
See Bourne, Randolph S(illiman)

Aurelius, Marcus 121-180 .... **CMLC 45**
See Marcus Aurelius
See also RGWL 2, 3

Aurobindo, Sri
See Ghose, Aurabinda

Aurobindo Ghose
See Ghose, Aurabinda

Austen, Jane 1775-1817 ...... **NCLC 1, 13, 19, 33, 51, 81, 95, 119; WLC**
See also AAYA 19; BRW 4; BRWC 1; BRWR 2; BYA 3; CDBLB 1789-1832; DA; DA3; DAB; DAC; DAM MST, NOV; DLB 116; EXPN; LAIT 2; LATS 1; LMFS 1; NFS 1, 14, 18, 20; TEA; WLIT 3; WYAS 1

Auster, Paul 1947- .... **CLC 47, 131**
See also AMWS 12; CA 69-72; CANR 23, 52, 75, 129; CMW 4; CN 7; DA3; DLB 227; MTCW 1; SUFW 2

Austin, Frank
See Faust, Frederick (Schiller)
See also TCWW 2

Austin, Mary (Hunter) 1868-1934 . **TCLC 25**
See Stairs, Gordon
See also ANW; CA 109; 178; DLB 9, 78, 206, 221, 275; FW; TCWW 2

Averroes 1126-1198 .... **CMLC 7**
See also DLB 115

Avicenna 980-1037 .... **CMLC 16**
See also DLB 115

Barbauld, Anna Laetitia
1743-1825 .... **NCLC 50**
See also DLB 107, 109, 142, 158; RGEL 2
Barbellion, W. N. P. .... **TCLC 24**
See Cummings, Bruce F(rederick)
Barber, Benjamin R. 1939- .... **CLC 141**
See also CA 29-32R; CANR 12, 32, 64, 119
Barbera, Jack (Vincent) 1945- .... **CLC 44**
See also CA 110; CANR 45
Barbey d'Aurevilly, Jules-Amedee
1808-1889 .... **NCLC 1; SSC 17**
See also DLB 119; GFL 1789 to the Present
Barbour, John c. 1316-1395 .... **CMLC 33**
See also DLB 146
Barbusse, Henri 1873-1935 .... **TCLC 5**
See also CA 105; 154; DLB 65; EWL 3;
RGWL 2, 3
Barclay, Bill
See Moorcock, Michael (John)
Barclay, William Ewert
See Moorcock, Michael (John)
Barea, Arturo 1897-1957 .... **TCLC 14**
See also CA 111; 201
Barfoot, Joan 1946- .... **CLC 18**
See also CA 105
Barham, Richard Harris
1788-1845 .... **NCLC 77**
See also DLB 159
Baring, Maurice 1874-1945 .... **TCLC 8**
See also CA 105; 168; DLB 34; HGG
Baring-Gould, Sabine 1834-1924 ... **TCLC 88**
See also DLB 156, 190
Barker, Clive 1952- .... **CLC 52; SSC 53**
See also AAYA 10, 54; BEST 90:3; BPFB
1; CA 121; 129; CANR 71, 111; CPW;
DA3; DAM POP; DLB 261; HGG; INT
CA-129; MTCW 1, 2; SUFW 2
Barker, George Granville
1913-1991 .... **CLC 8, 48**
See also CA 9-12R; 135; CANR 7, 38;
DAM POET; DLB 20; EWL 3; MTCW 1
Barker, Harley Granville
See Granville-Barker, Harley
See also DLB 10
Barker, Howard 1946- .... **CLC 37**
See also CA 102; CBD; CD 5; DLB 13,
233
Barker, Jane 1652-1732 .... **LC 42, 82**
See also DLB 39, 131
Barker, Pat(ricia) 1943- ..... **CLC 32, 94, 146**
See also BRWS 4; CA 117; 122; CANR 50,
101; CN 7; DLB 271; INT CA-122
Barlach, Ernst (Heinrich)
1870-1938 .... **TCLC 84**
See also CA 178; DLB 56, 118; EWL 3
Barlow, Joel 1754-1812 .... **NCLC 23**
See also AMWS 2; DLB 37; RGAL 4
Barnard, Mary (Ethel) 1909- .... **CLC 48**
See also CA 21-22; CAP 2
Barnes, Djuna 1892-1982 .... **CLC 3, 4, 8, 11,
29, 127; SSC 3**
See Steptoe, Lydia
See also AMWS 3; CA 9-12R; 107; CAD;
CANR 16, 55; CWD; DLB 4, 9, 45; EWL
3; GLL 1; MTCW 1, 2; RGAL 4; TUS
Barnes, Jim 1933- .... **NNAL**
See also CA 108, 175; CAAE 175; CAAS
28; DLB 175
Barnes, Julian (Patrick) 1946- . **CLC 42, 141**
See also BRWS 4; CA 102; CANR 19, 54,
115; CN 7; DAB; DLB 194; DLBY 1993;
EWL 3; MTCW 1
Barnes, Peter 1931-2004 .... **CLC 5, 56**
See also CA 65-68; CAAS 12; CANR 33,
34, 64, 113; CBD; CD 5; DFS 6; DLB
13, 233; MTCW 1
Barnes, William 1801-1886 .... **NCLC 75**
See also DLB 32

Baroja (y Nessi), Pio 1872-1956 .... **HLC 1;
TCLC 8**
See also CA 104; EW 9
Baron, David
See Pinter, Harold
Baron Corvo
See Rolfe, Frederick (William Serafino Austin Lewis Mary)
Barondess, Sue K(aufman)
1926-1977 .... **CLC 8**
See Kaufman, Sue
See also CA 1-4R; 69-72; CANR 1
Baron de Teive
See Pessoa, Fernando (Antonio Nogueira)
Baroness Von S.
See Zangwill, Israel
Barres, (Auguste-)Maurice
1862-1923 .... **TCLC 47**
See also CA 164; DLB 123; GFL 1789 to
the Present
Barreto, Afonso Henrique de Lima
See Lima Barreto, Afonso Henrique de
Barrett, Andrea 1954- .... **CLC 150**
See also CA 156; CANR 92
Barrett, Michele .... **CLC 65**
Barrett, (Roger) Syd 1946- .... **CLC 35**
Barrett, William (Christopher)
1913-1992 .... **CLC 27**
See also CA 13-16R; 139; CANR 11, 67;
INT CANR-11
Barrie, J(ames) M(atthew)
1860-1937 .... **TCLC 2**
See also BRWS 3; BYA 4, 5; CA 104; 136;
CANR 77; CDBLB 1890-1914; CLR 16;
CWRI 5; DA3; DAB; DAM DRAM; DFS
7; DLB 10, 141, 156; EWL 3; FANT;
MAICYA 1, 2; MTCW 1; SATA 100;
SUFW; WCH; WLIT 4; YABC 1
Barrington, Michael
See Moorcock, Michael (John)
Barrol, Grady
See Bograd, Larry
Barry, Mike
See Malzberg, Barry N(athaniel)
Barry, Philip 1896-1949 .... **TCLC 11**
See also CA 109; 199; DFS 9; DLB 7, 228;
RGAL 4
Bart, Andre Schwarz
See Schwarz-Bart, Andre
Barth, John (Simmons) 1930- ... **CLC 1, 2, 3,
5, 7, 9, 10, 14, 27, 51, 89; SSC 10**
See also AITN 1, 2; AMW; BPFB 1; CA
1-4R; CABS 1; CANR 5, 23, 49, 64, 113;
CN 7; DAM NOV; DLB 2, 227; EWL 3;
FANT; MTCW 1; RGAL 4; RGSF 2;
RHW; SSFS 6; TUS
Barthelme, Donald 1931-1989 ... **CLC 1, 2, 3,
5, 6, 8, 13, 23, 46, 59, 115; SSC 2, 55**
See also AMWS 4; BPFB 1; CA 21-24R;
129; CANR 20, 58; DA3; DAM NOV;
DLB 2, 234; DLBY 1980, 1989; EWL 3;
FANT; LMFS 2; MTCW 1, 2; RGAL 4;
RGSF 2; SATA 7; SATA-Obit 62; SSFS
17
Barthelme, Frederick 1943- ...... **CLC 36, 117**
See also AMWS 11; CA 114; 122; CANR
77; CN 7; CSW; DLB 244; DLBY 1985;
EWL 3; INT CA-122
Barthes, Roland (Gerard)
1915-1980 .... **CLC 24, 83; TCLC 135**
See also CA 130; 97-100; CANR 66; DLB
296; EW 13; EWL 3; GFL 1789 to the
Present; MTCW 1, 2; TWA
Barzun, Jacques (Martin) 1907- ..... **CLC 51,
145**
See also CA 61-64; CANR 22, 95
Bashevis, Isaac
See Singer, Isaac Bashevis

Bashkirtseff, Marie 1859-1884 .... **NCLC 27**
Basho, Matsuo
See Matsuo Basho
See also PFS 18; RGWL 2, 3; WP
Basil of Caesaria c. 330-379 .... **CMLC 35**
Basket, Raney
See Edgerton, Clyde (Carlyle)
Bass, Kingsley B., Jr.
See Bullins, Ed
Bass, Rick 1958- .... **CLC 79, 143; SSC 60**
See also ANW; CA 126; CANR 53, 93;
CSW; DLB 212, 275
Bassani, Giorgio 1916-2000 .... **CLC 9**
See also CA 65-68; 190; CANR 33; CWW
2; DLB 128, 177, 299; EWL 3; MTCW 1;
RGWL 2, 3
Bastian, Ann .... **CLC 70**
Bastos, Augusto (Antonio) Roa
See Roa Bastos, Augusto (Antonio)
Bataille, Georges 1897-1962 .... **CLC 29**
See also CA 101; 89-92; EWL 3
Bates, H(erbert) E(rnest)
1905-1974 .... **CLC 46; SSC 10**
See also CA 93-96; 45-48; CANR 34; DA3;
DAB; DAM POP; DLB 162, 191; EWL
3; EXPS; MTCW 1, 2; RGSF 2; SSFS 7
Bauchart
See Camus, Albert
Baudelaire, Charles 1821-1867 . **NCLC 6, 29,
55; PC 1; SSC 18; WLC**
See also DA; DA3; DAB; DAC; DAM
MST, POET; DLB 217; EW 7; GFL 1789
to the Present; LMFS 2; PFS 21; RGWL
2, 3; TWA
Baudouin, Marcel
See Peguy, Charles (Pierre)
Baudouin, Pierre
See Peguy, Charles (Pierre)
Baudrillard, Jean 1929- .... **CLC 60**
See also DLB 296
Baum, L(yman) Frank 1856-1919 .. **TCLC 7,
132**
See also AAYA 46; BYA 16; CA 108; 133;
CLR 15; CWRI 5; DLB 22; FANT; JRDA;
MAICYA 1, 2; MTCW 1, 2; NFS 13;
RGAL 4; SATA 18, 100; WCH
Baum, Louis F.
See Baum, L(yman) Frank
Baumbach, Jonathan 1933- .... **CLC 6, 23**
See also CA 13-16R; CAAS 5; CANR 12,
66; CN 7; DLBY 1980; INT CANR-12;
MTCW 1
Bausch, Richard (Carl) 1945- .... **CLC 51**
See also AMWS 7; CA 101; CAAS 14;
CANR 43, 61, 87; CSW; DLB 130
Baxter, Charles (Morley) 1947- . **CLC 45, 78**
See also CA 57-60; CANR 40, 64, 104;
CPW; DAM POP; DLB 130; MTCW 2
Baxter, George Owen
See Faust, Frederick (Schiller)
Baxter, James K(eir) 1926-1972 .... **CLC 14**
See also CA 77-80; EWL 3
Baxter, John
See Hunt, E(verette) Howard, (Jr.)
Bayer, Sylvia
See Glassco, John
Baynton, Barbara 1857-1929 .... **TCLC 57**
See also DLB 230; RGSF 2
Beagle, Peter S(oyer) 1939- .... **CLC 7, 104**
See also AAYA 47; BPFB 1; BYA 9, 10,
16; CA 9-12R; CANR 4, 51, 73, 110;
DA3; DLBY 1980; FANT; INT CANR-4;
MTCW 1; SATA 60, 130; SUFW 1, 2;
YAW
Bean, Normal
See Burroughs, Edgar Rice
Beard, Charles A(ustin)
1874-1948 .... **TCLC 15**
See also CA 115; 189; DLB 17; SATA 18

Benford, Gregory (Albert) 1941- ..... **CLC 52**
See also BPFB 1; CA 69-72, 175; CAAE
175; CAAS 27; CANR 12, 24, 49, 95;
CSW; DLBY 1982; SCFW 2; SFW 4

Bengtsson, Frans (Gunnar)
1894-1954 .... **TCLC 48**
See also CA 170; EWL 3

Benjamin, David
See Slavitt, David R(ytman)

Benjamin, Lois
See Gould, Lois

Benjamin, Walter 1892-1940 .... **TCLC 39**
See also CA 164; DLB 242; EW 11; EWL
3

Ben Jelloun, Tahar 1944-
See Jelloun, Tahar ben
See also CA 135; CWW 2; EWL 3; RGWL
3; WLIT 2

Benn, Gottfried 1886-1956 .. **PC 35; TCLC 3**
See also CA 106; 153; DLB 56; EWL 3;
RGWL 2, 3

Bennett, Alan 1934- .... **CLC 45, 77**
See also BRWS 8; CA 103; CANR 35, 55,
106; CBD; CD 5; DAB; DAM MST;
MTCW 1, 2

Bennett, (Enoch) Arnold
1867-1931 .... **TCLC 5, 20**
See also BRW 6; CA 106; 155; CDBLB
1890-1914; DLB 10, 34, 98, 135; EWL 3;
MTCW 2

Bennett, Elizabeth
See Mitchell, Margaret (Munnerlyn)

Bennett, George Harold 1930-
See Bennett, Hal
See also BW 1; CA 97-100; CANR 87

Bennett, Gwendolyn B. 1902-1981 .... **HR 2**
See also BW 1; CA 125; DLB 51; WP

Bennett, Hal .... **CLC 5**
See Bennett, George Harold
See also DLB 33

Bennett, Jay 1912- .... **CLC 35**
See also AAYA 10; CA 69-72; CANR 11,
42, 79; JRDA; SAAS 4; SATA 41, 87;
SATA-Brief 27; WYA; YAW

Bennett, Louise (Simone) 1919- .... **BLC 1;
CLC 28**
See also BW 2, 3; CA 151; CDWLB 3; CP
7; DAM MULT; DLB 117; EWL 3

Benson, A. C. 1862-1925 .... **TCLC 123**
See also DLB 98

Benson, E(dward) F(rederic)
1867-1940 .... **TCLC 27**
See also CA 114; 157; DLB 135, 153;
HGG; SUFW 1

Benson, Jackson J. 1930- .... **CLC 34**
See also CA 25-28R; DLB 111

Benson, Sally 1900-1972 .... **CLC 17**
See also CA 19-20; 37-40R; CAP 1; SATA
1, 35; SATA-Obit 27

Benson, Stella 1892-1933 .... **TCLC 17**
See also CA 117; 154, 155; DLB 36, 162;
FANT; TEA

Bentham, Jeremy 1748-1832 .... **NCLC 38**
See also DLB 107, 158, 252

Bentley, E(dmund) C(lerihew)
1875-1956 .... **TCLC 12**
See also CA 108; DLB 70; MSW

Bentley, Eric (Russell) 1916- .... **CLC 24**
See also CA 5-8R; CAD; CANR 6, 67;
CBD; CD 5; INT CANR-6

ben Uzair, Salem
See Horne, Richard Henry Hengist

Beranger, Pierre Jean de
1780-1857 .... **NCLC 34**

Berdyaev, Nicolas
See Berdyaev, Nikolai (Aleksandrovich)

Berdyaev, Nikolai (Aleksandrovich)
1874-1948 .... **TCLC 67**
See also CA 120; 157

Berdyayev, Nikolai (Aleksandrovich)
See Berdyaev, Nikolai (Aleksandrovich)

Berendt, John (Lawrence) 1939- ...... **CLC 86**
See also CA 146; CANR 75, 93; DA3;
MTCW 1

Beresford, J(ohn) D(avys)
1873-1947 .... **TCLC 81**
See also CA 112; 155; DLB 162, 178, 197;
SFW 4; SUFW 1

Bergelson, David (Rafailovich)
1884-1952 .... **TCLC 81**
See Bergelson, Dovid
See also CA 220

Bergelson, Dovid
See Bergelson, David (Rafailovich)
See also EWL 3

Berger, Colonel
See Malraux, (Georges-)Andre

Berger, John (Peter) 1926- .... **CLC 2, 19**
See also BRWS 4; CA 81-84; CANR 51,
78, 117; CN 7; DLB 14, 207

Berger, Melvin H. 1927- .... **CLC 12**
See also CA 5-8R; CANR 4; CLR 32;
SAAS 2; SATA 5, 88; SATA-Essay 124

Berger, Thomas (Louis) 1924- .. **CLC 3, 5, 8,
11, 18, 38**
See also BPFB 1; CA 1-4R; CANR 5, 28,
51, 128; CN 7; DAM NOV; DLB 2;
DLBY 1980; EWL 3; FANT; INT CANR-
28; MTCW 1, 2; RHW; TCWW 2

Bergman, (Ernst) Ingmar 1918- ...... **CLC 16,
72**
See also CA 81-84; CANR 33, 70; CWW
2; DLB 257; MTCW 2

Bergson, Henri(-Louis) 1859-1941 . **TCLC 32**
See also CA 164; EW 8; EWL 3; GFL 1789
to the Present

Bergstein, Eleanor 1938- .... **CLC 4**
See also CA 53-56; CANR 5

Berkeley, George 1685-1753 .... **LC 65**
See also DLB 31, 101, 252

Berkoff, Steven 1937- .... **CLC 56**
See also CA 104; CANR 72; CBD; CD 5

Berlin, Isaiah 1909-1997 .... **TCLC 105**
See also CA 85-88; 162

Bermant, Chaim (Icyk) 1929-1998 ... **CLC 40**
See also CA 57-60; CANR 6, 31, 57, 105;
CN 7

Bern, Victoria
See Fisher, M(ary) F(rances) K(ennedy)

Bernanos, (Paul Louis) Georges
1888-1948 .... **TCLC 3**
See also CA 104; 130; CANR 94; DLB 72;
EWL 3; GFL 1789 to the Present; RGWL
2, 3

Bernard, April 1956- .... **CLC 59**
See also CA 131

Bernard of Clairvaux 1090-1153 .. **CMLC 71**
See also DLB 208

Berne, Victoria
See Fisher, M(ary) F(rances) K(ennedy)

Bernhard, Thomas 1931-1989 ..... **CLC 3, 32,
61; DC 14**
See also CA 85-88; 127; CANR 32, 57; CD-
WLB 2; DLB 85, 124; EWL 3; MTCW 1;
RGWL 2, 3

Bernhardt, Sarah (Henriette Rosine)
1844-1923 .... **TCLC 75**
See also CA 157

Bernstein, Charles 1950- .... **CLC 142**
See also CA 129; CAAS 24; CANR 90; CP
7; DLB 169

Bernstein, Ingrid
See Kirsch, Sarah

Berriault, Gina 1926-1999 .... **CLC 54, 109;
SSC 30**
See also CA 116; 129; 185; CANR 66; DLB
130; SSFS 7,11

Berrigan, Daniel 1921- .... **CLC 4**
See also CA 33-36R, 187; CAAE 187;
CAAS 1; CANR 11, 43, 78; CP 7; DLB 5

Berrigan, Edmund Joseph Michael, Jr.
1934-1983
See Berrigan, Ted
See also CA 61-64; 110; CANR 14, 102

Berrigan, Ted .... **CLC 37**
See Berrigan, Edmund Joseph Michael, Jr.
See also DLB 5, 169; WP

Berry, Charles Edward Anderson 1931-
See Berry, Chuck
See also CA 115

Berry, Chuck .... **CLC 17**
See Berry, Charles Edward Anderson

Berry, Jonas
See Ashbery, John (Lawrence)
See also GLL 1

Berry, Wendell (Erdman) 1934- ... **CLC 4, 6,
8, 27, 46; PC 28**
See also AITN 1; AMWS 10; ANW; CA
73-76; CANR 50, 73, 101, 132; CP 7;
CSW; DAM POET; DLB 5, 6, 234, 275;
MTCW 1

Berryman, John 1914-1972 ... **CLC 1, 2, 3, 4,
6, 8, 10, 13, 25, 62**
See also AMW; CA 13-16; 33-36R; CABS
2; CANR 35; CAP 1; CDALB 1941-1968;
DAM POET; DLB 48; EWL 3; MTCW 1,
2; PAB; RGAL 4; WP

Bertolucci, Bernardo 1940- ...... **CLC 16, 157**
See also CA 106; CANR 125

Berton, Pierre (Francis Demarigny)
1920- .... **CLC 104**
See also CA 1-4R; CANR 2, 56; CPW;
DLB 68; SATA 99

Bertrand, Aloysius 1807-1841 .... **NCLC 31**
See Bertrand, Louis oAloysiusc

Bertrand, Louis oAloysiusc
See Bertrand, Aloysius
See also DLB 217

Bertran de Born c. 1140-1215 .... **CMLC 5**

Besant, Annie (Wood) 1847-1933 ..... **TCLC 9**
See also CA 105; 185

Bessie, Alvah 1904-1985 .... **CLC 23**
See also CA 5-8R; 116; CANR 2, 80; DLB
26

Bestuzhev, Aleksandr Aleksandrovich
1797-1837 .... **NCLC 131**
See also DLB 198

Bethlen, T. D.
See Silverberg, Robert

Beti, Mongo .... **BLC 1; CLC 27**
See Biyidi, Alexandre
See also AFW; CANR 79; DAM MULT;
EWL 3; WLIT 2

Betjeman, John 1906-1984 ...... **CLC 2, 6, 10,
34, 43**
See also BRW 7; CA 9-12R; 112; CANR
33, 56; CDBLB 1945-1960; DA3; DAB;
DAM MST, POET; DLB 20; DLBY 1984;
EWL 3; MTCW 1, 2

Bettelheim, Bruno 1903-1990 .... **CLC 79;
TCLC 143**
See also CA 81-84; 131; CANR 23, 61;
DA3; MTCW 1, 2

Betti, Ugo 1892-1953 .... **TCLC 5**
See also CA 104; 155; EWL 3; RGWL 2, 3

Betts, Doris (Waugh) 1932- ..... **CLC 3, 6, 28;
SSC 45**
See also CA 13-16R; CANR 9, 66, 77; CN
7; CSW; DLB 218; DLBY 1982; INT
CANR-9; RGAL 4

Bevan, Alistair
See Roberts, Keith (John Kingston)

Bey, Pilaff
See Douglas, (George) Norman

Brodkey, Harold (Roy) 1930-1996 .. **CLC 56;
TCLC 123**
See also CA 111; 151; CANR 71; CN 7;
DLB 130

Brodsky, Iosif Alexandrovich 1940-1996
See Brodsky, Joseph
See also AITN 1; CA 41-44R; 151; CANR
37, 106; DA3; DAM POET; MTCW 1, 2;
RGWL 2, 3

Brodsky, Joseph . **CLC 4, 6, 13, 36, 100; PC 9**
See Brodsky, Iosif Alexandrovich
See also AMWS 8; CWW 2; DLB 285;
EWL 3; MTCW 1

Brodsky, Michael (Mark) 1948- .... **CLC 19**
See also CA 102; CANR 18, 41, 58; DLB 244

Brodzki, Bella ed. .... **CLC 65**

Brome, Richard 1590(?)-1652 .... **LC 61**
See also DLB 58

Bromell, Henry 1947- .... **CLC 5**
See also CA 53-56; CANR 9, 115, 116

Bromfield, Louis (Brucker)
1896-1956 .... **TCLC 11**
See also CA 107; 155; DLB 4, 9, 86; RGAL
4; RHW

Broner, E(sther) M(asserman)
1930- .... **CLC 19**
See also CA 17-20R; CANR 8, 25, 72; CN
7; DLB 28

Bronk, William (M.) 1918-1999 .... **CLC 10**
See also CA 89-92; 177; CANR 23; CP 7;
DLB 165

Bronstein, Lev Davidovich
See Trotsky, Leon

Bronte, Anne 1820-1849 ..... **NCLC 4, 71, 102**
See also BRW 5; BRWR 1; DA3; DLB 21,
199; TEA

Bronte, (Patrick) Branwell
1817-1848 .... **NCLC 109**

Bronte, Charlotte 1816-1855 ...... **NCLC 3, 8, 33, 58, 105; WLC**
See also AAYA 17; BRW 5; BRWC 2;
BRWR 1; BYA 2; CDBLB 1832-1890;
DA; DA3; DAB; DAC; DAM MST, NOV;
DLB 21, 159, 199; EXPN; LAIT 2; NFS
4; TEA; WLIT 4

Bronte, Emily (Jane) 1818-1848 ... **NCLC 16, 35; PC 8; WLC**
See also AAYA 17; BPFB 1; BRW 5;
BRWC 1; BRWR 1; BYA 3; CDBLB
1832-1890; DA; DA3; DAB; DAC; DAM
MST, NOV, POET; DLB 21, 32, 199;
EXPN; LAIT 1; TEA; WLIT 3

Brontes
See Bronte, Anne; Bronte, Charlotte; Bronte,
Emily (Jane)

Brooke, Frances 1724-1789 .... **LC 6, 48**
See also DLB 39, 99

Brooke, Henry 1703(?)-1783 .... **LC 1**
See also DLB 39

Brooke, Rupert (Chawner)
1887-1915 ..... **PC 24; TCLC 2, 7; WLC**
See also BRWS 3; CA 104; 132; CANR 61;
CDBLB 1914-1945; DA; DAB; DAC;
DAM MST, POET; DLB 19, 216; EXPP;
GLL 2; MTCW 1, 2; PFS 7; TEA

Brooke-Haven, P.
See Wodehouse, P(elham) G(renville)

Brooke-Rose, Christine 1926(?)- ..... **CLC 40, 184**
See also BRWS 4; CA 13-16R; CANR 58,
118; CN 7; DLB 14, 231; EWL 3; SFW 4

Brookner, Anita 1928- .. **CLC 32, 34, 51, 136**
See also BRWS 4; CA 114; 120; CANR 37,
56, 87, 130; CN 7; CPW; DA3; DAB;
DAM POP; DLB 194; DLBY 1987; EWL
3; MTCW 1, 2; TEA

Brooks, Cleanth 1906-1994 . **CLC 24, 86, 110**
See also CA 17-20R; 145; CANR 33, 35;
CSW; DLB 63; DLBY 1994; EWL 3; INT
CANR-35; MTCW 1, 2

Brooks, George
See Baum, L(yman) Frank

Brooks, Gwendolyn (Elizabeth)
1917-2000 ... **BLC 1; CLC 1, 2, 4, 5, 15, 49, 125; PC 7; WLC**
See also AAYA 20; AFAW 1, 2; AITN 1;
AMWS 3; BW 2, 3; CA 1-4R; 190; CANR
1, 27, 52, 75, 132; CDALB 1941-1968;
CLR 27; CP 7; CWP; DA; DA3; DAC;
DAM MST, MULT, POET; DLB 5, 76,
165; EWL 3; EXPP; MAWW; MTCW 1,
2; PFS 1, 2, 4, 6; RGAL 4; SATA 6;
SATA-Obit 123; TUS; WP

Brooks, Mel .... **CLC 12**
See Kaminsky, Melvin
See also AAYA 13, 48; DLB 26

Brooks, Peter (Preston) 1938- .... **CLC 34**
See also CA 45-48; CANR 1, 107

Brooks, Van Wyck 1886-1963 .... **CLC 29**
See also AMW; CA 1-4R; CANR 6; DLB
45, 63, 103; TUS

Brophy, Brigid (Antonia)
1929-1995 .... **CLC 6, 11, 29, 105**
See also CA 5-8R; 149; CAAS 4; CANR
25, 53; CBD; CN 7; CWD; DA3; DLB
14, 271; EWL 3; MTCW 1, 2

Brosman, Catharine Savage 1934- ..... **CLC 9**
See also CA 61-64; CANR 21, 46

Brossard, Nicole 1943- .... **CLC 115, 169**
See also CA 122; CAAS 16; CCA 1; CWP;
CWW 2; DLB 53; EWL 3; FW; GLL 2;
RGWL 3

Brother Antoninus
See Everson, William (Oliver)

The Brothers Quay
See Quay, Stephen; Quay, Timothy

Broughton, T(homas) Alan 1936- ..... **CLC 19**
See also CA 45-48; CANR 2, 23, 48, 111

Broumas, Olga 1949- .... **CLC 10, 73**
See also CA 85-88; CANR 20, 69, 110; CP
7; CWP; GLL 2

Broun, Heywood 1888-1939 .... **TCLC 104**
See also DLB 29, 171

Brown, Alan 1950- .... **CLC 99**
See also CA 156

Brown, Charles Brockden
1771-1810 .... **NCLC 22, 74, 122**
See also AMWS 1; CDALB 1640-1865;
DLB 37, 59, 73; FW; HGG; LMFS 1;
RGAL 4; TUS

Brown, Christy 1932-1981 .... **CLC 63**
See also BYA 13; CA 105; 104; CANR 72;
DLB 14

Brown, Claude 1937-2002 ... **BLC 1; CLC 30**
See also AAYA 7; BW 1, 3; CA 73-76; 205;
CANR 81; DAM MULT

Brown, Dee (Alexander)
1908-2002 .... **CLC 18, 47**
See also AAYA 30; CA 13-16R; 212; CAAS
6; CANR 11, 45, 60; CPW; CSW; DA3;
DAM POP; DLBY 1980; LAIT 2; MTCW
1, 2; NCFS 5; SATA 5, 110; SATA-Obit
141; TCWW 2

Brown, George
See Wertmueller, Lina

Brown, George Douglas
1869-1902 .... **TCLC 28**
See Douglas, George
See also CA 162

Brown, George Mackay 1921-1996 ... **CLC 5, 48, 100**
See also BRWS 6; CA 21-24R; 151; CAAS
6; CANR 12, 37, 67; CN 7; CP 7; DLB
14, 27, 139, 271; MTCW 1; RGSF 2;
SATA 35

Brown, (William) Larry 1951- .... **CLC 73**
See also CA 130; 134; CANR 117; CSW;
DLB 234; INT CA-134

Brown, Moses
See Barrett, William (Christopher)

Brown, Rita Mae 1944- .... **CLC 18, 43, 79**
See also BPFB 1; CA 45-48; CANR 2, 11,
35, 62, 95; CN 7; CPW; CSW; DA3;
DAM NOV, POP; FW; INT CANR-11;
MTCW 1, 2; NFS 9; RGAL 4; TUS

Brown, Roderick (Langmere) Haig-
See Haig-Brown, Roderick (Langmere)

Brown, Rosellen 1939- .... **CLC 32, 170**
See also CA 77-80; CAAS 10; CANR 14,
44, 98; CN 7

Brown, Sterling Allen 1901-1989 ...... **BLC 1;
CLC 1, 23, 59; HR 2; PC 55**
See also AFAW 1, 2; BW 1, 3; CA 85-88;
127; CANR 26; DA3; DAM MULT,
POET; DLB 48, 51, 63; MTCW 1, 2;
RGAL 4; WP

Brown, Will
See Ainsworth, William Harrison

Brown, William Hill 1765-1793 .... **LC 93**
See also DLB 37

Brown, William Wells 1815-1884 ...... **BLC 1;
DC 1; NCLC 2, 89**
See also DAM MULT; DLB 3, 50, 183,
248; RGAL 4

Browne, (Clyde) Jackson 1948(?)- ... **CLC 21**
See also CA 120

Browning, Elizabeth Barrett
1806-1861 ... **NCLC 1, 16, 61, 66; PC 6;
WLC**
See also BRW 4; CDBLB 1832-1890; DA;
DA3; DAB; DAC; DAM MST, POET;
DLB 32, 199; EXPP; PAB; PFS 2, 16;
TEA; WLIT 4; WP

Browning, Robert 1812-1889 . **NCLC 19, 79;
PC 2; WLCS**
See also BRW 4; BRWC 2; BRWR 2; CD-
BLB 1832-1890; CLR 97; DA; DA3;
DAB; DAC; DAM MST, POET; DLB 32,
163; EXPP; LATS 1; PAB; PFS 1, 15;
RGEL 2; TEA; WLIT 4; WP; YABC 1

Browning, Tod 1882-1962 .... **CLC 16**
See also CA 141; 117

Brownmiller, Susan 1935- .... **CLC 159**
See also CA 103; CANR 35, 75; DAM
NOV; FW; MTCW 1, 2

Brownson, Orestes Augustus
1803-1876 .... **NCLC 50**
See also DLB 1, 59, 73, 243

Bruccoli, Matthew J(oseph) 1931- ... **CLC 34**
See also CA 9-12R; CANR 7, 87; DLB 103

Bruce, Lenny .... **CLC 21**
See Schneider, Leonard Alfred

Bruchac, Joseph III 1942- .... **NNAL**
See also AAYA 19; CA 33-36R; CANR 13,
47, 75, 94; CLR 46; CWRI 5; DAM
MULT; JRDA; MAICYA 2; MAICYAS 1;
MTCW 1; SATA 42, 89, 131

Bruin, John
See Brutus, Dennis

Brulard, Henri
See Stendhal

Brulls, Christian
See Simenon, Georges (Jacques Christian)

Brunner, John (Kilian Houston)
1934-1995 .... **CLC 8, 10**
See also CA 1-4R; 149; CAAS 8; CANR 2,
37; CPW; DAM POP; DLB 261; MTCW
1, 2; SCFW 2; SFW 4

Bruno, Giordano 1548-1600 .... **LC 27**
See also RGWL 2, 3

Castro (Ruz), Fidel 1926(?)- .... **HLC 1**
  See also CA 110; 129; CANR 81; DAM
  MULT; HW 2

Castro, Guillen de 1569-1631 .... **LC 19**

Castro, Rosalia de 1837-1885 ... **NCLC 3, 78;
PC 41**
  See also DAM MULT

Cather, Willa (Sibert) 1873-1947 . **SSC 2, 50;
TCLC 1, 11, 31, 99, 132, 152; WLC**
  See also AAYA 24; AMW; AMWC 1;
  AMWR 1; BPFB 1; CA 104; 128; CDALB
  1865-1917; CLR 98; DA; DA3; DAB;
  DAC; DAM MST, NOV; DLB 9, 54, 78,
  256; DLBD 1; EWL 3; EXPN; EXPS;
  LAIT 3; LATS 1; MAWW; MTCW 1, 2;
  NFS 2, 19; RGAL 4; RGSF 2; RHW;
  SATA 30; SSFS 2, 7, 16; TCWW 2; TUS

Catherine II
  See Catherine the Great
  See also DLB 150

Catherine the Great 1729-1796 .... **LC 69**
  See Catherine II

Cato, Marcus Porcius
  234B.C.-149B.C. .... **CMLC 21**
  See Cato the Elder

Cato, Marcus Porcius, the Elder
  See Cato, Marcus Porcius

Cato the Elder
  See Cato, Marcus Porcius
  See also DLB 211

Catton, (Charles) Bruce 1899-1978 . **CLC 35**
  See also AITN 1; CA 5-8R; 81-84; CANR
  7, 74; DLB 17; SATA 2; SATA-Obit 24

Catullus c. 84B.C.-54B.C. .... **CMLC 18**
  See also AW 2; CDWLB 1; DLB 211;
  RGWL 2, 3

Cauldwell, Frank
  See King, Francis (Henry)

Caunitz, William J. 1933-1996 .... **CLC 34**
  See also BEST 89:3; CA 125; 130; 152;
  CANR 73; INT CA-130

Causley, Charles (Stanley)
  1917-2003 .... **CLC 7**
  See also CA 9-12R; 223; CANR 5, 35, 94;
  CLR 30; CWRI 5; DLB 27; MTCW 1;
  SATA 3, 66; SATA-Obit 149

Caute, (John) David 1936- .... **CLC 29**
  See also CA 1-4R; CAAS 4; CANR 1, 33,
  64, 120; CBD; CD 5; CN 7; DAM NOV;
  DLB 14, 231

Cavafy, C(onstantine) P(eter) .... **PC 36;
TCLC 2, 7**
  See Kavafis, Konstantinos Petrou
  See also CA 148; DA3; DAM POET; EW
  8; EWL 3; MTCW 1; PFS 19; RGWL 2,
  3; WP

Cavalcanti, Guido c. 1250-c.
  1300 .... **CMLC 54**

Cavallo, Evelyn
  See Spark, Muriel (Sarah)

Cavanna, Betty .... **CLC 12**
  See Harrison, Elizabeth (Allen) Cavanna
  See also JRDA; MAICYA 1; SAAS 4;
  SATA 1, 30

Cavendish, Margaret Lucas
  1623-1673 .... **LC 30**
  See also DLB 131, 252, 281; RGEL 2

Caxton, William 1421(?)-1491(?) .... **LC 17**
  See also DLB 170

Cayer, D. M.
  See Duffy, Maureen

Cayrol, Jean 1911- .... **CLC 11**
  See also CA 89-92; DLB 83; EWL 3

Cela (y Trulock), Camilo Jose
  See Cela, Camilo Jose
  See also CWW 2

Cela, Camilo Jose 1916-2002 .... **CLC 4, 13,
59, 122; HLC 1; SSC 71**
  See Cela (y Trulock), Camilo Jose
  See also BEST 90:2; CA 21-24R; 206;
  CAAS 10; CANR 21, 32, 76; DAM
  MULT; DLBY 1989; EW 13; EWL 3; HW
  1; MTCW 1, 2; RGSF 2; RGWL 2, 3

Celan, Paul .... **CLC 10, 19, 53, 82; PC 10**
  See Antschel, Paul
  See also CDWLB 2; DLB 69; EWL 3;
  RGWL 2, 3

Celine, Louis-Ferdinand .. **CLC 1, 3, 4, 7, 9,
15, 47, 124**
  See Destouches, Louis-Ferdinand
  See also DLB 72; EW 11; EWL 3; GFL
  1789 to the Present; RGWL 2, 3

Cellini, Benvenuto 1500-1571 .... **LC 7**

Cendrars, Blaise .... **CLC 18, 106**
  See Sauser-Hall, Frederic
  See also DLB 258; EWL 3; GFL 1789 to
  the Present; RGWL 2, 3; WP

Centlivre, Susanna 1669(?)-1723 .... **LC 65**
  See also DLB 84; RGEL 2

Cernuda (y Bidon), Luis 1902-1963 . **CLC 54**
  See also CA 131; 89-92; DAM POET; DLB
  134; EWL 3; GLL 1; HW 1; RGWL 2, 3

Cervantes, Lorna Dee 1954- ..... **HLCS 1; PC
35**
  See also CA 131; CANR 80; CWP; DLB
  82; EXPP; HW 1; LLW 1

Cervantes (Saavedra), Miguel de
  1547-1616 .... **HLCS; LC 6, 23, 93; SSC
12; WLC**
  See also AAYA 56; BYA 1, 14; DA; DAB;
  DAC; DAM MST, NOV; EW 2; LAIT 1;
  LATS 1; LMFS 1; NFS 8; RGSF 2;
  RGWL 2, 3; TWA

Cesaire, Aime (Fernand) 1913- .... **BLC 1;
CLC 19, 32, 112; DC 22; PC 25**
  See also BW 2, 3; CA 65-68; CANR 24,
  43, 81; CWW 2; DA3; DAM MULT,
  POET; EWL 3; GFL 1789 to the Present;
  MTCW 1, 2; WP

Chabon, Michael 1963- ... **CLC 55, 149; SSC
59**
  See also AAYA 45; AMWS 11; CA 139;
  CANR 57, 96, 127; DLB 278; SATA 145

Chabrol, Claude 1930- .... **CLC 16**
  See also CA 110

Chairil Anwar
  See Anwar, Chairil
  See also EWL 3

Challans, Mary 1905-1983
  See Renault, Mary
  See also CA 81-84; 111; CANR 74; DA3;
  MTCW 2; SATA 23; SATA-Obit 36; TEA

Challis, George
  See Faust, Frederick (Schiller)
  See also TCWW 2

Chambers, Aidan 1934- .... **CLC 35**
  See also AAYA 27; CA 25-28R; CANR 12,
  31, 58, 116; JRDA; MAICYA 1, 2; SAAS
  12; SATA 1, 69, 108; WYA; YAW

Chambers, James 1948-
  See Cliff, Jimmy
  See also CA 124

Chambers, Jessie
  See Lawrence, D(avid) H(erbert Richards)
  See also GLL 1

Chambers, Robert W(illiam)
  1865-1933 .... **TCLC 41**
  See also CA 165; DLB 202; HGG; SATA
  107; SUFW 1

Chambers, (David) Whittaker
  1901-1961 .... **TCLC 129**
  See also CA 89-92

Chamisso, Adelbert von
  1781-1838 .... **NCLC 82**
  See also DLB 90; RGWL 2, 3; SUFW 1

Chance, James T.
  See Carpenter, John (Howard)

Chance, John T.
  See Carpenter, John (Howard)

Chandler, Raymond (Thornton)
  1888-1959 .... **SSC 23; TCLC 1, 7**
  See also AAYA 25; AMWC 2; AMWS 4;
  BPFB 1; CA 104; 129; CANR 60, 107;
  CDALB 1929-1941; CMW 4; DA3; DLB
  226, 253; DLBD 6; EWL 3; MSW;
  MTCW 1, 2; NFS 17; RGAL 4; TUS

Chang, Diana 1934- .... **AAL**
  See also CWP; EXPP

Chang, Eileen 1921-1995 .... **AAL; SSC 28**
  See Chang Ai-Ling; Zhang Ailing
  See also CA 166

Chang, Jung 1952- .... **CLC 71**
  See also CA 142

Chang Ai-Ling
  See Chang, Eileen
  See also EWL 3

Channing, William Ellery
  1780-1842 .... **NCLC 17**
  See also DLB 1, 59, 235; RGAL 4

Chao, Patricia 1955- .... **CLC 119**
  See also CA 163

Chaplin, Charles Spencer
  1889-1977 .... **CLC 16**
  See Chaplin, Charlie
  See also CA 81-84; 73-76

Chaplin, Charlie
  See Chaplin, Charles Spencer
  See also DLB 44

Chapman, George 1559(?)-1634 . **DC 19; LC
22**
  See also BRW 1; DAM DRAM; DLB 62,
  121; LMFS 1; RGEL 2

Chapman, Graham 1941-1989 .... **CLC 21**
  See Monty Python
  See also CA 116; 129; CANR 35, 95

Chapman, John Jay 1862-1933 .... **TCLC 7**
  See also CA 104; 191

Chapman, Lee
  See Bradley, Marion Zimmer
  See also GLL 1

Chapman, Walker
  See Silverberg, Robert

Chappell, Fred (Davis) 1936- .... **CLC 40, 78,
162**
  See also CA 5-8R; 198; CAAE 198; CAAS
  4; CANR 8, 33, 67, 110; CN 7; CP 7;
  CSW; DLB 6, 105; HGG

Char, Rene(-Emile) 1907-1988 .... **CLC 9, 11,
14, 55; PC 56**
  See also CA 13-16R; 124; CANR 32; DAM
  POET; DLB 258; EWL 3; GFL 1789 to
  the Present; MTCW 1, 2; RGWL 2, 3

Charby, Jay
  See Ellison, Harlan (Jay)

Chardin, Pierre Teilhard de
  See Teilhard de Chardin, (Marie Joseph)
  Pierre

Chariton fl. 1st cent. (?)- .... **CMLC 49**

Charlemagne 742-814 .... **CMLC 37**

Charles I 1600-1649 .... **LC 13**

Charriere, Isabelle de 1740-1805 .. **NCLC 66**

Chartier, Alain c. 1392-1430 .... **LC 94**
  See also DLB 208

Chartier, Emile-Auguste
  See Alain

Charyn, Jerome 1937- .... **CLC 5, 8, 18**
  See also CA 5-8R; CAAS 1; CANR 7, 61,
  101; CMW 4; CN 7; DLBY 1983; MTCW
  1

Chase, Adam
  See Marlowe, Stephen

Chase, Mary (Coyle) 1907-1981 .... **DC 1**
  See also CA 77-80; 105; CAD; CWD; DFS
  11; DLB 228; SATA 17; SATA-Obit 29

Cicero, Marcus Tullius
106B.C.-43B.C. .... **CMLC 3**
See also AW 1; CDWLB 1; DLB 211;
RGWL 2, 3

Cimino, Michael 1943- .... **CLC 16**
See also CA 105

Cioran, E(mil) M. 1911-1995 .... **CLC 64**
See also CA 25-28R; 149; CANR 91; DLB
220; EWL 3

Cisneros, Sandra 1954- .... **CLC 69, 118, 193;**
HLC 1; PC 52; SSC 32, 72
See also AAYA 9, 53; AMWS 7; CA 131;
CANR 64, 118; CWP; DA3; DAM MULT;
DLB 122, 152; EWL 3; EXPN; FW; HW
1, 2; LAIT 5; LATS 1; LLW 1; MAICYA
2; MTCW 2; NFS 2; PFS 19; RGAL 4;
RGSF 2; SSFS 3, 13; WLIT 1; YAW

Cixous, Helene 1937- .... **CLC 92**
See also CA 126; CANR 55, 123; CWW 2;
DLB 83, 242; EWL 3; FW; GLL 2;
MTCW 1, 2; TWA

Clair, Rene .... **CLC 20**
See Chomette, Rene Lucien

Clampitt, Amy 1920-1994 .... **CLC 32; PC 19**
See also AMWS 9; CA 110; 146; CANR
29, 79; DLB 105

Clancy, Thomas L., Jr. 1947-
See Clancy, Tom
See also CA 125; 131; CANR 62, 105;
DA3; INT CA-131; MTCW 1, 2

Clancy, Tom .... **CLC 45, 112**
See Clancy, Thomas L., Jr.
See also AAYA 9, 51; BEST 89:1, 90:1;
BPFB 1; BYA 10, 11; CANR 132; CMW
4; CPW; DAM NOV, POP; DLB 227

Clare, John 1793-1864 .. **NCLC 9, 86; PC 23**
See also DAB; DAM POET; DLB 55, 96;
RGEL 2

Clarin
See Alas (y Urena), Leopoldo (Enrique
Garcia)

Clark, Al C.
See Goines, Donald

Clark, (Robert) Brian 1932- .... **CLC 29**
See also CA 41-44R; CANR 67; CBD; CD
5

Clark, Curt
See Westlake, Donald E(dwin)

Clark, Eleanor 1913-1996 .... **CLC 5, 19**
See also CA 9-12R; 151; CANR 41; CN 7;
DLB 6

Clark, J. P.
See Clark Bekederemo, J(ohnson) P(epper)
See also CDWLB 3; DLB 117

Clark, John Pepper
See Clark Bekederemo, J(ohnson) P(epper)
See also AFW; CD 5; CP 7; RGEL 2

Clark, Kenneth (Mackenzie)
1903-1983 .... **TCLC 147**
See also CA 93-96; 109; CANR 36; MTCW
1, 2

Clark, M. R.
See Clark, Mavis Thorpe

Clark, Mavis Thorpe 1909-1999 ...... **CLC 12**
See also CA 57-60; CANR 8, 37, 107; CLR
30; CWRI 5; MAICYA 1, 2; SAAS 5;
SATA 8, 74

Clark, Walter Van Tilburg
1909-1971 .... **CLC 28**
See also CA 9-12R; 33-36R; CANR 63,
113; DLB 9, 206; LAIT 2; RGAL 4;
SATA 8

Clark Bekederemo, J(ohnson) P(epper)
1935- .... **BLC 1; CLC 38; DC 5**
See Clark, J. P.; Clark, John Pepper
See also BW 1; CA 65-68; CANR 16, 72;
DAM DRAM, MULT; DFS 13; EWL 3;
MTCW 1

Clarke, Arthur C(harles) 1917- .... **CLC 1, 4,**
13, 18, 35, 136; SSC 3
See also AAYA 4, 33; BPFB 1; BYA 13;
CA 1-4R; CANR 2, 28, 55, 74, 130; CN
7; CPW; DA3; DAM POP; DLB 261;
JRDA; LAIT 5; MAICYA 1, 2; MTCW 1,
2; SATA 13, 70, 115; SCFW; SFW 4;
SSFS 4, 18; YAW

Clarke, Austin 1896-1974 .... **CLC 6, 9**
See also CA 29-32; 49-52; CAP 2; DAM
POET; DLB 10, 20; EWL 3; RGEL 2

Clarke, Austin C(hesterfield) 1934- .. **BLC 1;**
CLC 8, 53; SSC 45
See also BW 1; CA 25-28R; CAAS 16;
CANR 14, 32, 68; CN 7; DAC; DAM
MULT; DLB 53, 125; DNFS 2; RGSF 2

Clarke, Gillian 1937- .... **CLC 61**
See also CA 106; CP 7; CWP; DLB 40

Clarke, Marcus (Andrew Hislop)
1846-1881 .... **NCLC 19**
See also DLB 230; RGEL 2; RGSF 2

Clarke, Shirley 1925-1997 .... **CLC 16**
See also CA 189

Clash, The
See Headon, (Nicky) Topper; Jones, Mick;
Simonon, Paul; Strummer, Joe

Claudel, Paul (Louis Charles Marie)
1868-1955 .... **TCLC 2, 10**
See also CA 104; 165; DLB 192, 258; EW
8; EWL 3; GFL 1789 to the Present;
RGWL 2, 3; TWA

Claudian 370(?)-404(?) .... **CMLC 46**
See also RGWL 2, 3

Claudius, Matthias 1740-1815 .... **NCLC 75**
See also DLB 97

Clavell, James (duMaresq)
1925-1994 .... **CLC 6, 25, 87**
See also BPFB 1; CA 25-28R; 146; CANR
26, 48; CPW; DA3; DAM NOV, POP;
MTCW 1, 2; NFS 10; RHW

Clayman, Gregory .... **CLC 65**

Cleaver, (Leroy) Eldridge
1935-1998 .... **BLC 1; CLC 30, 119**
See also BW 1, 3; CA 21-24R; 167; CANR
16, 75; DA3; DAM MULT; MTCW 2;
YAW

Cleese, John (Marwood) 1939- .... **CLC 21**
See Monty Python
See also CA 112; 116; CANR 35; MTCW 1

Cleishbotham, Jebediah
See Scott, Sir Walter

Cleland, John 1710-1789 .... **LC 2, 48**
See also DLB 39; RGEL 2

Clemens, Samuel Langhorne 1835-1910
See Twain, Mark
See also CA 104; 135; CDALB 1865-1917;
DA; DA3; DAB; DAC; DAM MST, NOV;
DLB 12, 23, 64, 74, 186, 189; JRDA;
LMFS 1; MAICYA 1, 2; NCFS 4; NFS
20; SATA 100; SSFS 16; YABC 2

Clement of Alexandria
150(?)-215(?) .... **CMLC 41**

Cleophil
See Congreve, William

Clerihew, E.
See Bentley, E(dmund) C(lerihew)

Clerk, N. W.
See Lewis, C(live) S(taples)

Cliff, Jimmy .... **CLC 21**
See Chambers, James
See also CA 193

Cliff, Michelle 1946- .... **BLCS; CLC 120**
See also BW 2; CA 116; CANR 39, 72; CD-
WLB 3; DLB 157; FW; GLL 2

Clifford, Lady Anne 1590-1676 .... **LC 76**
See also DLB 151

Clifton, (Thelma) Lucille 1936- .... **BLC 1;**
CLC 19, 66, 162; PC 17
See also AFAW 2; BW 2, 3; CA 49-52;
CANR 2, 24, 42, 76, 97; CLR 5; CP 7;
CSW; CWP; CWRI 5; DA3; DAM MULT,
POET; DLB 5, 41; EXPP; MAICYA 1, 2;
MTCW 1, 2; PFS 1, 14; SATA 20, 69,
128; WP

Clinton, Dirk
See Silverberg, Robert

Clough, Arthur Hugh 1819-1861 ... **NCLC 27**
See also BRW 5; DLB 32; RGEL 2

Clutha, Janet Paterson Frame 1924-2004
See Frame, Janet
See also CA 1-4R; 224; CANR 2, 36, 76;
MTCW 1, 2; SATA 119

Clyne, Terence
See Blatty, William Peter

Cobalt, Martin
See Mayne, William (James Carter)

Cobb, Irvin S(hrewsbury)
1876-1944 .... **TCLC 77**
See also CA 175; DLB 11, 25, 86

Cobbett, William 1763-1835 .... **NCLC 49**
See also DLB 43, 107, 158; RGEL 2

Coburn, D(onald) L(ee) 1938- .... **CLC 10**
See also CA 89-92

Cocteau, Jean (Maurice Eugene Clement)
1889-1963 ...... **CLC 1, 8, 15, 16, 43; DC**
17; TCLC 119; WLC
See also CA 25-28; CANR 40; CAP 2; DA;
DA3; DAB; DAC; DAM DRAM, MST,
NOV; DLB 65, 258; EW 10; EWL 3; GFL
1789 to the Present; MTCW 1, 2; RGWL
2, 3; TWA

Codrescu, Andrei 1946- .... **CLC 46, 121**
See also CA 33-36R; CAAS 19; CANR 13,
34, 53, 76, 125; DA3; DAM POET;
MTCW 2

Coe, Max
See Bourne, Randolph S(illiman)

Coe, Tucker
See Westlake, Donald E(dwin)

Coen, Ethan 1958- .... **CLC 108**
See also AAYA 54; CA 126; CANR 85

Coen, Joel 1955- .... **CLC 108**
See also AAYA 54; CA 126; CANR 119

The Coen Brothers
See Coen, Ethan; Coen, Joel

Coetzee, J(ohn) M(axwell) 1940- ..... **CLC 23,**
33, 66, 117, 161, 162
See also AAYA 37; AFW; BRWS 6; CA 77-
80; CANR 41, 54, 74, 114; CN 7; DA3;
DAM NOV; DLB 225; EWL 3; LMFS 2;
MTCW 1, 2; WLIT 2; WWE 1

Coffey, Brian
See Koontz, Dean R(ay)

Coffin, Robert P(eter) Tristram
1892-1955 .... **TCLC 95**
See also CA 123; 169; DLB 45

Cohan, George M(ichael)
1878-1942 .... **TCLC 60**
See also CA 157; DLB 249; RGAL 4

Cohen, Arthur A(llen) 1928-1986 ...... **CLC 7,**
31
See also CA 1-4R; 120; CANR 1, 17, 42;
DLB 28

Cohen, Leonard (Norman) 1934- ...... **CLC 3,**
38
See also CA 21-24R; CANR 14, 69; CN 7;
CP 7; DAC; DAM MST; DLB 53; EWL
3; MTCW 1

Cohen, Matt(hew) 1942-1999 .... **CLC 19**
See also CA 61-64; 187; CAAS 18; CANR
40; CN 7; DAC; DLB 53

Coppee, Francois 1842-1908 .... **TCLC 25**
    See also CA 170; DLB 217
Coppola, Francis Ford 1939- ... **CLC 16, 126**
    See also AAYA 39; CA 77-80; CANR 40,
    78; DLB 44
Copway, George 1818-1869 .... **NNAL**
    See also DAM MULT; DLB 175, 183
Corbiere, Tristan 1845-1875 .... **NCLC 43**
    See also DLB 217; GFL 1789 to the Present
Corcoran, Barbara (Asenath)
    1911- .... **CLC 17**
    See also AAYA 14; CA 21-24R, 191; CAAE
    191; CAAS 2; CANR 11, 28, 48; CLR
    50; DLB 52; JRDA; MAICYA 2; MAIC-
    YAS 1; RHW; SAAS 20; SATA 3, 77;
    SATA-Essay 125
Cordelier, Maurice
    See Giraudoux, Jean(-Hippolyte)
Corelli, Marie .... **TCLC 51**
    See Mackay, Mary
    See also DLB 34, 156; RGEL 2; SUFW 1
Corman, Cid .... **CLC 9**
    See Corman, Sidney
    See also CAAS 2; DLB 5, 193
Corman, Sidney 1924-2004
    See Corman, Cid
    See also CA 85-88; 225; CANR 44; CP 7;
    DAM POET
Cormier, Robert (Edmund)
    1925-2000 .... **CLC 12, 30**
    See also AAYA 3, 19; BYA 1, 2, 6, 8, 9;
    CA 1-4R; CANR 5, 23, 76, 93; CDALB
    1968-1988; CLR 12, 55; DA; DAB; DAC;
    DAM MST, NOV; DLB 52; EXPN; INT
    CANR-23; JRDA; LAIT 5; MAICYA 1,
    2; MTCW 1, 2; NFS 2, 18; SATA 10, 45,
    83; SATA-Obit 122; WYA; YAW
Corn, Alfred (DeWitt III) 1943- .... **CLC 33**
    See also CA 179; CAAE 179; CAAS 25;
    CANR 44; CP 7; CSW; DLB 120, 282;
    DLBY 1980
Corneille, Pierre 1606-1684 ... **DC 21; LC 28**
    See also DAB; DAM MST; DLB 268; EW
    3; GFL Beginnings to 1789; RGWL 2, 3;
    TWA
Cornwell, David (John Moore)
    1931- .... **CLC 9, 15**
    See le Carre, John
    See also CA 5-8R; CANR 13, 33, 59, 107,
    132; DA3; DAM POP; MTCW 1, 2
Cornwell, Patricia (Daniels) 1956- . **CLC 155**
    See also AAYA 16, 56; BPFB 1; CA 134;
    CANR 53, 131; CMW 4; CPW; CSW;
    DAM POP; MSW; MTCW 1
Corso, (Nunzio) Gregory 1930-2001 . **CLC 1,
    11; PC 33**
    See also AMWS 12; BG 2; CA 5-8R; 193;
    CANR 41, 76, 132; CP 7; DA3; DLB 5,
    16, 237; LMFS 2; MTCW 1, 2; WP
Cortazar, Julio 1914-1984 ... **CLC 2, 3, 5, 10,
    13, 15, 33, 34, 92; HLC 1; SSC 7**
    See also BPFB 1; CA 21-24R; CANR 12,
    32, 81; CDWLB 3; DA3; DAM MULT,
    NOV; DLB 113; EWL 3; EXPS; HW 1,
    2; LAW; MTCW 1, 2; RGSF 2; RGWL 2,
    3; SSFS 3, 20; TWA; WLIT 1
Cortes, Hernan 1485-1547 .... **LC 31**
Corvinus, Jakob
    See Raabe, Wilhelm (Karl)
Corwin, Cecil
    See Kornbluth, C(yril) M.
Cosic, Dobrica 1921- .... **CLC 14**
    See also CA 122; 138; CDWLB 4; CWW
    2; DLB 181; EWL 3
Costain, Thomas B(ertram)
    1885-1965 .... **CLC 30**
    See also BYA 3; CA 5-8R; 25-28R; DLB 9;
    RHW

Costantini, Humberto 1924(?)-1987 . **CLC 49**
    See also CA 131; 122; EWL 3; HW 1
Costello, Elvis 1954- .... **CLC 21**
    See also CA 204
Costenoble, Philostene
    See Ghelderode, Michel de
Cotes, Cecil V.
    See Duncan, Sara Jeannette
Cotter, Joseph Seamon Sr.
    1861-1949 .... **BLC 1; TCLC 28**
    See also BW 1; CA 124; DAM MULT; DLB
    50
Couch, Arthur Thomas Quiller
    See Quiller-Couch, Sir Arthur (Thomas)
Coulton, James
    See Hansen, Joseph
Couperus, Louis (Marie Anne)
    1863-1923 .... **TCLC 15**
    See also CA 115; EWL 3; RGWL 2, 3
Coupland, Douglas 1961- .... **CLC 85, 133**
    See also AAYA 34; CA 142; CANR 57, 90,
    130; CCA 1; CPW; DAC; DAM POP
Court, Wesli
    See Turco, Lewis (Putnam)
Courtenay, Bryce 1933- .... **CLC 59**
    See also CA 138; CPW
Courtney, Robert
    See Ellison, Harlan (Jay)
Cousteau, Jacques-Yves 1910-1997 .. **CLC 30**
    See also CA 65-68; 159; CANR 15, 67;
    MTCW 1; SATA 38, 98
Coventry, Francis 1725-1754 .... **LC 46**
Coverdale, Miles c. 1487-1569 .... **LC 77**
    See also DLB 167
Cowan, Peter (Walkinshaw)
    1914-2002 .... **SSC 28**
    See also CA 21-24R; CANR 9, 25, 50, 83;
    CN 7; DLB 260; RGSF 2
Coward, Noel (Peirce) 1899-1973 . **CLC 1, 9,
    29, 51**
    See also AITN 1; BRWS 2; CA 17-18; 41-
    44R; CANR 35, 132; CAP 2; CDBLB
    1914-1945; DA3; DAM DRAM; DFS 3,
    6; DLB 10, 245; EWL 3; IDFW 3, 4;
    MTCW 1, 2; RGEL 2; TEA
Cowley, Abraham 1618-1667 .... **LC 43**
    See also BRW 2; DLB 131, 151; PAB;
    RGEL 2
Cowley, Malcolm 1898-1989 .... **CLC 39**
    See also AMWS 2; CA 5-8R; 128; CANR
    3, 55; DLB 4, 48; DLBY 1981, 1989;
    EWL 3; MTCW 1, 2
Cowper, William 1731-1800 ..... **NCLC 8, 94;
    PC 40**
    See also BRW 3; DA3; DAM POET; DLB
    104, 109; RGEL 2
Cox, William Trevor 1928-
    See Trevor, William
    See also CA 9-12R; CANR 4, 37, 55, 76,
    102; DAM NOV; INT CANR-37; MTCW
    1, 2; TEA
Coyne, P. J.
    See Masters, Hilary
Cozzens, James Gould 1903-1978 . **CLC 1, 4,
    11, 92**
    See also AMW; BPFB 1; CA 9-12R; 81-84;
    CANR 19; CDALB 1941-1968; DLB 9,
    294; DLBD 2; DLBY 1984, 1997; EWL
    3; MTCW 1, 2; RGAL 4
Crabbe, George 1754-1832 .... **NCLC 26, 121**
    See also BRW 3; DLB 93; RGEL 2
Crace, Jim 1946- .... **CLC 157; SSC 61**
    See also CA 128; 135; CANR 55, 70, 123;
    CN 7; DLB 231; INT CA-135
Craddock, Charles Egbert
    See Murfree, Mary Noailles
Craig, A. A.
    See Anderson, Poul (William)

Craik, Mrs.
    See Craik, Dinah Maria (Mulock)
    See also RGEL 2
Craik, Dinah Maria (Mulock)
    1826-1887 .... **NCLC 38**
    See Craik, Mrs.; Mulock, Dinah Maria
    See also DLB 35, 163; MAICYA 1, 2;
    SATA 34
Cram, Ralph Adams 1863-1942 ..... **TCLC 45**
    See also CA 160
Cranch, Christopher Pearse
    1813-1892 .... **NCLC 115**
    See also DLB 1, 42, 243
Crane, (Harold) Hart 1899-1932 .... **PC 3;
    TCLC 2, 5, 80; WLC**
    See also AMW; AMWR 2; CA 104; 127;
    CDALB 1917-1929; DA; DA3; DAB;
    DAC; DAM MST, POET; DLB 4, 48;
    EWL 3; MTCW 1, 2; RGAL 4; TUS
Crane, R(onald) S(almon)
    1886-1967 .... **CLC 27**
    See also CA 85-88; DLB 63
Crane, Stephen (Townley)
    1871-1900 ...... **SSC 7, 56, 70; TCLC 11,
    17, 32; WLC**
    See also AAYA 21; AMW; AMWC 1; BPFB
    1; BYA 3; CA 109; 140; CANR 84;
    CDALB 1865-1917; DA; DA3; DAB;
    DAC; DAM MST, NOV, POET; DLB 12,
    54, 78; EXPN; EXPS; LAIT 2; LMFS 2;
    NFS 4, 20; PFS 9; RGAL 4; RGSF 2;
    SSFS 4; TUS; WYA; YABC 2
Cranmer, Thomas 1489-1556 .... **LC 95**
    See also DLB 132, 213
Cranshaw, Stanley
    See Fisher, Dorothy (Frances) Canfield
Crase, Douglas 1944- .... **CLC 58**
    See also CA 106
Crashaw, Richard 1612(?)-1649 .... **LC 24**
    See also BRW 2; DLB 126; PAB; RGEL 2
Cratinus c. 519B.C.-c. 422B.C. ..... **CMLC 54**
    See also LMFS 1
Craven, Margaret 1901-1980 .... **CLC 17**
    See also BYA 2; CA 103; CCA 1; DAC;
    LAIT 5
Crawford, F(rancis) Marion
    1854-1909 .... **TCLC 10**
    See also CA 107; 168; DLB 71; HGG;
    RGAL 4; SUFW 1
Crawford, Isabella Valancy
    1850-1887 .... **NCLC 12, 127**
    See also DLB 92; RGEL 2
Crayon, Geoffrey
    See Irving, Washington
Creasey, John 1908-1973 .... **CLC 11**
    See Marric, J. J.
    See also CA 5-8R; 41-44R; CANR 8, 59;
    CMW 4; DLB 77; MTCW 1
Crebillon, Claude Prosper Jolyot de (fils)
    1707-1777 .... **LC 1, 28**
    See also GFL Beginnings to 1789
Credo
    See Creasey, John
Credo, Alvaro J. de
    See Prado (Calvo), Pedro
Creeley, Robert (White) 1926- .. **CLC 1, 2, 4,
    8, 11, 15, 36, 78**
    See also AMWS 4; CA 1-4R; CAAS 10;
    CANR 23, 43, 89; CP 7; DA3; DAM
    POET; DLB 5, 16, 169; DLBD 17; EWL
    3; MTCW 1, 2; PFS 21; RGAL 4; WP
Crevecoeur, Hector St. John de
    See Crevecoeur, Michel Guillaume Jean de
    See also ANW
Crevecoeur, Michel Guillaume Jean de
    1735-1813 .... **NCLC 105**
    See Crevecoeur, Hector St. John de
    See also AMWS 1; DLB 37

Doolittle, Hilda 1886-1961 . **CLC 3, 8, 14, 31, 34, 73; PC 5; WLC**
See H. D.
See also AMWS 1; CA 97-100; CANR 35, 131; DA; DAC; DAM MST, POET; DLB 4, 45; EWL 3; FW; GLL 1; LMFS 2; MAWW; MTCW 1, 2; PFS 6; RGAL 4

Doppo, Kunikida .... **TCLC 99**
See Kunikida Doppo

Dorfman, Ariel 1942- .... **CLC 48, 77, 189; HLC 1**
See also CA 124; 130; CANR 67, 70; CWW 2; DAM MULT; DFS 4; EWL 3; HW 1, 2; INT CA-130; WLIT 1

Dorn, Edward (Merton)
1929-1999 .... **CLC 10, 18**
See also CA 93-96; 187; CANR 42, 79; CP 7; DLB 5; INT CA-93-96; WP

Dor-Ner, Zvi .... **CLC 70**

Dorris, Michael (Anthony)
1945-1997 .... **CLC 109; NNAL**
See also AAYA 20; BEST 90:1; BYA 12; CA 102; 157; CANR 19, 46, 75; CLR 58; DA3; DAM MULT, NOV; DLB 175; LAIT 5; MTCW 2; NFS 3; RGAL 4; SATA 75; SATA-Obit 94; TCWW 2; YAW

Dorris, Michael A.
See Dorris, Michael (Anthony)

Dorsan, Luc
See Simenon, Georges (Jacques Christian)

Dorsange, Jean
See Simenon, Georges (Jacques Christian)

Dorset
See Sackville, Thomas

Dos Passos, John (Roderigo)
1896-1970 ... **CLC 1, 4, 8, 11, 15, 25, 34, 82; WLC**
See also AMW; BPFB 1; CA 1-4R; 29-32R; CANR 3; CDALB 1929-1941; DA; DA3; DAB; DAC; DAM MST, NOV; DLB 4, 9, 274; DLBD 1, 15; DLBY 1996; EWL 3; MTCW 1, 2; NFS 14; RGAL 4; TUS

Dossage, Jean
See Simenon, Georges (Jacques Christian)

Dostoevsky, Fedor Mikhailovich
1821-1881 .. **NCLC 2, 7, 21, 33, 43, 119; SSC 2, 33, 44; WLC**
See Dostoevsky, Fyodor
See also AAYA 40; DA; DA3; DAB; DAC; DAM MST, NOV; EW 7; EXPN; NFS 3, 8; RGSF 2; RGWL 2, 3; SSFS 8; TWA

Dostoevsky, Fyodor
See Dostoevsky, Fedor Mikhailovich
See also DLB 238; LATS 1; LMFS 1, 2

Doty, M. R.
See Doty, Mark (Alan)

Doty, Mark
See Doty, Mark (Alan)

Doty, Mark (Alan) 1953(?)- .... **CLC 176; PC 53**
See also AMWS 11; CA 161, 183; CAAE 183; CANR 110

Doty, Mark A.
See Doty, Mark (Alan)

Doughty, Charles M(ontagu)
1843-1926 .... **TCLC 27**
See also CA 115; 178; DLB 19, 57, 174

Douglas, Ellen .... **CLC 73**
See Haxton, Josephine Ayres; Williamson, Ellen Douglas
See also CN 7; CSW; DLB 292

Douglas, Gavin 1475(?)-1522 .... **LC 20**
See also DLB 132; RGEL 2

Douglas, George
See Brown, George Douglas
See also RGEL 2

Douglas, Keith (Castellain)
1920-1944 .... **TCLC 40**
See also BRW 7; CA 160; DLB 27; EWL 3; PAB; RGEL 2

Douglas, Leonard
See Bradbury, Ray (Douglas)

Douglas, Michael
See Crichton, (John) Michael

Douglas, (George) Norman
1868-1952 .... **TCLC 68**
See also BRW 6; CA 119; 157; DLB 34, 195; RGEL 2

Douglas, William
See Brown, George Douglas

Douglass, Frederick 1817(?)-1895 ..... **BLC 1; NCLC 7, 55, 141; WLC**
See also AAYA 48; AFAW 1, 2; AMWC 1; AMWS 3; CDALB 1640-1865; DA; DA3; DAC; DAM MST, MULT; DLB 1, 43, 50, 79, 243; FW; LAIT 2; NCFS 2; RGAL 4; SATA 29

Dourado, (Waldomiro Freitas) Autran
1926- .... **CLC 23, 60**
See also CA 25-28R; 179; CANR 34, 81; DLB 145; HW 2

Dourado, Waldomiro Autran
See Dourado, (Waldomiro Freitas) Autran
See also CA 179

Dove, Rita (Frances) 1952- . **BLCS; CLC 50, 81; PC 6**
See also AAYA 46; AMWS 4; BW 2; CA 109; CAAS 19; CANR 27, 42, 68, 76, 97, 132; CDALBS; CP 7; CSW; CWP; DA3; DAM MULT, POET; DLB 120; EWL 3; EXPP; MTCW 1; PFS 1, 15; RGAL 4

Doveglion
See Villa, Jose Garcia

Dowell, Coleman 1925-1985 .... **CLC 60**
See also CA 25-28R; 117; CANR 10; DLB 130; GLL 2

Dowson, Ernest (Christopher)
1867-1900 .... **TCLC 4**
See also CA 105; 150; DLB 19, 135; RGEL 2

Doyle, A. Conan
See Doyle, Sir Arthur Conan

Doyle, Sir Arthur Conan
1859-1930 .... **SSC 12; TCLC 7; WLC**
See Conan Doyle, Arthur
See also AAYA 14; BRWS 2; CA 104; 122; CANR 131; CDBLB 1890-1914; CMW 4; DA; DA3; DAB; DAC; DAM MST, NOV; DLB 18, 70, 156, 178; EXPS; HGG; LAIT 2; MSW; MTCW 1, 2; RGEL 2; RGSF 2; RHW; SATA 24; SCFW 2; SFW 4; SSFS 2; TEA; WCH; WLIT 4; WYA; YAW

Doyle, Conan
See Doyle, Sir Arthur Conan

Doyle, John
See Graves, Robert (von Ranke)

Doyle, Roddy 1958(?)- .... **CLC 81, 178**
See also AAYA 14; BRWS 5; CA 143; CANR 73, 128; CN 7; DA3; DLB 194

Doyle, Sir A. Conan
See Doyle, Sir Arthur Conan

Dr. A
See Asimov, Isaac; Silverstein, Alvin; Silverstein, Virginia B(arbara Opshelor)

Drabble, Margaret 1939- ...... **CLC 2, 3, 5, 8, 10, 22, 53, 129**
See also BRWS 4; CA 13-16R; CANR 18, 35, 63, 112, 131; CDBLB 1960 to Present; CN 7; CPW; DA3; DAB; DAC; DAM MST, NOV, POP; DLB 14, 155, 231; EWL 3; FW; MTCW 1, 2; RGEL 2; SATA 48; TEA

Drakulic, Slavenka 1949- .... **CLC 173**
See also CA 144; CANR 92

Drakulic-Ilic, Slavenka
See Drakulic, Slavenka

Drapier, M. B.
See Swift, Jonathan

Drayham, James
See Mencken, H(enry) L(ouis)

Drayton, Michael 1563-1631 .... **LC 8**
See also DAM POET; DLB 121; RGEL 2

Dreadstone, Carl
See Campbell, (John) Ramsey

Dreiser, Theodore (Herman Albert)
1871-1945 .... **SSC 30; TCLC 10, 18, 35, 83; WLC**
See also AMW; AMWC 2; AMWR 2; BYA 15, 16; CA 106; 132; CDALB 1865-1917; DA; DA3; DAC; DAM MST, NOV; DLB 9, 12, 102, 137; DLBD 1; EWL 3; LAIT 2; LMFS 2; MTCW 1, 2; NFS 8, 17; RGAL 4; TUS

Drexler, Rosalyn 1926- .... **CLC 2, 6**
See also CA 81-84; CAD; CANR 68, 124; CD 5; CWD

Dreyer, Carl Theodor 1889-1968 ...... **CLC 16**
See also CA 116

Drieu la Rochelle, Pierre(-Eugene)
1893-1945 .... **TCLC 21**
See also CA 117; DLB 72; EWL 3; GFL 1789 to the Present

Drinkwater, John 1882-1937 .... **TCLC 57**
See also CA 109; 149; DLB 10, 19, 149; RGEL 2

Drop Shot
See Cable, George Washington

Droste-Hulshoff, Annette Freiin von
1797-1848 .... **NCLC 3, 133**
See also CDWLB 2; DLB 133; RGSF 2; RGWL 2, 3

Drummond, Walter
See Silverberg, Robert

Drummond, William Henry
1854-1907 .... **TCLC 25**
See also CA 160; DLB 92

Drummond de Andrade, Carlos
1902-1987 .... **CLC 18; TCLC 139**
See Andrade, Carlos Drummond de
See also CA 132; 123; LAW

Drummond of Hawthornden, William
1585-1649 .... **LC 83**
See also DLB 121, 213; RGEL 2

Drury, Allen (Stuart) 1918-1998 .... **CLC 37**
See also CA 57-60; 170; CANR 18, 52; CN 7; INT CANR-18

Dryden, John 1631-1700 ..... **DC 3; LC 3, 21; PC 25; WLC**
See also BRW 2; CDBLB 1660-1789; DA; DAB; DAC; DAM DRAM, MST, POET; DLB 80, 101, 131; EXPP; IDTP; LMFS 1; RGEL 2; TEA; WLIT 3

du Bellay, Joachim 1524-1560 .... **LC 92**
See also GFL Beginnings to 1789; RGWL 2, 3

Duberman, Martin (Bauml) 1930- ..... **CLC 8**
See also CA 1-4R; CAD; CANR 2, 63; CD 5

Dubie, Norman (Evans) 1945- .... **CLC 36**
See also CA 69-72; CANR 12, 115; CP 7; DLB 120; PFS 12

Du Bois, W(illiam) E(dward) B(urghardt)
1868-1963 ..... **BLC 1; CLC 1, 2, 13, 64, 96; HR 2; WLC**
See also AAYA 40; AFAW 1, 2; AMWC 1; AMWS 2; BW 1, 3; CA 85-88; CANR 34, 82, 132; CDALB 1865-1917; DA; DA3; DAC; DAM MST, MULT, NOV; DLB 47, 50, 91, 246, 284; EWL 3; EXPP; LAIT 2; LMFS 2; MTCW 1, 2; NCFS 1; PFS 13; RGAL 4; SATA 42

Dubus, Andre 1936-1999 ..... **CLC 13, 36, 97; SSC 15**
See also AMWS 7; CA 21-24R; 177; CANR 17; CN 7; CSW; DLB 130; INT CANR-17; RGAL 4; SSFS 10

Duca Minimo
See D'Annunzio, Gabriele

Ducharme, Rejean 1941- .... **CLC 74**
See also CA 165; DLB 60

du Chatelet, Emilie 1706-1749 .... **LC 96**

Duchen, Claire .... **CLC 65**

Duclos, Charles Pinot- 1704-1772 .... **LC 1**
See also GFL Beginnings to 1789

Dudek, Louis 1918-2001 .... **CLC 11, 19**
See also CA 45-48; 215; CAAS 14; CANR 1; CP 7; DLB 88

Duerrenmatt, Friedrich 1921-1990 ... **CLC 1, 4, 8, 11, 15, 43, 102**
See Durrenmatt, Friedrich
See also CA 17-20R; CANR 33; CMW 4; DAM DRAM; DLB 69, 124; MTCW 1, 2

Duffy, Bruce 1953(?)- .... **CLC 50**
See also CA 172

Duffy, Maureen 1933- .... **CLC 37**
See also CA 25-28R; CANR 33, 68; CBD; CN 7; CP 7; CWD; CWP; DFS 15; DLB 14; FW; MTCW 1

Du Fu
See Tu Fu
See also RGWL 2, 3

Dugan, Alan 1923-2003 .... **CLC 2, 6**
See also CA 81-84; 220; CANR 119; CP 7; DLB 5; PFS 10

du Gard, Roger Martin
See Martin du Gard, Roger

Duhamel, Georges 1884-1966 .... **CLC 8**
See also CA 81-84; 25-28R; CANR 35; DLB 65; EWL 3; GFL 1789 to the Present; MTCW 1

Dujardin, Edouard (Emile Louis) 1861-1949 .... **TCLC 13**
See also CA 109; DLB 123

Duke, Raoul
See Thompson, Hunter S(tockton)

Dulles, John Foster 1888-1959 .... **TCLC 72**
See also CA 115; 149

Dumas, Alexandre (pere) 1802-1870 .... **NCLC 11, 71; WLC**
See also AAYA 22; BYA 3; DA; DA3; DAB; DAC; DAM MST, NOV; DLB 119, 192; EW 6; GFL 1789 to the Present; LAIT 1, 2; NFS 14, 19; RGWL 2, 3; SATA 18; TWA; WCH

Dumas, Alexandre (fils) 1824-1895 ...... **DC 1; NCLC 9**
See also DLB 192; GFL 1789 to the Present; RGWL 2, 3

Dumas, Claudine
See Malzberg, Barry N(athaniel)

Dumas, Henry L. 1934-1968 .... **CLC 6, 62**
See also BW 1; CA 85-88; DLB 41; RGAL 4

du Maurier, Daphne 1907-1989 .. **CLC 6, 11, 59; SSC 18**
See also AAYA 37; BPFB 1; BRWS 3; CA 5-8R; 128; CANR 6, 55; CMW 4; CPW; DA3; DAB; DAC; DAM MST, POP; DLB 191; HGG; LAIT 3; MSW; MTCW 1, 2; NFS 12; RGEL 2; RGSF 2; RHW; SATA 27; SATA-Obit 60; SSFS 14, 16; TEA

Du Maurier, George 1834-1896 ..... **NCLC 86**
See also DLB 153, 178; RGEL 2

Dunbar, Paul Laurence 1872-1906 ... **BLC 1; PC 5; SSC 8; TCLC 2, 12; WLC**
See also AFAW 1, 2; AMWS 2; BW 1, 3; CA 104; 124; CANR 79; CDALB 1865-1917; DA; DA3; DAC; DAM MST, MULT, POET; DLB 50, 54, 78; EXPP; RGAL 4; SATA 34

Dunbar, William 1460(?)-1520(?) .... **LC 20**
See also BRWS 8; DLB 132, 146; RGEL 2

Dunbar-Nelson, Alice .... **HR 2**
See Nelson, Alice Ruth Moore Dunbar

Duncan, Dora Angela
See Duncan, Isadora

Duncan, Isadora 1877(?)-1927 .... **TCLC 68**
See also CA 118; 149

Duncan, Lois 1934- .... **CLC 26**
See also AAYA 4, 34; BYA 6, 8; CA 1-4R; CANR 2, 23, 36, 111; CLR 29; JRDA; MAICYA 1, 2; MAICYAS 1; SAAS 2; SATA 1, 36, 75, 133, 141; SATA-Essay 141; WYA; YAW

Duncan, Robert (Edward) 1919-1988 .... **CLC 1, 2, 4, 7, 15, 41, 55; PC 2**
See also BG 2; CA 9-12R; 124; CANR 28, 62; DAM POET; DLB 5, 16, 193; EWL 3; MTCW 1, 2; PFS 13; RGAL 4; WP

Duncan, Sara Jeannette 1861-1922 .... **TCLC 60**
See also CA 157; DLB 92

Dunlap, William 1766-1839 .... **NCLC 2**
See also DLB 30, 37, 59; RGAL 4

Dunn, Douglas (Eaglesham) 1942- .... **CLC 6, 40**
See also CA 45-48; CANR 2, 33, 126; CP 7; DLB 40; MTCW 1

Dunn, Katherine (Karen) 1945- .... **CLC 71**
See also CA 33-36R; CANR 72; HGG; MTCW 1

Dunn, Stephen (Elliott) 1939- .... **CLC 36**
See also AMWS 11; CA 33-36R; CANR 12, 48, 53, 105; CP 7; DLB 105; PFS 21

Dunne, Finley Peter 1867-1936 ...... **TCLC 28**
See also CA 108; 178; DLB 11, 23; RGAL 4

Dunne, John Gregory 1932-2003 ..... **CLC 28**
See also CA 25-28R; 222; CANR 14, 50; CN 7; DLBY 1980

Dunsany, Lord .... **TCLC 2, 59**
See Dunsany, Edward John Moreton Drax Plunkett
See also DLB 77, 153, 156, 255; FANT; IDTP; RGEL 2; SFW 4; SUFW 1

Dunsany, Edward John Moreton Drax Plunkett 1878-1957
See Dunsany, Lord
See also CA 104; 148; DLB 10; MTCW 1

Duns Scotus, John 1266(?)-1308 ... **CMLC 59**
See also DLB 115

du Perry, Jean
See Simenon, Georges (Jacques Christian)

Durang, Christopher (Ferdinand) 1949- .... **CLC 27, 38**
See also CA 105; CAD; CANR 50, 76, 130; CD 5; MTCW 1

Duras, Marguerite 1914-1996 . **CLC 3, 6, 11, 20, 34, 40, 68, 100; SSC 40**
See Donnadieu, Marguerite
See also BPFB 1; CA 25-28R; 151; CANR 50; CWW 2; DLB 83; EWL 3; GFL 1789 to the Present; IDFW 4; MTCW 1, 2; RGWL 2, 3; TWA

Durban, (Rosa) Pam 1947- .... **CLC 39**
See also CA 123; CANR 98; CSW

Durcan, Paul 1944- .... **CLC 43, 70**
See also CA 134; CANR 123; CP 7; DAM POET; EWL 3

Durfey, Thomas 1653-1723 .... **LC 94**
See also DLB 80; RGEL 2

Durkheim, Emile 1858-1917 .... **TCLC 55**

Durrell, Lawrence (George) 1912-1990 ..... **CLC 1, 4, 6, 8, 13, 27, 41**
See also BPFB 1; BRWS 1; CA 9-12R; 132; CANR 40, 77; CDBLB 1945-1960; DAM NOV; DLB 15, 27, 204; DLBY 1990; EWL 3; MTCW 1, 2; RGEL 2; SFW 4; TEA

Durrenmatt, Friedrich
See Duerrenmatt, Friedrich
See also CDWLB 2; EW 13; EWL 3; RGWL 2, 3

Dutt, Michael Madhusudan 1824-1873 .... **NCLC 118**

Dutt, Toru 1856-1877 .... **NCLC 29**
See also DLB 240

Dwight, Timothy 1752-1817 .... **NCLC 13**
See also DLB 37; RGAL 4

Dworkin, Andrea 1946- .... **CLC 43, 123**
See also CA 77-80; CAAS 21; CANR 16, 39, 76, 96; FW; GLL 1; INT CANR-16; MTCW 1, 2

Dwyer, Deanna
See Koontz, Dean R(ay)

Dwyer, K. R.
See Koontz, Dean R(ay)

Dybek, Stuart 1942- .... **CLC 114; SSC 55**
See also CA 97-100; CANR 39; DLB 130

Dye, Richard
See De Voto, Bernard (Augustine)

Dyer, Geoff 1958- .... **CLC 149**
See also CA 125; CANR 88

Dyer, George 1755-1841 .... **NCLC 129**
See also DLB 93

Dylan, Bob 1941- .... **CLC 3, 4, 6, 12, 77; PC 37**
See also CA 41-44R; CANR 108; CP 7; DLB 16

Dyson, John 1943- .... **CLC 70**
See also CA 144

Dzyubin, Eduard Georgievich 1895-1934
See Bagritsky, Eduard
See also CA 170

E. V. L.
See Lucas, E(dward) V(errall)

Eagleton, Terence (Francis) 1943- .. **CLC 63, 132**
See also CA 57-60; CANR 7, 23, 68, 115; DLB 242; LMFS 2; MTCW 1, 2

Eagleton, Terry
See Eagleton, Terence (Francis)

Early, Jack
See Scoppettone, Sandra
See also GLL 1

East, Michael
See West, Morris L(anglo)

Eastaway, Edward
See Thomas, (Philip) Edward

Eastlake, William (Derry) 1917-1997 .... **CLC 8**
See also CA 5-8R; 158; CAAS 1; CANR 5, 63; CN 7; DLB 6, 206; INT CANR-5; TCWW 2

Eastman, Charles A(lexander) 1858-1939 .... **NNAL; TCLC 55**
See also CA 179; CANR 91; DAM MULT; DLB 175; YABC 1

Eaton, Edith Maude 1865-1914 .... **AAL**
See Far, Sui Sin
See also CA 154; DLB 221; FW

Eaton, (Lillie) Winnifred 1875-1954 .... **AAL**
See also CA 217; DLB 221; RGAL 4

Eberhart, Richard (Ghormley) 1904- .... **CLC 3, 11, 19, 56**
See also AMW; CA 1-4R; CANR 2, 125; CDALB 1941-1968; CP 7; DAM POET; DLB 48; MTCW 1; RGAL 4

Eberstadt, Fernanda 1960- .... **CLC 39**
See also CA 136; CANR 69, 128

Echegaray (y Eizaguirre), Jose (Maria Waldo) 1832-1916 .... **HLCS 1; TCLC 4**
See also CA 104; CANR 32; EWL 3; HW 1; MTCW 1

Echeverria, (Jose) Esteban (Antonino) 1805-1851 .... **NCLC 18**
See also LAW

Echo
See Proust, (Valentin-Louis-George-Eugene) Marcel

Eckert, Allan W. 1931- .... **CLC 17**
See also AAYA 18; BYA 2; CA 13-16R; CANR 14, 45; INT CANR-14; MAICYA 2; MAICYAS 1; SAAS 21; SATA 29, 91; SATA-Brief 27

Eckhart, Meister 1260(?)-1327(?) ... **CMLC 9**
See also DLB 115; LMFS 1

Eckmar, F. R.
See de Hartog, Jan

Eco, Umberto 1932- .... **CLC 28, 60, 142**
See also BEST 90:1; BPFB 1; CA 77-80; CANR 12, 33, 55, 110, 131; CPW; CWW 2; DA3; DAM NOV, POP; DLB 196, 242; EWL 3; MSW; MTCW 1, 2; RGWL 3

Eddison, E(ric) R(ucker)
1882-1945 .... **TCLC 15**
See also CA 109; 156; DLB 255; FANT; SFW 4; SUFW 1

Eddy, Mary (Ann Morse) Baker
1821-1910 .... **TCLC 71**
See also CA 113; 174

Edel, (Joseph) Leon 1907-1997 .. **CLC 29, 34**
See also CA 1-4R; 161; CANR 1, 22, 112; DLB 103; INT CANR-22

Eden, Emily 1797-1869 .... **NCLC 10**

Edgar, David 1948- .... **CLC 42**
See also CA 57-60; CANR 12, 61, 112; CBD; CD 5; DAM DRAM; DFS 15; DLB 13, 233; MTCW 1

Edgerton, Clyde (Carlyle) 1944- ...... **CLC 39**
See also AAYA 17; CA 118; 134; CANR 64, 125; CSW; DLB 278; INT CA-134; YAW

Edgeworth, Maria 1768-1849 .... **NCLC 1, 51**
See also BRWS 3; DLB 116, 159, 163; FW; RGEL 2; SATA 21; TEA; WLIT 3

Edmonds, Paul
See Kuttner, Henry

Edmonds, Walter D(umaux)
1903-1998 .... **CLC 35**
See also BYA 2; CA 5-8R; CANR 2; CWRI 5; DLB 9; LAIT 1; MAICYA 1, 2; RHW; SAAS 4; SATA 1, 27; SATA-Obit 99

Edmondson, Wallace
See Ellison, Harlan (Jay)

Edson, Margaret 1961- .... **DC 24**
See also CA 190; DFS 13; DLB 266

Edson, Russell 1935- .... **CLC 13**
See also CA 33-36R; CANR 115; DLB 244; WP

Edwards, Bronwen Elizabeth
See Rose, Wendy

Edwards, G(erald) B(asil)
1899-1976 .... **CLC 25**
See also CA 201; 110

Edwards, Gus 1939- .... **CLC 43**
See also CA 108; INT CA-108

Edwards, Jonathan 1703-1758 .... **LC 7, 54**
See also AMW; DA; DAC; DAM MST; DLB 24, 270; RGAL 4; TUS

Edwards, Sarah Pierpont 1710-1758 .. **LC 87**
See also DLB 200

Efron, Marina Ivanovna Tsvetaeva
See Tsvetaeva (Efron), Marina (Ivanovna)

Egeria fl. 4th cent. - .... **CMLC 70**

Egoyan, Atom 1960- .... **CLC 151**
See also CA 157

Ehle, John (Marsden, Jr.) 1925- ...... **CLC 27**
See also CA 9-12R; CSW

Ehrenbourg, Ilya (Grigoryevich)
See Ehrenburg, Ilya (Grigoryevich)

Ehrenburg, Ilya (Grigoryevich)
1891-1967 .... **CLC 18, 34, 62**
See Erenburg, Il'ia Grigor'evich
See also CA 102; 25-28R; EWL 3

Ehrenburg, Ilyo (Grigoryevich)
See Ehrenburg, Ilya (Grigoryevich)

Ehrenreich, Barbara 1941- .... **CLC 110**
See also BEST 90:4; CA 73-76; CANR 16, 37, 62, 117; DLB 246; FW; MTCW 1, 2

Eich, Gunter
See Eich, Gunter
See also RGWL 2, 3

Eich, Gunter 1907-1972 .... **CLC 15**
See Eich, Gunter
See also CA 111; 93-96; DLB 69, 124; EWL 3

Eichendorff, Joseph 1788-1857 .... **NCLC 8**
See also DLB 90; RGWL 2, 3

Eigner, Larry .... **CLC 9**
See Eigner, Laurence (Joel)
See also CAAS 23; DLB 5; WP

Eigner, Laurence (Joel) 1927-1996
See Eigner, Larry
See also CA 9-12R; 151; CANR 6, 84; CP 7; DLB 193

Eilhart von Oberge c. 1140-c.
1195 .... **CMLC 67**
See also DLB 148

Einhard c. 770-840 .... **CMLC 50**
See also DLB 148

Einstein, Albert 1879-1955 .... **TCLC 65**
See also CA 121; 133; MTCW 1, 2

Eiseley, Loren
See Eiseley, Loren Corey
See also DLB 275

Eiseley, Loren Corey 1907-1977 .... **CLC 7**
See Eiseley, Loren
See also AAYA 5; ANW; CA 1-4R; 73-76; CANR 6; DLBD 17

Eisenstadt, Jill 1963- .... **CLC 50**
See also CA 140

Eisenstein, Sergei (Mikhailovich)
1898-1948 .... **TCLC 57**
See also CA 114; 149

Eisner, Simon
See Kornbluth, C(yril) M.

Ekeloef, (Bengt) Gunnar
1907-1968 .... **CLC 27; PC 23**
See Ekelof, (Bengt) Gunnar
See also CA 123; 25-28R; DAM POET

Ekelof, (Bengt) Gunnar 1907-1968
See Ekeloef, (Bengt) Gunnar
See also DLB 259; EW 12; EWL 3

Ekelund, Vilhelm 1880-1949 .... **TCLC 75**
See also CA 189; EWL 3

Ekwensi, C. O. D.
See Ekwensi, Cyprian (Odiatu Duaka)

Ekwensi, Cyprian (Odiatu Duaka)
1921- .... **BLC 1; CLC 4**
See also AFW; BW 2, 3; CA 29-32R; CANR 18, 42, 74, 125; CDWLB 3; CN 7; CWRI 5; DAM MULT; DLB 117; EWL 3; MTCW 1, 2; RGEL 2; SATA 66; WLIT 2

Elaine .... **TCLC 18**
See Leverson, Ada Esther

El Crummo
See Crumb, R(obert)

Elder, Lonne III 1931-1996 ..... **BLC 1; DC 8**
See also BW 1, 3; CA 81-84; 152; CAD; CANR 25; DAM MULT; DLB 7, 38, 44

Eleanor of Aquitaine 1122-1204 ... **CMLC 39**

Elia
See Lamb, Charles

Eliade, Mircea 1907-1986 .... **CLC 19**
See also CA 65-68; 119; CANR 30, 62; CD-WLB 4; DLB 220; EWL 3; MTCW 1; RGWL 3; SFW 4

Eliot, A. D.
See Jewett, (Theodora) Sarah Orne

Eliot, Alice
See Jewett, (Theodora) Sarah Orne

Eliot, Dan
See Silverberg, Robert

Eliot, George 1819-1880 ...... **NCLC 4, 13, 23, 41, 49, 89, 118; PC 20; SSC 72; WLC**
See Evans, Mary Ann
See also BRW 5; BRWC 1, 2; BRWR 2; CDBLB 1832-1890; CN 7; CPW; DA; DA3; DAB; DAC; DAM MST, NOV; DLB 21, 35, 55; LATS 1; LMFS 1; NFS 17; RGEL 2; RGSF 2; SSFS 8; TEA; WLIT 3

Eliot, John 1604-1690 .... **LC 5**
See also DLB 24

Eliot, T(homas) S(tearns)
1888-1965 ...... **CLC 1, 2, 3, 6, 9, 10, 13, 15, 24, 34, 41, 55, 57, 113; PC 5, 31; WLC**
See also AAYA 28; AMW; AMWC 1; AMWR 1; BRW 7; BRWR 2; CA 5-8R; 25-28R; CANR 41; CDALB 1929-1941; DA; DA3; DAB; DAC; DAM DRAM, MST, POET; DFS 4, 13; DLB 7, 10, 45, 63, 245; DLBY 1988; EWL 3; EXPP; LAIT 3; LATS 1; LMFS 2; MTCW 1, 2; NCFS 5; PAB; PFS 1, 7, 20; RGAL 4; RGEL 2; TUS; WLIT 4; WP

Elizabeth 1866-1941 .... **TCLC 41**

Elkin, Stanley L(awrence)
1930-1995 .. **CLC 4, 6, 9, 14, 27, 51, 91; SSC 12**
See also AMWS 6; BPFB 1; CA 9-12R; 148; CANR 8, 46; CN 7; CPW; DAM NOV, POP; DLB 2, 28, 218, 278; DLBY 1980; EWL 3; INT CANR-8; MTCW 1, 2; RGAL 4

Elledge, Scott .... **CLC 34**

Elliott, Don
See Silverberg, Robert

Elliott, George P(aul) 1918-1980 .... **CLC 2**
See also CA 1-4R; 97-100; CANR 2; DLB 244

Elliott, Janice 1931-1995 .... **CLC 47**
See also CA 13-16R; CANR 8, 29, 84; CN 7; DLB 14; SATA 119

Elliott, Sumner Locke 1917-1991 ..... **CLC 38**
See also CA 5-8R; 134; CANR 2, 21; DLB 289

Elliott, William
See Bradbury, Ray (Douglas)

Ellis, A. E. .... **CLC 7**

Ellis, Alice Thomas .... **CLC 40**
See Haycraft, Anna (Margaret)
See also DLB 194; MTCW 1

Ellis, Bret Easton 1964- ...... **CLC 39, 71, 117**
See also AAYA 2, 43; CA 118; 123; CANR 51, 74, 126; CN 7; CPW; DA3; DAM POP; DLB 292; HGG; INT CA-123; MTCW 1; NFS 11

Ellis, (Henry) Havelock
1859-1939 .... **TCLC 14**
See also CA 109; 169; DLB 190

Ellis, Landon
See Ellison, Harlan (Jay)

Ellis, Trey 1962- .... **CLC 55**
See also CA 146; CANR 92

Ellison, Harlan (Jay) 1934- ... **CLC 1, 13, 42, 139; SSC 14**
See also AAYA 29; BPFB 1; BYA 14; CA 5-8R; CANR 5, 46, 115; CPW; DAM POP; DLB 8; HGG; INT CANR-5; MTCW 1, 2; SCFW 2; SFW 4; SSFS 13, 14, 15; SUFW 1, 2

Ellison, Ralph (Waldo) 1914-1994 .... **BLC 1; CLC 1, 3, 11, 54, 86, 114; SSC 26; WLC**
See also AAYA 19; AFAW 1, 2; AMWC 2; AMWR 2; AMWS 2; BPFB 1; BW 1, 3; BYA 2; CA 9-12R; 145; CANR 24, 53; CDALB 1941-1968; CSW; DA; DA3; DAB; DAC; DAM MST, MULT, NOV;

DLB 2, 76, 227; DLBY 1994; EWL 3;
EXPN; EXPS; LAIT 4; MTCW 1, 2;
NCFS 3; NFS 2; RGAL 4; RGSF 2; SSFS
1, 11; YAW

Ellmann, Lucy (Elizabeth) 1956- ..... **CLC 61**
See also CA 128

Ellmann, Richard (David)
1918-1987 .... **CLC 50**
See also BEST 89:2; CA 1-4R; 122; CANR
2, 28, 61; DLB 103; DLBY 1987; MTCW
1, 2

Elman, Richard (Martin)
1934-1997 .... **CLC 19**
See also CA 17-20R; 163; CAAS 3; CANR
47

Elron
See Hubbard, L(afayette) Ron(ald)

Eluard, Paul .... **PC 38; TCLC 7, 41**
See Grindel, Eugene
See also EWL 3; GFL 1789 to the Present;
RGWL 2, 3

Elyot, Thomas 1490(?)-1546 .... **LC 11**
See also DLB 136; RGEL 2

Elytis, Odysseus 1911-1996 .... **CLC 15, 49,
100; PC 21**
See Alepoudelis, Odysseus
See also CA 102; 151; CANR 94; CWW 2;
DAM POET; EW 13; EWL 3; MTCW 1,
2; RGWL 2, 3

Emecheta, (Florence Onye) Buchi
1944- .... **BLC 2; CLC 14, 48, 128**
See also AFW; BW 2, 3; CA 81-84; CANR
27, 81, 126; CDWLB 3; CN 7; CWRI 5;
DA3; DAM MULT; DLB 117; EWL 3;
FW; MTCW 1, 2; NFS 12, 14; SATA 66;
WLIT 2

Emerson, Mary Moody
1774-1863 .... **NCLC 66**

Emerson, Ralph Waldo 1803-1882 . **NCLC 1,
38, 98; PC 18; WLC**
See also AMW; ANW; CDALB 1640-1865;
DA; DA3; DAB; DAC; DAM MST,
POET; DLB 1, 59, 73, 183, 223, 270;
EXPP; LAIT 2; LMFS 1; NCFS 3; PFS 4,
17; RGAL 4; TUS; WP

Eminescu, Mihail 1850-1889 .. **NCLC 33, 131**

Empedocles 5th cent. B.C.- .... **CMLC 50**
See also DLB 176

Empson, William 1906-1984 ... **CLC 3, 8, 19,
33, 34**
See also BRWS 2; CA 17-20R; 112; CANR
31, 61; DLB 20; EWL 3; MTCW 1, 2;
RGEL 2

Enchi, Fumiko (Ueda) 1905-1986 ..... **CLC 31**
See Enchi Fumiko
See also CA 129; 121; FW; MJW

Enchi Fumiko
See Enchi, Fumiko (Ueda)
See also DLB 182; EWL 3

Ende, Michael (Andreas Helmuth)
1929-1995 .... **CLC 31**
See also BYA 5; CA 118; 124; 149; CANR
36, 110; CLR 14; DLB 75; MAICYA 1,
2; MAICYAS 1; SATA 61, 130; SATA-
Brief 42; SATA-Obit 86

Endo, Shusaku 1923-1996 ..... **CLC 7, 14, 19,
54, 99; SSC 48; TCLC 152**
See Endo Shusaku
See also CA 29-32R; 153; CANR 21, 54,
131; DA3; DAM NOV; MTCW 1, 2;
RGSF 2; RGWL 2, 3

Endo Shusaku
See Endo, Shusaku
See also DLB 182; EWL 3

Engel, Marian 1933-1985 .... **CLC 36; TCLC
137**
See also CA 25-28R; CANR 12; DLB 53;
FW; INT CANR-12

Engelhardt, Frederick
See Hubbard, L(afayette) Ron(ald)

Engels, Friedrich 1820-1895 .. **NCLC 85, 114**
See also DLB 129; LATS 1

Enright, D(ennis) J(oseph)
1920-2002 .... **CLC 4, 8, 31**
See also CA 1-4R; 211; CANR 1, 42, 83;
CP 7; DLB 27; EWL 3; SATA 25; SATA-
Obit 140

Enzensberger, Hans Magnus
1929- .... **CLC 43; PC 28**
See also CA 116; 119; CANR 103; EWL 3

Ephron, Nora 1941- .... **CLC 17, 31**
See also AAYA 35; AITN 2; CA 65-68;
CANR 12, 39, 83

Epicurus 341B.C.-270B.C. .... **CMLC 21**
See also DLB 176

Epsilon
See Betjeman, John

Epstein, Daniel Mark 1948- .... **CLC 7**
See also CA 49-52; CANR 2, 53, 90

Epstein, Jacob 1956- .... **CLC 19**
See also CA 114

Epstein, Jean 1897-1953 .... **TCLC 92**

Epstein, Joseph 1937- .... **CLC 39**
See also CA 112; 119; CANR 50, 65, 117

Epstein, Leslie 1938- .... **CLC 27**
See also AMWS 12; CA 73-76, 215; CAAE
215; CAAS 12; CANR 23, 69; DLB 299

Equiano, Olaudah 1745(?)-1797 . **BLC 2; LC
16**
See also AFAW 1, 2; CDWLB 3; DAM
MULT; DLB 37, 50; WLIT 2

Erasmus, Desiderius 1469(?)-1536 ..... **LC 16,
93**
See also DLB 136; EW 2; LMFS 1; RGWL
2, 3; TWA

Erdman, Paul E(mil) 1932- .... **CLC 25**
See also AITN 1; CA 61-64; CANR 13, 43,
84

Erdrich, Louise 1954- .... **CLC 39, 54, 120,
176; NNAL; PC 52**
See also AAYA 10, 47; AMWS 4; BEST
89:1; BPFB 1; CA 114; CANR 41, 62,
118; CDALBS; CN 7; CP 7; CPW; CWP;
DA3; DAM MULT, NOV, POP; DLB 152,
175, 206; EWL 3; EXPP; LAIT 5; LATS
1; MTCW 1; NFS 5; PFS 14; RGAL 4;
SATA 94, 141; SSFS 14; TCWW 2

Erenburg, Ilya (Grigoryevich)
See Ehrenburg, Ilya (Grigoryevich)

Erickson, Stephen Michael 1950-
See Erickson, Steve
See also CA 129; SFW 4

Erickson, Steve .... **CLC 64**
See Erickson, Stephen Michael
See also CANR 60, 68; SUFW 2

Erickson, Walter
See Fast, Howard (Melvin)

Ericson, Walter
See Fast, Howard (Melvin)

Eriksson, Buntel
See Bergman, (Ernst) Ingmar

Eriugena, John Scottus c.
810-877 .... **CMLC 65**
See also DLB 115

Ernaux, Annie 1940- .... **CLC 88, 184**
See also CA 147; CANR 93; NCFS 3, 5

Erskine, John 1879-1951 .... **TCLC 84**
See also CA 112; 159; DLB 9, 102; FANT

Eschenbach, Wolfram von
See Wolfram von Eschenbach
See also RGWL 3

Eseki, Bruno
See Mphahlele, Ezekiel

Esenin, Sergei (Alexandrovich)
1895-1925 .... **TCLC 4**
See Yesenin, Sergey
See also CA 104; RGWL 2, 3

Eshleman, Clayton 1935- .... **CLC 7**
See also CA 33-36R, 212; CAAE 212;
CAAS 6; CANR 93; CP 7; DLB 5

Espriella, Don Manuel Alvarez
See Southey, Robert

Espriu, Salvador 1913-1985 .... **CLC 9**
See also CA 154; 115; DLB 134; EWL 3

Espronceda, Jose de 1808-1842 ..... **NCLC 39**

Esquivel, Laura 1951(?)- ... **CLC 141; HLCS
1**
See also AAYA 29; CA 143; CANR 68, 113;
DA3; DNFS 2; LAIT 3; LMFS 2; MTCW
1; NFS 5; WLIT 1

Esse, James
See Stephens, James

Esterbrook, Tom
See Hubbard, L(afayette) Ron(ald)

Estleman, Loren D. 1952- .... **CLC 48**
See also AAYA 27; CA 85-88; CANR 27,
74; CMW 4; CPW; DA3; DAM NOV,
POP; DLB 226; INT CANR-27; MTCW
1, 2

Etherege, Sir George 1636-1692 . **DC 23; LC
78**
See also BRW 2; DAM DRAM; DLB 80;
PAB; RGEL 2

Euclid 306B.C.-283B.C. .... **CMLC 25**

Eugenides, Jeffrey 1960(?)- .... **CLC 81**
See also AAYA 51; CA 144; CANR 120

Euripides c. 484B.C.-406B.C. .... **CMLC 23,
51; DC 4; WLCS**
See also AW 1; CDWLB 1; DA; DA3;
DAB; DAC; DAM DRAM, MST; DFS 1,
4, 6; DLB 176; LAIT 1; LMFS 1; RGWL
2, 3

Evan, Evin
See Faust, Frederick (Schiller)

Evans, Caradoc 1878-1945 ... **SSC 43; TCLC
85**
See also DLB 162

Evans, Evan
See Faust, Frederick (Schiller)
See also TCWW 2

Evans, Marian
See Eliot, George

Evans, Mary Ann
See Eliot, George
See also NFS 20

Evarts, Esther
See Benson, Sally

Everett, Percival
See Everett, Percival L.
See also CSW

Everett, Percival L. 1956- .... **CLC 57**
See Everett, Percival
See also BW 2; CA 129; CANR 94

Everson, R(onald) G(ilmour)
1903-1992 .... **CLC 27**
See also CA 17-20R; DLB 88

Everson, William (Oliver)
1912-1994 .... **CLC 1, 5, 14**
See also BG 2; CA 9-12R; 145; CANR 20;
DLB 5, 16, 212; MTCW 1

Evtushenko, Evgenii Aleksandrovich
See Yevtushenko, Yevgeny (Alexandrovich)
See also RGWL 2, 3

Ewart, Gavin (Buchanan)
1916-1995 .... **CLC 13, 46**
See also BRWS 7; CA 89-92; 150; CANR
17, 46; CP 7; DLB 40; MTCW 1

Ewers, Hanns Heinz 1871-1943 ..... **TCLC 12**
See also CA 109; 149

Ewing, Frederick R.
See Sturgeon, Theodore (Hamilton)

Exley, Frederick (Earl) 1929-1992 .... **CLC 6,
11**
See also AITN 2; BPFB 1; CA 81-84; 138;
CANR 117; DLB 143; DLBY 1981

Ferron, Jacques 1921-1985 .... **CLC 94**
   See also CA 117; 129; CCA 1; DAC; DLB
   60; EWL 3

Feuchtwanger, Lion 1884-1958 .... **TCLC 3**
   See also CA 104; 187; DLB 66; EWL 3

Feuerbach, Ludwig 1804-1872 ..... **NCLC 139**
   See also DLB 133

Feuillet, Octave 1821-1890 .... **NCLC 45**
   See also DLB 192

Feydeau, Georges (Leon Jules Marie)
   1862-1921 .... **TCLC 22**
   See also CA 113; 152; CANR 84; DAM
   DRAM; DLB 192; EWL 3; GFL 1789 to
   the Present; RGWL 2, 3

Fichte, Johann Gottlieb
   1762-1814 .... **NCLC 62**
   See also DLB 90

Ficino, Marsilio 1433-1499 .... **LC 12**
   See also LMFS 1

Fledeler, Hans
   See Doeblin, Alfred

Fiedler, Leslie A(aron) 1917-2003 ..... **CLC 4,**
   13, 24
   See also AMWS 13; CA 9-12R; 212; CANR
   7, 63; CN 7; DLB 28, 67; EWL 3; MTCW
   1, 2; RGAL 4; TUS

Field, Andrew 1938- .... **CLC 44**
   See also CA 97-100; CANR 25

Field, Eugene 1850-1895 .... **NCLC 3**
   See also DLB 23, 42, 140; DLBD 13; MAI-
   CYA 1, 2; RGAL 4; SATA 16

Field, Gans T.
   See Wellman, Manly Wade

Field, Michael 1915-1971 .... **TCLC 43**
   See also CA 29-32R

Field, Peter
   See Hobson, Laura Z(ametkin)
   See also TCWW 2

Fielding, Helen 1958- .... **CLC 146**
   See also CA 172; CANR 127; DLB 231

Fielding, Henry 1707-1754 .... **LC 1, 46, 85;**
   WLC
   See also BRW 3; BRWR 1; CDBLB 1660-
   1789; DA; DA3; DAB; DAC; DAM
   DRAM, MST, NOV; DLB 39, 84, 101;
   NFS 18; RGEL 2; TEA; WLIT 3

Fielding, Sarah 1710-1768 .... **LC 1, 44**
   See also DLB 39; RGEL 2; TEA

Fields, W. C. 1880-1946 .... **TCLC 80**
   See also DLB 44

Fierstein, Harvey (Forbes) 1954- ..... **CLC 33**
   See also CA 123; 129; CAD; CD 5; CPW;
   DA3; DAM DRAM, POP; DFS 6; DLB
   266; GLL

Figes, Eva 1932- .... **CLC 31**
   See also CA 53-56; CANR 4, 44, 83; CN 7;
   DLB 14, 271; FW

Filippo, Eduardo de
   See de Filippo, Eduardo

Finch, Anne 1661-1720 .... **LC 3; PC 21**
   See also BRWS 9; DLB 95

Finch, Robert (Duer Claydon)
   1900-1995 .... **CLC 18**
   See also CA 57-60; CANR 9, 24, 49; CP 7;
   DLB 88

Findley, Timothy (Irving Frederick)
   1930-2002 .... **CLC 27, 102**
   See also CA 25-28R; 206; CANR 12, 42,
   69, 109; CCA 1; CN 7; DAC; DAM MST;
   DLB 53; FANT; RHW

Fink, William
   See Mencken, H(enry) L(ouis)

Firbank, Louis 1942-
   See Reed, Lou
   See also CA 117

Firbank, (Arthur Annesley) Ronald
   1886-1926 .... **TCLC 1**
   See also BRWS 2; CA 104; 177; DLB 36;
   EWL 3; RGEL 2

Fish, Stanley
   See Fish, Stanley Eugene

Fish, Stanley E.
   See Fish, Stanley Eugene

Fish, Stanley Eugene 1938- .... **CLC 142**
   See also CA 112; 132; CANR 90; DLB 67

Fisher, Dorothy (Frances) Canfield
   1879-1958 .... **TCLC 87**
   See also CA 114; 136; CANR 80; CLR 71,;
   CWRI 5; DLB 9, 102, 284; MAICYA 1,
   2; YABC 1

Fisher, M(ary) F(rances) K(ennedy)
   1908-1992 .... **CLC 76, 87**
   See also CA 77-80; 138; CANR 44; MTCW
   1

Fisher, Roy 1930- .... **CLC 25**
   See also CA 81-84; CAAS 10; CANR 16;
   CP 7; DLB 40

Fisher, Rudolph 1897-1934 .... **BLC 2; HR 2;**
   SSC 25; TCLC 11
   See also BW 1, 3; CA 107; 124; CANR 80;
   DAM MULT; DLB 51, 102

Fisher, Vardis (Alvero) 1895-1968 .... **CLC 7;**
   TCLC 140
   See also CA 5-8R; 25-28R; CANR 68; DLB
   9, 206; RGAL 4; TCWW 2

Fiske, Tarleton
   See Bloch, Robert (Albert)

Fitch, Clarke
   See Sinclair, Upton (Beall)

Fitch, John IV
   See Cormier, Robert (Edmund)

Fitzgerald, Captain Hugh
   See Baum, L(yman) Frank

FitzGerald, Edward 1809-1883 .... **NCLC 9**
   See also BRW 4; DLB 32; RGEL 2

Fitzgerald, F(rancis) Scott (Key)
   1896-1940 ... **SSC 6, 31; TCLC 1, 6, 14,**
   28, 55; WLC
   See also AAYA 24; AITN 1; AMW; AMWC
   2; AMWR 1; BPFB 1; CA 110; 123;
   CDALB 1917-1929; DA; DA3; DAB;
   DAC; DAM MST, NOV; DLB 4, 9, 86,
   219, 273; DLBD 1, 15, 16; DLBY 1981,
   1996; EWL 3; EXPN; EXPS; LAIT 3;
   MTCW 1, 2; NFS 2, 19, 20; RGAL 4;
   RGSF 2; SSFS 4, 15; TUS

Fitzgerald, Penelope 1916-2000 . **CLC 19, 51,**
   61, 143
   See also BRWS 5; CA 85-88; 190; CAAS
   10; CANR 56, 86, 131; CN 7; DLB 14,
   194; EWL 3; MTCW 2

Fitzgerald, Robert (Stuart)
   1910-1985 .... **CLC 39**
   See also CA 1-4R; 114; CANR 1; DLBY
   1980

FitzGerald, Robert D(avid)
   1902-1987 .... **CLC 19**
   See also CA 17-20R; DLB 260; RGEL 2

Fitzgerald, Zelda (Sayre)
   1900-1948 .... **TCLC 52**
   See also AMWS 9; CA 117; 126; DLBY
   1984

Flanagan, Thomas (James Bonner)
   1923-2002 .... **CLC 25, 52**
   See also CA 108; 206; CANR 55; CN 7;
   DLBY 1980; INT CA-108; MTCW 1;
   RHW

Flaubert, Gustave 1821-1880 .... **NCLC 2, 10,**
   19, 62, 66, 135; SSC 11, 60; WLC
   See also DA; DA3; DAB; DAC; DAM
   MST, NOV; DLB 119, 301; EW 7; EXPS;
   GFL 1789 to the Present; LAIT 2; LMFS
   1; NFS 14; RGSF 2; RGWL 2, 3; SSFS
   6; TWA

Flavius Josephus
   See Josephus, Flavius

Flecker, Herman Elroy
   See Flecker, (Herman) James Elroy

Flecker, (Herman) James Elroy
   1884-1915 .... **TCLC 43**
   See also CA 109; 150; DLB 10, 19; RGEL
   2

Fleming, Ian (Lancaster) 1908-1964 . **CLC 3,**
   30
   See also AAYA 26; BPFB 1; CA 5-8R;
   CANR 59; CDBLB 1945-1960; CMW 4;
   CPW; DA3; DAM POP; DLB 87, 201;
   MSW; MTCW 1, 2; RGEL 2; SATA 9;
   TEA; YAW

Fleming, Thomas (James) 1927- ...... **CLC 37**
   See also CA 5-8R; CANR 10, 102; INT
   CANR-10; SATA 8

Fletcher, John 1579-1625 .... **DC 6; LC 33**
   See also BRW 2; CDBLB Before 1660;
   DLB 58; RGEL 2; TEA

Fletcher, John Gould 1886-1950 .... **TCLC 35**
   See also CA 107; 167; DLB 4, 45; LMFS
   2; RGAL 4

Fleur, Paul
   See Pohl, Frederik

Flooglebuckle, Al
   See Spiegelman, Art

Flora, Fletcher 1914-1969
   See Queen, Ellery
   See also CA 1-4R; CANR 3, 85

Flying Officer X
   See Bates, H(erbert) E(rnest)

Fo, Dario 1926- .... **CLC 32, 109; DC 10**
   See also CA 116; 128; CANR 68, 114;
   CWW 2; DA3; DAM DRAM; DLBY
   1997; EWL 3; MTCW 1, 2

Fogarty, Jonathan Titulescu Esq.
   See Farrell, James T(homas)

Follett, Ken(neth Martin) 1949- ...... **CLC 18**
   See also AAYA 6, 50; BEST 89:4; BPFB 1;
   CA 81-84; CANR 13, 33, 54, 102; CMW
   4; CPW; DA3; DAM NOV, POP; DLB
   87; DLBY 1981; INT CANR-33; MTCW
   1

Fontane, Theodor 1819-1898 .... **NCLC 26**
   See also CDWLB 2; DLB 129; EW 6;
   RGWL 2, 3; TWA

Fontenot, Chester .... **CLC 65**

Fonvizin, Denis Ivanovich
   1744(?)-1792 .... **LC 81**
   See also DLB 150; RGWL 2, 3

Foote, Horton 1916- .... **CLC 51, 91**
   See also CA 73-76; CAD; CANR 34, 51,
   110; CD 5; CSW; DA3; DAM DRAM;
   DFS 20; DLB 26, 266; EWL 3; INT
   CANR-34

Foote, Mary Hallock 1847-1938 .. **TCLC 108**
   See also DLB 186, 188, 202, 221

Foote, Shelby 1916- .... **CLC 75**
   See also AAYA 40; CA 5-8R; CANR 3, 45,
   74, 131; CN 7; CPW; CSW; DA3; DAM
   NOV, POP; DLB 2, 17; MTCW 2; RHW

Forbes, Cosmo
   See Lewton, Val

Forbes, Esther 1891-1967 .... **CLC 12**
   See also AAYA 17; BYA 2; CA 13-14; 25-
   28R; CAP 1; CLR 27; DLB 22; JRDA;
   MAICYA 1, 2; RHW; SATA 2, 100; YAW

Forche, Carolyn (Louise) 1950- .... **CLC 25,**
   83, 86; PC 10
   See also CA 109; 117; CANR 50, 74; CP 7;
   CWP; DA3; DAM POET; DLB 5, 193;
   INT CA-117; MTCW 1; PFS 18; RGAL 4

Ford, Elbur
   See Hibbert, Eleanor Alice Burford

Ford, Ford Madox 1873-1939 ... **TCLC 1, 15,**
   39, 57
   See Chaucer, Daniel
   See also BRW 6; CA 104; 132; CANR 74;
   CDBLB 1914-1945; DA3; DAM NOV;
   DLB 34, 98, 162; EWL 3; MTCW 1, 2;
   RGEL 2; TEA

Gertler, T. .... **CLC 34**
See also CA 116; 121

Gertsen, Aleksandr Ivanovich
See Herzen, Aleksandr Ivanovich

Ghalib .... **NCLC 39, 78**
See Ghalib, Asadullah Khan

Ghalib, Asadullah Khan 1797-1869
See Ghalib
See also DAM POET; RGWL 2, 3

Ghelderode, Michel de 1898-1962 ..... **CLC 6, 11; DC 15**
See also CA 85-88; CANR 40, 77; DAM DRAM; EW 11; EWL 3; TWA

Ghiselin, Brewster 1903-2001 .... **CLC 23**
See also CA 13-16R; CAAS 10; CANR 13; CP 7

Ghose, Aurabinda 1872-1950 .... **TCLC 63**
See Ghose, Aurobindo
See also CA 163

Ghose, Aurobindo
See Ghose, Aurabinda
See also EWL 3

Ghose, Zulfikar 1935- .... **CLC 42**
See also CA 65-68; CANR 67; CN 7; CP 7; EWL 3

Ghosh, Amitav 1956- .... **CLC 44, 153**
See also CA 147; CANR 80; CN 7; WWE 1

Giacosa, Giuseppe 1847-1906 .... **TCLC 7**
See also CA 104

Gibb, Lee
See Waterhouse, Keith (Spencer)

Gibbon, Edward 1737-1794 .... **LC 97**
See also BRW 3; DLB 104; RGEL 2

Gibbon, Lewis Grassic .... **TCLC 4**
See Mitchell, James Leslie
See also RGEL 2

Gibbons, Kaye 1960- .... **CLC 50, 88, 145**
See also AAYA 34; AMWS 10; CA 151; CANR 75, 127; CSW; DA3; DAM POP; DLB 292; MTCW 1; NFS 3; RGAL 4; SATA 117

Gibran, Kahlil 1883-1931 . **PC 9; TCLC 1, 9**
See also CA 104; 150; DA3; DAM POET, POP; EWL 3; MTCW 2

Gibran, Khalil
See Gibran, Kahlil

Gibson, William 1914- .... **CLC 23**
See also CA 9-12R; CAD 2; CANR 9, 42, 75, 125; CD 5; DA; DAB; DAC; DAM DRAM, MST; DFS 2; DLB 7; LAIT 2; MTCW 2; SATA 66; YAW

Gibson, William (Ford) 1948- ... **CLC 39, 63, 186, 192; SSC 52**
See also AAYA 12, 59; BPFB 2; CA 126; 133; CANR 52, 90, 106; CN 7; CPW; DA3; DAM POP; DLB 251; MTCW 2; SCFW 2; SFW 4

Gide, Andre (Paul Guillaume) 1869-1951 ..... **SSC 13; TCLC 5, 12, 36; WLC**
See also CA 104; 124; DA; DA3; DAB; DAC; DAM MST, NOV; DLB 65; EW 8; EWL 3; GFL 1789 to the Present; MTCW 1, 2; RGSF 2; RGWL 2, 3; TWA

Gifford, Barry (Colby) 1946- .... **CLC 34**
See also CA 65-68; CANR 9, 30, 40, 90

Gilbert, Frank
See De Voto, Bernard (Augustine)

Gilbert, W(illiam) S(chwenck) 1836-1911 .... **TCLC 3**
See also CA 104; 173; DAM DRAM, POET; RGEL 2; SATA 36

Gilbreth, Frank B(unker), Jr. 1911-2001 .... **CLC 17**
See also CA 9-12R; SATA 2

Gilchrist, Ellen (Louise) 1935- .. **CLC 34, 48, 143; SSC 14, 63**
See also BPFB 2; CA 113; 116; CANR 41, 61, 104; CN 7; CPW; CSW; DAM POP; DLB 130; EWL 3; EXPS; MTCW 1, 2; RGAL 4; RGSF 2; SSFS 9

Giles, Molly 1942- .... **CLC 39**
See also CA 126; CANR 98

Gill, Eric 1882-1940 .... **TCLC 85**
See Gill, (Arthur) Eric (Rowton Peter Joseph)

Gill, (Arthur) Eric (Rowton Peter Joseph) 1882-1940
See Gill, Eric
See also CA 120; DLB 98

Gill, Patrick
See Creasey, John

Gillette, Douglas .... **CLC 70**

Gilliam, Terry (Vance) 1940- .... **CLC 21, 141**
See Monty Python
See also AAYA 19, 59; CA 108; 113; CANR 35; INT CA-113

Gillian, Jerry
See Gilliam, Terry (Vance)

Gilliatt, Penelope (Ann Douglass) 1932-1993 .... **CLC 2, 10, 13, 53**
See also AITN 2; CA 13-16R; 141; CANR 49; DLB 14

Gilman, Charlotte (Anna) Perkins (Stetson) 1860-1935 ...... **SSC 13, 62; TCLC 9, 37, 117**
See also AMWS 11; BYA 11; CA 106; 150; DLB 221; EXPS; FW; HGG; LAIT 2; MAWW; MTCW 1; RGAL 4; RGSF 2; SFW 4; SSFS 1, 18

Gilmour, David 1946- .... **CLC 35**

Gilpin, William 1724-1804 .... **NCLC 30**

Gilray, J. D.
See Mencken, H(enry) L(ouis)

Gilroy, Frank D(aniel) 1925- .... **CLC 2**
See also CA 81-84; CAD; CANR 32, 64, 86; CD 5; DFS 17; DLB 7

Gilstrap, John 1957(?)- .... **CLC 99**
See also CA 160; CANR 101

Ginsberg, Allen 1926-1997 .... **CLC 1, 2, 3, 4, 6, 13, 36, 69, 109; PC 4, 47; TCLC 120; WLC**
See also AAYA 33; AITN 1; AMWC 1; AMWS 2; BG 2; CA 1-4R; 157; CANR 2, 41, 63, 95; CDALB 1941-1968; CP 7; DA; DA3; DAB; DAC; DAM MST, POET; DLB 5, 16, 169, 237; EWL 3; GLL 1; LMFS 2; MTCW 1, 2; PAB; PFS 5; RGAL 4; TUS; WP

Ginzburg, Eugenia .... **CLC 59**

Ginzburg, Natalia 1916-1991 .... **CLC 5, 11, 54, 70; SSC 65**
See also CA 85-88; 135; CANR 33; DFS 14; DLB 177; EW 13; EWL 3; MTCW 1, 2; RGWL 2, 3

Giono, Jean 1895-1970 .... **CLC 4, 11; TCLC 124**
See also CA 45-48; 29-32R; CANR 2, 35; DLB 72; EWL 3; GFL 1789 to the Present; MTCW 1; RGWL 2, 3

Giovanni, Nikki 1943- ...... **BLC 2; CLC 2, 4, 19, 64, 117; PC 19; WLCS**
See also AAYA 22; AITN 1; BW 2, 3; CA 29-32R; CAAS 6; CANR 18, 41, 60, 91, 130; CDALBS; CLR 6, 73; CP 7; CSW; CWP; CWRI 5; DA; DA3; DAB; DAC; DAM MST, MULT, POET; DLB 5, 41; EWL 3; EXPP; INT CANR-18; MAICYA 1, 2; MTCW 1, 2; PFS 17; RGAL 4; SATA 24, 107; TUS; YAW

Giovene, Andrea 1904-1998 .... **CLC 7**
See also CA 85-88

Gippius, Zinaida (Nikolaevna) 1869-1945
See Hippius, Zinaida (Nikolaevna)
See also CA 106; 212

Giraudoux, Jean(-Hippolyte) 1882-1944 .... **TCLC 2, 7**
See also CA 104; 196; DAM DRAM; DLB 65; EW 9; EWL 3; GFL 1789 to the Present; RGWL 2, 3; TWA

Gironella, Jose Maria (Pous) 1917-2003 .... **CLC 11**
See also CA 101; 212; EWL 3; RGWL 2, 3

Gissing, George (Robert) 1857-1903 .... **SSC 37; TCLC 3, 24, 47**
See also BRW 5; CA 105; 167; DLB 18, 135, 184; RGEL 2; TEA

Giurlani, Aldo
See Palazzeschi, Aldo

Gladkov, Fedor Vasil'evich
See Gladkov, Fyodor (Vasilyevich)
See also DLB 272

Gladkov, Fyodor (Vasilyevich) 1883-1958 .... **TCLC 27**
See Gladkov, Fedor Vasil'evich
See also CA 170; EWL 3

Glancy, Diane 1941- .... **NNAL**
See also CA 136; 225; CAAE 225; CAAS 24; CANR 87; DLB 175

Glanville, Brian (Lester) 1931- .... **CLC 6**
See also CA 5-8R; CAAS 9; CANR 3, 70; CN 7; DLB 15, 139; SATA 42

Glasgow, Ellen (Anderson Gholson) 1873-1945 .... **SSC 34; TCLC 2, 7**
See also AMW; CA 104; 164; DLB 9, 12; MAWW; MTCW 2; RGAL 4; RHW; SSFS 9; TUS

Glaspell, Susan 1882(?)-1948 ..... **DC 10; SSC 41; TCLC 55**
See also AMWS 3; CA 110; 154; DFS 8, 18; DLB 7, 9, 78, 228; MAWW; RGAL 4; SSFS 3; TCWW 2; TUS; YABC 2

Glassco, John 1909-1981 .... **CLC 9**
See also CA 13-16R; 102; CANR 15; DLB 68

Glasscock, Amnesia
See Steinbeck, John (Ernst)

Glasser, Ronald J. 1940(?)- .... **CLC 37**
See also CA 209

Glassman, Joyce
See Johnson, Joyce

Gleick, James (W.) 1954- .... **CLC 147**
See also CA 131; 137; CANR 97; INT CA-137

Glendinning, Victoria 1937- .... **CLC 50**
See also CA 120; 127; CANR 59, 89; DLB 155

Glissant, Edouard (Mathieu) 1928- .... **CLC 10, 68**
See also CA 153; CANR 111; CWW 2; DAM MULT; EWL 3; RGWL 3

Gloag, Julian 1930- .... **CLC 40**
See also AITN 1; CA 65-68; CANR 10, 70; CN 7

Glowacki, Aleksander
See Prus, Boleslaw

Gluck, Louise (Elisabeth) 1943- .. **CLC 7, 22, 44, 81, 160; PC 16**
See also AMWS 5; CA 33-36R; CANR 40, 69, 108; CP 7; CWP; DA3; DAM POET; DLB 5; MTCW 2; PFS 5, 15; RGAL 4

Glyn, Elinor 1864-1943 .... **TCLC 72**
See also DLB 153; RHW

Gobineau, Joseph-Arthur 1816-1882 .... **NCLC 17**
See also DLB 123; GFL 1789 to the Present

Godard, Jean-Luc 1930- .... **CLC 20**
See also CA 93-96

Gozzano, Guido 1883-1916 .... **PC 10**
See also CA 154; DLB 114; EWL 3
Gozzi, (Conte) Carlo 1720-1806 .... **NCLC 23**
Grabbe, Christian Dietrich
1801-1836 .... **NCLC 2**
See also DLB 133; RGWL 2, 3
Grace, Patricia Frances 1937- .... **CLC 56**
See also CA 176; CANR 118; CN 7; EWL
3; RGSF 2
Gracian y Morales, Baltasar
1601-1658 .... **LC 15**
Gracq, Julien .... **CLC 11, 48**
See Poirier, Louis
See also CWW 2; DLB 83; GFL 1789 to
the Present
Grade, Chaim 1910-1982 .... **CLC 10**
See also CA 93-96; 107; EWL 3
Graduate of Oxford, A
See Ruskin, John
Grafton, Garth
See Duncan, Sara Jeannette
Grafton, Sue 1940- .... **CLC 163**
See also AAYA 11, 49; BEST 90:3; CA 108;
CANR 31, 55, 111; CMW 4; CPW; CSW;
DA3; DAM POP; DLB 226; FW; MSW
Graham, John
See Phillips, David Graham
Graham, Jorie 1951- .... **CLC 48, 118; PC 59**
See also CA 111; CANR 63, 118; CP 7;
CWP; DLB 120; EWL 3; PFS 10, 17
Graham, R(obert) B(ontine) Cunninghame
See Cunninghame Graham, Robert
(Gallnigad) Bontine
See also DLB 98, 135, 174; RGEL 2; RGSF
2
Graham, Robert
See Haldeman, Joe (William)
Graham, Tom
See Lewis, (Harry) Sinclair
Graham, W(illiam) S(idney)
1918-1986 .... **CLC 29**
See also BRWS 7; CA 73-76; 118; DLB 20;
RGEL 2
Graham, Winston (Mawdsley)
1910-2003 .... **CLC 23**
See also CA 49-52; 218; CANR 2, 22, 45,
66; CMW 4; CN 7; DLB 77; RHW
Grahame, Kenneth 1859-1932 ...... **TCLC 64,
136**
See also BYA 5; CA 108; 136; CANR 80;
CLR 5; CWRI 5; DA3; DAB; DLB 34,
141, 178; FANT; MAICYA 1, 2; MTCW
2; NFS 20; RGEL 2; SATA 100; TEA;
WCH; YABC 1
Granger, Darius John
See Marlowe, Stephen
Granin, Daniil .... **CLC 59**
See also DLB 302
Granovsky, Timofei Nikolaevich
1813-1855 .... **NCLC 75**
See also DLB 198
Grant, Skeeter
See Spiegelman, Art
Granville-Barker, Harley
1877-1946 .... **TCLC 2**
See Barker, Harley Granville
See also CA 104; 204; DAM DRAM;
RGEL 2
Granzotto, Gianni
See Granzotto, Giovanni Battista
Granzotto, Giovanni Battista
1914-1985 .... **CLC 70**
See also CA 166
Grass, Guenter (Wilhelm) 1927- ... **CLC 1, 2,
4, 6, 11, 15, 22, 32, 49, 88; WLC**
See also BPFB 2; CA 13-16R; CANR 20,
75, 93; CDWLB 2; DA; DA3; DAB;
DAC; DAM MST, NOV; DLB 75, 124;
EW 13; EWL 3; MTCW 1, 2; RGWL 2,
3; TWA

Gratton, Thomas
See Hulme, T(homas) E(rnest)
Grau, Shirley Ann 1929- .... **CLC 4, 9, 146;
SSC 15**
See also CA 89-92; CANR 22, 69; CN 7;
CSW; DLB 2, 218; INT CA-89-92,
CANR-22; MTCW 1
Gravel, Fern
See Hall, James Norman
Graver, Elizabeth 1964- .... **CLC 70**
See also CA 135; CANR 71, 129
Graves, Richard Perceval
1895-1985 .... **CLC 44**
See also CA 65-68; CANR 9, 26, 51
Graves, Robert (von Ranke)
1895-1985 .. **CLC 1, 2, 6, 11, 39, 44, 45;
PC 6**
See also BPFB 2; BRW 7; BYA 4; CA 5-8R;
117; CANR 5, 36; CDBLB 1914-1945;
DA3; DAB; DAC; DAM MST, POET;
DLB 20, 100, 191; DLBD 18; DLBY
1985; EWL 3; LATS 1; MTCW 1, 2;
NCFS 2; RGEL 2; RHW; SATA 45; TEA
Graves, Valerie
See Bradley, Marion Zimmer
Gray, Alasdair (James) 1934- .... **CLC 41**
See also BRWS 9; CA 126; CANR 47, 69,
106; CN 7; DLB 194, 261; HGG; INT
CA-126; MTCW 1, 2; RGSF 2; SUFW 2
Gray, Amlin 1946- .... **CLC 29**
See also CA 138
Gray, Francine du Plessix 1930- ..... **CLC 22,
153**
See also BEST 90:3; CA 61-64; CAAS 2;
CANR 11, 33, 75, 81; DAM NOV; INT
CANR-11; MTCW 1, 2
Gray, John (Henry) 1866-1934 ...... **TCLC 19**
See also CA 119; 162; RGEL 2
Gray, Simon (James Holliday)
1936- .... **CLC 9, 14, 36**
See also AITN 1; CA 21-24R; CAAS 3;
CANR 32, 69; CD 5; DLB 13; EWL 3;
MTCW 1; RGEL 2
Gray, Spalding 1941-2004 .... **CLC 49, 112;
DC 7**
See also CA 128; 225; CAD; CANR 74;
CD 5; CPW; DAM POP; MTCW 2
Gray, Thomas 1716-1771 .... **LC 4, 40; PC 2;
WLC**
See also BRW 3; CDBLB 1660-1789; DA;
DA3; DAB; DAC; DAM MST; DLB 109;
EXPP; PAB; PFS 9; RGEL 2; TEA; WP
Grayson, David
See Baker, Ray Stannard
Grayson, Richard (A.) 1951- .... **CLC 38**
See also CA 85-88, 210; CAAE 210; CANR
14, 31, 57; DLB 234
Greeley, Andrew M(oran) 1928- .... **CLC 28**
See also BPFB 2; CA 5-8R; CAAS 7;
CANR 7, 43, 69, 104; CMW 4; CPW;
DA3; DAM POP; MTCW 1, 2
Green, Anna Katharine
1846-1935 .... **TCLC 63**
See also CA 112; 159; CMW 4; DLB 202,
221; MSW
Green, Brian
See Card, Orson Scott
Green, Hannah
See Greenberg, Joanne (Goldenberg)
Green, Hannah 1927(?)-1996 .... **CLC 3**
See also CA 73-76; CANR 59, 93; NFS 10
Green, Henry .... **CLC 2, 13, 97**
See Yorke, Henry Vincent
See also BRWS 2; CA 175; DLB 15; EWL
3; RGEL 2
Green, Julian (Hartridge) 1900-1998
See Green, Julien
See also CA 21-24R; 169; CANR 33, 87;
DLB 4, 72; MTCW 1

Green, Julien .... **CLC 3, 11, 77**
See Green, Julian (Hartridge)
See also EWL 3; GFL 1789 to the Present;
MTCW 2
Green, Paul (Eliot) 1894-1981 .... **CLC 25**
See also AITN 1; CA 5-8R; 103; CANR 3;
DAM DRAM; DLB 7, 9, 249; DLBY
1981; RGAL 4
Greenaway, Peter 1942- .... **CLC 159**
See also CA 127
Greenberg, Ivan 1908-1973
See Rahv, Philip
See also CA 85-88
Greenberg, Joanne (Goldenberg)
1932- .... **CLC 7, 30**
See also AAYA 12; CA 5-8R; CANR 14,
32, 69; CN 7; SATA 25; YAW
Greenberg, Richard 1959(?)- .... **CLC 57**
See also CA 138; CAD; CD 5
Greenblatt, Stephen J(ay) 1943- ...... **CLC 70**
See also CA 49-52; CANR 115
Greene, Bette 1934- .... **CLC 30**
See also AAYA 7; BYA 3; CA 53-56; CANR
4; CLR 2; CWRI 5; JRDA; LAIT 4; MAI-
CYA 1, 2; NFS 10; SAAS 16; SATA 8,
102; WYA; YAW
Greene, Gael .... **CLC 8**
See also CA 13-16R; CANR 10
Greene, Graham (Henry)
1904-1991 .... **CLC 1, 3, 6, 9, 14, 18, 27,
37, 70, 72, 125; SSC 29; WLC**
See also AITN 2; BPFB 2; BRWR 2; BRWS
1; BYA 3; CA 13-16R; 133; CANR 35,
61, 131; CBD; CDBLB 1945-1960; CMW
4; DA; DA3; DAB; DAC; DAM MST,
NOV; DLB 13, 15, 77, 100, 162, 201,
204; DLBY 1991; EWL 3; MSW; MTCW
1, 2; NFS 16; RGEL 2; SATA 20; SSFS
14; TEA; WLIT 4
Greene, Robert 1558-1592 .... **LC 41**
See also BRWS 8; DLB 62, 167; IDTP;
RGEL 2; TEA
Greer, Germaine 1939- .... **CLC 131**
See also AITN 1; CA 81-84; CANR 33, 70,
115; FW; MTCW 1, 2
Greer, Richard
See Silverberg, Robert
Gregor, Arthur 1923- .... **CLC 9**
See also CA 25-28R; CAAS 10; CANR 11;
CP 7; SATA 36
Gregor, Lee
See Pohl, Frederik
Gregory, Lady Isabella Augusta (Persse)
1852-1932 .... **TCLC 1**
See also BRW 6; CA 104; 184; DLB 10;
IDTP; RGEL 2
Gregory, J. Dennis
See Williams, John A(lfred)
Grekova, I. .... **CLC 59**
See Ventsel, Elena Sergeevna
See also CWW 2
Grendon, Stephen
See Derleth, August (William)
Grenville, Kate 1950- .... **CLC 61**
See also CA 118; CANR 53, 93
Grenville, Pelham
See Wodehouse, P(elham) G(renville)
Greve, Felix Paul (Berthold Friedrich)
1879-1948
See Grove, Frederick Philip
See also CA 104; 141, 175; CANR 79;
DAC; DAM MST
Greville, Fulke 1554-1628 .... **LC 79**
See also DLB 62, 172; RGEL 2
Grey, Lady Jane 1537-1554 .... **LC 93**
See also DLB 132

Hiraoka, Kimitake 1925-1970
See Mishima, Yukio
See also CA 97-100; 29-32R; DA3; DAM
DRAM; GLL 1; MTCW 1, 2

Hirsch, E(ric) D(onald), Jr. 1928- .... **CLC 79**
See also CA 25-28R; CANR 27, 51; DLB
67; INT CANR-27; MTCW 1

Hirsch, Edward 1950- .... **CLC 31, 50**
See also CA 104; CANR 20, 42, 102; CP 7;
DLB 120

Hitchcock, Alfred (Joseph)
1899-1980 .... **CLC 16**
See also AAYA 22; CA 159; 97-100; SATA
27; SATA-Obit 24

Hitchens, Christopher (Eric)
1949- .... **CLC 157**
See also CA 152; CANR 89

Hitler, Adolf 1889-1945 .... **TCLC 53**
See also CA 117; 147

Hoagland, Edward 1932- .... **CLC 28**
See also ANW; CA 1-4R; CANR 2, 31, 57,
107; CN 7; DLB 6; SATA 51; TCWW 2

Hoban, Russell (Conwell) 1925- ... **CLC 7, 25**
See also BPFB 2; CA 5-8R; CANR 23, 37,
66, 114; CLR 3, 69; CN 7; CWRI 5; DAM
NOV; DLB 52; FANT; MAICYA 1, 2;
MTCW 1, 2; SATA 1, 40, 78, 136; SFW
4; SUFW 2

Hobbes, Thomas 1588-1679 .... **LC 36**
See also DLB 151, 252, 281; RGEL 2

Hobbs, Perry
See Blackmur, R(ichard) P(almer)

Hobson, Laura Z(ametkin)
1900-1986 .... **CLC 7, 25**
See Field, Peter
See also BPFB 2; CA 17-20R; 118; CANR
55; DLB 28; SATA 52

Hoccleve, Thomas c. 1368-c. 1437 ...... **LC 75**
See also DLB 146; RGEL 2

Hoch, Edward D(entinger) 1930-
See Queen, Ellery
See also CA 29-32R; CANR 11, 27, 51, 97;
CMW 4; SFW 4

Hochhuth, Rolf 1931- .... **CLC 4, 11, 18**
See also CA 5-8R; CANR 33, 75; CWW 2;
DAM DRAM; DLB 124; EWL 3; MTCW
1, 2

Hochman, Sandra 1936- .... **CLC 3, 8**
See also CA 5-8R; DLB 5

Hochwaelder, Fritz 1911-1986 .... **CLC 36**
See Hochwalder, Fritz
See also CA 29-32R; 120; CANR 42; DAM
DRAM; MTCW 1; RGWL 3

Hochwalder, Fritz
See Hochwaelder, Fritz
See also EWL 3; RGWL 2

Hocking, Mary (Eunice) 1921- .... **CLC 13**
See also CA 101; CANR 18, 40

Hodgins, Jack 1938- .... **CLC 23**
See also CA 93-96; CN 7; DLB 60

Hodgson, William Hope
1877(?)-1918 .... **TCLC 13**
See also CA 111; 164; CMW 4; DLB 70,
153, 156, 178; HGG; MTCW 2; SFW 4;
SUFW 1

Hoeg, Peter 1957- .... **CLC 95, 156**
See also CA 151; CANR 75; CMW 4; DA3;
DLB 214; EWL 3; MTCW 2; NFS 17;
RGWL 3; SSFS 18

Hoffman, Alice 1952- .... **CLC 51**
See also AAYA 37; AMWS 10; CA 77-80;
CANR 34, 66, 100; CN 7; CPW; DAM
NOV; DLB 292; MTCW 1, 2

Hoffman, Daniel (Gerard) 1923- . **CLC 6, 13,
23**
See also CA 1-4R; CANR 4; CP 7; DLB 5

Hoffman, Eva 1945- .... **CLC 182**
See also CA 132

Hoffman, Stanley 1944- .... **CLC 5**
See also CA 77-80

Hoffman, William 1925- .... **CLC 141**
See also CA 21-24R; CANR 9, 103; CSW;
DLB 234

Hoffman, William M(oses) 1939- ..... **CLC 40**
See Hoffman, William M.
See also CA 57-60; CANR 11, 71

Hoffmann, E(rnst) T(heodor) A(madeus)
1776-1822 .... **NCLC 2; SSC 13**
See also CDWLB 2; DLB 90; EW 5; RGSF
2; RGWL 2, 3; SATA 27; SUFW 1; WCH

Hofmann, Gert 1931- .... **CLC 54**
See also CA 128; EWL 3

Hofmannsthal, Hugo von 1874-1929 ... **DC 4;
TCLC 11**
See also CA 106; 153; CDWLB 2; DAM
DRAM; DFS 17; DLB 81, 118; EW 9;
EWL 3; RGWL 2, 3

Hogan, Linda 1947- ..... **CLC 73; NNAL; PC
35**
See also AMWS 4; ANW; BYA 12; CA 120,
226; CAAE 226; CANR 45, 73, 129;
CWP; DAM MULT; DLB 175; SATA
132; TCWW 2

Hogarth, Charles
See Creasey, John

Hogarth, Emmett
See Polonsky, Abraham (Lincoln)

Hogg, James 1770-1835 .... **NCLC 4, 109**
See also DLB 93, 116, 159; HGG; RGEL 2;
SUFW 1

Holbach, Paul Henri Thiry Baron
1723-1789 .... **LC 14**

Holberg, Ludvig 1684-1754 .... **LC 6**
See also DLB 300; RGWL 2, 3

Holcroft, Thomas 1745-1809 .... **NCLC 85**
See also DLB 39, 89, 158; RGEL 2

Holden, Ursula 1921- .... **CLC 18**
See also CA 101; CAAS 8; CANR 22

Holderlin, (Johann Christian) Friedrich
1770-1843 .... **NCLC 16; PC 4**
See also CDWLB 2; DLB 90; EW 5; RGWL
2, 3

Holdstock, Robert
See Holdstock, Robert P.

Holdstock, Robert P. 1948- .... **CLC 39**
See also CA 131; CANR 81; DLB 261;
FANT; HGG; SFW 4; SUFW 2

Holinshed, Raphael fl. 1580- .... **LC 69**
See also DLB 167; RGEL 2

Holland, Isabelle (Christian)
1920-2002 .... **CLC 21**
See also AAYA 11; CA 21-24R; 205; CAAE
181; CANR 10, 25, 47; CLR 57; CWRI
5; JRDA; LAIT 4; MAICYA 1, 2; SATA
8, 70; SATA-Essay 103; SATA-Obit 132;
WYA

Holland, Marcus
See Caldwell, (Janet Miriam) Taylor
(Holland)

Hollander, John 1929- .... **CLC 2, 5, 8, 14**
See also CA 1-4R; CANR 1, 52; CP 7; DLB
5; SATA 13

Hollander, Paul
See Silverberg, Robert

Holleran, Andrew 1943(?)- .... **CLC 38**
See Garber, Eric
See also CA 144; GLL 1

Holley, Marietta 1836(?)-1926 .... **TCLC 99**
See also CA 118; DLB 11

Hollinghurst, Alan 1954- .... **CLC 55, 91**
See also CA 114; CN 7; DLB 207; GLL 1

Hollis, Jim
See Summers, Hollis (Spurgeon, Jr.)

Holly, Buddy 1936-1959 .... **TCLC 65**
See also CA 213

Holmes, Gordon
See Shiel, M(atthew) P(hipps)

Holmes, John
See Souster, (Holmes) Raymond

Holmes, John Clellon 1926-1988 ...... **CLC 56**
See also BG 2; CA 9-12R; 125; CANR 4;
DLB 16, 237

Holmes, Oliver Wendell, Jr.
1841-1935 .... **TCLC 77**
See also CA 114; 186

Holmes, Oliver Wendell
1809-1894 .... **NCLC 14, 81**
See also AMWS 1; CDALB 1640-1865;
DLB 1, 189, 235; EXPP; RGAL 4; SATA
34

Holmes, Raymond
See Souster, (Holmes) Raymond

Holt, Victoria
See Hibbert, Eleanor Alice Burford
See also BPFB 2

Holub, Miroslav 1923-1998 .... **CLC 4**
See also CA 21-24R; 169; CANR 10; CD-
WLB 4; CWW 2; DLB 232; EWL 3;
RGWL 3

Holz, Detlev
See Benjamin, Walter

Homer c. 8th cent. B.C.- .... **CMLC 1, 16, 61;
PC 23; WLCS**
See also AW 1; CDWLB 1; DA; DA3;
DAB; DAC; DAM MST, POET; DLB
176; EFS 1; LAIT 1; LMFS 1; RGWL 2,
3; TWA; WP

Hongo, Garrett Kaoru 1951- .... **PC 23**
See also CA 133; CAAS 22; CP 7; DLB
120; EWL 3; EXPP; RGAL 4

Honig, Edwin 1919- .... **CLC 33**
See also CA 5-8R; CAAS 8; CANR 4, 45;
CP 7; DLB 5

Hood, Hugh (John Blagdon) 1928- . **CLC 15,
28; SSC 42**
See also CA 49-52; CAAS 17; CANR 1,
33, 87; CN 7; DLB 53; RGSF 2

Hood, Thomas 1799-1845 .... **NCLC 16**
See also BRW 4; DLB 96; RGEL 2

Hooker, (Peter) Jeremy 1941- .... **CLC 43**
See also CA 77-80; CANR 22; CP 7; DLB
40

Hooker, Richard 1554-1600 .... **LC 95**
See also BRW 1; DLB 132; RGEL 2

hooks, bell
See Watkins, Gloria Jean

Hope, A(lec) D(erwent) 1907-2000 .... **CLC 3,
51; PC 56**
See also BRWS 7; CA 21-24R; 188; CANR
33, 74; DLB 289; EWL 3; MTCW 1, 2;
PFS 8; RGEL 2

Hope, Anthony 1863-1933 .... **TCLC 83**
See also CA 157; DLB 153, 156; RGEL 2;
RHW

Hope, Brian
See Creasey, John

Hope, Christopher (David Tully)
1944- .... **CLC 52**
See also AFW; CA 106; CANR 47, 101;
CN 7; DLB 225; SATA 62

Hopkins, Gerard Manley
1844-1889 .... **NCLC 17; PC 15; WLC**
See also BRW 5; BRWR 2; CDBLB 1890-
1914; DA; DA3; DAB; DAC; DAM MST,
POET; DLB 35, 57; EXPP; PAB; RGEL
2; TEA; WP

Hopkins, John (Richard) 1931-1998 .. **CLC 4**
See also CA 85-88; 169; CBD; CD 5

Hopkins, Pauline Elizabeth
1859-1930 .... **BLC 2; TCLC 28**
See also AFAW 2; BW 2, 3; CA 141; CANR
82; DAM MULT; DLB 50

Hopkinson, Francis 1737-1791 .... **LC 25**
See also DLB 31; RGAL 4

Jennings, Elizabeth (Joan)
1926-2001 .... **CLC 5, 14, 131**
See also BRWS 5; CA 61-64; 200; CAAS 5; CANR 8, 39, 66, 127; CP 7; CWP; DLB 27; EWL 3; MTCW 1; SATA 66

Jennings, Waylon 1937- .... **CLC 21**

Jensen, Johannes V(ilhelm)
1873-1950 .... **TCLC 41**
See also CA 170; DLB 214; EWL 3; RGWL 3

Jensen, Laura (Linnea) 1948- .... **CLC 37**
See also CA 103

Jerome, Saint 345-420 .... **CMLC 30**
See also RGWL 3

Jerome, Jerome K(lapka)
1859-1927 .... **TCLC 23**
See also CA 119; 177; DLB 10, 34, 135; RGEL 2

Jerrold, Douglas William
1803-1857 .... **NCLC 2**
See also DLB 158, 159; RGEL 2

Jewett, (Theodora) Sarah Orne
1849-1909 .... **SSC 6, 44; TCLC 1, 22**
See also AMW; AMWC 2; AMWR 2; CA 108; 127; CANR 71; DLB 12, 74, 221; EXPS; FW; MAWW; NFS 15; RGAL 4; RGSF 2; SATA 15; SSFS 4

Jewsbury, Geraldine (Endsor)
1812-1880 .... **NCLC 22**
See also DLB 21

Jhabvala, Ruth Prawer 1927- . **CLC 4, 8, 29, 94, 138**
See also BRWS 5; CA 1-4R; CANR 2, 29, 51, 74, 91, 128; CN 7; DAB; DAM NOV; DLB 139, 194; EWL 3; IDFW 3, 4; INT CANR-29; MTCW 1, 2; RGSF 2; RGWL 2; RHW; TEA

Jibran, Kahlil
See Gibran, Kahlil

Jibran, Khalil
See Gibran, Kahlil

Jiles, Paulette 1943- .... **CLC 13, 58**
See also CA 101; CANR 70, 124; CWP

Jimenez (Mantecon), Juan Ramon
1881-1958 .... **HLC 1; PC 7; TCLC 4**
See also CA 104; 131; CANR 74; DAM MULT, POET; DLB 134; EW 9; EWL 3; HW 1; MTCW 1, 2; RGWL 2, 3

Jimenez, Ramon
See Jimenez (Mantecon), Juan Ramon

Jimenez Mantecon, Juan
See Jimenez (Mantecon), Juan Ramon

Jin, Ha .... **CLC 109**
See Jin, Xuefei
See also CA 152; DLB 244, 292; SSFS 17

Jin, Xuefei 1956-
See Jin, Ha
See also CANR 91, 130; SSFS 17

Joel, Billy .... **CLC 26**
See Joel, William Martin

Joel, William Martin 1949-
See Joel, Billy
See also CA 108

Johann Sigurjonsson 1880-1919 .... **TCLC 27**
See also CA 170; DLB 293; EWL 3

John, Saint 10(?)-100 .... **CMLC 27, 63**

John of Salisbury c. 1115-1180 ..... **CMLC 63**

John of the Cross, St. 1542-1591 .... **LC 18**
See also RGWL 2, 3

John Paul II, Pope 1920- .... **CLC 128**
See also CA 106; 133

Johnson, B(ryan) S(tanley William)
1933-1973 .... **CLC 6, 9**
See also CA 9-12R; 53-56; CANR 9; DLB 14, 40; EWL 3; RGEL 2

Johnson, Benjamin F., of Boone
See Riley, James Whitcomb

Johnson, Charles (Richard) 1948- .... **BLC 2; CLC 7, 51, 65, 163**
See also AFAW 2; AMWS 6; BW 2, 3; CA 116; CAAS 18; CANR 42, 66, 82, 129; CN 7; DAM MULT; DLB 33, 278; MTCW 2; RGAL 4; SSFS 16

Johnson, Charles S(purgeon)
1893-1956 .... **HR 3**
See also BW 1, 3; CA 125; CANR 82; DLB 51, 91

Johnson, Denis 1949- . **CLC 52, 160; SSC 56**
See also CA 117; 121; CANR 71, 99; CN 7; DLB 120

Johnson, Diane 1934- .... **CLC 5, 13, 48**
See also BPFB 2; CA 41-44R; CANR 17, 40, 62, 95; CN 7; DLBY 1980; INT CANR-17; MTCW 1

Johnson, E. Pauline 1861-1913 .... **NNAL**
See also CA 150; DAC; DAM MULT; DLB 92, 175

Johnson, Eyvind (Olof Verner)
1900-1976 .... **CLC 14**
See also CA 73-76; 69-72; CANR 34, 101; DLB 259; EW 12; EWL 3

Johnson, Fenton 1888-1958 .... **BLC 2**
See also BW 1; CA 118; 124; DAM MULT; DLB 45, 50

Johnson, Georgia Douglas (Camp)
1880-1966 .... **HR 3**
See also BW 1; CA 125; DLB 51, 249; WP

Johnson, Helene 1907-1995 .... **HR 3**
See also CA 181; DLB 51; WP

Johnson, J. R.
See James, C(yril) L(ionel) R(obert)

Johnson, James Weldon 1871-1938 .. **BLC 2; HR 3; PC 24; TCLC 3, 19**
See also AFAW 1, 2; BW 1, 3; CA 104; 125; CANR 82; CDALB 1917-1929; CLR 32; DA3; DAM MULT, POET; DLB 51; EWL 3; EXPP; LMFS 2; MTCW 1, 2; PFS 1; RGAL 4; SATA 31; TUS

Johnson, Joyce 1935- .... **CLC 58**
See also BG 3; CA 125; 129; CANR 102

Johnson, Judith (Emlyn) 1936- .... **CLC 7, 15**
See Sherwin, Judith Johnson
See also CA 25-28R; 153; CANR 34

Johnson, Lionel (Pigot)
1867-1902 .... **TCLC 19**
See also CA 117; 209; DLB 19; RGEL 2

Johnson, Marguerite Annie
See Angelou, Maya

Johnson, Mel
See Malzberg, Barry N(athaniel)

Johnson, Pamela Hansford
1912-1981 .... **CLC 1, 7, 27**
See also CA 1-4R; 104; CANR 2, 28; DLB 15; MTCW 1, 2; RGEL 2

Johnson, Paul (Bede) 1928- .... **CLC 147**
See also BEST 89:4; CA 17-20R; CANR 34, 62, 100

Johnson, Robert .... **CLC 70**

Johnson, Robert 1911(?)-1938 .... **TCLC 69**
See also BW 3; CA 174

Johnson, Samuel 1709-1784 .... **LC 15, 52; WLC**
See also BRW 3; BRWR 1; CDBLB 1660-1789; DA; DAB; DAC; DAM MST; DLB 39, 95, 104, 142, 213; LMFS 1; RGEL 2; TEA

Johnson, Uwe 1934-1984 .. **CLC 5, 10, 15, 40**
See also CA 1-4R; 112; CANR 1, 39; CD-WLB 2; DLB 75; EWL 3; MTCW 1; RGWL 2, 3

Johnston, Basil H. 1929- .... **NNAL**
See also CA 69-72; CANR 11, 28, 66; DAC; DAM MULT; DLB 60

Johnston, George (Benson) 1913- .... **CLC 51**
See also CA 1-4R; CANR 5, 20; CP 7; DLB 88

Johnston, Jennifer (Prudence)
1930- .... **CLC 7, 150**
See also CA 85-88; CANR 92; CN 7; DLB 14

Joinville, Jean de 1224(?)-1317 ..... **CMLC 38**

Jolley, (Monica) Elizabeth 1923- ..... **CLC 46; SSC 19**
See also CA 127; CAAS 13; CANR 59; CN 7; EWL 3; RGSF 2

Jones, Arthur Llewellyn 1863-1947
See Machen, Arthur
See also CA 104; 179; HGG

Jones, D(ouglas) G(ordon) 1929- ..... **CLC 10**
See also CA 29-32R; CANR 13, 90; CP 7; DLB 53

Jones, David (Michael) 1895-1974 .... **CLC 2, 4, 7, 13, 42**
See also BRW 6; BRWS 7; CA 9-12R; 53-56; CANR 28; CDBLB 1945-1960; DLB 20, 100; EWL 3; MTCW 1; PAB; RGEL 2

Jones, David Robert 1947-
See Bowie, David
See also CA 103; CANR 104

Jones, Diana Wynne 1934- .... **CLC 26**
See also AAYA 12; BYA 6, 7, 9, 11, 13, 16; CA 49-52; CANR 4, 26, 56, 120; CLR 23; DLB 161; FANT; JRDA; MAICYA 1, 2; SAAS 7; SATA 9, 70, 108; SFW 4; SUFW 2; YAW

Jones, Edward P. 1950- .... **CLC 76**
See also BW 2, 3; CA 142; CANR 79; CSW

Jones, Gayl 1949- ...... **BLC 2; CLC 6, 9, 131**
See also AFAW 1, 2; BW 2, 3; CA 77-80; CANR 27, 66, 122; CN 7; CSW; DA3; DAM MULT; DLB 33, 278; MTCW 1, 2; RGAL 4

Jones, James 1921-1977 ...... **CLC 1, 3, 10, 39**
See also AITN 1, 2; AMWS 11; BPFB 2; CA 1-4R; 69-72; CANR 6; DLB 2, 143; DLBD 17; DLBY 1998; EWL 3; MTCW 1; RGAL 4

Jones, John J.
See Lovecraft, H(oward) P(hillips)

Jones, LeRoi .... **CLC 1, 2, 3, 5, 10, 14**
See Baraka, Amiri
See also MTCW 2

Jones, Louis B. 1953- .... **CLC 65**
See also CA 141; CANR 73

Jones, Madison (Percy, Jr.) 1925- ...... **CLC 4**
See also CA 13-16R; CAAS 11; CANR 7, 54, 83; CN 7; CSW; DLB 152

Jones, Mervyn 1922- .... **CLC 10, 52**
See also CA 45-48; CAAS 5; CANR 1, 91; CN 7; MTCW 1

Jones, Mick 1956(?)- .... **CLC 30**

Jones, Nettie (Pearl) 1941- .... **CLC 34**
See also BW 2; CA 137; CAAS 20; CANR 88

Jones, Peter 1802-1856 .... **NNAL**

Jones, Preston 1936-1979 .... **CLC 10**
See also CA 73-76; 89-92; DLB 7

Jones, Robert F(rancis) 1934-2003 .... **CLC 7**
See also CA 49-52; CANR 2, 61, 118

Jones, Rod 1953- .... **CLC 50**
See also CA 128

Jones, Terence Graham Parry
1942- .... **CLC 21**
See Jones, Terry; Monty Python
See also CA 112; 116; CANR 35, 93; INT CA-116; SATA 127

Jones, Terry
See Jones, Terence Graham Parry
See also SATA 67; SATA-Brief 51

Jones, Thom (Douglas) 1945(?)- ..... **CLC 81; SSC 56**
See also CA 157; CANR 88; DLB 244

Koch, Kenneth (Jay) 1925-2002 .... **CLC 5, 8, 44**
    See also CA 1-4R; 207; CAD; CANR 6, 36, 57, 97, 131; CD 5; CP 7; DAM POET; DLB 5; INT CANR-36; MTCW 2; PFS 20; SATA 65; WP

Kochanowski, Jan 1530-1584 .... **LC 10**
    See also RGWL 2, 3

Kock, Charles Paul de 1794-1871 . **NCLC 16**

Koda Rohan
    See Koda Shigeyuki

Koda Rohan
    See Koda Shigeyuki
    See also DLB 180

Koda Shigeyuki 1867-1947 .... **TCLC 22**
    See Koda Rohan
    See also CA 121; 183

Koestler, Arthur 1905-1983 ... **CLC 1, 3, 6, 8, 15, 33**
    See also BRWS 1; CA 1-4R; 109; CANR 1, 33; CDBLB 1945-1960; DLBY 1983; EWL 3; MTCW 1, 2; NFS 19; RGEL 2

Kogawa, Joy Nozomi 1935- .... **CLC 78, 129**
    See also AAYA 47; CA 101; CANR 19, 62, 126; CN 7; CWP; DAC; DAM MST, MULT; FW; MTCW 2; NFS 3; SATA 99

Kohout, Pavel 1928- .... **CLC 13**
    See also CA 45-48; CANR 3

Koizumi, Yakumo
    See Hearn, (Patricio) Lafcadio (Tessima Carlos)

Kolmar, Gertrud 1894-1943 .... **TCLC 40**
    See also CA 167; EWL 3

Komunyakaa, Yusef 1947- .. **BLCS; CLC 86, 94; PC 51**
    See also AFAW 2; AMWS 13; CA 147; CANR 83; CP 7; CSW; DLB 120; EWL 3; PFS 5, 20; RGAL 4

Konrad, George
    See Konrad, Gyorgy
    See also CWW 2

Konrad, Gyorgy 1933- .... **CLC 4, 10, 73**
    See Konrad, George
    See also CA 85-88; CANR 97; CDWLB 4; CWW 2; DLB 232; EWL 3

Konwicki, Tadeusz 1926- .... **CLC 8, 28, 54, 117**
    See also CA 101; CAAS 9; CANR 39, 59; CWW 2; DLB 232; EWL 3; IDFW 3; MTCW 1

Koontz, Dean R(ay) 1945- .... **CLC 78**
    See also AAYA 9, 31; BEST 89:3, 90:2; CA 108; CANR 19, 36, 52, 95; CMW 4; CPW; DA3; DAM NOV, POP; DLB 292; HGG; MTCW 1; SATA 92; SFW 4; SUFW 2; YAW

Kopernik, Mikolaj
    See Copernicus, Nicolaus

Kopit, Arthur (Lee) 1937- ...... **CLC 1, 18, 33**
    See also AITN 1; CA 81-84; CABS 3; CD 5; DAM DRAM; DFS 7, 14; DLB 7; MTCW 1; RGAL 4

Kopitar, Jernej (Bartholomaus) 1780-1844 .... **NCLC 117**

Kops, Bernard 1926- .... **CLC 4**
    See also CA 5-8R; CANR 84; CBD; CN 7; CP 7; DLB 13

Kornbluth, C(yril) M. 1923-1958 .... **TCLC 8**
    See also CA 105; 160; DLB 8; SFW 4

Korolenko, V. G.
    See Korolenko, Vladimir Galaktionovich

Korolenko, Vladimir
    See Korolenko, Vladimir Galaktionovich

Korolenko, Vladimir G.
    See Korolenko, Vladimir Galaktionovich

Korolenko, Vladimir Galaktionovich 1853-1921 .... **TCLC 22**
    See also CA 121; DLB 277

Korzybski, Alfred (Habdank Skarbek) 1879-1950 .... **TCLC 61**
    See also CA 123; 160

Kosinski, Jerzy (Nikodem) 1933-1991 .... **CLC 1, 2, 3, 6, 10, 15, 53, 70**
    See also AMWS 7; BPFB 2; CA 17-20R; 134; CANR 9, 46; DA3; DAM NOV; DLB 2, 299; DLBY 1982; EWL 3; HGG; MTCW 1, 2; NFS 12; RGAL 4; TUS

Kostelanetz, Richard (Cory) 1940- .. **CLC 28**
    See also CA 13-16R; CAAS 8; CANR 38, 77; CN 7; CP 7

Kostrowitzki, Wilhelm Apollinaris de 1880-1918
    See Apollinaire, Guillaume
    See also CA 104

Kotlowitz, Robert 1924- .... **CLC 4**
    See also CA 33-36R; CANR 36

Kotzebue, August (Friedrich Ferdinand) von 1761-1819 .... **NCLC 25**
    See also DLB 94

Kotzwinkle, William 1938- ..... **CLC 5, 14, 35**
    See also BPFB 2; CA 45-48; CANR 3, 44, 84, 129; CLR 6; DLB 173; FANT; MAICYA 1, 2; SATA 24, 70, 146; SFW 4; SUFW 2; YAW

Kowna, Stancy
    See Szymborska, Wislawa

Kozol, Jonathan 1936- .... **CLC 17**
    See also AAYA 46; CA 61-64; CANR 16, 45, 96

Kozoll, Michael 1940(?)- .... **CLC 35**

Kramer, Kathryn 19(?)- .... **CLC 34**

Kramer, Larry 1935- .... **CLC 42; DC 8**
    See also CA 124; 126; CANR 60, 132; DAM POP; DLB 249; GLL 1

Krasicki, Ignacy 1735-1801 .... **NCLC 8**

Krasinski, Zygmunt 1812-1859 .... **NCLC 4**
    See also RGWL 2, 3

Kraus, Karl 1874-1936 .... **TCLC 5**
    See also CA 104; 216; DLB 118; EWL 3

Kreve (Mickevicius), Vincas 1882-1954 .... **TCLC 27**
    See also CA 170; DLB 220; EWL 3

Kristeva, Julia 1941- .... **CLC 77, 140**
    See also CA 154; CANR 99; DLB 242; EWL 3; FW; LMFS 2

Kristofferson, Kris 1936- .... **CLC 26**
    See also CA 104

Krizanc, John 1956- .... **CLC 57**
    See also CA 187

Krleza, Miroslav 1893-1981 .... **CLC 8, 114**
    See also CA 97-100; 105; CANR 50; CDWLB 4; DLB 147; EW 11; RGWL 2, 3

Kroetsch, Robert 1927- .. **CLC 5, 23, 57, 132**
    See also CA 17-20R; CANR 8, 38; CCA 1; CN 7; CP 7; DAC; DAM POET; DLB 53; MTCW 1

Kroetz, Franz
    See Kroetz, Franz Xaver

Kroetz, Franz Xaver 1946- .... **CLC 41**
    See also CA 130; EWL 3

Kroker, Arthur (W.) 1945- .... **CLC 77**
    See also CA 161

Kropotkin, Peter (Aleksieevich) 1842-1921 .... **TCLC 36**
    See Kropotkin, Petr Alekseevich
    See also CA 119; 219

Kropotkin, Petr Alekseevich
    See Kropotkin, Peter (Aleksieevich)
    See also DLB 277

Krotkov, Yuri 1917-1981 .... **CLC 19**
    See also CA 102

Krumb
    See Crumb, R(obert)

Krumgold, Joseph (Quincy) 1908-1980 .... **CLC 12**
    See also BYA 1, 2; CA 9-12R; 101; CANR 7; MAICYA 1, 2; SATA 1, 48; SATA-Obit 23; YAW

Krumwitz
    See Crumb, R(obert)

Krutch, Joseph Wood 1893-1970 ..... **CLC 24**
    See also ANW; CA 1-4R; 25-28R; CANR 4; DLB 63, 206, 275

Krutzch, Gus
    See Eliot, T(homas) S(tearns)

Krylov, Ivan Andreevich 1768(?)-1844 .... **NCLC 1**
    See also DLB 150

Kubin, Alfred (Leopold Isidor) 1877-1959 .... **TCLC 23**
    See also CA 112; 149; CANR 104; DLB 81

Kubrick, Stanley 1928-1999 .... **CLC 16; TCLC 112**
    See also AAYA 30; CA 81-84; 177; CANR 33; DLB 26

Kumin, Maxine (Winokur) 1925- ..... **CLC 5, 13, 28, 164; PC 15**
    See also AITN 2; AMWS 4; ANW; CA 1-4R; CAAS 8; CANR 1, 21, 69, 115; CP 7; CWP; DA3; DAM POET; DLB 5; EWL 3; EXPP; MTCW 1, 2; PAB; PFS 18; SATA 12

Kundera, Milan 1929- . **CLC 4, 9, 19, 32, 68, 115, 135; SSC 24**
    See also AAYA 2; BPFB 2; CA 85-88; CANR 19, 52, 74; CDWLB 4; CWW 2; DA3; DAM NOV; DLB 232; EW 13; EWL 3; MTCW 1, 2; NFS 18; RGSF 2; RGWL 3; SSFS 10

Kunene, Mazisi (Raymond) 1930- ... **CLC 85**
    See also BW 1, 3; CA 125; CANR 81; CP 7; DLB 117

Kung, Hans .... **CLC 130**
    See Kung, Hans

Kung, Hans 1928-
    See Kung, Hans
    See also CA 53-56; CANR 66; MTCW 1, 2

Kunikida Doppo 1869(?)-1908
    See Doppo, Kunikida
    See also DLB 180; EWL 3

Kunitz, Stanley (Jasspon) 1905- .. **CLC 6, 11, 14, 148; PC 19**
    See also AMWS 3; CA 41-44R; CANR 26, 57, 98; CP 7; DA3; DLB 48; INT CANR-26; MTCW 1, 2; PFS 11; RGAL 4

Kunze, Reiner 1933- .... **CLC 10**
    See also CA 93-96; CWW 2; DLB 75; EWL 3

Kuprin, Aleksander Ivanovich 1870-1938 .... **TCLC 5**
    See Kuprin, Aleksandr Ivanovich; Kuprin, Alexandr Ivanovich
    See also CA 104; 182

Kuprin, Aleksandr Ivanovich
    See Kuprin, Aleksander Ivanovich
    See also DLB 295

Kuprin, Alexandr Ivanovich
    See Kuprin, Aleksander Ivanovich
    See also EWL 3

Kureishi, Hanif 1954(?)- .... **CLC 64, 135**
    See also CA 139; CANR 113; CBD; CD 5; CN 7; DLB 194, 245; GLL 2; IDFW 4; WLIT 4; WWE 1

Kurosawa, Akira 1910-1998 ..... **CLC 16, 119**
    See also AAYA 11; CA 101; 170; CANR 46; DAM MULT

Kushner, Tony 1956(?)- .... **CLC 81; DC 10**
    See also AMWS 9; CA 144; CAD; CANR 74, 130; CD 5; DA3; DAM DRAM; DFS 5; DLB 228; EWL 3; GLL 1; LAIT 5; MTCW 2; RGAL 4

Las Casas, Bartolome de
1474-1566 .... **HLCS; LC 31**
See Casas, Bartolome de las
See also LAW

Lasch, Christopher 1932-1994 .... **CLC 102**
See also CA 73-76; 144; CANR 25, 118;
DLB 246; MTCW 1, 2

Lasker-Schueler, Else 1869-1945 ... **TCLC 57**
See Lasker-Schuler, Else
See also CA 183; DLB 66, 124

Lasker-Schuler, Else
See Lasker-Schueler, Else
See also EWL 3

Laski, Harold J(oseph) 1893-1950 . **TCLC 79**
See also CA 188

Latham, Jean Lee 1902-1995 .... **CLC 12**
See also AITN 1; BYA 1; CA 5-8R; CANR
7, 84; CLR 50; MAICYA 1, 2; SATA 2,
68; YAW

Latham, Mavis
See Clark, Mavis Thorpe

Lathen, Emma .... **CLC 2**
See Hennissart, Martha; Latsis, Mary J(ane)
See also BPFB 2; CMW 4

Lathrop, Francis
See Leiber, Fritz (Reuter, Jr.)

Latsis, Mary J(ane) 1927(?)-1997
See Lathen, Emma
See also CA 85-88; 162; CMW 4

Lattany, Kristin
See Lattany, Kristin (Elaine Eggleston)
Hunter

Lattany, Kristin (Elaine Eggleston) Hunter
1931- .... **CLC 35**
See also AITN 1; BW 1; BYA 3; CA 13-
16R; CANR 13, 108; CLR 3; CN 7; DLB
33; INT CANR-13; MAICYA 1, 2; SAAS
10; SATA 12, 132; YAW

Lattimore, Richmond (Alexander)
1906-1984 .... **CLC 3**
See also CA 1-4R; 112; CANR 1

Laughlin, James 1914-1997 .... **CLC 49**
See also CA 21-24R; 162; CAAS 22; CANR
9, 47; CP 7; DLB 48; DLBY 1996, 1997

Laurence, (Jean) Margaret (Wemyss)
1926-1987 . **CLC 3, 6, 13, 50, 62; SSC 7**
See also BYA 13; CA 5-8R; 121; CANR
33; DAC; DAM MST; DLB 53; EWL 3;
FW; MTCW 1, 2; NFS 11; RGEL 2;
RGSF 2; SATA-Obit 50; TCWW 2

Laurent, Antoine 1952- .... **CLC 50**

Lauscher, Hermann
See Hesse, Hermann

Lautreamont 1846-1870 .. **NCLC 12; SSC 14**
See Lautreamont, Isidore Lucien Ducasse
See also GFL 1789 to the Present; RGWL
2, 3

Lautreamont, Isidore Lucien Ducasse
See Lautreamont
See also DLB 217

Lavater, Johann Kaspar
1741-1801 .... **NCLC 142**
See also DLB 97

Laverty, Donald
See Blish, James (Benjamin)

Lavin, Mary 1912-1996 . **CLC 4, 18, 99; SSC
4, 67**
See also CA 9-12R; 151; CANR 33; CN 7;
DLB 15; FW; MTCW 1; RGEL 2; RGSF
2

Lavond, Paul Dennis
See Kornbluth, C(yril) M.; Pohl, Frederik

Lawler, Ray
See Lawler, Raymond Evenor
See also DLB 289

Lawler, Raymond Evenor 1922- .... **CLC 58**
See Lawler, Ray
See also CA 103; CD 5; RGEL 2

Lawrence, D(avid) H(erbert Richards)
1885-1930 .... **PC 54; SSC 4, 19, 73;
TCLC 2, 9, 16, 33, 48, 61, 93; WLC**
See Chambers, Jessie
See also BPFB 2; BRW 7; BRWR 2; CA
104; 121; CANR 131; CDBLB 1914-
1945; DA; DA3; DAB; DAC; DAM MST,
NOV, POET; DLB 10, 19, 36, 98, 162,
195; EWL 3; EXPP; EXPS; LAIT 2, 3;
MTCW 1, 2; NFS 18; PFS 6; RGEL 2;
RGSF 2; SSFS 2, 6; TEA; WLIT 4; WP

Lawrence, T(homas) E(dward)
1888-1935 .... **TCLC 18**
See Dale, Colin
See also BRWS 2; CA 115; 167; DLB 195

Lawrence of Arabia
See Lawrence, T(homas) E(dward)

Lawson, Henry (Archibald Hertzberg)
1867-1922 .... **SSC 18; TCLC 27**
See also CA 120; 181; DLB 230; RGEL 2;
RGSF 2

Lawton, Dennis
See Faust, Frederick (Schiller)

Layamon fl. c. 1200- .... **CMLC 10**
See Laȝamon
See also DLB 146; RGEL 2

Laye, Camara 1928-1980 ..... **BLC 2; CLC 4,
38**
See Camara Laye
See also AFW; BW 1; CA 85-88; 97-100;
CANR 25; DAM MULT; MTCW 1, 2;
WLIT 2

Layton, Irving (Peter) 1912- .... **CLC 2, 15,
164**
See also CA 1-4R; CANR 2, 33, 43, 66,
129; CP 7; DAC; DAM MST, POET;
DLB 88; EWL 3; MTCW 1, 2; PFS 12;
RGEL 2

Lazarus, Emma 1849-1887 ...... **NCLC 8, 109**

Lazarus, Felix
See Cable, George Washington

Lazarus, Henry
See Slavitt, David R(ytman)

Lea, Joan
See Neufeld, John (Arthur)

Leacock, Stephen (Butler)
1869-1944 .... **SSC 39; TCLC 2**
See also CA 104; 141; CANR 80; DAC;
DAM MST; DLB 92; EWL 3; MTCW 2;
RGEL 2; RGSF 2

Lead, Jane Ward 1623-1704 .... **LC 72**
See also DLB 131

Leapor, Mary 1722-1746 .... **LC 80**
See also DLB 109

Lear, Edward 1812-1888 .... **NCLC 3**
See also AAYA 48; BRW 5; CLR 1, 75;
DLB 32, 163, 166; MAICYA 1, 2; RGEL
2; SATA 18, 100; WCH; WP

Lear, Norman (Milton) 1922- .... **CLC 12**
See also CA 73-76

Leautaud, Paul 1872-1956 .... **TCLC 83**
See also CA 203; DLB 65; GFL 1789 to the
Present

Leavis, F(rank) R(aymond)
1895-1978 .... **CLC 24**
See also BRW 7; CA 21-24R; 77-80; CANR
44; DLB 242; EWL 3; MTCW 1, 2;
RGEL 2

Leavitt, David 1961- .... **CLC 34**
See also CA 116; 122; CANR 50, 62, 101;
CPW; DA3; DAM POP; DLB 130; GLL
1; INT CA-122; MTCW 2

Leblanc, Maurice (Marie Emile)
1864-1941 .... **TCLC 49**
See also CA 110; CMW 4

Lebowitz, Fran(ces Ann) 1951(?)- ... **CLC 11,
36**
See also CA 81-84; CANR 14, 60, 70; INT
CANR-14; MTCW 1

Lebrecht, Peter
See Tieck, (Johann) Ludwig

le Carre, John .... **CLC 3, 5, 9, 15, 28**
See Cornwell, David (John Moore)
See also AAYA 42; BEST 89:4; BPFB 2;
BRWS 2; CDBLB 1960 to Present; CMW
4; CN 7; CPW; DLB 87; EWL 3; MSW;
MTCW 2; RGEL 2; TEA

Le Clezio, J(ean) M(arie) G(ustave)
1940- .... **CLC 31, 155**
See also CA 116; 128; DLB 83; EWL 3;
GFL 1789 to the Present; RGSF 2

Leconte de Lisle, Charles-Marie-Rene
1818-1894 .... **NCLC 29**
See also DLB 217; EW 6; GFL 1789 to the
Present

Le Coq, Monsieur
See Simenon, Georges (Jacques Christian)

Leduc, Violette 1907-1972 .... **CLC 22**
See also CA 13-14; 33-36R; CANR 69;
CAP 1; EWL 3; GFL 1789 to the Present;
GLL 1

Ledwidge, Francis 1887(?)-1917 .... **TCLC 23**
See also CA 123; 203; DLB 20

Lee, Andrea 1953- .... **BLC 2; CLC 36**
See also BW 1, 3; CA 125; CANR 82;
DAM MULT

Lee, Andrew
See Auchincloss, Louis (Stanton)

Lee, Chang-rae 1965- .... **CLC 91**
See also CA 148; CANR 89; LATS 1

Lee, Don L. .... **CLC 2**
See Madhubuti, Haki R.

Lee, George W(ashington)
1894-1976 .... **BLC 2; CLC 52**
See also BW 1; CA 125; CANR 83; DAM
MULT; DLB 51

Lee, (Nelle) Harper 1926- . **CLC 12, 60, 194;
WLC**
See also AAYA 13; AMWS 8; BPFB 2;
BYA 3; CA 13-16R; CANR 51, 128;
CDALB 1941-1968; CSW; DA; DA3;
DAB; DAC; DAM MST, NOV; DLB 6;
EXPN; LAIT 3; MTCW 1, 2; NFS 2;
SATA 11; WYA; YAW

Lee, Helen Elaine 1959(?)- .... **CLC 86**
See also CA 148

Lee, John .... **CLC 70**

Lee, Julian
See Latham, Jean Lee

Lee, Larry
See Lee, Lawrence

Lee, Laurie 1914-1997 .... **CLC 90**
See also CA 77-80; 158; CANR 33, 73; CP
7; CPW; DAB; DAM POP; DLB 27;
MTCW 1; RGEL 2

Lee, Lawrence 1941-1990 .... **CLC 34**
See also CA 131; CANR 43

Lee, Li-Young 1957- .... **CLC 164; PC 24**
See also CA 153; CANR 118; CP 7; DLB
165; LMFS 2; PFS 11, 15, 17

Lee, Manfred B(ennington)
1905-1971 .... **CLC 11**
See Queen, Ellery
See also CA 1-4R; 29-32R; CANR 2; CMW
4; DLB 137

Lee, Nathaniel 1645(?)-1692 .... **LC 103**
See also DLB 80; RGEL 2

Lee, Shelton Jackson 1957(?)- .. **BLCS; CLC
105**
See Lee, Spike
See also BW 2, 3; CA 125; CANR 42;
DAM MULT

Lee, Spike
See Lee, Shelton Jackson
See also AAYA 4, 29

Lee, Stan 1922- .... **CLC 17**
See also AAYA 5, 49; CA 108; 111; CANR
129; INT CA-111

Lee, Tanith 1947- .... **CLC 46**
See also AAYA 15; CA 37-40R; CANR 53,
102; DLB 261; FANT; SATA 8, 88, 134;
SFW 4; SUFW 1, 2; YAW

Lee, Vernon .... **SSC 33; TCLC 5**
See Paget, Violet
See also DLB 57, 153, 156, 174, 178; GLL
1; SUFW 1

Lee, William
See Burroughs, William S(eward)
See also GLL 1

Lee, Willy
See Burroughs, William S(eward)
See also GLL 1

Lee-Hamilton, Eugene (Jacob)
1845-1907 .... **TCLC 22**
See also CA 117

Leet, Judith 1935- .... **CLC 11**
See also CA 187

Le Fanu, Joseph Sheridan
1814-1873 .... **NCLC 9, 58; SSC 14**
See also CMW 4; DA3; DAM POP; DLB
21, 70, 159, 178; HGG; RGEL 2; RGSF
2; SUFW 1

Leffland, Ella 1931- .... **CLC 19**
See also CA 29-32R; CANR 35, 78, 82;
DLBY 1984; INT CANR-35; SATA 65

Leger, Alexis
See Leger, (Marie-Rene Auguste) Alexis
Saint-Leger

Leger, (Marie-Rene Auguste) Alexis
Saint-Leger 1887-1975 .. **CLC 4, 11, 46;
PC 23**
See Perse, Saint-John; Saint-John Perse
See also CA 13-16R; 61-64; CANR 43;
DAM POET; MTCW 1

Leger, Saintleger
See Leger, (Marie-Rene Auguste) Alexis
Saint-Leger

Le Guin, Ursula K(roeber) 1929- ..... **CLC 8,
13, 22, 45, 71, 136; SSC 12, 69**
See also AAYA 9, 27; AITN 1; BPFB 2;
BYA 5, 8, 11, 14; CA 21-24R; CANR 9,
32, 52, 74, 132; CDALB 1968-1988; CLR
3, 28, 91; CN 7; CPW; DA3; DAB; DAC;
DAM MST, POP; DLB 8, 52, 256, 275;
EXPS; FANT; FW; INT CANR-32;
JRDA; LAIT 5; MAICYA 1, 2; MTCW 1,
2; NFS 6, 9; SATA 4, 52, 99, 149; SCFW;
SFW 4; SSFS 2; SUFW 1, 2; WYA; YAW

Lehmann, Rosamond (Nina)
1901-1990 .... **CLC 5**
See also CA 77-80; 131; CANR 8, 73; DLB
15; MTCW 2; RGEL 2; RHW

Leiber, Fritz (Reuter, Jr.)
1910-1992 .... **CLC 25**
See also BPFB 2; CA 45-48; 139; CANR 2,
40, 86; DLB 8; FANT; HGG; MTCW 1,
2; SATA 45; SATA-Obit 73; SCFW 2;
SFW 4; SUFW 1, 2

Leibnlz, Gottfried Wilhelm von
1646-1716 .... **LC 35**
See also DLB 168

Leimbach, Martha 1963-
See Leimbach, Marti
See also CA 130

Leimbach, Marti .... **CLC 65**
See Leimbach, Martha

Leino, Eino .... **TCLC 24**
See Lonnbohm, Armas Eino Leopold
See also EWL 3

Leiris, Michel (Julien) 1901-1990 ..... **CLC 61**
See also CA 119; 128; 132; EWL 3; GFL
1789 to the Present

Leithauser, Brad 1953- .... **CLC 27**
See also CA 107; CANR 27, 81; CP 7; DLB
120, 282

le Jars de Gournay, Marie
See de Gournay, Marie le Jars

Lelchuk, Alan 1938- .... **CLC 5**
See also CA 45-48; CAAS 20; CANR 1,
70; CN 7

Lem, Stanislaw 1921- ...... **CLC 8, 15, 40, 149**
See also CA 105; CAAS 1; CANR 32;
CWW 2; MTCW 1; SCFW 2; SFW 4

Lemann, Nancy (Elise) 1956- .... **CLC 39**
See also CA 118; 136; CANR 121

Lemonnier, (Antoine Louis) Camille
1844-1913 .... **TCLC 22**
See also CA 121

Lenau, Nikolaus 1802-1850 .... **NCLC 16**

L'Engle, Madeleine (Camp Franklin)
1918- .... **CLC 12**
See also AAYA 28; AITN 2; BPFB 2; BYA
2, 4, 5, 7; CA 1-4R; CANR 3, 21, 39, 66,
107; CLR 1, 14, 57; CPW; CWRI 5; DA3;
DAM POP; DLB 52; JRDA; MAICYA 1,
2; MTCW 1, 2; SAAS 15; SATA 1, 27,
75, 128; SFW 4; WYA; YAW

Lengyel, Jozsef 1896-1975 .... **CLC 7**
See also CA 85-88; 57-60; CANR 71;
RGSF 2

Lenin 1870-1924
See Lenin, V. I.
See also CA 121; 168

Lenin, V. I. .... **TCLC 67**
See Lenin

Lennon, John (Ono) 1940-1980 .. **CLC 12, 35**
See also CA 102; SATA 114

Lennox, Charlotte Ramsay
1729(?)-1804 .... **NCLC 23, 134**
See also DLB 39; RGEL 2

Lentricchia, Frank, (Jr.) 1940- .... **CLC 34**
See also CA 25-28R; CANR 19, 106; DLB
246

Lenz, Gunter .... **CLC 65**

Lenz, Jakob Michael Reinhold
1751-1792 .... **LC 100**
See also DLB 94; RGWL 2, 3

Lenz, Siegfried 1926- .... **CLC 27; SSC 33**
See also CA 89-92; CANR 80; CWW 2;
DLB 75; EWL 3; RGSF 2; RGWL 2, 3

Leon, David
See Jacob, (Cyprien-)Max

Leonard, Elmore (John, Jr.) 1925- . **CLC 28,
34, 71, 120**
See also AAYA 22, 59; AITN 1; BEST 89:1,
90:4; BPFB 2; CA 81-84; CANR 12, 28,
53, 76, 96; CMW 4; CN 7; CPW; DA3;
DAM POP; DLB 173, 226; INT CANR-
28; MSW; MTCW 1, 2; RGAL 4; TCWW
2

Leonard, Hugh .... **CLC 19**
See Byrne, John Keyes
See also CBD; CD 5; DFS 13; DLB 13

Leonov, Leonid (Maximovich)
1899-1994 .... **CLC 92**
See Leonov, Leonid Maksimovich
See also CA 129; CANR 74, 76; DAM
NOV; EWL 3; MTCW 1, 2

Leonov, Leonid Maksimovich
See Leonov, Leonid (Maximovich)
See also DLB 272

Leopardi, (Conte) Giacomo
1798-1837 .... **NCLC 22, 129; PC 37**
See also EW 5; RGWL 2, 3; WP

Le Reveler
See Artaud, Antonin (Marie Joseph)

Lerman, Eleanor 1952- .... **CLC 9**
See also CA 85-88; CANR 69, 124

Lerman, Rhoda 1936- .... **CLC 56**
See also CA 49-52; CANR 70

Lermontov, Mikhail Iur'evich
See Lermontov, Mikhail Yuryevich
See also DLB 205

Lermontov, Mikhail Yuryevich
1814-1841 .... **NCLC 5, 47, 126; PC 18**
See Lermontov, Mikhail Iur'evich
See also EW 6; RGWL 2, 3; TWA

Leroux, Gaston 1868-1927 .... **TCLC 25**
See also CA 108; 136; CANR 69; CMW 4;
NFS 20; SATA 65

Lesage, Alain-Rene 1668-1747 .... **LC 2, 28**
See also EW 3; GFL Beginnings to 1789;
RGWL 2, 3

Leskov, N(ikolai) S(emenovich) 1831-1895
See Leskov, Nikolai (Semyonovich)

Leskov, Nikolai (Semyonovich)
1831-1895 .... **NCLC 25; SSC 34**
See Leskov, Nikolai Semenovich

Leskov, Nikolai Semenovich
See Leskov, Nikolai (Semyonovich)
See also DLB 238

Lesser, Milton
See Marlowe, Stephen

Lessing, Doris (May) 1919- ... **CLC 1, 2, 3, 6,
10, 15, 22, 40, 94, 170; SSC 6, 61;
WLCS**
See also AAYA 57; AFW; BRWS 1; CA
9-12R; CAAS 14; CANR 33, 54, 76, 122;
CD 5; CDBLB 1960 to Present; CN 7;
DA; DA3; DAB; DAC; DAM MST, NOV;
DFS 20; DLB 15, 139; DLBY 1985; EWL
3; EXPS; FW; LAIT 4; MTCW 1, 2;
RGEL 2; RGSF 2; SFW 4; SSFS 1, 12,
20; TEA; WLIT 2, 4

Lessing, Gotthold Ephraim 1729-1781 . **LC 8**
See also CDWLB 2; DLB 97; EW 4; RGWL
2, 3

Lester, Richard 1932- .... **CLC 20**

Levenson, Jay .... **CLC 70**

Lever, Charles (James)
1806-1872 .... **NCLC 23**
See also DLB 21; RGEL 2

Leverson, Ada Esther
1862(?)-1933(?) .... **TCLC 18**
See Elaine
See also CA 117; 202; DLB 153; RGEL 2

Levertov, Denise 1923-1997 .. **CLC 1, 2, 3, 5,
8, 15, 28, 66; PC 11**
See also AMWS 3; CA 1-4R, 178; 163;
CAAE 178; CAAS 19; CANR 3, 29, 50,
108; CDALBS; CP 7; CWP; DAM POET;
DLB 5, 165; EWL 3; EXPP; FW; INT
CANR-29; MTCW 1, 2; PAB; PFS 7, 17;
RGAL 4; TUS; WP

Levi, Carlo 1902-1975 .... **TCLC 125**
See also CA 65-68; 53-56; CANR 10; EWL
3; RGWL 2, 3

Levi, Jonathan .... **CLC 76**
See also CA 197

Levi, Peter (Chad Tigar)
1931-2000 .... **CLC 41**
See also CA 5-8R; 187; CANR 34, 80; CP
7; DLB 40

Levi, Primo 1919-1987 ...... **CLC 37, 50; SSC
12; TCLC 109**
See also CA 13-16R; 122; CANR 12, 33,
61, 70, 132; DLB 177, 299; EWL 3;
MTCW 1, 2; RGWL 2, 3

Levin, Ira 1929- .... **CLC 3, 6**
See also CA 21-24R; CANR 17, 44, 74;
CMW 4; CN 7; CPW; DA3; DAM POP;
HGG; MTCW 1, 2; SATA 66; SFW 4

Levin, Meyer 1905-1981 .... **CLC 7**
See also AITN 1; CA 9-12R; 104; CANR
15; DAM POP; DLB 9, 28; DLBY 1981;
SATA 21; SATA-Obit 27

Levine, Norman 1924- .... **CLC 54**
See also CA 73-76; CAAS 23; CANR 14,
70; DLB 88

Levine, Philip 1928- .. **CLC 2, 4, 5, 9, 14, 33, 118; PC 22**
See also AMWS 5; CA 9-12R; CANR 9, 37, 52, 116; CP 7; DAM POET; DLB 5; EWL 3; PFS 8

Levinson, Deirdre 1931- .... **CLC 49**
See also CA 73-76; CANR 70

Levi-Strauss, Claude 1908- .... **CLC 38**
See also CA 1-4R; CANR 6, 32, 57; DLB 242; EWL 3; GFL 1789 to the Present; MTCW 1, 2; TWA

Levitin, Sonia (Wolff) 1934- .... **CLC 17**
See also AAYA 13, 48; CA 29-32R; CANR 14, 32, 79; CLR 53; JRDA; MAICYA 1, 2; SAAS 2; SATA 4, 68, 119, 131; SATA-Essay 131; YAW

Levon, O. U.
See Kesey, Ken (Elton)

Levy, Amy 1861-1889 .... **NCLC 59**
See also DLB 156, 240

Lewes, George Henry 1817-1878 ... **NCLC 25**
See also DLB 55, 144

Lewis, Alun 1915-1944 .... **SSC 40; TCLC 3**
See also BRW 7; CA 104; 188; DLB 20, 162; PAB; RGEL 2

Lewis, C. Day
See Day Lewis, C(ecil)

Lewis, C(live) S(taples) 1898-1963 .... **CLC 1, 3, 6, 14, 27, 124; WLC**
See also AAYA 3, 39; BPFB 2; BRWS 3; BYA 15, 16; CA 81-84; CANR 33, 71, 132; CDBLB 1945-1960; CLR 3, 27; CWRI 5; DA; DA3; DAB; DAC; DAM MST, NOV, POP; DLB 15, 100, 160, 255; EWL 3; FANT; JRDA; LMFS 2; MAICYA 1, 2; MTCW 1, 2; RGEL 2; SATA 13, 100; SCFW; SFW 4; SUFW 1; TEA; WCH; WYA; YAW

Lewis, Cecil Day
See Day Lewis, C(ecil)

Lewis, Janet 1899-1998 .... **CLC 41**
See Winters, Janet Lewis
See also CA 9-12R; 172; CANR 29, 63; CAP 1; CN 7; DLBY 1987; RHW; TCWW 2

Lewis, Matthew Gregory
1775-1818 .... **NCLC 11, 62**
See also DLB 39, 158, 178; HGG; LMFS 1; RGEL 2; SUFW

Lewis, (Harry) Sinclair 1885-1951 . **TCLC 4, 13, 23, 39; WLC**
See also AMW; AMWC 1; BPFB 2; CA 104; 133; CANR 132; CDALB 1917-1929; DA; DA3; DAB; DAC; DAM MST, NOV; DLB 9, 102, 284; DLBD 1; EWL 3; LAIT 3; MTCW 1, 2; NFS 15, 19; RGAL 4; TUS

Lewis, (Percy) Wyndham
1884(?)-1957 .. **SSC 34; TCLC 2, 9, 104**
See also BRW 7; CA 104; 157; DLB 15; EWL 3; FANT; MTCW 2; RGEL 2

Lewisohn, Ludwig 1883-1955 .... **TCLC 19**
See also CA 107; 203; DLB 4, 9, 28, 102

Lewton, Val 1904-1951 .... **TCLC 76**
See also CA 199; IDFW 3, 4

Leyner, Mark 1956- .... **CLC 92**
See also CA 110; CANR 28, 53; DA3; DLB 292; MTCW 2

Lezama Lima, Jose 1910-1976 .... **CLC 4, 10, 101; HLCS 2**
See also CA 77-80; CANR 71; DAM MULT; DLB 113, 283; EWL 3; HW 1, 2; LAW; RGWL 2, 3

L'Heureux, John (Clarke) 1934- ...... **CLC 52**
See also CA 13-16R; CANR 23, 45, 88; DLB 244

Li Ch'ing-chao 1081(?)-1141(?) .... **CMLC 71**

Liddell, C. H.
See Kuttner, Henry

Lie, Jonas (Lauritz Idemil)
1833-1908(?) .... **TCLC 5**
See also CA 115

Lieber, Joel 1937-1971 .... **CLC 6**
See also CA 73-76; 29-32R

Lieber, Stanley Martin
See Lee, Stan

Lieberman, Laurence (James)
1935- .... **CLC 4, 36**
See also CA 17-20R; CANR 8, 36, 89; CP 7

Lieh Tzu fl. 7th cent. B.C.-5th cent. B.C. .... **CMLC 27**

Lieksman, Anders
See Haavikko, Paavo Juhani

Li Fei-kan 1904-
See Pa Chin
See also CA 105; TWA

Lifton, Robert Jay 1926- .... **CLC 67**
See also CA 17-20R; CANR 27, 78; INT CANR-27; SATA 66

Lightfoot, Gordon 1938- .... **CLC 26**
See also CA 109

Lightman, Alan P(aige) 1948- .... **CLC 81**
See also CA 141; CANR 63, 105

Ligotti, Thomas (Robert) 1953- ...... **CLC 44; SSC 16**
See also CA 123; CANR 49; HGG; SUFW 2

Li Ho 791-817 .... **PC 13**

Li Ju-chen c. 1763-c. 1830 .... **NCLC 137**

Liliencron, (Friedrich Adolf Axel) Detlev von 1844-1909 .... **TCLC 18**
See also CA 117

Lille, Alain de
See Alain de Lille

Lilly, William 1602-1681 .... **LC 27**

Lima, Jose Lezama
See Lezama Lima, Jose

Lima Barreto, Afonso Henrique de
1881-1922 .... **TCLC 23**
See also CA 117; 181; LAW

Lima Barreto, Afonso Henriques de
See Lima Barreto, Afonso Henrique de

Limonov, Edward 1944- .... **CLC 67**
See also CA 137

Lin, Frank
See Atherton, Gertrude (Franklin Horn)

Lin, Yutang 1895-1976 .... **TCLC 149**
See also CA 45-48; 65-68; CANR 2; RGAL 4

Lincoln, Abraham 1809-1865 .... **NCLC 18**
See also LAIT 2

Lind, Jakov .... **CLC 1, 2, 4, 27, 82**
See Landwirth, Heinz
See also CAAS 4; DLB 299; EWL 3

Lindbergh, Anne (Spencer) Morrow
1906-2001 .... **CLC 82**
See also BPFB 2; CA 17-20R; 193; CANR 16, 73; DAM NOV; MTCW 1, 2; SATA 33; SATA-Obit 125; TUS

Lindsay, David 1878(?)-1945 .... **TCLC 15**
See also CA 113; 187; DLB 255; FANT; SFW 4; SUFW 1

Lindsay, (Nicholas) Vachel
1879-1931 .... **PC 23; TCLC 17; WLC**
See also AMWS 1; CA 114; 135; CANR 79; CDALB 1865-1917; DA; DA3; DAC; DAM MST, POET; DLB 54; EWL 3; EXPP; RGAL 4; SATA 40; WP

Linke-Poot
See Doeblin, Alfred

Linney, Romulus 1930- .... **CLC 51**
See also CA 1-4R; CAD; CANR 40, 44, 79; CD 5; CSW; RGAL 4

Linton, Eliza Lynn 1822-1898 .... **NCLC 41**
See also DLB 18

Li Po 701-763 .... **CMLC 2; PC 29**
See also PFS 20; WP

Lipsius, Justus 1547-1606 .... **LC 16**

Lipsyte, Robert (Michael) 1938- ...... **CLC 21**
See also AAYA 7, 45; CA 17-20R; CANR 8, 57; CLR 23, 76; DA; DAC; DAM MST, NOV; JRDA; LAIT 5; MAICYA 1, 2; SATA 5, 68, 113; WYA; YAW

Lish, Gordon (Jay) 1934- ... **CLC 45; SSC 18**
See also CA 113; 117; CANR 79; DLB 130; INT CA-117

Lispector, Clarice 1925(?)-1977 .... **CLC 43; HLCS 2; SSC 34**
See also CA 139; 116; CANR 71; CDWLB 3; DLB 113; DNFS 1; EWL 3; FW; HW 2; LAW; RGSF 2; RGWL 2, 3; WLIT 1

Littell, Robert 1935(?)- .... **CLC 42**
See also CA 109; 112; CANR 64, 115; CMW 4

Little, Malcolm 1925-1965
See Malcolm X
See also BW 1, 3; CA 125; 111; CANR 82; DA; DA3; DAB; DAC; DAM MST, MULT; MTCW 1, 2

Littlewit, Humphrey Gent.
See Lovecraft, H(oward) P(hillips)

Litwos
See Sienkiewicz, Henryk (Adam Alexander Pius)

Liu, E. 1857-1909 .... **TCLC 15**
See also CA 115; 190

Lively, Penelope (Margaret) 1933- .. **CLC 32, 50**
See also BPFB 2; CA 41-44R; CANR 29, 67, 79, 131; CLR 7; CN 7; CWRI 5; DAM NOV; DLB 14, 161, 207; FANT; JRDA; MAICYA 1, 2; MTCW 1, 2; SATA 7, 60, 101; TEA

Livesay, Dorothy (Kathleen)
1909-1996 .... **CLC 4, 15, 79**
See also AITN 2; CA 25-28R; CAAS 8; CANR 36, 67; DAC; DAM MST, POET; DLB 68; FW; MTCW 1; RGEL 2; TWA

Livy c. 59B.C.-c. 12 .... **CMLC 11**
See also AW 2; CDWLB 1; DLB 211; RGWL 2, 3

Lizardi, Jose Joaquin Fernandez de
1776-1827 .... **NCLC 30**
See also LAW

Llewellyn, Richard
See Llewellyn Lloyd, Richard Dafydd Vivian
See also DLB 15

Llewellyn Lloyd, Richard Dafydd Vivian
1906-1983 .... **CLC 7, 80**
See Llewellyn, Richard
See also CA 53-56; 111; CANR 7, 71; SATA 11; SATA-Obit 37

Llosa, (Jorge) Mario (Pedro) Vargas
See Vargas Llosa, (Jorge) Mario (Pedro)
See also RGWL 3

Llosa, Mario Vargas
See Vargas Llosa, (Jorge) Mario (Pedro)

Lloyd, Manda
See Mander, (Mary) Jane

Lloyd Webber, Andrew 1948-
See Webber, Andrew Lloyd
See also AAYA 1, 38; CA 116; 149; DAM DRAM; SATA 56

Llull, Ramon c. 1235-c. 1316 .... **CMLC 12**

Lobb, Ebenezer
See Upward, Allen

Locke, Alain (Le Roy)
1886-1954 .... **BLCS; HR 3; TCLC 43**
See also BW 1, 3; CA 106; 124; CANR 79; DLB 51; LMFS 2; RGAL 4

Locke, John 1632-1704 .... **LC 7, 35**
See also DLB 31, 101, 213, 252; RGEL 2; WLIT 3

Lurie, Alison 1926- ..... **CLC 4, 5, 18, 39, 175**
See also BPFB 2; CA 1-4R; CANR 2, 17, 50, 88; CN 7; DLB 2; MTCW 1; SATA 46, 112

Lustig, Arnost 1926- .... **CLC 56**
See also AAYA 3; CA 69-72; CANR 47, 102; CWW 2; DLB 232, 299; EWL 3; SATA 56

Luther, Martin 1483-1546 .... **LC 9, 37**
See also CDWLB 2; DLB 179; EW 2; RGWL 2, 3

Luxemburg, Rosa 1870(?)-1919 ..... **TCLC 63**
See also CA 118

Luzi, Mario 1914- .... **CLC 13**
See also CA 61-64; CANR 9, 70; CWW 2; DLB 128; EWL 3

L'vov, Arkady .... **CLC 59**

Lydgate, John c. 1370-1450(?) .... **LC 81**
See also BRW 1; DLB 146; RGEL 2

Lyly, John 1554(?)-1606 .... **DC 7; LC 41**
See also BRW 1; DAM DRAM; DLB 62, 167; RGEL 2

L'Ymagier
See Gourmont, Remy(-Marie-Charles) de

Lynch, B. Suarez
See Borges, Jorge Luis

Lynch, David (Keith) 1946- ...... **CLC 66, 162**
See also AAYA 55; CA 124; 129; CANR 111

Lynch, James
See Andreyev, Leonid (Nikolaevich)

Lyndsay, Sir David 1485-1555 .... **LC 20**
See also RGEL 2

Lynn, Kenneth S(chuyler)
1923-2001 .... **CLC 50**
See also CA 1-4R; 196; CANR 3, 27, 65

Lynx
See West, Rebecca

Lyons, Marcus
See Blish, James (Benjamin)

Lyotard, Jean-Francois
1924-1998 .... **TCLC 103**
See also DLB 242; EWL 3

Lyre, Pinchbeck
See Sassoon, Siegfried (Lorraine)

Lytle, Andrew (Nelson) 1902-1995 ... **CLC 22**
See also CA 9-12R; 150; CANR 70; CN 7; CSW; DLB 6; DLBY 1995; RGAL 4; RHW

Lyttelton, George 1709-1773 .... **LC 10**
See also RGEL 2

Lytton of Knebworth, Baron
See Bulwer-Lytton, Edward (George Earle Lytton)

Maas, Peter 1929-2001 .... **CLC 29**
See also CA 93-96; 201; INT CA-93-96; MTCW 2

Macaulay, Catherine 1731-1791 .... **LC 64**
See also DLB 104

Macaulay, (Emilie) Rose
1881(?)-1958 .... **TCLC 7, 44**
See also CA 104; DLB 36; EWL 3; RGEL 2; RHW

Macaulay, Thomas Babington
1800-1859 .... **NCLC 42**
See also BRW 4; CDBLB 1832-1890; DLB 32, 55; RGEL 2

MacBeth, George (Mann)
1932-1992 .... **CLC 2, 5, 9**
See also CA 25-28R; 136; CANR 61, 66; DLB 40; MTCW 1; PFS 8; SATA 4; SATA-Obit 70

MacCaig, Norman (Alexander)
1910-1996 .... **CLC 36**
See also BRWS 6; CA 9-12R; CANR 3, 34; CP 7; DAB; DAM POET; DLB 27; EWL 3; RGEL 2

MacCarthy, Sir (Charles Otto) Desmond
1877-1952 .... **TCLC 36**
See also CA 167

MacDiarmid, Hugh .... **CLC 2, 4, 11, 19, 63; PC 9**
See Grieve, C(hristopher) M(urray)
See also CDBLB 1945-1960; DLB 20; EWL 3; RGEL 2

MacDonald, Anson
See Heinlein, Robert A(nson)

Macdonald, Cynthia 1928- .... **CLC 13, 19**
See also CA 49-52; CANR 4, 44; DLB 105

MacDonald, George 1824-1905 .... **TCLC 9, 113**
See also AAYA 57; BYA 5; CA 106; 137; CANR 80; CLR 67; DLB 18, 163, 178; FANT; MAICYA 1, 2; RGEL 2; SATA 33, 100; SFW 4; SUFW; WCH

Macdonald, John
See Millar, Kenneth

MacDonald, John D(ann)
1916-1986 .... **CLC 3, 27, 44**
See also BPFB 2; CA 1-4R; 121; CANR 1, 19, 60; CMW 4; CPW; DAM NOV, POP; DLB 8; DLBY 1986; MSW; MTCW 1, 2; SFW 4

Macdonald, John Ross
See Millar, Kenneth

Macdonald, Ross ..... **CLC 1, 2, 3, 14, 34, 41**
See Millar, Kenneth
See also AMWS 4; BPFB 2; DLBD 6; MSW; RGAL 4

MacDougal, John
See Blish, James (Benjamin)

MacDougal, John
See Blish, James (Benjamin)

MacDowell, John
See Parks, Tim(othy Harold)

MacEwen, Gwendolyn (Margaret)
1941-1987 .... **CLC 13, 55**
See also CA 9-12R; 124; CANR 7, 22; DLB 53, 251; SATA 50; SATA-Obit 55

Macha, Karel Hynek 1810-1846 .... **NCLC 46**

Machado (y Ruiz), Antonio
1875-1939 .... **TCLC 3**
See also CA 104; 174; DLB 108; EW 9; EWL 3; HW 2; RGWL 2, 3

Machado de Assis, Joaquim Maria
1839-1908 ...... **BLC 2; HLCS 2; SSC 24; TCLC 10**
See also CA 107; 153; CANR 91; LAW; RGSF 2; RGWL 2, 3; TWA; WLIT 1

Machaut, Guillaume de c.
1300-1377 .... **CMLC 64**
See also DLB 208

Machen, Arthur .... **SSC 20; TCLC 4**
See Jones, Arthur Llewellyn
See also CA 179; DLB 156, 178; RGEL 2; SUFW 1

Machiavelli, Niccolo 1469-1527 ... **DC 16; LC 8, 36; WLCS**
See also AAYA 58; DA; DAB; DAC; DAM MST; EW 2; LAIT 1; LMFS 1; NFS 9; RGWL 2, 3; TWA

MacInnes, Colin 1914-1976 .... **CLC 4, 23**
See also CA 69-72; 65-68; CANR 21; DLB 14; MTCW 1, 2; RGEL 2; RHW

MacInnes, Helen (Clark)
1907-1985 .... **CLC 27, 39**
See also BPFB 2; CA 1-4R; 117; CANR 1, 28, 58; CMW 4; CPW; DAM POP; DLB 87; MSW; MTCW 1, 2; SATA 22; SATA-Obit 44

Mackay, Mary 1855-1924
See Corelli, Marie
See also CA 118; 177; FANT; RHW

Mackenzie, Compton (Edward Montague)
1883-1972 .... **CLC 18; TCLC 116**
See also CA 21-22; 37-40R; CAP 2; DLB 34, 100; RGEL 2

Mackenzie, Henry 1745-1831 .... **NCLC 41**
See also DLB 39; RGEL 2

Mackey, Nathaniel (Ernest) 1947- .... **PC 49**
See also CA 153; CANR 114; CP 7; DLB 169

MacKinnon, Catharine A. 1946- .... **CLC 181**
See also CA 128; 132; CANR 73; FW; MTCW 2

Mackintosh, Elizabeth 1896(?)-1952
See Tey, Josephine
See also CA 110; CMW 4

MacLaren, James
See Grieve, C(hristopher) M(urray)

Mac Laverty, Bernard 1942- .... **CLC 31**
See also CA 116; 118; CANR 43, 88; CN 7; DLB 267; INT CA-118; RGSF 2

MacLean, Alistair (Stuart)
1922(?)-1987 .... **CLC 3, 13, 50, 63**
See also CA 57-60; 121; CANR 28, 61; CMW 4; CPW; DAM POP; DLB 276; MTCW 1; SATA 23; SATA-Obit 50; TCWW 2

Maclean, Norman (Fitzroy)
1902-1990 .... **CLC 78; SSC 13**
See also CA 102; 132; CANR 49; CPW; DAM POP; DLB 206; TCWW 2

MacLeish, Archibald 1892-1982 ... **CLC 3, 8, 14, 68; PC 47**
See also AMW; CA 9-12R; 106; CAD; CANR 33, 63; CDALBS; DAM POET; DFS 15; DLB 4, 7, 45; DLBY 1982; EWL 3; EXPP; MTCW 1, 2; PAB; PFS 5; RGAL 4; TUS

MacLennan, (John) Hugh
1907-1990 .... **CLC 2, 14, 92**
See also CA 5-8R; 142; CANR 33; DAC; DAM MST; DLB 68; EWL 3; MTCW 1, 2; RGEL 2; TWA

MacLeod, Alistair 1936- .... **CLC 56, 165**
See also CA 123; CCA 1; DAC; DAM MST; DLB 60; MTCW 2; RGSF 2

Macleod, Fiona
See Sharp, William
See also RGEL 2; SUFW

MacNeice, (Frederick) Louis
1907-1963 .... **CLC 1, 4, 10, 53**
See also BRW 7; CA 85-88; CANR 61; DAB; DAM POET; DLB 10, 20; EWL 3; MTCW 1, 2; RGEL 2

MacNeill, Dand
See Fraser, George MacDonald

Macpherson, James 1736-1796 .... **LC 29**
See Ossian
See also BRWS 8; DLB 109; RGEL 2

Macpherson, (Jean) Jay 1931- .... **CLC 14**
See also CA 5-8R; CANR 90; CP 7; CWP; DLB 53

Macrobius fl. 430- .... **CMLC 48**

MacShane, Frank 1927-1999 .... **CLC 39**
See also CA 9-12R; 186; CANR 3, 33; DLB 111

Macumber, Mari
See Sandoz, Mari(e Susette)

Madach, Imre 1823-1864 .... **NCLC 19**

Madden, (Jerry) David 1933- .... **CLC 5, 15**
See also CA 1-4R; CAAS 3; CANR 4, 45; CN 7; CSW; DLB 6; MTCW 1

Maddern, Al(an)
See Ellison, Harlan (Jay)

Madhubuti, Haki R. 1942- ... **BLC 2; CLC 6, 73; PC 5**
See Lee, Don L.
See also BW 2, 3; CA 73-76; CANR 24, 51, 73; CP 7; CSW; DAM MULT, POET; DLB 5, 41; DLBD 8; EWL 3; MTCW 2; RGAL 4

McCullers, (Lula) Carson (Smith)
1917-1967 .... **CLC 1, 4, 10, 12, 48, 100;**
SSC 9, 24; WLC
See also AAYA 21; AMW; AMWC 2; BPFB
2; CA 5-8R; 25-28R; CABS 1, 3; CANR
18, 132; CDALB 1941-1968; DA; DA3;
DAB; DAC; DAM MST, NOV; DFS 5,
18; DLB 2, 7, 173, 228; EWL 3; EXPS;
FW; GLL 1; LAIT 3, 4; MAWW; MTCW
1, 2; NFS 6, 13; RGAL 4; RGSF 2; SATA
27; SSFS 5; TUS; YAW

McCulloch, John Tyler
See Burroughs, Edgar Rice

McCullough, Colleen 1938(?)- .. **CLC 27, 107**
See also AAYA 36; BPFB 2; CA 81-84;
CANR 17, 46, 67, 98; CPW; DA3; DAM
NOV, POP; MTCW 1, 2; RHW

McCunn, Ruthanne Lum 1946- .... **AAL**
See also CA 119; CANR 43, 96; LAIT 2;
SATA 63

McDermott, Alice 1953- .... **CLC 90**
See also CA 109; CANR 40, 90, 126; DLB
292

McElroy, Joseph 1930- .... **CLC 5, 47**
See also CA 17-20R; CN 7

McEwan, Ian (Russell) 1948- .... **CLC 13, 66,**
169
See also BEST 90:4; BRWS 4; CA 61-64;
CANR 14, 41, 69, 87, 132; CN 7; DAM
NOV; DLB 14, 194; HGG; MTCW 1, 2;
RGSF 2; SUFW 2; TEA

McFadden, David 1940- .... **CLC 48**
See also CA 104; CP 7; DLB 60; INT CA-
104

McFarland, Dennis 1950- .... **CLC 65**
See also CA 165; CANR 110

McGahern, John 1934- ... **CLC 5, 9, 48, 156;**
SSC 17
See also CA 17-20R; CANR 29, 68, 113;
CN 7; DLB 14, 231; MTCW 1

McGinley, Patrick (Anthony) 1937- . **CLC 41**
See also CA 120; 127; CANR 56; INT CA-
127

McGinley, Phyllis 1905-1978 .... **CLC 14**
See also CA 9-12R; 77-80; CANR 19;
CWRI 5; DLB 11, 48; PFS 9, 13; SATA
2, 44; SATA-Obit 24

McGinniss, Joe 1942- .... **CLC 32**
See also AITN 2; BEST 89:2; CA 25-28R;
CANR 26, 70; CPW; DLB 185; INT
CANR-26

McGivern, Maureen Daly
See Daly, Maureen

McGrath, Patrick 1950- .... **CLC 55**
See also CA 136; CANR 65; CN 7; DLB
231; HGG; SUFW 2

McGrath, Thomas (Matthew)
1916-1990 .... **CLC 28, 59**
See also AMWS 10; CA 9-12R; 132; CANR
6, 33, 95; DAM POET; MTCW 1; SATA
41; SATA-Obit 66

McGuane, Thomas (Francis III)
1939- .... **CLC 3, 7, 18, 45, 127**
See also AITN 2; BPFB 2; CA 49-52;
CANR 5, 24, 49, 94; CN 7; DLB 2, 212;
DLBY 1980; EWL 3; INT CANR-24;
MTCW 1; TCWW 2

McGuckian, Medbh 1950- .... **CLC 48, 174;**
PC 27
See also BRWS 5; CA 143; CP 7; CWP;
DAM POET; DLB 40

McHale, Tom 1942(?)-1982 .... **CLC 3, 5**
See also AITN 1; CA 77-80; 106

McIlvanney, William 1936- .... **CLC 42**
See also CA 25-28R; CANR 61; CMW 4;
DLB 14, 207

McIlwraith, Maureen Mollie Hunter
See Hunter, Mollie
See also SATA 2

McInerney, Jay 1955- .... **CLC 34, 112**
See also AAYA 18; BPFB 2; CA 116; 123;
CANR 45, 68, 116; CN 7; CPW; DA3;
DAM POP; DLB 292; INT CA-123;
MTCW 2

McIntyre, Vonda N(eel) 1948- .... **CLC 18**
See also CA 81-84; CANR 17, 34, 69;
MTCW 1; SFW 4; YAW

McKay, Claude .... **BLC 3; HR 3; PC 2;**
TCLC 7, 41; WLC
See McKay, Festus Claudius
See also AFAW 1, 2; AMWS 10; DAB;
DLB 4, 45, 51, 117; EWL 3; EXPP; GLL
2; LAIT 3; LMFS 2; PAB; PFS 4; RGAL
4; WP

McKay, Festus Claudius 1889-1948
See McKay, Claude
See also BW 1, 3; CA 104; 124; CANR 73;
DA; DAC; DAM MST, MULT, NOV,
POET; MTCW 1, 2; TUS

McKuen, Rod 1933- .... **CLC 1, 3**
See also AITN 1; CA 41-44R; CANR 40

McLoughlin, R. B.
See Mencken, H(enry) L(ouis)

McLuhan, (Herbert) Marshall
1911-1980 .... **CLC 37, 83**
See also CA 9-12R; 102; CANR 12, 34, 61;
DLB 88; INT CANR-12; MTCW 1, 2

McManus, Declan Patrick Aloysius
See Costello, Elvis

McMillan, Terry (L.) 1951- . **BLCS; CLC 50,**
61, 112
See also AAYA 21; AMWS 13; BPFB 2;
BW 2, 3; CA 140; CANR 60, 104, 131;
CPW; DA3; DAM MULT, NOV, POP;
MTCW 2; RGAL 4; YAW

McMurtry, Larry (Jeff) 1936- .. **CLC 2, 3, 7,**
11, 27, 44, 127
See also AAYA 15; AITN 2; AMWS 5;
BEST 89:2; BPFB 2; CA 5-8R; CANR
19, 43, 64, 103; CDALB 1968-1988; CN
7; CPW; CSW; DA3; DAM NOV, POP;
DLB 2, 143, 256; DLBY 1980, 1987;
EWL 3; MTCW 1, 2; RGAL 4; TCWW 2

McNally, T. M. 1961- .... **CLC 82**

McNally, Terrence 1939- .... **CLC 4, 7, 41, 91**
See also AMWS 13; CA 45-48; CAD;
CANR 2, 56, 116; CD 5; DA3; DAM
DRAM; DFS 16, 19; DLB 7, 249; EWL
3; GLL 1; MTCW 2

McNamer, Deirdre 1950- .... **CLC 70**

McNeal, Tom .... **CLC 119**

McNeile, Herman Cyril 1888-1937
See Sapper
See also CA 184; CMW 4; DLB 77

McNickle, (William) D'Arcy
1904-1977 .... **CLC 89; NNAL**
See also CA 9-12R; 85-88; CANR 5, 45;
DAM MULT; DLB 175, 212; RGAL 4;
SATA-Obit 22

McPhee, John (Angus) 1931- .... **CLC 36**
See also AMWS 3; ANW; BEST 90:1; CA
65-68; CANR 20, 46, 64, 69, 121; CPW;
DLB 185, 275; MTCW 1, 2; TUS

McPherson, James Alan 1943- . **BLCS; CLC**
19, 77
See also BW 1, 3; CA 25-28R; CAAS 17;
CANR 24, 74; CN 7; CSW; DLB 38, 244;
EWL 3; MTCW 1, 2; RGAL 4; RGSF 2

McPherson, William (Alexander)
1933- .... **CLC 34**
See also CA 69-72; CANR 28; INT
CANR-28

McTaggart, J. McT. Ellis
See McTaggart, John McTaggart Ellis

McTaggart, John McTaggart Ellis
1866-1925 .... **TCLC 105**
See also CA 120; DLB 262

Mead, George Herbert 1863-1931 . **TCLC 89**
See also CA 212; DLB 270

Mead, Margaret 1901-1978 .... **CLC 37**
See also AITN 1; CA 1-4R; 81-84; CANR
4; DA3; FW; MTCW 1, 2; SATA-Obit 20

Meaker, Marijane (Agnes) 1927-
See Kerr, M. E.
See also CA 107; CANR 37, 63; INT CA-
107; JRDA; MAICYA 1, 2; MAICYAS 1;
MTCW 1; SATA 20, 61, 99; SATA-Essay
111; YAW

Medoff, Mark (Howard) 1940- .... **CLC 6, 23**
See also AITN 1; CA 53-56; CAD; CANR
5; CD 5; DAM DRAM; DFS 4; DLB 7;
INT CANR-5

Medvedev, P. N.
See Bakhtin, Mikhail Mikhailovich

Meged, Aharon
See Megged, Aharon

Meged, Aron
See Megged, Aharon

Megged, Aharon 1920- .... **CLC 9**
See also CA 49-52; CAAS 13; CANR 1;
EWL 3

Mehta, Gita 1943- .... **CLC 179**
See also CA 225; DNFS 2

Mehta, Ved (Parkash) 1934- .... **CLC 37**
See also CA 1-4R; 212; CAAE 212; CANR
2, 23, 69; MTCW 1

Melanchthon, Philipp 1497-1560 .... **LC 90**
See also DLB 179

Melanter
See Blackmore, R(ichard) D(oddridge)

Meleager c. 140B.C.-c. 70B.C. ...... **CMLC 53**

Melies, Georges 1861-1938 .... **TCLC 81**

Melikow, Loris
See Hofmannsthal, Hugo von

Melmoth, Sebastian
See Wilde, Oscar (Fingal O'Flahertie Wills)

Melo Neto, Joao Cabral de
See Cabral de Melo Neto, Joao
See also CWW 2; EWL 3

Meltzer, Milton 1915- .... **CLC 26**
See also AAYA 8, 45; BYA 2, 6; CA 13-
16R; CANR 38, 92, 107; CLR 13; DLB
61; JRDA; MAICYA 1, 2; SAAS 1; SATA
1, 50, 80, 128; SATA-Essay 124; WYA;
YAW

Melville, Herman 1819-1891 ..... **NCLC 3, 12,**
29, 45, 49, 91, 93, 123; SSC 1, 17, 46;
WLC
See also AAYA 25; AMW; AMWR 1;
CDALB 1640-1865; DA; DA3; DAB;
DAC; DAM MST, NOV; DLB 3, 74, 250,
254; EXPN; EXPS; LAIT 1, 2; NFS 7, 9;
RGAL 4; RGSF 2; SATA 59; SSFS 3;
TUS

Members, Mark
See Powell, Anthony (Dymoke)

Membreno, Alejandro .... **CLC 59**

Menander c. 342B.C.-c. 293B.C. .... **CMLC 9,**
51; DC 3
See also AW 1; CDWLB 1; DAM DRAM;
DLB 176; LMFS 1; RGWL 2, 3

Menchu, Rigoberta 1959- .. **CLC 160; HLCS**
2
See also CA 175; DNFS 1; WLIT 1

Mencken, H(enry) L(ouis)
1880-1956 .... **TCLC 13**
See also AMW; CA 105; 125; CDALB
1917-1929; DLB 11, 29, 63, 137, 222;
EWL 3; MTCW 1, 2; NCFS 4; RGAL 4;
TUS

Mendelsohn, Jane 1965- .... **CLC 99**
See also CA 154; CANR 94

Menton, Francisco de
See Chin, Frank (Chew, Jr.)

Minehaha, Cornelius
See Wedekind, (Benjamin) Frank(lin)
Miner, Valerie 1947- .... **CLC 40**
See also CA 97-100; CANR 59; FW; GLL
2

Minimo, Duca
See D'Annunzio, Gabriele
Minot, Susan 1956- .... **CLC 44, 159**
See also AMWS 6; CA 134; CANR 118;
CN 7

Minus, Ed 1938- .... **CLC 39**
See also CA 185
Mirabai 1498(?)-1550(?) .... **PC 48**
Miranda, Javier
See Bioy Casares, Adolfo
See also CWW 2
Mirbeau, Octave 1848-1917 .... **TCLC 55**
See also CA 216; DLB 123, 192; GFL 1789
to the Present
Mirikitani, Janice 1942- .... **AAL**
See also CA 211; RGAL 4
Mirk, John (?)-c. 1414 .... **LC 105**
See also DLB 146
Miro (Ferrer), Gabriel (Francisco Victor)
1879-1930 .... **TCLC 5**
See also CA 104; 185; EWL 3
Misharin, Alexandr .... **CLC 59**
Mishima, Yukio ... **CLC 2, 4, 6, 9, 27; DC 1;**
SSC 4
See Hiraoka, Kimitake
See also AAYA 50; BPFB 2; GLL 1; MJW;
MTCW 2; RGSF 2; RGWL 2, 3; SSFS 5,
12
Mistral, Frederic 1830-1914 .... **TCLC 51**
See also CA 122; 213; GFL 1789 to the
Present
Mistral, Gabriela
See Godoy Alcayaga, Lucila
See also DLB 283; DNFS 1; EWL 3; LAW;
RGWL 2, 3; WP
Mistry, Rohinton 1952- ...... **CLC 71; SSC 73**
See also CA 141; CANR 86, 114; CCA 1;
CN 7; DAC; SSFS 6
Mitchell, Clyde
See Ellison, Harlan (Jay)
Mitchell, Emerson Blackhorse Barney
1945- .... **NNAL**
See also CA 45-48
Mitchell, James Leslie 1901-1935
See Gibbon, Lewis Grassic
See also CA 104; 188; DLB 15
Mitchell, Joni 1943- .... **CLC 12**
See also CA 112; CCA 1
Mitchell, Joseph (Quincy)
1908-1996 .... **CLC 98**
See also CA 77-80; 152; CANR 69; CN 7;
CSW; DLB 185; DLBY 1996
Mitchell, Margaret (Munnerlyn)
1900-1949 .... **TCLC 11**
See also AAYA 23; BPFB 2; BYA 1; CA
109; 125; CANR 55, 94; CDALBS; DA3;
DAM NOV, POP; DLB 9; LAIT 2;
MTCW 1, 2; NFS 9; RGAL 4; RHW;
TUS; WYAS 1; YAW
Mitchell, Peggy
See Mitchell, Margaret (Munnerlyn)
Mitchell, S(ilas) Weir 1829-1914 ... **TCLC 36**
See also CA 165; DLB 202; RGAL 4
Mitchell, W(illiam) O(rmond)
1914-1998 .... **CLC 25**
See also CA 77-80; 165; CANR 15, 43; CN
7; DAC; DAM MST; DLB 88
Mitchell, William (Lendrum)
1879-1936 .... **TCLC 81**
See also CA 213
Mitford, Mary Russell 1787-1855 ... **NCLC 4**
See also DLB 110, 116; RGEL 2
Mitford, Nancy 1904-1973 .... **CLC 44**
See also CA 9-12R; DLB 191; RGEL 2

Miyamoto, (Chujo) Yuriko
1899-1951 .... **TCLC 37**
See also CA 170, 174
Miyamoto Yuriko
See Miyamoto, (Chujo) Yuriko
See also DLB 180
Miyazawa, Kenji 1896-1933 .... **TCLC 76**
See Miyazawa Kenji
See also CA 157; RGWL 3
Miyazawa Kenji
See Miyazawa, Kenji
See also EWL 3
Mizoguchi, Kenji 1898-1956 .... **TCLC 72**
See also CA 167
Mo, Timothy (Peter) 1950(?)- ... **CLC 46, 134**
See also CA 117; CANR 128; CN 7; DLB
194; MTCW 1; WLIT 4; WWE 1
Modarressi, Taghi (M.) 1931-1997 ... **CLC 44**
See also CA 121; 134; INT CA-134
Modiano, Patrick (Jean) 1945- .... **CLC 18**
See also CA 85-88; CANR 17, 40, 115;
CWW 2; DLB 83, 299; EWL 3
Mofolo, Thomas (Mokopu)
1875(?)-1948 .... **BLC 3; TCLC 22**
See also AFW; CA 121; 153; CANR 83;
DAM MULT; DLB 225; EWL 3; MTCW
2; WLIT 2
Mohr, Nicholasa 1938- .... **CLC 12; HLC 2**
See also AAYA 8, 46; CA 49-52; CANR 1,
32, 64; CLR 22; DAM MULT; DLB 145;
HW 1, 2; JRDA; LAIT 5; LLW 1; MAI-
CYA 2; MAICYAS 1; RGAL 4; SAAS 8;
SATA 8, 97; SATA-Essay 113; WYA;
YAW
Moi, Toril 1953- .... **CLC 172**
See also CA 154; CANR 102; FW
Mojtabai, A(nn) G(race) 1938- ..... **CLC 5, 9,**
15, 29
See also CA 85-88; CANR 88
Moliere 1622-1673 ..... **DC 13; LC 10, 28, 64;**
WLC
See also DA; DA3; DAB; DAC; DAM
DRAM, MST; DFS 13, 18, 20; DLB 268;
EW 3; GFL Beginnings to 1789; LATS 1;
RGWL 2, 3; TWA
Molin, Charles
See Mayne, William (James Carter)
Molnar, Ferenc 1878-1952 .... **TCLC 20**
See also CA 109; 153; CANR 83; CDWLB
4; DAM DRAM; DLB 215; EWL 3;
RGWL 2, 3
Momaday, N(avarre) Scott 1934- ...... **CLC 2,**
19, 85, 95, 160; NNAL; PC 25; WLCS
See also AAYA 11; AMWS 4; ANW; BPFB
2; BYA 12; CA 25-28R; CANR 14, 34,
68; CDALBS; CN 7; CPW; DA; DA3;
DAB; DAC; DAM MST, MULT, NOV,
POP; DLB 143, 175, 256; EWL 3; EXPP;
INT CANR-14; LAIT 4; LATS 1; MTCW
1, 2; NFS 10; PFS 2, 11; RGAL 4; SATA
48; SATA-Brief 30; WP; YAW
Monette, Paul 1945-1995 .... **CLC 82**
See also AMWS 10; CA 139; 147; CN 7;
GLL 1
Monroe, Harriet 1860-1936 .... **TCLC 12**
See also CA 109; 204; DLB 54, 91
Monroe, Lyle
See Heinlein, Robert A(nson)
Montagu, Elizabeth 1720-1800 .... **NCLC 7,**
117
See also FW
Montagu, Mary (Pierrepont) Wortley
1689-1762 .... **LC 9, 57; PC 16**
See also DLB 95, 101; RGEL 2
Montagu, W. H.
See Coleridge, Samuel Taylor

Montague, John (Patrick) 1929- ..... **CLC 13,**
46
See also CA 9-12R; CANR 9, 69, 121; CP
7; DLB 40; EWL 3; MTCW 1; PFS 12;
RGEL 2
Montaigne, Michel (Eyquem) de
1533-1592 .... **LC 8, 105; WLC**
See also DA; DAB; DAC; DAM MST; EW
2; GFL Beginnings to 1789; LMFS 1;
RGWL 2, 3; TWA
Montale, Eugenio 1896-1981 ... **CLC 7, 9, 18;**
PC 13
See also CA 17-20R; 104; CANR 30; DLB
114; EW 11; EWL 3; MTCW 1; RGWL
2, 3; TWA
Montesquieu, Charles-Louis de Secondat
1689-1755 .... **LC 7, 69**
See also EW 3; GFL Beginnings to 1789;
TWA
Montessori, Maria 1870-1952 ...... **TCLC 103**
See also CA 115; 147
Montgomery, (Robert) Bruce 1921(?)-1978
See Crispin, Edmund
See also CA 179; 104; CMW 4
Montgomery, L(ucy) M(aud)
1874-1942 .... **TCLC 51, 140**
See also AAYA 12; BYA 1; CA 108; 137;
CLR 8, 91; DA3; DAC; DAM MST; DLB
92; DLBD 14; JRDA; MAICYA 1, 2;
MTCW 2; RGEL 2; SATA 100; TWA;
WCH; WYA; YABC 1
Montgomery, Marion H., Jr. 1925- .... **CLC 7**
See also AITN 1; CA 1-4R; CANR 3, 48;
CSW; DLB 6
Montgomery, Max
See Davenport, Guy (Mattison, Jr.)
Montherlant, Henry (Milon) de
1896-1972 .... **CLC 8, 19**
See also CA 85-88; 37-40R; DAM DRAM;
DLB 72; EW 11; EWL 3; GFL 1789 to
the Present; MTCW 1
Monty Python
See Chapman, Graham; Cleese, John
(Marwood); Gilliam, Terry (Vance); Idle,
Eric; Jones, Terence Graham Parry; Palin,
Michael (Edward)
See also AAYA 7
Moodie, Susanna (Strickland)
1803-1885 .... **NCLC 14, 113**
See also DLB 99
Moody, Hiram (F. III) 1961-
See Moody, Rick
See also CA 138; CANR 64, 112
Moody, Minerva
See Alcott, Louisa May
Moody, Rick .... **CLC 147**
See Moody, Hiram (F. III)
Moody, William Vaughan
1869-1910 .... **TCLC 105**
See also CA 110; 178; DLB 7, 54; RGAL 4
Mooney, Edward 1951-
See Mooney, Ted
See also CA 130
Mooney, Ted .... **CLC 25**
See Mooney, Edward
Moorcock, Michael (John) 1939- ...... **CLC 5,**
27, 58
See Bradbury, Edward P.
See also AAYA 26; CA 45-48; CAAS 5;
CANR 2, 17, 38, 64, 122; CN 7; DLB 14,
231, 261; FANT; MTCW 1, 2; SATA 93;
SCFW 2; SFW 4; SUFW 1, 2
Moore, Brian 1921-1999 ... **CLC 1, 3, 5, 7, 8,**
19, 32, 90
See Bryan, Michael
See also BRWS 9; CA 1-4R; 174; CANR 1,
25, 42, 63; CCA 1; CN 7; DAB; DAC;
DAM MST; DLB 251; EWL 3; FANT;
MTCW 1, 2; RGEL 2

Mrozek, Slawomir 1930- .... **CLC 3, 13**
See also CA 13-16R; CAAS 10; CANR 29;
CDWLB 4; CWW 2; DLB 232; EWL 3;
MTCW 1

Mrs. Belloc-Lowndes
See Lowndes, Marie Adelaide (Belloc)

Mrs. Fairstar
See Horne, Richard Henry Hengist

M'Taggart, John M'Taggart Ellis
See McTaggart, John McTaggart Ellis

Mtwa, Percy (?)- .... **CLC 47**

Mueller, Lisel 1924- .... **CLC 13, 51; PC 33**
See also CA 93-96; CP 7; DLB 105; PFS 9,
13

Muggeridge, Malcolm (Thomas)
1903-1990 .... **TCLC 120**
See also AITN 1; CA 101; CANR 33, 63;
MTCW 1, 2

Muhammad 570-632 .... **WLCS**
See also DA; DAB; DAC; DAM MST

Muir, Edwin 1887-1959 . **PC 49; TCLC 2, 87**
See Moore, Edward
See also BRWS 6; CA 104; 193; DLB 20,
100, 191; EWL 3; RGEL 2

Muir, John 1838-1914 .... **TCLC 28**
See also AMWS 9; ANW; CA 165; DLB
186, 275

Mujica Lainez, Manuel 1910-1984 ... **CLC 31**
See Lainez, Manuel Mujica
See also CA 81-84; 112; CANR 32; EWL
3; HW 1

Mukherjee, Bharati 1940- ..... **AAL; CLC 53,
115; SSC 38**
See also AAYA 46; BEST 89:2; CA 107;
CANR 45, 72, 128; CN 7; DAM NOV;
DLB 60, 218; DNFS 1, 2; EWL 3; FW;
MTCW 1, 2; RGAL 4; RGSF 2; SSFS 7;
TUS; WWE 1

Muldoon, Paul 1951- .... **CLC 32, 72, 166**
See also BRWS 4; CA 113; 129; CANR 52,
91; CP 7; DAM POET; DLB 40; INT CA-
129; PFS 7

Mulisch, Harry 1927- .... **CLC 42**
See also CA 9-12R; CANR 6, 26, 56, 110;
DLB 299; EWL 3

Mull, Martin 1943- .... **CLC 17**
See also CA 105

Muller, Wilhelm .... **NCLC 73**

Mulock, Dinah Maria
See Craik, Dinah Maria (Mulock)
See also RGEL 2

Munday, Anthony 1560-1633 .... **LC 87**
See also DLB 62, 172; RGEL 2

Munford, Robert 1737(?)-1783 .... **LC 5**
See also DLB 31

Mungo, Raymond 1946- .... **CLC 72**
See also CA 49-52; CANR 2

Munro, Alice 1931- .... **CLC 6, 10, 19, 50, 95;
SSC 3; WLCS**
See also AITN 2; BPFB 2; CA 33-36R;
CANR 33, 53, 75, 114; CCA 1; CN 7;
DA3; DAC; DAM MST, NOV; DLB 53;
EWL 3; MTCW 1, 2; RGEL 2; RGSF 2;
SATA 29; SSFS 5, 13, 19; WWE 1

Munro, H(ector) H(ugh) 1870-1916 .... **WLC**
See Saki
See also AAYA 56; CA 104; 130; CANR
104; CDBLB 1890-1914; DA; DA3;
DAB; DAC; DAM MST, NOV; DLB 34,
162; EXPS; MTCW 1, 2; RGEL 2; SSFS
15

Murakami, Haruki 1949- .... **CLC 150**
See Murakami Haruki
See also CA 165; CANR 102; MJW; RGWL
3; SFW 4

Murakami Haruki
See Murakami, Haruki
See also DLB 182; EWL 3

Murasaki, Lady
See Murasaki Shikibu

Murasaki Shikibu 978(?)-1026(?) ... **CMLC 1**
See also EFS 2; LATS 1; RGWL 2, 3

Murdoch, (Jean) Iris 1919-1999 ... **CLC 1, 2,
3, 4, 6, 8, 11, 15, 22, 31, 51**
See also BRWS 1; CA 13-16R; 179; CANR
8, 43, 68, 103; CDBLB 1960 to Present;
CN 7; CWD; DA3; DAB; DAC; DAM
MST, NOV; DLB 14, 194, 233; EWL 3;
INT CANR-8; MTCW 1, 2; NFS 18;
RGEL 2; TEA; WLIT 4

Murfree, Mary Noailles 1850-1922 .. **SSC 22;
TCLC 135**
See also CA 122; 176; DLB 12, 74; RGAL
4

Murnau, Friedrich Wilhelm
See Plumpe, Friedrich Wilhelm

Murphy, Richard 1927- .... **CLC 41**
See also BRWS 5; CA 29-32R; CP 7; DLB
40; EWL 3

Murphy, Sylvia 1937- .... **CLC 34**
See also CA 121

Murphy, Thomas (Bernard) 1935- ... **CLC 51**
See also CA 101

Murray, Albert L. 1916- .... **CLC 73**
See also BW 2; CA 49-52; CANR 26, 52,
78; CSW; DLB 38

Murray, James Augustus Henry
1837-1915 .... **TCLC 117**

Murray, Judith Sargent
1751-1820 .... **NCLC 63**
See also DLB 37, 200

Murray, Les(lie Allan) 1938- .... **CLC 40**
See also BRWS 7; CA 21-24R; CANR 11,
27, 56, 103; CP 7; DAM POET; DLB 289;
DLBY 2001; EWL 3; RGEL 2

Murry, J. Middleton
See Murry, John Middleton

Murry, John Middleton
1889-1957 .... **TCLC 16**
See also CA 118; 217; DLB 149

Musgrave, Susan 1951- .... **CLC 13, 54**
See also CA 69-72; CANR 45, 84; CCA 1;
CP 7; CWP

Musil, Robert (Edler von)
1880-1942 .... **SSC 18; TCLC 12, 68**
See also CA 109; CANR 55, 84; CDWLB
2; DLB 81, 124; EW 9; EWL 3; MTCW
2; RGSF 2; RGWL 2, 3

Muske, Carol .... **CLC 90**
See Muske-Dukes, Carol (Anne)

Muske-Dukes, Carol (Anne) 1945-
See Muske, Carol
See also CA 65-68, 203; CAAE 203; CANR
32, 70; CWP

Musset, (Louis Charles) Alfred de
1810-1857 .... **NCLC 7**
See also DLB 192, 217; EW 6; GFL 1789
to the Present; RGWL 2, 3; TWA

Mussolini, Benito (Amilcare Andrea)
1883-1945 .... **TCLC 96**
See also CA 116

Mutanabbi, Al-
See al-Mutanabbi, Ahmad ibn al-Husayn
Abu al-Tayyib al-Jufi al-Kindi

My Brother's Brother
See Chekhov, Anton (Pavlovich)

Myers, L(eopold) H(amilton)
1881-1944 .... **TCLC 59**
See also CA 157; DLB 15; EWL 3; RGEL
2

Myers, Walter Dean 1937- .. **BLC 3; CLC 35**
See also AAYA 4, 23; BW 2; BYA 6, 8, 11;
CA 33-36R; CANR 20, 42, 67, 108; CLR
4, 16, 35; DAM MULT, NOV; DLB 33;
INT CANR-20; JRDA; LAIT 5; MAICYA
1, 2; MAICYAS 1; SAAS 2; SATA 2;
SATA 41, 71, 109; SATA-Brief 27; WYA;
YAW

Myers, Walter M.
See Myers, Walter Dean

Myles, Symon
See Follett, Ken(neth Martin)

Nabokov, Vladimir (Vladimirovich)
1899-1977 .... **CLC 1, 2, 3, 6, 8, 11, 15,
23, 44, 46, 64; SSC 11; TCLC 108;
WLC**
See also AAYA 45; AMW; AMWC 1;
AMWR 1; BPFB 2; CA 5-8R; 69-72;
CANR 20, 102; CDALB 1941-1968; DA;
DA3; DAB; DAC; DAM MST, NOV;
DLB 2, 244, 278; DLBD 3; DLBY 1980,
1991; EWL 3; EXPS; LATS 1; MTCW 1,
2; NCFS 4; NFS 9; RGAL 4; RGSF 2;
SSFS 6, 15; TUS

Naevius c. 265B.C.-201B.C. .... **CMLC 37**
See also DLB 211

Nagai, Kafu .... **TCLC 51**
See Nagai, Sokichi
See also DLB 180

Nagai, Sokichi 1879-1959
See Nagai, Kafu
See also CA 117

Nagy, Laszlo 1925-1978 .... **CLC 7**
See also CA 129; 112

Naidu, Sarojini 1879-1949 .... **TCLC 80**
See also EWL 3; RGEL 2

Naipaul, Shiva(dhar Srinivasa)
1945-1985 .... **CLC 32, 39; TCLC 153**
See also CA 110; 112; 116; CANR 33;
DA3; DAM NOV; DLB 157; DLBY 1985;
EWL 3; MTCW 1, 2

Naipaul, V(idiadhar) S(urajprasad)
1932- .... **CLC 4, 7, 9, 13, 18, 37, 105;
SSC 38**
See also BPFB 2; BRWS 1; CA 1-4R;
CANR 1, 33, 51, 91, 126; CDBLB 1960
to Present; CDWLB 3; CN 7; DA3; DAB;
DAC; DAM MST, NOV; DLB 125, 204,
207; DLBY 1985, 2001; EWL 3; LATS 1;
MTCW 1, 2; RGEL 2; RGSF 2; TWA;
WLIT 4; WWE 1

Nakos, Lilika 1903(?)-1989 .... **CLC 29**

Napoleon
See Yamamoto, Hisaye

Narayan, R(asipuram) K(rishnaswami)
1906-2001 . **CLC 7, 28, 47, 121; SSC 25**
See also BPFB 2; CA 81-84; 196; CANR
33, 61, 112; CN 7; DA3; DAM NOV;
DNFS 1; EWL 3; MTCW 1, 2; RGEL 2;
RGSF 2; SATA 62; SSFS 5; WWE 1

Nash, (Frediric) Ogden 1902-1971 . **CLC 23;
PC 21; TCLC 109**
See also CA 13-14; 29-32R; CANR 34, 61;
CAP 1; DAM POET; DLB 11; MAICYA
1, 2; MTCW 1, 2; RGAL 4; SATA 2, 46;
WP

Nashe, Thomas 1567-1601(?) .... **LC 41, 89**
See also DLB 167; RGEL 2

Nathan, Daniel
See Dannay, Frederic

Nathan, George Jean 1882-1958 .... **TCLC 18**
See Hatteras, Owen
See also CA 114; 169; DLB 137

Natsume, Kinnosuke
See Natsume, Soseki

Natsume, Soseki 1867-1916 .... **TCLC 2, 10**
See Natsume Soseki; Soseki
See also CA 104; 195; RGWL 2, 3; TWA

Natsume Soseki
See Natsume, Soseki
See also DLB 180; EWL 3

Norris, (Benjamin) Frank(lin, Jr.)
1870-1902 .... **SSC 28; TCLC 24**
See also AAYA 57; AMW; AMWC 2; BPFB
2; CA 110; 160; CDALB 1865-1917; DLB
12, 71, 186; LMFS 2; NFS 12; RGAL 4;
TCWW 2; TUS

Norris, Leslie 1921- .... **CLC 14**
See also CA 11-12; CANR 14, 117; CAP 1;
CP 7; DLB 27, 256

North, Andrew
See Norton, Andre

North, Anthony
See Koontz, Dean R(ay)

North, Captain George
See Stevenson, Robert Louis (Balfour)

North, Captain George
See Stevenson, Robert Louis (Balfour)

North, Milou
See Erdrich, Louise

Northrup, B. A.
See Hubbard, L(afayette) Ron(ald)

North Staffs
See Hulme, T(homas) E(rnest)

Northup, Solomon 1808-1863 ...... **NCLC 105**

Norton, Alice Mary
See Norton, Andre
See also MAICYA 1; SATA 1, 43

Norton, Andre 1912- .... **CLC 12**
See Norton, Alice Mary
See also AAYA 14; BPFB 2; BYA 4, 10,
12; CA 1-4R; CANR 68; CLR 50; DLB
8, 52; JRDA; MAICYA 2; MTCW 1;
SATA 91; SUFW 1, 2; YAW

Norton, Caroline 1808-1877 .... **NCLC 47**
See also DLB 21, 159, 199

Norway, Nevil Shute 1899-1960
See Shute, Nevil
See also CA 102; 93-96; CANR 85; MTCW
2

Norwid, Cyprian Kamil
1821-1883 .... **NCLC 17**
See also RGWL 3

Nosille, Nabrah
See Ellison, Harlan (Jay)

Nossack, Hans Erich 1901-1978 .... **CLC 6**
See also CA 93-96; 85-88; DLB 69; EWL 3

Nostradamus 1503-1566 .... **LC 27**

Nosu, Chuji
See Ozu, Yasujiro

Notenburg, Eleanora (Genrikhovna) von
See Guro, Elena (Genrikhovna)

Nova, Craig 1945- .... **CLC 7, 31**
See also CA 45-48; CANR 2, 53, 127

Novak, Joseph
See Kosinski, Jerzy (Nikodem)

Novalis 1772-1801 .... **NCLC 13**
See also CDWLB 2; DLB 90; EW 5; RGWL
2, 3

Novick, Peter 1934- .... **CLC 164**
See also CA 188

Novis, Emile
See Weil, Simone (Adolphine)

Nowlan, Alden (Albert) 1933-1983 ... **CLC 15**
See also CA 9-12R; CANR 5; DAC; DAM
MST; DLB 53; PFS 12

Noyes, Alfred 1880-1958 ...... **PC 27; TCLC 7**
See also CA 104; 188; DLB 20; EXPP;
FANT; PFS 4; RGEL 2

Nugent, Richard Bruce 1906(?)-1987 ... **HR 3**
See also BW 1; CA 125; DLB 51; GLL 2

Nunn, Kem .... **CLC 34**
See also CA 159

Nwapa, Flora (Nwanzuruaha)
1931-1993 .... **BLCS; CLC 133**
See also BW 2; CA 143; CANR 83; CD-
WLB 3; CWRI 5; DLB 125; EWL 3;
WLIT 2

Nye, Robert 1939- .... **CLC 13, 42**
See also CA 33-36R; CANR 29, 67, 107;
CN 7; CP 7; CWRI 5; DAM NOV; DLB
14, 271; FANT; HGG; MTCW 1; RHW;
SATA 6

Nyro, Laura 1947-1997 .... **CLC 17**
See also CA 194

Oates, Joyce Carol 1938- .. **CLC 1, 2, 3, 6, 9,
11, 15, 19, 33, 52, 108, 134; SSC 6, 70;
WLC**
See also AAYA 15, 52; AITN 1; AMWS 2;
BEST 89:2; BPFB 2; BYA 11; CA 5-8R;
CANR 25, 45, 74, 113, 129; CDALB
1968-1988; CN 7; CP 7; CPW; CWP; DA;
DA3; DAB; DAC; DAM MST, NOV,
POP; DLB 2, 5, 130; DLBY 1981; EWL
3; EXPS; FW; HGG; INT CANR-25;
LAIT 4; MAWW; MTCW 1, 2; NFS 8;
RGAL 4; RGSF 2; SSFS 17; SUFW 2;
TUS

O'Brian, E. G.
See Clarke, Arthur C(harles)

O'Brian, Patrick 1914-2000 .... **CLC 152**
See also AAYA 55; CA 144; 187; CANR
74; CPW; MTCW 2; RHW

O'Brien, Darcy 1939-1998 .... **CLC 11**
See also CA 21-24R; 167; CANR 8, 59

O'Brien, Edna 1936- ..... **CLC 3, 5, 8, 13, 36,
65, 116; SSC 10**
See also BRWS 5; CA 1-4R; CANR 6, 41,
65, 102; CDBLB 1960 to Present; CN 7;
DA3; DAM NOV; DLB 14, 231; EWL 3;
FW; MTCW 1, 2; RGSF 2; WLIT 4

O'Brien, Fitz-James 1828-1862 ...... **NCLC 21**
See also DLB 74; RGAL 4; SUFW

O'Brien, Flann .... **CLC 1, 4, 5, 7, 10, 47**
See O Nuallain, Brian
See also BRWS 2; DLB 231; EWL 3;
RGEL 2

O'Brien, Richard 1942- .... **CLC 17**
See also CA 124

O'Brien, (William) Tim(othy) 1946- . **CLC 7,
19, 40, 103; SSC 74**
See also AAYA 16; AMWS 5; CA 85-88;
CANR 40, 58; CDALBS; CN 7; CPW;
DA3; DAM POP; DLB 152; DLBD 9;
DLBY 1980; MTCW 2; RGAL 4; SSFS
5, 15

Obstfelder, Sigbjoern 1866-1900 .... **TCLC 23**
See also CA 123

O'Casey, Sean 1880-1964 .... **CLC 1, 5, 9, 11,
15, 88; DC 12; WLCS**
See also BRW 7; CA 89-92; CANR 62;
CBD; CDBLB 1914-1945; DA3; DAB;
DAC; DAM DRAM, MST; DFS 19; DLB
10; EWL 3; MTCW 1, 2; RGEL 2; TEA;
WLIT 4

O'Cathasaigh, Sean
See O'Casey, Sean

Occom, Samson 1723-1792 .... **LC 60; NNAL**
See also DLB 175

Ochs, Phil(ip David) 1940-1976 .... **CLC 17**
See also CA 185; 65-68

O'Connor, Edwin (Greene)
1918-1968 .... **CLC 14**
See also CA 93-96; 25-28R

O'Connor, (Mary) Flannery
1925-1964 ..... **CLC 1, 2, 3, 6, 10, 13, 15,
21, 66, 104; SSC 1, 23, 61; TCLC 132;
WLC**
See also AAYA 7; AMW; AMWR 2; BPFB
3; BYA 16; CA 1-4R; CANR 3, 41;
CDALB 1941-1968; DA; DA3; DAB;
DAC; DAM MST, NOV; DLB 2, 152;
DLBD 12; DLBY 1980; EWL 3; EXPS;
LAIT 5; MAWW; MTCW 1, 2; NFS 3;
RGAL 4; RGSF 2; SSFS 2, 7, 10, 19;
TUS

O'Connor, Frank .... **CLC 23; SSC 5**
See O'Donovan, Michael Francis
See also DLB 162; EWL 3; RGSF 2; SSFS
5

O'Dell, Scott 1898-1989 .... **CLC 30**
See also AAYA 3, 44; BPFB 3; BYA 1, 2,
3, 5; CA 61-64; 129; CANR 12, 30, 112;
CLR 1, 16; DLB 52; JRDA; MAICYA 1,
2; SATA 12, 60, 134; WYA; YAW

Odets, Clifford 1906-1963 ..... **CLC 2, 28, 98;
DC 6**
See also AMWS 2; CA 85-88; CAD; CANR
62; DAM DRAM; DFS 3, 17, 20; DLB 7,
26; EWL 3; MTCW 1, 2; RGAL 4; TUS

O'Doherty, Brian 1928- .... **CLC 76**
See also CA 105; CANR 108

O'Donnell, K. M.
See Malzberg, Barry N(athaniel)

O'Donnell, Lawrence
See Kuttner, Henry

O'Donovan, Michael Francis
1903-1966 .... **CLC 14**
See O'Connor, Frank
See also CA 93-96; CANR 84

Oe, Kenzaburo 1935- .. **CLC 10, 36, 86, 187;
SSC 20**
See Oe Kenzaburo
See also CA 97-100; CANR 36, 50, 74, 126;
CWW 2; DA3; DAM NOV; DLB 182;
DLBY 1994; EWL 3; LATS 1; MJW;
MTCW 1, 2; RGSF 2; RGWL 2, 3

Oe Kenzaburo
See Oe, Kenzaburo
See also EWL 3

O'Faolain, Julia 1932- .... **CLC 6, 19, 47, 108**
See also CA 81-84; CAAS 2; CANR 12,
61; CN 7; DLB 14, 231; FW; MTCW 1;
RHW

O'Faolain, Sean 1900-1991 ...... **CLC 1, 7, 14,
32, 70; SSC 13; TCLC 143**
See also CA 61-64; 134; CANR 12, 66;
DLB 15, 162; MTCW 1, 2; RGEL 2;
RGSF 2

O'Flaherty, Liam 1896-1984 .... **CLC 5, 34;
SSC 6**
See also CA 101; 113; CANR 35; DLB 36,
162; DLBY 1984; MTCW 1, 2; RGEL 2;
RGSF 2; SSFS 5, 20

Ogai
See Mori Ogai
See also MJW

Ogilvy, Gavin
See Barrie, J(ames) M(atthew)

O'Grady, Standish (James)
1846-1928 .... **TCLC 5**
See also CA 104; 157

O'Grady, Timothy 1951- .... **CLC 59**
See also CA 138

O'Hara, Frank 1926-1966 .... **CLC 2, 5, 13,
78; PC 45**
See also CA 9-12R; 25-28R; CANR 33;
DA3; DAM POET; DLB 5, 16, 193; EWL
3; MTCW 1, 2; PFS 8; 12; RGAL 4; WP

O'Hara, John (Henry) 1905-1970 . **CLC 1, 2,
3, 6, 11, 42; SSC 15**
See also AMW; BPFB 3; CA 5-8R; 25-28R;
CANR 31, 60; CDALB 1929-1941; DAM
NOV; DLB 9, 86; DLBD 2; EWL 3;
MTCW 1, 2; NFS 11; RGAL 4; RGSF 2

O Hehir, Diana 1922- .... **CLC 41**
See also CA 93-96

Ohiyesa
See Eastman, Charles A(lexander)

Okada, John 1923-1971 .... **AAL**
See also BYA 14; CA 212

Okigbo, Christopher (Ifenayichukwu)
1932-1967 .... **BLC 3; CLC 25, 84; PC 7**
See also AFW; BW 1, 3; CA 77-80; CANR
74; CDWLB 3; DAM MULT, POET; DLB
125; EWL 3; MTCW 1, 2; RGEL 2

Okri, Ben 1959- .... **CLC 87**
See also AFW; BRWS 5; BW 2, 3; CA 130;
138; CANR 65, 128; CN 7; DLB 157,
231; EWL 3; INT CA-138; MTCW 2;
RGSF 2; SSFS 20; WLIT 2; WWE 1

Olds, Sharon 1942- .. **CLC 32, 39, 85; PC 22**
See also AMWS 10; CA 101; CANR 18,
41, 66, 98; CP 7; CPW; CWP; DAM
POET; DLB 120; MTCW 2; PFS 17

Oldstyle, Jonathan
See Irving, Washington

Olesha, Iurii
See Olesha, Yuri (Karlovich)
See also RGWL 2

Olesha, Iurii Karlovich
See Olesha, Yuri (Karlovich)
See also DLB 272

Olesha, Yuri (Karlovich) 1899-1960 . **CLC 8;**
SSC 69; TCLC 136
See Olesha, Iurii; Olesha, Iurii Karlovich;
Olesha, Yury Karlovich
See also CA 85-88; EW 11; RGWL 3

Olesha, Yury Karlovich
See Olesha, Yuri (Karlovich)
See also EWL 3

Oliphant, Mrs.
See Oliphant, Margaret (Oliphant Wilson)
See also SUFW

Oliphant, Laurence 1829(?)-1888 .. **NCLC 47**
See also DLB 18, 166

Oliphant, Margaret (Oliphant Wilson)
1828-1897 .... **NCLC 11, 61; SSC 25**
See Oliphant, Mrs.
See also DLB 18, 159, 190; HGG; RGEL
2; RGSF 2

Oliver, Mary 1935- .... **CLC 19, 34, 98**
See also AMWS 7; CA 21-24R; CANR 9,
43, 84, 92; CP 7; CWP; DLB 5, 193;
EWL 3; PFS 15

Olivier, Laurence (Kerr) 1907-1989 . **CLC 20**
See also CA 111; 150; 129

Olsen, Tillie 1912- ... **CLC 4, 13, 114; SSC 11**
See also AAYA 51; AMWS 13; BYA 11;
CA 1-4R; CANR 1, 43, 74, 132;
CDALBS; CN 7; DA; DA3; DAB; DAC;
DAM MST; DLB 28, 206; DLBY 1980;
EWL 3; EXPS; FW; MTCW 1, 2; RGAL
4; RGSF 2; SSFS 1; TUS

Olson, Charles (John) 1910-1970 .. **CLC 1, 2,**
5, 6, 9, 11, 29; PC 19
See also AMWS 2; CA 13-16; 25-28R;
CABS 2; CANR 35, 61; CAP 1; DAM
POET; DLB 5, 16, 193; EWL 3; MTCW
1, 2; RGAL 4; WP

Olson, Toby 1937- .... **CLC 28**
See also CA 65-68; CANR 9, 31, 84; CP 7

Olyesha, Yuri
See Olesha, Yuri (Karlovich)

Olympiodorus of Thebes c. 375-c.
430 .... **CMLC 59**

Omar Khayyam
See Khayyam, Omar
See also RGWL 2, 3

Ondaatje, (Philip) Michael 1943- .... **CLC 14,**
29, 51, 76, 180; PC 28
See also CA 77-80; CANR 42, 74, 109; CN
7; CP 7; DA3; DAB; DAC; DAM MST;
DLB 60; EWL 3; LATS 1; LMFS 2;
MTCW 2; PFS 8, 19; TWA; WWE 1

Oneal, Elizabeth 1934-
See Oneal, Zibby
See also CA 106; CANR 28, 84; MAICYA
1, 2; SATA 30, 82; YAW

Oneal, Zibby .... **CLC 30**
See Oneal, Elizabeth
See also AAYA 5, 41; BYA 13; CLR 13;
JRDA; WYA

O'Neill, Eugene (Gladstone)
1888-1953 ... **DC 20; TCLC 1, 6, 27, 49;**
WLC
See also AAYA 54; AITN 1; AMW; AMWC
1; CA 110; 132; CAD; CANR 131;
CDALB 1929-1941; DA; DA3; DAB;
DAC; DAM DRAM, MST; DFS 2, 4, 5,
6, 9, 11, 12, 16, 20; DLB 7; EWL 3; LAIT
3; LMFS 2; MTCW 1, 2; RGAL 4; TUS

Onetti, Juan Carlos 1909-1994 ... **CLC 7, 10;**
HLCS 2; SSC 23; TCLC 131
See also CA 85-88; 145; CANR 32, 63; CD-
WLB 3; DAM MULT, NOV; DLB 113;
EWL 3; HW 1, 2; LAW; MTCW 1, 2;
RGSF 2

O Nuallain, Brian 1911-1966
See O'Brien, Flann
See also CA 21-22; 25-28R; CAP 2; DLB
231; FANT; TEA

Ophuls, Max 1902-1957 .... **TCLC 79**
See also CA 113

Opie, Amelia 1769-1853 .... **NCLC 65**
See also DLB 116, 159; RGEL 2

Oppen, George 1908-1984 ..... **CLC 7, 13, 34;**
PC 35; TCLC 107
See also CA 13-16R; 113; CANR 8, 82;
DLB 5, 165

Oppenheim, E(dward) Phillips
1866-1946 .... **TCLC 45**
See also CA 111; 202; CMW 4; DLB 70

Opuls, Max
See Ophuls, Max

Origen c. 185-c. 254 .... **CMLC 19**

Orlovitz, Gil 1918-1973 .... **CLC 22**
See also CA 77-80; 45-48; DLB 2, 5

Orris
See Ingelow, Jean

Ortega y Gasset, Jose 1883-1955 ...... **HLC 2;**
TCLC 9
See also CA 106; 130; DAM MULT; EW 9;
EWL 3; HW 1, 2; MTCW 1, 2

Ortese, Anna Maria 1914-1998 .... **CLC 89**
See also DLB 177; EWL 3

Ortiz, Simon J(oseph) 1941- .... **CLC 45;**
NNAL; PC 17
See also AMWS 4; CA 134; CANR 69, 118;
CP 7; DAM MULT, POET; DLB 120,
175, 256; EXPP; PFS 4, 16; RGAL 4

Orton, Joe .... **CLC 4, 13, 43; DC 3**
See Orton, John Kingsley
See also BRWS 5; CBD; CDBLB 1960 to
Present; DFS 3, 6; DLB 13; GLL 1;
MTCW 2; RGEL 2; TEA; WLIT 4

Orton, John Kingsley 1933-1967
See Orton, Joe
See also CA 85-88; CANR 35, 66; DAM
DRAM; MTCW 1, 2

Orwell, George ...... **SSC 68; TCLC 2, 6, 15,**
31, 51, 128, 129; WLC
See Blair, Eric (Arthur)
See also BPFB 3; BRW 7; BYA 5; CDBLB
1945-1960; CLR 68; DAB; DLB 15, 98,
195, 255; EWL 3; EXPN; LAIT 4, 5;
LATS 1; NFS 3, 7; RGEL 2; SCFW 2;
SFW 4; SSFS 4; TEA; WLIT 4; YAW

Osborne, David
See Silverberg, Robert

Osborne, George
See Silverberg, Robert

Osborne, John (James) 1929-1994 .... **CLC 1,**
2, 5, 11, 45; TCLC 153; WLC
See also BRWS 1; CA 13-16R; 147; CANR
21, 56; CDBLB 1945-1960; DA; DAB;
DAC; DAM DRAM, MST; DFS 4, 19;
DLB 13; EWL 3; MTCW 1, 2; RGEL 2

Osborne, Lawrence 1958- .... **CLC 50**
See also CA 189

Osbourne, Lloyd 1868-1947 .... **TCLC 93**

Osgood, Frances Sargent
1811-1850 .... **NCLC 141**
See also DLB 250

Oshima, Nagisa 1932- .... **CLC 20**
See also CA 116; 121; CANR 78

Oskison, John Milton
1874-1947 .... **NNAL; TCLC 35**
See also CA 144; CANR 84; DAM MULT;
DLB 175

Ossian c. 3rd cent. - .... **CMLC 28**
See Macpherson, James

Ossoli, Sarah Margaret (Fuller)
1810-1850 .... **NCLC 5, 50**
See Fuller, Margaret; Fuller, Sarah Margaret
See also CDALB 1640-1865; FW; LMFS 1;
SATA 25

Ostriker, Alicia (Suskin) 1937- .... **CLC 132**
See also CA 25-28R; CAAS 24; CANR 10,
30, 62, 99; CWP; DLB 120; EXPP; PFS
19

Ostrovsky, Aleksandr Nikolaevich
See Ostrovsky, Alexander
See also DLB 277

Ostrovsky, Alexander 1823-1886 .. **NCLC 30,**
57
See Ostrovsky, Aleksandr Nikolaevich

Otero, Blas de 1916-1979 .... **CLC 11**
See also CA 89-92; DLB 134; EWL 3

O'Trigger, Sir Lucius
See Horne, Richard Henry Hengist

Otto, Rudolf 1869-1937 .... **TCLC 85**

Otto, Whitney 1955- .... **CLC 70**
See also CA 140; CANR 120

Otway, Thomas 1652-1685 .... **DC 24**
See also DAM DRAM; DLB 80; RGEL 2

Ouida .... **TCLC 43**
See De la Ramee, Marie Louise (Ouida)
See also DLB 18, 156; RGEL 2

Ouologuem, Yambo 1940- .... **CLC 146**
See also CA 111; 176

Ousmane, Sembene 1923- ... **BLC 3; CLC 66**
See Sembene, Ousmane
See also BW 1, 3; CA 117; 125; CANR 81;
CWW 2; MTCW 1

Ovid 43B.C.-17 .... **CMLC 7; PC 2**
See also AW 2; CDWLB 1; DA3; DAM
POET; DLB 211; RGWL 2, 3; WP

Owen, Hugh
See Faust, Frederick (Schiller)

Owen, Wilfred (Edward Salter)
1893-1918 ... **PC 19; TCLC 5, 27; WLC**
See also BRW 6; CA 104; 141; CDBLB
1914-1945; DA; DAB; DAC; DAM MST,
POET; DLB 20; EWL 3; EXPP; MTCW
2; PFS 10; RGEL 2; WLIT 4

Owens, Louis (Dean) 1948-2002 .... **NNAL**
See also CA 137, 179; 207; CAAE 179;
CAAS 24; CANR 71

Owens, Rochelle 1936- .... **CLC 8**
See also CA 17-20R; CAAS 2; CAD;
CANR 39; CD 5; CP 7; CWD; CWP

Oz, Amos 1939- ...... **CLC 5, 8, 11, 27, 33, 54;**
SSC 66
See also CA 53-56; CANR 27, 47, 65, 113;
CWW 2; DAM NOV; EWL 3; MTCW 1,
2; RGSF 2; RGWL 3

Ozick, Cynthia 1928- .... **CLC 3, 7, 28, 62,**
155; SSC 15, 60
See also AMWS 5; BEST 90:1; CA 17-20R;
CANR 23, 58, 116; CN 7; CPW; DA3;
DAM NOV, POP; DLB 28, 152, 299;
DLBY 1982; EWL 3; EXPS; INT CANR-
23; MTCW 1, 2; RGAL 4; RGSF 2; SSFS
3, 12

Ozu, Yasujiro 1903-1963 .... **CLC 16**
See also CA 112

Peters, Joan K(aren) 1945- .... **CLC 39**
See also CA 158; CANR 109

Peters, Robert L(ouis) 1924- .... **CLC 7**
See also CA 13-16R; CAAS 8; CP 7; DLB 105

Petofi, Sandor 1823-1849 .... **NCLC 21**
See also RGWL 2, 3

Petrakis, Harry Mark 1923- .... **CLC 3**
See also CA 9-12R; CANR 4, 30, 85; CN 7

Petrarch 1304-1374 .... **CMLC 20; PC 8**
See also DA3; DAM POET; EW 2; LMFS 1; RGWL 2, 3

Petronius c. 20-66 .... **CMLC 34**
See also AW 2; CDWLB 1; DLB 211; RGWL 2, 3

Petrov, Evgeny .... **TCLC 21**
See Kataev, Evgeny Petrovich

Petry, Ann (Lane) 1908-1997 .. **CLC 1, 7, 18; TCLC 112**
See also AFAW 1, 2; BPFB 3; BW 1, 3; BYA 2; CA 5-8R; 157; CAAS 6; CANR 4, 46; CLR 12; CN 7; DLB 76; EWL 3; JRDA; LAIT 1; MAICYA 1, 2; MAIC-YAS 1; MTCW 1; RGAL 4; SATA 5; SATA-Obit 94; TUS

Petursson, Halligrimur 1614-1674 .... **LC 8**

Peychinovich
See Vazov, Ivan (Minchov)

Phaedrus c. 15B.C.-c. 50 .... **CMLC 25**
See also DLB 211

Phelps (Ward), Elizabeth Stuart
See Phelps, Elizabeth Stuart
See also FW

Phelps, Elizabeth Stuart
1844-1911 .... **TCLC 113**
See Phelps (Ward), Elizabeth Stuart
See also DLB 74

Philips, Katherine 1632-1664 . **LC 30; PC 40**
See also DLB 131; RGEL 2

Philipson, Morris H. 1926- .... **CLC 53**
See also CA 1-4R; CANR 4

Phillips, Caryl 1958- .... **BLCS; CLC 96**
See also BRWS 5; BW 2; CA 141; CANR 63, 104; CBD; CD 5; CN 7; DA3; DAM MULT; DLB 157; EWL 3; MTCW 2; WLIT 4; WWE 1

Phillips, David Graham
1867-1911 .... **TCLC 44**
See also CA 108; 176; DLB 9, 12, 303; RGAL 4

Phillips, Jack
See Sandburg, Carl (August)

Phillips, Jayne Anne 1952- .... **CLC 15, 33, 139; SSC 16**
See also AAYA 57; BPFB 3; CA 101; CANR 24, 50, 96; CN 7; CSW; DLBY 1980; INT CANR-24; MTCW 1, 2; RGAL 4; RGSF 2; SSFS 4

Phillips, Richard
See Dick, Philip K(indred)

Phillips, Robert (Schaeffer) 1938- .... **CLC 28**
See also CA 17-20R; CAAS 13; CANR 8; DLB 105

Phillips, Ward
See Lovecraft, H(oward) P(hillips)

Philostratus, Flavius c. 179-c. 244 .... **CMLC 62**

Piccolo, Lucio 1901-1969 .... **CLC 13**
See also CA 97-100; DLB 114; EWL 3

Pickthall, Marjorie L(owry) C(hristie)
1883-1922 .... **TCLC 21**
See also CA 107; DLB 92

Pico della Mirandola, Giovanni
1463-1494 .... **LC 15**
See also LMFS 1

Piercy, Marge 1936- .... **CLC 3, 6, 14, 18, 27, 62, 128; PC 29**
See also BPFB 3; CA 21-24R; 187; CAAE 187; CAAS 1; CANR 13, 43, 66, 111; CN 7; CP 7; CWP; DLB 120, 227; EXPP; FW; MTCW 1, 2; PFS 9; SFW 4

Piers, Robert
See Anthony, Piers

Pieyre de Mandiargues, Andre 1909-1991
See Mandiargues, Andre Pieyre de
See also CA 103; 136; CANR 22, 82; EWL 3; GFL 1789 to the Present

Pilnyak, Boris 1894-1938 . **SSC 48; TCLC 23**
See Vogau, Boris Andreyevich
See also EWL 3

Pinchback, Eugene
See Toomer, Jean

Pincherle, Alberto 1907-1990 ...... **CLC 11, 18**
See Moravia, Alberto
See also CA 25-28R; 132; CANR 33, 63; DAM NOV; MTCW 1

Pinckney, Darryl 1953- .... **CLC 76**
See also BW 2, 3; CA 143; CANR 79

Pindar 518(?)B.C.-438(?)B.C. .... **CMLC 12; PC 19**
See also AW 1; CDWLB 1; DLB 176; RGWL 2

Pineda, Cecile 1942- .... **CLC 39**
See also CA 118; DLB 209

Pinero, Arthur Wing 1855-1934 .... **TCLC 32**
See also CA 110; 153; DAM DRAM; DLB 10; RGEL 2

Pinero, Miguel (Antonio Gomez)
1946-1988 .... **CLC 4, 55**
See also CA 61-64; 125; CAD; CANR 29, 90; DLB 266; HW 1; LLW 1

Pinget, Robert 1919-1997 .... **CLC 7, 13, 37**
See also CA 85-88; 160; CWW 2; DLB 83; EWL 3; GFL 1789 to the Present

Pink Floyd
See Barrett, (Roger) Syd; Gilmour, David; Mason, Nick; Waters, Roger; Wright, Rick

Pinkney, Edward 1802-1828 .... **NCLC 31**
See also DLB 248

Pinkwater, Daniel
See Pinkwater, Daniel Manus

Pinkwater, Daniel Manus 1941- .... **CLC 35**
See also AAYA 1, 46; BYA 9; CA 29-32R; CANR 12, 38, 89; CLR 4; CSW; FANT; JRDA; MAICYA 1, 2; SAAS 3; SATA 8, 46, 76, 114; SFW 4; YAW

Pinkwater, Manus
See Pinkwater, Daniel Manus

Pinsky, Robert 1940- .... **CLC 9, 19, 38, 94, 121; PC 27**
See also AMWS 6; CA 29-32R; CAAS 4; CANR 58, 97; CP 7; DA3; DAM POET; DLBY 1982, 1998; MTCW 2; PFS 18; RGAL 4

Pinta, Harold
See Pinter, Harold

Pinter, Harold 1930- .. **CLC 1, 3, 6, 9, 11, 15, 27, 58, 73; DC 15; WLC**
See also BRWR 1; BRWS 1; CA 5-8R; CANR 33, 65, 112; CBD; CD 5; CDBLB 1960 to Present; DA; DA3; DAB; DAC; DAM DRAM, MST; DFS 3, 5, 7, 14; DLB 13; EWL 3; IDFW 3, 4; LMFS 2; MTCW 1, 2; RGEL 2; TEA

Piozzi, Hester Lynch (Thrale)
1741-1821 .... **NCLC 57**
See also DLB 104, 142

Pirandello, Luigi 1867-1936 .. **DC 5; SSC 22; TCLC 4, 29; WLC**
See also CA 104; 153; CANR 103; DA; DA3; DAB; DAC; DAM DRAM, MST; DFS 4, 9; DLB 264; EW 8; EWL 3; MTCW 2; RGSF 2; RGWL 2, 3

Pirsig, Robert M(aynard) 1928- ... **CLC 4, 6, 73**
See also CA 53-56; CANR 42, 74; CPW 1; DA3; DAM POP; MTCW 1, 2; SATA 39

Pisarev, Dmitrii Ivanovich
See Pisarev, Dmitry Ivanovich
See also DLB 277

Pisarev, Dmitry Ivanovich
1840-1868 .... **NCLC 25**
See Pisarev, Dmitrii Ivanovich

Pix, Mary (Griffith) 1666-1709 .... **LC 8**
See also DLB 80

Pixerecourt, (Rene Charles) Guilbert de
1773-1844 .... **NCLC 39**
See also DLB 192; GFL 1789 to the Present

Plaatje, Sol(omon) T(shekisho)
1878-1932 .... **BLCS; TCLC 73**
See also BW 2, 3; CA 141; CANR 79; DLB 125, 225

Plaidy, Jean
See Hibbert, Eleanor Alice Burford

Planche, James Robinson
1796-1880 .... **NCLC 42**
See also RGEL 2

Plant, Robert 1948- .... **CLC 12**

Plante, David (Robert) 1940- . **CLC 7, 23, 38**
See also CA 37-40R; CANR 12, 36, 58, 82; CN 7; DAM NOV; DLBY 1983; INT CANR-12; MTCW 1

Plath, Sylvia 1932-1963 ..... **CLC 1, 2, 3, 5, 9, 11, 14, 17, 50, 51, 62, 111; PC 1, 37; WLC**
See also AAYA 13; AMWR 2; AMWS 1; BPFB 3; CA 19-20; CANR 34, 101; CAP 2; CDALB 1941-1968; DA; DA3; DAB; DAC; DAM MST, POET; DLB 5, 6, 152; EWL 3; EXPN; EXPP; FW; LAIT 4; MAWW; MTCW 1, 2; NFS 1; PAB; PFS 1, 15; RGAL 4; SATA 96; TUS; WP; YAW

Plato c. 428B.C.-347B.C. ... **CMLC 8; WLCS**
See also AW 1; CDWLB 1; DA; DA3; DAB; DAC; DAM MST; DLB 176; LAIT 1; LATS 1; RGWL 2, 3

Platonov, Andrei
See Klimentov, Andrei Platonovich

Platonov, Andrei Platonovich
See Klimentov, Andrei Platonovich
See also DLB 272

Platonov, Andrey Platonovich
See Klimentov, Andrei Platonovich
See also EWL 3

Platt, Kin 1911- .... **CLC 26**
See also AAYA 11; CA 17-20R; CANR 11; JRDA; SAAS 17; SATA 21, 86; WYA

Plautus c. 254B.C.-c. 184B.C. ...... **CMLC 24; DC 6**
See also AW 1; CDWLB 1; DLB 211; RGWL 2, 3

Plick et Plock
See Simenon, Georges (Jacques Christian)

Plieksans, Janis
See Rainis, Janis

Plimpton, George (Ames)
1927-2003 .... **CLC 36**
See also AITN 1; CA 21-24R; 224; CANR 32, 70, 103; DLB 185, 241; MTCW 1, 2; SATA 10; SATA-Obit 150

Pliny the Elder c. 23-79 .... **CMLC 23**
See also DLB 211

Pliny the Younger c. 61-c. 112 ...... **CMLC 62**
See also AW 2; DLB 211

Plomer, William Charles Franklin
1903-1973 .... **CLC 4, 8**
See also AFW; CA 21-22; CANR 34; CAP 2; DLB 20, 162, 191, 225; EWL 3; MTCW 1; RGEL 2; RGSF 2; SATA 24

Plotinus 204-270 .... **CMLC 46**
See also CDWLB 1; DLB 176

Reiner, Max
See Caldwell, (Janet Miriam) Taylor (Holland)
Reis, Ricardo
See Pessoa, Fernando (Antonio Nogueira)
Reizenstein, Elmer Leopold
See Rice, Elmer (Leopold)
See also EWL 3
Remarque, Erich Maria 1898-1970 . **CLC 21**
See also AAYA 27; BPFB 3; CA 77-80; 29-32R; CDWLB 2; DA; DA3; DAB; DAC; DAM MST, NOV; DLB 56; EWL 3; EXPN; LAIT 3; MTCW 1, 2; NFS 4; RGWL 2, 3
Remington, Frederic 1861-1909 ..... **TCLC 89**
See also CA 108; 169; DLB 12, 186, 188; SATA 41
Remizov, A.
See Remizov, Aleksei (Mikhailovich)
Remizov, A. M.
See Remizov, Aleksei (Mikhailovich)
Remizov, Aleksei (Mikhailovich)
1877-1957 .... **TCLC 27**
See Remizov, Alexey Mikhaylovich
See also CA 125; 133; DLB 295
Remizov, Alexey Mikhaylovich
See Remizov, Aleksei (Mikhailovich)
See also EWL 3
Renan, Joseph Ernest 1823-1892 .. **NCLC 26**
See also GFL 1789 to the Present
Renard, Jules(-Pierre) 1864-1910 .. **TCLC 17**
See also CA 117; 202; GFL 1789 to the Present
Renault, Mary .... **CLC 3, 11, 17**
See Challans, Mary
See also BPFB 3; BYA 2; DLBY 1983; EWL 3; GLL 1; LAIT 1; MTCW 2; RGEL 2; RHW
Rendell, Ruth (Barbara) 1930- .. **CLC 28, 48**
See Vine, Barbara
See also BPFB 3; BRWS 9; CA 109; CANR 32, 52, 74, 127; CN 7; CPW; DAM POP; DLB 87, 276; INT CANR-32; MSW; MTCW 1, 2
Renoir, Jean 1894-1979 .... **CLC 20**
See also CA 129; 85-88
Resnais, Alain 1922- .... **CLC 16**
Revard, Carter (Curtis) 1931- .... **NNAL**
See also CA 144; CANR 81; PFS 5
Reverdy, Pierre 1889-1960 .... **CLC 53**
See also CA 97-100; 89-92; DLB 258; EWL 3; GFL 1789 to the Present
Rexroth, Kenneth 1905-1982 .... **CLC 1, 2, 6, 11, 22, 49, 112; PC 20**
See also BG 3; CA 5-8R; 107; CANR 14, 34, 63; CDALB 1941-1968; DAM POET; DLB 16, 48, 165, 212; DLBY 1982; EWL 3; INT CANR-14; MTCW 1, 2; RGAL 4
Reyes, Alfonso 1889-1959 .... **HLCS 2; TCLC 33**
See also CA 131; EWL 3; HW 1; LAW
Reyes y Basoalto, Ricardo Eliecer Neftali
See Neruda, Pablo
Reymont, Wladyslaw (Stanislaw)
1868(?)-1925 .... **TCLC 5**
See also CA 104; EWL 3
Reynolds, Jonathan 1942- .... **CLC 6, 38**
See also CA 65-68; CANR 28
Reynolds, Joshua 1723-1792 .... **LC 15**
See also DLB 104
Reynolds, Michael S(hane)
1937-2000 .... **CLC 44**
See also CA 65-68; 189; CANR 9, 89, 97
Reznikoff, Charles 1894-1976 .... **CLC 9**
See also CA 33-36; 61-64; CAP 2; DLB 28, 45; WP
Rezzori (d'Arezzo), Gregor von
1914-1998 .... **CLC 25**
See also CA 122; 136; 167

Rhine, Richard
See Silverstein, Alvin; Silverstein, Virginia B(arbara Opshelor)
Rhodes, Eugene Manlove
1869-1934 .... **TCLC 53**
See also CA 198; DLB 256
R'hoone, Lord
See Balzac, Honore de
Rhys, Jean 1894(?)-1979 ...... **CLC 2, 4, 6, 14, 19, 51, 124; SSC 21**
See also BRWS 2; CA 25-28R; 85-88; CANR 35, 62; CDBLB 1945-1960; CDWLB 3; DA3; DAM NOV; DLB 36, 117, 162; DNFS 2; EWL 3; LATS 1; MTCW 1, 2; RGEL 2; RGSF 2; RHW; TEA; WWE 1
Ribeiro, Darcy 1922-1997 .... **CLC 34**
See also CA 33-36R; 156; EWL 3
Ribeiro, Joao Ubaldo (Osorio Pimentel)
1941- .... **CLC 10, 67**
See also CA 81-84; EWL 3
Ribman, Ronald (Burt) 1932- .... **CLC 7**
See also CA 21-24R; CAD; CANR 46, 80; CD 5
Ricci, Nino (Pio) 1959- .... **CLC 70**
See also CA 137; CANR 130; CCA 1
Rice, Anne 1941- .... **CLC 41, 128**
See Rampling, Anne
See also AAYA 9, 53; AMWS 7; BEST 89:2; BPFB 3; CA 65-68; CANR 12, 36, 53, 74, 100; CN 7; CPW; CSW; DA3; DAM POP; DLB 292; GLL 2; HGG; MTCW 2; SUFW 2; YAW
Rice, Elmer (Leopold) 1892-1967 ...... **CLC 7, 49**
See Reizenstein, Elmer Leopold
See also CA 21-22; 25-28R; CAP 2; DAM DRAM; DFS 12; DLB 4, 7; MTCW 1, 2; RGAL 4
Rice, Tim(othy Miles Bindon)
1944- .... **CLC 21**
See also CA 103; CANR 46; DFS 7
Rich, Adrienne (Cecile) 1929- ... **CLC 3, 6, 7, 11, 18, 36, 73, 76, 125; PC 5**
See also AMWR 2; AMWS 1; CA 9-12R; CANR 20, 53, 74, 128; CDALBS; CP 7; CSW; CWP; DA3; DAM POET; DLB 5, 67; EWL 3; EXPP; FW; MAWW; MTCW 1, 2; PAB; PFS 15; RGAL 4; WP
Rich, Barbara
See Graves, Robert (von Ranke)
Rich, Robert
See Trumbo, Dalton
Richard, Keith .... **CLC 17**
See Richards, Keith
Richards, David Adams 1950- .... **CLC 59**
See also CA 93-96; CANR 60, 110; DAC; DLB 53
Richards, I(vor) A(rmstrong)
1893-1979 .... **CLC 14, 24**
See also BRWS 2; CA 41-44R; 89-92; CANR 34, 74; DLB 27; EWL 3; MTCW 2; RGEL 2
Richards, Keith 1943-
See Richard, Keith
See also CA 107; CANR 77
Richardson, Anne
See Roiphe, Anne (Richardson)
Richardson, Dorothy Miller
1873-1957 .... **TCLC 3**
See also CA 104; 192; DLB 36; EWL 3; FW; RGEL 2
Richardson (Robertson), Ethel Florence Lindesay 1870-1946
See Richardson, Henry Handel
See also CA 105; 190; DLB 230; RHW

Richardson, Henry Handel .... **TCLC 4**
See Richardson (Robertson), Ethel Florence Lindesay
See also DLB 197; EWL 3; RGEL 2; RGSF 2
Richardson, John 1796-1852 .... **NCLC 55**
See also CCA 1; DAC; DLB 99
Richardson, Samuel 1689-1761 ...... **LC 1, 44; WLC**
See also BRW 3; CDBLB 1660-1789; DA; DAB; DAC; DAM MST, NOV; DLB 39; RGEL 2; TEA; WLIT 3
Richardson, Willis 1889-1977 .... **HR 3**
See also BW 1; CA 124; DLB 51; SATA 60
Richler, Mordecai 1931-2001 .... **CLC 3, 5, 9, 13, 18, 46, 70, 185**
See also AITN 1; CA 65-68; 201; CANR 31, 62, 111; CCA 1; CLR 17; CWRI 5; DAC; DAM MST, NOV; DLB 53; EWL 3; MAICYA 1, 2; MTCW 1, 2; RGEL 2; SATA 44, 98; SATA-Brief 27; TWA
Richter, Conrad (Michael)
1890-1968 .... **CLC 30**
See also AAYA 21; BYA 2; CA 5-8R; 25-28R; CANR 23; DLB 9, 212; LAIT 1; MTCW 1, 2; RGAL 4; SATA 3; TCWW 2; TUS; YAW
Ricostranza, Tom
See Ellis, Trey
Riddell, Charlotte 1832-1906 .... **TCLC 40**
See Riddell, Mrs. J. H.
See also CA 165; DLB 156
Riddell, Mrs. J. H.
See Riddell, Charlotte
See also HGG; SUFW
Ridge, John Rollin 1827-1867 ...... **NCLC 82; NNAL**
See also CA 144; DAM MULT; DLB 175
Ridgeway, Jason
See Marlowe, Stephen
Ridgway, Keith 1965- .... **CLC 119**
See also CA 172
Riding, Laura .... **CLC 3, 7**
See Jackson, Laura (Riding)
See also RGAL 4
Riefenstahl, Berta Helene Amalia 1902-2003
See Riefenstahl, Leni
See also CA 108; 220
Riefenstahl, Leni .... **CLC 16, 190**
See Riefenstahl, Berta Helene Amalia
Riffe, Ernest
See Bergman, (Ernst) Ingmar
Riggs, (Rolla) Lynn
1899-1954 .... **NNAL; TCLC 56**
See also CA 144; DAM MULT; DLB 175
Riis, Jacob A(ugust) 1849-1914 ..... **TCLC 80**
See also CA 113; 168; DLB 23
Riley, James Whitcomb 1849-1916 .... **PC 48; TCLC 51**
See also CA 118; 137; DAM POET; MAICYA 1, 2; RGAL 4; SATA 17
Riley, Tex
See Creasey, John
Rilke, Rainer Maria 1875-1926 .... **PC 2; TCLC 1, 6, 19**
See also CA 104; 132; CANR 62, 99; CDWLB 2; DA3; DAM POET; DLB 81; EW 9; EWL 3; MTCW 1, 2; PFS 19; RGWL 2, 3; TWA; WP
Rimbaud, (Jean Nicolas) Arthur
1854-1891 ... **NCLC 4, 35, 82; PC 3, 57; WLC**
See also DA; DA3; DAB; DAC; DAM MST, POET; DLB 217; EW 7; GFL 1789 to the Present; LMFS 2; RGWL 2, 3; TWA; WP

Russell, (Henry) Ken(neth Alfred)
1927- .... **CLC 16**
See also CA 105
Russell, William Martin 1947-
See Russell, Willy
See also CA 164; CANR 107
Russell, Willy .... **CLC 60**
See Russell, William Martin
See also CBD; CD 5; DLB 233
Russo, Richard 1949- .... **CLC 181**
See also AMWS 12; CA 127; 133; CANR
87, 114
Rutherford, Mark .... **TCLC 25**
See White, William Hale
See also DLB 18; RGEL 2
Ruyslinck, Ward .... **CLC 14**
See Belser, Reimond Karel Maria de
Ryan, Cornelius (John) 1920-1974 ..... **CLC 7**
See also CA 69-72; 53-56; CANR 38
Ryan, Michael 1946- .... **CLC 65**
See also CA 49-52; CANR 109; DLBY
1982
Ryan, Tim
See Dent, Lester
Rybakov, Anatoli (Naumovich)
1911-1998 .... **CLC 23, 53**
See also CA 126; 135; 172; SATA 79;
SATA-Obit 108
Ryder, Jonathan
See Ludlum, Robert
Ryga, George 1932-1987 .... **CLC 14**
See also CA 101; 124; CANR 43, 90; CCA
1; DAC; DAM MST; DLB 60
S. H.
See Hartmann, Sadakichi
S. S.
See Sassoon, Siegfried (Lorraine)
Saba, Umberto 1883-1957 .... **TCLC 33**
See also CA 144; CANR 79; DLB 114;
EWL 3; RGWL 2, 3
Sabatini, Rafael 1875-1950 .... **TCLC 47**
See also BPFB 3; CA 162; RHW
Sabato, Ernesto (R.) 1911- .... **CLC 10, 23;
HLC 2**
See also CA 97-100; CANR 32, 65; CD-
WLB 3; DAM MULT; DLB 145; EWL 3;
HW 1, 2; LAW; MTCW 1, 2
Sa-Carneiro, Mario de 1890-1916 . **TCLC 83**
See also DLB 287; EWL 3
Sacastru, Martin
See Bioy Casares, Adolfo
See also CWW 2
Sacher-Masoch, Leopold von
1836(?)-1895 .... **NCLC 31**
Sachs, Hans 1494-1576 .... **LC 95**
See also CDWLB 2; DLB 179; RGWL 2, 3
Sachs, Marilyn (Stickle) 1927- .... **CLC 35**
See also AAYA 2; BYA 6; CA 17-20R;
CANR 13, 47; CLR 2; JRDA; MAICYA
1, 2; SAAS 2; SATA 3, 68; SATA-Essay
110; WYA; YAW
Sachs, Nelly 1891-1970 .... **CLC 14, 98**
See also CA 17-18; 25-28R; CANR 87;
CAP 2; EWL 3; MTCW 2; PFS 20;
RGWL 2, 3
Sackler, Howard (Oliver)
1929-1982 .... **CLC 14**
See also CA 61-64; 108; CAD; CANR 30;
DFS 15; DLB 7
Sacks, Oliver (Wolf) 1933- .... **CLC 67**
See also CA 53-56; CANR 28, 50, 76;
CPW; DA3; INT CANR-28; MTCW 1, 2
Sackville, Thomas 1536-1608 .... **LC 98**
See also DAM DRAM; DLB 62, 132;
RGEL 2
Sadakichi
See Hartmann, Sadakichi

Sade, Donatien Alphonse Francois
1740-1814 .... **NCLC 3, 47**
See also EW 4; GFL Beginnings to 1789;
RGWL 2, 3
Sade, Marquis de
See Sade, Donatien Alphonse Francois
Sadoff, Ira 1945- .... **CLC 9**
See also CA 53-56; CANR 5, 21, 109; DLB
120
Saetone
See Camus, Albert
Safire, William 1929- .... **CLC 10**
See also CA 17-20R; CANR 31, 54, 91
Sagan, Carl (Edward) 1934-1996 .... **CLC 30,
112**
See also AAYA 2; CA 25-28R; 155; CANR
11, 36, 74; CPW; DA3; MTCW 1, 2;
SATA 58; SATA-Obit 94
Sagan, Francoise .... **CLC 3, 6, 9, 17, 36**
See Quoirez, Francoise
See also CWW 2; DLB 83; EWL 3; GFL
1789 to the Present; MTCW 2
Sahgal, Nayantara (Pandit) 1927- .... **CLC 41**
See also CA 9-12R; CANR 11, 88; CN 7
Said, Edward W. 1935-2003 .... **CLC 123**
See also CA 21-24R; 220; CANR 45, 74,
107, 131; DLB 67; MTCW 2
Saint, H(arry) F. 1941- .... **CLC 50**
See also CA 127
St. Aubin de Teran, Lisa 1953-
See Teran, Lisa St. Aubin de
See also CA 118; 126; CN 7; INT CA-126
Saint Birgitta of Sweden c.
1303-1373 .... **CMLC 24**
Sainte-Beuve, Charles Augustin
1804-1869 .... **NCLC 5**
See also DLB 217; EW 6; GFL 1789 to the
Present
**Saint-Exupery, Antoine (Jean Baptiste
Marie Roger) de** 1900-1944 .... **TCLC 2,
56; WLC**
See also BPFB 3; BYA 3; CA 108; 132;
CLR 10; DA3; DAM NOV; DLB 72; EW
12; EWL 3; GFL 1789 to the Present;
LAIT 3; MAICYA 1, 2; MTCW 1, 2;
RGWL 2, 3; SATA 20; TWA
St. John, David
See Hunt, E(verette) Howard, (Jr.)
St. John, J. Hector
See Crevecoeur, Michel Guillaume Jean de
Saint-John Perse
See Leger, (Marie-Rene Auguste) Alexis
Saint-Leger
See also EW 10; EWL 3; GFL 1789 to the
Present; RGWL 2
Saintsbury, George (Edward Bateman)
1845-1933 .... **TCLC 31**
See also CA 160; DLB 57, 149
Sait Faik .... **TCLC 23**
See Abasiyanik, Sait Faik
Saki .... **SSC 12; TCLC 3**
See Munro, H(ector) H(ugh)
See also BRWS 6; BYA 11; LAIT 2; MTCW
2; RGEL 2; SSFS 1; SUFW
Sala, George Augustus 1828-1895 . **NCLC 46**
Saladin 1138-1193 .... **CMLC 38**
Salama, Hannu 1936- .... **CLC 18**
See also EWL 3
Salamanca, J(ack) R(ichard) 1922- .. **CLC 4,
15**
See also CA 25-28R; 193; CAAE 193
Salas, Floyd Francis 1931- .... **HLC 2**
See also CA 119; CAAS 27; CANR 44, 75,
93; DAM MULT; DLB 82; HW 1, 2;
MTCW 2
Sale, J. Kirkpatrick
See Sale, Kirkpatrick
Sale, Kirkpatrick 1937- .... **CLC 68**
See also CA 13-16R; CANR 10

Salinas, Luis Omar 1937- ... **CLC 90; HLC 2**
See also AMWS 13; CA 131; CANR 81;
DAM MULT; DLB 82; HW 1, 2
Salinas (y Serrano), Pedro
1891(?)-1951 .... **TCLC 17**
See also CA 117; DLB 134; EWL 3
Salinger, J(erome) D(avid) 1919- .. **CLC 1, 3,
8, 12, 55, 56, 138; SSC 2, 28, 65; WLC**
See also AAYA 2, 36; AMW; AMWC 1;
BPFB 3; CA 5-8R; CANR 39, 129;
CDALB 1941-1968; CLR 18; CN 7; CPW
1; DA; DA3; DAB; DAC; DAM MST,
NOV, POP; DLB 2, 102, 173; EWL 3;
EXPN; LAIT 4; MAICYA 1, 2; MTCW
1, 2; NFS 1; RGAL 4; RGSF 2; SATA 67;
SSFS 17; TUS; WYA; YAW
Salisbury, John
See Caute, (John) David
Sallust c. 86B.C.-35B.C. .... **CMLC 68**
See also AW 2; CDWLB 1; DLB 211;
RGWL 2, 3
Salter, James 1925- .. **CLC 7, 52, 59; SSC 58**
See also AMWS 9; CA 73-76; CANR 107;
DLB 130
Saltus, Edgar (Everton) 1855-1921 . **TCLC 8**
See also CA 105; DLB 202; RGAL 4
Saltykov, Mikhail Evgrafovich
1826-1889 .... **NCLC 16**
See also DLB 238:
Saltykov-Shchedrin, N.
See Saltykov, Mikhail Evgrafovich
Samarakis, Andonis
See Samarakis, Antonis
See also EWL 3
Samarakis, Antonis 1919-2003 .... **CLC 5**
See Samarakis, Andonis
See also CA 25-28R; 224; CAAS 16; CANR
36
Sanchez, Florencio 1875-1910 .... **TCLC 37**
See also CA 153; EWL 3; HW 1; LAW
Sanchez, Luis Rafael 1936- .... **CLC 23**
See also CA 128; DLB 145; EWL 3; HW 1;
WLIT 1
Sanchez, Sonia 1934- .... **BLC 3; CLC 5, 116;
PC 9**
See also BW 2, 3; CA 33-36R; CANR 24,
49, 74, 115; CLR 18; CP 7; CSW; CWP;
DA3; DAM MULT; DLB 41; DLBD 8;
EWL 3; MAICYA 1, 2; MTCW 1, 2;
SATA 22, 136; WP
Sancho, Ignatius 1729-1780 .... **LC 84**
Sand, George 1804-1876 ..... **NCLC 2, 42, 57;
WLC**
See also DA; DA3; DAB; DAC; DAM
MST, NOV; DLB 119, 192; EW 6; FW;
GFL 1789 to the Present; RGWL 2, 3;
TWA
Sandburg, Carl (August) 1878-1967 . **CLC 1,
4, 10, 15, 35; PC 2, 41; WLC**
See also AAYA 24; AMW; BYA 1, 3; CA
5-8R; 25-28R; CANR 35; CDALB 1865-
1917; CLR 67; DA; DA3; DAB; DAC;
DAM MST, POET; DLB 17, 54, 284;
EWL 3; EXPP; LAIT 2; MAICYA 1, 2;
MTCW 1, 2; PAB; PFS 3, 6, 12; RGAL
4; SATA 8; TUS; WCH; WP; WYA
Sandburg, Charles
See Sandburg, Carl (August)
Sandburg, Charles A.
See Sandburg, Carl (August)
Sanders, (James) Ed(ward) 1939- .... **CLC 53**
See Sanders, Edward
See also BG 3; CA 13-16R; CAAS 21;
CANR 13, 44, 78; CP 7; DAM POET;
DLB 16, 244
Sanders, Edward
See Sanders, (James) Ed(ward)
See also DLB 244

Service, Robert W(illiam)
1874(?)-1958 .... **TCLC 15; WLC**
See Service, Robert
See also CA 115; 140; CANR 84; DA;
DAC; DAM MST, POET; PFS 10; RGEL
2; SATA 20

Seth, Vikram 1952- .... **CLC 43, 90**
See also CA 121; 127; CANR 50, 74, 131;
CN 7; CP 7; DA3; DAM MULT; DLB
120, 271, 282; EWL 3; INT CA-127;
MTCW 2; WWE 1

Seton, Cynthia Propper 1926-1982 .. **CLC 27**
See also CA 5-8R; 108; CANR 7

Seton, Ernest (Evan) Thompson
1860-1946 .... **TCLC 31**
See also ANW; BYA 3; CA 109; 204; CLR
59; DLB 92; DLBD 13; JRDA; SATA 18

Seton-Thompson, Ernest
See Seton, Ernest (Evan) Thompson

Settle, Mary Lee 1918- .... **CLC 19, 61**
See also BPFB 3; CA 89-92; CAAS 1;
CANR 44, 87, 126; CN 7; CSW; DLB 6;
INT CA-89-92

Seuphor, Michel
See Arp, Jean

Sevigne, Marie (de Rabutin-Chantal)
1626-1696 .... **LC 11**
See Sevigne, Marie de Rabutin Chantal
See also GFL Beginnings to 1789; TWA

Sevigne, Marie de Rabutin Chantal
See Sevigne, Marie (de Rabutin-Chantal)
See also DLB 268

Sewall, Samuel 1652-1730 .... **LC 38**
See also DLB 24; RGAL 4

Sexton, Anne (Harvey) 1928-1974 ..... **CLC 2,
4, 6, 8, 10, 15, 53, 123; PC 2; WLC**
See also AMWS 2; CA 1-4R; 53-56; CABS
2; CANR 3, 36; CDALB 1941-1968; DA;
DA3; DAB; DAC; DAM MST, POET;
DLB 5, 169; EWL 3; EXPP; FW;
MAWW; MTCW 1, 2; PAB; PFS 4, 14;
RGAL 4; SATA 10; TUS

Shaara, Jeff 1952- .... **CLC 119**
See also CA 163; CANR 109

Shaara, Michael (Joseph, Jr.)
1929-1988 .... **CLC 15**
See also AITN 1; BPFB 3; CA 102; 125;
CANR 52, 85; DAM POP; DLBY 1983

Shackleton, C. C.
See Aldiss, Brian W(ilson)

Shacochis, Bob .... **CLC 39**
See Shacochis, Robert G.

Shacochis, Robert G. 1951-
See Shacochis, Bob
See also CA 119; 124; CANR 100; INT CA-
124

Shaffer, Anthony (Joshua)
1926-2001 .... **CLC 19**
See also CA 110; 116; 200; CBD; CD 5;
DAM DRAM; DFS 13; DLB 13

Shaffer, Peter (Levin) 1926- .. **CLC 5, 14, 18,
37, 60; DC 7**
See also BRWS 1; CA 25-28R; CANR 25,
47, 74, 118; CBD; CD 5; CDBLB 1960 to
Present; DA3; DAB; DAM DRAM, MST;
DFS 5, 13; DLB 13, 233; EWL 3; MTCW
1, 2; RGEL 2; TEA

Shakespeare, William 1564-1616 .... **WLC**
See also AAYA 35; BRW 1; CDBLB Be-
fore 1660; DA; DA3; DAB; DAC; DAM
DRAM, MST, POET; DFS 20; DLB 62,
172, 263; EXPP; LAIT 1; LATS 1; LMFS
1; PAB; PFS 1, 2, 3, 4, 5, 8, 9; RGEL 2;
TEA; WLIT 3; WP; WS; WYA

Shakey, Bernard
See Young, Neil

Shalamov, Varlam (Tikhonovich)
1907(?)-1982 .... **CLC 18**
See also CA 129; 105; DLB 302; RGSF 2

Shamloo, Ahmad
See Shamlu, Ahmad
Shamlou, Ahmad
See Shamlu, Ahmad
Shamlu, Ahmad 1925-2000 .... **CLC 10**
See also CA 216; CWW 2
Shammas, Anton 1951- .... **CLC 55**
See also CA 199
Shandling, Arline
See Berriault, Gina
Shange, Ntozake 1948- ... **BLC 3; CLC 8, 25,
38, 74, 126; DC 3**
See also AAYA 9; AFAW 1, 2; BW 2; CA
85-88; CABS 3; CAD; CANR 27, 48, 74,
131; CD 5; CP 7; CWD; CWP; DA3;
DAM DRAM, MULT; DFS 2, 11; DLB
38, 249; FW; LAIT 5; MTCW 1, 2; NFS
11; RGAL 4; YAW
Shanley, John Patrick 1950- .... **CLC 75**
See also CA 128; 133; CAD; CANR 83;
CD 5
Shapcott, Thomas W(illiam) 1935- .. **CLC 38**
See also CA 69-72; CANR 49, 83, 103; CP
7; DLB 289
Shapiro, Jane 1942- .... **CLC 76**
See also CA 196
Shapiro, Karl (Jay) 1913-2000 ...... **CLC 4, 8,
15, 53; PC 25**
See also AMWS 2; CA 1-4R; 188; CAAS
6; CANR 1, 36, 66; CP 7; DLB 48; EWL
3; EXPP; MTCW 1, 2; PFS 3; RGAL 4
Sharp, William 1855-1905 .... **TCLC 39**
See Macleod, Fiona
See also CA 160; DLB 156; RGEL 2
Sharpe, Thomas Ridley 1928-
See Sharpe, Tom
See also CA 114; 122; CANR 85; INT CA-
122
Sharpe, Tom .... **CLC 36**
See Sharpe, Thomas Ridley
See also CN 7; DLB 14, 231
Shatrov, Mikhail .... **CLC 59**
Shaw, Bernard
See Shaw, George Bernard
See also DLB 190
Shaw, G. Bernard
See Shaw, George Bernard
Shaw, George Bernard 1856-1950 ..... **DC 23;
TCLC 3, 9, 21, 45; WLC**
See Shaw, Bernard
See also BRW 6; BRWC 1; BRWR 2; CA
104; 128; CDBLB 1914-1945; DA; DA3;
DAB; DAC; DAM DRAM, MST; DFS 1,
3, 6, 11, 19; DLB 10, 57; EWL 3; LAIT
3; LATS 1; MTCW 1, 2; RGEL 2; TEA;
WLIT 4
Shaw, Henry Wheeler 1818-1885 .. **NCLC 15**
See also DLB 11; RGAL 4
Shaw, Irwin 1913-1984 .... **CLC 7, 23, 34**
See also AITN 1; BPFB 3; CA 13-16R; 112;
CANR 21; CDALB 1941-1968; CPW;
DAM DRAM, POP; DLB 6, 102; DLBY
1984; MTCW 1, 21
Shaw, Robert 1927-1978 .... **CLC 5**
See also AITN 1; CA 1-4R; 81-84; CANR
4; DLB 13, 14
Shaw, T. E.
See Lawrence, T(homas) E(dward)
Shawn, Wallace 1943- .... **CLC 41**
See also CA 112; CAD; CD 5; DLB 266
Shchedrin, N.
See Saltykov, Mikhail Evgrafovich
Shea, Lisa 1953- .... **CLC 86**
See also CA 147
Sheed, Wilfrid (John Joseph) 1930- . **CLC 2,
4, 10, 53**
See also CA 65-68; CANR 30, 66; CN 7;
DLB 6; MTCW 1, 2

Sheehy, Gail 1937- .... **CLC 171**
See also CA 49-52; CANR 1, 33, 55, 92;
CPW; MTCW 1
Sheldon, Alice Hastings Bradley
1915(?)-1987
See Tiptree, James, Jr.
See also CA 108; 122; CANR 34; INT CA-
108; MTCW 1
Sheldon, John
See Bloch, Robert (Albert)
Sheldon, Walter J(ames) 1917-1996
See Queen, Ellery
See also AITN 1; CA 25-28R; CANR 10
Shelley, Mary Wollstonecraft (Godwin)
1797-1851 ...... **NCLC 14, 59, 103; WLC**
See also AAYA 20; BPFB 3; BRW 3;
BRWC 2; BRWS 3; BYA 5; CDBLB
1789-1832; DA; DA3; DAB; DAC; DAM
MST, NOV; DLB 110, 116, 159, 178;
EXPN; HGG; LAIT 1; LMFS 1, 2; NFS
1; RGEL 2; SATA 29; SCFW; SFW 4;
TEA; WLIT 3
Shelley, Percy Bysshe 1792-1822 .. **NCLC 18,
93, 143; PC 14; WLC**
See also BRW 4; BRWR 1; CDBLB 1789-
1832; DA; DA3; DAB; DAC; DAM MST,
POET; DLB 96, 110, 158; EXPP; LMFS
1; PAB; PFS 2; RGEL 2; TEA; WLIT 3;
WP
Shepard, Jim 1956- .... **CLC 36**
See also CA 137; CANR 59, 104; SATA 90
Shepard, Lucius 1947- .... **CLC 34**
See also CA 128; 141; CANR 81, 124;
HGG; SCFW 2; SFW 4; SUFW 2
Shepard, Sam 1943- .... **CLC 4, 6, 17, 34, 41,
44, 169; DC 5**
See also AAYA 1, 58; AMWS 3; CA 69-72;
CABS 3; CAD; CANR 22, 120; CD 5;
DA3; DAM DRAM; DFS 3, 6, 7, 14;
DLB 7, 212; EWL 3; IDFW 3, 4; MTCW
1, 2; RGAL 4
Shepherd, Michael
See Ludlum, Robert
Sherburne, Zoa (Lillian Morin)
1912-1995 .... **CLC 30**
See also AAYA 13; CA 1-4R; 176; CANR
3, 37; MAICYA 1, 2; SAAS 18; SATA 3;
YAW
Sheridan, Frances 1724-1766 .... **LC 7**
See also DLB 39, 84
Sheridan, Richard Brinsley
1751-1816 .... **DC 1; NCLC 5, 91; WLC**
See also BRW 3; CDBLB 1660-1789; DA;
DAB; DAC; DAM DRAM, MST; DFS
15; DLB 89; WLIT 3
Sherman, Jonathan Marc .... **CLC 55**
Sherman, Martin 1941(?)- .... **CLC 19**
See also CA 116; 123; CAD; CANR 86;
CD 5; DFS 20; DLB 228; GLL 1; IDTP
Sherwin, Judith Johnson
See Johnson, Judith (Emlyn)
See also CANR 85; CP 7; CWP
Sherwood, Frances 1940- .... **CLC 81**
See also CA 146, 220; CAAE 220
Sherwood, Robert E(mmet)
1896-1955 .... **TCLC 3**
See also CA 104; 153; CANR 86; DAM
DRAM; DFS 11, 15, 17; DLB 7, 26, 249;
IDFW 3, 4; RGAL 4
Shestov, Lev 1866-1938 .... **TCLC 56**
Shevchenko, Taras 1814-1861 .... **NCLC 54**
Shiel, M(atthew) P(hipps)
1865-1947 .... **TCLC 8**
See Holmes, Gordon
See also CA 106; 160; DLB 153; HGG;
MTCW 2; SFW 4; SUFW

Sinclair, Andrew (Annandale) 1935- . **CLC 2, 14**
See also CA 9-12R; CAAS 5; CANR 14, 38, 91; CN 7; DLB 14; FANT; MTCW 1

Sinclair, Emil
See Hesse, Hermann

Sinclair, Iain 1943- .... **CLC 76**
See also CA 132; CANR 81; CP 7; HGG

Sinclair, Iain MacGregor
See Sinclair, Iain

Sinclair, Irene
See Griffith, D(avid Lewelyn) W(ark)

Sinclair, Mary Amelia St. Clair 1865(?)-1946
See Sinclair, May
See also CA 104; HGG; RHW

Sinclair, May .... **TCLC 3, 11**
See Sinclair, Mary Amelia St. Clair
See also CA 166; DLB 36, 135; EWL 3; RGEL 2; SUFW

Sinclair, Roy
See Griffith, D(avid Lewelyn) W(ark)

Sinclair, Upton (Beall) 1878-1968 ..... **CLC 1, 11, 15, 63; WLC**
See also AMWS 5; BPFB 3; BYA 2; CA 5-8R; 25-28R; CANR 7; CDALB 1929-1941; DA; DA3; DAB; DAC; DAM MST, NOV; DLB 9; EWL 3; INT CANR-7; LAIT 3; MTCW 1, 2; NFS 6; RGAL 4; SATA 9; TUS; YAW

Singe, (Edmund) J(ohn) M(illington) 1871-1909 .... **WLC**

Singer, Isaac
See Singer, Isaac Bashevis

Singer, Isaac Bashevis 1904-1991 .. **CLC 1, 3, 6, 9, 11, 15, 23, 38, 69, 111; SSC 3, 53; WLC**
See also AAYA 32; AITN 1, 2; AMW; AMWR 2; BPFB 3; BYA 1, 4; CA 1-4R; 134; CANR 1, 39, 106; CDALB 1941-1968; CLR 1; CWRI 5; DA; DA3; DAB; DAC; DAM MST, NOV; DLB 6, 28, 52, 278; DLBY 1991; EWL 3; EXPS; HGG; JRDA; LAIT 3; MAICYA 1, 2; MTCW 1, 2; RGAL 4; RGSF 2; SATA 3, 27; SATA-Obit 68; SSFS 2, 12, 16; TUS; TWA

Singer, Israel Joshua 1893-1944 .... **TCLC 33**
See also CA 169; EWL 3

Singh, Khushwant 1915- .... **CLC 11**
See also CA 9-12R; CAAS 9; CANR 6, 84; CN 7; EWL 3; RGEL 2

Singleton, Ann
See Benedict, Ruth (Fulton)

Singleton, John 1968(?)- .... **CLC 156**
See also AAYA 50; BW 2, 3; CA 138; CANR 67, 82; DAM MULT

Sinjohn, John
See Galsworthy, John

Sinyavsky, Andrei (Donatevich) 1925-1997 .... **CLC 8**
See Sinyavsky, Andrey Donatovich; Tertz, Abram
See also CA 85-88; 159

Sinyavsky, Andrey Donatovich
See Sinyavsky, Andrei (Donatevich)
See also EWL 3

Sirin, V.
See Nabokov, Vladimir (Vladimirovich)

Sissman, L(ouis) E(dward) 1928-1976 .... **CLC 9, 18**
See also CA 21-24R; 65-68; CANR 13; DLB 5

Sisson, C(harles) H(ubert) 1914-2003 .... **CLC 8**
See also CA 1-4R; 220; CAAS 3; CANR 3, 48, 84; CP 7; DLB 27

Sitting Bull 1831(?)-1890 .... **NNAL**
See also DA3; DAM MULT

Sitwell, Dame Edith 1887-1964 ..... **CLC 2, 9, 67; PC 3**
See also BRW 7; CA 9-12R; CANR 35; CDBLB 1945-1960; DAM POET; DLB 20; EWL 3; MTCW 1, 2; RGEL 2; TEA

Siwaarmill, H. P.
See Sharp, William

Sjoewall, Maj 1935- .... **CLC 7**
See Sjowall, Maj
See also CA 65-68; CANR 73

Sjowall, Maj
See Sjoewall, Maj
See also BPFB 3; CMW 4; MSW

Skelton, John 1460(?)-1529 ..... **LC 71; PC 25**
See also BRW 1; DLB 136; RGEL 2

Skelton, Robin 1925-1997 .... **CLC 13**
See Zuk, Georges
See also AITN 2; CA 5-8R; 160; CAAS 5; CANR 28, 89; CCA 1; CP 7; DLB 27, 53

Skolimowski, Jerzy 1938- .... **CLC 20**
See also CA 128

Skram, Amalie (Bertha) 1847-1905 .... **TCLC 25**
See also CA 165

Skvorecky, Josef (Vaclav) 1924- ...... **CLC 15, 39, 69, 152**
See also CA 61-64; CAAS 1; CANR 10, 34, 63, 108; CDWLB 4; DA3; DAC; DAM NOV; DLB 232; EWL 3; MTCW 1, 2

Slade, Bernard .... **CLC 11, 46**
See Newbound, Bernard Slade
See also CAAS 9; CCA 1; DLB 53

Slaughter, Carolyn 1946- .... **CLC 56**
See also CA 85-88; CANR 85; CN 7

Slaughter, Frank G(ill) 1908-2001 ... **CLC 29**
See also AITN 2; CA 5-8R; 197; CANR 5, 85; INT CANR-5; RHW

Slavitt, David R(ytman) 1935- ..... **CLC 5, 14**
See also CA 21-24R; CAAS 3; CANR 41, 83; CP 7; DLB 5, 6

Slesinger, Tess 1905-1945 .... **TCLC 10**
See also CA 107; 199; DLB 102

Slessor, Kenneth 1901-1971 .... **CLC 14**
See also CA 102; 89-92; DLB 260; RGEL 2

Slowacki, Juliusz 1809-1849 .... **NCLC 15**
See also RGWL 3

Smart, Christopher 1722-1771 . **LC 3; PC 13**
See also DAM POET; DLB 109; RGEL 2

Smart, Elizabeth 1913-1986 .... **CLC 54**
See also CA 81-84; 118; DLB 88

Smiley, Jane (Graves) 1949- ...... **CLC 53, 76, 144**
See also AMWS 6; BPFB 3; CA 104; CANR 30, 50, 74, 96; CN 7; CPW 1; DA3; DAM POP; DLB 227, 234; EWL 3; INT CANR-30; SSFS 19

Smith, A(rthur) J(ames) M(arshall) 1902-1980 .... **CLC 15**
See also CA 1-4R; 102; CANR 4; DAC; DLB 88; RGEL 2

Smith, Adam 1723(?)-1790 .... **LC 36**
See also DLB 104, 252; RGEL 2

Smith, Alexander 1829-1867 .... **NCLC 59**
See also DLB 32, 55

Smith, Anna Deavere 1950- .... **CLC 86**
See also CA 133; CANR 103; CD 5; DFS 2

Smith, Betty (Wehner) 1904-1972 .... **CLC 19**
See also BPFB 3; BYA 3; CA 5-8R; 33-36R; DLBY 1982; LAIT 3; RGAL 4; SATA 6

Smith, Charlotte (Turner) 1749-1806 .... **NCLC 23, 115**
See also DLB 39, 109; RGEL 2; TEA

Smith, Clark Ashton 1893-1961 .... **CLC 43**
See also CA 143; CANR 81; FANT; HGG; MTCW 2; SCFW 2; SFW 4; SUFW

Smith, Dave .... **CLC 22, 42**
See Smith, David (Jeddie)
See also CAAS 7; DLB 5

Smith, David (Jeddie) 1942-
See Smith, Dave
See also CA 49-52; CANR 1, 59, 120; CP 7; CSW; DAM POET

Smith, Florence Margaret 1902-1971
See Smith, Stevie
See also CA 17-18; 29-32R; CANR 35; CAP 2; DAM POET; MTCW 1, 2; TEA

Smith, Iain Crichton 1928-1998 .... **CLC 64**
See also BRWS 9; CA 21-24R; 171; CN 7; CP 7; DLB 40, 139; RGSF 2

Smith, John 1580(?)-1631 .... **LC 9**
See also DLB 24, 30; TUS

Smith, Johnston
See Crane, Stephen (Townley)

Smith, Joseph, Jr. 1805-1844 .... **NCLC 53**

Smith, Lee 1944- .... **CLC 25, 73**
See also CA 114; 119; CANR 46, 118; CSW; DLB 143; DLBY 1983; EWL 3; INT CA-119; RGAL 4

Smith, Martin
See Smith, Martin Cruz

Smith, Martin Cruz 1942- .. **CLC 25; NNAL**
See also BEST 89:4; BPFB 3; CA 85-88; CANR 6, 23, 43, 65, 119; CMW 4; CPW; DAM MULT, POP; HGG; INT CANR-23; MTCW 2; RGAL 4

Smith, Patti 1946- .... **CLC 12**
See also CA 93-96; CANR 63

Smith, Pauline (Urmson) 1882-1959 .... **TCLC 25**
See also DLB 225; EWL 3

Smith, Rosamond
See Oates, Joyce Carol

Smith, Sheila Kaye
See Kaye-Smith, Sheila

Smith, Stevie .... **CLC 3, 8, 25, 44; PC 12**
See Smith, Florence Margaret
See also BRWS 2; DLB 20; EWL 3; MTCW 2; PAB; PFS 3; RGEL 2

Smith, Wilbur (Addison) 1933- .... **CLC 33**
See also CA 13-16R; CANR 7, 46, 66; CPW; MTCW 1, 2

Smith, William Jay 1918- .... **CLC 6**
See also AMWS 13; CA 5-8R; CANR 44, 106; CP 7; CSW; CWRI 5; DLB 5; MAICYA 1, 2; SAAS 22; SATA 2, 68

Smith, Woodrow Wilson
See Kuttner, Henry

Smith, Zadie 1976- .... **CLC 158**
See also AAYA 50; CA 193

Smolenskin, Peretz 1842-1885 .... **NCLC 30**

Smollett, Tobias (George) 1721-1771 ... **LC 2, 46**
See also BRW 3; CDBLB 1660-1789; DLB 39, 104; RGEL 2; TEA

Snodgrass, W(illiam) D(e Witt) 1926- .... **CLC 2, 6, 10, 18, 68**
See also AMWS 6; CA 1-4R; CANR 6, 36, 65, 85; CP 7; DAM POET; DLB 5; MTCW 1, 2; RGAL 4

Snorri Sturluson 1179-1241 .... **CMLC 56**
See also RGWL 2, 3

Snow, C(harles) P(ercy) 1905-1980 ... **CLC 1, 4, 6, 9, 13, 19**
See also BRW 7; CA 5-8R; 101; CANR 28; CDBLB 1945-1960; DAM NOV; DLB 15, 77; DLBD 17; EWL 3; MTCW 1, 2; RGEL 2; TEA

Snow, Frances Compton
See Adams, Henry (Brooks)

Snyder, Gary (Sherman) 1930- . CLC 1, 2, 5, 9, 32, 120; PC 21
See also AMWS 8; ANW; BG 3; CA 17-20R; CANR 30, 60, 125; CP 7; DA3; DAM POET; DLB 5, 16, 165, 212, 237, 275; EWL 3; MTCW 2; PFS 9, 19; RGAL 4; WP

Snyder, Zilpha Keatley 1927- .... CLC 17
See also AAYA 15; BYA 1; CA 9-12R; CANR 38; CLR 31; JRDA; MAICYA 1, 2; SAAS 2; SATA 1, 28, 75, 110; SATA-Essay 112; YAW

Soares, Bernardo
See Pessoa, Fernando (Antonio Nogueira)

Sobh, A.
See Shamlu, Ahmad

Sobh, Alef
See Shamlu, Ahmad

Sobol, Joshua 1939- .... CLC 60
See Sobol, Yehoshua
See also CA 200; CWW 2

Sobol, Yehoshua 1939-
See Sobol, Joshua
See also CWW 2

Socrates 470B.C.-399B.C. .... CMLC 27

Soderberg, Hjalmar 1869-1941 ...... TCLC 39
See also DLB 259; EWL 3; RGSF 2

Soderbergh, Steven 1963- .... CLC 154
See also AAYA 43

Sodergran, Edith (Irene) 1892-1923
See Soedergran, Edith (Irene)
See also CA 202; DLB 259; EW 11; EWL 3; RGWL 2, 3

Soedergran, Edith (Irene)
1892-1923 .... TCLC 31
See Sodergran, Edith (Irene)

Softly, Edgar
See Lovecraft, H(oward) P(hillips)

Softly, Edward
See Lovecraft, H(oward) P(hillips)

Sokolov, Alexander V(sevolodovich) 1943-
See Sokolov, Sasha
See also CA 73-76

Sokolov, Raymond 1941- .... CLC 7
See also CA 85-88

Sokolov, Sasha .... CLC 59
See Sokolov, Alexander V(sevolodovich)
See also CWW 2; DLB 285; EWL 3; RGWL 2, 3

Sokolov, Sasha .... CLC 59

Solo, Jay
See Ellison, Harlan (Jay)

Sologub, Fyodor .... TCLC 9
See Teternikov, Fyodor Kuzmich
See also EWL 3

Solomons, Ikey Esquir
See Thackeray, William Makepeace

Solomos, Dionysios 1798-1857 .... NCLC 15

Solwoska, Mara
See French, Marilyn

Solzhenitsyn, Aleksandr I(sayevich)
1918- .. CLC 1, 2, 4, 7, 9, 10, 18, 26, 34, 78, 134; SSC 32; WLC
See Solzhenitsyn, Aleksandr Isaevich
See also AAYA 49; AITN 1; BPFB 3; CA 69-72; CANR 40, 65, 116; DA; DA3; DAB; DAC; DAM MST, NOV; EW 13; EXPS; LAIT 4; MTCW 1, 2; NFS 6; RGSF 2; RGWL 2, 3; SSFS 9; TWA

Solzhenitsyn, Aleksandr Isaevich
See Solzhenitsyn, Aleksandr I(sayevich)
See also DLB 302; EWL 3

Somers, Jane
See Lessing, Doris (May)

Somerville, Edith Oenone
1858-1949 .... SSC 56; TCLC 51
See also CA 196; DLB 135; RGEL 2; RGSF 2

Somerville & Ross
See Martin, Violet Florence; Somerville, Edith Oenone

Sommer, Scott 1951- .... CLC 25
See also CA 106

Sondheim, Stephen (Joshua) 1930- . CLC 30, 39, 147; DC 22
See also AAYA 11; CA 103; CANR 47, 67, 125; DAM DRAM; LAIT 4

Sone, Monica 1919- .... AAL

Song, Cathy 1955- .... AAL; PC 21
See also CA 154; CANR 118; CWP; DLB 169; EXPP; FW; PFS 5

Sontag, Susan 1933- .... CLC 1, 2, 10, 13, 31, 105
See also AMWS 3; CA 17-20R; CANR 25, 51, 74, 97; CN 7; CPW; DA3; DAM POP; DLB 2, 67; EWL 3; MAWW; MTCW 1, 2; RGAL 4; RHW; SSFS 10

Sophocles 496(?)B.C.-406(?)B.C. .... CMLC 2, 47, 51; DC 1; WLCS
See also AW 1; CDWLB 1; DA; DA3; DAB; DAC; DAM DRAM, MST; DFS 1, 4, 8; DLB 176; LAIT 1; LATS 1; LMFS 1; RGWL 2, 3; TWA

Sordello 1189-1269 .... CMLC 15

Sorel, Georges 1847-1922 .... TCLC 91
See also CA 118; 188

Sorel, Julia
See Drexler, Rosalyn

Sorokin, Vladimir .... CLC 59
See Sorokin, Vladimir Georgievich

Sorokin, Vladimir Georgievich
See Sorokin, Vladimir
See also DLB 285

Sorrentino, Gilbert 1929- .. CLC 3, 7, 14, 22, 40
See also CA 77-80; CANR 14, 33, 115; CN 7; CP 7; DLB 5, 173; DLBY 1980; INT CANR-14

Soseki
See Natsume, Soseki
See also MJW

Soto, Gary 1952- ... CLC 32, 80; HLC 2; PC 28
See also AAYA 10, 37; BYA 11; CA 119; 125; CANR 50, 74, 107; CLR 38; CP 7; DAM MULT; DLB 82; EWL 3; EXPP; HW 1, 2; INT CA-125; JRDA; LLW 1; MAICYA 2; MAICYAS 1; MTCW 2; PFS 7; RGAL 4; SATA 80, 120; WYA; YAW

Soupault, Philippe 1897-1990 .... CLC 68
See also CA 116; 147; 131; EWL 3; GFL 1789 to the Present; LMFS 2

Souster, (Holmes) Raymond 1921- .... CLC 5, 14
See also CA 13-16R; CAAS 14; CANR 13, 29, 53; CP 7; DA3; DAC; DAM POET; DLB 88; RGEL 2; SATA 63

Southern, Terry 1924(?)-1995 .... CLC 7
See also AMWS 11; BPFB 3; CA 1-4R; 150; CANR 1, 55, 107; CN 7; DLB 2; IDFW 3, 4

Southerne, Thomas 1660-1746 .... LC 99
See also DLB 80; RGEL 2

Southey, Robert 1774-1843 .... NCLC 8, 97
See also BRW 4; DLB 93, 107, 142; RGEL 2; SATA 54

Southworth, Emma Dorothy Eliza Nevitte
1819-1899 .... NCLC 26
See also DLB 239

Souza, Ernest
See Scott, Evelyn

Soyinka, Wole 1934- .. BLC 3; CLC 3, 5, 14, 36, 44, 179; DC 2; WLC
See also AFW; BW 2, 3; CA 13-16R; CANR 27, 39, 82; CD 5; CDWLB 3; CN 7; CP 7; DA; DA3; DAB; DAC; DAM DRAM, MST, MULT; DFS 10; DLB 125; EWL 3; MTCW 1, 2; RGEL 2; TWA; WLIT 2; WWE 1

Spackman, W(illiam) M(ode)
1905-1990 .... CLC 46
See also CA 81-84; 132

Spacks, Barry (Bernard) 1931- .... CLC 14
See also CA 154; CANR 33, 109; CP 7; DLB 105

Spanidou, Irini 1946- .... CLC 44
See also CA 185

Spark, Muriel (Sarah) 1918- ..... CLC 2, 3, 5, 8, 13, 18, 40, 94; SSC 10
See also BRWS 1; CA 5-8R; CANR 12, 36, 76, 89, 131; CDBLB 1945-1960; CN 7; CP 7; DA3; DAB; DAC; DAM MST, NOV; DLB 15, 139; EWL 3; FW; INT CANR-12; LAIT 4; MTCW 1, 2; RGEL 2; TEA; WLIT 4; YAW

Spaulding, Douglas
See Bradbury, Ray (Douglas)

Spaulding, Leonard
See Bradbury, Ray (Douglas)

Speght, Rachel 1597-c. 1630 .... LC 97
See also DLB 126

Spelman, Elizabeth .... CLC 65

Spence, J. A. D.
See Eliot, T(homas) S(tearns)

Spencer, Anne 1882-1975 .... HR 3
See also BW 2; CA 161; DLB 51, 54

Spencer, Elizabeth 1921- ... CLC 22; SSC 57
See also CA 13-16R; CANR 32, 65, 87; CN 7; CSW; DLB 6, 218; EWL 3; MTCW 1; RGAL 4; SATA 14

Spencer, Leonard G.
See Silverberg, Robert

Spencer, Scott 1945- .... CLC 30
See also CA 113; CANR 51; DLBY 1986

Spender, Stephen (Harold)
1909-1995 ...... CLC 1, 2, 5, 10, 41, 91
See also BRWS 2; CA 9-12R; 149; CANR 31, 54; CDBLB 1945-1960; CP 7; DA3; DAM POET; DLB 20; EWL 3; MTCW 1, 2; PAB; RGEL 2; TEA

Spengler, Oswald (Arnold Gottfried)
1880-1936 .... TCLC 25
See also CA 118; 189

Spenser, Edmund 1552(?)-1599 ..... LC 5, 39; PC 8, 42; WLC
See also BRW 1; CDBLB Before 1660; DA; DA3; DAB; DAC; DAM MST, POET; DLB 167; EFS 2; EXPP; PAB; RGEL 2; TEA; WLIT 3; WP

Spicer, Jack 1925-1965 .... CLC 8, 18, 72
See also BG 3; CA 85-88; DAM POET; DLB 5, 16, 193; GLL 1; WP

Spiegelman, Art 1948- .... CLC 76, 178
See also AAYA 10, 46; CA 125; CANR 41, 55, 74, 124; DLB 299; MTCW 2; SATA 109; YAW

Spielberg, Peter 1929- .... CLC 6
See also CA 5-8R; CANR 4, 48; DLBY 1981

Spielberg, Steven 1947- .... CLC 20, 188
See also AAYA 8, 24; CA 77-80; CANR 32; SATA 32

Spillane, Frank Morrison 1918-
See Spillane, Mickey
See also CA 25-28R; CANR 28, 63, 125; DA3; MTCW 1, 2; SATA 66

Spillane, Mickey .... CLC 3, 13
See Spillane, Frank Morrison
See also BPFB 3; CMW 4; DLB 226; MSW; MTCW 2

Spinoza, Benedictus de 1632-1677 .. LC 9, 58

Spinrad, Norman (Richard) 1940- ... CLC 46
See also BPFB 3; CA 37-40R; CAAS 19; CANR 20, 91; DLB 8; INT CANR-20; SFW 4

Spitteler, Carl (Friedrich Georg)
1845-1924 .... TCLC 12
See also CA 109; DLB 129; EWL 3

Sumner, Gordon Matthew .... **CLC 26**
See Police, The; Sting

Sun Tzu c. 400B.C.-c. 320B.C. ...... **CMLC 56**

Surrey, Henry Howard 1517-1574 ...... **PC 59**
See also BRW 1; RGEL 2

Surtees, Robert Smith 1805-1864 .. **NCLC 14**
See also DLB 21; RGEL 2

Susann, Jacqueline 1921-1974 .... **CLC 3**
See also AITN 1; BPFB 3; CA 65-68; 53-56; MTCW 1, 2

Su Shi
See Su Shih
See also RGWL 2, 3

Su Shih 1036-1101 .... **CMLC 15**
See also Su Shi

Suskind, Patrick .... **CLC 182**
See Sueskind, Patrick
See also BPFB 3; CA 145; CWW 2

Sutcliff, Rosemary 1920-1992 .... **CLC 26**
See also AAYA 10; BYA 1, 4; CA 5-8R; 139; CANR 37; CLR 1, 37; CPW; DAB; DAC; DAM MST, POP; JRDA; LATS 1; MAICYA 1, 2; MAICYAS 1; RHW; SATA 6, 44, 78; SATA-Obit 73; WYA; YAW

Sutro, Alfred 1863-1933 .... **TCLC 6**
See also CA 105; 185; DLB 10; RGEL 2

Sutton, Henry
See Slavitt, David R(ytman)

Suzuki, D. T.
See Suzuki, Daisetz Teitaro

Suzuki, Daisetz T.
See Suzuki, Daisetz Teitaro

Suzuki, Daisetz Teitaro
1870-1966 .... **TCLC 109**
See also CA 121; 111; MTCW 1, 2

Suzuki, Teitaro
See Suzuki, Daisetz Teitaro

Svevo, Italo .... **SSC 25; TCLC 2, 35**
See Schmitz, Aron Hector
See also DLB 264; EW 8; EWL 3; RGWL 2, 3

Swados, Elizabeth (A.) 1951- .... **CLC 12**
See also CA 97-100; CANR 49; INT CA-97-100

Swados, Harvey 1920-1972 .... **CLC 5**
See also CA 5-8R; 37-40R; CANR 6; DLB 2

Swan, Gladys 1934- .... **CLC 69**
See also CA 101; CANR 17, 39

Swanson, Logan
See Matheson, Richard (Burton)

Swarthout, Glendon (Fred)
1918-1992 .... **CLC 35**
See also AAYA 55; CA 1-4R; 139; CANR 1, 47; LAIT 5; SATA 26; TCWW 2; YAW

Swedenborg, Emanuel 1688-1772 ..... **LC 105**

Sweet, Sarah C.
See Jewett, (Theodora) Sarah Orne

Swenson, May 1919-1989 ...... **CLC 4, 14, 61, 106; PC 14**
See also AMWS 4; CA 5-8R; 130; CANR 36, 61, 131; DA; DAB; DAC; DAM MST, POET; DLB 5; EXPP; GLL 2; MTCW 1, 2; PFS 16; SATA 15; WP

Swift, Augustus
See Lovecraft, H(oward) P(hillips)

Swift, Graham (Colin) 1949- ...... **CLC 41, 88**
See also BRWC 2; BRWS 5; CA 117; 122; CANR 46, 71, 128; CN 7; DLB 194; MTCW 2; NFS 18; RGSF 2

Swift, Jonathan 1667-1745 ..... **LC 1, 42, 101; PC 9; WLC**
See also AAYA 41; BRW 3; BRWC 1; BRWR 1; BYA 5, 14; CDBLB 1660-1789; CLR 53; DA; DA3; DAB; DAC; DAM MST, NOV, POET; DLB 39, 95, 101; EXPN; LAIT 1; NFS 6; RGEL 2; SATA 19; TEA; WCH; WLIT 3

Swinburne, Algernon Charles
1837-1909 ... **PC 24; TCLC 8, 36; WLC**
See also BRW 5; CA 105; 140; CDBLB 1832-1890; DA; DA3; DAB; DAC; DAM MST, POET; DLB 35, 57; PAB; RGEL 2; TEA

Swinfen, Ann .... **CLC 34**
See also CA 202

Swinnerton, Frank Arthur
1884-1982 .... **CLC 31**
See also CA 108; DLB 34

Swithen, John
See King, Stephen (Edwin)

Sylvia
See Ashton-Warner, Sylvia (Constance)

Symmes, Robert Edward
See Duncan, Robert (Edward)

Symonds, John Addington
1840-1893 .... **NCLC 34**
See also DLB 57, 144

Symons, Arthur 1865-1945 .... **TCLC 11**
See also CA 107; 189; DLB 19, 57, 149; RGEL 2

Symons, Julian (Gustave)
1912-1994 .... **CLC 2, 14, 32**
See also CA 49-52; 147; CAAS 3; CANR 3, 33, 59; CMW 4; DLB 87, 155; DLBY 1992; MSW; MTCW 1

Synge, (Edmund) J(ohn) M(illington)
1871-1909 .... **DC 2; TCLC 6, 37**
See also BRW 6; BRWR 1; CA 104; 141; CDBLB 1890-1914; DAM DRAM; DFS 18; DLB 10, 19; EWL 3; RGEL 2; TEA; WLIT 4

Syruc, J.
See Milosz, Czeslaw

Szirtes, George 1948- .... **CLC 46; PC 51**
See also CA 109; CANR 27, 61, 117; CP 7

Szymborska, Wislawa 1923- ... **CLC 99, 190; PC 44**
See also CA 154; CANR 91; CDWLB 4; CWP; CWW 2; DA3; DLB 232; DLBY 1996; EWL 3; MTCW 2; PFS 15; RGWL 3

T. O., Nik
See Annensky, Innokenty (Fyodorovich)

Tabori, George 1914- .... **CLC 19**
See also CA 49-52; CANR 4, 69; CBD; CD 5; DLB 245

Tacitus c. 55-c. 117 .... **CMLC 56**
See also AW 2; CDWLB 1; DLB 211; RGWL 2, 3

Tagore, Rabindranath 1861-1941 .... **PC 8; SSC 48; TCLC 3, 53**
See also CA 104; 120; DA3; DAM DRAM, POET; EWL 3; MTCW 1, 2; PFS 18; RGEL 2; RGSF 2; RGWL 2, 3; TWA

Taine, Hippolyte Adolphe
1828-1893 .... **NCLC 15**
See also EW 7; GFL 1789 to the Present

Talayesva, Don C. 1890-(?) .... **NNAL**

Talese, Gay 1932- .... **CLC 37**
See also AITN 1; CA 1-4R; CANR 9, 58; DLB 185; INT CANR-9; MTCW 1, 2

Tallent, Elizabeth (Ann) 1954- .... **CLC 45**
See also CA 117; CANR 72; DLB 130

Tallmountain, Mary 1918-1997 .... **NNAL**
See also CA 146; 161; DLB 193

Tally, Ted 1952- .... **CLC 42**
See also CA 120; 124; CAD; CANR 125; CD 5; INT CA-124

Talvik, Heiti 1904-1947 .... **TCLC 87**
See also EWL 3

Tamayo y Baus, Manuel
1829-1898 .... **NCLC 1**

Tammsaare, A(nton) H(ansen)
1878-1940 .... **TCLC 27**
See also CA 164; CDWLB 4; DLB 220; EWL 3

Tam'si, Tchicaya U
See Tchicaya, Gerald Felix

Tan, Amy (Ruth) 1952- . **AAL; CLC 59, 120, 151**
See also AAYA 9, 48; AMWS 10; BEST 89:3; BPFB 3; CA 136; CANR 54, 105, 132; CDALBS; CN 7; CPW 1; DA3; DAM MULT, NOV, POP; DLB 173; EXPN; FW; LAIT 3, 5; MTCW 2; NFS 1, 13, 16; RGAL 4; SATA 75; SSFS 9; YAW

Tandem, Felix
See Spitteler, Carl (Friedrich Georg)

Tanizaki, Jun'ichiro 1886-1965 ... **CLC 8, 14, 28; SSC 21**
See Tanizaki Jun'ichiro
See also CA 93-96; 25-28R; MJW; MTCW 2; RGSF 2; RGWL 2

Tanizaki Jun'ichiro
See Tanizaki, Jun'ichiro
See also DLB 180; EWL 3

Tanner, William
See Amis, Kingsley (William)

Tao Lao
See Storni, Alfonsina

Tapahonso, Luci 1953- .... **NNAL**
See also CA 145; CANR 72, 127; DLB 175

Tarantino, Quentin (Jerome)
1963- .... **CLC 125**
See also AAYA 58; CA 171; CANR 125

Tarassoff, Lev
See Troyat, Henri

Tarbell, Ida M(inerva) 1857-1944 . **TCLC 40**
See also CA 122; 181; DLB 47

Tarkington, (Newton) Booth
1869-1946 .... **TCLC 9**
See also BPFB 3; BYA 3; CA 110; 143; CWRI 5; DLB 9, 102; MTCW 2; RGAL 4; SATA 17

Tarkovskii, Andrei Arsen'evich
See Tarkovsky, Andrei (Arsenyevich)

Tarkovsky, Andrei (Arsenyevich)
1932-1986 .... **CLC 75**
See also CA 127

Tartt, Donna 1963- .... **CLC 76**
See also AAYA 56; CA 142

Tasso, Torquato 1544-1595 .... **LC 5, 94**
See also EFS 2; EW 2; RGWL 2, 3

Tate, (John Orley) Allen 1899-1979 .. **CLC 2, 4, 6, 9, 11, 14, 24; PC 50**
See also AMW; CA 5-8R; 85-88; CANR 32, 108; DLB 4, 45, 63; DLBD 17; EWL 3; MTCW 1, 2; RGAL 4; RHW

Tate, Ellalice
See Hibbert, Eleanor Alice Burford

Tate, James (Vincent) 1943- ..... **CLC 2, 6, 25**
See also CA 21-24R; CANR 29, 57, 114; CP 7; DLB 5, 169; EWL 3; PFS 10, 15; RGAL 4; WP

Tauler, Johannes c. 1300-1361 ...... **CMLC 37**
See also DLB 179; LMFS 1

Tavel, Ronald 1940- .... **CLC 6**
See also CA 21-24R; CAD; CANR 33; CD 5

Taviani, Paolo 1931- .... **CLC 70**
See also CA 153

Taylor, Bayard 1825-1878 .... **NCLC 89**
See also DLB 3, 189, 250, 254; RGAL 4

Taylor, C(ecil) P(hilip) 1929-1981 .... **CLC 27**
See also CA 25-28R; 105; CANR 47; CBD

Taylor, Edward 1642(?)-1729 .... **LC 11**
See also AMW; DA; DAB; DAC; DAM MST, POET; DLB 24; EXPP; RGAL 4; TUS

Taylor, Eleanor Ross 1920- .... **CLC 5**
See also CA 81-84; CANR 70

Taylor, Elizabeth 1932-1975 ..... **CLC 2, 4, 29**
See also CA 13-16R; CANR 9, 70; DLB 139; MTCW 1; RGEL 2; SATA 13

Thorndike, Edward L(ee)
1874-1949 .... **TCLC 107**
See also CA 121

Thornton, Hall
See Silverberg, Robert

Thorpe, Adam 1956- .... **CLC 176**
See also CA 129; CANR 92; DLB 231

Thubron, Colin (Gerald Dryden)
1939- .... **CLC 163**
See also CA 25-28R; CANR 12, 29, 59, 95;
CN 7; DLB 204, 231

Thucydides c. 455B.C.-c. 395B.C. .. **CMLC 17**
See also AW 1; DLB 176; RGWL 2, 3

Thumboo, Edwin Nadason 1933- .... **PC 30**
See also CA 194

Thurber, James (Grover)
1894-1961 .. **CLC 5, 11, 25, 125; SSC 1,
47**
See also AAYA 56; AMWS 1; BPFB 3;
BYA 5; CA 73-76; CANR 17, 39; CDALB
1929-1941; CWRI 5; DA; DA3; DAB;
DAC; DAM DRAM, MST, NOV; DLB 4,
11, 22, 102; EWL 3; EXPS; FANT; LAIT
3; MAICYA 1, 2; MTCW 1, 2; RGAL 4;
RGSF 2; SATA 13; SSFS 1, 10, 19;
SUFW; TUS

Thurman, Wallace (Henry)
1902-1934 .... **BLC 3; HR 3; TCLC 6**
See also BW 1, 3; CA 104; 124; CANR 81;
DAM MULT; DLB 51

Tibullus c. 54B.C.-c. 18B.C. .... **CMLC 36**
See also AW 2; DLB 211; RGWL 2, 3

Ticheburn, Cheviot
See Ainsworth, William Harrison

Tieck, (Johann) Ludwig
1773-1853 .... **NCLC 5, 46; SSC 31**
See also CDWLB 2; DLB 90; EW 5; IDTP;
RGSF 2; RGWL 2, 3; SUFW

Tiger, Derry
See Ellison, Harlan (Jay)

Tilghman, Christopher 1946- .... **CLC 65**
See also CA 159; CSW; DLB 244

Tillich, Paul (Johannes)
1886-1965 .... **CLC 131**
See also CA 5-8R; 25-28R; CANR 33;
MTCW 1, 2

Tillinghast, Richard (Williford)
1940- .... **CLC 29**
See also CA 29-32R; CAAS 23; CANR 26,
51, 96; CP 7; CSW

Timrod, Henry 1828-1867 .... **NCLC 25**
See also DLB 3, 248; RGAL 4

Tindall, Gillian (Elizabeth) 1938- ...... **CLC 7**
See also CA 21-24R; CANR 11, 65, 107;
CN 7

Tiptree, James, Jr. .... **CLC 48, 50**
See Sheldon, Alice Hastings Bradley
See also DLB 8; SCFW 2; SFW 4

Tirone Smith, Mary-Ann 1944- .... **CLC 39**
See also CA 118; 136; CANR 113; SATA
143

Tirso de Molina 1580(?)-1648 .... **DC 13;
HLCS 2; LC 73**
See also RGWL 2, 3

Titmarsh, Michael Angelo
See Thackeray, William Makepeace

**Tocqueville, Alexis (Charles Henri Maurice
Clerel Comte) de** 1805-1859 .. **NCLC 7,
63**
See also EW 6; GFL 1789 to the Present;
TWA

Toer, Pramoedya Ananta 1925- ...... **CLC 186**
See also CA 197; RGWL 3

Toffler, Alvin 1928- .... **CLC 168**
See also CA 13-16R; CANR 15, 46, 67;
CPW; DAM POP; MTCW 1, 2

Toibin, Colm
See Toibin, Colm
See also DLB 271

Toibin, Colm 1955- .... **CLC 162**
See Toibin, Colm
See also CA 142; CANR 81

Tolkien, J(ohn) R(onald) R(euel)
1892-1973 .... **CLC 1, 2, 3, 8, 12, 38;
TCLC 137; WLC**
See also AAYA 10; AITN 1; BPFB 3;
BRWC 2; BRWS 2; CA 17-18; 45-48;
CANR 36; CAP 2; CDBLB 1914-1945;
CLR 56; CPW 1; CWRI 5; DA; DA3;
DAB; DAC; DAM MST, NOV, POP;
DLB 15, 160, 255; EFS 1; EWL 3; FANT;
JRDA; LAIT 1; LATS 1; LMFS 2; MAI-
CYA 1, 2; MTCW 1, 2; NFS 8; RGEL 2;
SATA 2, 32, 100; SATA-Obit 24; SFW 4;
SUFW; TEA; WCH; WYA; YAW

Toller, Ernst 1893-1939 .... **TCLC 10**
See also CA 107; 186; DLB 124; EWL 3;
RGWL 2, 3

Tolson, M. B.
See Tolson, Melvin B(eaunorus)

Tolson, Melvin B(eaunorus)
1898(?)-1966 .... **BLC 3; CLC 36, 105**
See also AFAW 1, 2; BW 1, 3; CA 124; 89-
92; CANR 80; DAM MULT, POET; DLB
48, 76; RGAL 4

Tolstoi, Aleksei Nikolaevich
See Tolstoy, Alexey Nikolaevich

Tolstoi, Lev
See Tolstoy, Leo (Nikolaevich)
See also RGSF 2; RGWL 2, 3

Tolstoy, Aleksei Nikolaevich
See Tolstoy, Alexey Nikolaevich
See also DLB 272

Tolstoy, Alexey Nikolaevich
1882-1945 .... **TCLC 18**
See Tolstoy, Aleksei Nikolaevich
See also CA 107; 158; EWL 3; SFW 4

Tolstoy, Leo (Nikolaevich)
1828-1910 . **SSC 9, 30, 45, 54; TCLC 4,
11, 17, 28, 44, 79; WLC**
See Tolstoi, Lev
See also AAYA 56; CA 104; 123; DA; DA3;
DAB; DAC; DAM MST, NOV; DLB 238;
EFS 2; EW 7; EXPS; IDTP; LAIT 2;
LATS 1; LMFS 1; NFS 10; SATA 26;
SSFS 5; TWA

Tolstoy, Count Leo
See Tolstoy, Leo (Nikolaevich)

Tomalin, Claire 1933- .... **CLC 166**
See also CA 89-92; CANR 52, 88; DLB
155

Tomasi di Lampedusa, Giuseppe 1896-1957
See Lampedusa, Giuseppe (Tomasi) di
See also CA 111; DLB 177; EWL 3

Tomlin, Lily .... **CLC 17**
See Tomlin, Mary Jean

Tomlin, Mary Jean 1939(?)-
See Tomlin, Lily
See also CA 117

Tomline, F. Latour
See Gilbert, W(illiam) S(chwenck)

Tomlinson, (Alfred) Charles 1927- .... **CLC 2,
4, 6, 13, 45; PC 17**
See also CA 5-8R; CANR 33; CP 7; DAM
POET; DLB 40

Tomlinson, H(enry) M(ajor)
1873-1958 .... **TCLC 71**
See also CA 118; 161; DLB 36, 100, 195

Tonna, Charlotte Elizabeth
1790-1846 .... **NCLC 135**
See also DLB 163

Tonson, Jacob fl. 1655(?)-1736 .... **LC 86**
See also DLB 170

Toole, John Kennedy 1937-1969 ..... **CLC 19,
64**
See also BPFB 3; CA 104; DLBY 1981;
MTCW 2

Toomer, Eugene
See Toomer, Jean

Toomer, Eugene Pinchback
See Toomer, Jean

Toomer, Jean 1894-1967 .. **BLC 3; CLC 1, 4,
13, 22; HR 3; PC 7; SSC 1, 45; WLCS**
See also AFAW 1, 2; AMWS 3, 9; BW 1;
CA 85-88; CDALB 1917-1929; DA3;
DAM MULT; DLB 45, 51; EWL 3; EXPP;
EXPS; LMFS 2; MTCW 1, 2; NFS 11;
RGAL 4; RGSF 2; SSFS 5

Toomer, Nathan Jean
See Toomer, Jean

Toomer, Nathan Pinchback
See Toomer, Jean

Torley, Luke
See Blish, James (Benjamin)

Tornimparte, Alessandra
See Ginzburg, Natalia

Torre, Raoul della
See Mencken, H(enry) L(ouis)

Torrence, Ridgely 1874-1950 .... **TCLC 97**
See also DLB 54, 249

Torrey, E(dwin) Fuller 1937- .... **CLC 34**
See also CA 119; CANR 71

Torsvan, Ben Traven
See Traven, B.

Torsvan, Benno Traven
See Traven, B.

Torsvan, Berick Traven
See Traven, B.

Torsvan, Berwick Traven
See Traven, B.

Torsvan, Bruno Traven
See Traven, B.

Torsvan, Traven
See Traven, B.

Tourneur, Cyril 1575(?)-1626 .... **LC 66**
See also BRW 2; DAM DRAM; DLB 58;
RGEL 2

Tournier, Michel (Edouard) 1924- .... **CLC 6,
23, 36, 95**
See also CA 49-52; CANR 3, 36, 74; DLB
83; EWL 3; GFL 1789 to the Present;
MTCW 1, 2; SATA 23

Tournimparte, Alessandra
See Ginzburg, Natalia

Towers, Ivar
See Kornbluth, C(yril) M.

Towne, Robert (Burton) 1936(?)- ..... **CLC 87**
See also CA 108; DLB 44; IDFW 3, 4

Townsend, Sue .... **CLC 61**
See Townsend, Susan Lilian
See also AAYA 28; CA 119; 127; CANR
65, 107; CBD; CD 5; CPW; CWD; DAB;
DAC; DAM MST; INT CA-
127; SATA 55, 93; SATA-Brief 48; YAW

Townsend, Susan Lilian 1946-
See Townsend, Sue

Townshend, Pete
See Townshend, Peter (Dennis Blandford)

Townshend, Peter (Dennis Blandford)
1945- .... **CLC 17, 42**
See also CA 107

Tozzi, Federigo 1883-1920 .... **TCLC 31**
See also CA 160; CANR 110; DLB 264;
EWL 3

Tracy, Don(ald Fiske) 1905-1970(?)
See Queen, Ellery
See also CA 1-4R; 176; CANR 2

Trafford, F. G.
See Riddell, Charlotte

Traherne, Thomas 1637(?)-1674 .... **LC 99**
See also BRW 2; DLB 131; PAB; RGEL 2

Traill, Catharine Parr 1802-1899 .. **NCLC 31**
See also DLB 99

Wagner, Linda W.
See Wagner-Martin, Linda (C.)

Wagner, Linda Welshimer
See Wagner-Martin, Linda (C.)

Wagner, Richard 1813-1883 ..... **NCLC 9, 119**
See also DLB 129; EW 6

Wagner-Martin, Linda (C.) 1936- .... **CLC 50**
See also CA 159

Wagoner, David (Russell) 1926- .... **CLC 3, 5, 15; PC 33**
See also AMWS 9; CA 1-4R; CAAS 3; CANR 2, 71; CN 7; CP 7; DLB 5, 256; SATA 14; TCWW 2

Wah, Fred(erick James) 1939- .... **CLC 44**
See also CA 107; 141; CP 7; DLB 60

Wahloo, Per 1926-1975 .... **CLC 7**
See also BPFB 3; CA 61-64; CANR 73; CMW 4; MSW

Wahloo, Peter
See Wahloo, Per

Wain, John (Barrington) 1925-1994 . **CLC 2, 11, 15, 46**
See also CA 5-8R; 145; CAAS 4; CANR 23, 54; CDBLB 1960 to Present; DLB 15, 27, 139, 155; EWL 3; MTCW 1, 2

Wajda, Andrzej 1926- .... **CLC 16**
See also CA 102

Wakefield, Dan 1932- .... **CLC 7**
See also CA 21-24R, 211; CAAE 211; CAAS 7; CN 7

Wakefield, Herbert Russell 1888-1965 .... **TCLC 120**
See also CA 5-8R; CANR 77; HGG; SUFW

Wakoski, Diane 1937- ...... **CLC 2, 4, 7, 9, 11, 40; PC 15**
See also CA 13-16R, 216; CAAE 216; CAAS 1; CANR 9, 60, 106; CP 7; CWP; DAM POET; DLB 5; INT CANR-9; MTCW 2

Wakoski-Sherbell, Diane
See Wakoski, Diane

Walcott, Derek (Alton) 1930- ... **BLC 3; CLC 2, 4, 9, 14, 25, 42, 67, 76, 160; DC 7; PC 46**
See also BW 2; CA 89-92; CANR 26, 47, 75, 80, 130; CBD; CD 5; CDWLB 3; CP 7; DA3; DAB; DAC; DAM MST, MULT, POET; DLB 117; DLBY 1981; DNFS 1; EFS 1; EWL 3; LMFS 2; MTCW 1, 2; PFS 6; RGEL 2; TWA; WWE 1

Waldman, Anne (Lesley) 1945- .... **CLC 7**
See also BG 3; CA 37-40R; CAAS 17; CANR 34, 69, 116; CP 7; CWP; DLB 16

Waldo, E. Hunter
See Sturgeon, Theodore (Hamilton)

Waldo, Edward Hamilton
See Sturgeon, Theodore (Hamilton)

Walker, Alice (Malsenior) 1944- .... **BLC 3; CLC 5, 6, 9, 19, 27, 46, 58, 103, 167; PC 30; SSC 5; WLCS**
See also AAYA 3, 33; AFAW 1, 2; AMWS 3; BEST 89:4; BPFB 3; BW 2, 3; CA 37-40R; CANR 9, 27, 49, 66, 82, 131; CDALB 1968-1988; CN 7; CPW; CSW; DA; DA3; DAB; DAC; DAM MST, MULT, NOV, POET, POP; DLB 6, 33, 143; EWL 3; EXPN; EXPS; FW; INT CANR-27; LAIT 3; MAWW; MTCW 1, 2; NFS 5; RGAL 4; RGSF 2; SATA 31; SSFS 2, 11; TUS; YAW

Walker, David Harry 1911-1992 ...... **CLC 14**
See also CA 1-4R; 137; CANR 1; CWRI 5; SATA 8; SATA-Obit 71

Walker, Edward Joseph 1934-2004
See Walker, Ted
See also CA 21-24R; 226; CANR 12, 28, 53; CP 7

Walker, George F. 1947- .... **CLC 44, 61**
See also CA 103; CANR 21, 43, 59; CD 5; DAB; DAC; DAM MST; DLB 60

Walker, Joseph A. 1935- .... **CLC 19**
See also BW 1, 3; CA 89-92; CAD; CANR 26; CD 5; DAM DRAM, MST; DFS 12; DLB 38

Walker, Margaret (Abigail) 1915-1998 .... **BLC; CLC 1, 6; PC 20; TCLC 129**
See also AFAW 1, 2; BW 2, 3; CA 73-76; 172; CANR 26, 54, 76; CN 7; CP 7; CSW; DAM MULT; DLB 76, 152; EXPP; FW; MTCW 1, 2; RGAL 4; RHW

Walker, Ted .... **CLC 13**
See Walker, Edward Joseph
See also DLB 40

Wallace, David Foster 1962- ... **CLC 50, 114; SSC 68**
See also AAYA 50; AMWS 10; CA 132; CANR 59; DA3; MTCW 2

Wallace, Dexter
See Masters, Edgar Lee

Wallace, (Richard Horatio) Edgar 1875-1932 .... **TCLC 57**
See also CA 115; 218; CMW 4; DLB 70; MSW; RGEL 2

Wallace, Irving 1916-1990 .... **CLC 7, 13**
See also AITN 1; BPFB 3; CA 1-4R; 132; CAAS 1; CANR 1, 27; CPW; DAM NOV, POP; INT CANR-27; MTCW 1, 2

Wallant, Edward Lewis 1926-1962 ... **CLC 5, 10**
See also CA 1-4R; CANR 22; DLB 2, 28, 143, 299; EWL 3; MTCW 1, 2; RGAL 4

Wallas, Graham 1858-1932 .... **TCLC 91**

Waller, Edmund 1606-1687 .... **LC 86**
See also BRW 2; DAM POET; DLB 126; PAB; RGEL 2

Walley, Byron
See Card, Orson Scott

Walpole, Horace 1717-1797 .... **LC 2, 49**
See also BRW 3; DLB 39, 104, 213; HGG; LMFS 1; RGEL 2; SUFW 1; TEA

Walpole, Hugh (Seymour) 1884-1941 .... **TCLC 5**
See also CA 104; 165; DLB 34; HGG; MTCW 2; RGEL 2; RHW

Walrond, Eric (Derwent) 1898-1966 .... **HR 3**
See also BW 1; CA 125; DLB 51

Walser, Martin 1927- .... **CLC 27, 183**
See also CA 57-60; CANR 8, 46; CWW 2; DLB 75, 124; EWL 3

Walser, Robert 1878-1956 ..... **SSC 20; TCLC 18**
See also CA 118; 165; CANR 100; DLB 66; EWL 3

Walsh, Gillian Paton
See Paton Walsh, Gillian

Walsh, Jill Paton .... **CLC 35**
See Paton Walsh, Gillian
See also CLR 2, 65; WYA

Walter, Villiam Christian
See Andersen, Hans Christian

Walters, Anna L(ee) 1946- .... **NNAL**
See also CA 73-76

Walther von der Vogelweide c. 1170-1228 .... **CMLC 56**

Walton, Izaak 1593-1683 .... **LC 72**
See also BRW 2; CDBLB Before 1660; DLB 151, 213; RGEL 2

Wambaugh, Joseph (Aloysius), Jr. 1937- .... **CLC 3, 18**
See also AITN 1; BEST 89:3; BPFB 3; CA 33-36R; CANR 42, 65, 115; CMW 4; CPW 1; DA3; DAM NOV, POP; DLB 6; DLBY 1983; MSW; MTCW 1, 2

Wang Wei 699(?)-761(?) .... **PC 18**
See also TWA

Warburton, William 1698-1779 .... **LC 97**
See also DLB 104

Ward, Arthur Henry Sarsfield 1883-1959
See Rohmer, Sax
See also CA 108; 173; CMW 4; HGG

Ward, Douglas Turner 1930- .... **CLC 19**
See also BW 1; CA 81-84; CAD; CANR 27; CD 5; DLB 7, 38

Ward, E. D.
See Lucas, E(dward) V(errall)

Ward, Mrs. Humphry 1851-1920
See Ward, Mary Augusta
See also RGEL 2

Ward, Mary Augusta 1851-1920 ... **TCLC 55**
See Ward, Mrs. Humphry
See also DLB 18

Ward, Peter
See Faust, Frederick (Schiller)

Warhol, Andy 1928(?)-1987 .... **CLC 20**
See also AAYA 12; BEST 89:4; CA 89-92; 121; CANR 34

Warner, Francis (Robert le Plastrier) 1937- .... **CLC 14**
See also CA 53-56; CANR 11

Warner, Marina 1946- .... **CLC 59**
See also CA 65-68; CANR 21, 55, 118; CN 7; DLB 194

Warner, Rex (Ernest) 1905-1986 ...... **CLC 45**
See also CA 89-92; 119; DLB 15; RGEL 2; RHW

Warner, Susan (Bogert) 1819-1885 .... **NCLC 31**
See also DLB 3, 42, 239, 250, 254

Warner, Sylvia (Constance) Ashton
See Ashton-Warner, Sylvia (Constance)

Warner, Sylvia Townsend 1893-1978 .. **CLC 7, 19; SSC 23; TCLC 131**
See also BRWS 7; CA 61-64; 77-80; CANR 16, 60, 104; DLB 34, 139; EWL 3; FANT; FW; MTCW 1, 2; RGEL 2; RGSF 2; RHW

Warren, Mercy Otis 1728-1814 ..... **NCLC 13**
See also DLB 31, 200; RGAL 4; TUS

Warren, Robert Penn 1905-1989 .. **CLC 1, 4, 6, 8, 10, 13, 18, 39, 53, 59; PC 37; SSC 4, 58; WLC**
See also AITN 1; AMW; AMWC 2; BPFB 3; BYA 1; CA 13-16R; 129; CANR 10, 47; CDALB 1968-1988; DA; DA3; DAB; DAC; DAM MST, NOV, POET; DLB 2, 48, 152; DLBY 1980, 1989; EWL 3; INT CANR-10; MTCW 1, 2; NFS 13; RGAL 4; RGSF 2; RHW; SATA 46; SATA-Obit 63; SSFS 8; TUS

Warrigal, Jack
See Furphy, Joseph

Warshofsky, Isaac
See Singer, Isaac Bashevis

Warton, Joseph 1722-1800 .... **NCLC 118**
See also DLB 104, 109; RGEL 2

Warton, Thomas 1728-1790 .... **LC 15, 82**
See also DAM POET; DLB 104, 109; RGEL 2

Waruk, Kona
See Harris, (Theodore) Wilson

Warung, Price .... **TCLC 45**
See Astley, William
See also DLB 230; RGEL 2

Warwick, Jarvis
See Garner, Hugh
See also CCA 1

Washington, Alex
See Harris, Mark

Washington, Booker T(aliaferro) 1856-1915 .... **BLC 3; TCLC 10**
See also BW 1; CA 114; 125; DA3; DAM MULT; LAIT 2; RGAL 4; SATA 28

Wilde, Oscar (Fingal O'Flahertie Wills)
1854(?)-1900 ..... **DC 17; SSC 11; TCLC 1, 8, 23, 41; WLC**
See also AAYA 49; BRW 5; BRWC 1, 2; BRWR 2; BYA 15; CA 104; 119; CANR 112; CDBLB 1890-1914; DA; DA3; DAB; DAC; DAM DRAM, MST, NOV; DFS 4, 8, 9; DLB 10, 19, 34, 57, 141, 156, 190; EXPS; FANT; LATS 1; NFS 20; RGEL 2; RGSF 2; SATA 24; SSFS 7; SUFW; TEA; WCH; WLIT 4

Wilder, Billy .... **CLC 20**
See Wilder, Samuel
See also DLB 26

Wilder, Samuel 1906-2002
See Wilder, Billy
See also CA 89-92; 205

Wilder, Stephen
See Marlowe, Stephen

Wilder, Thornton (Niven)
1897-1975 .. **CLC 1, 5, 6, 10, 15, 35, 82; DC 1, 24; WLC**
See also AAYA 29; AITN 2; AMW; CA 13-16R; 61-64; CAD; CANR 40, 132; CDALBS; DA; DA3; DAB; DAC; DAM MST, NOV; DFS 1, 4, 16; DLB 4, 7, 9, 228; DLBY 1997; EWL 3; LAIT 3; MTCW 1, 2; RGAL 4; RHW; WYAS 1

Wilding, Michael 1942- ...... **CLC 73; SSC 50**
See also CA 104; CANR 24, 49, 106; CN 7; RGSF 2

Wiley, Richard 1944- .... **CLC 44**
See also CA 121; 129; CANR 71

Wilhelm, Kate .... **CLC 7**
See Wilhelm, Katie (Gertrude)
See also AAYA 20; BYA 16; CAAS 5; DLB 8; INT CANR-17; SCFW 2

Wilhelm, Katie (Gertrude) 1928-
See Wilhelm, Kate
See also CA 37-40R; CANR 17, 36, 60, 94; MTCW 1; SFW 4

Wilkins, Mary
See Freeman, Mary E(leanor) Wilkins

Willard, Nancy 1936- .... **CLC 7, 37**
See also BYA 5; CA 89-92; CANR 10, 39, 68, 107; CLR 5; CWP; CWRI 5; DLB 5, 52; FANT; MAICYA 1, 2; MTCW 1; SATA 37, 71, 127; SATA-Brief 30; SUFW 2

William of Malmesbury c. 1090B.C.-c. 1140B.C. .... **CMLC 57**

William of Ockham 1290-1349 ..... **CMLC 32**

Williams, Ben Ames 1889-1953 ..... **TCLC 89**
See also CA 183; DLB 102

Williams, C(harles) K(enneth)
1936- .... **CLC 33, 56, 148**
See also CA 37-40R; CAAS 26; CANR 57, 106; CP 7; DAM POET; DLB 5

Williams, Charles
See Collier, James Lincoln

Williams, Charles (Walter Stansby)
1886-1945 .... **TCLC 1, 11**
See also BRWS 9; CA 104; 163; DLB 100, 153, 255; FANT; RGEL 2; SUFW 1

Williams, Ella Gwendolen Rees
See Rhys, Jean

Williams, (George) Emlyn
1905-1987 .... **CLC 15**
See also CA 104; 123; CANR 36; DAM DRAM; DLB 10, 77; IDTP; MTCW 1

Williams, Hank 1923-1953 .... **TCLC 81**
See Williams, Hiram King

Williams, Helen Maria
1761-1827 .... **NCLC 135**
See also DLB 158

Williams, Hiram Hank
See Williams, Hank

Williams, Hiram King
See Williams, Hank
See also CA 188

Williams, Hugo (Mordaunt) 1942- ... **CLC 42**
See also CA 17-20R; CANR 45, 119; CP 7; DLB 40

Williams, J. Walker
See Wodehouse, P(elham) G(renville)

Williams, John A(lfred) 1925- . **BLC 3; CLC 5, 13**
See also AFAW 2; BW 2, 3; CA 53-56, 195; CAAE 195; CAAS 3; CANR 6, 26, 51, 118; CN 7; CSW; DAM MULT; DLB 2, 33; EWL 3; INT CANR-6; RGAL 4; SFW 4

Williams, Jonathan (Chamberlain)
1929- .... **CLC 13**
See also CA 9-12R; CAAS 12; CANR 8, 108; CP 7; DLB 5

Williams, Joy 1944- .... **CLC 31**
See also CA 41-44R; CANR 22, 48, 97

Williams, Norman 1952- .... **CLC 39**
See also CA 118

Williams, Sherley Anne 1944-1999 ... **BLC 3; CLC 89**
See also AFAW 2; BW 2, 3; CA 73-76; 185; CANR 25, 82; DAM MULT, POET; DLB 41; INT CANR-25; SATA 78; SATA-Obit 116

Williams, Shirley
See Williams, Sherley Anne

Williams, Tennessee 1911-1983 . **CLC 1, 2, 5, 7, 8, 11, 15, 19, 30, 39, 45, 71, 111; DC 4; WLC**
See also AAYA 31; AITN 1, 2; AMW; AMWC 1; CA 5-8R; 108; CABS 3; CAD; CANR 31, 132; CDALB 1941-1968; DA; DA3; DAB; DAC; DAM DRAM, MST; DFS 17; DLB 7; DLBD 4; DLBY 1983; EWL 3; GLL 1; LAIT 4; LATS 1; MTCW 1, 2; RGAL 4; TUS

Williams, Thomas (Alonzo)
1926-1990 .... **CLC 14**
See also CA 1-4R; 132; CANR 2

Williams, William C.
See Williams, William Carlos

Williams, William Carlos
1883-1963 .... **CLC 1, 2, 5, 9, 13, 22, 42, 67; PC 7; SSC 31**
See also AAYA 46; AMW; AMWR 1; CA 89-92; CANR 34; CDALB 1917-1929; DA; DA3; DAB; DAC; DAM MST, POET; DLB 4, 16, 54, 86; EWL 3; EXPP; MTCW 1, 2; NCFS 4; PAB; PFS 1, 6, 11; RGAL 4; RGSF 2; TUS; WP

Williamson, David (Keith) 1942- ..... **CLC 56**
See also CA 103; CANR 41; CD 5; DLB 289

Williamson, Ellen Douglas 1905-1984
See Douglas, Ellen
See also CA 17-20R; 114; CANR 39

Williamson, Jack .... **CLC 29**
See Williamson, John Stewart
See also CAAS 8; DLB 8; SCFW 2

Williamson, John Stewart 1908-
See Williamson, Jack
See also CA 17-20R; CANR 23, 70; SFW 4

Willie, Frederick
See Lovecraft, H(oward) P(hillips)

Willingham, Calder (Baynard, Jr.)
1922-1995 .... **CLC 5, 51**
See also CA 5-8R; 147; CANR 3; CSW; DLB 2, 44; IDFW 3, 4; MTCW 1

Willis, Charles
See Clarke, Arthur C(harles)

Willy
See Colette, (Sidonie-Gabrielle)

Willy, Colette
See Colette, (Sidonie-Gabrielle)
See also GLL 1

Wilmot, John 1647-1680 .... **LC 75**
See Rochester
See also BRW 2; DLB 131; PAB

Wilson, A(ndrew) N(orman) 1950- ... **CLC 33**
See also BRWS 6; CA 112; 122; CN 7; DLB 14, 155, 194; MTCW 2

Wilson, Angus (Frank Johnstone)
1913-1991 . **CLC 2, 3, 5, 25, 34; SSC 21**
See also BRWS 1; CA 5-8R; 134; CANR 21; DLB 15, 139, 155; EWL 3; MTCW 1, 2; RGEL 2; RGSF 2

Wilson, August 1945- ... **BLC 3; CLC 39, 50, 63, 118; DC 2; WLCS**
See also AAYA 16; AFAW 2; AMWS 8; BW 2, 3; CA 115; 122; CAD; CANR 42, 54, 76, 128; CD 5; DA; DA3; DAB; DAC; DAM DRAM, MST, MULT; DFS 3, 7, 15, 17; DLB 228; EWL 3; LAIT 4; LATS 1; MTCW 1, 2; RGAL 4

Wilson, Brian 1942- .... **CLC 12**

Wilson, Colin 1931- .... **CLC 3, 14**
See also CA 1-4R; CAAS 5; CANR 1, 22, 33, 77; CMW 4; CN 7; DLB 14, 194; HGG; MTCW 1; SFW 4

Wilson, Dirk
See Pohl, Frederik

Wilson, Edmund 1895-1972 .. **CLC 1, 2, 3, 8, 24**
See also AMW; CA 1-4R; 37-40R; CANR 1, 46, 110; DLB 63; EWL 3; MTCW 1, 2; RGAL 4; TUS

Wilson, Ethel Davis (Bryant)
1888(?)-1980 .... **CLC 13**
See also CA 102; DAC; DAM POET; DLB 68; MTCW 1; RGEL 2

Wilson, Harriet
See Wilson, Harriet E. Adams
See also DLB 239

Wilson, Harriet E.
See Wilson, Harriet E. Adams
See also DLB 243

Wilson, Harriet E. Adams
1827(?)-1863(?) .... **BLC 3; NCLC 78**
See Wilson, Harriet; Wilson, Harriet E.
See also DAM MULT; DLB 50

Wilson, John 1785-1854 .... **NCLC 5**

Wilson, John (Anthony) Burgess 1917-1993
See Burgess, Anthony
See also CA 1-4R; 143; CANR 2, 46; DA3; DAC; DAM NOV; MTCW 1, 2; NFS 15; TEA

Wilson, Lanford 1937- ... **CLC 7, 14, 36; DC 19**
See also CA 17-20R; CABS 3; CAD; CANR 45, 96; CD 5; DAM DRAM; DFS 4, 9, 12, 16, 20; DLB 7; EWL 3; TUS

Wilson, Robert M. 1941- .... **CLC 7, 9**
See also CA 49-52; CAD; CANR 2, 41; CD 5; MTCW 1

Wilson, Robert McLiam 1964- .... **CLC 59**
See also CA 132; DLB 267

Wilson, Sloan 1920-2003 .... **CLC 32**
See also CA 1-4R; 216; CANR 1, 44; CN 7

Wilson, Snoo 1948- .... **CLC 33**
See also CA 69-72; CBD; CD 5

Wilson, William S(mith) 1932- .... **CLC 49**
See also CA 81-84

Wilson, (Thomas) Woodrow
1856-1924 .... **TCLC 79**
See also CA 166; DLB 47

Wilson and Warnke eds. .... **CLC 65**

Winchilsea, Anne (Kingsmill) Finch
1661-1720
See Finch, Anne
See also RGEL 2

Literary Criticism Series
Cumulative Topic Index

This index lists all topic entries in Gale's *Classical and Medieval Literature Criticism* (CMLC), *Contemporary Literary Criticism* (CLC), *Drama Criticism* (DC), *Literature Criticism from 1400 to 1800* (LC), *Nineteenth-Century Literature Criticism* (NCLC), *Short Story Criticism* (SSC), and *Twentieth-Century Literary Criticism* (TCLC). The index also lists topic entries in the Gale Critical Companion Collection, which includes the following publications: *The Beat Generation* (BG), and *Harlem Renaissance* (HR).

Topic Index

Topic Index

SSC Cumulative Nationality Index

Nationality Index

SSC-74 Title Index

ISBN 0-7876-8871-1

90000